THE CIVIL WAR AND RECONSTRUCTION

THE CIVIL WAR AND RECONSTRUCTION

SECOND EDITION, REVISED
WITH ENLARGED BIBLIOGRAPHY

J. G. RANDALL

Late Professor of History, University of Illinois

DAVID DONALD

Harry C. Black Professor of American History,
The Johns Hopkins University

D. C. HEATH AND COMPANY
A Division of Raytheon Education Company
Lexington, Massachusetts

MAPS BY RUSSELL LENZ

Library of Congress Number 74–76471

Preface

In this revision, the text of the 1961 edition of *The Civil War and Reconstruction* remains substantially unchanged, except for the correction of typographical and minor factual errors. While rereading it, I found that there were some points which I would now make differently and some emphases which I would change, but on the whole it has worn well. That it has done so is due, in no small measure, to the broad mastery which the late Professor Randall had over the entire mid-nineteenth century period; even in 1937 he accurately anticipated the direction which subsequent scholarship took. That the changes which I made for the 1961 edition have stood the test of time is attributable to the fact that much Civil War–Reconstruction scholarship in the last eight years has been devoted to exploring the leads previously given by the great scholars in the field, such as Bruce Catton, Avery Craven, Allan Nevins, Roy F. Nichols, Bell I. Wiley, and T. Harry Williams. I also had the inestimable advantage of drawing upon a number of studies still unpublished in 1961, many of them by the extraordinarily able graduate students with whom I had the privilege of working at Columbia and Princeton universities: William Dusinberre, Eugene D. Genovese, William Gillette, Stanley P. Hirshson, Ari A. Hoogenboom, Grady McWhiney, Samuel Shapiro, and Irwin Unger.

Since most of these works have subsequently been published, the bibliography of the 1961 edition has grown increasingly out of date, and I have greatly expanded it in this revision. Even so, it includes only the most significant titles from the enormous flood of literature published during the past eight years. In preparing this substantially new bibliographical essay, I have been struck by the fact that little new work has been done in some important areas during the past decade. Constitutional and diplomatic aspects of the Civil War and the Reconstruction years, neglected in 1961, continue to attract attention from only a handful of specialists. Discussions of "The Causes of the Civil War," once a historical perennial, are now rare. After the massive studies by Allan Nevins and Roy F. Nichols, few have ventured further exploration into the tangled politics of the 1850's. Aside from the work of Don E. Fehrenbacher, there have been few major contributions to Lincolniana. In 1961 it seemed that there was no end to the military studies of the Civil War, but since the close of the centennial observances in 1965 most of the guns have been silent. Though much important work has appeared on the years 1865–1867, the remaining decade of the Reconstruction era has drawn little interest from historians.

Interest in other aspects of the period has grown enormously. The history of the American Negro, whether in slavery, in war, or in freedom, has increasingly attracted students, and the abolitionists have remained a never-ending source of fascination, and of controversy. Oddly enough, in a time when the economic interpretation has become ever more unfashionable, some of the most exciting writings on the Civil War and Reconstruction period have been broadly conceived economic studies, such as those of Alfred H. Conrad, John R. Meyer, and Eugene D. Genovese for the ante-bellum era, of Thomas C. Cochran and Paul W. Gates for the war years, and of Robert P. Sharkey and Irwin Unger for the Reconstruction decade.

In exploring these, and other, currents of historical writing during the past eight years, I have been greatly assisted by the careful bibliographies prepared periodically for the *American Historical Review* by Wood Gray and for *Civil War History* by Ada M. Stoflet, as well as by the useful listings of articles in the *Journal of Southern History* and the *Journal of American History*. I have also profited from the suggestions of two of my colleagues in the Institute of Southern History, Professors Thomas B. Alexander and Joe M. Richardson. Whatever degree of accuracy the bibliography has must be credited to the careful typing of my secretary, Mrs. Alice Anderson, and to the thorough checking performed by four student assistants at The Johns Hopkins University: Michael A. Burlingame, E. Kenneth Grove, Douglass Sawyer, and Peter Wallenstein. My wife, Aïda DiPace Donald, has taken time from her own writing to help with the tedious checking of proofs. For whatever errors remain I, of course, am responsible, and I will be truly grateful to any reader who will take the time to point them out to me.

The Johns Hopkins University   *David Donald*

Contents

THE DIVIDED UNION

THE RESTORED UNION

Maps and Graphs

Illustrations

THE DIVIDED UNION

CHAPTER I

A Growing Nation

I

THE UNITED STATES in the 1850's was a growing nation. A land so vast in extent and so conglomerate in origin naturally was divided by significant local and sectional differences, but it was also united by the fact of its unprecedentedly rapid growth. Change and fluidity were the twin themes of American life, and they affected every aspect of the nation's economics, social structure, and political organization. There was a veritable poetry of motion about the expansion of the American people in the 1850–1860 decade. Having just acquired 188,520 additional square miles of territory in the 1840's, they were already beginning to fill up the land from a population that increased 35 per cent every ten years.[1] The decade after 1850 saw the total number of inhabitants of the United States rise from 23,000,000 to 31,000,000. Though all parts of the country were expanding, not all did so with equal rapidity. Minnesota's population grew by an incredible 2760 per cent in the 1850's, while Vermont showed an increase of only 0.31 per cent.[2] In general, the sparsely settled Pacific Coast states showed the greatest proportionate growth, but the largest numerical increase came in the great Middle West. The older states of the South and Northeast were about equal in population and showed growth rates of 24 and 23 per cent respectively.[3]

Though fecundity was high in that decade, much of the increase came direct from Europe. In the fifties the foreign-born element in the country almost doubled. Numbering 2,210,000 in 1850, it exceeded four million

[1] The total land area of the United States in 1840 was 1,754,622 square miles; in 1850 it was 2,943,142. The Gadsden Purchase of 1853 increased the total to 2,974,159. *A Century of Population Growth* (Bur. of the Census, 1909), 54. In the following pages the frequently cited *Mississippi Valley Historical Review* will be referred to as M.V.H.R. and the *Journal of Southern History* as J.S.H.

[2] J. C. G. Kennedy, *Preliminary Report on the Eighth Census, 1860*, 131.

[3] Calculated from figures in *Historical Statistics of the United States, 1789–1945*, 27.

in 1860. All parts of the country were affected by this huge influx. Though the South received fewer immigrants, proportionately, than any other region, by the end of the decade 21 per cent of Savannah's population was foreign-born, as was 31 per cent of that of Memphis.[4] Far heavier concentrations of the foreign-born appeared in the Middle West, where Wisconsin during this period became almost another Germany and Swedish beginnings in Minnesota suggested to Fredrika Bremer the term "New Scandinavia." The East, too, was swamped with immigrants: New York in 1855 contained 469,000 persons born in Ireland and 218,000 born in Germany, and these two groups constituted at the time nearly one-fifth of the Empire State. About 96 per cent of the immigrants entering the United States in the fifties came from the north and west of Europe (chiefly from Germany, Scandinavia, and the British Isles); while the contribution of southern and eastern Europe was negligible.

In the reaction of native America to this wave of foreign settlement there was much of violence and persecution, with inevitable results in the field of politics. While immigrants were being welcomed in the mass and some of the states (notably Wisconsin) were permitting them to vote while aliens, Kentucky showed a strong tendency to deny the vote even to naturalized citizens, and "nativism" became a veritable craze in certain areas. The thronging immigrants were not only different in language and appearance from native Americans; their outlook and social customs, as in the matter of Sabbath observance, were obviously foreign to the American type. Many of them were Roman Catholics. Of the various anti-Catholic and anti-foreign organizations that made themselves felt in this period the most striking was the "Knownothing" or "American" party. In certain localities the American movement amounted to a landslide. The 1855 elections in Maryland gave the Knownothings control of local offices in a majority of the state's counties, a clear majority of thirty-four in the lower house of the legislature, and four of the state's six congressmen. In March, 1856, the secret order won control of all branches of the government of New Orleans. The New York legislature in 1855 had a Knownothing speaker. This legislature was predominantly Whig; but sixty of the eighty who composed the Whig caucus had taken the Knownothing oath. By the election of 1854 Massachusetts became virtually a Knownothing state. Every state senator, a large majority of the lower house, and the governor were Knownothings; and the members of this anti-foreign party had no difficulty in putting their candidate, Henry Wilson, into the United States Senate. Organized in 1853, the party obtained in the national election of 1856 a popular vote of 874,000 for its candidate, this being over one-fifth of the total vote. The fact that an ex-President of the United States, Millard Fillmore, accepted nomination by this party, and that such politi-

---

[4] Ella Lonn, *Foreigners in the Confederacy*, 8.

cally influential men as Henry Winter Davis, Andrew Jackson Donelson, Edward Everett, Edward Bates, and John Bell joined the movement, showed how fully the party was associated with sentiments and principles of "staunch Americanism." Another fact significant of the times was the close association of the Knownothings with the Whigs. Indeed one of the greatest sources of embarrassment to Whig leaders in this period of party realignment was the uncomfortable necessity of taking a stand for or against the nativists.

2

Despite the abundance of fertile but unoccupied land, the labor of the farm in the United States hardly claimed a majority of those gainfully employed. Of the 5,210,047 white males in the whole country in 1850, only 2,298,870 were reported as engaged in agricultural pursuits.[1] In 1860, of the 8,287,000 whose occupations were given in the census, 3,305,000 were classed as farmers, farm laborers, or planters.[2] Yet a considerable majority of the whole population lived in a rural environment. Only one-eighth of the people lived in cities of eight thousand or over in 1850; by 1860 this proportion had increased to one-sixth. Agrarian influence was powerful; agitation for publicly donated homesteads was running high; and the government was taking an increasing share in agricultural development. The vast structure of the Federal department of agriculture, however, with its experiment stations and its elaborate dissemination of seeds and scientific information, was still in the future. It was in 1862 that the bureau of agriculture was created by Congress; it did not become a department until 1889.

In the decade preceding the Civil War the production of all basic agricultural crops was notably accelerated. Corn production leaped from 592,071,000 to 838,793,000 bushels; wheat, from 100,486,000 to 173,105,000 bushels; cotton, from 2,469,000 to 5,387,000 bales.[3] Illinois may be taken as representative of this fabulous expansion of agriculture. In 1849 the state produced nine million bushels of wheat; in 1859 the output was nearly twenty-four million. In the same period the price per bushel increased from $1.20 to $1.55. Increased immigration, improved transportation, abundance of cheap land, and developments in farm machinery were working a quickened prosperity on the Middle Border. Notable among these factors of growth was the McCormick reaper, produced in 1831, an epochal invention which caused many thousands of farmers to discard harvesting methods that had been in use from time

[1] *A Century of Population Growth* (Bur. of Census, 1909), 143.

[2] *U. S. Census, 1860,* "Population," 662, 670.

[3] In each case the figures are for 1849 and 1859. *Historical Statistics of the United States, 1789–1945,* 106, 109.

POPULATION OF THE UNITED STATES—1850

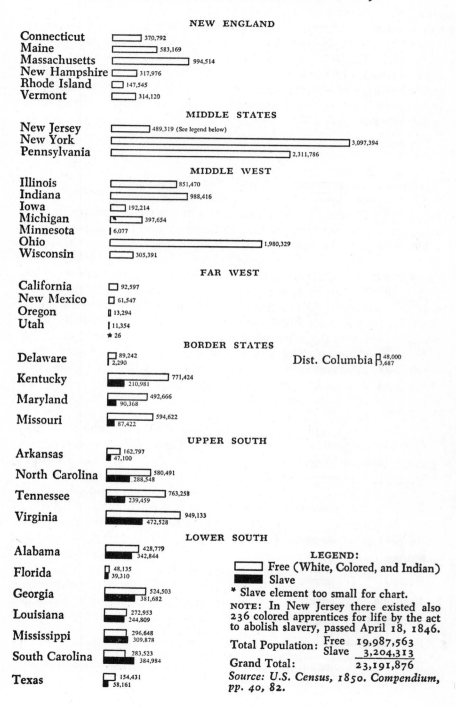

NEW ENGLAND

Connecticut	370,792
Maine	583,169
Massachusetts	994,514
New Hampshire	317,976
Rhode Island	147,545
Vermont	314,120

MIDDLE STATES

New Jersey	489,319 (See legend below)
New York	3,097,394
Pennsylvania	2,311,786

MIDDLE WEST

Illinois	851,470
Indiana	988,416
Iowa	192,214
Michigan	397,654
Minnesota	6,077
Ohio	1,980,329
Wisconsin	305,391

FAR WEST

California	92,597
New Mexico	61,547
Oregon	13,294
Utah	11,354
	★ 26

BORDER STATES

Delaware	89,242 / 2,290
Kentucky	771,424 / 210,981
Maryland	492,666 / 90,368
Missouri	594,622 / 87,422

Dist. Columbia 48,000 / 3,687

UPPER SOUTH

Arkansas	162,797 / 47,100
North Carolina	580,491 / 288,548
Tennessee	763,258 / 239,459
Virginia	949,133 / 472,528

LOWER SOUTH

Alabama	428,779 / 342,844
Florida	48,135 / 39,310
Georgia	524,503 / 381,682
Louisiana	272,953 / 244,809
Mississippi	296,648 / 309,878
South Carolina	283,523 / 384,984
Texas	154,431 / 58,161

LEGEND:
☐ Free (White, Colored, and Indian)
■ Slave
* Slave element too small for chart.
NOTE: In New Jersey there existed also 236 colored apprentices for life by the act to abolish slavery, passed April 18, 1846.

Total Population:
Free 19,987,563
Slave 3,204,313

Grand Total: 23,191,876

Source: U.S. Census, 1850. Compendium, pp. 40, 82.

POPULATION OF THE UNITED STATES—1860

NEW ENGLAND

Connecticut ▭ 460,147
Maine ▭ 628,279
Massachusetts ▭ 1,231,066
New Hampshire ▭ 326,073
Rhode Island ▭ 174,620
Vermont ▭ 315,098

MIDDLE STATES

New Jersey ▭ 672,017 (See legend below) 3,880,735
New York ▭
Pennsylvania ▭ 2,906,215

MIDDLE WEST

Illinois ▭ 1,711,951
Indiana ▭ 1,350,428
Iowa ▭ 674,943
Michigan ▭ 749,113
Minnesota ▭ 172,023
Ohio ▭ 2,339,511
Wisconsin ▭ 775,881

Kansas ▭ 107,204 * 2
Nebraska ▭ 28,826 * 15
Dakota ▭ 4,837

FAR WEST

California ▭ 379,994
New Mexico ▭ 93,516
Oregon ▭ 52,465
Utah ▭ 40,244 * .29

Colorado ▭ 34,277
Nevada ▭ 6,857
Washington ▭ 11,594

BORDER STATES

Delaware ▭ 110,418 * 1,798
Kentucky ▭ 930,201 / 225,483
Maryland ▭ 599,860 / 87,189
Missouri ▭ 1,067,081 / 114,931

Dist. Columbia ▭ 71,895 * 3,185

UPPER SOUTH

Arkansas ▭ 324,335 / 111,115
North Carolina ▭ 661,563 / 331,059
Tennessee ▭ 834,082 / 275,719
Virginia ▭ 1,105,453 / 490,865

LOWER SOUTH

Alabama ▭ 529,121 / 435,080
Florida ▭ 78,679 / 61,745
Georgia ▭ 595,088 / 462,198
Louisiana ▭ 376,276 / 331,726
Mississippi ▭ 354,674 / 436,631
South Carolina ▭ 301,302 / 402,406
Texas ▭ 421,649 / 182,566

LEGEND:
▭ Free (White, Colored, and Indian)
▬ Slave
* Slave element too small for chart.
NOTE: In New Jersey there remained, in addition to the 672,017 free, 18 colored apprentices for life by the act to abolish slavery, passed April 18, 1846.

Total Population: Free 27,489,561
Slave 3,953,760
Grand Total: 31,443,321
Source: U.S. Census, 1860. Population, pp. 598–599.

immemorial. Having worked out his invention in Virginia, McCormick enlisted the assistance of the railway magnate William B. Ogden and set up at Chicago a cluster of factory buildings which in the fifties covered 110,000 square feet of floor space. From these buildings over four thousand machines were turned out in a year.[4] The business methods of the McCormick company offered an early example of high-pressure salesmanship. Convincing advertising and easy conditions of payment brought golden returns and the firm was soon netting $300,000 a year, while its founder was hailed as one of the great men of the time, winning honors and profits abroad as well as in America. "No General or Consul drawn in a chariot through the streets of Rome [said William H. Seward in 1854] . . . ever conferred upon mankind benefits so great as he [McCormick] who thus vindicated the genius of our country at the World's Exhibition of Art in the Metropolis of the British Empire." [5]

In these years the lake ports—Milwaukee, Chicago, Toledo, Cleveland, Buffalo—showed enormous activity. In 1851 Milwaukee exported 317,000 bushels of wheat; ten years later its business had grown to thirteen million bushels. For the marketing of the huge grain surplus, methods characteristic of the capitalist system were soon fastened upon the agricultural world. The Merchants Grain Forwarding Association was formed in Chicago in 1857; and speculation was rife both at the Board of Trade and on the curb. "There many a fortune of twenty or thirty thousand dollars was made or lost within a few weeks." [6] At the same time the southward traffic on the Ohio and Mississippi rivers was reaching a new peak. Though the railroads were already beginning to be a serious challenge, it was "the golden age of steamboating in the Mississippi Valley," and 3566 steamboats arrived at New Orleans alone in 1860.[7] The annual commerce of the Mississippi-Ohio traffic was valued at $140,000,-000.[8] Business, like agriculture, was everywhere expanding in the fifties. Though a shrewd critic could have discovered unsound elements in the economy of young America, the tonic effect of increasing markets, European war, expanding wants, technological advance, and widespread exploitation of resources was unmistakable. It was the day of Stewart and his New York palace of merchandise; of the fabulously wealthy Astors; of August Belmont, New York agent of the Rothschilds; of Aspinwall and his Panama Railroad; of Corcoran and Riggs (Washington bankers); of Amos and Abbott Lawrence (Boston merchants); of Moses Grinnell, shipping magnate; of "Commodore" Vanderbilt, master of sundry steam-

---

[4] Yet by 1860 McCormick had more than a hundred rivals in the reaper machine business. *Dict. of Am. Biogr.*, XI, 607.

[5] W. T. Hutchinson, *Cyrus Hall McCormick: Seed-Time, 1809–1856*, 468.

[6] A. C. Cole, *The Irrepressible Conflict*, 102.

[7] Louis C. Hunter, *Steamboats on the Western Rivers*, 481, 645.

[8] Allan Nevins, *Ordeal of the Union*, II, 216.

boat and railway lines. "Throw down our merchants ever so flat [wrote a diarist of the period], they roll over once, and spring to their feet again. Knock the stairs from under them, and they will make a ladder of the fragments, and remount." [9] Visiting the "palace of labor" at Lowell the Scandinavian traveler Miss Bremer, who obviously did not see all, was inspired to rhetorical ecstasy at the glittering lights, the whirr of machines, and the procession of operatives. [10] At Lowell she had but a glimpse into the enterprise of a commercial and manufacturing state whose industry was producing annually nearly $300 per capita. One county in the Bay State (Middlesex) had a taxable valuation of all property in 1860 which exceeded the real estate valuation of the whole state of South Carolina. [11]

Not alone in Massachusetts, but also in Rhode Island and Connecticut, in lower New York, in the Delaware River area, along the Erie Canal, and in the areas of Pittsburgh, Cincinnati, Buffalo, Chicago, and St. Louis, were found the seats of America's industrial empire. Massachusetts was especially the seat of textile and shoe production; Maine of lumber mills; the Pittsburgh area of iron and coal; Connecticut of clocks and the ingenious devices of the peddler's cart. Though the South remained primarily an agricultural region, it too showed a keen interest in manufacturing during the 1850's. During the decade Southern manufacture of agricultural implements increased by 101 per cent, production of steam engines and machinery grew by 387 per cent, and output of boots and shoes mounted by 80 per cent. [12] Everywhere in the land it was the day of the capitalists, merchant princes, employers of thousands, financial promoters, and dwellers in Fifth Avenue mansions. Technology was moving apace. The Morse magnetic telegraph was invented in 1832 and well extended by the time of the Civil War; the pneumatic tire appeared in 1845; the sewing machine and rotary press in 1846; the hydraulic turbine in 1849; the electric locomotive in 1851; the Otis elevator in 1852; the Kelly steel process (later known as the Bessemer process) at about the same time. In the late fifties Cyrus Field was making great headway on his Atlantic cable project. Americans were exulting in the wonder of their contrivances—their heating systems, sleeping cars, river and ocean steamboats, engines, improved plows, Colt revolvers, Goodyear rubber patents, power looms, and typesetting machines. Standardization and technological automatic production were adding a stimulus to eco-

[9] *Diary of Philip Hone*, Aug. 11, 1845. Hone was a New York merchant, civic leader, and society lion whose diary is one of the finest records of American life from 1828 to 1851. The whole diary has never been published; the best edition is by Allan Nevins (1927).

[10] *America of the Fifties: Letters of Fredrika Bremer*, 79–80.

[11] The figure for 1855. Appleton's *American Annual Cyclopedia*, 1861, 449, 646.

[12] J. C. G. Kennedy, *Preliminary Report on the Eighth Census*, 1860, 169, 171, 185.

RAILROAD MILEAGE IN THE UNITED STATES, 1850 AND 1860

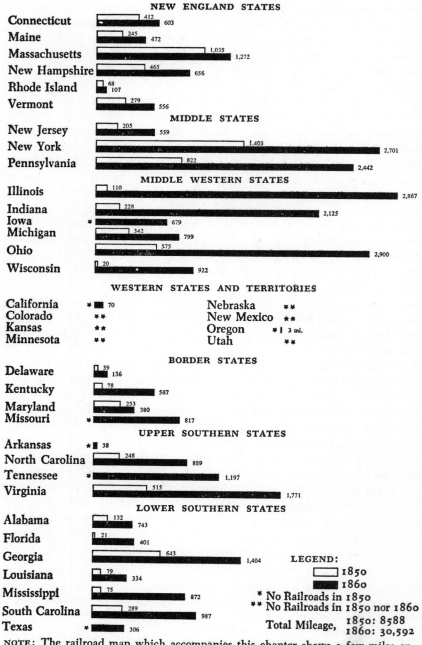

NEW ENGLAND STATES

Connecticut — 412 / 603
Maine — 245 / 472
Massachusetts — 1,035 / 1,272
New Hampshire — 465 / 656
Rhode Island — 68 / 107
Vermont — 279 / 556

MIDDLE STATES

New Jersey — 205 / 559
New York — 1,403 / 2,701
Pennsylvania — 822 / 2,442

MIDDLE WESTERN STATES

Illinois — 110 / 2,867
Indiana — 228 / 2,125
Iowa — * / 679
Michigan — 342 / 799
Ohio — 575 / 2,900
Wisconsin — 20 / 922

WESTERN STATES AND TERRITORIES

California — * 70
Colorado — **
Kansas — **
Minnesota — **
Nebraska — **
New Mexico — **
Oregon — * 3 mi.
Utah — **

BORDER STATES

Delaware — 39 / 136
Kentucky — 78 / 567
Maryland — 253 / 380
Missouri — * / 817

UPPER SOUTHERN STATES

Arkansas — * 38
North Carolina — 248 / 889
Tennessee — * / 1,197
Virginia — 515 / 1,771

LOWER SOUTHERN STATES

Alabama — 132 / 743
Florida — 21 / 401
Georgia — 643 / 1,404
Louisiana — 79 / 334
Mississippi — 75 / 872
South Carolina — 289 / 987
Texas — * / 306

LEGEND:
☐ 1850
■ 1860
* No Railroads in 1850
** No Railroads in 1850 nor 1860
Total Mileage, 1850: 8588
1860: 30,592

NOTE: The railroad map which accompanies this chapter shows a few miles operating in December 1850 which are omitted in the census and hence not shown on this chart.

Source: U.S. Census, 1860. "Miscellaneous," p. 333.

nomic life which was to go to the root of American philosophy. This was made easier by the fact that the basic maladjustments of the machine age had not developed. Production did not greatly outrun consumption; the laborer was not submerged by the machine; where abuses existed they were often unrealized or tolerated. Under these circumstances the fundamental tenets of the prevailing system of capitalist economy were hardly questioned except by a few doctrinaires and reformers.

In this technological and manufacturing development as well as in agricultural advance the railroad was playing a major part. While in 1850 there were only 8500 miles of railroad in the United States, the mileage in 1860 exceeded thirty thousand.[13] In the fifties over two thousand miles were built per year, construction being especially rapid in the Middle West and along those east-and-west lines which joined the nation's granary with its ports and hives of industry. New York and Philadelphia now displaced New Orleans as outlets of western trade; for a notable gap in prewar transportation was the lack of railroad construction in the South and the failure to connect the South with the upper Mississippi Valley. While in the Gulf states railroad mileage increased only from 287 miles to 2200 miles, the increase in the Northwest was from 1275 in 1850 to more than ten thousand in 1860. It is of interest to note the states in 1860 that were practically or wholly without railroads. Arkansas had only thirty-eight miles; Kentucky 569 miles (as compared with 2999 for Ohio); Minnesota none; Kansas none; Oregon three miles; California seventy miles.

This forward plunge of railroad building was impulsive and spasmodic rather than methodical. The mania of overbuilding brought competition, rate cutting, and depression in railroad securities, contributing largely to the panic of 1857. Accidents were frequent and travel was expensive and uncomfortable. Other difficulties arose from puritanical crusades against Sunday trains, struggles over the adoption of a standard gauge, annoying changes and long waits between trains, and dependence upon England for much of the technical equipment of the industry.

If one turns to shipping he finds in the fifties the golden age of the American merchant marine. In the whole period prior to the First World War American shipbuilding reached its peak in 1854–1855. During these two years over a million tons of ships were produced on American ways: never again till 1917 was that record equaled. As to sailing ships, their ultimate record for all time was reached in New England and New York in this decade. While in 1800 a vessel of three hundred tons was considered a sizable ship, the greatest of the Yankee clippers of the fifties were fifteen times as large (the *Great Republic* registering 4555 tons), while their mainmasts towered in the harbor skylines to a height of two

[13] *U. S. Census, 1860, "Statistics . . . ,"* 331. For slightly variant figures, see *Historical Statistics of the U. S.,* 200.

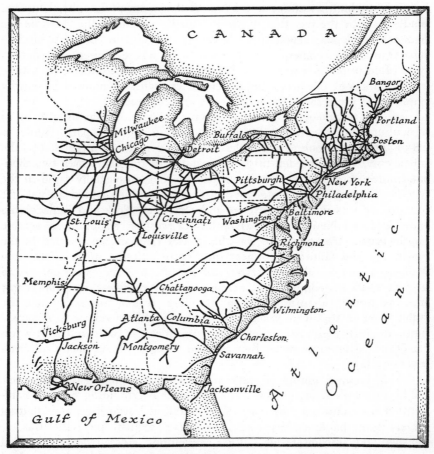

RAILROADS IN THE UNITED STATES, 1860

hundred feet. With their huge spread of canvas these square-rigged vessels were no less notable for speed than for size.

The day of the clipper began in 1845 when J. W. Griffith's *Rainbow* with its daring new design left the ways in the Smith and Dimon yards at New York and disappointed the croakers who had predicted that five minutes after launching it would be at the bottom of the East River. Fifteen years later the rapid decline of these sailing giants had begun. Though brief, the day of the clipper was one of record-breaking achievement in the maritime world. The *Rainbow* made the round trip from New York to China under wind power only between October and April. The *Sea Witch* flew over the fifteen thousand miles from New York to San Francisco in ninety-seven days; later the *Flying Cloud* (created by Donald

McKay, "Rembrandt of American builders") [14] did it in eighty-nine. The *Sovereign of the Seas* sailed from Honolulu to New York in eighty-two days; the *Lightning* on her voyage across the Atlantic in 1854 made a day's run of 436 miles, "the longest authenticated day's distance ever covered by a wind-propelled vessel," not exceeded even by steam until 1889. In eleven years following 1846 our shipping devoted to international trade increased from 943,000 to 2,268,000 tons. American ships were then carrying 70 per cent of our outbound cargoes, while our total tonnage of 5,299,000 nearly equaled that of Britain and her colonies, which amounted to 5,710,000.

Conditions of the time were favorable to American achievement in ship construction and operation. There was a long and honorable tradition of maritime greatness reaching back into colonial times. Large timbers were easily available. Raw materials generally were abundant. American shipwrights were unsurpassed; labor was efficient; owners and operators were closely associated with builders, being often united in the same person; foreign demand for American carriers was brisk. In these days Americans were producing "more ton-miles for a dollar" than any other nation. American shipping laws were favorable; foreign government reports admitted the superiority of American crews. Sailors were often college men; training in navigation was highly developed; American captains were often part owners and were on the whole better educated than those of England. America of that day was ship-minded; youths took avidly to seafaring careers; substantial citizens took pride in each new shipping triumph. Philip Hone, seeing an American packet ship launch on her maiden voyage, thought that John Bull would be "knocked in half" by "Yankee naval magnificence," and called to mind Tocqueville's prediction that "the Americans were born to rule the seas." [15] Though much has been said of the clipper, other types constituted the bulk of the nation's tonnage. "Ship for ship—clipper or ordinary merchantmen—the United States dominated the commerce of the world." [16]

Expansion in industry and transportation was naturally accompanied by expansion in American cities. While the country as a whole increased in population in the fifties by 35 per cent, and while rural sections increased 30 per cent, the cities showed an increase of 75 per cent. America's largest city in 1850 was New York with its population of 515,000. New York and Brooklyn together had 612,000; next came Philadelphia with 340,000; Baltimore was third with 169,000; Boston fourth with 136,000; Chicago twentieth with 29,000. The census of 1860 revealed enormous changes wrought in ten years: New York and Brooklyn now

[14] William Brown Meloney, *The Heritage of Tyre*, 68.
[15] *Diary of Philip Hone*, Sept. 16, 1843.
[16] Meloney, 89.

had 1,080,000 souls; Philadelphia 565,000; Baltimore 212,000; Boston 177,000; Cincinnati 161,000; St. Louis 160,000; and Chicago, having trebled its population, stood ninth with 109,000. Municipal improvements—street cars and "subterranean railways," pavements, sidewalks, water works, and sanitary systems—were actively pushed during the decade. It is true that New York was just emerging from the period when pigs wandered about on Broadway in full enjoyment of "life, liberty, and the pursuit of happiness"; [17] but the tempo of such emergence in New York and elsewhere was of breath-taking rapidity, and urban America was holding its head high in comparison with Europe.

Though wealth abounded in the fifties, it was inequitably distributed and much of it was insecurely grounded. The two factors that seem most striking in the business world of the time were prosperity that reached boom proportions and panic which broke in 1857, bringing paralysis to industry and misery to thousands. The business shock was both financial and industrial. James Buchanan attributed the malady entirely to our "vicious system of paper currency and bank credits, exciting the people to wild speculations and gambling in stocks"; [18] but the true explanation was found in a variety of interrelated factors such as undue expansion, excessive railroad building, speculative real estate booms, bubbles of business excitement resulting from gold discoveries, enormous loans, insecure banknotes, and rampant greed in the scramble for quick fortunes. In the one year 1857 liabilities in business failures in the United States amounted to $291,000,000.[19] It is significant that the failures in New York City and Brooklyn amounted to $135,000,000, showing how fully the metropolis had become the business and financial hub of the nation. In the South the failures amounted to only $26,000,000, of which amount 60 per cent belonged to the states of Louisiana, Missouri, and Maryland. These figures, however, must be read in the light of the small amount of industrial enterprise in the South; and they offer no measure of losses by thousands of Southern citizens owing to Northern failures.

The human aspects of the panic were seen in the struggles of bankrupt individuals with debts and foreclosures, in the forty thousand who were thrown out of work in New York City, in shivering crowds of city beggars, in violent hunger demonstrations, in decreased immigration, in the unrecorded misery that affected the working class, and in consequent labor unrest. The United States had in the fifties no national labor organization. Solidarity of feeling and comprehensive organization in the labor world were but little developed. The unionism of the period,

[17] *America in the 'Forties: The Letters of Ole Munch Raeder,* Trans. by G. J. Malmin, 78.

[18] Richardson, *Messages . . . of the Presidents,* V, 437.

[19] *Ann. Cyc., 1861,* 312. For purposes of comparison it may be noted that business failures in the country in 1859 involved liabilities of only $64,000,000.

an outgrowth of a movement dating chiefly from the presidency of Jackson, proceeded along local lines and by crafts; it did not embrace the great army of unskilled workers. Yet some of the earmarks of modern labor turbulence were evident in the insistence upon collective bargaining, in strikes and walkouts, in capitalists' counter organizations, in employers' appeals to the courts, in labor parades, in the use of troops to suppress labor opposition, and in the dismissal of a New England pastor for showing sympathy with strikers.

3

On the motives and tendencies manifest in the field of literature adequate comment is impossible within the space limitations of the present volume. The forties and fifties were the golden age of romanticism. Voices in literature were positive and vibrant; spirits were buoyant; production was prolific. Cynical sophistication was conspicuously lacking; and sentimental moralizing classics of the Longfellow type were the characteristic output of the time. Not a few of the prominent writers were women; as to "lesser authoresses and poetesses . . . they [were] legion." The vast number were sparrows, said Miss Bremer, with only here and there a thrush but never the full inspiration of the nightingale.[1]

The chief Southern writer, Edgar Allan Poe, died just before the decade opened (1849), but his gloomy Gothic style continued to be imitated by scores of later writers. The Middle States were also losing literary leadership. One of the most important figures in the history of the American novel, James Fenimore Cooper, whose ponderous triteness was as much a national characteristic as his fondness for authentic American settings, died in 1851. The supreme writer of the older school, Washington Irving, lived nearly through the decade (until November 28, 1859), but, unfortunate in his choice of themes, he had turned from those Knickerbocker chronicles and legendary sketches which constituted his forte to such heavy tasks as the two-volume life of Goldsmith and the monumental life of George Washington in five volumes. With the passing of Irving and Cooper, hegemony was shifting to Concord, Beacon Street, and Cambridge; and the genteel sway of New England immortals had by the close of the fifties reached its most impressive stage.

By 1860 Longfellow had produced his best-known poems and had obtained fame as a lovable lecturer in the Smith professorship of modern languages at Harvard. James Russell Lowell had served as first editor of the *Atlantic Monthly* (established in 1857), had produced *The Vision of Sir Launfal, The Biglow Papers,* and many other poems, and was Longfellow's successor in the Harvard chair. Dr. Oliver Wendell Holmes,

[1] *America of the Fifties: Letters of Fredrika Bremer,* 78.

witty, gently satirical, guiltless of the Puritan's dour seriousness, had achieved notably in both medicine and literature, had assisted Lowell in "making" the *Atlantic,* and had given to the world the Autocrat, the Professor, and enough lyrics to make him "poet laureate" of Boston. Emerson, approaching sixty, had issued the first and second series of his *Essays* and had produced the greatest of his lectures. His Concord neighbor Hawthorne, one of the finest of America's creative spirits, still lived, but his work was nearly finished. In 1850 had appeared *The Scarlet Letter;* in 1860 *The Marble Faun;* and in intervening years *The House of the Seven Gables, The Blithedale Romance,* and *Tanglewood Tales.* He was to live only till 1864, and in those few remaining years he was to be hastened to the grave by the black intolerance of civil war, the dishonoring of his political party, and the discrediting of his bosom friend, Franklin Pierce. Most original of the Concord group, Henry Thoreau had nearly completed in the Walden groves his fearless quest for the verities of life. To the individualistic nonconformity of the transcendentalists he had given a bold economic and spiritual interpretation; and for the restless urge to acquire riches he had substituted the simplest of lives in a cabin. Perhaps more than any other writer of his age he adopted a manner of living in accord with his teaching. In particular he made a daily application of Christian principles which was startling. Almost the equal of Lowell and Holmes in his early service to the *Atlantic,* John Greenleaf Whittier, Quaker bard and abolitionist poet, had by 1860 produced a whole literature of antislavery sermons in verse, had blazoned the craftsman's virtues in *Songs of Labor,* and, in the lines of *Parson Avery* and *Skipper Ireson,* had turned some of the neatest phrases of American balladry.

The journalism of the time was highly developed. Whether judged by the standard of literary merit, of personal force and picturesqueness, or of capitalistic enterprise, the editor-proprietors of the fifties were men of mark. By 1859 William Cullen Bryant had completed three remarkable decades as editor of the New York *Evening Post* and was destined to hold this position of eminence for nearly two decades more. Under his leadership, powerfully aided by the work of Parke Godwin, the *Post* grew steadily not alone as a daily newspaper of high reportorial and editorial tone, but even more as a medium of liberal thought. Of quite different breed than Bryant was James Gordon Bennett the elder (1795–1872), one of the boldest and coarsest spirits in American journalistic annals. Denounced by a Whig enthusiast as an "impudent disturber of the public peace," [2] Bennett lashed out savagely against reformers and scoffed at causes and crusades. Sparing neither pains nor expense in his ruthless search for news, he made his New York *Herald* one of the most widely read of the cheap dailies. With no scruples against the exploitation of

---

[2] *Diary of Philip Hone,* Feb. 14, 1842.

scandal he conducted his sensational sheet somewhat along the lines of the "yellow journal" of a later day.

Bennett's chief rival, Horace Greeley, had by 1860 made the *Tribune* a national institution. Animated by enthusiasms that tended toward fanaticism, and marred by personal eccentricities that laid him open to ridicule, this Yankee printer had risen from stark poverty to influence and power; and, as supporter of the Whig and later the Republican party, had demonstrated in areas widely distant from his sanctum the tremendous force of political journalism. With defects of character that were to grow with the years, he showed the finer idealism of his ardent nature in efforts to improve the workingman's lot, in generous support of movements for popular education, and in championship of progressive social movements generally. Charles A. Dana, Greeley's able teammate on the *Tribune,* George Jones and Henry J. Raymond of the *Times,* Thurlow Weed, political boss in New York and proprietor of the Albany *Evening Journal,* Samuel Bowles of the *Springfield Republican,* Joseph Medill of the Chicago *Tribune,* Murat Halstead of the Cincinnati *Commercial,* Thomas Ritchie of the Richmond *Whig,* Robert Barnwell Rhett of the Charleston *Mercury,* George W. Kendall of the New Orleans *Picayune,* and George D. Prentice of the Louisville *Journal* were but a few of the many other prominent journalists of this age, when newspapers were more than commercialized corporations and when the personality of the editor-proprietor was as essential as the very name of the paper.

4

In American thought and philosophy modern tendencies were struggling with orthodoxy, and conspicuous thinkers were notable for their liberal and optimistic humanitarianism. It was a day of intellectual renascence whose most memorable element was the flowering of transcendentalism. From Emerson's serene study at Concord there issued, in exalted stanzas that were essays and in essays that were poetry, a notable body of writings that scorned system but, as Carlyle said, stretched "far beyond all systems." Having broken with orthodoxy by resigning his pastorate in Boston because he could not conceal disbelief in traditional creeds, Emerson's emancipated spirit soared through a career that was spared the bitterness of most idealists. It was given to him to prove that a philosopher could reach the heights in intellectual adventuring and yet keep in tune with his times. His books were avidly read in America and abroad; distinguished men and women found their way to his home; and in language "chaste, strong and vigorous" [1] he unfolded to admiring lecture audiences his philosophy of confident individualism. The universal soul, one mind

---

[1] *Diary of O. H. Browning* (Ill. Hist. Colls., XX), I, 90.

common to all revealing itself in each individual's reaction, was his theme. Self-reliance, readiness to believe one's own thought, to watch that gleam that flashes across the mind, he counted real genius. To realize the divine in every man, to be a nonconformist, with virtues that were more than penances, to discard usages that signified slavery to sect or party, was his religion. Consistency he called the hobgoblin of little minds. To be great, he said, is to be misunderstood. Scorning an armchair philosophy he warned that our culture must not omit the heroic. With perfect urbanity to dare the gibbet and the mob, to have contempt for safety and be negligent of life and danger, was the sterner motif of his teaching.[2] Though keeping somewhat aloof from extravagant social experimentation he held an open mind toward each new crusade and became the guiding genius not only of transcendental thinking (which he modestly disavowed) but also of solid humanitarian reform. Trained in moral self-discipline, scion of ministerial families, he was the supreme product of Puritanism; but in his person the Puritan soul revealed itself in spiritual strength and insight rather than in self-righteous conformity. To know the best in New England character it must be remembered that there were many lesser Emersons and that he stands in American cultural history not only as philosopher and guide but as sample of a type. Had it been otherwise there could never have been so ready a welcome for his writings.

In the field of pure science the United States could point to the work of Asa Gray in botany, of Joseph Henry in physics, of Joseph LeConte in geology, of Matthew Fontaine Maury in oceanography, of James Dwight Dana in mineralogy, and of Louis Agassiz in natural history and geology. Savants in America were abreast of the latest developments in scholarship; often the literary men were half-scientists; and Darwin's *Origin of Species* (1859), so disturbing to those who staked their religious faith on a matter-of-fact misinterpretation of the Biblical story of creation, found a ready sale which caused the first American edition to be quickly exhausted.

In their hunger for mental stimulus Americans of the time eagerly formed their lecture programs and lyceum bureaus. Reaching remarkable proportions in the fifties the lecture movement satisfied the American craving for amusement, supplied a well-nigh universal demand for intellectual improvement, and catered to the American wish to gaze upon celebrities in the flesh. Though mere notoriety would draw a crowd, and though one of the most famous of professional lecturers (John B. Gough) was described as an "evangelical comedian" whose contortions were tolerated for the sake of his drollery;[3] the performances of such figures as Emerson, Parke Godwin, Thoreau, Thackeray, Fanny Kemble [Butler], the Shakespearean reader, and George William Curtis, were of distin-

[2] Paraphrased from the *Essays, passim.*
[3] T. W. Higginson in *Macmillan's Magazine*, XVIII, 54.

guished excellence. The American talent for organization expressed itself in lecture chains under central management, with connections reaching far into the pioneer West. Popular interest in things of the mind found expression not only in attendance at lectures but in numerous local literary societies, in organizations for historical or philosophical study, and in a lively sale for books. Public libraries were few; [4] but the Astor Library in New York illustrated the use of private fortunes for the endowment of institutions intended to raise the general intellectual level.

In the field of education, especially popular extension of education by government support, the period witnessed steady advance. The educational *credo* of America was epitomized by an English traveler in the fifties under the following four heads:

1st. That a general diffusion of education is essential to the success of republican institutions.

2nd. That it is the duty of the State governments to insist on provision being made for it.

3rd. That all sectarian teaching must be excluded in national seminaries [i.e., where education by government support is involved].

4th. That the Christian sects, if consistent and conscientious, should attend to the religious tuition of all the members of the community, both young and old. [5]

Though there were some dissenters, general assent was given to the concepts of Horace Mann, to whom the common school was an essential of democratic society not alone for its enlightenment of citizens but also for its tendency to obliterate class distinctions. Through the work of the state board of education of which he was president he had introduced revolutionary changes into the common school system of Massachusetts, placing that commonwealth in the forefront in that phase of educational development and producing widespread results by emulation in other states. By a movement started through his influence and pushed against the opposition of pedagogues, sectarians, and social conservatives, the United States advanced to the point where by 1860 its citizens were deemed "the most generally educated and intelligent people on the earth." [6] The extent of public school enterprise may be measured by the fact that in 1852 there were 862,000 children attending common schools in New York; 492,000 in Pennsylvania; 90,000 in Vermont; 152,000 in New Jersey; and 199,000 in Massachusetts. [7] The South, a relatively poorer region with a scattered population and bad roads, lagged behind the rest

[4] In 1860 the census takers discovered only sixty-five librarians in the whole country. *U. S. Census, 1860,* "Population," 666–667.

[5] William Edward Baxter, *America and the Americans,* 167–168.

[6] Statement by Bishop Fraser, cited in Cole, *Irrepressible Conflict,* 241.

[7] Baxter, *America and the Americans,* 160.

of the country, but it too was making enormous educational progress in the 1850's. North Carolina, under the prodding of Calvin J. Wiley, the first superintendent of education, established 3000 schools which enjoyed an annual revenue of $279,000; Alabama spent $474,000 in 1856 for the education of 90,000 students.[8]

Other significant educational tendencies paralleled the common school development. City high schools, emphasizing Latin and mathematics and conceived as fitting schools for the college or university, rapidly increased in numbers till in 1860 Massachusetts had seventy-eight; New York forty-one; and Ohio forty-eight.[9] In the South the place of the high school was taken by the secondary schools known as academies. "In 1850 there were 3000 academies in the South; a state as new as Arkansas had 90 such institutions." [10] All over the nation institutions for teacher training were considerably extended. In all sections of the country, too, there was an increasing number of colleges. Ohio in 1861 had seventeen that were to be permanent; Pennsylvania sixteen; New York fifteen; Illinois twelve; and the United States as a whole 182. In addition, there were many others that have not survived the years. Religious ascendancy in the college world was at a high stage. Yale was a "little temple" with "prayer and praise . . . the delight . . . of the students"; atheism was in retreat; and the "forces of irreligion, of rationalism, and of deistic thought were effectually checked on a hundred fronts." [11] Of the permanent denominational colleges founded before the Civil War the Presbyterians had the greatest number (forty-nine), having captured various institutions (e.g., Illinois College) launched under Congregational leadership. Next came the Methodists with thirty-four; the Baptists with twenty-five; the Congregationalists with twenty-one; the Catholics with fourteen; the Episcopalians with eleven. No other sect had more than six destined for permanency.

Separation of church and state having been worked out in the older states after famous struggles, the principle of such separation was fixed by constitutional provision in the twenty-one new states admitted before the Civil War, with the double result that state universities were now non-sectarian, while each denomination felt that it must take care of the training of its ministers and also of both the religious and secular education of its college youth. Twenty-one state universities had been established (in twenty of the thirty-four states) prior to the Civil War; some of the more notable being those of Georgia (1785), North Carolina (1789), Virginia (1819), Indiana (1828), Michigan (1837), Mis-

---

[8] Francis B. Simkins, *A History of the South*, 176.
[9] H. J. Carman, *Soc. and Econ. Hist. of the U. S.*, II, 377.
[10] Simkins, 171.
[11] D. G. Tewksbury, *The Founding of American Colleges and Universities Before the Civil War*, 67.

souri (1839), and Wisconsin (1848). To aid this movement Federal land grants had been voted by Congress, Tennessee receiving 100,000 acres, Wisconsin 92,000, Missouri 46,000, and most of the other states the same amount as Missouri. The content of college education is suggested by the courses which John Hay took at Brown University between 1855 and 1858, which consisted of chemistry, mathematics, rhetoric, physics, Latin, Greek, French, German, moral philosophy, declamation, history, intellectual philosophy, and political economy. Another phase of college life in a democracy was illustrated by the "horror . . . of the members of rival fraternities when they saw Hay come into chapel . . . wearing the *Shield* with the . . . letters $\theta\Delta X$, emblazoned on its sable field." [12]

5

It was an age when women were preferred as angels rather than amazons, home-makers rather than careerists; yet considerable advance was being made in the direction of woman's rights. Early aspects of feminism in America are usually associated with a famous incident at the World's Anti-Slavery Conference in London in 1840 when Lucretia Mott and Elizabeth Cady Stanton, duly chosen American delegates, were denied participation though permitted to observe and listen behind a screen in the gallery. In protest against this rebuff William Lloyd Garrison declined to speak as scheduled, but in a "beautiful gesture" took his place beside his sisters in the cause. In July of 1848 under the promotion of Mrs. Mott and Mrs. Stanton there was held at Seneca Falls the notable convention which inaugurated the woman's rights movement in the United States. In many fields women were advancing toward equality with men. Already, in strong contrast to England and the continent, the profession of elementary teaching was becoming a feminine affair. Mrs. Antoinette Brown Blackwell, educated at Oberlin, was preaching at South Butler, New York. Elizabeth Blackwell, having tried to practice medicine in New York City, was doing needful work through the New York Infirmary and College for Women. Margaret Fuller, Dorothea Dix, Fanny Wright, and many others were demonstrating the aptitude of women in the fields of literature and social reform. Codes were being liberalized to give women fuller legal rights. James Silk Buckingham, eminent British traveler, found women in America "always equal to the men, and often superior to them, in the extent of their reading and the shrewdness of their observations." [1] Slender beginnings were made in woman suffrage by the action of Kentucky in giving widow-mothers a limited vote in school elections. Women's colleges of the modern type were just beginning to

---

[12] W. R. Thayer, *Life and Letters of John Hay*, I, 35, 38–39.

[1] Allan Nevins, *American Social History as Recorded by British Travellers*, 313.

take the place of the older "female academies" and finishing schools; but the movement had only been launched. Mount Holyoke was founded in 1837; but other famous women's colleges of the North belonged to a later time: Vassar was founded in 1861; Radcliffe in 1879; Smith in 1871; Wells in 1868; Barnard in 1889; Bryn Mawr in 1880. In the South "Elizabeth Female Academy, a Methodist school at Old Washington in Mississippi, was chartered as a college in 1819, and in 1836 the Georgia Female College (now Wesleyan College) was authorized to give degrees." [2]

Toward the more striking forms of feminism, sentiment was unfavorable. Male leaders often refused to speak on the same platform with women; Bennett of the New York *Herald* insisted that women's votes should be polled only at the tea table; and more than a half-century was to elapse before equality at the polls was to be made nation-wide.

Reformers found many sore spots in the social body; and in its humanitarian striving the period was marked by the variety and intensity of its "movements." In temperance and liquor control, in the days before the W.C.T.U. and the National Prohibition party, the assault upon the demon rum was conducted by local temperance societies, campaigns of public education through lecturers and tracts, and prohibitory or licensing laws passed in the states. In 1851 Maine enacted state prohibition of the liquor traffic, and temperance forces soon succeeded in obtaining laws for some type of liquor control or prohibition in Vermont, New Hampshire, Rhode Island, Connecticut, New York, Illinois, Indiana, Michigan, Iowa, Wisconsin, Delaware, and Tennessee, though in some cases (e.g., in Illinois and Indiana) the experiment was abandoned soon after it was launched. This aspect of the movement may be largely traced to the vigorous efforts of Neal Dow, "father of the Maine law" and pioneer advocate of legislative prohibition. Urged by temperance songs and novels, by the popular agitation of such a lecturer as John B. Gough, and by the work of a crusading band of reformed drunkards known as the "Washingtonians," Americans of the period were becoming increasingly conscious of the physiological and social evils of drink. One feature of the crusade was the struggle for abolition of "grog and cat" from the navy of the United States. The cat-o'-nine-tails was abolished in the fifties; but spirits remained a part of the sailor's ration till the next decade.

There was alarm over lax Sunday observance, among foreign-born groups especially; and religious leaders were showing militant opposition to the activity of saloons and places of questionable amusement on the Sabbath day. One of the most persistent crusades was the movement led by Dorothea Dix for better treatment of the indigent insane by the removal of such unfortunates from prisons and for their special treatment in institutions provided for the purpose. The efforts of Miss Dix brought

[2] Simkins, 168.

success in the form of state insane asylums; but when in 1854 she procured the passage by Congress of a national law granting ten million acres of public land to the states for this purpose, thus offering a cause in which land speculators and philanthropists found a "mutual opportunity," [3] the bill met defeat through the veto of President Pierce, who braved humanitarian opposition in his refusal to make "the Federal Government the great almoner of public charity throughout the United States."

For many another crusade there was a Dorothea Dix or a Neal Dow. Nor were these movements always separate and distinct. The causes of the time beat often in the same breast. Charles Stuart, active in the antislavery movement, wrote to Theodore Dwight Weld in 1831: "Let me hear from you—about you—about Finney—Revivals—Temp[erance] 'Joe'—The Negroes—The missionaries and Indians in Georgia—The Colonization Society—The free coloured people—your family—Oneida Academy etc. . . ." [4] In prison reform, in charitable organization, in the cleaning up of tenements, in subscriptions to relieve foreign distress, in the efforts of S. G. Howe for relief of the blind, in societies for international peace, in utopian experiments such as Brook Farm and the Amana community in Iowa, the impulse to remake human society and stamp out social evils was finding increasing expression.

6

Though all these humanitarian crusades flourished chiefly in the wealthier and more populous Northern states, only one of these reform drives was confined to a single section, the antislavery movement. It had not always been so. In the early days of the republic George Washington, Thomas Jefferson, and Patrick Henry had made known their opposition to Negro slavery, and many other Southerners had looked toward the gradual eradication of the "peculiar institution." Antislavery activities in the first decades of the nineteenth century had known no sectional lines. The American Colonization Society, which sought to expatriate free Negroes to Africa, "drew its support from all sections of the country and from all classes of men—slaveholders and nonslaveholders, proslavery and antislavery advocates." [1] But by the 1830's the Southern states had come to believe that slavery was the necessary basis of their section's economy and, what is even more important, that it was the only way in which the allegedly inferior Negro race could be kept in subordination.

At the same time an important transformation was occurring in

---

[3] R. F. Nichols, *Franklin Pierce*, 349.

[4] Gilbert H. Barnes and Dwight L. Dumond, eds., *Letters of Theodore Dwight Weld, Angelina Grimké Weld, and Sarah Grimké, 1822–1844*, I, 49.

[1] Dwight L. Dumond, *Antislavery Origins of the Civil War*, 5.

Northern antislavery opinion. It is customary to date abolitionism (by which is meant the demand for the immediate, uncompensated emancipation of all slaves) from 1831, when William Lloyd Garrison founded his *Liberator* in Boston, but in fact Garrison's outbursts were only a part of a new and increasingly strident Northern attack upon the South's "peculiar institution" as a relic of barbarism and a species of sin. In discussing the rise of abolitionism many non-Garrisonian factors, especially evident in New York, Ohio, and the West generally, must be brought into the picture, such as the evangelistic labors of C. G. Finney, the organizing efforts and financial contributions of Arthur and Lewis Tappan, the reverberating effects of a notable debate among the students at Lane seminary (Cincinnati, 1834), the withdrawal of zealous antislavery students from Lane and their removal to Oberlin College, and the widespread antislavery agitation conducted by Theodore Dwight Weld. Garrison was primarily a free-lance agitator-journalist who offended influential leaders such as Lyman Beecher and who did not even retain the undivided support of New England abolitionists, who were (to mention only one factor) offended by his theological heresies and hostility to churches. He had no program except that his program was agitation. Methods of emancipation did not concern him. Indeed he realized that a discussion of methods of eradicating slavery, bringing into view social realities and revealing differences of opinion, would take the edge off his crusade. He denounced colonization, opposed compensation of slaveholders, and demanded (without any statement of how it should be done) that his goal of universal emancipation be reached immediately.

By 1833 Arthur Tappan and a vigorous group known as the "New York Committee" (Tappan's associates in antislavery organization) had laid plans for a national society. At this point Garrison, returning in a blaze of reflected glory from England where he was hailed as the apostle of American abolitionism, stole Tappan's thunder and promoted a premature and thinly attended meeting at Philadelphia at which there was launched the American Anti-Slavery Society, in which he was thenceforth to play such an important role. The fact that the actual organizing and financing of the antislavery crusade was the work of Finney, the Tappans, Weld, and their allies rather than that of Garrison has caused some recent scholars to minimize the importance of the New England wing of the abolition movement, but it should not be forgotten that Garrison, who was for twenty-two terms president of the American Anti-Slavery Society, was surely its most eloquent voice. In fact, in a certain sense he was a detriment to the cause he so devotedly served, for the extremism of his editorials and the vitriol of his attacks doubtless alienated many moderates in the North and certainly antagonized the slaveholders of the South.

The scorn of social disapproval North and South served to brand the abolitionists as a distrusted and persecuted sect. A mob in Boston in

1835 handled Garrison so roughly that he was put in jail as a protection. J. G. Birney, abolitionist of Alabama and later of Danville, Kentucky, was so menaced by opposition that he removed to the vicinity of Cincinnati, where in 1836 he founded the *Philanthropist*. Another case of exile from the South was that of the Grimké sisters, Angelina and Sarah. Having shifted from Episcopalian beginnings in her native Charleston, South Carolina, to Philadelphia and to Quakerism, Angelina published in 1836 a vigorous antislavery pamphlet. For so doing she faced the hazard of imprisonment if she should return to the city of her birth. In Alton, Illinois, in 1837 Elijah P. Lovejoy was murdered while defending his abolitionist printing establishment against aroused citizens who believed that his activity endangered the peace of the town and that he had not observed a pledge to discontinue publication. In August of 1845 a committee of citizens in Lexington, Kentucky, delivered to Cassius M. Clay, one of the most pugnacious abolitionists of his time, an ultimatum that he "discontinue the publication of . . . *The True American,* as . . . dangerous to the peace of our community. . . ." Defiantly refusing, Clay mounted two brass cannon to guard his doors, armed his little band of friends with rifles and shotguns, and prepared for battle. The Lexingtonians, however, avoiding blood and violence, held a dignified meeting and appointed a committee of sixty law-abiding men who quietly and with a sense of doing a painful duty dismantled the press and equipment of Clay's paper and packed it to the station for exportation from the state.[2]

It is important to distinguish degrees and groups among antislavery men, for they were not all stamped with the same die. There were the root-and-branch radical abolitionists of the Garrison type, listening to no compromise, using vituperative language, and demanding immediate action. Wendell Phillips, Gerrit Smith, T. W. Higginson, and Theodore Parker belonged to this school. They constituted a very small group when compared to the population of the Northern states; and there is no instance prior to the Civil War of an abolitionist of this type being appointed to a post in the President's cabinet or to any national position of comparable importance. It is also true that very few extreme abolitionists had positions of importance in any Northern state. The slender numerical strength of the Garrisonians is further suggested by the fact that the circulation of the *Liberator* at no time exceeded three thousand. There were men of pronounced antislavery views who were not technically abolitionists, such as Horace Mann. There were antislavery statesmen such as Salmon P. Chase and Charles Francis Adams, who avoided abolitionist excess while working through the Free Soil party to oppose the nationalization of slavery and restrict its spread. Of still different degree were men of moderate antislavery views—men such as Abraham Lincoln—who broke

---

[2] W. H. Townsend, *Lincoln and His Wife's Home Town,* 129–135.

openly with abolitionists and refused cooperation with Free-Soilers. Finally, there were Northerners such as Orville H. Browning of Illinois who were antislavery and yet whose activity against the institution was even milder. Browning, for instance, drew up a resolution in the Illinois senate condemning abolitionists on the ground that their efforts defeated the cause of gradual emancipation; yet he championed the legal rights of the slave, opposed the fugitive slave act, and argued for the exclusion of slavery from the territories.

There were also degrees among those of the North who opposed anti-slavery agitation. Their points of view ranged from that of Edward Everett (secretary of state, minister to Great Britain, president of Harvard), who maintained a merely colorless and negative attitude, being careful to avoid offending the South and keeping a dignified aloofness from this most troublesome question of the day, to that of Stephen A. Douglas, who sought in the arena of politics a compromise that would satisfy both North and South, or of James Buchanan or Franklin Pierce, who went farther than Douglas by becoming Northern allies of slaveholders.

Differences on the race question were reflected in the treatment of Negroes in the North. In 1860 this element numbered approximately 240,000 in the states north of the Mason and Dixon line, and there were many variations in the laws and practices concerning them. In Illinois fines were levied upon Negroes entering the state; and black men "seeking homes on the prairies . . . were put upon the block." [3] Elsewhere opportunities were open to them as barbers, waiters, and servants; and a beginning had been made in Negro schools and colleges, as in the schools of the New York Manumission Society, special Negro schools organized as part of the systems of public instruction in some states, and here and there a Negro college such as Wilberforce University, Xenia, Ohio, or Avery College, established by Charles Avery with a fund of $300,000 in Pittsburgh in 1849. The "caste system," however, with its neglect of Negro education by public authorities, was the rule; though an exception was found in Massachusetts, where in 1855 a law was passed owing to the agitation of such men as Charles Sumner and Wendell Phillips which opened the public schools of the state without distinction of race. Though there was much prejudice against the Negro in the North with many restrictions upon his lot, yet in the years before the Civil War a number of them attained prominence. Dr. James McCune Smith, with a medical degree from the University of Glasgow, practiced in New York City. William C. Nell and William Wells Brown were writers of considerable distinction. Negro newspapers such as *Freedom's Journal* and *The Colored American* revealed not only the ability of Negro leaders in journalism but also the fact that a considerable number of Negroes were able to read.

---

[3] Cole, *Irrepressible Conflict*, 264.

Freedom's Journal was established in 1827 by John B. Russwurm, graduate of Bowdoin, the first Negro to obtain a degree from an American college. Negro ministers were numerous, Alexander Crummell and Henry H. Garnett being among the best known. As a publicist and lecturer Frederick Douglass had in this period a reputation which made him the most distinguished Negro of his generation.

In its religious aspects the abolition movement had wide ramifications. The subject inevitably found its way into meetings of official church bodies, thus putting a stamp upon religious denominations as a whole. In England antislavery enthusiasm among evangelical sects had presented a striking contrast to the comparative indifference of the Episcopal Church. The established church had shown a friendliness to slavery interests which harmonized with its traditional support of the existing social and economic régime of which it was the beneficiary. Anglican bishops resisted abolitionist reform, which found ready acceptance in dissenting circles. In parliamentary struggles over the slavery question an analysis of the votes by shires shows that, where dissent was weakest, abolition votes were fewest.[4] For America no easy generalization fits the case as to the relation of the churches to abolitionism. In the South the religious defense of slavery was vigorous and widespread. What is not so generally recognized, however, is that slavery "found many defenders . . . [in the North] particularly in the colleges and the churches." [5] To a large extent antislavery agitation in the North was either an extra-church movement, or, as in the case of Weld and Finney, it was more associated with evangelism and a variety of propagandist efforts than with regular and normal church activity. Furthermore, the undoubted religious emphasis of Weld and Finney does not mean that they captured the churches. There were notable defenses of slavery written by Northern religious writers, while the antislavery resolutions passed in church assemblies tended often to be perfunctory or lukewarm.

An analysis of abolitionist leadership shows "a heavy Congregational-Presbyterian and Quaker preponderance." Among the leaders there were "many Methodists, some Baptists, but very few Unitarians, Episcopalians, or Catholics." [6] Not all abolitionist spokesmen belonged to any organized religious group; in Garrison's case his antagonism toward the churches was conspicuous and well known. Probably no other sect was so unanimous in its support of abolitionism as the Quakers, but, torn between their hostility to slavery and their traditional preference for peaceful rather than violent reform, they did not produce the principal leaders of the movement.

In the case of the Baptists, Methodists, and Presbyterians their general

---

[4] Adolf Lotz, *Sklaverei, Staatskirche und Freikirche* (Leipzig, 1929).

[5] Adelaide A. Lyons, "Religious Defense of Slavery in the North," *Historical Papers,* Trinity College Hist. Soc., Durham, N. C., 1919, p. 5.

[6] David Donald, *Lincoln Reconsidered,* 29.

distribution North and South presented a factor of great difficulty when-ever the slavery question came up in national gatherings. When in 1844 the general conference of the Methodist Church passed a resolution re-questing Bishop James O. Andrew of Georgia to desist from duties as bishop so long as he remained a slaveowner, the result was the formation of a Southern general conference which effected the complete separation of Southern and Northern Methodists. In the same year there was formed a "Southern Baptist Convention" because of differences with Northern brethren who opposed the appointment of missionaries who held slaves. That slavery should have been powerfully supported by the churches in the South should cause no surprise. The church exerted its spiritual leadership within the social order, not by advocating its overthrow. To contend for abolition in the South was to demand a specific concrete reform at home, with social consequences that were deemed revolutionary. To do so in Northern church circles might arouse opposition at home among those who deprecated abolition as a disturbing factor; but it was also true that antislavery preaching did not threaten to undermine the very basis of the Northern social and economic order.

7

In modes and styles America was in the spread-eagle age. A fashionable woman's dress in the fifties, following the Paris vogue via the Godey fashion plate, was an amazing combination of whalebone, steel, and crinoline, while the frippery of male attire was hardly less extravagant. Oratory was of the grandiloquent type. Sermons were long and high-flown. Architecture was departing from the chasteness of colonial and Georgian models to assume the resplendent grandeur characteristic of a romantic age. River steamers were floating palaces of elaborate filigree and glittering chande-liers. Historiography, glorifying the nation's past after the manner of George Bancroft, overstated American military achievement, catered to national boastfulness, and made overweening pride synonymous with patriotism. Music, art, poetry, and drama dripped with sentiment, not all of which has perished, for some of it bore the quality of genius. Taking inspiration from Negro spirituals and using an atlas to suggest an obscure Florida stream he had never heard of, Stephen Foster produced in 1851 the immortal "Swanee River," to be followed by "Massa's in the Cold, Cold Ground" and "My Old Kentucky Home."

America had no titles of nobility, yet throughout the older sections of the country swelling fortunes were creating an aristocracy of wealth, and the "better sort" were keenly aware of class distinctions. Though most Southern political and economic leaders were self-made men, the planta-tion owners continued to think of themselves as the descendants of the Cavaliers. Similarly in the Northeast, Boston Brahmins tended to forget that they were in most cases recently descended from yeomen and mechanics and affected social superiority. The West found its norms in the East but applied them with a difference: the "aristocracy of Keokuk" was both less pretentious and less exclusive than that of Charleston or New York. But the real flowering of the moneyed "aristocracy" was to come after the Civil War; as yet the nation was predominantly and comfortably middle-class. Democratic rights for all and opportunity for the lowliest were the themes of orators: these were at least the avowed ideals of the country. Simplicity of manners might impress some observers as a type of vulgarity; but to the Norwegian scholar Munch Raeder it appeared "in a form that is both venerable and noble, as befits a republic which claims to have its roots in the virtues of its citizens." [1]

It is true that American democracy in the raw was often a painful spectacle. English consuls in our cities found the rule of the people "utterly shocking," and the main impression which they recorded was "one of general lawlessness. . . ." [2] Having witnessed a "gang of . . . Loco-foco ruffians" parading the streets with clubs, Philip Hone concluded that universal suffrage would "not do for large communities." [3] The distinguished legal commentator Chancellor James Kent agreed with him and wrote that "universal suffrage and a licentious press are incompatible with government and security to property. . . ." [4] So absorbed were Americans in politics that business was likely to be suspended on election day; but their interest was in party success rather than in the purity of political principles. Nor were party violence and ribaldry confined to street ruffians. Discussion in Congress might lead to dignified duels, but they were as likely to result in a disgraceful mêlée among the grave and reverend.

Though seeing but fragments of Yankeedom, foreign travelers left their records of American society. To their detached eyes Americans seemed worshipers of the dollar. "How many dollars is a man worth?" was a common question. The excitability of Americans, their unbounded boastfulness, their frank hospitality, inquisitiveness, and love of novelty, were matters of comment. The habit of galloping at meals was noted. The American type was not of the healthiest: hollow chests and sallow cheeks showed too often the effects of bad cooking, hasty eating, poor diet, and lack of exercise. Morals were in general high; woman was exalted as lawgiver in matters of society and home; blue laws and puritanical restrictions were often irksome to the European. Yet cities had their gamblers and prostitutes, and metropolitan politicians collected filthy money for the protection of vice. When a foreigner of great name arrived—a Kossuth or a Dickens—Americans over-

[1] Raeder, *op. cit.*, 80.
[2] Laura A. White, "The United States in the 1850's as Seen by British Consuls," *M.V.H.R.*, XIX, 522.
[3] *Diary*, Nov. 3–4, 1840.
[4] Quoted in V. L. Parrington, *The Romantic Revolution in America*, 199.

whelmed the visitor with extravagant welcome. In the case of Dickens the Boz ball, the "tallest compliment ever paid to a little man," [5] was an "agony" of ornaments, waltzes, tableaus, and dining multitudes. When Dickens later wrote in *Martin Chuzzlewit* of "That republic . . . foul to the eye" it seemed to Philip Hone that we Americans "made fools of ourselves to do him honour." [6]

Yet other visitors to our shores were more friendly. Fredrika Bremer was especially kindly in her mirroring of the American scene in the fifties. She considered the "best men and women" in the United States distinguished by intelligence and kindness. To her a Yankee was a go-ahead, all-conquering young American who shrank from nothing and was stopped by no discouragement, an American forever building and starting afresh, trying many professions, confident of himself, lord of the earth, fraternal, and full of unbounded faith in his country.[7]

[5] *Diary of Philip Hone,* Feb. 15, 1842.
[6] *Ibid.,* Oct. 12, 1843.
[7] Paraphrased from Bremer, *op. cit.,* 92–94.

CHAPTER 2

The Old South

I

THE AMERICAN SOUTH of the ante-bellum period presented a spectacle of immense variety. Its climate ranged from semi-tropical areas of perpetual summer to elevated mountain reaches where snow fell at Easter. Low coastal plains, sandy-soiled tidewater areas, river valleys, deltas, piedmont stretches, sea islands, rice swamps, cattle ranges, the cotton "black belt," and pine barrens offered the most diverse physical patterns with their variations of weather, topography, and soil. Human elements were no less diverse. The South was at once a sophisticated civilization and a frontier. To pass from the spacious grandeur of the plantation to the poverty of the back country or the primitive crudity of the mountaineer was like entering a new world—a world whose outlook was as different as its dialect was strange and uncouth. The poor white was as isolated from the life of the planter as if he had inhabited another planet. "Indeed," as Avery Craven has remarked, "taken as a whole, a section which contained social and political elements as diverse as Arkansas and Charleston, eastern Tennessee and tidewater Virginia, upland North Carolina and western Texas, can hardly be thought of as forming a solid block of interests or ideas." [1]

It must also be remembered that this vast and varied region was, in many important respects, very similar to the rest of the United States in the 1850's. Certain basic likenesses are so obvious as to require no elaboration: The Old South, like the North and the West, was essentially Protestant in its religion, western European in its traditions, and English in its language, law, and governmental structure. Other similarities are less familiar, partly because historians of the Old South tend to follow stereotypes and to depict the region as either an Elysium where planters sipped mint juleps on spacious verandas or as a purgatory where Simon Legrees sadistically tortured Negro slaves.

If one looks at the contemporary evidence, he discovers that the history

[1] Craven, *The Coming of the Civil War,* 22.

of the Old South fits neither of these patterns but is instead "mainly the history of the roll of frontier upon frontier—and on to the frontier beyond." [2] Migration stripped the older states of the South of the ablest and most energetic portions of their population, white and black. By 1860 only 59 per cent of all persons born in South Carolina continued to live in that state; the rest had moved west, chiefly to Georgia, Alabama, Mississippi, Tennessee, and Texas. Consequently all the seaboard states were in a curiously unsettled, transient state. Houses were allowed to fall into disrepair because, as a contemporary wrote, "Nobody knows how long he will live where he is. . . ." [3] Land, once cultivated but no longer profitable in the face of Western competition, was permitted to become "old fields" and to revert to its native growth. The Northern traveler Frederick Law Olmsted portrayed the desolate state of much of Virginia in the 1850's: "For hours and hours one has to ride through the unlimited, continual, all-shadowing, all-embracing forest, following roads, in the making of which no more labor has been given than was necessary to remove the timber which would obstruct the passage of wagons; and even for days and days he may sometimes travel, and see never two dwellings of mankind within sight of each other; only, at long distances, often several miles asunder, . . . isolated plantation patriarchates." [4]

If much of the older part of the South was relapsing into a kind of primitive state, the newer areas to the southwest had never left it. The Gulf states presented a typical example of the booming frontier. While the population of South Carolina grew by only 5 per cent during the 1850's, that of Texas leaped by 184 per cent. Everything in this Gulf area was still unfinished, still to be exploited. It must be remembered that men who had helped settle Mississippi and Arkansas were still in full vigor in 1861. The entire southwestern area was not, "on the whole, more than a few steps removed from the frontier stage at the beginning of the Civil War." [5]

Many of the basic social traits of the Old South derived from this essentially frontier character of its life. As was natural in so new and changing a society, the "great body of Southerners belonged to the middle class in both an economic and a social sense." Three-fourths of all Southern families owned no slaves; most of them lived on farms containing less than 500 acres. These Southern counterparts "of Northern pioneer farmers, [and] small rural residents of the older sections" lived simple, uneventful, and moderately prosperous lives.[6] Generally unedu-

---

[2] W. J. Cash, *The Mind of the South*, 4.
[3] James C. Bonner, "Plantation Architecture of the Lower South on the Eve of the Civil War," *J.S.H.*, XI, 371 (Aug., 1945).
[4] Olmsted, *A Journey in the Seaboard Slave States* (London, 1856), 87.
[5] Cash, 10.
[6] Craven, 29.

cated, devoutly religious, and fiercely independent, these "plain folk of the Old South" exhibited deep loyalties and an ingrained conservatism. Professor Frank L. Owsley has described the life of the average Southern yeoman as centered "around a small farm, ranging from a fifty-acre to a five-hundred-acre tract, tilled by the owner, undriven by competition, supplied with corn by his own toil and with meat from his own pen or from the fields and forests. The amusements might be . . . the three-day break-down dances which David Crockett loved, or horse races, footraces, cock and dog fights, boxing, wrestling, shooting, fighting, log-rolling, house raising, or corn-shucking. It might be crude or genteel, but it everywhere was fundamentally alike and natural. The houses were homes, where families lived sufficient and complete within themselves, working together and fighting together. And when death came, they were buried in their own lonely peaceful graveyards, to await domesday together." [7]

Naturally in such a rural society individualism and democracy flourished—just as they did in other frontier areas. The older Southern states of the seaboard had originally been constituted as aristocratic commonwealths. In Virginia, for example, at the beginning of the nineteenth century the most important organs of the government were the thoroughly undemocratic county courts, which "had authority to levy taxes, to provide for the upkeep of county buildings, and to build new roads and repair old ones, . . . registered wills and deeds and supervised fiduciary relationships," and "possessed large judicial power, both in civil and criminal cases"; these bodies were, as Thomas Jefferson protested, "self-appointed, self-continued, holding their authorities for life, and with an impossibility of breaking in on the perpetual succession of any faction once possessed of the bench." But when newer states were organized in the southwest, a more democratic structure of government was agreed upon. Meanwhile the governments of the older states during the 1820's were subject to "vigorous domestic criticism," followed in the 1830's by "thoroughgoing constitutional reformation." [8] Though South Carolina continued to hold out against constitutional change, the other Southern states by the 1850's saw the triumph of democracy in the "establishment of white manhood suffrage, the abolition of property qualifications for office holders, the election of all officers by popular vote, and the apportionment of representation on population rather than on wealth, with periodic reapportionment." [9] The result of these changes was to bring new, democratic elements into political power in the South. W. J. Cash notes that "of the eight governors of Virginia from 1841 to 1861, only one was

[7] *I'll Take My Stand*, 71–72.
[8] Charles S. Sydnor, *The Development of Southern Sectionalism, 1819–1848*, 35, 40, 275.
[9] Fletcher M. Green, "Democracy in the Old South," *J.S.H.*, XII, 17–18 (Feb., 1946).

born a gentleman, two began their careers by hiring out as plowhands, and another (the son of a village butcher) as a tailor." [10]

Just as the Old South joined the rest of the nation in the democratic movement of the nineteenth century, so it participated in most of the humanitarian drives of the period. Antislavery was, by the 1840's, an exclusively Northern agitation, and Southerners, with the conservatism of a rural people, had little use for the woman's rights crusade. But most of the Southern states gave generous grants for the training of their deaf and dumb, and somewhat fewer made special provision for the blind. Before 1848 Louisiana, Kentucky, Maryland, South Carolina, Tennessee, and Georgia all spent considerable sums in endowing state hospitals for the care of the insane. There was a general improvement in the lot of the debtors, for many of the southwestern states prohibited imprisonment for debt, and vigorous efforts were made to better the condition of inmates of penitentiaries. The strong movement to improve public education in the South was a part of this general democratic striving.

If the ante-bellum South shared in the humanitarian and democratic aspirations of the age, it also exhibited something of "the personal and *puerile* attitude which distinguished the frontier outlook everywhere." [11] As in all turbulent, rapidly changing societies, violence became a way of life. The Old South as a section became noted for hot tempers and hair-triggered individualism. Fighting, whether the bloody eye-gouging of the frontier wrestling match or the ritualized assassination of the duel, touched every aspect of Southern culture. "Even those who sought careers in politics, agriculture, or elsewhere found it difficult to pursue the paths of peace," writes John Hope Franklin. "A fledgling lawyer might, and frequently did, carry a brace of pistols in his portfolio. A planter, however absorbed in his crops and Negroes, did not lose his early acquired skills with knives and pistols. A young editor, daily running the risk of offending someone with his pen, was most unwise if he neglected any of the honorable means of self-defense." [12] Nor was the Southern pattern of violence confined to individual combats. It made, on the one hand, for laudable pride in the South's contribution to the wars of the United States and, on the other, for unmitigated rowdyism and the prevalence of mob violence throughout the section.

2

Even though the South was an infinitely varied region within itself and though many of its traits were shared with other sections of the

[10] *The Mind of the South,* 37.
[11] *Ibid.,* 42.
[12] Franklin, *The Militant South, 1800–1861,* 19.

country, particularly with the frontier West, it did, after all, form a distinct section, with certain unique characteristics of its own. In speaking of the Old South it is proper, as Cash observes, to talk of "a fairly definite mental pattern, associated with a fairly definite social pattern— a complex of established relationships and habits of thoughts, sentiments, prejudices, standards and values, and associations of ideas, which, if not common strictly to every group of white people in the South, [was] still common in one appreciable measure or another, and in some part or another, to all but relatively negligible ones." [1] Yet to define this "Southernness" is less easy than to recognize its existence. Just as the name "Dixie" loses something of its haunting melody when subjected to etymological analysis, so the quality called "Southern," and identifiable on the instant, seems to dissolve into thin air when wiseheads fall to explaining it in terms of historical origins and conditioning factors.

Perhaps one should begin with negative characteristics. The South was clearly not an urban region. This is not to say that ante-bellum Southerners were totally unfamiliar with city ways. Buckingham, the English traveler, exhausted his rhetoric in describing the brilliance of Charleston, the urbanity of Richmond, and the charm of New Orleans.[2] In *Nouvelle-Orléans* was found the most cosmopolitan of American cities. Unique in its mixture of French, Spanish, and American elements, mart of the pioneer West as of the newer South, meeting place of flatboat and tall-masted ship, this Crescent City, otherwise called "the Paris of America," presented a combination of bustling activity, dreamy ease, and spirited adventure. With such streets as *rue de l'Amour* and Bagatelle, with architectural combinations of balcony, courtyard, patio, and cabildo, it offered a romantic setting for a high-strung people in whom the "habit of command acquired from the ownership of slaves, and the refining influence of well employed leisure, formed a sort of aristocracy from which the South derived some of its brightest intellects." It was a society in which the "women, bred . . . under a mother's jealous surveillance, . . . versed in arts and in letters" were treated by the men with "deferential gallantry," while "over men and women . . . ruled a supreme sense of dignity and honor." [3] Into the life of the city the Catholic Church was woven as "bone of her bone, moss of her oaks." [4] Here the *code duello* reached its height. A small gaucherie might bring a challenge to meet "under the dueling oaks"; and from this there was no evasion with honor. Punctilios of combat were rigidly enforced: seconds had their fateful duties; even insults were decorous; a gentleman would not fight except

[1] Cash, viii.
[2] J. S. Buckingham, *The Slave States of America*, I, 46–66, 316–369; II, 413–433.
[3] John Augustin, in *Library of Southern Literature*, XVI, 6–7.
[4] Basil Thompson, in *These United States*, ed. by E. Gruening, I, 207.

with a gentleman. "You could not fight a man whom you would not ask to your house." Dazzling and mysterious, brilliant in fête and carnival, gallant in manners, refined in the arts of music, dance, and opera, yet dark with its auction block, its *demi-monde,* and voodoo mysteries—such was "fabulous" New Orleans, "where tragedy and gaiety walked side by side in chivalrous converse." [5]

In old Charleston were found both a planter aristocracy and a distinguished urban society. Living chiefly on commerce, its traders had learned to combine politeness with business; and the warmth of its sophisticated life attracted the cotton planter who left his estate each year to enjoy for a season the pleasures of his city home. Flowering gateways, secluded gardens, magnolia petals, the grim Battery, the stately architecture of St. Michael's and St. Phillip's, the picturesque street names, the broad view toward the bay, gave a noble setting to the gallant life of proud families, whose local pride has never been surpassed in America. There was about Charleston more of an English flavor, even to the matter of accent and modes of speech, than in cities of the North. Nor was Virginia with its Alexandria, Fredericksburg, Richmond, Williamsburg, and Norfolk less noted for the rich background, the architectural beauty, or the cultural finish of its cities.

While one must not underestimate these urban factors in the Old South, he must beware of giving them too great importance. The section as a whole had no single urban focus. All these principal cities were on the periphery of the region; Baltimore, Louisville, and St. Louis faced North, and Norfolk, Wilmington, Charleston, Savannah, Mobile, New Orleans, and Galveston faced outward toward Europe. None of these cities had either the size or the importance in the life of the section which New York, Philadelphia, or Boston had for the Northeast.

Similarly, the beginnings of industrialism in the Old South do not refute the contention that the region was essentially agricultural. One must not neglect Southern factories, for they later became of incalculable importance in the life of the Confederacy, and it has already been noted that enormous progress was being made in the 1850's. The value of manufactured goods in the South "increased from thirty-four million dollars in 1840 to nearly a hundred million in 1860." In the manufacture of cotton there was an increase from $1,500,000 to $4,500,000 in the same period. Respectable industrial beginnings were found in Richmond, Petersburg, Charleston, Augusta, Graniteville, South Carolina, and Columbus, Georgia.[6] Even a new and very rural state like Mississippi showed a beginning of textile development, with the capital invested in factories rising from $50,000 to $345,000 in the decade of the 1850's and the number

[5] Augustin, *op. cit.,* 14, 6.
[6] Philip G. Davidson, "Industrialism in the Ante-Bellum South," *So. Atl. Quart.,* XXVII, 414–415.

of spindles increasing from 1500 to 8000.[7] As for railroads, the mileage in the South increased from four hundred in 1840 to more than nine thousand in 1861.

Nevertheless, this incipient industrialism never played a major role in the Southern economy. Capital in the South was mostly absorbed in slave-maintained plantations. It was non-fluid, not easily deflected into manufacturing pursuits; consequently the amount of capital invested in the average Southern factory was less than one-half of that invested in the typical New England plant. Labor was a constant problem with these Southern factories. Though Southern advocates of industrialism tried to argue that "a great good to society must result from the employment of thousands of idle and immoral persons, who are now consumers and not producers,"[8] the low wages paid did not sufficiently attract back-country whites and immigrants. Slaves were used on a limited scale, but the cost was prohibitive; besides, many Southerners felt that allowing "the slave to become a member of an industrial society was tantamount to giving him the weapon with which to gain his own freedom." Many Southern factories were forced into bankruptcy in the face of Northern competition, and such failures had a discouraging effect upon Southern industry as a whole. Furthermore, there was something in the social philosophy of the people which was unfriendly to industrialism. Despising "the filthy, crowded, licentious factories . . . of the North," many Southerners vigorously opposed "the efforts of those who, dazzled by the splendors of Northern civilization, would endeavor to imitate it," an imitation which, they earnestly warned, could be achieved "only by the destruction of the planter."[9]

3

Perhaps a more positive formulation of Southern traits should begin with the structure of the section's economy. It was a predominantly agricultural region, and, though thousands of Southern farmers made their livings by self-subsistent farming and grazing, the section as a whole depended heavily upon the production of staple crops for the market. Hemp was widely cultivated in the upper South; in 1859 "Kentucky and Missouri produced more than three-fourths of the 74,493 tons of hemp raised in the United States." Tobacco flourished in Virginia and Kentucky, with lesser production in Tennessee, Maryland, North Carolina, and Missouri. Rice

[7] John H. Moore, "Mississippi's Ante-Bellum Textile Industry," *Jour. of Miss. Hist.*, XVI, 81 (April, 1954).

[8] Richard W. Griffin and Diffee W. Standard, "The Cotton Textile Industry in Ante-Bellum North Carolina, Part II . . . ," *N. C. Hist. Rev.*, XXXIV, 155 (April, 1957).

[9] Fabian Linden, "Repercussions of Manufacturing in the Ante-Bellum South," *ibid.*, XVII, 321–322 (Oct., 1940).

was a major staple only in South Carolina, though it was also cultivated in Georgia, North Carolina, Louisiana, and other states on a less commercial basis. The production of sugar cane for the market was chiefly confined to Louisiana.[1]

Elsewhere the Old South was a "fabric of cotton." The production of this great staple, whose name became a magic word, was almost negligible before 1800; but from that date forward, and especially after 1820, the crop increased at an amazing rate, until it far surpassed tobacco, rice, indigo, and sugar in importance and became the leading export product of the nation. In 1791 cotton production in the country amounted to only 4000 bales. Two years later Yankee inventiveness made one of its contributions to the South in Eli Whitney's cotton gin; and by 1801 production had mounted to 100,000 bales. By 1811 the total had leaped to 167,000 bales, which was insignificant as compared with the production of 1,062,-000 bales in 1835. In 1849 the total had increased to 2,469,000 bales, but by the end of another decade this amount had been more than doubled.[2]

The importance of cotton in Southern economy and sentiment is suggested by the elaborate care devoted to the conditioning factors of its cultivation and marketing—to the relative advantages of the various grades; the selection of the soil; bedding up, hoeing, and thinning; drainage and the prevention of erosion; rotation; fertilization; the eradication of weeds; and the war against insect pests. The success of the South in conquering these difficulties, as well as the remarkable adaptation of Southern climate and soil to cotton culture, is shown by the dependence of European manufacturers on Southern cotton. From 1840 to the time of the Civil War, Great Britain drew from the Southern states of America about four-fifths of all her cotton imports.[3]

A traveler in the South in 1827 was overwhelmed by cotton on every side. Walking along the wharves at Charleston he saw them "piled up with mountains of Cotton, and all your stores, ships, steam and canal boats, crammed with . . . Cotton." The daily papers and the conversation of hotel boarders teemed with cotton. Riding through the streets, he had to dodge from side to side "to steer clear of the cotton waggons." Arriving in Augusta he found cotton boats crowding the river and cotton warehouses covering whole squares. And Hamburg was "worser," as one of the Negroes said; for it was hard to tell "which was the largest, the piles of cotton or the houses." Journeying through the country he overtook "hordes of cotton planters from North Carolina, South Carolina, and Georgia, with large gangs of negroes, bound to Alabama, Mississippi, and Louisiana;

[1] Lewis C. Gray, *History of Agriculture in the Southern United States to 1860*, II, 821, 757, 723, 748.
[2] *Historical Statistics of the U.S.*, 109.
[3] F. L. Owsley, *King Cotton Diplomacy*, 3–4.

'where the cotton land is not worn out.'" Continuing his travels to Mobile, and from there in a cotton-stuffed schooner to New Orleans, he attended a play in a cotton-press house, and, bethinking himself of a "Pharo Bank," he was told that he would "find one at the Louisiana Coffee-house, just below the cotton-press, opposite to a cotton ware-house," [4]

Neither travelers' records nor statistics, however, suffice to express the place of cotton in the Southern scheme. "For cotton," says a recent writer, "is something more than a crop or an industry; it is a dynastic system, with a set of laws and standards always under assault and peculiarly resistant to change. It is map-maker, trouble-maker, history-maker; . . . . It was cotton that made the South into a section. . . . On cotton, . . . the South built up a social and political economy essentially different from that prevailing in the rest of the country." [5] The full study of cotton in its relation to the life of the Old South, important and elaborate as are its agricultural aspects, is more than an agrarian study. It is a field in which politics, finance, business organization, economics, chemistry, and social psychology are elaborately intermingled. What we are dealing with here is a culture complex. Despite the fact that cotton growing and slaveholding directly involved only a minority, it was nevertheless true that standards, conditions, and patterns of society were set by the basic staple.

4

Socially as well as economically the ante-bellum South had a kind of unity. Again one must start by making exceptions, for there were unassimilable elements in the Southern social system. At the bottom of the social ladder were the "poor whites," a wretched class whom even the Negro despised.[1] Uninspired, physically deficient, occupying the pine barrens or the infertile back country, they lived a hand-to-mouth existence, mere hangers-on of a régime in which they had no determining part. Choosing a small tract where progress would not molest him, the "hill-billy" or "clay-eater" lived his unpromising days on the very margin of subsistence.

Here [writes Paul H. Buck] he would build a rude cabin of round

[4] *Documentary History of American Industrial Society*, I, 283–287.
[5] Anne O'Hare McCormick, in *N. Y. Times Magazine*, June 1, 1930, p. 1.

[1] Professor Frank L. Owsley warns that one must not consider most "piney-wood folk of the ante-bellum South" in this degraded category, though contemporary travelers often confused the two groups. Had these independent, moderately prosperous yeomen lived on the plains, Professor Owsley points out, "their livestock economy would have been apparent; but because of the great forests their herds of cows and droves of hogs were seldom to be seen by anyone passing hurriedly through the country. Nor could the economic importance of the subsidiary occupation of hunting and trapping be realized except by one who tarried long and learned the ways of these taciturn folk." Owsley, *Plain Folk of the Old South*, 36.

logs in the typical backwoods manner. "A few rickety chairs, a long bench, a dirty bed or two, a spinning-wheel, . . . a skillet, an oven, a frying-pan, a triangular cupboard in one corner and a rack . . . [for] the family rifle " might serve as an inventory of the contents of the cabin's single room. Food could be procured with a minimum of effort. "Wild hogs, deer, wild turkeys, squirrels, raccoons, opossums—these and many more are at [the] very doors [of the poor whites]; and they have only to pick up 'old Silver Heels' [the rifle], walk a few miles out into the forest, and return home laden with enough meat to last them a week." The yield of their rifles and fishing rods might be supplemented by corn and potatoes from their straggling gardens. Altogether it was a life without much effort and it produced a class of lazy, idle men who gained a universal reputation for shiftlessness.[2]

That these poor whites, living in such primitive fashion, were content with their lot and lacking in ambition, conveys only a partial impression of their degradation. The measure of their inferiority is further suggested by the practice of eating clay, a practice which was in fact a disease; while the prevalence of hookworm among them indicated a pathological condition which was both cause and result of their manner of life, and which has had to wait for recent science and philanthropy to find a cure.

Concerning the attitude of well-to-do Southerners toward the poor whites, it may be said that there was little contact between these two classes; that outside references to this lowly element as a symptom of depressing conditions in his social order served not at all to disturb the Southerner's complacency but tended rather to produce an attitude of self-justification; that the "plantation system . . . rendered superfluous the potential labor contribution of the poor white"; and that, recognizing the sandhiller's satisfaction with his meager lot, the Southerner felt that neglect did him no great harm.[3] Daniel R. Hundley, in his survey of Southern social problems, wrote that "there is no . . . method by which they can be weaned from leading the lives of vagrom-men, idlers, and squatters, useless to themselves and the rest of mankind." [4] The Southerner did not exploit or mistreat the poor white. If he ignored him, this was due not so much to a deliberately unsympathetic attitude as to the feeling that the environment of these less fortunate folk was not beneath their deserts and was not inappropriate to their character and manner of living. Mark Twain, portraying the misery of Huckleberry Finn when efforts were made to civilize him by compulsion, was after all touching upon a fundamental aspect of the problem. "The planter, satisfied with the plantation system, . . . was not concerned in the existence of a

[2] P. H. Buck, in *Am. Hist. Rev.*, XXXI, 43.
[3] *Ibid.*, 46–47.
[4] D. R. Hundley, *Social Relations in Our Southern States*, 119.

lower class that was unobtrusive and contented, whose chief sins were idleness and shiftlessness. And the poor white, simple in mind and attitude, was content to bask in the sunlight of indifference." [5]

Another group which had little contact with the rest of Southern society were the "highlanders," who lived in the inaccessible mountain regions. Here was an isolated part of America which maintained its racial purity and adhered tenaciously to the traditions and customs of a primitive day. Deflected from the current of progress, speaking a quaint brogue, untouched by the conventions of sophisticated society, they have been called "our contemporary ancestors." Ballads known long ago in Britain, passing down by oral transmission from generation to generation, still persist among these people, who have become a favorite source for specialists in American folklore. Fond of hunting and outdoor life, inured to hardship, strangers to the bathtub, quick on the trigger, they were nevertheless generous and hospitable; and if one begins at King's Mountain and comes down through later struggles to Sergeant York it appears that these sturdy mountain folk have helped to fight the nation's battles. The crude life of the mountaineer was not akin to the "shiftlessness" of the poor white: it signified rather a true preference for old traditions, a disdain of too much progress, a readiness to accept the narrow radius of a mountain cove as a sufficient world, a contempt for softness and over-refinement. It was not merely that economic conditions kept certain of the pioneers in mountain homes while "more fortunate" neighbors pushed on, nor that such an accident as the breaking of a lynchpin might cause a family to remain fixed in a mountain retreat. There was, among these highlanders, as among mountain people generally, a process of selection and adaptation which resulted in the harmonization of a type of men and women to their environment: the peopling of the mountains, in other words, was not a haphazard affair. As to matters political, the highlander could not understand the ways of courts; he felt no need of "law men" to regulate relations with his fellows; and he failed to think of the government as "ary thing but a president in a biled shirt who commands two-three judges and a gang o' revenue officers." [6]

5

Aside from these two small and relatively insignificant groups, Southern society found a central focus in the plantation system. This is not to suggest that great numbers of Southerners could consider themselves planters, for, as has been previously noted, most white Southerners were yeoman farmers of decidedly limited means. Nor is it to be inferred that a plantation "aristocracy" somehow controlled the political destinies of the

[5] P. H. Buck, in *Am. Hist. Rev.*, XXXI, 49.
[6] Horace Kephart, *Our Southern Highlanders*, 120.

region, for the current of democracy had eroded the powers of the gentry until "whatever influence the planters exercised over the political action of the common people was of a personal and local nature." [1] It is rather that by the 1850's the plantation had come to play an ever increasing role in the economic and social life of the Old South.

As to the economic importance of the plantation in the ante-bellum South, historians are not in agreement. Professor Frank L. Owsley and several of his students have published studies minimizing the role of the planters and emphasizing the importance of the yeoman farmers of the ante-bellum South. Arguing not merely that the small farmers were the more numerous class, they have attempted also to prove that these yeomen were comfortably off during the 1850's, that "nonslaveholders were acquiring land more rapidly than the slaveholders," [2] and that "generally . . . there does not seem to have been a marked difference in the fertility and the value of the lands of slaveholders and nonslaveholders." [3] Of great value in pointing up the numerical importance of the nonplanter middle class in the South and in stimulating a reconsideration of ante-bellum history, the Owsley school has been severely criticized for statistical inadequacy, and, on the whole, one is not able to agree with its conclusions.

A few facts and figures will suggest, instead, that the plantation during the 1850's was not merely a major but a growing element in the Southern economy. In terms of income, one thousand Southern planter families "received over $50,000,000 a year, while all the remaining 666,000 families received only about $60,000,000." [4] The same inequities prevailed in land ownership. In the Alabama black belt counties in 1850 "two-thirds of all acres . . . were held by 17 per cent of the farming population and were parts of plantations which claimed over 500 acres." The planter held not merely more land than the yeoman; he generally owned the more valuable land. A study of fifteen Alabama and Mississippi counties shows that the land of farmers who owned less than 50 acres was worth only $7.20 an acre, while that of planters who owned more than 2000 acres was worth $29.50 an acre. Furthermore, during the decade before the Civil War, Southern wealth was becoming increasingly concentrated into fewer hands. "During the fifties," Fabian Linden has pointed out, "the increase in the number of white families in the entire South exceeded the growth in the number of slaveholders by over 25 per cent. Thus we must conclude that the propertied classes of the

[1] Frank L. Owsley, *Plain Folk of the Old South*, 139.

[2] Frank L. and Harriet C. Owsley, "The Economic Basis of Society in the Late Ante-Bellum South," *J.S.H.*, VI, 41 (Feb., 1940).

[3] Frank L. and Harriet C. Owsley, "The Economic Structure of Rural Tennessee, 1850–1860," *J.S.H.*, VIII, 182 (May, 1942).

[4] W. E. Dodd, *The Cotton Kingdom*, 24.

Old South constituted a relatively shrinking segment of the population." [5]
Professor James C. Bonner, who has made a detailed study of a typical
Georgia county, agrees that the 1850's saw "an increase in the number
of slaves, a concentration of ownership, and a rise in land values," which
"undoubtedly had an adverse effect upon the fortunes of tenant farmers
and squatters, many of whom were forced to secure employment as wage
earners." [6]

Socially as well as economically the plantation played an enormously
important role in Southern life; for the entire region the plantation
gentry became "the model for social aspiration." [7] For the urban and professional classes the plantation seemed the one sure road to social reputa-
bility, and there was "a decided tendency for lawyer, doctor, carpenter,
merchant, and tailor to move into agriculture, as fast as the accumula-
tion of capital would permit." [8] Small farmers, too, identified with the
plantation system. Despite the "concentration of wealth, slaves, and power
in the hands of a few," Roger W. Shugg has found, "little resentment
was expressed by the less fortunate majority. The rich planters in the
black belt did not excite great envy among the overseers, woodcutters,
and poor farmers who surrounded them. To the contrary, a West Feliciana
[Louisiana] overseer boasted that all the land was 'owned by big bugs,'
among whom his employer was 'one of the biggest sort.' " [9] Poor farmers,
given the franchise, made no serious attempt to disrupt the plantation
economy or to strike down their wealthier neighbors. If there were yeomen who were disaffected, they migrated further west, to begin life
anew.[10] Those who remained saw the neighboring planters as somewhat
more successful but by no means superior beings, to whom they were
often related by blood or marriage. At bottom this absence of class antagonisms was a result of the slavery system. As Cash astutely remarks,
"If the plantation had introduced distinctions of rank and wealth among
men of the old backcountry, and, in doing so, had perhaps offended
against the ego of the common white, it had also . . . introduced that
other vastly ego-warming and ego-expanding distinction between the
white man and the black." [11]

[5] Linden, "Economic Democracy in the Slave South: An Appraisal of Some
Recent Views," *Jour. of Negro Hist.*, XXXI, 160, 172, 178 (April, 1946).

[6] Bonner, "Profile of a Late Ante-Bellum Community," *Amer. Hist. Rev.*,
XLIX, 666, 675 (July, 1944).

[7] Cash, 60.

[8] Bonner, "Profile of a Late Ante-Bellum Community," 672.

[9] Shugg, *Origins of Class Struggle in Louisiana*, 28.

[10] Note that 86.9 per cent of the nonslaveholders emigrated from Jefferson
County, Mississippi, during the 1850's, while only 16.7 per cent of the planters
who owned more than one hundred slaves emigrated. Linden, " Economic Democracy in the Slave South," 179.

[11] *Mind of the South*, 38.

6

In describing the life of the gentleman planters, it is difficult not to be sentimental or romantic. At its best, as in certain sections of Virginia, it was, as George Cary Eggleston remembered, "a soft, dreamy, deliciously quiet life, a life of repose, an old life, with all its sharp corners and rough surfaces long ago worn round and smooth." [1] To recapture its flavor one must visit some of the fine old Southern mansions which still stand today like monuments of a departed era. One finds them set on a hill, nestling in a park, or facing a river bend; and the distinction of their architecture bespeaks the taste and gentlemanly ease of their owners. Within the mansion the furniture, silver, coats-of-arms, and ancient portraits revealed a dominant characteristic of the planter—his family pride. In Virginia the Carter family had its "Nomini Hall" in Westmoreland County; the Byrd family had its "Westover" near Richmond; William Bolling had three plantations on the James ("Pocahontas," "The Island," and "Bolling Hall"); Washington had at "Mount Vernon" one of the most perfect of the mansions; while the stately distinction of Jefferson's "Monticello," crowning its little mountain, reflected the genius of its cosmopolitan owner. If one mentions also "Berkeley," ancestral seat of the Harrisons, "Kenmore," the elegant home of Fielding Lewis at Fredericksburg, Mason's "Gunston Hall," and the estates of the Nelsons, Prestons, Randolphs, Pages, Tylers, Lees, Pendletons, and scores of others among the F. F. V.'s, he has but made a beginning in a survey of Virginia aristocracy, which had its counterpart in each of the other Southern states.

Life in such nearly idyllic surroundings could have an elegance and an ease rarely to be found elsewhere in America. In depicting the characteristics of the ante-bellum planters a contemporary writer stated that, arbitrary though they were, they "extorted admiration by their good sense—and many of them by their genuine and hearty hospitality." Life had "made men of them"; hard experience was their *alma mater;* they "were learned in the practical things." Many were diligent readers; some knew the Federal and state constitutions by heart. They subscribed for their party organs—Whigs read the *National Intelligencer,* Democrats the *Globe.* Though sometimes awkward in speech they were wise in action. Behind the awkward word was vigor of thought. Slavery had accustomed them to expect implicit obedience; opposition they could not brook. In their dealings, if this writer observed correctly, they preferred "foreigners who had been trained to obsequiousness of manner, to their own countrymen, who would assert themselves." [2] This portrait from

[1] Eggleston, *A Rebel's Recollections,* ed. by David Donald, 27.
[2] Paraphrased from H. S. Fulkerson, *Random Recollections of Early Days in Mississippi,* 15–16.

life may serve to explain why the planter often performed better in state-craft than in politics: in office he would usually do well, but in artfully angling for votes among democratic constituents he might be less adept.

This planter class was an educated elite. In contrast to the South's general backwardness in public schools, great stress was placed upon higher education. "If college attendance is any test of an educated people," Frank L. Owsley has written, "the South had more educated men and women in proportion to [white] population than the North, or any other part of the world." [3] William E. Dodd has pointed out that just before the Civil War eleven thousand students "were enrolled in the colleges of the cotton States, while in Massachusetts, with half as many white people . . . there were only 1733 college students." As a whole the South had over 25,000 college students, and in the decade between 1850 and 1860, as Professor Dodd shows, "practically every college and university in the South doubled its attendance." [4]

Southern plantation life at its height is depicted in a vivid description of a huge sugar plantation in Louisiana by the famous English correspondent W. H. Russell. As far as the eye could see, he wrote, fence palings "guarded wide-spread fields of maize and sugar-cane." Through a leafy avenue he approached the house, "with clustering flowers, rose, jasmine, and creepers, clinging to the pillars supporting the veranda." The view, he said, was "one of the most striking . . . in the world." "If an English agriculturist could see six thousand acres of the finest land in one field, unbroken by hedges . . . and covered with the most magnificent crops . . . , as level as a billiard table, he would surely doubt his senses. But here is literally such a sight—six thousand acres, better tilled than the finest patch in all the Lothians, green as Meath pastures, . . . and yielding an average profit [at old prices] . . . of at least £20 an acre. . . . My host . . . had purchased this estate for £300,000 and an adjacent property . . . for £150,000. . . ." [5]

The planter at his best wore the prerogatives of organization and command with a sense of responsibility. On the highly exceptional plantation of Jefferson Davis these prerogatives were tempered by republican tendencies, slave juries being used for the trial of plantation offenses. It was the firm belief of masters generally that the plantation was a civilizing influence: in some of its aspects it was a school; again it may be regarded as a social settlement, or a parish. As Professor Phillips has pointed out, it was also a variety show. "The procession of plowmen at evening," he writes, ". . . the bonfire in the quarter with contests in clogs . . . ; the work songs in solo and refrain . . . ; the baptiz-

[3] Quoted in Simkins, *A History of the South*, 168.
[4] Dodd, *Cotton Kingdom*, 111.
[5] W. H. Russell, *My Diary North and South*, 103, quoted in *Doc. Hist. Am. Indust. Soc.*, I, 256–257.

ing . . . ; the torchlight pursuit of 'possum and 'coon, with full-voiced haloo to baying houn' dawg and yelping cur; . . . the husking bee, the quilting party, the wedding, the cock fight, the crap game, . . ."—these were the features of plantation life, all of them "highly vocal." [6]

But one must remember that Southern plantation life rarely lived up to these possibilities. If a good number of planters spoke of themselves as aristocrats, it is wholesome to remember that the Southern gentry was in fact mostly descended from yeoman stock—generally within a very few generations. Only an "insignificant" number of Cavalier families had taken part in the settling of Virginia,[7] and elsewhere there was even less justification for speaking of the planters' ancient lineage. In fact, as Cash points out, the Southern "ruling class as a body and in its primary aspect was merely a close clique of property." [8]

Nor did the average Southern planter dwell in elegant luxury. Though he may have aspired to build a mansion like those in Virginia or Natchez, his house was "generally a rude ungainly structure, made of logs, rough hewn from the forest," and there was usually "a garden of 60 feet by 40 in its rear, full of long collards (fit only for cows and then when steamed), the oaks cut down in front, a Spanish mulberry or China tree planted in their stead, under the shade of which is seen in the summer time a lazy pack of egg-sucking hounds, or noisy sheep-killing curs, half starved." [9] Supercilious Northern travelers "described the condition of the new slaveholders and the poorer planters as being very miserable," and stated that New York farmers worth $40,000 lived more comfortably than Louisiana planters worth $300,000.[10]

The average Southern planter's life was one of hard work. He was no idle aristocrat but a businessman who was, as U. B. Phillips has remarked, simultaneously the head of a hierarchy, a homestead, a conscript army, a factory, a pageant, a matrimonial bureau, a nursery, and a divorce court. The seasons dictated the rhythm of his activities. In the spring he saw to the breaking of the ground and the planting of his crops; in the summer he supervised the weeding and hoeing and thinning and the ceaseless care against insect pests; in the fall he directed the picking, the ginning, and the marketing of his cotton; in winter he looked after the repair of his houses, fences, and drainage ditches. Even when he had an overseer to assist him, his was the ultimate responsibility for keeping the plantation smoothly functioning. All the while he had to give close attention to the financing of his enterprise, and generally he strug-

[6] U. B. Phillips, *Life and Labor in the Old South*, 202–203.
[7] T. J. Wertenbaker, *Patrician and Plebeian in Virginia*, 23.
[3] *Mind of the South*, 21.
[9] Bonner, "Plantation Architecture of the Lower South on the Eve of the Civil War," *J.S.H.*, XI, 372, 374 (Aug., 1945).
[10] Frederick Law Olmsted, *The Cotton Kingdom*, II, 44, 48.

gled with account books which he hoped would prove that his efforts were profitable.

Nor was the planter's wife the dainty and delicate female of fiction. The ideal lady of the plantation was a domestic Martha Washington who arose early each day in order to supervise the manifold household activities: the cooking, candle making, sewing, weaving, churning, and jelly making. She must guide and teach her slaves, smooth out their troubles, and doctor them when they were sick. To do these things efficiently, and to fulfill the Southern gentleman's ideal of a Southern lady—to be a perfect hostess, to cultivate tact and gentle charm—constituted her liberal education.

It must not be disguised that there were hard, frequently repulsive aspects of Southern plantation life. Howard W. Odum, in turning from the "glory that was the South" to the "grandeur that was not," writes of the prevalence of drinking and gambling, the false virtue of dueling, stubborn individualism, non-cooperative habits, violent tempers, feuds, fighting, isolation. Though the Southern woman was eulogized and feted with praise, yet, says Odum, there were "many things she was not supposed to see, and if seeing, was not to record, and if recording, was not to let it see the light either in her own consciousness, or in the records of posterity." He mentions the "relationships of the master . . . with the women slaves" as among the "shadows of tragedy" behind the "veil of glory." [11] Southerners themselves admitted that there were many abuses in the institution of slavery. Unruly Negroes were sometimes branded with the hot iron; free Negroes were kidnapped; families were torn asunder; whippings were sometimes brutal. While domestic slaves might wear fine clothes and be treated with indulgence, armies of field hands were less fortunate; and the intimacy that existed between master and slave on the smaller plantation was less evident where one estate comprised a hundred or more slaves. Though the evils of absentee landlordism, with its detachment of master and slave, were exceptional in the South, and while in this respect American slavery was more humane than the institution as found in the British or Spanish West Indies, yet occasionally such absenteeism was to be found, as where South Carolinian planters lived in Charleston, leaving their plantations to managers or overseers. In short, like every other society, the South had its sordidness, abuse, narrowness of outlook, and tragedy.

Yet in arriving at his final verdict, the historian must be careful to judge both the dream and the reality of Southern life. If all too often the Southern "mansion" was a shack, the Southern "aristocrat" was a cotton snob, and Southern "chivalry" was bullying pretentiousness, one must recognize that social ideals and achievements rarely coincide. In addition

---

[11] Odum, *An American Epoch,* chap. iv.

to giving a unity to Southern life, the plantation system gave it a goal of aspiration, which played a major part in the mental make-up of Southern men and women. Though not always realized, the "creed of the Old South" [12] was not shallow hypocrisy, for it gave to the section a rightful name for hospitality, generosity, openness, frankness, and manly courage.

7

More important even than agriculture or the plantation system in defining the Old South was the fact that Southerners had a growing consciousness of their own Southernism. Long before the Civil War Southerners came to speak not of their state or their nation but of their section as their native land. "The South is my home—my fatherland," exclaimed Alexander H. Stephens, of Georgia. "There sleep the ashes of my sire and grandsires; there are my hopes and prospects; with her my fortunes are cast; her fate is my fate, and her destiny my destiny." More and more "Southrons" (as they proudly called themselves) felt that such regionalism in mind and spirit was the highest expression of men's loyalties. George Fitzhugh, the proslavery propagandist, rejoiced that his fellow Southerners should become "provincial, and cease to be imitative cosmopolitans." [1] By the 1850's, Rollin G. Osterweis writes, the Southerners had begun "to manifest a group consciousness suggestive of nineteenth-century European romantic nationalism." [2]

It had not always been thus. In the early days of the Republic, George Washington, James Madison, and John Marshall had been Americans first and Southerners afterward. The early liberalism of the South had received its fullest expression in Thomas Jefferson, whose interests included music, art, architecture, philosophy, science, law, and literature, whose friendships were worldwide, and whose concern for liberty embraced all mankind. At the beginning of the nineteenth century most intelligent Southerners expected the ultimate extinction of slavery, and many, like young John C. Calhoun, hoped to diversify the economy of their region by introducing manufactures similar to those of New England.

Nor was the development of an exclusive sectional feeling a thing quickly arrived at in the South. "Not until some four decades after the American Revolution," Francis B. Simkins writes, "did leaders of the Southern states become acutely and permanently aware that their people possessed peculiar virtues and ambitions that needed defense from Northern interference." [3] During these years Southerners were more often

[12] Basil L. Gildersleeve, *Creed of the Old South.*

[1] Franklin, *The Militant South,* 219, 221.
[2] Osterweis, *Romanticism and Nationalism in the Old South,* vii.
[3] Simkins, *History of the South,* 95.

divided among themselves than from Yankees. Even down into the 1840's "the South had a vigorous two-party system, an asset it has never since enjoyed." Against the tradition of associating the Democratic party with the South one finds that during most of its lifetime (1834–1854) the Whig party carried on with the support of influential Southern elements. The Southern people, observes Charles G. Sellers, Jr., "divided politically in these years over much the same questions as northern voters, particularly questions of banking and financial policy." Small farmers tended to be on the Democratic side; "urban commercial and banking interests, supported by a majority of the planters," were on the other.[4] Instead of casting their votes as a solid section, Southerners split them almost evenly between the two parties. In the five presidential elections from 1836 to 1852 inclusive, "the total popular vote of the Whig candidates [in the Southern states] was 1,745,884, that of the Democratic candidates was 1,760,452, or a majority for the Democrats of only 14,568." [5]

The forces which eroded these national patterns of behavior and sapped Southern attachment to the Union were complex. In part the change was due to the cotton gin, which had made slavery, once considered near extinction, enormously profitable. In part, too, it was a reaction to the long agricultural depression of 1819–1832, which "took the bottom out of the farmer's world and brought to a sharp end the old agricultural order which had existed for a century and a half." Resentful and suspicious, Southern farmers and planters believed they were being victimized by protective tariffs, ship subsidies, and internal improvement legislation designed to assist the North. Some portion of the growing sectional feeling was developed in order to curb internal criticisms within the South, where there was "dissatisfaction over representation, the franchise, and inadequate transportation and educational facilities . . . in areas where slaves were few." [6] And in no small measure this sectionalism, in its most extreme forms, was a response to Northern attacks upon the South and its "peculiar institution."

It is, impossible, of course, precisely to date this transformation in Southern attitudes, but by the 1830's the process was well under way. Calhoun's shift from nationalism to sectionalism, as exemplified in his "Exposition and Protest" against the tariff of 1828, the suppression of Nat Turner's fanatical group of insurrectionary slaves in Virginia in 1831, the defeat of gradual emancipation plans in the Virginia legislature in 1831–1832, and South Carolina's nullification of the tariff in 1832 are mileposts along the road to self-conscious Southernism.

---

[4] Sellers, "Who Were the Southern Whigs?" *Amer. Hist. Rev.*, LIX, 336, 346 (Jan., 1954).

[5] Green, "Democracy in the Old South," *J.S.H.*, XII, 20–21 (Feb., 1946).

[6] Craven, *Coming of the Civil War*, 42, 153.

Thereafter the history of the ante-bellum South is one of increasing sectionalism. Political unanimity was not achieved, even outwardly, until the outbreak of the Civil War, but in other fields regionalism ran rampant. The division of churches along sectional lines has previously been noted, as has the suppression of antislavery sentiment within the South. More and more the Southerners came to think of themselves as a people apart, characterized by a unique and superior culture. Incurably romantic, they often fancied themselves descendants of the Cavaliers and proudly practiced the cult of chivalry. Some of them actually organized jousts and tournaments, where gallant champions styling themselves "Brian de Bois Guilbert" or "Wilfred of Ivanhoe" vied in tilting, so that the victor could crown his mistress "The Queen of Love and Beauty." A far larger number took their chivalry vicariously, through reading the romantic novels of Walter Scott, who was unquestionably the favorite Southern author. Scott's influence upon Southern thinking was great; Mark Twain remarked, with characteristic exaggeration, "Sir Walter had so large a hand in making Southern character, as it existed before the war, that he is in great measure responsible for the war." [7]

As for slavery, Southerners ceased being apologists for a dying institution and became fervent defenders of a beneficent system justified on historical, Biblical, scientific, economic, and sociological grounds. Senator R. M. T. Hunter, of Virginia, argued, "There is not a respectable system of civilization known to history, . . . whose foundations were not laid in the institution of domestic slavery." [8] Southern clerics announced that the Bible justified slavery. "Had not the Jews practiced slavery under the watchful care of Jehovah? Did not the Ten Commandments mention 'servants' thrice? . . . Did not the Apostle Paul urge the fugitive Onesimus to return to his master?" [9] Using some craniological evidence, Dr. Josiah C. Nott, of Mobile, tried to prove that the Negro belonged to a different species from the white man, and Dr. J. H. Van Evrie showed the application of this scientific finding in his book titled *Negroes and Negro "Slavery": The First an Inferior Race: The Latter Its Normal Condition.* Other apologists proved that slavery was essential to the functioning of the Southern economy, which in turn was essential to that of the United States, because cotton was the chief American export, and to that of Great Britain, which depended upon Southern cotton. In *Cannibals All! or, Slaves Without Masters* George Fitzhugh tried to demonstrate that in free society there was inevitably an antagonism between capital and labor, which must result in "robber barons" and "pauper slavery," while in slave society, where capital and labor were happily united in the per-

[7] Osterweis, 3–5, 26.
[8] David Donald, *Charles Sumner and the Coming of the Civil War,* 349.
[9] Simkins, *History of the South,* 107.

son of the Negro, such antagonisms were avoided.[10] Supported by these arguments, Albert Gallatin Brown, of Mississippi, had no hesitation in informing the United States Senate that "slavery is a great moral, social, and political blessing—a blessing to the slave, and a blessing to the master." [11]

In rejecting criticisms of slavery Southerners closed their ears to all other criticisms of their society. They were sure they lived in the best of all possible worlds. These ante-bellum "Southrons," Charles S. Sydnor has wittily exclaimed, "rare among mortals, claimed that their own age was the golden age, and they claimed that its main foundation was Negro slavery." This "affirmation of Southern perfection" was precisely expressed in the title of an essay by one Reverend Iverson L. Brookes, published in South Carolina in 1850: *A Defense of the South against the Reproaches and Encroachments of the North; in Which Slavery is Shown to be an Institution of God Intended to Form the Basis of the Best Social State and the Only Safeguard to the Permanence of a Republican Government.*[12]

[10] Craven, *Coming of the Civil War,* 168, 170–171.
[11] Donald, *Sumner,* 348.
[12] Sydnor, *Development of Southern Sectionalism,* 338–339.

CHAPTER 3

Slavery

I

WOVEN INTO THE PATTERN of Southern life was the institution of slavery. It was an institution so involved in controversy and so productive of emotional reaction that the historical scholar finds it no easy task to reach fair and unbiased conclusions about it. The records for the study of Negro slavery are imperfect and must be regarded with suspicion. Most contemporary printed accounts were written with the admitted purpose of justifying or condemning the "peculiar institution." Most travelers in the ante-bellum South saw what they set out to find. Numerous business and family records kept by Southern slaveowners are still preserved, but these are not fully representative, for most of them relate to the management of large plantations. The handful of autobiographies by former slaves, such as Frederick Douglass, who ran away to the North and later distinguished themselves, are clearly not typical, yet there are almost no other ways of ascertaining how the Negroes themselves reacted to the system. Consequently the subject is one on which even the experts differ. Finding not merely "injustice, oppression, brutality and heartburning in the régime" but "also gentleness, kind-hearted friendship and mutual loyalty," the Southern-born scholar Ulrich B. Phillips concluded that "it is impossible to agree that its basis and its operation were wholly evil." [1] A more recent Northern-born student, Kenneth M. Stampp, on the other hand, says bluntly "that slavery had no philosophical defense worthy of the name—. . . it had nothing to commend it to posterity, except that it paid." [2]

The prewar South, especially before about 1830, was far from unanimous in supporting slavery; nor was the prewar North even approximately unanimous in opposing it. There were Southerners who deplored the institution, such as Jefferson, Lee, Washington, George Mason, and John Tyler; and there were active Southern abolitionists, such as

[1] Phillips, *American Negro Slavery*, 514.
[2] Stampp, *The Peculiar Institution*, 422.

J. G. Birney and Cassius M. Clay. On the other hand, supporters of slavery were numerous in the North. Illinois, for instance, Lincoln's own state, during most of the period from the acquisition of statehood to the Civil War possessed some of the characteristics of a slave state. Though the Ordinance of 1787, the fundamental charter for the new states between the Ohio and the Mississippi, forbade slavery, the people of Illinois in the earlier years interpreted the ordinance to permit slaves holding over from the period before 1787 to be held in bondage. The practice of indentured servitude was recognized in the Illinois constitution of 1818 and was made effective by statutes passed in 1819. It is probable that an out-and-out recognition of slavery would have been included in the constitution of Illinois in 1818 if it had not been feared that such recognition would defeat the admission of the state to the Union. There was a movement in 1823 to amend the constitution; and the animating purpose back of this movement was to legalize slavery. This was but natural, since most of the people of early Illinois were descendants of Southerners. As late as 1840 the United States census continued to report slaves in Illinois, the number in 1840 being given as 331.

In Indiana much the same situation existed. When in the session of the United States Congress for 1805–1806 a petition was received from the territory of Indiana asking for a suspension of that article of the Northwest Ordinance which forbade slavery, a committee of Congress reported in favor of the suspension, thus approving the policy of permitting slavery in Indiana. The suspension of the article, they urged, was "an object almost universally desired" by the people of the territory of Indiana. The issue as they saw it was not between slavery and freedom; it was merely a matter of moving slaves from one part of the country to another. The legalization of slavery, they argued, would tend to accelerate the population of the territory of Indiana, whose development had been retarded by the prohibition of slavery. Even the slaves themselves would profit, said the committee, because they would be more separated and diffused, so that each slaveholder would have fewer slaves with more room to look after them.[3] This recommendation that slavery be permitted in Indiana was not approved by Congress; but it is significant that such a recommendation could be made by a congressional committee in 1806 with the approval of the people concerned. In Ohio before the war the general attitude of the courts was favorable to slaveholders in the many cases that arose in Cincinnati and elsewhere upon the border concerning the recovery of fugitives. Sectional differentiation concerning the right or wrong of Negro bondage is not as clear-cut as has been supposed.

[3] W. O. Blake, *History of Slavery and the Slave Trade* (1860), 434; F. S. Philbrick, ed., *The Laws of Indiana Territory* (Ill. Hist. Colls., XXI), Intro., xxxviii.

2

The historical background of American slavery must be sought in the early slave trade of Europe, England, and New England. The institution in America did not develop as a direct inheritance from Europe. Negroes were but little known in European countries up to the time of the discovery of America. Slavery as found in Roman and Teutonic civilizations had given place to medieval serfdom, which in turn was gradually replaced by conditions of modern peasantry. The introduction of slavery came rather as an incident of the long process of discovery and colonization. Exploitation of African slave centers arose early in the history of Portuguese expansion in the fifteenth century and antedated by several decades the discoveries of Columbus and his contemporaries and the development of European colonies in the Western Hemisphere. A considerable importation of slaves into Portugal and Spain had taken place prior to the opening up of Hispaniola, Puerto Rico, Jamaica, and Cuba. Following an insignificant experimentation with a form of native slavery, extensive efforts were launched shortly after 1500 for the importation of Negro slaves into the Spanish West Indies. English sea captains found profitable employment in supplying Spanish-American settlements with slaves, John Hawkins being a conspicuous example; and after the establishment of England's own colonies in North America, these slave-trading efforts were naturally intensified.

In the American colonial period English slave-trading interests became increasingly active.[1] For a time the Royal African Company, founded in 1672, enjoyed a monopoly of the trade; then an imposing number of separate traders obtained rights from Parliament, disputing the Royal African ascendancy. Soon the trade, with its large profits, grew into an important "vested interest" and as such made powerful claims upon government support.

Gradually the number of slaves in the American colonies increased. Governor Berkeley of Virginia stated in 1671 that at that time there were only 2000 "black slaves" as compared to 6000 "Christian servants" in Virginia; but by 1750 there were about 300,000 slaves in British North America. By the year of independence the number of slaves in the American colonies had increased to about 500,000.[2] In the heyday of the slave trade from 40,000 to 100,000 Negroes were taken out of Africa each

---

[1] The magnitude of the trade is suggested by the statement that the slaves imported into Jamaica alone between 1702 and 1775 amounted to 497,736. Elizabeth Donnan, *Documents Illustrative of the History of the Slave Trade to America*, II, xl.

[2] C. M. Andrews, *Colonial Self-Government*, 290; E. B. Greene, *Provincial America*, 238; W. E. B. Du Bois, *Suppression of the African Slave-Trade*, chap. i; Frederic Bancroft, *Slave-Trading in the Old South*, 2.

year; [3] and the ultimate toll of the trade upon native African populations was of colossal proportions.

Though clothed with the sanction of government and religion, the foreign slave trade was an unspeakably brutal affair. Traders established stations on the coast; and by a system of barter, native slave-hunters would bring the Negroes to the coast in slave caravans through hundreds of miles of menacing jungle. Many died on the way from thirst, famine, or exhaustion. On arriving at the coast, the Negroes were selected and purchased by traders and then subjected to the horrors of the "middle passage." Herded like cattle in unsanitary slave ships with insufficient room, inadequate ventilation, and scant food and water, great numbers of these unfortunates perished miserably in tropical waters before reaching America. The realities of the middle passage were in fact so revolting that a writer of the present day hesitates to give such details to his readers. In relating the horrors of a single night on a slave ship, an eye-witness spoke of "400 wretched beings . . . crammed into a hold 12 yards in length . . . and only 3½ feet in height." He described "the suffocating heat of the hold" which caused a panic among the Negroes in their efforts to escape to the upper air; "the smoke of their torment"; and the "Fifty-four crushed and mangled corpses lifted up from the slave deck" next day. In a period of forty days, 175 slaves died on the ship while many others died after being landed. Slaves in passage were branded with the hot iron like cattle. They were held in chains and ruled by fear. Beatings and cold-blooded murder were among the disciplinary measures employed. Where mutiny threatened, a condition of warfare existed on the slaver and on one occasion it is recorded that two hundred slaves were shot to prevent escape. In reporting a series of slave-trading trips, a contemporary observer stated that, while four hundred slaves were usually carried, "40 died on every passage." [4] Describing the trip of the Dutch ship *St. John* in 1659, Professor Phillips relates that "from one to five died nearly every day"; and that from April to October the "slave loss had reached 110." Generalizing on the fatalities of the trade, Professor Phillips shows that the "mortality on the average ship may be roughly conjectured . . . at eight or ten per cent." [5] Nor did the motive of private gain induce slaver captains to take smaller cargoes and avoid the loss of so much property. Insurance companies bore part of the loss, and profits were so high that heavy risks were cheerfully assumed.

These barbarities, however, are not to be blamed upon the South. It is not sufficient to say that they were the natural accompaniment of slavery. It is true that slavery produced the slave trade; but American slavery did not necessarily produce the horrors and brutalities of the

[3] Du Bois, 5.
[4] Blake, *History of Slavery and the Slave Trade*, 284, 290.
[5] Phillips, *Am. Negro Slavery*, 37–38.

trade as actually conducted. While slavery existed alike in the North and South till the later part of the eighteenth century, American slave-trading interests were most extensive in the North; [6] and, as compared to the Yankee trade, the institution of Southern slavery was mild indeed.

It is a matter of interest that the United States was the first nation to pronounce a condemnation upon the guilty traffic by its law of March 2, 1807; but in the effective suppression of the trade the efforts of the United States lagged far behind those of other nations. In the colonial period efforts were made, notably in Virginia, for the prohibition of the traffic. Various bills designed to suppress the trade were passed by the Virginia House of Burgesses; but these attempts, as well as similar efforts of other colonies, were overruled by the King in Council. The King through his ministers instructed the royal government of Virginia to give "assent to no laws by which the importation of slaves should be in any respect prohibited or obstructed." [7] In writing the Declaration of Independence, Jefferson included a stirring passage in which he vigorously denounced George III for waging "cruel war against human nature itself, violating its most sacred rights . . . in the persons of distant people, who never offended him, captivating and carrying them into slavery in another hemisphere, or to incur miserable death in their transportation thither." [8] In deference, however, to certain Southern states which had not as yet attempted to suppress the trade and because of the susceptibilities of "our Northern brethren," that passage was deleted from the Declaration as adopted. On attaining independence, Virginia passed a law (1778) prohibiting the importation of slaves within her borders, thus antedating by three decades the national law on the subject. One by one other states followed suit; so that by 1807 the abolition of the foreign slave trade had been provided by every state of the Union; though in South Carolina the trade had been reopened. [9] In the Constitution of the

[6] Some Southerners, however, of excellent social standing, were engaged in some manner in the business of importing slaves (Bancroft, *Slave-Trading in the Old South,* 3). Referring to the trade in South Carolina before the Revolution, Miss Elizabeth Donnan (*Am. Hist. Rev.,* XXXIII, 810) writes: "Of Charleston merchants there were few, if any, whose names did not . . . appear affixed to notices of negro sales. Before the Revolution at least one hundred firms had offered cargoes for sale. . . ." She estimates the total importations into South Carolina for the years 1753–1773 at 55,538 (*Ibid.,* 809, n. 37).

[7] B. B. Mumford, *Virginia's Attitude toward Slavery and Secession,* 17. For British official instructions designed to promote the slave trade and to protect the rights of the Royal African Company, see L. W. Labaree, *Royal Instructions to British Colonial Governors, 1670–1776,* II, 665 ff.

[8] P. L. Ford, ed., *Writings of Thomas Jefferson,* II, 52.

[9] Between 1787 and 1802 South Carolina had passed a series of acts prohibiting the slave trade; but in 1803, at a time when the opening up of Louisiana and other factors offered "fortunes to planters and Charleston slave-merchants," the

United States it was provided that Congress should not prohibit the trade before 1808. As the year 1808 approached, President Jefferson began to urge that Congress prepare to exercise the prohibitory power. In his annual message to Congress in December of 1806 he congratulated his fellow citizens "on the approach of the period at which you may interpose your authority constitutionally, to withdraw the citizens of the United States from all further participation in those violations of human rights which have been so long continued on the unoffending inhabitants of Africa." [10] By an act passed in 1794 Congress had already prohibited the carrying on of the slave trade from the United States to any foreign country; and now on March 2, 1807, the importation of slaves into the United States was prohibited from and after January 1, 1808. The similar act of the British Parliament was dated March 25, 1807. In 1820 the importation of slaves was placed by Congress on the same footing as piracy and made punishable by death.

Though these laws commanded the moral support of the American people they proved to a large extent ineffective. Importation of slaves continued as an illicit traffic, the illegal trade being even worse and more brutal than the authorized trade. The suppression of the prohibited traffic became an onerous burden upon the Federal government. Large sums were appropriated and revenue cutters and cruisers were employed to hunt down slavers. Negroes were recaptured in considerable numbers from bootleg slave ships; and the government was then confronted with the problem of their disposition. Since the law forbade their importation into the country, it was necessary for the government to feed and care for them and provide medical treatment. Government Negro colonies were maintained in this country; and the blacks, after being temporarily kept in these stations, were transported at public expense to Africa. For this purpose the government used a district in Africa which later became Liberia, a colony founded as a philanthropic enterprise about 1827. Controversies with state governments resulted from this activity of the Federal government, as for instance when American slaveholders in the South were found to be purchasers of imported slaves. Such purchasers were liable to a Federal penalty; and the Federal courts were kept busy with the prosecution of guilty parties.

3

The illicit slave trade continued through the years to the Civil War In 1860 there was presented to Congress a report covering 648 pages

prohibition was repealed. W. E. B. Du Bois, *Suppression of the African Slave-Trade to the United States of America*, 86, 229 ff.

[10] P. L. Ford, ed., *Writings of Thomas Jefferson*, VIII, 492.

which dealt entirely with this subject. "Almost all the slave expeditions for some time past [it was stated] have been fitted out in the United States, chiefly at New York." [1] Large amounts of American capital were involved, a fact regarded abroad as an international scandal. England, having abolished the trade in her own empire in 1807, became the leader of a determined movement in the early decades of the nineteenth century to suppress the traffic internationally by means of general conventions and specific treaties. Through English efforts a declaration was made by the Congress of Vienna that the slave trade was to be abolished. A series of bilateral treaties was made between England and various nations, beginning with the Treaty of Ghent (1814) in which it was declared that "the traffic in slaves is irreconcilable with the principles of humanity and justice"; wherefore it was agreed that both contracting parties (England and the United States) should use their best endeavors to "promote its entire abolition." Efforts to make this abolition effective became a constant topic of diplomatic conversation between the United States and England in the earlier part of the century. Castlereagh in 1818 urged that the United States conclude a treaty to cooperate in the suppression of the trade internationally, but was informed that the processes proposed, involving the search of mechant vessels by warships in time of peace and the extension of Federal judicial power beyond our borders, were "not adaptable to the institutions . . . of the United States." [2]

While the controversy dragged on, the flag of the United States was used to protect a trade which the United States government had declared to be piracy. In many cases the American flag was fraudulently attached to non-American ships. A Spanish ship would sail to a Florida port, e.g. Key West, bring about a nominal sale to an American owner, and engage in the slave trade under American colors; or an American vessel sold in Havana would illegally retain its American registry. Since slave-traders were pirates, since they were under the ban of both national and international law, they had about the same regard for law as pirates; it was nothing for them to carry forged American papers or fly the American flag fraudulently. But this is not the whole story: a large number of genuine American ships, many of them sailing from New York, engaged in the traffic. In the 1840's the controversy between England and the United States touching this subject became acute; and Webster as secretary of state concluded a treaty with England (1842) by which each nation agreed to maintain a naval force of not less than eighty guns on the African coast "to enforce separately . . . the laws . . . and obligations of each of the two countries for the suppression of the slave-trade." [3]

[1] *House Ex. Doc. No. 7*, 36 Cong., 2 sess., 15.
[2] W. C. Ford, ed., *Writings of John Quincy Adams*, VI, 469–472; see also *Memoirs of John Quincy Adams*, IV, 150–152.
[3] Blake, 303.

English and American squadrons were to act independently, cooperating by mutual consultation as exigencies might arise.

The United States, however, did not agree to what England was requesting, i.e. the right to stop and search ships which a British captain might have reason to believe were illegally flying the American flag and using that flag to cover the slave trade. England did not consider the Webster treaty adequate. Lord John Russell, British foreign minister, sent to the United States a dispatch in 1860 in which he complained that "United States capital has been more and more employed in this traffic" and that where vessels sailed under the American flag, no British cruiser could touch them. "The master [of the slaver]," said Russell, "often taunts the captain of a British cruiser with his impunity [*sic*] from capture." [4]

It will thus be seen that the illicit trade as practiced through the ante-bellum period brought many domestic and international embarrassments. Though, as Professor Phillips says, the "importations [after 1808] were never great enough to affect the labor supply in appreciable degree," and though, "[so] far as the general economic régime was concerned, the foreign slave trade was effectually closed in 1808," [5] yet importations into the country were by no means the whole story, and the scandal of American capital and American ships being employed in carrying slaves to non-American shores, though the United States was solemnly pledged to suppress the traffic, continued to and beyond the time of the Civil War.

4

Evolving under the social conditions of provincial America, slavery took root both North and South. Negroes came first; slavery as an institution developed afterward; slave laws came still later. It is often erroneously stated that slavery was introduced in Virginia in 1619. What really happened was that to the tiny Jamestown colony there came in 1619 a "dutch man of warre [privateer] that sold us twenty Negars." [1] For some decades following this event Negro importations were slight, and those who were brought in were employed with white servants. Those first Negroes, as Phillips has pointed out, "were not fully slaves in the hands of their Virginian buyers, for there was neither law nor custom then establishing the institution of slavery in the colony." [2] After a period of experimentation and uncertain control, during which time the Negroes were usually called "servants," the legal institution of slavery gradually took

[4] *House Ex. Doc. No. 7,* 36 Cong., 2 sess., p. 389.
[5] Phillips, *Am. Negro Slavery,* 147–148.

[1] Statement by John Rolfe. See John Smith, **Generall Historie of Virginia,** Arber ed., 541.
[2] Phillips, *Am. Negro Slavery,* 75.

shape, the laws being the result of social practice.[3] Ultimately each of the American colonies, even the Quaker colony of Pennsylvania, developed some form of slave code.

So harsh do these laws appear on paper that writers who have confined themselves to a legalistic recital have painted a dismal picture. Indeed, it is clear that in the eyes of the law the slave, as Kenneth M. Stampp observes, "was less a person than a thing." "At the heart of every code," Professor Stampp adds, "was the requirement that slaves submit to their masters and respect all white men." The Louisiana code of 1806 expressed the idea lucidly: "The condition of the slave being merely a passive one, his subordination to his master and to all who represent him is not susceptible of modification or restriction . . . he owes to his master, and to all his family, a respect without bounds, and an absolute obedience, and he is consequently to execute all the orders which he receives from him, his said master, or from them." Slaves were denied standing in court and their testimony was not accepted in opposition to that of white witnesses. Certain crimes when committed by slaves were punished with a heavier penalty than if committed by whites. There were severe restrictions upon leaving the masters' premises. Slaves were forbidden "to beat drums, blow horns, or possess guns; periodically their cabins were to be searched for weapons. They were not to administer drugs to whites or practice medicine. . . . A slave was not to possess liquor, or purchase it without a written order from his owner. He was not to trade without a permit, or gamble with whites or with other slaves."[4] Slaves could not form secret societies; they must step off the sidewalk when whites wished to pass. Teaching a slave to read or write was forbidden. Slaves were the property of their masters; on their part they were not permitted to own property without the masters' consent. Though in some of the laws slaves were defined as "imported non-Christians," conversion to Christianity did not result in freedom. In general "all persons with a palpable strain of negro blood" were "presumed . . . to be slaves unless they could prove the contrary"; and possession by masters was regarded as "presumptive evidence of legal ownership."[5] Marriages among slaves, as well as divorces and rematings, required merely the approval of the master and were not matters of legal record. For ordinary offenses the master had the power of discipline over his slaves; for more serious offenses there were special slave courts. On the other hand limits were placed upon the number of hours per day that slaves might be forced to work; and owners were required to give them adequate care and refrain from mistreatment.

[3] Oscar and Mary F. Handlin, "Origins of the Southern Labor System," *William and Mary Quart.*, 3 ser., VII, 199–222 (April, 1950); Stanley M. Elkins, *Slavery: A Problem in American Institutional and Intellectual Life*, 37–40.

[4] Stampp, *The Peculiar Institution*, 193, 207–209.

[5] Phillips, *Am. Negro Slavery*, 499.

There was, however, such a vast difference between the laws on paper and the system that existed in reality that it would be unhistorical to judge the slave régime in the South by this or that severe law which might be found by digging up old codes. The laws, especially where they were most drastic, were not strictly applied. Slaves were, in fact, taught to read and write; they did go abroad in a manner forbidden by statute; they did congregate despite laws forbidding their assembling. Members of the legislatures satisfied their sense of social duty by passing severe laws; and the people paid as much or as little attention to the laws as they saw fit. It could not be said that either the laws themselves or the actual practices of the institution were primarily motivated by any intention to treat the Negroes harshly.

Along with much degradation there were some elements of benefit to the blacks. It is, however, a difficult problem for the social historian, whether dealing with elements of degradation or benefit, to distinguish between factors traceable to the institution of slavery and factors due to the mere presence of the dark race in the South. One must be careful not to romanticize the picture. If the plantation was a school, as Southerners so often declared, it must be remembered that it was a school without a graduating exercise or a diploma. To be sure, the Negro under slavery became, in a limited sense, Americanized, but only at the expense of his rich African heritage, which he soon forgot. In the case of the Gullah type, an island home off the South Carolinian coast, isolated from the main currents of Southern life, encouraged the preservation of African elements and the cultivation of a unique dialect; but in general, as Professor Stampp sharply comments, slavery, "far from . . . acting as a civilizing force, . . . merely took away from the African his native culture and gave him, in exchange, little more than vocational training." [6] When weighed against the hard limitations of his outlook, the record of the Negro under slavery was indeed creditable. Socially ostracized, denied intellectual advancement, the average slave had no broader horizon than a hand-to-mouth existence and a routine of toil; yet the lilt of the work song added an element of poetry to lowly tasks, while in the higher fields of effort a few notable Negroes showed real achievement in things of the mind. [7]

Throughout the history of American slavery there were free Negroes in considerable numbers in the South. Manumission by deed or will was a familiar practice. Professor Phillips points out that "John Randolph's will set free nearly four hundred in 1833; Monroe Edwards of Louisiana manumitted 160 by deed in 1840; and George W. P. Custis of Virginia

---

[6] Stampp, *The Peculiar Institution,* 364.

[7] For Negro preachers, physicians, inventors, etc., see C. G. Woodson, *The Negro in Our History,* 142 ff., 230–231; John Hope Franklin, *From Slavery to Freedom,* 196–197; Richard Bardolph, *The Negro Vanguard,* 42–61.

liberated his two or three hundred at his death in 1857." [8] The census showed 434,000 free Negroes in the United States in 1850 and 488,000 in 1860. For the South the total of free Negroes in 1860 was 250,000. More than half of them were in Virginia and Maryland. In the lower South they were not only comparatively few, but because of increasingly stringent Southern regulations designed to check manumission their number tended to increase at a considerably lower rate than that of the whole Negro population.

For reasons of social control the Southern states, while tolerating the presence of the free Negro, qualified his status by various restraints. He was not commonly a citizen in the South,[9] though he was a state citizen in some of the Northern states. He was entitled to trial by jury; yet this was small comfort, for verdicts were usually foregone conclusions in complaints of whites against blacks, and unprejudiced trials were exceptional. In Maryland free Negroes if found vagrant could be sold into temporary slavery. In Kentucky slaves could be emancipated only on condition of being removed from the state; [10] no deed or will of emancipation could confer freedom until such removal had been effected. Assemblages of free Negroes without white supervision were illegal under prevailing Southern laws; and migration from state to state or county to county was prohibited. At all times the free Negro was subject to the hazard of kidnapping, to arrest as a suspected fugitive, and to ultimate re-enslavement. If seized by an official and charged with being a runaway slave he was not permitted to testify in his own behalf and was at the mercy of unscrupulous officials who were rewarded by fees for his "recapture." Yet despite these hardships many of them grew prosperous, owned considerable property, in some cases held slaves of their own,[11] and enjoyed the benefits of schools maintained by benevolent whites or by blacks in defiance of law.

For the status of free Negroes in the lower South the case of Missis-

[8] Phillips, *Am. Negro Slavery*, 426–427.

[9] This was the general situation; in North Carolina, however, at the time of the adoption of the Constitution, free Negroes had the privileges of citizenship. J. S. Bassett, "Slavery in the State of North Carolina," *Johns Hopkins Univ. Studies*, XVII, 354.

[10] *Revised Statutes of Ky.*, 1860, II, 359 ff. To illustrate the working of this law, it was decreed in a Kentucky court in 1858 that a slave, emancipated by its owner's will without financial provision for removal from the state, be hired out to provide a sufficient fund for that purpose. Helen T. Catterall, *Judicial Cases concerning American Slavery and the Negro*, I, 431.

[11] "The majority of Negro owners of slaves had some personal interest in their property," John Hope Franklin points out. "Frequently the husband purchased his wife or vice versa; or the slaves were the children of a free father who had purchased his wife; or they were other relatives or friends who had been rescued . . . by some affluent free Negro. There were instances, however, in which free Negroes had a real economic interest in . . . slavery and held slaves in order to improve their economic status." Franklin, *From Slavery to Freedom*, 221.

FREE–COLORED POPULATION OF THE UNITED STATES,
1850 AND 1860

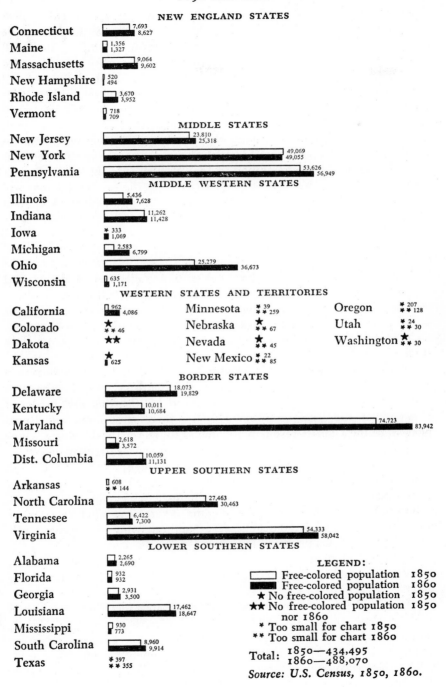

NEW ENGLAND STATES

Connecticut — 7,693 / 8,627
Maine — 1,356 / 1,327
Massachusetts — 9,064 / 9,602
New Hampshire — 520 / 494
Rhode Island — 3,670 / 3,952
Vermont — 718 / 709

MIDDLE STATES

New Jersey — 23,810 / 25,318
New York — 49,069 / 49,055
Pennsylvania — 53,626 / 56,949

MIDDLE WESTERN STATES

Illinois — 5,436 / 7,628
Indiana — 11,262 / 11,428
Iowa — *333 / 1,069
Michigan — 2,583 / 6,799
Ohio — 25,279 / 36,673
Wisconsin — 635 / 1,171

WESTERN STATES AND TERRITORIES

California — 962 / 4,086
Colorado — ★★ 46
Dakota — ★★
Kansas — ★ 625

Minnesota — *39 / **259
Nebraska — ★ / **67
Nevada — ★ / **45
New Mexico — *22 / **85

Oregon — *207 / **128
Utah — *24 / **30
Washington — ★ / **30

BORDER STATES

Delaware — 18,073 / 19,829
Kentucky — 10,011 / 10,684
Maryland — 74,723 / 83,942
Missouri — 2,618 / 3,572
Dist. Columbia — 10,059 / 11,131

UPPER SOUTHERN STATES

Arkansas — 608 / **144
North Carolina — 27,463 / 30,463
Tennessee — 6,422 / 7,300
Virginia — 54,333 / 58,042

LOWER SOUTHERN STATES

Alabama — 2,265 / 2,690
Florida — 932 / 932
Georgia — 2,931 / 3,500
Louisiana — 17,462 / 18,647
Mississippi — 930 / 773
South Carolina — 8,960 / 9,914
Texas — *397 / **355

LEGEND:
☐ Free-colored population 1850
■ Free-colored population 1860
★ No free-colored population 1850
★★ No free-colored population 1850 nor 1860
* Too small for chart 1850
** Too small for chart 1860
Total: 1850—434,495
1860—488,070
Source: U.S. Census, 1850, 1860.

sippi may be taken as an example. Though in Virginia in 1860 there were 58,042 free Negroes, and in Maryland 83,942; in Mississippi the number was only 773, as compared to 1366 in 1840. Legally all colored persons in Mississippi were presumed to be slaves; freedom for each individual had to be proved in court. Free blacks in the state faced the penalties of vagrancy if found outside their home counties; they could not sell goods except in incorporated towns; they were denied such employment as keeping houses of entertainment or typesetting. For circulating incendiary literature among Negroes the penalty was death. Emancipation was difficult; a special legislative act was necessary, and petitions were usually denied. Immigration of free Negroes into the state was prohibited; and when in 1831 certain citizens petitioned for the removal of free Negroes outside the state a law designed partially to effect such removal (with colonization in Liberia) was passed.

5

When the institution of slavery is examined closely it will be found that those features which involved harshness and brutality were in large part concerned with three aspects of the subject: (1) the problem of slave crimes, with which was associated the question of slave insurrection; (2) the problem of the runaway; and (3) the domestic or internal slave trade.

Though the whole history of American slavery exhibits surprisingly few instances of slave insurrections in the South, yet the Southerner's fear of possible servile uprisings conditioned his thinking and produced harsh social and legal arrangements. The three most important Negro plots were the Gabriel revolt in Richmond in 1800, the Denmark Vesey plot in Charleston in 1822, and the Nat Turner insurrection of 1831. The Gabriel and Vesey plots, while serious enough, were discovered in time to be frustrated; but the Turner conspiracy unfortunately resulted in the massacre of nearly sixty whites, most of whom were women and children, in Southampton County, Virginia. There were other, lesser plots, and down the long decades of slavery Southern whites were constantly fearful of further uprisings; but, faced with the overwhelming power in the hands of their masters, most discontented Negroes took out their ill feelings in malingering, in minor sabotage, in petty theft, or in running away.

In a study of runaways based upon newspaper files Professor Sydnor explains that, among other motives, the Negroes sought to renew family ties, to break away from professional traders or new masters, to escape heavy work in the cotton fields, to avoid punishment for misdeeds, or to follow the beckonings of apostles of freedom, whether white or black. The fugitive usually took nothing with him but the clothes on his back;

he ordinarily departed alone, though sometimes groups of four or five are mentioned; and he had only the vaguest notion as to where he would go. Dogs were only rarely used in the hunting of Negroes. Though the majority of slaveowners, says Sydnor, were "men of conscience," "there were undoubtedly some who were brutal. . . ." He adds that the "large majority [of the runaways] were ultimately returned to their . . . owners." [1]

The typical slave did not stray from the plantation. In part the problem of the runaway was similar to that of the tramp, in part that of the unwilling or discontented laborer. It was unusual for a sense of personal independence in Negroes to develop to such a point of defiance, not only of the master but of society itself, as to induce a bold stroke for freedom. Where slaves did break away, planters were much concerned: indeed the very essence of slavery demanded severity at this point. Southern states had drastic laws for apprehending absconding slaves; and they continually made demands for the rigid fulfillment of the Federal duty of remanding to servitude those who escaped from one state to another. Such were the abuses connected with the hunting of runaways that the cards were usually stacked against the fugitive, as well as against the free Negro accused of being a fugitive. Under the Federal fugitive slave law of 1850 a Negro suspected of escaping bondage had short shrift. Not only Federal marshals and their deputies but all good citizens were enjoined to help in catching absconders. When arrested a Negro would be taken before a Federal court or commissioner; and in the judicial hearing the statement of the man claiming ownership, though given *in absentia,* was taken as the main evidence, while the testimony of the alleged fugitive was not admitted.

In dealing with the domestic slave trade, a phase of Southern life that has produced a vast literature of denunciation, it is necessary to take account of economic pressures. Retardation in the older states coincided with phenomenal development in the new cotton states, with the result that great numbers of slaves were moved from Virginia and the Carolinas, where they were unprofitable, into Alabama, Mississippi, Louisiana, and Texas, where a rapid increase in the labor supply was demanded in order to keep pace with the opening of new lands. The legal prohibition of the importation of slaves left only two sources of supply open: bootleg importations from abroad, and the domestic trade. Without entering into the perplexing problems of estimates in a field where precise totals are unavailable, it may be noted that in 1857 a legislative committee in South Carolina reported that 234,638 slaves were exported from Maryland, Virginia, Kentucky, and the Carolinas during the decade 1840–1850, and that after correcting this estimate because of errors in method Frederic

[1] Charles S. Sydnor, "Pursuing Fugitive Slaves," *So. Atl. Quar.,* XXVIII, 152–164 (April, 1929).

Bancroft concludes that the probable total was approximately 180,000 for the decade. Bancroft also concludes that in the decade 1850–1860 the importations from other states into Alabama, Arkansas, Florida, Georgia, Mississippi, Louisiana, and Texas amounted to 230,335. When it is remembered that at the rate of $800 per slave this involved the enormous sum of $184,000,000, it will be seen that winnings in the trading business were more than commensurate with risks and that handsome profits were assured. For choice slaves much higher prices were obtained—e.g. $1500 for "No. 1 men," $1325 for "Best grown girls," and occasionally as high as $2500 for slaves of unusual value. So great was the differential between the prices paid by traders in obtaining the slaves in the old states and the prices received in the newer markets that substantial profits remained after deducting transportation costs, maintenance, depreciation, and other expenses. A single trading magnate was said to have made $500,000 in the business by 1834.[2]

That the trade brought hardship to thousands of hapless Negroes is not to be denied. Driven along the highways in coffles, marching and bivouacking in chains, urged on by whip and pistol, herded in stockades or slave pens, torn from their families and sold on the auction block as so many cattle, these creatures were snatched from districts where slavery was a dying institution, and where their presence might have tended to hasten emancipation, into regions where plantations were larger, where tasks were heavier, and where their bonds were at once more irksome and more permanent. One of the familiar topics of denunciation was the great activity of slave-traders in the District of Columbia, which caused John Randolph in 1816 to inveigh against daily practices "at which the despotisms of Europe would be horrorstruck. . . ."[3] It was not that the District was the largest trading center; it was rather the most conspicuous and notorious. Among other items of complaint was the use of public jails in the nation's capital for the convenience of traders.

The low caliber of many of the traders is evidenced by unethical practices to which they resorted and by the odium attaching to the trade in the Southern mind. Slaves were stolen; criminal slaves were sold on false assurances of character; free Negroes were kidnapped. Indeed it has been reasonably conjectured that the number of freemen kidnapped and subjected to slavery was equal to the number of slaves who escaped bondage. Though, as Bancroft shows, not a few Southerners of social standing were engaged in the trade,[4] yet one finds ample evidence of general disapprobation of the traffic. Said a lawyer in Mississippi: ". . . I can imagine a man . . . who would think it . . . right to own [slaves] . . . ,

[2] Frederic Bancroft, *Slave-Trading in the Old South,* 393–395, 117, 355, 60.
[3] *Ibid.,* 46.
[4] *Ibid.,* 3, 99, 167–168, 371, 376.

and yet . . . abhor . . . the speculator and the dealer, and . . . shun his society. And I can imagine a community of such men." [5] By the constitution of 1832 the importation of slaves into Mississippi from other states was prohibited, a prohibition which continued until 1846, when the constitution was amended.[6] The law was never properly enforced, and it led to intricate legal suits concerning the validity of promissory notes given for slaves illegally imported; but the mere fact that such a prohibition could exist in a state like Mississippi in the thirties and forties is a significant index of Southern feeling toward the traffic.

It is not necessary in these pages to enter upon the question of slave breeding or rearing for the market, except to say that extravagant abolitionist statements on this subject are to be read with skepticism. As Avery Craven has said: "The size of families and the age at which Negro women began bearing children do not seem to have been greatly affected by slavery. . . . Negro slaves differed little from the whites in these matters. Girls became mothers at about the same age. They bore about the same number of children and lost them at about the same fearful rate. Negro children, like white ones on Northern farms, were always welcome as potential laborers. The slave girl's value to her master, like that of the white girl to her husband, was, in part, measured by her capacity for motherhood. She was encouraged to bear children and sometimes rewarded with a new dress. In the matter of the dress she probably had an advantage over most of her equally fruitful white sisters." [7] Though the legend of "slave-breeding" must be dismissed, there is no denying that slave surpluses existed in Virginia and the upper South generally; nor must one forget that for many planters in that region "their most profitable product was the slave who could be sold." [8]

6

In its geographical distribution in the South the institution of slavery presented many inequalities. There were vast areas in which the slaves constituted less than one-tenth of the population, while there were other regions in which the ratio ran as high as 80 or 90 per cent. The highlands of the Appalachian Mountains, stretching southwestward from Pennsylvania to Alabama, formed a huge contiguous region in which slaveholding was rare, the Atlantic seaboard from Maryland to Florida an equally ex-

[5] Green *vs.* Robinson, 5 Miss. 80, 90. For a scathing denunciation of the trade by Robert J. Walker, see Groves et al. *vs.* Slaughter, 15 Peters 448, Appendix, 599–686.

[6] Catterall, *Jud. Cases,* III, 277–279.

[7] Craven, *Coming of the Civil War,* 83–84.

[8] Dodd, *Cotton Kingdom,* 9.

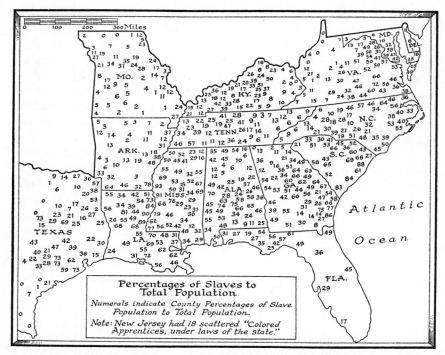

DISTRIBUTION OF SLAVE POPULATION, 1850

tensive region in which slavery was a dominant interest. In Virginia the slaves were concentrated in the eastern half of the state—i.e. in the region east of Lynchburg. In a section near Petersburg the percentage of Negroes in the population was 72; near Lexington the proportion was 30 per cent; in the mountainous regions the slaves numbered usually no more than 5 per cent of the population; while in the panhandle (the Wheeling region), the number of slaves was virtually reduced to zero.

In South Carolina physiographical characteristics were similarly re-flected in the statistics of slave distribution. In the Charleston region the percentage of slaves to the total population was 61; it was as high as 88 just north of Charleston, but as low as 21 in the back country. As a whole, however, the state of South Carolina presented a fairly continuous region of slave concentration. On the Georgia seacoast the percentage was over 80, while near Atlanta it was 16, and along the Tennessee line it was 2 or less. In central Alabama the percentage was about 70 near Selma and 65 near Montgomery, but as low as 4 or 6 per cent in some of the north-ern mountainous counties. Records for Mississippi show a belt along the Mississippi River in which the percentage of slave population ran as high as 93,[1] and one finds a fairly large slave population over most of the state; but in the northeastern corner the proportion was as low as 12 per cent. Beyond the Mississippi the state of Louisiana presented considerable areas where the slave ratio ran over half the total population; but in Arkansas and Missouri such areas were almost unknown. In Texas there were wide variations as to slave ratios, the chief concentration being in the lower courses of the Colorado River. Slavery would thus appear to be largely a matter of geography. Where climate, land, and soil features favored the institution by promoting the plantation system, slaves were plentiful; whereas in regions of barrenness, aridity, or mountain formations, slaves were not only few, but their proportion to the white population was very slight. That slavery occupied the best of the South, however, is a fact which emerges from a study of these geographical considerations.

NUMBER OF SLAVEHOLDERS IN THE UNITED STATES IN 1850

Holders of	1	slave each	68,820
	2– 4	slaves each	105,683
	5– 9		80,765
	10– 19		54,595
	20– 49		29,733
	50– 99		6,196
	100–199		1,479
	200–299		187
	300–499		56
	500 or more		11
Total number of slaveholders			347,525

The men of the South who had a proprietary interest in slaves constituted a minority, while those who owned enough Negroes to support sizable plantations were confined to a few thousand families. The total number of slaveholders in 1850 was only 347,525 out of a total white population of about six million in the slaveholding areas.[2] Half of these owned but four slaves or less; holders of more than 50 slaves numbered less than 8000, and holders of more than 100 slaves numbered less than 1800. About five-sevenths of the slaveowners of 1850 were small owners in that they owned nine slaves or less. In speaking therefore of the class known as "slave magnates," one is dealing with a group so small as to be comparable to the millionaires of the following century.[3] These few slave

[1] In 1860 five-sixths of the plantations of two hundred or more Negroes in Mississippi were in the river counties. Charles S. Sydnor, *Slavery in Miss.*, ch. viii.

[2] H. R. Helper, *Impending Crisis*, 144, 146. (This statement applies to the fifteen slave states and the District of Columbia.)

[3] In interpreting these statistics, however, it should be remembered that a slaveholder in the census meant usually a slaveholding family and accounted for perhaps five persons on the average when one includes simply the members of the owner's

SLAVEHOLDERS IN 1860

Total slaveholders compared with substantial slaveholders, with total white population, and with number of white families

BORDER STATES

Delaware
90,589
15,562
587
111

Kentucky
919,484
164,428
38,645
16,619

Maryland
515,918
94,855
13,783
5,410

Missouri
1,063,489
191,447
24,320
8,657

UPPER SOUTH

Arkansas
324,143
57,208
1,149
490

North Carolina
629,942
119,127
34,658
18,587

Tennessee
826,722
148,025
36,844
17,665

Virginia
1,047,299
190,939
52,128
26,773

LOWER SOUTH

Alabama
526,271
96,087
33,730
19,326

Florida
77,747
14,911
5,152
2,919

Georgia
591,550
109,283
41,084
23,550

Louisiana
357,456
70,994
22,033
11,798

Mississippi
353,899
62,882
30,943
18,254

South Carolina
291,300
56,695
26,701
16,684

Texas
420,891
76,651
21,878
10,536

LEGEND:
☐ Total white population
▨ Total white families (See note below)
▦ Total slaveholders
■ Substantial slaveholders (Possessing 5 or more slaves)

NOTE: For each state the census gives the precise average of persons per family. In North Carolina, for example, the average is 5.288 while the total white population is 629,942. Dividing the white population by 5.288 gives 119,127 as the estimated number of white families for North Carolina, though the census, in reporting free families, does not separate white and colored. Since in the census each slaveholder is normally a head of family, the significant comparison is not between slaveholders and total white population, but between slaveholders and the total number of white families.

magnates, however, had an influence far beyond their numbers. It was quite generally true among the states of the South that counties in which slaveholding predominated had more than a proportionate representation in the legislatures. Furthermore, the millions of non-slaveholding whites of the South were either indifferent to the institution or tenacious in defending it. Thought-patterns of the whole section were fixed by the upper four hundred; and it may well be questioned whether American social history has ever revealed such a concentration of wealth and social power in a few hands as existed in the ante-bellum South. Yet it would be irrational to conclude that such a concentration of wealth and position was merely the result of slavery; in large part it may be regarded as an incident of large-scale agricultural production.

7

On the individual plantation the régime of slavery involved a definite system of rules and an orderly regimentation. On the ordinary small plantation the owner himself saw to the carrying out of these regulations. On larger estates, however, the fulfillment of these rules fell to the overseer, who had general charge under the authority of the planter and functioned as a manager or steward of the plantation. Supervising the planting, cultivating, and harvesting of the crops, he had to be conversant with specialized forms of agriculture and capable of mastering the intricate details of rice, cotton, or sugar culture. Socially his place was inferior to that of the master of the big house. "He might belong to the same church with the planter, but he usually preferred some plain form of worship, as in the churches of Methodists or Baptists. If the two found themselves worshipping in the same place they sat apart. . . ." To the slaves the overseer was the "master's left hand," the "symbol of slavery." Ringing the plantation bell, keeping "his eye fixed on the workers," "punish[ing] the slothful," he stood "ever in the way of any slave who had liberal ideas of the comforts of bondage." "He rarely read a book," writes J. S. Bassett. "[He] looked out on a narrow horizon. . . . His words were apt to be severe, his epithets . . . strong, his standards of justice . . . crude." [1]

---

family, and for more if one counts the overseer and his family, together with other whites attached to the plantation. Writers sometimes overlook this and make out too strong a case in treating the numerical insignificance of Southern slaveholders. Further caution in using the census is necessary because the enumeration was taken by counties, so that a man with plantations in three counties would figure as three slaveholders. The number of holders is thus somewhat inflated and the full size of individual holdings not fully revealed. For slaveholding in relation to population, see chart, p. 68.

[1] J. S. Bassett, *The Southern Plantation Overseer as Revealed in His Letters*, 1–5.

General matters of labor control were under the overseers, whose journals, preserved among voluminous masses of plantation records, reveal the elaborate daily routine of the plantation. Under the overseer were placed slave-drivers chosen from among the better trained and more responsible slaves. The term "driver" should not be understood as connoting cruelty; the word merely denoted a position of authority in the maintenance of discipline and in labor management. Under the task system, for instance, it was the duty of the slave-driver, acting under the overseer, to give out the day's tasks to the slaves under his charge, and to be responsible for their performance.

"In food and housing," Allan Nevins writes, "the slaves fared ill compared with workmen and farmers of the Northern States, Canada, and Britain, but were not perceptibly worse off than common laborers or peasants of backward parts of continental Europe." [2] Cabins in the quarters were usually of logs; often they were dingy and windowless; seldom were they made of brick and set close to the mansion as at "Monticello"; not uncommonly the chimneys were of laths or split sticks, plastered with mud. Often the practice of feeding slaves in a common dining room and caring for children in a nursery caused the cabins to have less the quality of homes than of sleeping quarters. Clothing was adequate but cheap; both strong boots and lighter ones were provided; sufficient raiment was given so that, as Olmsted observed in Virginia, on "Sundays and holidays they usually look very smart, but when at work, very ragged and slovenly." [3] Their work of hoeing, plowing, planting, cultivating, picking, ginning, baling, et cetera, was organized by gangs, with set tasks performed under the drivers' eyes. Children began as quarter-hands; they advanced by stages to full hands; and they were relieved with declining strength until in old age field work was over. "Hours of labor were long," Professor Nevins concludes, "but not longer than those of the Iowa pioneer, the New York seamstress, or the Pawtucket factory hand." [4] Work generally began at daybreak and usually ended at sundown or shortly thereafter; noon rest extended from one to three hours. There were, however, many exceptions to this rule. Slaves in the southwest were worked harder than those in Virginia; slaves on large plantations were exploited more than those on small holdings. The work load depended also upon the season. "On the sugar plantations," Kenneth M. Stampp writes, "during the months of the harvest, slaves were driven to the point of complete exhaustion." [5]

On well managed plantations expectant mothers were excused from heavy work; Negro midwives presided at birth; after birth the mother

[2] Nevins, *Ordeal of the Union*, I, 427.
[3] F. L. Olmsted, *Cotton Kingdom*, I, 105.
[4] Nevins, *Ordeal of the Union*, I, 431.
[5] Stampp, *The Peculiar Institution*, 85.

was asked to do little but care for her baby. When ill, slaves were tended according to the medical usages of the time, with due regard for Negro faith in such "yarbs" as boneset and blackroot, and with due attention on the part of plantation physician, nurse, overseer, master, and mistress. The maintenance of infirmaries and hospitals for the slaves was not uncommon. Sometimes the sick were fed from the master's table. A family physician charged a Mississippi master $100 for attending a female slave.[6] Medical practice, for both whites and blacks, however, was in an extremely primitive stage, and it was "uncertain that even the most conscientious master would invariably prescribe better remedies than the superstitious slave healer." [7] Even more important is the fact that not all slave owners were concerned for the health of their slaves and that some willfully neglected their Negroes.

Slavery, Professor Stampp reminds us, "was above all a labor system." [8] Concerned with getting the maximum of effort out of their slaves, some masters resorted to force and ruthless exploitation. The more humane, who were also the more clever, recognized that morale "was no less needed than muscle if performance were to be kept above a barely tolerable minimum," [9] and used gifts, bonuses, and rewards as incentives. Others tacitly connived at relaxing the rigors of the black codes by teaching their slaves to read and write or by making systematic provision for religious worship, sometimes under a white minister, sometimes under a black. A handsome Gothic church was supplied on one unusual Mississippi plantation; and the sum of $1500 a year was spent to support a preacher for the master and his slaves.[10]

That such concessions often alleviated the slave's lot cannot be denied, but it must not be forgotten that he remained a chattel, subject to a rigorous and often brutal disciplinary system. This is not to argue that many slaveholders were sadists who deliberately adopted a policy of cruelty; it is rather to recognize "that controlling a gang of field-hands was at best a wretched business, and that a certain amount of savagery was inevitable." Manuscript plantation records painfully re-enforce contemporary abolitionist charges that slavery meant whippings, brandings, mutilations, and bloodhound pursuits. "It is a pity," one sensitive North Carolina planter wrote, "that . . . Slavery and Tyranny must go together and that there is no such thing as having an obedient and useful Slave, without the painful exercise of undue and tyrannical authority." [11]

[6] Munn *vs.* Perkins, 9 Miss. 415.
[7] Stampp, 307.
[8] *Ibid.*, 34.
[9] Phillips, *Life and Labor*, 198.
[10] *De Bow's Review*, VII, 221.
[11] Stampp, 184, 141.

8

In defending slavery on the economic front the Southerner had many arguments ready to hand. The importance of cotton in Southern economy was urged and the peculiar adaptation of Negro labor to the planting, cultivation, and harvesting of this major crop was stressed. Argument then proceeded from premise to conclusion about as follows: cotton is of controlling importance; large-scale production is more profitable than small-scale effort in cotton growing; such large-scale production is impossible without the Negro, for no other group can match his remarkable adaptation to subtropical labor; slavery is the best régime for the management of Negroes in large numbers; "the consolidation of domestic establishments, which slavery promotes, permits . . . economy in the purchase of supplies . . . [and] specialization of labor;" [1] hence slavery is indispensable for the maintenance of the whole Southern economic structure. Furthermore it was urged that slavery elevated the white master, making him proud of his race and tenacious of his liberty, and that it had an ennobling effect upon woman. Poverty, it was pointed out, was not only less prevalent under slavery than in Northern states, but where present it constituted less of a stigma; for race, not money, conferred honor. The bitter struggles between labor and capital as found in "free" industrial communities were contrasted with the spirit of kindness and cooperation between the Southern planter and his laborers, where the prosperity of the master constituted the happiness of the slave.

On the other hand, critics of slavery declared that it brought many economic evils in its train. Slaves were costly and land cheap; hence, said the critics, lands were exploited, soil exhausted, and new lands quickly taken up. There were sad predictions as to what would happen when new land was no longer available and when therefore the Southern plantation system should be forced back upon itself and confronted with the difficult problems of replenishment, of conservation, and of wringing profits out of older lands. Since slaves could cultivate more than they could harvest it was urged that the Southern planter was faced with the dilemma of planting less than his land and slaves could produce and raise, or of losing part of his crop at harvest time. This difficulty was only partially overcome by hiring additional hands for the stress of the harvest season.

A tendency for Southern capital to be absorbed in slaves and ever more slaves was pointed out as one of the evils inherent in the institution. In free communities, it was said, capital becomes embodied in soil development, in shops, buildings, and the manifold equipment of indus-

[1] Edmund Ruffin, paraphrased in Phillips, *Am. Negro Slavery*, 352.

try; while in slave communities, surplus wealth is put into the acquisition of increasing numbers of slaves. Much of the advantage of cotton profits, it was urged, was lost by reason of the ever mounting labor cost measured in terms of higher prices for field hands. A hundred thousand dollars transferred from Massachusetts to Illinois, said F. L. Olmsted, meant that saw mills, grist mills, and machinery would be introduced and that schools and other evidences of culture would take root; while if the same amount were transferred from South Carolina to Louisiana, nine-tenths of it would be put into the purchase of slaves.[2] An immense sum would be required to buy the slaves of a big plantation—$100,000, for instance, being enough for only a moderately large establishment—so that only the rich could become planters; hence the slave system tended more and more to monopoly and to the concentration of wealth, social position, and political control in a few hands. The Southern yeoman, unable to become a slaveholder, found his prospects growing less and less favorable; and the proportion of whites as compared to blacks in any community given over to great plantations was extremely small. This squeezing out of non-slaveholding whites was pointed to as one of the inescapable results in any régime made up of continuous plantations. It was urged that the perfection of the slave régime, if ever realized, would produce a situation similar to that of Jamaica, where elements extrinsic to slavery were almost unknown. "The destruction and expulsion of the white race are the legitimate effects of the plantation system," said a writer of the ante-bellum period.[3] Thus the benefits to slaveholders themselves in the institution of slavery were believed by its critics to be illusory, while the effect upon vast numbers of ill-favored whites, who were driven to the exhausted lands or the sand hills, was declared to be truly pitiable.

Historians have continued to debate the economic profitability of slavery, but the highly technical argument involves a good deal of semantic confusion. In terming slavery profitable or unprofitable, a writer should distinguish between the economic consequences of the institution to the large planter, to the small slaveholder, to the nonslaveholding white population, to the enslaved Negro, and to the sectional economy as a whole. In ascertaining levels of profitability, the problem is to find a suitable standard of comparison. Should the income from a Southern plantation operated by slaves be compared with that from a Southern farm worked by free labor, or with that from agricultural operations in the North and West, or with that derived from an equivalent amount of capital invested in banking securities or manufacturing stock? The analysis involves some technical questions of accounting, for a writer must decide whether in-

[2] F. L. Olmsted, *Cotton Kingdom*, II, 299–300.
[3] George M. Weston, *The Progress of Slavery in the United States*, 14.

terest upon the planters' investment in slaves is to be classified as a cost
of doing business or as a part of profits; [4] if it is properly the former, few
plantations made a profit, but if it is the latter a great many produced
reasonable incomes. In all his calculations the historian must recognize
that he is dealing with fictitious, if useful, concepts; there never was an
average planter or an average year, but, instead, "there were enormous
variations in the returns upon investments in slave labor from master to
master and from year to year." [5] Finally, an effort must be made to distinguish between the effects of slavery upon the South and those which
were the result of large-scale agriculture and to take into account the
many economic difficulties inherent in agricultural pursuits. [6]

In view of these difficulties, any conclusions must be made with
great caution, yet a few generalizations can be hazarded. No modern
writer believes that slavery was economically beneficial to the Negro; few
argue that it was beneficial to the nonslaveholding white; almost no one
maintains that it benefited the section as a whole. Even those who hold
that slavery was generally profitable to the planters admit that, from the
point of view of agricultural income, it was "unprofitable in regions in
the wake of expansion," such as the worn-out tobacco fields of Virginia
or the exhausted cotton plantations of South Carolina. [7] Virtually all
writers, on the other hand, agree that during the 1850's, a period of exceptional prosperity, slave plantations in the newly developed lands along
the Gulf brought in sizable profits. [8]

Attempting to reconcile these contradictions, two economists, Alfred H. Conrad and John R. Meyer, have produced what is perhaps the
most satisfactory statement about the profitability of slavery. They argue
that the ante-bellum South had not one but two productive functions.
The role of the lower South was the production of staples, chiefly cotton;
that of the upper South was the production of "slaves, exporting the increase to the staple-crop areas." If these two regions of the South are
considered as an economic unit, they argue, "Slavery was profitable to the
whole South, the continuing demand for labor in the Cotton Belt insur-

[4] Thomas P. Govan, "Was Plantation Slavery Profitable?" *J.S.H.*, VIII, 513–
535 (Nov., 1942).

[5] Stampp, 390.

[6] Robert R. Russel concludes: ". . . the importance of Negro slavery as a
factor determining . . . the economic development of the South has been greatly
overestimated. . . . compared with such great economic factors as climate, topography, natural resources, location with respect to the North and to Europe, means
of transportation, and character of the white population, Negro slavery was of
lesser consequence in determining the general course of Southern economic development." Russel, "The General Effects of Slavery upon Southern Economic Progress," *J.S.H.*, IV, 53–54 (Feb., 1938).

[7] L. C. Gray, *History of Agriculture in the Southern United States*, I, 478.
But cf. Stampp, 410–411.

[8] Nevins, *Ordeal of the Union*, I, 467–469.

ing returns to the breeding operation on the less productive land in the seaboard and border states. The breeding returns were necessary, however, to make the plantation operations on the poorer lands as profitable as alternative contemporary activities in the United States." [9]

If it can be accepted that slavery, in this limited sense, was profitable, the historian inevitably speculates upon the future of the institution. There appear to be no valid economic reasons for believing that the institution was about to die out. Though there was an increasing amount of antislavery feeling in the upper South, Allan Nevins writes, "Nowhere . . . did the emancipationist cause make verifiable and encouraging progress in the slaveholding area between 1840 and 1860"; [10] the slave trade, so necessary for sustaining the economy of that region, kept it firmly aligned with the cotton kingdom. There is some justification for believing that slavery had to expand, as inefficient methods of tillage used up the soil, and Professor Charles W. Ramsdell, pointing to the fact that there were no lands beyond Texas which were suitable for slave cultivation, maintained that the institution had by 1860 reached its natural limits. [11] But since there were vast areas of unexploited land within the South, there is no good reason to believe that self-strangulation was approaching. Indeed, when one reads that the amount of improved land in farms increased 61.5 per cent in the South Atlantic states between 1850 and 1910, 191.0 per cent in the East South Central states, and 1832.1 per cent in the West South Central states during the same period, he is obliged to conclude, with L. C. Gray, that "the lower South in 1860 contained land enough to admit of an increase of slave population for many decades." [12]

It is possible, of course, that the slave system might ultimately have been transformed through other economic processes. There were in 1860 about 400,000 slaves living in Southern cities and there were many additional thousands who were hired out by their owners. These Negroes "worked in sawmills, gristmills, quarries, and fisheries. They mined gold in North Carolina, coal and salt in Virginia, iron in Kentucky and Tennessee, and lead in Missouri. On river boats they were used as deck hands and firemen. Other slaves were employed in the construction and maintenance of internal improvements. . . . Town slaves worked in cotton presses, tanneries, shipyards, bakehouses, and laundries, as dock laborers and stevedores, and as clerks in stores." There were skilled slave artisans, "such as barbers, blacksmiths, cabinet makers, and shoemakers." A num-

[9] Conrad and Meyer, "The Economics of Slavery in the Ante Bellum South," *Jour. of Political Economy*, LXVI, 97, 121 (April, 1958).
[10] Nevins, *Ordeal of the Union*, I, 506.
[11] Ramsdell, "The Natural Limits of Slavery Expansion," *M.V.H.R.*, XVI, 151–171 (Sept., 1929).
[12] Gray, *History of Agriculture in the Southern United States*, II, 641–642.

ber of Southern factories employed slaves. "From its earliest beginnings the southern iron industry depended upon skilled and unskilled slaves." So did the "ropewalks" of Kentucky. After a strike by white workers in 1847 the famour Tredegar Iron Company of Richmond used "almost exclusively slave labor except as the Boss men." [13] Slaves also worked in some Southern textile mills. "The Saluda textile factory in South Carolina at one time employed ninety-eight slave operatives," and there were others "in the textile mills of Florida, Alabama, Mississippi, and Georgia." [14]

By the nature of their employments and the conditions of their service, as Richard B. Morris has pointed out, these urban and industrial slaves were a step removed from plantation servitude. Escaping the worst severities of its discipline, many of them were, despite numerous legal restrictions, "permitted to hold property, receive wages, make contracts, and assume supervisory responsibilities"; in addition, they possessed "some measure of mobility and occasionally a limited choice as to masters and occupations." "In industry slaves were customarily reimbursed for services performed beyond an accepted minimum," Professor Morris continues. ". . . slaves hired to others occasionally received directly a portion of the hiring wages. . . . Masters were often reluctant to force slaves to work as hirelings in occupations they disliked or for masters whom they found uncongenial." An increasing number of slaves were permitted to hire their own time—i.e., to work at whatever employment they pleased, paying their masters an annual rental. Such "nominal slaves " were able "to control their earnings, separate property, or occupational choices."

Lest one hastily decide that Southern slavery was tending toward at least quasi-freedom for the Negro, Professor Morris warns that the system gave these urban slaves no guarantees for "the physical security of the person, the right to a normal family life, and to freedom from arbitrary government"; even their limited economic freedom was at the pleasure of their masters. Moreover, the "trend toward upgrading slaves into a shadowland of quasi-freedom was actually offset by the deteriorating status of the free Negro," who "appears to have retrograded to a state of servitude or quasi-slavery." [15] That slavery was slowly changing can be admitted; that it was on the verge of transforming itself into freedom must be doubted.

In the ultimate analysis the attitude of the Southern people toward their "peculiar institution" was not determined by such economic forces. Slavery was for them part of a way of life; they saw it recognized all

[13] Stampp, 61–65.
[14] J. H. Franklin, *From Slavery to Freedom*, 196.
[15] Morris, "The Measure of Bondage in the Slave States," *M.V.H.R.*, XLI, 230–231, 233–234, 238–239 (Sept., 1954).

around them; they took it as a matter of course. It is not merely that the institution was defended economically; for as F. L. Olmsted has shown, "the vitality of slavery need be nowhere dependent on its mere economy as a labor system." [16] The sense of social stability, involving dislike of innovation and pride in the distinctiveness of Southern life, operated as a powerful determining force; and no argument was more potent than the question: What would happen if these millions of Negroes were to be turned loose upon society? Fearful Southerners, who like most Americans of the age thought that the Negro was innately inferior and incapable of genuine civilization, believed that beyond the problem of slavery lay "that of permanent race-adjustment," which "the abolition of slavery would only present . . . in a starker form." [17] Thus slavery as a matter of social control was always the vital consideration. The Negroes were in their midst. They had to be looked after; and any scheme of absolute and complete emancipation would involve such a departure in social structure as few statesmen of the time could envisage. Abolition according to the simple dicta of the Garrisons and Phillipses of the North was to the Southerner quite out of the question. It was contrary to the Southerner's sense of justice to consider emancipation without compensation to the owners. Even Lincoln in the midst of the Civil War, as well as at the end of the struggle, declared his conviction that any permanent emancipation scheme must involve compensation to slaveholders; and the burdens of such compensation, together with untold social difficulties that would emerge from any abolition program, could not be endured by the Southern ante-bellum mind. Through all his thinking on the subject the Southerner was conscious that slavery was, at any rate, his own problem. Outside advice, especially of the holier-than-thou variety, was resented. Above all he asked to be let alone.

[16] Broadus Mitchell, *Frederick Law Olmsted,* 74.
[17] Nevins, *Ordeal of the Union,* I, ix.

CHAPTER 4

Wedges of Separation

I

THUS FAR LITTLE has been said of sectional conflict. There were many individual friendships between Northerners and Southerners; Savannah and Charleston had common interests and friendly communication with Philadelphia and other Northern ports. To think of the prewar outlook of Boston or New York as one of hostility to the South would be a serious mistake. Southern editorials and legislative resolutions which singled out Garrison for denunciation as if he were typical of the North or representative of Boston were sadly misleading. On both sides of the Mason and Dixon line there existed a teeming civilization whose aspects were so numerous and whose interests so manifold that any suggestion of anti-Southernism as a dominant interest in the North, or of the opposite feeling as a controlling Southern motive, while perhaps agreeing here and there with certain factors selected for the purpose, would seem to belie hundreds of other elements so common and so obvious that they are likely to escape the historian's notice. Yet conflict did develop until it produced one of the hugest wars of history. The antecedents of that war will be traced in this and the following chapter. Since this portion of the narrative will necessarily involve frequent mention of antagonistic attitudes, it is important in the interest of straight thinking that one should avoid the facile assumption that these tendencies and attitudes represented majority sentiment or constituted at the time the leading phase of the nation's thought and life. The varied aspects that have been imperfectly suggested in the preceding chapters (literature, industry, humanitarian endeavor, etc.) ran concurrently with the sectional troubles now to be discussed; to single out these troubles for separate treatment is, after all, a mere literary device. One should not read back from the fact of war to the supposition that war-making tendencies were the nation's chief preoccupation in the fifties. In those years shipowners were interested in the merchant marine, writers in literature, captains of industry in economic enterprise; if any class was concerned chiefly with factors of sectional antagonism it would seem to have been certain groups of politicians and agitators.

With these preliminary considerations in mind it may be well at this point to examine two factors in the fifties that tended toward the placing of undue stress upon controversy and strife: (1) economic sectionalism, and (2) the intensification of the slavery issue by the singling out of one narrow aspect—slavery expansion in the territories—till it became, by a process of exaggeration and over-simplification, the equivalent of "Southern rights" when viewed by one set of leaders, while by another group the checking of such expansion was represented as synonymous with democracy and freedom.

Turning to the economic problem, one finds that the ante-bellum Southerner was encouraged to consider the science of Adam Smith and Ricardo as indeed the "dismal science." Reading the pages of *De Bow's Review,* or following the rhetorical portrayal of economic injustice by a certain boiling Kettell,[1] the patriotic Southern citizen must often have felt his fighting blood rising. Kettell marshaled an imposing array of data and statistics to show that the South was the great wealth-producing section, while the North, like an economic leech, sucked up the wealth of the South upon which it depended for raw materials and indeed for its very life. American commerce, according to this view, whether incoming or outgoing, drew fundamentally from the South. It was the South which supplied the bulk of exported products; and it was the South which bought the bulk of imported goods. Northern manufactures rested upon the production of Southern materials. Yet the North enjoyed the lion's share of the profits.

Elaborating this thesis, Kettell argued that this economic inequality resulted from the concentration of manufacturing, shipping, banking, and international trade in the North. For the marketing of export crops New York was the center. The Southern planter, sending his cotton to England, would draw upon the English importer a bill of exchange to be paid in sixty or ninety days. Not awaiting the arrival of his goods abroad, he would use this draft to obtain ready cash. The market for foreign bills of exchange, however, was in New York; it was there that ready money could be had for them. When the demand for such bills was low, this negotiable paper would be depressed; if the demand were high, some speculator rather than the Southern producer might reap the profit. The Southerner was as fully convinced of the prevalence of vicious speculation in cotton paper as the farmer today is convinced of the trickiness of methods that attend transactions in grain futures. The fact that the Northern broker assumed a risk in giving the planter ready money in exchange for a future claim was overlooked.

[1] T. P. Kettell, *Southern Wealth and Northern Profits.*

In addition to this monopoly of the foreign export business, the almost complete control of banking in the North worked a hardship on the South; and heavy tribute was paid to Yankee shipping interests which enjoyed the greater share of the ocean carrying trade of the country. Southerners were therefore saying: We must free ourselves from tl.is economic subservience. Manufacturing, banking, and international trade must be brought into Southern hands. New Orleans must supersede New York as the business hub of the nation. Look to the tariff! While the South has lacked the majority to determine the incidence of this unequal tax, yet her shoulders must bear the burden. Through the operation of unequal navigation laws passed by the Federal Congress, feudal palaces rise throughout New England and fleets of merchantmen crowd its ports. Let the South but assume her stand among the nations, and these palaces and fleets will vanish, and the seats of economic domination will be transferred to the harbors of the Chesapeake, to Charleston, Savannah, Mobile, or New Orleans. Great European liners will establish regular connection between Europe and the South, instead of having Boston, New York, or Philadelphia as the termini of the Atlantic lines.

In commerce and finance, as in literature, so the argument ran, we of the South have been hewers of wood and drawers of water for those who fatten on our prosperity while they rejoice at our misfortune. Unsound business conditions in Northern centers produce a "panic," and the South must suffer, not for any fault of its own, but because of its economic vassalage. Self-sufficient in essential matters, comparatively out of debt, indulging in none of the wild speculations of the day, controlling the great staple which is "King," the South is yet in a complete and thorough condition of serfdom. Producing the article which furnishes the basis of the world's trade, an article that rules the commerce of the whole civilized globe, the great producing region is yet powerless as a sick babe. Gamblers and money changers in New York, thieves and swindlers of Wall Street, sport with men's fortunes as children with toys; and within a few weeks cotton planters lose enough to equip a magnificent line of steamships.[2]

Northerners, of course, held a diametrically opposing view of these economic developments. Eager for "a liberal immigration policy to assure an abundance of cheap labor, ship subsidies for the promotion of commerce, internal improvements in the form of roads, canals, and harbor facilities, a sound monetary system to guarantee that loans and interest would be duly met in values at least equal to the nominal figure in the

---

[2] Condensed and paraphrased from various articles in *De Bow's Review*, esp. XX, 483 ff.; XXI, 308 ff.; XXII, 265 ff., 623 ff.; XXIII, 225 ff., 657 ff.; XXV, 220 ff. Though the tariff was a stock argument it is incorrect to regard this issue as an active Southern grievance against the Federal government in the prewar period. In the forties and fifties the tariff laws were passed with Southern votes.

bond, [and] high tariffs for industries," Northern businessmen complained that the backward, agrarian, feudalistic South dominated the national government. Southern votes had been chiefly responsible for the low Walker tariff of 1846, and Southern votes would back the still lower tariff of 1857, which greatly reduced rates and expanded the free list. In the days of Jackson and Van Buren it had been Southern votes which helped destroy the second Bank of the United States, thereby depriving the nation of central financial direction. Southern Congressmen defeated or retarded necessary appropriations for internal improvements. Southern jealousy held up federal assistance for the construction of a transcontinental railroad linking Chicago or St. Louis with the Pacific coast. Southern Congressmen repeatedly helped defeat homestead legislation which would have encouraged free-soil settlement of the national territories. To many irate Northern capitalists the South appeared to require that "the federal government was to do nothing for business enterprise while the planting interest was to be assured the possession of enough political power to guarantee it against the reënactment of the Hamilton-Webster program." [3]

These opposite economic arguments furnished agitators on each side abundant ammunition for rhetorical exercises in reciprocal denunciation. When submitted to scientific analysis, such arguments will be found to consist partly of solid truth and partly of fallacy. It was true that the South had an essentially colonial economy, from which heavy profits were drained off by Northern middlemen. It was also true that Southern political power, disproportionate to the section's economic strength, helped retard measures which Northern capitalists desired. Yet the Southerner usually erred in refusing to admit that the North was making a major contribution to the Southern economy, while the Northerner often failed to see how much of his profits depended upon the Southern trade. Those Southerners who demanded separation for economic reasons were not thinking sufficiently in terms of mutual dependence. Even if separation should come, yet physically, as Lincoln said, the sections could not separate: they would have to go on living side by side; and the many elements of economic interdependence would continue to operate.

Parallel with economic discontent there stood the slavery issue. Viewed in its manifold aspects, the subject of American slavery comprised, of course, a whole bundle of questions. Should slavery continue to exist on American soil? Should the United States in its international dealing continue to assume the attitude of a proslavery power? Should steps be taken toward cooperation with England in her efforts to stamp out international trade in human beings? What possibilities lay in the various projects for colonization? Were Negroes fitted to labor on planta-

[3] Charles A. and Mary R. Beard, *The Rise of American Civilization*, I, 664–665; II, 29.

tions as freemen for wages? Was slavery economically sound, or was it a drag upon agricultural and industrial progress in the South? What changes in domestic economy, in the social order, and in the political régime were likely if emancipation should be undertaken? Must the South always be a unit for slavery? If certain states found the institution unprofitable and wished to enter upon the adventure of emancipation, were they to be deterred by broad sentiments of the South as a section? Were not the Southern whites as well as the Negroes enslaved? Were they not bound to a rigid, unalterable social and economic order by chains of custom? Did not many individual planters feel that they were involved in a régime which they could not control, but which required them to carry on, more for the sake of their slaves than for their own welfare?

These larger phases of the slavery question, however, seemed to recede as the controversies of the fifties developed; for while the struggle sharpened, it also narrowed. As political conflicts between North and South unfolded, the attention of the country as a whole (as distinguished from certain crusading groups) became diverted from the fundamentals of slavery in its moral, economic, and social aspects; and the thought of the nation politically became concentrated upon the collateral problem as to what Congress should do with respect to slavery in the territories. Though the whole intricate complex of sectionalism must be taken into account, it was this narrow phase of the slavery question which became, or seemed, central in the succession of political events which actually produced the Civil War.

2

With *materia* of conflict ready to hand, it came about that a variety of disturbing circumstances produced in 1850 a sharp sectional crisis. The restless forties had been a period of notable expansion. Texas, Oregon, Utah, California—these words of thrilling import connote great episodes in the epic of western development which had wrought a new orientation in the American outlook and a new sense of national importance. Exuberant slogans and shibboleths ("Remember the Alamo," "Fifty-four forty or fight") brought war in Texas and sententious braggadocio as to Oregon. The repetition of such phrases as the "star of empire" and "manifest destiny" showed the impatient stirrings of a nationalistic spirit. What was called the Far West in 1840 had been but a vast expanse of unsettled country traversed by herds of buffalo, lightly peopled by a sparse Indian population, and known to only a handful of white traders and trappers. There were no roads worthy of the name; the aridity of the land presented unfamiliar problems to men of the humid East; there was great hazard where crude trails forded rivers or crossed mountain and desert. In the Southwest Sam Houston by 1836 had won a quick decision for independence as leader of American settlers in Texas; and by 1845 the force of expansion, aided and regularized by the American procedure of state making and state admission, had brought the great new commonwealth into the Union. In the far Northwest war had seemed to threaten with England; but Polk, once he was elected, forgot the excesses of campaign excitement and concluded a judicious treaty by which the Oregon claims were compromised on the line of the forty-ninth parallel. A curious migration had brought the nation of Mormons, fifteen thousand strong, to the shores of Salt Lake by June, 1848. In January of the same year the precious metal had been found on Sutter's ranch, and greedy humanity responded to the call of gold. By the close of the year 1849 California had a population of approximately 100,000.[1]

Through the doings of such men as Larkin and Frémont—Larkin the American consul at Monterey and Frémont the "Pathfinder"—events had moved rapidly toward making California an independent state with a prospect of annexation to the United States; while the war with Mexico came just in time to furnish the occasion for American naval "assistance" under Sloat and Stockton. With superlative vigor and state pride, comparable to that of Texas, Californians had set up impromptu local governments; they had managed the transition from the Mexican to the American legal régime; by extra-legal measures their vigilance committees had suppressed crime and instituted peace and order; and by September, 1849, they had perfected that ultimate device of American state making —a constitution—and were knocking for admission as a free state into the Union. Meanwhile, the Mexican War having been waged, the Treaty of Guadalupe Hidalgo had clinched the American claim to the Rio Grande boundary of Texas and had transferred to the United States a vast new territory which (in terms of later state names) was to comprise California, Utah, Nevada, large parts of Arizona and New Mexico, and portions of Colorado and Wyoming.

While the nation was accustoming itself to the new territorial horizon, an ominous flare-up of the slavery controversy caused thoughtful men to question whether the whole fabric of the republic was not to be shattered and whether there was to be one nation, or two, or several. Along with idealistic or partisan protests against the Mexican War as a "war of conquest," there had come loud complaints that it was a war of slavery expansion; and the "Wilmot proviso" had presented to the statesmen of the period the challenging problem of somehow quieting extremists on both sides, protecting Southern "rights," preventing war, and preserving a threatened Union. This proviso, which declared that slavery was to be prohibited in the whole of the territory to be acquired from Mexico, passed the House of Representatives, thus indicating the readiness of the lower house to approve a program which the South deemed intolerable;

[1] Various statistical estimates are given in Channing, *Hist. of the U. S.,* VI, 43 n.

and it was only prevented from becoming law by the failure of the Senate to act. Again and again the doctrine of the proviso re-emerged.[2] In 1849 the House voted to organize the territories of New Mexico and California on the Wilmot basis; and once more the restraining action of the Senate prevented the proviso from becoming law.

Meanwhile reaction from abolition attacks and a sense of outraged justice concerning the threatened exclusion of Southern "property" from the national territory combined to cause many Southerners to question the continuing value of the Union. To put the matter succinctly, it was becoming evident that the South would secede rather than submit to the Wilmot proviso. South Carolina was rightly the center of the drive for Southernism in 1850, but it was considered politic to have the movement apparently initiated elsewhere, and through the efforts of Calhoun a convention in Mississippi was induced to propose an all-Southern convention to be held at Nashville. Its purpose, the moderates said, was to consider what action should be taken in case essential Southern measures should fail in Congress; to the extremists the purpose was to strike at once for Southern independence regardless of Congress. Within South Carolina a struggle was being fought out between men who, like Robert Barnwell Rhett, favored secession by the state, and "cooperationists" such as Langdon Cheves, A. P. Butler, and R. W. Barnwell, who favored such secession undertakings as would move side by side with similar efforts in other states of the South. As for Unionism in South Carolina, it was at this time scarcely articulate; such men as J. L. Pettigru and Joel R. Poinsett, who were squarely against secession whether by "cooperation" or not, were already outside the main current of political agitation. The vital question in South Carolina in 1850 was not "Shall we secede?" but "Shall we secede independently?"[3] Though the aggressive tendency was less manifest in other states, mass meetings were being held in various parts of the South, and the Southern ear was becoming accustomed to the language of disunion.

Not the least disturbing factor in 1850 was the prospect that the

[2] The actual authorship of the proviso has sometimes been erroneously attributed to Jacob Brinkerhoff of Ohio; but Charles B. Going in his competent biography of Wilmot has shown that both its authorship and the initiative back of it were Wilmot's. It has been maintained by R. R. Stenberg (*Miss. Vall. Hist. Rev.*, XVIII, 535–541) that Wilmot, though an administration Democrat and even a "pro-Southern" man, had lost strength in protectionist Pennsylvania by his vote for the Walker tariff of 1846, and that in his proviso he sought to improve his position by means of antislavery support. But Avery Craven (*The Coming of the Civil War*, 224–225) shows that the proviso "did not, according to the local newspapers, add one vote" to Wilmot's strength and declares: "The general political disruption of the period suggests a better key to Wilmot's motives."

[3] N. W. Stephenson, "Southern Nationalism in South Carolina in 1851," *Am. Hist. Rev.*, XXXVI, 314–335.

exact numerical balance of free and slave states was about to be upset. In 1812 there were nine slave and nine free states. As the years passed, the admission of six more states in the North had been balanced, state by state, with six in the South; [4] so that in 1850 there were fifteen states on each side of the line. With the probable admission of California, however, the free states would have a majority; and the South saw no clear prospect of restoring the balance. Indeed the prospect was not only that the number of free states would increase, but that they would continually gain in population as compared with the South and thus (so it was feared) reduce that section to a position of distinct inferiority in the national Congress. If, in addition to this disturbing of the "balance," the Wilmot proviso should be made to apply to all future territory, thus shutting off the hope of admitting so much as a single additional slave state, the South would become "swallowed up," the maintenance of Southern "rights" in the Union would become hopeless, and disunion would offer the only hope of preserving a distinctly Southern culture. Such was the thought of many Southerners; and the transition from thought to action was an easy step.

3

With Southern separatism passing ominously from propaganda to programs, and with Northern extremists promoting measures of disunion, a troubled and divided Congress assembled (December, 1849) in one of the most stormy of its sessions. Such was the intensity of sectional feeling that for seventeen days the House could not choose a speaker; it was not until the sixty-third ballot that the deadlock between Robert C. Winthrop of Massachusetts and Howell Cobb of Georgia ended with the choice of Cobb by a plurality. The readiness to use intemperate language was illustrated by a species of cock-fight between R. K. Meade of Virginia and William Duer of New York. "If these outrages are to be committed upon my people," said Meade, "I trust . . . my eyes have rested upon the last speaker of the House of Representatives." On his words being challenged by Duer, a duel between the two was narrowly averted. Speaking of a piece of legislation objectionable to the South, Toombs of Georgia said: "If it should pass, I am for disunion"; upon which his colleague Alexander H. Stephens cried: "Every word of my colleague meets my hearty approval." If slavery should be excluded from the territories, Colcock of South Carolina asserted that he would offer a resolution declaring that this Union ought to be dissolved.

With such disruptive elements at work, it took real statesmanship to

---

[4] The Northern states added since 1812 were Indiana (1816), Illinois (1818), Maine (1820), Michigan (1837), Iowa (1846), and Wisconsin (1848). Those of the South were Mississippi (1817), Alabama (1819), Missouri (1820), Arkansas (1836), Texas (1845), and Florida (1845).

prevent an open break in 1850. Henry Clay had thought the matter through and was ready with a series of formulas by which he hoped that the ghost of disunion could be laid. The plan was: Let California come in as a free state; pass a severe fugitive slave law to please the South; organize the new territories of the Southwest without the Wilmot proviso; abolish the slave trade in the District of Columbia; give compensation to Texas for territory added to New Mexico. That Clay should have full credit for these compromise measures is, perhaps, unfair. His plan was not original; "he merely took over the various bills and resolutions then pending in Congress, revised them, made them his own, and presented them in one grand compilation." [1] Furthermore, Clay is not entitled to the principal credit for the adoption, in essential outlines, of his program. After a valiant attempt to secure the enactment of his "omnibus" bill, the old Whig leader, in failing health, was obliged to retreat to Newport in order to escape the torrid Washington summer, and the actual leadership of the compromise forces fell to Stephen A. Douglas. As Jefferson Davis rightly remarked at the conclusion of the protracted Congressional contest: "If any man has a right to be proud of the success of these measures, it is the Senator from Illinois." [2] At the same time one must be careful not to underestimate the importance of Clay's personal influence and prestige, both North and South, and of his concrete efforts toward practical legislation.

For ten weeks the great compromise was debated in an atmosphere of apprehension for the very life of the nation. Early in February Clay took the floor in favor of his resolutions. He urged that there was no need of the Wilmot proviso because slavery would not go into the new territories in any case. The North could concede what the South asked—laws favorable to slavery in the territories—without loss of any substantial interest. This being so, there was no need in the South for disunion. As the debate proceeded, all the leaders, great and small, took part. None was more gloomily impressive than Calhoun. On the verge of the grave, too weak to read his speech, he was yet able to attend the session of the Senate and have his words read by Senator James M. Mason of Virginia. His keynote was a lament over the growth of disunion sentiment and a feeling that to a large extent disunion had already been consummated, as shown by divisions in the churches. This disruptive tendency he attributed to the deplorable change in the nature of the general government, which had lost its original character as a federal republic and had taken on the nature of a consolidated democracy. He spoke of the development of

[1] George D. Harmon, "Douglas and the Compromise of 1850," *Journal*, Ill. St. Hist. Soc., XXI, 464 (Jan., 1929).
[2] Quoted in Holman Hamilton, "Democratic Senate Leadership and the Compromise of 1850," *M.V.H.R.*, XLI, 415 (Dec., 1954).

abolitionism as a serious menace to the South and urged that if the Union was to be saved the causes of Southern discontent must be removed.

Both sides in the debate were deploring sectionalism, which nearly every speaker was doing his bit to intensify by blaming the opposite section for the trouble. There were, however, some notable exceptions to this generalization: two outstanding Northerners, Douglas and Webster, were speaking for an understanding of Southern interests and denouncing the excesses of their own sections. Daniel Webster was now sixty-nine years of age, and his speech in this debate was the last great effort of his life. With galleries packed, and with a crowded Senate chamber breathless as he arose, he struck the note of conciliation in his first sentence: as his arguments unfolded, the thought of restraining the North and offering the olive branch to the South became evident as his dominant motive. Not "as a Massachusetts man, nor as a Northern man, but as an American," he spoke as one who had a part to play, a duty to fulfill, and that for the preservation of the Union.[3] He did not taunt the South with slavery, but treated it as a problem that faced both North and South, a problem to be solved not by recrimination and agitation, but by conciliation. Referring with sympathy to Southern grievances, he deplored the growth of agitation societies and expressed deep regret for journalistic violence in both sections, as well as for intemperate speeches in Congress, speeches so violent that he considered the vernacular tongue in danger of being corrupted by the style of congressional oratory. As to California and New Mexico, he held slavery to be excluded by the "law of nature"; he saw no reason to "reënact the law of God." Peaceable secession he declared to be unthinkable. "Why, sir," he said, "our ancestors . . . would . . . reproach us; and our children and grandchildren would cry out shame upon us, if we of this generation should dishonor these ensigns of the power of the Government and the harmony of the Union. . . ." It was soon seen at what personal cost Webster had dared to restrain the extremists among his own people when the antislavery poet Whittier scourged him with the scathing lines of "Ichabod." Though Whittier later regretted the severity of his awful lines, his denunciation of Webster stands as a fit example of the abolitionist attitude toward efforts that looked to moderation and conciliation.

Jefferson Davis spoke of disunion as inevitable if the balance of power between North and South should be destroyed. Yet he said of the

[3] At the same time Webster and his backers did have a secondary, more interested motive. As the Boston *Advertiser* explained: "It is thought that the passage of the Fugitive Slave Bill should place the South in a humor to favor some modification of the tariff, for the benefit of those Northern men who have jeoparded their political standing for conciliation." David D. Van Tassel, "Gentlemen of Property and Standing," *New England Quarterly*, XXIII, 319 (Sept., 1950).

American flag: "I look upon it with the affection of early love." Seward of New York gave a set speech in which he referred to the "higher law," a moral law above the Constitution which would one day destroy slavery. Salmon P. Chase of Ohio spoke vigorously in opposition to the compromise under consideration. Douglas, whose part in the debate was of primary importance, opposed the Wilmost proviso and urged the doctrine of "popular sovereignty," adding that the whole controversy over slavery in the territories was academic, because slavery would never actually find a foothold in the region obtained from Mexico. R. M. T. Hunter of Virginia gave a defiant speech, hinting plainly at disunion and declaring that if it should come he would "go with his state." Shields of Illinois, with whom Lincoln had quarreled almost to dueling, made his maiden speech, which was a plea for prohibition of slavery in national territory. Toombs of Georgia urged that there was in the North a fixed purpose to destroy Southern rights. His speech illustrated the manner in which Southerners were wont to generalize from a selected phase of the slavery question and to indulge in sweeping phrases of denunciatory rhetoric.

It must be remembered that in part these speeches were for home consumption. They had to do with prestige militantly interpreted, as in many another public discussion where nationalistic or sectional factors are at the fore. It should also be borne in mind that much of the practical work of Congress lies outside the debates and is to be traced in individual conference and committee deliberation behind the scenes. Nor in praising the disinterested efforts of compromise leaders should one neglect to note that there were also less elevated interests operating in the congressional lobbies. Holders of depreciated securities issued by the Republic of Texas anticipated great gains should the compromise pass, for Texas was to be given $10,000,000 to pay off their claims. These speculators included highly placed politicians and also the influential Washington banking firm of Corcoran & Riggs, which held more than $650,000 in Texas bonds and made from their redemption profits that "were enormous by the standards of that era." [4]

Thus it came about that, through a combination of selfish and public considerations, the conciliatory spirit of Douglas, Clay, and Webster prevailed. The compromise measures were enacted in September, 1850, with more Democrats than Whigs supporting them in both houses of Congress.[5] By these provisions, taken essentially from Clay's resolutions and put into separate bills, California was admitted to the Union as a free state; the territories of Utah and New Mexico were organized on the

[4] Holman Hamilton, "Texas Bonds and Northern Profits," *M.V.H.R.*, XLIII, 579–594 (Mar., 1957).
[5] Hamilton, "Democratic Leadership and the Compromise of 1850," *loc. cit.*, XLI, 408; id., "The 'Cave of the Winds' and the Compromise of 1850," *J.S.H.* XXIII, 350 (Aug., 1957).

basis of popular sovereignty,[6] later to be "received into the Union, with or without slavery, as their constitutions . . . [might] prescribe at the time of their admission"; adjustments of boundary were made between Texas and New Mexico with appropriate compensation to Texas; slave-trading in the District of Columbia was made unlawful, power being given to the local authorities to "abate, break up, and abolish any depot or place of confinement of slaves"; and a severe law for the recovery of fugitive slaves, a law well armed with "teeth," was enacted. This law greatly facilitated recapture and delivery, and by the same token made it hard for the suspected fugitive or anyone befriending him. Owners pursuing alleged fugitives were permitted to seize or arrest them without process; certificates claiming ownership, whether presented directly or indirectly, orally or in writing, were made conclusive upon the Federal courts or commissioners to whom jurisdiction in the premises was given; and the testimony of the alleged fugitive was not to be admitted in any trial. There were heavy penalties for helping fugitives or assisting their escape; Federal marshals were made personally liable in damages if responsible for such escape; and "all good citizens" were "commanded to . . . assist in the . . . execution of [the] law," power being given to officials to call bystanders to their aid, or to summon a *posse comitatus* for the purpose.[7]

Meantime the Nashville convention had met and adjourned without taking radical action. Though South Carolinian delegates wanted secession, the conservative element carried the day; and the convention contented itself with harmless resolutions whose chief item was the extension of the

[6] The territorial legislatures of New Mexico and Utah "might legislate on the subject of slavery either to prohibit it, or to establish it, or to regulate it," Robert R. Russel has proved, "subject to a possible veto by the governor or a possible disallowance by Congress." "What Was the Compromise of 1850?" *J.S.H.*, XXII, 296, 304 (Aug., 1956).

[7] *U. S. Stat. at Large*, IX, 462–465. In the Constitution (Art. IV, sec. 2) the provision for the rendition of slaves (persons "held to Service or Labour") fleeing from one state to another follows the clause concerning the extradition of fugitive criminals. The main difference in the two clauses is that the suspected criminal is to be delivered up "on Demand of the executive Authority of the State from which he fled," while the reclamation of the slave is to be merely "on Claim of the Party to whom such Service or Labour may be due." It may also be mentioned that the fugitive criminal is described as a person "charged . . . with . . . Crime," while the wording in the case of the suspected fugitive slave avoids any suggestion that his slave status may be merely suspected and makes no reference to a formal charge or legal accusation. Of more significance, however, than the distinction in constitutional provision is the variance in developed practice. As to recovery of criminals there has never been any application of Federal measures to compel observance. There is a striking contrast between the drastic Federal processes used to recover slaves and the hands-off policy concerning extradition which has caused it to remain purely a matter of interstate comity. See Kentucky *vs.* Dennison, 65 U. S. 107 ff.; J. G. Randall, *Constitutional Problems Under Lincoln*, 421.

Missouri line (36° 30′) westward to the Pacific. It is true that the convention issued an "address to the Southern people" drafted by the secessionist Rhett; yet among the vast majority of the Southern people the Compromise of 1850 was accepted as a settlement which obviated disunion. This is a significant fact. In Mississippi, for example, in 1851 the gubernatorial contest indicated the swing away from disunion sentiment. Quitman, running on a state-rights platform, was opposed by Foote, who endorsed the Compromise. So strong was the reaction against secession that Quitman withdrew; Jefferson Davis took his place on a platform renouncing secession; and in the outcome Foote was elected.

In South Carolina, it is true, the success of the Compromise and the "failure" of the Nashville convention (which was a failure only on the assumption that its purpose was immediate secession) did not by any means put an end to the secession movement. The Rhett faction in the state still worked for independent secession, while the Cheves-Butler-Barnwell faction continued to favor secession in cooperation with other states and looked to a "Southern Congress" to make such secession a reality. As between these two factions, the cooperationists won the day; and as the other states of the South did not choose to "cooperate," agitation for separation ended for the time in talk. The movement, however, remained dormant and was sure to reassert itself when again a "crisis" should arise.

Taking the country by and large, the general feeling at the end of 1850 was one of relief. People felt that a menace had been warded off; they trembled to think how narrowly the disruption of the Union had been prevented; they rejoiced that the turn for conciliation and adjustment of difference had been taken. The Compromise was hailed as an act of statesmanship; it was looked upon as a finality; it was considered almost treasonable to disturb it or reopen the slavery question. This phase, however, soon passed. In a few years the sectional controversy, with slavery in the territories as the focal point, was reopened with a roar; and there began a steady stream of circumstance which led on through the Kansas struggle and the realignment of parties to the Democratic split of 1860, the election of Lincoln, secession, and civil war.

4

For those who think in terms of presidential administrations, the years following the Compromise of 1850 may be regarded as the period of Pierce. There was now in the presidency a man whose political achievement was negligible. A handsome face, a military reputation, a ready oratory when descanting upon the glories of the flag, party regularity, and a slavery policy acceptable to the South were the chief qualifications of the candidate who in 1852 received the Democratic nomination on the forty-ninth ballot after the big leaders—Cass, Douglas, Buchanan, Marcy, and Butler—had defeated each other. As spokesman of the New England "Democracy" he had done service for his party against the disruptive forces of the abolitionists. As President his domestic policy was development of the West and conciliation of the South; abroad his keynote was expansion, with an embarrassing tendency to attract gasconading, intriguing "Young Americans" of the Sickles or Soulé type. It was the luckless lot of this quiet New Englander to be President in a time of transition and maladjustment. It was an age of urbanization, industrial growth, rushing European immigration, corporate development—a time of lobbies, pressure politics, and organized propaganda. In this hectic setting Franklin Pierce's pastoral ideals and his belief in Democracy as a panacea simply did not fit. The struggle of forces which caused the storm of conflict between the rural South and the industrial North to break during his presidency was as far beyond his ken as it was impossible for him to control. He would have liked to make his contribution in terms of reducing governmental favors to big business, resisting anti-Catholic bigotry, and promoting party unity; actually the two things for which his administration is remembered are the "Ostend Manifesto" and "bleeding Kansas."

The Ostend affair was part of an elaborate complex of factors involving American diplomacy and intrigue with reference to Cuba. Though one must discard many of the old-time generalizations as to the "slavocracy" angling for Cuba as an area of slave expansion, yet the strivings of diplomacy and the workings of international intrigue concerning the island were naturally a matter of concern to the South. It was a long story, much too complicated for detailed treatment here. England, laboring with Spain for an effective suppression of the international slave trade, could not forget that Cuba was an area of immense slave-trading activity. The acquisition of the island, as of other parts of Latin America, seemed at various times an objective of English diplomacy; while British effort toward the abolitionizing of Cuba angered the South and worried Calhoun as secretary of state. Dreams of British abolitionists looking toward the Africanization of Cuba as a sort of black military republic under British sponsorship, to be carried out by a policy of colonization and emancipation, frightened many Southerners. Bold spirits had sought to make history on their own account, and American intrigue in Cuba had found frequent expression in filibustering expeditions and in American sympathy extended to native insurgent movements. By the time the ardent French-Louisianian Pierre Soulé was appointed minister to Spain (1853), the Cuban issue had become acute, and Soulé himself had become prominently known as an advocate of Cuban acquisition and an apologist of filibusters. The most striking event of his turbulent and diplomatically useless mission to Madrid was the Ostend Report or "manifesto" (October, 1854), in which the explosive Pierre was joined by James Buchanan, minister to Great Britain, and John Y. Mason, minister to France. The more truculent passages of this document urged that the North American republic could never repose till Cuba was within its boundaries; that an effort should be made to purchase the island; and that, if Spain should refuse to sell it and if Spanish possession seriously endangered American peace and union, "then, by every law, human and divine, we shall be justified in wresting it from Spain if we possess the power." [1] This robber doctrine was repudiated, however, by Secretary of State Marcy; a flood of newspaper denunciation descended upon both Pierce and Soulé; and the latter's erratic mission ended with his resignation. If the expansionist diplomacy of Pierce had Cuba as a specific objective, it broke down completely; while as a diversion from sectionalism at home, it also failed to accomplish its purpose.

5

For the settlement of the territorial question three solutions were prominently urged. First, there was the Wilmot proviso, associated with the Free-Soilers and the Republican party: the doctrine that slavery in all national territory ought to be definitely prohibited by Congress. Second, at the other extreme there was the doctrine of the Southern Democracy that it was the duty of the Federal government to extend positive protection to slavery in the territories—i.e. not merely to permit it, but to maintain and protect it. This solution was soon to be powerfully supported by both the President and the Supreme Court of the United States. Third, there was the "popular sovereignty" program associated with the policy of Douglas and the anti-Buchanan Democrats. Briefly, its purport was that slavery should be neither positively established nor arbitrarily prohibited in any territory by national action, but that the issue should be settled on the broad American principle of local self-determination by leaving the people of each territory free to deal with the matter as the majority by conventional political processes should decide.[1]

It is to the last-mentioned program that attention must now turn. In

---

[1] A. A. Ettinger, *The Mission to Spain of Pierre Soulé*, 361–364. In any brief account which features its most fiery passages the Ostend Report must necessarily appear highly jingoistic. On a fuller study it will be seen that Mason and Buchanan distrusted the vociferous methods of Soulé and Sickles, that much of the trouble was due to the sensational account published by the New York *Herald,* and that the report never had the sanction of the Pierce administration. As to the passage touching seizure of Cuba, Roy F. Nichols writes (*Franklin Pierce,* 596): "It certainly is not a direct threat such as Soulé wanted. . . . It is a laborious . . . hint to Spain that, if she did not sell and did Africanize the island, then the United States ought to consider whether the law of self preservation required seizure. . . ." *Ibid.,* 586.

[1] There was, however, a fourth solution—i.e. not to treat all the national territory alike, but to give the West, at least nominally, a Mason and Dixon line by extending the Missouri Compromise line westward to the Pacific. This solution was often proposed, especially in the period from 1848 to 1850.

the slavery legislation of 1850 the principle of popular sovereignty had been applied to the Mexican acquisition; and now under Pierce a more famous instance of its application was to be seen in Douglas's Kansas-Nebraska bill of 1854. So truculent was the controversy waged concerning this piece of legislation that it is hard to penetrate the mists of vituperation and to isolate the causes and essential elements of the situation. A reappraisal of the much maligned Douglas will be of assistance in understanding the problem. Few men have presented so notable an example of rapid rise to political leadership. Born in Vermont, he struggled for some years as a lawyer in Illinois, became active in promoting the Democratic organization of his state, and served in the legislature simultaneously with Lincoln. For two years he was a member of the supreme court of Illinois; and the title "Judge Douglas" lasted through life. After serving briefly but brilliantly in the House of Representatives, he held the office of senator from Illinois during the critical years from 1847 to 1861, by which time he was the foremost Democrat of the North. His forthrightness, vigor, and aggressiveness, his force as a debater and talent as political strategist, had made a deep impression; and the breadth of his national vision had given him a peculiar distinction in an age when the sectionalism of many of the nation's leaders was all too evident.

Western problems and territorial issues had been a specialty of Douglas, who had since 1847 been chairman of the committee on territories of the United States Senate after having held a similar chairmanship in the House. Questions of territorial organization, involving far-reaching phases of the westward movement, necessarily awaited his action in the formulation and recommendation of policies. It has already been noted that his part in the Compromise of 1850 was as vital as that of Clay himself; in 1854 no man was more thoroughly conversant than he with the whole background of territorial politics. By this time the territorial organization of the vast "Platte country" was overdue.

Speaking for his committee, Douglas reported a bill for the territorial organization of the Platte country on January 4, 1854. Most of its provisions were conventional, but those concerning slavery attracted attention. Douglas declared that his bill was in tune with "certain great principles" which had already been enacted into law in 1850. "Your committee," he said, "deem it fortunate . . . that the controversy then resulted in the adoption of the compromise measures, which the two great political parties . . . have affirmed . . . and proclaimed . . . as a final settlement of the controversy and an end of the agitation." Briefly, these principles, as he stated them, were that the people, through their representatives in the legislature, should decide as to slavery in the territories with the right of appeal on matters of constitutionality to the Supreme Court of the United States.[2]

---

[2] *Sen. Rep. No. 15,* 33 Cong., 1 sess., p. 3.

Historians have long argued over Douglas's motives in introducing this measure, which seemed indirectly to repeal the Missouri Compromise ban on slavery in the Nebraska region [3] and thus reopened the sectional conflict. Some critics have maintained that Douglas had a material interest in the promotion of slavery, since his first wife had inherited a plantation with 150 slaves.[4] More frequently it has been argued that Douglas was angling for the Democratic presidential nomination in 1856 and hoped to win Southern support. Refuting these charges, friendly historians have suggested instead that Douglas wished to assist Senator David R. Atchison in his campaign for re-election in Missouri, that he desired to promote the building of a transcontinental railroad with eastern termini at Chicago and St. Louis, or that he hoped to give the floundering Democratic party a fresh issue upon which it could appeal to the voters.[5] Recently the argument has been settled by the discovery of a contemporary letter in which Douglas himself explained his motives. His purpose in introducing the Kansas-Nebraska bill, Douglas declared, was to remove the "barbarian wall" of Indian tribes checking further settlement in the central plains and "to authorize and encourage a continuous line of settlements to the Pacific Ocean." His central idea of continental expansion included railroad development. As he explained:

[3] In 1818–20 the problem of slavery in Missouri and ancillary questions had produced serious controversy. The House twice passed the Tallmadge amendment prohibiting further introduction of slavery into the state and freeing slave-born children at the age of twenty-five; but the Senate disagreed. A compromise was effected: Missouri was admitted as a slave state; Maine was admitted free; and it was provided that in all national territory north of 36° 30′ "slavery and involuntary servitude, otherwise than in the punishment of crimes . . . , shall be . . . forever prohibited." *Annals of Cong.*, 16 Cong., 1 sess., 427–430 (Feb. 18, 1820).

[4] George Fort Milton (*Eve of Conflict*, 34–35) explains that Douglas's wealthy father-in-law offered him a plantation in Mississippi with numerous slaves as a wedding gift, that Douglas declined it, being "totally ignorant of that species of property," and that when the father-in-law willed Mrs. Douglas the plantation with its slaves, he reminded her of her husband's wish not to own them and suggested that, if she should leave no children, the Negroes were to be colonized in Africa. The possession of these slaves by his wife was an embarrassment to Douglas; there is no evidence that his attitude as a public leader was affected in the direction of slavery by this property interest.

[5] Allan Nevins (*Ordeal of the Union*, II, 102) suggests that Douglas had in mind "the disorganized, discontented state of the Democratic party, lacking both leader and policy; the obligation resting upon 'Young America' for bold trenchant action; his own legitimate ambition to become President; the demand of the Northwest for a Pacific Railroad, with the consequent necessity for settling the Kansas-Nebraska country to furnish its future path; the fear of Missouri slaveholders lest they be surrounded on three sides by freesoil territory; Atchison's stubborn assertion that he would let Nebraska 'sink in hell' before he would see it organized on a basis excluding slaveholders with their property; and Atchison's ability to rally a solid block of Southern Senators behind him."

How are we to develope [*sic*], cherish and protect our immense interests and possessions in the Pacific, with a vast wilderness fifteen hundred miles in breadth, filled with hostile savages, and cutting off direct communication. The Indian barrier must be removed. The tide of emigration and civilization must be permitted to roll onward until it rushes through the passes of the mountains, and spreads over the plains, and mingles with the waters of the Pacific. Continuous lines of settlements with civil, political and religious institutions all under the protection of law, are imperiously demanded by the highest national considerations. These are essential, but they are not sufficient. . . . We must therefore have Rail Roads and Telegraphs from the Atlantic to the Pacific, through our own territory. Not one line only, but many lines, for the valley of the Mississippi will require as many Rail Roads to the Pacific as to the Atlantic, and will not venture to limit the number.[6]

Intent upon opening the West to further development, Douglas wished to ignore or by-pass the slavery question. Knowing that he had no chance whatever of getting a territorial bill adopted without Southern votes, he presented a deliberately ambiguous measure which did not explicitly exclude slavery from the area, but which almost certainly would have left the Missouri Compromise prohibition in effect during the territorial stage of its development. Personally hostile to slavery, Douglas did not think the South's peculiar institution could ever extend into the great plains; consequently he believed that his token concession to the South in no sense endangered liberty. "It is to be hoped," he argued, "that the necessity and importance of the measure are manifest to the whole country, and that so far as the slavery question is concerned, all will be willing to sanction and affirm the principles established by the Compromise measures of 1850."[7]

But once the measure was presented to the Senate, it became the object of intense political pressure. Excited Free Soilers attempted to add amendments reaffirming the Missouri Compromise ban on slavery. Angered by these maneuvers, Southerners informed Douglas that slavery must be permitted in the Nebraska country during the territorial phase of its organization. Reluctantly yielding to this latter pressure, Douglas on January 10 brought forward an additional section of his bill, which, he asserted, had previously been omitted through "clerical error"; it provided "that all questions pertaining to slavery in the Territories, and in the new States to be formed therefrom, are to be left to the people residing therein, through their appropriate representatives." Though this provision plainly implied the repeal of the Missouri Compromise, proslavery leaders were still not satisfied, and Douglas was obliged to add a further amendment declaring the Missouri Compromise "inoperative and void."

6 James C. Malin, "The Motives of Stephen A. Douglas in the Organization of the Nebraska Territory: A Letter dated December 17, 1853," *Kans. Hist. Quart.,* XIX, 351–352 (Nov., 1951).

7 *Ibid.*, 353.

At the same time his bill was modified in another important fashion by dividing the area under consideration into the two separate territories of Kansas and Nebraska. Thus the final version of the Kansas-Nebraska bill was not Douglas's alone; it was, as Roy F. Nichols has said, "the work of many hands and the fruit of much strategic planning." [8] Assisted by relentless pressure from the Pierce administration, the bill, after months of riotous debate, was passed; the fateful measure became law on May 30, 1854.

It was at once apparent that this legislation had let loose the dogs of war. While Southerners at first showed either indifference or resentment toward the act as one that offered them insufficient protection, they soon came enthusiastically to endorse it as "a measure . . . just in regards to the rights of the South, and . . . reasonable in its operation and effect." [9] In the North Douglas's bill furiously aroused antislavery sentiment, and free-soil men in both parties took steps to have the action of Congress repudiated. Chase of Ohio, a puritan in politics who had labored in the Liberty party of 1840 and with the Free-Soilers of '48, now headed a movement to capture the Democratic party for the cause of antislavery. In his "Appeal to the Independent Democrats" he denounced Douglas's action as a violation of a solemn pledge, predicted its dire effect upon immigration to the West, warned the country that freedom and union were in peril, and besought all Christians to rise in protest against this "enormous crime." [10] The vocabulary of abuse was exhausted in the attacks upon Douglas: "never before has a public man been so hunted and hounded." [11] As he himself declared, he could have traveled from Boston to Chicago by the light of his burning effigies. Even in his home state he was vigorously condemned. Both in Chicago and in downstate Illinois he encountered abuse and insult when he tried to defend his course, but he managed to strike home with his argument that it was the extremists on both sides, not himself, who were responsible for the storm of sectionalism.

In keeping with the prevailing tendency toward political realignment, and as a direct result of the Kansas-Nebraska act, a new political party now came into being. Wilmot-proviso sentiment caused various diverse elements here and there to fuse into organizations which sometimes bore the awkward designation of "anti-Nebraska" parties, but which soon came to be known as the "Republican" party. There has been some dispute as to the exact time and place where the party was "born." Coalition move-

[8] Nichols, "The Kansas-Nebraska Act: A Century of Historiography," *M.V.H.R.*, XLIII, 211 (Sept., 1956).

[9] Avery O. Craven, *The Growth of Southern Nationalism, 1848–1861,* 204.

[10] Chase's "Appeal" followed Douglas's report recommending the Kansas-Nebraska bill. *Cong. Globe,* 333 Cong., 1 sess., 281–282 (Jan. 19, 1854). Some Southerners, of course (e.g. Alexander H. Stephens), approved the bill, though Southern extremists later assailed Douglas. See *Am. Hist. Rev.,* VIII, 92.

[11] Washington *Union,* Mar. 4, 1854.

ments of a similar sort were afoot in many parts of the country at about the same time, and such a dispute is of little importance. The name "Republican" was adopted at a mass meeting on July 6, 1854, at Jackson, Michigan; prior to this, however, while the repeal of the Missouri compromise was pending in Congress, a similar mass meeting at Ripon, Wisconsin, had resolved that in the event of such repeal old party organizations would be discarded and a new party would be built "on the sole issue of the non-extension of slavery." Elsewhere in the country local conventions followed suit; and by late summer of 1854 the new party movement was well under way. Made up of old-line Whigs, many of whom, such as Bates of Missouri and Browning of Illinois, preserved the Southern conservative tradition, together with radical antislavery men such as Sumner and Julian, Knownothings, and free-soil Democrats such as Trumbull and Chase, the new party combined many diverse ingredients; the force that cemented them (at the outset) was common opposition to the further extension of slavery in the territories.

The outcome of Douglas's policy had been the opposite of his intentions. So far from allaying sectional conflict and uniting his party, he had reopened the strife which he himself had designated the "fearful struggle of 1850"; he had split the historic Democratic party; he had supplied the occasion for the entrance of a wholly sectional party onto the scene; and he had driven many Northern Democrats into the ranks of this sectional group.

6

Events in Kansas soon demonstrated the effect of the repeal of the Missouri compromise and of popular sovereignty when put into actual practice. It is significant that Nebraska, whose settlement belonged to the same period as that of Kansas, hardly enters into the national story until after the Civil War; while the Kansas story occupies the center of the picture in the fifties. In the heated passions of the time, the settlement of Kansas was envisaged not as a typical project of western pioneering, but as a matter of rescuing Missouri from contamination by abolition neighbors, of "saving" the South from "destruction" of its "rights," of promoting the Republican party, which soon came to be regarded as an end in itself, or of building bulwarks of freedom. Artificially stimulated emigration, fanatical outside interference, campaigns of propaganda, frontier brawls, violence in Congress, frantic debates of press and platform, election frauds, and partisan efforts to make political capital out of the Kansas situation—such were the factors which mark the development of this turbulent territory, and which make it difficult even yet for the historian to sift out the truth in tracing that development.

Present-day historians agree that the settlement of Kansas was not fundamentally dissimilar to that of other frontier states. The key to its development was land. The thousands of Missourians who poured into the territory as soon as it was opened "cared next to nothing about the question of slavery extension and still less about national politics. They simply wanted the land." [1] Most Northern immigrants had the same over-riding idea. Unfortunately the national government had failed to extinguish Indian titles and had neglected to provide for surveys before allowing settlers in. Consequently "on May 30, 1854, when Kansas territory was opened to settlement, not an acre of land was available for pre-emption or purchase." [2] Uncertainty over land titles played a major role in heightening tensions in an already highly dangerous situation.

The struggle in Kansas used to be depicted as a contest between pro- and antislavery forces, but, as Paul W. Gates reminds us, there were many "other causes of conflict, for example the patronage the new territories and states provided to political parties, the pleasures of distributing a rapidly multiplying number of offices paying generous salaries and profitable fees, the desire to control public offices such as territorial and educational institutions, a general hunger for lucrative mail, trucking, Indian, and army procurement contracts, and the granting of lands and loans to railroads." [3] Of key importance, too, was the location of county seats, for the interested speculator stood to profit enormously if his tract of land was selected as a governmental center.

This already complex situation was made more difficult through the activities of groups organized to promote pro- or antislavery immigration into Kansas. Even before the Kansas-Nebraska act was passed, Eli Thayer of Worcester, Massachusetts, had organized the Massachusetts Emigrant Aid Company (April, 1854) in order to "assist" emigrants to settle in the "West." When this organization proved defective it was soon superseded by the "New England Emigrant Aid Company." Thayer wished the project to be a profit-making enterprise, but such influential backers as A. A. Lawrence regarded it as a philanthropic undertaking and it is safe to say that the greater number of stockholders "considered subsidiary, if they did not ignore, the investment feature of their subscription." [4] Under the stimulus of the Thayer society some 1240 free-state settlers migrated to Kansas in 1854 and 1855. Though the numbers were small, the influence upon Kansas development was great. The activities of the New England Emigrant Aid Company, writes Samuel A. Johnson, "furnished the excuse, and some measure the provocation, for the Missouri invasion" of Kansas by proslavery "border ruffians"; the society gave "en-

[1] Samuel A. Johnson, "The Emigrant Aid Company in the Kansas Conflict," *Kans. Hist. Quart.*, VI, 21 (Feb., 1937).
[2] Paul W. Gates, *Fifty Million Acres: Conflicts over Kansas Land Policy*, 21.
[3] *Ibid.*, 2–3.
[4] Samuel A. Johnson, "The Genesis of the New England Emigrant Aid Company," *New England Quart.*, III, 118 (Jan., 1930).

couragement, advice and money" to the free-state leaders in Kansas; and "it was the officers of the company, if not the company itself, that armed the Free-State party." [5] By 1857 the New England Emigrant Aid Company had disappeared from the picture, its place being taken by various bodies organized throughout the free states to promote antislavery emigration to Kansas. In the South there was a counter agitation to send Southerners into the territory: its most striking result was an expedition of several hundred men from Georgia, Alabama, and South Carolina, led by Jefferson Buford of Alabama, an exuberant group who matched the Northerners in violence, with the addition of a few swashbuckling touches all their own.

The first governor of the territory, Andrew H. Reeder, arrived on the scene in October of 1854 to find that several thousand settlers were already on the ground and that they were carrying on without a government. During the period of his brief rule the proslavery element was particularly aggressive. When members of the territorial legislature were elected in March of 1855, several thousand armed intruders from Missouri marched into the territory and stuffed the ballot boxes with fraudulent votes. The legislature so chosen met at Shawnee Mission and adopted a drastic slave code by which office holding was limited to proslavery men, while imprisonment at hard labor was decreed for anyone who claimed that slavery did not legally exist in the territory. Reeder was soon removed as chief executive and was followed by a succession of governors—Shannon, Geary, Walker, Denver, and Medary—whose careers were turbulent and whose terms were short.

Repudiating the "bogus" Shawnee legislature, the free-state men, by equally irregular and extra-legal methods, held a constitutional convention at Topeka by which slavery was prohibited, had the constitution ratified by popular vote (in which the proslavery element took no part), and launched a state government with Charles Robinson as governor. When the year 1856 opened, Kansas presented the spectacle of two rival governments, both irregular, while it seemed hopeless to establish any government by orderly constitutional processes with the prospect that it would command the support of the proslavery and antislavery elements. Yet slavery was never a matter of any importance to Kansas itself. As A. A. Lawrence, one of the chief supporters of the New England Emigrant Aid Company, admitted in March, 1855: 'So far not a slave has been taken into the Territory (who staid more than a night), and I do believe there never will be one." [6] The census of 1860, taken after the territory had been legally open to slavery for six years, showed only two slaves in Kansas.

Nothing better illustrates the unsettled and partisan nature of the

[5] Johnson, "The Emigrant Aid Company in the Kansas Conflict," *Kans. Hist. Quart.*, VI, 32 (Feb., 1937).

[6] James C. Malin, *John Brown and the Legend of Fifty Six*, 509.

Kansas situation than the farcical but ominous "Wakarusa War." A free-state man named Dow was killed by a proslavery opponent in a private feud, whereupon the proslavery sheriff, instead of pursuing the murderer, collected a posse to apprehend one Branson, friend of the murdered man, on a charge of threatening revenge. Though the citizens of Lawrence disavowed any intention to make the cause of Dow or Branson their own, Governor Shannon stupidly declared the town of Lawrence to be "in rebellion" and the place was besieged by a motley force of "militia," many of whom came from Missouri with arms from the Federal arsenal at Liberty, which they had plundered. Under the leadership of James Henry Lane and Charles Robinson the free-state citizens or "rebels" of Lawrence collected a force armed with Sharp's rifles; and serious bloodshed seemed inevitable when the governor brought the *opéra bouffe* conflict to a close by a "treaty" negotiated with the Lawrence citizens. The "war" had fortunately terminated without fighting.

Some months later, however (May, 1856), a force of about eight hundred men, many of them from Missouri, invaded Lawrence in the capacity of "posses" led by the local sheriff and the Federal marshal to execute warrants for "treason." Despite the nonresistance of Lawrence citizens this invasion degenerated into a wanton raid, in the course of which the hotel of the Emigrant Aid Company was destroyed, helpless citizens were terrorized, newspaper presses were smashed, and Robinson's house was burned. The raid was almost bloodless, but the public mind was electrified by lurid descriptions which appeared in the Northern press; and the effect of the incident was heightened by two other acts of violence that occurred almost simultaneously—the Pottawatomie massacre and the Sumner-Brooks affair.

7

A grim, terrible man had now entered the story. Born in Connecticut in 1800, John Brown had tried tanning, land speculation, sheep raising, and various business ventures without success, meanwhile suffering family misfortunes, going through bankruptcy, and shifting about from Ohio to Pennsylvania, Massachusetts, and New York. By 1856 he had settled with his four sons at Osawatomie, Kansas, and had become a "captain" in the emergency force recruited by free-state citizens to defend the town of Lawrence. Up to this time killings in Kansas had been few; but on the night of May 24–25, 1856, a small party made up chiefly of Brown and his sons descended upon the cabins of proslavery families (named Doyle and Wilkinson) on Pottawatomie Creek, murdered five men in cold blood, and left their gashed and mutilated bodies—"a Free State warning to the proslavery forces that it was to be a tooth for a tooth, an eye for an eye . . . so far as one wing of the Free State party was concerned." [1] The motives for this fiendish atrocity are difficult to fathom and impossible to palliate. Professor James C. Malin, the closest student of Brown's Kansas career, maintains that the massacre was "political assassination, not merely private murder." With warped logic, Brown was merely carrying to an extreme the determination of the free-state men to disobey the "bogus" Shawnee legislature and to harass its law-enforcement officers. All of the murdered men were connected with the proslavery government's district court at Dutch Henry's Crossing, and Brown seems to have feared that they might convict him of "treason" in adhering to the rival Topeka régime. [2] The truth of these matters is very difficult to ascertain, for the congressional committee investigating matters in Kansas glossed over the outrage; Republican papers suppressed the facts; and the murderers were never prosecuted. Brown and his partisans, however, were attacked by several hundred proslavery men in what was called the "battle" of Osawatomie, in the course of which blood was shed on both sides, Brown's son Frederick was killed, and the little settlement was burned. Soon after, Brown left Kansas for the East.

On May 19–20, 1856, Charles Sumner of Massachusetts delivered on the floor of the Senate an intemperate and abusive speech which became famous under the title "The Crime against Kansas." It was, said Cass of Michigan, an "unpatriotic" and "un-American" speech such as he hoped "never to hear again." [3] With an exasperating attitude of superiority, Sumner not only inveighed against lawlessness in Kansas, but descended to ugly denunciation of South Carolina and to an offensive personal attack upon a proud South Carolinian, Andrew Pickens Butler, an absent member of the Senate. One of the South Carolinian members of Congress at this time was Preston S. Brooks, a relative of Butler. He was a courtly Southerner whose code of personal honor required that slander of a kinsman should not go unpunished. To his mind the chastisement of Sumner was an unpleasant duty. On May 22 he entered the Senate after adjournment when there were very few in the chamber, walked to Sumner's seat, faced him, explained that he had come to punish him for slandering an aged and absent relative, and then struck him repeatedly over the head with a cane. Brooks explained that he meant to "whip" Sumner, not to hurt him; but it took over three years for Sumner to recover, during which time the state of Massachusetts re-elected him to his seat in the Senate, which was kept vacant as a tribute.

The Sumner-Brooks incident was one of the outstanding events of the decade. The news set the North on fire, and it gave an awful advantage to antislavery leaders who denounced the barbarism of the South;

[1] Oswald Garrison Villard, *John Brown*, 148 ff.

[2] Malin, *John Brown and the Legend of Fifty Six*, 754–758.

[3] Sumner's speech is found in *Cong. Globe*, 34 Cong., 1 sess., App., 529–544; for Cass's reply, see *ibid.*, 544.

while in the South itself the "spirited" action of Brooks was applauded.[4] The assault mightily assisted the Republican party; and by making Sumner a martyr it greatly increased his prestige. The whole incident in its wider reactions and in its bearing upon social psychology reveals so much of the temper of North and South that it goes far to explain the Civil War.

8

In the heat of sectional controversy over the Kansas struggle the country faced the distractions of a presidential election. The venerable Whig party, whose leader had held the presidency so recently as 1853, had now virtually passed out of existence, so great had been the political overturn occasioned by the phenomenal rise of the Republican party. The American or Knownothing party, built chiefly on anti-foreign and anti-Catholic prejudice and championing the cause of "nativism," held its national council in Philadelphia in February, passed a noncommittal resolution concerning the burning question of slavery in the territories (thus offending the delegates of various Northern states who promptly withdrew), and, making their chief appeal to the South, chose as their candidates Millard Fillmore and Andrew Jackson Donelson.

Taking a definitely pro-Southern turn, the Democratic party in convention at Cincinnati took its stand on the principle of noninterference by Congress with slavery in state and territory; rejected Pierce, Cass, and Douglas; and nominated the dignified and "available" Buchanan of Pennsylvania. He had served in Congress as early as 1821. Though at first a Federalist, he had done battle as a Jackson Democrat in the United States Senate, had served as secretary of state under Polk, handling delicate and important matters of foreign policy, and had represented the United States at St. Petersburg and London. His Southern slant had been demonstrated in 1854, when he had joined with John Y. Mason and Pierre Soulé in promulgating the "Ostend Manifesto." Indeed his Southernism was a vital element in his career. The formulas for his political success were control of the Pennsylvania Democracy and the courting of Southern favor. The importance of Pennsylvania for the Democratic party was, of course, a large element in his presidential aspirations. In contrast to the opportunist Cameron, Buchanan was a man of real public spirit: to go down in history as a great and good man, to be a benevolent father to his people, was his ideal. By widespread personal contacts and an extensive correspondence, he kept in close touch with the political currents of the time. A few quotations from his writings and speeches may serve to suggest the trend of his thoughts. Writing to a friend on September 14, 1856, he referred to the apprehension "that the election of Fremont involves the

---

[4] In the House of Representatives, after an unsuccessful effort to expel him, Brooks defiantly resigned. He was then reelected by his district.

dissolution of the Union, & this immediately," and closed his letter with the words: "God save the Union! I do not wish to survive it." Speaking on November 6, 1856, he said, commenting on Democratic triumph in Pennsylvania and Indiana: "We had reached the crisis. The danger was imminent. Republicanism was sweeping over the North like a tornado. . . . The . . . Union . . . appeared to be tottering. . . . Had Pennsylvania yielded, had she become an abolition State, . . . we should have been precipitated into the yawning gulf of dissolution." [1] Born in 1791, Buchanan was now sixty-five years old, and age had weakened both his judgment and his will; yet his party showed little fear of his inadequacy in facing the crushing years that lay ahead. For the vice-presidency J. C. Breckinridge of Kentucky was named.

Since both the Democratic and American parties were marked by Southern tendencies and were considered "reactionary" and conservative, the new-fledged Republican party offered the only ballot to those numerous groups in the North who believed that slavery should not be extended. Playing on the Kansas note as the chief question before the country, the new party perfected its national organization at Pittsburgh in February, 1856, and held its first national nominating convention at Philadelphia in June. Though but two years old, the Republicans had acquired control of most of the state governments in the North, and they faced the coming contest with high confidence. Diversities within the party were illustrated by the various candidacies for the presidency. Those fired with antislavery zeal favored such men as Frémont or Chase; conservatives and "old fogies" preferred the aged McLean of Ohio, who, though a member of the Supreme Court of the United States for thirty years, had often been drawn into the current of political agitation. Many regarded Seward of New York as the logical standard-bearer; but Republican managers were now flirting with those Northern adherents of the American party who had "bolted the ticket" because of its proslavery tendencies, and it was considered undesirable to nominate a man who, like Seward, had been hostile to the Knownothings. There was, in fact, no serious contest; and on the first ballot Frémont was nominated. With a creditable army record and a dashing reputation in western exploration, the "Pathfinder," at the age of forty-three, though lacking in solid qualifications for the presidency, supplied those elements of romance and adventure which appealed to the youthful Republicanism of 1856. Senator William L. Dayton, an old-line Whig of New Jersey, was made vice-presidential candidate.

In their declaration of principles the Republicans took their stand against the repeal of the Missouri Compromise, opposed the extension of slavery, denounced the tyrannical and unconstitutional course of events in Kansas, favored its admission as a free state, denounced Southern ex-

[1] Buchanan, *Works,* ed. by J. B. Moore, X, 92, 96.

pansionism as represented in the Ostend Circular, and declared it the duty of Congress to stamp out those twin relics of barbarism—polygamy and slavery—from the territories. The party also went on record as favoring national aid for a Pacific railroad and congressional appropriations for local improvements. Nativism was vaguely denounced in a plank which favored "liberty of conscience and equality of rights." [2]

After these parties had entered the field and the political contest had taken shape, there met at Baltimore in September a feeble body known as the Whig convention. Under the chairmanship of Edward Bates of Missouri this obsolete party weakly ratified the nominations of the Knownothings. Declining to commit itself on the slavery question, the convention deplored the agitation that was shaking the country and declared: "It is enough to know that civil war is raging, and the Union is in peril."

In the campaign Douglas's "popular sovereignty" versus the Wilmot proviso doctrine of the Republicans occupied the chief attention. To the Northern Democrats popular sovereignty meant what Douglas meant, namely, that the people of a territory should decide the slavery question for themselves; while to the Southerners "noninterference" of the Federal government was understood to mean protection for slavery during the territorial stage, giving the people of the territory the privilege of choosing between slavery and freedom only at the time of making a state constitution and applying for admission to the Union. The public statements of Buchanan during the contest did not clarify the mystery that arose from this double interpretation of the platform.

In the result, the election of 1856 revealed much as to the state of sectionalism in the country. It was a pro-Southern democracy that gave Buchanan his narrow margin of victory. Though he obtained 174 electoral votes to Frémont's 114 and Fillmore's eight, he was chosen by less than an actual majority of all the popular votes cast, inasmuch as the votes of the people for Fillmore and Frémont considerably outnumbered his. Buchanan carried the entire South together with the border states, with the exception of Maryland, which cast its vote for Fillmore. In addition, he obtained the votes of Illinois, Indiana, California, New Jersey, and Pennsylvania. [3] The Republicans received negligible support in the South and on the border, which made their notable strength in the North seem the more ominous. They carried Connecticut, Maine, Iowa, Massachusetts, Michigan, New Hampshire, Ohio, New York, Rhode Island, Vermont, and Wisconsin, besides receiving large minority votes in Illinois, Indiana, New Jersey, and Pennsylvania. Of the three parties, only that of Fillmore could be regarded as nonsectional; for Southern radicals sup-

---

[2] E. Stanwood, *Hist. of the Presidency from 1788 to 1897*, 271–273.

[3] In Pennsylvania the popular vote of Frémont and Fillmore (229,686) almost equaled that of Buchanan (230,700). W. Dean Burnham, *Presidential Ballots, 1836–1892*, 704.

ported Buchanan and Northern radicals favored Frémont. As political post-mortems were held and the meaning of the contest was pondered it was borne in upon the country that slavery, in the words of the New York *Tribune,* was "the strongest bond and cement of our Union." So long as the Democratic party should preserve a policy friendly to slavery and at the same time retain the support of large numbers of Northern Democrats in the doubtful states, the Union seemed assured; but on the other hand the notable gains of the Republicans in the North, together with the growing discontent of Northern Democrats toward prevailing Southern tendencies in the party, gave the followers of Frémont a definite hope of success in 1860. Though in the sequel the Republican party was to make the Union its slogan, yet in 1856 they were denounced as the chief "disunionists" of the country. Unmoved by this taunt, they greeted the result with elation. With the control of state governments in most of the free commonwealths, they redoubled their efforts for the coming struggle; while the South, though conscious of a feeling of immediate relief, looked forward to the future with anxious concern.

CHAPTER 5

A House Divided

I

SECTIONALISM and strife on the economic, social, political, and constitutional fronts characterized the stormy years of Buchanan's administration. The solidarity of the South in defense of its social order grew mightily. Convinced that the Republican party intended "war against slavery, constitution or no constitution," more and more Southerners came to think "that separation was inevitable, that the South would ultimately be forced to secede or yield her way of life." Thoughtful leaders sought to defend their region against Northern "aggression" by promoting economic and intellectual sectionalism. J. D. B. DeBow, one of the most influential editors of the South, argued that the section must "build her own ships and conduct her own trade with foreign powers; manufacture at home every bale of cotton; diversify her industry, and build roads and railroads; cease the annual migrations to Northern watering places; educate all children at home and encourage a native literature." More radical spokesmen desired to strengthen the South's position by encouraging filibustering expeditions against Cuba and Central America, which were regarded as potential slave states, or by reopening the African slave trade. George Fitzhugh of Virginia argued on economic and sociological grounds that the slave society of the South was superior to the free society of the North. The latter was "a system of antagonism and war," where free laborers had "not a thousandth part of the rights and liberties of negro slaves." In the South, on the other hand, the slave laborer was always "cheerful, happy and contented, free from jealousy, malignity, and envy and at peace with all around him." [1]

At the same time a growing feeling of unity began to emerge in the North. Angered that the South was not satisfied with the concessions it had received in the Compromise of 1850 and the Kansas-Nebraska Act, many Northerners came to credit the abolitionist charge that the insati-

[1] Avery O. Craven, *The Growth of Southern Nationalism*, 247–248, 261–263.

able "slavocracy" intended further aggressions, that the magnates of the South would not be satisfied until slavery had been made legal in every state. Southern hostility to free homestead legislation caused many Northern mechanics and small farmers to cast their lots with the Republican party. When Southern congressmen, assisted by free-trade Democrats of the North, lowered the tariff again in 1857, powerful Eastern business interests came also to consider the Republican party as their only hope of capturing the Federal government for the cause of protection.

Sectional feeling in both the North and the South was increased by the serious financial panic of 1857. Northern businessmen believed that the depression was the inevitable consequence of Southern, low-tariff, Democratic domination of the nation's economic policy. In the South, where the impact of the panic was relatively slight, the sufferings of the Northern manufacturing community were taken as additional proof of the superiority of Southern economic institutions.

Growing sectionalism gave to many an agitator the chance to express his moral indignation, to battle for the right, and incidentally to serve his own sense of personal importance. In the South extremists tried to unite their section and to precipitate a dissolution of the union. Slavery, they argued, was a positive good. "That slavery is a blessing to the masters," shouted Albert G. Brown of Mississippi, "is shown by simply contrasting a Southern gentleman with a Northern abolitionist. One is courageous, high-bred, and manly. The other is cowardly, low-flung, and sneaking." Lawrence M. Keitt of South Carolina warned Southerners that "the Black Republican party, an amalgam of isms, a base conglomerate of opposing elements tied together by fanaticism," had pledged "its intention to abolitionize every department of the government and use them to the overthrow of slavery." The remedy, argued William L. Yancey of Alabama, was to form "Committees of Safety" throughout the states of the deep South. Through such means, he believed, "we shall fire the Southern heart—instruct the Southern mind—give courage to each other, and at the proper moment, by one organized concerted action, we can precipitate the Cotton States into a revolution." [2]

The North, too, had its agitators. Typical of the breed was Joshua R. Giddings of Ohio, who in 1859 completed twenty years of stormy service in the House of Representatives. A compelling persistence in pursuing an ideal was his outstanding characteristic, and with it extravagance of language, indifference to the niceties of courteous intercourse, and unshakable devotion to an objective. There was in his manner a standing-at-Armageddon attitude, not only battling for the Lord but hurling Olympian invectives and invoking almighty sanctions against opponents. Confident that his own motives were faultlessly pure, he was sure that all the right

[2] Allan Nevins, *The Emergence of Lincoln*, I, 405–409.

was on one side and that his adversaries' impulses were villainous and wicked. His speeches reveal that failure to see life whole, that lack of a sense of humor, that pertinacious meddling, and that tendency toward insulting bitterness, which mark the uncompromising crusader. Even more extreme than Giddings were the abolitionists who met at Worcester, Massachusetts, in January, 1857. Such men as William Lloyd Garrison, Wendell Phillips, Thomas W. Higginson, and Samuel J. May, spoke urgently for dissolution of the Union; and the convention resolved that "the sooner the separation takes place, the more peaceful it will be: but that peace or war is a *secondary consideration.*"

It cannot be said that the leading responsible statesmen of either the North or the South during these prewar years were of this uncompromising type, but as sectional conflict waxed hotter, the bad feelings which radicals in both sections stirred up became steadily more serious.

2

The Supreme Court of the United States, whose record for political impartiality has in general been maintained, but whose susceptibility to social and economic tendencies has ever been a factor in its decisions, did not escape entanglement in the sectional controversy. That the Court should make any decision in a matter affecting slavery meant inevitably that its action should be dramatized in the popular mind as taking sides; that it dealt in the Dred Scott case with the vexed question of slavery in the territories at the moment when excitement over this inflammatory issue was at its peak caused the Court, whose decision lent support to Southern doctrine, to be violently assailed as a champion of slavery.

Dred Scott, a Negro slave originally called "Sam," was purchased in 1832 or 1833 by John Emerson, a St. Louis doctor. When Emerson became a surgeon in the Federal army, he was ordered first to Rock Island, Illinois, and then to Fort Snelling, in Federal territory north of the line 36° 30', and he took his slave with him. Dred Scott had thus resided in a free state, and later in a portion of Federal territory in which slavery had been prohibited by the Missouri Compromise law of 1820. While at Fort Snelling he was married; in 1838 Dr. Emerson returned with him to Missouri.

The case in its legal details is exceedingly complicated; but the main steps may be briefly stated. In 1846, after Dr. Emerson's death, Scott, "having saved some money and having secured the interest and patronage of an army officer whom he had met in his military sojournings, applied to Mrs. Emerson to purchase his own and his family's freedom. She refused. Dred's case became known to a lawyer interested in such suits for humanitarian or financial reasons or both. Realizing that Dred had a good case, he brought suit" against Mrs. Emerson in the lower Missouri court at St. Louis.[1] Arguing that he was free because of residence in a free state and later in free territory, Scott obtained a judgment in his favor; but on appeal this decision was reversed by the state supreme court, which applied the rule that under Missouri law a slave, on returning voluntarily from residence in a free state, resumed his bonds.[2]

In November, 1853, the case entered a new phase. During the course of the earlier litigation Mrs. Emerson had met and married Dr. Calvin C. Chaffee, a Massachusetts politician of antislavery and Knownothing affiliations. "By her marriage," Vincent C. Hopkins has pointed out, "according to the laws of Missouri, she could no longer act in any capacity in regard to her first husband's estate, which had been left in trust for her daughter. . . ."[3] Her brother, John F. A. Sanford,[4] whom Dr. Emerson had named an executor of his will, had become the administrator of all the Emerson property, including the slaves. Since Sanford was a citizen of New York, Scott's lawyers claimed that the case should now be brought before the Federal courts, on the ground of diverse citizenship, and they brought an action for trespass against Sanford, with the object of securing Scott's freedom. Thus there arose the case of Scott *vs.* Sanford in the United States circuit court in Missouri. Sanford tried to quash the suit by arguing that Scott, being a Negro, was not a citizen of Missouri, and consequently that the circuit court did not have jurisdiction. Unimpressed by this defense, the court took jurisdiction; but when it came to instructing the jury, the Federal circuit judge, R. W. Wells, gave the ruling that the law was with Sanford.[5]

As expected and prearranged, the case was now appealed to the Supreme Court of the United States, where it was elaborately argued by learned counsel in February, 1856, and then reargued during the December term. In accordance with its custom, the Court deliberated on

[1] Vincent C. Hopkins, *Dred Scott's Case*, 182. "Why Mrs. Emerson refused to allow Dred to purchase his freedom can only be conjectured." *Ibid.*, 20.

[2] In giving judgment against Scott (15 Mo. 577) the supreme court of Missouri "based their opinion upon the ground that the laws of other states and territories had no extra-territorial effect in Missouri, except such as Missouri saw fit to give them." F. H. Hodder, in *M. V. H. R.*, XVI, 6. The same court, however, in eight previous cases, had held that a slave, after living in free territory, became free upon return to Missouri. It was now reversing its former rulings. See the article by Helen T. Catterall in *Am. Hist. Rev.*, XXX, especially pp. 65–68.

[3] Hopkins, *op. cit.*, 23.

[4] Misspelled "Sandford" in Howard's Reports.

[5] Judge Wells, who gave this decision in the circuit court, was willing enough to have his decision reversed, and wrote to Montgomery Blair, counsel for Scott before the United States Supreme Court, advising how this reversal might be obtained, pointing out that the Supreme Court would not be bound by local law as was the circuit court. Hodder, *op. cit.*, 8, n. 15.

February 15, 1857, as to how the case should be disposed of. In this conference it was agreed that the Court should entirely avoid the question as to the constitutionality of the Missouri Compromise and should decide the case against Scott on the ground that, by the law of Missouri, as now interpreted in the state supreme court, Scott remained a slave despite previous residence on free soil. Justice Nelson was directed to prepare the opinion of the Court to this effect.

It is not clear why the Court failed to accept Nelson's moderate opinion, which left untouched the two vexed issues of Negro citizenship and Congressional power over the territories. F. H. Hodder argued that the responsibility lay with McLean of Ohio and Curtis of Massachusetts, and he quoted a contemporary letter from Justice Grier, declaring that the determination of these two antislavery justices "to come out with a long and labored dissent, including their opinions and arguments on both the troublesome points, although not necessary to a decision of the case," compelled the proslavery majority of the Court "to express their opinions on the subject." [6] On the other hand, Allan Nevins has contended that Justice Wayne of Georgia "must be included among those whose share in bringing about a broad decision was greatest." Wayne, according to Justice Campbell, "stated that the case had been twice argued with thoroughness; that public expectation had been awakened and a decision of the important question looked for; that the Court would be condemned as failing in a performance of its duty, and that his own opinion was decided that the Chief Justice should prepare the opinion of the Court, and discuss all of the questions in the case." [7] Whoever forced the issue, the majority of the Court reversed their former intention and decided to give a broad opinion dealing with the whole question of Federal power over slavery in the territories.

In violation of judicial propriety, Justice Catron confidentially revealed to President Elect Buchanan the revised intention of the Court; whereupon Buchanan inserted in his inaugural address a prediction that the nation's highest tribunal would soon make a final judicial settlement of the vexed question of slavery in the territories. Buchanan's role in the Dred Scott decision was, however, even more intimate. Fearing that only the five slave state judges would join in the majority opinion declaring the Missouri Compromise unconstitutional, Buchanan, at Catron's urging, put pressure upon his old personal friend and political ally, Justice Grier of Pennsylvania, to join with the Southern judges. Grier agreed and, after showing Buchanan's letter to Taney and Wayne, wrote the President Elect: "We fully appreciate and concur in your views as to the desirableness . . . of having an expression of the opinion of the Court

[6] F. H. Hodder, "Some Phases of the Dred Scott Case," *M. V. H. R.*, XVI., 3–22.
[7] Nevins, *Emergence of Lincoln*, II, 473–477.

on this troublesome question." [8] As Roy F. Nichols has concluded: "Buchanan's, therefore, may well have been the deciding voice that determined the fateful Dred Scott decision. Had he not written to Grier, the latter might not have concurred; and had he not concurred, the five southern judges . . . might have finally refused to issue the dictum. Buchanan always had desired to be a member of the Supreme Court; in this instance he practically participated in their deliberations and influenced their judgment." [9]

Each of the nine justices issued a separate opinion. Technicalities make the case difficult and tiresome for the layman to follow, and this difficulty is heightened by diverse lines of reasoning pursued by the justices even when concurring. To discuss the case in all its legal aspects is out of the question here. Two important questions were "decided," or rather announced as decided,[10] by the majority of the Court: first, that a Negro "whose ancestors were . . . sold as slaves" [11] cannot become a member of the political community created by the Constitution and be entitled to the rights of Federal citizenship; second, that the Missouri Compromise law, prohibiting slavery in a part of national territory, was unconstitutional. It is because of these two fundamental points in the decision that the case possesses historical importance.

In developing the argument to support these points Taney declared that Negroes were not citizens of the several states at the time of the adoption of the Constitution and that the language of the Declaration of Independence did not embrace them as part of the "people" of the United States. He then proceeded as follows:

[8] *Ibid.*, I, 108–111.

[9] Nichols, *Disruption of American Democracy*, 66.

[10] The question as to Negro citizenship came up in connection with the defendant's "plea in abatement," i.e., Sanford's plea to abate the jurisdiction of the Federal district court on the ground that Scott, being a Negro, was not a citizen clothed with the right of access to Federal courts. Because of the manner in which this plea in abatement had been dealt with, there was a difference of opinion on the technical question whether it was rightfully before the Court on the writ of error. Thus, while six of the justices (Taney, Catron, Daniel, Wayne, Grier, and Campbell) concurred in holding that a Negro could not be a citizen of the United States, only three of these six (Taney, Wayne, and Daniel) expressed this view after holding that the plea in abatement was properly before the Court. It has therefore been technically maintained that, while the question of Negro citizenship was dealt with by a majority of the Court, yet this question was not in fact *judicially decided*. (G. T. Curtis, *Constitutional History of the United States*, II, 268 ff.) Because the Missouri Compromise question was taken up by judges who had previously held that the Court had no jurisdiction, it has been asserted that this problem also was not *judicially decided*. But see p. 113, n. 14.

[11] It should not be supposed that the slave ancestry of any particular Negro was involved: Taney was denying Federal citizenship to all Negroes, not merely to slaves or their descendants. His reference to ancestry should be read as a generalization concerning the dark race.

It is difficult at this day to realize the state of public opinion in relation to that unfortunate race, which prevailed in the civilized and enlightened portions of the world at the time of the Declaration of Independence, and when the Constitution of the United States was framed and adopted. But the public history of every European nation displays it in a manner too plain to be mistaken.

They had for more than a century before been regarded as beings of an inferior order, and altogether unfit to associate with the white race, either in social or political relations; and so far inferior, that they had no rights which the white man was bound to respect; and that the negro might justly and lawfully be reduced to slavery for his benefit. . . . This opinion was at that time . . . universal in the civilized portion of the white race. . . .

. . . . . .

The legislation of the different colonies furnishes positive and indisputable proof of this fact.[12]

There was at this time no constitutional definition of Federal citizenship, but the Constitution (Art. IV, sec. 2) provided that the "Citizens of each State shall be entitled to all Privileges and Immunities of Citizens in the several States." Taney, however, drew a distinction between "citizenship which a State may confer within its own limits, and the rights of citizenship as a member of the Union." A man might be a citizen of a state, he declared, but it did "not by any means follow . . . that he must be a citizen of the United States." Though the general rule was that Federal citizenship resulted from state citizenship, yet, said he, there was a limit to this rule, for "no State can . . . introduce a new member into the political community created by the Constitution of the United States." "It cannot," he said, "introduce any person, or description of persons, who were not intended to be embraced in this new political family, which the Constitution brought into existence, but were intended to be excluded from it." He therefore concluded that "Dred Scott was not a citizen of Missouri within the meaning of the Constitution of the United States, and not entitled as such to sue in its courts," and consequently that the circuit court had "no jurisdiction of the case."

Earlier in the case, the Chief Justice had summarized as follows:

1. Had the Circuit Court of the United States jurisdiction . . . ?
2. If it had jurisdiction, is the judgment it has given erroneous or not?[13]

This way of putting the matter implied that the second question should be entered upon only in case the first had been decided affirmatively. Later in the decision, however, having decided the first question negatively, the Chief Justice added: "We proceed, therefore, to inquire whether the facts relied on by the plaintiff entitled him to his freedom."

[12] 19 Howard (60 U. S.), 407–408.
[13] For quoted passages, see 19 Howard 405, 406, 427, 430, 400.

It was in this manner that he introduced the question of the constitutional validity of the Compromise act. Stressing the fact that slaves were property, and invoking the fifth amendment, which prohibits Congress from taking property without "due process of law," Taney declared that the "only power conferred" upon Congress by the Constitution in the matter of slavery in the territories was "the power coupled with the duty of guarding and protecting the owner in his rights." [14] The Compromise act, he declared, was "not warranted by the Constitution" and was "therefore void."

The scope of this book precludes the examination of the concurring opinions of Justices Campbell, Catron, Daniel, Grier, and Wayne. It is enough to note that each arrived at his conclusions by somewhat different processes of reasoning and that not all concurred with the Chief Justice's argument in all points. The opinion of Justice Nelson has special historical significance in the fact that it contains the original opinion of the Court itself before the case was reconsidered. Nelson avoided both the question of Negro citizenship and that of congressional power over slavery in the territories. He held that the case was controlled by Missouri law, and that, despite previous residence in regions where slavery did not exist, Scott resumed his status as slave on his return to Missouri.

There were two dissenting opinions, those of Justices McLean and Curtis, the latter being particularly important since it was widely circulated in the North and accepted by antislavery men as law and gospel. Curtis showed that before the adoption of the Constitution free Negroes were state citizens in New Hampshire, Massachusetts, New Jersey, New York, and North Carolina. He found "nothing in the Constitution which . . . deprives [them] of their citizenship"; and, in view of the reciprocal citizenship clause, he therefore concluded that such free Negroes were "also citizens of the United States." In his opinion the circuit court had jurisdiction; and, without the inconsistency attributed to Taney and the others of the majority, he proceeded to examine the case on its merits. He pointed out that, in the language of the Constitution, Congress is expressly granted the power to "make all needful Rules and

---

[14] Much has been made of the claim that Taney was going outside his province in declaring the Compromise act void after holding that the circuit court had no jurisdiction; and his announcement on this phase of the case has usually been regarded at *obiter dictum*. Even so, however, it was a solemn announcement of judicial doctrine by the Supreme Court of the United States; and it has been maintained by Professor E. S. Corwin that Taney's denial of the power of Congress to exclude slavery from the territories was not an *obiter dictum* at all, for a court is obliged to explore every pertinent phase of the case before it in order not to overlook any essential right that may be involved. Corwin further concludes, however, that in supporting his opinion Taney used irrelevant arguments, incorrectly invoked the principle of "vested rights," and misapplied the "due process of law" doctrine. *Am. Hist. Rev.*, XVII, 52–69.

Regulations respecting the Territory . . . belonging to the United States"; that the Constitution makes no exception to this power in the matter of slavery; that judicial construction for over fifty years would forbid such an exception; and that "it would . . . violate every sound rule of interpretation to force that exception into the Constitution upon the strength of abstract political reasoning."

In Republican and antislavery circles the decision was denounced as a "new and atrocious doctrine," a "deliberate iniquity," a "wilful perversion," "a *dictum* prescribed by the stump to the Bench," "the greatest crime in the judicial annals of the Republic," and "entitled to just so much moral weight as would be the judgment of a majority of those congregated in any Washington bar-room." On the other hand many influential newspapers in the North defended the decision, while in the South it was naturally accepted as the true interpretation.

3

Affairs in Kansas meanwhile contributed additional ammunition to the arsenals of Republican and antislavery agitation. Premature and *ex parte* efforts of an irregular nature were put forth on both sides to rush the territory into the Union, the proslavery faction being powerfully supported by the national administration under Pierce and Buchanan. In the House of Representatives a bill was presented to admit Kansas under a free-state constitution which had been adopted at Topeka in October of 1855, and "ratified" in a one-sided antislavery election. On July 3, 1856, this bill passed the House; but it was voted down in the Senate. Out of the confusion and strife which followed there developed a condition of civil war within the state. The free-state faction had elected a body which functioned as a "provisional" state legislature, choosing Lane and Reeder as United States senators; but the failure of the movement to have Kansas admitted under the Topeka constitution left this antislavery legislature stranded as a pretended government. In the absence of settled government, Kansas was now overrun by marauders and criminals who descended upon the homes of innocent settlers and subjected the inhabitants to repeated acts of violence. Under these circumstances President Pierce, who had attributed the troubles in Kansas to "propagandist colonization," and to the "spirit of revolutionary attack on the domestic institutions of the South," removed Governor Shannon and appointed John W. Geary of Pennsylvania, a vigorous and competent man, to establish order with the assistance of Federal troops. At the same time the President disavowed any intention of interfering with elections, declaring that the people are "all-sufficient guardians of their own rights." The President, he explained, had no power to "see to the regularity of local elections," and he added that if he had such power, the government would cease to be republican except in name. Governor Geary performed his task well, acting without partiality in suppressing lawlessness and doing much to restore order. In his annual message of December 2, 1856, Pierce expressed "unmingled satisfaction" in the establishment of a "peaceful condition" in Kansas, and stated that through the "wisdom and energy" of Governor Geary and the "prudence, firmness, and vigilance of the military officers on duty," "tranquillity [had] been restored without one drop of blood having been shed . . . by the forces of the United States." [1] Meanwhile Republican spokesmen were denouncing Pierce for what they regarded as proslavery interference.

Geary was succeeded in March, 1857, by Robert J. Walker, who had been reared in Pennsylvania, had gone South, and had achieved distinction in Mississippi politics, rising to the position of United States senator and later to cabinet rank as secretary of the treasury under Polk. The struggle for Kansan statehood now became acute with the controversy over what was known as the "Lecompton constitution." Under a census which omitted fifteen of the thirty-four counties of the state, a constitutional convention was chosen by less than a fourth of those listed as entitled to vote, inasmuch as the free-state element refrained from participating in what they regarded as a proslavery constitutional maneuver. Meeting at Lecompton, the convention so chosen (or rather a portion of it, for many of the delegates did not attend) adopted a slavery constitution in which it was declared that the "right of property is . . . higher than any constitutional sanction, and the right of the owner of a slave . . . is . . . as inviolable as the right of the owner of any property whatever." After a struggle within the convention it was decided not to submit the constitution to an untrammeled popular vote: the people were merely permitted to vote for the "constitution with slavery," or for the "constitution with no slavery." In case of the latter vote, slavery was to exist "no longer" in the state (so read the voting formula) "except that the right of property in slaves now in this Territory shall in no measure be interfered with." This meant that only the proslavery element had a ballot, and only such of them as favored the constitution, which, aside from the slavery matter, had various objectionable elements, such as provisions excluding free Negroes from the state and assigning "more than sixteen and a half million acres of land, approximately one-fifth of the territory," for the support of schools and favored railroad projects. [2] When the vote was taken (December 21, 1857), with the usual irregularities and frauds characteristic of Kansas elections in the fifties, the result, as officially announced, showed over six thousand votes for the "constitu-

---

[1] Richardson, *Messages and Papers of the Presidents*, V, 404–407.
[2] Nichols, *Disruption of American Democracy*, 125.

tion with slavery" as against less than six hundred for the constitution "with no slavery." Not only free-state men, but all who opposed the constitution, had abstained from voting.

Though the Lecompton constitution was clearly a swindle and a fraud, President Buchanan now urged Congress to admit the state. He defended the action of the Lecompton convention and stated that, had the convention submitted the whole constitution to the people, the free-state men, whom he denounced as adherents of a rebellious organization, would "doubtless have voted against it . . . not upon a consideration of [its] merits . . . , but simply because they have ever resisted the authority of the government authorized by Congress. . . ." Citing the Dred Scott decision, the President declared that "Kansas is . . . at this moment as much a slave State as Georgia or South Carolina." Speedy admission of Kansas, he said, would "restore peace and quiet to the whole country," while its rejection would be "keenly felt by the people of fourteen of the States of this Union, where slavery is recognized under the Constitution of the United States." [3]

In the congressional struggle which ensued when the question of admitting the state under the Lecompton constitution was presented, Douglas courageously opposed the administration and broke with the proslavery Democrats; as a result he was furiously attacked and was read out of the party by the Buchanan element. At this stage there was even talk of the Republicans taking up Douglas and making him their leader. The bill to admit Kansas with the Lecompton constitution passed the Senate (33 to 25), the vote finding Douglas in company with Seward, Wade, and Republicans generally. Since it was known that the bill could not pass the House, a compromise was struck in a measure known as the "English bill" (after William H. English, anti-Lecompton Democratic representative from Indiana) which received the support of both houses and became law on May 4, 1858. Under this act the Lecompton constitution was to be resubmitted as a whole to the people of Kansas in connection with a Federal land grant which should become available if the constitution were adopted. The measure was roundly denounced by the Republicans as a cunning bribe and was referred to as "the English swindle." Henry Wilson of Massachusetts called it "a conglomeration of bribes, of penalties, and of meditated fraud." [4] It had, however, the merit of providing a genuine popular vote on the constitution; and, as Professor Hodder has shown, it did not contain an exceptionally large offer of land but rather a grant identical with that offered to Minnesota the year before and analogous to those given to various states.[5] On August 2, 1858, the popular vote was taken as prescribed in the English bill, and the con-

[3] J. B. Moore, *Works of Buchanan*, X, 183, 190, 192.
[4] *Cong. Globe*, 35 Cong., 1 sess., 1874 (Apr. 29, 1858).
[5] F. H. Hodder, in *Annual Report*, Am. Hist. Assn., 1906, I, 201–210.

stitution was decisively rejected (11,300 to 1788). The rôle of Kansas in the sectionalization of the country had been played.

4

Amid this accompaniment of jarring sectionalism a note was struck in Illinois which vibrated through the coming years. " 'A house divided against itself cannot stand.' I believe this government cannot endure, permanently half *slave* and half *free*." [1] The occasion was the meeting of the Republican state convention at Springfield (June 16, 1858); the speaker was Abraham Lincoln, whom the convention chose as their candidate for the United States Senate. The new leader, now entering upon a hard-fought campaign with Douglas, was a rough-hewn product of pioneer Kentucky, his forebears reaching back among humble folk through Virginia, Pennsylvania, and Massachusetts to seventeenth century England. Shifting about in the streams of pioneer migration, Lincolns and Hankses had lived close to the soil in the backwoods manner without taking root; yet from their undistinguished lives and hardscrabble surroundings there had arisen the fire and sparkle of genius.

To Illinois in 1858, however, Lincoln was no genius but a familiar and effective politician. Personally known to the common people as rail-splitter, flatboatman, storekeeper, country postmaster, surveyor, and captain in the Black Hawk War, he had come up through the ranks as a self-made politician, had served four terms in the state legislature and one in Congress, and, as practicing lawyer, had traveled from county-seat to county-seat, mingling with the people on court days, amusing them with homespun stories and thrilling them with political speeches from the stump. Nor had he moved merely among the common people. He had married into one of the proud slaveholding families of the Kentucky aristocracy; he had risen to the top of the legal profession in his state; and from having been one of the most prominent Whigs of Illinois he had now taken his place as an outstanding Republican leader. With his homely, rugged face, his backwoods origin, his tall, awkward form, his reputation for honesty, his mental tenacity, his familiarity with the politician's craft, his innate conservatism shrewdly combined with crusading zeal, his Jeffersonian philosophy, his power of invective, and his mastery of terse, epigrammatic English, he stood out in 1858, not only as a formidable opponent of Douglas but as a vigorous spokesman of a new party that was profiting by the disruptive forces abroad in the land and gaining votes every day. After several years of slight political activity, he had returned to politics with redoubled earnestness in indignation at the repeal of the Missouri Compromise in 1854; he had become increasingly

---

[1] Roy P. Basler *et al.*, eds., *The Collected Works of Abraham Lincoln*, II, 461. Hereafter cited as: Lincoln, *Collected Works*.

prominent by his denunciation of Douglas's popular sovereignty; in 1856 the Republicans in national convention at Philadelphia had given him 110 votes for the vice-presidential nomination; and he now gained advantage and prestige by challenging the well-known Douglas to a series of joint debates at the time when Douglas was suffering by the party split between his own followers and the powerfully buttressed Buchanan faction. In truth Lincoln had been publicly debating Douglas for years; but there was something in this formal series of forensic encounters which seized the imagination of the country.

Opening at Ottawa on August 21, the joint debates continued with the fanfare of western campaigning at Freeport, Jonesboro, Charleston, Galesburg, and Quincy, closing at Alton on October 15. Douglas taunted Lincoln with his seemingly radical "house divided" declaration, accused him of promoting a war of sections, ridiculed the idea of state uniformity as to domestic institutions, hurled sneers at "black Republicans" whom he accused of demanding racial equality, expounded his own doctrine of letting the people decide the slavery question, and scored Lincoln and his followers for seeking to abolitionize the country and for defying the Supreme Court. Bitterly did he denounce the alliance which he declared to exist between the Republicans and the Buchanan Democrats for the purpose of defeating him with the aid of Federal patronage in order to satisfy Democratic revenge for his "having defeated" the Lecompton constitution. "What do you Republicans think," he said, "of a political organization that will try to make an unholy . . . combination with its professed foes to beat a man merely because he has done right? . . . You know that the axe of decapitation is suspended over every man in office in Illinois, and the terror of proscription is threatened every Democrat by the present administration unless he supports the Republican ticket in preference to my Democratic associates and myself." [2]

On Lincoln's side the debate revealed that combination of conservatism with moral indignation and reforming zeal which has been mentioned as one of his peculiar characteristics. No Garrisonian abolitionist, Lincoln shared some of the Southern attitudes toward the Negro. Though he denounced the Dred Scott decision for its doctrine that a Negro could not be a citizen, he said very frankly: ". . . I am not in favor of negro citizenship." [3] Similarly, he emphatically disclaimed the doctrine of social equality for the races; declined to advocate the repeal of the fugitive slave law; took no stand against the admission of further slave states; and qualified his "house divided" declaration by explaining that it contained no threat of radical violence or sectional strife. At the same time the passionate sincerity of his hostility to slavery gleamed through his rhetoric. "The difference between the Republican and the Democratic parties . . . [in]

[2] Lincoln, *Collected Works,* III, 211–212.
[3] *Ibid.,* III, 179.

this contest," he declared, "is, that the former consider slavery a moral, social and political wrong, while the latter *do not* consider it either a moral, social or political wrong. . . . The Republican party . . . hold that this government was instituted to secure the blessings of freedom, and that slavery is an unqualified evil to the negro, to the white man, to the soil, and to the State. Regarding it an evil, they will not molest it in the States where it exists . . . ; but they will use every constitutional method to prevent the evil from becoming larger. . . . They will, if possible, place it where the public mind shall rest in the belief that it is in the course of ultimate peaceable extinction, in God's own good time." [4]

Though the speeches on both sides were long and elaborate, they were largely taken up with repetition, or with half serious, half playful banter. While Lincoln dwelt at length on the moral wrong of slavery, his constructive proposals can be briefly summarized. Advocating no Federal interference with the institution in the states, he insisted that it be excluded from the territories (this being his most important proposal); in a qualified manner he favored exclusion from the District of Columbia; [5] he held that the Dred Scott decision, in denying to Congress the power to exclude slavery from the territories, was erroneous; and, while avoiding any attitude of radical defiance toward the Court, he declared his expectation that the decision would be reversed. With all his moderation and tolerance, however, Lincoln managed to inject enough fire and righteous denunciation into his speeches to inspire radicals; meanwhile his abolitionist partner, Herndon, kept in close and sympathetic touch with the antislavery wing.

Lincoln's shrewdness in proposing a set question to Douglas at Freeport, and Douglas's manner of answering it, were destined to have important consequences. "Can the people of a United States Territory," asked Lincoln, "in any lawful way . . . exclude slavery from its limits prior to the formation of a State Constitution?" If Douglas should follow the cue of the Supreme Court and answer *No,* he would disappoint many voters in his own state and in the North generally; should he answer *Yes,* he would offend his pro-Southern supporters in "Egypt" (Southern Illinois) and would alienate the slaveholding South. The chance that Douglas would lose the presidency in 1860 by an answer that would gain the senatorship in 1858 may not have been in Lincoln's mind; he was merely pursuing his relentless purpose, everywhere evident in the debates, of exposing the inconsistency between the Dred Scott doctrine and the

[4] *Ibid.,* III, 92–93.
[5] The prohibition of slavery in the District of Columbia was advocated by Lincoln in a guarded manner and with the same qualifying conditions which he had proposed in Congress: abolition was to be gradual; it was to be accompanied by compensation to slaveowners; and it was to be subject to popular referendum in the district.

principle of "popular sovereignty," and of widening the split between the Douglas and Buchanan wings of the Democratic party. Douglas replied:

> I answer emphatically . . . that in my opinion the people of a Territory can, by lawful means, exclude slavery from their limits prior to the formation of a State constitution. . . . It matters not what way the Supreme Court may hereafter decide as to the abstract question whether slavery may or may not go into a Territory under the Constitution, the people have the lawful means to introduce it or exclude it as they please, for the reason that slavery cannot exist a day . . . unless it is supported by local police regulations. Those police regulations can only be established by the local legislature; and if the people are opposed to slavery, they will elect representatives . . . who will by unfriendly legislation . . . prevent the introduction of it into their midst. If, on the contrary, they are for it, their legislation will favor its extension.[6]

By this answer, or rather by Douglas's whole career in the later fifties of which this answer was but a logical part, the "Little Giant" had made himself unavailable as a leader of Southern Democracy. As to the outcome of the election in Illinois, it presented a paradox not uncommon in American politics: Lincoln's party carried districts containing a larger population than those carried by the Democrats, but because of an inequitable apportionment (made under Democratic auspices) Douglas obtained a majority in the legislature, insuring his election.[7] Two outstanding results gave national significance to the debates: Douglas's position was so advertised and clarified as to intensify the rift in the Democratic party; and the Republicans had found a new leader, for Abraham Lincoln had achieved a national prominence which caused him soon to be mentioned for the presidency.

5

While the repeal of the Missouri Compromise, the Kansas struggle, the Dred Scott decision, and the Lincoln-Douglas debate were drawing attention to slavery in the territories, other factors served to emphasize another prolific source of unpleasantness in those clashes between the states which arose in connection with the escape of fugitive slaves. Though slaveowners recovered numerous runaways with a minimum of disorder, prominent instances of "rescues" or attempted rescues always attracted more notice than the unobstructed or forcible return of slaves. Salmon P. Chase in Ohio so often defended fugitives in the courts that he was dubbed the "attorney general for runaway negroes"; but he was regularly on the los-

---

[6] E. E. Sparks, ed., The Lincoln-Douglas Debates of 1858, 161.

[7] "The thirty-five Lincoln members of the House represent a larger population than the forty Douglas members; and the eleven Lincoln Senators represent a larger constituency than the fourteen Douglas and Buchanan Senators." Sparks, ed., Lincoln-Douglas Debates, 533. (Sparks quotes the Ill. State Jour.)

ing side, for the cases were decided against his clients both in Ohio and upon Federal appeal. Such was the case of one Van Zandt, seized in Ohio in 1842 in an attempt to rescue fugitive Negroes. The rescuer was subjected to heavy damages and penalties in the state courts which were sustained when the case was brought up to the Supreme Court of the United States. It was significant, however, that two of the coming statesmen of the Republican party, Chase and Seward, gave their services without compensation for the defense, and that both argued the invalidity of the fugitive slave act of 1793.

Fearless abolitionists could always be found who defied the law, often in the name of religion. Samuel J. May, a Unitarian minister in Syracuse active in the antislavery crusade, led a righteous mob which rescued a fugitive Negro named Jerry McHenry in 1851 from the officers of the law. The Negro was taken by friendly hands to Canada, and the participants in the "Jerry rescue" remained unpunished. In 1854, when a Virginia slave, Anthony Burns, sailed north as a stowaway and was recovered by his owner in Boston, no less a man than Richard Henry Dana handled his defense; the local "vigilance committee" swung into action; a Faneuil Hall crowd listened to inflammatory speeches by Theodore Parker and Wendell Phillips; and a mob led by Rev. Thomas Wentworth Higginson stormed the court house and did battle with Federal officers in an unsuccessful attempt at rescue. When Burns was put on board ship for Virginia 1100 soldiers escorted him to the wharf. The "Boston slave riot" and the Burns case remained vividly alive both in Southern and in abolitionist consciousness; the year after his return to slavery he was purchased by Boston citizens and set free.

One of the cleverest escapes was that of William Craft, who fled from Macon, Georgia. His quadroon wife under male disguise accompanied him as his supposed white owner, and the pair made their way to England with the assistance of the Boston vigilance committee. In another locality the affair of the Oberlin-Wellington rescue indicated the strong antislavery sentiment in the Western Reserve district in Ohio. At Wellington a crowd including a Sunday-school superintendent and an Oberlin professor rescued a Negro from slave-catchers. Various of the rescuers were prosecuted for violation of the Federal fugitive slave act of 1850, while prosecutions were instituted in the state courts against the slave-catchers on the charge of kidnapping. A compromise was struck and prosecutions on both sides dropped; but the incident left a marked impression. A similar incident at Christiania, in Lancaster County, Pennsylvania, resulted in a fatal riot in which Quaker bystanders, ordered to assist the Federal officer in the recovery of a fugitive, refused. They were prosecuted, but not convicted, on the excessive charge of "treason."

Most conspicuous in slave-rescuing enterprise was the "Underground Railroad." With its "agents" and "forwarding merchants" it zealously promoted the secret work of spiriting Negroes away from Southern masters, hiding them in barns or closets, moving them at night by definite "routes" and "stations," and landing them in Canada. There they were on free soil; international usage did not require their reclamation as in the case of fugitive criminals. Thousands of the "best people" of the free states were engaged in this humanitarian but law-defying work; on the other hand there were counter activities in the North about which less is known—sinister, clandestine plots to kidnap free Negroes or reclaim runaways by harsh methods which disregarded legal process.

A vexatious phase of the fugitive slave situation was the deliberate resistance which state governments in the North were offering to the recovery of slaves. Statutes known as "personal liberty laws" were passed to offer protection to Negroes seeking to evade or resist slave-catchers.[1] Many of the states denied the use of their jails for the detention of fugitives; state judges were forbidden to assist claimants; trial by jury was extended to Negroes claimed as slaves; and habeas corpus writs were directed to be issued by state authority for their release. States which had enacted laws of this general sort, though they differed in their provisions, were Maine, Vermont, Connecticut, Rhode Island, Massachusetts, New Hampshire, Indiana, Michigan, Wisconsin, Ohio, and Pennsylvania.[2]

Such action was denounced in the South as Northern state nullification, and in *Ableman* vs. *Booth* it received vigorous rebuke by the Supreme Court of the United States. The Booth case arose in Wisconsin. A fugitive slave had been rescued by an abolitionist editor (Sherman M. Booth), who was arrested and taken into custody by a Federal marshal for violation of the fugitive slave act of 1850. This Federal prisoner was defiantly declared to be discharged on habeas corpus writ issued under the judicial authority of the state of Wisconsin. The writ was unanimously sustained in a sententious decision of the state supreme court; and a serious jurisdictional controversy was thus engendered, involving the question whether a state court has the authority to release a prisoner held under the judicial author-

---

[1] Northern states were encouraged in the passage of such laws by a remark of Justice Story in what was known as the Prigg case. In this case the Supreme Court declared unconstitutional a Pennsylvania statute which made it a felony to remove a Negro by force for the purpose of slavery, on the ground that Federal power in the matter of fugitive slaves was exclusive. In delivering the Court's opinion, which was unanimous, Story remarked by way of *obiter dictum* that state officials were under no obligation to observe that part of the existing fugitive slave law which called for their assistance, and even that state legislatures might forbid them to do so. The decision was hateful to both proslavery and antislavery elements. 16 Peters 539.

[2] In addition to these states, it should be noted that the territory of Kansas had its personal liberty law, passed in 1858, and that a high court in New York had ruled that slaves became free by being taken into a non-slave state. Cole, *Irrepressible Conflict*, 274. Some of the states, having had earlier personal liberty laws, enacted new ones after the passage of the Federal fugitive slave law of 1850.

ity of the United States for the violation of the Federal law. Since the state court had rested its case on the invalidity of the fugitive slave act, and had sought by state judicial process to make that law of no effect in Wisconsin, and since this example was being applauded in certain Northern circles with the prospect that it would be emulated in other states, the issue from the standpoint of Federal supremacy was a grave one. It was essentially the same issue as that presented by "nullification" in South Carolina and Georgia during the administration of President Jackson. The defiance of the Wisconsin state judiciary was especially manifest when the United States Supreme Court issued a writ of error in the Booth case; for the state court directed its clerk to ignore the writ. Under these circumstances the slavery phase of the case dwindled in comparison with the issue of Federal integrity in the face of state recalcitrance. Despite the certainty of criticism for taking sides in the slavery controversy, Chief Justice Taney issued a ringing opinion (1859) in which he asserted that supremacy of Federal jurisdiction in Federal matters was fundamental in the Constitution and in congressional legislation, and that the maintenance of such supremacy against state interference was vital to the government. It was an ominous fact that abolitionists in the North, having praised the defiance of the Wisconsin court, now launched their darts against the Supreme Court of the United States, accusing that high tribunal of "usurpation" and of pro-slavery "conspiracy."

6

The potency of literature in the governance of men's minds was forcibly shown when in 1852 Harriet Beecher Stowe published her *Uncle Tom's Cabin*, a work of popular fiction which set up a Christian martyr in black skin as hero, idealized the Negro, stressed his unhappiness in the South, and presented harrowing pictures of brutality. The factual basis on which the author chiefly relied was an abolitionist tract entitled *Slavery As It Is, the Testimony of a Thousand Witnesses* (New York, 1839) which was compiled by Theodore Dwight Weld and extensively circulated by the American Anti-Slavery Society. It was related that Mrs. Stowe had the pamphlet in her work basket by day, and under her pillow by night. Her *Key to Uncle Tom's Cabin* (1853) contains many extracts from the Weld pamphlet. The book was universally read, 100,000 copies being sold within two months and 300,000 within a year. The South considered the book a slander, regarding it not incorrectly as an abolitionist tract. They knew that the public would forget those passages in which the kinder side of slavery was revealed and that thoughtless readers would take the murderous brutality of a Legree for the typical attitude of the Southern master. A Southern woman of spirit wrote of trying to read *Uncle Tom*, but added she "could not"; it was "too sickening." "Flesh and blood revolt," she said, at such details as a "man sending his little son to beat a human being tied to a tree." [1]

The significance of *Uncle Tom's Cabin,* as of similar mass attacks upon the popular mind, lay in the fact that the conflict of sections was becoming increasingly dramatized. Issues were becoming emotionalized; slogans were reducing public sentiment to stereotyped patterns; social psychology was approaching a hair-trigger instability. To this factor of mass psychology William H. Seward made a fateful contribution. Speaking at Rochester, New York, October 25, 1858, he said: "Shall I tell you what this collision means? They who think that it is accidental, unnecessary, the work of interested or fanatical agitators, and therefore ephemeral, mistake the case altogether. It is an irrepressible conflict between opposing and enduring forces, and it means that the United States must and will, sooner or later, become either entirely a slave-holding nation, or entirely a free-labor nation." [2] Seward was now one of the foremost senators of the country and an outstanding leader of the Republican party with a fair prospect of becoming their candidate for the presidency in 1860. His actual conservatism as a practical leader was obscured and the substance of his speeches in general forgotten; but the phrase "irrepressible conflict" burned itself into public consciousness.

A year after the speech was delivered old John Brown of Osawatomie broke out with an insane attack upon slavery in Virginia; and the sensitive mind of the South put the two together: Seward, the Republican spokesman, was preaching the "irrepressible conflict"; John Brown was giving the illustration of it in blood and servile war!

Scorning the "milk-and-water" abolitionists of the parlor variety, John Brown had said: "What is needed is action—action!" Long before his Kansas experience he had resolved to combat slavery by bloodshed and violence. Exalting this resolution to the self-immolating life-purpose of a martyr, he had sworn his sons to the support of his undertakings; and in the Pottawatomie massacre, albeit his complicity in this outrage was not generally known, he had demonstrated that murder in cold blood was part of his strategy. Writers who have studied the psychology of the man have called him insane; at the very least his mental condition was that of obsession and extreme, unbalanced fanaticism. Yet his strange, compelling personality, lacking as it did the ballast of practical reason, had an undoubted power over men of culture and education. Men such as Gerrit Smith, Theodore Parker, S. G. Howe, and T. W. Higginson, were induced to give assistance, as well as substantial men less known, such as George L. Stearns and Franklin B. Sanborn. Tireless in his determined efforts, Brown obtained money and arms from respectable antislavery sources; established

---

[1] Mrs. Chesnut, *Diary from Dixie,* 184.

[2] Frederic Bancroft, *Life of W. H. Seward,* I, 458–459; George E. Baker, ed., *Works of William H. Seward,* IV, 292.

himself in Canada with a band of twelve whites and thirty-four Negroes; held a "Convention" (misrepresented as a meeting to organize a colored Masonic lodge); drew up a document called "Provisional Constitution and Ordinances for the People of the United States"; and concocted a daring plan of violent emancipation. Briefly, his wild scheme was to liberate Southern slaves by violence; establish them in mountain fastnesses; defeat any military force, whether state militia or Federal troops, that might oppose them; organize the free blacks into a sort of government; teach them the mechanical and useful arts; take slaveholders as hostages; and force Southern commonwealths to adopt emancipatory measures. Having assembled his miniature army (twenty-one men in addition to Brown himself) at the Kennedy farm on the Maryland side of the Potomac across from Harpers Ferry, he devoted many weeks to waiting and preparation. It was from this point that, on the night of October 16, 1859, he led a forlorn and desperate band of eighteen followers, which included three of his own sons and five Negroes, to an assault upon Harpers Ferry, where he succeeded in capturing the Federal arsenal and armory and seizing some of the citizens of the town and surrounding countryside as hostages. There was no response on the part of Virginia slaves. Refusing to retreat to the mountains while the chance to do so in safety remained, Brown fortified himself in the engine-house, where his hopeless little force was routed by United States marines under Col. Robert E. Lee.

Virginia and the South responded to the raid in a frenzy of alarm out of proportion to the significance of so detached an incident; on the other side abolitionists were comparing Brown to Christ himself and were preparing for his apotheosis as saint and hero. Contempt of Virginia as of an inferior civilization was now the theme of antislavery speeches and editorials. Virginia, said Wendell Phillips, "is no government. . . . Virginia, the Commonwealth of Virginia! She is only a chronic insurrection. . . . She is a pirate ship, and John Brown sails the sea a Lord High Admiral of the Almighty with his commission to sink every pirate he meets on God's ocean of the nineteenth century." [3]

Amid furious popular excitement Brown and his conspirators were brought to trial; and on October 31 the jury found him guilty of treason against the state of Virginia, inciting slave rebellion, and murder. For these crimes he was hanged at Charles Town, December 2, 1859. Six of his followers suffered a like fate later; the rest had died or escaped.

The results of the John Brown raid are to be measured in terms of social psychology. Such an irresponsible and unsupported project presented no real menace to Southern civilization; but Southerners could not forget Santo Domingo, servile war was an unspeakable horror to them, rumor magnified the incident, and the whole effect was to dramatize anew the cause of Southern rights. There seemed a fateful unreadiness in the South

[3] *Speeches, Lectures, and Letters, by Wendell Phillips* (1864 ed.), 272.

to accept as typical the great mass of conservative Northern opinion which of course condemned the outrage. The attack was inextricably identified with the abolitionists who almost universally praised Brown; and responsibility was laid at the door of the Republicans. Even Douglas declared his "deliberate conviction that the Harpers Ferry crime was the . . . logical, inevitable result of the doctrines . . . of the Republican party." [4]

"John Brown's body" was to become a symbol and a shibboleth. In the superficial sense of a Northern nation going to war in the spirit of Brown's fanaticism the slogan has little meaning. If, however, one ponders those elements of misunderstanding between North and South which became associated with Brown's strangely inspired crime, and if one remembers how important were these misunderstandings in the irrational streams of thought that produced the Civil War, the gruesome shibboleth becomes a not inappropriate symbol of the American sectional tragedy.

[4] *Cong. Globe,* 36 Cong., 1 sess., 553.

CHAPTER 6

Secession of the Lower South

I

As THE YEAR 1860 opened it was evident that a struggle impended not only between parties but within parties. The disruptive force of sectionalism was proving stronger than the cement of party harmony. A purely sectional party—that of the Republicans—was looming ever larger on the horizon, while the historic Democratic party, the one best hope of saving the Union, was threatened with hopeless discord. No other party had both the likelihood of success if united and the ability to hold the country together if successful. With the Kansas struggle and the black horror of the John Brown raid fresh in memory, the South was now in fighting mood; and, while Southern devotion to the Union was far from dead, it was becoming a qualified devotion, for Southern Democrats were now less interested in conciliation than in a clear-cut statement of party principle in full accord with Southern doctrine.

The lower South was now at the fore in party strategy; and at the moment the spokesman of the lower South was William Lowndes Yancey. Gifted with personal force and oratorical power, Yancey had become socially identified with the planter class and was already known as the voice of Southern protest. Under his militant leadership Alabama, Georgia, Florida, and Virginia had in 1848 endorsed the "Alabama platform," which demanded that slavery in the territories be positively protected by Congress and insisted that no one out of accord with this view should be nominated by the Democrats for the presidency. When milder counsels prevailed and the Compromise of 1850 was adopted against his opposition, he withdrew into the background; but the situation in 1860 offered a perfect setting for his return to leadership. It was widely asserted in the deep South that Republican success would result in secession; and on February 24, 1860, the Alabama legislature resolved that the state would not submit to a "foul sectional party" and provided for the calling of a convention in the event of the election of a "black Republican" President. The reorganization of the military systems of this and other Southern states at this time was symptomatic of the general apprehension.

The factional struggle in the Democratic convention at Charleston focused on the wording of the platform, as if everything depended upon the precise phraseology which the party delegates should issue to the world. Two platform reports were submitted; they may be conveniently designated as the "Yancey platform" and the "Douglas platform." The former vigorously asserted that the Federal government, in all its departments, must protect slavery in the territories; the latter reaffirmed the Cincinnati platform, evaded the issue as to positive maintenance of slavery in the territories, and vaguely declared that the party would abide by the decisions of the Supreme Court. When the convention adopted the Douglas "non-intervention" platform, Yancey delivered an impassioned speech in which he attributed the existing discord to Northern invasion of Southern rights. Acting upon an instruction from his own state party convention he now presented not a mere demand but an ultimatum: either the platform of the lower South (approved by the majority of the platform committee) must be accepted, or the delegates from the lower South would withdraw. Since Douglas and his followers in the convention, constituting a majority of the delegates, would not accept any platform inconsistent with self-government in the territories, the break came. The convention adopted the Douglas platform; the Alabama delegation under the leadership of Yancey left the hall; the delegations from the cotton states, with but few exceptions, followed suit; and the disrupted convention, unable to choose a candidate, adjourned to meet in Baltimore.

Meanwhile at least one of the delegates at Charleston, W. B. Gaulden, a Georgia slave-trader, was convinced that the convention was missing the main issue. Declaring that the "theory" as to protection of slavery in the territories was a mere "abstraction," he asserted that the real trouble was the cutting off of the supply of slaves, and he vigorously demanded the reopening of the African slave trade. Referring to the African slave-trader as a "true missionary" and a "true Christian," he declared that slave trading in Virginia was "more immoral" and "more unchristian" than the African trade, and insisted that the legalizing of the international trade would stimulate the South by lowering the price of slaves and would act powerfully to preserve the Union.[1]

In the reassembled convention of the Democrats at Baltimore the seceding element reappeared, whereupon a fierce contest ensued between seceders and Douglas men over the seating of rival delegations. When the Douglas element won the contest another secession of Southern members occurred, after which the remaining fragment of the convention nominated Douglas for the presidency and Senator Benjamin Fitzpatrick of Alabama for the vice-presidency. Fitzpatrick having declined the nomination, it was conferred upon a Georgia moderate, Herschel V. Johnson. In addition,

[1] Greeley, *American Conflict*, I, 316–317.

conventions of Southern "bolters" were held at Baltimore and Richmond; for some of the Southern delegates had refused to go to Baltimore at all, while others conducted a rival convention in Baltimore. At both Baltimore and Richmond the Southern Democratic groups nominated John C. Breckinridge of Kentucky for President and Joseph Lane of Oregon for Vice-President.

In the interval between the conventions at Charleston and Baltimore the disruption of the party and attendant issues had become the theme of a rancorous debate in the United States Senate between Jefferson Davis and Stephen A. Douglas. A tiresome, legalistic discussion it was, each speaker trying to support his position by logic, history, the "laws of nature," legal citations, and *argumenta ad hominem*. What is the meaning of nonintervention? Can the people of a territory, as a territory, decide for or against slavery, or do they first become invested with this power of decision when forming a state constitution? What is the meaning of territorial sovereignty? Of sovereignty in general? Was the Ordinance of 1787 confirmed under the Constitution? What was the true meaning and result of the action taken at Charleston? Who is responsible for dividing the Democratic party? What are Democratic states? Are the Southerners denying the right of Illinois to be so regarded? Why cannot Mississippi and Alabama, which voted for Buchanan in 1856, support another candidate on the same platform in 1860? Such were the questions threshed out between the spokesmen of the Northern and Southern factions. The debate hinged upon a series of resolutions introduced by Davis on February 2, 1860, demanding Federal protection for slavery in the territories; and at the conclusion of the discussion the Senate affirmed the Davis doctrine by voting that neither Congress nor a territorial legislature could prohibit slavery in the territories, which were the "common possession" of all the states.[2] In this manner did the Democratic party (for such was the meaning of the Senate's action) repudiate Douglas on the eve of a presidential election in which he was, after all, the leading Democratic contender.

2

With all its high hopes the Republican party, in the pre-convention canvass, had only one unmistakably formidable contender for the nomination—Seward of New York. Chase, with his well-known antislavery zeal, had a radical reputation which hardly fitted the Republican mood of 1860. He lacked astute managers and even in Ohio he failed to muster the full support of the state delegation. Edward Bates of Missouri was conservative on the slavery question, enjoyed the powerful support of Greeley and the

[2] *Cong. Globe*, 36 Cong., 1 sess., 658, 2321–2322. The vote on this resolution was 35 to 21, the opposition being made up of twenty Republicans and the Douglas Democrat, Pugh of Ohio. Douglas was absent at the time of the vote.

Blairs, and if nominated would have drawn largely from the border states;
but he was weakened by his approval of Knownothing principles, and in
an election where the German-American element was a factor, this was
indeed a handicap. Cameron of Pennsylvania commanded little more than
the complimentary first ballot of his own state delegation. Lincoln's name
was commonly included in the calculation but was seldom mentioned with
prominence outside Illinois. That he was a "favorite son" signified that he
belonged to a numerous species of whom few have gained the prize. Until
the opening of convention week (May 13) his managers could not count
on more than the Illinois delegation, while at this stage Chase, Bates, and
Cameron each had more than twice as many delegates as Lincoln. McLean
of Ohio lacked the vigor which the new party demanded; and such men as
Wade of Ohio, Dayton of New Jersey, Cassius M. Clay of Kentucky, N. P.
Banks of Massachusetts, and Frémont of New York [1] had but minor and
scattered constituencies.

The case of Seward presented the familiar spectacle of an outstanding
leader whose very leadership over a long career made him less available as
a candidate than a smaller man. A prominent Whig and Republican, Seward had been in public life for over twenty years. He had served as governor of New York and as United States senator; he had been more the
acknowledged leader of the Republican party than its first presidential
candidate, Frémont; his antislavery principles were consistent without being too vociferous. In addition, he had an able manager in Thurlow Weed,
and was acceptable to the German-Americans by reason of his tolerance toward Catholics and his opposition to "nativism." On the other hand, his
phrase making had caused his name to be associated with the "higher law"
doctrine and the "irrepressible conflict"; and at the time of the nominating
convention he was embarrassed in his own state by the opposition of
Greeley.

Meanwhile Lincoln's star had been rising. The debate with Douglas
had given him a national reputation which was well capitalized by numerous speeches in Ohio, Indiana, Illinois, Iowa, Wisconsin, and Kansas, all
of which had served to advertise his effectiveness as a "literary statesman."
An important step toward the presidency was taken in his Cooper Union
speech in New York, February 27, 1860. Conservatively defining the
terms which the new party should offer to the country, he had carefully
avoided all excess, had repudiated Helper's book and the John Brown outrage, and had spoken in terms of sectional conciliation and broad nationalism. "It is exceedingly desirable," said he, "that all parts of this great Confederacy shall be at peace. . . . Let us Republicans do our part to have
it so. Even though much provoked, let us do nothing through passion and
ill temper. Even though the southern people will not so much as listen to

[1] Though Frémont had represented California in the United States Senate
(1850–1851), he was later a resident of New York. Bancroft, *Seward*, I, 418.

us, let us calmly consider their demands, and yield to them if, in our deliberate view of our duty, we possibly can. Judging by all they say and do, . . . let us determine . . . what will satisfy them." [2] Lincoln's attitude toward the Germans had been liberal and friendly. To many of them he was the second choice in case Seward could not be named. He was better able than any other candidate to muster the support of such diverse elements as the old-line Whigs and the crusading abolitionists; and, finally, he gained powerfully by the atmosphere and surroundings of the Chicago convention, where the "wigwam," a huge structure specially constructed for the convention's use, seemed to pulse with the spirit of the prairie West, and where resounding Lincoln "yawps" matched the lung power of the noisy Seward *claque.*

On the first ballot Seward led with 173½ votes to Lincoln's 102, Chase's 49, Cameron's 50½, and Bates's 48. Pennsylvania and Ohio gave Lincoln heavy support on the second ballot, in which he gained notably while Seward gained slightly. It was evident that "the field" against Seward was combining upon Lincoln; and when on the third ballot the transfer of four Ohio votes gave him the requisite majority for nomination, one delegation after another changed their votes amid wild shouts, and cannon boomed to an eager crowd the news of Lincoln's victory.

Differences within the party were skillfully suppressed in the convention, whose vote-getting platform vaguely reaffirmed the equality doctrine of the Declaration of Independence without defining it in terms of Negro citizenship. For the rest the platform deplored disunion; taunted the Democrats with sectionalism; recognized the power of each state to control its own domestic institutions; denounced Buchanan and the Lecompton constitution; and reaffirmed the Wilmot proviso, denying the authority of Congress or of a territorial legislature, or of any other power, to legalize slavery in the territories. Efforts to reopen the African slave trade were rebuked; the principle of a protective tariff was vigorously asserted; and support was pledged for such measures as a homestead law, internal improvements, a railroad to the Pacific, and the encouragement of aliens. With just enough emphasis upon a limited phase of the slavery issue, this sectional party, strongly supported by eastern business interests which were now weaning the Northwest away from its Southern alliance, looked forward confidently to success at the polls. Its candidate could carry virtually the whole North. Beyond that the road could not be so easily discerned.

One more party entered the lists. The former "American" or Knownothing party, now calling itself the "Constitutional Union" party, meeting in convention at Baltimore, took an evasive, middle-of-the-road course. Ignoring the slavery issue, and spurning the disruptive force of party platforms, they appealed to a distracted country on the sole issue of the Con-

[2] Lincoln, *Collected Works,* III, 547. In the original the passage quoted is in italics.

stitution, the Union, and the laws. With conservative candidates, John Bell of Tennessee and Edward Everett of Massachusetts, the party hoped to obtain both old-line Whig and Democratic support, its chief strength being found in the border states where Lincoln's support was negligible and where both Breckinridge and Douglas were largely avoided as being too factional.

In the four-sided contest that ensued each candidate protested devotion to the Union. "The Federal Union must be preserved," said Douglas. "The Constitution and the equality of the States," said Breckinridge, ". . . are symbols of everlasting union. Let these be the rallying cries." To Lincoln the "perpetual union" was fundamental; to Bell it was virtually the only issue.

As the campaign proceeded the war of factions between the two wings of the Democratic party grew bitter. Douglas accused Southern disunionists of desiring Lincoln's election so that it might be used as a signal for secession. "I do not believe that every Breckinridge man is a disunionist," he declared, "but I do believe that every disunionist in America is a Breckinridge man." [3] As for Lincoln, he avoided speeches during the campaign, allowing his contest to be conducted, with a well-filled party chest, by managers and campaigners, with vociferous parades and demonstrations, reminiscent of the roaring campaign for Harrison in 1840. Nor was the slavery issue greatly emphasized by the Republicans. Free land and American citizenship were offered to the Germans; the promise of homesteads was extended to the West and the agrarian element in general; protection for American industry was strongly urged in the manufacturing regions of the East; alluring prospects of American commercial expansion were held out as the happy result of Lincoln's elections; meanwhile in those regions where the prohibition of slavery in the territories was not a vote-getting issue, it was subordinated or ignored entirely.

While the South was fearing the worst from Lincoln, he made practically no effort to reassure them. In confidential letters he explained that his conservative opinions had often been stated, that persons honestly seeking his views would have no trouble in learning them, that "bad men . . . North and South" [4] would subject any new expression to further misrepresentation, and that consequently a reiteration of his policies would do no good. In this wise the representation of Lincoln as a "black Republican" and an enemy of the South continued throughout the campaign with no public effort on Lincoln's part to correct the impression.

John C. Breckinridge, leader of the Southern Democrats, though "sound" in his proslavery and state-rights views, was not a hotspur of the Yancey type. Deriving from the Kentucky aristocracy, he had been trained

---

[3] Speech of Douglas at Baltimore, Sept. 6, 1860. (For a newspaper report see N. Y. *Times*, Sept. 7, 1860, p. 1, c. 5.)

[4] Lincoln, *Collected Works*, IV, 135.

in the Jeffersonian tradition, had prepared for the law, had gone as major of volunteers to Mexico in 1847, had served in Congress (1851–55), and, as Vice-President under Buchanan, had presided impartially over the Senate during difficult years of sectional discord. His expressed views on the issue of slavery in the territories hardly jibed with the Southern Democratic platform of 1860; for in supporting the Kansas-Nebraska bill he had declared that it placed the decision as to slavery in the hands of the people of the territories; and he vigorously denied that the bill legalized slavery in Kansas or Nebraska. "The right to establish involves the right to prohibit," he declared; "and, denying both, I would vote for neither." [5]

When the votes were cast on November 6, it was found that Lincoln had 180 electoral votes; Breckinridge 72; Bell 39; and Douglas 12. Lincoln had a clear majority in the electoral college and was validly chosen President, thus obviating the strife and uncertainty that would have resulted if the election had been thrown into the House of Representatives, as many had feared. He had scored heavily over Douglas in the East; in the western states he had won by a narrow margin; as a result he had the electoral votes of every Northern free state except New Jersey.[6] Breckinridge "carried" the entire lower South; in the upper South and on the border he carried only Delaware, Maryland, and North Carolina. Douglas's twelve electoral votes came from Missouri and New Jersey. Bell carried Tennessee, Kentucky, and Virginia.

On a closer perusal of the election figures, significant facts emerge. As reported by Edward Stanwood, Lincoln's total popular vote throughout the whole country was only 1,866,452 as against 2,815,617 for all his opponents (Douglas 1,376,957; Breckinridge 849,781; Bell 588,879).[7] In ten of the Southern states Lincoln received not a single popular vote; the border states, taken as a section, placed him at the bottom of the list. The vote cast for Lincoln was the most sectional of all: Breckinridge received a far heavier vote in the North than did Lincoln in the South. Yet it is also significant that the Southern-rights candidate, Breckinridge, who has often been called the Southern "disunionist candidate" despite his pledges for the Union, failed to carry a majority of the popular votes of the whole South. In the slave states his total fell far short of the total given to his opponents. Taking Stanwood's figures for the fourteen slave states in which popular votes were taken (there being no popular vote in South Carolina), it appears Breckinridge had nearly 124,000 fewer votes than his opponents. When it is remembered that all Breckinridge's opponents were opposed to secession, and that Breckinridge himself was not an avowed se-

---

[5] Emerson D. Fite, *The Presidential Campaign of 1860*, 333.

[6] New Jersey gave four of her seven electoral votes to Lincoln and three to Douglas. Eugene H. Roseboom, *A History of Presidential Elections*, 183–184.

[7] Edward Stanwood, *History of the Presidency . . . to 1897*, 297. For variant totals, see W. Dean Burnham, *Presidential Ballots, 1836–1892*, 246.

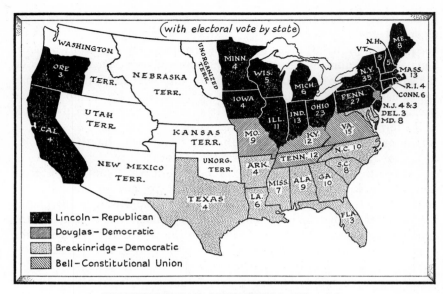

(with electoral vote by state)

Lincoln — Republican
Douglas — Democratic
Breckinridge — Democratic
Bell — Constitutional Union

PRESIDENTIAL ELECTION OF 1860

cessionist, it appears that if the election of 1860 registered any decision of the South as to secession, it was a negative decision. Since, however, these votes were virtually all anti-Lincoln votes, it may be said that they were chiefly votes to avoid secession by defeating Lincoln, and that such an anti-secessionist attitude was in many cases (we know not how many) consistent with a readiness to secede in the event of Lincoln's election.

Inasmuch as Lincoln's opponents received almost a million more votes than did Lincoln, it is evident that he was a "minority President." It seems but a corollary of this to say that he won merely because of a division among his opponents. A close study of the actual situation in the states, however, reveals the curious fact that Lincoln won not because of a lack of union among his rivals, but because of advantageous distribution of his votes among populous states where the large minority votes of his opponents, even if combined, would have failed to "carry" the states, and would thus have been wasted. As his biographers have pointed out: "If all the votes given to all the opposing candidates had been concentrated and cast for a 'fusion ticket,' . . . the result would have been changed nowhere except in New Jersey, California, and Oregon; Lincoln would have received but 11 fewer, or 169 electoral votes—a majority of 35 in the entire electoral college." [8]

[8] Nicolay and Hay, *Abraham Lincoln: A History* (cited hereafter as Nicolay and Hay, *Lincoln*), II, 295. See also Dumond, *Secession Movement*, 271 n.

3

The legislature of South Carolina, assembled at Columbia for the choice of presidential electors, received a communication from Governor Gist recommending that, in case of Lincoln's election, steps be immediately taken for summoning a convention of the sovereign people of the state for the purpose of severing their connection with the United States. Popular sentiment in the state, so far as it was vocal and demonstrative, was now overwhelmingly in favor of secession and of a Southern confederacy; and when the news came that Lincoln had actually been elected, the excitement and indignation of the crowds which thronged the streets of Charleston reflected the genuine determination of an enraged people to have done with the Union once and for all. Declining the suggestion of a few "co-operationists" who favored an all-Southern convention or at any rate sufficient delay to allow other Southern states to be heard from, the legislature, without a dissenting vote, passed a law (November 13) calling a convention to consider "the dangers incident to the position of the State in the Federal Union." The parades and fireworks, the marching of minute-men, the display of the palmetto flag, the mass meetings to "endorse" the action of the legislature, the flow of oratory and the noise of cheering—all attested the jubilant popular feeling that secession was an accomplished fact, even before the convention acted.[1] The feeling of the time was thus set down by a lady of South Carolina in her diary:

[Nov. 8, 1860.] Yesterday on the train . . . before we reached Fernandina a woman cried out—
"That settles the hash."
Tanny touched me on the shoulder.
—"Look out!—Lincoln's elected."
"How do you know?"—
"The man over there has a telegram"
        The excitement was very great. Every body was talking at the same time —One, a little more moved than the others stood up—saying despontly [*sic*]—

[1] On October 5, 1860, Governor Gist of South Carolina sent a confidential letter to each of the governors of the cotton states informing them that if Lincoln should be chosen South Carolina would call a convention, and asking whether the other states would cooperate. The governor of North Carolina replied that his people would not regard Lincoln's election as sufficient cause for disunion. The governor of Alabama answered that his state would secede if two or more others would set the example. The answer of the Mississippi executive was that if any state should move, Mississippi would go with her. The governor of Louisiana replied: "I shall not advise the secession of my State, and . . . I do not think the people of Louisiana will ultimately decide in favor of that course." The Georgia governor preferred to wait for an "overt act"; but from Florida the report was that the state was "ready to wheel into line with the gallant Palmetto State. . . ." Nicolay and Hay, *Abraham Lincoln: A History*, II, 306–314.

"The die is cast—No more vain regrets—Sad forebodings are useless. The stake is life or death—"

"Now did you ever!" was the prevailing exclamation, and some one cried out: "Now that the black radical Republicans have the power I suppose they will Brown us all." No doubt of it.[2]

Composed of distinguished men, the South Carolina convention, whose delegates were chosen in popular mass meetings, held its sessions first at Columbia and later at Charleston. On December 20, by a unanimous vote of 169 members, it passed a solemn "ordinance" declaring that "the union now subsisting between South Carolina and other States, under the name of the 'United States of America,' is hereby dissolved." To make it clear that South Carolina was not in rebellion, but was merely separating from "co-states," a document known as "a Declaration of the Immediate Causes which induce and justify the Secession of South Carolina from the Federal Union" was issued to the world. In 1776, this document explained, the American colonies asserted that they were "free and independent states." By the Articles of Confederation of 1778 each state retained "its sovereignty, freedom and independence"; and by the treaty of 1783 the British king acknowledged the former colonies to be "free, sovereign, and independent States." The Constitution of 1787 was formed as a "compact," with the states retaining "reserved powers." From this point, by reference to such matters as the "personal liberty laws" of the Northern states, and the fact that the non-slave states "have assumed the right of deciding upon the propriety of our domestic institutions; and have denied the rights of property established in fifteen of the States and recognized by the Constitution," it was affirmed that the ends of government as intended in the Constitution had been "defeated." A "sectional party," so the Declaration continued, has obtained the "election of a man to the high office of President of the United States whose opinions and purposes are hostile to slavery." This man has declared that the " 'government cannot endure permanently half slave, half free.' " On the 4th of March this sectional party will take control, whereupon the "slaveholding States will no longer have the power of self-government." Northern opinion "has invested a great political error with the sanctions of a more erroneous religious belief," and "all hope of remedy is rendered vain." For these reasons, the document concluded, the "People of South Carolina, . . . appealing to the Supreme Judge of the world for the rectitude of [their] intentions," solemnly declare that their union with "the other States of North America" is "dissolved."

South Carolina was now avowedly a separate nation. By its own statement it was separated not only from the North, but also from the South.

[2] This passage is found in *A Diary from Dixie,* by Mrs. Mary B. Chesnut. Except the last twenty-five words, the quotation is based on the facsimile facing p. xxii; the rest is from p. 1.

Dissolution having been declared, various practical questions arose. Did the simple announcement of secession automatically abrogate all Federal laws within the state? Could the severing of relations with co-states be so quickly accomplished? It was obvious that separate state secession was, after all, not the objective. Cooperation being the objective, why were co-operative methods deliberately avoided? What would be the good of South Carolina's secession if the state actually was to stand alone? Could the declarations as to isolated nationhood for the little commonwealth be taken at face value? If such nationhood really existed, then Federal functions would now become totally Carolinian functions; but how could this important change be effected? Having pulled down a structure that had stood for three-quarters of a century, were the people "houseless and homeless" while clearing away the rubbish and reconstructing their home? Was Federal money still legal tender? What was the status of the Federal forts in Charleston harbor? What of the everyday functions of the postoffice; what of Federal customs duties and other taxation? Were things to remain *in statu quo* in order to prevent confusion, awaiting the action of the legislature as to the abrogation of specific laws, provisional arrangements being made until the legislature could act; or did all laws of Congress, with the official functions deriving from them, fall instantly to the ground at the moment of secession? It was recognized that no converse existed with the government from which the state had withdrawn, and that on various matters commissioners would have to be appointed to "treat" with the general government; but as to temporary adjustments in the interval before such negotiation should be concluded, or as to the appropriate action in case the negotiations should prove ineffective, opinions differed. These questions, which were never settled, serve to illustrate the awkward and somewhat anomalous position of South Carolina in the weeks just following secession.

The situation in Georgia revealed a sharper difference of opinion among prominent leaders and a more vigorous opposition to secession than in South Carolina. The lack of unanimity in the state was illustrated in the national Democratic convention at Charleston in April of 1860 when only a portion of the Georgia delegation followed Yancey in his bolt. In the election of 1860, though the electoral vote of the state was cast for Breckinridge, the popular vote for Breckinridge fell short of the combined vote for Douglas and Bell. It must always be remembered, however, that a firm adherence to state rights, as firm indeed as that of South Carolina, was a powerful Georgia tradition, and belief in the "right of secession" was practically universal.

It happened that the governor of the state, Joseph E. Brown, was an aggressive secessionist; and he lost no time in moving for immediate action. Just after Lincoln's election, Brown addressed a message to the legislature, November 7, 1860, recommending the calling of a convention, accompanied by vigorous military measures.[3] The purpose of the convention, in Brown's mind, was to withdraw the state from the Union.

There was able leadership on both sides. In addition to Brown, the cause of immediate secession found aggressive promoters in Iverson, Toombs, T. R. R. Cobb, and Howell Cobb; of those who opposed immediate secession, while admitting the theoretical "right," the most prominent were Alexander H. Stephens, Benjamin H. Hill, and Herschel V. Johnson. When the legislature met at Milledgeville, the Breckinridge Democracy was, to use the words of Johnson, "rampant for immediate secession," and its manner was "impatient, overbearing, dictatorial and intolerant." Believing that the election of Lincoln was not "a sufficient cause to justify secession," [4] Johnson urged both an appeal to the nonslaveholding states and a consultation of other Southern states in place of independent secession by Georgia. The legislature was addressed by the fiery Toombs who spoke for immediate secession, after which the diminutive Stephens, emerging from political retirement, pleaded with much less force for "sober deliberation." He would not secede merely because of Lincoln's election; but was careful to add that the state's honor must be maintained, even though it required disunion. Won over by the secessionists, the legislature rejected the plan of an all-Southern convention and issued a call for a convention to meet on January 16.

In the interval before the assembling of the Georgia convention, three other states of the lower South (Alabama, Mississippi, and Florida) completed their secession from the Union. In Alabama a vigorous minority, drawing strength from the northern counties, opposed immediate secession, urging that the action of the state be delayed while awaiting a Southern convention. Though it seemed virtually certain that the convention would decide for secession as soon as the matter should be put to a vote, varying shades of opinion found expression in four days of discussion. On January 11 the convention was addressed by Yancey, who stressed the familiar, vague assertion that a sectional party was now in control of the government and would use its power to destroy the rights of the South. The ordinance of secession was now put to a vote and was passed, 61 to 39, though at an earlier stage the minority report to avoid immediate secession had been defeated by the closer vote of 54 to 45. Florida and Mississippi had already acted, and they did so almost simultaneously. The Mississippi convention,[5] meeting at Jackson, passed its ordinance of secession January

---

[3] In this message recommending a state convention, Brown advised against the projected convention of the slaveholding states. U. B. Phillips, *Georgia and State Rights, Annual Report, Am. Hist. Assn.,* 1901, II, 194.

[4] "From the Autobiography of Herschel V. Johnson, 1856–1867," *Am. Hist. Rev.,* XXX, 323.

[5] These secession conventions deserve more attention than can be given them here. Ralph A. Wooster, who has analyzed the membership of each of them, con-

9, by a vote of 84 to 15; the Florida ordinance was passed the following day, 62 to 7.

4

Four states of the lower South, constituting a majority of that section, had thus withdrawn. Conciliation schemes were now in the air. Buchanan's administration was wavering, meanwhile avoiding aggression; and the eight states of the upper South and the border, constituting a majority of all the slave states, were clinging to the Union and holding a moderate course. Under these circumstances there met, on January 16, one of the most important of all the Southern secession conventions, that of Georgia. In an atmosphere of revolution local mass meetings had been held, and able leaders had appeared on the stump. That union sentiment —i.e. a willingness to try further measures before appealing to secession as a "last resort"—was strong in the state, there can be no doubt. Some have maintained that this was the sentiment of the majority. Herschel V. Johnson held the opinion that "a fair and energetic canvass would have showed a large majority of the people against the policy [not the right] of secession." The speaking, he said, was mostly confined to the secessionists, who insisted that secession "would be peaceable—that it would not bring war —that if it should the Yankees were cowards and would not fight—and that, at the worst it would be a short war, in which the South would achieve an easy victory . . . ."[1]

When the convention met at Milledgeville, with the "fiery Spirits" much in evidence, such men as Hill, Means, Johnson, and Stephens used their influence in opposition to secession; though Stephens "failed to make a zealous fight."[2] Of great influence was the action of Toombs. Having

---

cludes: "Places of birth and occupations seem to have differed little between immediate secessionists in the conventions and those who favored some form of delay. The secessionists were slightly wealthier and younger and held more slaves than their combined opponents. The difference does not seem pronounced enough, however, to conclude that the slaveholders in the conventions formed a solid block for immediate separation. In Louisiana and Mississippi, for example, those favoring delay were the larger slaveholders. Too, the cooperationist faction had a slightly higher percentage of planters than did the immediate secessionists. The motives for supporting immediate withdrawal from the Union seem then to have had a deeper basis than personal characteristics of convention members alone." Wooster, "An Analysis of the Membership of Secession Conventions in the Lower South," *J.S.H.*, XXIV, 360–368 (Aug., 1958).

[1] "From the Autobiography of Herschel V. Johnson," *Am. Hist. Rev.*, XXX, 324.

[2] Johnson states that this was because Stephens had come to the conclusion that resistance to secession would be vain and would do more harm than good. *Ibid.*, 325–326.

changed his advice from time to time as he watched changing events in Washington, he came out on December 23 with a letter to the people of the state in which he said: "I tell you upon the faith of a true man that all further looking to the North . . . ought to be instantly abandoned. . . . Secession by the 4th of March next should be thundered from the ballot box by the unanimous voice of Georgia on the 2d of January next. Such a voice will be your best guaranty for liberty, security, tranquillity, and glory." [3]

Already the legislature had appropriated $1,000,000 for military defense and had provided for raising a state force of 10,000 troops. In anticipation of secession, the Federal stronghold, Fort Pulaski at Savannah, was seized by Governor Brown's order on January 3. When the crucial vote was taken in the Georgia convention on a motion to substitute "cooperation" for immediate secession, the count stood 133 to 164. It was thus by a narrow victory that the secessionists won; a change of sixteen votes in a total of 297 would have produced the opposite result.[4] Alexander H. Stephens stated that two-thirds of those voting for the ordinance expected a re-formation of the Union. The most powerful argument in the state campaign, he said, was that of T. R. R. Cobb: "We can make better terms out of the Union than in it." [5] In a spirit of harmony and state solidarity, the Georgia ordinance of secession, passed on January 19, 1861, was signed by nearly all the antisecessionists of the convention. "And so the Rubicon was crossed," records Herschel V. Johnson, "and . . . Georgia was launched upon a dark, uncertain and dangerous sea. Peals of cannon announced the fact, in token of exultation. The secessionists were jubilant. I never felt so sad before. The clustering glories of the past thronged my memory, but they were darkened by the gathering gloom of the lowering future." Commissioners were sent from Georgia to other slave states to urge secession; and Johnson was asked to serve as commissioner to Virginia. He had recently spoken in Richmond deprecating secession and urging that the Breckinridge policy would produce that result. He declined. "How could I have the face," he said, "with that speech fresh in

---

[3] U. B. Phillips, *Georgia and State Rights*, 200.

[4] After this test vote had registered the victory of the secessionists, the secession ordinance was passed by a vote of 208 to 89. *Ibid.*, 203. ". . . secession sentiment was strongest in the coastal area, in the newer cotton lands, and in the urban centers, while, on the other hand, delegates from North Georgia, the pine barrens, and the 'old cotton lands' manifested a disposition to cling to the Union." Horace Montgomery, *Cracker Parties*, 249–250.

[5] Phillips, *op. cit.*, 204. *Cf.* the speech of the "Commissioner from Mississippi" to citizens of Maryland at the time of South Carolina's secession, in which he stated that secession was not intended to break up the Union, but that the plan was to withdraw "for the present" in order to obtain guarantees concerning the rights of the South. Frank Moore, ed., *The Rebellion Record* (Diary), I, 3.

their memory, to urge Virginia to commit the same mistake which Georgia has done?" [6]

The action of two more states would now complete the secession of the lower South; and such action was not long delayed. The Louisiana convention passed its ordinance of secession on January 26. Though this ordinance was passed by a vote of 113 to 17, yet the popular vote for delegates to the convention showed a much smaller proportion of secessionists, the vote being 20,448 for secession as compared to 17,296 against it.[7] On February 1 the Texas convention decreed secession by a vote of 166 to 8. The distinguished governor, Sam Houston, was unwavering in his determination to adhere to the Union; but his vigorous efforts against secession were unavailing. On March 18, 1861, he was deposed for refusal to take the oath to support the Confederacy.

More than a month before the inauguration of Lincoln, secession had thus been voted in the seven states of the lower South. Once the movement had started, it gained momentum with each passing week until a vast, homogeneous section, with a similar climate and common economic interests, presented a united front to the outside world. The legal formula by which this was accomplished was simple; and the work of secessionist leaders was facilitated by having a convenient constitutional device ready to hand, the device of a state "convention." In constitutional theory all sovereign power rested in such a convention, which was elected by the people with the understanding that it should exercise ultimate and fundamental powers of government. Popular referendums to ratify the action of state conventions had been used somewhat in the process of state-making during the Revolution and also in the subsequent period; but Southern opinion inclined to the belief that the conventions themselves were entirely competent to take final action, and that such ratifications were unnecessary. In Texas alone of the states of the lower South was the secession ordinance submitted after its passage to popular vote; [8] but the delegates who voted secession in the other states had just been chosen by the people and empowered with specific authority to take final action in the premises.

[6] "From the Autobiography of Herschel V. Johnson," *Am. Hist. Rev.*, XXX, 327–328.

[7] Moore, *Rebell. Record* (Diary), I, 20; *Ann. Cyc.*, 1861, 431.

[8] Nicolay and Hay, *Lincoln*, III, 193. (In the case of Louisiana the popular vote above mentioned had to do with the election of delegates to the convention, not ratification of the ordinance.)

CHAPTER 7

Buchanan's Dilemma

I

THE FOUR-MONTH interval between Lincoln's election and his inauguration was a time of such confusion and excitement, with so many cross
currents moving at the same time, that it is hard to get a full picture of the
scene. While secession was progressing with confidence and rapidity from
state to state and the national structure was visibly crumbling, caution and
hesitation characterized the slow-moving efforts to avert war. The government at Washington, in the closing weeks under Buchanan and the first
few weeks under Lincoln, preserved a waiting attitude. Of the man who
was President in this crisis it is to be noted that he faced a harder situation,
perhaps, than any other President, and that he has been treated unkindly
by historians who have set off his "failure" as a foil for the conquering
and triumphant "success" of the administration which followed. Buchanan's critics have painted a damaging picture: secession leaders in
treasonable conspiracy with the "cabinet cabal"; powers of the Federal government willfully perverted to its own destruction; men in high Federal
office organizing "rebellion" weeks in advance of secession; Federal rifles
transmitted to the South and put into the enemy's hand; President Jackson's luminous example unheeded and General Scott's timely warning ignored; [1] occult influences at work to overawe a weak President; sophistical
legal reasoning employed to justify national suicide; the whole cause "given
away" while Lincoln was powerless to prevent disaster.

---

[1] On the ground that certain national forts in the South were in danger of being seized by the "insurgents," General Scott, in a letter of October 29, 1860, advised that six of them be immediately garrisoned to prevent seizure. Since Buchanan's whole course was to avoid a hostile demonstration against the South, he
dismissed Scott's suggestion as unwise. For this action Buchanan was severely criticized by Nicolay and Hay. On the other hand, Buchanan declared that Scott's advice
greatly excited the South, caused the seizure of various forts by the Southerners,
and had a most unfortunate effect in the border states, which at the moment were
not disposed to make common cause with South Carolina for the sake of disunion
per se. Nicolay and Hay, *Lincoln*, II, 339 ff.; P. G. Auchampaugh, *James Buchanan
and His Cabinet on the Eve of Secession*, 63–64.

In support of these criticisms one must admit that Buchanan was anything but a strong President, and history, as Allan Nevins has observed, cannot acquit him "of weakness, vacillation, and timidity, his inseparable faults." [2] Through the feebleness of his administration, the corruption of certain of his subordinates, and his own subservience to a proslavery cabal of Southern senators, he had forfeited much of the respect due to his high office. Now nearly seventy, tired and querulous, Buchanan spent the secession crisis "nervously hoping that the deluge might not descend until he was out of office." [3]

But though Buchanan is anything but a heroic figure in American history, it is unfair to indict him for having no policy for coping with the sectional crisis. As a lawyer and a student of arbitration Buchanan had a firm belief in the efficacy of peaceful measures as a substitute for force. Though maintaining an unwavering devotion to the Union, he had deeply sympathized with the South. When his unionism conflicted with his Southern sympathies he was indeed placed in an embarrassing position. It is true that Southerners had been his partisans, and that, up to the time of the break in 1860, Jefferson Davis had been regarded as his spokesman in the Senate. It is also true that he was profoundly displeased with Northern attacks upon the South. In 1849 he had written that "a little forbearance & moderation on the part of the North is all that is necessary." [4] To advocate Southern rights in the North as a means of allaying sectionalism had been with Buchanan a tradition and a policy for nearly half a century. With conflicting currents beating upon him, he knew that whatever steps he took would lead to bitter attacks from one quarter or another. Being thus friendly to the South and peacefully-minded, believing as he did that a policy of compromise would see the country through the crisis, Buchanan was determined that, whatever should happen, the North should not launch a war by committing an "overt act." He had reason to believe that violence on the part of the administration at Washington would precipitate war, while on the other hand he felt that a conciliatory policy would prevent the upper South and border states from joining the lower South in secession, and that when the leaders of the lower South should become convinced that they could not command even a majority of the slave states, secession schemes would break down.

It is mere speculation to say that Buchanan could have prevented war by acting in a warlike, Jacksonian manner against South Carolina; it is not improbable that the rest of the South would have made common cause with a sister state, and the war would merely have come under Buchanan instead of under Lincoln. To say that such an earlier clash at arms would have been fortunate by reason of giving the Union a greater advantage is

[2] Nevins, *The Emergence of Lincoln*, II, 342.
[3] Roy F. Nichols, *The Disruption of American Democracy*, 378.
[4] Auchampaugh, 17.

to dodge the whole issue as to the main question of the day, which was the prevention of war. Buchanan's motives, at any rate, were of the best; and, as Frank W. Klingberg has concluded: "In line with his heritage of compromise, with his concept of the importance of congressional representation of public opinion, with his belief in the bargaining rights of a minority, and his conviction that the Union could not be cemented by the blood of its citizens, it is difficult to see how Buchanan could have chosen another course." [5] His policy did avert war for the time, giving the various compromise efforts a chance to develop, and offering the incoming Republicans an opportunity to work out their own schemes of conciliation, should that be their intention. Avoiding any recognition of the Confederacy, he made no commitments that would seriously embarrass his successor.

Buchanan's message to Congress, December 3, 1860, was laboriously worked out through numerous cabinet consultations. He began by pointing out the responsibility of the abolitionists for the critical state of the country. The existing peril, he said, arose from incessant Northern agitation, by reason of which family security at the South had been shattered, so that "Many a matron throughout the South retires at night in dread of what may befall herself and her children before the morning." All that the South had contended for, he continued, was to be let alone to manage its domestic institutions. The late presidential election, he thought, did "not of itself afford just cause for dissolving the Union." Justice required that some overt act be awaited before resorting to such a remedy, especially in view of the fact that the President's power is limited, and that neither Congress nor the Supreme Court had been unfriendly to the South. Turning to the personal liberty laws of the Northern states, the President declared that they were in direct violation of the Constitution and that it would be the duty of the incoming executive to see that national law should be made effective over them, but that it should not be presumed in advance that he would fail in this duty.

Secession was not a valid remedy, the President urged, because the "Confederacy" (i.e., the United States) was not a rope of sand; the Union was "perpetual." By the supreme-law clause the Federal government acts directly upon the people, and "the Constitution of the United States is as much a part of the constitution of each State and is as binding upon its people as though it had been textually inserted therein." His next passage might have been written by Abraham Lincoln. It read: "This Government . . . is a great and powerful Government, invested with all the attributes of sovereignty over the special subjects to which its authority extends. Its framers never intended to implant in its bosom the seeds of its own destruction, nor were they at its creation guilty of the absurdity of providing for its own dissolution. It was not intended by its framers to be

[5] Klingberg, "James Buchanan and the Crisis of the Union," J.S.H., IX, 474 (Nov., 1943).

the baseless fabric of a vision, which at the touch of the enchanter would vanish into thin air, but a substantial and mighty fabric, capable of resisting the slow decay of time and of defying the storms of ages." [6] The framers, he said, did not imagine that the Constitution would be so interpreted as to enable any state, by its own act, to escape its Federal obligations.

Having denied the validity of secession, the President then entered upon the question of national authority to resist secession, and concluded that making war against a state was not only not a valid Federal power, but that, if the power existed, it would be unwise under existing circumstances to exercise it, for this would produce a fraternal conflict in which "a vast amount of blood and treasure would be expended, rendering future reconciliation . . . impossible." "The fact is," he said, "that our Union rests upon public opinion, and can never be cemented by the blood of its citizens shed in civil war. If it cannot live in the affections of the people, it must one day perish." The President then turned to another theme which was a central principle with Abraham Lincoln—the importance of the United States as a world example in self-control associated with popular government. By the shattering of the American republic, Buchanan said, "the hopes of the friends of freedom throughout the world would be destroyed, and a long night of leaden despotism would enshroud the nations. Our example for more than eighty years would not only be lost, but it would be quoted as . . . proof that man is unfit for self-government."

The message showed that the President had thought the matter through with his advisers and that he had a policy. At the time of the message, secession had not been actually consummated in a single state; and the President's policy was not to spring suddenly to truculent and warlike measures, but to try compromise and conciliation. There is little doubt that at the moment the majority of the American people wished for such conciliation to be tried. Peaceful adjustment being the purpose, the President could hardly have chosen a different course.

To the South Carolinian mind, however, conciliation was envisaged in terms of secession as a finality, while to Buchanan it was conceived in terms of the preservation of the Union. This was indeed a radical difference of view; and when "commissioners" appeared in Washington from South Carolina to "negotiate" on the assumption that the main issue had already been fully settled without a struggle, and that nothing remained beyond the adjustment of details on the basis of South Carolina's independent status as a foreign nation (and that, too, before any other Southern state had seceded), the President's pro-Southern tendencies were put to a severe strain; and just at this juncture a vexing complication arose in connection with the furious controversy over the status of the forts in

[6] Richardson, *Messages and Papers*, V, 626–637.

Charleston harbor. Buchanan refused to hand over the forts as South Carolina demanded; and Major Robert J. Anderson, in command at Fort Moultrie, was under instructions from the secretary of war (a Southerner, John B. Floyd) to do two things: (1) "carefully to avoid every act which would needlessly tend to provoke aggression"; but (2) to "hold possession of the forts" and if attacked to defend himself "to the last extremity." There being three forts (Castle Pinckney, Fort Moultrie, and Fort Sumter) and the garrison being too small for occupation of more than one, Anderson was under instruction to put his command into whichever fort he deemed most proper. With his double and conflicting duty before him and with Charlestonians in an inflamed state of mind, he secretly moved his force from Moultrie to Sumter, December 26, 1860. His reason for the change was the desire to avoid a clash and the conviction that possession of the more formidable Sumter would be likely to avert attack.

This proved one of the most vexing incidents of the whole unfortunate crisis. South Carolinians interpreted it as an aggression (though the intentions of the President, of the secretary of war, and of Anderson himself were the very negation of aggression); they at once seized Moultrie; and they demanded through their commissioners that the President evacuate Charleston harbor. Also, though this was inconsistent with evacuation, they demanded that Anderson be ordered back to Moultrie. On the 28th of December the commissioners harassed the President for two hours, but he refused, then and thereafter, to accede to their demands. An ominous clash of authority, and a sporting determination of each side to adhere to its "position," were now injected as disturbing factors in a situation which called for conference and adjustment rather than demands and threats.

2

To one who looks back after the war was begun, the Southern revolution seems a powerful, sweeping movement which engulfed the South and which moved on without possibility of hindrance to the formation of a confederacy of eleven states. In reality, however, the new Southern nation did not come suddenly into full-panoplied existence. It was not given the Buchanan administration to foresee the future, nor is it even yet evident that the bloody future, which was not of Buchanan's planning, was an inevitable necessity. In such a crisis every day and week has its important developments. What seemed an alteration in the very dimensions of time took place, so that a single hour was bigger with destiny than years of ordinary history. While the storm began to gather on November 6 with Lincoln's election, and while mutterings of coming storm had long been heard, it is impossible to name a date in all the remaining weeks of Buchanan's term when a statesman at Washington, viewing the whole scene, could have said with reasonable certainty that the game of compromise was not worth the candle, and that war was inevitable. Up to January 9 only one state had seceded.[1] If it be said that the secession of the others was certain, that is but reading backward. Only six states had seceded by the end of January; the formation of the confederacy of the lower South did not occur until February; and the close of the Buchanan administration found eight of the fifteen slave states remaining in the Union.

With measures afoot to avert civil war, with many Southerners still talking of what "terms" they could obtain, with Virginians looking askance at the precipitateness of the lower South, it seemed more statesmanlike to strive to hold the remaining Southern states by giving compromise efforts a trial than hopelessly to close the door to reunion, which, in Buchanan's view, would be the result of an aggressive policy. The key to the situation, in the view of moderates, was not at Charleston or Montgomery, but at Washington; it lay in the various efforts that were making to avert war. Buchanan's first hope for avoiding conflict and for restoring harmony in the country seemed to lie in the idea of a national convention. On this point Secretary Floyd made the following note in his diary, referring to a cabinet meeting of November 9:

His [Buchanan's] suggestion was that a proposition should be made for a general convention of the States as provided for under the constitution, and to propose some plan of compromising the angry disputes between the North and South. He said that if this were done, and the North or non-slaveholding States should refuse it, the South would be justified before the whole world for refusing longer to remain in a Confederacy where her rights were so shamefully violated. He said that he was compelled to notice at length [in his message to Congress] the alarming condition of the country, and that he would not shrink from his duty.[2]

In succeeding weeks the plan of a convention was much in the air. It was particularly urged by border-state men. If called by the President or Congress it was thought that it might shift the center of attention from the lower South to the national scene as a whole. Furthermore, it would have satisfied the American legal mind: no other body of men could so thoroughly have captured the respect of the American people as a regularly chosen convention of delegates from the states. Though the seceded states might not have participated, they would have been in the minority in the South and their nonparticipation would have robbed them of the advantage of declaring that every effort at redress had been tried without avail. There were those who felt that if such a convention had been called in November before any state had actually seceded, or at the first of the year, when South Carolina alone had completed its secession, it might have exercised a salutary and controlling influence on events. Other methods of conciliation

---

[1] For a recapitulation of the dates of secession, see below, p. 187 n.
[2] Quoted in Auchampaugh, 131.

occupied the stage, and the convention idea never matured into action; but the fact of its being under contemplation will go far toward explaining the reluctance of the Buchanan administration to take provocative steps which would jeopardize the efforts of peacemakers.

Congress was in session beginning December 3; and in a bungling, legalistic fashion it was going about the business of saving the country. Panaceas and compromise solutions piled up in such quantity that each house chose its committee to centralize the discussion, sift the numerous schemes, mediate between opposing points of view, and report such solution as seemed most hopeful of success. In the House of Representatives this function was performed by the "Committee of Thirty-three," a special "grand committee," one from each state, created at the suggestion of Representative Boteler of Virginia. On the one hand the committee was embarrassed by the attitude of radical Republicans, in Congress and elsewhere, who seemed intent upon blocking schemes of conciliation; on the other hand the work of adjustment was seriously impaired by caucuses of secessionist leaders who had already committed themselves to disunion and were loudly declaring that compromise was hopeless. The difficulty of the committee's task, as of all efforts toward harmony, will be appreciated if one remembers that on December 13, when its labors had just begun, a group of Southern members of Congress, before secession had yet been voted in any state, issued an address to their constituents which read as follows:

The argument is exhausted. All hope of relief in the Union, through the agency of committees, Congressional legislation, or constitutional amendments, is extinguished, and we trust the South will not be deceived by appearances or the pretence of new guarantees. The Republicans are resolute in the purpose to grant nothing that will or ought to satisfy the South. We are satisfied the honor, safety, and independence of the Southern people are to be found only in a Southern Confederacy—a result to be obtained only by separate State secession—and that the sole and primary aim of each slaveholding State ought to be its speedy and absolute separation from an unnatural and hostile Union.[3]

Just prior to this declaration of the impossibility of compromise, the committee of thirty-three had resolved that "reasonable . . . and effectual guarantees of their [i. e., Southern] . . . rights . . . should be promptly and cheerfully granted." In its final report to the House the compromise committee advocated the enforcement of the fugitive slave law, the repeal of the personal liberty laws of the Northern states, and the adoption of a constitutional amendment to protect the South against future interference with slavery in the states. The wording of this amendment was as follows:

No amendment shall be made to the Constitution which will authorize or give to Congress the power to abolish or interfere, within any State, with the

[3] McPherson, *Pol. Hist. of the . . . Rebell.*, 37.

domestic institutions thereof, including that of persons held to labor or service by the laws of said State.

Though this amendment presented something of a constitutional anomaly in that it sought for all time to restrain the American people from abolishing slavery by a nation-wide constitutional provision, yet it was adopted, with some Republican support, by the requisite two-thirds of both House and Senate.[4] Fast-crowding events, however, soon altered the whole horizon, and the amendment failed of ratification.

In the Senate the efforts toward compromise were officially centered in a "Committee of Thirteen," composed of able men including Crittenden of Kentucky, Seward of New York, Toombs of Georgia, Douglas of Illinois, Davis of Mississippi, and Wade of Ohio. Unfortunately the committee's efforts were fruitless, and it reported no compromise. The failure of the committee was attributed by the Republicans to Southern insistence upon the "Breckinridge platform"; by the Southerners it was attributed to the unwillingness of Republican leaders to accept compromise. It is a fact of vital importance that in this "fateful hour" responsible Republican leaders —notably Seward and Lincoln—refused to accept any compromise which did not recognize the impossible Wilmot proviso. Lincoln's position on this subject is exhibited in a letter of December 11, directed to William Kellogg, congressman from Illinois and member of the committee of thirty-three. He said: "Entertain no proposition for a compromise in regard to the *extension* of slavery. The instant you do, they have us under again; all our labor is lost, and sooner or later must be done over. . . . Have none of it. The tug has to come, & better now than later." On December 17 he wrote to Thurlow Weed: "Should the convocation of Governors . . . seem desirous to know my views on the present aspect of things, tell them you judge from my speeches that I will be inflexible on the territorial question; that I probably think either the Missouri line extended, or Douglas' . . . Pop[ular]. Sov[ereignty]. would lose us every thing we gained by the election; that filibustering for all South of us, and making slave states of it, would follow. . . . Also, that I probably think all opposition, real and apparant [sic], to the fugitive slave [clause] of the constitution ought to be withdrawn." [5] With extreme caution President-elect Lincoln was at this time avoiding speeches and public statements, but was guardedly permitting various spokesmen to express his views for him. That he should advise a spokesman to tell others what he "probably" thought, was un-

[4] *Cong. Globe,* 36 Cong., 2 sess., 1284–1285, 1403. The amendment was adopted by the House February 28, 1861 (133 to 65) and by the Senate March 2 (24 to 12). Many Republicans in the House (Sherman, Colfax, etc.) voted for the proposition; but the negative votes were, says Blaine, all Republican. In the Senate only twelve of the twenty-five Republicans voted in the negative. Blaine, *Twenty Years,* I, 266.

[5] Lincoln, *Collected Works,* IV, 150, 154.

satisfactory; but it should be remembered that Weed and Seward were at this time more powerful in the counsels of the Republican party than the newly elected President.

These statements of Lincoln referred broadly to the whole compromise discussion, but more particularly to the so-called "Crittenden compromise," presented to the Senate by the venerable John J. Crittenden of Kentucky. His plan in brief was as follows: Let slavery be prohibited in national territory north of the line 36° 30′, but let it be established and maintained by Federal protection south of that line; let future states, north or south of the line, come into the Union with or without slavery as they wish; restrain Congress from abolishing slavery in places within national jurisdiction which may be surrounded by slave states; where intimidation prevents Federal officials from arresting a fugitive slave, let the United States fully compensate the owner, recovering equivalent damages from the county in which the "intimidation, or rescue, was committed"; let the fugitive slave laws be vigorously enforced, and let Congress earnestly recommend the repeal of the personal liberty laws, which, though null and void by the provisions of the Constitution, have "contributed much to the discord . . . now prevailing." These compromise articles, when ratified, were to become amendments to the Constitution, and no future amendment was ever to be made which would authorize Congress to touch slavery in any of the states.[6]

The Southern Democratic members of the Senate compromise committee (Davis, Toombs, and Hunter) had, naturally enough, declared that no terms should be accepted by the South unless supported by the Republicans, the party which would control the incoming administration. When Republican support was withheld and Southern "terms" not adopted, these Southern leaders considered that adjustment had been tried and had failed, and that the failure was to be laid at the door of the Republicans. This phase of the matter is to be borne in mind in its effect upon Southern opinion.

Though Lincoln had little confidence in the Crittenden compromise (which, it was thought, might furnish a powerful incentive to slavery expansion into Cuba and Mexico), and though he stood firm in his refusal to give up slavery restriction in the territories, he was ready to offer concessions on other matters. He reiterated his fundamental belief in the right of the states to maintain slavery in their midst and explained that he intended no interference with that right. He favored enforcement of the fugitive slave law. Furthermore, though this was a difficult concession for him to make, he was willing to accept a constitutional amendment protecting existing state slavery. Not every phase of his attitude, however, was understood in the South, and he was dramatized as an opposer of all compromise.

Having failed to achieve his peaceful objective through the work of

[6] *Cong. Globe*, 36 Cong., 2 sess., 114.

the committee of thirteen, Senator Crittenden proposed (January 3) that the people of the whole country be asked to vote in a solemn referendum on his compromise. It may be questioned whether his terms were the best possible, but they were earnestly designed to satisfy the South on those aspects of the slavery question which were productive of discord; and, by a calculation based on the election of 1860, it was estimated that an overwhelming majority of the people of the country was "in favor of conciliation, forbearance, and compromise." [7] The referendum proposal, however, was novel in American constitutional procedure; a majority of the Republican senators did not favor it; and the chance for taking an appeal to the people was lost. In justice to the South, Republican responsibility for opposing this promising effort to avert war must not be overlooked.

3

One of the most ambitious efforts to avert war was that of the Peace Convention—a conference of twenty-one states which assembled in Washington on February 4 at the call of the Virginia legislature. The failure of this peace-making body was not due to lack of distinguished personnel. It was presided over by John Tyler, the ex-President, and it included among its delegates such men as William P. Fessenden, Lot M. Morrill, David Wilmot, Reverdy Johnson, W. C. Rives, Salmon P. Chase, Thomas Ewing, Caleb B. Smith, David Dudley Field, James A. Seddon, and Stephen T. Logan. Though held in secret, its debates and proceedings were elaborate; but its voluminous journal gives more evidence of disagreement and footless speech-making than of a genuine spirit of accommodation. The Convention was less formal and regular than if summoned by Congress; it was seriously weakened by the absence of all the states of the lower South and six others; [1] it assembled too late in the game to be of controlling influence; and it was embarrassed by the indifference or opposition of radicals on both sides who deliberately withheld cooperation. Southern secessionists were proceeding with the formation of their Confederacy while the Convention was in session; and they were displeased with the confidence which men of the border states placed in the prospect of compromise. Radical Republicans, on the other hand, made light of the Convention, or insisted that a "stiff" attitude be maintained by its Republican members.

On February 27 the Convention presented to Congress a plan of conciliation involving seven amendments to the Constitution. In general the plan resembled the abortive Crittenden compromise: the Missouri line to be extended westward; slavery to be protected in territory south of that

[7] *Ann. Cyc.*, 1861, 700.

[1] The states unrepresented were Arkansas, Michigan, Wisconsin, Minnesota, California, Oregon, and the seven states of the lower South.

line; no further territory to be acquired without the consent of a majority of the senators from the slave states; Congress never to have power over slavery in the states, not even by a future constitutional amendment; slave-owners to be compensated when prevented by intimidation from recovering fugitives.[2] Virginia leaders themselves repudiated the plan of the Convention; and it received but negligible support when brought to a vote on March 2 in the United States Senate.[3] This was a discouraging omen. If conference and deliberation among prominent representatives of the several states could not bring peace, the situation was indeed depressing.

It is now a pathetic exercise to look over the public statements made in and out of the Convention by those who held high hopes that it would lead the way to reunion and adjustment. The Convention was called "in an earnest effort to adjust the present unhappy controversies . . . ," the general assembly of Virginia had declared. "Our godlike fathers created," said its president, John Tyler, and he added: ". . . we have to preserve. They built up. . . . You have . . . a task equally grand . . . You have . . . to preserve the Government, and to renew and invigorate the Constitution. If you reach the height of this great occasion, your children's children will rise up and call you blessed." "Virginia steps in," said W. C. Rives, "to arrest the progress of the country on its road to ruin. . . . I have seen the pavements of Paris covered . . . with fraternal blood! God forbid that I should see this horrid picture repeated in my own country . . ." "Sir, I love this Union," said another Virginian, George W. Summers. "The man does not live who entertains a higher respect for this Government than I do. I know its history—I know how it was established. There is not an incident in its history that is not precious to me. I do not wish to survive its dissolution."[4] As a lasting evidence of the strength of unionism in the upper South and on the border the Peace Convention is of historical significance; but this significance has reference to hopes of what the Convention might do rather than to its actual doings as expressed in debates and resolutions.

The failure of the Convention is one of the tragedies of American history; yet in this failure the radicals of both sides rejoiced. Zachariah Chandler of Michigan, in a private letter while the Convention was in session, wrote that "no Republican State should have sent delegates," and that the "whole thing was gotten up against my judgment and advice, and will end in thin smoke." Then he added in a postscript: "Some of the manufacturing States think that a fight would be awful. Without a little blood-letting this Union will not, in my estimation, be worth a rush."[5]

[2] *Cong. Globe*, 36 Cong., 2 sess., 1254–1255.
[3] *Ibid.*, 1402.
[4] L. E. Chittenden, *Report . . . of the Conference Convention* [etc.], 9, 14, 135–136, 151.
[5] *Ibid.*, 468–469. The position of the lower South concerning the Convention

Meanwhile Buchanan's matured policy was becoming more clearly revealed. That it involved a considerable degree of "stiffening," which even anti-Buchanan writers admit, was due not so much to change in Buchanan's attitude as to events themselves. In other words, Buchanan's policy being one of conciliation *and union*, his government inevitably found itself at odds with leaders of the lower South to whom disunion was already a final consummation. By retirements, removals, and reappointments in his cabinet an added tinge of staunchness for the Union and for enforcing the laws in the South was imparted. Strangely enough, the most sensational of these cabinet changes—the resignation of Cass—has been hit upon as signalizing the opposite tendency. Cass resigned in mid-December when the question of the Charleston forts was under cabinet consideration; and his resignation has been usually represented as a bold, heroic refusal to remain in such bad company and an indignant withdrawal from a cabal of conspirators and traitors who were declining to resist insurrection. Representing a "Northern and loyal constituency, he could no longer without dishonor to himself and to them remain in such treasonable surroundings." Such was his own rationalization as paraphrased by Nicolay and Hay, who add that "he could not stand by and see premeditated dishonor done to the flag." [6]

The fact of the matter was that Cass's position in the cabinet was far from a commanding one, and that, on the day after sending in his letter of resignation, he requested Jacob Thompson to ask the President for its return. One who closely studies the whole complex situation finds it hard to take seriously the loud protestations as to the rectitude of Cass in contrast to the alleged treasonable weakness of Buchanan. The retirement of Cass did undoubtedly weaken Buchanan at the North, where some of the newspapers praised the secretary and called the President a traitor. Under these circumstances, as Dr. Auchampaugh has explained,[7] Buchanan felt that a return to the cabinet would be interpreted as a victory of Cass at the President's expense; but he also realized that there must be no repetition of such an incident, for in the last analysis his administration must rest upon conservative Northern opinion.

Other changes in Buchanan's cabinet had an explanation just the opposite of that falsely offered for Cass's withdrawal. Southern members retired; strong unionists took their place. Besides Cass, those who withdrew were Howell Cobb of Georgia, secretary of the treasury; Jacob Thompson of Mississippi, secretary of the interior; and John B. Floyd of Virginia, sec-

---

appears in the following editorial comment: "They [the seceded states] have . . . no longer the capacity to vote as States in the Union. . . . Whatever is done . . . in the way of conciliation, must be done without them, and submitted to them afterward. . . ." New Orleans *Daily Picayune*, Feb. 8, 1861, reprinted in Dumond, *Southern Editorials on Secession*, 449.

[6] Nicolay and Hay, *Lincoln*, II, 398–399.

[7] P. G. Auchampaugh, *James Buchanan and His Cabinet*, 72–73.

retary of war. Jeremiah S. Black of Pennsylvania, who favored "coercion" and the reinforcement of Sumter, was elevated from the position of attorney general to that of secretary of state; Edwin M. Stanton of Pennsylvania, a Democrat of staunch unionist sentiments, became attorney general; Joseph Holt of Kentucky, whose anti-Southern attitude was soon to become violent,[8] was transferred from the position of postmaster general to that of secretary of war; and John A. Dix of New York, a man thoroughly acceptable to unionists, became secretary of the treasury.[9] It was with this reconstructed cabinet that President Buchanan addressed himself in the later weeks of his administration, with increasing "firmness," to the task of upholding the tottering Union.

The stiffening of the Buchanan administration was made evident in the President's message to Congress of January 8, 1861. As one of the cabinet members recorded, it was "written paragraph by paragraph in the presence of the Cabinet, and discussed as it was prepared." [10] No state, said Buchanan, "has a right by its own act to secede from the Union or throw off its federal obligations at pleasure." The President, he said, had no right to recognize the independence of any seceded state; and as Chief Executive he had "no alternative . . . but to collect the public revenues and to protect the public property so far as . . . practicable under existing laws." Though he had no right to "make aggressive war upon any State," "the right and the duty to use military force defensively against those who resist the Federal officers . . . and . . . assail the property of the Federal Government" he held to be "clear and undeniable." Appealing first to patriotism, then to material considerations, he stressed the rich legacy of the Union, dwelt upon its advantages, and warned of the calamity which its destruction would bring to every portion of the country. Declaring that the secession movement had been "based upon misapprehension at the South of the sentiments of the majority in several of the Northern States," he said that if the question were referred to the ballot box the people themselves would give satisfaction to the South. "Time," he said, "is a great conservative power. . . . Would that South Carolina had been convinced of this truth before her precipitate action!" Then shifting to a sterner tone, he said: "I . . . appeal . . . to the people of the country to declare in their might that the Union must and shall be preserved by all constitutional means. . . . All other questions, when compared to this, sink into insignificance. The present is no time for palliations. Action, prompt action, is required. A delay in Congress to prescribe . . . a dis-

---

[8] At this time, however, Holt agreed with Buchanan on the desirability of preserving peace, and was not as "stiff" as Stanton or Black. Horatio King of Maine took Holt's position as postmaster general.

[9] For a brief period Philip F. Thomas had the treasury portfolio, between the resignation of Cobb and the accession of Dix.

[10] Statement of Philip F. Thomas. Auchampaugh, 174.

tinct and practical proposition for conciliation may drive us to a point from which it will be almost impossible to recede." To the end of the message this tone of firmness for the Union was maintained; at the conclusion the President announced that the duty of protecting the national capital at the time of the coming inauguration would be adequately performed.

The message was translated into action by the sending of a ship to reinforce the garrison at Sumter. At first favoring a powerful warship, the *Brooklyn,* for this purpose, the President yielded to the suggestion that the substitution of a merchant ship would give the expedition a less threatening character. A coasting steamer, the *Star of the West,* an unarmed merchant ship, was sent from New York harbor January 5 with two hundred men, together with arms and ammunition, the purpose being to put the government in a stronger defensive position and thus prevent trouble. On arrival in Charleston harbor the vessel was fired upon by South Carolina guns on Morris Island and in Fort Moultrie, whereupon Major Anderson was on the point of returning the fire from Sumter, thus inaugurating civil war, when the *Star of the West* turned back and steamed out of the harbor.

Thus not a shot was fired by the United States. As always in such incidents, each side considered the other the aggressor. Charleston resented the attempt to reinforce and deemed the expedition an invasion of an independent state by a foreign power. On the other hand the Washington government stressed the nonaggressive nature of the expedition, pointed out that no attack from Sumter was in any way contemplated, and resented the firing upon an unarmed ship. Though the incident might have been taken as throwing down the gage of battle then and there, ensuing negotiations enabled it to be passed over without precipitating war, though a similar expedition under Lincoln, an even less aggressive one, did bring war three months later.[11] The incident demonstrated two things: that there was dynamite in the Sumter situation, which became increasingly the pivotal point in prewar maneuvers; and that Northern sentiment applauded the President's determination to hold Sumter and maintain Federal authority in the South, while at the same time using every pacific resource within his reach.

James Buchanan was a sincere Christian; and at the turn of the year he summoned the people to a Christian altar for humiliation and prayer. Proclaiming the 4th of January as the day for this purpose, he called attention to the alarming and immediate danger threatening the Union and the

---

[11] On the day of the sailing of the *Star of the West,* an order to recall the ship was issued by the war department with the President's approval, because Anderson had suggested that reinforcements be sent later at the government's leisure; but the order came too late to prevent the ship's departure. The countermanding order has occasioned additional criticism of Buchanan; but it signified no weakening of the administration's general determination to hold Sumter. Nicolay and Hay, *Lincoln,* III, 96–97; Curtis, *Buchanan,* II, 447; Crawford, *Sumter,* 176.

"fearful" panic and distress which prevailed in the land. Indeed, said he, "hope seems to have deserted the minds of men." "In this, the hour of our calamity and peril," he continued, "to whom shall we resort . . . but to the God of our Fathers? . . . Let us implore Him to remove from our hearts that false pride of opinion which would impel us to persevere in wrong for the sake of consistency, rather than yield . . . to the unforeseen exigencies by which we are now surrounded." [12]

4

In contrast to the air of gloom which hung over Washington, a program of confident action was being unfolded at Montgomery, where a new and thrilling Southern adventure was being launched. It is true that at the moment there were varying views as to just what this adventure was. The "Southern cause" had long been conceived in terms of securing "Southern rights" in the Union; yet the Montgomery movement had significance only as an abandonment of the old roof and an erection of a new political structure. To some this new structure was viewed in terms of state rights; others envisaged a centralized Southern nation. The adventure started with high courage. Though revolution was in the air, its affairs were handled in an orderly way. Strong-arm methods were to come later; at the moment the emphasis was upon the Southerner's keen sense of democracy.

The convention at Montgomery was called not to consider whether the hazard of secession was to be entered upon, but to organize a Southern government. Even so the Montgomery meeting was not an all-Southern gathering, for at its assembling (February 4, 1861) it contained representatives from only six of the fifteen slave states (South Carolina, Georgia, Alabama, Mississippi, Florida, and Louisiana). The states had chosen their delegates in various ways. Each state sent a number equal to that of its delegation in the Congress at Washington; each state had one vote. The atmosphere at Montgomery was one of excitement and elation accompanied by the bustle of office-seeking and the stir of restless men maneuvering for position. As yet there was no war. The United States was quietly permitting this rival government to be organized in a peaceable manner. When plans should have been made for shipping out cotton, getting gold from Europe, and putting the Confederacy on an efficient war footing, the men of the Montgomery convention were devoting five weeks to the leisurely fashioning of a constitution. But the framers of the Southern Confederacy were emphasizing the peaceful nature of their program. In their minds the right to alter their forms of rule and to frame a government of their own choosing was undeniable; and the exercise of that right after con-

[12] Moore, *Rebell. Record* (Doc.), I, 17.

stitutional forms offered no just occasion for war. Under these circumstances, with the hazard of war in the offing, the absorbing new political venture was in the foreground.

Three main functions were performed by the convention: it made a constitution for the Confederate States; it chose the provisional President and Vice-President; and it acted as a provisional legislature for the new government pending the regular congressional elections. Constitution-making moved in old grooves; and in framing the new instrument for the Southern nation little originality was shown. In its general pattern the constitution closely resembled that of the United States; indeed at most points its wording was precisely the same. The main differences were in those features which looked to the guaranteeing of state rights, the safeguarding of slavery, and the instituting of minor improvements in governmental machinery.

The emphasis upon state rights was made evident at the outset; for the preamble recited that each state acted "in its sovereign and independent character, in order to form"—not a "more perfect union" but "a permanent federal government." The importance of the states was also recognized by a provision that any federal officer, acting solely within the limits of any state, might be impeached by the state legislature. On the other hand, state officers, as in the United States Constitution, were to be under oath to support the federal constitution; and, in the Confederate States as in the United States, the federal constitution, laws, and treaties were declared to be the "supreme law of the land," binding upon state judges and enforceable against contrary provisions in state constitutions or laws. Moreover, the provision for a supreme court was carried over without change,[1] and this was true of virtually the whole judicial article.

Restrictions upon the states were established in much the same terms as those of the United States Constitution. It was stipulated that no state should enter any alliance or confederation, coin money, pass any bill of attainder, or *ex post facto* law, or law impairing the obligation of contracts, grant any title of nobility, keep troops or warships in time of peace, form any compact with another state or a foreign power, or engage in war except in case of invasion or imminent danger. That a confederacy built upon state rights should place these limitations upon state governments is not so remarkable as might at first appear. State sovereignty was understood as the sovereignty of the people of the states; it was but an expression of this sovereignty when the people limited their own governments. A confederacy without state limitations would have been impossible, for in various spheres of governmental action federal authority would of necessity

---

[1] The constitution provided in Art. III, sec. 1: "The judicial power . . . shall be vested in one Supreme Court, and in such inferior courts as the Congress may . . . establish." As a matter of fact, however, no supreme court was actually created.

be exclusive. Though this might result in placing bounds upon state governments, yet in the Southern mind (so far as the matter had been thought out by the few who had carefully pondered the subject) this process did not impair the right of the people of the states to recover the powers which they had intrusted to their confederacy. The constitution was ordained, not by a consolidated people, but by "the people of the Confederate States, each State acting in its sovereign and independent character." It was no more a derogation upon state sovereignty for the people of the states to limit their state governments in the Confederate constitution than to do the same thing in their several state constitutions, which had long been the practice. In fine, "state sovereignty," as interpreted by Alexander H. Stephens, who wrote with unusual clarity on the subject, meant not the sovereignty of any government at all, but the sovereignty of the people of each state, considered severally. At some points the sovereign people would limit their state governments, at other points their federal government.[2]

Bestowing and distributing governmental powers as they wished, the people (or peoples) had also the right to recall what they had bestowed. This they might do by the process of amendment—or, if it should come to that, by secession. Consistency required that each of the states of the Confederacy retain the right of secession; and it is somewhat beside the point to urge that such right was nowhere specifically mentioned in the Confederate constitution. In the opinion of the Southern constitution-makers such mention was unnecessary, the "right of secession" being in no way vitiated by the lack of such mention in the Constitution of the United States.

The "peculiar institution" was well buttressed in the Southern constitution. No federal law "denying . . . the right of property in negro slaves" was to be passed. In all territory to be acquired by the Confederate States slavery was to be "recognized and protected by Congress and by the territorial government"; inhabitants of the several states were guaranteed the right to take their slaves into such territory. Whereas the Constitution of 1787 had employed a clumsy circumlocution which avoided the use of the word "slave," no such indirection was resorted to by the Southerners. The clause on reciprocal citizenship guaranteed to the citizen of any state the right of travel and sojourn with his slaves in any other state. Thus, while it was conceivable that one of the states of the Confederacy might have abolished slavery by state action, such abolition could not have impaired the slaveholding rights of citizens of sister states found within free-state borders. Proslavery sentiment, however, did not proceed to the point of legalizing the foreign slave trade. On the contrary the importation of slaves "from any foreign country other than the slaveholding

---

[2] A. H. Stephens, *Constitutional View of the War between the States*, summarized in Randall, *Constitutional Problems Under Lincoln*, 13 ff.

States or Territories of the United States of America" was distinctly prohibited in the constitution; and the possibility of retaliation against slave
states not joining the Confederacy was introduced by empowering Congress also to prohibit the importation of slaves from any such state.

The framers of the Confederate constitution improved upon the Constitution of the United States in a number of minor ways, designed to produce "the elimination of political waste, the promotion of economical government, and the keeping of each echelon of [the] complex government
within its appointed orbit." So effective were these changes that William M. Robinson, Jr., has termed the document "the peak contribution
of America to political science." [3] The process of amendment was altered.[4]
With certain exceptions Congress was not to appropriate money except
by two-thirds vote of both houses. The amount and purpose of each appropriation were to be precisely specified; and after the fulfillment of a public
contract Congress was not to grant any extra compensation to the contractor. "Riders" on money bills were discouraged by the provision that
the President might veto a given item of an appropriation bill without
vetoing the entire bill. Each law was to deal with "but one subject," to be
expressed in the title. A step toward effective cabinet government was
taken by providing that heads of executive departments might be granted
seats in either house of Congress; and a reference to the congressional
practice of asking heads of departments for estimates called attention to
the budgetary function of the executive. Expenses of the postoffice department were to be paid out of the department's revenue.[5] No bounties were
to be paid out of the treasury; and no protective tariff was to be passed.
The President was to be elected for the term of six years and was not
re-eligible. Strangely enough, the unsatisfactory electoral college, which
had not removed the selection of the President from the people as the
framers had expected, but had distorted the popular vote when translated
into final electoral votes, was carried over into the Montgomery document.

Without waiting for the constitution to become final and definitive
through the slow process of ratification, a full-fledged government was
quickly launched by measures easily taken by the Montgomery convention. Legislative functions were cared for by the convention constituting
itself the provisional legislature of the Confederate States; and the two

[3] Robinson, "A New Deal in Constitutions," *J.S.H.*, IV, 461 (Nov., 1938).

[4] Amendments were to be proposed by a convention of the states and to become effective when ratified either by two-thirds of the state legislatures, or by conventions in two-thirds of the states. Thus Congress was given no power of proposing
amendments, and ratification was made somewhat easier.

[5] This sounded well, but the history of Reagan's department showed that the
payment of expenses out of postal revenue was possible only by the curtailment of
service where particular postoffices proved unprofitable. See Walter F. McCaleb,
"The Organization of the Post-Office Department of the Confederacy," *Am. Hist.
Rev.*, XII, 66–74 (Oct., 1906).

elective officials of the executive department, President and Vice-President, were chosen provisionally by the convention.

The choice for President fell upon a man of high spirit. Though lacking the aristocratic ancestral background often associated with Southern leaders, Jefferson Davis rose to a career of wide influence and distinguished service. He was born in Kentucky in an unpretentious cabin, the tenth child of a pioneer family. His grandfather, Evan Davis, was a Welsh immigrant who had lived in Philadelphia and had moved later to Georgia. The father, Samuel Davis, had seen service in the Revolutionary War in Georgia, had lived near Augusta for a time, and had moved with his family to Christian County in central Kentucky, where he was making a modest living as tobacco planter and stock farmer when his son Jefferson was born on June 3, 1808. It was something of a coincidence that the birthplace of the Confederate leader was not more than a hundred miles from that of Abraham Lincoln. The personal histories of the two men owe much to the adventitious fact that Samuel Davis, during his son Jefferson's childhood, moved his family to Wilkinson County, Mississippi, while the Lincolns moved to Indiana and later to Illinois. Having obtained his education at Transylvania University (Lexington, Kentucky) and at West Point, Davis saw service in a Wisconsin army post and as a minor officer in the Black Hawk War. Then opened a new phase of his career when he left the army and became a Mississippi planter. His plantation "Brierfield," overlooking the Mississippi River, presented an example of slavery at its best, for Davis's manner was that of trustful kindness toward his Negroes, among whom he sought to introduce a régime of self-discipline. Having first married the daughter of Zachary Taylor (1835), who died after a few months, Davis took as his second wife Miss Varina Anne Howell, daughter of an aristocratic and wealthy Mississippi planter. As colonel of a volunteer regiment of Mississippi rifles in the Mexican War he distinguished himself at Monterrey and Buena Vista; and his mind was thereafter colored by a military pride which had been fed by the widespread praise which his exploits received.

Now began his political career. As senator from Mississippi (1847–1851) he opposed Clay's Compromise of 1850, tried hard to defeat the admission of California, and gave evidence of a leaning toward secession. Then he underwent a change. Serving as Pierce's secretary of war, he manifested a strong sense of nationalism with a considerable fondness for expansionist schemes in Cuba and Nicaragua. His national vision, albeit in Southern terms, was illustrated by his active efforts in behalf of a transcontinental railroad via a Southern route. It would appear that he now wanted something other than secession. His dream was that of a united South which would not withdraw from the Union, but would dominate the Union. As senator once more (1857–1861) he fought in deadly earnest against Douglas on the Kansas question; and, by joining with Rhett and

Yancey in preventing the nomination of Douglas at Charleston, he played his part in the breakup of the Democratic party. When, however, the prospect of Lincoln's election loomed in the campaign of 1860, he "went to Douglas and offered to withdraw Breckinridge and even Bell . . . if Douglas would also withdraw . . ." [6] so that a conservative could be chosen upon whom all opponents of Lincoln could unite, and the Union be saved. The secession movement of 1860 did not come of his choosing. On November 10, 1860, he wrote to Rhett that he doubted whether South Carolina ought to withdraw from the Union by herself and feared that Mississippi could not wisely follow her. He was not the only example of a leader prominent in the Confederacy who had been lacking in ardor for secession.

As provisional Vice-President the convention chose Alexander H. Stephens of Georgia, a member, until recently, of the national House of Representatives. Stephens, as we have seen, had opposed the secession of Georgia, but had no thought other than that of following his state, once secession had been decreed. President Davis took oath with high resolve and chose his cabinet; the provisional legislature passed an initial body of laws, which in various instances were but the re-enacting of those passed at Washington; [7] commissioners were appointed to treat with the government of the United States; negotiations were set afoot to bring other states within the fold; and in this manner the new nation at the South became a going concern.

Buchanan's closing weeks need not detain us long. Federal arsenals and forts in the South were in many instances seized; but the national government retained possession in the notable instances of Fort Pickens at Pensacola and Fort Sumter at Charleston. It is significant of the psychological importance of South Carolina to note that a so-called "truce" was arranged at Pickens which, had it been put into effect at Sumter, would have prevented a vast amount of trouble. The United States government was to land provisions in the Florida fort but was not to land additional troops; in return the Florida government agreed that its forces would not make an attack upon the fort. On the other hand, South Carolina opposed the landing of provisions and demanded Federal evacuation. The withdrawal of Southern members of the House and Senate intensified the impression of a crumbling union; and Southern oratory was tinged with tragedy and pathos as the seceders gave parting shots in "farewell ad-

[6] Dodd, *Statesmen of the Old South*, 229. See also Davis, *Rise and Fall*, I, 52; W. E. Dodd, *Jefferson Davis*, 189; Eckenrode, *Davis*, 94.

[7] On March 4, 1861, the Rules and Articles of War of the United States were adopted, with but few exceptions, for the Confederacy; on March 11 a committee was created "to revise the . . . laws of the United States, and report . . . such laws as are applicable to this Confederacy." *Journal*, Confed. Cong. (*Sen. Doc. No. 234*, 58 [U. S.] Cong., 2 sess.), I, 103–105, 124.

dresses." On February 11, Lincoln left Springfield and started east. He arrived in Washington on February 23, and his quarters at the Willard Hotel became, alike to serious statesmen and clamoring office-seekers, the temporary "White House." Approaching his seventieth birthday, the harassed Buchanan stepped out of office, not sure whether the challenging movement at Montgomery, or the lingering Peace Convention, which continued its sessions until nearly the end of his term, held the secret of the future.

CHAPTER 8

Lincoln and the Appeal to Arms

I

FEW PRESIDENTS have launched upon their tasks with prestige as slight as that of Abraham Lincoln on March 4, 1861. While the statesmanlike qualities of the "strange new man from Illinois" were still to be demonstrated, his superficial crudity was much in evidence. His homely appearance gave a handle to critics who ridiculed him as a "baboon" or "gorilla"; as to his probable conduct of the high office in which he had been placed by a minority of his country's votes he was altogether an enigma. In the East especially he was distrusted and regarded as inadequate to the crisis which confronted him. His career had been largely that of a politician; and his popularity had come in part from the people's delight in a man who met them on their own level, made no pretense to superiority, and— to borrow a phrase from Stephen Benét—looked "like people you know." Though not lacking in self-confidence, Lincoln at times showed acquiescence in the notion of his second-rate qualities. He agreed with his friend Browning that Bates was probably the "strongest and best man" [1] the Republicans could run in 1860; and after his nomination, in an autobiographical account prepared for the campaign, he acknowledged the "narrow circumstances" of his origin among the "second families." Such men as John A. Andrew, Charles Francis Adams, and Henry Ward Beecher distrusted Lincoln, and there were many who snobbishly dismissed him as a "simple Susan." His trip as President-elect added nothing to his reputation. His prudence in reserving his announcement of presidential policy for the inaugural address caused his speeches *en route* to seem colorless if not actually trivial; and the newspapers injured him by giving unfortunate publicity to minor incidents, as when the new leader, whose fine chin was now marred by a new-grown beard, publicly kissed a little girl as his train stopped at her town and explained that the facial decoration had been assumed at her request. In the vivid words of Charles Francis Adams, Jr.,

---

[1] Browning, *Diary*, I, 395.

while Seward, the "small, thin, sallow man, with . . . the everlasting cigar," was "laboring under a total misconception of . . . the logic of events," and while Sumner "talked like a crazy man, orating, gesticulating, . . . and doing everything but reason," Lincoln, an "absolutely unknown quantity," was "perambulating the country, kissing little girls and growing whiskers!" The outgoing President, thought Adams, made a better appearance on inauguration day than the incoming one. Despite his "wry neck and dubious eye," Buchanan was, he thought, "undeniably the more presentable man of the two; his tall, large figure, and white head, looked well beside Mr. Lincoln's lank, angular form and hirsute face; and the dress of the President-elect did not indicate that knowledge of the proprieties . . . which was desirable." [2] The new administration began with a secret night ride to Washington to which Lincoln reluctantly agreed under pressure from advisers who feared assassination. While opponents abused him for thus creeping into the capital, and while cartoonists rudely caricatured his alleged disguise upon changing cars at Baltimore, his friends were oppressed with a sense of humiliation. His preoccupation with hordes of office-seekers to the neglect of weightier matters, his social awkwardness, his caution, interpreted as timidity, in approaching critical problems, his inexperience in the management of great affairs, all contributed to the unfavorable impression. Many thought Lincoln would be President only in name, and that Seward would be the directing force in the new administration.

2

In the preparation of state papers, however, Lincoln possessed a real mastery. His inaugural address, delivered in an atmosphere of apprehension and military display, struck the note of gentle firmness and breathed the spirit of conciliation and of friendliness to the South. He made it clear that the government could not consent to its own destruction by recognizing secession, and that it must maintain its authority against the challenge of disunion. As to the Federal forts and property in the seceded states, he said: "The power confided to me, will be used to hold, occupy, and possess [he did not say "repossess"] [1] the property, and places belonging to the government"; but he added that "no bloodshed or violence" was involved in this policy. There "will be no invasion," he said, "no using of force against, or among the people anywhere." He further pledged that there would be

[2] *Charles Francis Adams (1835–1915): An Autobiography,* 79, 74, 80, 75, 82, 96–97. (This Adams was the son of the United States minister to Great Britain.)

[1] On the advice of O. H. Browning, Lincoln altered his inaugural address so as to omit the words expressive of a purpose to "reclaim the . . . places which have fallen." Nicolay and Hay considered this an exceedingly important modification. Browning, *Diary,* I, 455 n.

"no attempt to force obnoxious strangers among the people"; the sending of what came to be known later as "carpetbaggers" into the South was no part of his purpose.

"Physically speaking," he said, "we cannot separate." No "impassable wall" could be erected between the sections. They "cannot but remain face to face; and intercourse, either amicable or hostile, must continue between them." "Can aliens [he asked] make treaties easier than friends can make laws? . . . Suppose you go to war, you cannot fight always; and when, after much loss on both sides, and no gain on either, you cease fighting, the identical old questions . . . are again upon you."

As to slavery, he counseled the enforcement of all the laws, repeated his former declaration that he had "no purpose, directly or indirectly, to interfere with the institution of slavery in the States where it exists," and affirmed that ". . . the property, peace and security of no section are . . . in anywise endangered by the now incoming administration." He closed with an ardent appeal to the Southern people:

In *your* hands, my dissatisfied fellow countrymen . . . is the momentous issue of civil war. The government will not assail *you.* You can have no conflict without being yourselves the aggressors. *You* have no oath registered in Heaven to destroy the government, while *I* shall have the most solemn one to "preserve, protect, and defend" it.

. . . We are not enemies, but friends. We must not be enemies. . . . The mystic chords of memory, stretching from every . . . patriot grave to every living heart and hearthstone, all over this broad land, will yet swell the chorus of the Union, when again touched, as surely they will be, by the better angels of our nature.

For his cabinet Lincoln had brought together a somewhat ill-assorted group whose appointment had been dictated by a variety of motives— recognition of rivals within the party, recognition of that wing of the Republican party which had Democratic antecedents, regard for sections or states, and fulfillment of campaign pledges. The two ablest ministers were probably Seward and Chase—Seward chosen because of his commanding influence within the party; Chase because of antislavery leadership, ability, and prominence as a presidential rival. Welles of Connecticut was put in as a former Democrat and a New Englander. Cameron of Pennsylvania was reluctantly appointed in compliance with a prenomination bargain in which Lincoln personally had no part. It was plainly evident that this appointment went counter to Lincoln's better judgment. The official family was completed by the appointment of Edward Bates of Missouri as attorney general, Caleb Smith of Indiana as secretary of the interior, and Montgomery Blair of Maryland as postmaster general. Lincoln had earnestly wished to include within his cabinet some representative of the South (as distinguished from the border states), and had approached

John A. Gilmer of North Carolina on the subject; but his efforts in this direction did not succeed.

3

A dispassionate reading of Lincoln's inaugural address raises the question: Was there in Lincoln's policy and in the circumstances of his election any such menace to Southern rights as would justify disruption of the Union? It is not to be expected that historians will agree on this controversial subject; in these pages it would be most inappropriate to attempt any answer in the tone of finality. All that need be done is to note briefly some of the leading considerations on both sides.[1] To the Southerners it appeared that the Republican party had been rather thoroughly abolitionized. They could not forget that the party included Charles Sumner and that many of its devotees approved Helper's *Impending Crisis* [2] and proclaimed John Brown a hero. Nor could they overlook the fact that Republicans refused to accept the Dred Scott decision as final; that they had pushed their antislavery agitation with grim determination in the Kansas struggle; that the "personal liberty laws" of the North were largely their work; that Lincoln had been silent and noncommittal during the campaign of 1860; and that he had by no means answered the questions in the minds of Southerners in a reassuring manner. But even if the mildness of Lincoln's own purposes were to be admitted, Southerners thought of him as a Republican President: they feared increasingly radical tendencies within his party, which would draw him inevitably beyond his own desires or judgment. The radicalism of the Union government during the war and the orgy of vindictive rule after the war have since been offered as proof of the reasonableness of this apprehension as to the probable course of the Lincoln government. Many a Southerner refused to take seriously Lincoln's disclaimer of any intention to interfere with slavery in the states; many others, hearing only the talk concerning Lincoln that passed from mouth to mouth in the South, were unaware that he had made any such disclaimer. The controlling influence, the Southerner feared, would be that of such men as Henry Wilson, who promised to deliver the government from the grasp of the slave power. As for Lincoln, he showed but little leader-

[1] For a debate on this subject, see the two articles titled "Lincoln's Election an Immediate Menace to Slavery in the States?" by A. C. Cole, *Am. Hist. Rev.*, XXXVI, 740–767 (July, 1931), and by J. G. de R. Hamilton, *ibid.*, XXXVII, 700–711 (July, 1932). The discussion in the following paragraphs closely follows the reasoning of these two writers.

[2] *The Impending Crisis of the South: How to Meet It* was written by Hinton Rowan Helper, a middle-class nonslaveholder of North Carolina. The book was a violent denunciation of Southern policy, of Southern leaders, and especially of slavery, which the writer treated as a grievous economic curse. Appearing first in 1857, it was extensively reprinted in 1860. Though Lincoln disavowed it, many Republicans approved of it; indeed it served as a Republican campaign document.

ship in 1860; and the South in general was in almost total ignorance of the real character of the man. Republican policy seemed to be under the direction of others; and it was one of the unfortunate features of the situation that those others who were most prominently identified in the Southern mind with the Republican cause were of the threatening and intransigent type.

On both sides there was irrational inference: misrepresentations that beclouded the air seemed more potent than essential realities which the people were not permitted to understand. The nub of the matter was not so much the genuine intention of Lincoln's mind as it was the Southerner's fear or belief, unjustified though it may have been, that Lincoln's election signified an attack upon slavery in the states. Harboring such a belief, and remembering the "unsparing presentation of the evils of slavery in the Republican press," the Southerner tended to regard this election as a challenge to his social and economic system. With such a conviction in his mind it was but natural to exercise the fundamental right of altering his government and throwing off an alien rule.

In answer to these Southern contentions it has been urged that both Lincoln and the Republican party were fully committed to the policy of noninterference with slavery in the South; [3] that Republicans were ready to compromise any phase of the sectional conflict except that of slavery in the territories; that the states of the North stood ready to repeal their "personal liberty laws"; that abolitionizing the South was no part of Lincoln's plan; and that if such a plan had been tried the Southern states might have blocked it by their votes in Congress. In this connection the conservatism of Lincoln has been stressed. His Virginia ancestry and Kentucky birth, his many personal contacts with Southern friends or with Illinois friends of Southern antecedents, his marriage into an aristocratic slaveholding family, tended to make him a moderate and to draw him closer to the Southern point of view than to that of the New England antislavery extremists. Those who argue thus have urged that Lincoln was nominated as a brake upon radical tendencies, that he was deliberately chosen by the Republican convention in preference to men who were considered more extreme. During the campaign of 1860 Republican managers did their best to silence Sumner; they thought of his antislavery efforts as "rocking the boat." It has been urged that the Republican party during this period was making vigorous efforts to draw moderates within its ranks and to avoid repelling old-line Whigs, of whom Lincoln himself was a conspicuous example. With its "big business" alliances, it was placing little emphasis upon the slavery question in 1860; and "if the normal conditions of a

[3] Confederate diplomats, seeking in 1861 to influence English opinion, admitted (rather they emphatically declared) that Lincoln and the Republican party did not threaten slavery in the South. F. L. Owsley, *King Cotton Diplomacy*, 66–67.

peaceful Republican administration" had been realized, there was ground for expecting that "genuine abolitionists would have found themselves unable to make substantial headway with their crusade."

The "menace" of Lincoln's election has been elaborately studied by Professor A. C. Cole; and his conclusions should be pondered by anyone interested in a closer study of the problem. Lincoln's contacts, as Professor Cole shows, as well as his Whig connections, were among the many factors tending to make him conservative on the slavery question; and the "dread 'abolition' heresy" was no part of his political background. When the Republican party was formed Lincoln was reluctant to join it; and while campaigning for Frémont in 1856 he studiously avoided "referring to himself or to his party associates under the designation, 'Republican.'" Lincoln carefully explained that his house-divided speech could not be fairly interpreted as proclaiming a general abolition crusade; in his Peoria speech of October 16, 1854, he admitted his inability, "if all earthly power" were given him, to solve the slavery problem. Dr. Cole further points out that Southern unreadiness to listen to Lincoln had much to do with his silence in the campaign of 1860; for at the time a Charleston paper declared: "If Mr. Lincoln was to come out and declare that he held sacred every right of the South, with respect to African slavery, no one should believe him; and, if he was believed, his professions should have not the least influence on the course of the South." Instead of specifying concrete threats to their institutions, Southerners were accustomed to deal in "sublimated abstractions"; they declared they would "not tamely submit" and must "fight for their rights" without defining the submission demanded or the rights endangered.

As to Lincoln's presidential program, Professor David M. Potter has shown that it was as conciliatory as it could be without acquiescing in Southern independence. Paraphrasing the inaugural address, Professor Potter summarizes "the much vaunted 'firm' policy of Lincoln":

He would assert the Federal authority vigorously—but he would not exercise it. He would enforce the laws—where an enforcement mechanism existed. He would deliver the mails—unless repelled. He would collect the duties—offshore. He would hold the forts—at least the ones which Buchanan had held, and which seemed capable of holding themselves.[4]

It was natural for the South to be alarmed at Republican growth; yet in part it was the Southerners who gave the Republicans their opportunity. By splitting the Democratic party and abandoning their seats in Congress

---

[4] Potter, *Lincoln and His Party in the Secession Crisis*, 329. For the opposing view that Lincoln's inaugural meant a "rejection of compromise," which "might very well lead to conflict," and that the President "accepted that risk, and for that reason . . . took . . . enormous pains to absolve himself from the charge of aggression," see Kenneth M. Stampp, *And the War Came*, 209.

they contributed to Republican control. In the Thirty-Fourth Congress, whose second session opened in December, 1856, the Republicans had only 15 of the 62 senators, of whom the administration Democrats had 40; of the 234 representatives in this Congress the Republicans had 108, the Buchanan Democrats 83, and the Fillmore Americans 43. In the Thirty-Fifth Congress (1857–1859) the Republicans again failed to muster a majority in either house. Coming down to December of 1860 one finds that in the second session of the Thirty-Sixth Congress (elected in 1858) the membership was as follows: in the Senate 26 Republicans, 36 Democrats, 2 Americans, 2 vacancies; in the House 114 Republicans, 87 administration Democrats, 24 "South Americans" (members of the American party from Southern or border states), 6 anti-Lecompton Democrats, 6 vacancies. Thus in this session the Republicans with their anti-Lecompton allies had a slight majority, but only in the lower house. During this session the whole of the South Carolina delegation was absent from both houses, thus accounting for the six vacancies in the House and the two in the Senate.[5]

As for the Thirty-Seventh Congress, elected in November of 1860, it would not have been in Republican control if the Southern states had stayed in the Union and preserved their membership. Counting members elected and "to be elected" the Republicans could muster only twenty-nine in the Senate as compared to thirty-seven for the opposition; in the House the opposition could have mustered 129 to the Republicans' 108. Thus "in neither the House nor the Senate would the Republicans have [had] a majority." [6] Commenting on this situation Andrew Johnson of Tennessee stated on January 10, 1861, that if the Southern states remained in the Union the Democrats would command a majority in the Senate, that the opposition could block appointments and refuse appropriations, and that the incoming administration would come into office "handcuffed, powerless to do harm. . . ." [7]

4

The most important issues confronting the new President were the problem of conciliating the upper South so as to halt the secession movement, and the closely related problem of deciding what to do at Fort Sumter. Major Anderson, it will be recalled, had moved his force from Moultrie to Sumter, and his action was sustained by the Buchanan admin-

---

[5] For these figures see [N. Y.] *Tribune Almanac*, 1857, 16–17; 1858, 16–17; 1861, 16–18.

[6] Rhodes, II, 501.

[7] *Cong. Globe*, 36 Cong., 2 sess., 309 (Jan. 10, 1861). For a similar statement by A. H. Stephens as to Democratic control of both House and Senate, see his *Constitutional View of the War between the States*, II, 282 ff. See also Channing, *Hist. of the U. S.*, VI, 252.

istration. Supplies and reinforcements were sent, but were not landed because of the attack upon the *Star of the West*. To the end of his administration Buchanan refused to evacuate Sumter in compliance with the demands of South Carolina. One after another of the Federal strongholds and properties had fallen into Southern hands; but such incidents had been passed over by Buchanan without being treated as acts of war. Fort Moultrie and Castle Pinckney had been taken over by South Carolina late in December, 1860; and the state authorities had proceeded to the general strengthening of various defenses at Charleston. Fort Pulaski at Savannah was seized by Georgia state troops on January 3. Fort Morgan at Mobile was taken on January 4 by Alabama troops, and a strong garrison was put in charge. At Pensacola, though Fort Pickens was kept in Union possession, the Federal navy yard and Fort Barrancas were seized by Alabama and Florida troops, being surrendered by the Federal authorities (January 12) without a struggle. The most remarkable instance occurred in Texas, where nineteen Federal army posts were delivered to Texas authorities by General David E. Twiggs, U. S. A., commanding the Department of Texas. This business was transacted (February, 1861) while Twiggs was wearing the uniform of the United States army,[1] and it was done before the Texas ordinance of secession had been ratified.

In addition, a number of post offices, customhouses, hospitals, and other public property had been occupied; the mint at New Orleans had been taken over; United States revenue cutters and other ships had been seized; and batteries in Charleston harbor had fired on a schooner (the *R. H. Shannon*) displaying the Stars and Stripes. Of the forts in the seceded states the only ones remaining in Union hands in April, 1861, were Fort Sumter, Fort Pickens in Pensacola Bay, and two minor forts (Taylor and Jefferson) off the Florida coast. This Southern seizure of Federal forts, however, had occurred before Lincoln took office; and, while Lincoln had deliberately avoided threatening the repossession of places already taken, many in the North looked upon Sumter as a test of the President's

---

[1] The fact that, while in United States army service, Twiggs had secretly promoted the surrender by arrangements with Texan agents, led to his dismissal (March 1, 1861) from the army of the United States, the cause being described as "treachery to the flag . . . in having surrendered . . . , on the demand of the authorities of Texas, the military posts and other property of the United States . . . under his charge." Moore, *Rebell. Rec.* (Diary), I, 18. See also Robert Underwood Johnson and Clarence C. Buel, eds., *Battles and Leaders of the Civil War* (hereafter cited as *Battles and Leaders*), I, 33–39. In Twiggs's defense it is to be said that he considered the dissolution of the Union unavoidable and that his action was designed to avert violence. He was in sympathy with secession and had made it clear that he would not fire upon Southerners. He had asked to be relieved of command but the papers were delayed, and meanwhile, despite repeated requests for instructions, he was, says Douglas Freeman, "in the dark concerning the policy of the Government." See Douglas S. Freeman, *R. E. Lee*, I, 426–427.

adherence to his inaugural pronouncement that further surrenders would not take place.

In a peculiar sense the "two sides" faced each other at Sumter. Should measures be taken there which appeared aggressive, there was real danger that the lower South would become inflamed to the point of fighting, and that, once war was started, the upper South could no longer be held in the Union. Peace thus hung upon a trigger; and to make matters worse a time limit was added to the situation by the fact that Anderson's supplies were low and the garrison would have to withdraw, unless relieved, by the middle of April. For the President to withdraw the garrison was not so easy a solution as it seemed. It was sure to be heralded as an evidence of weakness, if not a deliberate evasion of presidential duty. By such a step the Executive would have sacrificed many of his best supporters in the North.

By March, 1861, a substantial body of Northern public opinion had crystallized against further concessions to the South. Kenneth M. Stampp has carefully analyzed the reasons for this change.[2] The dominant business interests of the Northeast, which earlier in the crisis had favored compromise, now were "forced back to the point where they found it necessary to 'take sides' for or against the Union." Holders of government securities "looked upon disunion as a menace to their investments"; other businessmen "believed that the reduction of the government to impotence would not only destroy its own credit but depress every form of private property"; those to whom Southerners owed money feared the secessionists would make "depreciated paper money legal tender in payment of private debts"; manufacturers thought that the Confederacy, under its free-trade policy, would no longer patronize Northern markets but would buy direct from Europe. Faced with these economic realities, businessmen, "like other Yankees, . . . overwhelmingly chose the Union—even at the cost of war."

More idealistic Northerners also opposed further compromise. Many Northern patriots felt that "only by preserving the Union could Americans fulfill the promise of their Manifest Destiny." They thought "the preservation of America's political greatness was more than a duty they owed to themselves; it was a duty to mankind. . . . Many in the free states believed that the sectional conflict was itself a struggle between democracy and despotism." Though some extreme antislavery spokesmen were willing to see the Southern states depart in peace from the Union, "there were more abolitionists who desired a war against slavery than there were who sought absolution from the national curse by speeding the departure of the South."

[2] Stampp, *And the War Came*, 205, 223, 226, 241, 245–246, 251, 156–157.

Northern politicians, too, had come to be increasingly hostile to compromise proposals. While, as Professor Stampp remarks, "it would be wrong to assume that most Republicans *consciously* placed party considerations above peaceful reunion," politicos could not but remember that the Whig party had been wrecked by its support of the Compromise of 1850. Seward's mild flirtation with compromise in December, 1860, was enough to show that radical antislavery Republicans would bolt the party rather than make further concessions. "I helped to make the Republican party," William H. Herndon, Lincoln's abolitionist law partner exclaimed, "and if it forsakes its distincuve ideas, I can help to tear it down, and help to erect a new party that shall never cower to any slave driver." Professor Stampp concludes: ". . . it was all too evident that reunion through compromise was impossible without the death of the Republican party, and there were few of its members who chose to make that sacrifice."

Despite this gradual hardening of Northern sentiment, Lincoln was most reluctant to abandon the idea of compromise; especially was he reluctant to force the issue at Fort Sumter. His closest advisers advocated concessions to the South. General Winfield Scott, veteran head of the army, argued that the sending of a sufficiently powerful provisioning or reinforcing expedition was impracticable. Turning to his cabinet, Lincoln found that only two of his ministers—Chase and Blair—favored an expedition intended to supply food to the garrison. Blair was sure that such an expedition would demonstrate the "firmness" of the administration; Chase, though approving the expedition, opposed such a move if it should inaugurate civil war. Seward blamed South Carolina for the "revolution," but declared that he "would not initiate war to regain a useless and unnecessary position. . . ." Cameron advised that an attempt to relieve the fort would be "unwise." Welles, Smith, and Bates also advised against a relief expedition.[3]

There is reason to believe that such advice, to which the inexperienced Lincoln paid more attention than he would in later years, caused the President seriously to reconsider his inaugural pledge "to hold, occupy, and possess the property and places belonging to the government" and to think of evacuating Fort Sumter. In conversation with unionist members of the Virginia secession convention who sought an interview with him, Lincoln is reported to have made a conditional suggestion that he would "evacuate Sumter if they would break up their convention, without any row or nonsense." [4] "A State for a fort," he said, "is no bad business." [5] At the

---

[3] The original poll of cabinet opinion as to the Sumter question was taken on March 15, 1861.

[4] Potter, *Lincoln and His Party*, 353.

[5] *Annual Report*, Am. Hist. Assn., 1915, 211. See also testimony of John B. Baldwin, Feb. 10, 1866, *House Report No. 30*, pt. 2, 39 Cong., 1 sess., pp. 102 ff., 115 ff.

same time he considered the possibility that he might yield at Sumter and still carry out his announced policy by remaining "firm" at Pickens, where the psychology of the situation was less threatening; [6] and indeed on March 12 he ordered the reinforcement of the Florida fort. During the early weeks of his administration there were several developments which gave the distinct impression that the government at Washington was planning the evacuation of Sumter. Indirect communications occurred between Seward, widely regarded as the "spokesman" of the administration, and the Confederate commissioners at Washington. Though Seward did not actually "recognize" the Confederacy by receiving these commissioners officially, he did deal with them through go-betweens, especially Justices Nelson and Campbell of the United States Supreme Court. To these men, who were going back and forth between the commissioners and himself, Seward gave assurances in harmony with his own sincere wish that Sumter should be evacuated. This was regarded by the commissioners and by Southern leaders generally as a "promise" that the garrison would be withdrawn, though Lincoln himself had given no such promise.

But during the last few days of March a series of developments compelled Lincoln to abandon any idea of yielding Sumter. Failure to hear whether his order for the reinforcement of Fort Pickens had been obeyed obliged him to contemplate a new course.[7] Perhaps he sensed the hardening of Northern opinion against further concessions to the South in the resolutions which Lyman Trumbull introduced in the Senate on March 28, to the effect that "it is the duty of the President to use all the means in his power to hold and protect the public property of the United States." [8] The same day his faith in his military advisers was shaken when General Scott, on political grounds, advised yielding both Pickens and Sumter to the Confederates. The next day, on polling the cabinet again, he found only Smith and Seward in favor of giving up the South Carolina fort, and the secretary of state forfeited much of Lincoln's confidence by proposing on April 1 to *"Change the question before the Public from one upon Slavery, or about Slavery,* for a question upon *Union* or *Disunion"* through making categorical demands upon Spain, France, Great Britain, and Russia, followed inevitably by war against the first two of those powers.[9]

Having tested the possibilities that lay in the policy of evacuation and

---

[6] In *The Lincoln Nobody Knows* (pp. 121–122), Professor Richard N. Current finds the story of Lincoln's negotiations with Virginia "questionable" and "casts doubt on the Lincoln version" of his willingness to surrender Sumter if he could keep Pickens.

[7] Lincoln, *Collected Works*, IV, 424–425. Not until April 6 did Lincoln learn that his order to reinforce Pickens had, through a misunderstanding of the local commander, not been executed. After new orders from the President, Pickens was reinforced on April 12 and remained in Union hands throughout the war.

[8] Potter, *Lincoln and His Party*, 360.

[9] Lincoln, *Collected Works*, IV, 317.

having sounded public opinion on the subject, Lincoln ordered two relief expeditions to be fitted out, one designed for Sumter and the other for Pickens. On April 4 he put Captain Gustavus Vasa Fox in command of the Sumter expedition and notified Anderson "the expedition will go forward." Two days later he ordered Robert S. Chew, a clerk in the state department, to proceed to South Carolina and to inform Governor Pickens: "I am directed by the President of the United States to notify you to expect an attempt will be made to supply Fort-Sumter [sic] with provisions only; and that, if such attempt be not resisted, no effort to throw in men, arms, or ammunition, will be made, without further notice, or in case of an attack upon the Fort." [10]

Did Lincoln anticipate that sending this expedition to provision Fort Sumter would precipitate a civil war? Even at the time there were those who claimed that Lincoln well knew the consequences of his action and deliberately tricked the Confederacy into firing the first shot. There is indeed some evidence to support this view. "You and I both anticipated," Lincoln wrote to Captain Fox in May, 1861, "that the cause of the country would be advanced by making the attempt to provision Fort-Sumpter [sic], even if it should fail; and it is no small consolation now to feel that our anticipation is justified by the result." [11] On July 3, the President told his friend Orville H. Browning: "The plan [sending supplies to Major Anderson] succeeded. They attacked Sumter—it fell, and thus, did more service than it otherwise could." [12] The distinguished Southern historian Charles W. Ramsdell has argued: ". . . Lincoln, having decided that there was no other way than war for the salvation of his administration, his party, and the Union, maneuvered the Confederates into firing the first shot in order that they, rather than he, should take the blame of beginning bloodshed." [13]

Yet many historians feel that this is a distortion of Lincoln's motives. One must grant, of course, that Lincoln was no pacifist and that he was willing to accept war rather than permit the dissolution of the Union. Yet

[10] *Ibid.*, IV, 323. The execution of the Sumter plan became involved in a serious muddle. Orders issued through Secretary Welles of the navy department assigned a powerful warship, the *Powhatan,* to the Sumter expedition; but Seward put through an order, which the President signed without reading, transferring the *Powhatan* to another fleet designed for Pickens. When Lincoln overruled Seward, directing him to restore the ship to the Sumter expedition, Seward bungled the matter by sending the new order in his own name; and the commander of the *Powhatan* refused to obey it in opposition to the previous order in the President's name. Thus the *Powhatan* did not sail with the Sumter expedition; and without it the expedition could not be successful.

[11] *Ibid.*, IV, 351.

[12] Browning, *Diary,* I, 476.

[13] Ramsdell, "Lincoln and Fort Sumter," *J.S.H.*, III, 259–288.

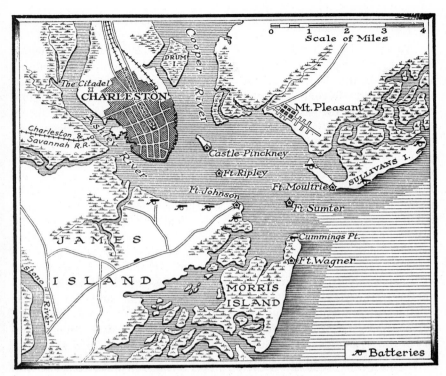

CHARLESTON HARBOR

it is hard to see how, short of acquiescing in Southern independence, he could have followed a more nonaggressive course. From the day of his inaugural to the time of the Confederate attack on Fort Sumter, he carefully refrained from any precautionary assembling of Federal troops, from any issuing of belligerent public statements, and from any attempts to repossess Federal possessions already taken over by the Confederacy. So far as Sumter was concerned, the approaching exhaustion of supplies in the fort made some change in the situation inevitable; but Lincoln's course offered the nearest approach to the preservation of the *status quo* which was possible. The expedition was directed not to reinforce but to provision Major Anderson's men; it was not stealthily sent, but due notice of its pacific purpose was given to the governor of South Carolina. Of course Lincoln was aware that sending provisions to Sumter might provoke hostilities, but that is not to say that he desired hostilities. And to argue that Lincoln meant that the first shot would be fired by the other side *if a first shot was fired* is by no means the same as arguing that he deliberately maneuvered to have the shot fired.

5

To the Southern mind Lincoln's plan to relieve Sumter seemed a threat, a challenge, and a breach of faith. After the Confederate cabinet had held an anxious consultation at Montgomery, the secretary of war, L. P. Walker, directed General Beauregard, in command at Charleston, to demand the evacuation of the fort, and, if the demand should be refused, to "reduce it." The excited temper of South Carolina made it seem inevitable that an attempt to provision the fort would precipitate an attack; and there was apprehension that, in the absence of orders from Montgomery, the state might take the initiative, thus embarrassing the infant Confederacy by a conflict of state and federal authority. On the afternoon of April 11 a boat carrying Col. James Chesnut, Jr., just resigned as United States senator from South Carolina, and Captain Stephen D. Lee, visited Fort Sumter under flag of truce and conveyed Beauregard's demand for its surrender. Anderson refused compliance, but remarked to the officers that he would "await the first shot" and that his garrison would be "starved out in a few days." [1] There has been much discussion as to whether this answer could not have been accepted as sufficient to avert an attack upon Sumter. Reluctance to fire the shot that would inaugurate war was manifest at Montgomery, as shown by the message which secretary of war Walker sent to Beauregard on the afternoon of April 11:

Do not desire needlessly to bombard Fort Sumter. If Major Anderson will state the time at which . . . he will evacuate, and agree that . . . he will not use his guns against us, unless ours should be employed against Fort Sumter, you are authorized thus to avoid the effusion of blood. If this, or its equivalent, be refused, reduce the fort. . . .[2]

During the night of April 11–12 three officers [3] visited the fort and informed Major Anderson of the instruction from Montgomery. After a consultation with his officers, Anderson directed the following reply to General Beauregard:

. . . cordially uniting with you in the desire to avoid the useless effusion of blood, I will, . . . evacuate Fort Sumter by noon on the 15th . . . , and . . . I will not in the meantime open my fires upon your forces unless compelled to do so by some hostile act . . . , should I not receive prior to that time controlling instructions from my Government or additional supplies.[4]

Without waiting to transmit this reply to Beauregard for further instructions, the aides, at 3:30 A.M., April 12, served notice upon Ander-

[1] *Battles and Leaders,* I, 75, 82.
[2] *Ibid.,* I, 75.
[3] Col. James Chesnut, Jr., Lt. Col. A. R. Chisolm, and Capt. Stephen D. Lee. Col. Roger A. Pryor accompanied the three on their trip but did not enter the fort.
[4] S. W. Crawford, *Hist. of the Fall of Fort Sumter,* 425.

son, by Beauregard's authority, that the general would open fire in one hour. Much has been made of this incident; and it has even been made to appear that these three young men, in their night conference, settled the fate of the country. The fact that the aides gave the order for the firing of the signal gun that was to begin the bombardment, instead of leaving the final order to Beauregard, does seem unsatisfactory; but the essential fact was that the Confederacy was demanding evacuation of a fort which Lincoln had decided not to evacuate, and to which he had dispatched a provisioning expedition which Southern authorities regarded as a ruse to permit strengthening of the garrison. Indeed, before the aides had departed on their night mission, word had come of the arrival of the Lincoln expedition. Thus the opening of the Civil War cannot be made to hinge upon the over-dramatized night conference of these Confederate aides.

At 4:30 A.M., April 12, the firing began; and Sumter was soon under cross fire from a number of batteries in the harbor. After a bloodless bombardment of forty hours, during which the walls were impaired, the ammunition nearly exhausted, and great damage done by fire, Major Anderson surrendered the fort on April 13, his garrison being permitted to depart after saluting the flag. Meanwhile the relief expedition commanded by Captain G. V. Fox, consisting of the *Baltic,* the *Pawnee,* and the *Harriet Lane,* but weakened by the absence of the *Powhatan* and unassisted by necessary tugs which had been detained by a gale, found itself powerless to do more than carry off Anderson and his men after the surrender.

6

Until the Sumter cannonade a waiting attitude on both sides had been maintained. Conflicting declarations had been made; but the evil day when declarations must be translated into violent action was delayed; and each day of postponement brought encouragement to the many who thought that compromise, i.e., peace with union, was yet possible. Certainly the upper South, the great border, and thousands of Southern sympathizers at the North thought so. The Sumter incident produced an instant change. On receipt of the news of the surrender of the fort, President Lincoln, on April 15, issued a proclamation calling forth "the militia of the several States of the Union, to the . . . number of seventy-five thousand," to suppress "combinations" in seven states "too powerful to be suppressed by the ordinary course of judicial proceedings." In the same proclamation the President summoned Congress to meet in special session July 4; soon after, he launched other war measures.[1]

Had there been a formal declaration of war, the effect could not have been more instantaneous and widespread. The President had, indeed, de-

[1] See below, pp. 274 ff., 293 ff.

clared an insurrection, which in practical effect, though not in legal
theory, was virtually declaring the existence of a state of war; and amid
the storm of indignation which shook both sections preparations for war
were vigorously pushed.

At the North the patriotic response was not confined to the President's
party. The attitude of Douglas was particularly significant. When campaigning for the presidency in 1860, he had been asked at Norfolk whether
he would advise resistance by force in case the South should secede on the
inauguration of Lincoln. He replied: "I answer emphatically that it is the
duty of the President of the United States, and all others in authority under
him, to enforce the laws . . . passed by Congress . . . ; and I, as in
duty bound by my oath of fidelity to the Constitution, *would do all in my
power to aid the Government of the United States in maintaining the supremacy of the laws against all resistance to them, come from what quarter
it might.*" On the question whether he would participate in an effort to dissolve the Union if Lincoln were elected, he answered: "I tell them, 'no—
never, on earth'!" [2]

Douglas's opposition had been directed equally against extremists on
both sides. On July 5, 1860, he had written to his friend Lanphier at
Springfield: "We must make the war boldly against the *Northern Abolitionists* and the *Southern Disunionists* and give no quarter to either." [3]
When South Carolina withdrew from the Union, Douglas at the same time
denounced secession and labored for conciliation. He supported the Crittenden plan, the Seward compromise resolutions, and the constitutional
amendment to protect slavery in the states. During March, while Lincoln's
course seemed to be one of vacillation, Douglas indicated "that he would
harass the Administration mercilessly unless it sacrificed almost everything
for peace." [4] At the same time he sharply rebuked the uncompromising
leaders of the South. When Breckinridge declared in the Senate that the
South must be conceded the right to emigrate into all the territories, or at
least an equitable partition of the national domain, Douglas answered that,
with Republican consent, the South already had that right. [5] When Senator

    [2] N. Y. *Times,* Aug. 29, 1860, p. 1; see also Milton, *Eve of Conflict,* 492–
493.
    [3] Frank E. Stevens, *Life of S. A. Douglas* (*Journal,* Ill. St. Hist. Soc., XVI),
625.
    [4] Allan Nevins, *The War for the Union,* I, 35.
    [5] Blaine expresses the matter thus: ". . . Douglas reminded him [Breckin-
ridge] that the South had, by the action of a Republican Congress, the full right to
emigrate into all the territory of the United States; and that, with the consent of the
Republican Congress, every inch of the territory of the United States south of the
thirty-seventh degree of latitude was at that hour open to slavery. 'So far,' said he,
'as the doctrine of popular sovereignty and non-intervention is concerned, the
Colorado Bill and the Nevada Bill and the Dakota Bill are identically the same with
the Kansas-Nebraska Bill, and in its precise language.' The answer was at once a

Wigfall of Texas demanded that Douglas state what he would advise the President to do with regard to Fort Sumter, Douglas parried with the question whether the Senator from Texas felt bound by his oath to support the Constitution of the United States.[6] On April 14 Douglas called upon President Lincoln and pledged his aid for the preservation of the Union.[7] He then devoted himself to the task of rallying his own state to the support of the government. His influence was everywhere felt throughout the "Democracy" of the North; in Illinois it operated powerfully in "Egypt," the southern region, where John A. Logan, later a distinguished Union general, was at that time conducting a campaign of resistance to the government at Washington.[8] The strain of his public efforts brought on a complication of maladies; and on June 3 Douglas died at Chicago. Public buildings were draped; stores were closed; the people went into mourning. His example became the guiding tradition of those "war Democrats" who, though opposed to Republican policies, joined in support of the war measures of the Lincoln administration.

---

complete destruction of the argument of Breckinridge, and a severe indictment of the Republican party. Never before in the existence of the Federal Government had its territory been so open, by Congressional enactment and by judicial decision, to the slave-holder as on the day that Abraham Lincoln assumed the office of President of the United States." J. G. Blaine, *Twenty Years of Congress*, I, 289. The point of Blaine's reference to the bills for Colorado, Nevada, and Dakota was that Congress organized these territories without any prohibition of slavery (February 28 and March 2, 1861). *U. S. Stat. at Large*, XII, 172, 209, 239. This was in the last days of the Thirty-Sixth Congress when the Republicans and their allies had a slight majority in the lower house. See above, p. 169. For Douglas's remarks in the Senate, in which he referred to the Republican abandonment of the Chicago platform, see *Cong. Globe*, 36 Cong., 2 sess., 1391 (Mar. 2, 1861). See also *ibid.*, 1460, 1503–1505.

  [6] Stevens, *Douglas*, 627–628.

  [7] Nicolay and Hay, *Lincoln*, IV, 80; Allen Johnson, *Douglas*, 475–476.

  [8] A. C. Cole states that Congressman John A. Logan was "opposed to the coercion of the southern states," and adds: "a speech in which he compared the secessionists with our forefathers struggling for liberty, was widely circulated." *Era of the Civil War*, 260.

CHAPTER 9

The Plight of the Upper South

I

THE SECESSION of Virginia and the rest of the upper South followed as a result of the appeal to arms. In the Old Dominion those who were ready to rush into secession as a thing desirable in itself were both less numerous and less influential than in the lower states. The strength of unionism in Virginia was shown by the election of 1860, which resulted in a plurality for Bell, who received the electoral vote of the state, and in a clear majority of Bell and Douglas over Breckinridge. On November 15 Governor Letcher summoned the legislature in special session; on January 7 he addressed the body in a message which sharply criticized the attitude of South Carolina; on January 14 the law providing for a convention was passed. In choosing delegates, the people voted that the action of the convention should not be binding until referred to the people for ratification.

Assembling at Richmond on February 13 the convention of 152 members contained a majority of unionists—but one must remember, with the historian of Virginia secession, "that the term 'Union' carried a different meaning in Virginia from what it did in the North." Virginia opponents of secession desired to preserve the Union, but at the same time most of them were unwilling to continue in it unless the North made concessions. "There will not be one man in [the Convention]," predicted one member, "who is not for a final separation of the states, in double quick time—unless there is reason to hope for a perfectly full, final and unqualified surrender of the slavery question to those to whom it concerns [i.e., to the Southerners]." [1] On another point, too, the convention's mind was made up— that of "coercing" a state. It was evident that the legislature, the convention, and the people of Virginia were of the opinion that the general government ought not to use force against a commonwealth that was attempting to secede. Motivated by these contradictory desires, the convention, instead of passing an ordinance of secession, as was usual in the lower

[1] Henry T. Shanks, *The Secession Movement in Virginia, 1847–1861,* 155–156.

South, proceeded to a real study of the situation, explored the possibilities of compromise, watched the efforts making at Washington in the direction of peace—especially those of the Peace Convention called by Virginia herself—and gave indication of avoiding precipitate action.

Lincoln's inuagural produced mingled feelings in the state. On March 9, John Letcher wrote to a friend: "Lincoln's Inaugural created quite a sensation here. The disunionists were wild with joy, and declared that if the Convention did not pass an ordinance of secession at once the State would be disgraced. They are again sobering down, being . . . satisfied . . . that the Conservatives intend to think calmly . . . before they announce their conclusion. The tendency now is to a conference with the border slaveholding States, accompanying that request with a platform on which Virginia can safely stand." [2]

While disapproving Lincoln's policy, the state in general was minded to stay in the Union if possible; but if the South were to be "coerced," or if war should come, Virginia could not choose otherwise than to come to the aid of sister states. Strength of Union sentiment on the one side, and essential Southernism on the other, were the conflicting forces. Virginians felt resentment both against Lincoln for his April policy and against South Carolina for her part in precipitating a conflict which ultimately involved Virginia, forcing her into a war not of her own choosing. Something of this feeling was expressed by Jubal A. Early when he said on March 5: "I do not approve of the inaugural of Mr. Lincoln . . . ; but, sir, I ask . . . if it were not for the fact that six or seven states of this Confederacy have seceded from this Union, if the declarations of President Lincoln that he would execute the laws in all the states would not have been hailed throughout the country as a guarantee that he would perform his duty . . . ? I ask why is it that we are placed in this perilous condition? And if it is not solely from the action of these states that have seceded from the Union without having consulted our views? " [3]

When commissioners from several of the seceded states of the lower South visited Richmond to induce Virginia to secede, the convention resisted their impassioned appeals. The convention's committee on federal relations, instead of reporting in favor of secession, recommended various constitutional amendments and compromises and favored a convention of the border states to meet at Frankfort, Kentucky, in May. On April 4 a motion to draw up an ordinance of secession was voted down, 88 to 45; and on April 8 the convention made a final effort to avert secession by sending a committee to confer with Lincoln at Washington and obtain a statement of his policy with reference to the seceded states. By the time

[2] John Letcher to J. D. Davidson, Richmond, March 9, 1861. Davidson MSS., McCormick Library, Chicago.

[3] Richmond *Enquirer*, Mar. 7, 1861, quoted in Munford, *Virginia's Attitude toward Slavery and Secession*, 266.

this committee (Alexander H. H. Stuart, George W. Randolph, and William Ballard Preston) reached Washington on April 12, having been delayed by a storm, the die was cast, and Sumter was at that very hour under bombardment. Lincoln's answer to the committee (April 13) was merely the President's justification of the policy which to Virginia meant coercion. If, said the President, "an unprovoked assault has been made upon Fort Sumter, I shall hold myself at liberty to repossess, if I can, like places which had been seized before the government was devolved upon me. And in any event I shall to the extent of my ability repel force by force." [4]

With the delivery in Richmond of this unsatisfactory reply there came the news of the Sumter attack and of the President's call for troops. "It was not the assault upon Fort Sumter, however momentous in its potency," writes a Virginia historian, "which impelled Virginia, but the proclamation of President Lincoln which followed." [5] There are various evidences that the proclamation of insurrection with the call for troops produced more of a shock in Virginia than the Sumter attack. Alexander H. H. Stuart stated that he had inferred from his conversation with Lincoln on April 13 that the holding of the forts was the President's specific purpose, and that nothing like a general war was intended to result from the Sumter situation. He stated also, without accusing Lincoln of "want of candor," that he was so surprised by the appearance of the proclamation that he refused at first to believe it genuine.

Whatever may be said in justification of the proclamation, its effect upon Virginia must be understood. After April 15 it was no longer a question of war or peace; it was a question "which side" Virginia should take. Should her militia respond to Lincoln's call, or should the "invasion" of Virginia and of the South by Federal troops be resisted? The answer was given on April 17 when the Richmond convention, by a vote of 88 to 55, adopted the ordinance of secession.[6] The date set for the popular referendum on the ordinance was May 23. By that time war was on in good earnest; and the Virginia convention (April 24) had entered into a league with the Confederate States in which Virginia agreed to place her entire military forces at the service of the President of the Confederacy.[7] In the

---

[4] A. F. Robertson, *Alexander H. H. Stuart,* 186.

[5] Beverly B. Munford, *Virginia's Attitude toward Slavery and Secession,* 284.

[6] After this vote had decided the issue, the question was again put, some of the members changed their votes, and the final vote stood 103 to 46.

[7] The extent to which Virginia's military league with the Confederacy committed the state to the Southern cause in advance of the popular vote is indicated in a public letter of J. M. Mason dated May 16, 1861. Mason explained that Virginia was already out of the Union, but that if the people should reject the ordinance of secession at the polls, the state would have to "change sides" and fight for the Union. Since this would involve capturing and turning over to the United States thousands of soldiers from South Carolina, Alabama, and other Southern states who had

circumstances ratification of the ordinance was foredoomed, and secession was approved by a substantial vote. Meanwhile the unionist leaders of the northwestern counties had taken matters into their own hands in defiance of Richmond, and the train of events which ultimately led to the formation of West Virginia had been set in motion.[8]

2

Elsewhere in the upper South one finds much the same interplay of forces as in Virginia. In Arkansas there was a determined struggle; for the unionists of the state, vigorous and numerically strong, had to cope with a powerful secessionist element which was persistent in its efforts and which counted the governor of the state among its ranks. Breckinridge carried the state in 1860; and the secessionists were so far successful as to obtain the passage of a bill calling for the election of a state convention. Meanwhile military preparation was being pushed and mass meetings kept up a constant agitation. When the members of the convention were elected the popular majority against secession (tested by the vote for delegates according to their previous stand) was 5699 in a total of 43,228. The convention assembled at Little Rock on March 4. Its sessions were turbulent; "there was much eloquence of the fervid type to which the South had long been accustomed"; and "outside pressure recruiting for the secessionists was strong."[1]

As in Virginia, it was Lincoln's April policy that produced secession. During the days from Lincoln's inauguration to the firing at Sumter the unionists held sufficient control to defeat a resolution condemning Lincoln's inaugural address and also to prevent the passage of a secession ordinance. It was evident, however, that the state would oppose "coercion"; and the secessionists, far from accepting defeat, were watching events, ready to make the most of any opening, while the unionists, thinking in terms of delay and hoping for peaceful proposals to be developed by the projected border-state convention to be held at Frankfort, were potential secessionists in that they were unwilling to join the Lincoln government against the South if war should come. With affairs in this situation, a compromise was struck in the convention by the passage of a resolution to hold a popular referendum as between cooperation and secession.[2] The date

---

marched to the aid of Virginia, the military league, in case of the rejection of the ordinance, would have been made "a trap to inveigle our generous defenders into the hands of their enemies. Edward McPherson, *Pol. Hist. of the . . . Rebellion,* 7.

   [8] See below, pp. 236–242.

   [1] David Y. Thomas, *Arkansas in War and Reconstruction,* 62.

   [2] "Cooperation" meant that "the convention should co-operate with the border slave states to secure a permanent . . . adjustment of the difficulty." *Ibid.,* 70.

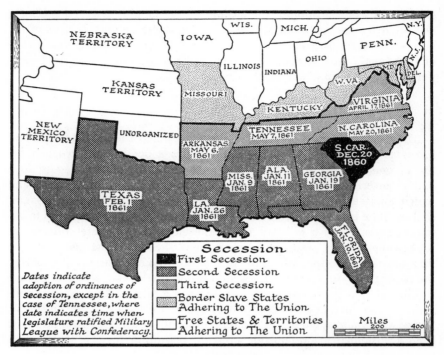

SECESSION

August 5 was set as the time for this referendum. Having done this, the Arkansas convention adjourned March 21, subject to call. It was only the slender hope that peace might be patched up between Lincoln and the lower South that held the state in the Union. Events at Sumter and the President's proclamation severed this hope; and when the call for militia reached Governor Rector he refused it as an insult. Various leaders in Arkansas now moved at once to support the Confederacy; and in the spirit of accepting the coercion of events, the reassembled convention on May 6 passed (65 to 5) the ordinance of secession which was signed the next day. An amendment to submit the question of secession to the people was voted down; and the convention "finished . . . its work by repealing the ordinance submitting the question of 'co-operation' or 'secession' to popular vote." [3]

In Tennessee the preponderant unionist purposes of the people were frustrated in part by events and in part by what has been called the "usurpation" of the legislature. In casting its electoral vote of 1860 for its own

[3] *Ibid.*, 81, 82.

leader, John Bell, Tennessee was animated by opposition to "both the extreme parties"; and, as explained by Dr. Fertig, the people were "disgusted and indignant" when the secession movement was launched by South Carolina. He adds, however: "In any conflict for what was regarded as Southern rights Tennessee was sure to go with the Gulf states, for she was bound to them by inseparable social and economic bonds." [4] This last statement, rather than emphasis upon unionism, is the key to the whole matter, not only as to Tennessee but as to the whole upper South.

The action of the Tennessee legislature in its special session of January, 1861, while opening the way for possible secession, was chiefly in favor of restoration. In a long message (January 7) Governor Isham G. Harris dwelt upon the slavery question, denounced the "threatened and actual aggressions [of the North] upon the . . . rights of the Southern citizen," and recommended the calling of a convention to determine what action Tennessee should take.[5] On January 19 the legislature in extra session called a convention, providing that the people should vote for delegates and should also vote on the question of a convention or no convention. Two steps, however, were taken by the same legislature looking toward peace. On January 16 it resolved to urge the President of the United States and each of the Southern states "that the *statu quo* [sic] . . . concerning the forts . . . be strictly maintained"; and on January 22 it provided that a convention of delegates from all the slaveholding states be held at Nashville on February 4 "to . . . define a basis upon which . . . the Federal Union and the Constitutional rights of the slave States may be . . . preserved," accompanying this resolution with an elaborate plan of adjustment.[6] But the people were more Union-minded than the legislature. The proposition to call a convention to consider secession was rejected by popular vote (69,675 to 57,798); while on the issue of secession or no secession the vote (as judged by delegates' commitments) was even more decisive—24,749 for, and 91,803 against.

Thus at the time of the Sumter outbreak Tennessee had no convention in session; furthermore the idea of holding such a convention had been decisively rejected by the voters. Under these circumstances, when Lincoln's call for militia came, the governor and legislature took matters into their own hands. Harris answered the militia call haughtily: ". . . in such an unholy crusade no gallant son of Tennessee will ever draw his sword." [7] On April 25 he addressed a new special session of the legislature, urging union with the Confederate States. On May 6 the assembly, deliberating

[4] J. W. Fertig, *The Secession and Reconstruction of Tennessee*, 15, 22, 25 ff.
[5] *Public Acts of . . . Tenn.* (extra sess., Jan., 1861), 1–13.
[6] *Ibid.*, 45, 49 ff.
[7] James Welch Patton, *Unionism and Reconstruction in Tennessee*, 14.

behind closed doors, directed that an election be held on June 8 to ratify or reject a declaration of independence and an ordinance dissolving the union between Tennessee and the United States. On May 1, however, Governor Harris had appointed commissioners who signed a military league with the Confederate States which provided that, in the interval before Tennessee should formally join the Confederate States, the state "shall be under the . . . direction of the President of the Confederate States, upon the same basis as if said state were now . . . a member of said Confederacy. . . ." This league was ratified by the legislature on May 7. Just before this, on May 6, the legislature authorized the governor to raise a force of 55,000 men, to be under the governor's control, bonds to be issued for the purpose.

. . . When the election day came [declares Dr. Fertig] the people went to the polls . . . conscious of the fact that they were no longer free to vote their sentiments. They saw that the Governor and the Legislature with the treasury in their hands . . . and a formidable army in their employ, had joined a conspiracy to overthrow the government, and whatever might be the wish of the people, the result would not be changed by their votes. Nothing that they could do would free them from the military government which had imposed itself upon them. . . . The secret session of the Legislature and the Military League had bound the state and had turned it over to the control of the Confederate army which immediately took possession. . . .[8]

The essential fact was that the people of Tennessee were not so much tricked by their legislature and governor as they were caught in an inescapable dilemma—the dilemma of the upper South—which gave them no chance to act as they wished (i.e., to proceed with measures for a peaceable restoration of the Union), but forced an immediate choice between two hateful alternatives. The vote on June 8 was more than two-to-one in favor of separation (104,913 to 47,238). Most of the unionist sentiment was in the eastern counties, where opposition to secession was so strong that a movement comparable to that of western Virginia seemed to be in the making. This movement, however, was never completed, partly because of Confederate forces which were soon in occupation. As will appear later, the secessionist government of Tennessee was short-lived; for with the fall of Fort Donelson in February, 1862, the capital at Nashville passed under the control of Governor Andrew Johnson, appointed military governor by Lincoln.

3

Nowhere was the contrast between upper and lower South better revealed than in the difference between the two Carolinas. It is significant that South Carolina was the first to pass an ordinance of secession, North

[8] Fertig, 26–27.

Carolina the last.[1] In North Carolina people and legislature repudiated secession in 1851; and this attitude continued to hold the state firmly in the Union until the actual outbreak of war. At Charleston in 1860 the North Carolina delegation favored cooperation with the Northern Democracy and, when the break came, refused to join the cotton states in bolting the convention. The campaign of 1860, while producing confusion in Democratic ranks, gave new life to the Whig party in its appeal to the Constitution and the Union; so that, while Breckinridge carried the state, his majority over Bell and Douglas was only 848.

North Carolina voters did not consider Lincoln's election a sufficient cause for secession. When the legislature, at the prodding of Governor John W. Ellis, submitted to the people a proposition for calling a convention to consider secession, it was defeated, on February 28, by a vote of 47,323 to 46,672. Unionist sentiment, however, gradually weakened as prospects for a peaceful settlement of the crisis waned. "I am a union man," wrote one of Zebulon B. Vance's correspondents, "but when they [i.e., the Lincoln administration] send men south it will change my notions. I can do nothing against my own people." Secessionist newspapers kept up their agitation, urging North Carolinians to *"dissolve all and every connection now and forever* from the vile, rotten, infidelic, puritanic, negro-worshipping, negro-stealing, negro-equality and Yankee-Union."

"The attack on Fort Sumter, Lincoln's call for troops, and the secession of Virginia," writes the historian of North Carolina secession, "almost instantly destroyed virtually all Union sentiment in North Carolina." Indignantly Governor Ellis replied to Lincoln's requisition of the militia: "I can be no party to this wicked violation of the laws of the country and to this war upon the liberties of a free people. You can get no troops from North Carolina." [2] Promptly he called the legislature in extra session to summon a convention. When the ordinance of secession was put to a vote in the convention, which had full power from the people for the purpose, it was passed (May 20) without a dissenting vote.

---

[1] The following are the dates of the passing of secession ordinances, except in the case of Tennessee, where the date indicates the time when the legislature ratified the military league with the Confederate States: S. C., Dec. 20; Miss., Jan. 9; Fla., Jan. 10; Ala., Jan. 11; Ga., Jan. 19; La., Jan. 26; Tex., Feb. 1.; Va., Apr. 17; Ark., May 6; Tenn., May 7; N. C., May 20. If popular votes are used as the key dates of secession, which is usually not the case, other dates must be given for several of the states, as follows: Tex., Feb. 23; Va., May 23; Tenn., June 8. Perhaps the best illustration of the fact that seceding states did not regard the popular vote as setting the effective date of secession is the case of Virginia, in which the league with the Confederacy was concluded April 24, a month in advance of the referendum. If, however, the popular vote be taken as marking the date, then Tennessee, not North Carolina, was the last state, there being no referendum in North Carolina.

[2] Joseph Carlyle Sitterson, *The Secession Movement in North Carolina,* 196–197, 238–240.

The correspondence of Jonathan Worth, a high-minded opponent of secession who declined to be a candidate for membership in the convention, reveals the anguished feelings of North Carolina unionists. Writing to a friend on the day the secession ordinance was passed, he said:

> I still firmly believe in the wisdom . . . of . . . the early promoters of our government and that no other *divided* government can ever be built up so good as the *United* one we are pulling down—and hence I abhor the Northern Abolitionist and the Southern Secessionist, both co-operating with different objects, to break up the Union, but the whole nation has become mad. The voice of reason is silenced. Furious passion and thirst for blood consume the air. . . . Nobody is allowed to retain and assert his reason. . . . The very women and children are for war. Every body must take sides with one or the other of these opposing factions or fall a victim to the mob. . . . I think the annals of the world furnish no instance of so groundless a war—but . . . let us fight like men for our own firesides.[3]

By different paths lower and upper South had thus arrived at the same goal. That the lower South had the advantage in the actual influencing of events is obvious: lack of initiative in the upper South is evident in the whole movement. Some of the South's best thinkers, in those critical months when war and peace hung in the balance, were thus denied the dominant rôle which their characters might well have justified. Whatever the differences of viewpoint in the upper South, there would seem to have been a prevailing pattern of unionist sentiment against a background of Southernism. What the upper South prayed for was very much like the consummation of Buchanan's policy: peace, conciliation, and respect for Southern rights within the Union. Resentment was therefore felt both against the secessionist agitator and the trouble-making abolitionist. Instead of a daring attitude of taking bold measures, this was a waiting attitude, motivated by the hope that time would cure the existing evils if only moderation could prevail alike in Washington and in the far South. In this phase the community of sentiment between the upper South and the border states is significant; but while the procedure that might have made this sentiment the dominant factor—e.g., a national convention or the border-state convention planned for Frankfort—was abortive, the procedure in the lower South (separate state secession and Confederate organization) was quick, convincing, and spectacular.

Throughout the whole situation one sees the unfortunate effect of Lincoln's April policy. Feeling that Lincoln should have given conciliation a better trial, that he should above all have avoided a crisis at Sumter, conservative Southerners were deeply outraged at what they deemed both a stroke of bad policy and a breaking of administration promises. As for his call for troops, it served in one flash to alienate that whole mass of Union

[3] J. G. de R. Hamilton, ed., *Correspondence of Jonathan Worth*, I, 150–151.

sentiment which, while not pro-Lincoln, was nevertheless antisecession-ist and constituted Lincoln's best chance of saving the Union without war. The attitude of Virginia and her neighbors, while conciliatory, had not been neutral; and when efforts toward peace failed, these states responded with a promptness that left no doubt of their Southernism, while in the days of conflict their ardor was manifest in the more than proportionate contribution of their war effort.

CHAPTER 10

The Campaigns: Earlier Phases

I

FOUR GHASTLY YEARS of war ensued. It was a war of confused issues and infinite complexity. So complicated was the struggle that the mind staggers under the effort to comprehend it and see it whole. Necessarily the chapters devoted to the military story must be detached from those which treat the political, diplomatic, financial, social, and economic phases. These conditioning factors, however, are separable only in abstract thought: in reality the various threads were interwoven. Problems of strategy did not exist in a vacuum.

When the alignment of states had become so stabilized that one could speak of a Northern and a Southern nation, the superior strength of the North became strikingly evident. The North had twenty-three states against eleven at the South.[1] Totaling the state populations and omitting Missouri and Kentucky, which were divided between North and South, one finds that the Union, with 20,700,000 people, confronted the Confederacy with 9,105,000. An important correction must at once be noted, however, for of the approximately nine million human beings in the South 3,654,000 were Negroes, mostly slaves. Though the place of these slaves in war economy was important, they were not, despite efforts in that direction late in the war, used as soldiers in the Southern armies. To estimate the military strength of the South these slaves should be subtracted; but there should also be a roughly proportionate subtraction of men necessary for the maintenance of agriculture, industry, and commerce in the North.

In economic strength as in manpower the Union was vastly superior to the Confederacy. In round numbers the North in 1860 had 110,000 manufacturing establishments, with 1,300,000 industrial workers; the South, 18,000 manufacturing establishments, with 110,000 workers. The value of the manufactures produced annually in the state of New

[1] In addition to the eleven states of the upper and lower South whose secession has been treated above, Kentucky and Missouri had members in the Congress at Richmond and were claimed by the Confederacy. See below, chap. 12.

York alone was more than four times as great as that of the entire Confederacy. The Southern states built only 4 per cent of all the locomotives produced in the United States in 1860 and manufactured only 3 per cent of the firearms. Of the 31,256 miles of railroads in the United States in 1861, the South contained only 9,283, or less than 30 per cent.[2] It was not merely that the North had greater financial resources; even Southern banking and foreign exchange had been centered in New York. The North had the existing government with its official machinery and with whatever of prestige this may have carried at home and abroad, while a national government had to be created by the Confederates.

Yet to contemporaries the war did not always appear so unequal as this superficial comparison would suggest. The Confederate general Beauregard said:

> No people ever warred for independence with more relative advantages than the Confederates; and if, as a military question, they must have failed, then no country must aim at freedom by means of war. . . . The South, with its great material resources, its defensive means of mountains, rivers, railroads, and telegraph, with the immense advantage of the interior lines of war, would be open to discredit as a people if its failure could not be explained otherwise than by mere material contrast.[3]

The nature of the war was such that the South needed fewer men: time and again Southern armies were able to stand off superior numbers. McClellan would necessarily require more men to assault and take Richmond than Lee would require to hold it. All comment on disparity of numbers between the sections, as T. L. Livermore has pointed out, must be read in the light of the defensive position of the South. Not only did the North have to spend heavily in battle losses; its task of enlarging the area of invasion and holding invaded territory "required many more men than mere battles upon equal terms would have required."[4]

The South had the advantage of fighting for independence—for something bold, positive, thrilling—while the North was too apt to appear in the rôle of subjugator. This gave the South, at least until emancipation, a distinct moral advantage. Confederate sentiment ran high in New York and many other Northern centers, while Union sentiment in the South, though by no means nonexistent, was stultified and inarticulate. The "best" of Washington "society" was Southern, and its sympathy with the Confederate cause was but too apparent. The difference between Northern and Southern morale was painfully evident from London and was keenly felt by young Henry Adams, who acted as secretary to his father, United States minister to England. Adams wrote of the despondency and apathy

[2] Nevins, *The War for the Union*, I, 424–426.
[3] *Battles and Leaders*, I, 222.
[4] T. L. Livermore, *Numbers and Losses in the Civil War*, 3.

of Northerners in England as contrasted with the vigor and exuberance of Southerners, inspired with ideals of liberty and independence.[5]

The South was more infused with the martial spirit than the North. Its young men had given more attention to military training and were handier with horse and rifle. Their generals were among the finest products of West Point. When to these factors it is added that many Federal forts and arsenals fell into their hands, that they fought with high courage on interior lines in their own country, and that much was expected from the international situation, it will be seen that they were not unreasonable in their hope of winning the war, if it should not be too long drawn out.[6] The unequal weight of resources against them was not so great as in the case of the American colonies in their fight against mighty England, nor of various other peoples who have achieved independence against heavy odds.

According to predictions the war which started at Sumter in mid-April was to be short. Lincoln's call for militia seemed to imply that the "insurrection" would be "suppressed" in three months; while in the South there were confident expectations of capturing Washington and driving out the "black Republicans" by early summer. Both sides were unprepared for a serious war of long duration. Neither side had a general staff or its equivalent, and the excited war preparations in the early months were more characterized by feverish bustle and patriotic flourish than by sound coordinated effort. The scenes that were enacted as the states of the North proceeded to respond to Lincoln's summons offered many a commentary upon the cross purposes, circumlocutions, and makeshifts of an unmilitary democracy struggling to improvise a war machine for an emergency. While demonstrating the courage of common men facing death at the call of their government, they illustrated also the blundering incompetence of politicians and the scheming ambition of greedy humanity scrambling for gain and self-promotion.

Popular response was genuine and enthusiastic as the seething crowds vented their pent-up feelings in that emotional release which followed as the psychological result of months of tense anxiety. Though the word was unfamiliar to the vocabulary of the time, public opinion was soon "mobilized." Mass meetings were everywhere held to listen to orators, great and small, who played upon popular emotion and prejudice. With reminiscence of the heroic days of the now idealized Revolution, men pledged their lives, their fortunes, and their sacred honor. There were, it is true, some dissenters. To the more earnest the thought of "civil war in our land"

[5] James Truslow Adams, *The Adams Family,* 274.
[6] Beauregard attributed the defeat of the South to the narrow military policy of the Confederate government, and the failure to attempt decisive strokes to be followed up to the end. *Battles and Leaders,* I, 222. For modern opinions on the subject, see David Donald, ed., *Why the North Won the Civil War.*

descended like a nightmare. "The shame, the folly, the outrage, seemed too great to believe," said General Jacob D. Cox of Ohio, "and we half hoped to wake from it as from a dream." [7] But "discordant notes" and thoughtful forebodings were lost in the general clamor. Volunteering, drilling, parading, forming their camps of instruction, the military men seized at once the center of the stage, while nonfighters rushed about in a hectic impulse to "do something." Anyone who wished could advertise his purpose to "raise a company," or perchance a regiment, and invite "all willing to join to come on a certain morning to some saloon, hotel or public hall." [8] In this unsystematic manner recruitment became largely a personal thing, and an amazing variety of military organizations sprang up. The "Excelsior Brigade," the "Buena Vista Guards," the "New York Fire Zouaves" (led by the dashing Ellsworth), the "Polish Legion," the "St. Patrick Brigade," the "Irish Volunteers," the "Steuben Volunteers," and the "Garibaldi Guards" were a few of these local units. Examples in Illinois were the "Quincy City Guards," "Plainfield Light Artillery," "Chicago Light Dragoons," "Grundy Tigers," "Yates Rangers," "Lincoln Guards," "Springfield Zouaves," "Chicago Zouaves," and "Pekin Grays." Naturally each of these units expected to be treated with dignity and to preserve its organization intact. [9]

The militia, though subject to Federal call and referred to in national laws, was in normal times a state institution so far as it had any existence at all; and in most of the states it was a nebulous affair with no effective organization. The regular army of the United States, though well trained and efficient, had a strength of only 13,000 officers and men in March, 1861; [10] and the haphazard method of raising the emergency force took no heed of the importance of using the regular army as a nucleus. Relying on the regular army as his mainstay in serious operations, General Scott refused the requests of young regular army officers who desired leaves of absence so that they could direct the organization of the state militia and volunteer units. [11]

[7] *Battles and Leaders,* I, 87.

[8] J. B. McMaster, *History of the People of the United States during Lincoln's Administration,* 39.

[9] The Illinois names are taken from the state archives at Springfield, the others from McMaster, *loc. cit.*

[10] In December, 1860, the United States army consisted of 16,367 officers and men; but on March 4, 1861, after some of the Southerners had withdrawn but before the upper South had seceded, the number stood at 13,024. *Battles and Leaders,* I, 7 n.; *Memoirs of Gen. W. T. Sherman,* II, 383. The United States army permitted its officers to resign with honorable discharges and take service with the Confederacy; this was a large factor in the military effectiveness of the South. The number of officers of the rank of brigadier general or higher who were furnished to the Confederacy from the army of the United States was 182. Upton, *Mil. Pol. of the U.S.,* 241.

[11] "The young regulars who asked leave to accept commissions in State regi-

The border and upper South would become the chief theaters of war. At the outset the war would be felt in Missouri; Kentucky and Tennessee would see bitter fighting in the West; Virginia, facing Washington and containing the capital of the Confederacy, would bear the brunt of the heavy campaigns in the East. Some of the earliest campaigning would be in that portion of the Old Dominion which bordered Ohio and Pennsylvania and became West Virginia. Thus the Southern sections which manifested the least enthusiasm for secession were destined to witness the severest fighting, though later in the struggle the devastating scourge was carried deep into the lower South. The North would seek to capture and hold Missouri, Kentucky, and Tennessee; contend for mastery of the Mississippi River, detaching the Southwest from the main portion of the Confederacy; keep a watchful eye for the protection of Washington; direct its most determined campaigns toward Richmond; blockade Southern coasts and push its gunboats up the inland rivers; and ultimately, by its "anaconda policy" and its campaign of "attrition" under Grant, would make crushing use of superior man power. On the principle that Providence favors the heaviest battalions, each side would seek, by scouting, rapid movement, and surprise maneuver, to confront its opponent at decisive points with superior numbers. Though the capture or destruction of armies would be the strategic objective, few battles were to be decisive in this sense; both Southern and Northern commanders usually found their troops too exhausted or were detained by other considerations from following up their victories. Thus after a battle had been won the defeated enemy would reorganize, shift his position, and re-form his lines, so that the whole business was to be done over again. Discouragement back home would naturally result as the seemingly senseless and purposeless character of an apparently interminable war was borne in upon the minds of the people.

Each side would seek to harass the other, raiding its territory, destroying its military stores, smashing its bridges, wrecking its railroads, cutting off its communications. Aside from such an exceptional case as that of Sherman in Georgia and the Carolinas, each army, when conducting major

---

ments were . . . refused, and were ordered to their own subaltern positions and posts. There can be no doubt that the true policy would have been to encourage the whole of this younger class to enter at once the volunteer service. They would have been field-officers in the new regiments, and would have impressed discipline and system upon the organization from the beginning. The Confederates really profited by having no regular army. They gave to the officers who left our service, it is true, commissions in their so-called 'provisional' army, to encourage them to expect permanent military positions if the war should end in the independence of the South; but this was only a nominal organization, and their real army was made up (as ours turned out practically to be) from the regiments of State volunteers. Less than a year afterward we changed our policy, but it was then too late to induce many of the regular officers to take regimental positions in the volunteer troops." General Jacob D. Cox in *Battles and Leaders*, I, 94.

military operations as distinguished from mere raids, would require a base, with telegraph, roads, railroads, and depots unbroken in its rear. The war would be waged over widely scattered areas. Sieges would be few; and trench warfare, while not unknown, would be exceptional. Instead of continuous, stable, fortified battle fronts, backed by carefully prepared secondary or reserve trenches, the usual situation would be that of open warfare, with frequent changes of base. Each distinct battle would ordinarily occupy no more than one or two days; but the number of battles would run into the hundreds, and there would be sniping, bushwhacking, guerilla fighting, and irregular neighborhood battles unrecorded by military historians. Cavalry, inferior in vital effectiveness to infantry and artillery, would usually play its rôle in scouting and raiding rather than in head-on charges. The use of balloons, reliance upon the telegraph, wire entanglements, and experimentation with submarines would make the war seem at the time very "modern"; to a later generation accustomed to airplanes, tanks, and rockets, it would seem antediluvian. High command would be a confused and halting thing on both sides; little military coordination would exist; public opinion would tyrannically interfere; meddling politicians and congressmen would take their fatal toll.

2

In the early weeks there was a panicky alarm in the North as to the safety of Washington. Unprotected as it was, with inadequate fortifications, with a sketchy militia, and with Confederate flags flying across the Potomac, the capital city was sadly exposed; and some authorities have declared that Beauregard missed a fine chance in not transferring his army rapidly northward from South Carolina after Sumter and seizing Washington before the Union troops had arrived and defensive outposts had been prepared, thus at small cost producing a major disaster for the North.[1] After the first panic had passed and especially after the arrival of the earliest military contingents—notably the Seventh New York Regiment and the Sixth Massachusetts—the President, government officials, and people breathed easier. An untoward event, however, occurred at Baltimore, where the Sixth Massachusetts on April 19 was mobbed as it passed through the city. In street fighting between the troops and the angry rioters, stones flew, men in uniform fired at will without orders, muskets were snatched from soldiers and turned against them, and, by the time the regiment had en-

[1] A hastily devised militia had been organized to defend the capital; but Beauregard could probably have descended upon Washington with 15,000 or 20,000 men at a time when General Scott considered that he could do no better than ward off a force of 10,000. Rhodes, *Hist. of the U. S.*, III, 375. Beauregard stated that he proposed just such a drive against Washington, but that Davis refused support. *Battles and Leaders*, I, 221–222.

trained, four of their number and probably nine or more of the citizens had been killed, many others wounded.[2] Arriving in Washington the soldiers were quartered in the capitol building; and the state of Maryland offered no further serious resistance to the passage of Federal troops.

Western Virginia, strong in its Unionist sentiment and exposed to easy Federal attack, now witnessed a campaign which, despite the triviality of the operations, produced a thrill of exultation in the North and brought to the fore a conquering hero of whom much was expected. Born in Philadelphia, educated at the University of Pennsylvania, and trained at West Point, George Brinton McClellan had served with distinction in the Mexican War, had engaged in far western explorations, and had acted as military observer in the Crimean War. Retiring to civil life, he had become a high officer of the Illinois Central Railroad and later president of the Ohio and Mississippi Railroad with headquarters at Cincinnati. At the opening of the war he was given the rank of major general and was put in command of the "military department of the Ohio."

A small Virginia force had seized Harpers Ferry with its valuable machinery and Federal arsenal. It was here that T. J. ("Stonewall") Jackson, temporarily in command at Harpers Ferry, saw his first service in the Civil War. The important Baltimore and Ohio Railroad, connecting Washington with the West, was temporarily cut, and Jackson managed to capture some much needed rolling stock for the South. He was then superseded by Joseph E. Johnston, who withdrew from Harpers Ferry to Winchester as a more tenable position; and Harpers Ferry was reoccupied by a Federal force under General Robert Patterson.

With about 20,000 men McClellan entered western Virginia in late June; and his campaign occupied a month. As compared with later movements it was a trivial episode, its chief features being minor encounters at Philippi and Rich Mountain, in neither of which did McClellan himself participate. Among other elements in the art of war, however, McClellan had learned how to advertise his exploits; and the Napoleonic flourish of the following address, coming when the nation was hungry for a winning general, had much to do (together with newspaper advertising) in establishing his reputation:

Soldiers of the Army of the West!

I am more than satisfied with you.

You have annihilated two armies, commanded by educated and experienced soldiers, intrenched in mountain fastnesses fortified at their leisure. You have taken five guns, twelve colors, fifteen hundred stand of arms, one thousand prisoners, including more than forty officers—one of the two commanders of

[2] The number of casualties has been variously reported and seems never to have been precisely ascertained. Nicolay and Hay, *Lincoln*, IV, 118; Rhodes, *Hist. of the U. S.*, III, 362; Moore, *Rebell. Rec.* (Doc.). I, 133–134.

the rebels is a prisoner, the other lost his life on the field of battle. You have killed more than two hundred and fifty of the enemy, who has lost all his baggage and camp equipage. All this has been accomplished with the loss of twenty brave men killed and sixty wounded on your part.

You have proved that Union men, fighting for the preservation of our Government, are more than a match for our misguided and erring brethren; more than this, you have shown mercy to the vanquished. You have made long and arduous marches, often with insufficient food, frequently exposed to the inclemency of the weather. I have not hesitated to demand this of you, feeling that I could rely on your endurance, patriotism, and courage. . . .

I am proud to say that you have gained the highest reward that American troops can receive—the thanks of Congress and the applause of your fellow-citizens.

Geo. B. McClellan,
Major-General, U. S. Army, Commanding.[3]

3

By mid-summer of 1861 the border states were, in general, saved for the Union. With the encouragement of Federal troops a Unionist government for Virginia was set up at Wheeling. Maryland, whose control was vital to the United States, was definitely stabilized as a Union state; for though the Confederates were to struggle for its "liberation," they were destined never to achieve that objective. In Kentucky and Missouri, Union sentiment contended with Confederate feeling on somewhat better than equal terms. The governors of both these states (Beriah Magoffin in Kentucky and Claiborne F. Jackson in Missouri) were active secessionists, and both replied with indignant refusals to Lincoln's call for militia; but they failed to swing their commonwealths into the Confederacy. The policy of "neutrality" was maintained in Kentucky long enough to prevent the passage of a secession ordinance; while in Missouri military action under such leaders as Francis P. Blair, Jr., and Nathaniel Lyon gave initial success to the Unionist movement. The Confederate camp near St. Louis was broken up and the Jackson government was turned out of the state capital and subjected to defeats which broke its prestige and left it but a weak contender for governmental control in the state. Such being the border situation generally in 1861,[1] the Virginia battle front, involving the protection of Richmond on the one side and of Washington on the other, became the most important area of war, and it remained so throughout the conflict.

In July, 1861, the Union general McDowell guarded the capital from a position near Centreville, about twenty miles southwest of Washington; while the main Confederate army under Beauregard was stationed near by

---

[3] *Offic. Rec.*, 1 ser., II, 236.

[1] For a discussion of developments in the border region see below, chap. 12.

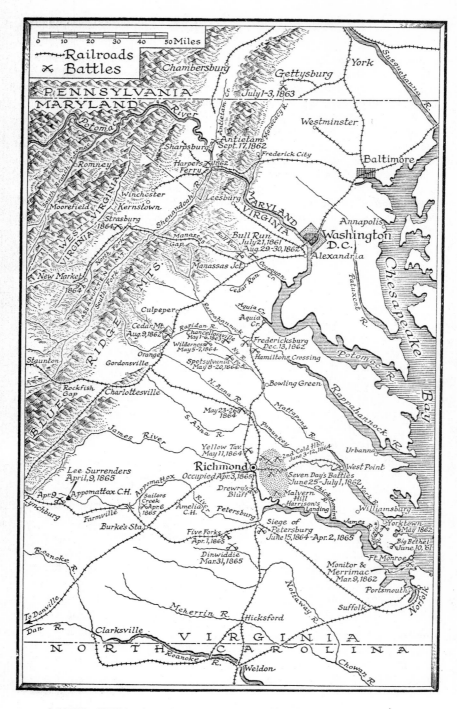

Railroads
× Battles

0 10 20 30 40 50 Miles

PENNSYLVANIA
MARYLAND

Chambersburg

Gettysburg
July 1-3, 1863

York

Susquehanna R.

Westminster

Potomac River

Baltimore

Sharpsburg

Antietam
Sept. 17, 1862

Monocacy R.

Antietam Cr.

Frederick City

Romney

Harpers
Ferry
1862

South Branch

Winchester

Leesburg

MARYLAND
VIRGINIA

Annapolis

Washington
D.C.

Moorefield
Kernstown

Shenandoah

Alexandria

WEST VIRGINIA

Strasburg
1864

Manassas
Gap

Bull Run
July 21, 1861
Aug. 29-30, 1862

Bull Run

Chesapeake

New Market
1864

North Fork

South Fork

MASSANUTTEN MTS.

Manassas Jct.

Occoquan Cr.

Cedar Run

Aquia Cr.
Aquia
Cr.

Patuxent R.

Culpeper

Rappahannock

Bay

Staunton

Cedar Mt.
Aug. 9, 1862

Rapidan R.

Chancellorsville
May 1-4, 1863

Fredericksburg
Dec. 13, 1862

Potomac R.

Orange

Wilderness
May 5-7, 1864

Hamiltons Crossing

Gordonsville

Spotsylvania
May 8-20, 1864

Rockfish
Gap

Charlottesville

N. Anna R.

Bowling Green

Rappahannock R.

BLUE RIDGE MTS.

James River

May 23-26
1864

S. Anna R.

Mattapony R.

Pamunkey

Yellow Tav.
May 11, 1864

2nd Cold H'br.
June 3-12, 1864

Urbanna

Lee Surrenders
April 9, 1865

Richmond
Occupied Apr. 3, 1865

West Point

Apr. 9

Appomattox C.H.

Appomattox River

Seven Day's Battles
June 25-July 1, 1862

York R.

Lynchburg

Sailors
Creek
Apr. 6
1865

Drewry's
Bluff

Malvern
Hill

Chickahominy

Williamsburg

Farmville

Amelia
C.H.

Petersburg

Harrison's
Landing

Yorktown
May 1862

Burke's Sta.

Five Forks
Apr. 1, 1865

Siege of
Petersburg
June 15, 1864-Apr. 2, 1865

James R.

Big Bethel
June 10, 61

Roanoke R.

Dinwiddie
Mar. 31, 1865

Ft. Monroe

Monitor &
Merrimac
Mar. 9, 1862

Portsmouth

To Danville

Meherrin R.

Nottaway R.

Suffolk

Norfolk

Dan R.

Clarksville

Hicksford

VIRGINIA

NORTH   CAROLINA

Roanoke R.

Weldon

Chowan R.

MAIN AREA OF EASTERN CAMPAIGNS, 1861–1865

at Manassas. Since at this point the Orange and Alexandria Railroad joined a line from the Shenandoah Valley, Beauregard's force, besides threatening Washington, was occupying a junction point which was vital for the protection of Richmond. Under pressure from popular clamor and newspaper agitation, McDowell planned a forward movement; and authorities agree that his plans were well laid. Though he had, for the most part, merely an aggregation of civilians in uniform, he had a few regulars, and his opponents' forces were as raw as his own. McDowell's campaign was based on the understanding that the Confederate force under Joseph E. Johnston, then at Winchester, was to be prevented from joining Beauregard. This was the task of General Patterson, who was expected to engage Johnston and keep him occupied. Even if defeated in such an engagement, he would have strengthened McDowell by preventing the reinforcement of Beauregard. Patterson's part in the campaign was not performed, however, and Johnston was allowed to slip away. His main force joined Beauregard on July 20.

Next day the attack was made by McDowell; and at first the Union forces dislodged the Confederates. Up to mid-afternoon the Federals had, in general, the better of the fight, having fought exceedingly well for raw troops. For a time Richmond was shaken by rumor of a Confederate *débâcle*. The Southerners, however, had several advantages. Their task was more that of defense and less of making long advances under fire than that of the Federals; and their cause was furthered by the arrival of reinforcements when most needed, and by short, quick assaults in which the Yankees were given to know the fury of the "rebel yell." In these operations the commands of Bee and Bartow, Kirby Smith, and T. J. Jackson particularly distinguished themselves. It was here that Jackson won his sobriquet "Stonewall." The conduct of this one commander did much to prevent a Confederate rout, while Johnston's reinforcements contributed the added factor needed for victory. It took desperate fighting to drive the Unionists from their position on Henry Hill; this having been done, McDowell was forced to retreat in the direction of Washington.

The retreat was at first orderly, and at Centreville the Federals blocked such limited pursuit as the Confederates attempted; but when the soldiers were fired upon in the road, becoming meanwhile entangled in a mass of camp followers, congressmen, and spectators, control was lost and the army disintegrated into a mob which rushed pell-mell into Washington.

There was never anything like it [wrote a spectator-congressman] for causeless, sheer, absolute, absurd cowardice, or rather panic, on this miserable earth before. Off they went, one and all; off down the highway, over across fields, towards the woods, anywhere, everywhere, to escape. Well, the further they ran the more frightened they grew, and although we moved on as rapidly as we could, the fugitives passed us by scores. To enable them better to run, they threw away their blankets, knapsacks, canteens, and finally muskets, cartridge-boxes, and everything else. We called to them, tried to tell them there was no danger, called them to stop, implored them to stand. We called them cowards, denounced them in the most offensive terms, put out our heavy revolvers, and threatened to shoot them, but all in vain; a cruel, crazy, mad, hopeless panic possessed them, and communicated to everybody about in front and rear. The heat was awful, although now about six; the men were exhausted—their mouths gaped, their lips cracked and blackened with the powder of the cartridges they had bitten off in the battle, their eyes starting in frenzy; no mortal ever saw such a mass of ghastly wretches.[2]

Though Bull Run seemed a smashing defeat for the Federals, yet, like most battles of the war, it was indecisive, producing no serious military disadvantage for the North nor gain, except in terms of pride and exultation, for the South. Indeed, since the grim realities of the battle served to stimulate war preparation in the North while causing relaxation in the South, the balance of benefit probably belonged to the Union side. The spirit in which the North received the humiliating news of the battle was typified by a memorandum in which President Lincoln outlined the "military policy suggested by the Bull Run defeat." This memorandum called for tightening the blockade, drilling the new volunteers, holding Baltimore with a "gentle but firm" hand, strengthening Patterson or Banks, reorganizing the forces lately engaged at Manassas, keeping the lines open from Washington to Manassas and from Harpers Ferry to Strasburg, and organizing a forward movement in the West which would shake the Confederate hold upon Tennessee.

Though McDowell had in fact served his country well, he was so discredited by Bull Run that a new commander was demanded. McClellan was promptly elevated to McDowell's command, and with the retirement of General Scott on November 1, 1861, he became general-in-chief of the army of the United States. At this time the matter of greatest concern to the Union government was the exposed and defenseless condition of Washington. On July 26, 1861, Edwin M. Stanton, who was convinced that the national "disgrace" was due to the "imbecility" of the Lincoln administration, wrote as follows: "The capture of Washington seems now to be inevitable; during the whole of Monday and Tuesday [July 22 and 23] it might have been taken without any resistance." McClellan found a few detached works and hasty intrenchments, but "in no sense . . . any general defensive line." Positions from which the enemy could have commanded the city of Washington were open for their occupation; and the city was "full of drunken men in uniform," [3] with McDowell's army so demoralized that its officers and men were leaving their camps at will. The

---

[2] Statement of A. G. Riddle, member of Congress from Ohio. Quoted by S. S. Cox in *Three Decades of Federal Legislation,* 158.
[3] *McClellan's Own Story,* 67–68.

two great tasks to which the new commander at once addressed himself, and for which he was peculiarly fitted, were the preparation of adequate defenses to protect the capital and, more especially, the drilling of the new levies. McClellan showed himself a brilliant organizer of an army, but so fully did these tasks occupy him that he attempted no forward movement until the spring of 1862. Fortunately for the cause of the United States, the Confederates, at this critical stage of the war, lost their "chance" to seize the capital.

In the South, according to Joseph E. Johnston, the army was "more disorganized by victory than that of the United States by defeat." [4] President Davis was accused of having blocked a concerted movement by Johnston and Beauregard which would have caught McDowell before his advance to Manassas, and also of preventing such a pursuit after Bull Run as would presumably have resulted in the capture of Washington and the "liberation" of Maryland. Davis's defenders, on the other hand, claimed that he "with much animation asserted the necessity for an urgent pursuit that night" but that Johnston "was decidedly averse to an immediate offensive, and emphatically discountenanced it as impracticable." [5] Authorities differ as to the ability of the Confederates to follow up their victory, but the sharpness of the controversy at the time and the bitterness of postwar recriminations reveal the disappointment with which Southern leaders realized the futility of their hard-earned victory.

4

There now ensued a period of inaction in the East, and meanwhile the war was brought home to the people of the West. In Kentucky, Lincoln's native state, communities and families were rent asunder, with brothers fighting on opposite sides. Some of Lincoln's Kentucky friends were now arrayed against him; the brother-in-law of Mrs. Lincoln (Ben H. Helm) was a Confederate colonel and was to become a brigadier general. George B. Crittenden was a major general in the Confederate army; his brother, Thomas L. Crittenden, held the same rank in the Union army. They were sons of John J. Crittenden, who had been untiring in his efforts to prevent war. Union recruits could be seen marching up one side of a street in Louisville while Confederate recruits marched down the other. When a train carrying a Union company to General William Nelson's camp took on board a company of Confederates on their way to Camp

[4] *Battles and Leaders,* I, 252.

[5] Hudson Strode, *Jefferson Davis, Confederate President,* 123–124. For the controversy on this subject, see *Offic. Rec.,* 1 ser., II, 504 ff.; *Battles and Leaders,* I, 198 ff.; D. S. Freeman, *Lee's Lieutenants,* I, 76–78; T. Harry Williams, *P. G. T. Beauregard: Napoleon in Gray,* 96–99; G. E. Govan and J. W. Livingood, *A Different Valor,* 59–60, 407.

Boone, a "treaty" was made by the opposing officers according to which the men were placed in separate cars.

While organization in the West was slowly proceeding to the point where armies were taking shape, an incident occurred which illustrated the miscalculations and blunders of the Union war administration. Chief command of the Union forces in Kentucky had been assigned to Brigadier General Robert Anderson of Sumter fame. Unable to endure the "mental torture" of his command, he relinquished it to General W. T. Sherman. Conferring with Secretary of War Cameron in Louisville in October of 1861, Sherman argued that, for effective offense, a force of 200,000 men would be needed in the West. Sherman's "insane" request was reported to the public; the general's "insanity" became a bit of stereotyped gossip which newspapers fostered; and Sherman was relieved of command of the Department of the Cumberland and placed in a subordinate position. The Union war department was at that time incompetent in its efforts to raise an army; and some of the regiments offered by Northern states were refused by a war ministry which could not keep up with the process of organizing them.

The year 1861 passed without a clash at arms on the Kentucky front; but in January, 1862, a minor engagement occurred between the Union commander, J. A. Garfield, and the Confederate general, Humphrey Marshall, near Prestonburg in the eastern part of the state. Both commanders withdrew from the field, each claiming victory; but the biographers of Garfield have hailed it as an important battle which established the Union hold upon eastern Kentucky. Shortly after this, one of the ablest of the Union commanders, George H. Thomas, defeated a Confederate force under General George B. Crittenden in the battle of Mill Springs. Though Thomas's victory opened the road for an invasion of eastern Tennessee, the difficulties of transportation and provisioning prevented such a movement. It was admitted by their own officers that the Confederates were placed at a disadvantage in this battle by desertion in their ranks.

Major operations in the West now opened, yielding such results as to give promise of ultimate Federal success in the vital "river war"—i.e., combined operations of armies and gunboats on large inland streams. Formidable posts were held by the Confederates at Columbus, Kentucky, on the Mississippi, Fort Henry on the Tennessee, and Fort Donelson on the Cumberland. The strategic value of these river positions is indicated by the fact that General Albert Sidney Johnston, Confederate commander in the West, was defending Nashville at Donelson. By a coordinated land-and-water effort under Grant for the army and Foote for the flotilla of armored vessels, Fort Henry was brought to surrender on February 6, 1862. While Grant was advancing his army toward the Confederate works, the capture was effected as the result of a short battle between the fort and the fleet, in

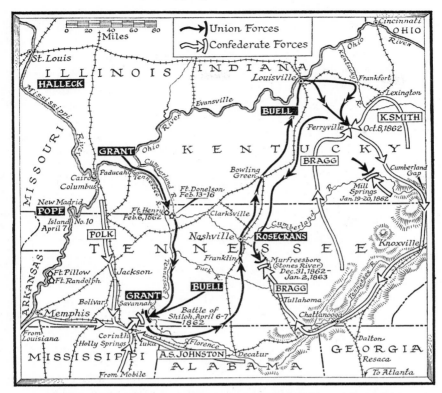

MAIN AREA OF WESTERN CAMPAIGNS, 1861–1862

which the losses were slight. The capture of Fort Donelson soon followed (February 16, 1862), but only after heavy fighting between Confederate forces under Pillow, Floyd, and Buckner, and Union forces under Mc-Clernand, Charles F. Smith, and Lew Wallace, with the cooperation of the flotilla under Foote.

The Federal victory at Donelson was promoted by a combination of factors. Confederate strategy was defective in permitting so many troops to be bottled up. There was noticeable lack of harmony between the Southern generals in command. The Confederates failed to attack before Grant's reinforcements arrived and they did not effectively use their own reinforcements which Johnston had sent. An important element in Union victory was the boldness of Grant, who, though absent during the earlier hours of fighting, came up at a time of Federal discomfiture, concluded that the enemy was in worse condition than he was, and ordered a charge upon the left. Though superior in the earlier stages of a combat which had opened on the 13th, the Confederates on the 15th had taken refuge within their works. That night their commanders (Floyd, Pillow, and Buckner) held a council of war at which it was decided that further resistance could only result in needless slaughter and that the fort must be surrendered. Floyd and Pillow fled during the night; and the surrender was left to Buckner, whose conduct in the emergency was dignified and high-minded.

On being requested by Buckner to state the conditions upon which he would accept capitulation, Grant sent the laconic response:

H^d Qrs. Army in the Field
Camp near Donelson, Feby 16th 1862

Gen. S. B. Buckner,
    Confed. Army,

Sir: Yours of this date proposing Armistice, and appointment of Commissioners, to settle terms of Capitulation is just received. No terms except an unconditional and immediate surrender can be accepted.

I propose to move immediately upon your works.

I am Sir: very respectfully

Your obt. sevt.
U. S. Grant
Brig. Gen.[1]

Buckner accepted these "ungenerous and unchivalrous terms" as he called them; and on the 16th Grant took over the fort, reporting the capture of a Confederate force of approximately 12,000 men and forty artillery pieces.

After months of discouragement the news of the river war sent a thrill throughout the North, and many thought the end near at hand. "After this, it certainly cannot be materially postponed," declared the New York *Times*. "The monster is already clutched and in his death struggle." [2] The fruits of Union victory now became evident with the evacuation of the Confederate position at Columbus and the retreat of Albert Sidney Johnston, ranking Confederate general in the West, who was forced not only to abandon his Kentucky front but to evacuate Nashville as well.[3]

5

With high optimism Grant now sought to consolidate the results of Henry and Donelson. So soon as a decisive Federal victory should be won he thought the "rebellion" would "collapse" in the West, and he consid-

---

[1] Facsimile in *Battles and Leaders*, I, 427. See also Grant, *Memoirs*, I, 311–312.

[2] New York *Times*, Feb. 17, 1862, p. 4.

[3] The Confederates evacuated Nashville by February 25, 1862; Columbus by March 2 (*Offic. Rec.*, 1 ser., VII, 426, 436–437).

ered Donelson such a victory. "The Tennessee and Cumberland rivers," he noted, "from their mouths to the head of navigation, were secured." [1] He was soon to find, however, that a new Confederate line was forming farther south, and that a powerful Confederate effort was now making to regain everything that was lost. Shiloh, the "severest battle fought at the West during the war," [2] was the result of this new effort. Though fought nearly a year after the war began, the battle was notable for the inexperience of the troops and the ease with which the whole Union war machine was thrown out of gear by a surprise attack. Few who engaged in the battle had any comprehensive picture of it in their minds; and the official reports, especially of the first day's fight, give an impression of disjointed Federal units which failed to support each other and which were thus severally and successively driven back by Confederate charges and flanking movements.

The attack found Grant unready. He was planning in terms of Union offensive, and was acting on his famous maxim that a successful general will think more about what he will do to the enemy than what the enemy will do to him. Although his main army was at Pittsburg Landing on the west bank of the Tennessee, he had his headquarters at Savannah nine miles down the river (i.e., farther north) on the opposite side. His army "had no line or order of battle, no defensive works of any sort, no outposts, properly speaking, to give warning, or check the advance of an enemy, and no recognized head during the absence of the regular commander." [3]

The most exposed position, at Shiloh Church, about three miles west of Pittsburg Landing, was held by the rawest of the troops, commanded by Sherman. At this point the Confederates suddenly struck in a sharp attack which constituted the main feature of the first day's battle. As Sherman explained, the place could easily have been made impregnable by defensive works; but in the inexperience which characterized the early period of the war this precaution was neglected, the more so because the invading army was conducting a forward movement. A hot and confused battle raged all day Sunday, April 6; and at the close of the day the Confederates were in occupation of the Union camps and the Federal line had been pushed a mile behind the position it had held in the morning. In disordered fighting the scattering troops lost touch with their units; fragments of broken regiments and companies joined such commands as they chanced to fall in with; only one of Sherman's brigades retained its organization. Many of the Union soldiers had just received their muskets and hardly knew how to load them. Two colonels, as Grant explained, "led their regiments from the field on first hearing the whistle of the enemy's bullets." [4] At one stage of the battle Grant found four or five thousand stragglers lying panic-

---

[1] *Battles and Leaders*, I, 485.
[2] *Ibid.*, I, 479.
[3] *Ibid.*, I, 487.
[4] *Ibid.*, I, 473.

stricken under cover of the river bluff. Union cavalry, useless in front, was employed to stop stragglers, who, recovering from their fright, would be quickly shifted to some part of the line where reinforcements were needed. Among other Federal difficulties in the Sunday fight was the delay of General Lew Wallace in bringing up reinforcements. Because of a confusion of orders he consumed the whole day in moving his force a short distance, and, though the explanation of the delay left no basis for discredit, arrived after the first day's battle was over.

Grant, who had recently suffered a painful fall from his horse, was at Savannah when the firing began, but he rushed to the front as soon as possible. Military historians differ heatedly over the effectiveness of his personal leadership in the battle. John Codman Ropes, arguing that the divisional commanders were left to their own devices during the fighting on the first day at Shiloh, maintains that Grant "seems . . . to have done little . . . except to show himself, and thus help to maintain confidence." [5] On the other hand, J. F. C. Fuller terms Ropes's charge "a gross calumny," finds Grant's leadership "quite wonderful," and concludes: ". . . had not this half-crippled man, who on the night of the 6th–7th slept among his men in torrents of rain and could get no rest because his ankle was much swollen, acted as he did, the battle would have been lost." [6]

Though victorious in the first day's battle, the Confederates suffered a serious loss in the death of their commanding general, Albert Sidney Johnston, who was hit in a leg artery and died from loss of blood. When the battle was resumed on Monday, Beauregard had succeeded Johnston and the Federals had been strengthened by reinforcements under Buell and Lew Wallace. With masses of fresh troops Grant was able, after ten hours of bitter struggle, to drive the enemy back upon Corinth; and Shiloh passed into history, to be refought endlessly in post-mortem reviews and divisional reunions.

Paralleling the Henry-Donelson-Shiloh campaign on the line of the Tennessee River, another Union army under General John Pope had been operating on the Mississippi, the whole being under the direction of General Henry W. Halleck, with headquarters at St. Louis. Naval cooperation was again supplied by the flotilla of gunboats and mortar boats under Admiral Foote. After the evacuation of Columbus, Kentucky, the Confederates took their stand just below Columbus on a bend of the river known as "Madrid Bend," with an army under Generals Polk and Pillow, and with batteries both on the shore and on Island Number Ten, so placed as to command the river. After a long and useless naval bombardment, part of the Union fleet was run past the batteries of the Island, while transports carrying the troops were moved through a specially cut canal. Pope's army of 20,000 was thus maneuvered into a commanding position below the

[5] Ropes, *Story of the Civil War*, II, 76.
[6] Fuller, *The Generalship of Ulysses S. Grant* (London, 1929), 113.

bend. Already partly cut off by the swampy approaches to the shore, the Confederates were caught in a *cul-de-sac,* so that New Madrid was abandoned March 14, and Island Number Ten, with its garrison of over 5000, was surrendered without bloodshed on April 7, 1862.[7] In addition to the garrison there fell into Union hands a considerable amount of artillery, ammunition, and provisions.

The continuation of the Shiloh campaign brought its further result when, Halleck having assumed personal command of the army, the Federal forces at the end of May captured Corinth,[8] the position which Beauregard had occupied following Shiloh. The place was weakly defended and would readily have fallen before the heavy guns and superior force of the Army of the Tennessee. Under these circumstances, by the secrecy of their withdrawal, which took the Unionists completely by surprise, the Confederates achieved a strategic success. The earlier phase of the western war, with its steady Union advance, now came to a close; and Federal arms suffered various delays and setbacks before winning further victories at Vicksburg and Chattanooga.

[7] According to the statement of William Preston Johnston, Col., C. S. A., son of Albert Sidney Johnston, the surrendering garrison at Island Number Ten numbered "6000 or 7000 men." *Battles and Leaders,* I, 549. Rear Admiral Henry Walke, U. S. N., gives the number as 5000. *Ibid.,* 445–446.

[8] *Offic. Rec.,* 1 ser., X, pt. 1, pp. 744, 762.

CHAPTER 11

The Virginia Front

I

ON THE EASTERN front there had been a long lull after Bull Run. When Lincoln singled out McClellan as the man of the hour he not only placed him directly over the Army of the Potomac, but intrusted him with full command of the armies of the republic. The new commander has properly been called "the problem child of the Civil War," for heated historical controversies have raged about nearly every aspect of his personality and career. "There was," T. Harry Williams remarks, "a duality in his character that made him at once honest and deceitful, simple and cunning, modest and arrogant, attractive and distasteful." [1] Some historians have seen the one McClellan, some the other; and, accordingly, they have defended or attacked him. Pro-McClellan writers have pointed out how he was able "to take command of a demoralized and formless army, work it into shape, direct the Union effort as general-in-chief for a period, lead a difficult operation against the South's finest commanders, see his plan wrecked not by enemy action but by interference at home, suffer displacement at the height of a great campaign, step down not because of defeat but because of hostile intrigue, step back when disaster befell his first successor, direct a desperate yet successful defense when Lee struck north via Maryland, prepare another advance (his second offensive and third major campaign in a year), and, at the moment of forward movement, fall a victim to a relentless political pressure which Lincoln could not resist." [2] Critics of the general have interpreted the same events as a sorry record of failures and have given the verdict: "McClellan was not a real general. McClellan was not even a disciplined, truthful soldier. McClellan was merely an attractive but vain and unstable man, with considerable military knowledge, who sat a horse well and wanted to be President." [3]

Even McClellan's critics, however, admit that he was "a fine organizer

[1] Williams, *Lincoln and His Generals*, 25.
[2] Randall, *Lincoln the President*, II, 70.
[3] K. P. Williams, *Lincoln Finds a General*, II, 479.

and trainer of troops." [4] From July, 1861, to March, 1862, he devoted his time and energies to organizing the army for an overwhelming advance that would end the war with a flourish. A trained army of a quarter-million, drilled and organized after European models, with a formidable fleet for support, was what he wanted. As months passed he concerned himself with drawing memoranda, devising general plans for western and naval operations as well as for those of his immediate army, giving advice as to foreign affairs, seeing to the defense of Washington, perfecting the divisions, brigades, and regiments of his infantry, studying the proportion of artillery pieces to each thousand men and the relation of field batteries to infantry units, building up his staff of adjutants and inspectors, marshaling his engineers, quartermasters, and commissaries, assembling his balloons and telegraph operators, and ordering all the infinite details which he deemed necessary before operations in the field could be thought of. His days were spent in the saddle, his nights in office work. He rode everywhere and saw everything. Much of his time was devoted to reports intended for posterity, putting things "on record" to show that the general in chief had left nothing undone. "Grand reviews established . . . the fact of progress in the equipment, instruction, and drill of the troops. At Bailey's Cross-roads might have been seen a rendezvous of 50,000 men, with all the paraphernalia of a campaign. . . . No such spectacle had ever been seen in the United States; . . . to a European not the least curious part of the pageant was the President, with his entire Cabinet, in citizens' dress, boldly caracoling at the head . . . and riding down the long lines of troops to the rattle of drums, the flourish of trumpets, and the loud huzzas of the whole army." [5]

All this time Lincoln, under pressure from the public and Congress, was pathetically eager that something be done; else, he is reported to have said, "the bottom would drop out of the whole concern." [6] Inexperienced as he was in such matters, he had been devouring military treatises, poring over maps, attending war councils, issuing repeated calls for troops, studying high military appointments, and engaging in an extensive correspondence regarding the affairs of the army. G. F. R. Henderson, the biographer of Stonewall Jackson, has argued that Lincoln's interference in these matters was a plague to the Union army, and John Codman Ropes agreed that the President possessed "an entire unfitness to have any general direction over military men," an "inaptitude for war" which he "retained to the end of his life." [7] General Colin Ballard, on the other hand, wrote a book to demonstrate *The Military Genius of Abraham Lincoln,* and T. Harry Wil-

[4] T. H. Williams, *Lincoln and His Generals,* 27.

[5] Philippe, comte de Paris, in *Battles and Leaders,* II, 118.

[6] Charnwood, *Abraham Lincoln,* 277.

[7] Ropes, "The Peninsular Campaign, General McClellan's Plans," *Mil. Hist. Soc. Mass.,* I, 77, quoted in K. P. Williams, *Lincoln Finds a General,* I, 140.

liams maintains that Lincoln was "a great natural strategist, a better one
than any of his generals," a President whose "larger strategy" did more
than "any general to win the war for the Union." [8]

McClellan, it is quite clear, agreed with the critics of Lincoln. He
found it "perfectly sickening" to be obliged to listen to the President's well
meant advice on military matters and concluded that his civilian superi-
ors were motivated by "hypocrisy, knavery, and folly." [9] Feeling the country's safety to be resting on his own shoulders, he bore himself toward his
chief with a marked assumption of superiority and showed what John Hay
called "unparalleled insolence of epaulettes" [10] in snubbing the President,
writing complaining letters, and disregarding his requests. With Congress
and the public stridently demanding an offensive, Lincoln decided to force
his slow-moving general into action. In January, 1862, he issued a special
command, designated as the "President's General War Order No. 1" for a
general forward movement of the Union forces to take place February 22.
At this time, as for months previous, Johnston's army was at Manassas,
while McClellan faced him near by, with a force three times as large. Lincoln, of course, expected a direct movement upon the Confederates; but
McClellan, ignoring the President's "war order," decided upon an oblique
advance to Richmond by way of the Peninsula between the York and James
rivers, a plan which offered military advantages but which Lincoln considered to have serious defects. A huge troop embarkation with the cooperation
of the Potomac flotilla now took place; and by May 1 McClellan was safely
on the Peninsula with an army of 112,000 and a firm hold on his base at
Fort Monroe.[11] All was now set for an advance upon the Confederate capital. His preliminary plans, however, had gone partly awry; for Lincoln, under pressure from McClellan's opponents and fearful that not enough
troops had been left to defend Washington, had relieved the general of supreme command, had reorganized the army under corps commanders, and
had withheld McDowell's corps,[12] thus materially weakening the peninsular
forces.

[8] T. H. Williams, *Lincoln and His Generals*, vii.

[9] Warren W. Hassler, Jr., *General George B. McClellan: Shield of the Union*,
115.

[10] Diary of John Hay, Nov. 13, 1861, quoted in W. R. Thayer, *Life . . . of
John Hay*, I, 124.

[11] On April 30, 1862, the total of the Army of the Potomac, present and absent,
was 130,378. The number present for duty was 112,392. *Offic. Rec.*, 1 ser., XI,
pt. 3, 130.

[12] Around this decision to withhold McDowell's corps rages "one of the greatest
controversies of the Civil War." For opposing views see Hassler, *op. cit.*, 78–81;
K. P. Williams, *op. cit.*, I, 159–160.

2

Yorktown would probably have yielded at once to Union assaults,[1] but McClellan devoted a month to a siege, after which, having occupied the abandoned Confederate works, he could write "Yorktown is in our possession" (May 4, 1862). Retiring up the Peninsula toward Richmond the Confederates checked the Union pursuit in the battle of Williamsburg (May 5), in which Longstreet, commanding the Confederate rear guard, fought off large Union numbers, dislocating McClellan's plan to fall upon the main Confederate force under Johnston. Norfolk fell into Union hands; and the James River was now open to those land-and-water operations in which the Unionists had been particularly successful. The Federal fleet, however, was halted at Drewry's Bluff near Richmond, and subsequent events rendered useless its whole effort on the line of the James.

With his base and headquarters at White House Landing, McClellan now planned a cautious advance upon Richmond, expecting a great decisive battle. Reporting that he had only 80,000 effectives, and desiring to overawe the "enemies of the Constitution" with the hugest possible force even though it might be more than necessary, he urged that his army be reinforced. An essential condition of success for his plans was cooperation in Washington, with the concentration under his command of available Federal forces in Virginia. Whether with this cooperation and augmented force he could have taken Richmond is a speculative problem on which authorities will forever differ. Kenneth P. Williams has cogently argued that "For a resolute and able commander the road to Richmond was open . . .";[2] but it can be replied that had McClellan broken into the Confederate capital, "Lee might have crashed into his rear, severed his communications, nullified his chance for naval support, and isolated his army," thus turning a brief Union triumph into "a death trap."[3]

Cooperation in Washington, however, was withheld; Lincoln and Stanton were taking counsel of their fears for the Federal capital. Lincoln thought the way to "cover" Washington was to keep McDowell directly between the two capitals: thinking in terms of strategy McClellan urged that the Confederates were not attacking Washington by way of Fred-

---

[1] Yorktown itself had strong defenses, but the Confederate fortified line from Yorktown across the Peninsula to the James River had weak points and could probably have been carried by assault.

[2] *Lincoln Finds a General*, I, 231.

[3] Randall, *Lincoln the President*, II, 97. Years after the war, Lee himself declared that McClellan could not have entered Richmond at this time, "that he [Lee] had taken every precaution to prevent it, . . . that it [Richmond] could not have been taken unless his own men had acted much worse than he had any reason to expect they would . . . , and that he was much stronger then than when Grant was before Richmond, as then he had only 45,000 men." Browning, *Diary*, II, 216–217. Cf. Emory Upton, *Military Policy of the U. S.*, 312 n.

ericksburg, that McDowell's service was to be measured in terms of interposition against an actually threatening Confederate army, and that Washington was virtually being defended on the Peninsula. McDowell with his
40,000 was indeed ordered to advance on Richmond, but his effective cooperation with McClellan never materialized.

McClellan being overruled, it was Lincoln and Stanton, with their
civilian advisers, against two of the ablest soldiers America has known—
Lee and Jackson; for with the wounding of J. E. Johnston at Seven Pines
(Fair Oaks) [4] Robert E. Lee had come into command of the forces protecting Richmond. Against the superior numbers of the enemy these brilliant Confederate commanders now made a striking use of brains, audacity, and swift movement, utilizing interior lines and taking advantage of
Union blunders and of McClellan's caution, which they read like an open
book. Jackson's task was to operate in the Shenandoah Valley, threatening
Washington by way of Harpers Ferry. Against his force (estimated at
16,000) the Federals brought into the Valley forces estimated at nearly
45,000,[5] while all the time McClellan on the Peninsula faced Richmond
with his more than 100,000. Jackson's strategy was not to fight a major
battle nor to win and hold this or that place, but to fall consecutively upon
the Union commanders before they could unite, create a panic as to the
safety of Washington, and thus prevent the one thing that would best defeat Lee—i.e., reinforcement of McClellan. In this purpose he was notably successful. By successive blows upon Shields, Milroy, Banks, and Frémont (in the battles of Kernstown, McDowell, Winchester, Cross Keys,
and Port Republic) he had the Union authorities mystified as to his movements, and caused Northern newspapers to shriek, "Washington is in danger." Lincoln was not frightened, but, thinking he saw a marvelous opportunity to trap Jackson in the Valley, he detached McDowell's corps from
McClellan's army. Though one of the President's admirers calls the order
"the first case of inspired warfare by the Federals in Virginia" since the
early days of the war,[6] the result was to deprive McClellan of 40,000 men

---

[4] See below, p. 213, n. 2.

[5] *Battles and Leaders,* II, 285 n. The student of Civil War campaigns soon
learns to attach a question mark to practically every statement as to numbers. Particularly in this Valley campaign, in which there was constant shifting of forces from
one command to another, there is general disagreement as to the strength of the
forces engaged. On May 25, 1862 (*Offic. Rec.,* 1 ser., XI, pt. 1, 31), Geary reported
Jackson's strength as 10,000; while it is stated in a Confederate source that his
strength was 13,000 to 15,000 (*Battles and Leaders,* II, 285). G. F. R. Henderson
(*Stonewall Jackson,* I, 413) and Frank E. Vandiver (*Mighty Stonewall,* 239) agree
on the figure 16,000. Federal reports estimated Jackson's force at Kernstown as
about 15,000 to Shields's 8000 (*Offic. Rec.,* 1 ser., XII, pt. 1, 335); at Winchester
(May 25, 1862) his force was estimated at 15,000 as compared to Banks's less than
4000 (*ibid.,* 528).

[6] K. P. Williams, *Lincoln Finds a General,* I, 213.

at the moment when his advance on the Confederate capital was about to materialize. Having kept Union forces away from Richmond to the extent of several times his own numbers, Jackson then joined Lee in time to add his strength to the main Confederate defense.

3

In June of 1862 the Confederates had about 85,000 men to defend Richmond, while McClellan had approximately 100,000 on the Peninsula, with about 40,000 elsewhere in Virginia.[1] The first main grapple in the peninsular campaign had occurred at Seven Pines (Fair Oaks) on May 31–June 1.[2] The Union army at this time straddled the Chickahominy, about one-third being north of that river. Johnston had struck, and there followed a severe and bloody encounter whose main results were that Johnston's force was driven back toward Richmond and Johnston himself was badly wounded.

In these difficult circumstances the Army of Northern Virginia, which was thenceforward to "carry the South on its bayonets," passed to the command of Robert E. Lee. Though at this time he was occupied with military administration at Richmond, active service as a high officer in the army better suited his genius and experience. Son of "Light Horse Harry" Lee, he was born in Westmoreland County near the birthplace of Washington,

[1] Freeman gives Lee's strength, after Jackson joined him, as 85,500 "of all arms" (Freeman, *Lee*, II, 116). Lee estimated the Union strength at this time at about 150,000 or more (*ibid.*, 117). On May 31 the aggregate present for duty in the Army of the Potomac under McClellan (i.e., on the Peninsula) was reported as 98,000 (*Offic. Rec.*, 1 ser., XI, pt. 3, 204). If the figures of Livermore are taken (*Numbers and Losses*, 86), it appears that Federals in the Seven Days' battles (June 25–July 1, 1862) had 91,169 "effectives engaged," while the Confederates had 95,481 "total engaged." McClellan's biographer states that the junction of Lee and Jackson at this time "gave them the largest army ever put into the field by the Confederacy" (W. S. Myers, *General George Brinton McClellan*, 295). See also T. G. Frothingham, "The Peninsula Campaign of 1862," *Proceedings*, Mass. Hist. Soc., vol. LVII.

[2] The battle of Seven Pines (Fair Oaks) was a hard-fought major engagement between the Confederate army under J. E. Johnston and Union forces under McClellan (May 31–June 1, 1862). Johnston's full strength was about 60,000 or 70,000, the full Union strength about 100,000. The three Union corps engaged had a force of about 50,000, the four Confederate divisions engaged about 39,000. Those "in close action" numbered about 12,000 Federals and 9500 Confederates. It is of interest that both R. E. Lee and Jefferson Davis were under fire in this battle, though Lee at this time had no field command, being on staff duty in the Confederate war department. The repulse of the Confederates at the gates of Richmond (the distance being about seven miles), and the feeling that the army had lost another Johnston, made the event a peculiarly bitter one for the South. The Federals lost in killed and wounded about 4300, the Confederates about 5700. *Battles and Leaders*, II, 220 ff.; Freeman, *Lee*, II, ch. vii.

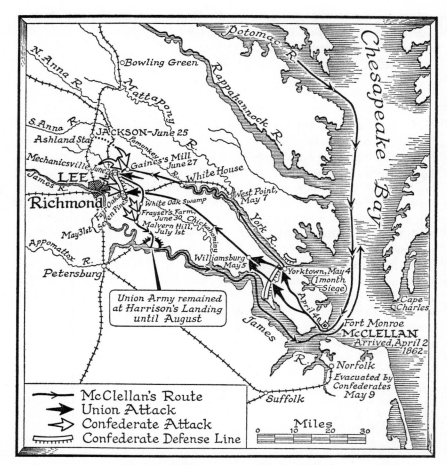

THE PENINSULA CAMPAIGN

graduated at West Point, served with the engineers of the regular army, and distinguished himself in twenty months of important service in the Mexican War. He served for a time as superintendent at West Point, and commanded the small Federal force which captured John Brown at Harpers Ferry in 1859. Having married Mary Custis, daughter of Washington's adopted son,[3] he was master of beautiful Arlington with its stately mansion opposite Washington. Just after Lincoln's call for troops he was offered the command of the armies of the United States; and much of the

---

[3] Mrs. Lee's father, George Washington Parke Custis, was the adopted son of George Washington (the grandson of Mrs. Washington). Arlington was Custis's home.

tragedy of the war was concentrated in the cup which he had to drink in resigning his commission. He had opposed both slavery and secession; but when Virginia seceded, the lifelong habits of his mind and the influence of his environment drew him to the South and to the defense of his state.

Douglas Freeman has called Lee's decision "the answer he was born to make." Finding himself in Texas on military duty while the secession crisis developed, he was so far out of sympathy with secessionists that he withdrew "into himself and . . . guard[ed] his tongue." While events "rushed on" and passion "continued high," "Lee still hoped." Long weeks before his resignation became necessary his position had become clear in his own mind: "if secession destroyed the Union, Lee intended to resign from the army and to fight neither for the South nor for the North, unless he had to act one way or the other in defense of Virginia." [4] As Freeman shows, his choice was not a matter of walking the floor in agonized uncertainty between two alternatives just prior to resignation, but of watching events to see if conflict of allegiance could be avoided, knowing well that if Virginia went with the South his only course would be to resign from the army and go with his state.[5]

Lee's dilemma (for so it may be called without implying any wavering in his own mind as to where duty lay) illustrated the plight into which Southern officers of the United States army and navy were forced by the War between the States. Admiral Farragut, George H. Thomas, and Winfield Scott are among the Southerners who faced the same question and decided it differently. Military men felt that muddling politicians had somehow got the country into a situation which forced a hateful duty upon them; nearly all the Southern officers interpreted that duty in the same light as Lee. It was a matter of conflicting loyalties, and decision had to be rendered in the court of individual conscience. Despite his wholehearted effort Lee was not one of those who felt after Appomattox that the South had "lost all." Having put his utmost into a war which he would have preferred to avoid, he was ready to accept the military decision. His spirit was thus to become a power and a guide for the "new South" as well as for the days of dark conflict.

Lee's exalted character has been aptly compared to that of Washington. His stature as a general is seen in his use of inferior numbers and resources for the protection of Richmond against McClellan and his successors, and in the spirit he infused into the Army of Northern Virginia. His tempered control of the army was not due to iron rigor; Lee's manner was not that of the mailed fist. His discipline depended rather on morale.[6]

---

[4] Freeman, *R. E. Lee*, I, 414–415, 422–423.

[5] When Virginia actually left the Union, Lee is said to have remarked that he could not "see the good of secession." *Ibid.*, I, 439.

[6] Douglas Freeman (*ibid.*, II, 335) refers to "the voluntary association known as the Army of Northern Virginia."

With an unusual memory for names and faces he knew and loved his army. Though viewing him at something of a distance his men reciprocated with an affection that amounted to hero worship.

After the union of Lee and Jackson for the defense of Richmond the opposing armies came to blows in what was known as the "Seven Days" (June 25–July 1, 1862). Beginning at Mechanicsville (Beaver Dam Creek, June 26) and proceeding through Gaines's Mill (June 27), Savage Station (June 29), and Frayser's Farm (June 30), the great armies struggled desperately as McClellan, retiring from the Chickahominy, changed his base from White House on the Pamunkey to Harrison's Landing on the James. Near Harrison's Landing at Malvern Hill there was fought on July 1 the final conflict of the Seven Days; and it proved one of the most terrible battles of the war. The engagement stands as a Union victory; yet McClellan had not taken Richmond, and this failure grievously disappointed Lincoln.

Lincoln now pondered the twin problems of replacing McClellan and of removing the Army of the Potomac from the Peninsula. Visiting McClellan's headquarters July 9 he subjected the generals to a barrage of questions. He inquired as to the health and numerical strength of the army, the whereabouts of the enemy, the desirability and practicability of "getting the army away from here," and the like. He was informed that McClellan had about 75,000 or 80,000 men, that the enemy was four or five miles away, and that the army was probably "safe" with the help of the navy. From his questioning he deduced that 160,000 men had gone into McClellan's army, that 86,500 remained, that no more than 23,500 had been killed or wounded, that 50,000 had "left otherwise," and that if these men could be brought back McClellan could go into Richmond in three days.

Lincoln's mind was now crowded with many problems: England's possible recognition of the Confederacy, compensated emancipation, the growing demand for a stroke against slavery, the passing of vindictive legislation in Congress, rumblings of Northern discontent, and anxiety for his party in the coming congressional election. McClellan had written and handed to the President in person a letter (the "Harrison's Landing letter," July 7, 1862) [7] which the general's enemies regarded as a "political document," giving advice on matters within the functions of President and Congress, opposing military excess, warning that arbitrary arrests could not be

[7] *McClellan's Own Story*, 487; William Starr Myers, *General George Brinton McClellan*, 306 ff. The letter was for Lincoln's "private consideration" (*ibid.*, 307). McClellan's course in writing this letter, which dealt principally with political, not military, matters, has been bitterly attacked (K. P. Williams, *Lincoln Finds a General*, I, 249–250) and warmly defended (Randall, *Lincoln the President*, II, 101–104; W. W. Hassler, *op. cit.*, 177–178).

tolerated, and counseling that war be conducted "upon the highest principles known to . . . civilization." It "should not be . . . a war upon population, but against armed forces and political organizations," said he. Confiscation of Southern private property should not be thought of, and especially "forcible abolition of slavery" should be avoided; for a radical antislavery policy would result in the disintegration of the armies.

Though McClellan had by no means failed, he had not attained his object, and Lincoln decided that the time had come to try new commanders in the Eastern theater. He brought John Pope from the West and placed him in command of the forces of Frémont, Banks, and McDowell, with orders to operate in central Virginia and in the Shenandoah valley. Relinquishing duties which he and Secretary of War Stanton had performed since March, he restored the rank of general in chief of the Union armies and conferred this office upon Halleck, who was fresh from victories in the West.[8] McClellan was reduced to a subordinate position and ordered to remove his army from the Peninsula to Aquia Creek on the Potomac, so that it could support Pope. In vain did McClellan protest against this move. His army was in fine condition, he asserted, and he was now planning a movement against Richmond by way of Petersburg. "Here," he said, is the "true defence of Washington"; in front of his army was the "heart of the rebellion." Withdrawal, in his opinion, would be disastrous.[9] His advice, however, was disregarded; and he was denied command of an active army.

The promotion of Pope to high command in Virginia was the result of pressure from Republican Radicals, who liked his talk of McClellan's "incompetency and indisposition to active movements," his promises to take "the most vigorous measures in the prosecution of the war," and his predictions that "Slavery must perish." [10] Though associated with easy victories in the West with the help of the fleet, his aptness for supreme command had by no means been demonstrated; and his supplanting of McClellan bore much the appearance of reward for ungenerous criticisms in which he had indulged and for boastful language used in testimony before the committee on the conduct of the war. He had confidently announced

[8] Most historians have been hostile to Halleck, quoting Lincoln's disillusioned remark that the general proved to be little more than "a first-rate clerk." (T. H. Williams, *Lincoln and His Generals*, 139.) K. P. Williams, on the other hand, argues that Halleck was a leader who "was a devoted student of military art and science and of the laws of war; who had an exalted sense of duty; who straightened out great confusion in Missouri . . . ; who for many months held a position in Washington harder than any other General in Chief or Chief of Staff has had; and whose telegrams had an enviable clarity." (*Lincoln Finds a General*, V, 282.)

[9] *McClellan's Own Story*, 497.

[10] David Donald, ed., *Inside Lincoln's Cabinet: The Civil War Diaries of Salmon P. Chase*, 97.

to this body that if matters had been placed in his charge in March nothing could have prevented his marching to New Orleans.[11]

The manner in which the Confederates disposed of Pope presents one of the most striking episodes of the war. It went far toward fixing Lee's reputation as a daring strategist who thought not alone of "rules of war," but of well-studied chances and probabilities. These chances were assessed in terms of Federal uncoordination, the backward look toward Washington, the likelihood that Pope would make mistakes, and the effectiveness of Jackson. It is doubtful whether similar methods would have worked against Grant or Sherman, or even against Pope without Jackson's cooperation. What happened can only be briefly suggested here: the full story is too elaborate. There was first a minor attack upon a detached portion of the Union army, then a flanking movement and a raid upon the rear, then a maneuvered engagement with the main host. At Cedar Mountain (August 9) Jackson, with superior numbers, struck Banks. The results of the hard-fought engagement were indecisive. Though Banks suffered heavier casualties and Jackson was left in possession of the field, tactically the Confederate leader "badly botched" the fighting and the Southerners received a "significant rebuff." [12] Undeterred, Jackson, by a remarkable march on Pope's right flank, involving a risky division of the Confederate forces, swept north (away from Lee) through Thoroughfare Gap in the Bull Run Mountains, reached Pope's rear, and assailed his communications. At this point a daring raid was made upon the Federal base at Manassas, this phase being intrusted to Stuart's cavalry. Seemingly this left the detached Confederates under Jackson open to an attack and trapping movement. This, however, Pope failed to accomplish; and, the Federals making a shift which Lee had anticipated, Jackson was allowed to slip back to precisely the point where Lee needed him for the business to follow.

In the two-day battle of August 29–30 (Second Manassas) gallant Federal assaults were sharply repulsed; a furious offensive action by Pope on the 30th failed chiefly because of Pope's errors, not for any lack of Union morale; and the struggle closed with a counter-stroke by Lee upon a retreating enemy. In these operations, McClellan's force at Aquia was left out of the argument, this being but one example of faulty Federal strategy.[13] In contrast to this, Confederate management had been at its best,

[11] Virtually all military historians condemn Pope. An exception is K. P. Williams, who denies that Second Bull Run was a Union debacle and maintains that "In every important particular Pope had shown himself superior to McClellan" (*Lincoln Finds a General*, I, 357–358).

[12] Vandiver, *Mighty Stonewall*, 344; K. P. Williams, *Lincoln Finds a General*, I, 301. Cf. Freeman, *Lee's Lieutenants*, II, 43–46. The engagement was also called the battle of Cedar Run.

[13] The responsibility for McClellan's failure to support Pope is heatedly argued. On the one hand, it has been suggested that Pope, taking credit to himself, wanted

enabling Lee to bring to a brilliant conclusion his campaign for the relief of Richmond. Contrasting the situation after Second Manassas with Southern prospects at the time Lee assumed command of the Army of Northern Virginia, Douglas Freeman points out that at the beginning of June, 1862, McClellan was in front of Richmond, Jackson was menaced in the Valley by three strong Union forces, and western Virginia was in Union hands; while at the end of August western Virginia was nearly evacuated, the main Union army was in full retreat on Washington, and, with insignificant exceptions, "the only Federals closer than 100 miles to Richmond were prisoners . . . and men . . . preparing to retreat. . . ." [14]

4

The state of the Union cause after the disaster of Second Manassas was critical in the extreme. The army of Pope, demoralized and badly whipped, was retiring toward Washington in disorder, with thousands of stragglers clogging the roads. Military control at Washington had fallen into confusion, with Secretary Stanton, General Halleck, and intriguing politicians urging their schemes upon the President and creating a situation in which coordinated command was impossible. Fearing that Lee would descend upon the capital, Lincoln and Halleck felt little confidence that they could save the distracted city. Pope being now discredited, the Union army was without a head; while the Confederate forces, in high morale from recent successes, were animated by the magnificent generalship of Lee and Jackson.

The choice of a successor to Pope admitted of no delay. McClellan, the best general then available to command the Union army in the East, had been shelved, having been reduced to the command of the meager forces assigned to the immediate defense of Washington. As a concession to circumstance Lincoln asked him to "accept command of all the forces"; but this action was taken with an embarrassing denial of moral support. Though the request came from the President, it was merely verbal; the only published order was that of September 2, which read: "Major-General McClellan will have command of the fortifications of Washington and of all the troops for the defense of the capital." Later McClellan was accused of "assuming command without authority"; and, to use his own words, he "fought the battles of South Mountain and Antietam with a halter around

---

to win the battle without McClellan's cooperation. On the other, it can be said that McClellan moved with even more than his customary slowness, that he spoke loftily of leaving Pope "to get out of his scrape" (*Offic. Rec.*, 1 ser., XII, 98), and that Lincoln thought McClellan "acted badly toward Pope" and "wanted him to fail" (Tyler Dennett, ed., *Lincoln and the Civil War in the . . . Diaries of John Hay*, 47).

[14] Freeman, *Lee*, II, 343.

[his] neck," for, he said, in case of defeat he might have been condemned to death. There was more than bragging in his statement: "I was fully aware of the risk I ran, but the path of duty was clear and I tried to follow it." The wild cheers that greeted him as he met the retreating force gave evidence of that confidence in "Little Mac" which the soldiers of the Army of the Potomac never lost. "Men threw their caps high into the air, and . . . frolicked like school-boys. . . . They cheered and cheered again. . . . It seemed as if an intermission had been declared in order that a reception might be tendered to the general-in-chief. A great crowd continually surrounded him, and the most extravagant demonstrations were indulged in. Hundreds even hugged the horse's legs and caressed his head and mane. . . . It was like a great scene in a play, with the roar of the guns for an accompaniment." [1]

With an audacity impossible to a man of smaller spirit Lee decided, despite the poor equipment of his ragged army, to invade the North. As he expressed it in his address to the people of Maryland, he was coming to liberate a "sister State" which had been "reduced to the condition of a conquered province" and to "aid" the state "in throwing off this foreign yoke." [2] Maryland, however, though largely sympathetic toward the Southern people, was not shaken from its Union allegiance.

Crossing the Potomac near Leesburg on September 5, Lee occupied Frederick, Maryland, on the 7th. Consternation shook the North as attacks upon Baltimore, Philadelphia, or Washington were momentarily expected and isolation of the capital feared. As McClellan slowly moved his force, interposing between Washington and the Confederate host, Lee took a dangerous risk. He had expected that Harpers Ferry, gateway to Maryland from the Shenandoah Valley, would be evacuated by the Unionists; but when this expectation was not fulfilled he divided his army in the face of a superior enemy, sending Stonewall Jackson in command of 25,000 men, with the cooperation of McLaws and J. G. Walker, to capture Harpers Ferry, while his own force proceeded toward Hagerstown.

It was McClellan's purpose to evacuate Harpers Ferry and use its garrison of 10,000 men as a reinforcement of his main army; but he was overruled by Halleck. Though according to the theory of warfare Halleck may have made a mistake, it was a most fortunate one for the Union side. "Halleck's bungle," as Warren Hassler has said, "helped unwittingly to place Lee at a disadvantage which went far toward causing the failure of his campaign," for he felt obliged to dislodge the Harpers Ferry garrison before concentrating west of the South Mountain range. [3] Lee's orders giving the disposition of his forces found their way into McClellan's hands, having been picked up by a Union private. Wrapped around three cigars, they

[1] *Battles and Leaders*, II, 549–552.
[2] Freeman, *Lee*, II, 357; Moore, *Rebell. Rec.* (Diary), V, 75.
[3] Hassler, *General George B. McClellan*, 238.

had been dropped by a Confederate officer. McClellan, however, still under delusions as to enemy strength, lost his chance of striking and possibly annihilating Lee's depleted army.

Confederate strategy at Harpers Ferry was to occupy the heights, surround the Union positions, and force a surrender without an assault; and it succeeded perfectly. On September 15 the Federals surrendered a force of over 11,000 men and 13,000 small arms, the garrisons at Winchester and Martinsburg being included. Lee, having learned of McClellan's discovery of his orders, was able to delay the Federal advance by a stiff engagement in the passes at South Mountain. Even so, however, he was caught in a serious situation. His force was far inferior to McClellan's; and he was facing battle with the river at his rear and with the danger of losing his whole force in case of defeat. Having pushed his plans for a victorious invasion of the North, Lee now realized these hazards so keenly that he was planning to withdraw across the Potomac into Virginia.

McClellan made the attack near Sharpsburg on the 17th; and a wholesale butchery resulted which made the battle of Antietam the heaviest engagement in American history up to that time. Though gory beyond description and terrific in its human cost, the fighting was so disjointed, so doubtful and shifting in its uncoordinated attacks, that McClellan's claim to "victory" has been seriously disputed. On the Union side the chief attacks were delivered by Hooker, Mansfield, Sumner, and (late in the battle) by Burnside, whose assault was quickly followed by repulse. The Confederate forces that saw the most action were those of McLaws, Hood, Jackson (returned from Harpers Ferry), D. H. Hill, and A. P. Hill.

The result has been defined as a "defeat for both armies." [4] McClellan had indeed stopped Lee's offensive; but, considering the disparity of forces and the possible stakes, this was a disappointing result compared to the smashing victory which many thought to be within his grasp. In the controversies that followed he was criticized, doubtless with some justice, for making inadequate use of his forces, failing to bring up Couch's division which had been left near Maryland Heights on the erroneous assumption that Jackson was still at Harpers Ferry, and keeping Porter's whole corps in reserve. Having struck with less than full effect, he failed to follow up the battle; Lee was permitted to cross the Potomac on the 18th and elude his grip. Lee had also failed, for an ambitious invasion had been brought to an inconclusive end. On the Confederate side, however, it was not a

[4] *Battles and Leaders*, II, 629. In a masterly review of Sharpsburg (Antietam) Douglas Freeman defends Lee's strategy but emphasizes the splendid work of McClellan in his organization of a demoralized army and his "unexpected rapidity" in directing Federal movements (Freeman, *Lee*, II, ch. xxvii). K. P. Williams, on the other hand, endorses the verdict of Peter S. Mitchie: "It does not seem possible to find any other battle ever fought in the conduct of which more errors were committed than are clearly attributable to the commander of the Army of the Potomac." *Lincoln Finds a General*, II, 463–464.

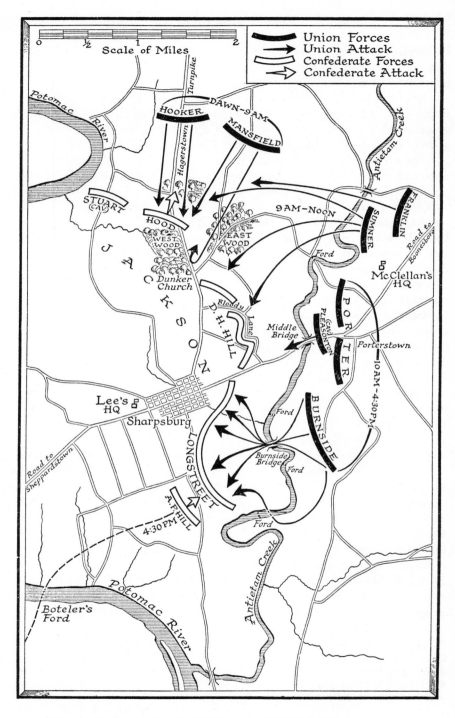

THE BATTLE OF ANTIETAM, SEPTEMBER 17, 1862

demoralizing failure. Lee had shown audacious courage. He retained "moral ascendancy." [5]

Battle after battle in the East with nothing settled! There seemed no end to the useless slaughter. And now at Antietam Creek the greatest battle to date had at least given the Federals a chance which was thrown away, said the critics, when McClellan allowed Lee's army to escape without pursuit. As McClellan himself explained it, "the national cause could afford no risks of defeat," [6] for Lee might have marched upon Washington, Baltimore, Philadelphia, or New York. In addition, the exhaustion of his men, the distance of his supply trains in the rear, the disorganized condition of his army, depleted as it was by extensive desertion, and the lack of sufficient morale for an offensive, were set down as excuses for delay. But did McClellan genuinely wish to crush the enemy? Gossip against McClellan in official circles was now furious and there arose in the President's mind a suspicion as to the general's intentions. At this time a certain Major John J. Key was dismissed from the Union service because he was reported to have said that it "was not the game" to bag the enemy after Sharpsburg, that the true policy for preserving the Union was to "tire the rebels . . . and ourselves," so that fraternal feelings could be restored and slavery saved.[7] Traducers of McClellan labored with the President, and comments reached his ears as to the general's alleged reluctance to hurt the enemy.

Confederate pluck in contrast to McClellan's caution was now made evident when "Jeb" Stuart, *beau sabreur* of the South, rode his cavalry round McClellan's whole army. He had done this trick before. During the peninsular campaign (June 12–15, 1862) he had made a complete circuit around McClellan's force. With a cavalry force of 1200, moving with great swiftness and secrecy, he had ridden round the Federal right far to the rear and had returned by the left flank. Doing what military critics considered a rash thing, he had nevertheless thrilled the South with his spectacular stunt, the more so as his exploit was exaggerated in the papers. The main purpose of the raid was to bring information to Lee as to the size and disposition of McClellan's forces; but, as Sir Frederick Maurice has remarked, "the dramatic element in Stuart's ride so struck men's imagination that the object of the expedition was forgotten, and the raid behind the enemy's rear came to be regarded as something of value in itself." He adds: "The damage which a body of cavalry can do behind an army can be quickly made good, and raids are of little advantage save when they furnish information which can be quickly used. . . . Where

---

[5] Sir Frederick Maurice, *Robert E. Lee the Soldier*, 154. For a criticism of McClellan's tactics, see *Battles and Leaders*, II, 656–658.

[6] *McClellan's Own Story*, 618.

[7] Lincoln, *Collected Works*, V, 442. On McClellan's alleged disloyalty see Myers, *McClellan*, 374–375; Browning, *Diary*, I, 538–539; Bates, *Diary*, 423.

they take cavalry away from a battlefield, they are . . . harmful, as Lee was soon to find." [8] Stuart's second raid round McClellan (October 10–12, 1862) carried him as far as Chambersburg and nearly to Gettysburg, then swiftly back to Lee's army. He brought useful information to the Confederate chieftain, but again the sporting quality of the raid caused it to be featured as an object in itself, for Stuart had covered eighty miles in twenty-seven hours with a loss of one wounded and two missing.

When, about this time, McClellan reported that his cavalry horses were too fatigued to move, Lincoln sarcastically asked "what the horses of your army have done since the battle of Antietam that fatigues anything?" [9] Obviously the President's patience was about to break. After long weeks of maddening delay, however, McClellan did at length move. He began his crossing of the Potomac on October 26; and by November 7 his army was massed in the neighborhood of Warrenton, ready for a stroke. In his memoirs he wrote: "I doubt whether, during the whole period that I had the honor to command the Army of the Potomac, it was in such excellent condition to fight a great battle." [10]

At this juncture McClellan's service with the army was suddenly terminated. By order of the President dated November 5 he was, on the eve of a forward movement, relieved from command of the Army of the Potomac and ordered to turn over the command to General A. E. Burnside. Just why Lincoln, having borne with McClellan so long, chose this particular occasion for dismissing him, is something of a mystery. The army was deeply aggrieved and almost mutinous at the news; but McClellan, taking his leave, was careful to bespeak their loyal support of Burnside and to assist his successor to seize the reins with the least delay and friction.

5

Mutterings of discontent as McClellan took his farewell were mingled with apprehension for the future; and such apprehension was soon amply justified. Less than six weeks after Burnside's accession to command he committed one of the colossal blunders of the war in bringing on the disastrous Union defeat at Fredericksburg. Missing his chance to strike Jackson and Longstreet (Lee's corps commanders) separately with advantage of position, he struck the united Confederate forces at Fredericksburg, where so great was the disadvantage of position that his preponderance of numbers was neutralized. The Confederates had established part of their force in an almost impregnable position on Marye's Heights west of the city, while the brigade of General T. R. R. Cobb, together with some of Kershaw's men and J. R. Cooke's North Carolinians, maintained an "unapproachable

[8] Maurice, *Robert E. Lee the Soldier,* 115. See also Freeman, *Lee,* II, 97 ff.; *Battles and Leaders,* II, 271 ff.
[9] Lincoln, *Collected Works,* V, 474.
[10] *McClellan's Own Story,* 648.

STATESMEN
OF COMPROMISE

DANIEL WEBSTER

HENRY CLAY

CHARLES SUMNER

ROGER B. TANEY   JOHN C. CALHOUN

A REPUBLICAN CAMPAIGN

BROADSIDE OF 1856

STEPHEN A. DOUGLAS

JEFFERSON DAVIS

Alexander Hessler

ABRAHAM LINCOLN

A UNION VOLUNTEER

The Library of Congress

PIERRE GUSTAVE TOUTANT BEAUREGARD

CONFEDERATE WINTER QUARTERS, CENTERVILLE, VIRGINIA,

MARCH, 1862

TWO SCENES FROM THE PENINSULA CAMPAIGN

FEDERAL WAGON PARK AT YORKTOWN, VIRGINIA

FEDERAL ARTILLERY PARK AT YORKTOWN, VIRGINIA

GEORGE B. McCLELLAN

PURSUING THE CONFEDERATE TROOPS AFTER THE EVACUATION OF YORKTOWN

FEDERAL THIRTEEN-INCH MORTARS
NEAR YORKTOWN, VIRGINIA, MAY, 1862

PROFESSOR T. S. C. LOWE
OBSERVING THE BATTLE
OF FAIR OAKS

THOMAS J. ("STONEWALL") JACKSON

ROBERT E. LEE

WHITE OAK SWAMP

Opposite page:

THE BATTLE OF SHILOH

CLEMENT L. VALLANDIGHAM

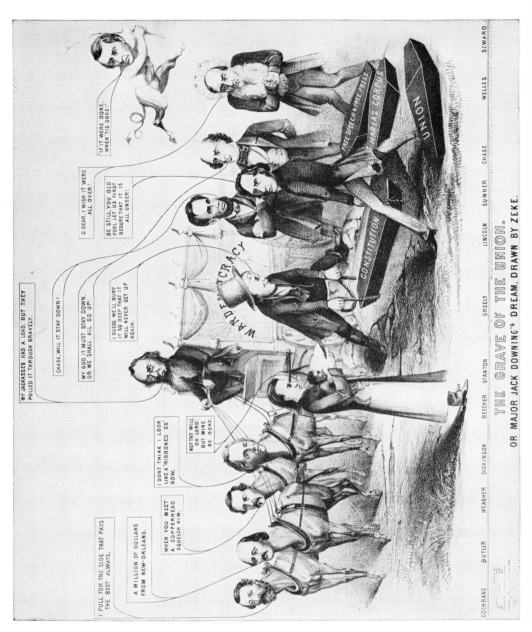

AN

ANTI-LINCOLN

CARTOON

New York Public Library

"CONTRABANDS" AT CUMBERLAND, VIRGINIA, MAY, 1862

COMPANY E, 4TH U.S. COLORED INFANTRY,
AT FORT LINCOLN, WASHINGTON, D.C.

The Library of Congress

The Library of Congress

NEGROES COMING INTO FEDERAL CAMP
AFTER THE EMANCIPATION PROCLAMATION

JAMES M. MASON

CHARLES FRANCIS ADAMS

RIVAL MINISTERS TO GREAT BRITAIN

HORACE GREELEY

The National Archives

WILLIAM H. SEWARD

The National Archives

CONTROVERSIAL FIGURES IN LINCOLN'S CABINET

EDWIN M. STANTON

SALMON P. CHASE

UNION SCOUTS
OBSERVING LEE'S TROOPS
CROSSING THE POTOMAC,
SEPTEMBER, 1862

The Library of Congress

PRESIDENT LINCOLN AND GENERAL McCLELLAN AT ANTIETAM, AROUND OCTOBER 2, 1862

FEDERAL SIGNAL TELEGRAPH TRAIN AT THE BATTLE OF FREDERICKSBURG

"GOING TO THE TRENCHES"—FEDERAL TROOPS IN 1862

HENRY W. HALLECK

AMBROSE E. BURNSIDE

BURNSIDE'S "MUD MARCH," JANUARY 21, 1863

When Pickets div. surrendered it grouped
around this Tree

A. R. Waud

Last Stand of Pickett

LAST STAND OF PICKETT'S MEN, GETTYSBURG, 1863

*ld be a wider interval betwee
arging lines, and perhaps a
ne broken —*

The Library of Congress

The National Archives

GEORGE E. PICKETT

JAMES LONGSTREET

J. E. B. STUART

The National Archives

BODIES OF THE DEAD

IN THE "WHEATFIELD," BATTLE OF GETTYSBURG

The Library of Congress

GEORGE G. MEADE

defense" [1] behind a stone wall in the "sunken road" at the base of the hill. The main battle resolved itself into a series of forlorn, desperate Union charges against the withering musketry and artillery fire of the Confederates. Hopeless as was their plight, the Federals charged on with magnificent determination until at nightfall they retired, leaving the field strewn with their dead, which in many cases were piled three deep.[2]

But these bloody Union assaults in front of Marye's Heights (the Confederate left) were only a part of the battle, for on the Confederate right there were heavy Union attacks against Jackson and desperate efforts were made to turn that side of Lee's line. "Quickly," writes Freeman, "the Confederate batteries opened in reply. Gaps were cut in the charging columns. Windrows of dead were left behind. In a long volley the Confederate infantry opened, claiming grievous toll in every regiment." [3] Burnside's force at Fredericksburg had numbered nearly 114,000 to Lee's 72,000; [4] but the Confederates were so placed that they could have succeeded had they been outnumbered two to one. Burnside lost 12,600 men, of whom 1284 were killed and 9600 wounded; Lee's killed numbered about six hundred and his total loss about 5300.[5]

With the failure at Fredericksburg the nadir of Northern depression seemed to have been reached. Sorrow caused by the death or mutilation of thousands of brave men turned into rage as the people wondered how so fine a fighting instrument as the Army of the Potomac had been used with such stupid futility. The slump in public credit was evident in the rise of gold to 134, involving the greatest depreciation of the greenback up to that date. Many urged that the South was ready for a reasonable peace and that it was only the obstinacy of the Lincoln administration which prolonged the war; others demanded a yet "more vigorous" policy, for which Lincoln was considered incompetent. Under bitter criticism for his emancipation proclamation and his suspension of the habeas corpus

---

[1] *Battles and Leaders*, III, 78. "The heights and the sunken road . . . constituted a death trap; were the Federals foolish enough to venture into it?" Freeman, *Lee*, II, 458.

[2] Referring to the impossibility of carrying the Fredericksburg position by direct assault, General Hooker, revisiting the scene after the war, said: "I never think of this ground but with a shudder." (*Battles and Leaders*, III, 215.) Describing Burnside's "mad determination to achieve the impossible" Douglas Freeman (*Lee*, II, 465) writes: "Each time the folly of the blind assault seemed more criminal."

[3] Freeman, *Lee*, II, 460.

[4] Livermore, *Numbers and Losses*, 96. These numbers must refer to army aggregates before the battle. As to Lee, for instance, it has been estimated that his effective strength at Fredericksburg was about 58,500, and that less than 20,000 were "actively engaged." *Battles and Leaders*, III, 147. Freeman (*Lee*, II, 452) writes of the situation before the battle: "Seventy-eight thousand men were ready for the worst that Burnside's 125,000 could do."

[5] Livermore, 96; Freeman, *Lee*, II, 471.

privilege, Lincoln was under attack from the moderates; and now the Radicals turned upon him and precipitated the most serious cabinet crisis of his administration.[6] With the army so distrustful of its commander that it seemed on the verge of disintegration, the luckless Burnside asked Lincoln to dismiss or degrade some of the best officers, including Brooks, Hooker, Newton, Cochrane, and Franklin. Their only offense was lack of faith in Burnside himself, a sentiment which pervaded the whole army. Burnside was now considering another thrust across the Rappahannock; but his chances were so doubtful that the President restrained him. Meanwhile Halleck's assistance in reaching a decision as to Burnside's proposed move had proved disappointing. The President wrote: "If in such a difficulty . . . you do not help, you fail me precisely in the point for which I sought your assistance. . . . Your military skill is useless to me if you will not do this." [7] Halleck tendered his resignation, which was not accepted; and Burnside's crossing of the Rappahannock was approved. It resulted in nothing except a wretched "mud march" which began on January 21, the army floundering in floods of rain and seas of sticky clay without making any progress in its purpose of attacking Lee. Another change was imperative. On January 25, 1863, Lincoln removed Burnside and put General Joseph Hooker in command of the Army of the Potomac.

The spring of 1863 came; and as the people looked back upon two years of bungling and sanguinary warfare neither of the struggling sections could point to gains comparable to the losses incurred. The conflict had reached proportions never dreamed of in 1861; fate had supplied a ghastly sequel to the confident predictions and generalizations in which the politicians of that far-off year had indulged. Adjustments that seemed easy in 1861 were out of the question now; neither side could see its way clear to a termination of the struggle. As to generals the advantage was clearly with the Confederacy. At a time when Southern enthusiasm for Lee and Jackson was unbounded, Lincoln wrote his new army chieftain a curious, fatherly letter in which he confessed that he was "not quite satisfied" with him, counseled him to "Beware of rashness," and wistfully besought him to "go forward, and give us victories." [8]

---

[6] See below, pp. 461–463.
[7] Lincoln, *Collected Works*, VI, 31.
[8] *Ibid.*, VI, 78–79.

CHAPTER 12

The Great Border

No ADEQUATE understanding of the issues of the Civil War is possible without a study of the border region. It is a striking fact that there was within the Union a huge section peculiarly in sympathy with the South, a section in which there was no will to fight the South on the issue of slavery, a region made up largely of Southerners and men of Southern parentage. Taking Edward Conrad Smith's formula as to the composition of this region (Kentucky, Missouri, western Virginia, and the southern portions of Ohio, Indiana, and Illinois) its white population as of 1860 numbered 4,967,000 [1] as compared to 5,451,000, the white population of the seceded states. Broaden the definition to include Maryland and Delaware, and the whites of the border considerably outnumbered those of the Confederate South. That the will of so extensive and populous an area should have been suppressed and overridden is one of the startling developments of the war; for both in the appeal to arms and in the manner of the conquest, as well as in political developments while the struggle progressed, this mighty border, though in a different sense, was as truly conquered as the South itself. To know the land of the border, its people, and its economic habits is to realize the truth of Dr. Smith's statement that the boundary between the sections was artificial. The Ohio River was less a barrier than a unifying factor; human elements on both sides were homogeneous; New Orleans was an outlet for Indiana and Illinois. It was from the border that the great compromisers—Clay, Benton, Crittenden, Douglas, Bell—had drawn their strength.

I

Nowhere were the peculiar problems of the border more clearly revealed than in Kentucky. Native state of both Lincoln and Davis, it was definitely of the South; yet its nationalism and its relations with the Northern border were of primary importance. So nearly was the balance

---

[1] Edward Conrad Smith, *The Borderland in the Civil War*, 3 n.

even between North and South that a slightly different turn of events might have drawn Kentucky into the Confederacy, making the Ohio River the boundary of the warring sections. Though Kentucky as a state was saved for the Union, yet, to use the language of E. M. Coulter, as "between the North and the South the finer feelings of sentiment bound the state to the latter"; [1] and after the war there was no part of the country where pro-Confederate feeling was more in evidence.

For that aspect of Southernism that was identified with secession in 1860–1861 Kentucky had no heart. Southerners had long realized that Kentucky was "different." Its favorite sons, such as Clay and Crittenden, had put the Union first and the state second; or, to put it more accurately, had thought of the state in terms of the Union. Nullification had been resented in the state, albeit the legislature in the famous resolutions of 1798–1799 had upheld state rights; and the pages of Kentucky history offer many a commentary on the thesis that Southernism was not incompatible with broad nationalism. It is true that slavery was strongly intrenched in the state and that much of the thought of the people was conditioned by their determination to conserve the slave régime; but as in Maryland, Delaware, and Missouri this adherence to slavery did not mean going the whole way with Southern "sister states." [2] Kentucky's significance as a bond between North and South is illustrated by the large number of Kentuckians in Northern states in 1860: 100,000 in Missouri; 60,000 in Illinois; 68,000 in Indiana; 15,000 in Ohio; 13,000 in Iowa. In all there were at this time 332,000 Kentuckians living in other commonwealths.

In the troublous campaign of 1860 Kentucky Democrats had refused to join with Southern "bolters"; and the vote of the state on all sides registered support of the Union. The combined Douglas and Bell vote of 91,000 was for the Union *par excellence;* and even many of the 52,800 votes for Breckinridge could be interpreted as pro-Union. As for Lincoln, he received only 1364 votes.

As the secession movement progressed, Kentucky showed itself more and more loath to choose between the Union and the South. Governor Magoffin, a man of Southern predilections, favored an all-Southern convention, while the labors of Senator Crittenden for a compromise that would avert the horror of civil war were expressive of the feelings of the people. Breckinridge himself opposed secession (though secessionists outside Kentucky looked to him as a leader) and used his influence to promote the Crittenden compromise. While a few active secessionists within the state maneuvered for a state convention which they hoped would sever the state from the Union, Unionists opposed the calling of a convention and Garrett Davis declared that the people ought to spring to armed re-

[1] E. Merton Coulter, *The Civil War and Readjustment in Kentucky,* 17.
[2] In 1860 Kentucky had 38,645 slaveholders, most of whom had small holdings; only seventy had fifty or more slaves. *Ibid.,* 7–8.

sistance if the legislature should pass a secession ordinance without submitting it to popular vote. Various suggestions such as a national convention or a convention of the border states were bruited about in such a way as to eclipse the talk of a Southern type of separate state convention; and the crisis passed with the Unionists keeping the saddle. Their victory was signalized by the adjournment of the legislature without summoning a state convention; furthermore the legislature did summon a convention of the border states.

Then came the firing at Sumter and Lincoln's call for militia, as a result of which there developed the short-lived policy of neutrality based upon the feeling that Kentucky should take no part in the insane war that was breaking out but should stand between the sections as a neutral and peace-promoting force. Of the efforts of Confederate agents to enlist Kentucky, of Magoffin's refusal to raise the state militia in response to Lincoln's call of April 15, of his like refusal to send troops to Harpers Ferry at the call of the Confederate secretary of war, and of his secret agreement to permit Confederate recruiting within the state, there is no room to treat. By May 20 both houses of the legislature had resolved in favor of Kentucky neutrality; and on that date Magoffin issued a proclamation announcing such neutrality to be legally operative.

Perhaps no party in the history of the state [writes E. M. Coulter after exhaustive research] ever announced more nearly the general desires of the people than the Union men did at this time in their neutrality stand. . . . Neutrality was logically and inevitably the result of the spirit of mediation and compromise; . . . it was assumed . . . [as] a last attempt to use these methods, and as a protest against being forced into a war abhorrent and detestable because it seemed to be criminally unnecessary.[3]

This condition of neutrality lasted from May to September, 1861. The difficulty of such an attitude, once war on a large scale had developed, is evident when one remembers that individuals within the state were enlisting for one side or the other, and that Kentuckians, though devoted to peace, were fighters. Those who supported neutrality with sufficient tenacity to fight for it—if one can admit such a paradox—would be in reality fighting for the Union.[4] In the special congressional election of June 20 [5] the Unionists won an overwhelming victory; and a little later a like victory

[3] Coulter, 41.

[4] Coulter writes (p. 91): "Neutrality meant at least the Union, and, hence, it expressed the dominant desire of Kentucky; but it was not difficult for many Kentuckians to be so strongly in favor of neutrality in theory that they were willing to fight for it, and this meant fighting for the Union. Various meetings over the state showed this strong Union feeling."

[5] This election was for the filling of vacancies, and was held with a view of completing Kentucky's representation in the special session of Congress which Lincoln had called for July 4.

was won in the choice of a new legislature. Meanwhile Lincoln had been besought to respect the neutrality of his native state. Declaring on April 26 that he had no military plan then in mind that required sending a force through Kentucky, he indicated that he would take no aggressive action against the state in case it should do nothing hostile to the national government. This cautious statement of policy was made more cautious by the following statement to J. J. Crittenden in July: ". . . I solemnly desire that no necessity for it [sending an armed force into Kentucky] may be presented; but I mean to say nothing which shall hereafter embarrass me in the performance of what may seem to be my duty." [6]

It was not that Kentucky seriously expected to be a sort of Switzerland between battling nations. In the neutrality phase there was registered the feeling of utter distaste with which the state contemplated the detestable quandary which was thrust upon a commonwealth which had neither any motive to leave the Union nor the slightest impulse to fight the South; there was revealed also the slowness of the state to accept the fact of war, the lingering feeling that war was not inescapable and that conciliatory efforts should still be tried. There was yet another aspect of the neutrality policy: it offered a temporary *modus vivendi* between the Union and Confederate elements within the state at a time when forces were recruiting and drilling on both sides in the same towns and confronting each other on every hand. Kentucky was indeed arming herself, but not entirely in the spirit of the neutrality resolution: the arming was in reality either for the Union or for the South. The time came when Lincoln denounced this neutral attitude which he said would "do for the disunionists that which . . . they most desire"; but it is none the less true that Union men supported the neutrality scheme, which has even been described as a trick by which the Unionists saved the day at a moment when no other device could have prevented secession.[7]

The rush of events, however, soon forced an abandonment of this interesting and high-minded policy of neutrality. Both belligerents were recruiting within the state; Kentuckians individually were taking sides;

[6] Coulter, 54, 99–100.

[7] The papers of John J. Crittenden in the Library of Congress throw a flood of light upon the difficult position of Kentucky. His mail in those trying days brought numerous last-minute proposals for adjustment, invitations to speak from admirers on both sides, expressions of the gratitude of American women for his compromise efforts, important communications from the Virginia convention, a letter from Louisiana signed "No North, no South, no East, no West, but my whole country," comments on the projected border-states convention, protests from Missouri against any arraying of the border states against the South, violent expressions of war feeling alternating with earnestly pacific declarations, proposals for an "armistice," suggestions that England or France should intervene for the sake of peace, expressions from Tennessee showing fear of secession and sympathy for Kentucky's neutrality, et cetera. As a guide to this correspondence, see C. N. Feamster, *Calendar of the Papers of John Jordan Crittenden*, esp. pp. 258 ff.

Kentucky Unionists brought about the establishment of a Union camp known as "Camp Dick Robinson" near Danville; soldiers of Kentucky took part on both sides in the battle of Bull Run; youthful military ardor was running high; and both Union and Confederate authorities were angling for so strategic a commonwealth. At a time when the Federals were suspected of being ready to seize some river position within Kentucky, the Confederates seized Columbus, and directly afterward Grant occupied Paducah. On September 11 the ghost of a neutrality already dead was laid when the legislature demanded the withdrawal of the Confederates. On the 18th the same body created a military force to expel the Confederates, thus placing the state unequivocally in the Union.

Even after this, however, the Union cause had hard sledding within the state. Nearly every town boasted flagpoles flying the banners of both North and South; families were sundered; and difficulty was encountered in raising the 42,000 Union volunteers asked for in '61 and '62.[8] A pro-Confederate state government for Kentucky was formed, which "continued its shadowy existence until Appomattox," despite the fact that it "was never quartered in the state long enough to develop any qualities of permanency." [9] As the war progressed complications concerning slavery and indignation at the arrest of leading Kentuckians kept the cauldron of anti-Lincoln feeling boiling; military developments led to the proclamation of martial law in the state; Kentucky Union Democrats found it a great embarrassment to be regarded as supporters of the administration at Washington; and denunciation of the Lincoln government became the order of the day. In the election of 1864 McClellan received 61,000 civilian votes to Lincoln's 26,000; [10] and the war ended with sentiment so strongly attached to the South that W. N. Haldeman, editor of the pro-Confederate Louisville *Courier,* an exile during the war, resumed his work at Louisville and was welcomed as a leader of the post-war Confederate Democracy.

2

The position of Maryland, nearly surrounding the capital city of the nation and standing between it and the North, was such that its loss to the Union cause could hardly have been conceived except in terms of Union defeat. Though the majority of its people were opposed to secession (as a course for Maryland to adopt), yet measures none too choice were

---

[8] In the aggregate Kentucky furnished 75,000 Union enlistments, as compared to 100,000 called for. *Offic. Rec.,* 3 ser., IV, 1269. To state with accuracy how many Kentuckians entered the Confederate army seems impossible because of incomplete records. A Confederate official source reported 7950 soldiers from Kentucky in February, 1862 (*ibid.,* 4 ser., I, 962), and there are indications that Confederate recruiting in the state after that time was slower than before.

[9] Coulter, 139.

[10] *Ibid.,* 187. The soldier vote was 3068 for McClellan, 1205 for Lincoln.

employed to insure the national allegiance of this strategically situated commonwealth. The strong Confederate sympathy in the city of Baltimore and the violence which attended the passage of Federal troops through that city at the outset of the war have already been noted.[1] In this opposition to the passage of troops one may glimpse not only Confederate sympathy but also a feeling akin to that of Kentucky—a feeling that continuing peace efforts should be made, even after Sumter, and that the state should take no hostile course toward either North or South.

The opponents of secession were fortunate in having Thomas Hicks as governor, for he was "a friend of the Union, though . . . hardly of that unflinching fearlessness needed in revolutionary emergencies." Fearing that "through some juggle Maryland would be forced into secession," Hicks refused to call the legislature into session until April, 1861, and then he convened it at Frederick, rather than at Baltimore, where secessionism was rife.[2] Despite these precautions, that body gave its official sanction to a go-in-peace policy. Protesting against the war and expressing sympathy "with the South in the struggle for their rights," the legislature resolved on May 10:

That Maryland implores the President . . . to cease this unholy war, at least until Congress assembles; that Maryland desires and consents to the recognition of the independence of the Confederate States. [That] the military occupation of Maryland is unconstitutional, and she protests against it, though the violent interference with the transit of Federal troops is discountenanced; that the vindication of her rights be left to time and reason, and that a Convention, under existing circumstances, is inexpedient.[3]

This friendliness to the South was reciprocated at Montgomery. A committee from the Maryland legislature had repaired to the Confederate capital; and they brought back a letter from Jefferson Davis voicing the hope that Maryland would join the Confederate States and echoing the wish for a cessation of hostilities.

In the course of the war the clash of interests because of the Southern sympathies of Maryland was evident on many occasions. Seizure of property, arrest of citizens, and suppression of newspapers kept alive the resentment of a proud people subjected to the indignity of military occupation. Typical of these troubles was the offense caused by the flamboyant and swashbuckling B. F. Butler, who, while in command of Federal troops at the outset of the war, took military possession of Annapolis and Baltimore. Butler's maladroitness and aptitude for producing irritating incidents was illustrated by his seizure of the Annapolis and Elk Ridge Railroad (to

---

[1] See above, pp. 195–196.
[2] Charles B. Clark, "Politics in Maryland during the Civil War," *Maryland Historical Mag.*, XXXVI, 240; XXXVIII, 230.
[3] N. Y. *Times*, May 11, 1861, p. 1.

prevent, as he said, the fulfillment of a threat that if his troops passed over the railroad it would be destroyed), and his threat of condign punishment growing out of a report that a Union private had been poisoned by food supplied by a local vender. His occupation of Baltimore proved particularly irritating. Since his measures were without authorization from Washington, he was supplanted by General George Cadwalader as commander of the Union military régime in the state.[4]

Keenly aware of the importance of Maryland to the Union cause, the Lincoln administration played a watchful and active role in the fall elections in that state. To support the unconditional Unionist candidate for governor, Augustus W. Bradford, Generals Banks and Dix, under orders from the secretary of war, kept the Maryland legislature under close military surveillance and placed nineteen of its members, along with Mayor Brown of Baltimore and other citizens, under arbitrary arrest. Maryland troops received three-day furloughs in order to go home and vote, and at the same time General Dix ordered the provost marshals to arrest any disunionists or Southern sympathizers who turned up at the polls. Bradford was elected by 57,502 votes to his opponent's 26,070. Though the Unionists might possibly have won a freely conducted election, they owed their victory to "intimidation, the illegal voting of soldiers, and the unlawful use of soldiery." The outcome of this 1861 election, writes Charles B. Clark, "destroyed practically all hope the State Rights party had of taking Maryland into the Confederacy, and many Maryland sympathizers with the Southern cause fled from the State after November, 1861. . . . After the election Maryland became in fact as well as in name a loyal state." [5]

As for Delaware, Harold Hancock points out, "while there was never any real danger of the state seceding, there was abundant pro-Southern feeling and a possibility that armed conflict might break out between friends of the North and South." Having extended to Judge Henry Dickinson, commissioner from Mississippi, the courtesy of listening to his address urging the state to join the proposed Southern Confederacy, the legislature, on January 3, 1861, unanimously expressed its "unqualified disapproval" of such a course. At the same time there were many influential persons, like the Delaware secretary of state, who were unwilling to "coerce" the seceded states and asked: "Why not let them depart in peace and save the horrors of a Civil War?" When the war did break out, communities were badly divided. "The boys, as well as the men, the grown up women as well as the young girls . . . , arrayed themselves against each other in bitter hostility," a contemporary recalled, "and it was some-

[4] See below, pp. 301–302, for a discussion of legal controversies growing out of Cadwalader's arrests.

[5] Clark, "Politics in Maryland during the Civil War," *loc. cit.,* XXXVII, 398–399.

times said, one half of the town did not speak or associate with the other half." [6] Gradually, however, Unionist sentiment triumphed. On April 26, 1861, Governor William Burton, in a manner none too enthusiastic, recommended the formation of "volunteer companies for . . . protection . . . of the people of this State against violence of any sort," adding that such companies might have the "option of offering their services to the general government for the defence of its capital and the support of the Constitution and laws of the country." [7] In all, Delaware supplied 12,000 enlistments to the Union cause. [8]

3

In Missouri the conflicts of unconditional Unionists, conservative Unionists, and secessionists produced unusual turbulence and governmental confusion. The governor, Claiborne F. Jackson, leading the movement for secession, was able to persuade the legislature to call a convention; but when the convention was chosen its personnel was so overwhelmingly Unionist that it adjourned on March 22 without passing the ordinance of secession which the governor had desired. The Jackson element and the Union element were soon armed in opposing groups, and forebodings of trouble were seen when a force accused of being pro-Confederate formed a camp at St. Louis ("Camp Jackson") while at the same time and in the same city the aggressive Nathaniel Lyon was in command of a pro-Union force which he had newly organized. Though the officers and men of Camp Jackson professed their support of the Union, Lyon, believing their protestations to be misleading, moved upon them in force, surrounded them with superior numbers, and compelled their surrender (May 10, 1861). Street fighting then occurred between Union soldiers and enraged citizens, resulting in twenty-eight deaths; and reports were spread of a "massacre" of defenseless persons, including women and children. Indignation at this "massacre" would have been enough to produce a reaction; but there were other elements in the complex situation. One factor was that of native Americanism versus foreigners. Since the Germans of Missouri, as elsewhere, were solidly Republican, antislavery, and Unionist, the force of anti-foreign prejudice, fanned so recently into flame by the Knownothings, a potent force with the populace, became a powerful ally of the anti-Unionists. Governor Jackson with his legislature now organized a state military force, putting it under the command of ex-Governor Sterling Price, a man of character and influence who had served

[6] Hancock, "Civil War Comes to Delaware," *Civil War Hist.*, II, 29–46 (Dec., 1956).
[7] Moore, *Rebell. Rec.* (Diary), I, 155.
[8] *Offic. Rec.* 2 ser., IV, 1269.

in the Mexican War. He had been a Unionist, presiding at the convention which had repudiated secession, but now he had become so outraged at the conduct of Lyon and the extreme Unionists as to join the secession ranks. Internecine war resulted.[1] At the battle of Wilson's Creek (August 10, 1861) Federal troops were defeated, but at Pea Ridge (March 6–8, 1862) they won a smashing victory and all except a small portion of the territory of the state fell under Unionist control.

For this result they paid a heavy price. It was not merely that they lost a vigorous leader in the death of Lyon at Wilson's Creek; their action had forced civil war in Missouri at a time when there was at least a chance that it might have been avoided. Neighborhood war, bushwhacking, sniping, and guerilla fighting now became rampant in Missouri. The situation grew worse through the intervention of troops from Kansas, where numbers of free-state men looked with fear and hostility upon their slaveholding neighbors across the border, remembered vividly the intervention of the Missouri "border ruffians" in Kansas affairs, and "were waiting for the opportunity to take revenge for real and fancied wrongs that had occurred in the five years before 1861." [2] Led by the notorious James H. Lane and the infamous Charles R. Jennison, these Kansas "jayhawkers" descended upon the Missouri border with the cry: "Everything disloyal . . . from a Durham cow to a Shanghai chicken, must be cleaned out." [3] Even Union officials in Missouri complained that these Kansas volunteers were "no better than a band of robbers." [4] Inevitably their actions drove many wavering Missouri Unionists into the secessionist camp and provoked guerilla warfare by pro-Southern "bushwhackers" of a most sanguinary sort. A "maelstrom of retaliation and counterretaliation built up," which culminated (August 21, 1863) when the bloodthirsty and heartless Confederate guerilla captain, William C. Quantrill, descended upon Lawrence, Kansas, and in a "wholesale and indiscriminate slaughter" killed 150 men and wounded 30 others in what has been called "the most atrocious act of the Civil War." [5] In revenge, Union authorities issued General Orders

---

[1] In order to avert such war, the "Harney-Price agreement" was negotiated on the side of the state troops by Price and on the Union side by General William S. Harney, who for the time commanded the Military Department of the West, and who, though a sincere Unionist, preferred conciliatory methods to force. The gist of this agreement was that Price would use his force merely to keep order in the state, and that in view of this Harney would not attack him. Various writers on Missouri history have regretted that the spirit of this agreement was not kept and that the radical leadership of Francis P. Blair, Jr., and Lyon, instead of that of Harney, prevailed. E. C. Smith, *Borderland*, 226–230, 245–246, 261.

[2] Richard S. Brownlee, *Gray Ghosts of the Confederacy*, 10.

[3] Albert Castel, *A Frontier State at War: Kansas, 1861–1865*, 53.

[4] Brownlee, 48.

[5] Castel, 63, 131, 136.

No. 11, which completed the ruin of western Missouri by forcing "the removal of all people in Jackson, Cass, Bates, and half of Vernon county, living more than a mile from Union military posts." [6]

Only through superior military power did the Federal government keep Missouri in the Union. Repeatedly portions of the state were placed under martial law; and military courts were busy with cases of civilians tried for bridge burning, tearing up railway and telegraph lines, and like offenses. The legal basis for the Union authority was the "state convention," which exercised constituent powers, emerging from time to time to perform fundamental functions as the spokesman of the people and continuing for so long a duration as to win the title "Long Convention." In the early summer of 1861 this convention declared the executive and legislative offices of the state vacant and filled the executive offices itself, after decreeing loyalty to the Union as a prerequisite of office-holding. A man of fine qualities, Hamilton R. Gamble, was chosen governor, and the Lincoln administration cooperated with him in a manner which avoided offense to state pride. When, for example, the governor organized the state militia as home guards, Lincoln selected the militia head as commander of the Federal military force in Missouri. The Lincoln government also supplied arms for state troops, together with the sum of $200,000 to be used in equipping and maintaining them. On the death of Gamble in January, 1864, his duties were assumed by Lt. Gov. Willard P. Hall, also appointed by the state convention.

Meanwhile the form if not the substance of a pro-Confederate state government had been maintained. General Jackson at New Madrid (August 5, 1861) proclaimed the independence of Missouri "as a sovereign, free, and independent republic"; and in November a remnant of the "deposed legislature" (less than a quorum in either house) met at Neosho, decreed the secession of Missouri from the United States, and set up a government which was recognized by the Confederate States and admitted to their fold. Jackson functioned as governor of this political entity till his death in 1862. The office was later held by Thomas C. Reynolds; and Missouri was thus stoutly represented as one of the states in the "Western section of the Confederacy" which would never "seek any destiny separate from that of our [Confederate] sisters east of the Mississippi." [7] The division of sentiment in the state is suggested by the fact that 109,000 men were furnished to the Union army; while about 30,000 fought with the South.

4

The formation of West Virginia was the result of irregular and illegal processes. Back of the wartime disruption there were decades of sectional

---

[6] Brownlee, 126.
[7] Moore, *Rebell. Rec.* (Doc.), VII, 406.

differences within the Old Dominion.[1] The tidewater, middle Virginia, the piedmont, and the Valley looked to the seaboard and the South; while in the montane counties of the northwest and those of the panhandle the flow of rivers and the general outlook was toward the Ohio. The region which has been loosely called "western Virginia" had in the course of time become aware of various grievances against the older counties, which had retained political power out of proportion to their numbers. Discrimination in favor of slaveholders in the matter of taxation, limitations as to voting, partiality in the distribution of governmental benefits—such were the complaints of the people of the Kanawha region, who felt that they were at a disadvantage as compared to the "aristocrats" of the East. Sectional differences equally serious, however, have existed in a number of other states without disrupting them; for example, the differences in Illinois between Chicago and downstate in taxation, political representation, poor relief, and constitutional change are as sharp as those within the Old Dominion of the ante-bellum period. Moreover, these differences had been partially adjusted, so that from 1851 to 1861 sectionalism within the state had become less acute. It is probable that, had war not supplied the impulse, no dismemberment of the state would have occurred. This, however, is not the whole story: the evidence also points clearly to the conclusion that, if during the war legal processes fully reflective of popular opinion had been employed, separate statehood would not have been established for any region corresponding to that which became West Virginia.

Since only a bare summary can be attempted here, the clearest method will be an enumeration, one by one, of the steps taken in state-making.

1. Union mass meetings were held directly after the secession of Virginia (April 17, 1861); and a mass meeting of special importance at Clarksburg on April 22 summoned a preliminary convention of delegates to meet at Wheeling to consider what emergency steps should be taken to uphold the Union in Virginia and strike down the heresy of secession.

2. This "May convention" assembled [2] at Wheeling. It passed resolutions denouncing secession and summoning a general convention to meet on June 11, also at Wheeling, to take fundamental political action for Virginia as a whole. In order to be fully representative of the entire state for which it presumed to act, the convention should have had delegates from all the 150 counties; instead it included delegates from only twenty-six of the fifty counties that became West Virginia. It was in reality a mass convention of delegates chosen by local Union mass meetings. That there

[1] For underlying causes see Charles H. Ambler, *Sectionalism in Virginia from 1776 to 1861*. A critical account of sources as well as secondary accounts pertaining to the West Virginia movement is found in the footnotes of chap. xviii ("The Partition of Virginia") in Randall, *Constitutional Problems Under Lincoln*, 433–476.

[2] May 13, 1861.

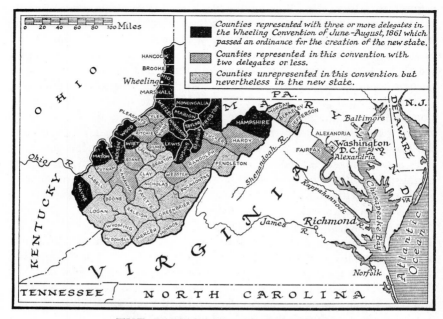

THE PARTITION OF VIRGINIA

was vital Union sentiment and indignant opposition to secession back of these meetings is clear; in the Richmond convention the members from the northwest had vigorously combated secession. What is not so clear is that the governmental measures taken in detail for the formation of a new state, as distinguished from the upholding of Unionism within the state, were backed up by majority opinion in the area concerned. Leaving aside the fact that many of those within the West-Virginian area were pro-Confederate, many of the Unionists were doubtful of the legality and wisdom of any action that would defy the authorities at Richmond, and many more were distrustful of any permanent disruption of the commonwealth. In view of the partial and one-sided nature of the May convention, it cannot be regarded as fully representative of the West-Virginian area.

3. After the ordinance for the secession of Virginia was ratified by popular vote there met at Wheeling (June–August, 1861) the convention which cast the die for separate statehood. It performed two principal functions: first, it passed an ordinance "reorganizing" the government of Virginia—i.e., Virginia as a whole—making loyalty to the Union the *sine qua non* of state office-holding, thus setting up a government rivaling that at Richmond; second, it adopted (August 20) another ordinance which decreed that "a new State, to be called the State of Kanawha, be formed and erected," to consist of forty-eight designated counties. This ordinance

was in reality the work of an active but limited group of separationists in the counties near Pennsylvania and Maryland. The whole atmosphere at Wheeling, which was within the Union lines, was favorable to the work of this group, just as the atmosphere at Richmond was favorable to the secessionists. A few of the leaders, with a map before them, drew the boundaries of the new state. The people of the area concerned had no opportunity, county by county, to determine whether they would adhere to Virginia or join the new commonwealth.[3] Their fate was determined by the whole vote cast some months later within the boundaries indicated by the convention. It is stated by J. C. McGregor that this plan was adopted to avoid "certain rejection in at least two thirds of the counties." [4] It is significant that half the area of the state-to-be was entirely unrepresented in the June convention which passed the ordinance for the new commonwealth and fixed its boundaries.

Those who were managing the secession movement at Wheeling at first assigned forty-eight counties to the new state: later the counties of Jefferson and Berkeley (in the region of Shepherdstown, Charles Town, and Harpers Ferry) were added in a manner whose irregularity was challenged by Virginia but upheld by the United States Supreme Court.[5] So strong, however, is the Virginian tradition in these two counties that they may be appropriately termed "Virginia Irredenta."

4. A body of men called the "reorganized legislature" of Virginia, constituted according to a pattern devised by the June convention, elected W. T. Willey and J. S. Carlile United States senators from Virginia (not West Virginia) in place of J. M. Mason and R. M. T. Hunter, adherents of the Confederacy, whose seats had been vacated.

5. A Unionist government for Virginia was put into operation at Wheeling. This was done by developing in detail the reorganization plan promulgated by the June convention, disqualifying existing office holders who would not take the Unionist oath and holding new elections in which only Unionists could qualify. The details of what went on in the launching of this "restored" government are extremely complex; if told in full they would reveal a condition of anarchy, uncertainty, and turbulence which has been almost lost from view in the war histories that hardly touch the surface of this political and social movement. The lacunae in civil government in the period of this awkward and puzzling transition brought bewilderment and distress to the honest-minded, at the same time opening the way to bandits, guerillas, and desperate men who roamed the country, lurked in the woods, shot citizens, ravaged the fields, broke into houses, and easily evaded the home guards and impromptu military forces which

[3] See below, p. 240, paragraph 6.
[4] *Disruption of Virginia,* 235–236.
[5] Virginia *vs.* West Virginia, 78 U. S. 39.

in the absence of adequate government were summoned to disperse them. In these circumstances, and in view of the coercion and social intolerance which accompanied the elections and the administering of oaths, many found life intolerable and took to flight, some of them finding their way within Confederate lines, others fleeing to Kentucky or Ohio. It was amid such conditions that Francis H. Pierpoint,[6] elected by the June convention, became "Governor of Virginia" at Wheeling.

6. On October 24, 1861, there was held, in accordance with the ordinance of the Wheeling convention, an election for a constitutional convention to frame an instrument of government for the new commonwealth. At the same election the people within the predetermined boundaries of the proposed new state voted (but not by counties) in a sort of referendum on the question whether the new state should be created. The vote was scattering and one-sided. It did not compare to the normal vote of the region, being virtually limited to Unionists, for Confederate sympathizers and anti-new-state men, speaking generally, did not vote at all. The result as announced was 18,408 yeas and 781 nays.

7. This convention met at Wheeling in November and after considerable labor formed a constitution for "West Virginia," dropping the picturesque name "Kanawha." On April 3, 1862, the people of the designated region voted (18,862 to 514) to ratify the constitution, which, incidentally, did not abolish slavery. In this election the anti-separationists, regarding all these proceedings as invalid and the election as unauthorized, did not vote. In contrast to a normal vote of 47,000 for the region, only 19,000 votes were cast in this election. In one county only 76 votes were cast, though there were 800 voters. McGregor has pointed out that the records of the West-Virginian constitutional convention were not printed because "the discussion had revealed so plainly the opposition of the people of West Virginia both to the North and to the new state that the publication of the debates might interfere with the admission of the state."[7]

8. On May 13, 1862, the "restored" state legislature at Wheeling, acting for all Virginia, gave its "consent" to the formation of the new state. This legislature consisted of about thirty-five members in the lower house and ten in the upper, though the full membership according to the Vir-

---

[6] "Pierpoint" was the wartime spelling and the wartime form of the man's own signature. Later the name appears as "Pierpont." Letters in the Pierpoint MSS. (Va. State Archives) address the man as: "Governor of Virginia," "Governor of West Virginia," "Governor . . . State West-Virginia," "the Governor of Loyal Virginia," "His Excellency the Governor of East Virginia, Alexandria, Virginia," "Military Governor of Eastern Virginia," "the Gov verner of west vir giney," "His Excellency Gov Pierpoint of the State of W^n Virginia," "Honerable F. H. Pierpoint, Governor of West Virginia," "Governor [sic] of the new Western Virginia State," "Governor of new Virginia." (It is to be noted that Pierpoint was never governor of West Virginia.)

[7] McGregor, p. ix.

ginia constitution should have been 152 delegates and fifty senators. Except for the "eastern shore" and a limited area opposite Washington, the constituencies represented were entirely of the northwest. Even in the northwest many of the counties were unrepresented; obviously Confederate Virginia was totally unrepresented. It was by this legal fiction that the "consent of Virginia" was obtained in nominal compliance with that provision of the Constitution of the United States which provides that no state shall be created within the limits of an existing commonwealth without the consent of the latter's legislature.

9. The matter now came up to the Federal Congress, which passed the bill admitting West Virginia to the Union, though many Virginia Unionists opposed such admission. Lincoln really disapproved of the bill and it was feared that he would veto it, though this fact has been generally overlooked.[8] His reluctant consent was, however, obtained; and on December 31, 1862, the bill became law, its provisions being so framed as to require the gradual abolition of slavery. From the wordy debates on the measure one bit may be selected for quotation here. Thaddeus Stevens spoke as follows: ". . . we may admit West Virginia . . . under our absolute power which the laws of war give us in the circumstances in which we are placed. I shall vote for this bill upon that theory, and upon that alone; for I will not stultify myself by supposing that we have any warrant in the Constitution for this proceeding." [9] It took some months to complete the conditions of statehood; and on April 20, 1863, President Lincoln issued a proclamation declaring the state of West Virginia admitted to the Union, setting the effective date of such admission at June 20.

10. The admission of the new state, whose capital was at Wheeling, left the Pierpoint government high and dry. It continued, however, to exist, and, transferring its seat to Alexandria across from Washington, sought bravely to carry on as the government of Virginia.

As for the war-born state of West Virginia, it was the offspring of a species of legal fiction. By assuming the consent of Virginia, which could only be asserted as a technical fact, the makers of the new state offered a kind of sophistry to excuse the non-fulfillment of a constitutional obligation. The whole proceeding presented an example of a measure which even its supporters did not wish to be emulated elsewhere or used as a precedent. The case is not fully covered by any statement of grievances or sectional considerations; for the question is not merely the need for a new state (which itself is seriously disputed), but the justification of the irregular process by which the new state was formed. Any normal and regular process of separation should have involved negotiation and agree-

---

[8] Senator Willey wrote to Pierpoint (December 17, 1862): "We have great fears that the President will veto the new State bill." Pierpoint Papers (MSS., Va. State Archives). See also Browning, *Diary,* I, 596; Welles, *Diary,* I, 191.

[9] *Cong. Globe,* 37 Cong., 3 sess., 50–51.

ment between the parent state and the new commonwealth as to details, such as the boundary, the division of the state debt, and the like. In these matters, however, Virginia's interests were cavalierly treated, as a result of which Berkeley and Jefferson counties were included in West Virginia contrary to the almost universal sentiment of the people of those counties; while as for the debt, it became a matter of long-drawn-out controversy owing to the refusal of the new state to assume its equitable share. Indeed it was not until 1920 that the new state gave satisfaction on this point, and then merely by way of reluctant and tardy compliance with a peremptory decree of the United States Supreme Court.[10]

[10] J. G. Randall, "The Virginia Debt Controversy," *Pol. Sci. Quar.*, XXX, 553 ff.; *Constitutional Problems Under Lincoln*, 476 n.

CHAPTER 13

Problems of the Confederacy

I

THE MOVEMENT for Southern nationhood and the organizing work of the Montgomery convention have been sketched above.[1] Approximately a month before Lincoln's inauguration the new nation was launched. In this phase the controlling agent was the convention in the Alabama capital; for with the assembling of that body the leaders had, so far as the lower South was concerned, accomplished their main purpose. In other words, the Montgomery convention had no *raison d'être* except in terms of Southern independence. It was not a convention to ponder the advisability of independence, but to put into effect the decision that a Southern confederacy be formed. Until the outbreak of war this confederacy numbered less than half the slaveholding states. The seven states within the fold prior to mid-April of 1861 contained less than five million souls (white and black), while the eight slaveholding states outside the Confederacy contained more than seven million.

Much could be written on what became of Southern unionism once the Confederacy was launched. The most obvious fact was that the new nation seized the imagination of the people; and as state after state joined it, there appeared the familiar phenomenon of a dominant and affirmative type of public opinion which bore the stamp of being "Southern," patriotic, and therefore sound; while the opposing type of opinion was that of dissent, doubt, and misgiving. Being negative this latter opinion was less thrilling than the dominant pattern. It was easily susceptible of denunciation by orators and editors, and soon came to be regarded as treasonable heresy. The attainment of quick popular support was the easier because the war factor was kept in the background. Not only did Southerners hope that war could be avoided; they were led to believe that, even if the Yankees did fight, they would not make any very determined effort to subjugate the South. "When the war first broke out said [Jefferson Davis] many of

[1] See pp. 127 ff., 156 ff.

our people could with difficulty be persuaded that it would be long or serious." [2] The nonaggressive nature of the whole Southern movement was emphasized; and it was possible to make the appeal to both those who turned readily to slogans of battle and those whose blood ran cold at the thought of a war of brothers. Similarly it was possible at the outset to enlist even Unionists in the Southern cause. This was done by the familiar argument for secession which predicted that "better terms" could be had by seceding, these terms being capable of interpretation in the sense of return to the Union. But perhaps the more common attitude of those Unionists who were brought over to the support of secession was the realization that, though they would have willed a different result, their states had acted otherwise, so that both the motive of state loyalty and the compelling necessity of maintaining law and public authority required acquiescence in a time of such emergency.

To rationalize the Southern movement in constitutional terms was easy; and much of the discussion of the time was devoted to this aspect. The justification of the legal "right of secession" was, in the South, virtually unanswerable. As a rule not even Unionists denied that the right existed; to them the vital question was not the legal right but the wisdom of separation. The most famous constitutional defense of secession was written by a Georgia Unionist, Alexander H. Stephens.[3] The state-rights arguments being ready to hand, the Southern constitutionalist did not have to invent them; he had only to reach for them. The abstract concept of "sovereignty" was exalted as the supreme thing in government; the people of the states (not precisely the state governments) were sovereign; with them resided ultimate authority. The supreme-law clause of the Federal Constitution, so the argument ran, did not make the national government sovereign over the people of the states. It was the people of the states who originated that supreme-law clause as part of the state-and-federal pattern. So long as government operated within that pattern, the supreme-law clause, properly applied, would hold good, for the people of the states had so willed; but that did not mean that the people could not alter a pattern which they themselves had made. That the people of all the states or of a sufficient number to make a constitutional amendment could alone change the pattern was not admitted. It was held that a few of the states, if their people so decreed, could set up for themselves, especially if the original pattern were distorted or abused. The Constitution being a "compact" (between state peoples), it was fitting that if some of the confederated parties violated its terms, the other parties, or any of them, could declare its dissolution.

It is, however, unnecessary in these pages to elaborate the constitu-

[2] This was embarrassing because the people were averse to long enlistments. Rowland, *Davis*, V, 205.

[3] *A Constitutional View of the Late War Between the States.*

tional arguments further. The cause of nationhood moved with the spirit of high adventure. It steeled men to keen endeavor; it became a holy cause; it presented the opportunity for heroism where life was otherwise a humdrum matter; it made dissent seem ignoble; it throbbed with the *élan* and verve of a popular crusade. Though it has been said that the aristocratic planters set the pace, yet, if this is true, it is merely a repetition of the same truth to add that the populace caught step. Certainly throughout the story of the Southern movement, as for instance with regard to dictatorial methods of war government, it was always necessary to reckon with the Southern sense of democracy. Anything like a directory or dictatorship would be out of line with Southern tendencies and would be sure to encounter obstacles.

2

The first régime being provisional, it was necessary to launch a permanent government. The two inaugurations of President Davis mark the distinction between the provisional and permanent phases. On February 18, 1861, Davis was inaugurated provisional President, that office having been conferred by the Montgomery convention; on February 22, 1862, he was inaugurated President under the permanent régime. Between these two dates had occurred the completion of the permanent constitution, which was adopted unanimously by the Montgomery Congress on March 11, 1861; the ratification of the constitution, which was not unanimous, by conventions in the seceding states; the general elections for Congress and for presidential electors in November, 1861; and the choice of President and Vice-President by the electors.

The Confederate government, provisional and permanent, was non-partisan. The question how long it could have continued so is an interesting speculation; but the only presidential election in Confederate history showed all the electoral votes, a total of 109, cast for Davis and Stephens. There had been no party nominations in this election.

The Montgomery government quickly became for the South the successor of the Federal government at Washington. A motion to "make known to the world the motives" of the people in forming the Confederacy was lost. A flag, the famous "Stars and Bars," was adopted for the new republic after study by a committee.[1] Commissioners were sent to Washington to

[1] The committee pointed out that the "keeping" of the flag of the United States would be a "political and military solecism." They added: "Whatever attachment may be felt . . . for 'the Stars and Stripes' (an attachment which your committee . . . do not all share) . . . we can not . . . without encountering . . . practical difficulties, retain the flag of the Government from which we have withdrawn." It was also stated that the battles of the Revolution had not been fought under the Stars and Stripes; and as to the glory of the South in more recent times, the committee declared that "history will preserve and commemorate the fact more imperishably than a mere piece of striped bunting." It was pointed out that our

negotiate for the delivery of Federal forts, arsenals, et cetera, within the Confederacy and to give assurance of the wish to "preserve the most friendly relations." Other men were chosen as commissioners to the European powers. The fabric of Federal legislation was dealt with by an act passed (against the vote of South Carolina) to continue in force all the laws of the United States as of November, 1860, so far as they were not inconsistent with the Confederate constitution, until they were repealed or altered by Congress. A committee was appointed to revise the statutes of the United States and refit them to the Confederacy. It was resolved that the Confederate Congress employ an "agent at Washington to furnish any documents or information which may be useful to this body"; and it was also voted to confirm existing customs officers in the South and continue them in office.[2] Thus the labors of creating a government *de novo* were remarkably simplified by taking over, with adaptations, the constitution of the Federal government, its laws, and even its official personnel.

It was natural also that the Confederate cabinet should follow the Washington pattern, the departments being the same as those at Washington, except that a department of justice was added [3] and no department of the interior was formed. Promptly appointed by President Davis and confirmed by the Montgomery Congress, the cabinet consisted of the following: Robert Toombs of Georgia, secretary of state; C. G. Memminger of South Carolina, secretary of the treasury; Leroy P. Walker of Alabama, secretary of war; Judah P. Benjamin of Louisiana, attorney general; S. R. Mallory of Florida, secretary of the navy; John H. Reagan of Texas, postmaster general. Toombs soon resigned to become a general in the Confederate army, and was succeeded by R. M. T. Hunter of Virginia. Other changes followed. Benjamin's chief service was as secretary of state. Thomas Bragg and George Davis, both of North Carolina, and Thomas H. Watts of Alabama served as attorney general. George A. Trenholm of South Carolina succeeded Memminger as secretary of the treasury. The office of secretary of war saw many changes, Walker's successors being Judah P. Benjamin, G. W. Randolph of Virginia, James A. Seddon of Virginia, and John C. Breckinridge of Kentucky. Mallory and Reagan, appointed at the beginning, retained their positions to the end. The state of Kentucky in 1865 had the distinction of being represented in both the Confederate and Union cabinets. When one considers Southern efforts to capture additional slaveholding states and Union efforts toward reconstruction in the South, it may be said that this distinction might conceivably have come to any of the states south of the Mason and Dixon line.

forefathers, though nurtured under the British flag, under which Washington won his spurs, separated with "no lingering, regretful looks behind." *Journal,* Confed. Cong. (*Sen. Doc. No. 234,* 58 [U. S.] Cong., 2 sess.), I, 101–102.

2 *Ibid.,* I, 52–53.

3 The department of justice of the United States was created in 1870.

Herschel V. Johnson wrote: "I thought Mr. Davis was unfortunate in the composition of his Cabinet." [4] Though the cabinet contained able men, yet it was rather conspicuous for the lack of men who had an importance in the South comparable to that of Seward or Chase in the North. The case of Toombs illustrates the preference of prominent and vigorous Southern leaders for military service.

Many problems crowded in upon the Confederacy in the early weeks. The tariff, the navigation of the Mississippi River, the coasting trade, the post office, the seizure of United States funds, the organization and procedure of the courts, appeals to the other slaveholding states to join the Confederacy, the control of Indian affairs, and the apprehension, restraint, and removal of citizens of Northern states as "alien enemies" occupied the lawmakers. An army and a navy were organized. One of President Davis's first steps was to send agents into the North with authorization "to make purchases and contracts for machinery and munitions," to "engage . . . for the establishment of a powder mill at some point in the limits of our territory," and to take similar precautions.[5] Such agents did their work efficiently, and this illustrates but one of many methods by which the North contributed to the war preparations of the South. In general, however, such preparations were not of a thoroughgoing nature; and, in conformity with the nonaggressive character of the Confederate movement as interpreted by its leaders, such preparations were deemed merely defensive.

One of the knottiest problems at the beginning was the Sumter situation. It was not only that the government of the United States did not accept the thesis that its retention of Sumter put it in the position of an invading power; there was the further difficulty that the Sumter situation might cause embarrassment between South Carolina and the Confederate government. This, indeed, was one of the earliest challenges confronting the Southern nation from the angle of state rights. There were strong evidences that South Carolina was determined to have her way; and when the Montgomery convention sought to restrain the state, and considered a resolution requesting the commonwealth to abstain from any hostile attack upon Sumter until the President of the Confederate states could be inaugurated, Mr. Chesnut, representing the state in the Confederate Congress, offered an amendment by which the Confederate government's control of the war power was to be held subject to that clause of the constitution which provided that no state should "engage in war, unless actually invaded, or in such imminent danger as will not admit of delay." [6] The Montgomery convention voted to take "under its charge the questions . . . relating to the occupation of the forts . . . and other public establish-

[4] *Am. Hist. Rev.*, XXX, 329.
[5] Jefferson Davis to Raphael Semmes, Feb. 21, 1861, Rowland, *Davis,* V, 54–56.
[6] *Journal,* Confed. Cong., I, 47, 904.

ments," [7] whereupon Governor Pickens of South Carolina (February 13, 1861) wired urging that "it is due to us under all the circumstances to get possession of Sumter at a period not beyond the fourth [of March]." [8] At the same time Pickens sent the president of the Congress a long letter in which he stated:

It has . . . been considered . . . necessary for this State to take possession of that fort as soon as the measures necessary for the accomplishment of that result can be completed. And it is now expected that within a short time all the arrangements will be perfected . . . for its certain and speedy reduction. . . .

. . . If war can be averted, it will be by making the capture of Fort Sumter a fact accomplished during the . . . present Administration, and leaving to the incoming Administration the question of an open declaration of war. . . . Mr. Buchanan can not resist, because he has not the power. Mr. Lincoln may not attack, because the cause of quarrel will have been, or may be considered by him, as past.[9]

As a Southern writer has stated, there was "much impatience at what the Carolina leaders looked on as the pacific and temporizing policy of the Montgomery government, and more than a little chance that if that government did not order the reduction of Fort Sumter the state government would. In a measure the situation forced the hands of the Confederate Cabinet." [10]

Despite this difficulty, however, the events of April 12–13 concerning Sumter became a ringing war slogan for the South. The Southern point of view was effectively stated by President Davis in his message to Congress, April 29, 1861. Southern commissioners, as Davis pointed out, had arrived in Washington March 5; they had on the 12th made overtures for negotiation with the secretary of state. Waiving questions of form, they had consented to unofficial intercourse with an intermediary by whom they had been assured of the intention to evacuate Sumter. "The crooked paths of diplomacy [said Davis] can scarcely furnish an example so wanting in courtesy, in candor, and directness as was the course of the United States Government toward our commissioners in Washington." The President then recounted the story of the Sumter expedition, the refusal of the Northern President and secretary of state to listen to Southern proposals, the wish of the Confederate government to avoid effusion of blood, and the refusal of Anderson to agree to peaceful proposals; after which, he said, there "remained . . . no alternative but to direct that the fort should be at once reduced," which order "was executed by General Beauregard." He then

[7] Ibid., I, 47.
[8] Ibid., I, 49.
[9] Ibid., I, 57–58.
[10] Robert S. Henry, Story of the Confederacy, 30–31.

recounted the extraordinary action of the President of the United States in calling "for an army of 75,000 men to act as a *posse comitatus* . . . in States where no courts exist whose mandates . . . are not cheerfully obeyed . . . by a willing people." [11]

In this war message the Confederate President, with unanswerable logic from the Southern viewpoint, presented the South as a peaceful nation drawn into a purely defensive war by aggression from without. When a bill was passed authorizing letters of marque and reprisal, a change of wording was effected by which it was declared that the "President of the Confederate States [was] . . . authorized . . . to *meet* [not to *wage*] the war thus commenced. . . ." [12] In this spirit of proud defense the Southern President, speaking for his people, protested that they desired peace "at any sacrifice, save that of honor and independence"; that they sought no conquest; and that all they asked was to be let alone and be free from subjugation. [13]

The Montgomery phase of the Confederacy soon ended. On May 21, 1861, the decision was made to transfer the capital to Richmond, and this transfer was effected in June. The importance and prestige of Virginia and the need for a vigorous defense of the Old Dominion offered strong motives for accepting the invitation of the Virginia convention which had been extended on April 27. "Strategically [writes Douglas Freeman] it was a serious mistake, for it placed almost on the frontier of the Confederacy . . . the capital that was so soon . . . to become the emblem of the Southern cause. . . ." When it came to such details as the transfer of the Virginia troops to the Confederacy, the "separate efforts" of Virginia and the Confederacy were "not . . . without friction." [14]

3

It promptly became clear that the most urgent task of the Confederacy would be to raise and equip an army. Indeed, even before the attack on Fort Sumter the Confederate Congress had acted to create both a regular army (which remained only a paper force throughout the conflict) and a provisional force which actually fought the war. The details of this legislation are complicated and confusing: the Confederate Congress initially authorized the recruiting of 100,000 troops to serve either six months or a year, but after war actually began, the number was increased to 400,000 who should serve either for three years or for the duration of the conflict. As E. Merton Coulter summarizes this complex legislation: "A person

---

[11] *Journal*, Confed. Cong., I, 163–165.

[12] Authors' italics. *Ibid.*, I, 177; *Stat. at Large of the [Confed.] Provisional Government* . . . (hereafter cited as *Stat. at Large*, C. S. A.), 100.

[13] *Journal*, Confed. Cong., I, 168–169.

[14] *R. E. Lee: A Biography*, I, 514.

might become a member of the Provisional Army either as a volunteer without passing through the hands of a governor or as a member of state militia offered by the governor; and his term of service might be for the duration of the war however long it might last, for the duration if not over three years, for three years, for twelve months, for six months, or possibly for any intermediate time." [1]

At the outbreak of the war the confusion and inconsistency of this legislation seemed of little importance, for it appeared that virtually every able-bodied man in the South was rushing to enlist. "All of us are . . . ripe and ready for the fight," one Virginian reported to his governor. "I shall be shoulder to shoulder with you whenever the fight comes off. I go for taking Boston & Cincinati [sic]. I go for wipeing them out." So great was the flood of volunteers that the government could not arm or equip them all. "From Mississippi I could get 20,000 men who impatiently wait for notice that they can be armed," President Davis reported. "In Georgia numerous tenders are made to serve for any time at any place and to these and other offers I am still constrained to answer, 'I have not arms to supply you.' " [2] Secretary of War Walker estimated that he was obliged to decline the services of 200,000 volunteers during the early months of the war.

Generally, volunteering followed a regular order. A prominent citizen would raise a company from among his neighbors and would initiate them into the mysteries of elementary army tactics. An election would be held to choose company officers, and usually the person most active in raising the company would be elected captain. The men brought whatever arms and equipment they could find, including shotguns, flintlocks, and even swords used in the Mexican and Revolutionary wars. An important aspect of this preliminary stage was the choosing of a company name. Bell I. Wiley lists a few characteristic ones: "Tallapoosa Thrashers; Baker Fire Eaters; Southern Avengers; Amite Defenders; Butler's Revengers; Bartow Yankee Killers; Chickasaw Desperadoes; Dixie Heroes; Clayton Yellow Jackets; Hornet's Nest Riflemen; Lexington Wild Cats; Green Rough and Readys; Racoon Roughs; Barbour Yankee Hunters; Southern Rejectors of Old Abe; Cherokee Lincoln Killers; Yankee Terrors; and South Florida Bull Dogs." [3] When organized and christened, the company tendered its services to the state governor or directly to the Confederate authorities, and, if accepted, marched away to the mingled cheers and tears of the womenfolk they left behind.

But after the first enthusiastic rush to the colors, volunteering slowed down to a trickle. The most devoted Southerners enlisted at the outset; those who remained behind lacked the intensity of sectional devotion or had inescapable duties at home. Many Southerners thought the war was

---

[1] Coulter, *The Confederate States of America*, 309.
[2] Bell I. Wiley and Hirst Milhollen, *They Who Fought Here*, 22–23.
[3] Wiley, *The Life of Johnny Reb*, 20.

won at First Bull Run and saw no further call for their services. Volunteering was also discouraged by reports from men in the army that soldiering was not all "fun and frolic" but was instead drill, spit-and-polish, military discipline, and more drill. As one disillusioned Alabama enlisted man wrote home: "A soldier is worse than any negro on Chatahooche [sic] river. He has no privileges whatever. He is under worse taskmasters than any negro. He is not treated with any respect whatever. His officers may insult him and he has no right to open his mouth and dare not do it." [4]

After the miserable winter of 1861–1862, when Northern and Southern armies faced each other in sullen idleness, many Confederate twelve-month volunteers prepared to return to their homes when their enlistments expired in the spring. At just the time when McClellan was about to begin his great Peninsula offensive it seemed likely that the Confederate armies would be virtually disbanded. So great was the crisis that the Southern Congress hurriedly passed an act to encourage re-enlistments by granting generous furloughs and bounties to veterans who promised once more to volunteer.

Even so, it was clear that the volunteer system was breaking down, and under pressure from President Davis, who declared compulsory service "absolutely indispensable," [5] the Southern Congress on April 16, 1862, passed the first conscription law, enforcing military service upon white men between the ages of eighteen and thirty-five. In September, 1862, this act was amended to extend the age limits from thirty-five to forty-five, and in February, 1864, there was a further modification which made the age limits seventeen and fifty. [6]

As an effective conscription system, these measures had numerous defects, the most objectionable being the provision which allowed a man to escape military service by hiring a substitute and the exemption of numerous categories, such as "schoolteachers of twenty pupils, ministers, college professors, druggists, mail carriers, postmasters, civil officers of state governments and of the Confederacy, employees of railroads, ferrymen, telegraph operators, employees in cotton and woolen mills, mines, furnaces, and foundries, shoemakers, blacksmiths, tanners, millers, saltmakers, printers, and one editor for each paper." The exemption which caused the greatest outcry was that of one overseer or slaveowner to every twenty slaves, a provision which actually freed only a few hundred men from military service but which caused the poorer classes to protest that it was "a rich man's war and a poor man's fight." [7]

[4] David Donald, "The Confederate as a Fighting Man," *J. S. H.*, XXV, 180 (May, 1959).

[5] *Ann. Cyc.*, 1862, 243.

[6] ". . . those under eighteen and over forty-five should constitute a reserve for state defense and not be required to serve beyond their state's limits." Coulter, *Confederate States*, 314–315.

[7] Clement Eaton, *A History of the Southern Confederacy*, 86.

It is difficult to judge just how effective Confederate conscription was. Though Richmond authorities claimed to be satisfied with the system, the constant modifications made in the laws indicate that the results left something to be desired. There is not space here to go into the details of this supplementary legislation. One can note, for example, that in December, 1863, the system of substitution was abolished; that in February, 1864, all industrial exemptions were ended (although soldiers were to be detailed to war industries) and other exemptions were drastically reduced; and that in the same month the "twenty Negro law" became the "fifteen Negro law," in a gesture to appease the smaller plantation owners. Precisely how many conscripts the draft laws brought into the Confederate armies can never be determined; in fact, a chief function of this legislation was not so much to draft men as to force them through volunteering to avoid the odium of being conscripted. Professor A. B. Moore concludes that, directly or indirectly, conscription was responsible for the enlistment of 300,000 soldiers, about one-third of the entire Confederate fighting force.[8]

4

It was almost as difficult for the Confederacy to supply these troops as to raise them. Rarely has a nation entered upon a war with so little in the way of arms and ammunition as the South had in 1861. At the beginning of the war the Confederacy had perhaps 190,000 stand of small arms of all descriptions seized from Federal arsenals in the South, and there were probably 300,000 more, "of varying degrees of antiquity and disrepair" which the states owned. In the entire South in 1861 there were only two small, inactive powder factories.[1]

That the South was not defeated by its shortages of arms and ammunition was largely the work of Josiah Gorgas, a Pennsylvanian who accepted appointment as the Confederacy's chief of ordnance. Quiet and unassuming, Gorgas was little known to the public, but because of his unostentatiously efficient labors the South rarely if ever lost a battle through want of munitions of war. During the first two years of the war imports from Europe formed a principal source of Confederate supply; in all, blockade runners brought in 330,000 stand of arms for the ordnance bureau and 270,000 for states and private individuals. Another source was the capture of Northern arms on the battlefield; Southern soldiers took about

[8] Moore, *Conscription and Conflict in the Confederacy,* 356–357. Cf. the conclusion of Robert Preston Brooks: ". . . conscription appears to have put into the army not more than twenty-five per cent of the total." "Conscription in the Confederate States of America, 1862–1865," *Bull. of the Univ. of Ga.,* XVII, 441 (Mar., 1917).

[1] Coulter, *Confederate States,* 200, 206.

35,000 Federal small arms in the Seven Days' battles and about 20,000 more at Second Bull Run.

Increasingly, however, the Confederacy relied upon its own manufactories for arms and ammunition. Through Gorgas's industry large arsenals were set up at Richmond, Fayetteville, Augusta, Charleston, Columbia, Macon, Atlanta, and Selma; foundries were erected at Macon, Columbus, Augusta, and elsewhere; and, under the expert supervision of Colonel George W. Rains, a huge powder mill was built at Augusta. In addition, government contracts were let to privately owned factories, notably to the Tredegar Iron Works at Richmond, which "made torpedoes, submarines, plates for ironclad ships, propeller shafts, cannon, the great Brooke rifled naval guns, machinery for war production, and many other things both great and small." [2] By 1863 Gorgas could say confidently, "We are now in a condition to carry on the war for an indefinite period." [3]

The quartermaster corps of the Confederate army was less well managed. Admittedly its problems were almost insuperable, but, under Abraham C. Myers, too much attention was given to red tape. One of Myers's chief duties was to procure millions of uniforms and shoes for the army. Since there were in the nonindustrial South no factories capable of handling orders of such magnitude, the Confederate government was obliged to set up its own clothing and shoe manufactories; by the fall of 1861 "army clothing was being made almost exclusively in the quartermaster's depots under military supervision." Some of these government-owned factories were "conspicuously well managed, especially those at Richmond, Augusta, Atlanta, and Columbus"; others were "less successful, sometimes because of the inexperience of the officials in charge, sometimes because of the difficulties inherent in their location, in a few cases perhaps because of dishonesty." [4]

Another of Myers's functions was to procure the horses and mules desperately needed in the Confederate army for the cavalry, for the artillery, and for general transport, a task that became increasingly difficult as Union forces conquered the horse-breeding areas of Kentucky and Tennessee. After the battle of Chancellorsville Lee's army "was never again adequately supplied" with horses; in late 1864 more than one-fourth of the Confederate cavalry were dismounted for want of horses. So desperate did the problem become that in February, 1865, General W. N. Pendleton, Lee's chief of artillery, protested, "The question of our horse supply is hardly second to that of supplying men for the army, or food for the men." [5]

[2] *Ibid.*, 207.

[3] Eaton, *History of the Southern Confederacy*, 135.

[4] C. W. Ramsdell, "The Control of Manufacturing by the Confederate Government," *M. V. H. R.*, VIII, 232–233 (Dec., 1921).

[5] Ramsdell, "General Robert E. Lee's Horse Supply, 1862–1865," *Amer. Hist. Rev.*, XXXV, 763, 775 (July, 1930).

As shortages grew pressing, discontent with Myers's administration spread. The officials of the quartermaster corps resorted to substitutes, such as using "wooden-soled, canvas-topped brogans" for army shoes—an arrangement which, as Frank E. Vandiver remarks, "seemed to please everybody but the infantrymen." [6] In August, 1863, dissatisfaction was so widespread that President Davis replaced Myers with General Alexander R. Lawton, of Georgia, who brought new vigor to his department but whose difficulties during the final months of the conflict were even more staggering.

The commissary general of the Confederate army, Lucius B. Northrop, was perhaps the most abused man in the Southern forces. To most Confederates it seemed preposterous that, in a great agricultural area like the South, there should be shortages of food for the armies, and they naturally blamed Northrop. George Cary Eggleston summarized their complaints:

At Manassas, where the army was well-nigh starved out in the very beginning of the war, food might have been abundant but for the obstinacy of this one man. On our left lay a country unsurpassed, and almost unequaled in productiveness. It was rich in grain and meat. . . . The obvious duty of the commissary-general, therefore, was to draw upon that section for the supplies which were both convenient and abundant. The chief of subsistence ruled otherwise, however, thinking it better to let that source of supply lie exposed to the first advance of the enemy, while he drew upon the Richmond *dépôts* for a daily ration, and shipped it by the overtasked line of railway leading from the capital to Manassas. It was nothing to him that he was thus exhausting the rear and crippling the resources of the country for the future. It was nothing to him that in the midst of plenty the army was upon a short allowance of food. . . . System was everything, and this was a part of his system. The worst of it was, that in this all-important branch of the service experience and organization wrought little if any improvement as the war went on, so that as the supplies and the means of transportation grew smaller, the undiminished inefficiency of the department produced disastrous results. . . . Red tape was supreme, and no sword was permitted to cut it.[7]

It must be admitted that Northrop was one of the least successful of President Davis's appointments, but in extenuation of his record it should be noted that he had to bring food to the armies over an imperfect and inefficient transportation system. The Confederate railroad network in 1861 was composed mostly of "short lines, inadequately financed by local capital, cheaply constructed, poorly equipped, and supplemented but very little by water transportation." [8] At the outbreak of the war very few leaders in the Confederacy had any comprehension of the role railroads would play

    [6] Vandiver, *Rebel Brass*, 101.
    [7] Eggleston, *A Rebel's Recollections*, ed. by David Donald, 158–159.
    [8] C. W. Ramsdell, "The Confederate Government and the Railroads," *Amer. Hist. Rev.*, XXII, 795 (July, 1917).

in the conflict; almost none understood, as did Brigadier General J. H. Trapier, that "Railroads are at one and the same time the *legs* and the *stomach* of an army." [9] The Davis administration, averse to meddling with private enterprise, sought to rely upon informal agreements with the railroad operators rather than to coerce them, but, despite the best intentions, railroad officials "representing a multitude of small lines, were never able to co-ordinate their policies and services. . . ." [10]

The result was a constant record of disagreements, of inefficiency, and of putting private interest before public welfare. Though the excellent officials appointed by President Davis to coordinate the railroads repeatedly proposed reasonable plans for pooling cars and engines and for controlling schedules and rates, political and business hostility scotched their programs. Again and again army officials urged the Confederate government to take over the carriers, but, as Robert C. Black writes, "the Confederacy was never to exert an effective supervision over its railways. Paper controls would receive the grudging acquiescence of Congress, but neither the Davis Administration, nor the successive military officers it placed in charge of the carriers, ever carried them thoroughly into effect. Everyone concerned, from the President down, appeared smitten by a fatal hesitation." Congress on May 1, 1863, passed a measure authorizing the President to seize railroads which failed to give priority to military shipments, but the act "lay unused in an obscure pigeonhole." [11]

Not until February 28, 1865, were vigorous steps taken, when Congress ordered that the transportation of troops, supplies, munitions, et cetera, "shall be under the immediate control of the Secretary of War," who was given power to place railroad and navigation companies under military officers and to furnish aid to the companies in "money, material, subsistence," and "other things . . . necessary to secure their efficiency," charging the roads for such aid in their settlement with the government, while compensating them for war damage.[12] By this time it was far too late, for the railroads which had not already been captured by Northern armies were slowly disintegrating. As Captain F. W. Sims, the railroad coordinator, sadly reported in February, 1865, "not a single bar of railroad iron has been rolled in the Confederacy since [the beginning of] the war, nor can we hope to do any better during the continuance." [13]

[9] Robert C. Black, III, *The Railroads of the Confederacy,* 137.
[10] C. W. Ramsdell, *Behind the Lines in the Southern Confederacy,* 118.
[11] Black, *op. cit.,* 63, 164.
[12] *Journal,* Confed. Cong., VII, 584.
[13] Ramsdell, "The Confederate Government and the Railroads," 805.

CHAPTER 14

Behind the Southern Lines

I

ALL THE PROBLEMS of the Confederacy were aggravated by its difficulties over finance. A basically agricultural region, without large stores of specie and without numerous banks, the South was obliged to confront some of the most difficult worries that ever faced a nation. It is easy to stress the failures of the Confederacy in these matters, without appreciating the magnitude of its problems. As a careful student has urged, one should "not emphasize the mistaken financial policy adopted by the government, but rather the fact that, in spite of it, the South maintained herself so long." [1]

When Christopher G. Memminger became Confederate secretary of the treasury in 1861, he encountered a desperate financial situation. The treasury had literally no money in it; he and his assistant had to furnish their office out of their own pockets. Only timely loans from the state of Alabama and from the banks of New Orleans made it possible for the Confederate States even to begin the war in solvency. Never was there time to work out a balanced, carefully constructed financial program for the South. Memminger, a South Carolinian of German birth, was obliged to rely upon his own rather limited experience as chairman of the House Ways and Means Committee in the South Carolina legislature and upon the advice of the principal bankers of the Confederacy in drawing up a make-shift policy. It is ironical that Memminger, who was at heart a hard-money advocate who favored stringent taxation, should have presided over a treasury administration which depended so heavily upon paper money.

Three principal methods were available to the Confederacy in financing the war: taxation, loans, and treasury notes. Despite the urging of Secretary Memminger, the Confederate Congress was reluctant to rely upon the first of these. Southerners had not been accustomed to paying heavy taxes; taxation might impose too heavy a strain upon loyalty to the Confederacy; and taxation was practically difficult since great segments of

[1] John Christopher Schwab, *The Confederate States of America*, 312.

the richest areas of the South were being overrun by Northern armies. Besides, many Confederates thought it unfair that they should have to do both the fighting and the paying for the war. As the editor of the Wilmington (N. C.) *Journal* declared: "The burden of taxation, State and Confederate, should be laid as lightly as possible on our suffering people. We of today are paying the price of our righteous war of defence in blood and wounds and death . . . , and it is but just and right that posterity should pay in money the price of that heritage of freedom, property, and glory which we will bequeath them." [2]

Taxation, consequently, was never a major resource for the Confederate treasury. The Northern blockade kept the import and export duties from bringing in much revenue. A direct tax, enacted on August 19, 1861, upon real estate, slaves, and other property,[3] was weakened by the provision that the states might avoid the incidence of the tax directly upon their citizens by making payments as state governments either in Confederate treasury notes or in specie. This unfortunate provision, together with slowness in getting the tax into operation, produced disappointing results; all told, only $17,500,000 was realized,[4] and, as J. C. Schwab states, "what robbed the tax entirely of its character was the general practice on the part of the States to avoid the payment of the tax by borrowing the amount due and transferring the proceeds to Richmond. They followed the precedent of the States during the Revolution in meeting their quota of the [continental] taxes . . . not by raising the amount by taxation, but by issuing bonds of paper money." [5]

Though the direct tax was obviously defective, Congress did not move to remedy the situation until 1863. So remiss was the legislature that one witnessed the extraordinary spectacle of people throughout the South actually begging to be taxed. As the Richmond *Enquirer* declared: "We are the advocates of taxation because we believe it to be the only mode . . . by which a nation can provide for its pecuniary necessities. . . . To ORIGINATE a tax bill is the duty of the House of Representatives, a duty wholly and shamefully neglected by that body; a dereliction of duty which cannot and shall not be forgotten. . . ." [6] Under such pressure the Congress finally did adopt a more comprehensive tax law on April 24, 1863, combining in one measure the features of an income levy, a license tax,

[2] Eugene M. Lerner, "The Monetary and Fiscal Programs of the Confederate Government, 1861–1865," *Jour. of Political Economy*, LXII, 509 (Dec., 1954).

[3] Such a tax law was possible because the Confederacy was still operating under its provisional Constitution. Its permanent Constitution prohibited the levying of direct taxes except in proportion to population.

[4] Only round figures can be given here. For precise statements of amounts raised by the Confederacy through taxes, loans, and paper issues, see Richard Cecil Todd, *Confederate Finance*.

[5] Schwab, 287.

[6] Albert D. Kirwan, ed., *The Confederacy*, 124.

and a general internal revenue measure. The duties imposed by this law included, among other things, an 8 per cent levy upon all naval stores, salt, wines, liquors, tobacco, cotton, wool, flour, sugar, molasses, syrup, rice, and all other agricultural products; a license tax, of varying amounts, upon bankers, brokers, auctioneers, wholesale and retail dealers in liquors, pawnbrokers, distillers, brewers, innkeepers, theater and circus owners, jugglers, butchers, bakers, apothecaries, physicians, tobacconists, peddlers, lawyers, photographers, and confectioners; and a graduated income tax, ranging (after an initial exemption of $1000) from one per cent on the first $1500 to 15 per cent on all incomes over $10,000. No tax was imposed directly upon land or slaves, because the Confederate Constitution required that such direct taxes be apportioned according to population; but to circumvent this difficulty a tax-in-kind was imposed. After reserving certain amounts of food for his own use, each farmer and planter was required to pay to the government one-tenth of his wheat, corn, oats, rye, buckwheat or rice, sweet and Irish potatoes, cured hay and fodder, sugar, molasses, cotton, wool, tobacco, beans, peas, and bacon.[7]

Though the new tax legislation did bring in both money and much needed supplies for the army, it was very unpopular, especially among the farmers, who compared their 10 per cent duties with the small levies against other incomes and protested that the tax-in-kind was "oppressive, and a relic of barbarism, which alone is practised in the worst despotisms."[8] In North Carolina there was vigorous, open opposition, but in the trans-Mississippi region on the other hand, there seems to have been little dissatisfaction with either the act or its administration.[9]

Later Confederate tax legislation can here be noted only briefly. A law of February 17, 1864, ostensibly strengthened and extended the tax schedules of the earlier measure, but in fact, through allowing rebates and permitting taxes to be paid in depreciated note issues, "practically deprived that act of all virility as a tax measure." On March 11, 1865, Congress moved to plug some of these holes, and on March 17 it "passed its last tax measure by levying a tax of 25% . . . on all coin, bullion, and foreign exchange in the Confederate States," but before any income could be realized from either of these measures the Confederacy collapsed.[10] All in all, the tax measures of the Confederacy can be summarized in the phrase "too little, too late." E. Merton Coulter concludes that "The Confederacy raised throughout its existence about one percent of its income in taxes."[11]

---

[7] For a careful summary of these and other provisions of this complicated legislation, see Todd, *Confederate Finance*, 140–141.

[8] *Ibid.*, 142.

[9] James L. Nichols, "The Tax-in-Kind in the Department of the Trans-Mississippi," *Civil War Hist.*, V, 388–389 (Dec., 1959).

[10] Todd, 150, 155.

[11] Coulter, *Confederate States*, 182.

2

Nor was the Confederacy much more successful in its loans. At the outset of the war there was not enough specie in the South to make large loan subscriptions possible; later, when there were vast quantities of depreciating paper money, "people would not tie up their credits in rigid bonds; they must have their resources in the fluidity of currency or else in gold or personal property and real estate." [1] The chief borrowing measures were the $15,000,000 loan, the $100,000,000 loan, the Erlanger loan, and the produce loans. The $15,000,000 domestic loan, authorized on February 28, 1861, was in general a success, being substantially subscribed by November of that year. It is significant that nearly two-fifths of the amount was taken up in the city of New Orleans. The loan was subscribed chiefly by banks; and its proceeds constituted one of the few sources of specie for the Confederate government. The $100,000,000 loan (August 19, 1861) was taken up chiefly by planters and was paid in part in paper money (treasury notes and bank notes) and in part in produce. Thus early in the war the idea of the "produce loan" was introduced into Southern fiscal schemes. In later loan measures this type of borrowing came to be a conspicuous factor. In the produce loans the planters, in effect, turned over their cotton and other commodities to the government in specified amounts in return for Confederate bonds. Because of the reluctance of some planters to part with their cotton for government paper, however, and also because of the difficulty of getting specie for cotton, the produce loans proved disappointing.[2]

The most famous of the borrowing measures of the Confederate government was the adventure in high finance essayed in 1863 in contract with a French financier named Erlanger. In return for Confederate bonds backed by cotton, Erlanger agreed to market a loan abroad, being secretly promised a handsome profit by an arrangement which permitted him to take over the bonds at 77 and sell them in foreign financial markets at 90.

[1] *Ibid.*, 170.

[2] Alexander H. Stephens proposed a daring plan for overcoming these difficulties and for using the cotton to benefit the Confederacy. "His theory was that by taking two million bales of the 1861 crop, paying $100,000,000 for them in 8 per cent bonds, and adding to them two million bales of the old crop at the same price, the Confederacy would be enabled to acquire fifty ironclad steamers to protect the cotton in transit to Europe. Once there, the staple would be stored until its price reached fifty cents a pound, when it would be sold for $1,000,000,-000, giving the Confederacy a clear profit of $800,000,000 in sterling." Rembert W. Patrick, *Jefferson Davis and His Cabinet*, 219–220. As Professor Patrick points out, this scheme was "visionary." There were not four million bales of cotton available in the Confederacy at the time; there is no reason to believe that the Union government would have sat idly by while the ironclad fleet was being prepared; and, had so much cotton been stored abroad, the price would certainly never have risen to fifty cents a pound.

Since the bonds were exchangeable for cotton at a price far below the current market price, the whole scheme bore the aspect of a gigantic cotton speculation. In addition the Erlanger firm was given a commission of 5 per cent and was further able to obtain Confederate funds with which to sustain the slipping market. Eventually the profits of the firm were enormous, running to something like thirteen and a half million francs.[3] Having fluctuated badly during the war the bonds became worthless after the collapse of the Confederacy, though the ever hopeful bondholders kept pushing their schemes for payment.

All in all, it is estimated that the Confederacy realized only about $712,000,000 from these various loans, a sum that amounted to approximately 39 per cent of its total revenues.[4]

3

Inevitably, therefore, as both loans and taxes proved insufficient, the Confederacy turned to its last resource, the printing press. At first only small sums of paper money were authorized in order to give the South necessary circulating medium and to pay outstanding debts of the new government. Virtually every responsible leader of the Confederacy realized the perils from fiat currency; Memminger himself declared that printing money was "the most dangerous of all methods of raising money." [1] Still, the business need for currency, the inadequacy of other fiscal measures, and the readiness of the Congress to take the easiest road led to the issue of immense quantities of treasury notes by which the Richmond government promised to pay a specified number of dollars to the bearer "two years after the ratification of a treaty of peace between the Confederate States and the United States of America." It is notable that Confederate paper money, unlike Northern greenbacks, was never made legal tender, for both Davis and Memminger believed these notes "did not need any assistance to enable them to perform the functions of legal tender, but that a law to compel their acceptance as such would create suspicion and distrust of the currency." [2]

As more and more of these treasury notes rolled from the printing presses, all other forms of currency were quickly driven into hiding. Small coins disappeared, and people tried, rather unsatisfactorily, to use postage stamps in their place. Shinplasters, "small paper notes, generally in denominations from five cents to fifty cents . . . , were issued illegally by merchants, railroads, taverns, saloons, butchers, bakers almost every other

[3] Schwab, 36.
[4] Todd, 84; Lerner, "Monetary and Fiscal Programs," 507.

[1] Lerner, 520.
[2] Patrick, 224.

kind of business, and even by individuals." [3] Inevitably there was a great deal of counterfeiting, both of these local and state currencies and of the Confederate treasury notes. For this last problem Memminger, hard pressed to grind out enough paper from his presses, hit upon a novel solution. He "recommended that the South resort to honoring counterfeits. Any person holding a bogus note should be able to exchange it for a 6 per cent call certificate. The counterfeits could then be stamped 'valid' by the Treasury and reissued." [4]

By the end of the war the Confederacy had issued $1,554,000,000 in such paper currency [5]—over three times the total amount of Federal greenbacks. While the gold value of these Confederate notes stood at 90 in 1861, they declined to 82.7 in early 1862, to 29.0 in early 1863, and to 4.6 in early 1864. [6] So desperate did the situation become that the Confederacy was obliged to resort to a kind of partial repudiation; a law of February 17, 1864, required treasury notes to be exchanged for 4 per cent bonds by April 1 (July 1 west of the Mississippi), and after that larger bills would be gradually reduced in value until they were worthless, while small bills could be exchanged at two-thirds of their face rate. A new, and presumably less depreciated, paper currency was meanwhile to be issued. The scheme gave the death blow to faith in the honesty of the Confederate treasury administration; at the same time the reduction of the currency did little permanent good because the Congress began promptly authorizing the further issuance of treasury notes. By early 1865 these were worth only 1.7 cents.

So great grew the outcry against Memminger that the secretary, weary with continued congressional hostility to his own fiscal plans and annoyed with being saddled with the responsibility for plans which he had not sponsored, resigned (June 15, 1864). History has, on the whole, been unkind to Memminger, but it is doubtful whether any other secretary could better have escaped the pitfalls that beset him. He was, to be sure, a somewhat stiff and difficult person, and he was not so forceful in urging taxes as he should have been. On the other hand, he did see to the heart of the South's financial problems, and he tried to erect a system for financing the war from taxation and loans. Reliance upon treasury notes was an error, but it was not one of Memminger's own choosing. [7]

Memminger's successor was George A. Trenholm, one of the wealthiest men in the South, who, as member of the financial firm of Fraser, Trenholm and Company of Charleston, had already had many dealings with the Southern treasury department and had become familiar with its

---

[3] Coulter, *Confederate States*, 154.
[4] Lerner, "Monetary and Fiscal Programs," 520.
[5] Todd, 120.
[6] Schwab, 172.
[7] The best appraisal of Memminger's work is in Patrick, 231–234.

problems. Trenholm did not basically alter Memminger's financial policies, but he did try to change the direction of the treasury's appeal. Instead
of aiming principally for "planter, merchant, and banker support," he
sought to cement "the natural alliance that exists between a people and
their treasury," and to bolster general public confidence.[8] It was, however,
far too late to remedy a bad situation. As Professor Patrick summarizes:
"George A. Trenholm undertook an impossible task in July, 1864, and as
was inevitable, he failed." [9]

4

This arid fiscal history is necessary to any understanding of the disturbed state of the Southern wartime economy. At a time when productiv-
ity was declining, because the South had overmobilized and had not left
a sufficient proportion of its able-bodied men to man its fields and factories, the Confederate treasury constantly increased the volume of the
currency. Inevitably there was inflation, which stimulated the more rapid
circulation of the currency and hence further inflation; men bought today, knowing that their money would be worth less tomorrow. Consequently prices steadily rose. "For thirty-one consecutive months, from
October, 1861, to March, 1864, the general price index of the Confederacy rose at an almost constant rate of 10 per cent a month." The partial
repudiation of the treasury notes in early 1864 was designed to check the
price spiral; in fact, the announcement of the plan caused Southerners to
reduce their cash balances by immediate spending, and the general price
index rose 23 per cent during the single month of February, 1864. The
funding measure did take hold in May, 1864, when "prices fell sharply
and remained stable for the next six months," but the alleviation was only
temporary. By December, 1864, with fresh currency issues, inflation was
on again, and by April, 1864, "the general price index had risen to
ninety-two times its prewar base." [1]

To make these impersonal figures meaningful one must think of the
human suffering caused by the fantastic prices. As early as July, 1862,
an outraged French consul at Richmond reported that, aside from potatoes, there were "no . . . vegetables except cabbages and one cabbage,
one single cabbage, costs $1.25." [2] In October, 1863, Robert Garlick Hill

---

[8] Ralph Louis Andreano, "A Theory of Confederate Finance," *Civil War Hist.*,
II, 27 (Dec., 1956).
[9] Patrick, 243.

[1] Eugene M. Lerner, "Money, Prices, and Wages in the Confederacy, 1861–
65," *Jour. of Political Economy*, LXIII, 23–24 (Feb., 1955); Lerner, "Monetary
and Fiscal Programs," 522.
[2] Gordon Wright, "Economic Conditions in the Confederacy as Seen by the
French Consuls," *J. S. H.*, VII, 211 (May, 1941).

Kean, head of the Confederate bureau of war, noted what inflation had done to his income:

My salary of $3000 goes about as far as $300 would do in ordinary times in purchasing all the articles of household necessity, the average of prices being about ten fold. The consequence is that with an income from all sources of at least $6000 and a good deal of help from my father-in-law, my family is reduced to two meals a day . . . and they are of the most plain and economical scale. Wood for fuel is $38 per cord, butter $4 per pound, coal $1.25 per bushel, calico $4.50 a yard.[3]

Seven months later another war department official recorded the following prices in Richmond: "boots, $200; coats, $350; pants, $100; shoes, $125; flour, $275 per barrel; meal, $60 to $80 per bushel; bacon, $9 per pound; no beef on the market; chickens, $30 per pair; shad, $20; potatoes, $25 per bushel; turnip greens, $4 per peck; white beans, $4 per quart . . . ; butter, $15 per pound; lard, same; wood, $50 per cord." [4] By the end of the war flour sold at $1,000 a barrel in the Confederate capital.

Except for debtors and speculators every class in the South suffered from the rampant inflation. Men on fixed salaries, such as government workers, were perhaps hardest hit. Planters, too, were affected, for their crops, normally exported, declined in real value. Creditors actually ran away from their debtors to avoid the payment of debts in worthless paper. Professional men were badly hurt; some doctors were forced to resort to a barter arrangement, offering their professional services at 1861 rates "to those who will furnish . . . grain or forage AT OLD PRICES." [5] Laborers were greatly injured, for real wages "declined to approximately one-third their prewar level." As one group of workingmen complained to Secretary Memminger, wages were "totally inadequate to afford us the merest necessities of life—plain food, shelter, fuel, and clothing. We are literally reduced to destitution." [6]

The families of soldiers were especially hard hit by inflation. "Unheard of prices . . . for provisions of almost every kind," lamented the *Eastern Clarion,* a Mississippi newspaper, in 1862, "are fast reducing a large class of our population to the condition of paupers." [7] State governments made valiant efforts to care for these indigent families; most of them appropriated large sums for direct relief and Louisiana "adopted a systematic pension system, providing for the payment of $10 monthly to wives or widows of soldiers . . . , the same amount to dependent par-

---

[3] Edward Younger, ed., *Inside the Confederate Government,* 108.

[4] J. B. Jones, *A Rebel War Clerk's Diary* (1866 ed.), II, 212.

[5] Kirwan, *The Confederacy,* 138.

[6] Lerner, "Money, Prices, and Wages," 33.

[7] Georgia Lee Tatum, *Disloyalty in the Confederacy,* 94. For further comment on hardships in the Confederacy, see below, pp. 516–520.

ents, and $5 each to children and dependent younger brothers and sisters of soldiers." But these were small sums in terms of purchasing power, and repeatedly the complaint rose:

There is no doubt an ample sufficiency of Corn in this county for its consumption; but holders can't be moved to sell for less than the most exorbitant prices & many women & children are entirely without. Now just let this news reach our Soldiers in the Army whose families are thus oppressed, & I should not be surprised to hear any day that many of them had laid by their arms and marched off home.[8]

5

There can be no doubt that such sufferings brought out the fundamental disunity of the Confederacy. The South, it will be recalled, was never unanimous in support of secession; every state, with the possible exception of South Carolina, had from the beginning a vigorous Unionist group. In the slave states of Delaware, Maryland, Kentucky, and Missouri Unionist sentiment was strong enough to prevent secession; throughout the great Appalachian mountain region opponents of the Confederacy were probably in the majority throughout the war.[1]

In other areas Unionists (or "Reconstructionists" as they were often styled), though in a minority, continued throughout the war to dissent from the Confederacy. In the hill country of Alabama, for example, there were hundreds who agreed with one small farmer's verdict that the war was a slaveholders' plot: "all they want is to git you pupt up and go to fight for there infurnal negroes and after you do there fighting you may kiss there hine parts for o [all] they care." [2] The Ozark region of Arkansas was strongly opposed to the war, and in Texas, which had a heavy infusion of antislavery Germans, it is estimated that one-third of the people "remained neutral and one-third, actively or passively, gave support to the Federal cause." [3]

In most parts of the South, however, at the outbreak of war Unionists agreed, with varying degrees of reluctance, to go along with their states in the experiment of independence; these areas required the hard shocks of war to bring latent, persistent grievances again to the fore. Next to inflation, the operation of the conscription act did most to turn Southerners against the Confederacy. The exemption of one slaveholder or overseer

[8] Charles W. Ramsdell, *Behind the Confederate Lines,* 62–68, 46.

[1] For the separate-state movements among Unionists in western Virginia and eastern Tennessee, see above, pp. 186, 236–242.

[2] Hugh C. Bailey, "Disloyalty in Early Confederate Alabama," *J. S. H.,* XXIII, 525 (Nov., 1957).

[3] Claude Elliott, "Union Sentiment in Texas, 1861–1865," *Southwestern Hist. Quart.,* L, 450 (April, 1947).

for every twenty (later fifteen) slaves was especially objectionable to the small farmers of the South. "Never did a law meet with more universal odium than the exemption of slave owners," wrote Senator James Phelan of Mississippi to Jefferson Davis; "its injustice, gross injustice, is denounced even by men whose position allows them to take advantage of its privileges. . . . It has aroused a spirit of rebellion . . . and bodies of men have banded together to desert." [4] Many outraged Southerners shared the opinions of a North Carolina draftee, who paid his respects to President Davis as he deserted:

Your happy conscript would go to the far-away North whence the wind comes and leave you to reap the whirlwind with no one but your father the devil to reap and rake and bind after you. And he's going. It is with intense and multifariously proud satisfaction that he gazes for the last time upon our holy flag— that symbol . . . of an adored trinity, cotton, niggers, and chivalry. . . . Behind he leaves the legitimate chivalry of this unbounded nation centered in the illegitimate son of a Kentucky horse-thief. . . . . And now, bastard President of a political abortion, farewell. . . . Except it be in the army of the Union, you will not again see the conscript. [5]

Sometimes these deserters formed guerilla bands, which hid out in the hill country of the Confederacy. In Washington County, in southwestern Virginia, deserters "roamed over the county and robbed citizens indiscriminately of money, clothing, horses, saddles, grain and forage." [6] In some counties in northwestern Georgia the conscription law was practically suspended for twelve months before the end of the war because "tories and bushwhackers" were in control and made the region "a theater for the lawless depredations of prowling bands of cavalry." [7] If Confederate enrolling officers halted these disloyal citizens and asked for their authority to be absent from their commands, they patted their guns and defiantly said, "This is my furlough." [8]

Deserters moved with impunity through the backwoods areas of the Confederacy because the large majority of the population in that region had come to share their disaffection toward the Richmond government. All over the South secret peace societies sprang up. In Arkansas the poor, nonslaveholding whites as early as 1861 banded together, vowing "they would never muster under the d—d nigger flag, but if any one would just come along with the stars and stripes that they would arise at midnight

---

[4] Tatum, 89.

[5] A. B. Moore, *Conscription and Conflict in the Confederacy*, 20–21.

[6] Henry T. Shanks, "Disloyalty to the Confederacy in Southwestern Virginia, 1861–1865," *N. C. Hist., Rev.*, XXI, 123 (Apr., 1944).

[7] T. Conn Bryan, *Confederate Georgia*, 155.

[8] Tatum, 124. For a fuller discussion of desertion in the Confederacy, see below, pp. 516–517.

and go to it, and they would fight for it too when they got there." [9] **The** Peace Society also flourished in Mississippi, Alabama, Georgia, eastern Tennessee, and perhaps Florida. Its members had elaborate rituals for recognizing each other. The signs were:

1, Salute with the right hand closed, thumb pointing back behind the shoulder; 2, If the person saluted was one of the faithful, he would then grasp his own left hand with his right, knuckles of the left hand down, of right hand up; 3, Both then looked one another in the eyes and each tapped his right foot with a stick; 4, One of them broke a small stick or like article and threw the pieces carelessly over the left shoulder.[10]

Similar societies flourished in Virginia and in the Carolinas. William W. Holden, the most influential editor in North Carolina and candidate for governor of that state in 1864, was a member of the secret peace society called the Order of the Heroes of America. Holden regularly used his newspaper, the Raleigh *Standard,* to attack the Confederate government and to advocate a separate peace. "North Carolina is true, and will be true to the Confederate government as it was formed, in its integrity and purity," he argued sophistically; "but she would not be bound by a government which had lost its original character and had been perverted to despotic purposes against her own rights and the rights and liberties of her citizens." [11]

Many disaffected Southerners expressed their disloyalty by simply refusing to serve in the Confederate armies or to obey Confederate laws. Others took more active steps of opposition, openly trading with the enemy or giving Federal troops information as to the whereabouts of Confederate forces. Some idea of the extent and importance of disloyalty in the Confederacy can be gained from the fact that after the war 22,298 persons put in claims for over sixty million dollars against the United States government for reimbursement for quartermaster and commissary supplies they declared they had furnished to the advancing Federal armies in the South. That disloyalty was by no means confined to the poor and humble classes of the South is evidenced by the fact that 701 of these professed pro-Union Southerners made claims totaling $10,000 or more each.[12]

6

Internal opposition within the Confederacy was evident on many fronts. Despite enthusiasm for the cause of Southern nationalism embodied

[9] Ted R. Worley, "The Arkansas Peace Society of 1861: A Study in Mountain Unionism," *J. S. H.,* XXIV, 454 (Nov., 1958).

[10] Tatum, 27.

[11] Horace W. Raper, "William W. Holden and the Peace Movement in North Carolina," *N. C. Hist. Rev.,* XXXI, 507 (Oct., 1954).

[12] Frank W. Klingberg, *The Southern Claims Commission,* 17–19.

in the government at Richmond, the very basis on which the Confederacy was founded, the principle of state rights, proved embarrassing in a war which rendered imperative a considerable degree of centralization. In one of its aspects the factor of internal opposition might be traced as a contest waged around President Davis; it could also be viewed in its connection with unpopular measures such as conscription, impressment, and the tax in kind; or it could be discussed with reference to this or that local region. The two states in which opposition was most conspicuous were Georgia and North Carolina; and much of the story can be read in the Confederate relations of the governors of these states—Joseph E. Brown of Georgia and Zebulon Vance of North Carolina—the two state executives who stood forth as the stoutest opponents of the Southern President.

Brown took state sovereignty very seriously. In the period just after the secession of Georgia, when technically it was an independent nation, he even sent a diplomatic officer abroad. On January 30, 1861, he appointed T. Butler King "commissioner to the Government of Queen Victoria, to the Emperor Napoleon III, and to the Government of the King of Belgium, with all the powers, and . . . duties" mentioned in accompanying instructions. In these instructions he was directed to explain Georgia's secession and to "ascertain from those Governments whether it will accord with their . . . policy, to immediately acknowledge the Government of Georgia as that of an independent State." On February 5 he ordered the seizure of all the ships in Savannah harbor belonging to citizens of the state of New York as a reprisal for the seizure of Georgia guns by the New York police. After Georgia's entrance into the Confederacy he was intensely loyal to the cause of Southern independence; but, as his verbose messages and papers show, he was frequently in controversy with the authorities at Richmond. His policy was that Georgia should look to her own defenses, raise huge war chests, develop her own foundries, raise and maintain state troops (referred to as "the Georgia regular army"), "prevent the Confederate tax-gatherers from making their appearance among us," [1] and in general promote the Southern cause by state measures with as little obedience to central direction as possible.

As the war dragged on, however, Brown's devotion to the Confederacy seriously diminished, and he began to contemplate making a separate peace treaty between Georgia and the United States. Brown's biographer speaks of the traits which kept him from working harmoniously with President Davis's government: "his provincialism and opportunism, which precluded his visualizing the Confederacy as a whole and caused him to view the war only insofar as it affected Georgia and his own political opportunities; his stubborn insistence on his own point of view in all times and under all circumstances . . . ; his supreme self-confidence which seems

[1] A. D. Candler, *Confederate Records of the State of Georgia*, II, 19–21, 24 ff., 107, 114.

to have led him for a time to believe that he might supplant Davis in the Presidency; and, finally, as the fortunes of the Confederacy waned, his propensity to be on the side in the ascendency, leading him to seek the favor of the enemy through opposition to his own government." [2]

In Governor Vance of North Carolina the Davis administration found a different kind of opponent. A soldier himself and a vigorous administrator, Vance never wavered in his loyalty to the Confederacy, even when Holden, his principal backer, and large segments of the Conservative party joined the peace movement. Announced the governor stoutly, "I will see this Conservative party blown into a thousand atoms and Holden and his understrappers in hell . . . before I will consent to a course which I think would bring dishonor and ruin upon both State and Confederacy." [3] At the same time that he supported the Confederacy, Vance insisted "that the Richmond authorities should exert their war power with due regard for the rights of North Carolina and with especial consideration for her civil law." [4] Whenever the governor thought that the Confederate government was infringing upon the sovereignty of his state or was mistreating her citizens, he exploded in heated protests to President Davis. At one point his language in objecting to alleged discriminations against North Carolina became so intemperate that the Southern President was obliged stiffly to reply, ". . . I must beg that a correspondence so unprofitable in its character, and which was not initiated by me, may here end, and that your future communications be restricted to such matters as may require official action." [5]

With such popular leaders ready at all times to enter the lists as champions of state rights it was certain that internal difficulties would arise whenever measures of a drastic sort, which would bear hard upon the people, should be essayed at Richmond. It was ominous of future developments that in the very early months of the war even the thoroughly loyal governor of Alabama, A. B. Moore, should refuse to permit state agents to collect taxes for the Confederacy, declaring, "The State should never concede to the General Government the exercise of powers not delegated in the Constitution, and they should never, except in cases of absolute necessity, consent to exercise powers or to perform duties which do not properly belong to them." [6]

Conscription was perhaps the most frequent source of conflict between

[2] Louise Biles Hill, "Governor Brown and the Confederacy," *Ga. Hist. Quart.*, XXI, 371–372 (Dec., 1937).

[3] Raper, "Holden and the Peace Movement," 508.

[4] Richard E. Yates, "Zebulon B. Vance as War Governor of North Carolina, 1862–1865," *J. S. H.*, III, 59 (Feb., 1937).

[5] Coulter, *Confederate States*, 389 n.

[6] Lerner, "Monetary and Fiscal Programs," 509.

Richmond and state officials. Governor Brown, for instance, argued that conscription was "a palpable violation of the Constitution," a "dangerous assault upon both the rights and the sovereignty of the State," which would reduce the country to a condition "bordering upon military despotism" and convert "free-born citizens" into the "vassals of the central power." [7] There ensued a wordy correspondence between Richmond and Milledgeville in the course of which President Davis, while courteously admitting that Brown's "noble State [had] promptly responded to every call," [8] vigorously repudiated the governor's argument against the law and asserted its validity and wisdom. With much grumbling, Brown submitted to the first conscription act, but when the second one was passed, on September 27, 1862, he "refused to allow the new act to be enforced in Georgia until the legislature had deliberated upon it." Not until the friends of the Davis administration had demonstrated powerful strength in the legislature and the state supreme court on November 11 had rendered a unanimous decision in favor of conscription did the governor reluctantly permit the law to go into effect.[9] Even then he used the exemption clauses to the fullest, declaring that some 15,000 persons, mostly in the militia, were indispensable state officers not subject to the draft.[10]

There was further trouble within the Confederacy because of the law of February 27, 1862, which gave the President the power to suspend the privilege of the habeas corpus writ. Though Davis was slow to use the power so conferred, yet conditions arose which caused suspension to be adopted in various localities. Portsmouth, for example, and also Salisbury, Norfolk, Mobile, Petersburg, New Orleans, and the state of Texas were at one time or another put under Confederate martial law. This subject became a favorite theme of denunciation by Brown and Vance. The following statement of Brown indicates the defiant nature of his attitude.

We were recently informed . . . that a [Confederate] military commander . . . had issued an order declaring the city of Atlanta . . . to be under *martial law,* and had appointed a Governor and his *aides* to assume the government of the city. . . . The order was issued without any conference with the Executive of this State . . . , and the Governor appointed by the General assumed the Government and control of the city. As you [i.e., the Georgia legislature] were soon to assemble, I thought it best to avoid all conflict . . . till the facts should be placed before you, ... I consider this and all like proceedings, on the part of Confederate officers not only high-handed usurpation . . . without the shadow of constitutional right, but dangerous precedence, which if acquiesced in by the people of this State, tend to the subversion of the govern-

7 Hill, 346–347.
8 Candler, III, 245.
9 Bryan, *Confederate Georgia,* 87.
10 Hill, *Joseph E. Brown and the Confederacy,* 96.

ment and sovereignty of the State, and of the individual rights of the citizen. This order of the commanding General was, after some delay, annulled by the War Department.[11]

State judges released prisoners held under Confederate authority. Chief Justice Pearson, for example, of the supreme court of North Carolina, granted writs to all who applied and "went on discharging man after man." In North Carolina, despite Justice Pearson, the supreme court upheld the habeas corpus act as constitutional. In Georgia, however, the legislature declared the act unconstitutional;[12] and J. L. M. Curry, commissioner to execute the act in 1864, stated that enforcement in Georgia was impossible.[13]

7

It is hard to arrive at an objective appraisal of the manner in which President Davis performed the duties of his difficult office. His opponents were vigorous in attacking him and in questioning his fitness for the post. T. R. R. Cobb called him the "embodiment and concentration of cowardly littleness," garnished over "with pharisaical hypocrisy"; James L. Alcorn agreed that the President was a "miserable, stupid, one-eyed, dyspeptic, arrogant tyrant"; [1] Linton Stephens, brother of the Vice-President of the Confederacy, termed Davis "a *little, conceited, hypocritical, snivelling, canting, malicious, ambitious, dogged* knave and fool." [2] Seeing his "country dying from the incompetency of its presumptuous chief," Congressman William W. Boyce lamented, "It looks to me like we were going under the Jeff Davis lead very fast over the precipice. His intermeddling with the armies is usually disastrous, and he has no diplomacy. I don't see how we can come out without ruin if the matter is left entirely to Davis. . . ." [3]

Some of the complaints against Davis appear to have been justified. For a man who had made an enviable record as secretary of war in the Pierce administration, he was an astonishingly bad administrator. He spent far too much time on details, on "little trash which ought to be dispatched by clerks in the adjutant general's office." [4] As Secretary Mallory thought, he "neither labored with method or celerity himself, nor permitted others to do so for him." Conducting a revolutionary enterprise as though it were

---

[11] Candler, II, 305–306. For Brown's later activities, looking toward a separate peace for Georgia, see below, pp. 521–522.

[12] McMaster, *Lincoln's Administration*, 474–475.

[13] Owsley, *State Rights in the Confederacy*, 190–191.

[1] Coulter, *Confederate States*, 374–375.

[2] James Z. Rabun, "Alexander H. Stephens and Jefferson Davis," *Am. Hist. Rev.*, LVIII, 307 (Jan., 1953).

[3] Rosser H. Taylor, ed., "Boyce-Hammond Correspondence," *J.S.H.*, III, 354 (Aug., 1937).

[4] Younger, ed., *Inside the Confederate Government*, 100.

a leisurely Southern debating society, Davis insisted upon holding prolonged cabinet meetings, but, as Mallory lamented, "from his uncontrollable tendency to digression,—to slide away from the chief points to episodical questions, the amount of business accomplished bore but little relation to the time consumed; and unfrequently [*sic*] a Cabinet meeting would exhaust four or five hours without determining anything; while the desk of every chief of a Department was covered with papers demanding his attention." [5]

Another of Davis's weaknesses was his attempt to combine civilian and military leadership of the Confederacy in his own person. He would have preferred a military command to his political position, and he never got over thinking that if he and Lee could jointly lead the armies they would sweep to victory. Whenever there was a battle impending near Richmond, he rushed to the front. Davis's "belief in himself as a competent field commander," Frank E. Vandiver writes, "inevitably complicated his administrative duties as President. Had he been able to be one or the other, things might have been different. The Constitution helped trap him by making him commander in chief of the army and navy. A strict constitutionalist, he found it difficult to yield any constitutional prerogative. The President was entrusted with military leadership, and he must exercise it. From his point of view, of course, it was fortunate that he had had professional soldierly training. In reality it was an inestimable curse." [6]

An equally serious defect was Davis's insensitivity to public opinion. Though he could be warm and even humorous in private conversation, his public manner was "chillingly, freezingly cold." [7] As Bell I. Wiley has said, "Davis neither realized the importance of cultivating good will nor was he willing to pay the price of being a popular leader." [8] Sure of his own rectitude and of the justice of his cause, he "scorned to believe it necessary to coax men to do their duty in the then condition of their country." [9]

Connected with this insensitivity was Davis's loyalty to his friends even after they had lost the confidence of the public at large. When Judah P. Benjamin, as acting secretary of war, came under severe congressional criticism after the loss of Forts Henry and Donelson in the West and Roanoke Island on the east coast, Davis, instead of sacrificing the secretary, promoted him to be secretary of state. "Thus," writes Rembert W. Patrick, "he salved his own conscience and made amends for the injustice done his friend and trusted adviser." [10] Similarly, Davis clung to unpopular commanders like Bragg and Pemberton, even after defeat had cost them

[5] Joseph T. Durkin, *Stephen R. Mallory, Confederate Navy Chief,* 176.
[6] Vandiver, *Rebel Brass,* 26–27.
[7] Durkin, 179.
[8] Wiley, *The Road to Appomattox,* 28.
[9] Durkin, 179.
[10] Patrick, *Jefferson Davis and His Cabinet,* 178.

the support both of the public and of the army, and he insisted upon keeping the notorious Lucius B. Northrop as commissary-general.

Other charges against Davis have far less justification. Though it has been argued that "he gave his attention to the most minute details of military affairs and neglected the people," [11] Davis, in fact, made more use of the written and spoken word than did Lincoln. He made various tours among his people, speaking effectively and with tremendous earnestness. For example, in the desperate days before the fall of Vicksburg the President returned to his home state of Mississippi and in a moving address to the state legislature urged them to continue the grim struggle against "a power armed for conquest and subjugation," vowing, "The South could never, never reunite with the North." [12]

The accusation that Davis lacked any over-all strategic plan for winning the war is not accurate. It is probably correct to say that the Confederate President was not the ideal leader for a revolutionary cause, because he was traditional in his ideas and precedent-minded in his actions. But Davis did have a comprehensive strategic plan for the Confederacy, as Frank E. Vandiver has pointed out; it was "the offensive-defensive," a technical phrase whose meaning is clear enough: "the Confederates would stand on the defensive because they had fewer men and feebler resources than the Yankees, but they would exploit every chance to counterattack, to take the initiative, to carry the war to the enemy." The program lacked daring originality, but, as Vandiver says, it was one justified by the best strategic theory of the day and one "consistent with Southern political and social thought and consistent with economic and military realities." [13]

That Davis was inept at getting along with people and that chronic neuralgia caused his temper at times to be short may be granted, but it does not follow that he was in the wrong in his frequent and protracted quarrels with such subordinates as Joseph E. Johnston and Beauregard. One needs only to read Hudson Strode's sympathetic biography of Davis to realize that these generals were independent to the point of insubordination and that they were deliberately playing to the grandstand of disaffected Confederate opinion. With a general like Lee, who understood both his own role and the necessary supremacy of the head of the government, Davis had no such problems.

On the positive side there is much to commend about Davis's leadership. No one ever questioned either his honesty or his courage. He played his role as head of the Southern nation with great dignity and restraint. He looked the part of the leader. As a Confederate lieutenant described him, "He bears the marks of greatness about him beyond all persons I have

[11] Clifford Dowdey, *The Land They Fought For,* 125.

[12] Hudson Strode, *Jefferson Davis: Confederate President,* 350.

[13] Vandiver, "Jefferson Davis and Confederate Strategy," in *The American Tragedy: The Civil War in Retrospect,* 20.

ever seen—A perfect head, a deep set eagle eye, an aquiline nose, and mouth and jaw sawed in *steel*—but above all, the *gentleman* is apparent, the *thorough, high-bred,* polished gentleman." [14]

Much of the criticism of the Confederate President fails to take into account the insuperable difficulties of his position and to realize that no other Southern political leader even approached Davis in stature. Rembert W. Patrick's conclusion is a judicious one:

Davis's claim to conspicuous ability as a leader is incontestable. Undeterred by physical handicaps, he went steadily forward, holding his people together long after they had become too weak to continue the war effectively. His energy, will, determination, and knowledge did much to enable a nation possessed of little in resources and military effectives to hold off for four years an enemy vastly superior in wealth, material, and man power. The final defeat of the cause he led has dimmed Davis's reputation for leadership. A world that ever applauds success, too often, as in his case, fails to appreciate the quality of leadership that falls short of attaining the goal. The leader's errors and the defects and limitations of his character are magnified and stand out as do a few spots of ink on a sheet of white paper. . . . The Confederacy chose as its President its most suitable citizen and he did everything in his power to establish its independence.[15]

[14] Wiley, *The Road to Appomattox,* 10.
[15] Patrick, *Jefferson Davis and His Cabinet,* 44–45.

CHAPTER 15

Men and Measures

I

AT THE NORTH an unwieldy democracy lumbered into war in a state of unpreparedness, met the crisis with half-way measures, left much to the states and local agencies, planned first for a "three-months' war," lost itself in intrigue and in legalistic discussions as to what the war was about, struggled with divisions at home while facing serious menace in its foreign entanglements, and gradually proceeded to more and more drastic measures and more vindictive legislation as the conflict raged on. Finding defects in its rather inefficient government, it was compelled often to tinker with the machine, though it seldom attempted drastic alterations in governmental structure. Swept by gales of hysteria and war frenzy, it was raised to heights of exaltation by the courage of heroic sacrifice and invigorated by newly tapped sources of energy and organization; yet it was also shamed by the shocking degradation of wartime aggrandizement and personal greed. As the war progressed it changed its character, so that all hope of restoring the *status quo ante* was doomed to disappointment. The simple patterns of Jeffersonian and Lincolnian democracy had been submerged in an irrevocable past.

In planning for a three-months' war, Lincoln acted in the absence of Congress. Though the war began in April, Congress was not assembled until July. For this unsatisfactory situation there was a variety of causes. Cooperation between the legislative and executive branches, conspicuous in a parliamentary government such as England's, has seldom been a distinguishing feature of the American system. Lincoln was new to the duties of high office and seemed reluctant to incur the embarrassment of a congressional session. It was felt that time was needed for the maturing of opinion at the North before the solons should assemble. Furthermore, a peculiar situation existed in Kentucky, where a special election was to be held for members of the Thirty-Seventh Congress; and Lincoln was glad to allow time for a full canvass in his native state, then wavering between North and South.

The interval of eighty days between the beginning of the war and the assembling of Congress gave the President a virtual monopoly of emergency powers. On April 15, in language reminiscent of Washington's at the time of the Whisky Insurrection, Lincoln declared on "insurrection" to exist, announced that Federal laws were being opposed in seven states "by combinations too powerful to be suppressed by the ordinary course of judicial proceedings, or by the powers vested in the marshals by the law," and summoned the militia of the states to the number of 75,000 to "suppress said combinations." By this proceeding the Civil War began without a declaration. This was natural enough, since the South considered secession a peaceable act, while according to the Union point of view such secession was null and required a defensive attitude on the part of the government with a readiness to strike in retaliation for any act of resistance to the national authority. This drifting policy, accompanied by conditions in the social mind which can only be described as pathological, had led to the Sumter crisis; and war was upon the country, with each side stoutly protesting that its actions were purely defensive and that the opponent was the aggressor.

Lincoln took many other war measures. He issued two proclamations of blockade: the first one, dated April 19, 1861, applied to South Carolina, Georgia, Alabama, Florida, Mississippi, Louisiana, and Texas; the second, April 27, applied to Virginia and North Carolina. It was these proclamations of blockade which were taken by the Supreme Court as marking the legal beginning of the war.[1] He decreed the expansion of the regular army on his own authority. Whereas the call of April 15 was a summoning of militia, which the President has the right to call out for the suppression of insurrection, a further call of May 3 was for recruits to the regular army beyond the total then authorized by law. Increasing the regular army is a congressional function. "I never met any one," said John Sherman, "who claimed that the President could, by a proclamation, increase the regular army."[2] The stir of patriotic activity, however, left no time for deliberation as to legal authority; and Lincoln did not wait till the constitutionality of his action could be settled. "These measures," he said in his message of July 4, 1861, "whether strictly legal or not, were ventured upon, under what appeared to be a popular demand, and a public necessity; trusting . . . that Congress would readily ratify them." It was in this spirit that he gave large powers unofficially to citizens of his own choosing who were to make arrangements for transporting troops and supplies and otherwise promoting the public defense. Doubting the loyalty of certain persons in government departments, he directed the secretary of the treasury to advance $2,000,000 of public money without security to John A. Dix, George Opdyke, and Richard Blatchford of New York, to

[1] Randall, *Constitutional Problems Under Lincoln*, 49–50.
[2] N. Y. *Tribune*, Aug. 23, 1861, p. 7.

pay the expenses of "military and naval measures necessary for the defence and support of the government." [3] Yet the Constitution provides that "No Money shall be drawn from the Treasury, but in Consequence of Appropriations made by Law." Lincoln himself admitted the irregularity of this proceeding, saying he was not aware that a dollar of the public funds "thus confided without authority of law to unofficial persons" was lost or wasted. In Lincoln's mind the honesty of his act and the emergency which occasioned it excused its illegality. He issued his first suspension of the habeas corpus privilege at this time,[4] thereby assuming a vast extent of presidential power. In a word, the whole machinery of war was set in motion by the President, with all that this meant in terms of Federal effort, departmental activity, state action, and private enterprise.

The Thirty-Seventh Congress met by presidential call July 4, 1861. Certain members appeared from Virginia and Tennessee; otherwise the states of the Confederacy were unrepresented. In the House of Representatives there were few names that rose above mediocrity. Thaddeus Stevens of Pennsylvania, unlovely but masterful, soon became one of the leading personalities of the lower house, guiding it toward harsh and vengeful measures. Others among the Republicans in the House were Owen Lovejoy of Illinois, brother of the abolitionist martyr; G. W. Julian and Schuyler Colfax of Indiana; F. P. Blair, Jr., of Missouri, befriended by Lincoln; E. G. Spaulding of New York, adept in financial matters; Ashley of Ohio, a vindictive of the Stevens brand; Bingham of Ohio; and, from Pennsylvania, W. D. Kelley and John Covode. Among the Democrats were such men as Richardson, McClernand, and John A. Logan of Illinois, the last soon to become a conspicuous general and a radical Republican; Voorhees of Indiana; Pendleton, Vallandigham, and S. S. Cox of Ohio; and Erastus Corning of New York. The greater portion, however, of the lower house consisted of men who followed the leaders and made little contribution to the development of policy.

The party distribution in the House followed sectional and geographic lines. The Republican party predominated in the New England, New York, and Pennsylvania delegations. The Democratic party showed some strength among the Illinois, Ohio, and Indiana delegations without controlling them; while the Democrats and old-line Whigs or "Americans" controlled the border states of Kentucky, Maryland, and Missouri. Among the moderates of the border states none was more notable than the venerable John J. Crittenden, whose service in the Senate "began the day that Madison left the Presidency, and ended the day of Lincoln's inauguration," [5] and who now carried into the lower house the pacific ideals of the Clay tradition and the Bell-Everett party.

In the Senate there was much the same party and sectional division.

[3] Lincoln, *Collected Works*, V, 242.
[4] To be treated later. See chap. 16.
[5] Blaine, *Twenty Years*, I, 330. (This service was not continuous.)

Most of the "free-state" senators (all except five from New Jersey, Indiana, Oregon, and California) were Republicans, with the New England group distinctly in the lead. The most important committee chairmanships were held by New Englanders; and the formulation of vital legislation was largely in their hands.[6]

Seward, Cameron, and Chase had left the Senate for the cabinet; of those who remained, Charles Sumner was the most prominent. In this eloquent son of Massachusetts one finds a blending of New England qualities in which the loveliest attributes were not always uppermost. In his own region Sumner gained sympathy from the Brooks attack and from his antislavery convictions. Emerson, borrowing a phrase from Bishop Burnet, called him "the whitest soul I ever knew," [7] and in 1874 L. Q. C. Lamar of Mississippi praised him in a memorable eulogy; [8] but to many of his colleagues the man seemed egotistical, pedantic, and artificial. To Southerners his Puritan zeal appeared sinister and insincere; in their eyes his antislavery sentiments seemed to carry more venom against the slaveholder than humanitarian interest in the Negro. Somewhat resembling Sumner in their radicalism were such men as Benjamin F. Wade of Ohio and Zachariah Chandler of Michigan. Lyman Trumbull of Illinois, a Republican of Democratic antecedents, was more often in alliance with the Radicals than the moderate nature of his mind would seem to suggest. William Pitt Fessenden of Maine was one of the ablest men of the Senate, especially prominent in financial legislation. Jacob Collamer of Vermont presented a fine example of a moderate, reasonable, and high-minded Republican. His venerable dignity and conservative counsel offered a pleasing contrast to the excitement and excess which so often characterized the debates. Cowan of Pennsylvania, Henderson of Missouri, Grimes of Iowa, and Browning of Illinois are to be linked with Collamer in the group of moderate-minded Republicans. Doolittle of Wisconsin was prominent among moderate senators and was conspicuous for his clear thinking and sound counsel.

The Democrats, so recently the dominant party, were not without able representatives in the Senate. John C. Breckinridge appeared in the upper house as a Democrat from Kentucky. It has been previously noted that he had favored the Union during his campaign for the presidency in 1860 and that in the winter crisis of 1860–61 he labored not for secession but for a compromise that would avert it. Now, however, "his loyalties, his

---

[6] Sumner of Massachusetts was chairman of the Senate committee on foreign relations; his colleague, Henry Wilson, headed the committee on military affairs; the naval committee was headed by J. P. Hale of New Hampshire; the finance committee, concerned with both revenue and expenditure, was under the chairmanship of W. P. Fessenden of Maine. The committees on postal affairs, pensions, claims, patents, public buildings, printing, and contingent expenses were also headed by New England senators. L. M. Morrill of Maine was the only New England senator without a chairmanship. Blaine, *Twenty Years*, I, 323–324.

[7] Emerson, *Miscellanies* (*Complete Works*, XI), 251.

[8] *Cong. Record*, 43 Cong., 1 sess., 3410–3411 (Apr. 27, 1874).

prejudices, and perhaps his ambition pulled him in diverse directions," and his trumpet gave forth an uncertain note. ". . . I infinitely prefer to see a peaceful separation of these States," he admitted, "than to see endless, aimless, devastating war, at the end of which I see the grave of public liberty and of personal freedom." [9] One of the dramatic incidents of the summer session of 1861 was a tilt between Breckinridge and E. D. Baker of Oregon, close friend of Lincoln, who appeared on the Senate floor in the full uniform of a colonel of the Union army and took Breckinridge vigorously to task for his aid and comfort to the enemy. Being pro-Confederate in his post-Sumter attitude, Breckinridge found himself in opposition to the prevailing policy of his own state, whose legislature requested him and his colleague, L. W. Powell, to resign their seats. Without the formality of such a resignation Breckinridge entered the Confederate military service; and the Senate (December 4, 1861) expelled him from its membership.[10] The full duty of a loyal Southerner in 1861 is often indicated by the expression "going with his state." Certainly in the case of Breckinridge a different interpretation of duty was adopted.

In contrast to Breckinridge, there sat in the Senate a vigorous Southerner who had opposed secession—Andrew Johnson of Tennessee. He had displayed both physical and moral courage in his opposition to the whole Confederate movement; he stoutly championed the homestead bill and similar help for the farmer, and, though self-made, was powerful in debate and altogether an admirable representative of the antislavery and non-aristocratic whites of the South. Few Americans have held as consistently to principle in public life as this man. While in the Senate, he enjoyed the friendship of men who in later years were to become fierce opponents.

The border-state senators, chiefly Democrats with here and there an "American" or old-line Whig, were of a conservative and moderate turn. Bayard and Saulsbury of Delaware, Pearce and Hicks of Maryland, and Garrett Davis of Kentucky were able and reasonable men. Theirs, however, was the ability of dissent; their voices were raised in opposition to the prevailing trend.

In a well-worded message of July 4, Lincoln reviewed the Sumter crisis, recounted the emergency measures he had taken, argued the justification of the war on the Union side, and appealed for ratification of his irregular acts, taken in absence of congressional authority.

This [said the President] is essentially a People's contest. On the side of the Union, it is a struggle for maintaining in the world, that form . . . of government, whose leading object is, to elevate the condition of men—to lift

[9] Frank H. Heck, "John C. Breckinridge in the Crisis of 1860–1861," *J. S. H.*, XXI, 346, 341 (Aug., 1955).

[10] On July 11, 1861, the Senate had voted to expel various other senators from the seceded states.

artificial weights from all shoulders—to clear the paths of laudable pursuit for all—to afford all, an unfettered start, and a fair chance, in the race of life. Yielding to partial, and temporary departures, from necessity, this is the leading object of the government for whose existence we contend.

. . . . . .

Our popular government has often been called an experiment. Two points in it, our people have already settled—the successful *establishing,* and the successful *administering* of it. One still remains—its successful *maintenance* against a formidable [internal] attempt to overthrow it. It is now for them to demonstrate to the world, that those who can fairly carry an election, can also suppress a rebellion—that ballots are the rightful, and peaceful, successors of bullets; and that when ballots have fairly, and constitutionally, decided, there can be no successful appeal, back to bullets. . . . Such will be a great lesson of peace; teaching men that what they cannot take by an election, neither can they take it by a war—teaching all, the folly of being the beginners of a war.

Commenting on the world significance of the existing struggle, Lincoln declared:

And this issue embraces more than the fate of these United States. It presents to the whole family of man, the question, whether a constitutional republic, or a democracy—a government of the people, by the same people— can . . . maintain its territorial integrity, against its own domestic foes. It presents the questions, whether discontented individuals . . . can . . . break up their Government, and thus practically put an end to free government upon the earth. It forces us to ask: "Is there, in all republics, this inherent, and fatal weakness?" "Must a government, of necessity, be too *strong* for the liberties of its own people, or too *weak* to maintain its own existence?" [11]

So viewing the issue, Lincoln felt that no choice was left but to call out the war power of the government; and so to resist force employed for its destruction, by force for its preservation. Heeding the President's request that his emergency acts be regularized, Congress responded with the following resolution:

. . . *be it . . . enacted,* That all the acts, proclamations, and orders of the President . . . [after March 4, 1861] respecting the army and navy of the United States, and calling out . . . the militia or volunteers from the States, are hereby approved and in all respects legalized and made valid . . . as if they had been issued and done under the previous express authority and direction of the Congress of the United States.[12]

In addition to this approval of the President's acts, the special session of July–August, 1861, was chiefly occupied with emergency war measures. It passed a law (July 13) recognizing that an "insurrection" existed, this

[11] Lincoln, *Collected Works,* IV, 438–439, 426.
[12] *U. S. Stat. at Large,* XII, 326.

being the nearest approach to a congressional declaration of war.[13] The effect of the disaster of Bull Run was instantly reflected in its proceedings. On the day after the battle, taking counsel of its fears as to border-state sentiment and its anxiety to win proslavery support for the Union, the House of Representatives passed (July 22, 1861) the "Crittenden resolution," which declared:

That the present deplorable civil war has been forced upon the country by the disunionists of the southern States, now in arms against the constitutional Government . . . ; that in this national emergency, Congress, banishing all feelings of mere passion or resentment, will recollect only its duty to the whole country; that this war is not waged on their part in any spirit of oppression, or for any purpose of conquest or subjugation, or . . . of overthrowing or interfering with the rights or established institutions of those States, but to defend and maintain the *supremacy* of the Constitution, and to preserve the Union with all the dignity, equality, and rights of the several States unimpaired; and that as soon as these objects are accomplished the war ought to cease.[14]

If this resolution meant anything, C. Vann Woodward remarks, it meant that, "so far as both President and Congress were able to formulate war aims, this was a war of narrowly limited objectives and no revolutionary purpose. It was to be a war against secession, a war to maintain the Union—that, and nothing more." [15] But this solemn declaration, though probably reflecting the prevailing sentiment of the nation at the time, marked but a passing phase in the development of legislative policy. Though in July the resolution passed the House with only two dissenting votes (121 to 2), yet in early December, by a vote of 71 to 65,[16] the House refused to reaffirm it.

Of more solid significance than the Crittenden resolution was another bit of legislation which passed Congress the day following the Bull Run débâcle. It was an act authorizing the enlistment of volunteers to the number of 500,000 for a period of not more than three years nor less than six months. Overnight the Congress had altered its conception of the struggle from a three-months' war to a three-years' war. Then a few days later (July 25, 1861) the question of the length of service was more satisfactorily solved by a supplementary act providing that volunteers be mustered in to serve "during the war."

[13] *Ibid.,* XII, 255.

[14] *Cong. Globe,* 37 Cong., 1 sess., 222–223. (A similar resolution also passed the Senate July 25. *Ibid.,* 265.)

[15] Woodward, "Equality: America's Deferred Commitment," *Am. Scholar,* XXVII (Winter, 1958), 460.

[16] Dec. 4, 1861. *Cong. Globe,* 37 Cong., 2 sess., 15.

2

The attention of the war Congress, however, was not limited to actual legislation. The manner in which it extended its investigational functions, as well as its quasi-judicial activities and its interference in executive matters, is illustrated by the organization known as the "committee on the conduct of the war." As an example of the meddling of politicians in military affairs, the committee has been criticized, but such criticism ignores the fact that in a democratic society civilians must exercise control over the military, even during times of war.

Pressure for the creation of this investigatory committee came from a group of "Radicals" ("Jacobins," as their enemies called them), who were angered during the autumn of 1861 by McClellan's failure to use his army of 190,000 to "push back the defiant traitors." They visited McClellan's camp, remonstrated with him, and voiced their complaints to Lincoln. Their feelings were further aroused by the disaster at Ball's Bluff, a minor engagement which occurred on October 21, 1861, when at a point on the Potomac some distance above Washington a portion of General Charles P. Stone's division, under the command of Col. E. D. Baker, was repulsed by a superior Confederate force and sacrificed in a seemingly needless slaughter. The Union casualties (49 killed, 158 wounded, 714 captured or missing) mark it as a small engagement; but the proximity to Washington, the reliance placed in Stone's division for the defense of the capital, the inevitable comparison of Ball's Bluff with Bull Run, and especially the death of E. D. Baker, a close friend of Lincoln who had been recently a member of the Senate, caused the Radicals to demand closer congressional oversight of the war effort.

On the convening of Congress (December 2, 1861) the House of Representatives unanimously passed a resolution introduced by Conkling of New York requesting the secretary of war to report on the Ball's Bluff disaster. Further resolutions calling for sundry investigations by Congress were presented, until finally a resolution was adopted by both houses creating a committee "to inquire into the conduct of the present war." The committee consisted of three senators appointed by the Vice-President (B. F. Wade of Ohio, Zachariah Chandler of Michigan, and Andrew Johnson of Tennessee) and four representatives appointed by the Speaker of the House (D. W. Gooch of Massachusetts, G. W. Julian of Indiana, John Covode of Pennsylvania, and Moses F. Odell of New York).[1]

Much of the work of the committee was unexceptional. Its members performed a useful service in the investigation of scandals in connection with such diverse matters as "light-draught monitors, ice contracts, heavy

[1] There were later changes. Andrew Johnson was succeeded by J. A. Wright of Indiana, then by B. F. Harding of Oregon, and by C. R. Buckalew of Pennsylvania; Covode of the House membership was succeeded by B. F. Loan of Missouri.

ordnance, employment of disloyal persons in government work, hospitals and the treatment of the wounded, and illicit trade with the Confederates." The committee, declares W. W. Pierson, "brought speed and efficiency into the conduct of the war; . . . they ferreted out abuses and put their fingers down heavily upon governmental inefficiency; and . . . they labored, for a time at least, to preserve a balance and effect a co-operation between the legislative and executive departments."

But all too often there was a distinctly partisan tinge to the committee's work. Not only did its members resent the importance given to Democratic generals; they labored to promote one flank of the Republican party, and that the flank opposed to Lincoln and his administration. The committee traveled extensively, summoned numerous witnesses, filled huge volumes with its hearings and reports, investigated Union disasters, and "considered themselves . . . a sort of Aulic Council clothed with authority to supervise the plans of commanders in the field, to make military suggestions, and to dictate military appointments." [2]

Illustrative of the worst features of the committee's work was its investigation of the alleged responsibility of General Stone for the Union defeat at Ball's Bluff. Stone had a fine military record. Coming of an excellent Massachusetts family, he had been trained at West Point, had served in the Mexican War, and had been a resident of California. He was in Washington when the trouble with the South showed signs of developing into war; and at the request of General Scott he was given the important commission of raising, organizing, and commanding the troops (militia and volunteers of the Federal district) upon whom the defense of the national capital first rested. His services were so well performed that he was later promoted to the rank of brigadier general and given command of a division under McClellan. The Ball's Bluff affair was chiefly due to the rashness of Colonel Baker, who had exceeded instructions; but a living scapegoat was demanded, and the Jacobins pounced upon Stone, who had become the target of a multitude of malicious rumors. In a manner which showed how wretchedly it used its quasi-judicial power, the committee on the conduct of the war conducted an *ex parte* investigation of Stone's conduct and listened solemnly to amazing tales of his alleged disloyalty, his treasonable correspondence with the enemy, and his supposed interviews with Confederate officers. Wade, as T. Harry Williams points out, "conducted the inquiry in a manner that showed he had prejudged the case." [3] The "evidence" was kept secret; Stone was not permitted to know the charges against him nor the names of the witnesses; and the whole atmosphere of the proceedings indicated that the legislative investigators had already determined the case against the unfortunate general. The com-

[2] W. W. Pierson, Jr., "The Committee on the Conduct of the Civil War," *Am. Hist. Rev.*, XXIII, 574–576, 566.
[3] Williams, "Investigation: 1862," *Am. Heritage*, VI, 19 (Dec., 1954).

mittee's "trial" or inquiry never reached any conclusion, and Stone's persistent demand for a proper military court of inquiry was refused; but on the strength of unsupported rumor and false testimony he was placed under arrest (February 8, 1862) by order of Secretary Stanton through General McClellan and was imprisoned without trial, first at Fort Lafayette, then at Fort Hamilton, for 189 days. Such imprisonment was contrary to the existing Articles of War, under which an officer, when arrested, was entitled to a prompt trial and a copy of the charges against him. Not until February of 1863 did the committee present Stone with a copy of its charges. The flimsiness of their evidence then appeared; and Stone answered each accusation with such convincing frankness that they were never again revived except by way of whisper and gossip. Stone was restored to command, which amounted to a governmental confession of the wrong perpetrated upon him. The defamation of character, however, could not be undone; petty persecution continued to plague him; and at last, finding his usefulness to the army destroyed, he resigned (September 13, 1864). Later he became chief of staff to the Khedive of Egypt.

For this episode the committee on the conduct of the war was chiefly to blame. Responsibility also falls upon Secretary Stanton, who gave the order for the arrest, evidently prejudged the case, delayed Stone's release, and ungraciously refused to acknowledge his error. The injury to this officer's reputation stands as an example of the intolerance of the congressional Radicals of the Wade stamp and an illustration of the injustice of placing inquisitorial powers in the hands of a legislative committee whose mere inquiry may produce the most serious damage to a man's name, but whose proceedings lack the fairness, impartiality, and publicity of a proper trial such as would be conducted by a judicial or even a military tribunal.[4]

3

From another angle the manner in which Congress approached its wartime task may be seen in connection with the Federal confiscation acts. In the summer session of 1861 Congress passed a half-way measure of confiscation (August 6, 1861) which provided for the seizure of all property used for "insurrectionary purposes." Only such property as was used "in aid of the rebellion" was seizable under this act. In the speeches of the Radicals who urged confiscation, the severity of the war mind found complete expression. The Radical slant was illustrated by the outburst of Thaddeus Stevens. "[I]f," said he, "their whole country [i.e., the South] must be

---

[4] The thoroughness of the committee's work is shown by the fact that it "investigated" the administration of all the generals in command of the Army of the Potomac except Grant. Not only Bull Run and Ball's Bluff were subjected to inquiry; but also Fredericksburg, Chancellorsville, Gettysburg, and the battle of the crater at Petersburg. In addition, testimony was taken on many campaigns other than those on the main eastern front.

laid waste, and made a desert, in order to save this Union from destruction, so let it be. I would rather, sir, reduce them to a condition where their whole country is to be repeopled by a band of freemen than to see them perpetrate the destruction of this people through our agency." [1]

In the long session of the Thirty-Seventh Congress the Radicals succeeded in passing a far more sweeping measure known as the "second confiscation act," one of the most drastic laws ever enacted by the American Congress. The law covered three main subjects: the punishment of treason, the confiscation of property, and the emancipation of slaves.[2] Persons convicted of treason against the United States were to be punished by death or fine and imprisonment; those concerned in "rebellion or insurrection" were to be subjected to fine, imprisonment, and the liberation of slaves. As to confiscation, the main provision was immediate forfeiture to the United States of all the property of officers of the Confederate government without warning and a similar forfeiture after sixty days' warning in the case of all other persons who supported the "rebellion."

It was "enemies' property" that was made seizable in the second confiscation act; and the harsh rule was adopted that all persons residing in the eleven "insurrectionary" states were enemies during the Civil War, a rule which was even extended to include foreigners and those who were in fact loyal to the Union flag.[3] It was held after the war that neither pardon nor universal amnesty could restore property rights when proceedings under the second confiscation act had been completed.[4] Thus the guilty thing during the war was mere *residence* in an "insurrectionary state." Yet the United States Supreme Court in another line of decisions held that insurrection and war do not loosen the bonds of society, and that ordinary acts of the individual Southern states were valid and binding. The Confederate States were held to be a government maintaining such actual supremacy during the war in the South that obedience to its authority, in civil and local matters, was both a necessity and a duty.[5] In seeking to understand the various interpretations of what the government at Washington required of the Southern people it might perhaps be said that they were expected to withhold support from their own governments insofar as such governments were acting against the United States, while giving support in "ordinary" civil matters. Such qualified support of any government, however, is difficult to defend in theory, while in practice it was utterly impossible.[6]

---

[1] *Cong. Globe,* 37 Cong., 1 sess., 415.
[2] For the relation of the act to emancipation, see below, pp. 372–373.
[3] *House Report No. 262,* 43 Cong., 1 sess., pp. 6 ff.
[4] Semmes *vs.* U. S., 91 U. S. 21, 25.
[5] Thorington *vs.* Smith, 75 U. S. 1.
[6] On this subject of legal theories and judicial pronouncements on the highly involved question of "rebel" status, see Randall, *Constitutional Problems Under Lincoln,* 48–117, 275 ff., 307 ff., 362.

In vain did such moderates as Browning of Illinois, Garrett Davis of Kentucky, Collamer of Vermont, and Henderson of Missouri urge that the drastic confiscation program was designed to ruin millions of unoffending civilians. Of no avail were the arguments that it was unjustifiable as a belligerent measure, that it was forbidden by the Constitution, that it amounted to a bill of attainder, that it would bear heavily upon men who really supported the Union. The final bill, after complicated parliamentary maneuvers, passed by decisive majorities in both chambers.

The moderate nature of Lincoln's mind as well as his tendency to defer to the influence of the Radicals is illustrated by his intended veto of this second confiscation bill. In an able veto message the President remarked that "the severest justice may not always be the best policy." He pointed out that the bill unconstitutionally declared forfeitures "beyond the lives of the guilty parties" and that, by proceedings *in rem,* it "forfeited property . . . without a conviction of the supposed criminal or a personal hearing . . . in any proceeding." By a peculiar rigmarole Congress rushed through an "explanatory joint resolution" to the effect that the law was not to work forfeiture beyond the life of the accused; and, though this met only part of his objections, the signature of Lincoln was obtained on a measure of which he fundamentally disapproved.[7]

After contemplating the lavish outpouring of oratory upon this bill during the period of its incubation in Congress and the extravagant predictions as to financing the war by means of forfeiture and sale of Southern property, one learns with surprise of the very meager enforcement of the act. Condemnation of property took place by proceedings in United States courts; only such "rebel" property as was subject to attachment by reason of location within the jurisdiction of some Federal court—i.e., Southern-owned property within Northern judicial reach—was legally confiscable. Actually, proceedings depended largely upon the attorney general, who made no serious effort to enforce the act, and as a result a relatively small amount of property was seized. In the end no useful object in the prosecution of the war was achieved by this attempt to appropriate the private property of unoffending citizens. The whole experience pertaining to confiscation was such as to condemn the policy of promoting war by harsh punitive measures for the coercion of individuals.

In the matter of tariff legislation the lawmakers began in 1861 a trend in the direction of government-aided industrialism which was in marked contrast to the tendency of preceding decades. Under pressure from New England manufacturers the United States Congress in the 1820's had embraced the "American system" of protection; and a considerable portion

---

[7] Strangely enough, though Lincoln's intended veto of the second confiscation bill was thus avoided and the measure was signed by him, he transmitted his veto message, and it became a matter of legislative record. *Journal,* House of Representatives, July 17, 1862, p. 1125.

of the American public had come to adopt a capitalistic creed which affirmed that it rested with the Federal government to control the course of economic development, that prosperity for the manufacturer worked a kind of magic which tended to produce prosperity all down the line, and that protection was a species of cure-all for economic ills. In the course of time this "protection" was to be curiously identified with the principle of rugged American individualism: the regulation of business enterprise was viewed as the fostering of individual initiative and self-reliance. For a number of years prior to 1833, the protective principle had been dominant. Duties of about 25 per cent *ad valorem* had been levied in the Dallas tariff of 1816 to continue in peace time the monopolistic advantage which industrialists had enjoyed because of the cutting off of foreign trade before and during the War of 1812. Various duties had been increased in the tariff of 1824 which Webster opposed in a "lucid and magnificent speech." [8]

A curious counterplay of sectional antagonism and political timidity on the eve of a presidential election produced in 1828 the "tariff of abominations" which further raised protective duties to a point where Southerners became desperate. By favoring the tariff of 1828, Daniel Webster, who had now struck his stride as the spokesman of New England, completely reversed his antiprotectionist position of 1824. Speaking for Southern agriculturists, McDuffie of South Carolina urged that the manufacturing states protect their own industrialists by taxes and bounties instead of begging Congress for a relief which imposed a serious burden upon the South. The revolt of South Carolina against the tariff of 1828 and the resulting "nullification controversy" produced a sort of bargain (the tariff compromise of 1833) sponsored by Clay and supported by Calhoun, by which through successive yearly reductions a tariff for revenue was gradually to be established. Thus by 1846 the country had become accustomed to moderate duties; and in that year was passed the Walker tariff,[9] a measure designed with a view to abandoning the principle of protection altogether. In 1857 the tariff was still further lowered owing to the ascendency of free-traders and the abundance of Federal revenue from existing duties. Except for the iron manufacturers, most Northern businessmen were reasonably content with the new rates; Southerners, of course, were happy with them.

The year 1861 marked a new orientation in the tariff. While a majority of Northern manufacturers were "indifferent or actually hostile to any further changes in the tariff," [10] the iron interests, hard hit by the panic of 1857, eagerly demanded protection. Their pleas gained plausi-

---

[8] Quoted in J. B. McMaster, *Daniel Webster*, 121.

[9] Originated by R. J. Walker, an advocate of free trade, who was secretary of the treasury under President Polk.

[10] Richard Hofstadter, "The Tariff Issue on the Eve of the Civil War," *Am. Hist. Rev.*, XLIV, 55 (Oct., 1938).

bility from the fact that mounting deficits called for increase in the Federal revenue. Learning to make political capital out of the old principle of protection which was part of their Whig inheritance, the Republicans adopted a platform promising duties which would "encourage the development of the industrial interests of the whole country." Their tactics were highly successful; "Republican and Democratic campaign managers agreed that the tariff issue enabled Lincoln to carry pivotal Pennsylvania." [11]

Under these circumstances there was passed in the closing days of the Buchanan administration (February 20, 1861) the Morrill tariff. Introduced by Justin S. Morrill of Vermont and favored by the Republicans, this measure could hardly have been enacted but for the withdrawal of the Southern members. It was thus a Republican measure, though passed before the accession of Lincoln. The protection it afforded was moderate. Indeed the law was framed largely with reference to increasing Federal revenue; it was not distasteful to low-tariff advocates; and it was described as a return to 1846, with such changes as were necessitated by a shift from *ad valorem* to specific duties. Even so the Morrill tariff provided an appreciable increase over the low duties of 1857.

Then came the war; and Congress, as part of the complex of war finance, was induced to change the tariff again and again, actuated first by the need for additional revenue, and later by the quite different principle of "compensatory" duties—i.e., high tariff rates to protect American manufacturers from foreign competition during the period when they were subjected to heavy internal taxes. The tariff act of August 5, 1861, with its levies upon coffee, tea, sugar, spices, india rubber, and other articles necessarily imported, was distinctly revenue-producing. The act of July 14, 1862, increased the rates on articles of non-American production, gave protective increases in the case of many articles which could be produced at home, and greatly reduced the free list. Compensatory protection because of wartime taxation was the chief feature of the tariff act of June 30, 1864. In the words of Edward Stanwood, manufacturers "found their opportunity in the necessity of the government"; they "had only to declare what rate of duty they deemed essential, and that rate was accorded to them." [12] The nature of this tariff may be partly judged by the fact that unmanufactured tobacco was taxed at 35 cents a pound, beer at 35 cents a gallon, and brandy at $2.50 a gallon. The war ended with some duties as high as 100 per cent and with the general average at about 47 per cent, considerably more than double the average as of 1857.

---

[11] Reinhard H. Luthin, "Abraham Lincoln and the Tariff," *ibid.*, XLIX, 622 (July, 1944).

[12] E. Stanwood, *American Tariff Controversies in the Nineteenth Century*, II, 129–130.

4

Despite the war, the development of the Far West, so notable in the 1850's, moved forward with liberal encouragement on the part of the Federal government. Railroad schemes were pushed; Indians were progressively "eliminated" as obstacles to settlement; bountiful help was given to the homesteader. Expansionist movements of the forties and fifties, the Mexican War, and the discovery of gold and silver in California and Colorado, together with the manifest-destiny psychology of the American people, had produced much talk of a far western railway that would some day link the East with the Pacific coast. Schemes for a transcontinental railway by a Southern route had been among the favorite projects of the Pierce administration. Under his presidency the strip known as the "Gadsden purchase" had been obtained by treaty from Mexico (1853), a handy bargain for Uncle Sam, as a result of which Santa Anna (President of Mexico) became so unpopular that his resignation and exile soon followed.[1] Pierce's secretary of war, Jefferson Davis, had vigorously promoted the project by an elaborate government survey and a voluminous report. Owing to sectional rivalry, however, no definite steps had been taken; for there was not only the competition of North and South to obstruct progress, but also the clamoring of particular cities—e.g., New Orleans, St. Louis, Memphis, Chicago—for selection as the eastern terminus. As noted above,[2] promotion of transcontinental railroads was one of Douglas's motives in introducing the Kansas-Nebraska act; and during the Buchanan administration the transcontinental railway plan had remained dormant. After the withdrawal of Southern members from Congress, however, the Republicans, committed to the policy of a transcontinental railway, were in a position to proceed by the Northern route. The plan finally adopted was to create a Federal corporation, the Union Pacific Railroad Company, charged with building a line westward from Omaha, then only a village; while at the same time a California railroad, the Central Pacific, was to push its line eastward till the tracks united. The purpose of this grand scheme was to "form a continuous line of railroad from the Missouri River to the navigable waters of the Sacramento . . . , and thereby to unite the railroad system of the Eastern States with that of California, strengthen the bonds of union between the Atlantic and Pacific coasts, develop the immense resources of the great central portion of the North American continent, and create a new route for commerce from the Atlantic and Europe to the Pacific and Asia." [3] Federal statutes were passed (July 1, 1862, and July 2,

---

[1] It is sometimes stated that Santa Anna was banished as a traitor; but H. I. Priestley (*Mex. Nation*, 321–322) speaks of his resignation and voluntary exile, mentioning the Gadsden purchase as the cause of bitter feeling against him.

[2] See pp. 94–95.

[3] *House Report No. 78*, 42 Cong., 3 sess., pt. 1, p. 1.

1864) by which governmental largess on a vast scale was extended to this railway enterprise. Right of way was guaranteed; Indian titles were extinguished by the government; intruding Indians were driven off by military force; the power of eminent domain was exercised; millions of acres of public land were donated; [4] and the corporation was further made the beneficiary of millions in Federal bonds. As a subsidy to private enterprise the project (when linked with the parasitic *Crédit Mobilier*) offered roseate opportunities to "promoters." Though framed as a great program to promote the public interest, the scheme, progressing little during the war, fell into corrupt hands and became one of the scandals of the postwar age.

5

A factor of unique importance in westward development was the homestead law. Through the decades the Federal government had become increasingly generous in the disposal of the public domain by sales to homemakers at low rates, while it had also, with less justification, permitted the private exploitation of its vast stores of timber and mineral wealth. The plan to "give every poor man a home" had seized the imagination of the pioneers, whether from older settlements in the United States or from Europe; and the Republicans had attracted many votes by the "homestead plank" in their platform of 1860. The importance of this factor in the West may be judged from an article in a Nebraska paper in September, 1860. Under the heading "Let It Be Remembered" the writer protested that neither the Douglas nor the Breckinridge party platform said "one word" about a homestead bill, and that the Douglas convention, while ignoring this vital subject, had passed a resolution favoring the acquisition of Cuba, thus "saying to the . . . farmer on the Western frontiers, 'we care nothing about you or your rights, all we desire is to extend the area of slave Territory.' " [1]

In 1860 a homestead bill had been passed; but it met the veto of President Buchanan, who doubted the power of Congress to give lands to individuals and who objected to the law as a discrimination against soldiers and old settlers whose property would be depressed in value, and against mechanics as compared to farmers. On May 20, 1862, however, the homestead act became law. A quarter section of unoccupied land was to be given to homesteaders on payment of nominal fees after five years of actual residence. During the year ending June, 1864, lands to the amount

---

[4] By the act of July 1, 1862, 6400 acres of public land were donated for each mile of road, amounting to fifteen and a half million acres. The law of July 2, 1864, doubled these donations. Report, Sec. of the Interior, Nov., 1862, *House Exec. Doc. No. 1*, vol. II, 37 Cong., 3 sess., p. 50; *U. S. Stat. at Large*, XII, 492; *ibid.*, XIII, 358.

[1] Nebraska City *People's Press*, Sept. 20, 1860.

of 1,261,000 acres [2] were taken under the operation of the act; and succeeding decades witnessed brisk activity in the settlement of the West by the homestead system. It is a system whose effect upon American social and economic life is still imperfectly understood. There are widespread misconceptions in this field of American development, one of the most persistent being the erroneous notion that by 1890 the West was pretty well filled up, the free land about gone, and the frontier at an end. As a matter of fact much more land has been deeded since 1890 than before. Also many offhand assertions as to the effect of western land-taking upon the labor surplus are now discredited. The thoughtless assumption that free western land sustained wages and kept laboring conditions healthy by making it possible for laborers everywhere to turn quickly to agriculture is without foundation. The fact that vast numbers of laborers had neither the understanding nor equipment for a sudden shift to agriculture must not be overlooked. The readiness of large numbers to make such a shift existed chiefly in the realm of theoretical economics.

Another wartime measure of permanent importance was the act of 1862 for the establishment of "agricultural and mechanical colleges" in the states through the aid of Federal land grants. The act embodying this scheme for the advancement of higher education was called the Morrill land-grant act after Justin S. Morrill of Vermont, who fostered the movement in Congress, though the bill finally passed was introduced by Senator Wade of Ohio. Back of the work of Morrill, however, were years of earnest agitation by an almost forgotten man, Jonathan B. Turner, professor in Illinois College, Jacksonville. Turner was the leading spirit in a series of farmers' conventions in Illinois whose original purpose was to apply the "seminary fund" of the state, accumulated through the sale of public lands, to the establishment of a general state industrial university instead of having it dissipated among various existing private institutions. There was formed for this purpose the "Industrial League of Illinois," and Turner as its leader issued in 1853 a pamphlet on "Industrial Universities for the People" in which he projected an ambitious plan for the state university, a plan which today reads as a worthy forecast of western state universities in general. In 1852 the league had memorialized Congress for a grant of land to each commonwealth to endow "a system of Industrial Universities, one in each state"; the legislature of Illinois voted on February 8, 1853, to recommend such action to Congress; and thus the "Illinois idea," championed editorially by Greeley of the *Tribune,* attracted comment throughout the country.

Three features of the Turner plan deserve special attention, for without them the appeal for Federal aid could hardly have succeeded at this

---

[2] Report, Sec. of the Interior, 1864, p. 4.

period: (1) the Federal government was asked for donations in land, not money; (2) all states were to be treated alike in proportion to population, the older states having the same consideration as those in which public lands were still unsold; (3) the movement was popularized by emphasis upon "practical" education for agricultural and industrial pursuits.

For five years (1857–62) Morrill struggled for the adoption of his measure in Congress. His bill passed the House on April 20, 1858; but it was delayed in the Senate by the opposition of such men as Pugh of Ohio, Jefferson Davis of Mississippi, Clay of Alabama, and Mason of Virginia. Clay denounced the bill in bitter terms, objecting particularly to the fact that it "treats the States as agents instead of principals, as the creatures, instead of the creators of the Federal government." Finally the bill passed the upper house (February, 1859) but was vetoed by President Buchanan, whose constitutional objections were intensified by the existing depression with its resulting governmental deficits. On July 2, 1862, however, the land-grant-college bill became law by the signature of Lincoln. By its provisions there were granted to each state thirty thousand acres of public land for each senator or representative in Congress. Though the benefits of the act were at first confined to the "loyal" states, its terms were later extended to all the commonwealths. The measure was to prove significant more as a stimulus to state effort for higher education than as a Federal bounty or an establishment of a national educational bureaucracy. It is only in those states that have promoted their public universities as state enterprises that the system has shown marked results. It is in the West that this development has been most notable; though, because of the comparative smallness of population as of 1860, many of the states of this section were at a disadvantage in their sharing of Federal land donations.

To strike a balance as to the merits and faults of wartime legislation, one must take account of the futility or unwisdom of many of the measures as compared with the permanent importance of a few beneficial ones. In its patriotic enthusiasm to do anything which might promote the speedy and successful termination of the war, Congress often became committed to wrong-headed policies. Its fantastic scheme of confiscation was as unwise as it was unworkable. Its committee on the conduct of the war did great harm along with some good. Congress during the Civil War was no more successful than were subsequent legislatures in later conflicts in its handling of the extraordinary problems of wartime finance. Some of its "emergency" measures had unexpected permanence: the high tariffs of war time were continued in subsequent decades of peace, and the national banking system remained essentially unaltered until the time of Wilson. To read the wartime debates (a species of punishment now chiefly confined to graduate students of history) is to be mystified concerning that hypothetical collective entity which is called the "intention of the legislators." Many spoke as if they had not read the bills they were discussing, and the authors of the bills often devoted their speeches to the correction of their colleagues' misconceptions.

Yet here and there one finds an enlightened note. The act for the Pacific railroad was described as "striking proof of the unconquerable determination of the nation and an unfaltering faith in its ability to preserve its territorial integrity." "Had it been deemed possible that our country could fall a prey to rebellion [said the secretary of the interior], and its dissevered parts become subjected to . . . separate and alien governments, the construction of such a work would never have been undertaken and its execution would have been impracticable." [3] While the spirit of war was showing many of its worst aspects in the national capital, yet in a republic threatened by disruption and ruin the lawmakers thought and planned in terms of an enduring nation.

[3] Report of the Secretary of the Interior, 1865, *House Ex. Doc. No. 1,* 39 Cong., 1 sess., p. xii.

CHAPTER 16

The Government and the Citizen

I

THE REACTION of the Lincoln administration to the war emergency produced many unusual situations. Governmental norms were abandoned. War powers overbore the rule of law, and extralegal procedures were instituted. Well-known distinctions of government were obscured. The line was blurred between state and federal functions, between executive, legislative, and judicial authority, and between civil and military spheres. Probably no President, not even Wilson nor Franklin Roosevelt, carried the presidential power, independently of Congress, as far as did Lincoln. As already suggested, he began his administration by taking to himself the virtual declaration of the existence of a state of war, for his proclamation of insurrection (April 15, 1861) started the war régime as truly as if a declaration of war had been passed by Congress.

In issuing this proclamation Lincoln committed the government to a definite theory of the nature of the war. While this subject has too many facets and too much technicality to be developed here, it may be noted that in strict theory the Union government declined to regard the struggle as analogous to a regular war between independent nations. The Confederacy was never officially and formally recognized; it was deemed a pretender, an unsuccessful rival, and a usurper. Instead of the struggle being regarded as a clash between governments, the Southern effort was denounced as an insurrection conducted by combinations of individuals against their constituted authorities. While war is not legally a coercion of individuals (being rather the exercise of force between organized belligerent communities), the United States *technically* held the Southerners guilty of rebelling against the government to which, from the Union standpoint, they owed allegiance. In contrast to this, the Southern view was analogous to that of the Americans in the Revolution. They maintained that the Confederacy was an independent nation, conducting war under a high-minded, responsible government, and entitled to the respect due to a people fighting off an invader. It might have been supposed that the gigantic proportions of the conflict would change the Northern theory, but not so; for long after the guns at Sumter had united the South in solid array, the Lincoln administration and the statesmen at Washington still spoke of the Southern movement as an "insurrection," a "rebellion," or a "private combination of persons." [1]

Care was taken by the Lincoln administration to avoid meeting the commissioners appointed by the Confederate President, in conformity with a resolution of the Confederate Congress, to deal diplomatically with the United States as a foreign power. These commissioners were not received in person by the secretary of state; they were not even considered as representatives of a *de facto* government. Relations with England were strained because of an unreasonable resentment against the Queen's proclamation of neutrality; for in Washington the view prevailed that the existing struggle was purely a domestic affair and should be so treated by foreign powers. So also later in the war when negotiations for peace with the Confederacy were proposed: there was no recognition of the Confederacy as a continuing government with which the United States could negotiate. A careful study of the details of the war will reveal many another example of the fact that the Lincoln administration, which did not think of itself as merely the agent of the North, was giving no official or formal recognition to that of the South. All governments are sensitive on this matter of status and sovereignty. To have recognized the Confederacy would have been to admit the consummation of disunion, whereas the fundamental principle of the Lincoln administration was that the Union could not be broken by such efforts as those making at the South, no matter how tremendous they were.

It must not, however, be supposed that the government under Lincoln consistently developed all the implications and consequences of the insurrectionary theory. So long as it did not have to make concessions formally in the matter of governmental status, it was willing to yield in matters touching the practical modification of the insurrectionary principle to prevent the unjustifiable punishment of individuals. Confederate soldiers when captured were treated as prisoners of war; crews of Confederate privateers were treated as naval prisoners, not as pirates; [2] Southern citizens supporting the war were not punished for treason; and the conflict in general, though with some exceptions, was conducted in accordance with the *jus belli*.

Unless this distinction between legal theory and governmental practice is remembered, the war will be misunderstood. Though those engaged in the so-called "rebellion" were technically traitors, by a governmental theory similar to that which made George Washington treasonable in the eyes of the British government, yet belligerent rights were "conceded" to the Con-

[1] Randall, *Constitutional Problems Under Lincoln*, 63–73.
[2] See pp. 448–449.

federate armed forces. For legitimate acts of war Confederate officers and soldiers were relieved of individual civil responsibility. In legislative halls and in the Northern press there was vociferous talk of punishing "red-handed" and "black-hearted" traitors; but this was the frenzied exaggeration of the war mind. As a working rule the government followed the line indicated by Representative Samuel S. Blair of Pennsylvania, who said in debate: "[W]hat are our relations to these rebellious people? They are at war with us, having an organized government . . . and an organized army . . ., and I hold that . . . we are compelled to act, in most respects, towards them as if they were a foreign government of a thousand years' existence, between whom and us hostilities have broken out." [3]

It remained for the Supreme Court to give an orthodox pronouncement concerning the legal entanglements involved in this matter of Southern status. Its decisions were fitted into a convenient pattern that may be called the double-status theory—i.e., that the United States "sustained [toward the enemy] the double character of a belligerent and a sovereign, and had the rights of both." [4] So far as consummated policy was concerned the traitor-status principle was of slight importance. Government action was never so severe as the utterings of Radical statesmen. Southerners engaged in the war were in general treated as belligerents—as under a recognized government conducting an organized war. That there was inconsistency in the variance of theory and practice is of the essence of the subject. One cannot understand the war at all if he constantly looks for consistency.

2

Lincoln's view of his own war powers was most expansive. He believed that in time of war constitutional restraints did not fully apply, but that so far as they did apply they restrained the Congress more than the President. Assuming to his presidential office a sort of monopoly of emergency powers, he planned to cure the defect, if such it was, by appealing to Congress for ratification of executive measures so far as, in his opinion, they trenched upon the legislative sphere. In making this appeal, however, he presented Congress with a *fait accompli;* by the time Congress had the opportunity to act the measures had been irrevocably taken. Thus not only was Lincoln so interpreting the "war powers" as to place most of them with the President rather than Congress, but even with regard to the powers which he conceded to be legislative (such as the enlarging of the army and the appropriation of money) he anticipated Congress by acting in the premises and then asking for retroactive legislative authorization.

Such procedure raised the whole question of the "legality" of the war in its beginning. In the *Prize Cases* (decided in 1863) the Supreme Court was confronted with the contention that the war measures taken between

---

[3] *Cong. Globe,* 37 Cong., 2 sess., 2299.
[4] Miller *vs.* U. S., 78 U. S. 306–307.

April 15, 1861, the date of Lincoln's proclamation of insurrection, and July 13, 1861, when Congress passed an act recognizing the existence of the insurrection, were illegal and void. The point at issue had to do with certain ships captured for violation of the blockade proclamations of April 19 and April 27. It was argued that the President had no right to issue such proclamations in the absence of a congressional declaration of war, that he had acted beyond his powers, that war did not legally exist when the captures were made, and that the vessels were not legally forfeit. While the case was pending R. H. Dana, Jr., wrote: "In all States but ours . . . the function of the Judiciary is to interpret the acts of the Government. In ours, it is to decide their legality. . . . Contemplate . . . a Supreme Court, deciding that this blockade is illegal! . . . It would end the war, and how it would leave us with neutral powers, it is fearful to contemplate!" [1]

In a five-to-four decision the Court held that domestic war may begin without a declaration, that the President was bound to meet the war as he found it without waiting for Congress to "baptize it with a name," and that the presidential proclamations of blockade were valid.[2] Four dissenting justices, however, including the Chief Justice, held that the President's power of suppressing an insurrection is not tantamout to the power of initiating a legal state of war and that civil war does not validly begin with an executive proclamation. This was heavy and powerful dissent. Indeed, considering both the duty of the Court to sustain the government and the well-known tradition that the Court does not enter upon the settlement of a political question, the even balance and exceedingly narrow majority might seem almost a defeat or rebuke to the Lincoln administration. The "fearful" situation, to use Dana's term, that would have resulted if one of the five had voted differently, together with the fact that one of those who sustained Lincoln was of the Deep South (Wayne) and might have been expected to vote otherwise, may well serve as a text for dramatic comment. It would be an error to overdramatize, however, because there was no likelihood that even the dissenters could have held that the war as of 1863 was illegal. The point on which the Court divided was the legality of the war measures between April and July, 1861. The whole Court agreed that from July 13, 1861, when Congress acted,[3] a legal state of war existed and the President was invested with belligerent powers appropriate to the executive.

---

[1] Quoted in Charles Warren, *Sup. Court in U. S. Hist.* (two-vol. ed.), II, 382.

[2] The Prize Cases, 67 U. S. 635. The majority opinion was sustained by Justices Swayne of Ohio, Miller of Iowa, Davis of Illinois, Wayne of Georgia, and Grier of Pennsylvania. Those who dissented were Chief Justice Taney of Maryland and Justices Nelson of New York, Catron of Tennessee, and Clifford of Maine. It is of interest to note that five of the justices had been born before 1800, Taney as early as 1777.

[3] The act of July 13, 1861, "for the Collection of Duties . . . , and for

Though in many respects Lincoln was a leader of men, such a description hardly fits the case when one is speaking of his relations with Congress. In July of 1861 he asked for legislative "ratification" of his acts; but such was not his usual practice. More commonly he went his way in what he conceived to be the executive sphere, assuming large powers to himself, justifying his actions by a liberal interpretation of presidential authority rather than seeking legislation to put powers into the President's hand.[4] One can point to very few legislative measures under Lincoln which were initiated by the President and put through by the exertion of his influence. His chief effort to bring about a reform by legislative act—his scheme for emancipation by the states with Federal compensation—resulted in mere paper approval by Congress; it was never carried to the point of application. On the other hand, Congress passed several measures, such as the West Virginia bill and the second confiscation act, of which Lincoln disapproved, but which he nevertheless signed. Under Lincoln there was nothing analogous to Wilson's quick assumption of leadership in the summoning of Congress in special session at the beginning of his administration. Lincoln, in fact, seemed to prefer a legislative recess; he regarded Congress often as an embarrassment. Finding himself opposed in House and Senate by a powerful element (the "Jacobins" or Radicals) within his own party, he yielded to them where necessary, sinking his own preferences in so doing and using his well-tempered tact to prevent them from taking authority too much out of his hands. Meanwhile far-reaching acts of executive authority were performed in disregard of the legislative branch.

3

In the treatment of "disloyal" practices the government under Lincoln carried its authority far beyond the normal restraints of civil justice. To put the subject in its legal setting one must remember that in Anglo-Saxon jurisprudence there is the fundamental conception of the "rule of law"— the concept that government itself is under the law, that it must not be arbitrary, and that its agents are punishable or liable to damages if they wrongfully invade private rights. Against this concept there is the doctrine

---

other Purposes" (sec. 5) gave authority to the President to declare a state of insurrection under certain conditions. *U. S. Stat. at Large*, XII, 255–258. Justice Nelson remarked in his dissenting opinion (67 U. S. 696) that this act "recognized a state of civil war. . . ."

4 As an illustration, one may note how Lincoln, disregarding the constitutional provision that Congress should "make Rules for the Government and Regulation of the land and naval Forces," authorized General Halleck, who was ably assisted by Professor Francis Lieber, to draw up and issue "General Orders No. 100: Instructions for the Government of the Armies of the United States in the Field." Frank Freidel, "General Orders 100 and Military Government," *M. V. H. R.*, XXXII, 541–556 (Mar., 1946).

of "military necessity" with its maxim "necessity knows no law." Those who assume that the whole subject of governmental restraint in time of war can be dismissed by repeating such maxims are unaware of much of the nation's legal history. A government at war, according to a long line of American precedent and interpretation, must restrain itself in various ways. It must not overstep international law; it must not violate treaties; it must keep within what are called the "laws of war"; it must not ignore certain rights of enemy citizens when conducting a régime of military occupation; it must not destroy civil rights among its own people.

American interpretation does not readily run to the justification of military dictatorship or summary procedure. Martial law has no recognized niche in the constitutional framework of the United States; it does not come within the constitutional power of Congress to make rules to govern the armies. Just as in England grave disturbances (e.g., the Gordon riots of 1780, the Chartist disturbances of 1839 and 1848, and the Fenian outbreak in 1867) have been suppressed without martial law, so in the United States civil justice has usually proved sufficient to cope with insurrectionary violence and disloyalty. In the Whisky Rebellion Washington's government avoided instituting a military régime, and those prosecuted were dealt with in the regular civil courts. This precedent was followed in the case of the Burr conspiracy. Though General Andrew Jackson showed an opposite tendency during the War of 1812, seeking to overpower judges by military force, his action was judicially condemned and he was fined for his aggression. Certain of the states, especially in labor disputes, have resorted to martial law, but such resort by the Federal government has been most rare. At the time of the Civil War there was a decided preponderance of precedent in the opposite direction.[1]

That so mild a President as Abraham Lincoln, a man thoroughly imbued with Anglo-Saxon principles of civil liberty, should have used methods that smacked of despotism may seem strange; but such alleged despotism became a familiar topic of denunciation among his opponents. To comment intelligently upon the matter one must study the nature of practices in the North which were called "disloyal" and note how thoroughly they were entangled with political activities and partisan agitation. One of the angles of the problem is to be seen in connection with Democratic attempts, associated with such names as Vallandigham and Voorhees, to defeat the Republican party. Before the war there were groups of progressive Democrats who looked to a future of reform and enlightened development under the aegis of liberal Democracy. These men were strong in the states of Ohio, Indiana, and Illinois; they were friendly to the South; and they bitterly regretted the war, which they blamed upon Republican politicians. Their regret was compounded of distress at the thought of a brothers' war,

---

[1] Randall, *Constitutional Problems Under Lincoln*, especially 140 ff.

disappointment at the postponement of peaceful development, and displeasure at the party in power; it was powerfully reinforced by agrarian disgruntlement over the Eastern industrialists' apparent domination of the nation's economic policies.[2] In Indiana Lincoln's opponents obtained control of the legislature, so that Governor Morton had to find unofficial means of obtaining funds. In Illinois the "Copperheads" (to use the contemporary term of reproach for those Democrats who were outspoken in their opposition to the Lincoln administration) controlled the legislature of 1863. Though they denounced secession and supported the Union they so embarrassed Governor Yates by their agitation for an armistice that the Governor prorogued the body.

The fact that these anti-Republican groups formed secret organizations, with all the mystery and dark rumor that accompany such orders, led to misapprehension as to their essential purposes. While Republicans were forming their Union Leagues, some of the Democrats in certain localities, especially in Ohio, Indiana, and Illinois, established an organization known as the "Knights of the Golden Circle," then as the "Order of American Knights," and later as "Sons of Liberty." With the mummery and passwords that characterize secret orders, they held their lines together and carried on their activities with supposed secrecy; though as a matter of fact both the Federal and state governments had spies or detectives who reported their activities. It is clear now that the main purpose of the "Knights" was to promote the success of the Democratic party, and careful historians do not accept the view that they were a dangerous organization of a thoroughly treasonable nature. As to the situation in Indiana, it has been said that Governor Morton was "more afraid that his Democratic opponent, Joseph E. McDonald, would defeat him for Governor in the October election of 1864 than that the Sons of Liberty would rise and depose him from power."[3]

As it is made to appear from the report of the judge advocate general, these secret societies, which were said to comprise hundreds of thousands of members, were in communication with the enemy, seeking to promote Union defeat, and endeavoring to overthrow the government at Washington. Such things as aiding desertion, discouraging enlistment, resisting arrests, destroying enrollment lists, and circulating disloyal literature were among the charges against them. More serious accusations referred to such matters as recruiting for the enemy, distributing arms and ammunition so that "rebel" raids in the North might be assisted from the rear, plotting the release of Confederate prisoners, and planning the detachment of a "Northwest Confederacy" which by dividing the North was to promote Confederate success. Though some of the bolder schemes of the Knights seemed

[2] Frank Klement, "Middle Western Copperheadism and the Genesis of the Granger Movement," *M. V. H. R.*, XXXVII, 679–694 (Mar., 1952).

[3] Rhodes, *Hist. of U. S.*, V, 319–320.

to slant toward treason, their leaders ('such as Vallandigham) vigorously combated disloyal activity, and the main interest of the order was in party agitation against Republican rule and in mass meetings to urge peace (with union) by negotiation. In addition to these Southern sympathizers there were also agents of the Confederacy at various places in the North who were suspected, or in some cases caught in the act, of committing outrages upon Unionists, stealing military supplies, destroying bridges, engaging in bushwhacking, mapping fortifications, carrying treasonable correspondence, intimidating voters, or otherwise assisting the enemy.

For the controlling of such activities Lincoln concluded that the laws were insufficient and the courts inadequate. Congress passed the conspiracies act of July 31, 1861, and the treason act (known also as the second confiscation act) of July 17, 1862; but neither of these laws proved effective for the punishment of antiwar activities in the North. The conspiracies act decreed fine and imprisonment for those who conspired to "overthrow the government" or oppose governmental authority. The treason act softened the penalty for treason from death, as it stood in existing law, to an alternative of death or imprisonment and fine. Judicial activity in the enforcement of the treason and conspiracies acts in the North was slight.[4] Zealous grand juries brought indictments, but the typical procedure was to keep them on the docket from term to term, the offenders meanwhile being free on recognizance; and after a time the indictments were dropped. Attorney General Bates had no interest in such prosecutions. He resented the use of the courts for this type of business.

Courts do not automatically enforce the law: the extent of punishment depends rather upon the executive. If the government's prosecutors—the district attorneys acting under the President through the attorney general—are lukewarm in promoting prosecutions, convictions will be few; and such a lukewarm attitude was decidedly manifest under Lincoln. The administration knew not only that conviction in such a technical judicial proceeding as treason would be difficult to obtain, but that such a verdict, by rendering the victim a martyr, might be more embarrassing than acquittal.

Instead of enforcing statutes and conducting prosecutions in the courts, Lincoln followed a course which has led to widespread discussion and criticism: he suspended the habeas corpus privilege and resorted to summary arrest by executive authority assumed in disregard of both Congress and the judiciary. In the early part of the war such suspension was restricted to definite localities specified in presidential proclamations, beginning with that of April 27, 1861, covering the line from Washington to

[4] It is a striking fact that not until 1947 was a life forfeited or a sentence of fine and imprisonment ever carried out in any judicial prosecution under the Federal laws for treason against the United States. Randall, *Lincoln the Liberal Statesman*, 126–127, 234–235.

Philadelphia. In 1861 Secretary Seward had charge of these arrests, which were conducted on a scale that seems astonishing when one recalls that he was in charge of foreign affairs and that his official acts frequently invaded the domain of other departments and even of the President. Seward had his secret service organization, with confidential agents placed at strategic points to obtain the arrest of suspected persons. Passports were demanded of persons entering or leaving the country and those considered dangerous were intercepted. Prisoners were not told why they were seized. As to many of them Seward's department "never made up its case." [5]

In February of 1862 two important steps were taken. A sweeping order provided for the wholesale release of political prisoners, and the control of arrests was transferred from the state to the war department. A special commission, consisting of Judge Edwards Pierrepont and John A. Dix, was appointed to operate under the secretary of war for the examination of individual cases. On recommendation of this commission many releases were effected in February, 1862, and succeeding months.

On September 24, 1862, despite previous action seeking to prevent arbitrary arrests from getting out of hand, Lincoln issued a general proclamation providing that during the existing "insurrection" all persons discouraging enlistment, resisting the draft, or guilty of any disloyal practice, were subject to martial law and liable to trial by courts-martial or military commissions. Touching such persons the suspension of the habeas corpus privilege was authorized. The number of these arrests, involving the withholding of normal constitutional guarantees, mounted into the thousands. The estimate of Alexander Johnston that they ran up to 38,000 [6] seems an exaggerated guess; but over 13,000 cases are listed in the records of the Federal commissary general of prisoners, and to this number one must add those arrested under the navy and state departments and confined in penitentiaries or in prisons maintained by the several states. [7]

4

A famous controversy resulted from the arbitrary arrests. One Merryman, officer of a secessionist drill company, was arrested in Maryland, [1] taken into military custody by order of General Cadwalader, commander of the department, and confined in Fort McHenry. A petition for a writ of

[5] Frederic Bancroft, *Life of W. H. Seward*, II, chap. xxxiv. The above treatment is based on extensive research in the *Official Records* (especially 2 ser., II) and in the "domestic correspondence" of the department of state.

[6] Alexander Johnston, in *Cyc. of Pol. Sci.* [etc.], ed. by J. J. Lalor, II, 432–434.

[7] Randall, *Constitutional Problems Under Lincoln*, 152.

[1] The arrest occurred May 25, 1861, near Cockeysville, Maryland. Merryman was accused of being "an active secessionist sympathizer." David M. Silver, *Lincoln's Supreme Court*, 28 ff.

habeas corpus was presented to Chief Justice Taney. Hearing the petition in chambers while on circuit duty, Taney caused the writ to be served directing Cadwalader to produce Merryman in court so that the cause of his imprisonment might be judicially examined. Cadwalader's instructions, however, were to hold persons whose offenses were such as Merryman's and to decline to produce prisoners where habeas corpus writs were issued. He showed no truculence toward the judiciary as did Jackson in the War of 1812, but in a respectful return to the writ stated the cause of Merryman's apprehension, cited the President's suspension of the privilege of the writ, and declined to produce the prisoner. Taney then issued a writ of attachment for contempt against the general; but the marshal seeking to serve this writ was refused entrance to the fort and (to suppose an entirely hypothetical situation) would have encountered superior force had he attempted by a *posse comitatus* to compel the general's obedience to the judicial mandate. Having met resistance in pursuance of duty the Chief Justice prepared an opinion vigorously denying the President's right to "suspend the writ," put the proceedings on record in the circuit court, and caused a copy to be transmitted to the President, leaving to that "high official" the obligation of causing the "civil process of the United States to be . . . enforced." The right to suspend, he declared, belonged only to Congress; the President had no power to effect such suspension himself; and his action in this and thousands of similar cases was without legal warrant. Since the courts were holding sessions and conducting business, Taney maintained that any suspected treason should have been reported to the district attorney and dealt with by judicial process. Denouncing Lincoln's act as usurpation, he put it up to him to maintain constitutional guarantees.

Though the Merryman case had not reached the Supreme Court of the United States,[2] that tribunal was asked to pass judgment in one of the most prominent of the wartime cases involving the suspension of civil liberties— that of Clement L. Vallandigham, a Democratic politician of Ohio whose name became a slogan for thousands of Lincoln's opponents. Indeed the whole movement for constitutional guarantees seemed to be focused in this

---

[2] The mistake is sometimes made of attributing the Merryman decision to the Supreme Court of the United States; but it was the opinion of one member of the court while on circuit duty (17 *Fed. Cas.* 144). When rendered it was not regarded as a settlement of the matter. Though Taney's opinion was issued in May, 1861, there were various later apprehensions as to a possible decision by the Supreme Court on the President's suspending power. Attorney General Bates, writing confidentially to Stanton, January 31, 1863, expressed such apprehension, and declared that a decision pronouncing the arbitrary arrests illegal would "do more to paralyze the Executive . . . than the worst defeat our armies have yet sustained." Stanton Papers (MSS., Libr. of Cong.), no. 52223. See also Welles, *Diary*, II, 242, 245–246.

cause célèbre. On May 1, 1863, Vallandigham made a political speech at Mount Vernon, Ohio, asserting that the war could easily have been concluded by negotiation or by the acceptance of French mediation, but that the administration was needlessly prolonging the bloodshed. The war, he said, was not for the Union, but for the liberation of the blacks and the enslavement of the whites. Vallandigham was accused of violating "General Order No. 38" issued by General A. E. Burnside (April 19, 1863) while in command of the Department of the Ohio with headquarters at Cincinnati. This order announced that "the habit of declaring sympathies for the enemy [would] be no longer tolerated" and threatened that offenders would be punished by military procedure.[3]

It was stated by S. S. Cox that Vallandigham had used no denunciatory epithets toward Burnside, that he did not advocate resistance to military orders nor attack conscription, but that he counseled resistance to the Lincoln administration by means of the ballot and free discussion.[4] Nevertheless by Burnside's order the orator was placed under military arrest, which of course enhanced his importance, was denied the habeas corpus privilege, and was tried by military commission. Though he refused to plead, denying the jurisdiction of the military court, the judge advocate entered a plea of not guilty, and the trial proceeded with such safeguards for the accused as are customary in military commissions. The commission found Vallandigham guilty of declaring disloyal opinions with the object of weakening the government, and he was sentenced to close confinement during the war. Making full use of his dramatic opportunity for publicity, he issued from "a military bastile" at Cincinnati (May 5, 1863) a stirring appeal "To the Democracy of Ohio" in which he epitomized his attitude in the following words: "I am a Democrat—for the Constitution, for law, for the Union, for liberty—this is my only 'crime.' "

The President was embarrassed. There were thousands of Vallandighams, and severe treatment would but help their cause. Lincoln himself wrote to Burnside: "All the cabinet regretted the necessity of arresting . . . Vallandigham, some perhaps, doubting, that there was a real necessity for it. . . ."[5] On the other hand the administration wished to guard against the effect of a hasty release that might be interpreted as weakness. Lincoln extricated himself from the dilemma by commuting Vallandigham's sentence from imprisonment to banishment within the Confederate lines. From this point, by turning the pages of Vallandigham's voluminous biography written by his brother,[6] one reads of the exile's ride under military escort to the Confederate outposts; his "proposition" that he address Union

---

[3] Randall, *Constitutional Problems Under Lincoln*, 176 ff.
[4] J. L. Vallandigham, *Life of Clement L. Vallandigham*, 277 ff.
[5] Lincoln, *Collected Works*, VI, 237.
[6] J. L. Vallandigham, *Life of Clement L. Vallandigham.*

soldiers who would be moved by his words to "tear Lincoln . . . to pieces"; his nomination for the governorship of Ohio on the Democratic ticket; his escape from the South by running the blockade; his sojourn at Windsor, Canada, whence he issued addresses to the people denouncing the despots at Washington; and his determination to "recover the liberties of which he had been deprived, . . . or perish in the attempt." In Falstaffian disguise, aided by a thick mustache and a pillow, he returned to the United States; then, throwing off the disguise, he took a conspicuous part in the political campaign of 1864. After this return from Elba his speeches were as violent as before, but Lincoln's moderation and sense of humor allowed the man to go unmolested, though the terms of banishment involved reimprisonment in case of return.

Meanwhile the Vallandigham case had been brought up to the Supreme Court on a motion to review the sentence of the military commission. In the argument of defense counsel it was urged that the prisoner had been tried on a charge unknown to the law; that the military commission had exceeded its jurisdiction; and that the Supreme Court of the United States, as the only remedy for such excess of authority, had the power to review the proceedings. In an opinion taken bodily from the argument of Judge Advocate General Joseph Holt, the Supreme Court refused (February, 1864) to review the case, declaring that its authority, derived from the Constitution and the judiciary act of 1789, did not extend to the proceedings of a military commission.[7]

After the war, however, an opposite opinion was issued by the Supreme Court.[8] The case originated in the arrest at Indianapolis (October 5, 1864) of L. P. Milligan, who with several associates was condemned by military commission and sentenced to be hanged. The accusation was conspiracy to release "rebel" prisoners and to march into Kentucky and Missouri in cooperation with Confederate forces in an expedition directed against the United States. It was shown that the prisoners were members of the Order of American Knights, whose activities have been described above. The date of the hanging was fixed at May 19, 1865, but execution was postponed pending appeal to the United States Supreme Court. On April 3, 1866, there was issued from that tribunal an opinion written by Justice David Davis which has become famous as one of the bulwarks of American civil liberty. The Court decided that Milligan's trial by military commission was illegal. "Martial law [it was held] cannot arise from a *threatened* invasion. The necessity must be actual and present; the invasion real, such as effectually closes the courts and deposes the civil administration. . . . Martial rule can never exist where the courts are open, and in the proper and unobstructed exercise of their jurisdiction. It is . . . confined to the locality of actual war." After this decision Milligan

[7] *Ex parte* Vallandigham, 68 U. S. 243.
[8] *Ex parte* Milligan, 71 U. S. 2.

was released. Later he was successful in an action for damages against General Hovey, under whose order he had been arrested, though the damages awarded were nominal.[9]

5

In line with his habit of treating the opposition with respect Lincoln defended his extralegal measures in his message to Congress of July 4, 1861, as well as in certain carefully worded letters, especially the "Birchard letter" and the "Corning letter." His main defense was to argue the desperateness of the emergency, the force of the war power, and the inability of the courts to deal with organized rebellion. When a meeting of citizens protested against the arrest of an agitator, Lincoln referred to the death penalty for deserters and then asked: "Must I shoot a simple-minded soldier boy who deserts, while I must not touch a hair of a wiley [sic] agitator who induces him to desert?" Summary methods, Lincoln showed, were not for partisan advantage, not even for punishment, but for a precautionary purpose. In contrast to judicial prosecutions intended for quiet times as punishments for deeds committed, he urged that arrests in cases of "rebellion" were made "not so much for what has been done, as for what probably would be done." The purpose, he explained, was "preventive," not "vindictive." [1]

On legal and constitutional points the President's acts are defended in the official opinion of his attorney general, and in the writings of a distinguished lawyer, Horace Binney, who justified the President's course in an elaborate pamphlet.[2] According to these arguments there was no violation of the Constitution, since that instrument permits suspension of the habeas corpus privilege when the public safety requires it during a rebellion, and does not specify what branch of the government is to exercise the suspending power. From this point of view the case is not analogous to English law and procedure, where the purpose is to limit the King and where under the habeas corpus act of 1679 Parliament may suspend at any time regardless of whether there is rebellion or not. It was urged that the case was not covered by constitutional construction according to context; for, though the habeas corpus clause appears in the legislative article, this was no evidence that the constitution makers meant such suspension to belong exclusively to Congress, inasmuch as the clause was debated in the constitutional convention in connection with the judiciary and was merely grouped with the legislative clauses as an afterthought by the committee on style.

[9] 71 U. S. 127; Warren, *Supreme Court* (two-vol. ed.), II, 427. For the relation of the Milligan decision to the postwar situation, see below, pp. 643–644.

[1] Lincoln, *Collected Works*, VI, 260–269, 300–306.

[2] Summarized in Randall, *Constitutional Problems Under Lincoln*, 120–127.

This question of arbitrary arrests was far from clarified by the habeas corpus act of March 3, 1863, a measure which was tardily passed after much wrangling and which left the main issue—the President's right to suspend—precisely where it had been before. This law provided that "during the present rebellion, the President of the United States, whenever, in his judgment, the public safety may require it, is authorized to suspend the privilege of the writ of habeas corpus in any case throughout the United States, or any part thereof." [3]

Some thought this meant that Congress was not conferring upon the President the right to suspend, but merely recognizing that he had that right. Others thought that by giving the authority Congress was implying that the President did not possess it of his own power or prerogative. The intention of the act was to effect a compromise between camp and bench and to introduce a *modus vivendi* by which the authority of the courts would be respected without too seriously restricting the executive and military authorities. On the one side the President's authority to suspend was recognized; on the other hand lists of political prisoners were to be sent to the Federal courts, and if grand juries found no indictments against them they were to be released. Whereas arrests and releases had previously been at the discretion of the executive, it was now intended that the further holding of prisoners should depend upon judicial procedure. If lists were not furnished, the law declared that a Federal judge might discharge the prisoner on habeas corpus. The essential fact, however, is that the habeas corpus act was virtually ignored and that the arrest, confinement, and release of prisoners continued as if it had not been passed. In the Vallandigham case, for example, it offered no remedy. Executive authorities were negligent in furnishing lists of prisoners to the courts, and the latter did not in fact control the situation.

A most sensational treatment of this subject of political prisoners, in which the arrests are discussed in harrowing detail, appears in a book called the *American Bastile,* written by the officially appointed historian of an association of prisoners of state.[4] A careful study, however, reveals that comforts were not in general denied to prisoners, that they could carry on correspondence and receive visitors, and that there was no deliberate policy of governmental abuse directed against them. Such hardships as they suffered were due to general conditions of prison administration. While arbitrarily taken into prison, they were as arbitrarily released. Their imprisonment was, of course, a serious matter. The terms of confinement, however, were usually short, and the ultimate effect was much milder than if opponents of the administration had been subjected to such a thing as the French Revolutionary Tribunal or the English Star Chamber with

[3] *U. S. Stat. at Large,* XII, 755.
[4] John A. Marshall, *American Bastile: A History of the Illegal Arrests and Imprisonments during the Late Civil War* (Phila., 1869).

all the steps completed, including trial, conviction, and execution. In the vast majority of cases there was no trial at all, the military commission being as a matter of usual practice confined to the legitimate function of dealing with citizens in military areas charged with military crimes. Where, for instance, civilians in proximity to the Union army were engaged in sniping or bushwhacking, in bridge-burning or the destruction of railroad and telegraph lines, they were tried by military commission. This has occasioned little comment, though there were hundreds of instances. The prominence of the Vallandigham and Milligan cases should not obscure the fact that these prosecutions were exceptional. In other words, the military trial of citizens for nonmilitary offenses in peaceful areas was far from typical. So far as the period of the war was concerned, it was a rare use of the military commission that was denounced by the Supreme Court in the Milligan decision. That decision derives much of its importance from the postwar setting in which it was delivered.

Lincoln's practice fell short of dictatorship as the word is understood in the twentieth century. He did not think of suppressing his legislature and ruling without it. He did not pack his Congress, nor eject the opposition. There was nothing in his administration comparable to a Napoleonic *coup d'état* or a Cromwellian purging of Parliament. No party emblem was adopted as the flag of the country. No rule for the universal saluting of Lincoln was imposed. There was no Lincoln party constituting a super-state and visiting vengeance upon political opponents. Criminal violence was not employed *sub rosa* after the fashion of modern dictatorships. No undue advantage was taken of the emergency to force arbitrary rule upon the country or to promote personal ends. Lincoln half expected to be defeated in 1864. The people were free to defeat him if they chose at the polls. The Constitution was indeed stretched, but it was not subverted.

Freedom of speech and of the press were not extinguished under Lincoln. Though Vallandigham was banished in 1863 for making a speech, he spoke frequently and with equal violence in 1864 without molestation. Being without restraint, his utterings were less effective. In this matter one must avoid the historical fault of generalizing from selected instances. There were, it is true, a number of newspaper suppressions or suspensions by officers acting under Lincoln. The Chicago *Times,* an anti-Lincoln sheet, was suspended by military order of General Burnside (June, 1863) because of "disloyal and incendiary sentiments," but Burnside's act was not promoted by the Lincoln administration. The order was promptly revoked by the President, the paper being permitted to resume. In May, 1864, the New York *World* and the *Journal of Commerce* were suspended for publishing a bogus proclamation of the President calling for 400,000 men and naming a day of public humiliation and prayer. The perpetration of this hoax was not so much a deliberate falsifying by the management of the papers (though their anti-administration bias was evident) as it was a trick by one Howard to rig the stock market.[5] On the third day after the suspension the papers were allowed to resume. Various other newspapers, including the Louisville (Kentucky) *Courier,* the New Orleans *Crescent,* the *South* of Baltimore, the Baltimore *Gazette,* and the Philadelphia *Evening Journal,* were suppressed or suspended. The larger fact, however, is that the government as a general rule refrained from control of news, both on the positive and on the negative sides. It did not pursue the policy of forcing the publication of "inspired" articles; nor did it maintain a censorship. Scores of newspapers throughout the country, including some that were very prominent, continually published abusive articles during the Lincoln administration without encountering the suppressing hand of government. Lincoln's view as to the appropriate course to be taken toward newspapers was expressed as follows in a letter to General Schofield: ". . . you will only arrest individuals, and suppress assemblies, or newspapers, when they may be working *palpable* injury to the Military in your charge; and, in no other case will you interfere with the expression of opinion in any form, or allow it to be interfered with violently by others. In this, you have a discretion to exercise with great caution, calmness, and forbearance." [6]

Ignoring the papers, allowing them to "strut their uneasy hour and be forgotten" as President Wilson expressed it,[7] proved as a rule effective in regions where pro-Lincoln sentiment was active; while in localities where the opposite sentiment prevailed, suppression would have failed of its purpose by promoting sympathy for the victims. The Civil War was fought, as a recent writer has pointed out, "with the enemy at our gates and powerful secret societies in our midst without an Espionage Act." [8]

Criticism of the Lincoln administration resolves itself into a question of standards and ideals, viewed in the light of Anglo-Saxon traditions and with reference to conditions which subjected the government to difficulties of the most serious nature. As the Civil War was unique in its proportions and intensity, so was the Lincoln administration unique in its methods. That it swerved from the course of democratic government and departed from the forms of civil liberty is obvious; that it stretched and at times seemed to ignore the Constitution is evident. The arbitrary arrests cannot be passed over lightly: to do so would allow too small a value to civil guarantees. On the other hand a search of the full record will show that anything like a drastic military régime was far from Lincoln's thoughts. The harshness of war regulations was often tempered by leniency. The President was generous in releasing political prisoners, whom he refused to

---

[5] For the *World* and other anti-Lincoln papers, see also pp. 494 ff.

[6] Lincoln, *Collected Works,* VI, 492.

[7] Speech of President Wilson before Congress, Dec. 4, 1917, *Cong. Rec.,* 65 Cong., 2 sess., 21.

[8] Z. Chafee, *Freedom of Speech,* 116.

treat as war criminals, and in the suppression of anti-governmental activity the government under Lincoln was milder than that of Wilson, though facing greater provocation. As for dictatorships after recent European models, the pattern simply does not fit the Lincoln government. The word "dictator" in its twentieth-century connotation would be utterly inappropriate if applied to the Civil War President.

CHAPTER 17

The Raising of the Army

I

FOR THE HEAVY demands of a nation entering upon a stupendous war both the army and the war department in April of 1861 were inadequate and unprepared.[1] The regular army was especially small; laws for its rebuilding would have to be passed by Congress; much of it was scattered among western posts. The clerical staff of the war department was insufficient, poorly housed, and bound down by antiquated methods. Under Buchanan's secretary of war, John B. Floyd, the army had been weakened for the emergency. The canard as to Floyd's supplying the South with large stores of federally owned arms and ammunition with intent that these arms should be used against the United States is now discredited, and the historian of today does not accept the familiar charge that the secretary sold war supplies to Southern states on easy terms for a similar purpose. Yet, to quote an impartial scholar, "his sins of omission and commission were numerous," and one "cannot but be impressed in nearly all that Floyd did with the looseness of his methods, his lack of judgment in caring for na-

---

[1] Just what would have been the effect of greater prewar preparedness on the conduct and outcome of the war is a matter that cannot be treated here. To a considerable extent such preparedness (under Southern secretaries of war) would have helped the South as well as the North; whether it would have shortened the war or promoted Union victory is a matter of speculation. By the middle of 1862 the Army of the Potomac was fairly well organized and prepared; yet defeat followed defeat and the war dragged on indecisively. Something else was lacking besides preparedness. Furthermore, considering the enormous proportions of the Civil War, any preparation adequate for the conflict (or measurably so) would have been out of keeping with American habits and policies in the ante-bellum era. The United States was under no menace of foreign attack; and it is rather hard to conceive the picture of any responsible statesman heading a powerful movement of preparation for the event of civil war. Certainly the political implications of such a prewar movement should not be overlooked. To mention only one factor, the state-rights philosophy of the South would have been involved. In 1860 the United States was (or were) not a nation in the full sense.

tional interests and his frequent disregard of the law." [2] Congress had neglected to act in the closing weeks of Buchanan's administration to protect the United States government and to build up its military forces.

There were three branches of military service as established by law and by practice in previous wars. (1) There was the regular army, recruited by voluntary enlistment and consisting of professional soldiers. This normal Federal army was, according to General Winfield Scott, inadequate even for "peace-time troubles with the Indians." [3] At the outbreak of the War of 1812 it had numbered less than 7000 men, many of whom were inexperienced, intemperate, and ignorant. When the Mexican War opened, the army did not exceed 9000. At the beginning of 1861, before the withdrawal of Southerners, it numbered 16,402 men and officers.[4]

(2) In case of war the traditional method of expanding the forces was through a system of volunteering into an emergency national army. In contrast to the regular army these volunteers were citizens coming to their country's defense in time of need and expecting to return to civil life once the need had passed. For the Mexican War the "volunteers" numbered about 73,000, while the regular army had been increased, but only temporarily, to 31,000.[5]

(3) From early times there had existed, first in the colonies and then in the states, the organization known as the militia. It was at once a state and a Federal institution. The militia forces were created by state law; their officers were appointed by state authority; and their services were at the command of the state governor. The state recruited the force and paid its expenses while in state service, the governor constituting the commander-in-chief of the militia as a state institution. The state militia, however, was also the "uniform militia," invested with a national character and available for extraordinary national uses. Though drilled, governed, and commanded by state authority, it was under a uniform system of drill and organization prescribed by Congress. The Federal Constitution made distinct references to the militia as a national institution,[6] and from this source has been derived the congressional power to standardize the force on a uniform pattern and to provide for calling it forth to execute the law, suppress insurrection, or repel invasion. The actual calling forth for such national purposes has been a presidential function exercised through the state governors. When so called out, the militia loses its character as a state institution, being un-

---

[2] A. Howard Meneely, *The War Department, 1861*, 40, 49.

[3] *Ibid.*, 23.

[4] Of this total as of January 1, 1861, only 14,657 men and officers were reported as present. It is to be noted that the total included 1098 commissioned officers (727 of whom were present), and that 313 of these officers left the army to go with the South. The number of privates who did so was negligible. *Offic. Rec.*, 3 ser., V, 605.

[5] Emory Upton, *Military Policy of the United States*, 216, 218.

[6] *U. S. Constitution*, art. I, sec. 8, cl. 15; art. II, sec. 2, cl. 1.

der the discipline, courts-martial, pay, and authority of the nation. It should not be supposed, however, that the state governors are, as to this matter, the subordinates of the President. At any given time a militia force is either in state or in Federal service. For the former case the governor is commander; for the latter the President. At no time is the militia under the command of both the President and the governor. Though the President issues his call for the militia to the governors, this is not analogous to the President's issuing an order to a subordinate Federal officer—e.g., to a marshal directing him to stay an execution. The order is *upon* the citizens *through* the governor. It is a relation of comity, rather than one of superior and inferior. By a series of Federal laws, chiefly those of 1792 and 1795,[7] national arrangements concerning the militia had been determined. On paper it consisted of "every free able-bodied white male citizen of the respective states" between the ages of eighteen and forty-five, this being the law of May 8, 1792.

As was to be expected, the Lincoln government operated within the limits of these three grades of military service. The vast bulk of the Union forces consisted of specially recruited units of "U. S. Volunteers." It is chiefly in these troops that one sees the response of the Northern democracy to the crisis. In addition, the regular army was increased, first by presidential fiat, then by act of Congress. The militia was also expanded and modified, and to the process of voluntary enlistment there was added, midway in the war, a clumsy form of conscription.

At the outset of the war the militia, considered as a national institution, was a somewhat hazy affair, since the states had neglected to give it life and effectiveness. Lincoln's first call, April 15, 1861, was for the militia of the several states of the Union to the number of 75,000. Approximately 80,000 troops were raised under this call. If, however, the government was to continue to use the militia as an efficient instrument, it was necessary to adapt it to the purposes of national army making. With this in view there was passed an unsatisfactory measure known as the militia act of 1862.[8] When calling the militia into Federal service the act provided that the President might specify the period of such service (not to exceed nine months) and issue regulations for enrolling the militia and putting the act into execution where this should be necessary to cover de-

[7] *U. S. Stat. at Large*, I, 119, 264, 271, 403, 424, 522, 576; II, 207.
[8] Act of July 17, 1862, *ibid.*, XII, 597. Of course, only a small part of the militia was ever called into the national service. Between 125,000 and 200,000 men in the organized state militias provided a useful supplement to the Federal troops by serving, "either separately or in conjunction with Federal forces, to garrison fortifications, guard the coastline and Canadian frontier, man lines of communications, protect industrial establishments important for the war effort, guard camps in which Confederate prisoners were held, and protect the Indian frontier." Robert S. Chamberlain, "The Northern State Militia," *Civil War Hist.*, IV, 107 (June, 1958).

fects in state laws. Universal military liability was recognized in the act by the provision that the militia "shall . . . include all able-bodied male citizens between the ages of eighteen and forty-five," while the President's authority to issue regulations, a power generously applied, involved the use of a process of national conscription. Thus arose the "draft of 1862." Where the states had systems of their own for enrolling and drafting the militia, which was usually not the case, these local systems were to be employed; but deficiencies in state law or practice were to be made up by regulations of the Federal war department.

The militia act, with its limping draft, exhibited many defects when carried into practice. A critic of American military policy, after discussing the "impotent and extravagant" nature of the law, remarks that Congress in passing this measure "exercised the power to support armies, but the power to raise them it conferred on the governors." [9] When applied in Indiana, for example, the draft of 1862 under the militia act followed a scheme devised by Governor Morton, the lists to be made up by a commissioner in each county and a deputy commissioner in each township, these being appointed by the governor. By this system the ardent Morton used his own appointees to deal with widespread disaffection without relying upon local sheriffs.

In general, the act proved a failure. Leaving much to the President and his secretary of war, it opened the way for "presidential legislation"; it had the weakness of resting upon state authority and proceeding within state regulations where such existed; it was based on the theory that a slight modification of the militia would suffice to create a huge emergency army; and it produced judicial puzzles and legal difficulties when put into practice.[10]

2

It was not until 1863 that the Federal government passed, one should not say an effective, but at least a definitely national, conscription law.[1]

[9] Emory Upton, *Military Policy of the United States*, 434, 436.

[10] The regulations issued by the war department under the President's authority for executing the militia act of 1862 named the quotas of the states and called upon the governors to fill them. If no state system of conscription existed, the regulations prescribed that designated state officials appointed by the governor, chiefly sheriffs and commissioners, were to make the enrollment, consider exemptions, and conduct the draft. Provost marshals in the states, appointed by the war department at Washington on nomination of the governors, were to deal with disorders, enforce attendance at rendezvous, keep the men in custody, and perform similar duties. *Offic. Rec.*, 3 ser., II, 291, 333–335; Randall, *Constitutional Problems Under Lincoln*, 252 ff.

[1] The primary factor in the adoption of conscription was the inadequacy of volunteering. Senator Henry Wilson said: "Volunteers we cannot obtain, and everything forbids that we should resort to the temporary expedient of calling out the

By this act (March 3, 1863) all able-bodied male citizens between twenty
and forty-five, besides alien declarants, were "to constitute the national
forces," and were declared liable to military service. Exemptions were extended to the mentally or physically unfit, certain high officials of the Federal government and the states, the only son of a dependent widow, and
the only son of infirm parents. Federal machinery of enforcement was elaborately provided, including enrollment officers organized by congressional
districts, boards of enrollment, provost marshals, and, over all, a provost
marshal general in Washington.[2]

Men so enrolled were subject to be "called into the military service of
the United States" but their service was not to exceed three years. Conscripts were to have the same advance pay and the same Federal bounties
as three-year volunteers. In calls issued by the President state quotas were
fixed; opportunity was given for volunteering; and such volunteer enlistments were to be taken into account, so that only the "deficiency" was to
be made up by conscription. This was for the double purpose of stimulating voluntary enlistment and equalizing the burden as between states. By
harking back to practices used in old militia systems, two provisions of a
questionable nature were included—those pertaining to substitutes and
commutation money. If a drafted man furnished an acceptable substitute
he might be exempt from service; such exemption could also be bought out-
right for $300.[3]

Conscription as practiced and enforced, evaded and obstructed, under
this act became one of the crying scandals of the war. To a certain extent
the law itself was to blame: the government waited two years before a
truly national system of conscription was attempted; the country was
blanketed with a costly and inquisitorial system of Federal officials; the
government's enrolling officers made the lists; state pride was offended; the
conscript was stigmatized (conscription being used as a sort of penalty or
last resort); great disturbances were encountered; a vicious bounty system

---

militia." *Cong. Globe,* 37 Cong., 3 sess., 976. Lincoln argued that in contending
with an enemy who made use of every able-bodied man it would be unwise to
"waste time to re-experiment with the volunteer system, already deemed by congress, and palpably, in fact, . . . inadequate. . . ." Lincoln, *Collected Works,*
VI, 370. The whole story of the conscription bill in Congress, however, shows little
effort to create an efficient system, while it reveals much as to the readiness of
politicians to accept a kind of conscription that would enable a man to buy his
way out of the service and would otherwise bear lightly on the people. Shannon,
Organization and Administration of the Union Army, II, 31.

[2] The complexity of the system can only be suggested here. Each state, for
example, had an acting assistant provost marshal general. Shannon, II, 106; *Offic.
Rec.,* 3 ser., V, 613.

[3] The commutation clause was materially modified in 1864; thereafter it applied only to conscientious objectors. Substitution, however, was retained to the end
of the war. Shannon, *Union Army,* II, 87; and see below, pp. 318–319.

was used; an undignified scheme of bargaining in substitutes and commutation money was engendered; and as a final result about 46,000 conscripts and 118,000 substitutes, making about 6 per cent of the Union forces, were actually pulled into the army by the conscript net.[4]

The enforcement of the act of 1863 produced numerous difficulties and vexations. Military government was brought home to the people, with provost marshals making arrests, drafted boys sentenced as deserters for failing to appear at rendezvous, and troops ordered to quell popular disturbances. Secret societies organized for the encouragement of desertion and for resistance to the draft. Obstruction was manifest in widely separated parts of the country, and disaffection spread wide and deep. Enrolling officers were rudely handled and some were shot in performance of duty. The property of others was destroyed. The drawing of names from the wheel, a public proceeding, often resulted in violence, while the making of an arrest was likely to create a riot. Where riotous conditions became desperate, however, Federal troops or state militia would be called to the scene, and at their appearance, mob resistance usually evaporated.

To recount the instances of draft disturbance is not possible in these pages. To take a few widely scattered examples, an "insurrection" in Holmes County, Ohio, was suppressed; many arrests were made for resistance to conscription in Columbia County, Pennsylvania; and there was similar trouble in Bucks County in the same state.[5] There were outbreaks in Kentucky which required a special military force to protect enrolling officers.[6]

In Wisconsin [writes William B. Hesseltine], Governor Salomon's troubles were more serious: in one county the boxes containing names of potential draftees were destroyed, and it became extremely hazardous for the draft officers to serve notices personally. In Ozaukee County a mob assaulted a commissioner. Salomon issued a special proclamation to Milwaukeeans, warning them not to resist the draft and assuring them that he would enforce the draft at any cost. Salomon begged [Secretary of War] Stanton for 600 troops and for permission to serve notices by publication. The Governor arrested citizens until he had one hundred and fifty of them. Then he urged Stanton to take them out of the state.[7]

[4] The provost marshal general in summarizing the results of the Civil War draft stated that 86,724 escaped military service by payment of commutation, leaving 168,649 "actually drafted." The number of substitutes was 117,986, leaving 50,653 "whose personal service . . . was conscripted"; but of this number only 46,347 actually entered the ranks of the army. Second Report of the Provost Marshal General, Dec. 20, 1918 (Wash., Gov. Ptg. Office, 1919), 376–377; *Offic. Rec.*, 3 ser., V, 720, 730 ff.

[5] For these instances see *Offic. Rec.*, 1 ser., XXIII, pt. 1, 395–397; 1 ser., XLIII, pt. 1, 973; McMaster, *Lincoln's Administration*, 406; Shannon, *Union Army*, II, 175–243.

[6] *Offic. Rec.*, 1 ser., XXXIX, pt. 2, 35.

[7] Hesseltine, *Lincoln and the War Governors*, 280.

There was rioting in Troy, Albany, and Newark. In Missouri there was serious violence owing to peculiar border conditions, pro-Southern feeling, and the activity of guerillas. Also there was a great deal of disturbance in Ohio, Indiana, and Illinois, where secret orders were strong and pro-Southern sentiment active.

It was, however, in New York City that the gravest trouble occurred. From the beginning of the war there had been a vigorous strain of Southern sympathy in the city, and powerful papers such as the *World* and the *Journal of Commerce* were outspoken in their criticism of Lincoln and the Union government. The New York Irish were notoriously hostile to the Negro and averse to abolition. Politics at its worst was rife within the municipality, where Tammany leaders such as Fernando Wood and A. Oakey Hall were active against Lincoln and where W. M. Tweed was entering upon his unsavory career through the door of the volunteer fire department, with the political *credo* that politics were always corrupt in New York, that one could always buy an alderman, and that a rising politician must "take things" as he found them. There was, of course, much genuine disapproval of the brothers' war and sincere sympathy with Southerners. The governor of New York, Horatio Seymour, was politically opposed to Lincoln, was strong for local rights, and was not to be expected to ignore the powerful anti-war sentiment in city and state. In a party speech at Albany on July 4, 1863, he attacked the Lincoln government for its alleged violation of individual liberty. In forum, press, and barroom there was talk of the conscription act's being unconstitutional, of Democratic districts furnishing more than their share of conscripts while Republicans got off lightly; of ballot boxes stuffed with bogus soldier votes; and of Negro suffrage being manipulated for party gain. The people were also led to believe that the country was helpless and that the government could not protect itself.

The drawing of the first draftees' names, on July 11, 1863, set off what has been called "New York's bloodiest week." As one reads of these riots in contemporary newspapers, he gains the impression that the city was turned over to bloodthirsty looters. First the provost marshal's headquarters at Third Avenue and 46th Street were stoned and burned. Then telegraph wires all over the city were cut. The mob engaged in pitched battles with the police. When Police Superintendent John Kennedy tried to calm the rioters, they "beat him, dragged him through the streets by his head, pitched him into a horsepond, rolled him into mud-gutters, dragged him through piles of filth indescribable." Crying "Down with the rich!" the mob plundered fine houses and rifled jewelry stores. Negroes were the special object of attack. "A Negro cartman, trying to escape under cover of darkness, was caught by a gang of men and boys and hanged from one of the fine spreading chestnut trees on Clarkson Street." [8] Another Negro "was

[8] Lawrence Lader, "New York's Bloodiest Week," *Am. Heritage*, X, 44–49, 95–98 (June, 1959).

hanged by a gang of murderers who put a cigar in his mouth, stuffed his nostrils with matches, put a beer mug in his hand, and stuck a sign on his coat reading 'Black Dutchman.' " [9] The rioters first sacked, then burned the Colored Orphan Asylum. The newspapers tell of an entire city given over to anarchy, of the impotence of the city government, and of the hundreds of casualties.

In fact, such a picture is an exaggeration, made for partisan purposes. As Seymour's scholarly biographer, Stewart Mitchell, points out, the rioting, though certainly a serious and disgraceful episode, lasted for only three days (July 13–15), and it affected only a small part of the city. Some of the "destruction" attributed to the mob was invented later, when the city offered to reimburse those who had suffered from the riots. Far from being paralyzed, the city government did its best to quell the disturbance, and Governor Seymour, who promptly came to the scene, pleaded with the people to be orderly and peaceful, promising that their rights would be protected and announcing that he had requested the postponement of the draft. And as for casualties, Mitchell reports, after a close examination of the vital statistics, there is "no evidence that any more than seventy-four possible victims of the violence of three days died anywhere but in the columns of partisan newspapers." [10] By July 16, army units rushed home from the Gettysburg campaign, in cooperation with the police, militia, and naval forces, and with the help of a company from West Point, stopped the rioting and dispersed the mob.

Though it is certainly unjust to blame Horatio Seymour for the draft riots, it must be admitted that the New York governor did little to make Lincoln's task of raising a national army easier. Politically opposed to the President, convinced that the conscription was unequal, fraudulent, and a disgrace to the American people, Seymour asked Lincoln to suspend the draft until it could be judicially tested; he also demanded that New York's quotas be drastically lowered. Anxious to avoid further conflict, Lincoln reduced the number of conscripts required of New York and consented to a commission, with Democrats predominating, to study the draft in New York. On August 19, 1863, the New York draft was resumed,[11] and it proceeded without interference, Governor Seymour meanwhile advising on the one hand peaceful submission to conscription and on the other a testing of the constitutionality of the law.[12]

Disaffection and violence in these matters are not to be glibly explained. Social complexes inducing such popular demonstrations were made up of

[9] Robert Ernst, *Immigrant Life in New York City, 1825–1863*, 291.

[10] Mitchell, *Horatio Seymour of New York*, 330–334.

[11] The state of New York ultimately furnished 448,000 enlistments.

[12] The United States Supreme Court never passed upon the constitutionality of the conscription act of 1863, but under Wilson a unanimous court sustained the selective service act. 245 U. S. 366; Randall, *Constitutional Problems Under Lincoln*, 268–274.

many elements. Party feeling, race prejudice, agitation for peace, disgust
with the oft-mentioned "incompetence" of the Lincoln administration, belief in the hopelessness of subjugating the South, resentment born of blunders in the conscription act and the manner of its execution, outraged personal independence reacting against an effort to force a man into a service
contrary to his sympathies and convictions, anger at the "rich man's war"
with its frauds and profiteering—these were among the motives which resulted in mass obstruction of the draft. Such opposition was not due to
cowardice. The quickest way to get into a fight was to resist the draft, and
for one who wished to escape the draft without a fight there were many
methods of evasion which were practiced.

3

In enacting and enforcing conscription there arose the problem of the
conscientious objector. In the case of Quakers and similar sects it was recognized that a lofty ethical sense and a more than superficial acceptance of
Christianity caused an attitude toward war which, if pushed to the extremity, might challenge the whole authority of the state. No people were more
peaceable and law-abiding. If driven to the wall in this matter, however,
defying the state was to the serene Quaker a lesser offense than violating
conscience and flouting God's will by killing one's fellow men. If the government's position on conscription were to be enforced in an unqualified
manner, individual will would have to be overridden: this would be very
much like forcing men at the point of the bayonet to kill other men.[1] In
the militia draft of 1862 the problem of the objector was relegated to the
states; and, to take Indiana as an example, exemption was permitted to
such persons on payment of $200 commutation money.[2] There being no
legal sanction for this practice, however, the money was later refunded.
In the conscription act of 1863 no provision was made for excusing even
ministers,[3] and there was no clause by which one could claim exemption
on religious grounds. Objectors, of course, could avoid service by furnishing substitutes or paying $300 commutation money as in the case of any
drafted person. This, however, failed to touch the essential factor—to wit,
sincere conscientious objection to war—which was very different from a
selfish individual desire to escape service. Individual exemption by the
commutation or substitute method, indeed, took no account of the true

---

[1] In addition to the Quakers, there were other sects which made opposition to
war a part of their recognized creed, such as the Mennonites (among whom there
were many branches), Dunkers, Shakers, Schwenkfelders, Christadelphians, Roger-
enes, and those of the Amana persuasion.

[2] Randall, *Constitutional Problems Under Lincoln,* 260–261.

[3] "Under the original act embarrassment frequently arose in the attempt to
secure, as required by law, military service under the draft from ministers of the
gospel, but more especially from . . . 'Friends, or Quakers.'" Statement of the
provost marshal general, Mar. 17, 1866, *Offic. Rec.,* 3 ser., V, 633.

position of the Friends. They were therefore officially opposed to the attitude of the war department at Washington, which issued the instruction that under the law of 1863 exemption in the case of those not coming within the excused classes could only be had by the money commutation or the right of substitution. As the war progressed the respectful tone of Quaker memorials and the staunch attitude of many of the drafted objectors caused increasing embarrassment. In the case of one Cyrus Pringle, a Vermont Quaker, for example, army officers had to deal with a drafted man who not only flatly refused to serve but also declined to hire a substitute or to buy his freedom. No amount of force could shake him; he was literally ready to die rather than conform to military authority. Finally, after refusing this and that type of camp duty, declining to receive a gun, and resisting military discipline, this inflexible Quaker was released and sent home by government order.[4]

On the part of officials there was, as a general rule, no wish to deal harshly with such as Pringle, and on December 15, 1863, there was issued a war department instruction providing that conscientious objectors opposed to paying commutation money and hiring substitutes "shall . . . be put on parole . . . , to report when called for." [5] A further step was taken on February 24, 1864, when in the amendment to the enrollment act it was provided that genuine religious objectors were to be considered "noncombatants" when drafted, and were to be assigned to duty in hospitals, or in the care of freedmen, or were to pay $300 for the benefit of sick and wounded soldiers.

It must not be inferred that no Quakers complied with the unamended law. A goodly number did military service under protest, for which they met lenient treatment by their brethren; some escaped the dilemma by money payment; and many did service in noncombatant capacities, which, even before the law of February, 1864, had been made available to them as a matter of executive policy. Very little attention was paid to those whose conscientious objections to military service were based on nonreligious grounds.

4

The relation of the war department to the army on the one side and the contractors on the other is a sorry tale. Whether it was a matter of uniforms, food, horses, guns, or munitions, the service was made to suffer while ill-gotten wealth was gathered in by shameless profiteers. Some of the trouble, of course, was due to inevitable difficulties in the supplying of *matériel*. Sudden demand for equipment, competition with Confederate as well as Northern state agents in the European market, misinformation

[4] E. N. Wright, *Conscientious Objectors in the Civil War*, 165; Shannon, *Union Army*, II, 255–256; Rufus M. Jones, ed., *The Record of a Quaker Conscience: Cyrus Pringle's Diary*.

[5] *Offic. Rec.*, 3 ser., III, 1173.

and wild rumor as to government funds available for army purchases, claims of rival producers, the bewildering effect of newly invented models, the strain of pressure production as factories were overwhelmed with a rush of orders, the operations of sharp-eyed speculators—such factors would have brought sleepless nights to any secretary of war.

Unfortunately, Lincoln's first secretary of war was poorly fitted for his post. Simon Cameron was a self-made businessman and politician who had "played the game" in Pennsylvania, had become a sort of "boss" in the Democratic party, and who, because of factors that cannot be detailed here, had shifted to the Republican party, winning for himself the senatorship from Pennsylvania in 1857.

Cameron's party somersaulting was now at an end [writes Dr. Meneely]; he remained a Republican for the rest of his life, and gave generously of his time, his energy and experience to the building up of a smooth-running party machine. In the management and control of it he was unequaled. Thaddeus Stevens, David Wilmot, William Kelley, Andrew Curtin and others might dispute his leadership, force a set-back, administer a defeat, but none ever succeeded in permanently supplanting him in his position. . . . No politician of his generation understood the science of politics better than Simon Cameron; none enjoyed greater power; none had more success. . . . His methods were often circuitous, the means employed were often questionable, but the end in view was always clear. . . . By patronage he was able to build up a political despotism in Pennsylvania; with it he rewarded his friends and punished his foes.[1]

By bargains made in the nominating convention at Chicago Lincoln was committed against his will to the conferring of some cabinet post upon this man. No selection caused Lincoln more hesitation and embarrassment. At the inauguration the war secretaryship was unfilled; and even today the details of what went on behind the scenes pertaining to the appointment are obscure. The records available, however, prove without question the reluctance of Lincoln to make the appointment. After offering Cameron a cabinet chair without specifying which one, he repented and besought him to "decline"; then he requested his consent to a "recall" of the offer; finally he ended by taking him into the cabinet (March 5, 1861) as secretary of war.

The situation which prevailed under Cameron's administration of the war department produced one of the sharpest controversies of the Lincoln administration. While officials in the national capital struggled in a net of red tape, governors "became war lords" and pushed ahead "as if there was not an inch of red tape in the world."[2] Such governors as Andrew of Massachusetts and Morton of Indiana simply took over the functions that should have been centered at Washington. So slightly had the proper ad-

[1] Meneely, 82–83.
[2] *Ibid.*, 141.

justment between Washington and the states been made by January of 1862 that Governor David Tod of Ohio wrote in that month to Stanton asking the following questions: (1) What control had the governor over state troops in camp or in the field after they had been mustered into the Federal service? (2) What were his duties in the procuring or issuing of military supplies? (3) Would the Federal government refund to the states "*all* the money expended directly and indirectly in the raising, equipping, sustaining and mustering of the troops?" (4) What control did the governor have over military prisoners sent to the state for safekeeping? [3] The fact that such a letter could be written by a governor to the secretary of war nine months after the firing at Sumter shows both the extent of the governor's activities and the vagueness of the relationships involved.

To a large extent the Union forces were raised by and through the states. The governors directed the raising of the militia quotas in response to Lincoln's first call and in compliance with the militia act of 1862. As to "U. S. Volunteers" the governors usually directed their recruitment, though they did not have the exclusive function of so doing, and they appointed the regimental officers. In addition to this, state delegations in Congress possessed a sort of unofficial right of consultation and recommendation in the President's selection of generals in the volunteer service.[4] At times United States regiments were raised by state action in advance of Federal calls and in a spirit of impatience at the delay and incompetence of the administrators at Washington. While Yates of Illinois was working energetically to raise Union regiments, Cameron sent word to him: "Let me earnestly recommend to you . . . to call for no more than twelve regiments, of which six only are to serve for three years or during the war, and if more are already called for, to reduce the number by discharge." [5] Governor Morton insisted upon furnishing six regiments though the call was for four.[6] Cameron accepted only three of the ten regiments offered by Ohio, and a similar situation existed with regard to Massachusetts and other states.[7]

Governors even had their state agents abroad. The activities of Robert Dale Owen as "State Agent for Indiana" early in the war offer a case in point. Acting for Governor Morton, he was energetic in purchasing rifles and carbines, sabres, and revolvers abroad; forwarding arms from New York to Fort Monroe as well as to Indianapolis; procuring greatcoats, blankets, and equipment; visiting Indiana regiments in the field; making contracts for Indiana, though the bills were ultimately paid by the Federal government; and doing many things which transcended state functions.

[3] Paraphrased from Tod's letter to Stanton, Jan. 28, 1862, Stanton Papers (MSS., Libr. of Congr.), no. 50513.
[4] Browning, *Diary*, I, 487 (July 27, 1861).
[5] *Report of the Adjutant-General of Illinois* (1886), I, 10.
[6] W. D. Foulke, *Life of O. P. Morton*, I, 128.
[7] H. G. Pearson, *Life of John A. Andrew*, I, 224, 225.

On one occasion he wrote to Morton: "I fear that if you trust wholly to the [Federal] Government to send you what more guns we may need, you will be likely to get trash. I hear very poor accounts of the purchases made by the Government agent in Europe." One of the objects for which Owen exerted himself was to have the arsenal at Indianapolis continued when national interests seemed to require its discontinuance.[8] The far-reaching efforts of such state agents seriously embarrassed the Washington authorities. Bidding against the Federal government in the foreign arms markets they not only added to the expense which the treasury at Washington had to bear, but laid the basis for a complicated mass of postwar claims which arose when the national government made good its pledge of compensating the states for war expenditures.[9]

The other side of the story, of course, is that to a large extent the governors—Andrew, Morton, Curtin, Morgan, Yates, and the rest of them—bore the brunt of the immediate emergency. Andrew's zeal was especially conspicuous as he directed the recruiting of the early Massachusetts regiments, the appointment of the officers, the examination and equipment of the troops, the chartering of steamers and railroad facilities for their transportation, and the raising of emergency funds by which the first bills were paid. For a time, since Massachusetts had prematurely sent forward 4000 men, the state had to maintain them in the field in semihostile territory 450 miles distant. Though producing administrative tangles, the early action of the states brought results. Within two weeks after Lincoln's first call 55,000 men were either in Washington, on the way, or ready to entrain.[10] In the hurried dash to get things done there was no time to quibble about authority; men assumed responsibility in confidence that their actions would later receive ratification and support.

5

Whatever may be said of Cameron personally, it is a matter of record that shameful frauds were permitted during his secretaryship. The des-

[8] Morton Correspondence (State Archives, Indiana State Libr.); Randall, *Constitutional Problems Under Lincoln*, 410 n.; Meneely, 150.

[9] Laws were passed by the Federal Congress on July 17 and July 27, 1861, concerning this matter (*U. S. Stat. at Large*, XII, 261, 276). The sum of $10,-000,000 was set aside to be refunded to the states for their expenses in raising volunteer forces, and a general obligation for further reimbursement was incurred. Many appropriation acts were passed after the war for this purpose. Over $42,-000,000 had been returned to the states by 1880, with nearly $9,000,000 still unpaid. In 1880 the Federal examiner of state claims wrote: ". . . it would probably be beyond the power of the judges . . . in the Court of Claims . . . to memorize or collate the administrative rulings or precedents that underlie the departmental actions touching allowances . . . on these claims." Randall, *Constitutional Problems Under Lincoln*, 426–427; *Sen. Ex. Doc. No. 74*, 46 Cong., 2 sess., pp. 6, 199.

[10] Pearson, *Andrew, passim;* Shannon, *Union Army*, I, 34.

perate need for haste in outfitting the armies, coupled with the outmoded procurement procedures followed by the war department, afforded a bonanza for shrewd speculators who were not too proud to gain from their country's misfortunes. The case of Frémont in Missouri is instructive. In his military district rules and regulations "went by the board"; and an orgy of expenditure made it necessary for Lincoln to appoint a commission to investigate. Among the transactions described by the commission we find a total of $191,000 on a contract to build five forts, $111,000 of which went as profit to the contractor.[1] One must not, however, blame Frémont himself for this mismanagement; as Allan Nevins, his most careful biographer, observes, "the waste was chiefly attributable to the frenzied haste and War Department inefficiency." St. Louis had to be defended, and Frémont's ill-equipped troops had to be armed. The failure of the national treasury promptly to supply the necessary funds compelled the general to rely on credit and as soon as that happened, "control over prices passed into the hands of banks, brokers, speculators, and moneyed merchants, the intermediary links between the army and its sources." [2]

Everywhere under Cameron's régime the dealings of the administrators of the war department with sharp and cunning businessmen exhibited similar looseness. Thousands of pistols were sold to the government at $25 each, though the fair price on a proper competitive basis would not have exceeded $14.50. Horses which could be bought for $60 or less were sold to the government for $117. "Out of one lot of 252 [horses] . . . inspected at Chicago, all but twenty-seven were found to be diseased, maimed, or otherwise unfitted for use." Austrian muskets, rejected by the ordnance bureau at a price of $5.50, were bought by a government agent at $6.50. Enfield rifles purchasable for $20 were bought for the government at $26.50; Colt's revolvers worth $15 were paid for at $35.[3]

Administrative practices under Cameron were brought up to the United States Supreme Court in the case of *Tool Company* vs. *Norris,* a case in which a lobby "agent" was to receive $3 per gun, or a total of $75,000, merely for the use of his "influence" in obtaining a contract. Concerning such practices Justice Field wrote in this case:

Considerations as to the most efficient and economical mode of meeting the public wants [in the letting of contracts] should alone control . . . the action of every department of the Government. No other consideration can lawfully enter into the transaction, so far as the Government is concerned. . . . [Agreements such as the one under consideration] tend to introduce personal solicitation, and personal influence, as elements in the procurement of contracts; and thus directly lead to inefficiency in the public service, and to unnecessary expenditures of the public funds.[4]

1 Meneely, 269–271.
2 Allan Nevins, *Frémont: Pathmarker of the West* (1957 ed.), 647.
3 Meneely, 263–265, 274, 275–276; Shannon, I, 64, 69, 120.
4 69 U. S. 45, 54; see also Meneely, 262–263.

Finally embarrassment due to Cameron became so acute that a change became inevitable. To let him down gracefully Lincoln accepted the resignation of Cassius M. Clay as minister to Russia (Clay being anxious to return home for military service); and Cameron, resigning the war portfolio (January 11, 1862), was appointed to this diplomatic post. He seems not to have intended to serve long in Russia; as a matter of fact he resigned the ministership in November, 1862. His conduct was condemned by the House of Representatives in the following words:

Resolved, That Simon Cameron, late Secretary of War, by investing Alexander Cummings with the control of large sums of the public money, and authority to purchase military supplies, without restriction . . . , and by involving the Government in a vast number of contracts with persons not legitimately engaged in the business pertaining to . . . such contracts, . . . has adopted a policy highly injurious to the public service, and deserves the censure of the House.[5]

On January 20, 1862, Edwin M. Stanton took charge of the war department. Though he had serious faults, yet in such matters as contracts and inspection the situation was greatly improved under his administration.

---

[5] Resolution of House of Representatives, April 30, 1862, *Cong. Globe,* 37 Cong., 2 sess., 1888.

CHAPTER 18

Army Administration

I

To UNDERSTAND what manner of army it was that fought the battles of the Union one must read the spirited accounts of Bruce Catton and Bell I. Wiley, along with the caustic criticisms of Fred A. Shannon and General Emory Upton.[1] Here there is space for a consideration only of some of the basic problems which confronted the new armies. In the first enthusiasm of volunteering, there grew up the practice of permitting individuals to take the initiative in raising regiments, and thus overnight to become colonels, with brigadier-generalships thereafter easily attainable. On August 6, 1861, it was officially stated that the war department "had accepted twice as many regiments from independent agencies as from state executives." This was usually done to please friends of those in power or to recognize known military ability. The governors opposed the practice; but, though it was pointed out that "the numerous skeleton organizations created unnecessary competition and resulted in no regiments being enlisted to full strength," [2] the war department continued the policy. The clear-sighted Governor Andrew of Massachusetts was one of those who protested; and his imbroglio with General B. F. Butler well illustrates the baneful results of the system. Against Andrew's wishes Butler obtained an order authorizing him to raise six regiments in the New England states. A serious deadlock ensued because of clashes of authority between the state governors, whose power to appoint officers of volunteers was recognized by the Federal government, and General Butler, whom the war department placed in command of the "Department of New England" with six states under his jurisdiction for recruiting purposes. It was only with the resignation of Cameron and the abolition of the "Department of New England" that this Butler-Andrew quarrel was adjusted.

One aspect of Union military policy was the failure to make effective

[1] Catton, *Mr. Lincoln's Army, Glory Road,* and *A Stillness at Appomattox;* Wiley, *The Life of Billy Yank;* Shannon, *Organization and Administration of the Union Army* (2 vols.); Upton, *Military Policy of the United States.*
[2] Meneely, 210.

use of the existing regular army. General Upton has pointed out that "the difficulties of recruiting regulars in competition with volunteers, would have suggested the reduction of the line of the Army to a cadre,[3] and the dispersion of its officers as commanders and instructors among the new troops." "Had this course been adopted," he adds, "every regiment of volunteer infantry, cavalry, and artillery might have had a regular officer for a leader, and with these to guide the instruction, three months would have sufficed to give us an army in fair drill and discipline." [4] There was, indeed, a law of Congress which authorized (but did not direct) the commanding general to make such use of regular army officers,[5] but not being mandatory it was permitted to remain a dead letter. Statistics reveal that "while only one-quarter of the . . . graduates [of West Point] in service [when the war broke out] rose to the rank of general officer, more than one-half of those [graduates] who came back from civil life attained the same grade. . . ." Upton's conclusion is that the preference for amateurism in the army and the departure from military standards prolonged the war, entailing a "useless sacrifice of life and treasure," and that for this result "our military counselors at Washington were chiefly responsible." [6]

Another mistake was that of permitting the men to elect their officers. Though this was not the usual method, yet the practice, especially as to officers below the rank of colonel, was "widespread," and was "recognized by both state and federal governments." [7] By the act of July 22, 1861, this unmilitary method was written into Federal law. For the filling of vacancies in the volunteer forces, this act provided that each company should vote for officers as high as captain, above which vacancies were to be filled by the votes of the commissioned officers.[8] This provision, said General Upton, incorporated the "worst vice known in the military system of any of the States," for it "tempted every ambitious officer and soldier to play the demagogue." [9] In an army where such practices prevailed, it was but natural that "the politician, lawyer, or tradesman, if an officer, looked upon his men as clients, customers, constituents, or rivals." [10] On August 6, 1861, this section was repealed; [11] and in the later years of the war there was a noticeable tightening of discipline.

In such vital matters as food, clothing, and bedding the Union soldier was well supplied by the standards of the period. They had "the most abundant food allowance of any soldiers in the world" at that time, infi-

[3] A skeleton military establishment.
[4] Upton, 235.
[5] Act of July 29, 1861. U. S. Stat. at Large, XII, 281.
[6] Upton, 235–237.
[7] Shannon, I, 159.
[8] U. S. Stat. at Large, XII, 270.
[9] Upton, 260.
[10] Shannon, I, 169.
[11] U. S. Stat. at Large, XII, 318.

nitely more than the Confederates had. Bread, meat, and coffee were the staples of army diet. Like all soldiers in all wars, Union troops complained vigorously about the quality of their victuals. "The boys say that our 'grub' is enough to make a *mule* desert, and a *hog* wish he had never been born," an Illinois corporal wrote in 1862. Almost with pride another soldier counted "32 worms, maggots &c" in a single piece of his hardtack. Their salt pork, which they called "sowbelly" or "salt horse," seemed at times "so strong it could almost walk its self." During the early days of the war and during all periods of rapid movement and active fighting there was some basis for these grumblings, but on the whole the Union soldier seldom suffered from hunger.[12] During the first months of the war many army uniforms were made of "shoddy," which, to quote a contemporary writer, consisted of "the refuse stuff and sweepings of the shop, pounded, rolled, glued, and smoothed to the external form and gloss of cloth." Naturally during the first rainstorm the soldiers "found their clothes, overcoats, and blankets, scattering to the winds in rags, or dissolving into their primitive elements of dust."[13] But after the first year or so, these supply contracts were cleaned up, and thenceforth "Billy Yank had relatively little ground for complaint as to the quality of clothing received from the quartermaster."[14]

As to munitions, at the outset the Union army was supplied with virtually every kind of small firearm in existence. So difficult was it to purchase equipment, thousands of men were initially given smoothbore muskets, hastily converted from flint to percussion locks; others received outmoded European firearms. As the war continued, however, the standard infantry weapon became the Springfield or Enfield rifle. These were accurate and reliable but difficult to load. Robert V. Bruce has described the "tedious process a soldier had to go through to load and fire the regulation Springfield muzzle-loading rifle":

Reaching into his cartridge pouch, the soldier took out a paper cartridge containing the powder charge and the bullet. Holding this between his thumb and forefinger, he tore it open with his teeth. Next he emptied the powder into the barrel and disengaged the bullet with his right hand and the thumb and two fingers of the left. Inserting the ball point up into the bore, he pressed it down with his right thumb. Then he drew his ramrod, which meant pulling it halfway out, steadying it, grasping it again and clearing it. He rammed the ball halfway down, took hold of the ramrod again, and drove the ball home. He then drew the ramrod out and returned it to its tube, each movement again in two stages. Next he primed his piece by raising it, half cocking it, taking off the old cap, taking a new one out of the pouch and pressing it down on the nipple.

[12] Wiley, *Life of Billy Yank*, 224, 226, 238, 240.
[13] *Harper's Monthly Magazine*, XXIX, 227–228, quoted in Shannon, I, 94–95.
[14] Wiley, 60–61.

At last he cocked the gun, aimed it and fired. And if he had a particular target in mind, which was unlikely in all the excitement, he probably missed it clean.[15]

Breech-loading rifles were not supplied, except in small numbers and to select groups of sharpshooters and cavalrymen. It has been seriously argued that had the war department introduced the breech-loader the war might have been ended in the first year.[16] Certainly President Lincoln kept up an insistent pressure upon his stubbornly conservative Chief of Ordnance, James W. Ripley, to adopt the new weapon.[17] But, in defense of the war department, it must be noted that in 1861 the breech-loader was an untested and imperfect weapon, which, in any case, could not be mass-produced in either America or Europe. Though highly useful for mobile troops, the breech-loader, at this stage of its development, had serious disadvantages for the ordinary infantryman. "It was not the breech-loader alone," Kenneth P. Williams observes, "but the breech-loader plus smokeless powder that completely altered infantry combat. With a breech-loader a man could load while lying down. That was a great gain, but the smoke from the black powder quickly revealed his position." [18]

One of the most flagrant blunders in the army was the introduction of the bargaining or mercenary factor by an elaborate system of bounties. At the beginning of the war city and state authorities began the practice of offering money bonuses to recruits; and it was not long before the Federal government adopted the practice. Sanctioning a war department practice already in use, Congress on July 22, 1861, added a bounty of $100 over and above the regular pay of volunteers; and by 1864 the Federal bounty for new recruits had increased to $300, with an additional $100 for veterans.[19] When conscription was introduced, the "peculiar horror of the draft" [20] which pervaded the country served powerfully to stimulate the bounty system, which eventually reached amazing proportions and produced serious consequences. With cities, counties, states, the national government, and private organizations bidding for recruits, the sums spent for this purpose reached enormous figures. Cook County in Illinois,

[15] Bruce, *Lincoln and the Tools of War*, 99–100.

[16] Shannon, I, 128–142. Professor Shannon refutes the war department objection that the breech-loading mechanism was too intricate by noting that muzzle-loaders became "almost totally unmanageable in the hands of an excited soldiery." He adds: "A reliable army officer stated that of 27,574 muskets collected from the field, after the battle of Gettysburg, 24,000 were loaded, 12,000 contained two charges each, and 6000 were charged with from three to ten loads each. . . . [The] excited soldier was unlikely to realize that his charge had not exploded and would continue to reload. . . . With even one unexploded charge in a gun it was useless. . . . Such a condition was impossible with the breech loader. . . ."

[17] Bruce, Chap. 7.

[18] Williams, *Lincoln Finds a General*, II, 782–785.

[19] Ella Lonn, *Desertion during the Civil War*, 140.

[20] Shannon, II, 57.

for instance, spent $2,801,239 for bounties; Henry County, $260,548; Bureau County, $616,862; and all the counties of Illinois, $13,711,389. In addition they spent considerable sums for transportation, subsistence, and the relief of soldiers' families.[21] In New Jersey there were more than one hundred laws passed at one session of the legislature authorizing various districts to incur obligations for this purpose.[22] New York spent over $86,000,000; the total for the states and localities for the latter half of the war was in excess of $286,000,000; that of the national government more than $300,000,000. To figure the grand total of the country's mercenary bill would require the inclusion of various other items such as substitute fees; it is the estimate of Dr. Shannon that this total "could not be far short of three-quarters of a billion dollars." [23]

Nor can it be said that the results of the bounty system justified the means. On the contrary the results were pernicious, raising the price of substitutes, retarding enlistment (for prospect of a higher bounty would cause men to hold back, if money was the motive), producing a low class of men known as "bounty brokers," and creating the practice of "bounty jumping." With no intention of serving in the army, a man would enlist in one locality, collect the cash bounties there, desert, and enlist under a different name in another locality, and repeat the practice as long as he could evade detection. Some bounty jumpers "enlisted as many as twenty times and received as much as $8000 per man." [24] In one case a man "confessed to having 'jumped the bounty' thirty-two times." [25]

Meanwhile the pay of the soldier, though high in comparison with that in European armies, was far below prevailing wage scales. At the beginning of the war the pay was $11 a month; by 1864 it was increased to $16, but the increase was more than offset by the depreciation of the greenback.[26] The enormous amounts spent for bounties, if the intention was actually to put the money to the use of soldiers or their families, might better have been devoted to increasing the soldier's regular pay.[27]

In view of the conditions which prevailed in the war department and in the Union army, it is not surprising that desertion was a common fault. Even so the actual extent of it, as shown in official reports, comes as a distinct shock. Though the determination of the full number is a bit complicated, the total would seem to have been well over 200,000.[28] From New

[21] *Report of Adjutant General of Illinois* (1886), I, 198–209.

[22] Randall, *Constitutional Problems Under Lincoln*, 249.

[23] Shannon, II, 80.

[24] James Barnett, "The Bounty Jumpers of Indiana," *Civil War Hist.*, IV, 431 (Dec., 1958).

[25] *Offic. Rec.*, 3 ser., V, 725.

[26] Shannon, I, 246.

[27] For comment on the hopelessness of the bounty system and the urgent need for reform, see N. Y. *Times*, July 23, 1862, p. 4.

[28] On September 11, 1865, the provost marshal general estimated the total number of desertions from the army to be 195,255, not including drafted men who

York there were 44,913 deserters according to the records; from Pennsylvania, 24,050; from Ohio, 18,354. The daily hardships of war, deficiency in arms, forced marches (which sometimes made straggling a necessity for less vigorous men), thirst, suffocating heat, disease, delay in pay,[29] solicitude for family, impatience at the monotony and futility of inactive service, and (though this was not the leading cause) panic on the eve of battle— these were some of the conditioning factors that produced desertion. Many men absented themselves merely through unfamiliarity with military discipline or through the feeling that they should be "restrained by no other legal requirements than those of the civil law governing a free people"; and such was the general attitude that desertion was often regarded "more as a refusal . . . to ratify a contract than as the commission of a grave crime." [30]

The sense of war weariness, the lack of confidence in commanders, and the discouragement of defeat tended to lower the morale of the Union army and to increase desertion. General Hooker estimated in 1863 that 85,000 officers and men had deserted from the Army of the Potomac, while it was stated in December of 1862 that no less than 180,000 of the soldiers listed on the Union muster rolls were absent, with or without leave.[31] Abuse of sick leave or of the furlough privilege was one of the chief means of desertion. Other methods were: slipping to the rear during a battle, inviting capture by the enemy (a method by which honorable service could be claimed), straggling, taking French leave when on picket duty, pretending to be engaged in repairing a telegraph line, et cetera. Some of the deserters went over to the enemy not as captives but as soldiers; others lived in a wild state on the frontier; some turned outlaw or went to Canada; some boldly appeared at home; in some cases deserter gangs, as in western Pennsylvania, formed bandit groups.

To suppress desertion the extreme penalty of death was at times applied, especially after 1863; but this meant no more than the selection of a few men as public examples out of many thousands equally guilty. The commoner method was to make public appeals to deserters, promising pardon in case of voluntary return with dire threats to those who failed to return. That desertion did not prevent a man posing after the war as an

---

failed to report. *Offic. Rec.*, 3 ser., V, 109. On December 31, 1865, it was stated that 278,644 desertions had been reported, but that many of those reported had been sick on the march, injured without official knowledge, or otherwise justifiably absent. According to the same report the monthly desertions in 1863 averaged 4647; in 1864 they averaged 7333. *Ibid.*, 757–758. See also Shannon, II, 179 n., and, for a general treatment of the whole subject, Ella Lonn, *Desertion during the Civil War.*

[29] The N. Y. *Times* of Oct. 11, 1862, complained (p. 4) that some of the troops had not been paid since June.

[30] *Offic. Rec.*, 3 ser., V, 678.

[31] Lonn, 151; N. Y. *Times*, Dec. 2, 1862, p. 1.

honorable soldier is evident by a study of pension records. The laws required honorable discharge as a requisite for a pension; but in the case of those charged with desertion Congress passed numerous private and special acts "correcting" the military record.[32]

2

As to the central directing force in control of the army, the story is one of slow and confused evolution. Under the Constitution the President is named commander-in-chief of the army and navy of the United States, but Lincoln did not, of course, take to the battlefield in person.[1] The President's principal military adviser at the outbreak of the war was General Winfield Scott, for whose "most distinguished character, as a military captain" Lincoln had great respect.[2] Scott was, however, older than the national capitol and was physically incapable of commanding an army in the field. Consequently he was obliged to entrust actual battle operations to his subordinates, such as General Frémont in Missouri and General McDowell in Virginia. The staff of the army, if it can be so called, consisted of Scott and a few heads of departments and bureaus, such as the quartermaster general, the adjutant general, and the chief of ordnance. Civilian direction of the war effort would normally have fallen to Cameron, but the secretary of war was so inefficient that he shoved many of his duties off on Chase, the ambitious and able secretary of the treasury. As Chase later explained: "The President and Secretary of War committed to me for a time the principal charge of what related to Kentucky and Tennessee, and I was very active also in promoting the measures deemed necessary for the safety of Missouri. . . . While he was Secretary of War, General Cameron conferred much with me. I never undertook to do any thing in his department, except when asked to give my help, and I gave it willingly." [3]

The first battle of Bull Run showed the consequences of this system of divided responsibilities, and, as previously noted, Lincoln brought McClellan to Washington. For a time McClellan worked under Scott's direction, but the "Little Napoleon" soon came to regard the old general as "a fearful incubus" who "always comes in the way, . . . understands nothing, appreciates nothing," and he began dealing directly with the President and the cabinet, ignoring his military superior.[4] Finally, on

[32] W. H. Glasson, *Federal Military Pensions in the United States*, 276 n.

[1] Lincoln did take part in the Union operations which led to the capture of Norfolk in May, 1862. J. W. Schuckers, *The Life and Public Services of Salmon Portland Chase*, 366–374. In addition he came under enemy fire during Early's raid upon Washington in 1864. J. H. Cramer, *Lincoln Under Enemy Fire, passim.*

[2] Lincoln, *Collected Works*, IV, 137.

[3] David Donald, ed., *Inside Lincoln's Cabinet*, 12.

[4] C. W. Elliott, *Winfield Scott: The Soldier and the Man*, 735–736.

November 1, 1861, McClellan forced Scott to retire and himself assumed the double roles of general-in-chief of all the Union armies and commander-in-chief of the forces in northern Virginia.

But as winter passed into spring and McClellan failed to move against the Confederates, his enemies began to agitate against him. The first six months of 1862 saw a gradual whittling away of the general's extraordinary powers. On March 8 Lincoln, against McClellan's wishes, reorganized the Army of the Potomac by grouping its divisions into corps. The four corps commanders were not special friends of McClellan's but were chosen by the President from among "those elder generals whose point of view was similar to his own." [5] Three days later, as McClellan was about to begin the Peninsula campaign, Lincoln relieved him of his duties as general-in-chief, restricting his role to that of commander of the Department of the Potomac. The same order showed that the new secretary of war had taken over from Chase the reins of civilian administration; it required "all the commanders of departments" to send "prompt, full, and frequent reports" to Stanton, rather than to McClellan.[6] Though there was much political hostility and personal jealousy behind these anti-McClellan moves, they were entirely justified. The general had attempted to do far more than any one man could have accomplished.

While McClellan was fighting on the Peninsula, Lincoln and Stanton attempted personally to exercise a central direction over the war effort, notably in their effort to trap Stonewall Jackson in the Shenandoah Valley. Painfully aware that he was "the depository of the power of the government and had no military knowledge," the President in March, 1862, sought to make a mentor of the elderly, retired, and ailing General Ethan Allen Hitchcock, who, much against his will, accepted an ill-defined staff appointment as adviser to Stanton and Lincoln.[7] The administrative machinery was further complicated when Stanton created an "army board" composed of chiefs of various bureaus of the war department.[8]

There was now great confusion in army control—no unity of command; no general-in-chief; Stanton and his bureau heads in exercise of functions which a general-in-chief should have performed; Lincoln, under political pressure, proclaiming army movements which were never carried out and withdrawing large units from McClellan's main force; corps commanders reporting first to the President, then to the secretary of war, then to the army board; councils of generals distant from the field being called into consultation on difficult operations; and, through it all, the committee on the conduct of the war exerting a never-failing interference.

[5] N. W. Stephenson, *Lincoln*, 229–230.

[6] Lincoln, *Collected Works*, V, 155.

[7] W. A. Croffut, ed., *Fifty Years in Camp and Field: Diary of Major-General Ethan Allen Hitchcock, U.S.A.*, 437–443; Randall, *Lincoln the President*, II, 84–85.

[8] Upton, 289–293; Stephenson, *Lincoln*, 233–234.

Order began to emerge from the chaos when Lincoln, on July 11, 1862, appointed General Halleck "to command the whole land forces of the United States as General-in-Chief." [9] Though Halleck exhibited neither the daring nor the decisiveness which Lincoln had desired, he did have "the happy faculty of being able to communicate civilian ideas to a soldier and military ideas to a civilian and make both of them understand what he was talking about." [10] His tiny office, which initially had only seven officers and sixteen enlisted men, did serve in some measure to give a central strategic direction to the war. Increasingly Secretary Stanton was allowed to devote his abundant energies to problems of procurement and supply. There was still a great deal of confusion and working at cross-purposes, for the President was not a man to revere any table of organization; moreover, after four months of personal command, he was not "satisfied to sit back and merely watch attentively." [11]

It was not until 1864 that the problem of organizing and administering the Union armies was satisfactorily solved. On March 12 Lincoln brought in Grant from the West and, naming him Lieutenant General, assigned him "to the command of the Armies of the United States." Halleck, relieved of his duty as general-in-chief, became "Chief of Staff of the Army, under direction of the Secretary of War and the Lieutenant General commanding." [12] Though not entirely free from flaws, the new arrangement did work. As T. Harry Williams remarks: "The arrangement of commander in chief, general in chief, and chief of staff gave the United States a modern system of command for a modern war. It was superior to anything achieved in Europe until von Moltke forged the Prussian staff machine of 1866 and 1870." [13]

3

The discussion of practices concerning prisoners in the Civil War has become so largely the theme of vituperation and recrimination on both sides that it may well give pause to the historian. Harrowing stories of suffering among prisoners can be produced *ad nauseam;* volumes of abuse, growing out of the desperate feeling engendered by such suffering, were poured forth on both sides. Professor Channing concludes that "each government cared for its enemy prisoners about as well as . . . for its own soldiers"; while Dr. Hesseltine has pointed out that each side displayed mismanagement, congestion, and unfitness in officer personnel, and that in the North as well as the South one finds disease, filth, depression, disorder, vermin, poor food, lack of elementary sanitation, and, as a result,

[9] Lincoln, *Collected Works,* V, 312–313.
[10] T. Harry Williams, *Lincoln and His Generals,* 301.
[11] K. P. Williams, *Lincoln Finds a General,* V, 277.
[12] Lincoln, *Collected Works,* VII, 239.
[13] Williams, *Lincoln and His Generals,* 302–303.

intolerable misery and death on an appalling scale.[1] Had the struggle not been between sections of a once-united country a system for the exchange of prisoners might have been worked out which would have mitigated the evil by greatly reducing the number of prisoners held. As it was, this problem, though a matter of frequent negotiation, became so entangled with the issue of Confederate status, and so involved in recriminating and retaliatory declarations, that efforts toward a consistent general policy broke down; and, though exchanges and releases on parole did take place to a certain extent especially earlier in the war, there was never any enduring plan for such exchange and release worked out by the belligerents.

Early in the war the threat to treat Confederate privateersmen as pirates, which involved the penalty of death, was met by Southern counter threats of retaliation against selected Northern hostages; and until this was adjusted by the Northern decision that privateersmen were to be dealt with as prisoners of war, no general cartel could be reached. If during this period captives were exchanged or released, it was done on the basis of some special understanding between commanders. As the war progressed and the number of captives increased, the demand for some general plan of exchange became insistent; and a cartel was arranged on July 22, 1862, by General John A. Dix for the United States and General D. H. Hill for the Confederacy. The purpose was to effect the release of all prisoners of war [2] and to deal with the problem of an excess on one side or the other by having surplus prisoners released under parole not to take up arms again, while prisoners released on the basis of even exchange were not denied further military service.[3]

While this cartel was in force the general situation regarding prisoners was in far better case than later in the war; but there arose many obstacles to the continuance of the arrangement. Camps of paroled prisoners were maintained in order to keep the men under surveillance and release them for service when exchanged, such camps being located, for instance, at Columbus, Ohio (Camp Chase), at Benton Barracks, Missouri, and at Annapolis. When certain Iowa men among the paroled prisoners at Benton Barracks were placed on guard duty in their own camp, thereby releasing a force of men for service in the field, Iowa authorities protested that such duty was inconsistent with their paroles, and that, in addition to the point of honor involved, if the men were caught by the enemy they would be severely handled. As a result it was ordered at Washington that such service should be discontinued. But this was only one of many complications. It was discovered that order in the parole camps was hard to keep; that paroled prisoners expected to be sent home, not to camps; that guerillas

---

[1] E. Channing, *Hist. of the U. S.*, VI, 439; W. B. Hesseltine, *Civil War Prisons: A Study in War Psychology, passim.*

[2] Moore, *Rebell. Rec.* (Doc.), V, 341–342; E. A. Pollard, *Lost Cause*, 618–620.

[3] Hesseltine, 32–33.

presented a special problem; and that, with the prospect of being paroled, men would purposely fall into the hands of the enemy.[4]

While the exchange system was thus under constant strain, military severity, followed by retaliation and counter-retaliation, caused a breakdown. On June 7, 1862, General B. F. Butler, in occupation of Louisiana, caused a Southern citizen, Mumford by name, to be executed by sentence of a military commission for tearing down the Union flag in New Orleans.[5] This brutal and needlessly severe act, coming at a time when Confederate authorities were charging Union commanders with similar severities elsewhere, brought sorry consequences to both North and South and contributed materially to the discontinuance of the cartel. On December 23, 1862, President Jefferson Davis proclaimed Butler (known in the South as "Beast Butler") a felon, an outlaw, and an enemy of mankind; and ordered that in the event of his capture "the officer in command of the capturing force do cause him to be immediately executed by hanging." In the same proclamation Davis also ordered "that no commissioned officer of the United States, taken captive, shall be released on parole, before exchange, until the said Butler shall have met with due punishment for his crime." [6]

Butler's vicious act and Davis's hot retaliation had injected a new element into the cartel situation. On December 28, 1862, Stanton ordered the exchange of commissioned officers to be discontinued.[7] Further difficulties arose because of the use of Negro troops by the United States, refusal of Confederate authorities to exchange these Negro soldiers and their white officers as prisoners of war, and misunderstanding as to Southern prisoners released on parole at Vicksburg and Port Hudson. Grant charged the Confederates with bad faith in later using these paroled men as soldiers, while the Confederate authorities answered that the paroles were irregular and invalid.

As a result of all this, the system of exchanges under the cartel broke down; and from 1863 forward the number of prisoners on each side enormously increased. There were, it is true, some exchanges later in the war; there was a Confederate attempt to negotiate a new cartel through Vice-President A. H. Stephens; and there was endless negotiation between Robert Ould, Confederate agent of exchange, and W. H. Ludlow, Union agent for the same purpose. All this, however, failed to bring a restoration of any such system as the Dix-Hill cartel. Then in 1864 another factor arose—the grim, fight-it-out attitude of General Grant, who ordered on April 17, 1864,[8] that no more exchanges of Confederate prisoners be permitted until the Confederates should cease discriminating against colored

4 *Ibid.*, 76 ff.
5 *Offic. Rec.*, 2 ser., III, 673.
6 Moore, *Rebell. Rec.* (Doc.), VI, 291–293.
7 *Offic. Rec.*, 2 ser., V, 128; Rhodes, *Hist. of U. S.*, V, 485.
8 *Offic. Rec.*, 2 ser., VII, 62–63.

prisoners and should release enough Union prisoners to offset the paroled men of Vicksburg and Port Hudson who in his view had violated their paroles. Various proposals for even exchange, man-for-man and officer-for-officer, were now being put forward by the Confederates; but they were rejected until January, 1865, when Grant, realizing that the war was nearly over, consented to the policy of even exchange.[9]

This subject of the exchange of prisoners, bothersome as it is, is at the heart of the problem and must be understood before any comment on the treatment of prisoners can be attempted. Amazing numbers of prisoners were taken and held. According to official reports as analyzed by J. F. Rhodes, the Confederates captured 211,000 Federal soldiers, of whom 16,000 were released on the field; while the Federals captured the enormous number of 462,000, of whom 247,000 were paroled on the field. Subtracting those paroled on the field, the Confederates took nearly 195,000 Unionists and the Unionists about 215,000 Confederates. The embarrassment of the South, especially in the latter part of the war, in attempting to care for these hordes of captives at a time when its own transportation and supply system was breaking down, when Sherman and Grant were hammering at the gates, and when effective officers and men were desperately needed at the front, must be remembered in judging the admittedly frightful conditions which existed at Andersonville, Belle Isle, and Salisbury.

The Andersonville prison, until the soldiers built huts for themselves, was but a stockaded enclosure of sixteen and a half acres in southwestern Georgia. Mosquito-infested tents; myriads of maggots; pollution and filth due to lack of sanitation; soldiers dying by thousands; men desperately attempting to tunnel their way to freedom; prison mates turn'ng on their fellows whom they suspected of treachery or theft; unbaked rations; inadequate hospital facilities; escaping men hunted down by bloodhounds—such are the details that come down to us from incontrovertible sources. The causes of such conditions are to be found in the sheer inability of officers in charge to cope with the immense number of prisoners pouring in on them before preparations could be made to receive them, the insurmountable difficulties in obtaining supplies and equipment, and the poverty of the Confederacy in material resources. Union prisoners at Andersonville were in no worse case than many of the soldiers of Lee's army; and it should be remembered that "the prisoners received the same rations as . . . the soldiers who were guarding them." [10] On this point of the food furnished to prisoners the following statement appears in a Southern official report:

The evidence proves that the rations furnished to prisoners of war in Richmond and on Belle Isle, have been never less than those furnished to the Confederate soldiers who guarded them, and have at some seasons been larger in

9 Rhodes, V, 500.
10 Hesseltine, 137.

quantity and better in quality than those furnished to Confederate troops in the field. This has been because, until February, 1864, the Quartermaster's Department furnished the prisoners, and often had provisions or funds, when the Commissary Department was not so well provided. Once and only once, for a few weeks, the prisoners were without meat, but a larger quantity of bread and vegetable food was in consequence supplied to them. How often the gallant men composing the Confederate Army, have been without meat, for even longer intervals, your committee do not deem it necessary to say. . . . It is well known that this quantity of food [given the prisoners] is sufficient to keep in health a man who does not labour hard. [The statements issued by the Northern Sanitary Commission] are merely conjectural . . . , and cannot weigh against the positive testimony of those who superintended the delivery of large quantities of food, ... according to a fixed ratio, for the number of men to be fed.[11]

It was in February of 1864 that prisoners began to arrive at Andersonville; in May the number had reached 15,000; by the close of July there were over 31,000. In the one month of August nearly three thousand prisoners are reported to have died (approximately one hundred a day). Some of the figures are unreliable, but one may note that prisoners' graves in the Andersonville cemetery number 12,912. The sickening story of Andersonville, however, is not to be set down, in the manner of lurid prison literature, as a chapter in Confederate cruelty; it is the tragedy of an impossible situation forced by the barbarity of war. Of Libby prison at Richmond, of Belle Isle (a misnamed island in the James at Richmond), and of minor Southern prisons at Macon, Salisbury, and Columbia, at Millen, Charleston, Savannah, and Florence, there is no room to speak. In most of these prisons conditions were better than at Andersonville, some of the evils that did exist being traceable to the vicious character of the prisoners themselves; for Northern bummers, criminals, and bounty-jumpers were among the Union men captured. As Dr. Hesseltine points out, the harrowing personal memoirs of prisoners, which generally follow a set pattern, are to be taken *cum grano salis;* [12] and the careful student will tend to agree with him in rejecting the legend of willful Southern atrocities.

Among the prisons of the North were Johnson's Island (in Lake Erie near Sandusky), some barracks at Elmira, New York, various forts (e.g., Castle Williams and Fort Lafayette) in New York harbor, Fort Warren (Boston), Fort McHenry (Baltimore), Point Lookout (St. Mary's County, Maryland), Rock Island Prison (Rock Island, Illinois), Benton Barracks (Missouri), and various "Camps" named for this or that statesman, such as Camps Morton (Indianapolis), Chase (Columbus), Randall (Madison, Wisconsin), Douglas (Chicago), and Butler (Springfield, Illinois). To

[11] Report of Committee of Confederate Congress, E. A. Pollard, *Lost Cause,* 636–637.
[12] Hesseltine, 248 ff.

describe in detail the varying conditions in these many prisons would require a volume for each one; it is enough, perhaps, to observe with Bruce Catton that "Northern camps killed their full quota of Southerners." At Elmira, for instance, 775 of the 8347 prisoners died of disease within three months, and no wonder, for the river that flowed through the grounds was "green with putrescence, filling the air with its messengers of disease and death." At Rock Island doctors reported "a striking want of some means for the preservation of human life which medical and sanitary science has indicated as proper." At Camp Douglas "Filth, poor drainage, and overcrowding created a horror. . . ." [13]

On the other hand, if one were minded to consider the less gruesome aspects of the situation, it could be shown that prisoners were permitted to receive gifts from friends; that often they were given better clothing than they had when captured; that Confederate officers in uniform "continued to wander the streets of Columbus and to register at the best hotels"; that Southern officers at Camp Chase were "permitted to retain their negro servants"; that time and again efforts were made to improve conditions; and that genuine kindness was shown by prison officials, as in the case of Col. Richard D. Owen (in charge of Camp Morton), who has been honored by an inscription now to be seen in the Indiana State House, in which Southern soldiers under his charge pay tribute to his generosity.

It should not be forgotten that in treating the subject of prisoners one is dealing with some of the most venomous aspects of war psychosis. In this state of mind shocking tales of atrocities were deliberately circulated and widely believed. Harrowing stories of prisoners' sufferings appeared in the daily papers. Secretary of War Stanton announced: "The enormity of the crime committed by the rebels towards our war prisoners . . . cannot but fill with horror the civilized world when the facts are revealed. There appeared to have been a deliberate system of savage and barbarous treatment and starvation." [14] Public opinion in the North was fed upon stories of Southern vindictiveness, and Northern readers were informed of the superiority of Union prisons in the treatment of Southerners. Conversely in the South there were fierce denunciations of Yankee brutality. E. A. Pollard, for example, wrote of the Yankees' "cruel purpose to let their prisoners rot and die," while on the other hand he blames conditions in Southern prisons upon the authorities at Washington.[15] As already explained, the Confederates resented the failure of the United States government to cooperate in the exchange of prisoners, such failure being attributed to a deliberate purpose to inflict suffering upon enemy captives in disregard of the woes of Northern as well as Southern soldiers.

[13] Catton, "Prison Camps of the Civil War," *Am. Heritage*, X, 8, 96 (Aug., 1959).
[14] T. Harry Williams, *Lincoln and the Radicals*, 344–345.
[15] Pollard, *Lost Cause*, 625.

To pursue the subject fully would be to examine mountains of testimony, to note wide variations between different prisons, to support many accusations while refuting others, to record the effects of threatened retaliation, and to observe the apparent inability of the statesmanship of the period to deal adequately with a problem which was unavoidably vexatious. In so complex a field any offhand generalization must break down; and after following the subject to its farthest limits the fair-minded observer, though he may find many a commentary on the hideous realities of war, will be likely to discountenance any sweeping reproach by one side upon the other, and to conclude that whatever be the message of the dead at Andersonville and Rock Island, that message is not to be read as a mandate for the perpetuation of sectional blame and censure.

CHAPTER 19

The War Treasury

I

IN STRUGGLING to finance the war, the government of the United States faced apparently insuperable difficulties. Two economists have summarized these problems: "The American economy was overwhelmingly agricultural. The national income was low (estimated at $4.3 billion, or $140 per capita), and savings were not available in large enough quantities to make it easy for the government to obtain large funds. Moreover, the revenue system, being based on customs, sales of public land, and miscellaneous sources, lacked the elasticity required for overnight expansion. Excise taxes had not been levied for a generation, and the income tax was unknown. The methods of borrowing were not much more efficient. . . . The Federal government had no central bank which could act as its fiscal agent, and not having had any contact with banks for nearly twenty years, it did not know how to deal with them in placing loans. The banking business was conducted by 1600 state banks, each going its own merry way; 7000 different kinds of bank notes circulated, with more than half being spurious." [1]

Until these difficulties could be cleared up, the Federal government had to resort in hit-or-miss fashion to every available method of raising money: borrowing, taxing, issuing paper money, and creating markets for Union bonds through a new federal banking system. Speaking broadly, the government financed itself during the war chiefly by loans and paper money; in comparison to the amount obtained from these sources, the sums collected in taxes were small. In the first year of the war, loans exceeded taxes more than eightfold. As the war progressed, however, the ratio of loans to taxes decreased, until in the last year of the war it was less than three to one. [2] The war loans took various forms, constituting a sort of hodgepodge of miscellaneous indebtedness which required a thorough "refunding" after the war.

[1] Paul Studenski and Herman E. Krooss, *Financial History of the United States,* 137.
[2] D. R. Dewey, *Financial Hist. of the U. S.,* 299.

The most noticeable features of the wartime borrowing are the immense issues of paper money (which cannot be dissociated from other phases of public credit) and the considerable volume of short-term loans at high interest. The obligations which ran for three years and bore 7.30 per cent interest,[3] as will be seen in the table on pages 342–343, ran to an immense figure. It is obvious that terms so disadvantageous to the government added considerably to the cost of the war. The total amount received from loans, including treasury notes, during the war—i.e., for the four fiscal years 1862–1865 inclusive—was 2621 million [4] dollars as compared to 667 million received from taxes.[5]

2

For the treasury portfolio Lincoln had made a political choice. Salmon P. Chase of Ohio, a strait-laced but high-minded statesman, was an antislavery leader, a Free-Soil organizer, and an anti-Douglas Democrat who had turned to the Republican party on the slavery issue. Chase no sooner took office than he discovered that the treasury faced an alarming crisis. Since 1857 declining tariff revenues had obliged the government to resort to deficit financing, and so great had been the distrust of Buchanan's administration in financial circles that Chase's predecessors had been obliged to make "short-term borrowing . . . the predominant feature of government finance." [1] Confronted with a virtually empty treasury and a mounting pile of requisitions to be paid, Chase promptly learned the arduous extent of his responsibilities; though not a financial expert, he was expected to advise with congressmen as to the framing of financial bills, to obtain money from keen-minded bankers and investors, to prepare estimates of revenue and expenditure in a time of great uncertainty and of unscientific budgets, to devise new schemes of currency and banking, and to direct the administration of unusual measures, such as the law for the seizure of captured and abandoned property in the South.

Chase's first report as secretary of the treasury had an unfortunate effect. Bankers had hoped that he would outline an adequate tax program; but when instead of this he indicated that borrowing would be the government's main reliance, there developed in financial circles a doubt as to the secretary's competence and a misgiving as to the nation's credit. The storm over the *Trent* affair, with its menace of war with England, broke at this time; and, though this was entirely beyond his control, Chase found himself face to face with a sharp financial crisis. As has been explained by

[3] The rate of 7.30 per cent was adopted because of convenience. On a one-hundred-dollar note the interest would be two cents a day.

[4] On July 1, 1861, the public debt of the United States stood at $90 million. Report, Sec. of Treas., 1865, *House Ex. Doc. No. 3*, 39 Cong., 1 sess., p. 253.

[5] Dewey, *Financial Hist. of the U. S.* (6th ed.), 299.

[1] Robert T. Patterson, "Government Finance on the Eve of the Civil War," *Jour. of Ec. Hist.*, XII, 43–44 (Winter, 1952).

CIVIL WAR LOANS OF THE UNITED STATES GOVERNMENT [1]

Date of the act	Nature of the loan, term, and rate of interest	Amount issued (or authorized; see n. [2] below)	Amount outstanding June 30, 1865
Acts of July 17, 1861, and Aug. 5, 1861	Bonds redeemable after 20 years. Interest, 6%	$ 50,000,000	$ 50,000,000.00
	Treasury notes, 3 years. Interest, 7.30%	139,999,750	139,155,650.00
	Demand notes without interest . . .	60,000,000	472,603.00
Act of Aug. 5, 1861	Twenty-year bonds. Interest, 6%. Exchangeable for 7.30% treasury notes		431,300.00
Act of Feb. 25, 1862	"Five-twenties"—i.e., bonds redeemable after 5 years and payable 20 years from date. Interest, 6%. . .	514,780,500	514,780,500.00
Acts of Feb. 25, 1862, July 11, 1862, Jan. 17, 1863, and Mar. 3, 1863	U. S. notes—i.e., paper money ("greenbacks") irredeemable and non-interest-bearing	450,000,000 [2]	432,687,966.00
Acts of Feb. 25, 1862, Mar. 17, 1862, July 11, 1862, June 30, 1864	Short, temporary loans, not less than 30 days. Interest, 4, 5, and 6% . .	150,000,000 [2]	89,717,061.40
Acts of Mar. 3, 1863, and June 30, 1864	"Ten-forty" bonds, running not less than 10 nor more than 40 years, issued at premium of 4.13%. Interest, 6%	75,000,000	75,000,000.00
Act of Mar. 3, 1863	Interest-bearing treasury notes, payable in one or two years. Interest, 5%	211,000,000	42,338,710.00
Act of Mar. 3, 1863	Same, payable in 3 years. Interest, 6%	17,250,000	15,000,000.00

[1] Condensed and rearranged from Report of the Secretary of the Treasury, 1865, *House Exec. Doc. No. 3*, 39 Cong., 1 sess., pp. 50 ff.

[2] These were the amounts authorized, the amounts issued not being given in this report.

W. C. Mitchell, national credit declined; government securities could not be sold through the banks; depositors withdrew their funds; and specie became alarmingly scarce. "It was all outgo now, and no income. The end was but a question of time. After standing the strain upon their reserves

CIVIL WAR LOANS OF THE UNITED STATES GOVERNMENT (*Continued*)

Date of the act	Nature of the loan, term, and rate of interest	Amount issued	Amount outstanding *June 30, 1865*
Act of Mar. 3, 1864	"Ten-forties." Interest, 5%	$172,770,100	$ 172,770,100.00
Acts of Mar. 1, 1862, and Mar. 3, 1863	One-year certificates of indebtedness. Interest, 6%		115,772,000.00
Acts of July 17, 1862, and Mar. 3, 1863	Postal currency	20,192,456	9,915,408.66
Same laws as for preceding item	Notes of fractional parts of one dollar	[Not specified]	15,090,420.10
Act of June 30, 1864	"Five-twenties"—bonds running not less than 5 nor more than 20 years. Interest, 6% . . . . : .	91,789,000	91,789,000.00
Act of June 30, 1864	Interest-bearing treasury notes, payable in 3 years. 6% compound interest	178,756,080	178,756,080.00
Act of June 30, 1864	Interest-bearing treasury notes, payable in 3 years. Interest, 7.30% . .	234,400,000	234,400,000.00
Acts of July 1, 1862, and July 2, 1864	Thirty-year bonds to Central Pacific R. R. Co. Interest, 6%	1,258,000	1,258,000.00
Act of Mar. 3, 1865	Three-year treasury notes. Interest, 7.30%	437,210,400	437,210,400.00
Total indebtedness of the U. S., June 30, 1865 [1]			2,682,593,026.53

[1] This total includes the items shown in the table, and in addition various items of debt outstanding in 1861.

for two weeks, the New York banks were compelled . . . to suspend specie payments on the thirtieth day of December [1861]. Banks in other cities speedily followed suit. The suspension of the national Treasury was entailed as a necessary consequence of the suspension of the banks. Thus the first day of the new year 1862 saw the collapse of the whole scheme of national finance." [2]

[2] White, *Money and Banking* (5th ed.), 109, citing Wesley C. Mitchell in *Jour. of Pol. Econ.*, VII, 289–326 (June, 1899).

After encountering serious difficulties in marketing government bonds, Secretary Chase made the powerful firm of Jay Cooke and Company the sole subscription agent for the distribution of the bonds of the United States. Cooke thus came to be known as the "financier of the Civil War." With his sub-agencies throughout the country, his lavish use of newspaper advertising, and his vivid appeals to workingmen to put their savings into government bonds, the loans were quickly marketed. Some thought, however, that it was unsatisfactory to have the government represented in these matters by one who was not its official, and whose commission was merely a matter of informal exchange of letters with the secretary of the treasury. Nor was the floating of the bonds entirely a matter of Cooke's promotional sagacity. Bankers and men of wealth were the chief subscribers; the bonds and interest-bearing treasury notes were good investments; and Chase squirmed considerably under the terms and conditions to which the government was subjected.

Owing to the expectation of a short war and the reluctance of Congress to place burdens upon the people, the levying of taxes was at first inadequate. Since customs duties served as a small source of revenue, the chief taxes were internal. One of the most curious of the wartime levies was the "direct tax" law of August 5, 1861. Each state was given its quota of the tax, the apportionment being based on population, as provided by the Constitution. It is generally held by authorities in public finance that ability to pay, not numbers, is the proper criterion for taxation; and it may be noted that Congress in passing this direct tax was using an obsolescent method of taxation, a method soon to be entirely abandoned. The law called for $20,000,000 to be raised in this fashion by the states; but the tax ultimately yielded only $17,000,000. It does not loom large in the history of Civil War finance, but it has a curious interest derived from the fact that the Federal government actually made determined attempts to collect the tax in the South and enforce penalties for its nonpayment by Southerners.

Another of the minor sources of revenue was the income tax law of August 5, 1861. From the wording of the measure it would seem that this act should have served as the mainstay of the treasury. As first passed it fixed a tax of 3 per cent on incomes in excess of $800 a year,[3] the rate being later increased so that by act of June 30, 1864, incomes up to $5000 bore 5 per cent, the exemption being reduced to $600; while on higher incomes the rate on the excess was 7½ per cent on amounts from $5000 to $10,000, and 10 per cent on amounts over $10,000.[4]

This was the first income tax ever levied by the United States government. It had a place in the Federal budget for ten fiscal years (1863–

[3] There was an $800 exemption, the amount of the excess above $800 being taxed at 3 per cent. *U. S. Stat. at Large*, XII, 309.

[4] *Ibid.*, XIII, 223, 281.

1872), the total amount received in this decade being $346,911,760.[5]
The sum collected during the war years (1863–1865), however,
amounted to only $55,000,000. The measure stands as an interesting ex-
periment in public finance, whose merits deserved more postwar consideration than they received.

The most important of the wartime taxes were the various internal
revenue duties. The excise was a subject on which the American people
had a "complex"—an adverse attitude reaching back though the Whisky
Rebellion into colonial days, when English ministries were given to understand that internal taxation was taboo so far as the mother country was
concerned. Yet despite this adverse background it was a huge excise which
provided the bulk of the Federal revenues. The internal revenue law of
July 1, 1862, has been broadly described as an attempt to tax everything.
With regard to a carriage, for instance, the leather, cloth, wood, and metal
would be taxed as raw materials; the manufacturer was taxed for the
process of putting them together; the dealer was taxed for selling the carriage; and the purchaser, having paid a price sufficient to cover these various levies, was taxed in addition for its ownership. So also with other
luxuries. All sorts of manufactures were made to contribute their share.

. . . Spirituous and malt liquors and tobacco were relied upon for a very
large share of revenue; a considerable sum was expected from stamps; . . . .
Manufactures of cotton, wool, flax, hemp, iron, steel, wood, stone, earth, and
every other material were taxed three per cent. Banks, insurance and railroad
companies, telegraph companies, and all other corporations were made to pay
tribute. The butcher paid thirty cents for every beef slaughtered, ten cents for
every hog, five cents for every sheep. Carriages, billiard-tables, yachts, gold
and silver plate, and all other articles of luxury were levied upon heavily. Every
profession and every calling, except the ministry of religion, was included
within the far-reaching provisions of the law and subjected to tax for license.
Bankers and pawn brokers, lawyers and horse-dealers, physicians and confectioners, commercial brokers and peddlers, proprietors of theatres and jugglers
on the street, were indiscriminately summoned to aid the National Treasury.
The law was so extended and so minute that it required thirty printed pages
of royal octavo and more than twenty thousand words to express its provisions.[6]

This wide range of schedules having been established in 1862, consumers and producers became accustomed to the new taxes, so that later
in the war it was merely necessary to increase the rates. This having been
done, the internal revenue system, including the income tax, produced
for the year 1864–1865 a yield of $209,000,000.[7] Used to a restricted
Federal government in the days of Buchanan, the people were rapidly ac-

[5] Richardson, *Messages and Papers*, X, 415.
[6] Blaine, *Twenty Years*, I, 433.
[7] Report, Sec. of the Treas., 1865, *House Ex. Doc. No. 3*, 39 Cong., 1 sess.,
p. 18.

customing their eyes to the spectacle of a leviathan state, a giant whose tendency has been to grow enormously with every emergency and somehow to keep his growth after the emergency has passed.

3

In addition to taxes and loans the government had recourse to large amounts of paper money, for the dislocation occasioned by the suspension of specie payments at the end of 1861 caused congressional financiers to look elsewhere than to hard-money methods for the solution of fiscal problems. With the treasury nearly empty, financial markets shaken, foreign bankers unsympathetic, taxation inadequate, and loans unmarketable except at a discount, the door of escape by way of paper money seemed most tempting. Without consulting the treasury department, Representative E. G. Spaulding of New York introduced a bill for the issue of treasury notes to be made legal tender in payment of all debts. What it amounted to was that the United States government was "making money" by means of the printing press. Though not "fiat money" in the bald sense, this paper currency had features which resembled fiat money. Some of its advocates, indeed, regarded such money as sound and proper.

Many questions were raised in debate concerning this measure of financial extremity. Was it necessary? Would the people fail the government in the matter of taxes and loans? Would not the patriotic impulse supply the treasury as it was filling the armies? Was not the issuing of irredeemable paper money as legal tender a breach of contract? Since gold was virtually the prewar money of the country, would it not be bad faith to introduce paper for the payment not only of government obligations but of private debts as well? What about the rights of creditors who had paid out gold and were to be repaid in paper? Was it not bad ethics to permit a man to pay off his debts at a discount, and in so doing to have all the force of the government and its courts at his disposal? Was it not a forced loan? Would not such action injure public credit; would it not seriously embarrass sounder schemes of finance which the treasury might attempt? And would not this display of "governmental bankruptcy" embolden and encourage the enemy? Besides, where was the constitutional power in Congress to make paper money legal tender?

In support of the measure it was argued that there was no choice. The bill was a necessity, said its advocates. The treasury was facing staggering expenditures. The government would be sadly hampered in the war if this important power were withheld. As to the alternative plan being worked out by the treasury department with leading bankers, it was held that this would take too long to mature,[1] and that the banks would not take the

---

[1] While the legal tender bill was pending in Congress, Chase was in consultation with representative bankers; and a "plan" was worked out involving some of the features of the later national banking system but avoiding the necessity of making

notes unless they were made legal tender. The bill was defended as a war measure—a drastic remedy that would not be thought of as part of a sound, permanent policy—yet it was pointed out that the danger of using this medicine as food in normal times was a real menace and should be stoutly resisted. The law was passed in a period of unsound bank currency; and it was argued that the paper notes, with the faith of the government and the wealth of the nation behind them, were preferable to the flood of irredeemable banknotes with which the country was then plagued.[2]

As passed into law on February 25, 1862, the legal tender act authorized the issue of $150,000,000 of non-interest-bearing "United States notes," soon to be dubbed "greenbacks." Such notes were vague promises to pay hard money; but no provision was made for their actual, specific redemption on demand, nor at any indicated time. They were receivable for internal taxes to the United States and for obligations of the United States except interest on bonds, which was to be paid in coin. The notes were declared to be "legal tender in payment of all debts, public and private, within the United States, except duties on imports and interest [on the public debt]." When received into the treasury they were to be reissued. The same law provided for $500,000,000 of "five-twenty" bonds bearing 6 per cent; and the legal tender notes were made convertible in fifty-dollar lots into such bonds.[3]

In the earlier phases of the proceedings concerning the legal tender bill the attitude of Secretary Chase was uncertain and it was thought that he opposed the measure. To set these doubts at rest he sent a letter to the committee on ways and means of the House (January 29, 1862) stating that because of the government's financial difficulties he considered that "it had become necessary that we should resort to the issue of United States notes." Chase had indeed opposed the measure at first; and when circumstances overbore this opposition, his approval was given with reluctance. In a few months he asked Congress for more paper money, and Congress responded with the act of July 11, 1862, authorizing an additional $150,000,000 of greenbacks and lowering the minimum denomination from five dollars to one dollar. A further increase was approved in 1863,

---

the United States notes legal tender. Chase's conferences with the bankers are of interest as showing that he was seeking to avert the legal tender act, while the slight attention of the lawmakers to the treasury's efforts is illustrative of that poor coordination between the legislative and executive branches which has ever characterized the American system of government.

[2] The bill was supported by Spaulding, Thaddeus Stevens, Fessenden, Wilson of Massachusetts, and Sherman of Ohio. Among its opponents were Collamer, Owen Lovejoy, Justin S. Morrill, King, Powell, and Saulsbury. Blaine, *Twenty Years*, I, 411–425.

[3] This convertibility feature was soon dropped. By the act of March 3, 1863, such conversion was withheld as to further issues, while the right to obtain bonds for previously issued notes was withdrawn unless exercised by July 1, 1863.

so that by the close of the war a total of $450,000,000 of legal tender notes had been authorized. Actual issues reached $432,000,000.

4

The inevitable differentiation between this type of currency and gold produced a complex of problems bound up with operations on the "Gold Exchange." An importer of goods would have to pay his foreign creditor in gold, or, what amounts to the same thing, in a bill of exchange on a gold basis. The requirements of international trade, involving contracts to pay in gold at the expiration of sixty or ninety days, created a legitimate demand for future gold; and a class of brokers naturally arose to handle these dealings in "gold futures." Though speculative, such dealings were not the equivalent of mere gambling. The essence of gambling is that an artificial and unnecessary risk is created. In gold speculation the element of risk was inherent in the situation. The value of gold in terms of the greenback was an uncertain and fluctuating quantity; so that if gold brokers had not assumed the risk in gold futures, such risk would have fallen back upon dealers, importers, and any in fact who had need for gold in future business operations. Gold traders, presumably equipped with specialized aptitude and experience, enabled dealers to plan with reference to a definite future price of such gold as they might contract for.

The first appearance of the premium on gold came as a result of the suspension of specie payments; with the advent of the greenback it became a regular and necessary factor in business. Finding their shops swamped, with customers overflowing to the sidewalks, the Wall Street brokers who dealt in foreign currencies obtained the use of a restaurant; then a more suitable building was occupied and the Gold Exchange organized, with a Gold Exchange Bank as its adjunct. The gold room was a wartime phenomenon which continued for seventeen years. As explained by Horace White the method of clearing was as follows: "Each transaction was noted on a 'ticket of advice' signed by both buyer and seller. All the tickets were passed into the bank. If Mr. A. had bought $1,000,000 worth of gold from various persons at various prices and had sold $999,000, then instead of receiving from and paying to all these people he would settle only with the bank. He would receive at the close of the day $1000 in gold and would pay whatever sum in greenbacks was due from him as the resultant of all his transactions. The usual daily amount of such clearings was $60,000,-000 to $70,000,000."

All the foreign trade of the country, both imports and exports [continues Mr. White], was regulated by the daily and hourly quotations of the Gold Room. This trade could not have been carried on otherwise. The wholesale prices of all importable and exportable commodities were regulated by the quotations. Retail prices were affected at longer range. That is, the retail dealers were obliged to fix their prices high enough to cover fluctuations and to save themselves from loss. The consumer was not able to buy at the lowest price that the law of competition would, under other circumstances, have made. Commodities not of an exportable or importable kind were affected in less degree and at still longer range, but were not exempt from the influence. In short, the whole trade of the country, both external and internal, pivoted on the Gold Exchange. Gold being the universal liquidator of commerce, it was necessary to know where and at what price it could be obtained in any desired quantity. The Gold Exchange gave the answer to this question daily and hourly, and was accordingly indispensable.[1]

In addition to this element of legitimate service which the gold brokers performed, the system opened the way for abuse and speculation. By a fortunate estimate of future fluctuations a broker could make handsome gains; furthermore anyone might take his chance on the gold market as on the stock or grain markets with the hope of heavy killings if the dice should fall as he wished. There seemed no way of limiting gold operations to the necessary uses of commerce. So widespread and open was the trading, and so disastrous were its effects upon public morale and government credit, that Congress decided to intervene. On June 17, 1864, when the ratio of paper to gold was about two to one, Congress passed the "gold bill," forbidding any purely speculative trading in gold futures, and making it unlawful for anyone to contract for subsequent delivery of gold unless he possessed gold to this amount at the time the contract was made. For violation of the act penalties of fine and imprisonment were imposed.[2]

Confusion worse confounded was the result of this act. On June 18, 1864, the gold premium stood at 95¼, i.e., it would require $1.95¼ in paper to purchase one dollar in gold. By June 29 the premium had risen to 150, making it necessary to pay $2.50 for each gold dollar. An intolerable situation had arisen; the legislators were deluged with complaints; and on July 2, fifteen days after it had been passed, the gold act was repealed.[3]

By reference to the military situation it will be seen that the furor over the gold act synchronized with a period of panic as to national safety. Jubal A. Early was pressing on through Maryland; by July 11 he was at the doors of Washington. On that day the paper price of gold reached $2.84. In January, 1862, according to the statement of the comptroller of the currency, gold in New York was at the very low premium of 1½ per cent. "On the 1st of January, 1864 [continued the comptroller], it opened at 52, went up to 88 on the 14th of April, and fell to 67 on the 19th of the same month. . . . On the 1st of July it was forced up to 185, but on the day following (the gold bill having been repealed) it fell to 130. On the 11th of the same month it went up again to 184; on the 15th it fell to

1 Horace White, *Money and Banking*, 5th ed., 126–127.
2 *U. S. Stat. at Large*, XIII, 132–133.
3 Dewey, *Financial Hist. of the U. S.*, 296–297.

144, and after various fluctuations dropped on the 26th of September to 87. . . ." [4]

It should of course be added that there were numerous other influences that produced gold fluctuations: indeed the gold market was about as thoroughly sensitized to the whole political and economic pulse of the country as the stock market. Changing currents of fiscal policy, debates in Congress, international crises, market fluctuations in United States bonds, changes in the personnel of government, pre-election news, and many other factors affected the price of gold, or, to put it in different words, influenced the degree of depreciation of the greenback.

5

At the time of the Civil War the country lacked a uniform system of banking and banknote currency, and one of the important matters of war finance was the creation of such a system. Chase had early seen the need of reform in this field; and in his report of December, 1862, he outlined his plan for national banks and national bank currency. In view of the criticism of his treasury administration it may be well to note the favorable comment which this report evoked from the mayor of New York City. Mayor George Opdyke wrote to Chase that the report was "admirable both in matter and manner, superior . . . to any state paper that has ever emanated from the Treasury Department. It is clear in statement, sound in theory, logical in argument, and most comprehensive in its grasp." [1]

What Chase proposed was a system of national banking associations under Federal supervision, which would issue banknotes based upon United States bonds and guaranteed by the Federal government. In making this proposal he had in mind especially the evils of the existing state banknotes. These were of bewildering variety and great redundancy; the security back of them was flimsy; they were subject to wide and eccentric fluctuations; and so long as such wildcat currency existed, any plan for an adequate national currency was doomed.

The delays and complications of legislative procedure which followed when Congress sought to meet Chase's suggestions need not be noted here. The measure was promoted by such men as E. G. Spaulding, Samuel Hooper, and John Sherman; it was opposed by Collamer, Carlile, Howard of Michigan, and other conservatives. It became law on February 25, 1863; but this law had certain defects, so that Congress faced the whole problem afresh and reframed the statute. It is therefore to the law of June 3, 1864, that one must turn for the legislative basis of the national banking system as it emerged from the Civil War. Banking associations under national charters were to be created anywhere in the United States, their or-

---

[4] Report, Sec. of the Treas., 1864, *House Exec. Doc. No. 3*, 38 Cong., 2 sess., pp. 52–53.

[1] Opdyke to Chase, Dec. 14, 1862. Chase Papers (MSS., Libr. of Cong.).

ganization and management to be supervised by a bureau of the treasury department, headed by a newly created officer to be known as the comptroller of the currency. The minimum capital for each association was specified, varying with the population of the city or town in which the bank might be founded. Each shareholder was made doubly liable for the obligations of his bank. Every such bank was required to purchase United States bonds to an amount not less than $30,000, nor less than one third of its paid-in capital, these bonds to be deposited in the Federal treasury. A new form of currency was created known as "national banknotes." The comptroller of the currency was to issue the notes to the national banks, and they were to be equal in amount to 90 per cent of the value of the United States bonds received. The maximum amount of such banknotes was fixed at $300,000,000.

Other provisions of the act were concerned with the maintenance of a required reserve against both banknotes and deposits; the depositing of such reserve in "reserve cities" (which permitted the concentration of bankers' funds in New York City); the appointment of receivers under national supervision in the case of failed banks; and the use of the banks as depositaries and financial agents for the government. As a method of stimulating, or rather forcing, the sale of United States bonds, the national-bank act became an essential feature of Civil War finance.

Organization of banks under the national banking act at first proceeded slowly. Initially New York, Boston, Philadelphia, and Baltimore financiers were strongly hostile to the new arrangement. As Robert P. Sharkey points out, their "large eastern banks which depended very little upon note issues for their profits simply had very little to gain and something to lose in joining the system." As late as 1864 the New York Clearing House resolved that "all National Bank currency be treated as uncurrent money unless the bank [in question] redeem at par through a member of this Association." Many western bankers, who "saw that the system would raise serious obstacles to their profitable privilege of issuing notes without restraint," were also slow to favor the national banking system.[2] Not until Congress on March 3, 1865,[3] placed a tax upon state banknote issues did most of the state banks see the handwriting on the wall and make plans to join the national system. During 1865, 1014 new national banks were organized, bringing the total number to 1601.

When fully in operation, the national banking system did much to bring order and a degree of stability out of the previous financial chaos. The new national banknotes, based upon adequate reserves, were in every sense superior to the fluctuating and unreliable state note issues which they replaced. On the other hand, "the arbitrary limit placed on the amount

[2] Sharkey, *Money, Class, and Party,* 299, 226–227.
[3] Act of Mar. 3, 1865, to become effective July 1, 1866. *U. S. Stat. at Large,* XIII, 484.

of the national bank-note circulation," "the irredeemability of that circulation," and, especially, the concentration of "a large part of the nation's banking reserve in New York for use on the call loan market" contributed heavily to the periodic financial panics in the postwar decades.[4] Another of the inequities of the system as actually administered was the favoritism shown after the war to the eastern states, which received the lion's share of the $300,000,000 of banknote circulation assigned by law as the maximum for the whole country. As explained by George LaVerne Anderson, each state in the New England and Middle Atlantic regions obtained an amount of banknotes in excess of its quota, while not a state in the South received an amount equal to its quota. "Massachusetts [writes Anderson] received the circulation which would have been necessary to raise Virginia, West Virginia, North and South Carolina, Louisiana, Florida and Arkansas to their legal quotas. . . . The little state of Connecticut had more national bank circulation than Michigan, Wisconsin, Iowa, Minnesota, Kansas, Missouri, Kentucky and Tennessee. . . . Massachusetts had more than the rest of the Union exclusive of the New England and Middle Atlantic states."

Interesting comparison [he continues] can be made between comparatively small New England towns and the Southern states. Thus Woonsocket, Rhode Island, had more national bank circulation than North and South Carolina, Mississippi and Arkansas; Waterville, Maine, had nearly as much as Alabama; New Haven, Connecticut, had more than any single Southern state. Bridgeport in the same state had more than North and South Carolina, Alabama and Texas. Similar comparisons could be made, but enough have been suggested to show the true nature of the question.

The *per capita* figures are just as astonishing. Rhode Island had $77.16 for each inhabitant, Arkansas had 13 cents. No state in the Middle Atlantic or New England group had less than $11 *per capita* and no state outside of those groups, with the exception of Nevada, had more than $8.

If it be said in answer to these facts that distributing circulation according to population is absurd . . . it should be kept in mind that not a single Southern state had obtained, by October, 1869, its legal share of the $150,000,-000 which was to have been apportioned according to existing banking capital, wealth and resources. Louisiana was entitled to $7,200,000 on this basis and received $1,094,589; Georgia was entitled to $4,470,000 and received $1,234,100; South Carolina was entitled to $4,185,000 and received $192,500.[5]

With some modifications the national banking system continued for half a century. Though it had some merit, it created an inelastic currency,

[4] Sharkey, *op. cit.*, 229–231.
[5] George LaVerne Anderson, *The National Banking System, 1865–1875: A Sectional Institution* (MS. doctoral dissertation, Univ. of Ill., 1933), 111 ff. Cf. Anderson, "Western Attitudes toward National Banks, 1873–1874," *M. V. H. R.*, XXIII, 205–216 (Sept., 1936).

tended toward the concentration of bank resources in New York, opened the way for serious abuse in the speculative exploitation of bank funds, and contributed to the sharp financial flurry of 1907. Proving inadequate as a nation-wide control of currency and banking, it was tardily superseded by an improved plan in the federal reserve act of 1913.

6

It is difficult to arrive at a sound appraisal of Chase's performance as secretary of the treasury. All authorities admit that he was energetic, and virtually all stress his incorruptibility.[1] But later economists have generally condemned his financial policies, particularly his share in the movement for putting out great issues of paper money, his objection to the option by which the holder of legal tender notes could exchange them for six-percent government bonds payable in gold, and his refusal to insist upon prompt, stiff taxation. Chase's annual reports, declares Sidney Ratner, reveal "no adequate grasp of the serious financial situation."[2] In his learned *History of the Greenbacks,* Wesley C. Mitchell blamed Chase's ignorance and inexperience for the decision to issue legal-tender notes, which "increased the debt incurred during the war by a sum running into hundreds of millions."[3] Don C. Barrett agreed that Chase did not bring to his office "those larger considerations of a finance minister which would lead to a proper anticipation of future needs and to a comprehensive and well-digested scheme of finance."[4] Even more harsh was Albert S. Bolles's verdict: "Unskilled in finance, unwilling to learn, and, when going astray, persisting in his course, Mr. Chase's failure was inevitable."[5]

In Chase's defense it must be pointed out that such criticisms often fail to take account of the magnitude and urgency of the problems which the secretary faced; he "was operating with untested assistants to meet unascertained demands from uncertain resources."[6] Moreover, much of the abuse of Chase comes from writers who have made sound money and a balanced budget cardinal articles of economic faith and have accordingly denounced Civil War finance as an unwholesome aberration. Recent experiences during the New Deal and the Second World War in managed currency and in deficit financing have caused some economists to revise upward their judgment of Chase. For, when compared with World War I

---

[1] An exception is the debunking biography, *So Fell the Angels,* by Thomas Graham Belden and Marva Robins Belden, which attempts to prove, upon the basis of insufficient evidence, that Secretary "Chase decided that he could no longer afford the luxury of a fastidious conscience" (p. 36) and engaged in "improper bonding, bribery, and favoritism" (p. 143).

[2] Ratner, *American Taxation,* 68.

[3] Mitchell, *A History of the Greenbacks,* 419.

[4] Barrett, *The Greenbacks and Resumption of Specie Payments,* 36.

[5] Bolles, *The Financial History of the United States,* 116.

[6] Donald, *Inside Lincoln's Cabinet,* 35–36.

and World War II, the Union debt incurred during the Civil War does not appear to have been excessive, nor does the interest charge upon it seem to have been exorbitant.[7] On the whole, the threat of inflation was more effectively curbed during the Civil War than during the First World War.[8] Indeed, as John K. Galbraith has observed, it is remarkable that, without rationing, price controls, or central banking, Chase could have managed the Federal economy so well during the Civil War.[9]

[7] Marshall A. Robinson, "Federal Debt Management: Civil War, World War I, and World War II," *Am. Ec. Rev.*, XLV, 389 (May, 1955).

[8] Milton Friedman, "Price, Income, and Monetary Changes in Three Wartime Periods," *ibid.*, XLII, 614 (May, 1952).

[9] Galbraith, paper read before the First Annual Civil War Conference at Gettysburg College, Nov. 19, 1957.

CHAPTER 20

The American Question Abroad

IN EUROPEAN chancelleries the quarrel across the Atlantic was designated as "the American question." When the full story of the European view of this question is told it will be realized that in the 1860's the Atlantic was, as to ideas, no less a separating gulf than in the 1770's or the Napoleonic years, and yet, as to international complications, not so much an ocean of isolation as a sea highway in which international interests jostled and clashed. Such were the controversies and intrigues affecting North and South that a summary of European *mores* and stereotypes might be built around the story of diplomatic developments touching America. To an unstable Europe, steeped in aristocracy and fearful of revolution, there came the necessity of making adjustments in a conflict where statesmen saw differently just how democracy, revolution, and economic self-interest were involved. Sensitive to revolt, torn by feuds and predatory conquest, unhappy on its own borders, heading toward serious wars, Europe in the sixties was just emerging from the Metternichian period in which the concept of legitimate monarchy, resistance to new political ideas, and joint intervention for the suppression of popular movements were cardinal principles. It was a time when the word "intervention" came readily to the lips of European statesmen, a period when the countries of most concern to America—England and France—were under leaders (Palmerston and Napoleon III) to whom the affairs of remote and unrelated portions of the globe had become somewhat of a specialty.

The American question could not be evaded. Between neutrality and intervention a choice had to be made; yet either choice would involve a whole series of further choices.[1] To grapple with the question was partly a problem of reading the true situation amid the demands and threats of enraged belligerents, partly of guessing the future, partly of balancing one interest against another at home. In the outcome, while neutrality was the

[1] To speak accurately neither side wanted Great Britain to be strictly neutral. What the United States desired was a denial of belligerent status to the Confederacy (a very different thing from neutrality in maritime matters). The Confederacy desired unneutral assistance and intervention.

course adopted all round, yet, as a commentary on the proverbially unhappy situation of a neutral in any quarrel, it is significant that the war drew to its close with both belligerents nursing major grievances against England and France, neither side being satisfied with the conduct of those powers.

I

European attitudes toward the Civil War were destined profoundly to affect its ultimate outcome, yet at the outbreak of the conflict most foreigners were poorly informed about the United States. As Leslie Stephen said in 1865: "The name of America five years ago, called up to the ordinary English mind nothing but a vague cluster of associations, compounded of Mrs. Trollope, *Martin Chuzzlewit,* and *Uncle Tom's Cabin."* [1] Influenced by the rabidly pro-Southern London *Times,* most upper-class Englishmen tended promptly to side with the Confederacy. For years the Old South had been close to Great Britain in both business and society, and it was easy to see in the Southern planters an equivalent of the English gentry. British aristocrats like the Marquis of Lothian, the Marquis of Bath, Lord Robert Cecil, and Lord Wharncliffe thought that the success of the Confederacy would give a much needed check to democracy, both in America and in Europe. More liberal Englishmen, too, could favor the South, supposing its desire to escape Northern "tyranny" was something comparable to the fulfillment of Italian and German national aspirations. The character of the leaders of the Southern Confederacy inspired respect abroad, and the chivalric bearing of Robert E. Lee and Stonewall Jackson enlisted the Englishman's deepest admiration. From the outset of the war, therefore, the "great body of the aristocracy" in England was "anxious to see the United States go to pieces." [2]

Though at first not so articulate, there were, in fact, large segments of British opinion which favored the Union cause. Many English manufacturers and shippers had strong commercial ties with the North. The powerful British humanitarian movement, especially the antislavery societies, found it hard to sympathize with the Confederacy. Friends of democracy and proponents of republicanism saw in the United States a model to be cherished. Powerful John Bright, leader of the British radicals, spoke eloquently of the "odious and . . . blasphemous" attempts of the Confederates to divide the United States and looked to the day when America, with "one people, and one language, and one law, and one faith," should become "the home of freedom, and a refuge for the oppressed of every race and of every clime." [3] The principal leaders of the British labor movement were "firmly on the side of the North," for they saw in the pro-Southern sympathies of the "millionaire aristocrats, venal politicians, and some of

[1] *The History of the* [London] *Times,* II, 359.
[2] Worthington C. Ford, ed., *A Cycle of Adams Letters, 1861–1865,* I, 220.
[3] Randall, *Lincoln the Liberal Statesman,* 237.

the press, led by the great bully *The Times*," a "hatred to freedom, jealousy of the growing power of the United States, and a desire to see democratic or republican institutions overthrown or brought into disrepute." [4]

At the outbreak of the war it was far from clear that these latter sentiments, resting on the profound pro-Unionism of the British masses, would triumph. At first it seemed that the North muffed every opportunity to enlist British support. Already fearful of Northern economic competition, which threatened the supremacy of the British merchant marine and challenged the pre-eminence of British manufactures, the English middle classes were alienated when the Republicans adopted the Morrill tariff of 1861. Northern appeals to British idealism were undercut when Seward, early in the war, explicitly declared that the conflict was not being waged over slavery and would not disturb the South's peculiar institution. Even a stanch friend of the Union like the Duke of Argyll was obliged to conclude "that the North is not entitled to claim *all* the sympathy which belongs to a cause which they do not avow; and which is promoted only as an indirect consequence of a contest which (on their side at least) is waged for other objects, and on other grounds." [5]

The English viewed the leaders of the Northern cause with suspicion. Lincoln was an unknown quantity, whom even the friendly Richard Cobden characterized as "a backwoodsman of great sturdy common sense, but . . . unequal to the occasion." [6] It was assumed that the administration would be run by Seward, who was widely distrusted abroad. From careless words spoken during his prewar trip to England he had acquired "a heavy load of obloquy" abroad. [7] Englishmen repeated the story that Seward had boasted to the Duke of Newcastle, during the Prince of Wales's American visit in 1860, of his intention to twist the lion's tail once he assumed high office. When news leaked out of his incredible April 1, 1861, memorandum, proposing to demand categorical explanations from Great Britain, France, and Spain, followed by war against the two latter powers, [8] European fears were confirmed.

It was, therefore, with reasonable hope of success that the infant Confederacy looked to Europe for recognition and assistance. A month before the war (March 16, 1861) William L. Yancey, Pierre A. Rost, and A. Dudley Mann were sent on an introductory mission to England, France, Russia, and Belgium. Their instructions from Secretary Toombs were to present to these governments the nature and purposes of the Southern cause, to open diplomatic intercourse, and to "negotiate treaties of friend-

[4] J. R. Pole, *Abraham Lincoln and the Working Classes of Britain*, 15.

[5] Duke of Argyll to W. E. Gladstone, Aug. 23, 1861, Gladstone MSS., British Museum.

[6] Randall, *Lincoln the President*, II, 32.

[7] Thurlow Weed to Archbishop John Hughes, Dec. 22, 1861, Seward MSS., Univ. of Rochester Lib.

[8] See above, p. 173.

ship, commerce and navigation. . . ." [9] This was the first of a series of diplomatic or commercial missions which, as the war progressed, were sent by the Confederacy not only to the countries mentioned, but to Spain, to the Pope, to the States of the Church, to the United States of Mexico, to the Empire of Mexico, to individual states within Mexico, and to imperial dependencies or dominions such as Canada, Ireland, and various West Indian colonies.

In the diplomatic game the enterprising Confederates took the first trick. On May 13, 1861, Queen Victoria issued her proclamation of neutrality, recognizing the Confederates as having belligerent rights. The significance of this initial "concession to the South" is best to be measured by the disappointment it produced at Washington, where Seward asserted that the war was a domestic question and that belligerency should not be accorded the pretended Southern government, as the Washington authorities regarded it. That the Queen's proclamation, a proper one under international law which was imitated in other countries, did involve a recognition of Confederate belligerency, however, was a fact that could not be gainsaid: to the eyes of Europe the government of the South, though not yet a member of the "family of nations," was a responsible government conducting war. As such it was deemed entitled to the rights and subject to the obligations of a belligerent in international law. The matter of status being fundamental, the refusal of Europe to adopt the Northern interpretation of the war as a mere irresponsible insurrection was of real significance; it has even been said that by this recognition of belligerent status "the South almost realized its ambitions of drawing England in upon its side." [10]

Fortunately for the Union cause Lincoln had made one of his best appointments for the post at London. Indeed when all the facts are considered it must be admitted that the character and ability of Charles Francis Adams were as valuable as Union military victories in contributing to ultimate success in the war. As a boy he had witnessed stirring events in Europe; in the company of his mother he had taken the long and arduous winter journey by carriage from St. Petersburg to Paris to join his father, John Quincy Adams. Passing through the Allied lines, he reached Paris just after Napoleon's return from Elba. After a preliminary education at a drab English boarding school whose master made an unpleasant impression on him, he graduated at Harvard, and studied law under the great Webster. By 1861 he had served as legislator in Massachusetts, had become prominent as a leader of the "conscience Whigs" and the Free-Soilers, and had achieved the position of an influential member of the national House of

[9] Offic. Rec. (Nav.), 2 ser., III, 191–195. Treaties then in force between the United States and Great Britain were to be assumed as between the Confederacy and Britain, with one exception. The Confederacy, though prohibiting the African slave trade, was not prepared to assist other countries in promoting that object, as was provided by the Webster-Ashburton treaty.

[10] F. L. Owsley, King Cotton Diplomacy (1959 ed.), 58–59.

Representatives, where his main contribution was as a moderate Republican earnestly engaged in the work of avoiding war. Though depressed at the nomination of Lincoln, whom he never fully admired, he accepted appointment as minister to England and gave of his best as a loyal servant of the Lincoln administration. "No man in American public life [writes Worthington C. Ford] was by inheritance, training and matured convictions, so well fitted to occupy this office at so delicate and critical a time. . . . Facing perils where a misstep would have involved catastrophe, . . . he made no mistake . . ., no concession of right or principle." [11]

Arriving in England on the day of the Queen's proclamation of neutrality (one of the things he sought to prevent), Adams had hardly time to settle in London when another serious matter claimed his attention. It was Seward's "bold remonstrance" (Dispatch No. 10) of May 21. In this dispatch Seward gave Adams the impossible instruction to have no relations whatever with the British government so long as they continued to interfere in American domestic questions, and to discontinue relations if Russell should continue to hold intercourse with Confederate diplomats.[12] The dispatch had fortunately been softened by Lincoln; and Adams, without binding himself to a literal compliance with Seward's instructions, handled the matter so deftly as to avoid a clash, and also to win from Russell the statement that he intended no more interviews with the Southern commissioners.

During the life of the Yancey-Rost-Mann mission [13] March, 1861, to January, 1862, the South scored several points, but was unsuccessful in its main undertakings. The commissioners found entrée into London society, seized the attention of a considerable public, and obtained recognition of belligerency; but they failed to secure full recognition of the Confederate government, sought in vain for a treaty of amity and commerce, met disappointment in their demand that England denounce the blockade, were denied the use of foreign ports for Confederate privateers, and saw their hopes deferred in the matter of intervention. Though Russell granted interviews to the commissioners on May 3 and May 9, the conversations were unofficial, and on seeking further interviews the Southerners were requested (August 7) to put their communications in writing. As time passed Yancey developed a feeling of bitterness toward England and asked to be relieved of his duties. The commissioners had differed among them-

---

[11] Ford, ed., *A Cycle of Adams Letters,* I, ix.

[12] E. D. Adams *Great Britain and the American Civil War,* I, 126; Bancroft, *Seward,* II, 169 ff.

[13] In colorful characterizations Owsley indicates that Yancey was a poor choice in view of his qualities as a "fire eater" and his prominence as a defender of slavery; that Rost, a Louisiana judge of French birth, was without serious qualifications; and that Mann "spoke like a Polonius, full of words and wind," and was "harmless either at home or abroad." *King Cotton Diplomacy,* 52.

selves; they had somewhat the feeling of being officially snubbed; and, with the arrival of new commissioners in January, 1862 (Mason and Slidell), their mission came to an end. Yancey returned to the South; Mann turned up in Belgium; Rost was transferred to Madrid.

2

Turning from preliminary maneuvers to more settled diplomacy the Confederate government selected for the most important foreign capitals two distinguished men—James Murray Mason of Virginia for London, and John Slidell of Louisiana for Paris. Of these men it may be said that their diplomatic activities were of less significance than their initial voyage, which raised such serious questions as to bring England and the United States to the brink of war. At the Spanish port of Havana the commissioners had taken passage on a British merchant ship, a mail packet named the *Trent*. The day after leaving port (November 8, 1861) the vessel was stopped by the conventional signal, a shot across the bow, by a warship of the United States, the *San Jacinto* under Captain Charles Wilkes; and the two commissioners, with their secretaries, were arrested and removed to the *San Jacinto*. The searching party "met with some difficulty" as stated in Wilkes's report, and "a force became necessary to search" the ship. Though the envoys were "treated with every possible courtesy by Captain Wilkes and his officers" [1] they were political prisoners and were placed in confinement in Fort Warren, Boston Harbor. The effect of this seizure was immediate and sensational. No international incident better illustrates the stupid thoughtlessness of popular clamor, which was fortunately in striking contrast to the caution and moderation of those who guided international policy. With unintelligent exultation and in ignorance of the merits of the controversy, the act of Captain Wilkes was vociferously applauded at home. He was banqueted at Boston and elsewhere; his exploit was approved by the secretary of the navy; American newspapers treated him as a hero; and the House of Representatives joined in the general acclaim by a ringing resolution.

Amid the noise and jubilation, however, the more serious-minded began to develop doubts. What after all was to be gained by sustaining Wilkes's act? Since he had acted without instructions, was it not fortunate that the government could save its face by disowning the act altogether? Did America not have an embassy in London and was there not a British ambassador at Washington? What was diplomacy for if not to deal with just such a situation? As for going to war with England while the tremendous conflict raged at home, would this not be an act of the utmost rashness, especially on an issue where the United States would appear to be renouncing its traditional defense of neutral rights at sea? If such a war should be the outcome, would not Mason and Slidell have accomplished, from the

[1] Statement of Mason. *Offic. Rec.* (Nav.), 2 ser., III, 296, 484.

standpoint of Confederate intentions, infinitely more than they were likely to accomplish by proceeding on their mission?

As to the merits of the legal question, the point at issue was not a mere matter of searching a neutral ship. The right of search, ancillary to the right of capture where contraband is found or violation of a blockade involved, was clearly recognized.[2] Nor was the right to seize and condemn contraband on board a neutral vessel a matter of question. The offense to England consisted in the fact that certain individuals had been "forcibly taken from on board a British vessel . . . while such vessel was pursuing a lawful and innocent voyage—an act of violence which was an affront to the British flag and a violation of international law." [3] The act of Wilkes was not properly an exercise of the right of search: it was rather an impressment of persons from the deck of a neutral ship. Even admitting the right of the United States to take Mason and Slidell (on the doubtful ground that persons could be deemed contraband), it was clear that Wilkes's method was faulty. If any part of the ship's "cargo" was to be condemned this could be done only by sailing the ship into a port of the United States, submitting the case to a prize court, and carrying out the forfeitures as the result of a regular judicial decree in compliance with the substance and procedure of international law. The nub of the matter was that "Wilkes had undertaken to pass upon the issue of a violation of neutrality on the spot, instead of sending the *Trent* as a prize into port for . . . adjudication." [4]

Yet the act of Wilkes was more than a breach of international usage. It was an affront and a challenge to England's sense of national honor. When he heard the news, Palmerston blazed out in cabinet meeting: "You may stand for this but damned if I will!" [5] The mass of the English people appeared to share his rage. War preparations were carried to the point of sending 8000 troops and war material to Canada, putting a steam fleet in readiness, and prohibiting the exportation of munitions. Henry Adams wrote from England to his brother: "This nation means to make war." A "few weeks [he said] may see us . . . on our way home. . . ." The American minister was "indescribably sad" as he witnessed "the exultation in America over an event which [bade] fair to be the final calamity in this contest"; while the son wrote of the "bloody set of fools" that were applauding Wilkes.[6]

Despite jingoistic manifestations, however, the affair was satisfactorily adjusted. The first letter of instructions from the British cabinet to Lord

[2] The American jurist, Story, declared that the right of search was "allowed by the general consent of nations, in time of war." The Marianna Flora, 24 U. S. 41.

[3] Statement of Earl Russell, quoted in J. B. Moore, *Principles of American Diplomacy,* ed. of 1918, 114–115.

[4] E. D. Adams, I, 212.

[5] Allan Nevins, *The War for the Union,* I, 388.

[6] *Cycle of Adams Letters,* I, 76, 81, 83.

Lyons was softened by the royal tact of the Prince Consort, then on the eve of death. Lincoln's deficiencies in the refinements of international law were more than offset by a common sense which caused his thoughts to turn to arbitration if diplomacy should fail; yet he was determined that governmental reason and tact should not fail. In a timely exchange of letters Sumner in America and Bright and Cobden in England made known the wish of reasonable men on both sides that a friendly settlement be reached. As the weeks passed, suggestions continued to be made that the matter might be adjusted without war. Seward and Adams made it clear that Wilkes had acted without authorization. The cabinet in England, having avoided an ultimatum, first demanded an apology, but was led to reconsider even that demand and accept in lieu of an apology (which might have implied that the American government was originally in the wrong) an assurance that Wilkes had acted without authority. Finally the matter was threshed out in a meeting of Lincoln's cabinet (December 25, 1861), in which Sumner read his friendly letters from Bright and Cobden. After long discussion "all yielded to the necessity [i.e., to the conviction that war with England must be avoided], and unanimously concur[r]ed in Mr. Sewards letter to L[or]d. Lyons. . . ." [7]

In this letter Seward closed the incident by a statement that the prisoners would be "cheerfully liberated," but not without irritating touches intended for home effect. After elaborately analyzing the pertinent questions of international law, he readily conceded the main point by declaring that Wilkes had erred in arresting the prisoners instead of sending the vessel into port for adjudication. This concession, however, was so phrased as to put England in the wrong as regarded her traditional contention for impressment and to call attention to America's high-minded rôle as a champion of freedom of the seas. Finally, in a saucy passage that his biographer has characterized as "sheer impudence," he needlessly stated that "if the safety of this Union required the detention of the captured persons it would be the right and duty of this government to detain them." [8]

So completely did the release of the envoys close the incident that by the end of January, when they arrived in England, there was "an almost complete disappearance" of public interest in them.[9] The sense of relief felt in the American legation in London best appears in the Adams letters. Late in December Henry Adams had feared that "our stay here is at an end." Then came the settlement and the minister wrote on January 10: "Captain Wilkes has not positively shipwrecked us. . . . The first effect of the surrender of Messrs. Mason and Slidell has been extraordinary. The current which ran against us with such extreme violence six weeks ago now seems to be going with equal fury in our favor." [10]

[7] Bates, *Diary*, 216.
[8] Bancroft, *Seward*, II, 241–242.
[9] E. D. Adams, I, 234.
[10] *Cycle of Adams Letters*, I, 93, 99.

3

Through all the diplomatic maneuvers there ran the central question of recognition of the Confederacy and the related questions of mediation, intervention, and the demand for an armistice. Had the South won on any of these points, victory would have been well-nigh assured. With Confederate commissioners clamorously pleading for recognition while Minister Adams was under instruction to break relations if this should happen, the British cabinet was confronted with a delicate situation. Recognition having been avoided in 1861 and the *Trent* affair having been satisfactorily adjusted, the prospects of "Lincoln, Seward and Co." in England in the early months of 1862 seemed distinctly brighter; but by the summer of that year it was evident that on this very question of recognition, which was then being seriously considered by the British cabinet, a crisis was approaching. By September of 1862 Palmerston and Russell's deliberations had reached the point where, in view of the failures of McClellan and Pope and the prospects of Lee's offensive, Palmerston suggested "an arrangement upon the basis of separation" (i.e., Southern victory); while Russell, the foreign minister, wrote in answer that in his opinion the time had come "for offering mediation . . . with a view to the recognition of the independence of the Confederates." He added that in case of the failure of mediation, England should on her own part recognize the South.[1] At this point Russell did in fact tentatively launch a mediation plan involving joint action by England, France, and Russia. Though there was little doubt of French support, Russian support could not be obtained; and just at this juncture there came a bombshell in the speech of the chancellor of the exchequer, W. E. Gladstone, at Newcastle (October 7) in which he said: "Jefferson Davis and other leaders of the South have made an army; they are making, it appears, a navy; and they have made what is more than either,—they have made a nation. . . . We may anticipate with certainty the success of the Southern States so far as regards their separation from the North."[2] Delivered offhand without approval by the ministry, this speech served to forecast a policy which had not matured; nevertheless it had the effect of stimulating Russell's efforts to bring British interposition in the American question to a head, for on October 13 the foreign minister sent a memorandum to the cabinet members proposing an armistice so that the weighty questions of peace could be calmly considered. E. D. Adams has stated that this mediation plan of Russell constituted "the most dangerous crisis in the war for the restoration of the Union."[3] For such a mediation plan to have developed to the point of an official program in Great Britain would probably have meant a severance of rela-

---

[1] E. D. Adams, II, 38.
[2] Quoted in C. F. Adams, *Charles Francis Adams*, 280.
[3] E. D. Adams, II, 73.

tions between Washington and London; had it been followed by intervention to stop the conflict, war with the United States would, according to all indications, have been the result.

At this critical point, however, various factors acted as a brake upon British policy. Lee's repulse at Antietam and Lincoln's emancipation proclamation (though its significance was discounted by the cabinet) were having their effects; Cornewall Lewis, a member of the cabinet, made a speech in answer to Gladstone in which he urged a continuance of strict neutrality; Cobden, Bright, and Forster backed him up; and Palmerston, having doubts of the unconquerableness of the Confederacy, held back, advising on October 22 that "we must continue . . . to be lookers-on till the war shall have taken a more decided turn." [4] A cabinet consideration of the question, set for October 23, was postponed; and by October 31 the tenseness between the United States and England had so far been relaxed that J. P. Benjamin referred to the conviction at Richmond "that there exists a feeling on the part of the British ministry unfriendly to this [the Confederate] Government." [5] On this date he advised Mason to address a formal protest to Earl Russell (on another matter) and hinted that the Confederacy was considering the propriety of expelling the British consuls. That the crisis of October passed was also due in large part to Charles Francis Adams, who, keeping in the background his instructions to depart if England recognized the Confederacy, made just enough reference to packing his carpetbag and trunks to make Russell cautious. In the matter of mediation Adams made it unmistakably clear that an affirmative answer from Washington was impossible.

4

In July, 1862, there steamed down the Mersey a powerful warship known as the *Enrica* or the "290." Not yet supplied with war equipment, the ship had left Liverpool supposedly on a "trial trip," but had headed for sea. Reaching an appointed rendezvous off the Azores this English-built vessel took on English-supplied arms, provisions, and coal, was boarded by Admiral Raphael Semmes, and, as the illustrious *Alabama,* launched upon her career as a Confederate cruiser specializing in commerce destruction.

The full story of the proceedings concerning this vessel and others like her offers one of the most serious chapters in Anglo-American diplomacy. England's neutrality law (the foreign enlistment act of 1819, modeled on the American neutrality law of 1818) [1] was designed to prevent or punish

[4] *Ibid.,* II, 54–55.
[5] *Offic. Rec.* (Nav.), 2 ser., III, 587.

[1] American influence upon the neutrality laws of England is generally recognized by the authorities. Not only was the English law of 1819 based on the American act of 1818, but in 1870, profiting by the difficulties arising over the *"Alabama* claims," England greatly strengthened her law. T. J. Lawrence, *Principles of International Law,* 4th ed., 595.

unneutral activities within English jurisdiction. The law forbade the fitting out, equipping, or arming of vessels for warlike operations in a war in which England was neutral; but it was interpreted by a type of legerdemain which in American parlance would be termed a "joker." According to this attenuated interpretation the law was not contravened if the equipping and arming of the vessel were accomplished as distinct operations separate from the building, even though the whole procedure were planned and accomplished as a connected program involving English aid throughout. The building of the *Alabama,* along with other warships, had been promoted by Captain Bulloch of the Confederate navy, who was in England for the purpose; and so transparent was the concealment that there had never been any real mystery about the ship, whose character as a Confederate cruiser had been unmistakable. Nor was the *Alabama* an isolated case. In March of 1862 the *Oreto* (*Florida*) had been allowed to depart from Liverpool, had disappeared for a time, and was later to turn up at Nassau and receive her equipment and arms from English sources.[2] Adams at London and Dudley, United States consul at Liverpool, had laid the evidence before the British ministry; but, on advice from the Queen's law officers that "sufficient proof" had not been presented, the government had neglected to seize or detain the ships. To legal evasion were added delay and circumlocution. While work went on swiftly on a project that threatened a break between England and the United States, and while Captain Bulloch was kept sufficiently in touch with developments to predict the attitude of the British government and choose his time for the flight of the *Alabama,* Russell meanwhile advising Adams with perfect truth that the matter had been referred to the "proper authorities," the papers in the case at the most critical stage of the proceedings lay in the home of one of the Queen's advocates whose nerves had so far given way as to incapacitate him for serious work. Adams persisted, however; and at length the proof became so irresistible that the law officers recommended the seizure of the vessel "without loss of time." On the basis of this advice Russell ordered the *Alabama* detained (July 31); but this order arrived too late to prevent departure of the ship, and under all the circumstances it was but natural that at the time the American authorities, with such vital interests at stake, should characterize the attitude of the British government as one of negligence, and even connivance.[3]

[2] "Registered as an English ship, in the name of Englishmen, commanded by an Englishman, . . . and . . . marked . . . under the direction of the board of trade, she [the *Manassas,* formerly the *Oreto,* later the *Florida*] seems . . . secure against capture . . . until an attempt be made to arm her or change the flag . . . at sea." Bulloch to Mallory, March 21, 1862, *Offic. Rec.* (Nav.), 1 ser., I, 754.

[3] Connivance was the American charge; but, as Rhodes has pointed out, "at least four cabinet ministers—the Duke of Argyll, Sir George Cornewall Lewis, Milner Gibson, and Earl Russell—regretted deeply the escape of the *Alabama.*" In later years Charles Francis Adams himself cleared Russell of the charge of ill-will to the United States, or unworthy motives of any sort. Rhodes, IV, 90–91.

Yet, viewing the question in the full light of historical evidence, it does not appear that the actual motives of the British ministry justified Northern resentment; indeed Confederate exultation was soon to give place to disappointment. By arrangements conducted by Bulloch two powerful ironclads had been contracted for with the Laird firm; and it was obvious that these ships would be ready for delivery in 1863. If these "Laird rams," intended to "raise the blockade . . . and thus secure for the Confederacy foreign recognition," had been allowed to depart, following upon the cases of the *Florida* and *Alabama,* then indeed a diplomatic break, not improbably followed by war, would have seemed inevitable. The seriousness of the matter appears in the advice of Assistant Secretary Fox of the Union navy to stop the rams "at all hazards," [4] in the fear that the rams could "lay under contribution any of the loyal cities on the coast or could break the blockade at any point," [5] and in Union anxiety concerning the destructiveness of the *Alabama,* then in full career. Fundamental in Seward's policy was the conviction that England dreaded a war with the United States; and in keeping with this divination of British motives he sent Adams the instruction (April 10, 1863) to inform Great Britain that the proceedings relative to the fitting out of ships for the Confederacy "complicate the relations between the two countries in such a manner as to render it difficult . . . to . . . preserve friendship between them. . . ." [6]

Another serious factor in the situation was the privateering bill passed by the United States Congress [7] which was designed to offset the rams by providing a "flood of privateers" which, operating widely on the seas, might aid the blockade by seizing blockade-runners.[8] If in so doing they committed indignities upon British ships, here was an ominous menace of war. In this situation much depended upon the temper and conduct of two men — Adams and Russell. The fact that both were reasonable men and that in the main they spoke the same language was a factor of the greatest significance. An important step was taken on April 5, 1863, when the British government ordered the seizure of the *Alexandra* (a raider intended for the Confederacy), an act which has been described by E. D. Adams as a "face-about on declared policy." [9] This seizure indicated a serious attempt

---

[4] C. F. Adams, *Charles Francis Adams,* 316, 321.

[5] Bancroft, *Seward,* II, 388.

[6] *House Exec. Doc. No. 1,* 38 Cong., 1 sess. (Papers relating to Foreign Affairs), pt. 1, 243–244.

[7] This measure became law on March 3, 1863. See p. 448.

[8] It should also be noted that an attempt was made to buy the rams for the United States navy, in which case the government at Washington (probably on the theory that, if neutral violations were to continue, the United States might as well profit from them) would have been a party to the very type of proceedings against which the Lincoln administration was earnestly contending. Nothing, however, came of the attempt. C. F. Adams, *Charles Francis Adams,* 320–321.

[9] The *Alexandra* was seized on the ground that it was "apparently intended"

by the British government to make effective its neutrality. As to the Laird rams, however, it still seemed possible that they might escape on the pretext that they were intended for France or for the government of Egypt; and it was not until five months after the *Alexandra* seizure that the matter was disposed of. Within these months the Union victories of Gettysburg and Vicksburg occurred; the Roebuck parliamentary motion for a recognition of the South came to naught; and, through it all, Adams kept presenting affidavits of the true intent of the rams, at the same time emphasizing the serious nature of the controversy as it affected Anglo-American relations. The matter was finally settled to the complete satisfaction of the United States government when, on September 9, the rams were placed under surveillance, to be seized in October and purchased by the British government.

To those who prefer to think in terms of heroics this compliance by the British government has been attributed to a famous letter of Adams to Russell under date of September 5, 1863. The letter was written on the eve of the expected departure of the rams, at a time when Adams had just been informed by Russell (September 1) that the government could not detain the ships on existing information, but would be ready to stop them if trustworthy evidence should show any proceeding contrary to statute. The crisp phrase which made this letter of Adams memorable was the statement: "It would be superfluous in me to point out to your lordship that this is war." [10] As a check upon the traditional heroics, however, it may be noted that if Earl Russell had been in London at the time the matter could have been easily settled by interview with Adams, that the affair was complicated by the writing of notes which crossed each other, and that in reality Russell and Adams were thinking alike. E. D. Adams has pointed out that Russell had moved in the direction of detaining the rams before receiving Adams's note of the 5th; that the foreign secretary had in fact arrived at his new policy in its essential aspects five months earlier in the *Alexandra* affair; and that Adams was under a misapprehension in supposing that this April policy had been abandoned. Stressing the friendliness of Seward (despite his official instructions), the same writer throws out a caution against the account traditionally given by American historians by the use of American sources, and states that the "correct understanding . . . is the recognition that Great Britain had in April given a pledge and performed an act which satisfied Seward and Adams that the Rams would not be permitted to escape." Later apprehension arose from a fear that the pledge might not be carried out; but this was due to lack of

---

for the Confederacy, whereas the *Alabama* and *Florida* had been allowed to escape for lack of "conclusive" evidence that they had been so intended. E. D. Adams, II, 136–137.

[10] *House Exec. Doc. No. 1,* 38 Cong., 1 sess. (Papers relating to Foreign Affairs), pt. 1, p. 418.

full knowledge as to the steps taken by Russell for the detention of the ships.[11]

Though the international outlook of the North and South was mainly concerned with England and France, the attitude of Russia was of considerable significance. Baron de Stoeckl, Russian minister in Washington, had contempt for what he considered the demagogy of American politicians, but a long-standing friendship had existed between Russia and the United States; and Prince Gortchakov, Russian foreign minister, was outspoken in his expressions of good will. The sending of Russian warships to American waters, though motivated by European considerations, had the effect of emphasizing this friendship. Several ships under Rear Admiral Lisovskii arrived at New York in September, 1863; in the following month a squadron under Rear Admiral Popov put into San Francisco harbor. Both squadrons were ordered home in April, 1864.

The European situation leading to these naval visits was bound up with the perennial Polish question, which (because of factors that cannot be detailed here) occasioned a joint remonstrance against Russia (April, 1863) by England, France, and Austria. Anticipating the possibility of war, Russian statesmen considered it unwise to have their ships in home waters where they might be trapped by the British navy. A visit to some friendly neutral country was indicated; and American ports, in addition to other advantages, offered a point of departure for operations against enemy commerce in case war should break out, as well as for possible attacks upon enemy colonies. In addition it was hoped that such a placing of Russian ships would exercise a restraining influence upon war tendencies in England.

To speak of the American Civil War as the occasion of the sending of the Russian ships would be incorrect, and even at the time there were some Americans who suspected that more selfish motives were behind the Russian move. Yet, as Thomas A. Bailey has proved, "a majority of interested citizens at the time—and certainly an overwhelming majority later—appear to have accepted the visit of the fleets as primarily a gesture of friendship, with the strong possibility of an alliance and open assistance against common enemies." [12] Americans made much of the Russian visitors; Welles extended the courtesies of the Brooklyn navy yard to Lisovskii; and Popov's assistance in extinguishing a fire at San Francisco ingratiated him with the people of that city. Indeed, since Popov was ready if necessary to act against Confederate cruisers, "Russia came very near becoming our active ally." [13]

Thus midway in the war the stakes of diplomacy had been won by the United States. The full effect, however, of Southern international failure

[11] E. D. Adams, II, 141–147.

[12] Bailey, "The Russian Fleet Myth Re-Examined," *M. V. H. R.*, XXXVIII, 90 (June, 1951).

[13] F. A. Golder, "The Russian Fleet and the Civil War," *Am. Hist. Rev.*, XX, 809 (July, 1915).

was not yet evident, and future events in the foreign sphere would depend upon a combination of factors. While diplomatic maneuvers and the personal conduct of diplomats were never unimportant, the outcome abroad continually reflected events at home. Step by step the influence of Lincoln's emancipation policy and of Northern military advances was manifest abroad. Further aspects of the long struggle must therefore be examined before resuming the diplomatic story.

CHAPTER 21

Slavery and the War

I

THE INSTITUTION of slavery, closely associated with the causation of the war, became the subject of swift-changing policy on many fronts while the struggle progressed. To one who approaches the problem with the view that the North fought the war to suppress slavery in the South, the disclaimers of such a purpose by the Washington government may seem surprising. Lincoln made such a disclaimer in his inaugural of 1861, putting this topic first in his address. Referring to Southern apprehension on this point he said: "There has never been any reasonable cause for such apprehension. Indeed, the most ample evidence to the contrary has all the while existed. . . . It is found in nearly all the published speeches of him who now addresses you. I do but quote from one of those speeches when I declare that 'I have no purpose, directly or indirectly, to interfere with the institution of slavery in the States where it exists.' " In announcing this policy of hands off as to slavery in the states, Lincoln was acting in harmony with the program of his party, for the Republican platform of 1860 declared that "the maintenance inviolate of the rights of the States, and especially the right of each State to . . . control its own domestic institutions . . . exclusively, is essential to that balance of power on which the perfection and endurance of our political fabric depend. . . ." As noted in a previous chapter, Congress uttered a similar disclaimer in the Crittenden resolution (July 22, 1861), in which it was announced that the war was not being prosecuted with the intention of overthrowing the "established institutions" of the states.

Back of these disclaimers was the fundamental concept, prevalent North and South in 1861, that the sphere of Federal authority was marked by the Constitution and usage, that "domestic institutions" belonged exclusively to the states, and that slavery was such an institution. An analogous case at the present day would be the question of marriage and divorce. Nor was it the intention of the Republican party to change existing arrangements and make slavery a matter of national legislation, except to limit the extension of slavery in national territory; but even here the judicial doctrine of the Dred Scott case stood in the way.[1]

With such declarations and disclaimers the war began. It was not long, however, before the fact of war over an extended front with a slaveholding region inevitably forced upon the Union government certain practical problems touching slavery and the colored people. One of these was the problem of fugitive slaves finding their way within Union lines. Confronted with this question in Virginia, General B. F. Butler, commanding at Fort Monroe, refused (May 24, 1861) to give up three such Negro slaves, declaring that he needed workmen, that the slaves were being employed in the erection of enemy batteries, and that the fugitive slave act of the United States did not affect a foreign country, which Virginia claimed to be.[2]

The manner in which the events of war threatened to wrest the slavery problem from Lincoln's hand was illustrated by the action of General Frémont, who published on August 30, 1861, a remarkable proclamation instituting martial law throughout the state of Missouri and proclaiming as to all persons resisting the United States that their property was confiscated and their "slaves . . . declared freemen." Lincoln's secretaries treat this action as a clumsy bid for popular favor at a time when the general's prestige was waning. On the other hand it has been urged that the occasion for the proclamation was a local military situation arising especially from a most alarming and crippling guerilla warfare within Union lines. Whatever may have been Frémont's motives, however, he had exceeded his military authority in dealing with far-reaching matters of policy belonging to the general government at Washington. Lincoln promptly ordered him to show leniency as to martial law, allowing no man to be shot without the President's consent, and to modify the confiscatory and emancipating order so as to conform to existing law.

The Frémont episode had wide repercussions. Lincoln himself stated that the "Kentucky Legislature would not budge till that proclamation was modified," and that "on the news of General Fremont having actually issued deeds of manumission, a whole company of our Volunteers threw down their arms and disbanded."[3] Lincoln's overruling of the proclamation was not intended as a rebuke to Frémont, much less as an occasion for his dismissal; but the President was embarrassed by the general's defiance, together with complaints of military incompetence, and on November 2,

[1] In abolishing slavery in the territories (see p. 372), Congress passed and Lincoln signed an unconstitutional law, according to Supreme Court doctrine.

[2] The term "contraband," applying to slaves captured by Union military forces and as a slang word to Negroes generally, has been traced to Butler's action on this occasion. Nicolay and Hay disputed Butler's authorship, but Butler declared that " 'contraband' was the ground upon which I refused to release" the slaves. In the correspondence at the time, however, the word "contraband" did not occur. B. F. Butler, *Butler's Book*, ch. vi; Nicolay and Hay, *Lincoln*, IV, 387–389.

[3] Lincoln, *Collected Works*, IV, 532.

1861, he was removed from command at St. Louis. Lincoln's policy of not permitting military commanders to force his hand in the matter of emancipation was again illustrated in May, 1862, when he overruled an order of General Hunter freeing "persons in . . . Georgia, Florida, and South Carolina—heretofore held as slaves. . . ." Problems of military emancipation, said the President, "are questions which, under my responsibility, I reserve to myself. . . ." [4]

2

While the President was thus embarrassed by the exigent nature of the slavery question, Congress was nibbling and whacking at the problem in its own way. In the confiscation act of August 6, 1861, it was provided that, when slaves were engaged in hostile military service, all owners' claims to the labor of such slaves were forfeited. The law was vague as to the manner of forfeiture; yet it marked a stage in the early development of legislative policy touching emancipation. The second confiscation act of July 17, 1862, went further. It provided that, if anyone committed treason, his slaves were free; as to all persons supporting the "rebellion" it proclaimed that their slaves should be "forever free of their servitude, and not again held as slaves." In addition, slave-soldiers of enemy ownership, together with their families, were freed by the militia act of July 17, 1862; and later in the war freedom was also extended to slave-soldiers of "loyal owners," with bounties to the owners.[1] By act of March 13, 1862, Congress took to itself the vexed military question of fugitive slaves finding their way within Union lines, prohibiting the use of the military power for their return. A further step was taken on July 17, 1862, when the delivery of escaping slaves, unless to a loyal owner, was prohibited and slaves of "rebel" owners coming within Union lines were declared free.[2]

Still other emancipatory measures were passed by Congress. Slavery in the District of Columbia was abolished, with compensation to the owners, on April 16, 1862; and emancipation in the territories, without compensation, was provided by act of June 19 of the same year. Steps had also been taken in the international sphere: on May 20, 1862, there occurred in London the exchange of ratifications which made effective a treaty nego-

[4] *Ibid.*, V, 222.

[1] In the confiscation act of 1862 no procedure was specified by which emancipation was to be effected, the confiscating sections of the act (providing for the "sale" of "property") being obviously inapplicable to slaves who were to be freed. The emancipatory clause of the act was a bit of imperfect and ill-studied legislation which was not enforced. Randall, *Constitutional Problems Under Lincoln*, 357–364.

[2] The continued existence of slavery within the framework of the United States government was illustrated by the fact that the fugitive slave acts of 1793 and 1850 remained on the statute-books until June 28, 1864, when they were repealed by Congress. *U. S. Stat. at Large*, XIII, 200.

tiated by the Lincoln administration with England for the suppression of the slave trade. "Disguise it as we may," declared the New York *Times,* "we cannot escape the charge, before the civilized world, of having been, to a great extent, one prime cause of the immunity offered, for many years past, to this accursed traffic. . . . Henceforth the Government of the United States washes its hands completely of all complicity in the Slave-trade. . . ." [3] On February 21, 1862, there had occurred in New York the execution of Captain Nathaniel P. Gordon, who had commanded a slave ship. Since 1820 the importation of slaves into the United States had been punishable by death; [4] but lax enforcement had made the law seem a dead letter. Apropos of the Gordon case the New York *Times* commented on the previous failure to prosecute slave-traders, setting off the sternness of Lincoln by contrast. According to the *Times,* the public had thought, "They dare not hang him." [5]

The issuance of the emancipation proclamation by the President, and the manner in which it seized the popular imagination, caused these emancipatory acts of Congress to be almost overlooked; and it is seldom realized that before Lincoln's proclamation was issued in September, 1862, Congress had done as much, at least on paper, as was done by the proclamation. Indeed, when one considers the limitations in the proclamation, it will be seen that that edict fell short of the emancipating clause in the confiscation act of July 17, 1862, [6] which declared that "all slaves of persons who shall hereafter be engaged in rebellion against the Government of the United States, or who shall in any way give aid . . . thereto, . . . being within any place occupied by rebel forces and afterwards occupied by the forces of the United States . . . shall be forever free. . . ." Such, however, was the ineffectiveness of this legislation, and such the lack of coordination between President and Congress, that Lincoln in issuing his edict acted as if Congress had done nothing, and as if he were attacking the problem anew.

3

As the war progressed Lincoln pondered the slavery question in its bearing on the war and in its legal and ethical implications; and out of this pondering there evolved a plan of constructive statesmanship. It must be remembered that the emancipation proclamation did not embody Lincoln's main policy toward slavery: his fundamental and permanent solution was

[3] N. Y. *Times,* May 2, 1862, p. 4, c. 4. For the treaty, see W. M. Malloy, *U. S. Treaties* [etc.], I, 674.

[4] See above, p. 55.

[5] New York *Times,* Feb. 22, 1862, p. 4, c. 3.

[6] The peculiar legal reasoning of the Union authorities was that all who resided in "rebel" territory were "rebels." (*House Report No.* 262, 43 Cong., 1 sess., 6 ff.; and see above, chap. 15, sec. 3.) The confiscation act of 1862 declared slaves of rebels to be free. It was not qualified by the hundred-day warning nor the extensive territorial exceptions of the emancipation proclamation.

rather in terms of "compensated emancipation," a very different matter. Richard N. Current has concisely summarized the five elements in Lincoln's own solution to the slavery problem:

First, the states themselves must emancipate the slaves, for in his opinion slavery was a "domestic" institution, the concern of the states alone. Second, slaveowners must be paid for the chattels of which they were to be deprived. Third, the Federal government must share the financial burden by providing Federal bonds as grants-in-aid to the states. Fourth, the actual freeing of the slaves must not be hurried; the states must be given plenty of time, delaying final freedom as late as 1900 if they wished. Fifth, the freed Negroes must be shipped out of the country and colonized abroad, but they must be persuaded to go willingly.[1] Federal aid, gradual emancipation, and voluntary colonization—these were the indispensable features of the Lincoln plan.[2]

In an effort to put his plan to a trial Lincoln drafted an act to be passed by the Delaware legislature, freeing the slaves of that state with Federal compensation at the rate of $400 per slave; but opposition in Delaware proved too strong for its passage.[3] He then called a conference of the congressmen from the Union slave states of Maryland, Delaware, "Virginia," [4] Kentucky, and Missouri. He pleaded with these men of the border to give honest consideration to a measure which, to his mind, had large possibilities for the shortening of the war and the decent burial of a dying institution. At about the same time [5] he answered one of the chief objections to his scheme, i.e., the huge expense involved. He showed that compensation at the rate of $400 each for all the slaves of Delaware ($719,-200) was insignificant in comparison with one day's cost of the war, which amounted to $2,000,000, while eighty-seven days' cost of the war ($174,-

---

[1] Space is here wanting to discuss Lincoln's continuing interest in colonization of ex-slaves. In August, 1862, he told a deputation of free Negroes: "You and we are different races. . . . your race suffer very greatly . . . by living among us, while ours suffer from your presence. . . . [O]n this broad continent, not a single man of your race is made the equal of a single man of ours. . . . It is better for us both, therefore, to be separated." Lincoln, *Collected Works*, V, 371–372. Lincoln was greatly interested in the unsuccessful project of a free Negro colony at Chiriquí, in Central America, and in the disastrous attempt of some four hundred Negroes to settle at Isle à Vache, in Haiti.

[2] Current, *The Lincoln Nobody Knows*, 221–222.

[3] In the heated partisanship of the time it was made to appear that proponents of the emancipation measure had plotted "to 'put one over' on the people of Delaware, ..." H. Clay Reed, "Lincoln's Compensated Emancipation Plan and Its Relation to Delaware," *Delaware Notes*, seventh series (Univ. of Del., 1931), 44.

[4] The separate-state movement in Virginia had not yet been completed, and slavery had not yet been abolished in that portion which became West Virginia. As to "restored Virginia" (to be distinguished from West Virginia), see pp. 236–242, 555.

[5] Lincoln, *Collected Works*, V, 160.

ooo,ooo) would more than provide compensation at $400 each for all the slaves of Delaware, Maryland, the District of Columbia, Kentucky, and Missouri. He urged that Southern leaders expected, having established their independence, to add the other slave states to their Confederacy, but that, once a scheme was initiated [6] looking toward abolition in these states, this hope would disappear. "To deprive them of this hope," he declared, "substantially ends the rebellion. . . ."

The result of the border-state conference, however, was disappointing. As Lincoln's secretaries expressed it, the tone of the Union slave-state members was "one of doubt, of qualified protest, and of apprehensive inquiry." [7] Lincoln did indeed induce Congress to pass a resolution (April 10, 1862) approving his plan in principle, and he was gratified to see definite action taken in the adoption of compensated emancipation in the District of Columbia as above noted; but his scheme of state emancipation with Federal compensation failed. In the joint resolution of April 10, 1862, the wording was that "the United States ought to cooperate with any State which may adopt gradual abolishment of slavery, giving to such State pecuniary aid. . . ." That this pledge was never fulfilled by a grant of money to any state was due chiefly to three causes: a swift change of events which soon gave a new aspect to the slavery issue; the tenacity of some of the border states in conserving slavery; and the parliamentary accident by which affirmative action in both houses of Congress giving financial aid to Missouri became ineffective because the House and Senate, in the short session ending March, 1863, passed their bills in different forms and did not have time to put the same bill through both houses. In the House bill Federal bonds for $10,000,000 were provided as compensation for Missouri, while the Senate bill called for bonds up to $20,000,000 on the condition that emancipation be completed by July 4, 1865.[8]

The bitterness of the President's disappointment in this failure was but the measure of his earnestness in promoting a program which was peculiarly his own and in which he saw an equitable and permanent solution of the slavery issue. Expressing this intensity of feeling the President spoke as follows in a further appeal to the border states:

I intend no reproach . . . when I assure you that in my opinion, if you all had voted for the resolution in the gradual emancipation message of last March, the war would now be substantially ended. . . . You and I know what the level of their power is. Break that lever . . . and they can shake you no more . . . . [F]or the sake of the whole country I ask "Can you, for your states, do better than to take the course I urge?["] . . . The incidents of the war can not be avoided. If the war continues long, . . . the institution in your

6 "I say 'initiation' because, in my judgment, gradual, and not sudden emancipation, is better for all." *Ibid.*, V, 145.

7 Nicolay and Hay, *Lincoln*, V, 213.

8 Randall, *Constitutional Problems Under Lincoln*, 366; *Cong. Globe*, 37 Cong., 3 sess., 209; *Senate Journal*, Feb. 12, 1863, 243.

states will be extinguished by mere friction and abrasion. . . . It will be gone, and you will have nothing valuable in lieu of it. Much of it's [*sic*] value is gone already. . . .

. . . . .

You are patriots and statesmen; and, as such, I pray you, consider this proposition; and, at the least, commend it to the consideration of your states and people. As you would perpetuate popular government for the best people in the world, I beseech you that you do in no wise omit this. Our common country is in great peril, demanding the loftiest views, and boldest action to bring it speedy relief. . . .[9]

4

Lincoln was later to return to this compensation scheme, but meanwhile those influences which produced the emancipation proclamation claimed his attention. Beset as he was by the clamorings of abolitionists, he was never permitted to forget the slavery issue; but until the summer of 1862 his prevailing attitude was that of caution in avoiding offense to the border states and unwillingness to allow extremists to force his hand. Sometimes he took the ground that power to overthrow slavery did not lie within his grasp. Replying to a religious delegation from Chicago he said: "What *good* would a proclamation of emancipation from me do . . . as we are now situated? I do not want to issue a document that the whole world will see must necessarily be inoperative, like the Pope's bull against the comet." [1] Or again he took the ground that slavery was incidental, while the cause of the Union was primary and vital. When Horace Greeley, in his "Prayer of Twenty Millions," reproached the President for not boldly striking at slavery,[2] Lincoln, overlooking "assumptions of fact which [he knew] to be erroneous," gave out a public statement of his policy as to the Union and slavery. "My paramount object," he said, "*is* to save the Union, and is *not* either to save or to destroy slavery. . . . What I do about slavery, and the colored race, I do because I believe it helps to save the Union; and what I forbear, I forbear because I do *not* believe it would help to save the Union." Having struck this note of expediency as to his emancipation policy, the

[9] Lincoln, *Collected Works*, V, 317–319.

[1] *Ibid.*, V, 420.

[2] ". . . Mr. President, there is not one . . . intelligent champion of the Union cause who does not feel that all attempts to put down the Rebellion and at the same time uphold its inciting cause are preposterous and futile. . . . [A]n immense majority of the Loyal Millions of your countrymen require of you . . . a frank . . . execution of the laws of the land, more especially of the Confiscation Act. . . . The Rebels are . . . using the late anti-negro riots in the North . . . to convince the slaves that they have nothing to hope from a Union success—that we mean . . . to sell them into . . . bondage to defray the cost of the war. . . . We must have scouts, . . . teamsters, diggers and choppers from the Blacks of the South . . . or we shall be baffled and repelled." Horace Greeley in N. Y. *Tribune*, Aug. 20, 1862.

President closed with a repetition of his *"personal* wish that all men every where could be free." [3]

Yet, at the time of this Greeley letter, and also of the bull-against-the-comet declaration, Lincoln had in fact made up his mind to issue the proclamation of military emancipation.[4] According to the statement of Gideon Welles, he informed both Welles and Seward on July 13, 1862, that he "had about come to the conclusion" that a proclamation of emancipation was "absolutely essential for the salvation of the Union"; [5] and Secretary Chase records that at the cabinet meeting of July 22, 1862, the President announced his intention to issue an order "proclaiming the emancipation of all slaves within States remaining in insurrection on the first of January, 1863." [6] By this time the increasing radicalism of the war mind, the presence of thousands of slaves attending the armies in the field, and the growing recognition of foreign antislavery sentiment in its bearing upon the war had produced their effect in overcoming the President's conservatism and caution.

Lincoln could not fail to recognize that the international aspects of slavery policy were of pressing importance. Motley wrote emphatically to Seward that European dependence upon slave-produced cotton had no weight against the overwhelming sentiment for abolition.[7] Cyrus Pitt Grosvenor, who was in England to awaken interest in the colored people of America, wrote as follows to Secretary Chase: "The government cannot succeed in the attempt to put down rebellion with the left hand while supporting slavery with the right hand as it is now doing." Commenting on the general attitude of good feeling toward America which he observed in England, he added that Northern prejudice against the Negro race was the only thing that lessened the ardor of this friendship, and described a meeting attended by the "élite of London society" in which black men spoke on the same platform with distinguished gentlemen and were heard with respect.[8]

---

[3] Lincoln, *Collected Works,* V, 388–389.

[4] Why the President should have publicly argued and defended a policy of noninterference with slavery after he had abandoned this policy may seem hard to explain. Richard N. Current (*The Lincoln Nobody Knows,* 225–226) argues that, until after the battle of Antietam, Lincoln had "made no irrevocable commitment, even to himself. Here and there he dropped hints that he might issue the proclamation—and then again might not. Apparently his purpose was to prepare his hearers for the possibility that he might call the whole thing off. He was waiting for a decisive victory, but if that kind of victory had come, he might have forgotten about the proclamation. . . . If McClellan had administered a crushing defeat, the proclamation might have stayed in its pigeonhole."

[5] Welles, *Diary,* I, 70.

[6] Donald, ed., *Inside Lincoln's Cabinet,* 99.

[7] Bancroft, *Seward,* II, 336.

[8] C. P. Grosvenor to S. P. Chase, July 28, 1862. Chase Papers (MSS., Libr. of Cong.).

Thus by the close of summer in 1862 governmental policy at the North had advanced noticeably toward vigorous remedies in the matter of slavery. Congress had altered its policy of noninterference. War had wrought its inevitable change. Measures of emancipation were being placed upon the national statute-books. Internationally the United States had sharply reversed its traditional rôle of conservator of slavery. At home the denationalization of slavery, formulated in Wilmot's fateful proviso, expounded by Lincoln, and demanded by the Republicans, had been written into law by the hand of war. That aspect of the slavery issue which had received such strident emphasis on both sides during the years of increasing sectional tension had reached its violent conclusion. The settlement of this matter, however, was of less importance than the manifest congressional purpose to strike, though at first by ineffective statutes, against slavery in the states. Meanwhile the inappropriateness of the war situation as a setting for conservative, statesmanlike legislation such as that projected by Lincoln in his emancipation scheme had become clear. Equitable adjustment of property rights might loom large in Lincoln's mind; moderate influences might appear in state papers issuing from the White House. Nonetheless the clumsy directness of wartime action would brush aside moderate sensibilities. On the border a middle course might be emotionally desirable and might constitute a popular demand; but the failure of Lincoln's emancipation scheme had demonstrated the inability of border sentiment to express itself in practical statesmanship. In emancipation as in other quarters radicalism was to find its war-born opportunity.

CHAPTER 22

Lincoln and Emancipation

I

LINCOLN HAD LAID aside his proclamation waiting for a victory.[1] He waited two months, meanwhile giving out public statements based on his previous noncommittal attitude: then on September 22, after Lee's invasion had been foiled at Antietam, he issued the preliminary proclamation. That this proclamation was far from an abolition document is shown by a careful reading of its provisions. The President began by reiterating that the purpose of the war was the restoration of the Union and reaffirming his intention still to labor for compensated emancipation. This was certainly a far cry from the Garrisonian program. He then declared that on January 1, 1863, slaves in rebellious states or parts of states should be "then, thenceforward, and forever free"; and he added, perhaps indiscreetly, that "the executive government of the United States . . . will do no act . . . to repress such persons . . . in any efforts they may make for their actual freedom."

This clause was open to misinterpretation as an incitement to servile insurrection, and it was almost universally so interpreted in the South. The authors, however, have not found a shred of evidence that Lincoln actually sought to encourage social war or Negro uprisings among the Southern people; indeed in one of his public papers he referred to the massacre of noncombatants as among the "barbarous" methods that are excluded in time of war.[2] The only method by which he meant for Negroes to fight for their freedom was as soldiers within the Union army acting within the rules of war. As to supporting their efforts toward actual freedom, he had in mind that a "promise, being made, must be kept," not in terms of encouraging servile war, but of guaranteeing freedom to Negro soldiers

[1] According to a fairly reliable report Lincoln was persuaded by Seward to withhold the proclamation so that it could be issued on the morrow of victory and thus not appear as "our last *shriek* on the retreat." Statement of Lincoln to the artist F. B. Carpenter, Feb. 6, 1864. John G. Nicolay and John Hay, eds., *Abraham Lincoln: Complete Works*, II, 479.

[2] Lincoln, *Collected Works*, VI, 408.

generally and to slaves finding their way into Union lines. To place the matter beyond doubt, he declared as follows in his final proclamation of January 1, 1863: "And I hereby enjoin upon the people . . . declared . . . free to abstain from all violence, unless in necessary self-defence. . . ."

The proclamation was not expressive of any general antislavery policy. Nowhere did it signify personal vindictiveness toward slaveholders: rather the President was still clinging to his compensated-emancipation scheme as the permanent solution; the reimbursement of Southern owners for the loss of their slaves was still part of his active policy. That the proclamation marked a departure in Lincoln's program toward slavery as announced at the outset of his administration is not to be interpreted as a breach of faith. It is the nature of wars to produce unforeseen measures. Lincoln's promise in his inaugural of 1861 that he would not touch slavery in the states was not a prediction of governmental policy in the event of civil war, but rather a pledge based on the assumption that the slave states should remain in the Union. No state remaining normally in the Union was affected by his proclamation when issued. That Lincoln, even in war, gave honest trial to his noninterference policy is shown by the following statement which he made in 1863: "There was more than a year and a half of trial to suppress the rebellion before the proclamation [was] issued. . . ." [3]

On January 1, 1863, the definitive proclamation was issued, its chief provision being that in regions then designated as "in rebellion" (with certain notable exceptions) all slaves were declared free. So famous has this proclamation become, and so encrusted with tradition, that a correct historical conception of its actual effect is rarely found in the voluminous literature which the subject has evoked. The stereotyped picture of the emancipator suddenly striking the shackles from millions of slaves by a stroke of the presidential pen is altogether inaccurate. On this point one should carefully note the exceptions in the proclamation itself. The whole state of Tennessee was omitted; none of the Union slave states was included; and there were important exceptions as to portions of Virginia and Louisiana, those being the portions within Union military lines. In fact freedom was decreed only in regions then under Confederate control. "The President has purposely made the proclamation inoperative [declared the N. Y. *World*] in all places where we have gained a military footing which makes the slaves accessible. He has proclaimed emancipation only where he has notoriously no power to execute it. The exemption of the accessible parts of Louisiana, Tennessee, and Virginia renders the proclamation not merely futile, but ridiculous." [4] As to the effect of the proclamation the *World* declared:

[3] *Ibid.*, VI, 408.
[4] Editorial, N. Y. *World*, Jan. 7, 1863.

Immediate practical effect it has none; the slaves remaining in precisely the same condition as before. They still live on the plantations, tenant their accustomed hovels, obey the command of their master . . . , eating the food he furnishes and doing the work he requires precisely as though Mr. Lincoln had not declared them free. . . . [The state courts] do not recognize the validity of the decree on which he [the slave] rests his claim. So long . . . as the present . . . status continues, the freedom declared by this proclamation is a dormant, not an actual, freedom.

. . . . .

The proclamation is issued as a war measure, as an instrument for the subjugation of the rebels. But that cannot be a *means* of military success which presupposes this same . . . success as the condition of its own existence. . . . A war measure it clearly is not, inasmuch as the previous success of the war is the thing that can give it validity.[5]

"We show our sympathy with slavery," Seward is reported to have said, "by emancipating slaves where we cannot reach them and holding them in bondage where we can set them free." [6] The London *Spectator* declared (October 11, 1862): "The government liberates the enemy's slaves as it would the enemy's cattle, simply to weaken them in the . . . conflict. . . . The principle is not that a human being cannot justly own another, but that he cannot own him unless he is loyal to the United States." On the same date the *Saturday Review,* in a caustic article, denounced the proclamation as a crime, and declared that Lincoln's "desperate efforts to procure military support will probably precipitate the ruin of his cause." [7] Earl Russell in England declared: "The Proclamation . . . appears to be of a very strange nature. It professes to emancipate all slaves in places where the United States authorities cannot exercise any jurisdiction . . . but it does not decree emancipation . . . in any States, or parts of States, occupied by federal troops . . . and where, therefore, emancipation . . . might have been carried into effect. . . . There seems to be no declaration of a principle adverse to slavery in this proclamation." [8]
It will be noted that Lincoln justified his act as a measure of war. To uphold his view would be to maintain that the freeing of enemy slaves was a legitimate weapon of war to be wielded by the President, and that a proclamation for the purpose would be somewhat analogous to a presidential proclamation blockading an enemy's coast, the legal principle being that a state of war puts the whole enginery of belligerent measures within the control of the President. In the new attitude toward slavery which the

[5] *Ibid.,* Jan. 3, 1863.
[6] Donn Piatt, *Memories of Men Who Saved the Union,* 150 (cited in Horace White, *Life of Lyman Trumbull,* 222).
[7] Bancroft, *Seward,* II, 339–340.
[8] Russell to Lyons, Jan. 17, 1863, Henry Wheaton, *Elements of International Law,* ed. by W. B. Lawrence (1863), suppl., 37.

war produced it was natural to find considerable support for the view that slavery was a legitimate target of the war power; but it is a matter of plain history that prior to the Civil War the United States had emphatically denied the "belligerent right" of emancipation. Indeed John Quincy Adams, who has been credited by his grandson with having originated the idea of the emancipation proclamation,[9] declared officially while secretary of state in 1820 that "No such right [emancipation of slaves] is acknowledged as a Law of War by writers who admit *any* limitation." [10]

A close study of the contemporary situation gives added point to Lincoln's concept of his proclamation as a war measure. That he really favored emancipation by state action with Federal compensation to owners has already been shown. The proclamation was by no means a touchstone for his whole abolition policy. In the period prior to the proclamation he had been "emphatic in denouncing any interference by the General Government with the subject." [11] The cabinet agreed with him in considering slavery a local, domestic question; and the adoption of the proclamation in contrast to these conceptions of public policy could only be thought of in terms of an emergency or extraordinary measure. He issued the proclamation "by virtue of the power in me vested as Commander-in-Chief of the Army and Navy . . . and as a fit and necessary war measure." He characterized it as an act "warranted by the Constitution *upon military necessity*." [12] This interpretation took the proclamation out of the pattern of normal constitutional procedure and gave it a certain irregularity for which the justification was to be found in the existing state of war, and more especially in Lincoln's interpretation of measures appropriate for such a state of war. It is pertinent therefore to remember that Lincoln's view of his war powers gave wide latitude to the President's choice of means for destroying enemy resistance. Interpreting his powers as wartime leader he once said: "I think the constitution invests its commander-in-chief, with the law of war, in time of war. . . . Armies, the world over, destroy ene-

---

[9] Speaking in the House of Representatives in 1842 John Quincy Adams asserted that an army commander had the right to emancipate slaves in invaded territory. He was no longer the official spokesman of a great slaveholding nation in its foreign policy and was speaking as congressman from Massachusetts. He seems to have had in mind a possible situation in which people of the free states would be called upon to aid in suppressing slave insurrection in the South, in which case he held military emancipation to be justified. Though this was a situation which differed materially from that of the Civil War, Charles Francis Adams, his grandson, advanced the contention that John Quincy Adams originated the principle back of Lincoln's famous proclamation. C. F. Adams, "John Quincy Adams and Martial Law," *Mass. Hist. Soc. Proceedings,* second series, XV, 436–478; Randall, *Constitutional Problems Under Lincoln,* 343–347, 374–376.

[10] U. S. Ministers' Instructions (MSS., Dept. of State), IX, 57.

[11] Welles, *Diary,* I, 71.

[12] The words in italic were inserted by Lincoln in a passage suggested by Chase. Rhodes, *Hist. of the U. S.,* IV, 213 n.

mies' property when they cannot use it; and even destroy their own to keep it from the enemy. Civilized belligerents do all in their power to help themselves, or hurt the enemy, except a few things regarded as barbarous or cruel." To Lincoln's mind the war emergency justified things normally unconstitutional. "I felt that measures, otherwise unconstitutional," he said, "might become lawful, by becoming indispensable to the preservation of the constitution, through the preservation of the nation." [13]

This placing of the proclamation strictly on the basis of military necessity had embarrassing aspects. It seemed a confession that the proclamation lacked law-worthiness. It served to discountenance any extension of the area of the proclamation later in the war; for if military necessity did not require the inclusion of Tennessee and of certain portions of Virginia and Louisiana at the beginning of 1863, there was even less necessity of including them later. Yet as the struggle progressed and abolition came to be regarded as a major war aim, this extension of military emancipation was precisely what the antislavery element demanded. Furthermore, the appeal to military necessity as the legal justification of the proclamation caused Lincoln's act to smack of irresponsible dictatorial power, and this aspect of the matter gave him no little concern. All these embarrassing features of the edict in its legal aspects were noted by Lincoln in a draft of a letter to Chase which appears among his published writings under date of September 2, 1863. Referring to the difficulties in the way of extending the area of the proclamation, he said:

. . . The original proclamation has no . . . legal justification, except as a military measure. . . . If I take the step must I not do so, without the argument of military necessity, and so, without any argument, except . . . that I think the measure . . . expedient and . . . right? . . . Would I not thus be in the boundless field of absolutism? . . . Could it fail to be perceived that without any further stretch, I might do the same in Delaware, Maryland, Kentucky, Tennessee, and Missouri; and even change any law in any state? Would not many of our own friends shrink away appalled? Would it not lose us the elections, and with them, the very cause we seek to advance? [14]

To follow further the legal questions presented by the proclamation is impossible here. There were strong grounds for disputing its law-worthiness, whether under the Constitution or under the laws of war; and these grounds of dispute seem the more convincing when one remembers the expansiveness of Lincoln's theory of the presidential war power and the seriousness of his doubts as to the proclamation despite this expansive theory. In sum, the edict of freedom would seem to illustrate Lincoln's willingness, with prudent caution and on due provocation, to seize extralegal weapons.

[13] Lincoln, *Collected Works*, VI, 408; VII, 281.
[14] *Ibid.*, VI, 428–429.

2

Though the legal bearings of the proclamation are of historical interest, its actual effects are of greater significance. In this field a study of realities based upon contemporary sources must be substituted for offhand or obvious conclusions. One must consider not merely the language of the proclamation, but also the manner in which certain meanings were read into the document by the popular mind. Especially is this true as to the bearing of the proclamation upon war aims. According to the strict wording of the proclamation it would appear that no change in war aims was intended. Preservation of slavery in nonrebellious regions was clearly implied; and (to assume an outcome at variance with possibilities) if the Southern states had done all that Lincoln asked in September of 1862, i.e., if they had come back into the Union, there was nothing in the emancipating declarations of Lincoln to prevent the war ending with slavery still maintained. Thus it cannot be said that Lincoln's proclamations specifically made abolition a war aim of the North; indeed the September proclamation forbade such a construction, since it proclaimed restoration of the Union, not abolition, as the object of the struggle. Yet the truth of the matter was that the proclamation became a species of slogan or shibboleth; its dramatization in the popular mind was of more effect than its actual provisions. Despite the absence in the proclamation of any express design to produce such a result, it came to be pretty generally assumed that in September of 1862 the war somehow took a new turn, and that thenceforward it was being prosecuted as a war against slavery. It was with this interpretation that the abolitionists favored the edict, and that those indifferent or unfriendly to emancipation opposed it.

That Lincoln by no means regarded his edict as a solution of the slavery question is evident in his annual message to Congress of December 1, 1862, in which he argued at great length the adoption of a constitutional amendment making effective his compensated-emancipation scheme by the issue of Federal bonds to such states as should abolish slavery by a gradual process to become complete by the year 1900. The President turned the proposition over and examined it in all its facets, elaborately exploring its economic, cultural, financial, constitutional, and ethical aspects. Never was Lincoln more in earnest. Referring deferentially to the greater age and public experience of some of those in Congress, he said: "Yet I trust that in view of the great responsibility resting upon me, you will perceive no want of respect to yourselves in any undue earnestness I may seem to display." [1]

It does not appear that Lincoln ever showed such enthusiasm concerning the proclamation. Late in the war he spoke of its legal inadequacy, saying: "A question might be raised whether the proclamation was legally

[1] Lincoln, Collected Works, V, 537.

valid. It might be urged, that it only aided those that came into our lines, and that it was inoperative as to those who did not give themselves up; or that it would have no effect upon the children of slaves born hereafter; in fact, it would be urged that it did not meet the evil." [2]

Upon the Negroes of the South the proclamation itself had but little immediate effect. This is not to argue that slaves were indifferent to the course of the war. Though most of the Negroes in the interior sections of the Confederacy remained faithful to their masters and though there were cases of unfailing slave loyalty elsewhere, most Negroes, as Federal troops neared, began exhibiting increasing restiveness, became impudent to their masters, and refused to work or to submit to punishment for their misdoings. When the Union army actually appeared on the scene, Bell I. Wiley writes, the Negroes generally engaged in the "seizure and distribution of property, and a general celebration of the advent of freedom." But the emancipation proclamation did not initiate, or even notably stimulate, these reactions. It did not lead to a general servile insurrection in the South. The Confederates detected a few plots among the slaves, but "actual outbreaks were fewer still, and these were immediately suppressed." "That the slaves in the interior did not 'rise up' against their masters," adds Professor Wiley, "is not surprising when one takes into consideration their lack of facilities for rapid communication and concerted action, the affection which the most intelligent ones had for their master's families, the fear inspired by the summary execution of those whose plots to rebel were detected, and the tremendous advantages which the whites had over them in every respect, save that of numbers." [3]

Nor did the proclamation create the phenomenon of Negroes appearing within Union lines. Prior to its issuance fugitive slaves within their camps had been a familiar sight to Union commanders; and such Negroes were by law free. Indeed the proclamation added hardly at all to what Congress had done, at least on paper, by its acts freeing fugitive slaves within Union lines, emancipating slave-soldiers, and freeing "rebel"-owned slaves by the confiscation act of 1862. On the morrow of Lincoln's edict Union generals in the South did not suddenly face an entirely new problem: it was rather that they now found it necessary to provide more formally and elaborately for the increasing numbers of Negroes who were no longer to be regarded merely as self-invited guests within their midst.

Grant's army in Tennessee and Mississippi found that, with the abandonment of plantations on the approach of Union forces, Negroes "flocked in vast numbers—an army in themselves—to the camps of the Yankees." Here was a slave population "springing from . . . barbarism, . . . for-

[2] The words quoted (apparently not verbatim) are taken from Lincoln's speech of Jan. 31, 1865, as published in Nicolay and Hay, eds., *Abraham Lincoln: Collected Works*, II, 633–634. For a further statement of the legal effect of the proclamation, see Randall, *Constitutional Problems Under Lincoln*, 378–385.

[3] Wiley, *Southern Negroes, 1861–1865*, 73–75, 77, 82–83.

saking its local traditions and all the associations . . . of the old plantation life, . . . with feet shod or bleeding, individually or in families . . . —an army of slaves and fugitives, pushing its way irresistibly
toward an army of fighting men, perpetually on the defensive and perpetually ready to attack. The arrival among us of these hordes was like the on-
coming of cities. There was no plan in this exodus, no Moses to lead it.
Unlettered reason or the mere inarticulate decision of instinct brought
them to us." [4]

To deal with this problem Grant ordered Chaplain John Eaton of the
Twenty-Seventh Ohio Infantry Volunteers to "take charge of the contrabands." As Grant explained, his own troops had to be protected from disease, and humane considerations dictated that care be given to these helpless folk.[5] For these purposes Eaton established Negro camps, cared for the
sick, organized the able-bodied for military labor, set them to work gathering and baling cotton, employed them as teamsters and in many other kinds
of service, dealt with Negro exhorters, kept Negro families together as best
he could, and made heroic efforts to transform shiftless bondsmen into self-
sufficing members of society. By July, 1864, Eaton had 113,650 freedmen under his supervision. Most of these were earning their own subsistence, 41,150 in military service as soldiers, laundresses, cooks, officers'
servants, or laborers, 62,300 in private employment as mechanics, dray-
men, hackmen, barbers, hired laborers, and the like; the remainder depended in whole or in part upon the government for support.[6] General
B. F. Butler in 1863 created a comparable system of Negro administration
in parts of Virginia and North Carolina, appointing a "general superintendent of negro affairs" with a number of superintendents under him and
directing these officials to take a colored census, provide shelter, medical
care, and other charity to freedmen, supervise labor contracts, allot lands
to Negroes, and attend to their training.[7]

These are but a few of the many instances of military action to deal
with the elaborate problems of the freedmen: they show clearly enough
that, whether by reason of the proclamation or not, Union commanders had
immense numbers of slaves (or ex-slaves) on their hands. As the armies
advanced in the South, especially in 1864–1865, the problem became
more pressing. The Negroes had but a hazy notion of the meaning of Lincoln's proclamation, in which haziness the whole country shared; but they

[4] John Eaton, *Grant, Lincoln, and the Freedmen* [etc.], 2. It was stated on
December 1, 1863, by a committee representing freedmen's aid societies that "the
late glorious victory near Chattanooga has, probably, loosed fifty thousand freedmen," and that for every mile of Grant's advance "ten thousand freedmen drop
their chains." This was obviously a mere offhand statement. *Sen. Doc. No. 1,* 38
Cong., 1 sess., p. 2.
   [5] Eaton, 5, 13.
   [6] Wiley, *op. cit.,* 227.
   [7] *Offic. Rec.,* 3 ser., III, 1139–1144.

soon knew of it and looked upon the Union military line as the line of freedom.

> The advance of Sherman's army [wrote General H. W. Slocum] . . . was known far and wide many miles in advance of us. It was natural that these poor creatures [the slaves], seeking a place of safety, should flee to the army, and endeavor to keep in sight of it. Every day, as we marched on we could see, on each side of our line of march, crowds of these people coming to us through roads and across the fields, bringing with them all their earthly goods, and many goods which were not theirs. Horses, mules, cows, dogs, old family carriages, carts, and whatever they thought might be of use . . . were . . . brought to us. They were allowed to follow in rear of our column, and at times they were almost equal in numbers to the army they were following.[8]

In the process of military emancipation, however, Lincoln's proclamation was but one of various factors; nor was it an unmixed blessing. It encouraged the rush of Negro refugees into Union lines, stimulated military action in dealing with freedmen, promoted abolition measures in some of the Union slave states, and prepared the way for the final eradication of slavery by constitutional amendment. On the other hand it complicated military adjustments between the United States and the Confederate States (e.g., with reference to the exchange of prisoners), opened the way to Southern retaliation, launched an angry wave of resentment in the South at what was considered a capital grievance, and gave to Lincoln's prestige a setback among certain elements of Northern opinion which proved a serious loss to the President and his party.

3

At the South the proclamation produced a reaction of indignant hostility. The Richmond *Whig* (October 1, 1862) denounced the "fiend's new programme," describing the proclamation as "a dash of the pen to destroy four thousand millions of our property, and . . . a bid for the slaves to rise in insurrection. . . ."[1] To the Richmond *Examiner* it seemed the "most startling political crime . . . yet known in American history." Servile insurrection seemed to this journal the "sole purpose" of the proclamation.[2] Referring to the proclamation in his message to the Confederate Congress on January 12, 1863, President Davis declared that "a restitution of the Union has been rendered forever impossible by the adoption of a measure which . . . neither admits of retraction nor can coexist with union."[3] The "entire newspaper press of the Confederacy," said a Richmond editor, "echoed the sentiment of the President."[4]

---

[8] *Battles and Leaders,* IV, 688–689.

[1] Quoted in Moore, *Rebell. Rec.* (Diary), V, 89.

[2] *Ibid.* (Diary), VI, 32.

[3] *Ibid.* (Doc.), VI, 381.

[4] Pollard, *Lost Cause,* 360.

E. A. Pollard described the proclamation as the "triumph of fanaticism under a false pretence." He declared that at first it had no effect, being worth "no more than the paper on which its bold iniquity was traced," but denounced its fundamental principle and referred to the "misrepresentation of the emancipation proclamation, as a deed of philanthropy" as "absurd." "A candid world," he said, interpreted it as "an act of malice towards the master rather than one of mercy to the slave." Animating the South to desperate exertion, he said, it "secured a new lease of war." [5]

In the North there was no general unanimity of feeling. Sentiment varied from unqualified endorsement to dissatisfaction, doubt, and resentment. Wendell Phillips spoke of the liberation and arming of the slaves as the salvation of the republic; and Charles Sumner endorsed the proclamation in an elaborate speech at Boston. Abolitionists generally, while disappointed at the limitations of the proclamation, gave it their approval. By the firing of guns, mass meetings, and other demonstrations, the event was widely hailed as an occasion for jubilation. The New York *Times* (September 23, 1862) referred to the President's decree as the most far-reaching document ever issued by the government, saying its wisdom was unquestionable, its necessity indisputable. Commenting on the first month of the proclamation on October 22, 1862, the *Times* declared that it was well received in the loyal states, that the border states had not been alienated, that the army was not offended, that Southern leaders feared the new policy, and that the chord of approval had been struck in Europe. In the Northern Congress, though there were outbursts against the edict, the votes taken were mostly favorable to it. A resolution of G. H. Yeaman of Kentucky, denouncing the proclamation as not calculated to hasten peace and not well chosen as a war measure, was tabled in the House (94 to 45); [6] and the resolution of S. C. Fessenden of Maine approving the resolution as well adapted to hasten peace was adopted, though by a narrower vote (78 to 51). [7]

There was some effort in Congress to "give effect" to the proclamation, i.e., to enact it as a law. Representative Arnold of Illinois introduced into the House of Representatives a bill to carry the proclamation "into more immediate execution" by prohibiting the re-enslavement of any person whom the proclamation declared to be free. [8] When the Wade-Davis bill was under consideration Sumner moved an amendment providing that the emancipation proclamation "is hereby adopted and enacted as a statute of the United States, and as a rule . . . for the government of the military and naval forces thereof." "I wish to see emancipation of the rebel States," said Sumner, "placed under the guarantee of an act of Congress. I do not

---

[5] *Ibid.*, 359–360.
[6] *Cong. Globe*, 37 Cong., 3 sess., 76 (Dec. 11, 1862).
[7] *Ibid.*, 92 (Dec. 15, 1862).
[8] *Cong. Globe*, 38 Cong., 1 sess., 20 (Dec. 14, 1863).

wish to see it left to float on a presidential proclamation." [9] Willard Saulsbury of Delaware, one of the border-state moderates, seized upon Sumner's amendment as a confession that the proclamation was without legal effect in itself, adding that he had not supposed the President's friends would so soon make open confession that his acts were illegal. Though these proposals were not adopted, both houses of Congress did pass in the Wade-Davis bill of 1864 a provision that "all persons held to involuntary servitude . . . in the [seceded] states . . . are hereby emancipated and discharged therefrom, and they and their posterity shall be forever free." Owing to Lincoln's veto this bill never became law; indeed one of his objections was this very clause, for he did not believe that Congress possessed even in war the power to abolish slavery in the South by ordinary statute. In this respect he felt that the President's war power exceeded that of Congress.

Many Northern individuals either opposed the proclamation or expressed disappointment in it. Thurlow Weed declared: ". . . it has strengthened the South and weakened the North. . . ." [10] The elder Francis P. Blair said that the President "had ruined himself by his proclamations, and it was necessary to do something to regain the confidence of the people." [11] The effect of the proclamation upon Orville H. Browning of Illinois is of considerable interest. Opposed to slavery, Browning had enlisted enthusiastically with the anti-Nebraska movement of 1854 and had become one of the leading Republicans of Illinois. His character and public acts offer an excellent study of the effect of Lincoln's increasing radicalism upon Republican moderates. He vigorously opposed the drastic confiscation act of 1862 and was offended when Lincoln signed it: the emancipation proclamation met with his strong disapproval and made a marked difference in his attitude toward Lincoln's policies and toward the Republican party. In his diary he revealed his views as follows: "Had conversation [October 14, 1862] with Judge Drummond [Federal justice in Illinois] upon public affairs. He agrees fully with me in my views— . . . Thought the Presidents proclamation unfortunate—He was not satisfied of its constitutionality but to say nothing of that, it was ill advised as it could do no possible good, and certainly would do harm in uniting the rebels more firmly than ever, and making them fight with the energy of despair." [12]

This Republican senator was asked to address a Union meeting in his home town, Quincy, Illinois, on the night before the election of November 4, 1862. According to the Quincy *Whig* he "appeared, began his speech by . . . pronouncing the issues more momentous tha[n] . . . in any election in this country and then astonished his hearers by the sage

[9] *Ibid.*, 3460.
[10] Seitz, *Greeley*, 244.
[11] Browning, *Diary*, I, 601.
[12] *Ibid.*, I, 578.

advice that they should . . . vote for the *best ticket,* leaving it to be inferred that he did not know which was the best ticket. Gov. Wright, a Democrat, had an opinion and gave it; Mr. Browning gave none, . . . fell back into the confiscation rut, and wound up with a sneer at proclamations." [13] It does not appear that Browning, friend of Lincoln though he was, ever again gave real support to the Republican party after the proclamation.

Many other examples of this dissent could be cited. Thomas Ewing "said the Presidents emancipation and Habeas Corpus proclamations had ruined the Republican party in Ohio." [14] The adverse verdict upon the Lincoln administration given in the election of 1862, and the part of the proclamation in contributing to this verdict, will be noted later.[15] As to the anti-Lincoln Democrats, their attitude was expressed by Vallandigham's denunciation of a war to free the blacks and enslave the whites. In Illinois the proclamation was denounced by Democrats as a "gigantic usurpation," as "unwarrantable in military [and] civil law," and as properly called a "war measure," for it would "protract the war indefinitely." [16] Similar expressions could be repeated at great length. It should, however, be noted *per contra* that such support as came to the administration in Illinois in the election of 1862 was attributed by the Chicago *Tribune* to the emancipation proclamation and the removal of General Buell; [17] that Grimes of Iowa considered the proclamation a source of strength in his state; [18] and that a similar view as to Missouri was expressed by the *Missouri Democrat.*[19]

As to the effect of the proclamation abroad it is not easy to generalize. It is true that there was in Europe and England an overwhelming anti-slavery sentiment and that enthusiastic applause was received from English abolitionists; but at the same time many felt that it was not the humanitarian motive which had actuated Lincoln and that the proclamation as issued was unfortunate. Various British newspapers scored the measure, declaring that it was without legal force, that it was a high-handed proceeding, and that it betrayed Lincoln's waning power.[20] On the other hand there were many foreign expressions of opinion distinctly favorable to the Lincoln administration. John Bigelow wrote to Seward (October 10,

[13] Quincy *Whig,* Nov. 10, 1862.
[14] Browning, *Diary,* I, 592.
[15] See below, pp. 456–461.
[16] Quoted in Cole, *Era of the Civil War,* 300.
[17] Chicago *Tribune,* Nov. 6, 1862, p. 1, c. 1.
[18] William Salter, *Life of James W. Grimes,* 218; O. B. Clark, *Politics of Iowa during the Civil War and Reconstruction,* 168–169.
[19] *Missouri Democrat,* Nov. 5, 6, 7, 1862.
[20] For a brief summary of British press opinion, see J. B. McMaster, *Lincoln's Administration,* 292. For French opinion see Lynn M. Case, *French Opinion on the United States and Mexico, 1860–1867,* and W. Reed West, *Contemporary French Opinion on the American Civil War.*

1862) that France was "unanimously for emancipation" and that the Union cause would "daily grow in grace" in that country. Among humanitarians in England the proclamation produced, as Frederic Bancroft has said, a "surprising awakening," being hailed in public meetings addressed by prominent speakers.[21] On January 29, 1863, an emancipation meeting in Exeter Hall, London, was so crowded that a second and a third meeting were held to accommodate the overflow. Telegrams were read reporting meetings in other places; the name of Lincoln was cheered and the cause of the South denounced.[22] So greatly were the Confederate agents worried at this time because of "the universal hostility of Europe to slavery and the . . . warnings that Europe would never recognize . . . a slave-power" that Judah P. Benjamin, Confederate secretary of state, has been described as "in profound despair" and ready to concede that "spades were trumps." New instructions for the Confederate commissioners were prepared: they were now ready to propose Southern emancipation of the Negroes if they could thus improve their prospects of recognition.[23] The fact that recognition was not obtained, though shortly previous to this it seemed highly probable, is in large part attributable to Lincoln's proclamation.

4

A natural accompaniment of emancipation was the use of colored men as Union soldiers. Though most Northerners were willing to accept Negroes as laborers in the army, there was, at the outset, much opposition to the idea of Negro troops, and even Lincoln "thought that the organization, equipment and arming of negroes, like other soldiers, would be productive of more evil than good." [1] But after the emancipation proclamation sentiment for Negro soldiers grew. Indeed, several Federal commanders had not waited for the President to act but, on their own initiative, had for several months been recruiting colored troops. On April 12, 1862, General David Hunter in command of the Department of the South had organized the first official regiment of Negro troops, composed of former slaves from Georgia, Florida, and South Carolina; but this proved a bad beginning, for the blacks were, according to one account, "driven like cattle" into the regiment, "kept for several months in camp, and then turned off without a shilling, by order of the War Department." [2] In July General John W. Phelps began outfitting "three regiments of Africans" in his Louisiana command, but friction with his superior officer, Benjamin F. Butler, soon led to his resignation. On August 22 Butler him-

---

21 Bancroft, *Seward*, II, 340–341.

22 Moore, *Rebell. Rec.* (Diary), VI, 40–41.

23 F. L. Owsley, *King Cotton Diplomacy*, 552, 554.

1 Donald, ed., *Inside Lincoln's Cabinet*, 99–100.

2 T. W. Higginson, *Army Life in a Black Regiment*, 15.

self called on the free colored militiamen of Louisiana to enroll in the volunteer forces of the Union. In theory, all who joined Butler's regiments had been free, but in practice, an observer remarked, "nobody inquires whether the recruit is (or has been) a slave. As a consequence the boldest and finest fugitives have enlisted. . . ." Meanwhile, General James H. Lane in Kansas had, from the very beginning of the war, enrolled Negroes into his forces, and "small units and companies of Kansas colored troops fought in the first engagements in the Civil War in which American Negroes were permitted to fight for the Union." [3]

On August 25, 1862, the war department gave official sanction to the policy of recruiting Negro soldiers by authorizing General Rufus Saxton in the Department of the South "to arm, uniform, equip, and receive into the service of the United States, such number of volunteers of African descent as [he] may deem expedient, not exceeding 5,000." Lincoln's final emancipation proclamation of January 1, 1863, also sanctioned the newly freed Negroes being received into the armed force of the United States; and thenceforward the formation of colored military units became common. In August, 1864, Lincoln stated that there were nearly 150,000 colored men in the Union service; [4] by the end of the war the number reached the high total of 178,895. [5] On widely separated fronts these Negro warriors saw action—in South Carolina and Florida, at Port Hudson, at Olustee, at Petersburg, and elsewhere.

Cautious at first as to Negro troops, Lincoln came to speak of them in eulogistic terms. Writing to General Dix on January 14, 1863, he said that since the disadvantages of the emancipation proclamation had to be endured, its benefits should also be grasped. In March, 1863, he spoke of colored troops as "very important, if not indispensable." Soon after, he expressed satisfaction at the conduct of colored troops at Jacksonville, Florida; again he said, "The raising of colored troops . . . will greatly help every way." Some, he said, considered "the emancipation policy and the use of the colored troops . . . the heaviest blow yet dealt to the rebellion, ..." [6] He pointed out that he could not give up these troops and could not abandon the forts garrisoned by black men; nor could he take 150,000 men from "our side" and let them be used "against us." He emphatically declared that these black soldiers should not be re-enslaved. "Should I do so," he said, "I should deserve to be damned in time and eternity." [7]

[3] Dudley T. Cornish, The Sable Arm: Negro Troops in the Union Army, 1861–1865, 59, 66, 78.

[4] Nicolay and Hay, eds., Abraham Lincoln: Complete Works, II, 562.

[5] "The whole number of colored troops recruited and organized during the war is usually given as 186,017, but since that figure includes 7,122 officers, a more nearly correct total is 178,895." Cornish, op. cit., 288.

[6] Lincoln, Collected Works, VI, 154, 158, 440, 409.

[7] Nicolay and Hay, eds., Abraham Lincoln: Complete Works, II, 562.

Negro soldiers were generally under white officers.[8] Perhaps the most famous of these was T. W. Higginson of Massachusetts, who in November, 1862, was invited to take command of the first regiment raised by General Saxton. "Had an invitation reached me to take command of a regiment of Kalmuck Tartars," wrote Higginson, "it could hardly have been more unexpected." Accepting the colonelcy of this slave regiment, which carried over the name of Hunter's abortive organization and was known as the "First Regiment of South Carolina Volunteers," Higginson trained it and led it in unimportant raiding operations up the St. Marys and Edisto rivers. He records this unique experience with enthusiasm and with extraordinary praise of these black soldiers. He writes of the "absurdity of distrusting the military availability of these people," who were almost entirely black, with scarcely a mulatto among them. His enthusiasm, however, was that of an extremist who could write: "I had been an abolitionist too long, and had known and loved John Brown too well, not to feel a thrill of joy at last on finding myself in the position where he only wished to be." [9]

Another son of Massachusetts who achieved fame in command of Negro troops was Robert Gould Shaw, youthful colonel of the Fifty-Fourth Massachusetts, the "first colored regiment of the North to go to the war." [10] In an ill-advised attack upon Battery Wagner, Charleston harbor (July 18, 1863), Shaw met death at the head of his troops, whose losses were heavy. Like Higginson, he had left a promising post in command of white troops in order to lead the blacks.

Throughout the war Negro soldiers were under discrimination in the matter of pay, bounties, and the like. According to Higginson, a definite assurance by the war department that colored soldiers should receive the same pay as white troops was violated.[11] Up until 1864 even Negro non-commissioned officers were paid only $7 a month, precisely what colored privates received. As a result of "sustained effort by prominent officers of Negro troops, with help from governors, newspaper editors, and senators," a partial victory was achieved in the army appropriation act of 1864, but not until after the war was over did the Federal government fully abandon its "shortsighted and parsimonious policy toward the pay of colored troops." [12]

Naturally the use of Negro troops produced sharp threats of retaliation at the South, where the practice was denounced as a departure from the

---

[8] "War Department policy was distinctly unfavorable to the appointment of Negro officers. In spite of this, about one hundred Negroes held commissions at various times during the Civil War, over three-fourths of these in the Department of the Gulf, where Butler mustered in the first three Louisiana regiments." Cornish, *op. cit.*, 214.

[9] Higginson, *Army Life*, 2, 10, 4.

[10] Rhodes, IV, 332.

[11] Higginson, *Army Life*, appendix.

[12] Cornish, *The Sable Arm*, 184, 192, 195.

laws of war and a measure of brutal barbarity. On August 21, 1862, President Jefferson Davis proclaimed that the Union generals Hunter and Phelps should be treated not as public enemies but as outlaws and should be executed as felons, on account of their use of slaves in armed service.[13] In his proclamation of December 23, 1862, Davis declared that in view of the efforts of the President of the United States to "excite servile war within the Confederacy," slave soldiers and Federal commissioned officers serving with them should be turned over to the states of the South to be dealt with according to the laws of said states,[14] which meant being put to death.[15] A modified treatment was decreed by the Confederate Congress, which regarded the matter as a problem for the Confederacy, not the states, and which provided (April 30, 1863) that white officers commanding Negro soldiers should be "deemed as inciting servile insurrection" and should, if captured, be "put to death or be otherwise punished, at the discretion of the court." [16]

Against these severe decrees an order of counter-retaliation was issued by Lincoln, who proclaimed (July 30, 1863) that for every Union soldier killed in violation of the laws of war, "a rebel soldier shall be executed," and for every one enslaved "a rebel soldier shall be placed at hard labor . . . and [so] continued . . . until the other shall . . . receive the treatment due to a prisoner of war."

It was not that these threats were put into effect: it appears rather that on both sides the retaliatory declarations were intended primarily to soften the war by putting an end to uncivilized practices; they are distinctly to be regarded as threats rather than as the basis of completed policy. Lincoln handled alleged Confederate atrocities against Negro soldiers with great caution and restraint, even the brutal affair at Fort Pillow, Tennessee, where on April 12, 1864, General N. B. Forrest was alleged to have refused quarter to surrendering Negro troops who constituted a part of that garrison and was reported to have massacred several hundred of them instead of taking them prisoners. A United States Senate investigating committee angrily charged that the Confederates had murdered 300 Union men "in cold blood after the post was in possession of the rebels, and our men had thrown down their arms." [17] Despite the aroused state

[13] Moore, *Rebell. Rec.* (Diary), V, 62.

[14] *Offic. Rec.*, 2 ser., V, 797.

[15] In South Carolina, for instance, by an act passed in 1805, Negroes caught in arms against whites were subjected to the penalty of death. *S. C. Statutes at Large*, V, 503.

[16] *Journal, Confed. Cong.*, III, 386–387.

[17] *Sen. Rep. No. 63*, 38 Cong., 1 sess.; see also Moore, *Rebell. Rec.* (Doc.), VII, 1 ff. The facts about the Fort Pillow affair are still in dispute. John L. Jordan argues ("Was There a Massacre at Fort Pillow? " *Tenn. Hist. Quart.*, VI, 99–133 [June, 1947]) that the Federal garrison was drunk at the time of the attack and failed to haul down the flag or to give up their arms in evidence of their surrender. But Dudley T. Cornish (*The Sable Arm*, 173–174) concludes that, while the ex-

of Northern opinion, Lincoln remained calm. In a public statement made six days after the "massacre" he declared: "We do not to-day *know* that a colored soldier, or white officer commanding colored soldiers, has been massacred by the rebels when made a prisoner. . . . We are having the Fort-Pillow affair thoroughly investigated. . . . If . . . it shall turn out that there has been no massacre at Fort-Pillow, it will be almost safe to say there has been none, and will be none elsewhere." [18] It is significant that, in spite of Northern indignation over this incident there was no retaliation by the Union government. As explained by Nicolay and Hay and by Rhodes, this may have been due to the rush of events, or, more probably, to the realization that the incident grew out of the heat of war, and that retaliation would only make the matter far worse.[19]

5

The actual consummation of freedom in American law and practice was less a matter of presidential proclamation than of state action and constitutional amendment. In West Virginia a clause providing gradual emancipation was included in the new-state constitution of 1863 in order to fulfill one of the requirements of admission to the Union. Immediate abolition was provided by constitutional amendment in Tennessee in February, 1865. In Maryland liberation was provided by an ordinary law which merely "repealed" the slave code of the state concerning Negroes, this code being but an enactment of the legislature. A still different method was adopted in Missouri, where slavery was abolished by ordinance passed by a state convention (January 11, 1865). Two of the border states, however, Delaware and Kentucky, clung tenaciously to the dying institution; and the war ended with slavery still a state matter, though seriously interfered with by national authority.[1]

For the final disposition of a problem which had been handled piecemeal by the President, the states, and Congress, and which in consequence was left in considerable confusion, it came to be recognized that a constitutional amendment was a legal necessity. Such an amendment was therefore reported from the Senate committee on the judiciary by Trumbull of Illinois. It was the first example of the use of the amending process to accomplish a specific reform on a nationwide scale, outside what may be called the strictly constitutional function of determining the composition and functions of government. There were grave doubts as to such use of the Constitution. Some felt that domestic institutions were so thoroughly a matter of state jurisdiction that a change such as the proposed thirteenth

---

tent of the "massacre" has been exaggerated, there was in fact " 'indiscriminate slaughter' of Union troops, particularly of Negroes, after the fort had fallen."

[18] Lincoln, *Collected Works*, VII, 302–303.

[19] Nicolay and Hay, *Lincoln*, VI, 479–481; Rhodes, V, 512–513.

[1] Randall, *Constitutional Problems Under Lincoln*, 385–390.

amendment should be resisted as a revolutionary alteration of the basic American federal system. There was also considerable doubt whether the national Constitution could be legally amended during the Civil War; and in this doubt Senator Trumbull himself, when discussing another matter, had shared. Such was the opposition to the amendment when first proposed that, though the Senate adopted it (April 8, 1864) by a vote of 38 to 6,[2] the lower house (June 15, 1864) failed to muster the necessary two-thirds, the vote being 93 to 65, with 23 not voting.[3] The representatives, however, were moved by the election of 1864 and the progress of the war to a change of heart; and on January 31, 1865, the amendment was carried, 119 to 56, 8 not voting.[4]

The story of the ratification of the amendment is bound up with the early stages of postwar reconstruction under President Johnson. Of the thirty-six states in 1865, three-fourths of which were necessary for ratification, more than one-fourth (eleven) had been seceded states of the Confederacy, while two of the Union states, Delaware and Kentucky, refused to ratify. It was thus necessary to count in some of the seceded states in order to obtain ratification; and as a matter of fact Secretary Seward, in the proclamation which declared the amendment in force (December 18, 1865), did include eight of the former Confederate States, as shown in the table on the following page.

That these eight Southern states should be considered competent to ratify the antislavery amendment, such ratification being essential to its enactment, and yet be rejected by Congress and not considered states in the Union, is but one of the many anomalies of reconstruction. They were the "Johnson governments" of the South, brought into being under President Johnson's direction in compliance with his generous plan of restoration, but were denied recognition by the vindictives who controlled Congress. Some of the Radicals had suggested in 1865 that the Southern states be left out of the count in the matter of ratifying the amendment, and that only the Union states be considered to constitute the total, three-fourths of which would have to give their ratification. In fact, Lincoln's secretaries and biographers have fallen into the error of saying that the amendment was "ratified by 21 out of the 26 States," [5] whereas it was actually ratified, as shown by Seward's proclamation of December 18, 1865, by twenty-seven of the thirty-six states. After the amendment was declared in force, various states added their ratifications, so that all doubts of its validity were removed.

Lincoln did not live to see emancipation legally consummated. Moreover, an important part of his emancipation policy was doomed to failure—

[2] *Cong. Globe*, 38 Cong., 1 sess., 1490.
[3] *Ibid.*, 2995.
[4] *Ibid.*, 38 Cong., 2 sess., 531.
[5] *Works* (12 vol. ed.), X, 352 n.

ADOPTION OF THE THIRTEENTH AMENDMENT, DECEMBER 18, 1865

(Stars indicate those states whose ratifications were counted in Seward's proclamation of December 18, 1865, declaring the amendment in force.)

Free States of the Union			Slave States of the Union	States of the Former Confederacy	
Cal.	* Md.	* Ohio	Del.	* Ark.	* La.
* Conn.	* Mich.	Ore.	Ky.	* Tenn.	Miss.
* Ill.	* Minn.	* Pa.		* N. C.	* Ala.
* Ind.	* Mo.	* R. I.		* Va. (See note	* Ga.
Ia.	* N. H.	* Vt.		below)	* S. C.
* Kan.	N. J.	* W. Va.		Tex.	
* Me.	* N. Y.	* Wis.		Fla.	
* Mass.	* Nev.				
Total, 23			Total, 2	Total, 11	

Total of all the States, 36

Note. The United States government recognized the "restored government" of Virginia; and that state was, rather fictitiously, represented in the Federal Congress in the early part of the war. It was not, however, considered to be in the Union in 1865.

that of compensation to slaveholders. In passing the British emancipation act of 1833 the Parliament granted the amount of £20,000,000 as compensation for the destruction of slave property. Not only did the Parliament consider the cash value of the slaves, but it also considered such factors as the value of slave-worked land and the prospective value of children to be born. Lincoln labored valiantly for compensation to Southern owners. At the Hampton Roads Conference (February, 1865) he is reported to have said that he "would be willing to be taxed to remunerate the Southern people for their slaves"; that he "believed the people of the North were as responsible for slavery as the people of the South"; and that he would be in favor "of the Government paying a fair indemnity for the loss to the owners." [6]

After the war, however, compensation for slaveholders not only received little thought but was opposed to the prevailing view. The joint resolution of Congress expressing a willingness in 1862 to compensate any state that would free its slaves represents simply a stage in a rapidly changing policy. It was natural to suppose that the offer should not hold good indefinitely, since promptness on the part of the states was desired in order to hasten peace. During the brief period when this compensation policy was presumably active, the border-state governments contributed their part

[6] Alexander H. Stephens, *War between the States,* II, 617. (Stephens reports the conference from his own personal observation as one of the commissioners.)

to the burial of the project: otherwise such efforts as those of Maryland in
1865 to obtain compensation on the basis of the Federal pledge might be
viewed with more sympathy. When at the end of the war a new policy—
abolition by constitutional amendment—had been put forth, the claims of
those few states whose independent abolition of slavery occurred just before the adoption of the nation-wide amendment were lost from sight. Finally the matter was settled by the fourteenth amendment to the Constitution, which declared that "neither the United States nor any State shall
assume or pay . . . any claim for the loss or emancipation of any slave."

CHAPTER 23

The Middle Phase:
Gettysburg, Vicksburg, Chattanooga

I

IN MILITARY operations the year 1863, though opening inauspiciously, proved in both the East and the West to be a period of significant Union achievement. On the Confederate side the victory of Fredericksburg had not been followed up. It is the view of E. A. Pollard that Burnside with "his shattered army . . . cowering beneath the houses of Fredericksburg" was at "an appalling extremity," and, he added, the Southern public "waited with impatience to hear that Gen. Lee had assumed the offensive." Pollard considered the annihilation of Burnside's army possible.[1] Lee, however, feared further assaults; he was loath to abandon his defensive position; and, whether rightly or not, he withheld his counterattack. Though facing a superior foe, he again divided his army, sending Longstreet on a minor enterprise against Suffolk.[2] Thus he gave a great advantage to Hooker, who had about 130,000 facing Lee's 60,000.[3] The Federal army was once more in fine condition, desertion having been largely checked and morale running high. Hooker divided his forces:

---

[1] E. A. Pollard, *The Lost Cause,* 345.

[2] Federals under General John J. Peck occupied Suffolk, Virginia, with a force of 15,000, which for a short time was increased to about 29,000. (*Offic. Rec.,* I ser., XVIII, 281–282.) In the belief that this position was being developed as a base for a movement against Richmond, Longstreet with a large force (estimated by Federals at about 30,000) was detached from Lee's main army facing Hooker and interposed between Suffolk and the Confederate capital. Unable to take the place by assault, he sat down to a siege, though he also described his purpose as that of collecting supplies from this eastern area. When Hooker attacked, Longstreet was ordered on April 29 to rejoin Lee; but Chancellorsville had been fought before his army reached Richmond. *Offic. Rec.,* I ser., XVIII, 267–341; *Battles and Leaders,* III, 244; IV, 533 n. Freeman (IV, 167) notes this as one of Lee's mistakes.

[3] *Battles and Leaders,* III, 237–238. Freeman's estimate (II, 506) is 138,000 for Hooker and 62,500 for Lee.

Sedgwick was to threaten Lee's right below Fredericksburg; Hooker's own forces were to strike at Lee from the direction of Chancellorsville (west of Fredericksburg); Stoneman with his cavalry was to imitate the redoubtable Stuart, executing a sweep to the rear of the Confederate force and wrecking their communications with Richmond. The Union commander had "divided his army into two wings, and the enemy, no ordinary enemy, lay between them." [4] Aware of Hooker's positions and designs, Lee showed his audacious contempt of superior Union strength by still further dividing his force, sending Stonewall Jackson with about 30,000 men on a wide flanking movement to strike Hooker's detached right under Howard, while Lee himself, with a force of about 15,000, was to hold Hooker. Jackson succeeded brilliantly, surprising Howard, whose men, with arms stacked, were cooking supper. Separated from the main force under Hooker, Howard was caught with greatly inferior numbers and was rolled up in a sharp attack in front, side, and rear by Jackson's crack troops. Here was an example of Confederate numerical superiority in an engagement despite general superiority of the whole Union force over the Confederate. In the confusion of this wilderness combat Jackson's charging troops struck suddenly and pursued for a mile as the Federals showed increasing resistance in their retreat. Meanwhile Lee's demonstration with a "thin line" farther to the east had deterred Hooker from sending troops to resist Jackson.[5] Blame for the Union defeat must fall partly upon Howard, who, in the words of his biographer, deserves "severe criticism" for his failure to reconnoiter his position and to anticipate Jackson's attack,[6] but it rests even more heavily upon Hooker, who, as two careful British soldiers tersely remark, "had under his command a larger force than he was capable of handling." [7]

Chancellorsville was Jackson's last battle (May 2, 1863). He had ridden out with staff officers beyond his lines; on returning his party was mistaken for Federals and he was shot by his own men. On May 10, 1863, he died, having received Lee's congratulations on the "victory, which is due to your skill and energy." [8] Such generals as Jackson could not be replaced. The Confederacy had suffered a stunning blow; Lee, now at "high noon," had lost his "right arm." [9]

The battle of Chancellorsville raged on from the 1st to the 5th of May; and by the 6th Lee had whipped back the splendid host which Hooker

---

[4] *Battles and Leaders*, III, 157. See also 152, 172.

[5] Freeman, *Lee*, II, 530–531.

[6] John A. Carpenter, "O. O. Howard: General at Chancellorsville," *Civil War Hist.*, III, 59 (Mar., 1957).

[7] W. Birkbeck Wood and James E. Edmonds, *The Civil War in the United States*, 36.

[8] *Recollections and Letters of General Robert E. Lee*, by his son, Captain R. E. Lee, 94.

[9] Freeman, *Lee*, II, chs. xxxiv, xxxv.

had described as "the finest army on the planet." Like so many other battles of the war, however, it was indecisive; and Hooker, putting the blame of defeat upon subordinates, was still a formidable foe in command of a powerful army. Another grapple between the Army of the Potomac and the Army of Northern Virginia necessarily impended. For Lee the main questions were whether to fight south of the Potomac or carry the war into enemy country, and whether to send a part of his troops west to relieve Pemberton and Bragg and try to save Vicksburg from Grant's closing vise.

2

Lee decided to invade the North and not to send troops west. To those who deal in hypothetical strategy it appeared that the Southern capital might at this point have been seized by Hooker. On the other hand, Lee could have taken Washington about as easily as Hooker Richmond. This "swapping of queens" was not to occur; the objective of each commander was the army of the other. The month of June was occupied in marching and maneuvering; and by the end of the month Lee had swung his three great corps under Longstreet, Ewell, and A. P. Hill into Pennsylvania, where on the first three days of July there was fought at Gettysburg the greatest battle of the war. That the armies met and gave battle at Gettysburg was without premeditation on either side. Lee was simply moving north to threaten Washington and other cities, even planning at one stage to push Ewell as far as Harrisburg; while Hooker had marched north over a more easterly route to keep his forces interposed between Washington and the Confederates. Detached forces accidentally came to blows just outside Gettysburg on July 1, and the battle was precipitated.

On the eve of the battle Lincoln removed Hooker and put the army and the nation's safety in the hands of George G. Meade, whose rise to high command was as much of a surprise to himself as to the army, which had gone wild with jubilation over a rumor that McClellan had been reinstated as their leader. Meade had been trained at West Point, had distinguished himself in the Virginia campaigns, and was soon to prove his soldierly qualities. The Union force under his command was about 88,000 to Lee's 75,000. On Meade's side the strategic object was to force Lee to fight before he could cross the Susquehanna. To Lee a battle was a necessity. He was conducting an offensive with a confident army; he could not retreat without fighting. It was Meade's game to see that the locus and conditions of the battle should be as favorable as possible to the Union side.

Lee had given up his Harrisburg project, had recalled Ewell, and was concentrating his forces at Cashtown when, on July 1, Heth's (Confederate) division of Hill's corps met and engaged Buford's (Union) cavalry together with the advance infantry of the Federals led by Reynolds, Meade's second in command. Other troops, Union and Confederate, were now rapidly approaching Gettysburg, so that each hour revealed important changes in the positions of corps, divisions, and brigades. On the first day the Union forces, in a sharp engagement, were overpowered by superior Confederate numbers; but by falling back in fair order they rallied on Cemetery Hill south of the town, and with the help of new troops under Howard and Hancock were able to hold that important position. In this first day's fight the Unionists sustained a grievous loss in the death of General Reynolds, who had exposed himself in the woods near the Chambersburg road west of Gettysburg and was brought down by a sharpshooter. He was succeeded by Winfield Scott Hancock, a soldierly leader trained at West Point and seasoned by service on the Peninsula, at Antietam, at Fredericksburg, and at Chancellorsville. He was one of the keenest and most alert of the Union commanders.

In the country around Gettysburg flat fields alternate with ridges, rock formations, hills, and small mountains. West of the town stands the Lutheran seminary, from which there extends north and south a stretch of high ground called "Seminary Ridge." About a mile east of this position is "Cemetery Ridge," these parallel ridges being but slightly higher than the intervening plain. The cemetery is just south of the town, this location being called "Cemetery Hill"; farther to the east is "Culp's Hill." About two miles south of Cemetery Hill are two small mountains of conical shape, called "Round Top" and "Little Round Top." When the Union position was developed after much shifting, it presented a fish-hook formation with the eye of the hook (the Union left) on Round Top, the main extent of the position along Cemetery Ridge, and the right (the barb of the hook) on Culp's Hill. It was a strong defensive position, assumed more by the accident of war than by the foresight of Union generals. Opposite, on Seminary Ridge, stood the Confederates. Instead of giving battle under such circumstances, Longstreet urged Lee to swing round the Union left and, by interposing between the Union army and Washington, dislodge Meade, select a good position, force Meade to make the attack, and beat the Federals as at Fredericksburg. Lee, however, overruled Longstreet's plan as impracticable. In this decision, says Freeman, he has been "sustained by nearly all military critics." [1]

The incidents of the second day were concerned chiefly with the right and left of the Union positions. On the left Longstreet and A. P. Hill hurled their forces against the exposed Union position below the Round Tops, and there followed furious fighting in the Peach Orchard and Devil's Den in which the Confederates were successful; so that the Den and the field at the foot of the Round Tops were held by the Confederates. The Round Tops themselves, however, were secure in Union hands. This was the work of General Warren, to whom Meade had intrusted the operations on his left. He found Little Round Top unoccupied, deemed it the "key of the whole position," and asked Meade for troops to be sent to this

[1] Freeman, *Lee,* III, 82.

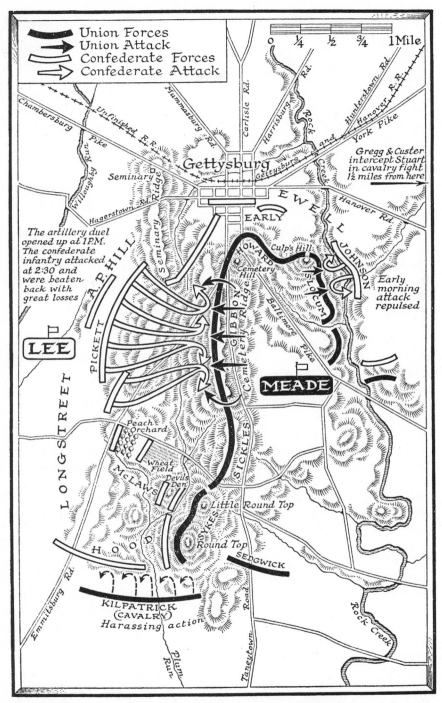

Legend:
- Union Forces
- Union Attack
- Confederate Forces
- Confederate Attack

0 ¼ ½ ¾ 1 Mile

Chambersburg Pike

Willoughby Run Rd.

Unfinished R.R.

Mummasburg Rd.

Carlisle Rd.

Harrisburg Rd.

Rock Creek

Gettysburg and Hanover R.R.

Hunterstown Rd.

Hanover Pike

York Pike

Gettysburg

Seminary

Hagerstown Rd.

Seminary Ridge

Gettysburg

Gregg & Custer intercept Stuart in cavalry fight 1½ miles from here

EARLY

EWELL

JOHNSON

Howard

Cemetery Hill

Culp's Hill

Slocum

Hanover Rd.

Early morning attack repulsed

The artillery duel opened up at 1 P.M. The confederate infantry attacked at 2:30 and were beaten back with great losses

A. P. HILL

PICKETT

GIBBON

Cemetery Ridge

Baltimore Pike

LEE

MEADE

LONGSTREET

Peach Orchard

Wheat Field

McLAWS

Devils Den

SICKLES

Little Round Top

SYKES

Round Top

Round Top

SEDGWICK

HOOD

Emmitsburg Rd.

KILPATRICK (CAVALRY) Harassing action

Plum Run

Taneytown Road

Rock Creek

THE BATTLE OF GETTYSBURG: THE THIRD DAY, JULY 3, 1863

point. Infantry and artillery were rushed to the height under pressure; they arrived in time to beat the Confederates back in a close encounter; and both Round Tops were in Union possession.

It has been asserted that the failure of the Confederates to shake the Union left on July 2 was due to Longstreet, whose attack did not occur until mid-afternoon. Maurice, writing in glowing terms of Lee's generalship, joins in the criticism of Longstreet; Freeman writes of his obstinacy, insubordination, and failure to cooperate.[2] On the other hand, Colonel Donald B. Sanger has shown that such critics have not studied the actual route which Longstreet's men had to take in order to get into the line of battle. "Considering the distance and the type of march," he writes, "arrival in position for attack could not be expected before 2 P.M. and might be extended to about 6 P.M. Anything between these extremes may be assumed with equal propriety." [3] It is worth remembering that the later complaints over Longstreet's alleged dilatoriness did not originate with Lee himself; the Confederate commander contented himself in his official report with the statement that "Longstreet's dispositions were not completed as early as was expected." [4] At the other end of the battle line, at the close of the second day, Ewell's troops assaulted the Union right. Early struck on East Cemetery Hill without capturing the position. Johnson's [5] division did better, seizing the Union intrenchments at Culp's Hill; this position, however, was recovered next day.[6]

On the night of the second day at Gettysburg Meade held a council of war at which it was decided to hold the existing Union position, remain on the defensive, and await Lee's attack. That attack was directed against the Union center; it was delayed until afternoon (July 3) and marked the climax of the battle. Again Longstreet urged that this frontal attack be avoided and that an attempt be made to turn the Federal position by a maneuver on Meade's left. He was overruled; and the attack by Pickett's division was ordered in the hope that by a supreme effort the Union center could be broken and the army put to rout. Meade had anticipated the attack on his center. He had concentrated his first and second corps there with

[2] *Ibid.*, III, chs. vi, vii, ix.

[3] Donald B. Sanger and Thomas R. Hay, *James Longstreet*, 176.

[4] *Offic. Rec.*, 1 ser., XXVII, pt. 2, 320. Lee also admitted that his army was "much embarrassed by the absence of the cavalry" under "Jeb" Stuart (*ibid.*, 321). For a defense of Stuart, see biography by J. W. Thomason, Jr., 427.

[5] Major General Edward Johnson, C. S. A.

[6] Space is lacking in which to treat the "Meade-Sickles controversy." It is charged that Meade's attention was concentrated on his right to the neglect of his left, and on the other hand that Sickles committed a costly error in advancing to the Emmitsburg road on the afternoon of the 2nd, breaking connection with the rest of the Union army and leaving Little Round Top undefended—an error which produced useless slaughter and nearly caused a major disaster by giving the Confederates an opening for the seizure of the Round Tops. *Battles and Leaders*, III, 406–419.

Hancock in command; the position was made secure by defensive works and artillery placements; reserves were ready to be rushed in; and cavalry were stationed in the rear with orders to shoot stragglers. About one o'clock the Confederate guns opened fire with such a cannonade as had never been witnessed in any American battle; whereupon answering Union batteries caused the scene to resemble a "furious thunderstorm." [7] Confederate ammunition was low, however, and Meade's artillery was far from silenced. Though it "seemed madness to launch infantry into that fire," [8] Pickett's division, supported by troops under Pettigrew, Wilcox, and Trimble—about 15,000 men—moved forward. Their advancing lines crumpled, re-formed, and pressed ahead under terrific fire from Union batteries; as they approached the Union position they were struck by concentrated infantry volleys aimed with precision, the work of the sharpshooters being especially effective. As life poured out like water the flower of Southern manhood was sacrificed in a ghastly slaughter. At the peak of the attack General Armistead fell at the moment when, with a hundred men, he had momentarily pierced the Union position at "bloody angle" on the crest of the ridge. The bleeding fragments of Pickett's division staggered back to Seminary Ridge; Lee, whose thoughts may have anticipated Appomattox, met them with self-composed dignity; Meade withheld the countercharge which the Southerners expected; and the battle of Gettysburg was over.[9] Next day the armies lay facing each other "like spent lions nursing their wounds"; [10] Meade still avoided attack; and Lee began his orderly retreat to Virginia (July 4). Having halted his army at Williamsport, where he waited for the Potomac to subside, he crossed on the night of the 13th. Meade's opportunity to strike a counter blow and catch Lee at a disadvantage, with a swollen river at the back of his retreating army, was lost. Thus the huge stakes possible as a result of Gettysburg, so Meade's critics said, were permitted to elude Union grasp.

3

Events on the western front must now be brought into the story. On the Union side the Henry-Donelson-Shiloh campaign and the Pope-Foote campaign, as already noted, had demonstrated the effect of joint military and naval operations on the western rivers, a factor whose importance in

[7] Freeman, *Lee*, III, 119.
[8] Statement of General E. P. Alexander, C. S. A., *Battles and Leaders*, III, 364.
[9] In reviewing Gettysburg Freeman points out that Stuart "violated orders and deprived Lee of his services when most needed," that the failure of Ewell to take Cemetery Hill at the end of the first day was a serious mistake, that Lee's extended line made coordination difficult, that Longstreet's delay was exceedingly costly, that the "reorganized army did not fight as a single machine," and that in Pickett's charge insufficient troops were thrown in to support the assault. Freeman, *Lee*, III, 147 ff.
[10] Thomas Nelson Page, *Lee*, 349.

the war can hardly be overestimated. After these campaigns, which left
the Cumberland and Tennessee rivers and the upper Mississippi in Union
control, there followed a series of changes in army command. Halleck,
reaping credit for western advance, was transferred to Washington and
made general-in-chief of all the land forces of the United States in July,
1862. This brought promotion to Grant, who had been relegated to an unimportant place and had even, for a time, been under arrest. He was now
put in general command of the forces in western Tennessee and northern
Mississippi.[1] Besides leading his own Army of the Tennessee he had authority over Rosecrans, who succeeded Pope as commander of the Army
of the Mississippi. D. C. Buell, commanding the Army of the Ohio, was
intrusted with operations in central and eastern Tennessee, the latter region being especially in Lincoln's eye because of its Unionism and its
readiness to cooperate in civil reconstruction.

The keys to western strategy were Chattanooga and Vicksburg. Chattanooga was so placed in topography and rail connections as to form a door-
way between Richmond and the nearer Southwest; Vicksburg not only
commanded the Mississippi River, but formed the rail connection with the
farther Southwest, especially Texas, where the blockade was of limited
efficiency, and where food and munitions were obtained for the Confederate armies in the East. Whatever might be the political importance of Kentucky as a prize for which the Confederates would be tempted to strike, the
loss of Chattanooga or Vicksburg would amount to the severing of vital
arteries; and the Union seizure of both these places in 1863 had as much
to do with sealing the doom of the Confederacy as the repulse of Lee at
Gettysburg.

On the Confederate side Bragg had succeeded Beauregard as general
commander of the forces between Virginia and the Mississippi River. He
now transferred his own army to Chattanooga, leaving the defense of
Vicksburg and the operations in northeastern Mississippi to Van Dorn and
Price. Other Confederate armies in the West were those of Humphrey
Marshall, soon to move into Kentucky from western Virginia, and E. Kirby
Smith, who commanded an important force at Knoxville and stood ready
to cooperate with Bragg on the fronts of eastern Tennessee and Kentucky.

Buell, whose business was to operate against Bragg, was embarrassed
because of his tenuous hold upon central Tennessee. Though he held Nashville and Murfreesboro, his communications via the Louisville and Nashville Railroad were difficult to maintain in a region of hostile civilians and
guerilla bands; and he was especially hampered by the destructive operations of two Confederate cavalry commanders, Generals J. H. Morgan and
N. B. Forrest. With 2000 cavalry Forrest descended upon Murfreesboro
(July 13, 1862) and captured a force of about brigade proportions under
General T. T. Crittenden. At about the same time Morgan's cavalry struck

---

[1] Ropes, *Story of the Civil War*, II, 386 (but see Upton, 274).

the line of the Louisville and Nashville in Kentucky, surprising small Union detachments, cutting railway tracks, wrecking bridges, capturing or destroying military stores, interrupting telegraph communications, intercepting Union dispatches, conveying false messages over the wire to the enemy, terrorizing small villages, and creating general havoc and confusion along the widely stretched Federal lines. This raid by Morgan (July 4–28) was followed by another smashing raid in August in the vicinity of Nashville, in which isolated Federal forces were dispersed or captured and a large Union cavalry command under General R. W. Johnson was routed, many of them being made prisoners.[2] Meanwhile the Union forces in Tennessee, and noncombatants as well, were annoyed by bushwhackers and guerillas who, in disregard of the rules of war, engaged in uncontrolled plunder, assassination, and terrorism.

The elaborate western campaigns of the summer and fall of 1862 were of a confused nature; the fighting was indecisive; and no clear-cut strategic plan was executed by either side. This portion of the war resolved itself into three main phases: (1) Bragg's invasion of Kentucky; (2) the Iuka-Corinth campaign of Rosecrans against Price and Van Dorn; and (3) unsuccessful strokes of Grant and Sherman against Vicksburg.

On August 28, 1862, Bragg began a northward march from Chattanooga which developed into an ambitious invasion of Kentucky. Reaching Glasgow, Kentucky, in mid-September, he pressed on and seemed on the point of taking Louisville; then he allowed himself to be diverted, and swung his columns toward Lexington. Buell promptly entered Louisville, where his army was augmented by fresh recruits. Bragg, on the other hand, was strengthened by the force under Kirby Smith which had proceeded from Knoxville, entered Kentucky in the region of Cumberland Gap, and defeated a Federal force at Richmond, Kentucky.

The climax of this campaign occurred in the battle of Perryville (October 8, 1862). On the eve of the battle Bragg was absent from his army, having gone to the capital, Frankfort, to participate in the inauguration of Richard Hawes as provisional (secessionist) governor of Kentucky. The approach of the Federal army rudely interrupted this ceremony; and "Governor" Hawes was soon in flight from the state. In the Perryville engagement three of Bragg's divisions under General (Bishop) Leonidas Polk attacked part of Buell's army, the brunt of the attack falling upon the corps of McCook, whose troops were surprised in a furious assault by superior numbers and driven back with terrific loss. A portion, however, of the Union line in this battle stood fast. The center, under P. H. Sheridan, secure in its intrenchments on Chaplin Heights, remained unshaken against violent Confederate assaults and delivered powerful counterblows.

[2] For these raids see *Battles and Leaders*, III, 3, 28, 37, 451, 484; comte de Paris, *Civil War in Amer.*, II, 365; *Offic. Rec.*, 1 ser., XVI, pt. 1, 731–784, 815–819, 871–882.

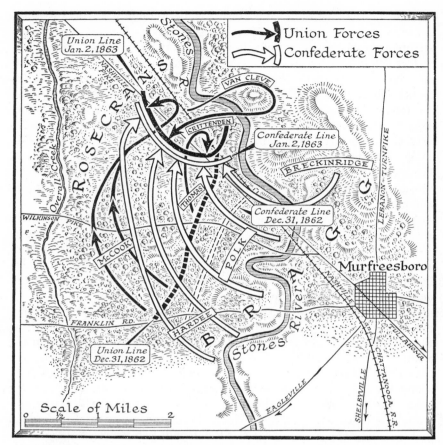

THE BATTLE OF MURFREESBORO, DECEMBER 31, 1862

Half the Federal army did not take part; for although the battle began at two o'clock, Buell did not know of the fight until four, so that the additional force which he sent arrived too late. The battle was severe and sanguinary, the Unionists suffering about 800 killed and 2800 wounded, the Confederates 500 killed and 2600 wounded.[3] Though neither side could count the battle a clear victory, the advantage was with the North. The Unionists failed to crush Bragg; on the other hand the Confederates now abandoned Kentucky, whose people had given an indifferent response to Confederate "liberation." The opposing armies went their way over widely separated routes, Bragg entering Tennessee by way of the Cumberland Gap, and Buell, who was soon to be superseded by Rosecrans, making for Nashville.

[3] Livermore, *Numbers and Losses*, 95.

The campaign just sketched had been accompanied by operations of Rosecrans which prevented Price from crossing the Tennessee River and effecting a junction with Bragg. In the battle of Iuka (September 19, 1862) Rosecrans defeated Price; then in the battle of Corinth (October 3–4) he defeated the combined forces of Price and Van Dorn. Dissatisfaction with Buell, who had failed to anticipate Bragg's invasion of Kentucky and neglected to pursue him after Perryville, now caused him to be supplanted by Rosecrans, who on October 30, 1862, became commander of the Army of the Ohio.[4]

The last day of 1862 saw another hard-fought engagement in the West. Rosecrans, commanding what was now called the Army of the Cumberland, moved out of Nashville on December 26 to strike Bragg's forces near Murfreesboro, the latter having just been weakened by the detachment of a whole division for operations in Mississippi.[5] Rosecrans had about 41,000 effectives; Bragg about 34,000.[6] The engagement begun on the 31st was one of the fiercest of battles.[7] Bragg lost 1294 killed and 7945 wounded; while Rosecrans lost 1677 killed and 7543 wounded.[8] It was a drawn battle, producing on neither side a result commensurate with the cost. Since it resulted in Bragg's evacuation of Murfreesboro and his retirement from middle Tennessee it has been claimed as a Union triumph; but the Union army which achieved the "victory" did not strike again for six months.

4

The main episode in the West in 1863 was Grant's remarkable Vicksburg campaign—an enterprise which only a daring and resourceful general could have conceived and carried to a successful conclusion. Vicksburg on its high bluff commanded a hairpin bend in the Mississippi, the surrounding topography making it virtually unapproachable except from the south and east. On the west the river approach was blocked by Confederate batteries, while on the north the region of the Yazoo delta constituted an intricate and hopeless tangle of back-water areas, lakes, swamps, creeks, bayous, and wooded bluffs. In May–June, 1862, a naval expedition under Farragut and Porter tried unsuccessfully to reduce and capture the city. Memphis was seized in the naval battle of June 6, 1862; then in December Sherman tried an impossible approach via Chickasaw Bayou.

---

[4] Buell had some excellent qualities. Succeeding Sherman in November, 1861, as commander of the Army of the Ohio, he organized and developed it into a well-disciplined fighting machine. Its later success as the Army of the Cumberland is in part a tribute to Buell's organizing ability.

[5] *Battles and Leaders,* III, 604, 474.

[6] Livermore, 97.

[7] Known as the battle of Murfreesboro or Stone's River (Dec. 31–Jan. 3, 1862–1863).

[8] Livermore, 97.

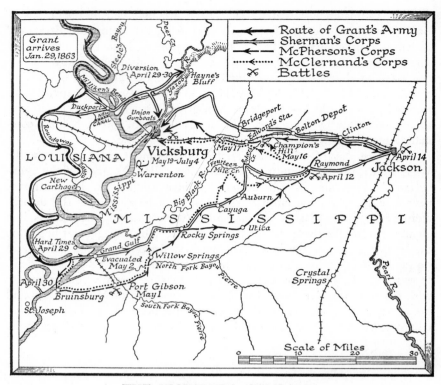

THE VICKSBURG CAMPAIGN

According to Union plans the Confederate force under Pemberton near Grenada was to be kept occupied by Grant while Sherman and Porter surprised Vicksburg. In this enterprise Grant's efforts were nullified by a Confederate drive in his rear under Van Dorn which destroyed his depot at Holly Springs; the navy had a sorry struggle in maneuvering its vessels in the narrow passages; and Sherman found that any attempt on Vicksburg from the Yazoo was "hopeless." [1] In his assault at Chickasaw Bluffs (December 29, 1862) the Union troops behaved valiantly, losing 1200 killed and wounded; but they were essaying the impossible. Still other efforts to get a force in front of Vicksburg, including the construction of a canal to divert the Mississippi River and the breaking of a levee to form a channel from the Mississippi to the Yazoo, were tried without success.[2]

[1] Sherman, *Memoirs*, I, 294.

[2] On January 11, 1863, a Union land-and-water expedition captured the Confederate works at Arkansas Post. In late January and February Sherman engaged in what might be aptly described as fighting the Mississippi River, vainly seeking to divert the mighty stream through a canal cut across the peninsula opposite

Finally Grant threw military theories aside, cut loose from his distant base at Memphis, and launched upon the arduous campaign which stands as his greatest achievement.[3] He moved his army to Milliken's Bend above Vicksburg, met the fleet, crossed the river to the Louisiana side, and marched south through a labyrinth of bayous and lakes to a point far below Vicksburg. There he awaited the fleet whose business it was to run the Vicksburg batteries. This difficult task was accomplished with little loss; and by the end of April Porter's gunboats and transports were ready to transfer Grant's force of 20,000 to the Mississippi side of the river at Bruinsburg.

Grant was now cut off from his supplies, operating in enemy country over a difficult terrain; yet within twenty days he mastered the whole Vicksburg area in a series of brilliant victories and closed in upon Pemberton with a grip that could not be broken. In the action at Port Gibson on May 1 he defeated Bowen, after which Grand Gulf was seized. General Gregg was defeated in the battle of Raymond, May 12; Jackson, capital of Mississippi, was captured, May 14; and on May 16 and 17 Grant met Pemberton and defeated him in the battles of Champion Hill and Big Black River Bridge. Joseph E. Johnston, operating near Jackson, and Pemberton, defending Vicksburg, were now divided. Their strategy has generally been regarded as faulty. By May 19 Grant had Vicksburg "completely invested"; on the 19th and 22nd of May he assaulted Pemberton's works; failing in this he sat down to a siege. For over six weeks the two armies faced each other at a distance of six hundred yards or less. There was much fraternizing and exchange of amenities and not a little Confederate desertion to the Union lines. After mines had been pushed nearer and nearer to the Confederate fortifications, a deposit of powder was exploded on June 25. Meanwhile the inhabitants of Vicksburg had been living largely underground; people and soldiers were on short rations; mules and rats had been used as food; and the city had been bombarded from the gun-

---

Vicksburg. Then he and Porter made a combined attempt to push through the bayous to the Yazoo River above Haynes's Bluff. This expedition not only failed of its object but was barely able to extricate itself.

[3] Grant's Vicksburg operations were embarrassed by the intrigues of John A. McClernand, who visited Washington and on October 21, 1862, obtained from Stanton a confidential order (which Grant learned of accidentally) authorizing him to recruit and organize troops for the capture of Vicksburg. The giving of such an order without notifying Grant, who was making his own preparations against Vicksburg with full authority to do so as commander of the Department of the Tennessee, can only be described as gross political meddling. As the campaign progressed McClernand's efforts to get all the credit for the Vicksburg enterprise and his noncooperation with Grant, who was his superior in command, produced an intolerable situation. Finally, when McClernand published an order in the newspapers congratulating his own troops and doing injustice to other commanders, Grant removed him from command and ordered him back to Springfield. *Battles and Leaders*, III, 451 n., 526.

boats and Grant's artillery. Finding himself bottled up by land, and prevented by the fleet from escaping via Louisiana, Pemberton surrendered
his whole force (over 30,000) on July 4, 1863.[4] Grant gave the necessary
rations to Pemberton's troops, which, instead of being taken captive, were
released as prisoners of war under parole. The fall of Vicksburg, coming
simultaneously with the Union victory at Gettysburg, gave heart to the
North, impressed Europe with the strength of the United States, and put
an entirely new face on the war, which in May had seemed virtually won
by the Confederates.[5]

5

Ranking in importance with the Vicksburg campaign was the Chattanooga–Chickamauga–Missionary-Ridge campaign, which made the year
1863 memorable as one of decisive Union advance in the West. After
months of inactivity Rosecrans in June, 1863, moved his army out of
Murfreesboro, and by September 9 he had maneuvered Bragg out of Chattanooga and had occupied the town without a battle. Bragg did not have
the confidence of his soldiers or subordinate generals; he lacked the resourcefulness, dash, and craftiness of Lee; his system of scouts was inefficient; and he was perplexed by the appearance of Rosecrans's various units
in different places and bewildered by "the popping out of the rats from so
many holes." [1] Confederate critics have found in his evacuation of Chattanooga a theme of criticism and an occasion for contrast with the bolder
strategy of Lee.[2] By this time Buckner had been drawn out of Knoxville,
which was promptly occupied by Burnside, now in command of the Department of the Ohio. Burnside, however, had failed to join Rosecrans,

[4] *Offic. Rec.,* 1 ser., XXIV, pt. 1, 57.
[5] A minor episode in the West in the summer of 1863 (simultaneous with the
Gettysburg and Vicksburg operations) was the "Ohio raid" of General John Hunt
Morgan. With about 2500 mounted infantry he pushed rapidly northward through
central Kentucky (via Burkesville, Lebanon, Springfield, and Bardstown, to Bran-
denburg on the Ohio), cut a swath in southern Indiana (touching Corydon, Lexington, and Vernon), swept through the suburbs of Cincinnati, and headed east. Tearing rapidly from town to town his men pillaged and plundered, captured horses,
destroyed bridges, and used clever ruses to elude pursuit. Their career as a raiding
force ended toward the end of July not far from Blennerhassett's Island on the
upper Ohio, where pursuit finally caught up with them. A few hundred escaped
and many were drowned; but most of the force, including the leader, were confined to Northern prisons. Escaping from prison at Columbus, Ohio (November,
1863), Morgan again made his way south. He met death near Greenville, Tennessee (September, 1864), in an attempt to escape from Northern troops. Though
Morgan "and his men" became romantically famous, the raid accomplished virtually
nothing for the Confederate cause. A more successful raid was that of Col. B. H.
Grierson of the Sixth Illinois Cavalry (April, 1863), cutting through hundreds of
miles of enemy territory from LaGrange, Mississippi, to Baton Rouge, and aiding
Grant materially in the Vicksburg campaign.

[1] *Battles and Leaders,* III, 644.
[2] *Ibid.,* III, 641.

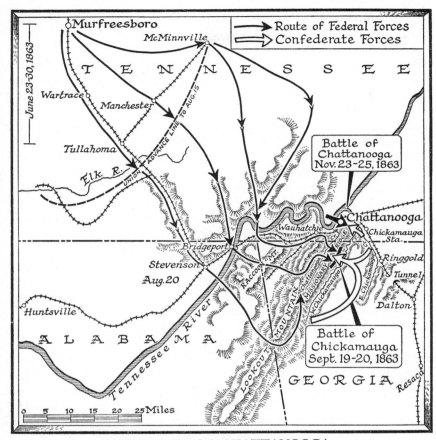

THE AREA OF CHATTANOOGA

while Buckner did join Bragg. Bragg's need now led to a measure which was unusual on the part of Confederate military leaders—the detachment of a large force from the East to the West; Lee sent Longstreet by rail with 11,000 troops.

On September 19–20 the armies met on the field of Chickamauga. With a wild yell Longstreet's troops struck a weak portion of the Federal right, made a gap, broke through, and drove two whole corps (those of Crittenden and McCook) off the field. Rosecrans himself was swept into the retreating current and made his way to Chattanooga, where he prepared to receive his defeated army and reorganize it for another stand. This phase of the battle was a Federal rout analogous to the first Bull Run. There was, however, another phase. Thomas, unaware of the reverse on the Union right, stood fast against terrific assaults by superior numbers and saved the Union army from complete disaster. It was, however, the strengthening of **Thomas which had weakened Rosecrans's right and let Longstreet through.**

As a slaughterhouse the battle was comparable to Gettysburg or Antietam. The Federals lost 1600 killed and about 16,000 in all; the Confederates a total of nearly 18,000, with 2300 killed.[3] Costly as it was, Chickamauga was a barren victory for the Confederates. Bragg now commanded the railroads entering Chattanooga and had his enemy penned up, so that the plight of Rosecrans made Washington extremely nervous; but events soon followed which were to change the whole situation. Another great Union fighter had now emerged from the smoke of war. At the moment when Rosecrans, paralyzed by the effect of Chickamauga, seemed to be supinely waiting for his army to starve, George H. Thomas, "the Rock of Chickamauga," superseded him as commander of the Army of the Cumberland. At the same time Grant was elevated to supreme command of Union operations in the West.[4]

At the opening of the Grant-Thomas campaign the Federals were practically besieged in Chattanooga. They were short of food and supplies, and Jefferson Davis was predicting that they would soon be compelled to evacuate the place. The Confederates had the great advantage of occupying the main heights facing the city—Missionary Ridge and Lookout Mountain—together with extended positions which blocked Union navigation of the Tennessee. Grant's first problem was to relieve the army of its beleaguered condition and open up a line of supplies; his next was to bring up his scattered forces; his third, to strike the Confederate army under Bragg. It is only by studying the arduous details of his preparatory movements that the full measure of the Union achievement can be appreciated. The river line of supplies via Bridgeport was opened up by means of a minor operation at Brown's Ferry below Chattanooga, an engagement planned by General William Farrar Smith, chief engineer of the Army of the Cumberland, and calling for the maximum of engineering enterprise with the minimum of fighting. Steamers could now ply this part of the Tennessee River; the army had its "cracker line." Sherman worked his way eastward from Memphis, his advance being largely a matter of railroad building, for the enemy had wrecked the tracks, captured or destroyed cars and locomotives, and demolished the bridges. All the manifold operations of railroad construction had to be pushed at top speed. This phase of the campaign was chiefly the work of General G. M. Dodge, who had "every branch of railroad building . . . going on at once." [5] The Army of the Potomac in Virginia was inactive; and two corps of this army were now sent by rail under Hooker to cooperate in the Chattanooga campaign.

While Grant was thus consolidating his forces, affairs on the Con-

---

[3] Livermore, 105–106. These totals include killed, wounded, and missing. See also *Battles and Leaders*, III, 673–675.

[4] There was one exception to Grant's command; he was not in authority over the operations conducted by N. P. Banks.

[5] *Personal Memoirs of U. S. Grant*, II, 48.

federate side were mismanaged. A fierce controversy sprang up between Bragg and his subordinate generals over the conduct of the recent battle. Speaking for himself and Generals Polk and D. H. Hill, Longstreet wrote the Confederate secretary of war: "I am convinced that nothing but the hand of God can help us as long as we have our present commander." [6] In the hope of settling the quarrel, President Davis himself visited the army but, after hearing the complaints of Bragg's subordinates, he kept the general in command. Clifford Dowdey has vigorously criticized Davis's "deranged support" of Bragg in these circumstances,[7] but the Confederate President's most careful biographer explains his action in terms of the "want of a better alternative" and of Davis's reluctance "to be unjust to a victorious officer to please the populace and boost his own popularity." [8] Most of Bragg's critics were relieved of command or posted elsewhere. In a fateful decision to divide Bragg's already small force, Longstreet, at Davis's suggestion, was sent off with one-third of the troops in an effort to capture Burnside's army at Knoxville. From the outset this campaign was bungled. Longstreet "allowed himself to go off on an expedition into an unknown part of the country with less than fifteen thousand men in an attempt to capture or defeat a larger force, with little or no control over transportation and less over the system of supply." [9] As might have been anticipated, he was repulsed before Knoxville. Meanwhile Grant attacked the main body of Bragg's army in the three-day battle of Lookout Mountain-Missionary Ridge, November 23–25, 1863. Grant had now assembled about 60,000 troops to Bragg's 40,000.[10] The battle had three main phases: (1) Sherman, having crossed the Tennessee at Brown's Ferry and marched east of Chattanooga, assaulted the Confederate right at the north end of Missionary Ridge. (2) Hooker struck the opposite extreme flank of the Confederates on Lookout Mountain, and in the so-called "battle above the clouds" repulsed a few Confederate skirmishers, whose resistance to overwhelming numbers did them great credit, and carried this mountain position. Bragg's army was now concentrated on Missionary Ridge; Sherman's operations had not shaken the Confederates seriously; and by midafternoon of November 25 the battle as planned had not been won. (3) The main engagement of the battle developed at 3:30, November 25. Two of Thomas's divisions (Sheridan's and T. J. Wood's) moved out for what was intended to be a "demonstration" to assist Sherman by relieving the pressure in this area.[11] Their orders were to carry the rifle pits at the

---

[6] Sanger and Hay, *James Longstreet*, 212.
[7] Dowdey, *The Land They Fought For*, 299.
[8] Hudson Strode, *Jefferson Davis: Confederate President*, 481.
[9] Sanger and Hay, *op. cit.*, 223.
[10] Rhodes, IV, 407, n. 3.
[11] According to Grant's plan, the movements of Thomas against the Confederate center and Hooker against the left were to be subordinate to those of Sherman against the right. The main effort was expected to be that of Sherman.

foot of the ridge. This done, the men pushed on without orders to the surprise of their generals. It was a sudden impulse which no commander could have either created or restrained. After the Union divisions forced their way over rough ground up the ridge a panic seized the Confederates at the top; and by one of those unexplainable turns of fortune the panting and exhausted Unionists, after severe fighting, carried the crest against troops who could seemingly have stopped them by a slight effort.[12] A Federal colonel stated that after the battle General Granger rode along the Union lines, calling to the troops: "I am going to have you all court-martialed! You were ordered to take the works at the foot of the hill, and you have taken those on top! You have disobeyed orders, all of you . . . !" [13] The outcome of the battle was the flight of Bragg's shattered army and the occupation of the ridge by the Federals. Chattanooga and Tennessee generally were now in Union hands.

[12] Among other documents revealing confusion and disorder within Confederate ranks the Bragg papers contain the penciled draft of a letter to Jefferson Davis, dated at Dalton, Georgia, December 1, 1863, in which Bragg comments on his "shameful discomfiture" in the Chattanooga campaign. "The disaster [he writes] admits of no palliation, and is justly disparaging to me as a commander." He adds: "I fear we both erred in the conclusion for me to retain command here after the clamor raised against me. . . ." Bragg MSS., Western Reserve Hist. Soc., Cleveland, Ohio.

[13] *Battles and Leaders,* III, 726 n.

ULYSSES S. GRANT

BENJAMIN F. BUTLER

DAVID G. FARRAGUT

FARRAGUT'S FLEET ASCENDING THE MISSISSIPPI, APRIL 17, 1862

ANDREW H. FOOTE

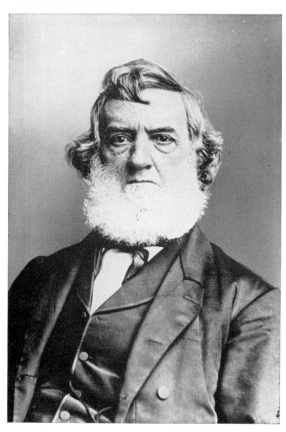

GIDEON WELLES

WRECK OF A BLOCKADE RUNNER
OFF SULLIVAN'S ISLAND, SOUTH CAROLINA

DECK VIEW OF THE U.S.S. "MONITOR"
SHOWING THE EFFECTS OF FIRE FROM THE C.S.S. "VIRGINIA"

CONFEDERATE IRONCLAD RAM "STONEWALL"
AT WASHINGTON, D.C., JUNE, 1865

THE C.S.S. "ALABAMA" AND THE "BRILLIANTE"

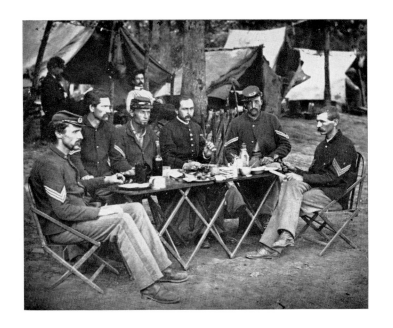

NONCOMMISSIONED OFFICERS' MESS, COMPANY D,
93RD NEW YORK INFANTRY NEAR BEALTON, VIRGINIA, AUGUST, 1863

The Library of Congress

HEADQUARTERS, 1ST BRIGADE, U.S. HORSE ARTILLERY,
BRANDY STATION, VIRGINIA, FEBRUARY, 1864

CONFEDERATES OPENING FIRE UPON FEDERAL CAVALRY
AT REED'S BRIDGE OVER THE CHICKAMAUGA

GEORGE H. THOMAS

FEDERAL TROOPS EXAMINING PASSES
AT GEORGETOWN FERRY

PHILIP H. SHERIDAN

WILLIAM T. SHERMAN

Opposite page:

PULPIT ROCK,

THE SUMMIT OF

LOOKOUT MOUNTAIN

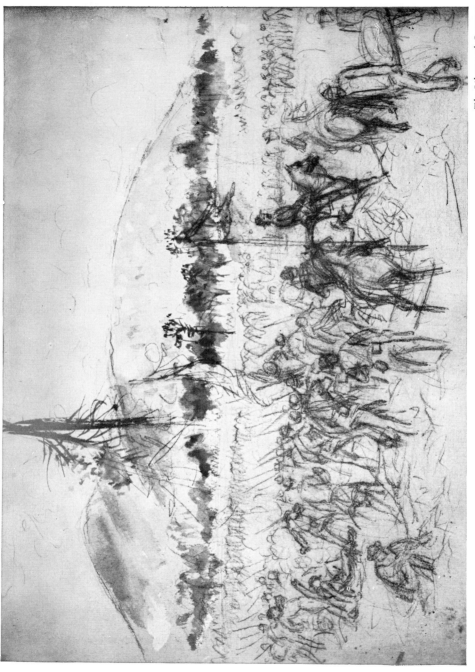

TWO SCENES OF THE BATTLE OF KENESAW MOUNTAIN, JUNE 27, 1864

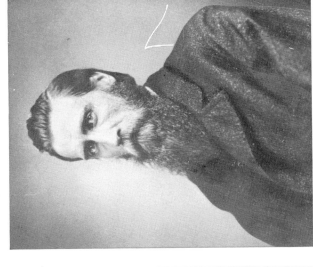

JOSEPH E. JOHNSTON

JOHN B. HOOD

WILDERNESS CAMPAIGN:
FEDERAL PONTOON BRIDGE
ACROSS THE
NORTH ANNA RIVER,
MAY, 1864

The Library of Congress

BRIGADIER GENERAL FRANCIS BARLOW'S CHARGE
AT COLD HARBOR, JUNE 3, 1864

The Library of Congress

Opposite page:

CONFEDERATE SOLDIER OF EWELL'S CORPS
KILLED IN ATTACK OF MAY 19, 1864

The Library of Congress

POLITICAL CARICATURE Nº 2.

MISCEGENATION
OR THE MILLENNIUM OF ABOLITIONISM.

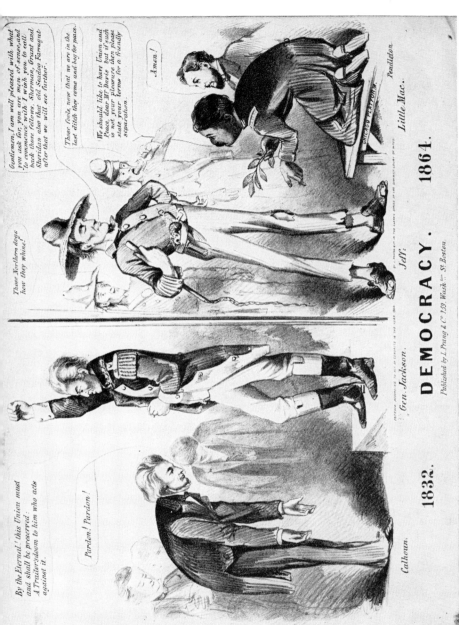

REPUBLICAN CAMPAIGN POSTER, 1864

PENNSYLVANIA SOLDIERS VOTING AT HEADQUARTERS, ARMY OF THE JAMES, 1864

ENGINE OF U.S. MILITARY RAILROAD AT CITY POINT, VIRGINIA

THE LAST TRAIN FROM ATLANTA

RUINS OF CHARLESTON

CONFEDERATE FORTIFICATIONS AROUND PETERSBURG

FEDERAL THIRTEEN-INCH MORTAR "DICTATOR"
IN FRONT OF PETERSBURG

The Library of Congress

Opposite page:

A DEAD CONFEDERATE SOLDIER

The Library of Congress

RUINS OF RICHMOND

LEE LEAVING THE McLEAN HOUSE AT APPOMATTOX

CONFEDERATES TAKING THE OATH
OF ALLEGIANCE TO THE UNION, 1865

EXECUTION
OF THE LINCOLN
ASSASSINATION
CONSPIRATORS
The Library of Congress

CHAPTER 24

Military Campaigns of 1864

I

WITH THE SPRING of 1864 the war entered a new phase. Union victories in the West had cut deeply into the economic and military strength of the Confederacy. They had done more, for they had associated the names of Grant and his lieutenants with a habit of mind which connoted aggressiveness, strategy on a large scale, and victory. It was not that Grant was a supreme master of the "science of war," nor even that he merited full credit for the victories under his command; indeed some of the movements completed under Grant had their inception under Rosecrans, and such a thing as the impulsive charge at Missionary Ridge was an unpredictable development for which no general should claim credit. It was rather that a situation was now reached where, with Northern recruiting, Confederate depletion, and Grant's sledge-hammer blows, the essential conditions of Union triumph had been presented. It was therefore a fact of great importance that on March 9, 1864, President Lincoln in the presence of his cabinet handed Grant a commission as lieutenant-general, a rank newly restored by Congress, and gave him general command of the Union armies. Almost immediately the final grand strategy of the war began to unfold itself, a strategy by which Grant used his numerical superiority and plunged ruthlessly ahead in Virginia, losing an enormous number of men, but wearing out the Confederates by sheer attrition; while in the lower South Sherman attained unenviable laurels by destroying vast amounts of food and other supplies in his "march" through Georgia and the Carolinas. It was by these unceasing blows at the heart of the Confederacy that the war, which had dragged on indecisively for three years, was brought to an end in 1865.

As Grant viewed the situation in the spring of '64 he found both hopeful and disheartening signs. The Mississippi River was in Union hands; Tennessee, West Virginia, and Virginia north of the Rapidan were held by Federal forces; most of the coast fortresses along the Atlantic and the Gulf were in Northern control; Louisiana was largely in Union occupation. On the other hand the vast bulk of the Confederacy was still unshaken;

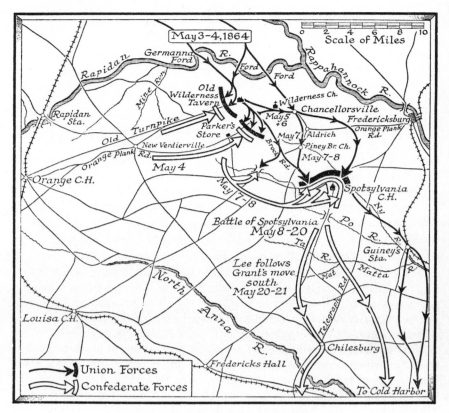

THE WILDERNESS CAMPAIGN

Southern arms held the rich Shenandoah Valley; and two powerful armies—Lee's in Virginia and Johnston's in northwestern Georgia—were ready to do battle against the Yankee invader. The campaigns of 1864 can be more readily visualized if it is remembered that while Grant accompanied Meade, who continued to command the Army of the Potomac operating against Lee, Sherman moved against Johnston, and Sheridan was occupied in reducing and devastating the Shenandoah Valley. The minor operations of Banks in the Southwest hardly entered the central picture.

As to Grant's own part (in company with Meade) the first episode was a series of bloody encounters in the tangled and wooded region near Fredericksburg. These tragic days have passed down as the Battle of the Wilderness. At the outset of this Virginia campaign Grant's main forces, assembled north of the Rapidan with headquarters at Culpeper, numbered approximately 118,000; while B. F. Butler was at Fort Monroe in command of about 36,000. Lee faced Grant's main host with about 60,000 effectives, while Beauregard commanded a supporting force of some 30,000 in the region of Richmond and Petersburg.[1]

On the early morning of May 4, 1864, the Army of the Potomac, inactive since Gettysburg except for maneuvering in the "bloodless game of Kriegsspiel," [2] started to move across the Rapidan. Grant had hoped to get through the Wilderness into clear country before giving battle; but wagon trains delayed his movements, and on the 5th and 6th, in dense thickets where orderly battle plans were impossible, the two armies came to grips in a series of engagements so complicated that any description in terms of corps and divisions is impracticable in these pages. Union losses approximated 18,000, of whom over 2000 were killed; the Confederate loss probably exceeded 10,000. Undeterred by the fearful slaughter, Grant launched another forward movement; in the judgment of W. T. Sherman this was "the supreme moment of his life." [3] In the terrible assaults of the coming weeks it seemed that the Union army was courting punishment. As a Confederate writer expressed it:

. . . surprise and disappointment were the prevailing emotions . . . when we discovered, after the contest in the Wilderness, that General Grant was not going to retire . . . and permit General Lee to carry on a campaign against Washington in the usual way, but was moving to the Spotsylvania position instead. We had been accustomed to a programme which began with a Federal advance, culminated in one great battle, and ended in the retirement of the Union army, the substitution of a new Federal commander for the one beaten, and the institution of a more or less offensive campaign on our part. . . . But here was a new Federal general, fresh from the West, and so ill-informed as to the military customs in our part of the country that when the battle of the Wilderness was over, instead of retiring to the north bank of the river and awaiting the development of Lee's plans, he had the temerity to move by his left flank to a new position, there to try conclusions with us again. We were greatly disappointed with General Grant, and full of curiosity to know how long it was going to take him to perceive the impropriety of his course.[4]

In the fighting from May 5 to May 12, much of which was hand-to-hand, Grant is said to have lost over 26,000 in killed and wounded.[5] Yet with the grim resolve to fight it out on that line "if it . . . [took] all summer," [6] he pushed on to Cold Harbor, where he brought on the severest fighting moments of the war and committed a costly error. With Lee's

[1] *Battles and Leaders*, IV, 152–153, 182–184, 187, 196 n., 198 n.

[2] Steele, *American Campaigns*, I, 468. The minor engagement at Bristoe Station and the threatened battle at Mine Run in the latter part of 1863 must be omitted from these pages. See Freeman, *Lee*, III, 176 ff., 198 ff.

[3] *Battles and Leaders*, IV, 248.

[4] George Cary Eggleston in *ibid.*, IV, 230 n.

[5] This week (May 5–12) was occupied with the battles of the Wilderness and Spotsylvania. For the losses, see Livermore, 113.

[6] *Offic. Rec.*, 1 ser., XXXVI, pt. 2, 627.

army squarely blocking the way behind strong intrenchments, Grant hurled three corps against an enfilading fire of the enemy (June 3, 1864), losing more men in the eight minutes of hottest fighting than in any similar period in the war. The 12,000 killed and wounded [7] in this attack produced a shudder in the North, intensified the peace movement and the opposition to Lincoln, and created in Union ranks an impression of reckless insanity in their commander combined with a suicidal willingness to follow. Facing death in obedience to fatal orders, many of the men had written their names and addresses on strips of paper and pinned them to their coats for the identification of their dead bodies. Cold Harbor was a ghastly mistake. Grant is reported to have said that he would not have fought it again under the circumstances; in his memoirs he expresses regret that the assault was ever made. [8]

In Lee's ranks there was less fear of Grant than of that grim enemy, hunger. George Cary Eggleston reports the rigid economies in food which his men practiced; then he adds:

Hunger to starving men is wholly unrelated to the desire for food as that is commonly understood and felt. It is a great agony of the whole body and of the soul as well. It is unimaginable, all-pervading pain inflicted when the strength to endure pain is utterly gone. It is a great despairing cry of a wasting body—a cry of flesh and blood, marrow, nerves, bones, and faculties for strength with which to exist and to endure existence. It is a horror which, once suffered, leaves an impression that is never erased from the memory, and to this day the old agony of that campaign comes back upon me at the mere thought of any living creature's lacking the food it desires, even though its hunger be only the ordinary craving and the denial be necessary for the creature's health. [9]

In the whole campaign from the Wilderness to Cold Harbor, the Union losses were approximately 55,000,[10] nearly as much as Lee's whole army. Grant, however, could find new recruits; he was amply reinforced; and he had no embarrassment from the lack of food and equipment. As a defensive accomplishment in fighting off superior numbers, the campaign stands as a significant chapter in Confederate annals.[11] The nature of this

[7] Livermore, 114.
[8] Grant, *Memoirs*, II, 276.
[9] *Battles and Leaders*, IV, 231.
[10] *Ibid.*, IV, 182.
[11] This is the usual conclusion, but to Grant the odds seemed not so uneven. Reviewing the campaign in after years he stated that Lee had 80,000 at the beginning of the campaign, with reinforcements "about equal to ours." "He was on the defensive," adds Grant, "and in a country in which every stream, every road . . . was familiar to him and his army. . . . Rear guards were not necessary for him, and having . . . a railroad at his back, large wagon trains were not required. All circumstances considered we did not have any advantage in numbers." Grant, *Memoirs*, II, 291. (Grant's estimate of Lee's strength was obtained by adding together the forces of Lee and Beauregard.)

accomplishment is indicated by the following comment of an officer of Lee's staff:

. . . The struggle from the wilderness to this point [i.e. to Grant's removal of his army south of the James] covers a period of about one month, during which time there had been an almost daily encounter of hostile arms, and the Army of Northern Virginia had placed *hors de combat* of the army under General Grant a number equal to its entire numerical strength at the commencement of the campaign, and, notwithstanding its own heavy losses and the reinforcements received by the enemy, still presented an impregnable front to its opponent, and constituted an insuperable barrier to General Grant's "On to Richmond." [12]

Confederate losses in the Wilderness campaign were proportionally heavier than those of Grant, behind whom stood the North with its numbers, wealth, organization, and equipment. Lee's chance of conquering the Northern armies had gone. His only chance now was in the doubtful hope that a stout and desperate defense, if continued long enough, would wear down the Northern will to fight, produce Lincoln's defeat in the election of 1864,[13] and by the sheer force of war weariness bring peace on terms acceptable to the South.

2

Grant's determination to fight it out "on this line" now underwent a reconsideration. The chance of defeating Lee north of Richmond having been proved impractical in forty days of frightful human sacrifice, he boldly transferred his whole army south of the James with the purpose of moving upon the Confederate capital from the rear. This crossing of unbridged rivers (the Chickahominy and the James) in the face of possible attack by Lee, requiring difficult engineering and involving the advance of immense numbers over marshy terrain with insufficient guides and maps, may be set down as one of the most important feats of the Army of the Potomac. Beginning the crossing on June 12, Grant had completed it by the 16th. He had taken Lee by surprise,[1] something his predecessors in Virginia had not been able to achieve; and on the 17th his warriors were surging against the defenses of Petersburg.

[12] Col. Walter H. Taylor, in *Recollections . . . of . . . R. E. Lee,* by his son, 129.
[13] Naturally the Confederates thought they would profit in case of Lincoln's defeat. But see below, pp. 477–479.
[1] According to Beauregard, Lee did not realize on June 16 that Grant had crossed the James, but supposed that certain Federal tugs and transports reported to him belonged to Butler's corps. (*Battles and Leaders,* IV, 541.) Grant's army, says Freeman, had "marched away so quietly that the Confederate pickets had not observed its departure." He also writes, however, that Lee expected Grant to cross the James, and that he knew the enemy's approximate position on June 14. (Freeman, *Lee,* III, 402, 441.)

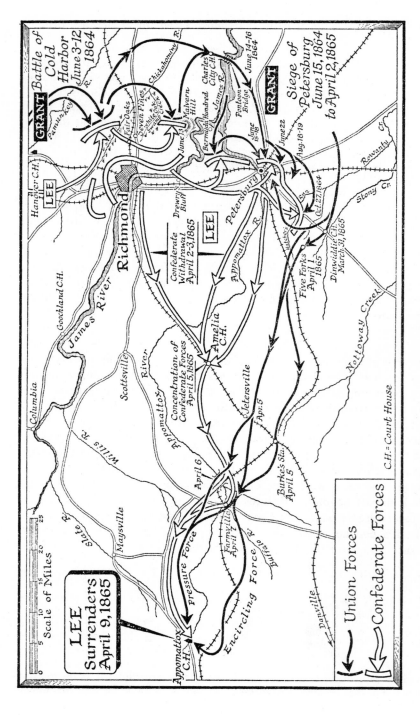

THE VICINITY OF RICHMOND, 1864–1865

LEE Surrenders April 9, 1865

Scale of Miles
0 5 10 15 20 25

Battle of Cold Harbor June 3–12 1864

Siege of Petersburg June 15, 1864 to April 2, 1865

GRANT

GRANT

LEE

LEE

Confederate Withdrawal April 2–3, 1865

Concentration of Confederate Forces April 5, 1865

Hanover C.H.

Richmond

Drewry's Bluff

James River

Goochland C.H.

Columbia

Scottsville

Appomattox River

Willis R.

Slate R.

Maysville

Appomattox C.H.

Pressure Force

Encircling Force

Farmville April 7

Buffalo R.

Danville

Burke's Sta. April 5

April 6

April 5

Jetersville

Amelia C.H.

Appomattox R.

Petersburg

Five Forks April 1 1865

Dinwiddie C.H. March 31, 1865

Stony Cr.

Nottoway Creek

Rowanty Cr.

Oct. 27, 1864

Aug. 18–19

June 22

June 15–18

Pontoon Bridge

Bermuda Hundred

June 14–16 1864

Charles City C.H.

James R.

Malvern Hill

June 1

Seven Pines

Fair Oaks

White Oak Creek

Chickahominy R.

Pamunkey R.

Union Forces

Confederate Forces

C.H. = Court House

While the main armies under Lee and Grant had been grappling with each other north of Richmond, a subsidiary campaign had been in progress below Richmond, where B. F. Butler was operating against Beauregard. Grant had expected Butler to advance up the James, approach Richmond, prevent reinforcements from reaching Lee, and break Confederate communications. His advance was timed to coincide with Grant's forward movement through the Wilderness, and was conceived as an essential factor in the Union strategy of 1864. Butler's incompetence proved as striking as his pompous self-importance. He advanced from Fort Monroe, easily seized City Point and Bermuda Hundred, and moved up as far as Drewry's Bluff, consuming enough time in the process to permit Beauregard to assemble his forces. Then he withdrew upon Beauregard's attack and intrenched at Bermuda Hundred in a neck of land between the James and the Appomattox, where he was penned in by the Confederates who intrenched against him. His army was secure in its unimportant position, but was "as completely shut off from further operations directly against Richmond as if it had been in a bottle strongly corked. It required but a comparatively small force of the enemy to hold it there." [2] Butler's release came only when the Confederates, hard pressed by the main Union drive south of the James, themselves uncorked the bottle.

The defense of Petersburg now became a dire necessity for the Southerners; and they were barely able to assemble their forces and stop the Union advance. Had Butler struck vigorously before this assembling of troops had been effected, there was a reasonable expectation that the place could have been seized. For four days (June 15–18) the Confederate lines at Petersburg were heavily assaulted by Union forces under Smith, Burnside, Warren, and Hancock. In desperate resistance against heavy odds Beauregard's men held their positions; Lee soon arrived with his army; and for the time Petersburg and Richmond were saved for the Confederacy. Then the "spade took the place of the musket"; [3] and Grant settled down to a long siege of Petersburg as the gateway to Richmond. His last large-scale battle with Lee had been fought.

An elaborate mine was now constructed from the center of Burnside's position to a point well within the Confederate works. Plans were laboriously laid, the mine was cut to the length of five hundred feet; eight thousand pounds of powder were deposited; and the fuses were touched off. As huge masses of earth shot into the air, "men, guns, carriages, and timbers" [4]

---

[2] This statement appeared in Grant's official report of July 22, 1865 (*Battles and Leaders*, IV, 147). In his memoirs (II, 152) he generously "corrected" the statement, saying it was his desire to "rectify all injustice" he may have done to a gallant general. As a matter of fact he was much provoked by what he regarded as Butler's failure in the task assigned to him. For failures less serious other commanders had been removed.

[3] *Battles and Leaders*, IV, 544.

[4] *Ibid.*, IV, 551.

were hurled aloft and buried in a shapeless ruin (July 30, 1864). The explosion left a "crater" thirty feet in depth and 170 in length. In the desperate battle which followed the explosion,[5] where the fighting was at close range and much of it hand-to-hand, the Confederates in frenzied combat repulsed the Federal attack. The Southerners' fury was greatly increased by the use of Negro soldiers in the assault. Lee's men were at their bravest here, and Burnside's troops were unable to carry the Confederate position. The whole operation, which cost the Union side almost 4000 men, was set down by Grant as a "stupendous failure." [6] The month of August opened with Richmond in Confederate possession, Lee's army holding fast, and no obvious or striking result to show an angry North for the thousands whom Grant had led to the slaughter.

3

While Lee in Virginia was resisting the crush of Grant's legions and the pinch of hunger, another distinguished Confederate commander, almost the peer of Lee in defensive generalship, was guarding the gateway to the lower South against Sherman's veterans. Joseph E. Johnston, reporting about 53,000 men,[1] stood at Dalton, Georgia, facing Sherman's 98,000 at Chattanooga.[2] The comradeship of Sherman and Grant bespoke

[5] In this battle, as well as in other Confederate operations in Virginia late in the war, important leadership fell to General William Mahone, whose military services have not generally received merited emphasis. After the war he turned Readjuster, supported the Republicans, and was hated by conservative Virginia Democrats.

[6] Grant, Memoirs, II, 315. According to official reports the Union loss was 504 killed, 1881 wounded, 1413 captured or missing. Battles and Leaders, IV, 560.

[1] The eternal controversy as to Confederate numbers is illustrated in the reports concerning Johnston's army at the opening of the Atlanta campaign. Steele (Am. Campaigns, I, 535–536) estimates Johnston's force at 60,000 and Sherman's at 98,000. Johnston reported his "effective total" on April 30, 1864, as 37,652 infantry, 2812 artillery, and 2392 cavalry, making a total of 42,856. (Battles and Leaders, IV, 261.) It will throw light on the variation in totals if one remembers the distinction between "effectives" and those "present for duty." The report of the same day, signed by Johnston and filed in the war department, indicated 52,992 (41,279 infantry, 8436 cavalry, 3277 artillery) as "present for duty." (Ibid., IV, 281.) Major E. C. Dawes (53d Ohio regiment) has explained that a large number of the horses were grazing in the rear, ready to be brought to the front when needed; hence an "effective" total of only 2392 cavalry when 8436 officers and men were "present for duty." When needed, the additional men could have been brought up. (Ibid., IV, 281.) According to Dawes's estimate Johnston had 75,000 men at the battle of New Hope Church (ibid., IV, 282), the odds against him being but five to four. Dawes also states that between April 30 and June 10 Johnston had to account for 84,328 men available for battle. (Ibid., IV, 281.)

[2] In addition to his field force of approximately 100,000, Sherman had an equal number of "guards of his large depots and long line of supply." Battles and Leaders, IV, 294.

a high morale in Union ranks. They were "as brothers," [3] said Sherman, both trained as professional soldiers but "made" on the anvil of war, both associated with western victories, each generously giving credit to the other and ready to cooperate in the closing strokes of a well-planned, comprehensive campaign.

It is far from the truth to suppose that Sherman hacked his way easily into the South by brute force. He was operating in rough country where such a matter as marching a hundred thousand men through a narrow mountain defile was slow business. His lines of communication, extending over a shaky railroad five hundred miles to Louisville, were, as he expressed it, exposed to the "guerrillas of an 'exasperated people.' " [4] At the beginning of May, when Grant moved south from the Rapidan, Sherman moved against Johnston and launched the strenuous campaign which resulted in the capture of Atlanta on September 2. At first he was held in check by the defensive skill of Johnston, with whom he fought a series of severe battles at Resaca (May 13–16), New Hope Church (May 25–28), and Kenesaw Mountain (June 27). By retreating slowly and in good order, destroying bridges and railway track, keeping his antagonist constantly on the move, avoiding open warfare, fighting him at advantage behind prepared intrenchments, and not permitting him to attack with his superior numbers, Johnston had given Sherman increasing grief as the campaign wore on; and in mid-July he was ready to strike the Yankees "on terms of advantage while they were divided in crossing Peach Tree Creek," [5] after which he intended to stand within the citadel of Atlanta. His resistance to Sherman was comparable to Lee's performance in delaying Grant. At this stage, however, the Confederate government rendered Sherman valuable service by removing Johnston. Mindful only of the fact that Sherman had been allowed to approach Atlanta instead of being pushed back into Tennessee, and that Johnston had expressed "no confidence" that he "could defeat or repel" his antagonist, the war department at Richmond required Johnston to hand his command over (July 17, 1864) to J. B. Hood, a brave man, but less skillful and cautious. Hood left his intrenchments to fight a losing battle (Peach Tree Creek, July 20). He then withdrew to the defensive line outside Atlanta. Almost immediately, upon attack by W. J. Hardee, the armies were again at grips in the battle of Atlanta (July 22), the advantage being won by the Army of the Tennessee.[6]

---

[3] W. T. Sherman, in *ibid.*, IV, 250.

[4] *Ibid.*

[5] *Ibid.*, IV, 333.

[6] Its commander, however, J. B. McPherson, one of Sherman's ablest, was struck dead on the battlefield. The command passed temporarily to General J. A. Logan, a politician of southern Illinois who, after some hesitation, had become an enthusiastic supporter of the Union cause in opposition to the pro-Southern sympathies of his region. He had left the House of Representatives for the army, but had shown more ability than the typical politician in uniform. After Logan's tem-

As the weeks wore on, Sherman extended his lines around Atlanta and succeeded at length in cutting off all rail communication. The "backing, digging, and constant service in the trenches" [7] had injured Hood's morale; Confederate desertion was becoming serious; and state-and-federal difficulties had arisen between Governor Brown of Georgia and President Davis at Richmond. In these circumstances, Atlanta was evacuated by Hood on September 1 and occupied by Sherman the following day. It is hard to exaggerate the effect of this news. To the average Northerner, weary with hope deferred after years of frightful loss, it seemed the most important achievement of Union arms in the year 1864. To Lincoln and the Republicans, under blame for a blundering and "hopeless" war, it was a godsend; for it promoted Republican success in the presidential election, this being a type of success which to many minds was as important as the suppression of the "rebellion."

The military situation which ensued upon the Confederate evacuation of Atlanta is one of the curiosities of the war. The main armies, so long at grips, now separated and withdrew in divergent directions, Sherman launching upon his Georgia campaign and Hood invading Tennessee. Hood believed that if he operated in Sherman's rear and struck his lines of communication he would, even if unable to beat him, at least be able to change the direction of the pursuit and prevent a deeper invasion of the South. Incidentally the failure of Sherman to capture Hood's army showed that his main objective had not been won. That army now numbered about 40,000; its morale improved when it took the offensive; and it caught something of Hood's confidence as he dreamed of drawing Sherman after him into Tennessee and Kentucky and even of defeating him in battle.[8]

Correspondence passed between Grant and Sherman, and in early November the latter's "march to the sea" was launched. As to the advisability of this plan Lincoln was "anxious, if not fearful";[9] while Grant thought Hood should be ruined before Sherman struck south.[10] Sherman, however, felt that he could not turn back; he judged that "no single army [could] catch Hood";[11] and he was convinced that his best game was to thwart Jefferson Davis's plan of maneuvering him out of Georgia. Abandoning his lines of communication and supply, he would lighten his baggage,

---

porary command of the Army of the Tennessee, O. O. Howard was assigned by President Lincoln as McPherson's successor and took command on July 27, 1864. When in 1865 Howard became head of the freedmen's bureau, Logan succeeded him.

[7] *Battles and Leaders*, IV, 335.

[8] Had Sherman joined Grant, Hood expected to march through Cumberland Gap to reinforce Lee. *Battles and Leaders*, IV, 427.

[9] Lincoln, *Collected Works*, VIII, 181.

[10] Grant to Sherman, Nov. 1, 1864. Sherman, *Memoirs*, II, 164. That Grant and Sherman differed on this point was obvious.

[11] Sherman, *Memoirs*, II, 165.

plunder as he went, and live off the country. As for Hood, he assigned Thomas the task of pursuing him.

In some of the Southern papers Sherman's campaign was treated as a confession of failure and as a fine opportunity for the Confederates to destroy his army. The Richmond *Enquirer* spoke as follows:

Never was there presented an opportunity so promising for the ruin of an army as Sherman now offers in Georgia. He has abandoned Atlanta, not by retreating backward toward his former base, but by a forward movement to a new base on the coast. It is . . . a confession that Atlanta could not be retained. . . . Rather than make the open confession of a failure by a retreat into Tennessee, the enemy have determined to keep up appearances and to march on, not to subjugation and conquest, but to devastation and ruin, as far as possible, and to a new base on the coast.

. . . Sherman has taught them [the Georgians] how he makes war; he has given them to understand that what he leaves behind him will be of very little use to them; cinders and ashes alone mark the site of Atlanta, and her exiled people are wandering among their friends. The same fate awaits every other city . . . that may fall into his hands.[12]

4

With no major Confederate army opposing him Sherman's famous march began November 10. His forces, "detached from all friends," numbered about 60,000. By field orders his army, stripped of noncombatants, would advance by four parallel roads fifteen miles a day, foraging on the country, destroying mills, houses, and cotton gins, and, if obstructed by guerillas, enforcing a "devastation more or less relentless." [1] Soldiers were forbidden to enter the dwellings of the inhabitants and were ordered to avoid trespass and refrain from abusive or threatening language, endeavoring to leave with each family a reasonable portion for their maintenance.

Once Atlanta was lost from sight, however, a devil-may-care attitude pervaded the troops, and the march through Georgia became a wild holiday. There was a discrepancy between the commander's orders and the performance of his men. Yet every commander must take responsibility for lack of discipline in his ranks, and Sherman's name inevitably bore the odium for the abuses in his army. Atlanta, an important city, was in large part burned, all citizens having been ordered to leave.[2] Milledgeville, the

---

[12] Richmond *Enquirer*, Nov. 21, 1864 (copied in N. Y. *Times*, Nov. 25, 1864). The *Enquirer* advised the Southerners to destroy their property before retreating, thus depriving Sherman of necessary supplies.

[1] Sherman, *Memoirs*, II, 171–172, 175.

[2] "Sixty thousand of us witnessed the destruction of Atlanta, while our post band and that of the 33d Massachusetts played martial airs and operatic selections. . . . At last came the familiar 'Fall in'; the great 'flying column' was on the march, and the last regiment in Atlanta turned its back upon the smoking ruins." Daniel Oakey, Captain, 2d Massachusetts Volunteers, in *Battles and Leaders*, IV, 672. (Between 1860 and 1870 Atlanta grew from 9554 to 21,789.)

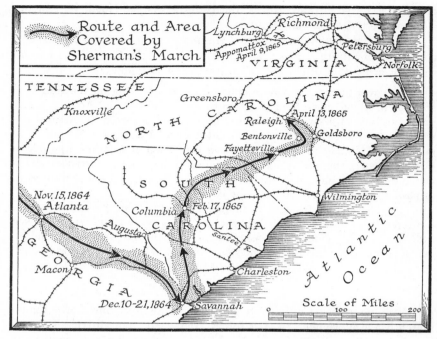

SHERMAN'S MARCH TO THE SEA

capital, fared better. It was entered November 23, and Yankee officers amused themselves by holding a mock session of the Georgia legislature in which they repealed the ordinance of secession. Some public buildings, including the arsenal, were destroyed; but private homes and property were respected.

The army as it proceeded, having little or no fighting to do, devoted itself to organized plunder. A Georgia news-writer pictured the scene as follows:

Dead horses, cows, sheep, hogs, chickens, corn, wheat, cotton, books, paper, broken vehicles, coffee-mills, and fragments of nearly every species of property that adorned the beautiful farms of this county, strew the wayside, monuments of the meanness, rapacity, and hypocrisy of the people who boast that they are not robbers and do not interfere with private property.

. . . The Yankees entered the house of my next door neighbor, an old man of over three score years, and tore up his wife's clothes and bedding, trampling her bonnet on the floor, and robbing the house and pantry of nearly everything of value.[3]

[3] N. Y. *Times,* Dec. 4, 1864 (quoting Augusta *Chronicle* and *Sentinel*).

The business of destroying material susceptible of warlike use was done with the thoroughness of an expert. In destroying a railroad, for instance, the rails were loosened from the ties; the ties were placed in piles with the rails on top; the piles were set on fire; and the heated rails were bent and twisted with specially constructed hooks till they were beyond hope of restoration except by re-rolling. Bridges were destroyed, cars burned, driving wheels and trucks broken, axles bent, boilers punctured, cylinder heads broken and cast into deep water, connecting rods bent and hidden away.[4] General Jacob D. Cox gives the following summary of this destruction:

The extent of line destroyed was enormous. From the Etowah River through Atlanta southward to Lovejoy's, for a hundred miles nothing was left of the road. From Fairburn through Atlanta eastward to Madison and the Oconee River, another hundred miles, the destruction was equally complete. From Gordon southeastwardly the ruin of the Central road was continued to the very suburbs of Savannah, a hundred and sixty miles. Then there were serious breaks in the branch road from Gordon northward through Milledgeville, and in that connecting Augusta and Millen. So great a destruction would have been a long and serious interruption even at the North; but the blockade of Southern ports and the small facilities for manufacture in the Confederate States made the damage practically irreparable. The lines which were wrecked were the only ones which then connected the Gulf States with the Carolinas, and even if Sherman had not marched northward from Savannah the resources of the Confederacy would have been seriously crippled. The forage of the country was also destroyed throughout a belt fifty or sixty miles in width. Both armies cooperated in this; the Confederate cavalry burning it that it might not fall into the hands of the National Army, and the latter leaving none that they could not themselves use, so that wagon transportation of military supplies across the belt might be made more difficult.[5]

Public buildings were often destroyed; foodstores were taken; horses, mules, and livestock were removed. Importance was attached to the removal of horses; for such supplies as were left were useless for military purposes if they could not be hauled. Special details were sent out to "forage," the men selected for the purpose being significantly called "bummers." Along with the systematic business of foraging there was a shocking amount of downright plunder and vandalism. Dwellings were needlessly burned; family plate was seized; wine cellars were raided; property that could not be carried away was wantonly ruined. It was a sorry chapter of the war, made worse than Sherman's intentions; for the army was in harum-scarum spirit and, being recruited in part by conscription, it included Northern riff-raff, drifters, vagabonds, and even criminals. That

---

[4] *Offic. Rec.*, 1 ser., XLVII, pt. 1, p. 804; *ibid.*, pt. 3, p. 116; *Battles and Leaders*, IV, 686 n.
[5] Jacob D. Cox, *The March to the Sea*, 36.

the worst element of his army should be uppermost in the work of plunder was hardly to be avoided.

Sherman's name became a byword in the South. Though told that Yankees were brutes and barbarians, many Southerners had discounted such stories as Confederate propaganda. But when Sherman came through, the deeds of his "bummers" made it seem that the Yankees were trying to justify their unsavory reputation. The elaborate story as to irregular methods of warfare (on both sides) during the Civil War cannot be sketched here; nor is this the place for rationalization concerning the use of such methods as distinguished from battles and sieges. If the war was ever to end otherwise than by a draw, if it was to be terminated by a military decision, its final aspects would unavoidably present to the invaded area an intolerable cup of bitterness. The dragon's teeth had been sown in years past; the war had been raging for three and a half years; and by the autumn of 1864 it was believed by both governments that it could not be ended by the attainment of any partial objective or the acceptance of any compromise. Indeed, once the appeal to arms had been made, the motive of winning, and winning completely, became the dominant purpose on both sides; and such was the grim nature of American resolution North and South that the wretched struggle had to go on from slaughter to slaughter until one side or the other was down and out. To fight to the end and die in the last ditch might make even defeat honorable; but to quit while there still remained a shaky line of ragged troops would seem a dishonor. The Civil War was not comparable to such a conflict as that of 1812 with England, in which neither side conquered and neither won even a measurable partial objective, but in which both saw the folly of continued struggle and were ready to make a treaty which said hostilities should cease and said little more. The factors being as they were in 1864, such a peace seemed impossible for the North and South. In these circumstances, on the eve of his "march to the sea" Sherman wrote:

. . . I propose to act in such manner against the material resources of the south as utterly to negative Davis's boasted threat and promises of protection. If we can march a well-appointed army right through his territory, it is a demonstration to the world—foreign and domestic—that we have a power which Davis cannot resist. This may not be war, . . . ; nevertheless, it is overwhelming to my mind that there are thousands of people abroad and in the south who will reason thus: If the north can march an army right through the south, it is proof positive that the north can prevail in this contest, leaving only open the question of its willingness to use that power. Now, Mr. Lincoln's election, (which is assured,) coupled with the conclusion thus reached, makes a complete logical whole. Even without a battle, the results, operating upon the minds of sensible men, would produce fruits more than compensating for the expense, trouble, and risk.[6]

⁶ Sherman to Grant, Nov. 6, 1864: "Supplemental Report, Com. on Conduct of the War," *Suppl. to Sen. Rep. no. 142*, 38 Cong., 2 sess., I, 261.

It cannot be denied that Sherman's march was marred by unjustifiable excess; yet his campaign, being directed against property and Southern resources, was conceived as a substitute for further human slaughter. That it did in fact contribute materially to ending the war is the opinion of most authorities. Sherman was in the South with the sorry job of helping to conquer the South. To gallant Southerners, animated by pride of country and praying for success to Confederate arms, that was, after all, the most detestable thing about him. Furthermore, the fact that he was operating, not against substantial armies but against Southern morale and upon the people, made his presence particularly offensive. Beyond the attainment of a military decision, however, Sherman had no desire to persecute the South, nor to promote a hateful policy of reconstruction.

In the impersonal military history which generalizes as to campaigns, armies, advances, and victories, the stench and agony of war does not appear; but in their effect upon human flesh and nerves and upon the human mind, these strictly "regular" campaigns and victories were brutal tragedies; while outside the sphere of regular military effort there was waged a different war—guerilla activities, sniping, assassination, banditry, devastation, and starvation. Of such elements, as well as of highly respectable profiteering and graft, the Civil War produced a prolific crop. Sherman's campaign is neither to be praised nor used as a text for sweeping generalizations as to Northern barbarity. The offender was war itself. War, which added the drunkenness of rage to that of liquor, regularized human slaughter, and compelled unnatural deeds of enmity among honorable men where no reasonable enmity existed, was the arch criminal.

Records of the time show that those inhabitants who remained in their homes fared better than those who abandoned them on approach of the Yankees. Also it appears that while pilfering, "souvenir hunting," and theft contrary to orders occurred to a disgusting degree, outrages on persons were rare. Though admitting that jewelry was taken from women and that acts of pillage and violence were committed by the bummers, Sherman wrote: "I never heard of any cases of murder or rape." [7]

A South Carolinian lady whose house was visited by Sherman's army has left the following record:

A crowd had burst in and, disregarding our remonstrances, spread themselves over everything, and from that time until morning a roaring stream of drunkards poured through the house, plundering and raging, and yet in a way curiously civil and abstaining from *personal insult.* Unhappily, they found plenty to plunder, for . . . I had in charge a number of trunks belonging to friends of mine, which were in the house. These they fell upon, and tore to pieces. . . .

. . . . .

They generally spoke to us as "lady" and, although they swore horribly, they seldom swore *at us.* Then, too, if a number of men were fighting over a

[7] *Memoirs,* II, 183.

trunk or a closet, spoiling more than they stole, and I would go and stand by, not saying a word, but looking on, they would become quiet, would cease plundering, and would sometimes stop to tell me they were sorry for the women and children, but South Carolina must be *destroyed*. South Carolina and her sins was the burden of their song. . . .

. . . . .

. . . By this time I was satisfied that they had orders not to hurt the woman [*sic*], and, moreover, *drunk or sober, every man in that army was acting under orders,* and obeying them, so I told them that I had endured the whole night to save the house for my children, and that if they burnt it they would burn a woman in it. They stamped about and swore a good deal, but at last told me I was "damned plucky," and went. That was the worst.[8]

As for the higher officers in Sherman's command, such men as O. O. Howard, J. A. Mower, J. W. Geary, Jeff. C. Davis, H. W. Slocum, and in fact the generality of his division and brigade commanders, conducted themselves as gentlemen; but accounts agree in singling out the cavalry commander Judson Kilpatrick as a glaring exception. On this point General J. D. Cox writes as follows: "Discipline in armies . . . is apt to be uneven, and among sixty thousand men there are men enough who are willing to become robbers, and officers enough who are willing to wink at irregularities or to share the loot to make such a march a terrible scourge to any country. A bad eminence in this respect was generally accorded to Kilpatrick, whose notorious immoralities and rapacity set so demoralizing an example to his troops that the best disciplinarians among his subordinates could only mitigate its influence." [9]

By way of contrast one may set down the following resolutions passed by Savannah citizens at a meeting called by Mayor R. D. Arnold:

Resolved, that Major-Gen. Sherman having placed as Military Commander of this post, Brig.-Gen. Geary, who has by his urbanity as a gentleman, and his uniform kindness to our citizens, done all in his power to protect them and their property from insult and injury, it is the unanimous desire of all present that he be allowed to remain in his present position, and that for the reasons above stated, the thanks of the citizens are hereby tendered to him and the officers under his command.[10]

It was doubtless as a recognition of Geary's conduct, and also as a gesture toward easing the burden of hostile occupation, that the following ad-

[8] Record of Mrs. St. Julien Ravenel in *South Carolina Women in the Confederacy* (edited and published by Mrs. Thomas Taylor and others, Columbia, S. C., 1903), I, 325, 327.

[9] J. D. Cox, *The March to the Sea*, 40.

[10] Savannah *Republican*, Dec. 29, 1864, copied in N. Y. *Times*, Jan. 5, 1865. General Geary was appointed to take command in Savannah "as a sort of governor," and Sherman (*Memoirs*, II, 236) commends the government which he established, pointing out that schools and stores were reopened and the destitute relieved.

monition appeared in a Savannah paper: "Let our conduct be such as to win the admiration of a magnanimous foe, and give no ground for complaint or harsh treatment on the part of him who will for an indefinite period hold possession of our city." [11]

Sherman's headquarters had been established in Savannah by December 22. If this was his objective, he reached it promptly enough; and his presentation of the city as a "Christmas-gift" to Lincoln [12] sent another thrill throughout the North. If, however, the small force opposing him was an objective, his purpose was not fulfilled, for Hardee's army was permitted to escape.

5

After a month in Savannah, Sherman struck north for his campaign through the Carolinas. From the Yankee point of view, South Carolina, the chief offender in causing the war, deserved more vengeful treatment than Georgia.

Somehow [wrote Sherman], our men had got the idea that South Carolina was the cause of all our troubles; her people were the first to fire on Fort Sumter, had been in a great hurry to precipitate the country into civil war; and therefore on them should fall the scourge of war in its worst form. Taunting messages had also come to us, when in Georgia, to the effect that, when we should reach South Carolina, we would find a people less passive, who would fight us to the bitter end, daring us to come over, etc.; so that I saw and felt that we would not be able longer to restrain our men as we had done in Georgia.

Personally I had many friends in Charleston, to whom I would gladly have extended protection and mercy, but they were beyond my personal reach, and I would not restrain the army lest its vigor and energy should be impaired; and I had every reason to expect bold and strong resistance at the many broad and deep rivers that lay across our path.[1]

Halleck had written to Sherman: "Should you capture Charleston, I hope that by *some* accident the place may be destroyed; and if a little salt should be sown upon its site, it may prevent the growth of future crops of nullification and secession." [2] In answer Sherman wrote: "I will bear in mind your hint as to Charleston, and don't think salt will be necessary. . . . The truth is the whole army is burning with an insatiable desire to wreak vengeance upon South Carolina." [3] It turned out, however, that Charleston, being off the main line of the march northward, was happily avoided by Sherman's force. As in Georgia, destruction marked his

[11] Savannah *Republican*, Dec. 21, 1864 (copied in N. Y. *Times*, Dec. 29, 1864, p. 1, c. 6).
[12] Sherman, *Memoirs*, II, 231.

[1] *Ibid.*, II, 254.
[2] Report of Gen. Sherman, in Report of Com. on Conduct of the War, suppl. to *Sen. Rep. no.* 142, 38 Cong., 2 sess., vol. I, 287.
[3] Sherman to Halleck, Dec. 24, 1864: *Offic. Rec.*, 1 ser., XLIV, 799.

path in South Carolina, the following towns being burned in whole or in part: Robertsville, Grahamville, McPhersonville, Barnwell, Blackville, Orangeburg, Lexington, Winnsboro, Camden, Lancaster, Chesterfield, Cheraw, and Darlington.[4] The worst destruction was by the disastrous fire which swept a large part of the city of Columbia, capital of the state. Sherman explained in his memoirs that the fire was accidental and that it began with the cotton which the Confederates under General Wade Hampton had set fire to on leaving the city. He then made the damaging admission that in his official report he deliberately charged the fire to Hampton "to shake the faith of his people in him." [5]

Hampton emphatically denied that any cotton was fired in Columbia by his order; [6] and Sherman's account is at various points disputed by a voluminous mass of Southern testimony, which is partly to the effect that the city was deliberately burned by Sherman's order and partly that it was done by the incendiary soldiers of his army, aided by escaped prisoners. The controversy still rages over this *cause célèbre;* and as late as 1930 an extensive mass of evidence was written into the *Congressional Record* [7] with special reference to the burning of the Washington Methodist Church and the Ursuline convent, representing Sherman's promise of protection as a beguilement and tending to stamp his men as incendiaries. The evidence on the subject is given in great volume, from eye-witnesses, in detail, and with close particulars. These Southern reports have been summed up by William Gilmore Simms, who writes that discipline ceased after the troops entered the city, that a "saturnalia" and "reign of terror" then began, and that the drunken soldiers carried cotton soaked with combustible liquids from dwelling to dwelling. "It was," he said, "a scene for the painter of the terrible. It was the blending of a range of burning mountains stretched in a continuous series for more than a mile." [8] Conclusions and judgments concerning the fire must still be partly conjectural; but it seems not unfair to state that, though the burning was not the deliberate act of Sherman himself, nor due to his orders, yet lax discipline and drunkenness among his soldiers were contributing factors that cannot be ignored.

6

Meanwhile, as part of Grant's strategy, there developed in Virginia elaborate cavalry operations which involved such Confederate leaders as

[4] This list is given by Col. J. W. Davidson in *So. Hist. Soc. Papers,* VII, 190.

[5] Sherman, *Memoirs,* II, 287. See also the paper entitled "Who Burned Columbia?" by J. F. Rhodes, in *Am. Hist. Rev.,* VII, 485–493.

[6] *So. Hist. Soc. Papers,* VII, 156.

[7] *Cong. Record,* May 15, 1930, 8981–9026.

[8] William Gilmore Simms, "The Sack and Destruction of Columbia" (first published in the Columbia *Daily Phoenix*), cited in *Cong. Record,* May 15, 1930, pp. 8986–8987.

Stuart, Early,[1] and Mosby; and on the Federal side Sheridan, Hunter, and Custer. When Grant launched his campaign of the Wilderness against Lee, Sheridan moved south from the Rapidan in a swift raid toward Richmond with the design of getting behind Lee's army, cutting his communications, drawing off Confederate cavalry, and contributing to Grant's success in the major attack. In this raid (May 9–24, 1864) [2] he took a course directly toward Richmond. Stuart at first pressed upon his rear; then, as the Union cavalry advanced toward the Confederate capital, he gave up pursuit and by a change of course and a hard march placed his force between Sheridan and Richmond at Yellow Tavern, six miles north of the city. At this point in a sharp engagement (May 11) the Confederates were attacked by superior numbers. They held the Unionists in check; but it was a day of bitterness, for "Jeb" Stuart, having "saved Richmond," was killed.

Sheridan did not push his raid into the city of Richmond, where great excitement and anxiety prevailed; but, penetrating the outer works of the capital, he swept east and south, reached the James at Haxall's Landing (May 14), turned his prisoners over to Butler, and started on his return march to join the Army of the Potomac, not knowing where he would find it nor what its fortunes had been in his absence. Crossing the Pamunkey on an improvised bridge, he rejoined the main army (May 24) on its march from North Anna to Cold Harbor. He had worried Lee's rear, had partly relieved Grant of molestation by the enemy's cavalry, had destroyed provisions and munitions, had broken up the railroads between Lee and Richmond, and had done much to restore the balance between Confederate and Union morale.

Sheridan's "Richmond raid" was followed by his "Trevilian raid" (June, 1864) north and west of Richmond, whose main accomplishment was the cutting of important railroads.[3] In the Shenandoah Valley the Federals under Franz Sigel had been operating in a minor campaign whose chief event was at New Market (May 15, 1864), where the Confederates under J. C. Breckinridge handled him roughly in an engagement which has loomed large in Confederate story because of a gallant charge by four companies of cadets from the Virginia Military Institute.[4] After this encounter, instead of his intended advance up the Valley, Sigel retreated to a position behind Cedar Creek (near Strasburg). Then followed a campaign

[1] Though heavily engaged against Sheridan, Early was an infantry commander and one of Lee's ablest. It is of some interest to note that he had stoutly opposed secession.

[2] *Offic. Rec.*, 1 ser., XXXVI, pt. 1, 789–792.

[3] *Battles and Leaders*, IV, 233 ff.

[4] For a classic account of this battle by a beardless cadet with a zest for life and a flair for writing, see chapter xix ("The Most Glorious Day of My Life") in *The End of an Era*, by John S. Wise.

between David Hunter, successor to Sigel, and Jubal A. Early, whom Lee had detached with a corps from the main Confederate army to drive Hunter from in front of Lynchburg, which he had invested on June 16. As Hunter withdrew along the Kanawha toward West Virginia, Early seized the opportunity for a bold raid upon Washington. Crossing the Potomac into Maryland, he turned east for a descent upon the Federal capital. At Monocacy near Frederick (July 9, 1864) he was met by a hastily improvised Federal division under Lew Wallace, who led a forlorn hope, but whose defeat is said to have saved Washington, for it gained valuable time for the troops which Grant dispatched to protect the seat of government. Early got within sight of the capitol, but hearing of the approach of troops sent by Grant and finding "impregnable" works "as far as the eye could reach" [5] he gave up hope of capturing Washington. Having given the Federal authorities a "terrible fright," he marched back to the Valley. It has been conjectured that Early "could have taken" Washington at this time. Though the Confederates would soon have been driven out by Grant, it was hoped at the South that a temporary capture would exercise a powerful effect upon Northern morale, upon the presidential election, and upon movements then afoot for concluding the war.

Despite energetic efforts to protect the seat of government, the people and the authorities were suffering from panic, uncertainty of news, and plenitude of rumor. On July 10 President Lincoln wired a group of Baltimore citizens: "Let us be vigilant, but keep cool. I hope neither Baltimore nor Washington will be sacked." At the same time his messages to Grant told of the "hundred day-men,[6] and invalids" who were defending Washington, the "odds and ends" assembled under Wallace, the troops "scarcely . . . worth counting" from New York and Pennsylvania, the "vague rumors" reaching the capital, and the urgency of Grant's coming "personally" to protect the city. Grant was then investing Petersburg. The troops which he sent (the Nineteenth Corps just arrived from New Orleans and two divisions of the Sixth Corps) came up in time to meet Early in the suburbs of Washington and drive him back to Virginia.

Grant now sent his ablest cavalry commander, Sheridan, into the Valley to dispose of Early and to carry on an extensive work of devastation. After sharp fighting at Winchester (Opequon Creek, September 19, 1864) and Fisher's Hill (September 22), in which the Federals had the better of the argument, Early retired up the Valley. It was a campaign of strenuous movement and fighting: "in twenty-six engagements, aside from the battles, the [Union] cavalry lost an aggregate of 3205 men and officers." [7] Sheridan made a quick trip to Washington for consultation with Halleck

---

[5] *Battles and Leaders*, IV, 497–498.
[6] To meet the menace of Early's invasion, Lincoln had called upon the governors of New York, Pennsylvania, and Massachusetts for hundred-day men.
[7] *Battles and Leaders*, IV, 513.

and Stanton; returning, he found his troops surprised and driven back, with hundreds of stragglers revealing the extent of Union confusion. Hearing the noise of distant battle at Winchester, where he had stopped overnight, he rode to meet his retreating force and succeeded in rallying his unhurt but demoralized men, who gave him a wild cheer as they re-formed their lines for a new attack which reversed the tide of battle and brought Union triumph. Inevitably this ride was magnified and embroidered in song and story. The spectacle of one commander turning defeat into victory by a rush to the rescue, a timely arrival, and the electric effect of his sudden appearance on the battlefield caught the imagination; and the poem immortalizing "horse and man" has been much admired by those who enjoy that type of martial poetry. As a footnote to the poem it may be pertinent to observe that Sheridan's men had been thoroughly surprised; that Early showed pluck and skill in his attack upon superior numbers; that the Confederate loss of victory after they had seemingly won it was due partly to their demoralization in plundering the Union camps; that the Southern generals were not able fully to control their troops, who judged for themselves "when it was proper to retire"; [8] and that Sheridan's losses far exceeded those of Early, the "wreck" of whose army carried off 1500 Union prisoners and subsequently faced Sheridan's whole force north of Cedar Creek without his attacking it.

After this battle [9] Sheridan and Early confronted each other without serious fighting until winter came on. Aside from fighting, Sheridan's efforts in the Valley were occupied with a devastation comparable to that of Sherman in the lower South. The burning of houses and barns, the destruction of food, and the removal of Negroes and animals were done with systematic thoroughness until the smiling valley presented a scene of grim waste and ruin. Violence to persons was, however, avoided; and it was far from true that the people were left utterly without subsistence. The Federal excuse for this destruction, which was ordered by Grant, was the accusation that the region was honeycombed with bushwhackers and guerillas who had operated against the Union forces by irregular means and had resorted to cold-blooded assassination of officers and men off guard.

The war had now entered its final phase. With Grant undermining the Confederate hold upon Petersburg, with Sherman swinging north to subdue Johnston and join Grant if necessary, with Sheridan's forces about to turn from destructive raids to cooperation in the main theater of war against Lee, with the Confederacy blockaded and Union forces supreme on the water, the surrenders of Lee and Johnston, signifying the military ending of the war, were not far distant.[10]

---

[8] *Ibid.*, IV, 529.
[9] The battle of Cedar Creek, October 19, 1864.
[10] For the end of the war, see below, pp. 523–527.

CHAPTER 25

The Naval War

I

IN THE NAVAL war the contrast between North and South was evident on all fronts; and so vital was this factor that Union victory without the naval contribution seems inconceivable. The Confederacy began the war without a navy and, apparently, without the means of constructing one. The South, as Joseph T. Durkin has observed, "had neither shipyards (save Norfolk, which was soon lost, and Pensacola, which was inadequate and also, finally, captured) nor workshops, steam mills or foundries, except on the most limited scale. . . . There was not, in the whole Confederacy, the means of turning out a complete steam engine of a size suitable for ships. The timber for the potential Confederate ships still stood in the forests; the iron required was still in the mines . . . ; the hemp required for ship ropes had actually to be grown. . . . There was not a rolling mill capable of turning out two-and-a-half inch plate. There was not a sufficient force of skilled mechanics." [1]

In confronting these apparently insuperable deficiencies the Southerners displayed remarkable ingenuity. The Confederate secretary of the navy, Stephen R. Mallory, was a man of unusual ability and of great force. As senator from Florida before the war, he had been chairman of the naval affairs committee and in "striving for a rehabilitation of the navy" had demonstrated his "alertness to new advances in naval design and ordnance." "Filled with a passion for learning his job," Mallory "possessed in regard to naval affairs a kind of impulsive progressivism, which, although it sometimes led him astray, enabled him in other instances to recognize and to develop with boldness sound new principles." [2] Quickly he came to understand his complex responsibilities. Briefly summarized, Confederate naval strategy involved defending the 3500 miles of Southern coastline against Union attack,[3] challenging the Federal blockade of Southern ports,

---

[1] Durkin, *Stephen R. Mallory: Confederate Navy Chief,* 150.
[2] *Ibid.,* 64–65, 133, 135.
[3] C. O. Paullin, "A Half-Century of Naval Administration in America . . . ," *U. S. Naval Institute Proceedings,* XXXIX, 165 (1913). The actual blockading

and, through the activities of privateers and cruisers, wreaking enough destruction upon the Northern merchant marine so that "the Federal government would be forced to withdraw numerous ships from the blockading squadrons in order to pursue the 'highwaymen of the sea.' " [4]

In all these fields of activity Mallory, ably assisted by other Confederate naval leaders such as Buchanan, Tattnall, Bulloch, and Semmes, achieved notable success. If "judged from the point of view of what was actually accomplished in the face of lack of material and financial resources," a careful student remarks, Mallory's "results were little short of phenomenal." [5] Recognizing that the only way in which the Confederates could challenge Northern superiority would be through novel approaches to naval war, Mallory consistently lent his support to daring and original methods of sea warfare. In defending the Confederate coastline, for example, he and his torpedo bureau developed elaborate systems of mines and underwater explosives, which "kept the U.S. Navy outside the harbors where blockade runners plied to Bermuda; and Wilmington, North Carolina, Charleston, and Mobile on the Gulf thrived as never before as ports." [6] The Southerners even devised a primitive submarine, the *C. S. Hunley,* whose attack on the Federal blockading sloop *Housatonic* outside Charleston harbor in February, 1864, marked "the first sinking of a warship by a submarine" in history.[7] Mallory very early saw that ironclads would have an immense advantage over the wooden ships in the Federal blockading fleet, and he made the construction of an ironclad fleet "his master principle of strategy, in relation to shipbuilding." [8] Some of these ironclads, such as the *Merri-*

---

problem, of course, was not a matter of the number of miles of coast line on the map, but of the limited number of points where cargoes could land and make contact with interior facilities of transportation. Also the distinction must be made between important trading operations and trivial smuggling. Much of the latter, while not of the most vital concern to the Union navy, was carried on in defiance of Southern customs officials, and was thus in opposition to both governments.

[4] Durkin, *op. cit.,* 168–169.

[5] Philip Melvin, "Stephen Russell Mallory, Southern Naval Statesman," *J. S. H.,* X, 156 (May, 1944).

[6] Clifford Dowdey, *The Land They Fought For,* 243–244.

[7] Lydel Sims, "The Submarine That Wouldn't Come Up," *Am. Heritage,* IX, 110 (April, 1958).

[8] Mallory, far earlier than Gideon Welles, became aware that the Civil War was being waged in an era of transition in naval architecture and fighting methods. In the half-century preceding the war "no less than five great naval revolutions were under way—steam, shell guns, the screw propeller, rifled ordnance, and armor. It was the shell gun that upset the balance between offense and defense and sounded the knell of the unarmored wooden ship." C. O. Paullin, in *Am. Hist. Rev.,* XXXIX, 126. The *Demologos,* an American vessel built in 1814 at a cost of $320,000, has been referred to as "the first steam warship"; but steam in naval architecture made little progress until the advent of the screw propeller (for which chief credit is due to Francis Pettit Smith and John Ericsson). Besides other advantages, the screw "made it possible to place the engines and boilers below the

mac (rechristened the *Virginia*), were fitted out in Southern shipyards, but Mallory looked to Europe for the heavy rams and cruisers which he hoped would finally break the blockade and drive the Northern fleet from the seas.

The task of the United States navy was, naturally, just the reverse of that of the Confederates. Upon it fell the heavy demands of maintaining the blockade, conducting operations on the Southern coasts combatting Confederate cruisers and privateers, and protecting the ocean commerce of the United States. The Union navy started the war with less advantage in completed ships than is often supposed. On March 4, 1861, the vessels of all classes in the navy numbered only ninety. Most of these were obsolescent sailing ships which, if available at all, would require overhauling before being made effective for war purposes. More than half the ninety ships were in ordinary, leaving only forty-two vessels in commission at the opening of Lincoln's administration; and most of these were on foreign stations, with no cable in existence to recall them quickly.[9]

The responsibility for making this feeble force into a powerful fighting navy fell upon Secretary Gideon Welles and his able assistant, Gustavus V. Fox. Though slighting remarks were made of the bewhiskered "Old Man of the Sea" whom Lincoln appointed partly for political and geographical reasons to head his navy department, the fact was that Gideon Welles of Connecticut was an able and vigorous administrator. C. O. Paullin, who has made a close study of naval administration, shows that, while Welles had none of the dashing qualities of some secretaries and made no pretensions to a technical knowledge of the navy, he was an efficient executive who distributed honors fairly, applied the law fearlessly, gave generous praise to gallant conduct, prepared clear and readable reports, expanded the navy with remarkable vigor, and struggled effectively with difficult and

---

water line." The importance of shell guns is indicated by the fact that even the old wood ships "could withstand a terrific hammering from solid shot." Shell guns led in turn not only to the introduction of the iron ship, which was not invulnerable to shells, but to the use of armor plate. "The first American iron warship, *U. S. S. Michigan*, . . . served on the Great Lakes from 1844 to 1923. . . ." French experimentation with ironclads under Napoleon III was of great importance, and the "first seagoing iron fleet" (the *Gloire* and others) was that of France in the fifties. Despite the conservatism of the Admiralty, Great Britain, stirred by French competition, had made a substantial beginning in the use of ironclads before the Civil War. The manner in which one invention led to another was further exemplified by the use of rifled ordnance as the effective means of attacking armor. For a scholarly treatment of these details, as well as of the whole subject, see J. P. Baxter, 3rd, *The Introduction of the Ironclad Warship* (1933). For the portions quoted in this note, see *ibid.*, 10, 11, 17, 41, 92 ff., 125.

[9] C. B. Boynton, *Hist. of the Navy during the Rebellion*, I, 100; *House Exec. Doc. No. 1*, 37 Cong., 3 sess., vol. III, p. 24. The report of the navy department, July 4, 1861 (*Sen. Exec. Doc. No. 1*, 37 Cong., 1 sess., p. 86) erroneously reports the number in commission on March 4, 1861, as twenty-four.

unprecedented tasks. His suspicious nature and ungenerous attitude toward colleagues appear in his deadly diary. That he was no master of international law was evident. For this and other reasons he was embarrassed by the interference of Seward in naval affairs.[10]

When the emergency arose every available vessel on the navy's idle list was repaired and fitted out; merchant ships were purchased or chartered; and construction of new warships was rapidly pushed in the navy yards. As compared to the forty-two ships of March, 1861, the secretary reported eighty-two vessels in commission July 4, 1861; 264 in December, 1861; 427 in December, 1862; 588 in December, 1863; and 671 in December, 1864.[11] The vessels purchased by the government were said to include every type of ship "from Captain Noah to Captain Cook." [12] In addition to acquiring the ships, many wartime tasks confronted the navy department. Fighting and cruising needs had to be anticipated in order to determine the design of vessels whose keels were yet to be laid. New designs would necessarily involve radical departures from old models; for sailing ships were rapidly giving way to steamers, ironclads were displacing wooden vessels, and notable inventors of the type of Ericsson were revolutionizing naval and marine construction. Expenditures and contracts had to be watched; naval bureaus and branches had to be reorganized; skilled mechanics had to be found; men and officers to man the new navy had to be recruited and drilled. Special difficulties presented themselves in the case of Southern officers in the United States navy whose sense of duty required them to go, as did Lee, with their states, i.e., into the Confederate service.[13] A further obstacle was found in the fact that, beyond its own coasts, the United States possessed at the time of the Civil War not a single coaling station in the world. Against such a handicap the navy's best resource was the construction of large, swift steam-and-sail cruisers which would be economical of coal, carrying a plentiful supply, and yet be capable of speed and deadly action when operating upon ocean highways.

From the outset of the war the Federal navy undertook to blockade the

[10] For a readable summary of naval administration during the Civil War, see C. O. Paullin, "A Half-Century of Naval Administration in America. . . ," *U. S. Naval Institute Proceedings*, 38: 1309–1336 (1912) and 39: 165–195 (1913). Paullin shows (38: 1310) that annual naval expenditures increased during the war from $12,000,000 to $123,000,000.

[11] Boynton, I, 139.

[12] Paullin, *op. cit.*, 39: 169.

[13] There are varying statements as to the number of officers who shifted from the Federal to the Confederate navy. Boynton (I, 104) places the number at 259; Welles at 332 (Paullin, *op. cit.*, 38: 1328); and there are other estimates. Though Federal ships were abandoned and fell into Southern hands, the factor of officers shifting both themselves and their ships to the Confederate service was negligible. Major William M. Robinson, Jr., states (memorandum to J. G. Randall, Oct. 6, 1935) that "there was a scrupulous . . . honor on the part of every Southern officer to disembarrass himself of all U. S. property for which he was responsible."

entire extensive coast of the Confederacy. At the beginning the Union fleet was obviously unable to make its blockade effective, and as late as 1864 there was still much running of supplies into the South; [14] but Welles justly believed that his ships were cutting off the Confederacy's trade in most heavy goods. With Yankee assurance, and with a bit of exaggeration, he reported on December 1, 1862, the activities of his four blockading squadrons:

> These squadrons have been incessantly maintaining a strict blockade of such gigantic proportions that . . . foreign statesmen . . . denounce[d] it as "a material impossibility;" and yet after this most imposing naval undertaking had been for a period of eighteen months in operation . . . from the outlet of the Chesapeake to the mouth of the Rio Grande, the same eminent authorities, with a list in their hands of all the vessels which had evaded . . . our blockading forces, could not refuse . . . to admit . . . that the proof of the efficiency of the blockade was conspicuous and wholly conclusive, and that in no previous war had the ports of an enemy's country been so effectually closed by a naval force. But even such testimony was not needed. The proof of the fact abounds in the current price of our southern staples in the . . . marts of the world, and . . . in the whole industrial and commercial condition of the insurgent region.[15]

2

Early in 1862, when in general the war was beginning in good earnest, the importance of the ironclad was signalized in the famous Hampton Roads combat. The Confederates had seized a powerful steam frigate, the *Merrimac* (sunk by the Federals on the evacuation of the Norfolk navy yard and promptly raised by the Confederates); and by March of 1862 the vessel had been armored with iron plate and a cast-iron ram added to its stem. On March 8 this iron giant, renamed the *Virginia,* steamed down the Elizabeth River under command of Captain Franklin Buchanan for an attack upon the Union blockading squadron in Hampton Roads. Its deadly work soon struck consternation in the hearts of the Unionists, for in the unequal contest the fire from the Federal wooden ships had little or no effect upon the "rebel" monster. With astonishing ease the *Virginia* rammed and shelled the *Cumberland,* whose crew stuck heroically to the sinking vessel and went down with flags flying. The *Congress* was then destroyed by hot shot with heavy casualties. The *Virginia* was but slightly injured (hardly at all by enemy fire), and the Southern people were jubilant as their newspapers predicted the raising of the Union blockade, the reduction of Washington, the leveling of New York, Boston, and Philadelphia, and the termination of the war by Confederate naval victory. Though the vessel was unseaworthy, its patched-up engines being unfit for an ocean

[14] See below, pp. 501–503.
[15] Report of the Sec. of the Navy, December 1, 1862, *House Exec. Doc. No. 1,* 37 Cong., 3 sess., vol. III, p. 3.

cruise, the news of the destruction of the *Cumberland* and *Congress* caused panic among officials in Washington and residents of Northern seaboard cities.

It happened, however, that the Union secretary of the navy had early in the war made contracts for several new types of ironclads; and one of these, the *Monitor,* now made its appearance in the nick of time.[1] Though the vessel presented a simple appearance, like a "tin can on a shingle," [2] its construction revealed advanced engineering technique. Its distinguishing features were its small size, the low flat hull but a few inches above the water line (the deck being awash in a gale), its shallow immersion and great mobility, and the ingeniousness of its central revolving gun turret which proved impregnable against ten-inch shot at close range. This new naval model, which was used for various ships so that the word "monitor" became a generic term, was the work of a brilliant inventor and builder, John Ericsson. On March 9 the *Virginia,* now under the command of Lieutenant Catesby ap R. Jones,[3] returning to the attack with the intention of destroying the *Minnesota* and the rest of the Union ships below Fort Monroe, was challenged by Ericsson's pigmy commanded by Lieutenant John L. Worden; [4] and there followed a hotly fought duel at close quarters in which the *Monitor* protected the *Minnesota* from the onslaught of the Confederate ironclad. Neither vessel did much damage to the other, and after several hours of fighting, with only one casualty, both quit as if by mutual agreement. The *Monitor* withdrew temporarily because its commander, Worden, was partially blinded by a shell; the leaking *Virginia,* whose commander probably considered the day's work done and the enemy whipped, turned back to Norfolk at about the same time.[5]

The subsequent fate of the two vessels deserves a word. After the evacuation of Norfolk by the Confederates (May 10, 1862) it was decided to lighten and repair the *Virginia,* whose unwieldy weight and deep immersion made it liable to running aground during a battle. The vessel was to be taken up the James to assist in the defence of Richmond. When the work of lightening had proceeded to the point where the hull was exposed below the armor, thus becoming unfit for action, but not sufficiently to make the passage up the James, its commander, Tattnall, decided that the menace of Federal attack, from both the *Monitor* and the Union batteries at Newport News, had put him under the painful necessity of destroying

[1] The *Monitor* was launched on January 30, 1862, and commissioned February 25, its keel having been laid October 25, 1861. Baxter, *Ironclad,* 265–266.

[2] William Chapman White and Ruth White, *Tin Can on a Shingle.* Cf. Robert S. McCordock, *The Yankee Cheese Box.*

[3] Jones had succeeded Buchanan, who had been severely wounded.

[4] Later Rear Admiral, U. S. N.

[5] Whether the *Monitor* returned to the combat before the *Virginia* made for Norfolk is uncertain. Baxter, *Ironclad,* 294. Subsequent to the famous fight the *Virginia* more than once offered battle to the *Monitor,* but, to the disgust of Ericsson, the latter did not accept the challenge.

his ship. She was consequently run ashore and burned after the disembar-
kation of her crew. This news brought distress and indignation in the South
and resulted in aspersions against Tattnall, who, however, was sustained
by court martial as an officer who had acted wisely and with resolution in
a difficult situation. After the destruction of the *Virginia,* its officers and
crew proceeded to Drewry's Bluff on the James, where batteries and naval
guns were quickly established for the defense of Richmond. On May 15,
1862, an effective stand was made by the Confederates at this point,
forcing the retirement of a small Federal naval force, including the ironclads *Galena* and *Monitor* and accompanying gunboats.

The *Monitor* accompanied the Union squadron which operated up
the James River in cooperation with McClellan's peninsular campaign.
When McClellan withdrew from the Peninsula, the vessel went to Hampton Roads, then to Washington for repairs, then back to Hampton Roads.
During the night of December 30–31, 1862, while bound for Beaufort,
North Carolina, the famous ship went down in a gale off Cape Hatteras,
part of its crew being saved, while four officers and twelve men were
drowned.

Though the "epoch-making" character of the *Monitor-Merrimac* duel
has been exaggerated, yet it did mark a definite trend in the naval war. The
Union fleets had been saved at a time of deadly menace; more ironclads
were added to the Union than to the Confederate navy; the value of the
turret (though not a new idea) was amply demonstrated; and Federal supremacy on the water remained unbroken.

3

In addition to its other tasks, the Union navy achieved the capture of
important positions on the Southern coasts. In August, 1861, a joint military and naval expedition seized Forts Clark and Hatteras; and the inlets
to Pamlico Sound were under Union control. In February–March, 1862,
another combined force of the army and navy under General A. E. Burnside and Commodore L. M. Goldsborough seized the fortified positions of
the Confederates on historic Roanoke Island and at New Berne; and with
these inner coastal positions in Union hands a much tighter blockade of
North Carolina could be maintained than by operations outside the sound.[1]
By these exploits Burnside acquired a reputation which, sadly for him and
for Union arms, led to his transfer to the main seat of war in Virginia. The
Port Royal entrance, including the town of Beaufort, South Carolina, together with valuable sea islands (Hilton Head, St. Helena, etc.), was
placed in Union hands in November, 1861, by an expedition under Flag
Officer Samuel F. DuPont.[2] Fort Pulaski, commanding the city of Savan-

---

[1] In the Goldsborough naval expedition to the North Carolina sounds S. C.
Rowan had an important part.
[2] Later Rear Admiral, U. S. N.

nah at the mouth of the Savannah River, fell to the Federals in April, 1862; and the Unionists had then nearly mastered the coast, where the chief ports still in Confederate control were Charleston, Mobile, and Wilmington.

The most striking of all these land-and-water expeditions was that which effected the capture of New Orleans in April, 1862. Not alone the wealth and size of this greatest of Southern cities, but its unique position as a mart of ocean and river commerce gave it a strategic importance which was duly appreciated by both sides. To seize the city by a land attack from the North was chimerical; on the other hand a mere naval assault would not suffice, for the city would have to be held by an occupying army. Though the Union navy department did not at first realize this, the undertaking called for a combined military and naval expedition. The city was defended by an army of 3000 under General Mansfield Lovell of the Confederate army, while the Gulf approach involved the reduction or passing of two powerful forts (St. Philip and Jackson) on either side of the river seventy-five miles below the city and also an encounter with a Confederate fleet of armed steamers and ironclads. In addition, Confederate fire rafts offered a further menace; and obstructions across the river were designed to hold enemy ships under fire from the shore guns.

The attacking squadron was placed under the command of Flag Officer D. G. Farragut, a Spanish-American Southerner. He was born in Tennessee, and had spent his early years in New Orleans. Having become the adopted son of Captain David Porter of the United States navy, he entered the naval service at the age of nine and as a midshipman saw service on the *Essex* under Porter and later in the Mediterranean. As a young officer he served in the "mosquito fleet" against the Caribbean pirates. After many years of uneventful naval service the outbreak of the war found him at Norfolk, where the influence of his associates, as well as his Southern antecedents, would have tended to draw him into the Confederate service. With no thought, however, of detaching himself from the United States navy, he applied to Washington for orders, and was given a "desk job" as a member of the naval "retiring board," whose duty it was to weed out incompetent officers.

Though sixty years old when appointed to the command of the "West Gulf Blockading Squadron," he was in fine fettle; no more fit leader could have been chosen for the hazardous enterprise. Commander D. D. Porter accompanied him with a fleet of mortar vessels, while Major General B. F. Butler, with an army of 18,000, stood in readiness to hold the city, once it had been seized, and to conduct the multifarious and vexatious details of hostile occupation. Farragut sailed from Hampton Roads on February 2, and spent two months in preparation, having great difficulty in maneuvering his heavy vessels across the bar at the mouth of the Mississippi River. For six days beginning April 18, Porter's mortar flotilla blazed away at

Forts St. Philip and Jackson with disappointing effect; after which Farragut, as he had all along intended, proceeded in the early hours of the 24th to "run the forts," pushing his vessels against a strong current under the terrific fire of a hundred shore guns and giving battle to the Confederate fleet, two of whose vessels, the *Louisiana* and the *Manassas,* were especially troublesome enemies. Farragut's flagship, the *Hartford,* having run upon a shoal, was set aflame by a fire raft, being at the same time engaged by the guns of Fort St. Philip. The ship was struck thirty-two times with a loss of three men killed and ten wounded; but Farragut extinguished the fire and led his fleet up the river and out of danger. His casualties before and during the action of the 24th were 39 killed and 171 wounded. Having passed the forts and the fleet, the latter being destroyed, Farragut steamed up the river and on the 25th his squadron confronted the proud city of New Orleans. Forts Jackson and St. Philip now surrendered; Lovell with his army withdrew; and by the 29th the city was in Union possession. Though an angry crowd of civilians confronted the landing force, street fighting was fortunately avoided; and by May 2 General Butler, conceiving himself to be a sort of avenging deity, had landed his troops and begun his notorious occupation.

On the inland rivers, as above noted, Union leaders had learned the valuable lesson of close cooperation between military and naval forces. Union success had been powerfully promoted by naval operations at Forts Henry and Donelson and at New Madrid and Island Number Ten, while the cooperation of the fleet in the elaborate Vicksburg campaigns was of decisive importance. The seizure of Memphis, the expedition against Arkansas Post, the movement on the Yazoo, the attempt of Farragut to force his way up the Mississippi, the successful operation of Porter in running the Confederate batteries at Vicksburg and in transporting Grant's army across that stream, illustrated the remarkable activity of the Union flotillas on the western waters. With the fall of Port Hudson on July 9, 1863, it was obvious midway in the war that the battle for the opening of the Mississippi had been won by the North.

4

Since the Confederate navy lacked not only ships but the materials to build and equip them, it expended its effort chiefly upon privateers and a few crack cruisers. As Jefferson Davis expressed it:

. . . At the inception of hostilities the inhabitants of the Confederacy were almost exclusively agriculturists; those of the United States, to a great extent, mechanics and merchants. We had no commercial marine, while their merchant vessels covered the ocean. We were without a navy, while they had powerful fleets. The advantage which they possessed for inflicting injury on our coasts and harbors was thus counterbalanced in some measure by the exposure of their commerce to attack by private armed vessels. . . . The value and efficiency of [the privateer] . . . is [*sic*] strikingly illustrated by the terror inspired among the commercial classes of the United States by a single cruiser of the Confederacy.[1]

It was in this situation that the South found the justification and necessity of privateering. Though in 1861 a dying institution, abolished by international agreement in the Declaration of Paris in 1856, yet, so far as the attitude of the United States was concerned, this weapon of maritime war was still reputable. The United States had declined to adhere to the Declaration of Paris; and the resort to privateering (not an inhumane weapon, merely an obsolescent one) was no exception to the rule that the officials of the Confederacy were careful to conduct their war at sea on a high-minded and civilized basis. In explaining that the Confederacy agreed to abide by all the principles of the Congress of Paris except that relating to privateering, President Davis said:

. . . As the right to make use of privateers was one in which neutral nations had, as to the present war, no interest; as it was a right which the United States had refused to abandon . . . ; as it was a right of which we were already in actual enjoyment, and which we could not be expected to renounce *flagrante bello* against an adversary possessing an overwhelming superiority of naval forces, it was reserved with entire confidence that neutral nations could not fail to perceive that just reason existed for the reservation. . . .[2]

The act of the Southern Congress concerning privateering became law on May 6, 1861. It authorized the President to issue letters of marque and reprisal against "the vessels, goods and effects of the government of the United States, and of the citizens or inhabitants of the states . . . thereof. . . ." Conforming in part to the Declaration of Paris, the law recognized the doctrine of "free ships, free goods" (i.e., that noncontraband private property of the enemy on a neutral ship was exempt from capture), and it also recognized the exemption of noncontraband neutral property if found on an enemy vessel. Thirty days' grace was allowed for the departure of private vessels of the enemy then in Confederate ports; privateersmen were enjoined to deal with enemy vessels and their crews with "justice and humanity"; neutral rights were safeguarded; and, to prevent any tendency toward piracy, each master of a privateer was required to keep a journal of his cruises and to deliver it to a Confederate collector of customs upon landing at a Southern port.

Romance, patriotism, thirst for adventure, and the hope of profit combined to stimulate privateering enterprise; and ships of the most diverse sorts, from the tiny *Sea Hawk* with its crew of nine to the formidable *Isabella* with its force of over two hundred, responded to the call of the Confederate government. The promised profit was a tempting bait; for the gov-

[1] *Journal*, Confed. Cong., VI, 13.
[2] *Ibid.*, 14.

ernment asked only one-twentieth of the proceeds of the captured prizes, the rest to go to the owners, crews, and officers according to a stipulated proportion. Privateering activity, however, was chiefly confined to the year 1861. After that year, not only were Confederate ports closed to Southern privateers by Federal fleets, but such was the menace of the blockade in shutting off foreign markets that Southern ships could perform both a more gainful and a more patriotic service by running the blockade as cargo carriers than by acting as privateers. If engaged in marine transportation there would be less uncertainty in their operations; and the goods they could bring in would command higher prices and contribute more to the nation's needs than the prizes they might be able to take and dispose of as privateers. The slow and awkward sailing vessels which were almost without exception the quarry of privateers were of little commercial or fighting value and it was a matter of chance whether their cargoes would be of service.

A distinction has usually been drawn between the North and South on the score of privateering. The nub of the matter was simply that the practice was of slight importance to the Federal cause, because of the effectiveness of the Federal navy and the small amount of Southern seagoing commerce which Federal privateers might have captured. Despite this, however, the Northern Congress passed and Lincoln signed (March 3, 1863) a law which authorized the issuing of letters of marque; it was merely an incidental fact that none were actually granted. On both sides, as in the case of the *Quaker City* fitted out by private citizens of New York at the outset of the war, certain vessels did the work of privateers without letters of marque. They were analogous to bushwhackers on land, who were by no means uncommon in the Civil War.

5

It has been said that the Civil War was *sui generis*. Its peculiar nature gave birth to a prolific offspring of sententious theories and conflicting notions, all of which caused serious discussions as to the treatment of captured privateersmen. Both warring governments were extremely sensitive in the matter of status, the Confederacy being proudly insistent upon full recognition of its attributes of independence, which on the other hand the United States government was reluctant to concede. Many of the more obvious statements that have appeared on this controversial subject are misleading and inaccurate.[1] Through some of the earlier declarations indicated otherwise, the United States government, after its policy had time to mature, did, in most important respects, treat the Southern government

[1] For the legal aspects of the war, with special reference to the status of the Confederacy, the Northern insurrectionary theory, and the treatment of Confederate leaders, see Randall, *Constitutional Problems Under Lincoln*, chaps. iii, iv, v, x, xx; and see above, pp. 293–295.

as a public belligerent.[2] In many of its public declarations, however, the Lincoln government showed a marked reluctance to commit itself officially and definitively to the conception of full belligerent status, and various paper threats were made as to punishing Southerners for treason or "piracy." President Lincoln unfortunately issued a proclamation (April 19, 1861) which declared the crews and officers of Confederate warships and privateers to be pirates, and there were several abortive trials of a few captured privateersmen; but a storm of abuse broke out in Europe when this was known, and Northern individuals were seized by the Confederate government and held as hostages, to be treated in accordance with the actual disposition made in the case of the captured crews. From every angle (not the least from that of Lincoln's humanitarian impulses) it was intolerable to treat privateersmen as pirates; and Federal judicial officers concerned with these cases found them highly embarrassing and distasteful. In the case of the *Petrel*, a Confederate privateer whose crew were indicted for piracy at Philadelphia in 1861, Justice Grier of the United States Supreme Court exclaimed:

I do not intend to try any more of these cases. . . . I have other business to attend to, and do not mean to be delayed here from day to day in trying charges against a few unfortunate men . . . out of half a million that are in arms against the government. Why should this difference be made between men captured on land and on the sea?

. . . . .

. . . Why not try all those taken on land and hang them? That might do with a mere insurrection; but when it comes to civil war, the laws of war must be observed, or you will lay it open to the most horrid reactions that can possibly be thought of. . . . I will not sit on another case. I am not going to have the whole civil business of the court . . . set aside for useless trifling.[3]

It was found that actual prosecutions under the piracy indictments would put the government in an impossible situation; to carry the cases through to conviction and enforce the death penalty was unthinkable. In the end, the trials were dropped and the crews sent south.[4]

[2] This working attitude must be distinguished from some of the formal declarations, and it found frequent illustration in the actual conduct of the war. It was in the exchange of prisoners that legal theory and sensitiveness as to status did the greatest practical harm. Various concessions as to the belligerent character of the Confederacy were approved and recognized by the Supreme Court of the United States. Randall, *op. cit.*, 65–73.

[3] Report of proceedings in U. S. Circuit Court at Philadelphia, Nov. 4, 1861, enclosure in letter of J. H. Ashton to Attorney General Edward Bates, same date. Attorney General's Papers (MSS., Libr. of Cong.).

[4] Despite this action, "Union officials . . . never . . . got over their fondness for applying the epithets 'pirate' and 'piratical' to everything naval in the South. . . ." W. M. Robinson, Jr., *The Confederate Privateers*, 151. For Union inconsistency on legal aspects of the war, see above, pp. 294–295.

6

Of the Confederate cruisers the earliest was the *Sumter,* a screw steamer of five hundred tons which was the "first 'ship of war' to fly the new Confederate flag on the high seas." [1] After cruising for six months in the Caribbean and Atlantic, receiving hospitable treatment in neutral ports and capturing eighteen vessels (eleven of which were released, ransomed, or recaptured), the ship was blockaded at Gibraltar by pursuing Union warships and abandoned by her officers after the discharge of her crew. She was later sold, was put under the English flag as a merchant vessel, did her bit at blockade-running, and was finally lost in the North Sea.

Her commander, Raphael Semmes, was the most distinguished fighter in the Confederate navy. Appointed midshipman by President Adams in 1826, he had long been an officer in the United States navy, had seen action in the Mexican War, had resigned (February 15, 1861) to go with his state (Alabama), and, prior to the outbreak of war, had done service for the Confederate navy in touring the principal workshops of New York, Connecticut, and Massachusetts, purchasing large quantities of munitions and powder. No officer was more ardent in his Southern sympathies, none more savage in his denunciation of Yankees one and all, than this doughty sea fighter. His great cruise was with the famous *Alabama.* This vessel, chiefly notable for the international controversy which it occasioned, had been built at Liverpool under an arrangement made by Captain James D. Bulloch, Confederate naval agent in England. Scrupulous care had been taken to keep secret the intention to transfer the vessel to Confederate service. It was a crack ship of a thousand tons, over 200 feet long, armed with eight guns and equipped with two engines of 300 horsepower each. Its crew, usually about 24 officers and 120 men, "made up from all the seafaring nations of the globe, with a large sprinkling of Yankee tars," [2] was mostly English and included very few Southerners. The vessel left Liverpool as a private ship, the *Enrica,* and sailed to the Azores, where (on the high seas) she received her equipment, her complement of men, and her stores, the munitions and supplies having been also transported to the Azores, an appointed rendezvous, in an English ship. Off the island of Terceira on August 24, 1862, Captain Semmes took command of the vessel, putting it formally into commission as a Confederate cruiser; and for two years she ranged over widely separated seas playing havoc with Yankee commerce. Her famous cruise took her to the Newfoundland Banks, to the Caribbean, to the vicinity of Galveston, to the Cape of Good Hope, then through Oriental waters as far as Singapore, back to Cape Town, again to the Azores, and finally to the French coast. In the course of this roving career the *Alabama* fought and sank the U. S. S. *Hatteras* (one hundred

[1] Colyer Meriwether, *Raphael Semmes,* 110.
[2] Statement of John McIntosh Kell, *Battles and Leaders,* IV, 603 n.

tons larger than herself) and captured sixty-two merchant ships, most of which were burned. In the matter of burning and sinking merchant ships (noncombatants in war) the persons on board—officers, crew, and passengers—were carefully removed out of danger; and where this was not possible the ship was usually released on "ransom bond," the master of the vessel in the name of the owner agreeing to pay a sum "unto the President of the Confederate States of America . . . within thirty days after the conclusion of the present war. . . ." [3] During these cruises the *Alabama* received many courtesies as well as solid aid and comfort in friendly English ports, where Captain Semmes obtained fuel and supplies, discharged prisoners, made repairs, and was made socially welcome.

Finally the vessel was trapped by a Union cruiser, the *Kearsarge,* commanded by Captain Winslow, in the port of Cherbourg; and in the ensuing fight, famous in naval annals, the *Alabama* was sent to the bottom (June 19, 1864). "Of her roster of 147–149, twenty-six were killed and drowned, seventy wounded and sound were taken to the *Kearsarge,* while forty-two were placed on the *Deerhound* [a British steam yacht cruising in the vicinity of the fight], and nine on a French pilot boat." [4] Other Confederate cruisers, such as the *Shenandoah, Florida, Tallahassee,* and *Georgia,* did a similar work of destruction. [5] The actual burning of specific vessels was but a small part of the damage done by Confederate cruisers and privateers: far more serious was the general hazard which raised insurance rates, caused over seven hundred American vessels to transfer to the British flag to avoid capture, and, together with other factors, gave the American merchant marine a setback from which it did not recover till the time of the first World War.

7

Coastal operations in the latter part of the war called forth some of the most determined efforts of the Union navy. Though important steps had been taken in the seizure of outer positions on Pamlico Sound, the operations against Roanoke Island and New Berne, the reduction of Port Royal and Fort Pulaski, the seizure of Norfolk, the occupation of Florida ports, and the reduction of New Orleans, yet the year 1864 opened with four important ports—Charleston, Mobile, Wilmington, and Galveston—still in Southern hands. It is true that each of these ports was blockaded; but their conquest and occupation was an essential element in Federal naval strategy. The ability of the Confederates to hold them as long as they did is one of the surprising features of the war.

[3] *Offic. Rec.* (Nav.), 1 ser., I, 782. It has been estimated that the *Alabama* destroyed property worth $10,000,000. Paullin, *op. cit.,* 39: 167.

[4] Meriwether, 285.

[5] International complications arising from England's connection with Confederate cruiser operations are discussed in chapters 20, 29, and 38.

In the case of proud Charleston, Union effort met conspicuous failure. Powerfully intrenched on the land side, the famous city was well supplied with harbor defenses, which included Forts Sumter, Moultrie, and Johnson, and Castle Pinckney. On April 7, 1863, DuPont opened attack upon Sumter with a fleet of monitors; but he encountered such deadly fire from Confederate batteries that he withdrew his squadron. This result, so different from Northern expectation (for the Union navy department had placed great reliance upon the monitors, which it regarded as invincible),[1] produced a distinct shock at a time when the military situation gave cause for general gloom in Union ranks. Other attempts, military and naval, were made against Charleston in July and August, 1863. A squadron of monitors under Dahlgren, successor to DuPont, made a vigorous attack; a military force under General Gillmore sought to reduce the city by siege operations and plucky infantry assaults upon Battery Wagner; the city itself was placed under fire; and Sumter was subjected to a seven-day military bombardment. None of these efforts, however, succeeded. Beauregard's men held fast; the assaults upon intrenched positions held by Confederate infantry and artillery were frustrated with severe loss; the exaggerated menace of submarine mines and torpedoes caused the defense to be considered even more formidable than it was; and, though Sumter was shattered and its guns silenced, the Confederates held the ruins till February, 1865, when the position was abandoned as an incident of Sherman's final campaign.

Further naval operations were concerned with such matters as the Red River expedition, the assault upon Mobile, and the belated reduction of Fort Fisher. The Red River expedition of March, 1864, though one of the elaborate episodes in the river war, proved a costly fiasco for the Union side. It was a huge land-and-water enterprise under General Banks and Admiral Porter whose main object was, by proceeding up the Red River, to clamp the Union vise upon Louisiana and East Texas and perchance to dampen the ardor of the French Napoleon in his Mexican schemes; while an incidental purpose was the seizure of quantities of cotton. In its strategic object the expedition failed utterly; as for the cotton, it was largely destroyed by the Southerners themselves on the approach of the Union forces. The army units in this expedition numbered about 30,000, while the navy used a score of ironclads and gunboats in addition to a large number of transports. Between the time when Porter's fleet entered the mouth of the Red River on March 12, 1864, escorting a detachment of Banks's army, until May 21, when the squadron and transports returned crestfallen to the Mississippi, fearful obstacles had been encountered by this "most formidable force that had ever been collected in the western waters." In part the difficulties of the expedition were due to the "treacherous nature of this

[1] The "navy" generally (not the department) disliked the monitors, which had disadvantages for navigation in a heavy sea.

crooked, narrow, and turbid stream, whose high banks furnished the most favorable positions for artillery and for the deadly sharp-shooter." Considering the ambitious nature of the enterprise, its outcome presented a sorry anticlimax. Shreveport had not been captured; the Southern military force was undefeated (Kirby Smith did not surrender until May, 1865); and Confederate strength in the Southwest had hardly been shaken. Sherman had, however, been deprived of a powerful force in his Atlanta campaign; Banks had suffered two defeats (Sabine Cross Roads and Pleasant Hill); the fleet had narrowly missed stranding in the falling river; the horde of speculators accompanying the army had retired furiously indignant "without their sheaves"; and a "bitter crop of quarrels" [2] among officers ensued.

Mobile, powerfully defended by shore forts and a fleet including the famous ram *Tennessee,* was captured after a hot fight (the battle of Mobile Bay, August 5, 1864) in which Farragut forced his large wooden ships, monitors, and gunboats up the difficult channel in disregard of torpedoes, while his flagship, the *Hartford,* with the old admiral lashed to its rigging, was swept by a fatal storm of shot and shell. The fact that the *Tennessee* failed to ram any of the Union vessels indicated the success of Farragut's sheering and maneuvering, nor did the torpedoes do much execution; but the fire of the Confederate fleet and of Fort Morgan fell with butchering precision upon the Union decks, piling them with mangled fragments of humanity.

For the reduction of Fort Fisher, which guarded Wilmington harbor, a formidable military and naval attack was planned. In December, 1864, the North Carolinian garrison with its elaborate coast defenses held out against a combined effort by the navy under Porter and the army under B. F. Butler and Godfrey Weitzel (this being one of Butler's many failures); but a second expedition in January, 1865—a huge armada under Porter and a military force of nearly 8000 under General A. H. Terry—reduced the fort, chiefly by a bombardment which silenced its guns. "Its capture [wrote its Southern defender], with the resulting loss of all the Cape Fear River defenses, and of Wilmington, the great importing depot of the South, effectually ended all blockade-running. Lee sent me word that Fort Fisher must be held, or he could not subsist his army." [3] Since, however, the capture of Fort Fisher was delayed till nearly the end of the war, the value of this Union success was less than had been expected. The war came to its end with the Stars and Bars still floating at Galveston. This port of the far Southwest did not surrender till June 2, 1865. Its fall may be regarded as the final act in the naval war.

[2] *Battles and Leaders,* IV, 361–362.
[3] *Ibid.,* IV, 642.

CHAPTER 26

Wartime Politics to 1864

I

IN ITS POLITICAL manifestations the Civil War brought profound transformations. Down to 1864, with the exception of Washington, in whose election all parties joined, none but a Democrat had been re-elected to the presidency.[1] A party strong and vibrant in 1856 was now so shaken that in the seven succeeding decades only two of its candidates reached the White House. A new-fledged party, uncertain of its future and precarious in its tenure in 1860, grew to such proportions because of what happened during the war and the period of reconstruction that it became, to millions of Americans, almost synonymous with the government itself; while the dominant party of the ante-bellum era, the party of Jefferson, Monroe, Jackson, Benton, Calhoun, Douglas, Toombs, and Davis, was reduced to secondary rank, if measured in terms of available strength in presidential elections. To measure the effect of the war in promoting this development one needs to remember that the Democracy of the North was of such strength in 1862 that it could have seized the Federal Congress had the South been restored in that year to the Union, but that as the war progressed this party of compromise lost its hold on the political machinery; while, without the American people being apparently conscious of what was going on, a limited group within the Republican party, the "Radicals," seized the reins, even claiming Lincoln himself, with reservations, as an unwilling adherent.

How far the American people willed the political result which came out of the war is a question that may well be pondered. Those political views which manifested themselves in the election of 1862 were hostile to the main result which flowed from the war, and so strong were these political views in 1864, at least down to September of that year, that many Republicans including Lincoln himself expected defeat. Defeat did not come: but the support which brought success was composite; it was not all of a piece. Many who voted for Lincoln in 1864 were supporting with some reluctance a party which was being transformed contrary to their desires.

[1] Indeed for thirty-two years no President of any party had been re-elected. Jackson was the last to be so honored.

This transformation of the Republican party and its attainment of dominating power was one of the major political developments of American history.

2

Difficulties within the Republican party had been manifest from the outset of Lincoln's presidency. It must always be remembered that Lincoln's nomination had produced poignant disappointment in influential quarters, and that the events associated with his taking office, as for instance his secret night ride to Washington above mentioned, had made an unfortunate impression. Just before his inauguration Lincoln had been seriously embarrassed by factional differences among the Republicans. Some of the Radicals (if the term may be used at that early date) were demanding the elimination of Seward, who had become a veritable storm center, being vigorously supported by certain groups but hotly opposed by others. The forces working behind the scenes cannot be detailed here; but they reached such a pass that on March 2, 1861, a group of Seward's supporters informed Lincoln that the New Yorker "could not serve in the Cabinet with Chase." For a President-Elect on the eve of inauguration this intransigency of the Seward-Weed faction produced a sorry dilemma. At this point Seward actually asked Lincoln's leave to withdraw from the cabinet. Lincoln, shrewdly realizing that the very existence of the Seward-Chase rift made it politic to have both factional chiefs in his official family, and being unwilling for Seward to "take the first trick," insisted that Seward countermand the withdrawal; and the administration was thus launched with a "compound Cabinet" [1] which Seward regarded as a doubtful experiment.

These factional dissensions, which had their ramifications throughout the North, were enhanced by the incident of Frémont's proclamation, treated in a previous chapter.[2] When Lincoln, mindful of border-state sentiment, at first overruled Frémont and then removed him, he went far toward splitting his party wide open. His friend O. H. Browning, though a conservative, warned him that Frémont's removal would be "damaging both to the administration and the cause." [3] At this time a prominent Ohioan wrote to Chase of the "consternation and wrath" caused by Lincoln's interference, declaring that public opinion was "entirely with General Frémont." In continuing he referred to suggestions he had heard as to Lincoln's impeachment and added that loyal men were giving their lives to no end "if the imbecility of Buchanan's administration is to be surpassed thus." While he is "conciliating the contemptible State of Kentucky," he added, let Lincoln remember "that the free States may want a little conciliation. . . ." Declaring that Frémont was the favorite of the

[1] Bancroft, *Seward*, II, 43, 45.
[2] Above, pp. 371–372.
[3] Browning, *Diary*, I, 503.

Northwest, he asserted that he would displace Lincoln if a presidential election were to be held at the time.[4]

In 1862 the opposition to the Lincoln administration was even more intense. Military failure increased the impression of incompetence at Washington. The peninsular episode, the Seven Days, Second Manassas, the failure to consolidate the results of Antietam, the calls for immense numbers of additional volunteers, the muddle as to Halleck's authority, and the general lack of coordination in the direction of army operations—all these developments had their political repercussions as the wretched months dragged on. Furthermore, while loosening the attachment of anti-slavery men to his cause and alienating those who were for pushing a vigorous war, Lincoln was also under fire from the opposite camp; his arbitrary arrests and summary methods were giving a handle to opponents who accused him of suppressing civil liberty.

3

Such was the general situation when in September of 1862 Lincoln startled the country with his "proclamations," the proclamation of emancipation (September 22) and that of September 24 by which a general suspension of the habeas corpus privilege was authorized and the use of military trials in suppressing disloyalty announced. By these edicts the President gave serious offense to conservatives, both within his own party and among the Democrats. Such support as he gained among vociferous abolitionists was more than offset by the defection of those who favored restoring the Union and letting other questions alone. John T. Stuart of Illinois, Lincoln's former law partner, considered the proclamations "most unfortunate"; while Senator Fessenden regarded the emancipation proclamation as *brutum fulmen* and deplored the habeas corpus edict as "an exercise of despotic power" and "very dangerous."[1]

As the congressional election approached, expressions of discontent became ominous. Grimes of Iowa wrote: ". . . we are going to destruction as fast as imbecility, corruption, and the wheels of time, can carry us."[2] Trumbull thought the war would never end unless a different tack were taken, and complained of the "lack of affirmative, positive action & business talent in the cabinet."[3] To Governor Andrew of Massachusetts it seemed that "the President [had] never yet seemed quite sure that we were in a war at all."[4] And the equable Lowell was sufficiently upset to declare:

---

[4] Rhodes, III, 473 n.

[1] Browning, *Diary*, I, 585, 587–588.

[2] William Salter, *Life of James W. Grimes*, 156; Winfred A. Harbison, "The Opposition to President Lincoln within the Republican Party," MS. doctoral dissertation, University of Illinois, 1930, 77.

[3] Harbison dissertation (see preceding note), 77; *Journal*, Ill. St. Hist. Soc., II, 48–49.

[4] Pearson, *Andrew*, II, 3; Harbison, 78.

"Mr. L. seems to have a theory of carrying on war without hurting the enemy." [5]

It would indeed be hard to name any faction in the fall of 1862 that was pleased with Lincoln. Many of the root-and-branch abolitionists, though partially appeased by the proclamation of September 22, attacked the administration for what they regarded as weakness and incompetence; they revealed in the confiscation debates and in countless other ways that they wanted even stronger measures. Within this group there were not a few who subordinated every other consideration to the extermination of slavery. A clergyman-professor in Illinois College, for example, in October, 1862, "asserted, with a great deal of pomposity, that all who clamored for the Constitution and the Union were traitors, or sympathizers with rebellion." [6] To say that Lincoln had won the support of these men by partially agreeing with them as to slavery would be far from the truth. The preliminary emancipation proclamation, accompanied by the President's promise of compensation to slaveowners, was far from satisfying them. What it amounted to was that the harassed President, without winning the hearty support of abolitionists, had alienated moderate Republicans and war Democrats. As for the opposition Democrats, he had put excellent ammunition into their hands.

A close student of the period has pointed out that, disregarding the Democratic press, Republican newspapers may be classified under three headings on the basis of their attitude toward Lincoln: (1) "administration journals" which supported the President (e.g., the Washington *Chronicle,* the Philadelphia *Inquirer,* the *Illinois State Journal*), this group being of less than major importance the country over; (2) "conservative papers which, on the whole, supported the general conduct of the war but did not hesitate to condemn particular acts or methods of the President" (e.g., the New York *Times,* the Cincinnati *Commercial*); (3) Radical journals which "not only censured the President for particular acts but also opposed his general war policy" (e.g., the New York *Tribune,* the New York *Evening Post,* the *Independent,* the Chicago *Tribune,* the *Missouri Democrat*).[7]

Speaking generally regarding most of the states, the "war Democrats" coalesced with the Republicans under the name "Union party," this development having been well launched in 1861. This factor in the political situation inured to the benefit of the Republicans, whose postwar attitude involved little of gratitude to the Democrats for wartime support. The main avowed purposes of this Union party were the vigorous prosecution of the war and the suppression of the "rebellion." These, indeed, were the broad purposes of the Northern people; they served admirably as party slogans. In opposition to this party stood the regular Democrats, who were outspoken

[5] Scudder, *James Russell Lowell,* II, 29; Harbison, 78.
[6] Browning, *Diary,* I, 576–577.
[7] Harbison, 155.

opponents of the administration. Since they refused to go with the "war Democrats," preferring to preserve their organization intact and to wrest control from those in power, there has arisen the misapprehension that they were anti-Union (or non-Union) Democrats. This was not generally true, though the misapprehension resulted naturally from the appropriation of broad national aims as party aims. The regular Democrats supported the government of the United States as against the Confederacy; but in the wish to follow a different direction in the prosecution of the war they sought to overthrow the existing Republican administration. Indeed they declared that Union success in the war could never come along the lines of the Lincoln government.

4

It was only by the slenderest margin that the party associated with Lincoln retained control of Congress in the election of 1862. Five important states which Lincoln had carried in 1860 now sent Democratic delegations to the House of Representatives, while a sixth sent an evenly balanced delegation.[1] For the Thirty-Seventh Congress (as it stood after the withdrawal of the Southern members) the [New York] *Tribune Almanac* reported the representatives as follows: Republicans, 106; Democrats, 42; Unionists, 28. For the Thirty-Eighth Congress elected in 1862 the figures become somewhat confusing because of an increase in total membership and also because of the consolidation of Unionists and Republicans. For its issue in 1863 the *Tribune Almanac* gave an incomplete statement showing 80 Republicans and 71 Democrats. Later, after the border states were added, it reported 102 "Republicans and Unconditional Unionists," 75 Democrats, and 9 border-state men. From Kentucky, Maryland, Missouri, and West Virginia the Republican-Unionist group mustered fifteen members chosen in the election of 1862; but even then (and despite increases in California, Connecticut, Iowa, and Minnesota) their majority was measurably diminished.[2]

When popular election statistics in the states are analyzed the extent of Republican loss becomes more evident. In Pennsylvania a Republican majority of 59,000 in 1860 was transformed into a Democratic majority of 3500 in 1862. For other states there was a similar reversal of majorities, as follows: New York, from 50,000 Republican to 10,700 Democratic; Ohio, from 20,700 Republican to 5500 Democratic; Indiana, from 5900 Republican to 9600 Democratic; Illinois, from 11,900 Republican to 16,500 Democratic. In New Jersey the Democratic popular majority grew

[1] The five states were New York, Pennsylvania, Ohio, Indiana, and Illinois; the Wisconsin delegation elected in 1862 contained three Democrats and three Republicans.

[2] For the figures above given see [N. Y.] *Tribune Almanac*, 1862, p. 18; 1863, p. 19; 1864, p. 24.

from 4400 in 1860 to 14,500 in 1862; while in states which remained Republican the decline in popular majorities as between 1860 and 1862 may be illustrated as follows: in Maine, from 24,700 to 6000; in New Hampshire, from 9100 to 1800; in Massachusetts, from 43,800 to 28,200; in Michigan, from 22,100 to 6600.[3] For the narrow margin of eighteen votes in the House of Representatives which the President's party retained, the border states, strangely enough, were largely responsible; and in producing this result the use of Federal troops was an important factor. "But for the aid of the Border slave States [wrote J. G. Blaine] the anti-slavery position of Mr. Lincoln might have been overthrown by a hostile House of Representatives." [4] In Kentucky the Lincoln administration took no chances. Federal military power was freely used; arrest and prosecution were threatened for anyone seeking office on a platform of hostility to the administration at Washington; votes were referred to as a "kind of Military Census, telling how many loyal men there are in a county"; and as a result the Union ticket was uniformly successful.[5]

Lincoln's defeat in his own state was one of the features of this election. In September, 1862, an anti-Lincoln organ at Springfield denounced the "party of unscrupulous demagogues" which "have the control of the United States Congress"; [6] and much was said as to the reign of terror in the North which the administration was promoting by its illegal arrests. The most striking phase of the election in Illinois was the contest in the eighth congressional district, where John Todd Stuart, former law partner of Lincoln, stood as the Democratic candidate against Leonard Swett, the Republican nominee. Stuart was one of those Whigs who in the recasting of party lines had not joined the Republicans. He had supported Fillmore in 1856 and Bell in 1860; now, in 1862, while supporting the war and professing undiminished personal respect for Lincoln, whose political mentor and ardent friend he had been, he differed with him as to policies, urging the maintenance of the Constitution and the Union without "resort to revolutionary means." [7] On such an announcement of policy he was accepted by the Democratic convention as their candidate. Here, then, were two of Lincoln's close friends at odds: Stuart opposing Lincoln the statesman while admiring Lincoln the man; Swett fully championing Lincoln's policies. In a heated campaign a flood of pamphlets denounced Lincoln's

[3] In these calculations the votes of 1860 are presidential, while those of 1862 are in state elections, usually for governor, but in some cases for auditor, treasurer, or secretary of state. Figures for state elections in 1862 naturally indicate the general political trend. [N. Y.] *Tribune Almanac*, 1863, 50 ff.

[4] *Twenty Years of Congress*, I, 444.

[5] E. M. Coulter, *Civil War and Readjustment in Kentucky*, 155.

[6] *Illinois State Register*, Sept. 9, 1862, quoted by H. E. Pratt in *Journal*, Ill. St. Hist. Soc., XXIV, 129.

[7] Paul M. Angle, *One Hundred Years of Law*, 39–40.

suppression of civil liberty, while the fires of race hatred were fanned over a local issue as to excluding Negroes from the state.[8] In the election the vote stood: Stuart, 12,808; Swett, 11,443. For Illinois as a whole five Republicans were chosen as against nine·Democrats; in addition, the opponents of Lincoln obtained control of the Illinois legislature. "Badly beaten by the Democrats," wrote O. H. Browning. "Just what was to be expected from the insane ravings of the Chicago Tribune, Quincy Whig, ed [sic] id omne genus." [9]

In summing up the causes for the administration's reverses in the congressional campaign of 1862 one must take account of such factors as the conservative reaction to Lincoln; opposition to the emancipation proclamation; disaffection aroused by arbitrary arrests and by such extreme measures as the confiscation act of 1862; factional discords within the Republican party; the menace of conscription; and, above all, military failure. The defeats inflicted upon the army by a numerically inferior enemy caused the people to feel a maddening sense of frustration—an unabated determination to win combined with a sense of helplessness under existing leaders. The prevalent feeling was thus expressed by a New Englander: ". . . The people ask what do our rulers mean? Are they only deceiving us? We cannot much longer endure the suspense. They say the determination of the Pres. and his Cabinet is not steady, bold, calculated to inspire us, and we fear the worst. Some of our truest men talk in this way. There is a deep undercurrent among the people, of dissatisfaction, and it will in the course of a few months . . . beat against the administration most angrily." [10] Much the same feeling was expressed by the New York *Times* in its issue of November 5, 1862:

> The heaviest load which the friends of the Government have been compelled to carry through this canvass has been the inactivity and inefficiency of the Administration. . . . The country has given the Government over a million of men, and all the money they could possibly use. . . .
>   . . . The fate of the nation must no longer be committed to Generals who, like Essex in the English Revolution, "next to a great defeat, *dread a great victory*."

[8] In 1862 a new constitution for Illinois was drawn up in a convention controlled by Democrats. Though it was defeated at the polls, the article prohibiting immigration of Negroes into the state was approved by a majority of 100,000 votes. Army officials were shipping Negroes to Cairo; farmers were being urged by Republicans to welcome this form of cheap labor; and in opposition to this the Democrats were furiously denouncing the Africanization of the state. H. E. Pratt in *Journal*, Ill. St. Hist. Soc., XXIV, 137. See also Arthur C. Cole, "President Lincoln and the Illinois Radical Republicans," *M.V.H.R.*, IV, 417–436 (Mar., 1918).
[9] Browning, *Diary*, I, 582.
[10] G. A. Oviatt to Gideon Welles, Somers, Conn., Sept. 26, 1862, Welles Papers (MSS., Libr. of Cong.).

Under the headline "The Vote of Want of Confidence" the *Times* declared on November 7:

> . . . The very qualities which have made Abraham Lincoln so well liked in private life— . . . his kindheartedness, his concern for fair play, his placidity of temper— in a manner unfit him for the stern requirements of deadly war. Quick, sharp, summary dealings don't suit him at all. He is all the while haunted with the fear of doing some injustice, and is ever easy to accept explanations. The very first necessity of war is extreme rigor, and yet every impulse of our constitutional Commander-in-Chief has been to get rid of it. . . . There is not a purer patriot in the land. And yet there is something beyond this which we miss—the high sacred vehemence, inspired by the consciousness of infinite interests at stake, ...

That the *Times* should have spoken thus signified a distrust of Lincoln's administration on the part of his friends, who felt that by their urging they might fortify his determination and intensify his vigor. There was in this situation the possibility of his friends becoming reluctant opponents, or at least inactive and indifferent supporters. By the same token his political antagonists were gaining in power.

5

If the congressional election of 1862 brought woe to the Lincoln forces, further grief was soon to follow. When Burnside's succession to McClellan's command was followed by the ghastly blunder of Fredericksburg, discontent broke out afresh. One expression of this displeasure was the action of a caucus of Republican senators which sought to wrest important matters of state from Lincoln's hands and to make significant changes in his cabinet. Could not something be done to assure the public and energize the government? Must disaster follow disaster until the cause was hopelessly lost? Where was the trouble? Should not the Senate formally express its want of confidence in Seward and demand his withdrawal? Was not Stanton also largely responsible for repeated military failures? Ought not the whole Senate to go in a body to the President and demand a new deal and a more effective program? Was it not essential that Republican generals be put in command? Were not the President's methods too loose; did he in fact have a cabinet; should there not be closer cooperation among the secretaries? And beyond all this, was not the real difficulty in the President himself? Might it not be best to go to him and tell him frankly of his defects? [1] Such were the questions raised in this senatorial caucus whose deliberations resulted in the selection of a committee to wait upon the President and urge "such selections and changes [in the cabinet] . . . as

---

[1] For the caucus ponderings suggested and paraphrased in this paragraph, see Browning, *Diary*, I, 596 ff.; Francis Fessenden, *Life . . . of William Pitt Fessenden*, I, 231–236.

will secure to the country unity of purpose and action, . . ." [2] This being interpreted meant the displacement of the Seward element and the enhancement of the political influence of Chase. One of the senators thus wrote of the designs of the Chase men: ". . . their game was to drive all the cabinet out—then force . . . the recall of Mr. Chase as Premier, and form a cabinet of ultra men around him." [3]

This cabinet crisis placed Lincoln in a dilemma. Though giving little outward evidence of emotion he revealed his inward distress to his intimate friend Browning, who has quoted him as saying: "What do these men want? . . . They wish to get rid of me, and I am sometimes half disposed to gratify them. . . . Since I heard . . . of the proceedings of the caucus I have been more distressed than by any event of my life." [4]

His manner of meeting the issue, however, showed the characteristic Lincolnian touch in the handling of those personal situations which often put statesmen to the test. Just in advance of his first meeting with the senatorial committee Lincoln received word of the resignation of his secretary of state. When the committee met him the venerable Collamer read a paper in which the Republican members of the Senate urged a vigorous and successful prosecution of the war and a uniform construction of the cabinet agreeing with the President in political principle and general policy—a condition which, as the Senate believed, did not then exist. In conclusion it was urged that the cabinet "be exclusively composed of statesmen who are the cordial, resolute, unwavering supporters of the principles and purposes first above stated"—i.e., prosecuting the war with energy and suppressing a "causeless and atrocious rebellion." [5]

Seward's resignation now seemed irrevocable; other secretaries might take the cue to resign; the Radicals seemed on the point of seizing the reins and remaking the cabinet; plainly the President's leadership (to mention but one factor) was at stake. Lincoln's next move was to contrive another meeting of the senatorial delegation to confer with him. On assembling they were surprised to find that the President had shrewdly arranged to have the whole cabinet except Seward present. The significance of this will be appreciated when it is remembered that Chase was reported to have talked freely with some of the senators concerning the untoward conditions which affected the cabinet and especially of the harmful influence of Seward. Nor was this a mere matter of sordid intrigue or of personal ambition; Chase's correspondence and diary show that he honestly differed with Lincoln, chafed at the President's inaction and lax methods as he regarded them, found it hard to suppress his impatience at repeated instances of costly military blundering, and probably came to believe in his own superior ability to conduct the nation's affairs. Though never reaching the

[2] Fessenden, I, 239.
[3] Browning, *Diary*, I, 604.
[4] *Ibid.*, I, 600–601.
[5] Fessenden, I, 239.

point of actual disloyalty to his chief, he was fast becoming, by reason of his personality, position, and views, the inevitable center of anti-Lincoln movements. Confronted with his colleagues, the senators, and the President, Chase found it necessary to state "that the cabinet were all harmonious"; though previously he is reported to have said to these same senators "that Seward exercised a back stair and malign influence upon the President, and thwarted all the measures of the Cabinet." [6] The upshot of the whole matter was that Chase as well as Seward resigned; Lincoln promptly refused to accept either resignation; and the crisis passed with a "milder spirit" prevailing,[7] the cabinet continuing as before, the senators somewhat chagrined, Chase embarrassed, and the President holding the tricks.

6

On the political front the developments of the year 1863 were not propitious to the Lincoln administration.[1] In March there came simultaneously the conscription law and the habeas corpus act. As to the latter, it became evident that, while not restraining arbitrary arrests as intended, it did contain an indemnity feature by which Federal officials committing wrongs upon citizens' rights within a state were exempted from existing judicial penalties.[2] On conscription Horace Greeley, then growing in importance as pundit of the Radical North, declared as follows: "It is folly to close our eyes to the signs of the times. The people have been educated to the idea of individual sovereignty, & the principle of conscription is repugnant to their feelings and cannot be carried out except at great peril to the free States. . . . The entire system must be changed. . . . Drafting is an anomaly in a free State; it oppresses the masses. Like imprisonment for debt . . . it must and will be reformed out of our systems of political economy." [3] That the law was poorly framed and badly administered has been noted above; naturally it became a favorite theme of denunciation not only by those who felt as Greeley did but also by liberal Democrats and supporters of individual liberty. To friends of state rights the law was an offense: they argued that it was unconstitutional, trenched upon the militia function of the states, and offered a precedent for a dangerous increase of despotic central power. Indeed to those who thought in terms of the original American federal system the whole tendency toward increasing centralization of governmental powers seemed an ominous thing.

[6] "I asked Judge Collamer how Mr. Chase could venture to make such a statement. . . . He answered 'He lied.' " Browning, *Diary*, I, 603.

[7] Bates, *Diary*, 270.

[1] By this time the more extreme wing of the Democratic party, known as the "Copperheads," had reached a considerable development, especially in the Middle West. For the tradition of Democratic "disloyalty," see pp. 478–479.

[2] On the indemnity act see Randall, *Constitutional Problems Under Lincoln*, chap. ix.

[3] Greeley to Stanton, June 12, 1863. Stanton Papers (MSS., Libr. of Cong.).

Conscription, arbitrary arrests, centralized banking control, huge measures of national taxation, clumsy Federal interference in intra-state struggles, Federal stimulus in the creation of West Virginia, national pressure in state elections, high judicial approval for irregular and questionable measures, the employment of Federal martial law or military rule within a state, drastic action by provost marshals under the control of the war department—these and similar measures of national control seemed to be part of a preconceived and deliberate pattern; and unless checked in time it was feared that they would introduce a new governmental era in which state autonomy would be but a feeble thing. It is now a commonplace to say that this new nationalism was one of the outstanding results of the war. As H. G. Pearson has remarked, it "is a fact of our national history that the Civil War put the separate states definitely and irrevocably in subordination to the central government, ..."[4]

To an anxious nation awaiting the outcome of another major battle in the East there came in May the sickening news of Chancellorsville, adding Hooker to the growing list of Union military failures and further discrediting Lincoln's ability in the choice of commanders. July brought a brighter prospect with Gettysburg and Vicksburg, but it also brought the draft riot in New York City and a sense of frustration on Meade's failure to crush Lee. Results in the matter of abolition were proving disappointing to Radicals as they realized how little the emancipation proclamation had actually accomplished; and when at the end of the year Lincoln launched his amnesty policy and his plan for easy restoration of the Southern states, he stirred up such factional opposition in his own party that his program on this front proved impossible of fulfillment.

This, in briefest outline, was the political setting as the year 1864 opened. Though hope came to the Union cause in September, the prospects up to that time made the spring and summer of this election year an exceedingly gloomy period. Yet by the inflexible American political system a presidential election had to be waged, so that all the elements of political dissatisfaction were to become enmeshed in the web of politics, with factional leaders capitalizing every source of discontent for campaign purposes. As the time for the Republican nomination approached it was evident that the Radicals were at the point of open break with Lincoln on the important issue of reconstruction. Soon this discontent took the form of the "Chase boom." In his intimate correspondence Chase had written in 1863: ". . . I think a man of different qualities from those the President has will be needed for the next four years. I am not anxious to be regarded as that man; and I am quite willing to leave that question to the decision of those who agree in thinking that some such man should be chosen."[5] By this

---

[4] Pearson, *Andrew*, II, 122.

[5] Chase to ex-Governor Sprague, his son-in-law, Nov. 26, 1863. J. W. Shuckers, *Life and Public Services of S. P. Chase*, 494.

time many earnest Union men, such as William Cullen Bryant, Theodore Tilton, and Horace Greeley, had reached an attitude that was not mere disaffection: it was a deep-seated conviction that the Lincoln administration was largely a failure and that, in words attributed to John Sherman, "there are better men for President than Lincoln." [6]

With awkward political strategy the Chase boom was launched by a group of congressmen acting under the sponsorship of Senator S. C. Pomeroy of Kansas.[7] Perhaps without consulting Chase himself this group distributed a paper known as the "Pomeroy Circular," which declared that the re-election of Lincoln was practically impossible, that his "manifest tendency toward temporary expedients" would become stronger during a second term, and that Chase united more of the needful qualities than any other available candidate.[8] An irritating incident now brought further embarrassment to the Chase movement. On February 27, 1864, Francis P. Blair, Jr., who had left his place in the army to promote the President's policies in Congress, delivered in the House of Representatives a vicious assault on the secretary of the treasury.[9] The incident almost led to Chase's resignation, and when Lincoln befriended Blair after this attack by restoring him to the army command in the West which he had given up late in 1863 on being called for political service to Washington,[10] the President's

[6] H. M. Dudley, in *M.V.H.R.*, XVIII, 501.

[7] As early as December 9, 1863, the day after Lincoln's announcement of his policy concerning the restoration of the South, a meeting was held in Washington to launch Chase's name as candidate for the presidency. Memorandum bearing the endorsement "Organization to make S P Chase President, December 9, 1863, Important" (MS., Libr. of Cong.).

[8] Writing of the distribution of the Pomeroy Circular, James M. Winchell, the secretary of the committee, declared: *"Mr. Chase was informed of this proposed action and approved it fully."* Thomas Graham Belden and Marva Robins Belden, *So Fell the Angels*, 113. Chase himself asserted that he was not consulted in the organization of the committee and the issuing of the Pomeroy Circular. This does not mean, however, that he had no part at all in the conversations concerning the nomination. (Warden, *Chase*, 573–574.) As noted above, he had not hesitated to criticize the President orally and in correspondence. He referred to the "so-called" cabinet, considered its meetings "useless," and expressed mortification at the conduct of affairs. (*Ibid.*, 539, 553.) Welles thought that the treasury was the source of mischievous remarks in the Senate (*Diary*, I, 525); and in general the evidence seems to show that Chase was in that attitude of mind which politicians describe as a "receptive mood."

[9] On May 23, 1864, Chase wrote to Col. A. P. Stone of Ohio: "I have not written a word to Ohio . . . on the . . . malignant, and lying assault of the Blairs—for the Congressional general was only the mouthpiece of the trio—and its apparent indorsement by Mr. Lincoln." Warden, 594–595.

[10] The President's restoration of Blair to his post in Sherman's army was done in fulfillment of a promise. Lincoln had proposed (Nov. 2, 1863) that Blair put his military commission in the President's hands and undertake to organize the House of Representatives along Lincolnian lines. It was expected that Blair might be elected speaker; if not, said Lincoln, he might return to the army. Lincoln, *Collected Works*, VI, 554–555; Nicolay and Hay, *Lincoln*, IX, 80.

motives were misconstrued as a rebuke to the Radicals and to Chase himself.

Lincoln's own statement of his attitude in the matter was that, while he knew of "secret issues" afoot and "secret agents" working along the lines of the Pomeroy committee, he "[knew] just as little of these things as [his] friends . . . allowed [him] to know." "They bring the documents to me," he said, "but I do not read them—they tell me what they think fit to tell me, but I do not inquire for more." [11] In this spirit, when Chase made his embarrassed explanation to the President protesting his passivity in the matter, Lincoln refused to accept the resignation which Chase offered to give and managed shrewdly to keep the secretary in the cabinet, where he could do the least harm to the Lincoln cause. It was not long before the boom collapsed. Powerful as was the anti-Lincoln movement, clumsiness of management and other factors prevented the success of efforts to close the ranks behind Chase as a leader.

[11] Lincoln, *Collected Works*, VII, 213.

CHAPTER 27

Peace Movements
and the Election of 1864

I

EVENTS OF MAY and early June, 1864, an important period because of the approach of presidential nominations, were not such as to increase the prestige of the administration. As to the effect of Grant's new drive against Lee, opinions differed. Some hailed his battles as great victories; to others it seemed that after the terrific losses of the Wilderness and Cold Harbor he was as far from Richmond as McClellan in '62. On May 18 a great stir had been made by the publication in the New York *World* and *Journal of Commerce* of a bogus proclamation of President Lincoln which gloomily recalled recent disasters, set a day of humiliation and prayer, and called for 400,000 men. The two papers, which had innocently enough published the forged document, foisted upon them by a man named Howard and slipped to the night force of the newspapers as a trick for rigging the stock market, were seized by military force and their publication was suspended. Though in three days the papers were allowed to resume, there was much ado about the matter in the city courts, and the subject continued for months to occupy columns in the daily press.

The movement to put forth a Republican rival of Lincoln spent itself with small result. In Cleveland on May 31 there met in convention a few disaffected Radicals [1] under the sponsorship of B. Gratz Brown and Wendell Phillips and supported vigorously by German extremists from the Middle West. What these men lacked in political *savoir faire* they made up in denunciatory enthusiasm. Their efforts to control the regular Republican machinery in the states had failed. In Illinois, for example, the "radical German opposition" had sought to have the Republican or Union dele-

---

[1] It is not to be inferred that the Radicals generally supported Frémont's hopeless effort. Their leaders (e.g., Chase, Wade, and Greeley) had too much political sagacity to throw away their chances in this fashion. What they wanted was control of the Republican (Union) party.

gates instructed to vote for Frémont; failing in this, they joined the independent Frémont movement and sent delegates to Cleveland. The general tone of the Cleveland convention was indicated in an informal speech delivered to that body by John Cochrane of New York and in a letter to the convention from Wendell Phillips, both bitterly denouncing the existing administration. On May 31 Frémont and Cochrane were nominated on a radical platform. In his letter of acceptance Frémont took his nomination seriously and violently criticized the Lincoln government.

Meanwhile Lincoln's managers had been active. They had the advantage of controlling the regular Republican (Union) party in which they held the managerial positions; they had the patronage, including provost marshals, postmasters, and Federal employees the country over; they had the disposal of contracts; and they worked through state conventions in which delegates to the national convention were instructed for Lincoln. When the Republican convention met at Baltimore on June 7 the effectiveness of organization and regularity in American politics was impressively demonstrated. Though something of a ripple was caused by the presence of an anti-Lincoln Radical delegation from Missouri, yet every vote was recorded for Lincoln.[2] When one remembers the opposition within the party and the last-minute hope of many that Grant could be made the nominee,[3] the ease with which this unanimity was obtained becomes a matter of wonder.

Outwardly Lincoln kept his hands off the convention, but his private secretary, J. G. Nicolay, was on the ground at Baltimore, functioning as a sort of Lincoln scout and taking care that nothing distasteful to the President be done on such matters as the platform and the vice-presidency. While behind the scenes Lincoln has been reported as favoring Andrew Johnson of Tennessee to supplant Hamlin, officially the President took the attitude that the convention must settle this question entirely for itself.[4] Largely through the shrewdness of Henry J. Raymond matters were so

[2] Missouri at first cast 22 votes for Grant; but on the question of making Lincoln's nomination unanimous Missouri's vote was changed and unanimity obtained. Nicolay and Hay, *Lincoln*, IX, 72.

[3] While some Radicals favored Frémont for President, others thought that the best ticket would be Grant and Frémont. Grant gave no encouragement to this effort, being a loyal Lincoln man; but a meeting called for June 4 at New York City to express gratitude for the general's services was regarded as a scheme to launch a Grant boom in opposition to Lincoln. Unable to attend this meeting, Lincoln sent a letter praising Grant and his "brave soldiers" for their "remarkable campaign." *Lincoln, Collected Works*, VII, 374.

[4] Lincoln's role in the nomination of Andrew Johnson later became a matter of acrimonious dispute. For a summary of the conflicting evidence on this point, stressing the President's support of Johnson, see J. G. Randall and Richard N. Current, *Lincoln the President*, IV, 130–134. For the opposing view, see James Glonek, "Lincoln, Johnson and the Baltimore Ticket," *Abraham Lincoln Quart.*, VI, 255–271 (Mar., 1951).

maneuvered that Johnson's name was presented at the right juncture; and when his nomination was made unanimous there came an outburst of enthusiasm growing out of the feeling that the ticket had been strengthened by the recognition at once of the war Democrats and of the South.

The platform was sufficiently broad to accommodate diverse elements. It is customary to say that the Radicals wrote the party manifesto. The truth is that the document had a radical flavor, but no Radical planks. Phrased in a tone of patriotic unction and heroic appeal, it demanded unity of effort to quell the "rebellion," denounced slavery as the cause of the war, and demanded its complete extirpation. Thanking people and soldiers for their sacrifices, it promised soldier relief, declared only supporters of the administration to be worthy of confidence, and then advocated specific measures, such as the protection of colored soldiers from violations of the laws of war, the encouragement of immigration, and the construction of a railroad to the Pacific.

Just following the President's renomination, opposition within his party broke out afresh. It was at this stage that the Jacobins pushed through the Wade-Davis reconstruction bill, a measure which Lincoln could not approve because of its severity and its obvious tendency to perpetuate wartime bitterness and hinder restoration. Lincoln seldom used the veto; in this case, however, he applied the pocket veto, which required no veto message and gave Congress no opportunity to override the President. The further details of this episode are treated elsewhere; [5] what concerns us here is that, by his veto and his later proclamation developing his policy of reconstruction, Lincoln had come to a hopeless deadlock with the Radicals on one of the major issues of the time, that of bringing the South back when the war should close. So bitter was the opposition that the two prominent Radicals whose names were associated with the bill issued a scathing denunciation of the President who had just been renominated. It had the caustic sting of a campaign diatribe; yet its authors were of the same party as the chief whom they were mercilessly denouncing.

There came now the long-heralded withdrawal of Chase from the cabinet. On former occasions he had offered to resign but had been urged to remain; now he once more put his resignation into Lincoln's hands, and to his chagrin, it was accepted. The occasion was a matter of patronage: in reality relations between President and secretary had been growing steadily more embarrassing. As Lincoln put it: "Of all I have said in commendation of your ability and fidelity, I have nothing to unsay; and yet you and I have reached a point of mutual embarrassment in our official relation which it seems cannot be overcome, or longer sustained, consistently with the public service." [6]

[5] See below, pp. 552–553.
[6] The date of Chase's resignation was June 29, 1864; it was accepted next day. Lincoln, *Collected Works*, VII, 419.

2

As the weeks dragged on during the summer of 1864, with their increasing military disappointments and sense of Union discouragement culminating in the Early raid and the narrowly averted capture of Washington, the clouds of depression, defeatism, and political opposition thickened and darkened. The Democrats played a waiting game, postponing their convention to the last of August but ominously gathering their forces. Meanwhile various forms of peace agitation and efforts toward negotiation were taking shape. C. L. Vallandigham, having escaped from the South and returned via Canada to Ohio, was attacking Lincoln and urging peace; in Illinois James W. Singleton and others were planning similar demonstrations. Singleton promoted a convention at Peoria (August 3, 1864) which was denounced as a copperhead movement to make "peace with traitors" (though many who participated did so, like Singleton, with sincere and honest purposes); and under like sponsorship a "peace pow-wow" was held at Springfield on August 18. It was not without significance that these efforts were closely associated with political opposition to the Lincoln government, and the connection of the movement with the "Sons of Liberty" served still further to identify the peacemakers with those who would overthrow the existing administration.

In a larger sense, however, the spread of the peace movement was an inevitable expression of a war-weary and heartsick nation; sincere Northern patriots yearned for an end to the fratricidal slaughter. Even the calm Charles Francis Adams, in faraway London, was willing to grasp at almost any hope for peace. Early in 1864 he entered into unofficial discussions with one Thomas Yeatman of Tennessee, who pledged that Jefferson Davis would step aside as President of the Confederacy in order to allow the Southern states to re-enter the Union, provided the Lincoln administration adopted a gradual plan of compensated emancipation. When Yeatman's indiscreet behavior and his failure to produce authoritative credentials as a Confederate peace envoy caused Seward to drop the negotiations, Adams grieved that his government had failed to pursue "the heroic policy which would have smoothed the path to reconciliation." [1]

Adams's explorations were kept secret, but when the more excitable Horace Greeley associated himself prominently with the peace movement, the attention of the whole North was focused upon the subject. Earnest though he was in his abolitionism and his denunciation of the South, Greeley had more than a trace of pacific idealism. On learning from a self-constituted envoy named Jewett that "two ambassadors of Davis & Co. are now in Canada, with full and complete powers for a peace," and being ad-

---

[1] Harriet Chappell Owsley, "Peace and the Presidential Election of 1864," *Tenn. Hist. Quart.*, XVIII, 3–19 (Mar., 1959). John Scott Russell, an English merchant, served as intermediary between Adams and Yeatman.

vised that "the whole matter [could] be consummated by me, you, them, and President Lincoln," [2] the editor of the *Tribune,* eager for peace but craving no personal connection with a possibly unpopular negotiation, referred the matter to President Lincoln, as in fact he should have done. "I venture to remind you [wrote Greeley to the President] that our bleeding, bankrupt, almost dying country also longs for peace; shudders at the prospect of fresh conscriptions, of further wholesale devastations, and of new rivers of human blood. And a widespread conviction that the government and its . . . supporters are not anxious for peace . . . is doing great harm. . . ." [3]

Lincoln, then harassed by Early's raid toward Washington, replied to Greeley on July 9 promising to meet "any person anywhere professing to have any proposition of Jefferson Davis in writing, for peace, embracing the restoration of the Union and abandonment of slavery. . . ." [4] At the same time he made the embarrassed Greeley the intermediary for conveying the government's declaration of its purpose to receive responsible negotiators. When days passed and nothing was done Lincoln became more emphatic and wrote to Greeley on the 15th: "I not only intend a sincere effort for peace, but I intend that you shall be a personal witness that it is made." [5] To show good faith the President extended to C. C. Clay, Jacob Thompson, J. P. Holcombe, and G. N. Sanders, the Southern "commissioners" in question, a formal letter of safe conduct to Washington. It has been maintained that the purpose of these Confederate agents in Canada was to harass the Lincoln government, promote the Confederate cause in certain Northern districts, and stir up peace sentiment among the Northern people. [6]

Caught up in a plan for which he had no relish, Greeley made the trip to Niagara only to find that the advertised diplomats had no credentials. Their mission was unofficial; they offered, however, if granted safe conduct to Washington and Richmond, to obtain the needed authorization. It appears that the agents had no authority to negotiate for peace at all, being interested rather in peace agitation (a very different matter); but that they had to guard against an unfortunate effect upon the people of the South if it were made to appear that Lincoln was ready for peace while the South was not. Informed of this development, Lincoln made public the following announcement:

To Whom it may concern:
  Any proposition which embraces the restoration of peace, the integrity of the whole Union, and the abandonment of slavery, and which comes by and

---

[2] W. C. Jewett of Colorado Territory wrote as above to Greeley from Niagara Falls on July 5, 1864, after conferring on the Canadian side with G. N. Sanders of Kentucky.
  [3] E. C. Kirkland, *Peacemakers of 1864,* 76.
  [4] Lincoln, *Collected Works,* VII, 435.
  [5] *Ibid.,* VII, 442.
  [6] Kirkland, 73.

with an authority that can control the armies now at war against the United States will be received and considered by the Executive government of the United States, and will be met by liberal terms on other substantial and collateral points. . . .[7]

Lincoln's memorandum was no mere gesture: he was ready to do precisely what he said. Since, however, reunion meant defeat in the Southern mind, his terms were impossible, while the lack of official credentials made the Southern agents useless as negotiators.

Thus the Greeley fiasco ended. It was soon followed by another unofficial peace effort which seemed more promising, the Jaquess-Gilmore mission. Jaquess was a preacher-soldier of Illinois, a Methodist college president who had become colonel of a volunteer regiment. Shocked that fellow Christians North and South should be killing each other, he obtained a furlough from military duty and journeyed to Fort Monroe, where he was afforded the facilities of a boat to enter the Confederate lines under flag of truce. He did this without government authority, though Lincoln unofficially approved the mission, even going so far as to say that it promised good if freed from difficulties. Though his mission broke down because of the refusal of Jefferson Davis to interview him, he persisted. J. R. Gilmore [8] had become associated with him in the enterprise; and in July, 1864, Lincoln was induced to consent to a new peace mission conducted by these two men. To Lincoln's mind it was an experiment. While carefully avoiding official connection with it, he saw no reason to prevent it. It may be also that Lincoln wished to expose the "political" purposes of the various peace efforts afoot and to bring into prominence the Southern attitude toward terms of peace. In Richmond the peacemakers conferred with President Davis and Secretary Benjamin on July 17, 1864; but, as in all similar cases, the undertaking broke down when the Confederate leaders indicated that Southern independence was indispensable. With an eye to war publicity the Boston *Evening Transcript* printed on July 22, 1864, an account of the Jaquess-Gilmore mission in which Jefferson Davis was quoted as saying: "This war must go on till the last of the generation falls in his tracks . . . *unless you acknowledge our right to self-government.*" Much the same result ensued at Toronto in August, 1864, when J. S. Black met Jacob Thompson, his former colleague in the Buchanan cabinet. Again the Southern *sine qua non* of independence closed discussion and gave no opening for a consideration of collateral points such as amnesty, state restoration, and compensation to slaveowners, on which Lincoln stood ready to offer generous pledges.

[7] Lincoln, *Collected Works*, VII, 451.

[8] Gilmore had combined business with literature in an unusual career which included ventures in cotton trading, travels in the South, editorial activities, and writings under the name of Edmund Kirke. He was a friend of Greeley and shared both his dreams of peace and his distrust of the Lincoln administration. See J. R. Gilmore, *Personal Recollections of Abraham Lincoln and the Civil War*.

3

A strange movement now developed—an effort within the Republican party to get rid of their chosen nominee, i.e., to force the withdrawal of Lincoln in favor of a "more vigorous" candidate. Whether viewed from the angle of Greeley's pacifism or of Wade's aggressiveness, the national prospect under existing management seemed, in the dark summer of 1864, nearly hopeless. Grant seemed to be accomplishing nothing; Lee appeared invincible; three years of war and hundreds of thousands of casualties had gone for naught; Sherman was apparently getting nowhere; Early had almost seized Washington. Lincoln was at odds with his own party on war aims and reconstruction and had offended his Congress. Prominent men kept denouncing the "imbecility" of the administration; the government's financial credit was ebbing; further calls for troops but emphasized the futility of Union effort; and meanwhile the people were made to believe that the South was anxious to negotiate but was rebuffed by a stubborn administration at Washington. On August 9 Greeley wrote: "I firmly believe that, were the election to take place tomorrow, the Democratic majority in this State and Pennsylvania would amount to 100,000, and that we should lose Connecticut also. Now if the Rebellion can be crushed before November it will do to go on; if not, we are rushing on certain ruin." [1]

Under these circumstances a "call" was confidentially circulated by dissenting Republicans who set September 28 as the date for a convention to meet at Cincinnati "to consider the state of the nation and to concentrate the union strength on some one candidate who commands the confidence of the country, even by a new nomination if necessary." [2] It was the intention to circulate the "call" secretly and then, if sufficient sentiment seemed ready to consolidate back of the movement, to bring the project into the open at what was deemed an opportune time.

Though the projected convention never met, the call evoked letters from men high in Republican councils which one reads today with considerable wonderment. Horace Greeley wrote: "Mr. Lincoln is already beaten. He cannot be elected. And we must have another ticket to save us from utter overthrow. If we had such a ticket as could be made by naming Grant, Butler, or Sherman for President, and Farragut as Vice, we could make a fight yet. And such a ticket we ought to have anyhow, with or without a convention." Henry Winter Davis wrote: "My letters from Maryland say Lincoln can do nothing there, even where the Union party is most vigorous, and everybody is looking for a new candidate. . . ." He added:

---

[1] Nicolay and Hay, *Lincoln*, IX, 196–197.

[2] N. Y. *Sun*, June 30, 1889, p. 3. (In this issue of the *Sun* a collection of documents was published to illustrate the "secret movement to supersede Abraham Lincoln in '64.") Among those associated with the movement were Horace Greeley, David Dudley Field, H. W. Davis, George Opdyke, and John Austin Stevens.

"I think we have a pretty good start in New York and the N. E. States, Pa., Del., and Ohio and Michigan. If a *break* be made *there,* it compels Lincoln's surrender." To Richard Smith, writing from the *Gazette* office in Cincinnati, it seemed that the success of the Democrats would be the ruin of the nation, that the "peace party" was of dangerous proportions, that the "people regard[ed] Mr. Lincoln's candidacy as a misfortune," and that the best course would be the withdrawal of Lincoln and Frémont and "the nomination of a man that would inspire confidence and infuse life into our ranks." Whitelaw Reid wrote on September 2: "That which I could do has been done in inducing the *Gazette* to come out for Mr. Lincoln's withdrawal." [3]

With this feeling of trepidation in Republican ranks, the Democratic delegates met at Chicago on August 29. The convention represented a union of war Democrats and peace Democrats: to please the war Democrats McClellan was nominated for the presidency, his running mate being Pendleton of Ohio; while the drafting of the platform was assigned to the so-called "peace faction," of which C. L. Vallandigham was the outstanding leader. After referring to "four years of failure to restore the Union by the experiment of war," the platform demanded the cessation of hostilities "to the end that at the earliest possible moment peace may be restored on the basis of the Federal Union of the States."

This was not a peace-at-any-price declaration; it proclaimed reunion as the condition of peace. Its weakness lay not in the aims and objectives that were visioned, but in the easy assumption that an undefeated Confederacy, having achieved an armistice on the basis of what would have been deemed Southern victory, would give up the main purpose for which they were fighting and consent to abdication by the Southern government.

Shortly prior to this convention, President Lincoln had set down on paper, chiefly as a way of formulating his own purpose, the following memorandum: "This morning . . . it seems exceedingly probable that this Administration will not be re-elected. Then it will be my duty to so cooperate with the President elect, as to save the Union between the election and the inauguration; as he will have secured his election on such ground that he can not possibly save it afterwards." In the diary of John Hay it is recorded that when Lincoln wrote this memorandum he obtained the signatures of his cabinet secretaries without showing them the contents, and that at the cabinet meeting of November 11 just after his re-election the President read the memorandum and stated that it had been his resolve, in case of McClellan's election, to "talk matters over with him" and say: "General, the election has demonstrated that you . . . have more influence . . . than I. Now let us together, you with your influence and I with . . . the executive power . . . , try to save the country. You raise as many troops as you possibly can . . . , and I will devote all my

[3] These quotations are from the N. Y. *Sun,* as above cited.

energies to assist and finish the war." "At least," said Lincoln, "I should have done my duty and have stood clear before my own conscience." [4]

Embarrassed by the peace plank, McClellan cut the knot by laying the strongest emphasis on the Union in his letter accepting the nomination. He thus went before the country as a war leader: indeed his war record was the reason for his candidacy. Nor did McClellan stand apart from other leading Democrats in his insistence on the preservation of the Union as the object of the war; the same emphasis was found in the general conduct of the Democratic campaign in the North. Democratic speakers generally, while avoiding mention of the "peace plank" of the platform, inveighed against Lincoln's policies, denounced his so-called acts of usurpation, and urged Republican unfitness for the task of restoring the Union.

Until the beginning of September the political horoscope seemed to presage Democratic victory. On September 2 three important editors— Greeley, Theodore Tilton, and Parke Godwin, representing the *Tribune, Independent,* and *Evening Post,* all of New York—joined in letters to Northern governors, seeking to promote the movement to discard Lincoln for some other candidate.[5] Suddenly, however, the horizon changed. The Democrats had stirred up resentment by their peace paragraph, which the Republicans used with telling effect, denouncing what they chose to call the "Copperhead platform." Then followed in quick succession the fall of Atlanta, giving Lincoln the military victory he needed, and Republican triumph in the elections held in Maine and Vermont. With remarkable rapidity the plans for the Cincinnati convention melted away. Frémont withdrew from the race (September 22). At the same time anti-Lincoln Radicals were appeased by the retirement of Montgomery Blair from the cabinet and the appointment of William Dennison, war governor of Ohio, in his place.[6] Even Wade and Davis, seeing the hopelessness of displacing Lincoln, decided that it was expedient to support him; Republican ranks were closed behind the President; and the "multitudes . . . rushing to McClellan" which had caused Henry Winter Davis so much concern [7] were halted.

[4] Nicolay and Hay, *Lincoln,* IX, 251 n.

[5] Pearson, *Andrew,* II, 162; Welles, *Diary,* II, 135.

[6] There is not room in these pages to enter upon the question whether the withdrawal of Frémont simultaneously with the retirement of Blair was the result of a "bargain" between Lincoln's managers and Frémont's friends. See W. E. Smith, *Blair Family,* II, 284; Rhodes, IV, 529; Nevins, *Frémont,* 578 ff. Nevins questions the "bargain" tradition. Charles R. Wilson ("New Light on the Lincoln-Blair-Frémont 'Bargain' of 1864," *Am. Hist. Rev.,* XLII, 71–78) further challenges the bargain theory and states that "Frémont came very close to withdrawing in favor of McClellan and the Democrats rather than in favor of the Republicans."

[7] N. Y. *Sun,* June 30, 1889, p. 3.

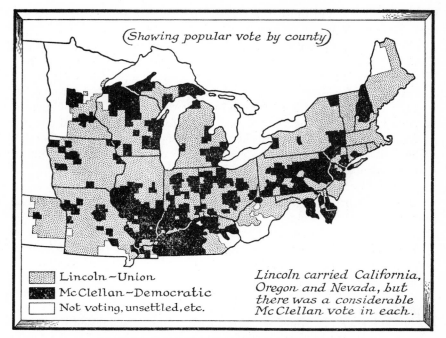

(Showing popular vote by county)

Lincoln – Union
McClellan – Democratic
Not voting, unsettled, etc.

Lincoln carried California, Oregon and Nevada, but there was a considerable McClellan vote in each.

PRESIDENTIAL ELECTION OF 1864

4

Only the Union states were counted, though elections were also held in Louisiana and Tennessee, which Lincoln carried. Just prior to the election Nevada was added to the Union. Earlier in the year, when radical Republican votes were needed in the Senate for reconstruction purposes, Congress had passed enabling acts for Colorado and Nevada (March 21, 1864). In Colorado the process was delayed, but in Nevada it worked according to design. The Nevada constitutional convention completed its work at so late a date that the constitution had to be telegraphed to Washington so that the state might be admitted prior to the election. It was on October 31, 1864, just eight days before the election, that Lincoln proclaimed the admission of the new commonwealth. Lincoln carried the state by a comfortable majority; and though much was made of its "argentiferous leads," there were those who suspected that its two Republican senators constituted its chief product.

Of these Union states, all except three (Kentucky, Delaware, and New Jersey) gave Lincoln their electoral vote, while in the popular ballots Lincoln had a majority of 400,000 over McClellan. In a careful analysis of the election returns, William Frank Zornow concludes: ". . . Lincoln won the election because of the support given him by the agricultural areas inhabited largely by native-born citizens, former Bell-Everett voters, and the skilled urban workers and professional classes. McClellan drew his best support from the immigrant proletariat and from rural areas in which the foreign element predominated. Those who supported Breckinridge in 1860 seem in a large measure to have voted for McClellan in 1864. Most Protestant denominations urged support of the administration, while the Irish element of the Catholic church supported McClellan." [1]

Though the election was hailed as a Lincoln "landslide," the large minorities for McClellan in New York, Pennsylvania, Ohio, Indiana, and Illinois gave point to those indications which seemed in August to foretell Democratic success. According to a contemporary observer (John D. Caton of Illinois), Democratic failure in 1864 was due to the ambiguous expressions in their platform and to the questionable principles of some who figured in the Chicago convention. The Democrats, supporting the war but condemning the "radicalism of Lincoln," won the election of 1862; then in 1864, thought Caton, they failed because they took up the cry of peace, denounced all others as abolitionists, organized secret societies, and wrote a platform to conciliate a minor group that had assumed leadership. [2]

It may be well to inquire into the validity of the familiar tradition regarding the election of 1864. The stereotyped picture is that Lincoln and McClellan were opposites, that McClellan personified a movement in opposition to Lincoln's main objectives, that Democratic victory would have brought defeat in the war and failure to the Union cause, and that only by the election of Lincoln were the purposes of the people in terms of "restoration" salvaged. The patent fact, however, is that all parties in the North in 1864 were Union parties. The Union (i.e., Republican) party under Lincoln, the Democratic party under McClellan, and the radical anti-Lincoln party under Frémont (whose ticket disappeared before election day), all favored the restoration of the Union as the chief point at issue. Writing from the contemporary Southern viewpoint E. A. Pollard commented as follows on the relation of war issues to the campaign:

> This struggle [of 1864] did not turn upon a sufficiently tangible issue to give it importance. As a Union party, the great body of the opposition [i.e., Democratic] party was committed to the war as the only practicable means of preserving and restoring the Union. . . . It would have been vain to expect success upon the principles of the very few Democrats . . . who believed . . . that the war had been unrighteous . . . in its leading object. . . . The great body of the opposition concurred with Gen. McClellan in the opinion that secession was unwarrantable . . . and that it ought to be resisted by all the power of the Union.

• • • • • •

Except in the important particular that the Government party proposed, in its amended platform, to abolish slavery by an extra-constitutional means,

---

[1] Zornow, *Lincoln & the Party Divided*, 214–215.

[2] John D. Caton to G. B. McClellan, Ottawa, Ill., Dec. 18, 1864, Caton MSS., quoted in H. E. Pratt, "Life of John Dean Caton" (MS.), chap. viii.

there was no great difference between the positions of these two parties in regard to slavery itself. . . . By the summer of 1864, however, the fate of slavery had . . . been sealed. It probably could not have existed if the Confederacy had been established.[3]

The false emphasis upon the "peace plank" adopted at Chicago comes largely from party propaganda directed against the Democrats.[4] It is to be noted in the first place that the peace declaration (in its reference to the war as a "failure") did not represent even a majority of the opposition party, and that if the Democrats had won the election, their victory would have been obtained under McClellan's leadership, not that of Vallandigham. Such a victory could have been fairly interpreted only as a mandate to do as McClellan said, i.e., to prosecute the war as a conflict whose object was restoration of the Union. Had McClellan been chosen, it is more reasonable to suppose that he would have held true to his own war record and his declarations in the campaign and would consequently have refused peace on terms of Union surrender, than to suppose that he and his advisers would have consented to such surrender. Not even the peace Democrats—the Vallandigham element—favored a peace of this nature.[5] Even the "Copperhead plank," so roundly denounced, declared for peace on the basis of reunion. The main difference between Vallandigham and McClellan was as to the efficacy of an armistice in promoting suitable peace terms.

On the main issues of the day Lincoln and McClellan were not opposites. They agreed in considering secession iniquitous and the war righteous; they agreed essentially as to reconstruction. The differences between them were more a matter of shading than of glaring contrast. Perhaps these can best be defined in terms of the support which each candidate drew. Though the great body of the Democrats in 1864 was formed of unquestionably loyal citizens who favored the vigorous prosecution of the war, the McClellan ticket also received the backing of the small but noisy anti-war faction; and so powerful was this group that, as we have seen, Lincoln

[3] Pollard, *Lost Cause*, 571–572.

[4] This emphasis is false in two respects: (1) it incorrectly imputes treasonable motives to those who actively labored for the adoption of the plank, forgetting that Vallandigham favored not treason but a regular armistice with ultimate restoration of the Union; (2) it misrepresents the main body of Democrats who stood with McClellan for a vigorous prosecution of the war.

[5] The "bloody shirt" tradition, which in postwar elections represented all Democrats as "Copperheads" and traitors, requires further research. One of the difficulties is the lack of data connecting individual party affiliation with army service. For Illinois the subject has been elaborately studied by two students, A. R. Hoeflin and Myron G. Armstrong. Comparing county voting records with county army statistics, they have concluded that Union army service was given no less freely in Democratic areas than in Republican areas. Military service was measured by the number of volunteers in proportion to the number properly subject to military duty.

thought it would control McClellan should he be elected. On the other hand, most Republicans in 1864 were undoubtedly moderates who desired nothing more than the restoration of peace and the Union; but the vigorous Radical minority, which wanted a social revolution in the South, was also a part of Lincoln's following, and, as the previous years had demonstrated, the President could be pushed into a gradual acceptance of their Radical views.

CHAPTER 28

The North in Wartime

I

THE NORTHERN people, having a more diverse civilization and being farther removed from the scene of battle, felt the conflict less directly than did the people of the South. Yet their suffering should not be minimized. Illinois with a population of 1,711,000 furnished 259,000 enlistments; Massachusetts with 1,231,000 furnished 146,000; Connecticut with 460,000 furnished 55,000; Michigan with 749,000 furnished 87,000; and other states in like proportion.[1] As the weary weeks dragged on the struggle was dramatized as a contest between Richmond and Washington, and the main interest was steadily on the Virginia front. With interest thus centered, the course of the war proved discouraging in the extreme. First came the humiliation of Bull Run, then long months of inaction. This was early in the struggle; yet people were already asking whether McClellan would ever fight and whether the war would ever end. At last McClellan moved; he came to the very outskirts of Richmond and was held back. Then a maddening series of defeats: the second Bull Run, Fredericksburg, Chancellorsville. Even the brighter news of Antietam and Gettysburg was considerably offset by the extent of Northern loss, the failure to pursue, and the fact that the North had been invaded and had suffered narrow escapes in a contest where, if ultimate victory was to come, the armies of the Union must be kept on the offensive. To understand what the Northern people felt as they lived through all this, one must supply the sense of duration, of time suspense, of hope endlessly deferred while increasing sacrifices were demanded; this indeed is one of the major psychological aspects of the war.

Economically the early months of the conflict were months of business depression and dislocation. The crisis of 1860–1861 was a period of industrial and financial recession; and this general condition continued until the year 1862. Business failures in the Northern states in 1861 were

---

[1] The figures are for enlistments, not for men furnished; many reenlistments are included. For numbers and losses in general, see below, pp. 529–531.

numbered at 5935 with liabilities up to $178,000,000. This depression was, however, brief. In what might be considered a classic demonstration of Keynesian economic theory, the activities of the Federal government in cutting off imports, through high tariff walls, and in pouring money into war contracts produced a speedy recovery. By 1862 business failures involved only $23,000,000.[2] Then came, in almost indecent proportions, the phenomenon of war prosperity. While profits mounted and while much of the profit was crooked, the conduct of the nation's war business was planless, chaotic, and ruinously individualistic. The editor of the New York *Times* declared in 1863 that "the greatest disadvantage of the war" was "the prosperity of the country."[3] It was literally true that thousands were fattening on the war and selfishly desired it to continue. The New York *Herald,* recalling that yearly or semi-yearly dividends had been the custom, called attention in 1864 to the monthly dividends being paid by a Colorado gold mine and playfully predicted that the country might yet hear of weekly or daily dividends. Railroad earnings were enormously increased. The earnings of the Erie Railroad, for example, leaped from $5,000,000 in 1860 to $10,000,000 in 1863, while its stock rose in three years from 17 to 126½. Money changers and war profiteers were growing rich; Old Hartford was waxing fat, as Mrs. Stowe observed; and people of the money-getting type were interested in army operations not from the patriotic motive but for their effect upon the stock market.

Despite the hundreds of thousands of men in the armies, crop production was well sustained. Areas open to grain production were increased in the western states; and where men were lacking, women and children did the heavy field work. Labor-saving machinery also helped replace the absent soldiers, a process which incidentally brought enormous profits to the manufacturers of reapers, threshers, and similar devices. In May, 1864, Cyrus H. McCormick, the reaper magnate, encouraged one of his Illinois salesmen: "Don't be so blue over the prospects. Remember 20,000 militia have to leave this state . . . and these men will have to come, many or a large share of them, from the farms."

Unusual war conditions promoted agricultural experimentation as in the efforts to produce cotton in Kentucky, Missouri, and the southern portions of Illinois and Indiana, in the beginnings of beet-sugar experiments, in increased sorghum production, and in the importation of sugar from Cuba. The shortage of raw materials obtainable from the South was not without its compensating features, as in the stimulation of wool production as well as that of flax and hemp as substitutes for cotton. Crop deficiency

[2] The figures of R. G. Dun and Company. They do not include the border states. *Ann. Cyc.,* 1861, p. 312; N. Y. *Herald,* Jan. 1, 1863, p. 3, cs. 1–2 and p. 4, c. 4. See also E. D. Fite, *Soc. and Indus. Conditions . . . during the Civil War,* 105–106.

[3] Editorial, July 2, 1863.

in Europe increased the foreign demand for American grain; and condi- tions in general gave satisfaction to Isaac Newton, first commissioner of the newly created bureau of agriculture, who, in summarizing the produc- tion of the basic crops, was able to report an increase in their total value from 955 million dollars in 1863 to 1440 million in 1864.[4] Between January and December of 1862 wheat rose from $1.52 a bushel (maxi- mum) to $1.75; corn from 68 cents to 95 cents; barley from 80 cents to $1.55.[5]

This inflation of agricultural prices was part of the general wartime trend. As the following table shows, all prices were rising:

PRICE INDEXES FOR THE CIVIL WAR YEARS

	General Price Index	Wholesale Farm Price Index
1860	100	100
1861	99	97
1862	111	112
1863	135	147
1864	182	210
1865	179	192

Source: Recalculated from Historical Statistics of the United States, 1789–1945, Table L 1–14.

2

It was customary to find newspapers bursting into superlatives in their comments upon material progress in the North. It was remarked by the New York Times in 1864 that in "the midst of the most gigantic civil war the world [had] yet seen" the people of the North were never better fed, sheltered, or clothed. The Illinois Central Railroad, built across a prairie ten years before, now traversed a "boundless cultivated field." Farm land valueless a decade ago was now worth from $10 to $100 an acre. Sales of the road's domain bade fair to cover the whole cost of its construction. Re- ceipts from this source were reported at $150,000 net per month.[1]

In such inflationary times businessmen were actually averse to demand- ing payment of debts due to them. As an agent wrote to the McCormick brothers, manufacturers of the reaper: ". . . I have not dared collect any- thing as the currency is in such bad shape, it is not safe to take it, and a large share is today worth only 50 or 60 cents on the dollar." When money did come in, capitalists attempted speedily to reinvest it in nonperishable goods. "I have felt that paper money kept on deposit was unwise and have bought nearly 3000 tons of pig iron," William McCormick reported to his

[4] Report of the Commissioner of Agriculture for the Year 1865, 10.
[5] Ann. Cyc., 1862, 5.
[1] New York Times, Mar. 1, 1864.

brother Cyrus in November, 1862. "Our pig iron is piled up high. . . . Now we are asked in St. Louis $40! for pig iron that we bought at $23 and so it is in other things and so you can see I have actually saved tens of thousands by having gone ahead early and bought these things. . . ." The McCormick brothers also invested their profits in farm lands and in Chicago lots, in the hope of hedging against inflation.[2]

Rising prices, mounting dividends in industrial production, and gold fluctuations combined with the artificial flush of war psychology to produce sensational scenes on the stock market and the gold exchange. One of the vicious aspects of the gold speculation was that bad news increased the price of gold, whereas good news diminished it; hence the bull speculator in gold would profit by disaster or threatened disaster to the country, as in the summer of 1864 when Washington seemed on the point of capture. As for the bear speculator his operations would tend to cause national military success to be associated with deflation, in both the monetary and the investment sense. While people realized that the speculative wave was probably temporary, that fact tended rather to increase their gambling operations. Warnings were issued; a revulsion was forecast; it was predicted that the war might end with startling suddenness; and people were told to beware of the coming crash. They were, however, also advised to "buy now"; and easy fortunes made before their eyes had more influence on speculative investors than sober admonitions. Women as well as men caught the mania; and in commenting on "Crinoline in Wall Street" the *Herald* noted that ladies were fully alive to per cent, and were talking stocks with an animation the reverse of agreeable to those who took an old-fashioned view of woman's sphere.[3] The new-made rich were conspicuous in purple and fine linen; and expenditures for luxuries were described as "unexampled, even in the history of our wasteful people." [4] New York City, it was said, had never been "so gay, . . . so crowded, so prosperous." [5]

The stimulation of business and the military drain upon man power naturally produced a condition of labor shortage, from which, however, only moderate results in the betterment of labor were obtained. The most obvious source of new labor supply was by the encouragement of immigration, which in the early part of the war showed a marked decline as compared with the fifties. Immigrants entering the country amounted to only 142,000 in 1861, 72,000 in 1862, and 132,000 in 1863, as compared to 427,000 in 1854.[6] Capitalists and industrialists became alarmed at the falling off; and in his annual message of December 8, 1863, Lincoln

[2] Eugene M. Lerner, "Investment Uncertainty during the Civil War—A Note on the McCormick Brothers," *Jour. of Ec. Hist.*, XVI, 35, 38 (Mar., 1956).

[3] N. Y. *Herald*, Mar. 24, 1864.

[4] N. Y. *Times*, Mar. 19, 1864.

[5] N. Y. *Herald*, Mar. 1, 1864.

[6] *New International Encyclopedia*, XII, 9. (For the sixties the figures are for fiscal years.)

reported that "there is still a great deficiency of laborers in every field of industry," and asked for governmental encouragement of immigration; whereupon Congress responded with a law (July 4, 1864) by which contract labor could be imported in conformity to regulations fixed by a commissioner of immigration, future wages and homesteads being mortgaged to repay the cost of emigration to America. The immigration figures for 1864 and 1865 (191,000 and 180,000 respectively) registered in part the effect of this law and in part the natural response to economic opportunity; but they fell considerably short of the postwar figure (332,000 for the fiscal year 1866). While many aliens were promptly advanced on the road to citizenship or entered the army as aliens, it should be remembered that those foreigners who had not voted nor declared an intention of becoming citizens were exempt from military duty.[7]

Labor suffered heavily from the paralysis of business which followed the outbreak of the war, and unemployment was heavy during 1861. But as wartime prosperity spread and as more and more workingmen enlisted in the armies, there soon came to be jobs for all. Wages gradually increased: carpenters' wages rose from an old daily minimum of $1.75 to $2.25; blacksmiths' from $1.50 to $2.25; harness makers' from $1.40 to $2.00; machinists' from $2.00 to $2.50; drug clerks' from $30 to $50 (a month).[8] This apparent increase in labor income was, however, largely deceptive, for the cost of living mounted even more rapidly; real wages (i.e., wages defined in terms of purchasing power) consequently declined. As a result there was much exploitation of labor, with sweatshop conditions and starvation wages especially manifest in the factories that employed large numbers of women.

At the beginning of the war labor was almost wholly unorganized, for the few small national unions were in a sad way and many of the local unions had never recovered from the depression of 1857. As prosperity increased, the movement for organizing labor was renewed. One of the earliest signs of a revival was the formation of a city trades' assembly in Rochester, New York, on March 13, 1863.[9] By December, 1863, some twenty

[7] It is often asserted that this contract-labor law "compensated the industrial capitalists for their contributions in taxes to the government and for the favors given to the farmers in the Homestead Act of 1862," e.g., Ratner, *American Taxation*, 91. A recent study, however, concludes that the act "did not result from a general pressure from industrialists" and that the promoters of contract labor "did not succeed in obtaining the whole-hearted support of American industrial capitalists." The American employer on the whole disliked contract-labor because of "the scarcity of skilled labor [among the immigrants], his unwillingness to train it, the difficulties of recruiting it abroad, and the unsatisfactory results in trade-unions when he did." Charlotte Erickson, *American Industry and the European Immigrant 1860–1885*, vii, 7, 63.

[8] *Ann. Cyc.*, 1863, 413.

[9] Norman J. Ware, *The Labor Movement in the United States, 1860–1895*, 1–2.

trades had been organized; by December, 1864, 53 trades were organized, with 203 locals; and by November, 1865, 69 trades, with 300 locals. National unions also sprang up, among them "the sons of Vulcan (iron puddlers), locomotive engineers, plasterers, cigarmakers, ship carpenters, coachmakers, house carpenters, bricklayers and masons, tailors, painters, and heaters." By 1864–1865 total union membership was estimated at 200,000. In September, 1864, twelve delegates representing eight city trades' assemblies met in Louisville and formed an abortive national labor organization which called itself the International Industrial Assembly of North America.[10]

NORTHERN WAGES DURING THE CIVIL WAR

	Wage Indexes for Non-agricultural Employments	Real Wage Indexes
1860	100.0	100 (January)
		100 (July)
1861	100.8	102 (January)
		104 (July)
1862	102.9	102 (January)
		101 (July)
1863	110.5	89 (January)
		86 (July)
1864	125.6	81 (January)
		71 (July)
1865	143.1	67 (January)
		97 (July)

Sources: The first column is from *Historical Statistics of the United States, 1789–1945*, Table D–108; the second is from Wesley Clair Mitchell, *A History of the Greenbacks*, 342.

None of these labor gains were made without bitter opposition from employers. Capital "called to its aid every possible form of cheap labor." The use of Negroes as strikebreakers was an element in the ugly race riots which occurred in New York, Brooklyn, and Cincinnati. In Illinois, under pressure from organized businessmen, the legislature enacted the "La Salle Black Laws," which "declared any person who by threat, intimidation, or otherwise sought to prevent another person from working, guilty of crime"; they were a potent weapon against strikes. Similar legislation in New York and Massachusetts was defeated only through labor pressure. Throughout the war federal troops were frequently called in to break strikes, such as those of the gun workers in Cold Springs, New York, the engineers on the Reading Railroad, and the miners in Tioga County, Pennsylvania. General

[10] Joseph G. Rayback, *A History of American Labor*, 111–112; John R. Commons et al., *History of Labor in the United States*, II, 33–37.

Rosecrans, who commanded the Union forces in Missouri in 1864, positively forbade the unionization of men engaged in war production, and his orders were used against "striking coal miners, machinists, printers, and tailors." On the whole it is safe to conclude that labor had a meager share of the wartime prosperity and that at the end of the conflict the workingman's condition was "undoubtedly worse than in 1860." [11]

3

Enhanced prosperity was reflected in the festivities and amusements of the time. Immense crowds nightly filled the theaters. Barnum's "colossal museum and menagerie" was thriving; Washington was gay with dinners, receptions, and elegant parties; organized baseball was on the increase; band music was given the public in Central Park. According to a contemporary account the quality of entertainment in New York playhouses did not deserve the crowds that blocked the aisles to the point where the theaters became fire traps.[1] Comedy was the vogue, though the New York Academy of Music in its offering of German grand opera was making a brave effort to compete with animal curiosities and Negro minstrels. One of the events of the time was the wedding of "General" Tom Thumb and his midget bride, a social affair at a Broadway church attended by General Burnside and followed by a reception at the Metropolitan Hotel at which the happy couple, perched on a piano, received their guests. In saloons, winter gardens, skating carnivals, billiard tournaments, burlesque shows and cock fights, and in Bowery theaters where the unwashed gathered to eat peanuts, whistle, and yell, the populace was either seeking to forget the war or showing indifference to it.

Even worse than indifference was the shocking story of corruption. Unbelievable profits were possible in cotton, which in 1864 could be had in the South at 20 cents or less and would bring $1.90 at Boston, and much of the trading in this commodity was illicit. Such was the situation under General Butler at New Orleans that soldiers wanted to go home, "not wishing to risk their lives to make fortunes for others." It was stated by a treasury official in 1862 that Col. Andrew J. Butler, brother of the Union general, was in Louisiana "for the sole purpose of making money." The general asserted that he had no interest in the transactions of his brother, whose profits, he said, amounted to "less than two hundred thousand dollars." [2] It was generally believed, however, that they were several times that figure.

That the government was swindled in its army contracts has already been shown. The enormous commissions paid to men who merely obtained

---

[11] Fite, 184–187; Rayback, 110, 113.

[1] A *Herald* writer stated: ". . . We have pushed our way down town, dropping in at all the places of amusement, and seeing them all jammed." N. Y. *Herald*, Jan. 25, 1864.

[2] Rhodes, V, 290, 304–306.

contracts for producing firms constituted a national scandal. After persistent exposures the New York *Herald* in June, 1864, was emphatic in condemning the "gross corruption prevailing in nearly every department of the government." [3] Much of the profiteering was in whiskey, which sold in New York in 1865 for $2.24 a gallon as compared with 39 cents in 1863.[4] By levying a tax of $1.50 a gallon in June, 1864, with notice in advance that the tax would be raised to $2.00 in February, 1865, without being retroactive as to existing stocks, the government stimulated an accumulation of liquor stocks "without precedent," with profits that had "probably no parallel . . . in this country" and could not be estimated at less than $50,000,000.[5] Trade with the enemy offered many scandals. The prohibition of such trade in accordance with the usual laws of war was qualified by regulations which permitted it for certain objects under presidential license. Even the "legitimate" trade was often questionable, while much of the traffic amounted to smuggling and giving aid to the enemy, evoking indignant comment by Union generals. General S. A. Hurlbut wrote that the practice was "perfectly demoralizing" and added that "bribery and corruption seem to go into every branch of service." [6] Grant thought that any trade at all with the enemy was a serious weakness. Both he and Sherman sought to have it suppressed. Restrictions to regulate the traffic, by making it unprofitable, served as Grant said to cause only dishonest men to go into it. He ventured to state that "no honest man has made money in West Tennessee in the last year [1862–1863], while many fortunes have been made there during the time." [7]

Yet in contrast to the many instances of profiteering and dishonesty, other instances could be presented of men in high place such as General Montgomery C. Meigs, quartermaster general of the United States, who made a fine record of supplying the army with the strictest honesty so far as the activities of his office were concerned. Secretary Chase of the treasury department is another example of an official who refused to use the war for personal gain; and, to take the case of one of the leading businessmen, mention may be made of W. H. Aspinwall of New York City, who sent to the government a check for over $25,000 as his portion of the profit obtained on arms purchased by Howland and Aspinwall for the war department.[8] The question of private profits during the war involves so many thousands of instances that generalization is difficult. The facts that seem to stand out are that the system in vogue as to governmental transactions with private firms permitted "legitimate" profits out of all proportion to

[3] June 21, 1864.
[4] *Ann. Cyc.,* 1865, 349.
[5] Statement of David A. Wells in 1866, quoted in Rhodes, V, 273 n.
[6] *Offic. Rec.,* 1 ser., XXII, pt. 1, 230.
[7] *Ann. Cyc.,* 1863, 199.
[8] Moore, *Rebell. Rec.* (Diary), V, 41. (But see N. Y. *Herald,* July 20, 1862.)

service rendered; that lobbying for government business was very active in Washington, being indulged in by public men of high respectability; and that downright swindling was a serious evil which took many diabolical forms. All this, of course, is consistent with the further generalization that the nation's business in the mass, public and private, was performed with honesty. As to the record of the Lincoln administration J. F. Rhodes has pointed out that the country had "an honest man for President and honest men at the heads of the departments"; that the extent of corruption, bad as it was, has been "much exaggerated"; and that "Of men high in administrative office after the resignation of Cameron, [he had] discovered only one implicated in dishonest transactions—one of the Assistant Secretaries of War." [9]

4

It does not appear from general statistics that crime was on the increase the country over during the war; [1] but if one turns from statistics to contemporary comment in metropolitan centers he finds many statements comparable to that of a New York newspaper in 1864 in which it was asserted that crimes recently committed in that city "would shock a congregation in Pandemonium." The writer went on to specify cold-blooded murders, revolting atrocities, burglaries, and attempted assassinations, and concluded that a few good city missionaries were needed, "even if we have to import or raffle for them." [2] Crooked politicians protected vice; [3] drunken brawls were common; concert saloons were scenes of debauchery; and prostitution was flagrant both in the cities and in the vicinity of army camps.

While the ugly face of war was disgustingly visible, and while, as Lincoln said, "Every foul bird [came] abroad, and every dirty reptile [rose] up," [4] another side of the picture was manifest in the humanitarian enterprise and welfare activity of the time. The Union government itself devoted far greater attention to the hospitalization and general care of the troops than in former wars; but the burden was too great for the government, and private initiative made a memorable contribution in the work of the United States Sanitary Commission. [5] Under its public-spirited president and secretary (H. W. Bellows and Frederick Law Olmsted) the commission served as a valuable civilian auxiliary to the medical bureau of the war department in tending the wounded and ministering to the morale and comfort of the soldiers. It may be regarded as the forerunner of the

[9] Rhodes, V, 219–221.
[1] Fite, *Social and Industrial Conditions . . . during the Civil War*, 305.
[2] N. Y. *Herald*, Feb. 27, 1864.
[3] *Ibid.*, Jan. 5, 1864.
[4] Lincoln, *Collected Works*, VI, 500.
[5] Among the women who did distinguished work in caring for wounded soldiers during the Civil War were Clara Barton and Dorothea L. Dix.

Red Cross; and like the later and more famous organization its ministrations were not confined to one flag. Many a Southern soldier left on the battlefield without surgeon, medicine, food, or nurse was supplied and cared for by Northern mercy through the work of the commission. Contributions to the commission were voluntary, systematic drives being conducted to obtain funds, chiefly by "sanitary fairs" in the cities. At the fair in Chicago in September, 1863, the sum of $78,000 was raised; at Brooklyn in October, 1864, the sum of $400,000; at New York in December, 1863, $1,000,000. Private funds for soldier relief were also raised by relief associations formed by workers who agreed to set aside regular portions of their wages, and by clubs, ballrooms, and theaters which gave benefit performances. Many private hospitals were opened for the admission of sick and wounded soldiers; and with their volunteer nurses they greatly supplemented the work of government hospitals. Not only did the commission tend those who suffered casualties; its work extended to soldiers generally and served to supply comforts which army regulations did not offer. Supplementing the welfare work of the Sanitary Commission was the Christian Commission, a project of the Young Men's Christian Associations, which provided religious ministration (though this function was more regularly performed by army chaplains), distributed Bibles, offered various forms of diversion to relieve the ennui of camp life, supplied magazines, and sent soldiers' money home to families.

5

The shaping and distorting of opinion during the war was partly the work of voluntary propagandist groups and partly the inevitable product of war psychology. As to official propaganda, i.e., governmental utilization of the press, platform, theater, and the like for the dissemination of stereotyped ideas and interpretations, it was not steadily and regularly practiced by the authorities either of Richmond or of Washington, except in the attack upon opinion abroad. Both the United States and the Confederate States did have their regular propaganda service for the influencing of foreign sentiment. The work of Hotze and of the *Index* for the Southern cause will be noted in the next chapter. As for the United States, the Lincoln government sent in the fall of 1861 a propaganda commission to Europe for the purpose, as Frederic Bancroft has stated, of "trying to influence the two great governments [England and France] by bringing the press and the clergy, and then the people, to a correct understanding of the causes and purposes of the Civil War." [1] For this commission it was desired to have men of high distinction and character. It was at first intended to send Edward Everett, J. P. Kennedy, Archbishop Hughes of the Roman Catholic Church, Bishop McIlvaine of the Protestant Episcopal Church, and Robert C. Winthrop. Not all these men accepted service, however;

[1] Bancroft, *Seward*, II, 220.

and the mission actually sent consisted of Archbishop Hughes, Bishop McIlvaine, and Thurlow Weed. McIlvaine was to make his appeal to the English clergy; the Archbishop was to win the support of the Papacy, of Napoleon, and of other Catholic rulers; Weed was to labor with journalists and public leaders in order to counteract Confederate journalistic enterprise abroad. The arrival of the mission coincided with the *Trent* affair; and when Weed published in *The Times* of London a long conciliatory comment on the affair, he managed to put in a suggestion as to a protracted paper negotiation which did not suit English taste. Nevertheless Charles Francis Adams the younger, in commenting on Weed, speaks of his "rare tact, shrewd judgment, and quick insight into men," and declares that he was useful both in Great Britain and on the Continent. As to other emissaries he was less enthusiastic. "These emissaries [writes Adams] were of four . . . types: (1) the roving diplomat, irregularly accredited by the State Department; (2) the poaching diplomat, accredited to one government, but seeking a wider field of activity . . . ; (3) the volunteer diplomat, not accredited at all . . . ; and (4) the special agent, sent out by some department . . . [for] a particular object." As examples of the last-named group, the navy department had sent J. M. Forbes and W. H. Aspinwall to buy the rams in England in 1863; and for other specific objects W. M. Evarts and Robert J. Walker were sent to England. Such emissaries, who were "addicted to the columns of the 'Times,' in which their effusions appeared periodically," [2] caused the American minister considerable annoyance.

At home, instead of governmentally directed propaganda, the beating of the tom-tom for the Union cause took many volunteer forms. Union mass meetings were common and some of them were enormous affairs. The speeches at such meetings ranged from the polished and cultured orations of Edward Everett to the ravings of Parson Brownlow of Tennessee, who lashed the Southerners with bitter invective and who roared on one occasion that after the rebels had been driven like the scriptural hogs into the sea, "England and France might come on, and we would lick them both." [3] Among other speakers of whom much was heard were Wendell Phillips, H. W. Beecher, W. M. Evarts, and Andrew Johnson. With the American propensity for organization it was inevitable that propaganda clubs should spring into existence; and of these the best known was the Union League. Beginning in Philadelphia in November, 1862, the League movement spread to New York and Boston. Soon it appeared in Baltimore, Washington, and San Francisco. Within a year it had not only spread over eighteen Northern states but had made its appearance among the Unionists of the South. Primarily the League was a rallying point for citizen-support

---

[2] C. F. Adams, *Charles Francis Adams*, 353–354.
[3] This coarse speech was made under the auspices of the Young Men's Republican Union. N. Y. *Times*, May 16, 1862.

of the Union cause. Masses of war literature were distributed; money was raised for soldier relief; recruiting of both white and Negro troops was promoted; and leadership of voluntary effort in an emergency was assumed, as in Pennsylvania at the time of the Gettysburg campaign. At the very beginning, however, and increasingly as time passed, the efforts of the League were chiefly "political," the very word "Union," denoting the cause of the Northern people, having been appropriated by a party. It was active in support of Governor Curtin as against Judge Woodward in Pennsylvania in 1863, and of Lincoln against McClellan in 1864. After the war its main motive was to combat the policies of President Johnson, whom it had helped to elect, and to function as an adjunct of the Radical wing of the Republican party.

Propaganda activity in the North appeared also in the work of the Loyal Publication Society of New York and of a similar society in New England. The New York society, under the leadership of Charles King and Francis Lieber, raised $30,000 during the three years of its existence, published ninety pamphlets "noteworthy on the whole for their logical approach and careful moderation," and distributed 900,000 documents. Frank Freidel has showed how its efforts were directed toward key groups in the North. "Especial appeals were made to Midwesterners, New Englanders, and New Yorkers; farmers, merchants, and bankers; Catholics and Protestants; people proud of their American ancestry, and recent German, Irish, and French immigrants. Even women were the subject of an especial appeal." [4] Such organizations, by their distribution of printed matter, "determined the content of [newspaper] editorials" and "rendered an important service to the maintenance of Northern morale." [5] It may also be said that the sanitary fairs, bond-selling campaigns, and recruiting drives served as mediums for war propaganda.

In the poetry of the war the motifs of intolerance, vengeance, and self-righteous hate of the *Gott strafe* variety, were played up in repetitious and undistinguished scribblings. To spare the reader, only a very few samples will be given to illustrate the type:

> Avenge thou Massachusetts' gore,
> That stains the name of Baltimore,
>
> . . . . .
>
> I herewith petition the "powers that be,"
> To give Davis and his followers, all,
> A *deep grave* reception—a home quite as free
> As Satan had after his fall.
>
> . . . . .
>
> Chieftains! our hearts beat high, in haste
> To plunge the rebel heart!

[4] Freidel, "The Loyal Publication Society: A Pro-Union Propaganda Agency," *M.V.H.R.*, XXVI, 364 (Dec., 1939).
[5] Cole, *Irrepressible Conflict*, 334.

Who could not glory in the deed
To drive them to death's mart?

. . . . .

We have Butterfield the daring, and we've Martindale the cool:
Where could we learn the art of war within a better school?
Add Morell to the list of names, and we must all agree,
We have the finest general in the army of the free.[6]

In the public drives for recruits the call of country was mingled with appeals to divers other motives. Pride of race was invoked as in a New York advertisement in which Irishmen, whose enlistment in the Phoenix regiment, Corcoran Zouaves, was sought, were urged to give their "patronage" to such good and true officers as Murphy, O'Reilly, Sullivan, and O'Rourke.[7] Throughout the recruiting campaigns there was constant emphasis on the bounty element. It is significant that in 1862, before the national draft was started, the city council of Buffalo appropriated $80,000 in order to give a bounty of $75 to each recruit;[8] Boston appropriated $300,000 ($100 to each volunteer);[9] Hartford in town meeting appropriated $100,000 for aiding soldier families and for promoting enlistments;[10] and the board of supervisors of Rensselaer County, New York, voted $75,000 as bounty money to be paid to enlisted men with the object of avoiding a draft in the county.[11] In Orleans County in the same state a cow was given to the wife of every married man who enlisted.[12] Meanwhile Northern newspapers reported Southern opinion of Northern recruits and of the reluctance of Northern men "to go on an aggressive war against a people who only ask to be let alone. . . ."[13] Newspapers also carried such notices as the following: "Those wishing to avoid being drafted can be informed the way to do so by addressing, enclosing $5, Counseller, box 149 Herald office."[14] Or the following: "I have engaged for myself and friends more substitutes than we shall require, and will assign, to a reliable . . . party, who is willing to pay $100 in advance and $150 more if he is drafted, a first rate substitute . . . who will doubtless be accepted when offered."[15]

[6] These random samples are from Moore, *Rebellion Record* (Poetry and Incidents), V, 20; VI, 12, 13, 14. The one which blazons the glories of Butterfield, Martindale, and Morell is the division song of Porter's division, Army of the Potomac. The songs that have a rollicking, semi-humorous camp flavor are the most pardonable of the wartime output. The great mass of it is intolerable drivel. See Moore, *passim*, for hundreds of examples.
[7] N. Y. *Herald*, July 2, 1862.
[8] *Ibid.*, July 9, 1862.
[9] *Ibid.*, July 15, 1862.
[10] *Ibid.*, July 20, 1862.
[11] *Ibid.*, Aug. 20, 1862.
[12] *Ibid.*, Aug. 1, 1862.
[13] *Ibid.*, July 30, 1862 (reprinted from Richmond *Enquirer*, July 25).
[14] *Ibid.*, Aug. 22, 1862.
[15] *Ibid.*, Aug. 23, 1862.

ENLISTMENTS IN THE UNION ARMY AND NAVY

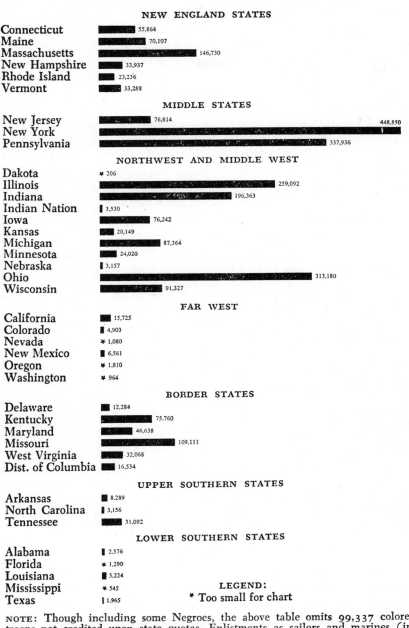

NEW ENGLAND STATES

Connecticut	55,864
Maine	70,107
Massachusetts	146,730
New Hampshire	33,937
Rhode Island	23,236
Vermont	33,288

MIDDLE STATES

New Jersey	76,814
New York	448,850
Pennsylvania	337,936

NORTHWEST AND MIDDLE WEST

Dakota	* 206
Illinois	259,092
Indiana	196,363
Indian Nation	3,530
Iowa	76,242
Kansas	20,149
Michigan	87,364
Minnesota	24,020
Nebraska	3,157
Ohio	313,180
Wisconsin	91,327

FAR WEST

California	15,725
Colorado	4,903
Nevada	* 1,080
New Mexico	6,561
Oregon	* 1,810
Washington	* 964

BORDER STATES

Delaware	12,284
Kentucky	75,760
Maryland	46,638
Missouri	109,111
West Virginia	32,068
Dist. of Columbia	16,534

UPPER SOUTHERN STATES

Arkansas	8,289
North Carolina	3,156
Tennessee	31,092

LOWER SOUTHERN STATES

Alabama	2,576
Florida	* 1,290
Louisiana	5,224
Mississippi	* 545
Texas	1,965

LEGEND:
* Too small for chart

NOTE: Though including some Negroes, the above table omits 99,337 colored troops not credited upon state quotas. Enlistments as sailors and marines (included in the state figures given above) aggregated 105,963. Of this total, Massachusetts supplied 19,983, New York 39,920, and Pennsylvania 14,307.

Total enlistments: 2,778,304. There were many more "enlistments" than individual soldiers.

Source: War of the Rebellion . . . Official Records, 3 ser., IV, 1269–1270.

President Lincoln's activity in promoting morale and winning support for his administration did not take the form of deliberate propaganda efforts; nor was there any organized "White House publicity." His typical manner of speaking to his public was by a well-timed letter to an individual, delegation, or group, which was in reality intended for the nation's ear. His August, 1863, letter to the unconditional Union men at Springfield, Illinois, his reply to Governor Seymour declining to suspend the draft, and his correspondence with Greeley concerning emancipation reveal Lincoln's pithy, epigrammatic style and common-sense reasoning at their best. On the rare occasions during the war when Lincoln made public addresses, he sought to unite the Northern people upon the fundamental principles for which the conflict was being fought. His brief address on November 19, 1863, at the dedication of the national cemetery at Gettysburg is a model of clear, subtle Lincolnian prose which gave meaning to the seemingly senseless carnage of war:

Four score and seven years ago our fathers brought forth on this continent, a new nation, conceived in Liberty, and dedicated to the proposition that all men are created equal.

Now we are engaged in a great civil war, testing whether that nation, or any nation so conceived and so dedicated, can long endure. We are met on a great battle-field of that war. We have come to dedicate a portion of that field, as a final resting place for those who here gave their lives that that nation might live. It is altogether fitting and proper that we should do this.

But, in a larger sense, we can not dedicate—we can not consecrate—we can not hallow—this ground. The brave men, living and dead, who struggled here, have consecrated it, far above our poor power to add or detract. The world will little note, nor long remember what we say here, but it can never forget what they did here. It is for us the living, rather, to be dedicated here to the unfinished work which they who fought here have thus far so nobly advanced. It is rather for us to be here dedicated to the great task remaining before us—that from these honored dead we take increased devotion to that cause for which they gave the last full measure of devotion—that we here highly resolve that these dead shall not have died in vain—that this nation, under God, shall have a new birth of freedom—and that government of the people, by the people, for the people, shall not perish from the earth.[16]

6

Newspapers in the North in wartime were as a rule free agents, conducted according to the purposes and predilections of their editor-proprietors; and the extent of their activity was enormous. The war for the

[16] Lincoln, *Collected Works*, VII, 23. For other drafts of the Gettysburg address, see *ibid.*, VII, 17–22. On the actual delivery of this address and contemporary reactions to it, see William E. Barton, *Lincoln at Gettysburg . . .* and J. G. Randall, *Lincoln the President*, II, Chap. 28. It should be noted that there is no foundation for the myth, so often repeated, that the speech was unappreciated by contemporaries. See Randall, *op. cit.*, II, 311–312.

Union was the heyday of the special reporter. Only occasionally, as under Sherman's orders, were journalists excluded from military areas; ordinarily they were made welcome and given special privileges. Government passes were extended to them. They had the use of government horses and wagons; they were given transportation with baggage on government steamers and military trains. Enjoying the confidence of admirals and army commanders, they were seldom at a loss to obtain the information they desired. They heard an immense deal of officers' talk and could pick up, along with casual chatter, snatches of military intelligence. One of the *Herald* correspondents had a pass which entitled him "to accompany naval expeditions in any staff capacity to which the commanders might appoint him provided they did not interfere with the regulations of the Navy." At Antietam a special *Tribune* writer carried several of Hooker's messages and orders. We read of correspondents writing from the battlefield, entering the service as nurses or signal officers, adopting clever ruses to evade guards or outwit rivals, or eavesdropping on secret conversations.

Despite the increased cost of newspaper reporting and publishing, the leading papers kept their staffs regularly with the armies and were lavish in their expenditures, which in the case of the New York *Herald* amounted to half a million dollars for its "war department." Regularly the Northern papers reprinted items from the South, for Southern newspapers reached them by various methods. They were obtained by spies, found in deserted Southern camps, sent by generals, or regularly transmitted by the Adams Express Company or the American Letter Express Company.[1] The censoring function, while not absent, was never carried very far by the government. For a time this function was exercised by the state department; then it was transferred to the war department; but at no time did it amount to more than a rather ineffective effort to prevent leakage of official information which the government wished to keep secret and the supervision of telegraphic communication which was under government control.

The best proof of governmental leniency in news control was the continual publication of all sorts of matter harmful to the government and unfriendly to the Lincoln administration. Such papers as the *World, Journal of Commerce,* and *Daily News* of New York, the Chicago *Times,* and the Columbus (Ohio) *Crisis* regularly indulged in vicious attacks upon the Lincoln government, while more friendly papers engaged in practices harmful to the government and the cause. They printed casualty lists at length; revealed the composition, location, and destination of military units; gave information as to preparations for military and naval expeditions; indicated the place of rendezvous of supply vessels; and in fact functioned almost as Confederate spies within the Union lines. It was Lee's

[1] Postal communication between the North and South was discontinued and the carrying of letters prohibited; but orders to this effect were evaded by various means. McMaster, *Lincoln's Administration,* 158 ff.

regular practice to peruse the Northern newspapers; and his confidential dispatches of the time indicate many items of valuable information which he obtained from them.[2] In addition to revealing military information the papers hurt the cause by undermining confidence in some of the best generals, who were wary of reporters, puffing the reputations of others less worthy who courted the press, peddling camp gossip, reporting the irresponsible talk of disgruntled officers, describing an army as a rabble of ruffians, sowing discontent among commanders, predicting military events, and keeping up such a clamor for "action" as to bring on ill-advised and disastrous engagements.

One may speak of the Northern papers as instruments of propaganda chiefly in the sense that they disseminated the opinions and thought patterns of this or that group, depending upon the management of the paper, as a rule uninfluenced by governmental pressure or restraint. As to propagandizing for a political party, American papers during the Civil War acted no differently than in normal times. Such propaganda is a regular and normal feature of the American press. Naturally the papers of the war period bore the partisan stamp of the particular groups which they represented. Naturally also they contained expressions of the war mind which become nauseating when read in cold print today. The significant point which becomes evident on a thorough study of sources is that the press was neither positively nor negatively a propaganda agency of the government at Washington. If Lincoln spoke to the nation, he did so by formal message, by letter over his own signature, or in a public speech, not as a rule by inspired editorials [3] nor by using the press as a government organ. The most diverse shades of opinion found free expression in speech and print; and while there were instances of suppressive action as noted above,[4] there were many times more examples of governmental restraint where hurtful newspaper activity was tolerated. Anti-Lincoln journals were vicious in their excessive ridicule and vituperation. The New York *World*, in discussing the President's emancipation policy, denounced the "crazy radicals" who were advising the President and the "miserable balderdash" by which, as the editor said, the country was governed.[5] The New York *Daily News*, apropos of a reported case of branding by a surgeon examining recruits, declared: "This war is rapidly driving us into barbarism. The Black Republican thirst for blood appears to have brutalized all the better feelings of the people. . . . So deeply are we becoming enslaved and bru-

---

[2] Douglas S. Freeman and Grady McWhiney, eds., *Lee's Dispatches*, 51, 223, 265, 329.

[3] Lincoln's private letter to Raymond of the New York *Times*, asking for a reconsideration of certain statements and "another article," was exceptional, not typical. Lincoln, *Collected Works*, V, 153.

[4] See above, pp. 307–308.

[5] Editorial, N. Y. *World*, Feb. 7, 1863.

talized by the terms of Mr. Lincoln's 'military necessity' that the whole country does not [demand] . . . punishment of the wretches who could practice such a system of Russian cruelty on a free-born American." [6] At the time of Lincoln's second inaugural the Chicago *Times* did not "conceive it possible that even Mr. Lincoln could produce a paper so slipshod, . . . so puerile, not alone in literary construction, but in its ideas, its sentiments, its grasp." "By the side of it, [added the editor] mediocrity is superb." [7] Such extracts, when read today, have significance chiefly as evidence that criticism of the government and its rulers, even to the point of coarse vituperation, was permitted. These instances are taken from anti-abolitionist papers; but it must also be remembered that much was endured from the abolitionists as well.

Abolition propaganda was dangerous to the Union cause in that it threatened to alienate border-state and conservative Northern sympathy; but despite this danger it was allowed to run its course. So also with the literature of defeatism. The government not only tolerated the holding of mass meetings and printing of numerous articles to protest against the continuation of the war; the President treated the leading exponents of these views with respect, and by passes through the lines and other assistance the government facilitated their self-inspired efforts to conduct negotiations and bring peace. In a large sense the press of the country, as well as other instruments of publicity, was but the reflection of sentiment. The best antidote was not governmental repression; because it was realized that such repression in a community hostile to the administration would only aggravate the evil by directing sympathy to victims of governmental injustice, whereas in a community friendly to the administration the people themselves took care of the situation by banishing, worrying, or doing violence to unpopular editors.[8] Sometimes, indeed, the government might seize a newspaper not to suppress it but to protect it from popular wrath; and it may be said in general that the public authorities did far less than enthusiastic Union men of the time would have wished in controlling the press. When the situation is viewed in the large it appears that the government neither forced nor suppressed sentiment.[9]

[6] Editorial, N. Y. *Daily News*, Aug. 23, 1864.

[7] Editorial, Chicago *Times*, Mar. 6, 1865.

[8] For numerous instances of spontaneous popular violence against newspapers, see *Ann. Cyc.*, 1864, 393–394.

[9] For conditions pertaining to the recruitment and administration of the army, see above, pp. 310–339; for other Northern problems during the war, see pp. 227 ff., 274 ff., 293 ff., 340 ff.

CHAPTER 29

The Failure of Cotton Diplomacy

I

AFTER THE SETTLEMENT of the affair of the rams in September–October, 1863, relations between the United States and Great Britain moved more smoothly, and by the same token the Confederacy became increasingly displeased with London. In retrospect it appears that the year 1863 marked a definite turn in the American question abroad; and it is at least an interesting coincidence that the failure of the effort to obtain Parliamentary support for Confederate recognition came simultaneously with the double victory of Gettysburg and Vicksburg. Lindsay and Roebuck, conspicuous champions of the Confederate cause in Parliament, had been in frequent consultation with Mann, and had essayed the rôle of amateur diplomats in visiting Napoleon III, who granted them various encouraging interviews.[1] This was the situation when on June 30, 1863, the Confederate question was debated in Parliament. Roebuck urged joint recognition by England and France in a burst of overenthusiasm in which he told more of the conference with Napoleon than was discreet. When the ministry replied that no advices consonant with Roebuck's statements had been received from France, the member's veracity was called into question. As the debate continued, a difficulty as to procedure developed among the advocates of the Confederacy, some of whom opposed Roebuck's motion; while on the contrary side Bright and Forster delivered powerful arguments against recognition. It developed that the opposition would not sponsor the motion of Roebuck, whose private venture in the realm of diplomacy had proved a farce. So the Roebuck motion was withdrawn by its author (July 13), whereupon Palmerston delivered a stinging rebuke to the self-employed diplomat.

The full effect of Roebuck's efforts had been far from helpful to the South. Caricatured by *Punch* as "Don Roebucco, the smallest man 'in the

[1] Joint recognition by England and France, or, failing that, independent French recognition, was the proposal urged in this informal negotiation.

House.' " [2] this gentleman, whom Henry Adams described as "rather more than three-quarters mad," offended "genuine sons of John Bull" by talking to the House of Commons "in a French sense"; in so doing he only succeeded in diverting attention from the problem of intervention to one of veracity as between himself and the Emperor.[3]

2

In their efforts to win popular sympathy and combat Northern propaganda, the Confederates had established such agencies of publicity as their resources would permit. English writers were employed in the newspaper and magazine field; spokesmen in Parliament were sought; pamphlets and books were published and freely distributed; news agencies were presented with prepared material; and a special newspaper, the *Index*, was set up by the chief Confederate propaganda agent, Henry Hotze. Through these channels, and through the utterings of Southern diplomats, foreign readers were advised of the unconquerable strength of the Confederate cause. It was pointed out that the Confederacy comprised "13 separate and sovereign States," with 870,610 square miles of territory and twelve millions of population.[1] The historical background of the Southern movement, the confederate nature of the Union, the legal right of secession, were duly elaborated. The vastness of the South, its enormous stretches of arable land, its advantages of soil, rivers, minerals, and climate, were stressed, and its attractiveness as a market for European goods was emphasized. The cardinal importance of cotton was shown by impressive statistics. Confederate military strength was emphasized; Southern victories were featured; Union victories denied or disparaged. The perfidy and hypocrisy of the Lincoln government were exhibited; and incidents such as Butler's "woman order" (misunderstood in Europe) were represented as typical and as if directed from Washington. The United States in general was stigmatized as "a country, if it deserves to be so called, which is capable of committing the most unscrupulous atrocities . . . ; a country that is a reproach to . . . civilization. . . ." Slavery was given little attention; but the ideals of self-government, resistance to oppression, and independence were presented as the issues at stake. The impossibility of conquering the South was constantly pointed out. The sections were represented as psychologi-

[2] A reproduction of the *Punch* cartoon appears in *A Cycle of Adams Letters,* II, 48.

[3] *A Cycle of Adams Letters,* II, 40–43. (It appears that Roebuck correctly reported Napoleon's readiness to join England in action favorable to the South; but the Emperor's failure to send official confirmation of the report served to discredit the whole Roebuck effort. E. D. Adams, II, 172 ff.)

[1] Southern statistics differed in the various accounts as to population, territory, and number of states. These figures appear in a letter of J. M. Mason to Earl Russell, July 24, 1862. *Offic. Rec.* (Nav.), 2 ser., III, 500.

cally incompatible. Sometimes the arguments in this field included expressions by Southern leaders as to essential terms to be insisted on in the making of peace and conditions that would follow when independence had been achieved. It was stated that no peace could be accepted without including within the Confederate States the commonwealths of Maryland, Kentucky, and Missouri and the territories of New Mexico and Arizona. Again it was brought out that, after independence, the "Northern States . . . must be to us henceforth as though they were without a place upon the earth's surface. . . . Let the Northern shipowners starve . . . rather than allow them to convey one pound of our staples to Europe. . . . In this manner we shall wield an overpowering and humiliating influence over them." Mindful of foreign resentment against filibustering in the past, the Southerners were careful to state that, once independence was achieved, there would be no wish for foreign territory; schemes of expansion would disappear; and, moreover, the "balance of power" in North America would be assured.[2]

A fundamental motive in Southern diplomacy was reliance upon the economic magic of "King Cotton." Confident of the commanding importance of the cotton industry upon which nearly five million people in England were dependent, an industry which "appeared to underlie the whole industrial and economic system of Great Britain," [3] the Southerners elevated the King Cotton theory to an importance comparable to that of the state-rights doctrine, and "King Cotton became a cardinal principle upon which all the men who were to lead the South out of the Union and to guide its destiny through the Civil War were almost unanimously agreed." David Christy had argued the controlling importance of cotton as a factor in international affairs in his book *Cotton Is King: or Slavery in the Light of Political Economy* (1855), and Owsley shows how the "phrase was soon on every tongue" when in 1860 there appeared another volume under the awkward title *Cotton Is King and Pro-slavery Arguments,* comprising Christy's book with a collection of arguments by various Southern writers in defense of slavery.[4] The subject was naturally taken up by DeBow in his *Review;* and the well-known doctrine took its place as one of the orthodox thought patterns of the Southland.

This belief in the wizardry of quick results from cotton control produced what has been called an "attempt at economic coercion" in the Southern cotton embargo of 1861. Eager to translate economic theory into solid fact the advocates of the embargo sought to obtain an embargo law by the Confederate Congress; but they failed to obtain any effective legislation. The problem was therefore handled as a matter of state law and even more of public agitation, reinforced by extralegal pressure from citizen

[2] *Ibid.,* 410, 333, 406–407, 474.
[3] Owsley, 6.
[4] *Ibid.,* 17, 15.

committees. The extraordinary difficulty of getting cotton out of Southern ports in 1861 justified in part the Southern representations abroad that an "air-tight embargo" on the export of cotton had been put into effect. In addition there was a widespread effort of Southerners to cut down the supply by restricted planting and even by deliberate burning of cotton as a patriotic duty. As a result of this campaign only "about a million and a half bales were produced [in 1862] as compared with four and a half million for 1861." [5]

Against the Union blockade of the South the Confederates made constant complaint. It was urged that the blockade hurt both the South and Europe and was therefore a major grievance, since by the Southern interpretation it was illegal. On the other hand this very illegality depended upon the contention that the blockade was ineffective; and on this basis the Confederate leaders accused the Lincoln government of using a discredited weapon—a "paper blockade"—while they also upbraided European governments for supporting the blockade by considering it regular, recognizing it in international law, and submitting when European vessels were caught and condemned for its violation.

On this point of ineffectiveness the Confederates presented impressive data. Secretary Benjamin, referring to the situation at the outset of the war, stated that the United States was operating the blockade with an average of one ship for every three hundred miles of coast. He estimated that Charleston was conducting in 1863 an annual foreign trade of $21,000,000, whereas in 1858 its annual commerce had amounted to less than $19,000,000. He added that steamers operated by the Confederate ordnance bureau had made forty-four voyages through the blockade between January and September, 1863, without a single loss by capture. Protesting against international recognition of a blockade that guarded "seven ports" over an extent of three thousand miles of coast with "189 openings," he sharply criticized the "contradictory" statements of the British foreign office on the matter, suggesting that Britain had "some unconfessed interest" in the continuance of the blockade. [6]

The blockade was, in fact, "far from a completely effective measure." [7] The Confederates smuggled in vast supplies of "food, boots, buttons, cloth for uniforms, thread, stockings, civilian clothes, medicines, drugs, salt, boiler iron, shoes, steel, copper, zinc, and chemicals." [8] More important, the South was able to import much of its firearms, artillery, and ammunition from Europe. The most careful student of the subject concludes that

[5] *Ibid.*, 23, 46.
[6] *Offic. Rec.* (Nav.), 2 ser., III, 884–886.
[7] Frank E. Vandiver, ed., *Confederate Blockade Running through Bermuda*, xli.
[8] Daniel O'Flaherty, "The Blockade That Failed," *Am. Heritage*, VI, 40 (Aug., 1955).

"All told, . . . 260,000 to 330,000 or more stand of small-arms were imported by the Confederacy." [9] Surprisingly few of the blockade-runners were seized by the Union fleet. One vessel, the *Kate*, "chalked up 44 trips through the blockade." Owsley summarizes as follows: "It seems from all the evidence that the captures ran about thus: 1861, not more than 1 in 10; 1862, not more than 1 in 8; 1863, not more than 1 in 4; 1864, not more than 1 in 3; 1865, . . . 1 in 2. This is an average for the war of about 1 capture in 6." [10]

As to profits of blockade-running it has been shown that the receipts of the *Banshee No.* 2 for one trip amounted to £85,000, and that two successful trips would serve to compensate the owners for the loss of the vessel on the third. [11]

It was but natural that Benjamin should denounce such a blockade as a fictitious affair; while Owsley concludes that Lincoln, to "gain a doubtful advantage," "flew in the face of all American precedents" and "vitiated the principles in the Declaration of Paris. . . ." [12] In answer to all this it has been maintained on the Union side that the cargoes brought in were "not such as either to disprove the efficiency of the blockade or to supply the needs of the Confederacy." [13] Statistics which emphasize the number of blockade-runners that succeeded as compared to those that were lost do not tell the whole story. It should be remembered that the Civil War blockade-runner was a small specialized ship of low hull and light construction, and that few vessels of the type that bore the bulk of ocean commerce were concerned in the traffic. The full effect of the blockade is to be measured not merely in terms of the stoppage of blockade-runners, but even more in terms of the many large ships that did not even attempt to brave the blockading squadrons. The facts that Confederate cruisers did not have access to their own ports, that Southern-bound cargoes were capturable anywhere on the ocean, and that great dependence was placed upon neutral ports such as Nassau and Matamoros are significant of the power of the blockade. It is to be noted that English importations of cotton dropped heavily during 1861 and 1862 and that, as L. B. Schmidt has pointed out, the Union blockade "threatened the English manufacturers with a cotton famine." [14]

One may conclude that, while allowing extensive evasion, the imperfect blockade was a solid factor in Northern sea power which increased in

[9] William Diamond, "Imports of the Confederate Government from Europe and Mexico," *J.S.H.*, VI, 478 (Nov., 1940).

[10] Owsley, 244, 261.

[11] Rhodes, V, 401.

[12] Owsley, 267.

[13] Bancroft, *Seward*, II, 375.

[14] L. B. Schmidt, "The Influence of Wheat and Cotton on Anglo-American Relations during the Civil War," *Iowa Jour. of Hist. and Pol.*, XVI, 400 ff. (esp. 409–410). For statistics of cotton importations in England, see below, p. 503, n. 2.

strength as the war progressed and which came well within Earl Russell's definition by being "sufficient to create an evident danger" where attempts were made to enter Confederate ports. To put the case in different words, it did not comport with Russell's definition of an ineffective blockade as one "sustained by a notoriously inadequate force." [15]

3

In the diminishing prospects of the Confederacy abroad after the summer of 1863 one may read in part the effect of Union victory, and in part the breakdown of the whole economic doctrine of King Cotton. It was not merely that economic determinism has its limitations as an agent in national affairs; it was also true that the cotton shortage, even at its height, fell short of its desired consequences in terms of foreign intervention, and that other economic factors entered the situation to offset the governmental effect of this shortage. The cotton surplus at the beginning of the war was, to begin with, a factor unfavorable to Southern expectations. From the large crops of 1858 and 1859 there was an accumulated abundance which would serve at least to delay the shortage, especially since excessive stocks of manufactured cotton goods in England were faced with depleted markets. The shortage came, however, in 1862, so that by July of that year the "stock in England was only 200,000 bales as compared with 1,200,000 in 1861; and only 70,000 bales were American as compared with 830,000 bales of American cotton in 1861." In 1862 and 1863 serious distress did occur because of the closing down of English cotton mills. By the end of 1862 it appeared that "only 121,129 of the 533,959 operatives were working full time, . . . while 247,230 were entirely out of work with no prospect of employment." In those days the loss of wages and the burden of poor relief were alarming. Adding those who were partly unemployed, those thrown out in ancillary industries, and dependents, it has been estimated that approximately two million people were without self-support when the "cotton famine" was at its peak at the end of 1862.[1] The industry picked up in 1863, however, owing to such factors as high prices, opening of non-American sources of supply,[2] and readjustment of industry to the new conditions. In December, 1863, the number on poor relief in England was only 180,000 as compared to 485,000 in December, 1862. By December, 1864, the figure had declined to 130,-

---

[15] *Offic. Rec.* (Nav.), 2 ser., III, 888.

[1] Owsley, 137, 142, 145.

[2] In discussing non-American sources of supply as an offset to the threatened cotton famine in England, Dr. Schmidt (*op. cit.*, 419) shows that, while American importations of cotton into England decreased from 2,580,000 bales in 1860 to 72,000 in 1862, and to 132,000 in 1863, non-American importations increased from 785,000 bales in 1860 to 1,445,000 in 1862, to 1,932,000 bales in 1863, and 2,587,000 in 1864.

ooo; and by May, 1865, it fell to 75,000, as compared to 48,000 in normal times.[3]

The pinch in cotton supply, whose effect was much less serious after 1863, was but one of various material factors influencing the British government. This very shortage in cotton gave a speculative profit to many mill owners who found it more profitable to hold their cotton stocks for a rise than to continue to operate their mills. Furthermore, the sudden ending of the war would offer an actual menace in the dumping of American cotton in large quantities on the market. As for the laborers, they were partially taken care of by poor relief both public and private; and in the notable case of John Bright, a mill operator in Lancashire, sympathy for the North was combined with a willingness to bear the burden of relief in the care of his own workers. There were, of course, other factors than cotton to be considered. England had need of wheat from the North as well as of cotton from the South.[4] Linen and woolen industries gained at the expense of cotton. English manufacturers of munitions reaped handsome profits from their sales to both belligerents. Certainly the men so engaged would not agitate for English intervention to bring the war to a close. In addition, the merchant marine of England, having faced the serious menace of American competition in the 1850's, was decidedly benefited by the rapid decline of the American merchant marine which the war brought.

On balance, then, neither economic interest nor sympathy for the South was strong enough to cause Britain to align herself on the Southern side. British neutrality, as Max Beloff has said, was "a case of traditional diplomacy, unheroic and unmoved by sentiment." [5] Palmerston was aware

[3] Owsley, 147.

[4] L. B. Schmidt urges that "Great Britain's dependence on American wheat was most acute when the cotton famine was at its height," that pro-Southern demonstrations in England were offset by protests against recognition, and that "an *adequate* and *cheap* food supply concerned the masses of the people . . . no less . . . than . . . the cotton supply" (*op. cit.,* 431, 435, 439). E. D. Adams (*op. cit,* II, 14), with little examination of economic data, notes the absence of wheat in diplomatic communications and refuses to accept Schmidt's thesis. Eli Ginzberg ("The Economics of British Neutrality during the American Civil War," *Agricultural Hist.,* X, 152–153 [Oct., 1936]) also rejects Schmidt's arguments, noting: "In 1858–1860 there was available annually 5.0 bushels of wheat per capita for the population of the United Kingdom, and the average price was 5s. 1od. The corresponding average for 1860, 1861, and 1862 was 5.7 bushels, and the price approximately 6s. 9d. If Great Britain had not imported a single quarter of wheat from the United States during the critical years, the supply would have permitted the per capita consumption to remain at the same level as in 1858–1860."

[5] Beloff, "Great Britain and the American Civil War," *History,* XXXVII, 47 (Feb., 1952). It is hard to judge what role pro-Union working-class opinion played in determining British policy. Lincoln thought the numerous mass meetings and the giant petitions they endorsed of great importance to the Union cause, and he praised the laborers' "sublime Christian heroism" in favoring the United States when support of the Confederacy would end the cotton famine from which they

that recognition of the South, with its attendant danger of war with the United States, might easily upset the precarious European balance of power and precipitate a world war. He was under no political pressure to intervene, for his opponents in the Conservative party, while giving "a detached, innocuous sympathy" to the South, had adopted their traditional policy of neutrality with regard to the American conflict and "the responsible men in their party were not only extremely careful to be neutral in their official utterances but they exercised a restraining influence over the pro-Southern members of their party." [6] At the same time, Palmerston realized that intervention would badly split his own Liberal party and probably would topple his cabinet.

Furthermore, it was powerfully brought home to Palmerston that the British national interest would best be served by declining "to press neutral rights to a point which might later embarrass the exercise of British sea power." [7] By a remarkable stroke of fortune, the United States government, hitherto an ardent defender of the rights of neutrals, especially on the high seas, had "completely reversed its former position . . . and stumbled unintentionally but irrevocably upon the side of the Mistress of the Seas." [8] Specifically, British jurists noted that recognition of the imperfect Union blockade of the South would form a useful precedent in a future war, whereas accepting the Confederate view of the illegality of such a blockade "would be to blunt in advance a weapon [Great Britain] might well need again." Moreover, had England continued to outfit Confederate raiders, she would have set a damaging precedent and in a future war might have to face the "prospect of limitless numbers of commerce-raiders being fitted out in American or other neutral ports." [9]

A powerful supplement to these forces working for peace was the suc-

---

were suffering. Lincoln, *Collected Works*, VI, 63–65. But Owsley (p. 565) points out that such "meetings, whether pro-northern or pro-southern, were not spontaneous, but were drummed up by well-subsidized leaders and were frequently packed by the liberal use of small coin." Moreover, since most British workers did not have votes, it is not clear that their voices were much heeded by the cabinet. It seems safe to conclude with Martin P. Claussen ("Peace Factors in Anglo-American Relations, 1861–1865," *M.V.H.R.*, XXVI, 522 [Mar., 1940]): "At most British labor had the same immediate goal as the shipowners who feared the ruin of their merchant marine [in the event of a war with the United States]. Both agreed on the economic consequences and the economic fallacy of war, and on the necessity for peace with the Union; but it was the commercial groups who probably had the ear of the government."

[6] Wilbur Devereux Jones, "The British Conservatives and the American Civil War," *Am. Hist. Rev.*, LVIII, 542–543 (April, 1953).

[7] James P. Baxter, 3rd, "Some British Opinions as to Neutral Rights, 1861 to 1865," *Amer. Jour. of Int. Law*, XXIII, 517 (July, 1929).

[8] Frank L. Owsley, "America and the Freedom of the Seas, 1861–1865," in Avery O. Craven, ed., *Essays in Honor of William E. Dodd*, 195.

[9] Beloff, *op. cit.*, 42.

cess of Union arms. It is significant that the two most dangerous threats of European intervention came at the height of Confederate military success, in the early fall of 1862 and in the summer of 1863. Union victories at Antietam and at Gettysburg were instrumental in blunting these threats. Confederate envoys abroad openly admitted that such Northern successes could not "fail to exercise an unfavorable influence on the question of recognition." [10] The fact that the relations of the United States with England were distinctly easier after the summer of 1863 was largely traceable to the general trend of the war from that time forward.

So serious indeed were the difficulties between England and the Confederacy in 1863 that a break came late in the year. The detention of the ironclads and the failure of recognition had much to do with this break; but another factor was an acrid controversy over the conduct and status of British consuls in Southern cities. These consuls—e.g., Bunch at Charleston, Cridland at Mobile, Moore at Richmond, and Fullerton at Savannah—occupied an anomalous position because of the lack of diplomatic relations between England and the Confederacy. Despite the irregularity of their status their continued service within the Confederacy was approved; but serious quarrels had arisen not only between them and the state department at Richmond, but also with state governors in the South who more than once assumed far-reaching functions in the international field. In the case of Cridland a quarrel occurred because he had been influential in forwarding a shipment of specie from Mobile to England in payment of interest due British citizens on the public debt of Alabama. Lord Lyons seriously objected to this, and the incident ended by the British government removing Cridland, who was replaced by an appointee of Lyons. This brought into view one of the major objections of the Confederate authorities to the activities of the British consuls—namely, the fact that they took orders from British diplomatic officials accredited to an enemy country, i.e., the United States. [11]

Meanwhile another serious issue had arisen because of repeated protests by British consuls against the drafting of British citizens into the Confederate army, and because, by assuming to extend British protection over their own nationals in the South, Her Majesty's government was, according to the Southern interpretation, assuming an unwarranted jurisdiction within Confederate territory. The most serious offender in this respect was Consul Moore at Richmond; in his case the trouble reached the point of expulsion by the Confederate government on June 5, 1863. His exequatur had been issued by the government of the United States; it had been tolerated by the Confederacy on the ground that it had been issued "by a former Government which was at the time of the issue the duly authorized agent for that purpose of the State of Virginia." Now, however (June 5,

[10] *Offic. Rec.* (Nav.), 2 ser., III, 855.
[11] *Ibid.*, 923.

1863), by letters patent Moore's exequatur was revoked and annulled by President Davis. Finally in October, 1863, President Davis expelled all the British consular agents from the South. In explaining this drastic action Secretary Benjamin referred to the "unwarrantable assumption . . . of jurisdiction within our territory," and to "offensive encroachment on the sovereignty of the Confederate States." [12]

A study of the public papers of the Confederacy in 1862 and 1863 reveals many a bitter comment on the attitude of England and of Europe generally. As early as March 8, 1862, there was introduced into the Confederate Congress a resolution calling for the withdrawal of Southern commissioners from England on the ground that that country declined to recognize the Confederacy.[13] On May 29 of the same year Mann complained that European neutrality did not exist and that European diplomacy was "notoriously one sided." Slidell complained (July 25, 1862) that England had adopted "a tortuous, selfish, and time-serving policy." Mann wrote (January 16, 1863) that "the conduct of the two western powers [Great Britain and France] toward us has been extremely shabby" and deplored their lack of spirit "against the arrogant pretensions of the insolent Washington concern." On March 19, 1863, Mason lamented bitterly that he had "no intercourse, unofficial or otherwise, with any member of the Government" in England. Not long afterward (June 22, 1863) Benjamin paid an unwilling compliment to his Northern opponent, admitting "the sagacity with which Mr. Seward penetrated into the secret feelings of the British cabinet, and the success of his policy of intimidation. . . ." Three days later Mann stated that the time had come when the Confederacy could be indifferent to recognition.[14] In his message to Congress on December 8, 1863, President Davis referred to the attitude of European nations as "positively unfriendly." [15] Yet while all these evidences of Confederate disappointment were piling up. Hotze, the Confederate propagandist, was reporting that in England there was "scarcely a man eminent in letters, in politics, or in society, who dares profess friendship for the North." [16]

Even before the expulsion of the British consuls the Confederate government had come to the decision that Mason's mission to England ought to be terminated. On August 4, 1863, Secretary Benjamin informed him of the President's desire that he consider his mission at an end. The following month (September 30) he left London for Paris, having given up his residence and removed the diplomatic archives.[17]

Though disappointed in specific matters of policy, such as the blockade

12 *Ibid.*, 789–790, 922 ff.
13 *Journal*, Confed. Cong., V, 71.
14 *Offic. Rec.* (Nav.), 2 ser., III, 440, 485, 659, 715, 817–818.
15 *Journal*, Confed. Cong., VI, 497.
16 *Offic. Rec.* (Nav.), 2 ser., III, 946.
17 *Ibid.*, 852, 934.

and the peaceful solution of the *Trent* affair, the Confederates were chiefly offended in the matter of status. Their greatest source of distress was the continued refusal of the European powers to recognize their official existence. By refusing to recognize Southern independence, said President Davis, foreign nations gave such encouragement to the United States as to prolong the carnage; the historian of the future, he declared, would therefore be unable to absolve them from responsibility for the myriads of human lives needlessly sacrificed.[18]

4

The conduct of Napoleon III touching the American question had been of a piece with the flamboyant diplomacy of that notorious monarch. The Emperor's oft-expressed sympathy with the cause of the South struck in part a responsive chord among the French people; but the strong antislavery sentiment in France, the dread of war with America, and the tendency to follow England's lead worked the other way. In the sequel the caution of the Emperor in seeming to hedge on every action he proposed left the Confederates with the impression that they had been duped. As in England, the Confederate cause looked most hopeful in France in 1861 and 1862. Napoleon gave support to England in the *Trent* affair; and the French cabinet "formed a group of propagandists for the recognition of the Confederacy." [1] In July of 1862 Mason wrote on good authority that Napoleon was "ready and anxious" to take some step equivalent to recognition of the Southern government.[2] As early as May 14, 1862, Thouvenel, minister of foreign affairs, had given Slidell an interview "decidedly frank and cordial" which left the Southerner with the inference that, "if New Orleans had not been taken and we suffered no very serious reverses in Virginia and Tennessee, . . . recognition would very soon have been declared. . . ." [3] Always in the French game as to the South, however, there loomed the question of England as well as the danger to his Mexican scheme should the Emperor become involved in war with the United States; and at all points one finds the reluctance of Napoleon to play, as to this matter, a lone hand. While delaying definite action the Emperor received Slidell with marked cordiality; and on November 10, 1862,[4] he sent to the English and French governments a proposal that these nations join in suggesting a six-months' armistice accompanied by a cessation of the blockade. Such an offer would have been highly acceptable to the

[18] *Journal,* Confed. Cong., VII, 251.

[1] Owsley, 171.
[2] *Offic. Rec.* (Nav.), 2 ser., III, 491.
[3] Reported in Slidell's letter of May 15, 1862, to Secretary Benjamin. *Ibid.,* 420.
[4] November 10 was the date of the formal offer. It had been indicated by preliminary conversations, however, and was known some time in advance.

South, but would have been indignantly rejected by the United States. To this suggestion the English government replied in the negative.[5]

Early in the next year (February 3, 1863) Mercier, French minister at Washington, while urging the Emperor's sincere friendship for the United States, gave an offer of mediation, proposing that Union and Confederate representatives meet on neutral territory for the discussion of terms of peace.[6] This offer was quickly disposed of by Seward, who replied that the Federal government had not the least thought of giving up the war for the Union by such a relinquishment of its authority in the South as the peace conference would imply.[7] In emphatic terms Seward's position was reinforced by Congress when both houses joined (March 3, 1863) in a resolution denouncing mediation as "foreign interference," expressing regret for the encouragement of the "rebellion" which derived from the hope of foreign sympathy, and reaffirming their "unalterable purpose" to suppress the Southern movement.[8]

Too often this mediation offer is treated by historians as if it existed in a vacuum; seldom does one find an adequate examination of its background or actuating causes. Now, however, it is possible on the basis of French archival sources compiled by Lynn M. Case to generalize reliably concerning French opinion on the American question. After an elaborate study Dr. Case writes that official reports to Paris from French provinces included complaints "about the suffering in French cotton and exporting industries caused by the American conflict," and he adds that these complaints were accompanied by pleas for action to stop the conflict and "by an almost unanimous expression of sympathy for the South." When the mediation project failed, writes Dr. Case, "the French public seemed more bitter toward England and Russia for declining to cooperate with France's mediation plan than toward the United States for spurning France's good offices." [9] When in the summer of 1863 the question of Napoleon's attitude was interjected into the Parliamentary debate in England as above noted,[10] the general effect, as before, was an injury to the Southern cause.

The hopes of the Confederacy as to the building of warships in France were also disappointed, though Confederate agents had been given ample

[5] E. D. Adams, *Great Britain and the American Civil War*, II, 65.

[6] "When the mediation proposal was published, it met with the approval of all parties [in France]. . . . It was interpreted by the Débats as a renunciation of the previous proposal of an armistice. . . ." W. Reed West, *Contemporary French Opinion on the American Civil War*, Johns Hopkins Univ. Studies in Hist. and Pol. Sci., ser. XLII, no. 1 (1924), 97.

[7] McPherson, *Pol. Hist. of the . . . Rebellion*, 345.

[8] *Cong. Globe*, 37 Cong., 3 sess., 1497–1498, 1541.

[9] Lynn M. Case, ed., *French Opinion on the United States and Mexico, 1860–1867: Extracts from the Reports of the Procureurs Généraux*, 257–258.

[10] See pp. 498–499.

food on which to nourish such hopes. With Napoleon's consent and with the specific authorization of the French minister of marine, contracts were made for the building of four cruisers at Nantes and Bordeaux. It was expected that the vessels would be ready in 1864 and that they would prey powerfully, as did the *Alabama,* upon ocean-going ships of the United States. Arrangements were also concluded for building two ironclad rams. It was to be asserted by the most transparent pretense that these warships were not for the Confederacy, but were intended for some neutral government. In the event, however, Confederate hopes for the delivery of these ships were unfulfilled. Through Bigelow and Dayton [11] the facts became known to the American government; Seward sent polite though vigorous protests; the English government purchased the Laird rams (which had been transferred to a French firm while still destined for the South); and Napoleon, facing the menace of war with the United States when the military situation was undergoing a turn favorable to the North, turned completely about in his attitude toward the Confederate agents and disposed of the matter by arranging that the cruisers be turned over to European governments. They were acquired in 1864 by Denmark and Prussia, then at war with each other, thus showing that the obligations of a neutral under international law rested but lightly upon the French government. On Denmark's refusal to accept one of the ships, the *Sphinx,* it found its way into Confederate hands; but this occurred so near the end of the war that Southern agents got little comfort from it. Though encouraging the South by glowing promises, France gave less aid and comfort to the Confederacy in the building of its navy than did England.

5

One of the most troublesome of the foreign complications that arose during the Civil War was the episode of French intervention in Mexico. Since the end of Spanish rule in 1821, Mexico had not only been torn by political factions, but had been hampered by peonage, aristocratic privilege, enormous land holdings by the clergy which had become an ally of reactionary politics, and foreign entanglements in the matter of governmental debts and otherwise. After repeated revolutions a situation existed in 1859 and 1860 in which the native leader Juarez stood at the head of the Liberal party (advocating religious toleration, confiscation of church property, civil marriage, and abolition of religious orders) in opposition to the politically powerful Church party, which the Liberals denounced as the heir of Spanish absolutism. By an election in the spring of 1861 Juarez was successful in opposition to Miramon, the Church-party leader. In July of 1861 the Juarez administration, being financially embarrassed and considering the

---

[11] John Bigelow was consul general at Paris; William L. Dayton of New Jersey was the American minister to France, 1861–1864. In April, 1865, Bigelow became minister.

government obligations contracted by the opposing party fraudulent and void, declared a two-year suspension of payments to foreign creditors. By existing treaty agreements customs receipts could be attached for such default; and on October 31, 1861, a convention was concluded by France, Spain, and England looking toward joint forcible collection of Mexican claims. Asked to join this convention, the United States declined; and Seward scored a point by obtaining from the three powers an express disclaimer of any intention to acquire territory or exercise political control in Mexico.

By January, 1862, the three nations had sent 10,000 troops to Mexico; in so doing they had recognized the Juarez government, had negotiated with it, and had sent that government a note disavowing any intention to meddle in Mexico's internal affairs. In May, 1862, having obtained satisfaction from Juarez on the matter of the debt, England and Spain withdrew their forces. France, however, not only held on, but sent additional troops and made impossible demands upon Juarez, requiring among other things an indemnity, French occupation of Vera Cruz and Tampico until specified conditions should be fulfilled, and the payment of certain discredited Mexican bonds floated by a Swiss-French banker named Jecker, which allowed such an enormous profit to the banker that they can only be described as a swindle.

French troops were soon augmented to the number of 35,000. With this force they made war upon Juarez, who fought back in guerilla fashion; and in June of 1863 Mexico City was occupied by the French. A French-made form of government was now set up; and the unhappy Maximilian, archduke of Austria, misled as to conditions and fondly expecting more Mexican support than he had solid reason to hope for, consented, under pressure from Napoleon, to assume the title of Emperor of Mexico. He and his wife Charlotte landed at Vera Cruz on May 28, 1864, made their way to the capital, and were greeted by a carefully manufactured popular demonstration. By this time it had become evident that Napoleon, seeking schemes of conquest to rival those of his uncle, attracted by Mexico's wealth (combined with weakness), and fearing annexation to the United States, had made it a policy of his reign to launch in Mexico a French-protected empire that would serve as a bulwark of Latin peoples in opposition to Anglo-Saxon expansion.[1]

During 1862 and the major part of 1863 there was but little protest from the United States; but on September 26, 1863, the American position was stated in a long dispatch to Dayton in which Seward expressed

[1] On the general Mexican situation as it affected the United States, see "The Present Condition of Mexico . . ." (Apr. 14, 1862), *House Exec. Doc. No. 100,* 37 Cong., 2 sess. For the convention of October 31, 1861, between France, Spain, and England, with its disclaimer of intent to acquire territory or political control (Article II), see *ibid.*, 134–137.

American interest in the maintenance of republics free from foreign domination in the western hemisphere, and warned that continued intervention would "scatter seeds . . . which might ultimately ripen into collision between France and the United States and other American republics." Referring to rumors of French desire to seize Texas, he wrote: "The President apprehends none of these things. He does not allow himself to be disturbed by suspicions so unjust to France . . . ; but he knows . . . that such suspicions will be entertained . . . by this country . . . ; and he knows, also, that it is out of such suspicions that the fatal web of national animosity is most frequently woven." [2] As the war dragged on Seward continued his warnings and protests, making clear the American position that French intervention was distasteful to the United States, while avoiding specific reference to the Monroe doctrine. After the war, as will be seen later, these warnings were to be reinforced by a definite threat of force on the border.[3]

The main interest of Confederate diplomacy with reference to the Mexican imbroglio was to use Mexico as a kind of pawn in the drive to obtain recognition. Their best argument, which was pressed by Benjamin, Slidell, and others, was that Napoleon's Mexican state could not possibly succeed except on the basis of Confederate success in the war; and on this basis the Confederate government offered to extend its support to Maximilian in return for French recognition of the Confederacy. In an interview with de Haviland, a friend of Jefferson Davis on business abroad for the South (November, 1863), Maximilian showed marked sympathy for the Confederacy and expressed the view that English and French recognition of the independence of the Confederacy ought to be assured before he accepted the Mexican title. Slidell worked toward the same end; but, apparently because of Napoleon's interference, efforts in this direction were nullified and an interview between Slidell and Maximilian was prevented. In tentative conversations on the subject the sympathy of the Confederacy for the French empire in Mexico was made clear. This amounted to an abandonment of the Monroe doctrine by the Confederacy (unless one could accept the fiction that Maximilian's government was based on the consent of the Mexican people); and this abandonment was further indicated by the appointment of William Preston by President Davis as "envoy extraordinary and minister plenipotentiary" to "His Imperial Majesty, Maximilian." It also appears that Confederate diplomats were willing to surrender another important element in the traditional foreign policy of the United States in that they stood ready to make an actual alliance with France. A. Dudley Mann wrote on August 15, 1863, that he would "gladly see [his] Government entering into an offensive and defensive treaty with

---

[2] *House Exec. Doc. No. 1*, 38 Cong., 1 sess. (Papers relating to Foreign Affairs), 781–783.

[3] See below, p. 649.

the Emperor of the French." [4] On the other hand, if efforts toward French cooperation failed, Confederate diplomats threatened combined action with the United States after the war to drive the French from Mexico, in which case the Monroe doctrine would have been invoked. Thus the famous doctrine of Monroe (directed against efforts by any European country to acquire territory or to extend political control in the western hemisphere) was not treated by the Confederates as a firm principle to be asserted without equivocation, but rather as a sort of pawn, a thing to be withheld or applied as the exigencies of war diplomacy should seem to require.

From the autumn of 1863 until the end of the war there was a notable relaxation of tension between the United States and England, and in foreign affairs generally. By the withdrawal of Mason, said Charles Francis Adams, Jr., the adversary had "abandoned the field." [5] Instead of anxious comment on threatened war or an approaching termination of the mission in London, the letters of Henry Adams in 1864 recount a dinner at a London guild-hall or an outing at Wenlock Abbey, while in diplomacy "quiet . . . reign[ed] supreme." Commenting in July, 1864, on a breakfast conversation concerning "Bokhara and the inhabitants of central Asia," he wrote: "I revelled in Tartaric steppes, and took a vivid interest in farthest Samarcand." [6] Under these circumstances statesmen felt that the American question had been thoroughly canvassed, and no advantage came to the Confederacy by playing its last desperate card in offering to abolish slavery if by this means recognition by England could be procured. Having reached this decision, Secretary Benjamin sent Duncan F. Kenner of Louisiana as a messenger to Mason, who, returning to London, was granted an interview of more than an hour with Lord Palmerston at Cambridge House on March 14, 1865. In guarded fashion, while avoiding an "open proposition" and showing an unwillingness to put his offer in plain words, Mason managed to convey the desired impression. In the face of impending Confederate defeat, however, it was too late to make diplomatic capital of any emancipation offer. [7] The incident is of historical interest not for any significance in London but rather as evidence of the effect of war pressure upon Confederate policy and as a reluctant admission by Confederate leaders that the institution of slavery was a serious drawback to the South in its long search for foreign support.

[4] *Offic. Rec.* (Nav.), 2 ser., III, 968–970, 1057–1059, 1063–1065, 484, 155, 871.
[5] C. F. Adams, *Charles Francis Adams,* 350.
[6] *Cycle of Adams Letters,* II, 200, 165–166.
[7] Owsley, 552 ff.

CHAPTER 30

Collapse of the Confederacy:
End of the War

I

IN COUNTLESS WAYS the war came closer to the people of the South than to those of the North. Huge Southern areas were actually within Union lines; other immense districts were torn and trampled and fought over by the shifting armies; Winchester changed hands so often that it became a kind of shuttlecock between contending forces. The Union occupation of Southern districts, especially Tennessee, Louisiana, parts of Virginia, and various coastal areas, was more than an ordinary matter of hostile military occupation. Prosecuting the war to "repossess" and "restore" territory seized by those in "insurrection," United States forces sought to recover the South once and for all from Confederate control. They did not consider themselves to be merely in enemy country, and Southern regions under the Union flag were administered in large part, though not entirely, as part of the United States.[1] The occupation of New Orleans, beginning in 1862, was not analogous to the occupation of Tampico by the United States in 1847. American authorities in Tampico looked forward to the relinquishment of their authority after the conclusion of the war by treaty; but in the case of New Orleans and other occupied districts of the South no treaty was anticipated, but rather the destruction of the Confederate government and the reclamation of territory held in its grasp, with such ultimate restoration of local authority as would comport with re-establishment of Federal rule.

To make a bad situation worse, in the most conspicuous case of all Lincoln was unfortunate in his choice of a commander. B. F. Butler's administration at New Orleans has been represented by eulogists as a régime designed to maintain order, prevent hardship, extend charitable relief, and

[1] Randall, *Constitutional Problems Under Lincoln,* 221 ff.

promote sanitation.[2] On the other hand the Southern attitude toward Butler is indicated by Mrs. Chesnut's characterization of him as this "hideous, cross-eyed beast." [3] Butler's provoking personality offers perhaps the chief explanation of Southern detestation, though any man in a like situation would have been unpopular. As already noted, there was more than suspicion that Butler's brother reaped ungodly millions of profit in cotton; and in general the people were outraged by the commander's boastful and sententious declarations and by vexatious incidents of his rule. Among the more serious of these incidents were the execution of Mumford, treated above,[4] and a notorious order which was interpreted as an insult to the women of New Orleans.[5] There were, however, many other extraordinary features of Butler's occupation. Under his orders Episcopal clergymen were required to include in the morning prayer the words "for the President of the United States and all in civil authority." When Dr. Goodrich, rector of St. Paul's, sought to evade the order by omitting the morning prayer altogether, the church was closed by an officer of Butler's staff.[6] Using the mansion of General Twiggs as a residence, Butler kept the people in constant excitement by his arrest of prominent citizens, suppression of newspapers, seizure of property, and like measures. Taking the Federal confiscation acts seriously, and overlooking the attorney general's preference for a slight enforcement through the Federal courts where the matter properly belonged, Butler issued sweeping orders of confiscation and set up a sequestration commission by which public sales of goods taken from "rebels" were conducted and the administration of estates by "loyal" owners promoted. It was asserted by President Davis that his sequestration policy would condemn a quarter of a million human beings to punishment by starvation.[7] Such details will serve to suggest the reasons for the extraordinary order by President Davis declaring Butler an outlaw [8] and ordering his execution as a felon. It is of interest to note that at the time this order was issued (December 23, 1862) the bellicose general had been removed by President Lincoln and superseded (December 17) by General N. P. Banks.

[2] James Parton, *General Butler at New Orleans, passim.* Butler's own defense is given in *Butler's Book* (1892).

[3] *Diary from Dixie*, 165.

[4] See p. 335.

[5] Basing his action on reports of repeated insults to his men and officers by women in New Orleans, Butler issued a notorious order (which he maintained was interpreted in a manner entirely foreign to his intention) providing that any female insulting a Union soldier or officer would "be regarded and held liable to be treated as a woman of the town plying her avocation." (Butler, *Private and Offic. Corresp.*, I, 490.) The order was denounced at home and abroad as an unspeakable infamy, and some of the English comment generalized to the point of renouncing kinship with a people in whose name such an order could be issued.

[6] *National Intelligencer*, Oct. 29, 1862.

[7] Moore, *Rebell. Rec.* (Docs.), VI, 292.

[8] See above, p. 335.

Butler's administration illustrates the excesses of a military régime in which civil government is subordinated to the whim of military officers. His high-flown notions of martial law, as revealed in his correspondence, are worth quoting in this connection. "Now, my theory of the law martial is this [he wrote]—that it is a . . . well-defined part of the common law of this country, . . . recognized in its proper place by the Constitution, and that proper place . . . is in the camp and garrison. Now, the best definition of martial law that I have ever heard was that by Sir Arthur Wellesly [sic], afterwards Duke of Wellington, . . .: 'The Will of the Comdg. General exercised according to . . . natural equity.' . . . Thus civil government may well exist in subordination to martial law . . . when . . . efficient to the end desired. When [not] . . ., that government is . . . to be cast aside." [9]

Other Union commanders in the South usually showed more discretion and less truculence than Butler. Andrew Johnson, for example, military governor of Tennessee, though resorting to arrest, seizure, and other severe measures, gave less occasion for widespread complaint; and such administrations as those of Banks at New Orleans and Geary at Savannah were conducted with moderation and restraint.

2

Desertion at the South, though less extensive than in the North, was a factor of large significance; and a study of the causes that produced it goes far toward revealing the conditions which made the war intolerable to thousands among people and soldiers. As explained by Miss Lonn, backwoodsmen and crackers were drawn into the army who had no sympathy with slavery and no interest in the issues of a struggle which they did not understand. The conscript net gathered in even Northerners and Mexicans, whose tendency to desert was natural enough. Many of the deserters were mere boys. Poor food and clothing, lack of shoes and overcoats, and insufficient pay inevitably produced disaffection. Sometimes the pay was fourteen months behind; often a soldier on leave could not pay the transportation to return to his command. Unsanitary camp conditions had their debilitating effect. Soldiers kept in unwholesome inaction were more than commonly subject to homesickness and depression. Often the alternative was abandonment and neglect of wife and children or departure from the army—in other words a choice between two kinds of desertion, a dilemma in facing conflicting loyalties. Men felt that their services were actually more needed at home than in the army. Not a few Southern soldiers found themselves in the situation of an Alabaman who deserted the army when his wife wrote him: "We haven't got nothing in the house to eat but a little bit o meal. . . . I don't want you to stop fighting them Yankees . . .

[9] *Private and Official Correspondence of Gen. B. F. Butler . . . , IV, 579.*

but try and get off and come home and fix us all up some and then you can go back." [1] Some Arkansas soldiers deserted when informed that Indians were on a scalping tour near their homes. Indignant at extortioners and profiteers, soldiers would become disgruntled at the "rich man's war and the poor man's fight." There were occasions when "whole companies, garrisons, and even regiments decamped at a time." In some cases deserters banded together, roamed the country, fortified themselves in the mountains, and made raids upon settlements, stealing cattle and robbing military stores. Some lived in caves. Forces had to be detached from the Confederate armies to run down such groups, whose retreats were inaccessible and whose courage in fighting off attack was formidable. Had it not been for Mosby's Rangers, as Miss Lonn had pointed out, many defenseless residents in Virginia's debatable land between the shifting armies "would have been at the mercy of the roving bands of deserters, turned bushwhackers, who had been left in the wake of both armies. . . ." At critical times in the war the extent of desertion prevented the South from following up victories or half-victories in the field; it was both the cause and effect of lowered morale; the amount was "appalling, incredible." Many who withdrew from the army "had little conception of the gravity of their offense." For such men desertion bore no stigma; and, in sum, it appears that this factor (which, after all, was but a reflection of many other factors) "contributed definitely to the Confederate defeats after 1862 and . . . [to] the catastrophe of 1865." [2]

On the nature and extent of devastation at the South the historian's sources present a sad record. By the end of the war the eleven seceding states had 32 per cent fewer horses than in 1860, 30 per cent fewer mules, 35 per cent fewer cattle, 20 per cent fewer sheep, and 42 per cent fewer swine. The economic consequences of four years of conflict, according to James L. Sellers, were "a shortage in agricultural capital, a reduced area under cultivation, diminished agricultural production, depreciated land value, stifled industry, demoralized commerce, [and] totally inadequate banking and currency facilities with a correspondingly high rate of interest." Omitting slave property from his calculations, Professor Sellers concludes that "southern wealth in 1860 had shrunk in value at the end of the war by 43%." [3]

At home the women bore a double burden as they struggled to manage and work the farms and plantations, supply vital war needs, and offer comfort to fighting men. Commenting on the manner in which grief kills women in war, Mrs. Chesnut wrote: "I know how it feels to die. . . . For instance, some one calls out, 'Albert Sidney Johnston is killed.' My

---

[1] Bessie Martin, *Desertion of Alabama Troops* . . . , 148.

[2] Ella Lonn, *Desertion during the Civil War*, 23, 119, 123–124.

[3] Sellers, "The Economic Incidence of the Civil War in the South," *M.V.H.R.*, XIV, 183–184, 189 (Sept., 1927).

heart stands still. I feel no more." She relates how the sexton at church would deliver messages to worshippers telling of relatives who had been brought in wounded, dying, or dead.[4] It was an exceptional woman, said Mrs. Jefferson Davis, who did not nurse in a hospital. Mrs. Arthur F. Hopkins of Alabama (née Juliet Ann Opie of Jefferson County, Virginia) was under fire while ministering to the wounded on the battlefield and received a wound at Seven Pines which lamed her for life. Maintaining their stricken households, kept tense by hourly apprehension, supplying social gaiety as in "starvation parties" to give pleasant diversion to soldiers, some even driving a team or following a plow so that men could be released for fighting, the women of the South, while witnessing daily the backwash and ruin of war, showed often a sustained morale and cheerfulness exceeding that of the men.

3

The pinch of the blockade together with the general disruption of normal pursuits made of the whole South a beleaguered nation. There was sporting glamor in the hazardous game of blockade-running, but there was a prejudice against the flaunting extravagance of men who profited by the business. Many thought that blockade-runners were not helping the Confederate cause so much as they were amassing personal profit; indeed the trade had some of the aspects of bootlegging and there was agitation for bringing it under public regulation. The blockade was a minor factor in the food shortage; but such shortage was an increasing source of distress, even in localities distant from the scene of war.

Mary Elizabeth Massey, who has made a thorough study of shortages in the South, concludes that "the poor people of the Confederacy found it extremely difficult to get enough to eat." By the end of the war many staples had permanently disappeared from the Southern diet; in 1864 "an ounce of meat per person daily was considered ample for the times." "Rats," Miss Massey continues, "had become an item in the diet of many. President Davis was quoted as saying that he saw no reason for not eating them, for he thought they would be 'as good as squirrels.' . . . Rats, however, never became the item of diet that mule-meat did." [1] Poor transportation facilities, the closing of the Mississippi River, Federal occupation of productive areas, Union raids, and campaigns of destruction had much to do in tightening the pinch of hunger; and there was the further factor of food speculation within the South. Indignation against speculators who accumulated stocks for extortionary purposes led to food riots at Salisbury, Atlanta, Mobile, and Richmond. It was reported that at Mobile the women assembled under such banners as "Bread or Blood," "Bread and Peace,"

[4] *Diary from Dixie,* 182, 245.

[1] Massey, *Ersatz in the Confederacy,* 57, 61–62.

and, "armed with knives and hatchets, marched down Dauphine street, breaking open the stores . . . and taking for their use such articles of food or clothing as they were in urgent need of."[2]

Tea was usually not available at all, and coffee became a rare luxury, being superseded by unsatisfactory substitutes concocted from "parched corn, rye, wheat, okra seed, . . . acorns, dandelion roots, sugar cane, parched rice, cotton seed, sorghum molasses, English peas, peanuts, . . . and beans."[3] The scarcity of clothing was evident from the angry raids upon clothing shops and from the tatterdemalion appearance of the troops, whose supply of blankets, uniforms, and socks was woefully deficient. Yet the diarist Jones of the Confederate war department thought that supplies in large quantities could be had if "the government would wake up." He referred to "the people here [Richmond] almost in a state of starvation in the midst of plenty, brought on by the knavery or incompetency of government agents." The government, he said, allowed forty thousand bushels of sweet potatoes to rot in depots between Richmond and Wilmington.[4] On one occasion the diarist mentioned a huge seizure of leather to prevent its falling into enemy hands and added that in his opinion there was abundance of leather in the South, but that it was "held, like everything else, by speculators, for extortioner's profits," and that government bureaus only aggravated the evil by "capricious seizures, and tyrannical restrictions on transportation."[5] The poor suffered grievously, yet there was at least some little evidence of comfortable living among the favored classes, for Mrs. Chesnut noted the contrast between the elegance of rich ladies "in their landaus . . . with tall footmen in livery" and the shabbiness of "poor soldiers' wives . . . on the side-walks."[6] Not all the blame could be put upon the Yankees. Referring to the distress of the poor when the war was not half over, Governor Vance of North Carolina wrote: ". . . the demon of speculation and extortion seems to have seized upon nearly all sorts and conditions of men, and all the necessaries of life are fast getting beyond the reach of the poor."[7]

In the shortage of minerals extensive search was made to discover new ore deposits, especially of iron and saltpeter. Much of the supply of common salt for the Confederacy came from the remote hamlet of Saltville in

[2] Moore, *Rebell. Rec.* (Diary), VII, 48.

[3] Massey, *op. cit.*, 72–73.

[4] J. B. Jones, *A Rebel War Clerk's Diary*, II, 89–90. (This famous diarist was sour and often quite extreme in his comments.)

[5] *Ibid.*, I, 196.

[6] *Diary from Dixie*, 155.

[7] Message of Governor Vance to the general assembly, Nov. 17, 1862, *Offic. Rec.*, 4 ser., II, 181. Earlier Vance had written that extortion was so great that it would be impossible to provision the army without "a most enormous outlay and submitting to most outrageous prices." *Ibid.*, 85–86.

southwestern Virginia, where the salt works were destroyed by Union attack in 1864.[8]

Such conditions of disorganization, profiteering, and devastation were continually reflected in the condition of the Southern soldier. Having witnessed 10,000 men marching along the turnpike near Richmond in August, 1863, Mrs. Chesnut recorded their painful contrast to the spick-and-span regiments she had formerly seen. "Such rags and tags as we saw now [she wrote]. Nothing was like anything else. Most garments and arms were . . . taken from the enemy. Such shoes as they had on. . . . Such tin pans . . . tied to their waists. . . . Anything that could be spiked was bayoneted and held aloft." [9]

4

The crushing effect of Union military advance in 1864–1865 brought diverse manifestations in the South, intensifying the zeal of thousands, producing in some an almost fanatical purpose to fight on, yet causing peace agitation and clamor for reunion, bringing talk of a dictator, and undermining confidence in high executive authority. In areas where individualism and backwoods self-sufficiency were strong factors, as in the piney woods of Jones County, Mississippi, the Confederacy encountered spirited opposition. Agitation for peace without realization of Southern war aims was a notable factor in North Carolina. By 1863 the legislature was "ripe for reconstruction" and Jonathan Worth "could say that on a recent trip nearly every man he met was for reconstruction on the basis of the old constitution." Peace efforts "ranged from ostensibly legitimate endeavors to overthrow the Davis government and . . . make . . . peace with the North, to secret plots and conspiracies to overthrow the Confederacy." [1]

One of the symptoms of approaching collapse was the tightening of governmental action against conspiracy. On November 9, 1864, President Davis advised his Congress that "a dangerous conspiracy exists in some of the counties of southwestern Virginia, and in the neighboring portions of North Carolina and Tennessee, which it is found impracticable to suppress by the ordinary course of law," [2] and he referred further to "serious embar-

---

[8] Ella Lonn, *Salt as a Factor in the Confederacy*.

[9] *Diary from Dixie*, 231.

[1] A. Sellew Roberts, in *M.V.H.R.*, XI, 190–199. There is a tradition that Jones County "seceded" from Mississippi and formed the "Republic of Jones," but in fact no such secession occurred. "The county was certainly in the hands of outlaws, who might well have . . . seceded," writes John K. Bettersworth. "Actually, they did . . . agree not to pay taxes. . . ." But "Anarchy rather than government prevailed in this 'free state' during the war; and one must look in vain for anything like an organized movement of counter-secession, even though the fact that the majority of the people were in one way or another disloyal to the Confederacy is fairly well established." *Confederate Mississippi*, 227–236.

[2] *Journal*, Confed. Cong., VII, 266–267.

rassment . . . at Mobile, Wilmington, and Richmond, on account of . . . persons against whom the testimony was sufficient to give full assurance that they were spies or holding treasonable communication with the enemy. . . ." Despite strenuous opposition by those who insisted that the habeas corpus privilege was one of the great bulwarks of freedom whose suspension was not justified under the circumstances, it had become necessary in February of 1864 to pass the third act for the suspension of the writ.[3] This law, in describing the practices to be stamped out, specified combinations to subvert the government of the Confederate States, conspiracies to resist the lawful authorities, communicating intelligence to the enemy, attempting to liberate Northern prisoners in the South, desertion and the aiding of deserters, trading with the enemy, advising or inciting others to abandon the Confederate cause, and attempting to destroy arsenals, foundries, or other property of the Confederate States. In commenting on this legislation, which he opposed, Herschel V. Johnson of Georgia wrote that it was intended mainly to imprison spies and traitors in Richmond and to arrest the disloyal movement of Holden in North Carolina. Johnson's biographer in this connection writes of the "defiant attitude of the states" and the "chaotic condition" which "resulted in the loss of confidence . . . and the earnest desire for the end of the war although without a victorious peace." He adds that this "decline in morale . . . led to the formation of peace societies for the purpose of furthering the cessation of hostilities." [4]

It was perhaps inevitable that in these circumstances the opposition to Davis should become more pronounced. What seems remarkable, however, is the role which the Vice-President, Alexander H. Stephens, played in efforts to unhorse the President. A strict constitutionalist and a devotee of state rights, Stephens opposed every attempt to give Davis the emergency powers so desperately needed in the conduct of the war. If Davis should again be given the right to suspend the writ of habeas corpus, he predicted in 1864, "constitutional liberty will go down, never again to rise on this continent." "Far better that our country should be overrun by the enemy, our cities sacked and burned, and our land laid desolate," the Vice-President gloomily announced, "than that the people should thus suffer the citadel of their liberties to be entered and taken by professed friends." Holding these views, Stephens saw nothing wrong in initiating a peace conspiracy in Georgia, and he heartily endorsed Governor Brown's talk "about re-establishing the principles of the Declaration of Independence—'the *right of all self-government and the sovereignty of the States,*' by which [Brown] meant, as he later said, that each state, Northern and Southern, should 'determine for herself what shall be her future connection, and who her future allies.' " Nothing concrete came of Stephens's peace ma-

[3] *Ibid.,* VI, 805–806; Flippin, *Herschel V. Johnson of Georgia,* 244–245.
[4] Flippin, 246–247.

neuvers, but it is clear that by deliberately schooling "a large fraction of the Southern people to hold the President responsible for their sufferings" he and his associates weakened the Confederate will to fight.[5]

There were, late in the war, suggestions that Lee be made dictator, though that term need not be understood in all its sinister connotations. If not dictator, it was at least obvious that Lee ought to be made supreme commander of all the Confederate forces. President Davis was among the last to realize this. In January, 1865, the Congress passed by substantial majorities a bill to appoint a general-in-chief of the armies, defeating an amendment which would have guarded against interference with the military rights and duties of the President. On February 6, 1865, Lee was appointed to the supreme military office. Thus the Confederacy was almost a year behind the Union government in conferring unified command. When the action was taken, however, it was plainly too late: the "seed corn of the Confederacy had already been ground."

The stress of military pressure in the South was revealed in legislation for the use of Negro troops. On November 7, 1864, President Davis went so far as to approve employment of slave-soldiers as preferable to subjugation, and on February 20, 1865, the Confederate House of Representatives voted that if the President should not be able to raise sufficient troops otherwise, he was authorized to call for additional levies "from such classes . . ., irrespective of color, . . . as the . . . authorities . . . may determine." [6] The final stages of legislation on this subject required considerable time; and the law did not go into effect until March 20, 1865. There was no mistaking the meaning of this action. The fundamental social concept of slavery was slipping; an opening wedge for emancipation had been inserted. Lee's opinion agreed with that of the President and Congress. On January 11, 1865, he wrote advising the enlistment of slaves as soldiers and the granting of "immediate freedom to all who enlist, and freedom at the end of the war to the families of those who discharge their duties faithfully. . . ." [7] This fact, together with other indications, suggests that, even if the Confederacy had survived the war, there was a strong possibility that slavery would be voluntarily abandoned in the South. Southern experiments in the use of slave-soldiers and in emancipation, however, were not put to the test. The law was passed on the eve of surrender and though a few Negro troops were recruited, none actually served in battle.

[5] James Z. Rabun, "Alexander H. Stephens and Jefferson Davis," *Amer. Hist. Rev.*, LVIII, 308, 311 (Jan., 1953); E. Merton Coulter, *The Confederate States of America*, 540.

[6] *Journal*, Confed. Cong., VII, 255, 611–612.

[7] *Offic. Rec.*, 4 ser., III, 1012–1013. Cf. also *ibid.*, 1 ser., XLVI, pt. 3, 1356–1357: letter of Lee (Mar. 27, 1865) to the Confederate secretary of war advising the "raising and organizing [of] the colored troops. . . ." And see Freeman, *Lee*, III, 544.

5

The military decision was not long delayed. As the year 1865 opened, the only operations which could have a bearing upon the main outcome of the war were those in Virginia and the Carolinas. By this time the Hood-Thomas campaign in Tennessee had been terminated. Hood had been pursuing Thomas during the progress of Sherman's Georgia march and the end of November found the armies in the vicinity of the Tennessee capital. In the battle of Franklin (November 30, 1864), about eighteen miles south of Nashville, Hood struck part of the Union army under Schofield in a series of desperate assaults which proved a costly but valorous Southern failure. Schofield lost over 2000 men; Hood over 6000. Hood then put the Unionists under siege in Nashville; and the lack of decisive action on the part of Thomas with his superior numbers caused increased impatience at Washington and at Grant's headquarters. Grant kept sending urgent but unheeded orders to Thomas demanding a battle, and finally sent Logan to supersede him. At this juncture, however, just in time to forestall Logan's actual assumption of command,[1] Thomas finally attacked and pushed his operations against Hood's lines in the two-day battle of Nashville (December 15–16), followed by a vigorous pursuit. Despite magnificent Confederate valor the result was a disastrous defeat for Hood, who had difficulty in making his escape across the Tennessee with a sorry remnant of the fine army which Johnston had turned over to him at Atlanta. One of Lee's chief measures as Confederate general-in-chief was to reinstate Johnston, whose Atlanta campaign against Sherman was now viewed with less disapproval in the light of Hood's failure; and Johnston was now assigned the task of stopping Sherman's advance through the Carolinas.

The advance of Sherman's columns, however, was irresistible. Leaving Savannah February 1, he reached Columbia, South Carolina, on February 17. By March 10 he was in Fayetteville. Up to this point his direction had been toward Raleigh; now he shifted to a more easterly course toward Goldsboro, near which point on March 19 he fought a sharp engagement with Johnston at Bentonville. Sherman did not overwhelm Johnston's inferior force; but he did drive him back, obtaining possession of Goldsboro and of railroads connecting with Wilmington and Beaufort. Fort Fisher had been reduced as noted above; Wilmington had been evacuated (February 22); Sherman's "march" had terminated. Further action by his well-placed army awaited conference with Grant and developments in the Petersburg-Richmond sector.

In the midst of these final campaigns, with Sherman pressing Johnston and with Grant threatening Lee at Petersburg, there occurred a peace con-

[1] On reaching Louisville with orders to take over Thomas's command Logan "found that the work intended for him was already done—and came no farther." *Battles and Leaders*, IV, 456.

ference of high officials. Following an unofficial visit of F. P. Blair, Sr., to Richmond, Lincoln consented to receive Southern agents within Union lines and talk of peace. He had already made clear his principal peace terms in the previous year and had indicated that reunion and abolition were indispensable. On January 12, 1865, President Davis wrote to the informal mediator Blair expressing willingness to enter into conference "with a view to secure peace to the two countries." On seeing the letter Lincoln wrote of his readiness to bring "peace to the people of our one common country." [2] Thus neither war weariness at the North nor approaching collapse at the South served to weaken either side in its concept of fundamental war aims.

Despite this deadlock as to purpose, the conference was held (February 3, 1865) between Lincoln and Seward for the United States and A. H. Stephens, R. M. T. Hunter, and J. A. Campbell for the Confederacy. The scene of the conference was the Union transport *River Queen* lying in Hampton Roads. Lincoln's terms were again set in writing just before the conference. They included three points: (1) reunion; (2) no receding as to emancipation; (3) no cessation of hostilities short of an end of the war and the disbanding of all forces hostile to the government. The last point was one of important difference; Confederate leaders were sparring for an armistice, were thinking of a "suspension" of hostilities if full peace could not be had, and were ready to postpone all matters of negotiation if such suspension could be obtained.

Various matters were discussed by the commissioners: the possibility of an armistice; the postponement of the question of separation; the possible diversion of attention to some extrinsic policy for a period, so that passions might subside; the antislavery policy of the United States; Southern representation in Congress; the attitude to be taken toward punitive measures; and the like. On collateral issues Lincoln showed generosity, assuring the Southerners that executive policy would be lenient and remarking that he would, for himself, be willing to consider compensation to slaveholders. He continued to insist, however, that the Union was a *sine qua non* and that the disbandment of Southern armies was indispensable. Thus the conference adjourned without agreement of views. Lincoln sent the correspondence and records to his Congress and informed them that the Southern commissioners neither assented to reunion nor refused assent, but desired "a postponement of that question, and the adoption of some other course first, which, as some of them, seemed to argue, might, or might not, lead to re-union, but which course, we thought, would amount to an indefinite postponement." [3] The Southern President also made a report to his Congress. He advised them that "the enemy refused to enter into negotiations

---

[2] Lincoln, *Collected Works*, VIII, 275–276.
[3] *Ibid.*, VIII, 279, 285.

with the Confederate States, . . . or to give to our people any other terms . . . than our unconditional submission to their rule. . . ." [4]

During the period of this conference Union troops had been advised that there was no let-up in the war and that they were to be kept in readiness to move on short notice. When the conference broke up in failure, Grant launched his final offensive with a view to hastening the military decision. His efforts before Petersburg had been devoted to extending his lines and guarding against Lee's escape. All the Union forces under Sherman, Sheridan, and Meade, with Grant in supreme command, were now ready to cooperate in the closing campaign, details of which were discussed when Lincoln met Grant and Sherman in a memorable conference on the *River Queen* in the James River at City Point (March 27–28). At this time Lincoln deplored further bloodshed and insisted that generous terms be offered the South.

6

The final campaign was a "study in attenuation." [1] Lee's long line in defense of Richmond was now so thinly manned that a break was inevitable, while Grant was strengthened by the arrival of Sheridan, who had shifted his army southward from Winchester and effected junction with the Army of the Potomac. In the last important battle of the war at Five Forks (April 1) Lee's army was overwhelmed, and this was at once followed by vigorous assaults upon the Confederate lines covering Petersburg, in which large numbers of Confederate prisoners were taken. It was now obvious that Petersburg was untenable and that with it Richmond must also fall. On the afternoon of April 2 Lee gave the order for the evacuation of Petersburg, which was accomplished that night. The next day the Union forces moved in and took possession of the city. It was now a matter of retreat and pursuit. Lee managed his escape well, getting away with nearly all his artillery. He directed his course toward Lynchburg; and Grant feared that from this point, via the Richmond and Danville Railroad, he might escape into North Carolina and join Johnston. Some of the most rapid movement of the war now occurred, with hard marching, sharp cavalry skirmishes, rear-guard actions, and sudden encounters at crossroads and bridges. The Confederate President and cabinet were now in flight; the government had in fact collapsed; regular contact between the President and the army was broken. There was confusion in the army itself, with destruction of reports and public papers, and with many of Lee's companies entirely without officers.

[4] Rowland, *Davis*, VI, 466.

[1] Freeman, *Lee*, IV, 67–73. Freeman writes (IV, 71): "The country had already been stripped of food and of provender. It was worse than a disappointment; it was a catastrophe. Often the loyal old army had been hungry, but now starvation seemed a stark reality."

Grant pushed his columns to the point where Lee's escape was cut off. The diminishing Confederate army was not only trapped but was almost without food. Meanwhile notes had been exchanged between Grant and Lee concerning surrender. On April 7 General Lee, reciprocating Grant's desire to avoid useless effusion of blood, asked for terms. On Sunday the 9th of April in the McLean house in the village of Appomattox Courthouse the opposing commanders met in conference. Grant was not dressed to comport with his rank; his mud-spattered uniform, except for the shoulder-straps, resembled that of a private; his appearance was careless; his brown hair and beard showed no touch of gray. Lee's distinguished gray-bearded head, erect military bearing, and faultless uniform presented a striking contrast.

Terms of surrender, which Grant had put in writing, were discussed. Officers and men of Lee's command were to be released on giving their paroles not to take arms against the United States until exchanged; arms, artillery, and public property were to be turned over. Then Grant added: "This will not embrace the side arms of the officers, nor their private horses or baggage." According to an eye-witness, Lee was visibly touched by this concession, which he said would have a happy effect upon his army; but he had a further point to mention. Not only his officers but his private soldiers in cavalry and artillery owned their own horses; he inquired whether they also could retain them. Grant replied that he would give orders that all the men who claimed to own a horse or mule would be permitted to take them home "to work their little farms." Grant had been generous in his terms; he had avoided any appearance of exultation; he had shown a fine respect for the feelings of his foe. The sword of Lee was not surrendered. Lee did not tender it; Grant did not demand it.[2]

The number of men surrendered by Lee was something over 28,000 as reported by Grant in his memoirs; though the number has been given elsewhere as about 26,000, and the number of rations supplied by Grant to the Confederates was 25,000.[3] In the days preceding surrender Lee's force had rapidly dwindled owing to battle losses, captures, straggling, and the abandonment of the army by many who anticipated the end of the war and were eager to get home. Lee issued an address to his army

[2] *Battles and Leaders,* IV, 738; Grant, *Memoirs,* II, 494; Freeman, *Lee,* IV, 142 n.

[3] Grant, *Memoirs,* II, 500. Grant states (*ibid.*) that in addition to the 28,000 paroled at Appomattox the Federals had captured over 19,000 Confederates between March 29 and the date of surrender, "to say nothing of Lee's other losses. . . ." Rhodes (V, 129) gives the number surrendered as 26,765. According to Lee's statement, confirmed by Taylor of his staff, he had on April 2 a total of 33,000 men from the Chickahominy to Dinwiddie Courthouse. Meade stated that at this time he had over 50,000 south of the James. Freeman, *Lee,* IV, 153. See also *Battles and Leaders,* IV, 742.

expressing appreciation of their "unsurpassed courage and fortitude." Riding back to camp he bade them a personal farewell, then set out for Richmond.

The Confederate capital, meanwhile, had fallen. President Davis and nearly all his cabinet departed by train on the night of Sunday, April 2. Next day they reached Danville. There they lingered a week before making their way southward, the fugitive President and secretaries constituting virtually the only remnant of the civil government of the Confederacy. On April 3 Union troops under Weitzel occupied Richmond, replacing the Stars and Bars with the Stars and Stripes. Fire broke out, and soon a considerable part of the downtown district was in ruins. The distracted city was put under martial law, and Weitzel occupied the mansion just vacated by Jefferson Davis. There was, however, little friction. "The military was for the most part courteous and the people gladly cooperated . . . to restore order." [4] Lincoln arrived April 5, passed through the streets unmolested, visited the erstwhile Confederate White House, conferred with Weitzel, John A. Campbell, and various others, and made clear his wish for peaceable readjustment.

The President returned to Washington and there learned of Lee's surrender. His mind was now occupied with problems of peace and reunion. Just a few weeks prior to this he had been inaugurated for his second term. His inaugural address was notable both for what it contained and what it lacked: he made no attempt to review the events and accomplishments of his administration; he included not a word of bitterness against the enemy; on the contrary he counseled his people to "judge not that we be not judged." Forgiveness and good will were the theme of his peroration: "With malice toward none; with charity for all; . . . let us strive on to finish the work we are in; to bind up the nation's wounds; . . . to do all which may achieve and cherish a just and lasting peace. . . ." On April 11 he delivered one of the principal speeches of his administration, treating the problem of reconstruction in a broad and generous spirit of conciliation.[5] The emancipation amendment to the Constitution had already been passed in Congress. Slavery being virtually gone, Lincoln asked only reunion, and this he would make easy by avoidance of any persecution of the Southern people. On April 14 he held a cabinet meeting at which he expressed the wish that there be no persecution, no bloody work after the war. It was reported that he spoke kindly of Lee and others of the Confederacy.[6] Next day the President lay dead. On the night of April 14 at Ford's Theater he had been shot by a desperate assassin, John Wilkes Booth. Secretary Sew-

[4] Mary N. Stanard. *Richmond: Its People and Its Story,* 209.
[5] See below, pp. 556–557.
[6] There are various records of this last cabinet meeting. See Rhodes, V, 137–138.

ard, recently injured in a carriage accident, was severely wounded by one of Booth's fellow conspirators. Another conspirator, detailed to kill Vice-President Johnson, had withheld his blow.

Assassination night and the following days were a time of rage, horror, dread, and wild rumor. Satisfaction at the end of the war was spoiled by this tragedy. Feelings of good will, difficult enough to foster after four years of hatred and strife, were further endangered by the removal of Lincoln's influence and by gross injustice to Confederate leaders who were falsely accused of complicity in the assassination.

News was now awaited from Sherman. Moving forward from Goldsboro he occupied Raleigh (doing no violence to its people) on April 13. Johnston's army facing him was not surrounded; it might, conceivably, have escaped and joined other Confederate forces in the Southwest. Yet Johnston as well as Sherman felt that to continue the war was useless slaughter. The fugitive Confederate President thought otherwise. On April 4 he had issued an address to the Southern people in which he spoke of continuing the war by "operating in the interior . . ., where supplies are more accessible, and where the foe will be far removed from his own base. . . ." He asked his people for that unquenchable resolve which alone was needed to "render our triumph certain." The very day of the surrender at Appomattox he had written Lee of his anxiety to "win success North of the Roanoke." After Appomattox his thoughts turned to the trans-Mississippi where he thought the Confederate government and army could continue the struggle. Reaching Greensboro he conferred with Johnston and Beauregard. He still talked in military terms and thought the enemy could be whipped. In his letter to Johnston on April 11 he wrote that the important question was "at what point shall concentration be made, in view of the present position of the two columns of the enemy, ..." [7] In contrast to this, Johnston at the Greensboro conference gave the President some plain talk, telling him that the Southern people were tired of war, that his men were rapidly deserting, and that the true course was to consult Sherman as to terms.

There followed a meeting between Johnston and Sherman (April 13–18) at which Sherman presented terms of capitulation so broadly phrased as to cover political reconstruction. Not a lawyer or a politician, Sherman thought he was following the spirit of Lincoln's generous program of reconstruction, which had so recently been conveyed to him at City Point by the President himself. In fact, however, Sherman's terms of peace went far beyond anything Lincoln could have contemplated, for they inadvertently "guaranteed property in slaves, left a chance for the payment of Confederate war debts, recognized insurgent state governments, and might well have put in question the authority of . . . Union state governments"

[7] Rowland, *Davis*, VI, 530, 541, 544.

already set up in the South.[8] Naturally President Johnson and his cabinet promptly overruled the general, and Secretary Stanton sternly ordered him to set aside the agreement he had drawn up. Sherman then arranged another conference with Johnston at the Bennett house near Durham Station, North Carolina (April 26),[9] where terms of capitulation similar to those accorded Lee at Appomattox were signed. In the Southwest, General James H. Wilson had pursued Forrest and captured Selma and Montgomery when news came of Johnston's surrender. The final disbandment of the remaining Confederate forces followed almost automatically. On May 4 at Citronelle, Alabama, the Confederate general Richard Taylor surrendered to E. R. S. Canby what remained of the forces east of the Mississippi, including those of Forrest's command. Three weeks later (May 26) Kirby Smith at New Orleans [10] surrendered to Canby the forces beyond the Mississippi; and with this capitulation Southern military resistance to Federal control of the South was at an end.[11]

7

Because of the lack of reliable and comparable records it may never be possible to say, except by more or less reasonable conjecture, actually how many men served in the Union and Confederate armies. Many Southerners have been inclined to accept the estimate that the Confederate armies numbered 600,000, while those of the Union numbered 2,778,304.[1] General Marcus J. Wright of the Confederate service, employed by the United States war department in the collection of Confederate archives, considered the best estimate of the Confederate total to be 600,000 to 700,000 men.[2] There have been numerous studies of the subject, both investigational and controversial. T. L. Livermore, who has made elaborate calculations, ar-

---

[8] Raoul S. Naroll, "Lincoln and the Sherman Peace Fiasco—Another Fable?" *J.S.H.*, XX, 483 (Nov., 1954).

[9] W. K. Boyd, *The Story of Durham: City of the New South*, 41 ff.

[10] The conference concerning Smith's surrender occurred at Baton Rouge; the surrender at New Orleans. *Ann. Cyc.*, 1865, 74.

[11] General Stand Watie, a Cherokee chieftain, was one of the last Confederate officers to surrender, not yielding up his sword until June 23, 1865.

[1] Estimate of Cazenove G. Lee, *So. Hist. Soc. Papers*, XXXII, 46.

[2] *Ibid.*, XIX, 254. Other statements worth noting are the "Consolidated Abstract from returns of the Confederate forces on or about Dec. 31, 1862 (compiled from such returns as are on file in the War Department)" showing 449,439 names (*Offic. Rec.*, 4 ser., II, 278), and the tabular statement of the Confederate bureau of conscription giving 566,456 as the number of volunteers and conscripts in January, 1864, from only six of the eleven Confederate states, namely Virginia, the Carolinas, Georgia, Alabama, and Mississippi (*ibid.*, 4 ser., III, 102). This statement is seriously at variance with the estimate of 600,000 for all the states of the Confederacy for the whole period of the war. H. J. Eckenrode places the approximate Confederate total at 800,000 (*Jefferson Davis*, 339).

rives at "1,227,890 as the total number of [Confederate] enlistments opposed to the 2,898,304 enlistments in the Union army during the war." This conclusion is obtained by the somewhat doubtful method of multiplying the known number of regular regiments (849) by the estimated average per regiment (1330) and then adding 98,720 for irregular organizations not officially enrolled.[3]

It must be remembered that there were more "enlistments" than individual soldiers, since many of the men enlisted several times, and also that an "enlistment" is not a definite unit of comparison because of wide variations in length of service. Some Union enlistments were for two or three weeks, many were for three months, others for three years. Many were the occasions when whole regiments re-enlisted. Desertion and bounty-jumping, as above noted,[4] accounted for many repeaters. There is a further complication owing to the fact that Union enlistments exceeded the number of soldiers to a greater extent than did Confederate enlistments.[5] Though there were 2,898,304 enlistments in the Union army and navy, it has been estimated by a careful military statistician (Col. W. F. Fox) that "[over] 300,000 [Federal] men enlisted just before the close of the war, few of whom, if any, participated in . . . active service."[6] Colonel Fox adds: "It is doubtful if there were 2,000,000 individuals actually in [Union] service during the war." Livermore, however, places the estimate at 2,300,000 individuals.[7]

Reducing the number of soldiers with their varying terms to equivalent numbers for a three-year term, Livermore gives 1,556,678 as the Union figure, while he estimates 1,082,119 as the total Confederate levies on this three-year basis.[8] These calculations have been adopted by Rhodes, but not by Channing.[9] The present writers are inclined to take Livermore's work as one of the important exhibits in the testimony rather than as a definitive verdict on the whole case. A significant fact, showing the man power still unexhausted at the North, is that at the end of April, 1865, the number of Federal men in the field amounted to about 1,000,000, while the "national forces" not yet called out by the Union government exceeded 2,000,000. It is also worth noting that according to official reckoning there were more men in the "loyal" states "properly subject" to military call at the end of the war than at the beginning.[10]

[3] Thomas L. Livermore, *Numbers and Losses in the Civil War* . . . , 2nd ed. (1901), 39.
[4] See above, pp. 328–331.
[5] T. L. Livermore, in *Proceedings*, Mass. Hist. Soc., 2 ser., XVIII, 440.
[6] W. F. Fox, *Regimental Losses in the American Civil War, 1861–65* (1889), 527.
[7] *Proceedings*, Mass. Hist. Soc., 2 ser., XVIII, 441.
[8] *Numbers and Losses*, 50, 61.
[9] Rhodes, *Hist. of the U. S.*, V, 186 ff.; Channing, *Hist. of the U. S.*, VI, 431.
[10] *Offic. Rec.*, 3 ser., V, 620.

There is another body of evidence that should not be ignored. The census of 1890 recorded 432,020 Confederate and 1,034,073 Union veterans then living.[11] To reconcile this evidence with the Southern estimate of 600,000 Confederates to 2,778,000 Federals would imply that over seventy per cent of the Confederate soldiers lived until twenty-five years after the war, while only thirty-seven per cent of the Federal soldiers survived for that period. One need not enter upon the question of the padding of veterans' rolls after the war, which doubtless occurred on both sides, but the census figures have been regarded by competent authorities as worthy of attention.[12]

If writhing and gasping men can be reduced to "reports" and statistics, it may be noted that the war cost a million casualties. Total deaths in the Union army have been figured at 360,222,[13] of which 110,070 were from battle wounds. Wounded Federals have been said to number 275,175. On the Confederate side the number of wounded survivors seems too uncertain to record here, but the Confederate dead have been estimated at 258,000, of whom 94,000 are estimated to have been killed or fatally wounded in battle. If the Confederate wounded be placed at no more than half the Federal, it will be seen that the grand total of the military casualties exceeds a million.

The complete cost of the war would include a variety of other factors: billions of treasure (Federal, Confederate, state, local, and unofficial), untold retardation of economic development, ruined homes, roads, buildings and fields, billions of dollar-value in slaves wiped out, a shattered mer-

[11] *U. S. Census,* 1890 ("Population," pt. II), 803–804. Livermore gives the census total incorrectly, omitting Union Negroes. *Proceedings,* Mass. Hist. Soc., 2 ser., XVIII, 441.

[12] The following further citations concerning comparative numbers may be noted: *Offic. Rec.,* 3 ser., IV, 1269; "War Debts of the Loyal States," *House Report No. 16,* 39 Cong., 1 sess., 5–6; "Confederate Handbook" (Confederate Museum, Richmond); article by "Our Special Correspondent," N. Y. *Tribune,* June 26, 1867, pp. 1–2; articles in various issues of the *So. Hist. Soc. Papers* (II, 6–21; VII, 287–290; XX, 238–259; XXXII, 46–50); Randolph H. McKim, *Numerical Strength of the Confederate Army* . . . (1912); A. B. Casselman, "The Numerical Strength of the Confederate Army," *Century,* Mar., 1892, 792–796; *Battles and Leaders of the Civil War,* IV, 767–768; A. B. Casselman, in *Current History,* Jan., 1923, 653–657; Arthur H. Jennings, *ibid.,* Apr., 1924, 113–115; *World Almanac,* 1959, 741. Nicolay and Hay, *Lincoln,* X, 339; Edward Atkinson, in *Forum,* Oct., 1888, 133; *The Medical and Surgical History of the War of the Rebellion* (6 vols., Washington); W. F. Fox, *op. cit.; House Exec. Doc. No. 1,* 39 Cong., 1 sess. For a good summary and bibliography, see Channing, *Hist. of the U. S.,* VI, 430–434. Channing writes (p. 434) that presumably 800,000 "at one time or another served in the armed forces of the seceded States." He notes that 300,000 Southern whites are "supposed to have served in the Union armies" (p. 434).

[13] This figure (360,222 grand aggregate Union deaths) is given in *Battles and Leaders,* IV, 767 n. The main facts as to costs and casualties are summarized in *ibid.,* IV, 767–768.

chant marine, and a wretched intangible heritage of hate, extravagance, corruption, truculence, partisan excess (lasting for decades), and intolerance.[14] It has become traditional to strew flowers over these wretched memories and to assume that the vast holocaust was either a necessary sacrifice for the Union or so gallant an adventure as to constitute a justifiable failure. These are sentiments and they lie outside the scope of this book. The proven fact is the failure of statesmen North and South to manage the crisis of 1860–1861, when, for instance, the device of a fully representative official national convention, earnestly recommended by moderates, was not tried, while truculent shoutings and strident declarations, having produced the impression that bloodshed was inevitable, made it a reality.

[14] Fred A. Shannon (*America's Economic Growth*, 3rd ed., 325–326) places the total financial cost of the Civil War, including Confederate war expenses, cancellation of title to property in slaves, destruction of property by armies, state war debts, pensions to 1917, and interest on the Federal debt, at around twenty billion dollars.

THE RESTORED UNION

CHAPTER 31

Presidential Reconstruction

THE RECONSTRUCTION period is one of the most controversial eras in American history. During the twelve years after the Civil War basic changes took place which were fundamentally to alter the future course of American history. It is from the reconstruction period that one dates the dominance of industrial over agrarian forces in the American economy. These same years saw the final repudiation of the theory that the American government rested upon state rights and the emergence of the omnicompetent Federal government. The period also witnessed the formal rejection of caste as the basis for the American social order and the inclusion in the Constitution of a pledge that henceforth "race, color, or previous condition of servitude" should not disqualify a man from full participation in the benefits of that society. Inevitably such drastic changes, coming so closely together, aroused bitter hostility among contemporaries, a feeling which later historians of the era have all too often shared.

Since writers have so frequently spoken of the reconstruction period as "The Tragic Era" or "The Age of Hate," it is helpful at the outset to remember that the treatment given the South after the war was, in James Ford Rhodes's words, "the mildest punishment ever inflicted after an unsuccessful Civil War." The North required of the South, as Paul H. Buck has said, recognition of "three general positions as logical consequences of the war. First, the doctrine of secession was renounced and the Union was recognized . . . to be one and indissoluble. Secondly, the institution of slavery was forever destroyed. And thirdly, it was more or less tacitly recognized that the prewar leadership of the Southern slavocrat in national politics was permanently to be replaced in favor of Northern direction." [1]

To many white Southerners these conditions seemed oppressively severe, but they must be measured against the crushing reparations, the mass deportation of peoples, and the genocide which have followed later wars. With the exception of Major Henry Wirz, commander of the notorious

[1] Buck, *The Road to Reunion* (Vintage ed.), 9.

Andersonville prison, who was hanged, no Confederate was executed for "war crimes." [2] Only a few Southern political leaders were even imprisoned for their part in the "rebellion," and, except for Jefferson Davis, their release was prompt.[3] Though slavery was abolished during the war, the reconstruction period saw no mass confiscation of the property of ex-Confederates.[4] Despite the fourteenth and fifteenth amendments to the Constitution, which remained largely impotent to protect the Negro, no direct assault was made upon "the greatest obstacle to the Negroes' salvation, the Southern caste system." It is, therefore, as Francis B. Simkins remarks, a capital blunder to treat the period "like Carlyle's portrayal of the French Revolution, as a melodrama involving wild-eyed conspirators whose acts are best described in red flashes upon a canvas." Instead, as Professor Simkins reminds us, during these postwar years the life of both Negroes and whites in the South "remained relatively wholesome and happy; there was little of the misery, hatred, and repression often sweepingly ascribed to it by writers." [5]

It is also important to remember that the reconstruction period cannot properly be understood in terms of legal or constitutional issues. It was, in fact, an abnormal time and, like all anomalous situations, it forced the principal participants into ambiguous and self-contradictory positions. After having fought heroically for their independence, Southerners, in defeat, now claimed that they had never legally been out of the Union. On the

[2] In addition, Professor Buck has found, one "obscure private was convicted of manslaughter and sentenced to a term in prison." *Ibid.*, 49.

[3] Among the Confederates briefly imprisoned were Vice-President A. H. Stephens, J. A. Campbell, B. H. Hill, S. T. Mallory, J. H. Reagan, and George A. Trenholm. Southern military chieftains were generally unmolested. On Davis, see below, pp. 646–648.

[4] No effort is here being made to minimize the severe sufferings of the South after 1865 (see below, pp. 543–546), but it must be emphasized such economic losses as the abolition of slavery, the repudiation of the Confederate debt, and the failure of Southern banks were due not to reconstruction policies but to the South's defeat in the war. There was, however, some confiscation of Confederate property, chiefly during the war years. Cotton worth about $30,000,000 was seized by United States treasury agents during and after the war under the captured property act. Randall, "Captured and Abandoned Property during the Civil War," *Am. Hist. Rev.*, XIX, 65–79. In addition, some Confederate homes and other property were seized. For example, the mansion and grounds of Arlington, Lee's proud estate across the Potomac from Washington, had been taken over by the Federal government and made into a national cemetery primarily for soldiers. Later the Lee heirs were paid $150,000 for this property. Randall, *Constitutional Problems under Lincoln*, 320–322. Perhaps the harshest economic measure of the reconstruction period directed specifically against the South was the special cotton tax of two and one-half cents a pound (increased to three cents in 1866), which extracted from the prostrate ex-Confederate states about $68,000,000. E. Merton Coulter, *The South during Reconstruction*, 10.

[5] Simkins, "New Viewpoints of Southern Reconstruction," *J. S. H.*, V, 56, 51, 53–54 (Feb., 1939).

other hand, Radical Republicans, who had been bending every effort to keep the South in the United States, now announced that the Confederate states had in fact seceded, thereby committing suicide or reverting to a territorial status. In the ensuing quarrel between President and Congress, both antagonists sought to give respectability to their arguments by invoking the Constitution, but in fact the President, by appointing military governors for the Southern states, and the Congress, by imposing conditions upon the suffrage there, were both behaving in an extra-Constitutional fashion. As William A. Russ, Jr., has soundly observed, "Neither Congress nor the President was helped much by an appeal to the Constitution, because the Fathers in 1787 had not envisioned such a situation as the rebellion presented." [6]

These perplexities and ambiguities, too often interpreted as willfulness or malignancy on the part of politicians of the period, reflected the almost insoluble intricacy of the reconstruction problem. On the basic outlines of that problem virtually everybody, North and South, agreed. Somehow the seceded states must be brought back into a proper relation with the rest of the Union; somehow the war-torn economy of the South had to be rebuilt; somehow the newly freed Negro had to be protected in his rights; and, most important but most difficult, somehow a feeling of loyalty to the American Union must be restored among white Southerners. Such was the problem. It was only about the solutions that disagreement arose.

I

Had the entire nation given its full attention to the problem of restoring the former Confederate states, the difficulties would still have been all but insurmountable, but, despite the amount of oratory devoted to the subject in the halls of Congress, this was not the sole, or even the primary, concern of most Americans in the years following the war. The real temper of the people was reflected not in the angry speeches in the Senate but in the rapid demobilization of the wartime armies. Southern forces disintegrated promptly after the surrenders of Lee and Johnston. The Northern armies went to pieces almost as quickly. The Union legions tramped in grand review along Pennsylvania Avenue in Washington on May 23–24, 1865. After that display the disbandment of the military forces proceeded rapidly. By August, 1865, 640,000 men had been mustered out; by November 15, over 800,000.[1] By September 30, 1867, the army had a total strength of only 56,815 officers and men. "Of the great volunteer army . . . [wrote the adjutant general] there then remained in the serv-

[6] Russ, "The Struggle between President Lincoln and Congress over Disfranchisement of Rebels," *Susquehanna Univ. Studies,* III, 229 (Mar., 1948).

[1] *Ann. Cyc.,* 1865, 33.

ice but 203 officers, and no enlisted men." [2] A year later the regular army numbered only 43,741 (soon to be considerably reduced); and the traditional military policy of the United States (involving a small standing army, no peace-time conscription nor universal service, absence of a general staff, no system of inducting new men continuously into the army nor of using the professional force for the training of reserves, reliance upon special recruiting and possible wartime conscription for an emergency force) remained the basic army pattern of a spirited but unmilitarized people.

Tired of war, most Americans wanted to get back to the business of making a living. To many the economic slump which immediately followed the peace seemed of as much importance as the future of the ex-Confederate states. Rendigs Fels has pointed out some of the difficulties in making the economic transition from war to peace: "A federal budget deficit of almost one billion dollars in the fiscal year 1865—perhaps one seventh of national income—dropped to less than zero in 1866. The wartime speculative boom in wholesale prices collapsed early in 1865. . . . Pig-iron production [geared to war contracts] . . . fell from 1,136 thousand long tons in 1864 to 932 in 1865. One and a half million men who had been directly or indirectly engaged in prosecuting the war were released to the working force. In addition, the working force had to absorb a stream of 300,000 immigrants in each of the fiscal years 1866 and 1867, compared to 180,000 in 1865." [3] In consequence, the cyclical contraction which began in April, 1865, continued until December, 1867. It was, however, relatively mild and was followed by a period of great prosperity. Between 1866 and 1878 agricultural output doubled in the United States. The number of miles of railroad operated in the United States leaped from 35,085 in 1865 to 81,747 in 1878. [4] Until 1873, therefore, the energies and attention of the country were directed not so much toward the problem of reconstruction as toward the enjoyment of prosperity; after that date, the prolonged depression of 1873–1879 absorbed most men's attention.

These postwar years saw the emergence of unprecedented consolidations in fields of basic industry. Notable among the examples of this movement were the consolidations in steel and oil. The period preceding the Civil War had witnessed an expansion of iron products, the production of pig iron increasing fivefold from 1830 to 1860. Then came the perfection of the Kelly-Bessemer process of steel blasting; but it was not till the Grant period that the extensive use of this epochal improvement was evident in the formation of huge steel works. In one of his trips to England after the war Andrew Carnegie gazed on a Bessemer converter and was en-

[2] *Ibid.*, 1867, 56.
[3] Fels, *American Business Cycles, 1865–1897*, 92.
[4] *Hist. Statistics of the U. S.*, 200.

tranced. "Give it thirty thousand pounds of common pig iron, and presto! the whole mass was blown into steel." [5] Funds were assembled; the firm of Carnegie, McCandless, and Company was organized with a capital of $700,000; the Edgar Thompson Steel Works were soon in operation; railroad deals were negotiated; and the Carnegie syndicate soon commanded a group of consolidations including rolling mills, bridge works, and steel plants which constituted the largest system of steel properties ever mobilized under one management. In 1874 one Carnegie mill set a world record by turning out a hundred tons of iron in one day.

Meanwhile a world empire of oil had seen its bold beginnings when John D. Rockefeller at the age of twenty-six formed in 1865 a Cleveland firm which was reorganized in 1870 as the Standard Oil Company of Ohio with a capital of $1,000,000. From that point the business expanded by such leaps that in ten years it controlled ninety per cent of the refining business of the country. The later history of the enterprise as a huge consolidation under the title of Standard Oil Company of New Jersey with numerous subsidiaries does not concern us here. What is relevant to the present theme is that the reconstruction era witnessed the germination of those methods by which the oil trust extended its power. Separate businesses, according to these methods, were assembled under a set of trustees, a perfect formula for unimpeded control by a few at the top. Rivals were snuffed out by underselling campaigns in certain areas and by other practices none too choice. Crude oil sources and transportation systems were extensively acquired, huge selling organizations were set up, a species of pool known as the South Improvement Company was launched, and special rebates in freight charges were obtained by secret arrangements with railroads. Other branches of industry were not slow to catch step. Pillsbury applied the new capitalism in flour milling, Armour and Swift in meat packing, Jay Cooke in finance, Vanderbilt, Huntington, and others in railroads, Wells and Fargo in western express service. Practices of the Lincoln age were already outmoded. A race of industrial kings was coming upon the American scene.

The cessation of war made it possible to restore scientific progress and renew the projects of ambitious inventors. Conspicuous among these was the Atlantic cable. This enterprise, promoted by such choice spirits as Cyrus and David Dudley Field, Peter Cooper, S. F. B. Morse, Moses Taylor, and various Englishmen, had achieved only momentary success in 1858. After the war the project was vigorously renewed. In 1865 the *Great Eastern* laid down twelve hundred miles of cable in the ocean, but the cable parted, and a fresh beginning had to be made. Success finally came in 1866, and on July 27 of that year oceanic telegraph connection between America and Europe was achieved, never again to be broken.

[5] Herbert N. Casson, *The Romance of Steel: the Story of a Thousand Millionaires,* 83.

Engineering wonders such as the Brooklyn bridge (1872–1883) and the Eads bridge at St. Louis (1874) were altering both the visible and the spiritual horizon of the people. Inventions such as the telephone and type-writer were revolutionizing business methods. City life was quick to catch the tempo. Chicago, laid in ruins by a mammoth fire in 1871, was promptly rebuilt in brick and stone and from that time forward progressively lifted from the prairie mud and reclaimed from Lake Michigan. It rapidly be-came not only the business hub for the great Middle West but the focusing point of culture and (with sorry exceptions in politics) a center of inspir-ing endeavor. Though at the end of the reconstruction period the cities were backward in community planning and the substitution of paving systems for cobblestones and mud, and while many were boss-ridden, the measure of their progress in material things—in street lamps, palatial hotels, department stores, plate glass, elevators, elevated railroads, refrigerators, streetcars, and hackney cabs—was indeed generous. The multiplication of private mansions in the cities to be tenanted by social nobodies suddenly raised to wealth demonstrated that social standards were becoming less a matter of inheritance and background and more a matter of hard cash. Multimillionaires were numerous enough to cause Ward McAllister to feel concern for the fine old families and to bethink himself of erecting new barriers against those who sought to crash the gates of exclusive New York society by means of wealth alone.

The West, too, shared in this phenomenal postwar expansion. Thou-sands of immigrants poured into the North Central states, eager to find their fortunes on the farm. Between 1865 and 1890 there was a "great surge of Canadians in Iowa, Minnesota, Kansas, Nebraska, and the Da-kotas." Immigration from the three Scandinavian countries "reached 10,000 a year by 1865, and attained a peak of 105,326 in 1882"; most of them settled in the Middle West. Some bought land directly from the government; others purchased farms from the railroads, to which the Fed-eral government gave huge grants; and still others took advantage of the homestead system. By 1900, according to Fred A. Shannon, "possibly 400,000 families, totaling 2,000,000 people, got free land from the gov-ernment and kept it for themselves." The production of wheat nearly tripled during the reconstruction years, leaping from 152,000,000 bush-els in 1866 to 420,000,000 in 1878. By 1880 the two North Central re-gions were producing 71.6 per cent of the total wheat crop of the United States.[6]

With the expansion of agriculture and the extension of railroads the process of "eliminating" the Indians was notably quickened. On the part of the red man there were violence and savage retribution. Much of this, however, was due to shameless exploitation of the natives by white settlers.

[6] Shannon, *The Farmer's Last Frontier,* 47, 49, 55, 417, 162.

While thoughtful statesmen sought to deal with the problem by peaceful negotiation and such observance of contracts as would insure justice to the natives and protection to the pioneers, vicious forces were at work to defeat these ends by military encroachment, squatter violence, corruption among Indian agents, avarice in trading, shameful cheating, border feuds, and various "wars." When George A. Custer fell with more than 250 of his men at the climax of the Sioux War in 1876, the tragedy of the Black Hills illustrated the desperation of the more warlike tribes in resisting expatriation, loss of tribal lands, white depredation, and destruction of independence. It was not alone Custer's last stand: it marked the transition of the Indian problem from the day of heroics to that of commonplace reservation life. Already even in the West the Indian was becoming somewhat of a museum piece. It is an amusing misconception, prominent abroad and in the East, which has pictured western America as one vast Indian and buffalo country. The total number of Indians in the United States in 1871 was estimated at only 321,000. It was a dwindling number, for in 1885 the Indian population outside Alaska was mentioned as 260,000; [7] and the sight of a Comanche or Sioux unattached to a reservation or Wild West show was a rare event.

In no field was the postwar business boom more evident than in railroad building. The famous "driving of the last spike" near Ogden, Utah, on May 10, 1869, indicated with characteristic American flourish the completion of the first continental line. What followed was a veritable mania of railroad construction. It is significant that many of the prominent men of the time turned in some form to railroad effort, as in the case of Charles Francis Adams (brother of Henry), George B. McClellan, Robert Todd Lincoln, C. M. Depew, and John A. Dix. Princely fees were being paid by the roads for the services of such a lawyer as William M. Evarts. Not only lines, but huge transportation systems, were built up. Leland Stanford and Collis Huntington in the Far West, Vanderbilt, Thompson, and Gould in the East, and numerous others in between, demonstrated the "killings" and fortunes obtainable in railroad enterprise. With Jay Gould and his confederate Jim Fisk capitalistic enterprise became a matter of manipulation, market rigging, and vicious plunder. While consolidations were rapidly promoted to the accompaniment of rebates, pools, and discriminatory practices, and while the public was mulcted by huge frauds in the investment field, Federal regulation lagged and unethical practices even received governmental encouragement as in the Crédit Mobilier scandal and excessive donations of public land and Federal bonds.

The zeal with which the building of roads outran the needs of population and business was little short of fantastic. The expansive optimism

[7] Oberholtzer, III, 384; Richardson, *Messages and Papers*, VIII, 355.

of Mark Twain's Colonel Sellers in projecting his grand schemes on a shoe-string becomes more than fiction when one turns to the census report on railroads and finds in sober official print scores of lines such as the "Horn Pond Branch Railroad Company," the "Bells Gap Railroad Company," the "Duck River Valley N. G. Railroad Company," or the "Paw Paw Railroad Company." [8] In 1870 there were 49,000 railroad miles for thirty-eight million people in America; in 1880 there were 87,000 for fifty million. Five years later, with 125,000 miles in operation, the United States had more than forty-five hundredths of the railway mileage of the world.[9] Not only the magnitude but also the equipment of the lines, with their Pullman cars and Westinghouse brakes commanded admiration. On the other hand, lack of regulation, haphazard planning, shallow and vicious capitalistic promotion, irresponsible management, disregard of the public and the stockholder, unnecessary construction, fraudulent finance, and many abuses were causing painful shock and indignant inquiry on the part of an outraged public.

Confronting these economic developments, most Northerners in the post-Civil War decade could give but half an ear to the South and its difficulties; they were instead absorbed with "social and economic disputes as old as the nation itself, in which the Civil War was but an interlude." [10] One group of historians has viewed these economic conflicts as a continuation of an age-old struggle between West and East, between agrarianism and industrialism. It is argued that Northeastern businessmen, who had greatly profited during the war and who were now protected by high tariffs, were benefiting from the national banking system, and were drawing interest in gold upon bonds for which they had paid in depreciated greenbacks, were threatened by Western farmers, who banded together in the Granger movement [11] to combat what William H. Herndon, Lincoln's former law partner, called "Your tariffs for protection, your exclusive banking system—your monopolies—your granted exclusive privileges—your building up of classes at the expense of the general man." [12] In this economic struggle, it is alleged, the South was a pawn. Western agrarian Democrats, hoping for allies among Southern white farmers, favored

[8] Other roads bore such names as "Suncook Valley," "Eel River," "Ruby Hill," and "Pioche and Bullionville." *Report . . . on Transportation,* Census Office, Wash., 1883, 310 ff.

[9] Report of the Senate select committee on interstate commerce, *Sen. Report No. 46,* 49 Cong., 1 sess., p. 5.

[10] Howard K. Beale, "The Tariff and Reconstruction," *Am. Hist. Rev.,* XXXV, 276 (Jan., 1930).

[11] In 1867 Oliver Hudson Kelley, a clerk in the department of agriculture, helped organize the Patrons of Husbandry, generally known as the Grange. Originally a social and educational organization, it came by the 1870's to be interested in political action and sponsored anti-monopoly legislation.

[12] Donald, *Lincoln's Herndon,* 261.

speedy readmission of the Southern states; Eastern business Republicans, fearing "a blended Copperhead and Rebel ascendency," which "could not help assailing the National Debt, disturbing the safeguards of our National Industry, and many other things equally provocative," demanded that stringent conditions be met before the ex-Confederate states were readmitted.[13] As Howard K. Beale has concisely expressed this view, "If Southern economic interests had coincided with those of the rising industrial groups of the North, there would have been no Radical reconstruction." [14]

Though there is an element of truth in this picture, it is largely a distortion, for neither Western farmers nor Eastern businessmen formed anything like a solid political bloc. On each of the principal economic issues before the country, Eastern business views were characterized by "diversity . . ., not uniformity"; [15] while farmers, basking in postwar prosperity, did not attempt "large-scale organization to achieve their economic and political objectives" until after the panic of 1873.[16] On the whole it is more accurate to view the economic struggles of the reconstruction period not so much as a clearcut sectional or even class fight but as "a contest between opposing banking, investing, mercantile, industrial, labor, and agricultural interests that was fought out on intra-sectional as well as inter-sectional lines." [17] The point here to emphasize, however, is that these economic controversies both affected Northern views of the Southern question and kept the best brains in the nation from squarely facing the problems of reconstruction.

2

That the South in these postwar years desperately needed the best thought the country could give was only too apparent. The South had been broken by the war. Lands were devastated. Proud plantations were now mere wrecks. Billions of economic value in slaves had been wiped away by emancipation measures without that compensation which Lincoln himself had admitted to be equitable. Difficult social problems presented themselves in the sudden elevation of a servile race to the status of free laborers and enfranchised citizens. Accumulated capital had disappeared. Banks were shattered; factories were dismantled; the structure of business intercourse had crumbled. In Atlanta, Columbia, Mobile, Richmond, and many other places great havoc had been wrought by fire.

The interior of South Carolina, in the wake of Sherman's march,

---

13 New York *Tribune*, quoted in Beale, *loc. cit.*, 280.
14 Beale, *The Critical Year*, 225.
15 Irwin Unger, "Business Men and Specie Resumption," *Political Science Quart.*, LXXIV, 69 (Mar., 1959).
16 Sharkey, *Money, Class, and Party*, 104.
17 Chester M. Destler, *American Radicalism*, 49.

"looked for many miles like a broad black streak of ruin and desolation—
the fences all gone; lonesome smoke stacks, surrounded by dark heaps of
ashes and cinders, marking the spots where human habitations had stood;
the fields along the road wildly overgrown by weeds, with here and there a
sickly looking patch of cotton or corn cultivated by negro squatters. In the
city of Columbia . . . a thin fringe of houses encircl[ed] a confused mass
of charred ruins of dwellings and business buildings, which had been destroyed by a sweeping conflagration." [1] The Tennessee valley, according to
the account of an English traveler, "consists for the most part of plantations in a state of semi-ruin, and plantations of which the ruin is for the
present total and complete. . . . The trail of war is visible throughout
the valley in burnt up gin-houses, ruined bridges, mills, and factories, of
which latter the gable walls only are left standing, and in large tracts of
once cultivated land stripped of every vestige of fencing. . . . Borne
down by losses, debts, and accumulating taxes, many who were once the
richest among their fellows have disappeared from the scene, and few
have yet risen to take their places." [2]

Many of the people had no homes. "From Winchester to Harrisonburg
scarce a crop, fence, chicken, horse, cow, or pig was in sight. . . . Extreme destitution prevailed throughout the entire valley. All able-bodied
negroes had left; only those unfit to work remained. The country between
Washington and Richmond was . . . like a desert." [3] Southerners were
without adequate currency. They had put their wealth into Confederate
bonds or had given their produce for such bonds; now these securities, together with Confederate money, were utterly worthless. Prominent men,
including Confederate generals, were "asking what they could do to earn
their bread." The city of Richmond may be taken as an example. A Federal
relief commission was formed; the city was divided into thirty districts;
and house-to-house visiting was instituted. By April 21, 1865, rations to
the number of 128,000 had been issued; and it was estimated that 15,000
persons had been given relief.[4] A report of the time stated that 35,000 persons in the region near Atlanta were dependent for subsistence upon the
Federal government, and that in Atlanta itself there were 15,000 recipi-
ents. Many Confederate soldiers, just discharged from Northern prisons,
were given rations. A Southern soldier remarked that "it must be a matter of
gratitude as well as surprise, for our people to see a Government which was
lately fighting us with fire, and sword, and shell, now generously feeding

[1] *Reminiscences of Carl Schurz*, III, 167.

[2] Robert Somers, *The Southern States Since the War* (1871), 114. Somers
was an English traveler in the South after the war.

[3] McMaster, *Lincoln's Administration*, 637.

[4] Mary N. Stanard, *Richmond: Its People and Its Story*, 212. See also *Offic.
Rec.*, 1 ser., XLVI, pt. 3, pp. 882–884.

our poor and distressed. . . . There is much in this that takes away the bitter sting . . . of the past." [5]

The war, as already noted, killed a quarter of a million soldiers of the South. The number of civilians that perished as a by-product of the struggle cannot be estimated. What had taken place was the collapse of a civilization. In one community in South Carolina, wrote a contemporary observer, "lived a gentleman whose income, when the war broke out, was rated at $150,000 a year. . . . Not a vestige of his whole vast property of millions remains today. Not far distant were the estates of a large proprietor and a well-known family, rich and distinguished for generations. The slaves are gone. The family is gone. A single scion of the house remains, and he peddles tea by the pound and molasses by the quart, on a corner of the old homestead, to the former slaves of the family, and thereby earns his livelihood." [6]

A Louisiana citizen told a United States senator of a postwar visit to sugar plantations on the Bayou Teche—the "garden spot of Louisiana." In prewar days, he said, with the "Devil of Slavery" in the land, this region presented a picture of fully cultivated fields, neatly whitewashed cabins for the hands, and sugar houses of the best construction, making the whole scene a "paradise to the eye." Now, with the devil of slavery gone, sugar houses had been destroyed, fences burned, weeds and brush were taking possession, and not a plantation was in decent order. Planters were without money or credit, could not borrow, and had no means of hiring or maintaining hands. A Louisiana planter who in 1861 had a sugar crop worth $125,000 was brushing his own shoes and dispensing with house service in postwar days.[7] From High Shoals, North Carolina, came an eye-witness account of conditions in that state: "almost thorough starvation from the failure of the last years crop"; "ten beggars here to one in Washington"; "whole families . . . coming in from South Carolina to seek food and obtain employment"; "agriculturists . . . entirely stripped by the Confederacy and . . . forced into the ranks to return to their poor wives and children destitute and unable to get any work." Summing up the situation, this writer said: "A more completely crushed country I have seldom witnessed." "The great majority," he added, "are as loyal to the Union as I could wish to see them." [8]

Areas lately within the Confederacy were treated as conquered prov-

[5] *Ann. Cyc.*, 1865, 392–393.

[6] J. S. Pike, *The Prostrate State: South Carolina under Negro Government*, 118–119.

[7] W. G. Eliot to John Sherman, Feb. 25, 1867, Sherman MSS. (Libr. of Congress).

[8] Captain Charles Wilkes to O. H. Browning, Aug. 17, 1866, Letters of O. H. Browning (MSS), Ill. State Hist. Libr.

inces and Federal troops were kept in occupation of the principal towns. The presence of these Federal soldiers, many of them Negroes, at a time when Southern armies had been disbanded and the wearing of the Southern uniform prohibited, was referred to by the Alabama legislature as "a constant source of irritation to the people . . . [which had] doubtless provoked at various times unpleasant collisions." [9] It was not merely that violence and even death resulted from clashes between the soldiers and ex-Confederates; the white people felt shocked and insulted by Negro troops in their midst, being "jostled from the sidewalks by dusky guards" among whom they recognized, in some cases, their former servants.[10]

Transportation, meager and primitive enough before the war, was now in a pitiful state after the destruction incidental to military operations. Roads had fallen into disrepair; horses and mules, and the food to support them, became "scarce and dear"; "wagons and ambulances were about the only vehicles which remained fit." [11] On Mississippi's main north-and-south line "the stations were burned, the rolling stock had disappeared, and most of the roadbed and the bridges had been destroyed." [12] The thoroughness of railroad destruction in Georgia has already been noted. The Charleston and Savannah road was "a mere wreck; every bridge and trestle was destroyed, including the magnificent and costly bridges over the Ashley, Edisto, and Savannah rivers; the depot in Charleston was burned, as well as the depots and buildings at eleven of the way stations, and nearly the whole track torn up." The close of the war found the Greenville and Columbia Railroad a sad victim not only of Federal invasion but of requisition by the government at Richmond, as compensation for which the road "had the bonds and notes of a fallen government." These instances were but typical of conditions throughout the South. Railroad facilities were in need of thorough rebuilding; but "unstable political conditions, fraud, mismanagement, trade conditions, and lack of financial resources" [13] made the work of rehabilitation slow and difficult.

If space permitted, it would be of interest to note the reaction of particular individuals in the South to the changed situation after Appomattox. To some the outcome was not a shock at all, but a relief. "I was not disappointed at the result of the war [wrote H. V. Johnson of Georgia]—I feared defeat and disaster from the beginning—I believed slavery would fall with the Confederacy. . . ." [14] In an address to his fellow citizens in September, 1865, Alexander H. H. Stuart of Virginia stated his position. He had

[9] Fleming, Doc. Hist., I, 49 (Acts of . . . Ala. [1865–1866]).
[10] Whitelaw Reid, After the War: A Southern Tour (quoting a New Orleans editorial), 422 n.
[11] F. B. Simkins and R. H. Woody, South Carolina during Reconstruction, 9.
[12] Allan Nevins, The Emergence of Modern America, 4.
[13] Simkins and Woody, 193–194, 202, 223.
[14] Flippin, Herschel V. Johnson of Georgia, 263.

been "inflexibly opposed" to the secession of Virginia and refused to change his vote cast in convention against the ordinance. After hostilities opened he voted to ratify the ordinance, he said, "not because I approved it, but because I believed that [otherwise] . . . we should have an internecine war added to the civil war which had already been inaugurated." During the war he usually abstained from public affairs; and "all assistance I gave to the Confederate cause [he declared] was by feeding the hungry" and otherwise assisting in soldier relief. His sympathies were, however, naturally with his own people and he was proud of their wartime gallantry and honor. After the surrender of Lee he prepared and signed a call for a mass meeting in Augusta County in order to facilitate restoration; later in the same year he was chosen by his district for membership in the Federal Congress in a campaign in which he urged his opposition to secession as a reason for his choice in the hope that it would appeal to conservative men in the North.[15]

There were many Johnsons and Stuarts; but on the other hand there were conspicuous cases of Southerners to whom defeat seemed unbearable. General Early first betook himself to Mexico; then he went to Canada; after that he sought unsuccessfully to promote the emigration of ex-Confederates to New Zealand. The scientist Matthew Fontaine Maury sought after the war to bring about a similar colonization of former Confederates in Mexico; J. P. Benjamin, escaping through Florida and the Bahamas, made his way to England, where he became Queen's counsel and practiced law with distinction. Breckinridge departed to Europe via the Florida Keys and Cuba. Edmund Ruffin, bequeathing unmitigated hatred of Yankees to Southerners yet unborn, ended his life by a pistol shot.

3

For most Southerners Lee's surrender did not mark the end of life but the beginning of a difficult period of readjustment to new conditions. The section's most urgent problems were not political but economic. The Southern transportation system had been totally disrupted; Southern banks and insurance companies were bankrupt; Southern industry had collapsed; Southern lands were worn out. In 1866, it is estimated, the average value of land in the Carolinas, Georgia, the Gulf states, and Arkansas, was less than one-half of that in 1860.[1]

With astonishing alacrity Southerners of both races set about rebuilding their war-torn section, and the speed of their recovery was impressive. Railroad building went on apace. Not merely were the dilapidated pre-

[15] A. F. Robertson, *A. H. H. Stuart*, 239–250. (As with other congressmen elected in the South in 1865, Stuart was denied a seat.)

[1] Theodore Salutos, "Southern Agriculture and the Problems of Readjustment, 1865–1877," *Agr. Hist.*, XXX, 61 (Apr., 1956).

war lines entirely rebuilt, but between 1865 and 1879 some 7,000 additional miles of railroad were constructed in the South—nearly 5,000 miles in the states east of Texas.[2] Manufacturing also flourished. In 1860 there had been about 300,000 cotton spindles in the South, and most of these were worn out during the war; by 1880, the South "had a total of 158 [cotton] mills, with 533,000 spindles, 11,800 looms, and a total investment of $17,000,000."[3] To counteract the customary depressing picture of the reconstruction era, it is helpful to remember that in a devastated state like Tennessee during the single decade 1860–1870 the number of manufacturing establishments increased from 2,572 to 5,317 that the total number of workers employed leaped from 12,500 to 19,400, and that the value added to goods by manufacturing mounted from $8,000,000 to $15,000,000.[4] In the South as a whole the number of manufacturing establishments increased by 80.8 per cent between 1860 and 1880, and the value of Southern manufactured products grew by 54.6 per cent during the same period.[5]

Promising as this rehabilitation was, it did not keep up with the phenomenal industrial progress of the rest of the country. Investment uncertainties and political disorders frightened Northern capital out of the South during the reconstruction period, and Southerners had to lift themselves by their own bootstraps. As a result their gains, though impressive when viewed as the single-handed accomplishment of a defeated and exhausted people, did not equal the economic growth of other sections. Despite extensive construction, the Southern percentage of the total national railroad mileage dropped from 26 per cent in 1856 to 19 per cent in 1879. Similarly the Southern proportion of the total number of manufacturing establishments dropped from 14.7 per cent in 1860 to 11.5 per cent in 1880; capital invested in Southern plants declined from 9.5 per cent of the national total in 1860 to 4.8 per cent in 1880.[6]

Such figures meant that the South was, and would remain, an essentially agricultural region, and it was in this field that the most important economic transformations and the most sweeping recovery in the postwar years were accomplished. The nature of this agricultural revolution in the South has often been misunderstood. Since the census reports show that between 1860 and 1880 the number of Southern farms was doubled, in-

[2] Carter Goodrich, "Public Aid to Railroads in the Reconstruction South," *Political Science Quart.*, LXXI, 438 (Sept., 1956).

[3] Coulter, *The South during Reconstruction,* 268.

[4] Constantine G. Belissary, "The Rise of the Industrial Spirit in Tennessee, 1865–1885," (MS. doctoral dissertation, Vanderbilt Univ., 1949), 37.

[5] Eugene M. Lerner, "Southern Output and Agricultural Income, 1860–1880," *Agr. Hist.*, XXXIII, 123 (July, 1959).

[6] *Ibid.*; Goodrich, "Public Aid to the Railroads in the Reconstruction South," 438.

creasing from 549,109 to 1,252,249, and their average size was cut in half, from 365 to 157 acres, historians have frequently been misled into asserting that the reconstruction period saw the widespread abandonment of the plantation system and the division of large estates into small holdings. In fact, such figures must be regarded with great skepticism, since the census takers listed all owners, renters, and sharecroppers in the South as separate farmers. Generalization on this subject is hazardous, because the evidence is scattered and few studies have been made, but there actually appears to have been a further concentration of land ownership during the postwar years. Professor Coulter points out that "from 1860 to 1880 . . . there was a large increase in the number of farms over 100, over 500, and over 1,000 acres" in the South.[7] Using tax rolls, which are far more reliable than census returns, Roger W. Shugg has shown that, in nine parishes of Louisiana, the proportion of land in plantations larger than 100 acres more than doubled between 1860 and 1880.[8] Undoubtedly the hardships of the reconstruction era brought some changes in land ownership, but they did not disrupt the traditional Southern pattern of large plantations.

In other ways, however, the collapse of the Confederacy did produce a marked change in the structure of Southern agricultural life. Although the Negroes did not to any considerable extent become independent landowners,[9] they were reluctant to stay in their communal quarters of slave days and, almost immediately after the war, were able to force "white competitors, for their labor in the expanding cotton fields, to establish them on separate farms in houses scattered over the land." "This abandonment of the communal character of the Southern plantation," Francis B. Simkins observes, "bestowed upon the Negroes the American farmer's ideal of independent existence." [10]

The Negro was economically independent only in a limited sense, however, for the huge majority of the colored race remained on the farms as laborers. The end of slavery meant that some new scheme for the employment of the freedmen had to be worked out, and the years immediately after the war saw much experimentation with rival labor systems. "In general," as Oscar Zeichner has shown, "during the first few years after 1865, wage labor prevailed on the plantations." At first the average wage varied from two to eighteen dollars a month in the old cotton country on

[7] Coulter, 214.

[8] Dr. Shugg's figures show 31.29 per cent of all land in these parishes held in plantations of over 100 acres in 1860 and 68.21 per cent in such holdings in 1880. Shugg, *Origins of Class Struggle in Louisiana,* 240.

[9] For example, in Georgia in 1880, "Negroes . . . owned 586,664 acres out of a total area of 37,700,000 acres." Coulter, 112.

[10] Simkins, "New Viewpoints of Southern Reconstruction," *J.S.H.,* V, 52 (Feb., 1939).

the seaboard, with slightly higher rates prevailing in the west. In 1867 wages rose to between $100 and $158 a year, but, after the bad crop failure of that year, there was a marked decline in 1868. Neither whites nor Negroes were satisfied with the system. The freedmen complained that food rations were not merely "of the cheapest sort, but they were also rather scanty. Plantation discipline was especially harsh. . . . The failure of the planter to pay his hands adequate wages . . . also made the laborer more restless." Employers, on the other hand, found wage payments a drain on their meager stores of capital, a problem that became more acute after the poor crops of 1866 and 1867; they complained that the Negroes would draw their pay during the slack months only to abscond when the cotton had to be picked; and, in general, they declared that the wage system failed to give them adequate control of their labor force.[11]

As a result, the practice of cropping gradually developed in the South. In general the system meant that the employer furnished the land, seed, tools, and direction, that the employees (usually Negroes) supplied the labor, and that the two divided in a fixed ratio whatever crop was produced. "Ordinarily," writes Rosser H. Taylor, "when the landlord furnished the tools, team, and tenement, the cropper was given one-half of the crop. . . . While sharecropping was the most common form of dependent land tenure, there were various other types of tenancy. 'Standing rent' involved the renting of land for a specified amount of produce—usually lint cotton. There was also cash rent which was accounted standing rent. Under another form, known as 'the third and fourth arrangement,' the tenant furnished tools, team, and provisions and turned over one-third or one-fourth of the crop to the landlord. . . . More often than not, the landlord furnished the sharecropper a stipulated sum of money payable in monthly installments until the crop was 'laid by.' In lieu of money, the landlord frequently would make arrangements with a time merchant to furnish the cropper provisions within certain limits. In either case, the landlord was secured by a prior lien on the crop." "It is obvious," Dr. Taylor adds, "that all the contracts were drawn with a view to safeguarding the interests of the landlord."[12]

This sharecropping system also made "important changes in the internal trade" of the South. Before the war planters had bought supplies in bulk for themselves and for their slaves. Now, as the Negroes scattered from the old slave quarters and became semi-independent croppers, "planters lost much of their centralized control over purchasing." Their place was taken by country storekeepers, eager to advance the croppers necessities upon credit, taking a lien against the anticipated crop. "Coun-

[11] Zeichner, "The Transition from Slave to Free Agricultural Labor in the Southern States," *Agr. Hist.*, XIII, 22–32.

[12] Taylor, "Post-Bellum Southern Rental Contracts," *ibid.*, XVII, 121 (April, 1943).

try storekeepers knew when each man would pick his crop; and when a sharecropper weighed his cotton, both planter and storekeeper were waiting to collect their portions." Observing the rise of this new mercantile middle class in the South, a rural editor remarked, "The country storekeeper has risen to the dignity of the country merchant." [13]

Just as the cropper had to go into debt to the planter and the storekeeper, so the landowner had to borrow money from the merchant and the banker, who soon replaced the ante-bellum cotton and tobacco factor in Southern economic life. "Thus," Professor Shannon remarks, "there arose the crop-lien system, under which the farmer pledged his crop, to be handled by the merchant when it was harvested." The system was a vicious one from every point of view. "Low prices for cotton, and high costs of all provisions, got the farmer into a perpetual state of indebtedness, so year after year he merely struggled to clean the slate for a new start. Until this could be done, he was wholly at the mercy of the merchant as to what he might buy and how much, what he should grow and the acreage of it, and how he should manage each detail of his work." [14] One should not, however, imagine that the system enormously enriched the merchants and bankers of the South, for low prices, crop failures, and absconding laborers drastically cut into their profits; besides, they were heavily in debt themselves to Northern investors and banking houses.

The principal result of the system was to make the South more than ever a one-crop economy. Because of the piled-up debts, the banker pressed the planter, and the planter pressed the cropper to produce only crops that had a ready money value, chiefly tobacco, sugar, and, especially, cotton. In terms of total output of these staples the South made a remarkable recovery in the reconstruction period. The number of bales of cotton produced in 1859 had been 4,508,000; in 1870, despite all the uncertainties of the postwar adjustment, it was 4,025,000; in 1880, it reached 6,357,000.[15] Even in agriculture, however, Southern output fell relative to that of the rest of the country, and the section as a whole remained desperately poor.

4

This social and economic rehabilitation of the South naturally did not await upon political adjustment, for the background of which one must go back to the efforts of the Lincoln administration in the midst of war. Characteristically, Lincoln approached the difficult problems of reconstruc-

[13] William E. Highsmith, "Louisiana Landholding during War and Reconstruction," *La. Hist. Quart.*, XXXVIII, 51 (Jan., 1955).

[14] Fred A. Shannon, *The Farmer's Last Frontier*, 90–91.

[15] *Hist. Statistics of the United States*, 108–109. The year 1859 has been chosen rather than 1860 because the crop in the former was more typical of the prewar Southern output.

tion with an open mind and an absence of commitment. As Federal troops overran the South, some sort of civil government had to be re-established, and the President, as commander-in-chief, had to act. In the later, unskillful hands of his successor Lincoln's tentative proposals were converted into dogmas, but it is important to remember that while Lincoln was alive his views on reconstruction were constantly changing. A shrewd observer like James G. Blaine felt "that Mr. Lincoln had no fixed plan for the reconstruction of the States." [1]

Lincoln's initial experiment with reconstruction came early in the war in his dealings with the border states. In both Maryland and Kentucky he learned that Federal troops were needed to uphold Unionist governments, and in Missouri, after Governor Claiborne Jackson joined the Confederates, Federal commanders reassembled the Missouri convention, which then declared state offices vacant and proceeded to fill the governorship with Hamilton R. Gamble.[2] From this experience, as Professor William B. Hesseltine points out, Lincoln derived his basic conception of reconstruction procedure, "the idea of installing a new governor under military auspices and with whatever popular support he could marshal." [3] The President further adapted this basic idea in 1862, when he appointed Andrew Johnson military governor of Tennessee and gave him "such powers as may be necessary and proper to enable the loyal people of Tennessee to present such a republican form of State government, as will entitle the State to the guaranty of the United States therefor, and to be protected under such State government, by the United States against invasion and domestic violence." [4]

In his proclamation of December 8, 1863, Lincoln undertook a more general formulation of reconstruction procedures. He offered pardon, with certain exceptions, to any adherents of the Confederacy who would take the oath to support "the Constitution of the United States, and the union of the States thereunder." Whenever in any state a loyal nucleus equal to one-tenth of the votes cast at the presidential election of 1860 should qualify by such oath-taking and establish a state government with abolition of slavery, Lincoln promised executive recognition of such government.[5]

Radicals who did not agree with Lincoln, though belonging to his party, opposed his plan of easy restoration and succeeded in thwarting it. Under the leadership of Henry Winter Davis, Benjamin F. Wade, Chandler, Julian, Stevens, and Sumner, these men brought about the passage (July 2, 1864) of the Wade-Davis bill, a severe measure which made

---

[1] Donald, *Lincoln Reconsidered,* 138–139.
[2] See above, pp. 227–236.
[3] Hesseltine, *Lincoln's Plan of Reconstruction,* 25.
[4] Lincoln, *Collected Works,* V, 469.
[5] *Ibid.,* VII, 53–56.

restoration difficult by intrusting the reconstruction of a state not to a minority ready for future loyalty, but to a majority whose Unionism was a matter of past conduct. Under authority of the provisional governor an enrollment of white male citizens was to be made. If the persons taking oath to support the Constitution of the United States should amount to a majority of those enrolled, the loyal people were to be invited to choose a constitutional convention for the launching of a new state government; but no one who had held office, state or Confederate, "under the rebel usurpation," or had voluntarily borne arms against the United States, should be permitted to vote or serve as delegate at such election.[6] In the new governments to be set up slavery was to be prohibited, the "rebel" debt was to be repudiated, and no office-holder under the "usurping power" (with minor exceptions) should "vote for or be a member of the legislature or governor."[7]

So fundamental was the difference between Lincoln and his Congress on this matter that a deadlock resulted between the executive and legislative branches. By a pocket veto the President prevented the Wade-Davis bill from becoming law. He then issued a rather eccentric proclamation announcing that while he was unprepared to approve the bill (thus making it the only possible plan of restoration and causing his new-formed governments in Louisiana and Arkansas to be held for naught) he was nevertheless satisfied with the measure "as one very proper plan for the loyal people of any State choosing to adopt it."[8] He stood ready to direct military governors to proceed according to the bill in such states as might wish to comply with its provisions. By this proclamation the President signified his readiness to give effect to a mere proposal—a bill that never became law—and he left the Southern people with two alternatives: they might take his plan, which involved no disfranchisement of their leading citizens, or that of Congress which involved that and other distasteful features.

None of the Southern states accepted the alternative of coming in under the Wade-Davis bill; but under Lincoln's various schemes reconstruction was started and carried forward to his own satisfaction in Tennessee, Louisiana, Arkansas, and Virginia. The President watched with particular care the progress of his plan in Louisiana, which had been under military occupation since the spring of 1862. There in April, 1864, a convention created a constitution under which slavery was prohibited. The

[6] The privilege of voting for delegates to the state constitutional conventions was limited by this bill to those who would swear that they had never voluntarily borne arms against the United States, nor given aid to persons in armed hostility thereto, nor had voluntarily supported any hostile "pretended government." This oath originally appeared in the Federal act of July 2, 1862, and reappeared in various pieces of later legislation. It was known as the "iron-clad" test oath. *U. S. Stat. at Large,* XII, 502.

[7] Richardson, *Messages and Papers,* VI, 223–226.

[8] Lincoln, *Collected Works,* VII, 433.

popular vote in favor of this constitution was 6836 as compared to 1566 for rejection.[9] The affirmative vote being more than ten per cent of the voters in 1860, Lincoln extended his support to the new state government; and on his part the state was treated as if restored to the Union. The Federal conscription act was enforced in the state in 1864. Elections to state and Federal offices were held the same year; but their validity even under state law was challenged. Uncertainty concerning the Louisiana question continued till Lincoln's death; ultimately the state found it necessary to go the road of reconstruction which Congress was later to prescribe.

Lincoln's ten-per-cent plan in Arkansas was likewise unsuccessful. A restoration movement was launched in that state to satisfy the President's wishes, and in March, 1864, a Unionist constitution was carried by 12,177 to 226 votes as compared with 54,000 voters in 1860.[10] Both the convention and the election, however, were irregular; and, according to T. S. Staples, "conditions were such in March, 1864, that a perfectly regular election was out of the question." [11] Slavery was abolished, and a working "free state government" was launched that served for state purposes, but that government never proved satisfactory to Congress. On June 29, 1864, the United States Senate, after prolonged debate, concluded that Arkansas was not entitled to representation; and accordingly Messrs. Fishback and Baxter were denied seats as senators.[12]

In Tennessee steps had been taken by the close of the war which were claimed by one faction to be a full compliance with Lincoln's ten-per-cent plan, while another faction branded the measures as irregular. A civil government under Union control had existed in that state since the appointment of Andrew Johnson as military governor in 1862; and ordinary functions of state government had been performed under Johnson's direction with Federal military aid throughout the remainder of the war. A state convention met in Nashville in September, 1864, followed by a second convention in January which claimed constituent powers; but a large element in the state considered all these proceedings irregular and regarded the conventions as mere bodies of private citizens with no valid authority to originate constitutional provisions. By the convention method certain constitutional amendments were recommended by which slavery was abolished and secession repudiated. At an election held on February 22, 1865, these amendments were ratified, and on March 4 W. G. ("Parson") Brownlow, a noisy Unionist agitator, was chosen governor. Just before assuming the vice-presidency Andrew Johnson issued a proclamation recognizing that

---

[9] *Ann. Cyc.*, 1864, 479.

[10] *Ibid.*, 30.

[11] T. S. Staples, *Reconstruction in Arkansas*, 43.

[12] *Cong. Globe*, 38 Cong., 1 sess., 3360–3368. In the House the question of admitting representatives from Arkansas was laid on the table (*ibid.*, 3390–3394).

Tennessee had met Lincoln's conditions as to reconstruction. Presidential electors for Lincoln and Johnson had been chosen somewhat irregularly in November, 1864, thus emphasizing the efforts of a portion of the state to return to the Union. These electors, however, were not counted in the electoral vote as received in 1865, albeit Andrew Johnson, a citizen of Tennessee, was declared to be duly elected Vice-President. A somewhat anomalous situation existed as to Tennessee's representation in Congress. The state had members in the lower house of the Thirty-Seventh Congress (1861–1863); but in the Thirty-Eighth (1863–1865) it had neither congressmen nor senators. Lincoln's plan to have Johnson as military governor appoint senators was not carried out; [13] and when the Thirty-Ninth Congress assembled in December of 1865 representation was again denied the state, though its citizen was then President.

In Virginia also a situation existed which, by ignoring realities and accepting legal fictions, could be interpreted as offering a nominal Unionist government. The "restored government" of Virginia (to be distinguished from the government of West Virginia) had, as stated above,[14] endured as a straw government with its capital at Alexandria; and it went so far as to formulate a new state constitution under which slavery was abolished, Unionism established, and the franchise altered. Full recognition of this government at Washington was sought in the later stages of the war, but representation was for the most part denied in Congress. In the Thirty-Eighth Congress (1863–1865) Virginia was not represented in the lower house, while in the Thirty-Ninth and Fortieth Congresses it had no representation in either house.[15] When reconstruction was finally effected for Virginia it was done by a process which ignored the "restored government" of Francis H. Pierpoint despite the fact that this government had been considered competent to consent to the creation of the new state, and has for certain other purposes (e.g., the fixing of the boundary and the apportionment of the state debt) been recognized in later years by both Virginia and the United States.[16] Thus it appears that the only states within the Confederacy which had any representation in the Federal Congress during the war were Virginia and Tennessee, and in the case of both representation was partial.

Lincoln never succeeded in putting his plan of reconstruction into full effect in any state. The ineffectiveness of his well-meant efforts is emphasized by the concessions he made to the Radicals of Congress. Not only did he give partial recognition to the Wade-Davis plan in his proclamation

[13] Randall, *Constitutional Problems Under Lincoln,* 223 n.

[14] See pp. 236–242.

[15] Randall, *op. cit.,* 463 ff.

[16] The attitude of the Virginia courts in the postwar period has been to recognize the legal validity of the Unionist (Pierpoint) government. Virginia *vs.* West Virginia, 11 Wallace 39; J. G. Randall in *Pol. Sci. Quar.,* XXX, 553 ff.

of July, 1864, accepting it as one method of reconstruction; he signed under protest the joint resolution which excluded from the electoral count of 1865 all the eleven states of the former Confederacy, including those which had complied with the requirements of his own plan of restoration.[17] In a letter to certain citizens of Tennessee he stated (October 22, 1864) that "the President is charged with no duty in the conduct of a presidential election in any State"; and in a tone which contrasts strikingly with his confident assumption of authority in other fields, he declared that the determination as to the counting of electoral votes belonged "not to the military agents, nor yet to the Executive Department, but exclusively to another department of the Government," i.e., Congress.[18] His pleading for support toward the close of the war shows a feeling of apprehension that his plan would encounter serious obstacles in the legislative branch.

It is a relief to turn from these futile details to the general principles of reconstruction as Lincoln expounded them. In a speech at Washington three days before the assassination (April 11, 1865) he reviewed the whole subject. The question whether the seceded states were in the Union or out of it he dismissed as a "pernicious abstraction," "good for nothing at all." "We all agree [he said] that the . . . States . . . are out of their proper practical relation with the Union; and that the sole object of the government . . . is to again get them into that proper practical relation." He would have all join in the restoration and each indulge his own opinion as to whether the states were being brought back into the Union or had never left it. He dwelt upon the case of Louisiana and answered objections to the new government set up in that commonwealth. As to the denial of the vote to colored men he said that he would have preferred enfranchising the "very intelligent" and the Negro soldiers. But in his opinion it was beside the point to complain because the new Louisiana government was not all that might be desired. He would take it as it was and improve it rather than reject it and dishearten the loyal element. He would encourage the thousands who had just voted for the new government to fight for their work and "ripen it to a complete success." For the sake of broad purposes to be accomplished he would recognize Unionist minorities and would tolerate irregularities. "Concede [he said] that the new government of Louisiana is only . . . as the egg is to the fowl, we shall sooner have the fowl by hatching the egg than by smashing it." What was said regarding Louisiana he would apply to the South as a whole. Yet his concept did not involve uniformity for all the states; for, said he, "so great peculiarities pertain to each state . . ., and withal, so new and unprecedented is the whole case that no . . . inflexible plan can safely be prescribed. . . ." He closed

[17] In signing this resolution, by which Congress again asserted the invalidity of Lincoln's reconstruction procedure, Lincoln disclaimed that he had expressed any opinion on its merits. Lincoln, *Collected Works*, VIII, 270.
[18] *Ibid.*, VIII, 72.

with the significant statement that he was at that time considering "some new announcement to the people of the South." [19]

Assassination, coming soon after, prevented this announcement from being made, and even its general tenor is a matter of speculation. It is clear that on the last day of Lincoln's life he again discussed reconstruction with his cabinet and that some of his advisers were unwilling to approve a settlement upon very lenient terms. Stanton presented to the cabinet "a project for military occupation as a preliminary step toward the reorganization of the Southern states, Virginia and North Carolina to be combined in a single military district." Welles strongly objected to this proposed destruction of the individuality of the states, and Lincoln sustained him, without, however, completely repudiating Stanton's proposal. Instead, he urged his Secretary of War to revise his plan and to present it at the next cabinet meeting.[20] Those present at the conference disagreed as to what the President's own views were. Seward later declared that Lincoln was contemplating a move similar to President Johnson's proclamation of May 29, 1865.[21] On the other hand, Attorney-General Speed thought the President was coming to accept Radical views and quoted him as admitting that he "had perhaps been too fast in his desires for early reconstruction." [22]

Efforts toward reconstruction during the war did not serve to further the cause materially nor to clarify the principles involved. As often happens in the American system of government, President and Congress had worked at cross purposes, and nothing substantial had been accomplished. Lincoln's purpose had been to anticipate the need for reconstruction, to have a definite method formulated, to bring this method progressively into operation as military success brought more and more territory under Union control, to prepare the people for the resumption of statehood in the Union as a thing to be taken for granted when hostilities ceased, and to have the movement sufficiently under way so that the completion of the further steps at the end of the war would be easy and natural. He would countenance imperfections for the sake of a speedy and generous restoration of the states. On such matters as pardon, cessation of punitive measures, confiscation of property, and even compensation of slaveholders, he would be generous both to the leaders and to the rank and file in the South. Persecution and vindictiveness were out of the picture so far as his plans were concerned. His scheme was offhand and practical rather than legally perfect, and it rested upon extraordinary (though benevolent) uses of executive and military power in the South; but such national executive power he hoped soon to replace by complete home rule. In its viewing of fundamentals the plan

[19] *Ibid.*, VIII, 399–405.

[20] Randall and Current, *Lincoln the President*, IV, 362.

[21] *House Report No. 7*, 40 Cong., I sess., 78–79 (first pagination), 401 (second pagination).

[22] Donald, ed., *Inside Lincoln's Cabinet*, 268.

was motivated by a magnanimous purpose to restore normal relations at the earliest possible moment. The opposition of Congress, however, left the whole subject in deadlock; and the opportunity to bring the states back, while the sentiment for quick restoration was strong on both sides, was definitely lost.

5

Lincoln's successor did not dally in his efforts to bring about a prompt restoration of the South to the Union. The change of administration was effected as quietly as the excited times would permit and the cabinet remained unchanged. The new President's views on the treatment of the Southerners underwent modifications; but by a month after Lincoln's assassination they had crystallized into a form which they retained throughout the coming struggles. His first comments had a radical tone. "Treason is a crime," he said to a New Hampshire delegation soon after assuming office, "and must be punished as a crime. . . . It must not be excused as an unsuccessful rebellion to be . . . forgiven. It is a crime before which all other crimes sink into insignificance. . . ." [1] These vindictive expressions, however, represented only a passing phase. After Johnson had settled down to the heavy duties of his new task, he attempted to carry out what he understood to be Lincoln's policy, omitting, however, the ten-per-cent aspect of his predecessor's program. In his proclamations, letters, messages, and speeches he showed that reconstruction in its manifold phases had assumed in his mind a definite pattern. To Johnson the war had had only two objectives, Union and freedom; he never subscribed to what C. Vann Woodward has called the "third war aim," the Radicals' demand for equality.[2] As the war had ended slavery, he considered the preservation of the Union as the cardinal tenet upon which emphasis should constantly be focused in the era of postwar adjustment. Loyalty must be insisted upon, and the loyal element must be recognized in the rebuilding of the states. Secession was a principle he had always opposed; but after the South had given it up and after Southern armies had been disbanded, he would not overlook the fact of Union victory and assume the continuance of a rebellion that no longer existed. To deal with a whole people in a spirit of revenge for the past he regarded as not only unjust but impossible. Though in his opinion the states of the South had erred, the success of Union armies should not be the occasion for concentrating all power in the hands of a few at the national capital. Like Lincoln, he viewed the restoration of the Southern states as an executive, not a legislative, function; but while his predecessor had moved with great adroitness and flexibility, Johnson was rigid, stubborn, and inept.

[1] *Ann. Cyc.*, 1865, 801.
[2] Woodward, "Equality: America's Deferred Commitment," *Am. Scholar*, XXVII, 463 (1958).

Various summaries of his policy are to be found; but perhaps the most complete is his regular message to Congress under date of December 6, 1865.[3] The message dwelt in extravagant terms, after the manner of American political leaders, upon the perfection of the Constitution, the greatness of the American system of republican government, and the superior wisdom of its framers. For the preservation of the government, he said, the rights of the states were essential. Finding the states broken from the effects of civil war, with Federal armies in occupation in the seceded commonwealths, the President had at the first to decide whether military rule in the South was to be continued. The indefinite prolongation of military rule he considered intolerable. Such a course would divide the people into vanquished and vanquishers, engender hatred, entail incalculable expense, discourage immigration, and foist upon the South a host of dependents upon the Federal government extracting profit from the miseries of their fellow citizens and extending over a vast population such a widespread power of national patronage as he, himself, would be most reluctant to exercise. In sum, the motive actuating his course was that of restoring the "rightful energy of the General Government and of the States."

Assuming office in April, the new President faced a long recess of Congress, and in the months from April to December, when Congress would convene in regular session, he was free to act without congressional "interference." One of the matters that are usually given central place in historical discussions concerning reconstruction is the tiresome controversy as to whether restoration was a "presidential function" or a "congressional function." The amount of editorial ink and political oratory devoted to this controversy is amazing. This phase of the dispute was prominent in the struggle between Lincoln and his Congress; it was given the greatest emphasis in the complex squabbles of the Johnson administration. Even more important in many minds than the solemn issue whether the states had "perdured" or whether they had, as Sumner said, committed the crime of state suicide [4] was the question whether Congress or the President should control the restoration of the Union. Writers have usually taken this subject seriously as a substantial question of real importance which had to be answered by *Yes* or *No*. Yet sound governmental principles would seem clearly to have demanded that reconstruction be regarded as a matter on which President and Congress should cooperate. The function could hardly be considered either presidential or congressional. Lincoln seems to have given

[3] *Cong. Globe,* 39 Cong., 1 sess., app., 1–5. The message fairly expressed the President's thoughts, though historians accept the conclusion of Professor Dunning that it was penned by George Bancroft. *Proceedings,* Mass. Hist. Soc., XIX, 395–405 (Nov., 1905).

[4] ". . . the State being, according to the language of the law, *felo-de-se,* ceases to exist." Resolution offered by Charles Sumner, U. S. Senate, Feb. 11, 1862. *Cong. Globe,* 37 Cong., 2 sess., 736–737.

insufficient heed to the function of Congress in the admission of the states; and Congress in Lincoln's day was needlessly aroused in its insistence on its own authority. Unless the executive and legislative branches could work together on reconstruction, efforts toward governmental action would be largely futile.

This weakness, which would seem to be an inherent defect in the American system as distinguished from the parliamentary system of government, was a leading factor in that unfortunate deadlock and delay which ended ultimately in a series of congressional measures that proved a failure when applied to the South. Not the least of the afflictions from which the country suffered during reconstruction was that governmental paralysis which resulted from lack of coordination between the executive and legislative departments. Substantial objects and issues were beclouded by a confusion of authority which in a parliamentary form of government would never have existed. The logic of the situation in April, 1865, called for a special session of Congress; but the President viewed the situation otherwise, and there was little in the temper of congressional leaders to encourage him. Seeking to steal a march on his legislature, and to confront them with a *fait accompli* on the assembling of Congress, he found antagonism so solidified that his whole program was set aside.

The steps taken in 1865 under the President's direction covered the whole process of state remaking; and by December every one of the seceded states except Texas had fulfilled the President's requirements, had elected Federal representatives and senators (most of whom had arrived in Washington), and stood ready for recognition. Resting fundamentally on Lincoln's plan, Johnson's method applied also some of the features of the Wade-Davis bill. His first proclamation was in regard to the situation in Virginia. On May 9 he declared all "rebel" authority in that state null, directed the re-establishment of national authority, and pledged Federal aid to Francis H. Pierpont in restoring peace and state authority throughout the commonwealth.[5] Next came the proclamation of May 29, which announced the President's policy on two fundamental factors: pardon and amnesty, and reconstruction procedure.

Pardon was applied as a preliminary to restoration. The traditional policy at the end of civil conflicts has been to extend oblivion and forgiveness to former "rebels" on condition of renewed allegiance. This tradition was in general followed in a series of proclamations by Presidents Lincoln and Johnson. In Lincoln's proclamation of December 8, 1863, a limited pardon was extended. An oath of allegiance was required; and it was declared that pardon did not restore rights as to slaves nor as to confiscated property where claims of third parties had intervened. Moreover various classes were excluded from the benefits of pardon, including all who had

[5] *Ann. Cyc.*, 1865, 815.

held civil office under the Confederate government and those who had mistreated prisoners. Pardon was again announced in Johnson's proclamation of May 29, 1865,[6] with exceptions similar to those of Lincoln; and a new condition was made: general amnesty did not automatically include those whose taxable property exceeded $20,000. To those excepted from general pardon, however, there remained the possibility of special pardon by petition; and much of Johnson's time was occupied in the granting of thousands of these special pardons, his policy in this respect being quite liberal. Later proclamations of general pardon indicated a relaxation of the conditions; and finally the presidential process of unconditional pardon was made complete by the proclamation of December 25, 1868, in which President Johnson declared "unconditionally, and without reservation, . . . a full pardon and amnesty for the offence of treason against the United States, or of adhering to their enemies during the late civil war, with restoration of all rights, privileges, and immunities under the Constitution and the laws. . . . "[7]

6

Simultaneously with the amnesty edict (May 29, 1865) came the President's important proclamation appointing W. W. Holden provisional governor of North Carolina. In this document the President's scheme of restoration was outlined. The provisional governor was instructed to call a convention to be chosen by the "loyal" people of the state to make constitutional changes and prepare the state for Federal restoration. The amnesty oath (to support the Constitution of the United States) was to be required of the delegates and those electing them;[1] but when the convention should assemble it was to prescribe permanent voting and officeholding qualifications for the state. The President definitely stated that the determination of these qualifications was "a power [which] the people of the . . . States . . . have rightfully exercised from the origin of the Government to the present time." Temporarily civil government for the state was to be administered under the authority of the provisional governor, while Federal functions, executive and judicial, were to be resumed by the proper officials.[2] In view of later developments it is important to remember that, according to Stanton's statement, this reconstruction policy was not a mere

---

[6] Richardson, *Messages and Papers,* VI, 310–312.

[7] *U. S. Stat. at Large,* XV, 711. It should be noted, however, that this presidential amnesty was largely ineffectual, since under the Fourteenth Amendment the pardoning power was vested in Congress. J. T. Dorris, *Pardon and Amnesty under Lincoln and Johnson,* 356–361.

[1] The amnesty oath was a pledge "henceforth" to support the Constitution and the Union, together with the laws concerning emancipation. It is not to be confused with the "iron-clad" test oath prescribed by Congress.

[2] Richardson, *Messages and Papers,* VI, 312–314.

creation of Johnson's brain. It was fully discussed in the cabinet, no member of which expressed "a doubt of the power of the executive branch of the government to reorganize state governments which had been in rebellion without the aid of Congress." [3]

Identical proclamations were issued for the other seceded states, and in each state the process of political and constitutional restoration was soon launched by the provisional governors. Taking the state of Alabama as an example, Governor Parsons (provisional governor) issued regulations prescribing in detail the method of procedure under the President's orders. Existing laws of Alabama, except in the matter of slavery, were kept in force. Extralegal agencies for punishing offenders, not authorized by the laws of the state, such as "vigilance committees," were prohibited; and the people were reminded that Federal military rule could not be withdrawn until orderly resumption of civil government had been effected. [4]

In general the provisional governors avoided any tone of oppression and struck the note of friendly cooperation. "Every generous heart," said Governor Hamilton in his proclamation to the people of Texas, "will feel . . . that the Government of the United States seeks not, and never has sought, to humiliate the people of the South. It but asks them to be friends rather than enemies." [5] In this mood the transitional steps were in general quietly taken. In keeping with the President's theory that the people of each Southern state had been "deprived . . . of all civil government" [6] by reason of the rebellion, existing governors and legislatures (those belonging to the régime of the Confederacy) ceased to function, especially as most of the legislatures were not then in session. Immediately upon assuming power in each state, the provisional governor used his appointive power to continue in office such existing state officers as judges, treasurers, sheriffs, tax collectors, etc., on condition of taking the oath, or to appoint others in their stead. Decrees of the state courts in ordinary civil and criminal matters were confirmed. Martial law during the transitional process was continued in each state, but without any of the attributes of terrorism, violence, or menace to the tranquillity of the people. Federal troops remained in occupation; and besides the provisional governor there was also for each state a military governor. His duty was to serve as head of the processes of military occupation, while the function of the provisional governor was primarily to direct the transitional steps necessary to launch a regular state government.

Elections were held in the Southern commonwealths and delegates chosen for those conventions which Johnson's proclamation prescribed.

[3] *House Report No. 7*, 40 Cong., 1 sess., 401.
[4] *Ann. Cyc.*, 1865, 11–12.
[5] *Ibid.*, 786.
[6] Proclamation appointing L. E. Parsons provisional governor of Alabama, June 21, 1865, *ibid.*, 11.

In general these conventions made null or repealed the ordinances of secession, abolished slavery, and repudiated such part of the state debt as was contracted for the prosecution of the war. State governments were so reorganized as to comply with Johnson's program, dates being set for the election of new state officers and for representatives in Congress. The newly chosen legislatures met, ratified the antislavery amendment to the Federal Constitution, and chose United States senators. When in each state the necessary steps had been completed to the satisfaction of the government at Washington, Secretary of State Seward issued a proclamation retiring the provisional governor whose functions were surrendered to the regular governor chosen by the people.

Such were the main steps by which the states put the President's plan into operation. It was a program that did not disfranchise the ex-Confederates. The fundamental principle was that the new governments were based not upon a denial of political rights because of past conduct, but upon a policy which recognized a return to Federal allegiance as a sufficient prerequisite to political enfranchisement. That the American system should return to its normal functioning was the President's purpose. The process involved direct personal cooperation between the President and the leaders of state reorganization in the South. Southern delegations conferred with Johnson in person, acquainting him with local conditions, presenting unforeseen problems, and receiving his direct pledges of reconciliation.

7

On the question of Southern readiness for loyal participation in the Union there was a conflict of evidence. After a tour of the South in November–December, 1865, General Grant, who, according to his own testimony, had never been an abolitionist, nor even "antislavery," reported that "the mass of thinking men of the South accept the present situation of affairs in good faith." His observations led him to the conclusion "that the citizens of the Southern States are anxious to return to self-government within the Union as soon as possible." He regretted that there could not be a greater "commingling . . . between the citizens of the two sections, and particularly of those intrusted with the lawmaking power." [1] Benjamin C. Truman, a newspaper correspondent who made a report to the President on conditions in the South, emphatically denied the charge that Northern men in the South were being persecuted. "For some unknown cause [he wrote] a large number of persons are engaged in writing and circulating falsehoods. For some unpatriotic purpose or other, reports of an incendiary character concerning the southern people are transmitted north." Referring to conditions early in 1866, Truman declared his belief that "the south—the great, substantial, and prevailing element—is more

[1] *Ann. Cyc.*, 1865, 809.

loyal now than it was at the end of the war—more loyal to-day than yester-day, and that it will be more loyal to-morrow than to-day." [2]

Other witnesses, however, came to diametrically opposite conclusions. One North Carolina observer in early 1866 asserted that "the feelings of by far the larger proportion of the people of this State are disloyal to the Govt—and enamored by the bitterest hatred toward the North." [3] J. T. Trowbridge, a Northern newspaperman, was told in South Carolina:

They are all Rebels here—all Rebels! . . . They are a pitiably poverty-stricken set; there is no money in the place, and scarcely anything to eat. We have for breakfast salt fish, fried potatoes, and treason. Fried potatoes, treason, and salt fish for dinner. At supper the fare is slightly varied, and we have treason, salt fish, fried potatoes, and a little more treason. . . . The war feeling here is like a burning bush with a wet blanket wrapped around it. Looked at from the outside, the fire seems quenched. But just peep under the blanket and there it is, all alive, and eating, eating in. [4]

Carl Schurz, whom President Johnson sent on a long trip through the South in 1865, agreed that the ex-Confederates had yet to accept defeat; he wrote of the "incorrigibles" of the South, of the detestation of Yankees, of the fact that treason did not appear odious, of the Southerner's lack of "communion with the progressive ideas of the times," of the want of "hearty attachment to the great republic," and of a "self-admiration" that resented criticism. [5]

Though apparently contradictory, these witnesses were, in fact, all partly correct. Different segments of Southern society responded in differing ways to the disaster that had befallen them. Furthermore, the problem is largely a semantic one of knowing what is meant by "accepting defeat." There can be no doubt that virtually all white Southerners agreed that they had been defeated in the war and that further efforts in support of state rights or slavery were worse than futile. The Macon (Ga.) *Journal and Messenger* succinctly expressed the dominant mood of the South when it declared, "We had much rather raise corn, meat and cotton, and do what we can to repair our dilapidated fortunes, than to take a hand in any new revolution." [6] At the same time, very few white Southerners were prepared to recognize that military defeat required them to repudiate the past and to change their attitudes toward the present. "Refusing to see that a

[2] Report of B. C. Truman, transmitted to the Senate May 7, 1866. *Sen. Ex. Doc. No. 43*, 39 Cong., 1 sess., 5–6.

[3] Jack B. Scroggs, "Southern Reconstruction: A Radical View," *J. S. H.*, XXIV, 408 (Nov., 1958).

[4] Trowbridge, *The Desolate South*, 41.

[5] *Sen. Ex. Doc., No. 2*, 39 Cong., 1 sess., pp. 5, 13.

[6] William A. Russ, Jr., "Was there Danger of a Second Civil War during Reconstruction?" *M. V. H. R.*, XXV, 39 (June, 1938).

mighty cataclysm had shaken the profound depths of national life," as E. Merton Coulter has said, "they did not expect that many things would be made anew but rather looked for them to be mended as of old—that Humpty Dumpty might after all be put back on the wall in the South, even if not in the nursery rhyme." [7]

[7] Coulter, *The South during Reconstruction*, 46.

CHAPTER 32

Johnson and the Radicals

I

WHEN CONGRESS assembled in December, 1865, Johnson's reorganized states of the South had completed their civil governments and were asking readmission to the Union. The Democrats, joined by a very few extremely conservative Republicans, were ready to welcome the Southern representatives, and such men as Ten Eyck, Powell, Grider, and Hendricks denounced attempts to impose further conditions upon the South. Said Ten Eyck of New Jersey: ". . . I thought that this whole war, the expenditure of thousands of millions of dollars and of oceans of blood, was for the very purpose of restoring this Union and bringing back these shooting stars to their ancient orbits." [1] "I believe that the States in revolt are still States of the Union [said Powell of Kentucky]: I believe . . . that when they choose to lay down their arms . . . and to send members to the House of Representatives, and Senators to this chamber, they . . . ought to be permitted to do so." [2] "All the . . . powers under the Constitution are conservative, none destructive [was the resolution offered by Grider of Kentucky]; wherefore all the States have been and are always in the Union." [3] "The States have not been regarded as in rebellion," said Hendricks of Indiana. "That has not been the language of the Executive proclamations; it has not been the language of Congress . . . in regard to the insurrection. . . . The State [of Virginia] was never declared to be in rebellion as a State; but the inhabitants of portions of the State . . . were declared to be in rebellion. Why, at the close of the war, . . . shall we adopt language that was not used during the . . . war . . . —legislative language . . . to give a character to the rebellion which it has not had heretofore? . . . I believe that in law the States are in the Union, and

---

[1] *Cong. Globe,* 38 Cong., 2 sess., 555 (Feb. 2, 1865).
[2] *Ibid.,* 557 (Feb. 2, 1865).
[3] Resolution of Jan. 17, 1866, *ibid.,* 39 Cong., 1 sess., 287.

that all that is needed is to give them practical relations to the Federal Government in every respect." [4] To the minds of these conservatives the statesmanlike course was to follow the program which Lincoln had urged and ratify the steps which had been taken by President Johnson in fulfillment of Lincoln's essential purpose. This would merely have involved accepting the senators and representatives from the reorganized states who had already arrived in Washington, admitting the states to the electoral college, and re-establishing normal state and federal relations.

Whether motivated by high-minded generosity or by a desire to rehabilitate the Democratic party, such spokesmen failed to take into consideration the dominant state of opinion in the North. During four bitter years of war Northern hatred of the South had been deliberately encouraged, and there had grown up a profound distrust of the Southerners and their way of life. Henry Ward Beecher expressed a common belief when he declared in early 1865 that the whole section must be strongly suspected. "Its products are rotten," he asserted. "No timber grown in its cursed soil is fit for the ribs of our ship of state or for our household homes. The people are selfish . . . brittle, and whoever leans on them for support is pierced in his hands. Their honor is not honor, but a bastard quality. . . . and for all times the honor of the supporters of slavery will be throughout the world a by-word and a hissing." Determined that these untrustworthy Southerners should not trick them out of the fruits of victory, Northerners wanted their government to take the utmost care in readmitting the "rebels" to the bonds of fellowship. Public opinion strongly approved James Russell Lowell's assertion, "We have the same right to impose terms and to demand guarantees . . . that the victor always has." [5]

On the nature of these terms and guarantees, the Republican party was not a unit. A very few Republican congressmen, such as Cowan and Doolittle, accepted the Democratic view and favored immediate, unconditional restoration, but they were without influence in the party's councils. A large majority were moderates, favoring speedy readmission of the Southern states but believing that rigid conditions should be imposed to prevent the re-emergence of treason. They did not want to bring about a social revolution in the South, but they did desire to prevent the former leaders of the Confederacy from reassuming political leadership of the section. As John Sherman declared, "We should not only brand the leading rebels with infamy, but the whole rebellion should wear the badge of the penitentiary, so that for this generation at least, no man who has taken part in it would dare to justify or palliate it." [6] Moderates also agreed with Lyman Trumbull that their party had a duty toward the freedman, be-

[4] *Ann. Cyc.*, 1866, 175–176.
[5] Buck, *Road to Reunion,* 23–25.
[6] *Ibid.,* 14.

lieving that he would "be tyrannized over, abused, and virtually reenslaved without some legislation by the nation for his protection." [7]

Smaller in numbers but highly influential were the Republican Radicals, who had originated the Wade-Davis bill and who had fought Lincoln's plan for readmitting Louisiana. At first it appears that this group expected much from Johnson and thought that he would cooperate with their schemes. Angered at Lincoln's opposition to their program, some of them even hailed the President's removal by assassination as a fortunate event. Referring to the day of Lincoln's death, G. W. Julian of Indiana wrote: "I spent most of the afternoon in a political caucus, held for the purpose of considering the necessity for a new Cabinet and a line of policy less conciliatory than that of Mr. Lincoln; and while everybody was shocked at his murder, the feeling was nearly universal that the accession of Johnson to the Presidency would prove a godsend to the country. Aside from Mr. Lincoln's known policy of tenderness to the Rebels, . . . his . . . views of the subject of reconstruction were as distasteful as possible to radical Republicans." Later, when Johnson showed his preference for Lincoln's policy in opposition to that of the Radicals, Julian wrote of him as a "genius in depravity." He added: "He was not simply 'an irresolute mule,' as General Schenck had styled him, but was devil-bent upon the ruin of his country. . . ." [8]

Initially only a tiny fraction of the entire Republican strength in Congress, the Radicals, because of the precipitancy of Johnson's overtures to the South and the zeal with which ex-Confederates responded to them, later came to dominate the party and to dictate its reconstruction program. Sumner, Wade, Chandler, Ashley, Boutwell, Julian, Butler, Morton, Wilson, and Yates were principal figures in the group, but its unquestioned leader was Thaddeus Stevens, that strange mixture of disinterested philanthropy and partisan vindictiveness. Of the various descriptions of Stevens's dour personality, that of Schurz, who agreed with his fundamental policies, may be selected for quotation here. "I once heard him make a stump-speech [wrote Schurz] which was . . . remarkable for argumentative pith and sarcastic wit. But the impression his personality made upon me was not sympathetic; his face long and pallid, topped with an ample . . . wig which was at the first glance recognized as such; . . . keen eyes . . . which sometimes seemed to scintillate with a sudden gleam, the underlip defiantly protruding; the whole expression usually stern; his figure would have looked stalwart but for a deformed foot which made him bend and limp. His conversation, carried on with a hollow voice devoid of music, easily disclosed a well-informed mind, but also a certain absolutism of opinion with contemptuous scorn for adverse argument. . . . What he him-

---

[7] Eric L. McKitrick, *Andrew Johnson and Reconstruction*, 292.
[8] G. W. Julian, *Political Recollections, 1840 to 1872*, 255–256, 314.

self seemed to enjoy most in his talk was his sardonic humor, which he made play upon men and things like lurid freaks of lightning." [9] The quality of his humor is illustrated by his reference (May 8, 1866) to "the late lamented Andrew Johnson of blessed memory." [10]

Stevens single-mindedly dedicated himself to the humiliation of the "rebels." As an old man of seventy-five, he stated in Congress that he desired to devote the "small remnant" of his life to "the punishment of traitors." [11] Demanding that the Southerners pay the cost of the war, he bitterly fought all propositions of amnesty. Why is it, he said, "that we are so anxious to proclaim universal amnesty? Is there danger that somebody will be punished? . . . The President has already . . . pardoned these rebels, and restored . . . their property . . . , and he has done it in defiance of law. . . . Sir, God helping me and I live, there shall be a question propounded . . . to this nation whether a portion of the debt shall not be paid by the confiscated property of the rebels." [12] With more realism than most of his contemporaries, Stevens recognized that the power of the former slaveholders in the South would not be broken so long as they retained economic power over the freedmen, and he favored the "thorough" policy of taking all the public lands of the seceded states as well as the private property of all "rebels" and distributing it to ex-slaves, giving to each head of a family a homestead of forty acres, with further gifts of money and buildings, pensions, etc. "Forty acres . . . and a hut," he bluntly declared, "would be more valuable . . . than the . . . right to vote." [13]

Later historians have been shocked by the candor with which Stevens avowed partisan motives for the Radical program. He openly asserted that his policies "would insure the ascendency of the Union [Republican] party." He continued: "Do you avow the party purpose? exclaims some horror-stricken demagogue. I do. For I believe . . . that on the continued ascendency of that party depends the safety of this great nation. If impartial suffrage [by which Stevens meant Negro suffrage] is excluded in the rebel States then every one of them is sure to send a solid rebel representative delegation to Congress, and cast a solid rebel electoral vote. They, with their kindred Copperheads [he meant Democrats] of the North, would always elect the President and control Congress. . . . For these, among other reasons, I am for negro suffrage in every rebel State. If it be . . . necessary, it should be adopted; if it be a punishment to traitors, they deserve it." [14] Again he said: "I know there is an impatience to bring in these

[9] *Reminiscences of Carl Schurz*, III, 214.
[10] *Cong. Globe*, 39 Cong., 1 sess., 2460.
[11] *Ann. Cyc.*, 1867, 251.
[12] *Cong. Globe*, 39 Cong., 2 sess., 1317 (Feb. 18, 1867).
[13] *Ibid.*, 39 Cong., 1 sess., 2459 (May 8, 1866).
[14] *Cong. Globe*, 39 Cong., 2 sess., 252 (Jan. 3, 1867).

chivalric gentlemen [the Confederates] lest they should not be here in time to vote for the next President. . . . Sir, while I am in favor of allowing them to come in as soon as they are fairly entitled, I do not profess to be very impatient to embrace them. I am not very anxious to see their votes cast along with others to control the next election of President and Vice President. . . ." [15]

Such utterances were characteristic of the man, yet they must not be taken as mere cynicism. In Stevens's eyes—and, indeed, in the eyes of most Northerners of the period—there was an identity between the welfare of the Republican party and that of the nation. Labeling the Northern Democrats, as "Copperheads" and the Southern whites as "traitors," the Radicals genuinely felt that the continuing security of the Union depended upon the triumph of their political faction.

2

Seeing Northern victory as the golden opportunity for "humiliating and destroying the influence of the Southern aristocracy," such Radicals as Ben Wade were from the outset suspicious of President Johnson's reconstruction measures.[1] During the summer of 1865 Stevens and Sumner exchanged anxious letters over the "insane course of the President" toward the South. "If something is not done," Stevens predicted, "the President will be crowned king before Congress meets." Reconciliation with the President seemed impossible, and the only salvation would be for the Radicals to take control of the Republican party. "Could we collect bold men enough," Stevens asked Sumner, "to lay the foundation of a party to take the helm of this government, and keep it off the rocks?" [2]

A large number of moderate Republicans were also seriously worried over the President's course. They grew concerned over reports that the "faces in the ante-chamber of the President look very much as they would if a Democratic administration were in power" and over stories that Johnson was "outspoken on the subject of State rights & old fashioned democracy." Still, most Republicans in 1865 clung to faith in the President's "stubborn democracy" and in his "hatred of the slave aristocracy" and were willing to let him try his lenient policy. Lot M. Morrill precisely expressed the moderate attitude when he wrote Sumner in July, 1865: "The Prest. is trying to demonstrate his theory of 'restoring states.' . . . It will fail of course. . . . Nobody approves it. Still, it is but an experiment—let him try it." [3]

[15] *Ibid.*, 1317 (Feb. 18, 1867).

[1] McKitrick, 60.
[2] R. N. Current, *Old Thad Stevens*, 211, 216.
[3] McKitrick, 70–71, 78–79.

A series of developments in 1865–1866 undermined this moderate attitude of forbearance. The conventions which Johnson's provisional governors summoned in the several Southern states exhibited a remarkable indifference to Northern opinion. Required by the President's proclamations to repudiate the acts of secession, only a few of the conventions followed North Carolina in unanimously declaring that the "supposed ordinance" of secession "is now, and at all times hath been, null and void." The Alabama convention rejected a similar resolution and merely declared that the ordinance was "null and void," without the implication that it had never been valid, and South Carolina "repealed" its ordinance of secession.[4] The South Carolina convention also raised objections to ratifying the thirteenth amendment, and Mississippi refused to ratify, on the ground that the amendment was unnecessary, since she had already abolished slavery within her boundaries. There was strong opposition in all the conventions to the repudiation of Confederate war debts, which the President required. Every one of the Southern conventions rejected Johnson's suggestion that the vote be extended to a few substantial and intelligent Negroes, and political power was firmly maintained as a white monopoly.

The elections held in these Southern states under Johnson's program were likewise not calculated to encourage Northern faith in the "experiment." Showing a total disregard of public opinion in the victorious section, Southern whites chose to office the natural leaders of their section, men who had been conspicuous in the military or civil service of the Confederacy. Thus, as William A. Dunning writes, "the newly chosen governor of South Carolina had been a Confederate senator; the governor of Mississippi had been a brigadier-general in the Confederate army; a late major-general in that army was elected a congressman in Alabama; and the legislature of Georgia elected as United States senator no less distinguished a personage than Stephens, late vice-president of the Confederacy." [5] In Alabama, moreover, "three-fourths of the members of the legislature had been either officers or privates in the Confederate army. Candidates with other records were denounced as 'traitors to the South,' and were 'premeditatedly and overwhelmingly defeated.' " [6]

Aroused by all these apparent evidences of Southern reluctance to accept defeat, Northerners were outraged when the newly assembled legislatures under the Johnson program adopted "black codes" for the regulation of the Negro population. In the minds of the Southern whites the intent was not to defy the North but to handle a very urgent problem. Slavery had been abolished, but the Negro remained. While in many cases the whites

[4] *Ann. Cyc.*, 1865, 16–17, 758–759.
[5] Dunning, *Reconstruction, Political and Economic*, 44–45.
[6] Oberholtzer, I, 125.

found their former slaves cheerful, willing to work, and evincing "good behavior . . . beyond all expectation," [7] in many others they had to cope with a disorganized and disoriented labor force. With emancipation many Negroes promptly left the plantations where they had always worked. Some joined in the general westward drift of the Southern population, which rapidly filled up Arkansas in the postwar years and made Texas the most populous state in the South by 1880. Others congregated in the cities and towns of the South, where they formed an idle and indigent population. In Alabama, for example, such counties as Mobile, Montgomery, and Dallas (containing the city of Selma) showed marked increases in the black population, with proportionate decrease in the rural counties.

It is impossible to generalize about the behavior of the freedmen as a whole. From one point of view the most striking thing about their emancipation was the absence of violence accompanying it; far from attempting to destroy their former masters, the freedmen paid them the greatest compliment of all by attempting to imitate them. In this sense, as Francis B. Simkins has pointed out, "Reconstruction can be interpreted as a definite step forward in the Anglicization or the Americanization of the blacks, certainly not their Africanization." [8] On the other hand, it must be admitted that many Negroes, unprepared for freedom, confused liberty with license. Their vagrancy and lack of responsibility proved trying to the Southern whites. Even Schurz, partial as he was to the freedmen, described their crowding around the military posts, their carousals, their religious paroxysms, and their straying from the plantations "just at the time when their labor was most needed to secure the crops of the season." [9]

In these circumstances, Southern whites believed they faced a social and economic necessity in enacting new codes of legislation for the Negro. The domestic relations of the freedman, his position in court, his obligations to his employer, his relationship to labor contracts, his liability in case of vagrancy or pauperism—all such things had to be dealt with as matters of social legislation. Had the Southern states not passed some legislation on these subjects, chaos would have resulted, and there would have been occasion for just rebuke in the North, on the ground that the Negro, while technically free, was denied the rights which freedom implies. Drawing upon their own experience as former slaveholders, upon the vagrancy codes of the Northern states, and upon precedents set in the British West Indies after emancipation, Southern legislators attempted to construct a new legal status for the freedmen.

[7] *Sen. Ex. Doc. No. 6,* 39 Cong., 2 sess., 156.
[8] Simkins, "New Viewpoints of Southern Reconstruction," *J.S.H.,* V, 59 (Feb., 1939).
[9] *Reminiscences,* III, 175.

3

To summarize the laws for all the states is beyond the scope of this book; but South Carolina may be taken as an example, the more so because in that state one finds the new provisions reduced at an early period to a comprehensive code. Existing marriages among persons of color in South Carolina were regularized; and all such persons thereafter desiring to become husband and wife were required to have the contract duly solemnized. Marriage between the races was prohibited; marriage of an apprentice was conditioned upon the master's approval; abandonment was made punishable as a misdemeanor. Parents were responsible for the maintenance of children whether born in regular wedlock or not. Compulsory apprenticeship of dependent colored children was regulated, as well as voluntary apprenticeship of others, masters being under obligation to supply food, clothing, and suitable training. Regulations regarding labor contracts were prescribed and the daily details of agricultural work specified. Servants were not to be absent from the premises without the master's permission. Contracts for labor were enforceable through appropriate penalties by public magistrates. A servant whose rights were not respected by the master might leave his service. No person of color might enter employment other than agricultural without a license from a judge, nor practice any mechanical trade without having served an apprenticeship. Eviction of helpless former slaves from their plantation quarters was prohibited; but trespassers were removable and future occupancy by Negroes was in general made subject to lease contracts. Unemployed or disorderly persons, peddlers, gamblers, those in disreputable occupations, unlicensed strolling players, and sturdy beggars were grouped as "vagrants" and made liable to imprisonment, hard labor, or both.[1]

The definition of civil rights, of access to the courts, and of criminal liability, constituted an important feature of these codes. Existing laws in Alabama concerning persons of color were repealed and the former slaves were given a new judicial status. They could sue and be sued, plead and be impleaded, on the same basis as whites. Their right to testify in court was restricted in the new Alabama code to cases in which persons of color were concerned; but in other states, as for instance in Tennessee [2] and South Carolina,[3] the Negro's right to act as witness was also recognized in cases

[1] This summary is taken from *Acts of the Gen. Assembly of S. C.*, 1864–1865, pp. 291 ff. See also Fleming, *Doc. Hist.*, I, 294–310.

[2] *Acts of . . . Tenn.*, 1865–1866, ch. xl.

[3] The law provided: ". . . all . . . free persons of color shall have the right to make and enforce contracts, to sue, be sued, to be affiants, and give evidence, to inherit, . . . hold . . . real and personal property, make wills and testaments, and to have full and equal benefit . . . of all remedies . . . , as white persons now have. . . ." *Acts of the Gen. Assembly of S. C.*, 1866, 393–394. See also Simkins and Woody, 59.

involving whites alone, or whites and blacks. In recommending to the legislature the removal of former discriminations as to Negro testimony Governor Orr of South Carolina pointed out that the old distinction was "indefensible," since it rested upon "prejudice against the caste of the negro." "With intelligent judges [he said] and discriminating juries, correct conclusions will be more certainly attained by hearing every fact, whatever . . . the . . . color of the witness." [4] In recognition of this liberalization of its laws the commanding general in South Carolina, D. E. Sickles, by order of October 15, 1866, turned over to the regular courts of the state the trial of all civil and criminal cases, announcing that the previous régime of military commissions was no longer necessary. Under the new laws, as reported by General Sickles, white men had been convicted of crimes upon Negro testimony; Negroes under charges brought by whites had been acquitted upon Negro testimony; and in one instance a freedman had been acquitted on his own testimony.[5] In general, these codes treated Negroes as inferior, or at least as separate from whites, being designated as a particular class in the community. Segregation of the races in schools and public places was commonly provided. Landowning by Negroes was restricted sometimes to the country, sometimes to towns. They were forbidden to carry arms. Especially did the "binding out" features of these laws occasion wide comment. For vagrancy, faithlessness to employment, and other offenses, the Mississippi law provided that Negroes might be subjected to fines; and it was made the duty of the county sheriff, if a vagrant Negro could not pay his fine, "to hire out said freeman . . . to any person who will, for the shortest period of service, pay said fine . . . and . . . costs." [6] In this provision especially, Northerners thought they saw an opening wedge for the re-establishment of slavery, and they became increasingly fearful that Johnson's hasty restoration procedures were giving away the fruits of their hard-won victory.

[4] *Ann. Cyc.*, 1866, 707–708. In Tennessee, however, Negroes were excluded from juries. *Acts of . . . Tenn.*, 1865–66, ch. xl.

[5] Report of the Sec. of War, Nov. 14, 1866, *House Exec. Doc. No. 1*, 39 Cong., 2 sess., pp. 59 ff., esp. p. 66. "The admission of negro testimony in courts was attended with more than the expected success [in South Carolina]. The colored witnesses appeared to be fully impressed with the obligations placed upon them, and their evidence was generally given with a manifest desire to tell the truth." *Ann. Cyc.*, 1866, 708.

[6] *Laws of . . . Miss.*, 1865, ch. vi, p. 90. Extracts from the postwar laws of Southern states concerning the Negro are given in *Sen. Exec. Doc. No. 6*, 39 Cong., 2 sess., 170–230.

CHAPTER 33

The Critical Year

I

DURING THE TWELVE months after the assembling of the Thirty-Ninth Congress, in December, 1865, moderate Republicans gradually drifted into an acceptance of a Radical program of reconstruction. The transition was slow and often reluctant, but the inflexibility of the President, the recurrence of violence in the South, and the constant, skillful pressure from Radical leadership compelled the change. When Congress met, the huge Republican majorities which dominated both houses were unwilling to break with the President, yet at the same time they were unhappy with the results of his construction efforts in the South. To register their disapproval they had agreed in caucus not to recognize the Johnson régimes in the ex-Confederate states, and when the clerk of the House of Representatives, Edward McPherson, called the roll on December 4 he carefully and by prearrangement passed over the Southern congressmen who were seeking readmission.

After taking this negative step, the Republican congressmen proceeded in a more positive fashion to assert that they, as well as the President, had a part to play in reorganizing the Southern states. Even before Johnson could send in his annual message, they pushed through a resolution creating a joint committee on reconstruction, consisting of nine members of the House of Representatives and six senators, to which all resolutions and bills pertaining to reconstruction should be referred. Democrats naturally attacked this "revolutionary tribunal," this "directory" or "star chamber," and subsequent historians have all too frequently accepted their charges that this was a piece of Radical partisan machinery. In fact, however, the proposal to create the joint committee was endorsed by both moderates and Radicals; in caucus the scheme was adopted by a vote of 129 to 35.[1] The moderate William Pitt Fessenden, of Maine, was one of the principal defenders of the proposal to create this committee. He approved of it, he told the

[1] Oberholtzer, I, 125.

Senate, "simply for this reason: that this question of the readmission . . .
of these confederate States, so called, . . . I conceived to be of infinite
importance, requiring calm and serious consideration, and I believed that
the appointment of a committee, carefully selected by the two Houses, to
take that subject into consideration, was not only wise in itself, but an imperative duty resting upon the representatives of the people in the two
branches of Congress." [2] Though the Radical Thaddeus Stevens was to
play an important role in the work of the joint committee, it must be remembered that that body was not initially dominated by Radicals. The
Senate, for example, refused to put Sumner on the committee, though he
greatly desired the place as a pulpit from which he could expound his Radical views, and instead named such moderates as Fessenden and Grimes. [3]

2

Hoping to avoid a conflict with the President yet unwilling to accept
the Southern governments he had created, the Republicans during the first
months of the session sought to work out some compromise that would
guarantee the rights of the Negroes and that would at the same time be
acceptable to Johnson. They believed they had found a suitable agency in
an already existing institution, the Freedmen's Bureau, which had been
first created by the act of March 3, 1865, and had since been doing indispensable work in the feeding and care of Southern refugees, white and
black. Operating under the war department, the bureau had an elaborate
organization in every Southern state, and its work was of a varied character.
Employment was found for former slaves. The bureau supervised labor
contracts entered into by freedmen, established them on public lands under the homestead law, fixed their wages and terms of employment, and
provided transportation to new-found homes. Colonies of Negroes were
sometimes formed; hospital service was extended; schools were widely established. Care was taken by the bureau to obtain justice for the Negro and
to protect him from discrimination as to civil rights in Southern communities. Its relief and educational activities were of real importance in a
period when certain groups known as "Jayhawkers," "Regulators," and
"Black-horse Cavalry" were striking terror to Negro hearts.

On the other hand, the bureau was not without its critics. Though its
head, General O. O. Howard, was a man of the finest character, many of
the bureau officers were corrupt, and its agents sometimes exceeded their

---

[2] McKitrick, *Andrew Johnson and Reconstruction*, 275.

[3] The House members were Thaddeus Stevens (Pa.), Elihu B. Washburne
(Ill.), Justin S. Morrill (Vt.), Henry Grider (Ky.), John A. Bingham (Ohio),
Roscoe Conkling (N. Y.), George S. Boutwell (Mass.), Henry T. Blow (Mo.), and
Andrew J. Rogers (N. J.). The senators were W. P. Fessenden (Me.), J. W.
Grimes (Ia.), Ira Harris (N. Y.), J. M. Howard (Mich.), G. H. Williams (Ore.),
and Reverdy Johnson (Md.). *Ann. Cyc.*, 1866, 139–140.

powers or misappropriated funds. Its daily control of important matters of domestic economy as well as the wide jurisdiction of its special courts in the adjustment of freedmen's claims, and more especially the activities of the bureau in consolidating Republican control, caused it to be widely distrusted by Southern whites. In fact, however, as George R. Bentley points out, "such southern opponents of the Bureau despised it more for what it stood for than for what it had done. . . . Generally . . . they did not think of the Freedmen's Bureau in terms of 'its best.' To most of them it was virtually a foreign government forced upon them and supported by an army of occupation. They resented its very existence, regardless of what it might do, for it had power over them and it was beyond their control." [1]

To moderate Republicans this seemed the ideal instrumentality for guarding the rights of the Southern Negroes without overtly antagonizing the President. Sponsored by the moderate Lyman Trumbull, of Illinois, and endorsed by the moderate Fessenden, a bill was introduced providing "that the Freedmen's Bureau should continue its work indefinitely, and that its authority should be extended to refugees and freedmen in all parts of the country." More controversial were the provisions, designed to counteract the "black codes," which gave the bureau the power "to 'extend military protection and jurisdiction' over all cases involving discrimination against persons on account of race, color, or previous condition of slavery. Any person who should, by reason of state or local law, or regulation, custom, or prejudice, cause any other person to be deprived of any civil right was to be liable to punishment by one year's imprisonment or one thousand dollars' fine or both. And the Freedmen's Bureau was 'to take jurisdiction of . . . all offenses committed against this provision; and also of all cases affecting . . . persons who are discriminated against. . . .' " [2]

Although the framers of the measure thought they had secured the President's prior approval of their bill, Johnson believed it to be an unwarranted continuance of the war power in time of peace. In his veto message he argued that state courts were peacefully functioning and that adequate protection was being given to freedmen without any such law. Conflicts of jurisdiction would inevitably arise, he thought, between military and civil authorities if the law were passed. He saw in the bill a dangerous extension of military jurisdiction, entailing the denial of jury trial and allowing court-martial penalties unauthorized by law. He deemed it better to intrust the rights of citizens to the civil courts "presided over by competent and impartial judges, bound by fixed rules of law and evidence, . . . than to the caprice . . . of an officer of the bureau, who, it is possible, may be entirely ignorant of the principles that underlie the just administration of the law." He feared that freedmen would be exploited by the officers, and

[1] Bentley, *A history of the Freedmen's Bureau*, 104–105.
[2] *Ibid.*, 116–117.

that an unnecessary continuance of the bureau "would inevitably result in fraud, corruption, and oppression." [3]

The President's veto message aroused great antagonism in Congress, but it was for the time being sustained, since two-thirds of the Senate could not be mustered to override it. By revealing the President's total intransigence, the veto helped convince many moderates that they could no longer work with Johnson, and increasingly they came to look with favor upon the program of the Radicals. In reply to the President's message, the joint Committee of Fifteen proposed a resolution declaring that in order "to close disturbing agitation no senator or representative from any of the eleven insurgent states should be admitted to either branch of Congress" until both houses had "declared such state entitled to such representation." Bitterly fought by the Democrats and a few conservative Republicans, it was adopted by the combined strength of the moderates and the Radicals. [4]

3

Three days after his veto of the Freedmen's Bureau Act, President Johnson further alienated moderate support in Congress by his injudicious remarks to some serenaders who came to the White House on the occasion of Washington's birthday. Forgetting the dignity due to his position, Johnson reverted to the rough-and-tumble political practice of frontier Tennessee, where orators exchanged violent personalities, crude humor, and bitter denunciations. Allowing hecklers in his audience to draw from him angry charges, he told the crowd: "I fought traitors and treason in the South; now when I turn around, and at the other end of the line find men—I care not by what name you call them—who will stand opposed to the restoration of the Union of these States, I am free to say to you that I am still in the field."

During the "great applause" which followed, a nameless voice shouted, "Give us the names at the other end. . . . Who are they?"

"You ask me who they are," Johnson retorted. "I say Thaddeus Stevens of Pennsylvania is one; I say Mr. Sumner is another; and Wendell Phillips is another." Increasing applause urged him to continue. "Are those who want to destroy our institutions . . . not satisfied with the blood that has been shed? . . . Does not the blood of Lincoln appease the vengeance and wrath of the opponents of this government?" [1]

The President's remarks were as impolitic as they were untrue. Not only was it manifestly false to assert that the leading Republican in the House and the most conspicuous Republican in the Senate were opposed

---

[3] *Cong. Globe,* 39 Cong., 1 sess., 3838–3839.
[4] Oberholtzer, I, 166.

[1] Donald, "Why They Impeached Andrew Johnson," *Am. Heritage,* VIII, 23–24 (Dec., 1956).

to "the fundamental principles of this government" or that they had been responsible for Lincoln's assassination; it was incredible political folly to impute such actions to men with whom the President had to work daily.

Johnson's failure to realize that the President of the United States cannot afford to be a quarreler was to cost him dearly. The intemperateness of his remarks stiffened the antagonism of the Radicals, and, what is more significant, it further weakened moderates' faith in the President.

Though the breach between the President and his party was now wide, it was not yet irreparable. Continuing to hope that Johnson would approve some measure which would guarantee minimal rights, under federal protection, to the freedmen, moderate Republicans joined with the Radicals in backing the civil rights bill introduced by Trumbull. The measure offered the first federal statutory definition of citizenship and asserted the right of the federal government to intervene in state affairs where necessary to protect the rights of United States citizens. Persons born in the United States and not subject to any foreign power were in general declared citizens of the United States, with the exception of Indians not taxed. Such persons "of every race and color" were declared to have the right in every state to sue, to give evidence, to inherit, hold, and convey property, and to be entitled "to full and equal benefit of all laws and proceedings for the security of person and property, as is enjoyed by white citizens." For depriving citizens of equal rights the offender in every state was made punishable by fine and imprisonment, and Federal courts were given exclusive jurisdiction over such offenders. Federal military and naval forces were made available for the enforcement of the measure; and it was declared, unnecessarily, that upon all questions arising under the act a final appeal might be taken to the Supreme Court of the United States. The bill received the virtually unanimous support of the entire Republican party in Congress; only three Republican votes were cast against it in the Senate.

Though moderates from all over the nation urgently appealed to Johnson to approve this measure and though every member of his cabinet, except Welles, advised him to sign it, the President was unyielding. He sent to Congress a strongly worded veto message. The subject matter of the measure he conceived to lie properly within state polity, and he objected to the bill as one which invaded both the legislative and the judicial power of the states, subjecting their judges to Federal penalties. The president reminded Congress that Federal judicial powers are fixed in the Constitution and that the bill authorized "the exercise of powers that are not, by the Constitution, within the jurisdiction of the courts of the United States." [2]

Even more than his veto of the Freedmen's Bureau Act or his impolitic words on Washington's birthday, Johnson's rejection of the Civil Rights Act drove the great body of moderate Republicans in Congress into the

2 Richardson, *Messages and Papers,* VI, 410–411.

Radical camp. On April 9, 1866, most of them joined the Radicals in passing the Civil Rights Act over the presidential veto. A few weeks later they passed a second version of the Freedmen's Bureau Act. When the President vetoed it, all but three Republicans in the Senate voted to override the executive's negative.

4

Even while Congress was enacting the Civil Rights Act and extending the life of the Freedmen's Bureau, the joint committee on reconstruction was preparing a constitutional amendment to govern the restoration of the Southern states. Often treated as a kind of conspiratorial procedure, the drafting of what became the fourteenth amendment was in fact the response to very urgent necessities in the complex reconstruction situation. Some arrangements obviously had to be made for the restoration of the seceded states to the Union, but virtually all Republicans felt that recognition of the Johnson governments in those states would be a course fraught with peril. Ironically enough, the Southern states, though defeated in the war, would have to come back into the Union with increased representation in Congress; the end of slavery automatically abolished the old three-fifths clause, and consequently the South as a whole would henceforth gain about fifteen additional representatives. If one remembers that the Johnson régimes in all of the Southern states were under leaders opposed to the Republican party, who were already making overtures to the Northern Democrats, it is easy to understand why Republicans, still largely in the grip of wartime hysteria, feared disastrous consequences. If readmitted, the Southerners, aided by their Northern allies, would be able to repeal the Civil Rights Act and to end the Freedmen's Bureau; they might attempt to return the Negro to virtual slavery; they could even possibly repudiate the Federal war debt or require the nation to assume that of the Confederacy. Even to moderate Republicans the prospect looked ominous, and so cautious a politician as John Sherman felt obliged to vow: ". . . never by my consent shall these rebels gain by this war increased political power and come back here to wield that power in some other form against the safety and integrity of the country." [1]

Gradually more and more Northerners had come to believe that an additional constitutional amendment was needed to safeguard the fruits of their Civil War victory. Nearly all agreed that there must be some irrepealable guarantee of the rights of the freedmen. Virtually all Republicans also thought that something must be done to prevent the return of the former Southern slaveowners to political power in their section. Radicals had already concluded that enfranchisement of the Negro would be the best solution of this problem. To men like Chase and Stevens, who had

[1] Joseph B. James, *The Framing of the Fourteenth Amendment*, 69–70.

devoted their lives to battling for the Negro's rights, impartial suffrage seemed obviously just. Sumner hesitated before advocating the enfranchisement of the largely illiterate Negro population of the South but soon came to the conclusion that there was "no substantial protection for the freedman except in the franchise." "He must have this," Sumner argued, "(1) For his own protection; (2) For the protection of the white Unionist; and (3) For the peace of the country. We put the musket in his hands because it was necessary; for the same reason we must give him the franchise." [2] Moderate Republicans were more reluctant to advocate Negro suffrage—a proposal which would certainly have adverse political repercussions in the various Northern states which still restricted the Negro's franchise; instead, they hoped to work out some system which would reduce the representation of the ex-Confederate states in Congress unless they were safely under Republican control.

Such were some of the pressures which beat upon the joint committee as it drafted a new constitutional amendment. There is not space here to discuss the elaborate negotiations which took place between groups and leaders in the actual designing of the proposed amendment. It is enough to suggest that it should properly be regarded as a compromise between moderate and Radical desires, not entirely satisfactory to either faction but ambiguous enough to permit each to support it. Thus Stevens and Sumner, though both protesting the inadequacies of the measure, finally voted for it. So also did John Sherman, who was able to boast to his constituents: "They talk about radicals; why, we defeated every radical proposition in it." [3]

Since this amendment was to mark a significant change in American constitutional history, its wording deserves careful attention. Its first section attempted a definition of American citizenship and of the rights belonging to citizens of the United States. As it then stood the Constitution, in the bill of rights, prohibited Congress from interfering with fundamental rights of civil liberty (freedom of speech, the right to fair trials, etc.); but these constitutional provisions offered no Federal limitations upon the states in such matters. As announced by its framers, the first purpose of the new amendment, therefore, was to create a Federal constitutional prohibition upon the states which would prevent them from denying equal protection of the laws to the millions of new-made citizens. The following definition of citizenship constituted the first part of the amendment: "All persons born or naturalized in the United States, and subject to the jurisdiction thereof, are citizens of the United States and of the State wherein they reside." Following the citizenship clause there came the provision which in subsequent constitutional interpretation has proved most important, that which prohibited a state from abridging the privileges and immunities of citizens of the United States, depriving "any person" of life,

[2] E. L. Pierce, *Memoir and Letters of Charles Sumner,* IV, 275.
[3] James, 167.

liberty, or property, without "due process of law," or denying to "any person" the equal protection of the laws.

These rather cryptic phrases, which constitutional lawyers now regard as the chief part of the amendment, have been the subject of much later litigation and historical controversy. Their ambiguity was intentional. There can be no doubt that, in the minds of most of the framers and supporters of the amendment, this first clause was "meant to apply neither to jury service, nor suffrage, nor antimiscegenation statutes, nor segregation." [4] In particular, there is nothing to suggest that the framers thought they were outlawing segregation in the public schools.[5] Thus it was chiefly an amendment embodying moderate Republican views. It was not, however, wholly unacceptable to the Radicals, for to those veterans of the antislavery contest "due process" and "equal protection of the laws" evoked memories of "the constitutional heritage of a quarter of a century of abolitionism," when these same phrases had been "the familiar instruments for the establishment and protection of the civil and personal rights of men." [6] Radicals saw that, with favorable circumstances, a broader interpretation of the Negro's rights might be possible. The clause was thus, as Alexander M. Bickel has suggested, a compromise. It permitted the moderates to "go forth and honestly defend themselves against charges that on the day after ratification Negroes were going to become white men's 'social equals,' marry their daughters, vote in their elections, sit on their juries, and attend schools with their children." But Radicals also benefited by it, obtaining "what early in the session had seemed a very uncertain prize indeed: a firm alliance, under Radical leadership, with the Moderates in the struggle against the President, and a good, clear chance at increasing and prolonging their political power." [7]

Since in subsequent years this section of the amendment was widely invoked to protect the rights of corporations, which were considered legal "persons," against state regulation, some historians have upheld a "conspiracy theory" of the Fourteenth Amendment. Charles A. and Mary Beard, for example, maintained that the true intent of the framers was to restore "to the Constitution the protection for property which Jacksonian judges had whittled away" by making "every act of every state and local government which touched adversely the rights of persons and property . . . subject to review and liable to annulment by the Supreme Court at Wash-

[4] Alexander M. Bickel, "The Original Understanding and the Segregation Decision," *Harvard Law Review,* LXIX, 1 (Nov., 1955).

[5] *Ibid.,* 58; but cf. A. H. Kelly, "The Fourteenth Amendment Reconsidered: the Segregation Question," *Mich. Law Rev.,* LIV, 1049–1086 (1956).

[6] Jacobus tenBroek, *The Antislavery Origins of the Fourteenth Amendment,* 125. For Radical interpretations of the equal protection clause, see John P. Frank and Robert F. Munro, "The Original Understanding of 'Equal Protection of the Laws,'" *Columbia Law Review,* L, 167–168 (Feb., 1950).

[7] Bickel, 62.

ington." [8] This argument has now been thoroughly discredited. There is not room here to summarize the voluminous literature on the subject, but it is enough to note that all recent, careful scholars agree with Joseph B. James that "there is no indication in contemporary records" that the framers of the Fourteenth Amendment "had any deliberate purpose to protect [corporations] by constitutional safeguards." As a matter of fact, Professor James notes, "corporations in 1865 were in no great need of special protection. Their growing influence in all branches of many state governments was recognized and criticized by some of the very people who are responsible for the amendment that later redounded to corporate advantage." [9] It is clear that the framers of the Fourteenth Amendment were thinking of their immediate postwar problems and that in the protection of "persons" and citizens they had human beings primarily in mind, especially the emancipated Negroes, for whose welfare they had earnest solicitude.

The second section of the amendment put forth a new formula of representation, eliminating the mixed basis (the three-fifths ratio for slaves) which the original Constitution prescribed. Despite Radical urging, Negro suffrage was not positively imposed by this amendment. Reconstruction leaders were still acting upon the principle that suffrage rested with the states; and they were not yet ready (or able) to write Negro suffrage unequivocally into the Constitution. Where, however, a state denied suffrage to any of its citizens 'except for . . . rebellion, or other crime," it was provided that there should be a proportionate reduction of representation in the lower house.

This section had a twofold purpose. In the first place it offered a possible check to the increased representation that would result from the emancipation of the Negroes of the South. In addition, in the words of Senator Howard of Michigan, it was so drawn "as to make it the political interest of the once slaveholding States to admit their colored population to the right of suffrage." [10]

Democrats objected, with some justice, that Republicans were afraid of making a clear-cut political issue of Negro suffrage and hence adopted this rather backhanded way of coercing the Southern states. With considerable logic they pointed out that the provision, in order to be equitable, ought also to reduce the representation of Northern states which had a heavy non-voting, alien population. "The section [said Senator Hendricks] does not rest upon the proposition that those whom the States treat as unfit to vote shall not be represented, for it is so framed as to continue to the northern and eastern States their twenty Representatives that are based

---

[8] Charles A. and Mary R. Beard, *Rise of American Civilization*, II, 113–114.
[9] James, 31, 186.
[10] *Cong. Globe*, 39 Cong., 1 sess, 2767.

upon a non-voting population. . . . You say that if the States treat the negroes as unfit to vote, . . . no representation shall be allowed for them; then, I ask, if in some of the northern States the foreigner is denied a vote . . . why shall he be voted for [i.e., represented]?" [11] In fact, neither the fears of the opponents of this clause nor the expectations of its supporters were justified. No state ever had its representation reduced as a penalty for denying suffrage, and the entire section lost most of its significance in 1870 when the Fifteenth Amendment (also futile in practice) was adopted.

The third section of the amendment imposed disabilities upon ex-Confederates. It was provided that those who had engaged in insurrection or rebellion against the United States after having sworn officially to support the Constitution were disqualified from holding any office, civil or military, state or Federal. There were those who wished such disqualification to be made perpetual and beyond the reach of pardon; but there was fortunately included a clause making the disability removable by two-thirds vote of each house of Congress. The objective of the section was to take away the pardoning power from the President, for Republican congressmen thought Johnson's amnesty proclamations and his thousands of special pardons showed premature willingness to grant relief and oblivion to the leaders of the Confederacy.

In its fourth section the amendment declared illegal and void all debts "incurred in aid of . . . rebellion against the United States" and invalidated all claims for emancipated slaves. At the same time the validity of the existing public debt of the United States was confirmed. That the Constitution should have to be amended in order to put beyond question the validity of the national debt seemed hard to comprehend; and it was urged that this clause, by suggesting doubt as to the government's good faith, might actually injure public credit. The fact that the claims of bondholders should be singled out for special constitutional guarantee was also the subject of adverse comment.

In June, 1866, the amendment was adopted by both houses of Congress, and Secretary Seward passed it on to the states for consideration. The President's signature is not necessary for a congressional resolution submitting a constitutional amendment; but Johnson took occasion to voice his protest and to express doubt as to whether any amendment to the Constitution ought to be proposed by Congress and pressed upon the state legislatures until after the admission to Congress of Southern representatives.[12] At first attempt the amendment failed of ratification when presented to the states. By March, 1867, twelve of the thirty-seven states (Delaware and Kentucky in addition to all the seceded states except Tennessee) had re-

[11] *Ibid.*, 2939.
[12] *Cong. Globe,* 39 **Cong.,** 1 **sess.,** 3349.

jected the amendment, which meant that ratification was defeated, since the negative action of ten states would have sufficed.[13] The decisive action of the Southern states was attributable in large measure to President Johnson's hostility toward the amendment. In the North it was widely interpreted as evidence of continuing Southern unwillingness to accept the results of the war. Inevitably, therefore, the amendment became a primary campaign issue in the fall elections.[14]

Frequently during the debates on this proposed amendment, both in Congress and in the state legislatures, it was asked whether it represented the final terms which Congress intended to impose upon the defeated South before readmitting it to the Union. Many moderate Republicans believed that ratification of the amendment would mark the end of reconstruction. As the Boston *Advertiser* declared, "There can be no question that the amendment was proposed with the distinct intention of submitting it as the final condition of restoration." On the other hand, Sumner, Stevens, Butler, and other Radicals, believing the amendment was too lenient, favored imposing further conditions.[15] The amendment itself was a compromise on this as upon so many other subjects; its deliberate vagueness marks, as Professor McKitrick suggests, a decision on the part of both moderate and Radical Republicans "to refrain for the time being from coming to any further decisions" on reconstruction. But "as a release from the embarrassments of non-action in committing Congress on the other states," [16] the Republican majority did move to readmit Tennessee, which, it was claimed, had ratified the amendment. In point of fact, the Tennessee ratification was dubious, for, even after voting qualifications partial to the Republicans had been set up, it was only by the forcible arrest of two opponents that a quorum was obtained in the legislature. In announcing the result to the secretary of the United States Senate the Radical governor "Parson" Brownlow, added: "Give my respects to the dead dog of the White House." [17] The resolution of Congress declaring Tennessee's readmission was worded with an eye to putting the President in a dilemma. Knowing Johnson's intense wish to have his own state restored, the leaders prefaced the resolution with a preamble designed to give legal regularity to congressional reconstruction. Johnson, however, met the trick with equal cleverness: he signed the resolution, but accompanied his signature with an able message in which he reviewed Southern measures in compliance

[13] Counting all the states North and South there were thirty-seven at this time. The principle had already been adopted in connection with the thirteenth amendment that the full number should be counted for the purpose of ratifying a constitutional amendment, regardless of the fact that some were yet "unreconstructed."

[14] For the subsequent ratification of the amendment, see below, 633–637.

[15] James, 172–174.

[16] McKitrick, 361.

[17] *Cong. Globe*, 39 Cong., 1 sess., 3957.

with his own plan of restoration, emphasized the delay of Congress in adopting a plan, stressed his earnest wish for reconciliation, denied that Tennessee had given valid ratification to the fourteenth amendment, and avoided committing himself to the propositions of the preamble, which he treated as "no legislation," but "simply . . . statements." [18] In this manner, by the passage of a joint resolution of Congress signed by the President, the state of Tennessee was restored to the Union in July, 1866. Its case was unique; the account of its restoration does not fit into the main reconstruction story.

5

President Johnson did not passively accept the defeat of his reconstruction program. A man of absolute integrity, with great native ability and force, he defended his policy with the same fearless independence which he had earlier demonstrated when battling the slaveholders and the secessionists of Tennessee. His powerful and often eloquent messages to Congress attracted to his support not merely the white Southerners but influential groups throughout the land which were eager to put an end to the sectional strife. Among his most powerful backers were New York businessmen, for "Johnson's movement to decentralize the war-bloated federal power was in keeping with the New York merchant's desire for a quick return to private enterprise over the traditional channels of Southern trade and thus the restoration of pre-war business conditions." [1]

On the other hand, Johnson was under many powerful disadvantages in his contest with Congress. His elevation to the presidency was the result of the accident of Lincoln's death; never chosen to his high position, he lacked his predecessor's enormous prestige. Johnson was also deficient in the flexibility and political adroitness which had characterized Lincoln. There was a temperamental coldness about this plain-featured, grave man that kept him from easy, intimate relations with even his political supporters. His massive head, dark, luxuriant hair, deep-set and piercing eyes, and cleft square chin seemed to Charles Dickens to indicate "courage, watchfulness, and certainly strength of purpose," but it was a grim face, with "no genial sunlight in it." Johnson knew none of the arts of managing men; sure of his own rectitude, he was indifferent to the demands of expediency. Once he had made a decision, his mind was immovably closed, and he then defended his course with fierce obstinacy.

Johnson was further handicapped by the fact that on the occasion of his inauguration as Vice President he had made a sorry, drunken spectacle of himself. Historians now know that he was not a heavy drinker. At the

[18] Richardson, *Messages and Papers*, VI, 395–397.

[1] George R. Woolfolk, *The Cotton Regency: The Northern Merchants and Reconstruction, 1865–1880*, 42.

time of his inaugural display, he was just recovering from a severe attack of typhoid fever. Feeling ill just before he entered the Senate chamber, he asked for some liquor to steady his nerves, and either his weakened condition or abnormal sensitivity to alcohol betrayed him. Never again was Johnson seen under the influence of liquor, but his one lapse allowed his congressional opponents to circulate gross misrepresentations of his character.

The President was also placed under a disadvantage by the nature of the support which his reconstruction plan attracted. Naturally his lenient views on the restoration of the seceded states aroused the greatest enthusiasm among white Southerners and among Northern Democrats, who saw the prospect of a speedy restoration to political power. Yet these were the very groups which most Northerners thought to be tainted with treason. Only a handful of extremely conservative Republicans could stomach these new allies; most moderates and all Radicals were repelled by them.

The behavior of Johnson's Southern supporters during the summer of 1866 served further to alienate the masses of the Republican party from the President. After electing ex-Confederates to Congress, adopting the "black codes," and rejecting the Fourteenth Amendment, the Southern whites seemed to exhibit a vindictive ferocity toward the newly freed Negroes. In May, 1866, a quarrel between a Memphis Negro and a white teamster led to a riot in which the city police and the poor whites raided the Negro quarter and burned and killed promiscuously. Far more serious was the disturbance in New Orleans two months later. The Republican party in Louisiana was split into pro-Johnson conservatives and Negro suffrage advocates. The latter group determined to hold a constitutional convention, of dubious legality, in New Orleans, in order to secure the ballot for the freedmen and the offices for themselves. Through imbecility in the war department,[2] the Federal troops occupying the city were left without orders, and the mayor of New Orleans, strongly opposed to Negro equality, had the responsibility for preserving order. There were acts of provocation on both sides, and finally, on July 30, a procession of Negroes marching toward the convention hall was attacked.

"A shot was fired . . . by a policeman, or some colored man in the procession," General Philip Sheridan reported. "This led to other shots, and a rush after the procession. On arrival at the front of the Institute [where the convention met], there was some throwing of brick-bats by both sides. The police . . . were vigorously marched to the scene of the disorder. The procession entered the Institute with the flag, about six or eight remaining outside. A row occurred between a policeman and one of these

_____

[2] The military commander in New Orleans wired Washington for instructions. Secretary of War Stanton, who favored Negro suffrage, withheld the telegram from the President, who would, as he later declared, have ordered the troops to disperse the convention. Beale, *Critical Year*, 349–350.

colored men, and a shot was again fired by one of the parties, which led to an indiscriminate firing on the building, through the windows, by the policemen. This had been going on for a short time, when a white flag was displayed from the windows of the Institute, whereupon the firing ceased and the police rushed into the building. . . . the policemen opened an indiscriminate fire upon the audience until they had emptied their revolvers, when they retired, and those inside barricaded the doors. The door was broken in, and the firing again commenced when many of the colored and white people either escaped out of the door, or were passed out by the policemen inside, but as they came out, the policemen who formed the circle nearest the building fired upon them, and they were again fired upon by the citizens that formed the outer circle." [3]

Thirty-seven Negroes and three of their white friends were killed; 119 Negroes and seventeen of their white sympathizers were wounded. Of their assailants, ten were wounded and but one killed. President Johnson was, of course, horrified by these outbreaks, but the Memphis and New Orleans riots, together with the "black codes," seemed to most Northerners devastating illustrations of how the President's policy, if left unchecked, would actually operate in the South. [4]

So great was Northern antagonism to the President in the summer of 1866 that many sober men feared a renewal of civil strife. It was in these hectic days that the veterans organized their Grand Army of the Republic, which held its first national encampment at Indianapolis in November, 1866. Though primarily a huge club of ex-soldiers, the G. A. R. promptly revealed that it had an ax to grind. Soldier preference in Federal appointments soon became a fact, and pension claims were actively pushed. The tradition that the Republican party had saved the country, together with the constant emphasis upon the enormous debt that the country owed to the ex-soldiers, and the further important fact that it was the Republicans who had favors to grant, caused the order to stray from its initial policy of non-partisanship: indeed it was charged that the organization functioned as an adjunct of the Republican party. At least there was no doubt that Republicans were angling for the soldier vote and capitalizing the motives of military patriotism for partisan uses, just as in the South a similar emphasis was being promoted by the Democrats. It was even feared that the furious antagonism of the G. A. R. to President Johnson, the wide distribution of arms, and the defenselessness of the national capital, presented the menace of a military *coup d'état,* though such a thing is utterly foreign to American tradition and experience.

[3] *Ibid.,* 351–352.

[4] It is not to be inferred that the majority of Southern whites approved of these riots. The important thing, for the present purpose, is to note how these unfortunate developments were interpreted in the North.

6

It was amid such commotions and alarms that the campaign of 1866 for the choice of a new Congress was waged. The President threw himself vigorously into the campaign; and in a "swing around the circle" (August 28 to September 15) he visited many of the leading cities, including Philadelphia, New York, Albany, Buffalo, Cleveland, Chicago, Indianapolis, Louisville, Cincinnati, and Pittsburgh. In the rough-and-ready manner of a campaigning politician he made a number of speeches, or, as Welles said, "essentially but one speech often repeated." [1] It was a humiliating spectacle. At a number of places the President was heckled and hooted at; losing his temper he lashed back in language not always refined or discreet. The main burden of his speeches was an exposition and defense of "My Policy" as it was derisively called; but his statements were "misquoted and burlesqued by the Radicals," [2] and the whole effect was to disgust many Americans who were shocked to see the high office of President outraged and belittled. The humiliation of Johnson's friends was expressed in a private letter by Doolittle, who deplored the "fatal mistake of the President in making extemporaneous speeches," adding: "He falls into the . . . error of supposing it possible for him to lay aside his official character and [speak] as a private citizen about public affairs. It is simply *an impossibility*." It was Doolittle's view that the Washington Birthday speech had "lost to our cause" 200,000 votes.[3] The President's formal speeches and messages brought high praise from men of critical judgment, and he had real oratorical power on the stump; but the unfortunate effect of his tour bears out the opinion of Doolittle.

One of the features of the campaign of 1866 was the effort to create a new political party which would back the presidential reconstruction program, a movement which centered in the National Union Convention at Philadelphia in August, 1866. It had the avowed approval of the President, and its object was to elect a Congress that would uphold his policy. It was hoped that this consolidation of conservative sentiment would unite "Douglas Democrats" and conservative Republicans in opposition to the extremes of the Radical group. Among the men connected with the movement were such Northerners as Doolittle, Dix, A. W. Randall, O. H. Browning, Edgar Cowan, Reverdy Johnson, Frank P. Blair, Jr., and Henry J. Raymond; while on the Southern side the list included Governor James L. Orr of South Carolina, B. F. Perry of the same state, and Alexander H. Stephens of Georgia. It was the first truly national political convention held in six years; it called forth many expressions of hearty approval; and its delibera-

[1] Welles, *Diary*, II, 647.

[2] E. P. Oberholtzer, *Hist. of the U. S. since the Civil War*, I, 409.

[3] Doolittle to O. H. Browning, Oct. 7, 1866, quoted in Browning, *Diary*, II, 93 n.

tions were marked by good sense and judgment. Southern leaders who attended expressed readiness to return loyally to the Union, repudiate the Southern debt, and do justice to the emancipated Negro. They did not agree to submit to the fourteenth amendment; but they were enthusiastically willing to cooperate in all steps which the President considered needful for restoration. Only one factor seemed to mar the prevailing note of harmony—the presence of such men as Fernando Wood and C. L. Vallandigham; but there was "a very general disposition . . . to exclude them from the Convention," and the matter was adjusted without a rumpus by their withdrawal. The most striking incident of the gathering was the entrance of the Massachusetts and South Carolina delegations arm in arm. "On their appearance the vast assemblage rose to their feet and gave cheer after cheer for the Union. Many were moved to tears." As if harmony were a thing to be despised, the Radicals sarcastically dubbed the gathering the "arm-in-arm" convention.[4]

In its resolutions and "address" the convention implored the voters to remember that the war had ended with the authority of the Federal government vindicated, and reminded them that an earlier Congress had defined the purpose of the war as maintenance of the Union without impairment of state rights. Denouncing congressional usurpation and partisanship the convention urged a prompt restoration of the states, expressed confidence in President Johnson, and called for the election of congressmen who would cooperate with him. Though the assemblage resembled a "Johnson rally," no personal ambition of the President was involved. There seems no reason to doubt the President's statement to Browning that "his only ambition was to bring all the states back to their proper relations to the general government, and give unity, tranquility and prosperity to the Country, and he was then ready to retire." [5]

The Philadelphia movement, however, failed. The President was unable to capture the imagination of the Northern masses. The Republican campaign against Johnson was skilfully organized and brilliantly managed. Realizing that economic issues would divide their party, its managers soft-pedaled such questions as a proposed increase in the tariff, which, it was said, would kill the Republican candidates in Indiana, Illinois, and Iowa.[6] Instead, they constantly harped on the charge that "the fixed purpose" of Johnson and his allies was "to transfer the entire government from the control of the loyal men to Copperheads and rebels." With sentiments so aroused, the campaign was naturally marked by wild vituperation. In Ohio Republicans charged that the President did "not intend a dollar of additional bounty shall be paid a Union soldier or his family"; in Wiscon-

[4] Browning, *Diary*, II, 89.
[5] *Ibid.*, II, 79.
[6] Beale, "The Tariff and Reconstruction," *Am. Hist. Rev.*, XXXV, 293 (Jan., 1930).

sin the allegation was that "Johnson was guilty of the assassination of President Lincoln"; in New York the "calamitous and traitorous Executive was called an "insolent, drunken brute, in comparison with whom Caligula's horse was respectable." [7]

Such tactics abundantly paid off at the polls. When the campaign of 1866 was over and the votes were counted it was found that the President's friends had been disastrously defeated. The Republicans, who henceforth came more and more to follow Radical leadership, obtained more than a two-thirds majority in both houses, carrying every "Union state" except Delaware, Maryland, and Kentucky. On the day of the election (November 6) the New York *Tribune,* typical of the Radical press, harped on Civil War emotions and invoked the "spirits of the martyred dead" in its appeal for Republican votes. This paper hailed the result with satisfaction; [8] but Secretary Welles, expressing the view of conservatives, greatly deplored the election. To him it seemed that the real political questions had not been discussed and that the result was determined by passion, prejudice, and hate.[9] Just after the election Doolittle wrote to Browning: "The elections are over and we are beaten for the present. But our cause will live." By their excesses he hoped that the Radicals would bring defeat upon themselves in the next presidential election.[10]

[7] Beale, *Critical Year,* 360–361, 370.
[8] N. Y. *Daily Tribune,* Nov. 6, 1866, p. 4; Nov. 10, 1866, p. 4.
[9] Welles, *Diary,* II, 616.
[10] Doolittle to Browning, Nov. 8, 1866, Letters of O. H. Browning (MSS., Ill. St. Hist. Libr.).

CHAPTER 34

The Fabric of
Reconstruction Legislation

I

"I WAS A CONSERVATIVE in the last session of this Congress," Thaddeus Stevens announced in December, 1866, "but I mean to be a Radical henceforth." [1] Indeed, the Radicals were in control as the new session of Congress convened. The Democrats constituted "a hopeless, demoralized, and suspected minority," [2] unable to do much more than denounce the Radical program. The conservative Republicans, never numbering more than a handful of congressmen, had been emphatically repudiated in the recent election. The large moderate majority of the Republican party found itself falling increasingly under Radical leadership. Able to thwart the more extreme Radical proposals, such as Stevens's plan to divide up Southern estates or Sumner's effort to abolish all segregation, they were, nevertheless, dragged along into adopting new and severe measures toward the South.

In viewing the evolution of the congressional plan of reconstruction it will be of advantage first to examine those measures designed to put Congress in control of governmental functions and to insure within Congress the ascendency of the Radical group, in other words to perfect the Radical machine. After elaborate debate the two houses resolved that no member from any of the insurrectionary states should be admitted into either Senate or House until Congress should have declared such state entitled to representation. This made Congress the dominating agency in the process of restoration and opened the way for any conditions that the Radicals might wish to impose upon states seeking readmission. Control of the electoral college was taken in two laws: an act of February 8, 1865, which enumerated the eleven seceded states and excluded their electoral votes; and, for the election four years later, the Edmunds resolution of July 20,

---

[1] Oberholtzer, I, 422.

[2] Albert V. House, Jr., "Northern Congressional Democrats as Defenders of the South during Reconstruction," *J. S. H.*, VI, 48 (Feb., 1940).

1868, which excluded from the electoral college all states which should not have been recognized according to the congressional formula.[3] Congressional control of the army was attempted by the army appropriation act of March 2, 1867, which prescribed that all military orders emanating from the President or the secretary of war should be issued through the general of the army, whose headquarters were to be at Washington and who was not to be removed nor assigned to duty outside Washington without the approval of the Senate.[4] Contrary orders were declared void, and officers issuing or heeding them were made heavily punishable as guilty of misdemeanors. The act also declared the militia of the seceded states disbanded and forbade their organization or use except as authorized by Congress.

In declaring certain military orders of the President void, this law, in the opinion of competent authorities, infringed upon his constitutional power as commander-in-chief of the army, while it also involved a destruction of state militia functions. The significance of the law will be better appreciated when one recalls how far reconstruction was formulated along the lines of a military program. Grant as general of the army was counted upon to cooperate with the Radicals; and all the circumstances of the time show that the purpose of the act was to tie the President's hands by preventing him from removing the general or controlling the army through him.

By another law Congress seized control of its sessions. The first regular session of the Fortieth Congress, elected in 1866, would normally have begun in December, 1867. By act of January 22, 1867, however, an additional session of that and succeeding Congresses was provided, to begin on the 4th of March following the election.[5] Though the legality of this session was not successfully challenged, it was the opinion of Attorney General Stanbery that this first session of the Fortieth Congress was unconstitutional, since according to his view Congress had no authority to create an additional term, and the function of calling Congress into extra session belonged to the President. In addition to its other extraordinary measures Congress undertook control of the process of amending the Constitution. The method by which the fourteenth amendment was put through was not the untrammeled procedure indicated in the Constitution, but a special procedure in which the national legislature did more than merely "propose" an amendment as the Constitution contemplated.[6]

Congress also brought the cabinet within its control by the tenure-of-office act, to be discussed later, and proceeded far in the control of the Supreme Court by so limiting its appellate jurisdiction as to avert a deci-

[3] *Cong. Globe*, 40 Cong., 2 sess., 4236 (July 20, 1868).
[4] *U. S. Stat. at Large*, XIV, 486–487; Richardson, *Messages and Papers*, VI, 472.
[5] *U. S. Stat. at Large*, XIV, 378.
[6] See below, pp. 633–637.

sion which might overrule the reconstruction acts. Finally, by the political
use of the impeachment process the men on Capitol Hill narrowly missed
seizing the presidency itself. As the successive features of the congressional
program unfolded, there loomed the specter of congressional dictatorship;
and conservatives feared some kind of revolution, with civil commotions
more serious than those of the war through which the country had just
passed.

Viewed from another angle, this matter of congressional control involved not merely laws but various types of political manipulation. If the
Radicals were to carry out their program, it was essential that they have a
two-thirds Radical majority (not merely a Republican majority) in both
houses; and the story of the methods by which this majority was obtained
would require considerable excursions into the field of partisan strategy.
Radical managers took advantage of every opening to reshape the membership of the legislative chambers. Democratic congressmen elected in Kentucky were denied seats in 1867 on the ground that "loyal voters" had been
"overawed," that the "elections were carried by . . . returned rebels," and
that "several" of the representatives-elect from that state were "alleged" to
be "disloyal." After refusal to permit these men to be sworn in, an investigation revealed that the charges were unsustained. By this method certain
members were excluded while important reconstruction measures were
passed, though they were later found to be entitled to their seats.[7] According to Thaddeus Stevens it was with the same motive that Daniel Voorhees,
a Democrat from Indiana, was unseated [8] in the House of Representatives.
The Senate unseated John P. Stockton of New Jersey ostensibly on the
ground that the state legislature had chosen him by a plurality instead of
a majority vote of the two houses; but the motive seems to have been the
elimination of a member who did not support the Radical program. Where
legislators could not be unseated or silenced in their opposition, they were
marked for later vengeance. For supporting Johnson's policy Senator Cowan
of Pennsylvania was punished by the Senate's refusal to confirm him when
appointed minister to Austria. The New York *Tribune* referred to the rejection as a "hint to Mr. Johnson that the Senate does not intend to reward
the men who abandoned their party in order to serve the President." [9]

When these measures and party devices had been completed, the Radicals were ready to impose their will upon the South and upon the country.
The functioning of the legislative machine having been made effective,

---

[7] *House Jour.*, July 3, 1867, p. 161; "Kentucky Elections . . . ," *House
Misc. Doc. No. 47*, 40 Cong., 1 sess.; *Biog. Dir. of Amer. Cong.* (*House Doc. No.
783*, 69 Cong., 2 sess.), 295.

[8] Concerning the charge of political motives in unseating Voorhees, Stevens
said: "I had been more earnest than usual . . ., inasmuch as at this moment
every vote which was fairly ours should be considered." *Cong. Globe*, 39 Cong.,
1 sess., 1003 (Feb. 23, 1866); C. G. Bowers, *The Tragic Era*, 107–108.

[9] N. Y. *Semi-Weekly Tribune*, Mar. 15, 1867, p. 5.

and preliminary measures having been passed in 1866, Congress at last proceeded to pass the main body of reconstruction legislation in 1867 and 1868.

2

The original reconstruction act was largely the work of John Sherman; for it was his substitute, not the earlier bill presented by Thaddeus Stevens, that was passed. Nonetheless the hand of Stevens was evident in the whole process. The law proceeded on the premise that no lawful governments existed in the seceded states and that they might be governed under the authority of Congress until restored by congressional decree. Temporary military rule and drastic reorganization of state governments on the basis of Negro suffrage were the main features of the bill. The ten states still deemed to be unreconstructed were divided into five military districts and placed under Federal commanders who were clothed with functions superior to the state governments, being empowered to make arrests, conduct trials by military commissions, and direct the agencies and processes of civil government as well as of constitution making. Elections for state constitutional conventions were to be held in which persons of color were authorized to vote, while those disqualified under the proposed fourteenth amendment for supporting the Confederacy were excluded from voting. It was further prescribed that Negro suffrage and disqualification of ex-Confederate leaders must be permanently written into the newly formed state constitutions, which were to be ratified by a majority of qualified voters. When these steps had been taken in any state, when in addition its legislature had ratified the fourteenth amendment, and when that amendment had become a part of the Federal Constitution, the state might (if the Radicals so willed) "be entitled to representation in Congress." [1] Meanwhile existing civil governments in the Southern states were declared provisional only, being "subject in all respects to the paramount authority of the United States." Disqualified ex-Confederates were not to be permitted to hold office under these provisional, temporary governments.

In vetoing the bill President Johnson referred to the measure as one "without precedent and without authority, in palpable conflict with the plainest provisions of the Constitution, and utterly destructive to those great principles of liberty . . . for which our ancestors . . . have shed so much blood. . . ." [2] The bill was promptly passed over his veto, the roll call showing a vote of 135 to 48 in the House, and 38 to 10 in the Senate. [3]

[1] The act merely outlined a method. It left for the future the declaration whether that method had been complied with in particular states. For any state to be readmitted to the Union still required a special act of Congress as to that state. *U. S. Stat. at Large*, XIV, 428–429.

[2] Richardson, *Messages and Papers*, VI, 500.

[3] *Cong. Globe*, 39 Cong., 2 sess., 1733, 1976.

The South had waited in anxious suspense while Congress dallied and debated; now at last when a reconstruction law had been passed after a delay of two years, its main effect was to plunge the Southern mind into a maze of uncertainty. Who in particular were disfranchised? Why was this disfranchisement extended to thousands who had been Unionists following the close of the war? Were state governments in the South immediately to be annulled? How was a constitutional convention to be called? Would Congress later provide further details concerning these conventions? Did the Sherman bill embrace county officers (sheriffs, clerks, judges, etc.) in its disqualifying provisions, or only executive, legislative, and judicial officers of the state? How could competent men be obtained in the South for the new governments, with safe Southern men disfranchised and extremely few Southerners available who could take the prescribed oath? Must Southern governments be put into the hands of so-called Union men who were in fact disloyal and who had become "blatant Union men" from motives of gain and duplicity? Were Negroes eligible for office under the new bili? Would not those proscribed be finally pardoned? These were a few of the questions which the reconstruction act provoked.

Southerners had drunk the cup of surrender and had disbanded their armies. They had repudiated the Southern debt, had solemnly renounced secession, had accepted the antislavery amendment. This they thought would be the end. New governments, loyal to the United States, had been set up. The President had recognized them, and their representatives had made their appearance in Washington, to be denied recognition in Congress. The next phase was a long delay, with wrangling and voluminous debating. Then came the fourteenth amendment. Here the Southerners balked. Their legislatures refused ratification. But even if ratification had been given, what assurance did the South have that this would be a finality? The people regarded such men as Stevens and Wade as leaders at Washington; and these men had hinted of further conditions to be imposed. Now in March of 1867, when a supposedly comprehensive reconstruction bill was passed, Southern citizens were not only mystified as to its meaning, but were left in doubt as to whether, after all these new conditions had been fulfilled, they would then actually be readmitted to the Union.[4]

In addition to uncertainty as to ambiguities in the law, there was also evident in the South an attitude of indignation and defiance which was in part a carry-over from wartime ardor, in part a distrust of Northern notions as to Negro rule, and in part a stout resentment against the proscription of Southern leaders. Thus with the passage of the reconstruction bill the Southern people did not know where they stood. There seemed a strong possibility that the Supreme Court would declare the law unconstitutional;

[4] This summary of Southern questioning is based closely upon actual letters written to Senator John Sherman. Sherman MSS. (Libr. of Cong.), *passim,* especially nos. 27155, 27260, 27266.

but even without this added uncertainty the terms of the law itself seemed impossible to interpret in any manner conformable to Southern ideas of law and order. "After two years [wrote a Virginia editor], . . . we are just launched on the path of . . . reconstruction. Perhaps the bill means that the present government of Virginia is not even provisional—but void. Perhaps we shall not even have a 'provisional' government until there is an election under the . . . bill. If so, all the . . . legislation of the past six years are [sic] void; and we are . . . in perfect chaos." [5]

Of itself the reconstruction act accomplished nothing except to create puzzlement, confusion, and resentment in the South. Though declaring terms upon which new Southern governments were to be formed, the act was deficient in providing the initial impetus for launching such governments. The process of calling conventions according to the congressional model was left to the people. If, however, the people took no steps toward reorganization, they would remain under their existing state governments (formed on the Johnson model) subject to military rule. It soon became evident that the Southern whites elected to remain in this condition, where their state officials were in sympathy with dominant Southern aims, rather than wreck their existing governments, intrust governmental functions to the Negro, and proscribe those whom they regarded as typical Southerners and competent leaders. To quote a declaration by conservative whites in Arkansas, reconstruction by the congressional plan was "an impossibility." Any reconstruction such as contemplated by the Radicals would result "in the certain degradation, prostration and complete ruin of the State." [6]

To deal with this situation the Radicals in Congress resolved to set the wheels moving by their own outside impulse. For this purpose there was passed the supplemental reconstruction act of March 23, 1867. Under this law the Federal military commanders in the South were directed to take the initiative and to launch the necessary proceedings as to registration of voters, election of delegates, assembling of conventions, and adoption of state constitutions. President Johnson, of course, vetoed the bill, pointing out that governments existed in the South which had been made in the accustomed way and were conformable to the "acknowledged standards of loyalty and republicanism." He denounced the Federal imposition of universal Negro suffrage, which was a matter that belonged to the states; and he could not approve "this legislative machinery of martial law, military coercion, and political disfranchisement." [7]

[5] Charlottesville (Virginia) *Chronicle*, Feb. 26, 1867.

[6] Fleming, *Doc. Hist.*, I, 423–424.

[7] Richardson, *Messages and Papers*, VI, 533. The veto was overridden the very day it was received (March 23, 1867). The vote in the House was 114 to 25 (25 not voting), in the Senate 40 to 7.

3

The South, thus reduced to "conquered provinces," was organized into five military districts, each under the command of a major general. The assigning of generals to these commands belonged to the President; but Johnson's performance of this painful duty was hardly more than a matter of accepting the advice of the general-in-chief of the army. Schofield was appointed for the district comprising Virginia; Sickles for North and South Carolina; Pope for Georgia, Alabama, and Florida; Ord for Mississippi and Arkansas; Sheridan for Louisiana and Texas. There were numerous changes in these appointments: Stoneman, A. S. Webb, and Canby were the successors of Schofield; Meade followed Pope; and a series of generals succeeded to other commands.[1] Among the less objectionable to Southerners were Hancock and Meade; the more objectionable included Sheridan, Sickles, and Pope.

Perhaps the greatest disturbance appeared under Sheridan in Louisiana, where the suppression of civil government by military rule presented analogies to the wartime situation under Butler. Sheridan arbitrarily removed sundry officials, including a city judge, a city treasurer, the mayor of New Orleans, the attorney general of the state, and a board of levee commissioners who controlled the disbursement of $4,000,000. He also removed J. Madison Wells, governor of Louisiana, and appointed B. F. Flanders in his place. Further trouble arose in the matter of the registration of Negro voters and the denial of registration to whites. Finally such was the disorder and agitation under Sheridan that Johnson transferred him to another area and assigned the command over Louisiana and Texas to W. S. Hancock, whose administration proved less provocative.

Confronted with practical problems in the enforcement of the reconstruction acts, President Johnson sought advice from his attorney general, Henry Stanbery, who gave an opinion (June 20, 1867) that the military commanders were not authorized to promulgate codes in defiance of civil governments in the states, but were to cooperate with the existing governments, which, it will be remembered, had been set up under Johnson's plan. Stanbery's opinion was intended to offer guidance to the President in his difficult position; and the President through the adjutant general issued a series of instructions to the commanders in the South indicating the manner in which recent acts of Congress should be applied. At this point, however, the Radicals of Congress, seeing in the President's instructions an attempt to undo their work, arranged for a reassembling of Congress in July, at which time they passed a "third reconstruction act," calculated to interpret and make effective their preceding legislation.

This third reconstruction act resolved itself largely into a statement of

---

[1] *Ann. Cyc.*, 1867, 736; Fleming, *Sequel of Appomattox*, 140 n.

the "true intent and meaning" of the preceding measures, thus piling up an accumulated mass of supplemental, explanatory, and interpretative legislation that only a Philadelphia lawyer could grasp. Congress now declared that existing state governments in the South were "not legal" and were fully subject to the military commanders and the paramount authority of Congress. The general of the army and the commanders of the military districts were directed to remove any state official who should "hinder, delay, prevent or obstruct the due and proper administration" of the reconstruction acts. Registration boards prescribed by the act of March 23 were empowered to deny registration on suspicion that oath-taking was not in good faith; and the provisions concerning the oath were given a stricter interpretation, so that participation in the "rebellion" could be established by parol evidence, without the requirement of record evidence. Registration officers were directed to revise registration lists in keeping with the new "interpretation," and the removal of such officers was authorized whenever "needful." To further emphasize the supremacy of the military power through Congress, it was provided that no military commander, nor any officer acting under him, should be bound "by the opinion of any civil officer of the United States." Finally there was added a curious clause which "enacted" that the reconstruction laws should "be construed liberally, to the end that all the intents thereof may be fully and perfectly carried out." This last clause was less a matter of legislation than a mandate as to the interpretation of legislation. Congress was introducing a distinction between the law and the "intent" of the law, and was appealing to executory officers to follow only a specified course in "construing" legislation whose purpose and meaning were continually undergoing restatement by Congress itself.

Three reconstruction acts had now been passed, two of them supplemental to the first. Some months elapsed; and it then became evident that the legislative machinery was not even yet accomplishing the purpose of the Radicals. As the law then stood (act of March 23, 1867, supplemental to the act of March 2, 1867) the adoption of a new constitution in a Southern state required a majority of all registered voters, not merely a majority of the votes cast. Seeing in this situation a chance to defeat the newly proposed Radical constitution in Alabama, framed by delegates said to represent merely the Negroes and non-residents, a conference of conservative men, assembled at Montgomery, issued an appeal to the people of the state advising those opposed to the constitution to refrain from voting. Conservatives knew that the law was so framed against them that they could not defeat the constitution at the election; and by refraining from voting they hoped to accomplish more than by going to the Radical-controlled polls and trying to cast negative votes, because their known attitude would cause the whole vote to be lighter, and the Radicals, being under the necessity of changing their own law so as to permit the constitution to be adopted by a mere majority of the votes cast, would thus "exhibit . . .

the fact that the constitution they impose is not the constitution of the people of Alabama, but . . . of a minority . . ., and that, a negro minority." [2] When the constitution was voted on (February 4, 1868) it was defeated by reason of the fact that the affirmative vote of about 70,000 amounted to less than half the number of registered voters, which was about 167,000.

Because of this situation Congress now passed the "fourth reconstruction act," by which a majority of the votes actually cast was made sufficient to put a new constitution into force, no matter how small the minority taking part in the election. This meant that the cards were stacked in favor of the Radicals, whose intention to force their type of government upon the South was emphasized by another provision of law, which gave the franchise to any voter who had resided in the election district for ten days preceding the election, "upon presentation of his certificate of registration, his affidavit, or other satisfactory evidence," under regulations made by the district commander.[3] This fourth reconstruction act became law on March 11, 1868, without the President's signature, by the operation of the ten-days rule.

Thus by March of 1868 the Radical party had, three years after the close of the war, built up its structure of legislation and supplemental legislation. The reconstruction acts were now launched; minorities, though made up of outsiders and Negroes, were sufficient to establish new governments; district military commanders, with power to set up military commissions in the place of the civil courts, were in possession with "sufficient military force . . . to . . . enforce . . . authority"; [4] opposition to the "directory" at Washington was ineffective; and the readiness to pile statute upon statute indicated a determination of the Radicals to permit no defeat of their purposes even by the provisions of their own laws.

[2] *Ann. Cyc.*, 1868, 15–16.
[3] *U. S. Stat. at Large*, XV, 41.
[4] Reconstruction act of March 2, 1867, sec. 2, *U. S. Stat. at Large*, XIV, 428.

CHAPTER 35

The President Impeached

THE EFFORT to remove President Johnson by impeachment was of a piece with the rest of the Radical program. The full story reveals the absence of the judicial attitude in House and Senate. The impeachment movement of 1867, proceeding by way of an investigation as a necessary preliminary to an impeachment resolution, resulted in defeat on the part of the impeachers; then in 1868, with no prior investigation and without even any charges to give colorable pretext to its action, the House passed the impeachment resolution, to be *followed* by articles of impeachment, after which the President was put on trial for his official life and reputation before a Senate made up chiefly of his outspoken enemies. In the end, however, the Radicals failed of conviction by one vote. The final outcome was to fix the precedent that the weapon of Federal impeachment, which is not merely a "method of removal," shall not be degraded to partisan purposes.

I

On January 7, 1867, the House passed a resolution offered by Ashley of Ohio by which the judiciary committee was instructed to investigate accusations gainst the President. The resolution read: "I [i.e., James M. Ashley] do impeach Andrew Johnson, Vice President and acting President of the United States, of high crimes and misdemeanors. I charge him with usurpation of power [etc.]. . . . Therefore, Be it Resolved, That the Committee on the Judiciary be . . . authorized to inquire into the . . . conduct of Andrew Johnson," [1] etc.

In the ensuing months the House judiciary committee conducted an elaborate "investigation" in which they dealt with a heterogeneous mass of charges touching such matters as Johnson's action in returning property to Southern railroads, his pardons, his restoration of private property to "rebels," his alleged corrupt use of the veto and appointing powers, his reluctance to prosecute Jefferson Davis, his so-called "treason" during the war, and his falsely rumored guilt in connection with the assassination of Lincoln. The committee hearings descended to cheap sensationalism in

[1] *Cong. Globe,* 39 Cong., 2 sess., 320.

connection with the "testimony" of one Conover, *alias* Dunham, who offered, for a money consideration, to produce "evidence" of Johnson's complicity in the assassination. Even after Conover was imprisoned for perjury (which, he said, had been induced by the President's impeachers), Ashley sought him in prison and offered to procure his release in return for a further letter concerning the fantastic charge that Johnson had a guilty preknowledge of the assassination.[2] In this testimony-hunting it developed that the sum of $25,000 was named as the amount demanded for fabricated letters implicating the President.[3] It is significant that Ashley, after all his talk of evidence in his possession against the President, was forced to admit before the committee that his "evidence" was not of a "legal character," that it was "not that kind of evidence which would satisfy the great mass of men, especially the men who do not concur with me in my theory about this matter," but that it nevertheless "satisfied" him, and that he "could come [to] a conclusion to which impartial men, holding different views, could not come." [4]

The judiciary committee at first opposed the impeachment, judging that sufficient grounds did not exist. One of the members, however, Churchill of New York, changed his position; and by a five-to-four decision the committee recommended to the House that the President be impeached and held to answer before the Senate. No articles of impeachment were prepared by the committee. The gravamen of their accusations against Johnson consisted of various "omissions of duty" and "usurpations of power" in connection with pardons, restoration of property, vetoes, and the like.[5] The keynote of the proceeding is found in the committee's own statement that all the President's offenses are referable "to the one great overshadowing purpose of reconstructing the . . . rebel States in accordance with his own will, in the interests of the great criminals who carried them into the rebellion." [6] Impeachment, according to the committee's concept, was not confined to crimes nor to offenses indictable under the statutes. It referred, they said, "not so much to moral conduct as to official relations"; [7] yet it was for crimes and misdemeanors that the President was to be impeached as recommended in the resolution which they framed and presented. Dissenting members of the committee stated that the report of the majority resolved all presumptions against the President and affirmed statements "in support of which there is not a particle of evidence before us which would be received by any court in the land." [8]

[2] *House Report No. 7*, 40 Cong., 1 sess., 1197 (second pagination).
[3] *Ibid.*, 1193.
[4] *Ibid.*, 1198–1199.
[5] *Ibid.* (first pagination), 58.
[6] *Ibid.* (first pagination), 2.
[7] *Ibid.* (first pagination), 50–51.
[8] *Ibid.* (first pagination), 59.

When put upon its passage in the House, the committee's resolution to impeach the President was voted down, 57 to 108.[9] Thus the "first impeachment" failed. Then came the controversy over Stanton's removal, giving an entirely new turn to the impeachment effort. The tenure-of-office act, passed by the Radicals of Congress on March 2, 1867, had made the removal of cabinet officers subject to the consent of the Senate, its violation being punishable as a "high misdemeanor." Though there was uncertainty and quibbling as to the meaning of the law and even as to the purpose of Congress in passing it,[10] the mooted statute acquired importance from its use as a means of preventing the President's removal of the secretary of war, and more especially as a statutory basis for declaring the Chief Executive a violator of law. Every member of the cabinet disapproved of the bill; and Stanton himself assisted in preparing the President's veto message denouncing the act as unconstitutional. Indeed, according to the diary of O. H. Browning, "Mr. Stanton was more earnest and emphatic in . . . his objections than any member of the Cabinet." The President, adds Browning, requested Stanton to prepare the veto message; and the secretary of war, though declining to do so because of a rheumatic arm, made suggestions "of the points of the veto" to Seward, who prepared the message.[11]

2

As legatee of the Lincoln administration, Johnson had long hesitated to make changes in the ill-assorted cabinet of the war President. For a long period he avoided asking the resignation of those members who were causing him embarrassment; but he had taken advantage of voluntary resignation to bring into the cabinet men of his own views: A. W. Randall in place of Dennison in the post office department; Henry Stanbery to succeed Speed as attorney general; and O. H. Browning (an Illinois conservative and friend of Lincoln) to take Harlan's post in the interior department. These changes, completed in the latter part of 1866, had given the President a harmonious cabinet with the exception of Secretary of War Stanton, whose failure to cooperate and whose alliance with the Radicals had placed a great strain upon the President's forbearance, a quality which Johnson possessed to a greater degree than is usually supposed. His patience at length exhausted, the President, during a recess of Congress, suspended Stanton from office (August 12, 1867) and authorized Grant to act as secretary of war ad interim.

Grant accepted, thus plainly implying that the President had his confidence and support; but his wavering attitude soon drew him into an em-

[9] Dec. 7, 1867. *Cong. Globe,* 40 Cong., 2 sess., 68.
[10] See below, p. 612.
[11] Browning, *Diary,* II, 132, 190; "Notes of Colonel W. G. Moore," *Am. Hist. Rev.,* XIX, 110; Welles, *Diary,* III, 50, 52, 54; Bancroft, *Seward,* II, 465.

barrassing and equivocal position. His postwar conduct had followed no
clear-cut policy, not even the Sherman policy of avoiding politics. As conquering hero in an age when army laurels were emphasized he found himself after the war the most popular man in the North. Not only for this,
but also because he was head of the army, the general was besieged by the
Radicals on one side and by Johnson's friends on the other, being meanwhile cheered, fêted, banqueted, obsequiously courted by politicians, and
showered with costly gifts. He participated in cabinet sessions under both
Lincoln and Johnson and was generally supposed to favor a generous restoration of the South. With Farragut he had accompanied Johnson in his
speaking tour of 1866, though at this time he was accessible to Radical
blandishments. On political matters he tried to be noncommittal; but by
the time reconstruction measures had matured in Congress he was co-
operating with the Radicals and with Stanton in the suppressive use of
military power in the South.

President Johnson of course supposed that Grant's acceptance of a
place in his cabinet meant that he could rely on his cooperation. On one
point in particular he found such cooperation essential. Anticipating the
Senate's refusal to confirm Stanton's suspension and desiring to test the
constitutionality of the tenure act in the courts, the President sought an
understanding with Grant. An elaborate controversy later developed as to
what this understanding was; certainly the President believed that Grant
agreed either to remain at the head of the war department until a court
decision could be obtained or to resign before the Senate acted, so that the
President could appoint someone who would retain the office.[1]

As expected, the Senate refused to concur in Stanton's removal, whereupon Grant, having held the office of secretary ad interim up to this point,
now surrendered it to Stanton. The President regarded this as a violation
of a solemn promise. After trying in vain to induce General W. T. Sherman to accept the office, Johnson appointed General Lorenzo Thomas. On
February 21, 1868, he sent Stanton a letter removing him from office as
secretary of war and directing him to yield the office to Thomas, to whom
he sent an official commission. There followed a serio-comic scene between
Thomas, who demanded the office, and Stanton, who refused to surrender;
after which Thomas withdrew and Stanton barricaded his rooms. From
this time forward Stanton kept the "office" (not only the rooms where official business was conducted, but also the bulk of the functions of secretary
of war), while Thomas attended cabinet meetings and enjoyed a nominal
recognition by the President as secretary of war ad interim.

With the tenure act and the removal of Stanton in mind as the basis

---

[1] For a summarization of the mass of material (in the Johnson papers and
elsewhere) bearing upon this question, see *Diary of O. H. Browning*, II, 178 n.,
180 n. Hesseltine (*Grant*, 107 n.) considers that the evidence against Grant on this
point is "flimsy."

for a new effort, the leaders of the House now returned to the attack upon the President; and by a vote of 126 to 47 they procured the passage (February 24, 1868) of the Covode resolution "That Andrew Johnson, President of the United States, be impeached of high crimes and misdemeanors in office." [2] The resolution was passed with no specific accusation whatever pending before the House in the form of an indictment or article of impeachment. It was well understood that the matter of Stanton's removal was the legal ground for the revival of the impeachment movement; the failure of the President's opponents to obtain a vote against him on general grounds of corruption and the like was an event fresh in memory. Yet the resolution of impeachment was the subject of spectacular debate in which the President was slandered and denounced on general principles and in which the former discredited charges were repeated and used to swing votes.

One could vote for this loose and sweeping resolution even though doubting the sufficiency of the Stanton affair as a basis for removing the President. As J. M. Ashley said: ". . . this [the removal of Stanton] is one of the smallest of the crimes of the President." "If Mr. Johnson had been guilty of no impeachable offense until his removal of Mr. Stanton, no one believes that a majority of this house could be induced to vote for his impeachment now." [3] This was a significant admission. Ashley, as we have seen, had failed to obtain an impeachment on his extravagant charges, and such charges were not before the House; yet they were undoubtedly used to influence the vote on the impeachment resolution. The remarks of Representative Lawrence of Ohio may be compared to those of Ashley. Lawrence asserted that the removal of the secretary was by no means the highest of Johnson's crimes and added: "Prior to his attempted removal [4] of Secretary Stanton . . . he had violated the Constitution in that wicked . . . attempt to create . . . governments in . . . the rebel States, . . . and to organize those States as members of the Union." [5]

Articles of impeachment were now sought and produced; but since the House had voted to impeach the President (with no accusation pending) the discussion of articles was in no sense a deliberation as to whether the President had committed an impeachable "crime," nor was the debate on specific articles a matter of reconsidering the vote to impeach. All the emphasis, as shown by a study of the record, was now placed upon the

[2] *Cong. Globe*, 40 Cong., 2 sess., 1400.
[3] *Ibid.*, 1361.
[4] The use of the phrase "attempted removal" is significant. Stanton had not been physically removed: indeed he had not been effectually ousted from the office. It was not until the conclusion of the impeachment trial by the acquittal of the President that Stanton, on May 26, 1868, relinquished charge of the war department. *Ann. Cyc.*, 1868, 743; and see below, p. 611.
[5] *Cong. Globe*, 40 Cong., 2 sess., 1549 (Feb. 29, 1868).

framing of charges in such a way as to avoid difficulties in the procuring of evidence (for which reason the charges were not to be made too severe), and to insure the success of the prosecution before the bar of the Senate. In order to facilitate prosecution some of the articles bore the *ad hominem* feature, being designed to put a senator in an inconsistent position, in view of previous commitments, if he voted for acquittal. The members were considering not justice to Johnson, but the value of each article in promoting conviction. In the adoption of the articles (the essence of the impeachment function) the House in its proceedings bore less the character of a grand jury than of a group of lawyers for the prosecution.

If a study of impeachments elsewhere in American history be made in comparison with the Johnson case, the defects of procedure in 1868 become even more clear. Normal procedure involves a preliminary resolution calling for an investigation preparatory to the preparation of articles; then, if the investigation warrants it, the presentation of definite charges, on which there should be real deliberation. After this comes the vote on impeachment, which cannot properly be defined otherwise than as a vote on the articles. In the first unsuccessful impeachment effort, the House did pass (January 7, 1867) a preliminary resolution to determine whether Johnson's conduct required "the interposition of the constitutional power of this House." [6] In 1868, however, proceedings began not with an investigation, not even with the presentation of charges, but with the Covode resolution that Johnson "be impeached of high crimes and misdemeanors"; and this resolution was referred not to the committee on the judiciary, but to the committee on reconstruction, by whose chairman (Stevens) it was reported to the House (February 22) with the recommendation that it be adopted.[7]

Two days later it was passed; and the next step should be carefully noted. While as yet no specific charges against Johnson had been adopted by the House, or had even been prepared, that body passed, under a suspension of the rules, the motion of Thaddeus Stevens that a committee of two be appointed to impeach Andrew Johnson at the bar of the Senate and to inform the Senate that the House would in due time "exhibit particular articles of impeachment . . . *and make good the same.*" [8] The committee was further instructed to demand that the Senate provide "for the appearance of . . . Andrew Johnson to answer to said impeachment." At the same time the House voted that a committee of seven be appointed, not to investigate, but to "report articles of impeachment" against Johnson. The committee of seven was designated in the record as a "Committee to declare Articles of Impeachment against the President of the United States," and it consisted of George S. Boutwell (Massachusetts), Thaddeus Stevens

[6] *Cong. Globe,* 39 Cong., 2 sess., 320.
[7] *Ibid.,* 40 Cong., 2 sess., 1336.
[8] Italics added. *Ibid.,* 1400.

(Pennsylvania), John A. Bingham (Ohio), James F. Wilson (Iowa), John A. Logan (Illinois), George W. Julian (Indiana), and Hamilton Ward (New York).[9] Every one of these seven had voted for the impeachment resolution; all were of the faction hostile to Johnson; five of them became impeachment managers in the trial.

After the articles were prepared they were presented to the House by Boutwell, who remarked upon their "artistic structure," adding that with such charges "we may safely go to the Senate and the country for the final judgment of guilty against the person accused." [10] The articles were debated under a special procedure designed to facilitate their passage, with frequent suspension of the rules; but the House refused to suspend the rules to permit the reading of a paper in which various members protested against the action of the majority.[11]

3

Ultimately the House adopted eleven verbose articles (March 2–3, 1868) whose sentences are so stilted and so stupidly tautological that the mind balks at reading them through. The first eight articles pertained to the attempted removal of Stanton. With various permutations of legalistic phrasing the President was charged with "unlawfully" removing Stanton and appointing Thomas secretary ad interim. It was affirmed in Articles 2 and 3 that Thomas was appointed "with intent to violate the Constitution of the United States"; and in Article 8 the President was charged not only with intent to violate the Constitution and the tenure act, but also to control unlawfully the disbursement of public moneys. In Articles 4, 5, 6, and 7 (the "conspiracy articles"), the President was accused of conspiring with Lorenzo Thomas and others to hinder a "duly appointed" officer from performing his duties, thus incurring the penalties of the wartime conspiracies act of July 31, 1861. The ninth article, known as the "Emory article," affirmed the President's intention to induce General Emory to violate the army act of March 2, 1867, so as to further enable Johnson to violate the tenure act.

After these nine articles had been adopted (on March 2) the President's foes were not satisfied. On the next day the "Butler article" (Article 10) was passed. In language reminiscent of the sedition act of 1798 (long since defunct) it charged the President with having delivered "inflammatory, and scandalous harangues" by which he attempted to bring the Congress into disgrace and hatred. It is significant that in this, the longest of the articles, no mention is made of the violation of any law; but Johnson was charged with having degraded the Presidency "to the great scandal of all good citizens," and was declared "guilty of a high misdemeanor in of-

---

[9] *Ibid.*, 1400–1402.
[10] *Ibid.*, 1544.
[11] *Ibid.*, 1633.

fice." [1] The eleventh and last of the charges (the "omnibus article") repeated in slightly different words the various earlier accusations touching
the removal of Stanton and added a charge that the President had referred
to the Thirty-Ninth Congress as "a Congress of only part of the States,
thereby denying, and intending to deny, that the legislation of said Congress was valid. . . ." Touching as it did a spot on which many senators
were sensitive, this article was designed to capture votes which the other
charges might not draw. After affirming that the President in denouncing
Congress had disregarded the Constitution and the laws, the eleventh
article further declared that he had attempted to prevent the execution of
three acts—the tenure act, the first reconstruction act, and the army act of
March 2, 1867. The multiplication of counts in the accusation and the
elaboration of the impeachment articles to a point where their bulk was
out of all proportion to their content were a matter of design on the part
of the impeachment promoters. They knew that if the President were convicted on any one of the eleven articles, the whole purpose of the attack
upon him would be accomplished. Yet the net result of all their zeal was a
set of charges which could be narrowed down to the removal of Stanton,
the assertion of authority over the army (of which the President is commander-in-chief), non-cooperation in congressional reconstruction, and
criticism of Congress.

Not once did the articles include the charge of corruption. The adverb
"unlawfully" was used; but the word "corruptly" did not appear. Unwittingly a tribute was paid to the President's probity: had actual evidence of
corruption been at hand, it would undoubtedly have been presented. The
attempt to find such evidence in 1867 had failed; and now in 1868 the opponents of the President, instead of accusing him of heinous or corrupt
acts, were taking the legalistic ground that things easy to prove, such as
criticism of Congress and attempted removal of a cabinet officer, were impeachable offenses.

4

Before the trial opened in the Senate, that body had taken measures
for increasing the number of Radical, anti-Johnson senators. By a renewal
of an effort launched the previous year, bills were passed in 1867 to create
two more states, Colorado and Nebraska. Proceedings on these bills came
to a vote just after the launching of the impeachment drive of 1867. Opposition by President Johnson, however, caused Radical hopes to be only half
fulfilled; for, both bills having been vetoed, only the Nebraska bill was
passed over the veto. On March 1, 1867, six years later than its territorial
twin (Kansas), Nebraska thus became the thirty-seventh state in the
Union. The Colorado case presented a different result. President Johnson,

---

[1] Very seldom are the articles printed in full. See *Ann. Cyc.*, 1868, 352 ff.

in his first veto of the Colorado bill (May 15, 1866), expressed doubt as to the need for statehood for a region whose population was estimated by optimists at no more than 40,000, though the ratio for representation in Congress was one for every 127,000. The veto was sustained; but on January 16, 1867, the bill was revived and again passed by Congress. Again, however (January 28, 1867), the bill was vetoed by the President, and once more the attempt to override the veto failed. Not until August, 1876, did Colorado become a state in the Union. Assuming that the admission of Colorado would have meant two more votes for the President's conviction, the failure to admit the state in 1867, when the "first impeachment" was in its early stages, was a factor of importance.[1] In this connection it is to be noted that both the Nebraska senators, Thayer and Tipton, voted for Johnson's conviction.

The Senate's anticipatory action was concerned also with the adoption of a set of twenty-five rules for the conduct of the trial and with efforts of the presiding officer, Chief Justice Chase, to see that the proceedings should be as nearly as possible judicial in character, in which his success was only partial and for which he was furiously denounced as favoring the President.

On March 5 and 6 the oath was administered to the senators, and the trial continued till May 26. An interesting point was presented when the name of Wade was reached in the oath-taking roll call. Under the law as it then stood, Wade, as president pro tempore of the Senate, would become President in the event of Johnson's removal. Since the Constitution specifically prevents the Vice-President (the President's successor) from having a part in an impeachment trial when the President is at bar, and since Wade's participation in the trial would involve sitting in judgment on a matter in which he had a strong personal interest, some thought it was ethically and legally improper for him to be sworn as a member of the senatorial court. After a full discussion, however, Wade was sworn in.[2] His vote for Johnson's conviction was a foregone conclusion.

The Radicals asserted that the Senate was not a court, but was acting in a political capacity when trying an impeachment case. Once when B. F. Butler, by a slip of the tongue, spoke of getting a bit of testimony "before the court," he was caught up by Stanbery and at once corrected himself, saying he wanted to get the point "before the Senate." [3] Sumner's opinion was that "this proceeding . . . is political in character—before a political body—and with a political object. . . . I have . . . called it one of the last great battles with slavery." [4]

[1] D. M. DeWitt, *Impeachment of Johnson,* 179.

[2] *Cong. Globe,* 40 Cong., 2 sess., 1671–1681, 1696–1701 (Mar. 5–6, 1868).

[3] *Ibid.,* 40 Cong., 2 sess., suppl., 151.

[4] Opinion of Charles Sumner, *Trial of Andrew Johnson* (Washington, 1868), III, 256.

The President was spared the humiliation of being dragged before the Senate. Though summoned to answer the charges, his appearance by counsel was accepted, and he was represented by Stanbery, Curtis, Groesbeck, and Evarts; while the prosecution was conducted by House managers, of whom Butler, Boutwell, and Stevens were the most prominent.[5] Much of the proceedings consisted of a sparring between attorneys as to the admissibility of evidence, all such questions being referable in the first instance to the Chief Justice, whose ruling might, at the request of any senator, be submitted to vote of the whole body. Debate was freely permitted; and the frequent remarks of senators served to prolong the trial. Much of the evidence for the President, going directly to the question of his "intent" as featured in the impeachment articles, was suppressed by vote of the Senate; but the President's counsel ultimately succeeded in presenting the testimony of General Emory, which demolished the ninth article, and that of General Sherman, who showed that the purpose of the President in the removal of Stanton was to test the constitutionality of the tenure act in the courts.[6] On this testimony it could be urged that he had not deliberately plotted to "violate the Constitution."

The opening argument for the prosecution was presented by Butler on March 30. The process of impeachment, he said, was neatly fixed by the Constitution and only one factor was left to implication—i.e., "the offenses or incapacities which are the groundwork of impeachment." He then proceeded to define an impeachable high crime or misdemeanor as an act "subversive of some fundamental or essential principle of government or highly prejudicial to the public interest." The Senate, he urged, had none of the attributes of a court, but was merely convened to determine whether Johnson "is longer fit to retain the office of President. . . ." Much of Butler's argument was occupied with denunciation of Johnson's speeches in which, for instance, the President referred to "a Congress factious and domineering," and to "a Radical Congress which gave origin to another rebellion." Denouncing the Chief Executive as one who had succeeded to the presidency "by murder most foul," and calling him the "elect of an assassin," Butler informed the senators that the "hopes of free institutions" waited upon their verdict. We of the House have done our duty, he said. "We have brought the criminal to your bar, and demand judgment at your hands for his so great crimes."[7]

Stevens's argument for the prosecution was brief; and his feebleness made it necessary for Butler to take the manuscript and conclude the reading. Like Butler, he urged that crime was not involved. "No corrupt or wicked motive [he said] need instigate the acts for which impeachment is brought. It is enough that they were official violations of law." Would any

[5] The other managers were Bingham, Wilson, Thomas Williams, and Logan.
[6] *Cong. Globe,* 40 Cong., 2 sess., suppl., 78–90, 173.
[7] *Ibid.,* 29–51.

senator dare to vote for the President's acquittal? threatened Stevens. "Neither for . . . the President nor . . . any one else would . . . [a senator] suffer himself to be tortured on the gibbet of everlasting obloquy." [8] The oral arguments of other managers (Boutwell, Bingham, and Williams) and the brief of Logan, filed as part of the record, need not be reviewed here.

Of the speeches in the President's defense, that of William M. Evarts was the most notable. The people, said Evarts, watch their President and view the office with attachment. When he is accused of high crimes they inquire whether he has betrayed a fortress, surrendered a fleet, or sold public favors; and they are told that he has removed a member of his cabinet. How comes this removal to be a crime? Stanton is secretary still. No force was used. It was all on paper. Why this effort to expel all ideas of a court of justice? What is it but an avowal that if it be a court there is no sufficient ground for judgment against the accused? If you senators are not sitting as a court, said Evarts, you are enacting a bill of attainder. To violate an unconstitutional law, he said, is not a crime. It is the right of every citizen to violate an invalid statute and get the matter into the courts. Criminal laws always look to the animus or intent of the act. But the evidence shows no evil intent on the President's part. He did no more than did Lincoln, who took various steps without legal authority. Remove the President, warned Evarts, and the constitutional division of powers will cease. We must then swing into the omnipotence of Congress and recur to the exploded experiment of the Confederation, when Congress was executive and legislature all in one.

Commenting on the spirit of the times, Evarts expressed regret that the vast problems of reconstruction should have to be settled at a time "when so great passions were enlisted, . . . when so great discontents had urged the controversy," and when "dangerous politics have been brought to the head in which these names of 'traitor' and of 'rebel,' which belong to war, have been made the current phrases of political discussion." Producing an article from Greeley's *Tribune* he showed that the denunciation of the President in the "forum of politics" was being so intermingled with the impeachment question as to constitute a confession that the formal "crimes" of the articles were of paltry consideration. [9]

Turning to the Senate's share in the removal power, Evarts pointed out that the debates in the First Congress and the practice of previous administrations from Washington onward had fixed the custom of independent removal on the part of the President. He reminded the senators of earlier proceedings touching cabinet tenure in which leading Republicans had expressed views precisely in accord with the position of Johnson. When

[8] *Ibid.,* 322–323.
[9] *Ibid.,* 349.

during the war it was thought desirable to purge Lincoln's cabinet of a dissentient member, various Republican senators signed a memorial contending that "the theory of our Government . . . is that the President should be aided by a Cabinet . . . agreeing with him in political principle and general policy," and that "such . . . changes in its members should be made as will secure . . . unity of purpose and action" among the President's advisers.[10] Among the signatures to this memorial were those of Sumner, Wilson, Chandler, and John Sherman.

Some of the most telling portions of Evarts's argument were those which reviewed the record on the passage of the tenure act. This review revealed two things: the ambiguity of the act as applying to cabinet secretaries holding over from the Lincoln administration, and the emphatic statements of senators (e.g., Sherman and Doolittle) that the act was not intended to qualify Johnson's power of removal in the case of these holdovers. The act gave tenure to cabinet members "for . . . the term of the President by whom they may have been appointed and for one month thereafter, subject to removal by . . . consent of the Senate." At the time of its passage the act was construed as giving Lincoln's appointees no statutory tenure during Johnson's term and as offering in reality (despite the purpose of some of the senators) no protection to the secretary of war against the President's independent removal.[11] When the bill was being debated Senator Doolittle called attention to its ambiguity and declared that, though the purpose had been to force Johnson to retain the Lincoln secretaries against his will, yet the bill was so clumsily worded that it would fail to accomplish that object; whereupon Sherman of Ohio emphatically stated that no such purpose existed in the minds of the conference committee of the House and Senate. Sherman expressed agreement with Doolittle's interpretation of the effect of the act, i.e., "that it would not prevent the present President [Johnson] from removing the Secretary of War, the Secretary of the Navy, and the Secretary of State." "And if I supposed [said Sherman] that either of these gentlemen was so wanting in manhood . . . as to hold his place after the politest intimation by the President . . . that his services were no longer needed, I . . . would consent to his removal at any time, and so would we all." [12]

5

Final action on the case was taken in the Senate on May 16 and May 26. For reasons which appealed to the President's opponents it was

[10] Reprinted in *Cong. Globe*, 40 Cong., 2 sess., 1610.

[11] In the case of Stanton, said Senator Grimes, no protection from the President's independent removal was conferred, because his "term" had ended with Lincoln's death two years before the tenure act was passed. *Cong. Globe*, 40 Cong., 2 sess., suppl., 421.

[12] *Ibid.*, 39 Cong., 2 sess., 1516 (Feb. 18, 1867).

decided to vote first on the eleventh article, which touched most nearly the pride of the Senate and which was regarded as most likely to bring conviction. When on May 16 the vote was called on the question whether the President was guilty of a misdemeanor as charged in this article, thirty-five senators voted "Guilty" and nineteen "Not Guilty," after which, on motion of one of the House managers, the Senate adjourned till May 26. There followed ten days of intense effort to obtain the needed vote, in the course of which terrific pressure was brought to bear upon individual senators. Senator Ross in particular was unmercifully badgered by the Radicals; and when, in response to a telegram from a thousand Kansans, he stated that he would act in accordance with his oath and the dictates of his judgment, he was notified that his motives were suspected and that Kansas repudiated him.

On reconvening (May 26) the Senate voted on the second and third articles with the same division (35 to 19) on each vote. At the final roll call the scene was intensely dramatic, interest being centered on Ross of Kansas. With but one more vote needed for conviction beyond those of whose support the managers were certain, and with the audience listening as for the "crack of doom," Ross voted "Not Guilty"; and the contest was virtually closed.[1] Meanwhile at the White House the cabinet, including General Thomas, was holding its regular meeting. "The President," wrote Browning in his diary, "was calm and self possessed . . ., and the Cabinet proceeded with business as usual." The diary record continues as follows:

We were in telegraphic communication with the Senate, despatches being sent to Willards, and thence to the White House by courier, so that every motion and vote were transmitted as soon as they transpired "They have refused to proceed with a vote upon the articles in their order"—"They have resolved to take a vote on the second article"— "The vote is being taken." "Ross stands firm and has voted right"—"The article is beaten 35 to 19"—"They are voting on the third article" "The vote is closed and the article beaten 35 to 19." "A motion has been made to adjourn the Court *sine die*" "The motion has prevailed and the Court is dissolved" As all these despatches were brot in handed to the President, and read, I watched him. He was calm, dignified, placid and self possessed with no outward sign of agitation, what ever passions may have glowed in his breast When the final result was announced, when we knew that the atrocity was ended—that the President was acquitted of all— that the Court was dissolved, without daring to take a vote on the main charge, the removal of Stanton, he received the congratulations of his Cabinet with the same serenity and self possession which have characterized him throughout this terrible ordeal.[2]

The acquittal of the President was made possible by the votes of seven Republicans, added to those of the Democrats, the seven being Fessenden,

---

[1] DeWitt, 544–545, 552–553.
[2] Browning, *Diary*, II, 199.

Fowler, Grimes, Henderson, Ross, Trumbull, and Van Winkle. Having been under pressure to coerce their vote, these men were now savagely denounced as Copperheads and traitors. The agitation had extended to the field of religion: the general conference of the Methodist Church had appointed an hour to pray that senators be saved from "error," and that their decision should be "in truth and righteousness." [3]

6

Each senator was allowed to file an opinion on the case; and we thus have a record, not necessarily of the mental processes and motives by which the decisions were reached, but of the individual senator's formal rationalization of his vote. Trumbull urged that the President had authority to remove Stanton, that proof had not been brought forward to justify conviction, and that, if an example were once set of impeaching and removing a President on insufficient grounds, no President would be safe when opposed by a majority of the House and two-thirds of the Senate. Grimes also believed that Stanton held office during the pleasure of the President and that the latter violated no law in removing him. Reverdy Johnson argued in detail that the President had acted properly, and indignantly spurned the suggestion, openly made, that a senator's judgment should be influenced by party considerations. Garrett Davis of Kentucky, in explaining his vote of acquittal, commented on the intent of the constitutional provisions regarding impeachment and insisted that the Senate was necessarily a court, and like other courts was bound by the law and the evidence.

Of those who voted for conviction, it may suffice to comment on the opinions of two only: Sumner because of his prominence as a Radical leader, and Sherman because of the admissions which he made. Sumner referred to Johnson as "the impersonation of the tyrannical Slave Power." To spare Johnson, he declared, would be to desert the Unionists of the South. The Senate in dealing with impeachment charges was not, in his opinion, a court; and the only matter before it was the question: Shall Andrew Johnson be expelled from office? Impeachment, he thought, is not confined to crimes and misdemeanors, but is "broad as the Constitution itself" and applies to any "act of evil example or influence." His duty, he added, if the rules permitted, would be to vote "Guilty of all [the offenses charged] and infinitely more." [1]

John Sherman's opinion is of interest for the reason that he voted for conviction in spite of his previously expressed view that the tenure act did not protect Stanton and that Johnson had a perfect right to remove him. Nor was this all: Sherman was Johnson's friend of long standing. They had sat together in the Senate and had campaigned together for the Union

[3] DeWitt, 530–531.

[1] *Cong. Globe*, 40 Cong., 2 sess., suppl., 463–465, 473.

ticket in 1864. Sherman sympathized with Johnson in the hard struggles of the war, and "admired his courage" when acting as governor of Tennessee. He had vigorously defended Johnson the President, declaring that he was but carrying out the policy of Lincoln and the mandate of the people as expressed in the election of Lincoln and Johnson in 1864.[2] Gradually, however, Sherman came to turn against the President. The seeming revival of a rebellious spirit in the South, the intransigence of Johnson, and the remorseless pressure from the Radical leaders left him no alternative but to go along with the majority of his party.

Much of the reconstruction story is revealed in the obvious inconsistency of Sherman's vote for conviction. The President's abuse of individual senators, he said in after years, was the reason for this change of front. Yet at the time of this abuse Sherman had deplored the coarse attacks upon the President and had declared that a man who had "never turned his back upon a foe" could not have been expected, because he was President, to submit to insult.[3] As above noted, Sherman had subscribed to the view that a President should have a free hand in making and remaking his cabinet, and he had said emphatically that the removal of Stanton by Johnson would be justified and would not be a violation of the tenure act. By a process of labored reasoning, however, he argued that Johnson's offense was not the removal of Stanton, but the appointment of Thomas in his place, constituting an effort to make an appointment without the Senate's consent. He thus "felt bound," he said, "with much regret," to vote "Guilty," but was "entirely satisfied with the result of the vote, brought about by the action of several Republican Senators."[4] Considering all his own statements, one may well doubt whether Sherman voted his true convictions when he answered "Guilty." In his *Recollections* he states his belief that the first action of the House in rejecting the impeachment resolution of 1867 was "entirely justified."[5]

It requires but a perusal of the record to discover the many inconsistencies of the attack upon the President. The impeachment was only nominally based upon the "articles"; managers and promoters had in mind the President's reconstruction policy. Conviction was sought on the assertion that Johnson's acts were "crimes," while at the same time it was argued that no proving of a crime was necessary. The President was tried under limited accusations, thus greatly simplifying the finding of evidence; but his conviction was sought, as Evarts put it, under the "wider indictment of the newspaper press."[6] All manner of irrelevant accusations unmentioned in the articles were dragged into the prosecuting speeches. It is

[2] *Ibid.*, 39 Cong., 1 sess., append., 126.
[3] *Ibid.*, 129.
[4] John Sherman, *Recollections*, I, 432.
[5] *Ibid.*, I, 414.
[6] *Cong. Globe*, 40 Cong., 2 sess., suppl., 350,

surprising how little these speeches were concerned with the evidence presented at the trial and how largely they were grounded on the conception that no trial in the judicial sense was necessary. The convicting senators, in "explaining their votes," descanted at length upon Stanton's removal, overlooking the fact that those articles which pertained directly to this removal were precisely the ones on which votes in the senatorial court had been avoided.[7]

If the reader will consult those works of political science which compare the American and British governments, he will note that the United States does not have the parliamentary system and that the President is not politically responsible to Congress. To make him virtually so by a process of impeachment, as a matter of custom outside the Constitution, would make the presentation of evidence as to "crimes" largely a matter of form, and would impose an ugly stigma and a lifetime disqualification from office-holding upon a President who might be opposed for merely political reasons. By such a policy the distractions and sensationalism of an impeachment would be injected into a contest between parties or factions. Having read the statements of the impeachment managers and of the majority senators that the President could be removed for unfitness, one may turn to the Constitution itself. There it will be found that civil officers "shall be removed from Office on Impeachment for, and Conviction of, Treason, Bribery, or other high Crimes and Misdemeanors," that judgment in a case of impeachment, involving removal and disqualification, is preliminary to prosecution in the courts, and that the severity of an adverse verdict in an impeachment proceeding is increased by the fact that the pardoning power does not extend to such cases.

Because of the importance of the presidential office it is not deemed wise to try a man for a crime while he is President. If an accusation of crime is involved, the President is to be removed (because of the crime) and then, when he is no longer President, tried for the crime in the ordinary courts. Under these circumstances the removal proceeding itself requires a trial. Except in the case of acquittal there are in fact two trials. The situation that would result if a President should be removed by the impeachment process and then acquitted in the courts would be anomalous; but such is the constitutional procedure, and the possibility of this situation but adds to the solemn importance of the Senate's judicial function. If it be felt that the President ought to be subject to political removal by Congress through a method dissociated from the taint of crime, thus making his position analogous to that of an English prime minister, the answer would seem to be that this should be accomplished by an amendment to

[7] Articles II and III related to the appointment of Lorenzo Thomas as secretary ad interim; the eleventh article was concerned chiefly with Johnson's speeches as they pertained to Congress, and only indirectly with the Stanton matter. These were the only articles voted on.

the Constitution, but that the constitutional framework as it stands intentionally makes the President independent of Congress.

The Myers postmaster case (1926),[8] in which the United States Supreme Court upheld the President's independent power of removal without the Senate's consent (despite an act of Congress limiting that power), has generally been regarded as a vindication of President Johnson. The tenure question and the Stanton removal are now generally regarded as a mere excuse for getting rid of Johnson; so that one might disagree with the Court's opinion in the Myers case and yet hold that the cabinet question did not constitute sufficient ground for Johnson's removal under stigma of crime. As the House voted to impeach before adopting or even framing any article of impeachment, so various senators voted "Guilty" though disapproving of the form in which the articles were cast, while Sherman voted "Guilty" though agreeing with Johnson in the Stanton matter. The sweeping language of Sumner's opinion indicates that even flimsier charges would have brought this senator's vote for conviction.

[8] 272 U. S. 52. The whole subject of the President's power of removal was elaborately reviewed in the Myers case; but this is not the Court's last word on the subject. In Rathbun v. U. S. (55 Sup. Court Reporter 869), decided on May 27, 1935, the Court held that Congress has the constitutional power to limit presidential removal in such a matter as membership in the federal trade commission. In this decision the removal of W. E. Humphrey from the commission was held illegal. (Rathbun was Humphrey's executor.) Between the Myers case and the Humphrey case there is a field of doubt which the Court did not try to clear up; but the reasoning and pronouncements in the Humphrey case obviously were not intended to apply to the position of a cabinet officer.

CHAPTER 36

Black Reconstruction

I

THE PROCEEDINGS by which the states of the South found their way into the Union, after undergoing the process of Radical remodeling, belong chiefly to the year 1868, though the last of the states was not received until 1871. The exceptional readmission of Tennessee in 1866 has already been noted; and the main fabric of reconstruction legislation in 1867–1868 has been reviewed. The process of reconstruction in the South was put into effect in the states by outside impulse, after which, state by state, Congress considered the question of readmission. For Arkansas the readmission act was passed in June, 1868. It declared that Arkansas, having complied with the reconstruction acts, having formed a republican government, and having ratified the fourteenth amendment, was admitted to Congress upon the fundamental condition that the constitutional provision for Negro suffrage in the state should be perpetual.[1] The new Arkansas constitution required voters to take oath accepting the "civil and political equality of all men" and renouncing any attempt to deprive any person of any civil right or immunity because of color. If the voters of many of the states of the North and West, said President Johnson, "were required to take such an oath . . ., there is reason to believe that a majority of them would remain from the polls."[2] The President's veto was overridden; and the act became law June 22, 1868.[3] Senators and representatives from Arkansas (the first state admitted under the "reconstruction acts") took their seats June 23 and 24. In subsequent years the "fundamental condition" which

[1] The wording of the condition was "that the Constitution shall never . . . deprive any . . . class of citizens . . . of the right to vote who are entitled to vote by the constitution herein recognized, except . . . for . . . crimes. . . ." U. S. Stat. at Large, XV, 72.

[2] Cong. Globe, 40 Cong., 2 sess., 3331 (June 20, 1868).

[3] In the House the vote for overriding the veto was less than two-thirds of those present. There were 111 yeas, 31 nays, and 48 not voting. Ibid., 3331 (June 20, 1868).

Congress imposed with so much unction has been disregarded. Senator Sherman had stated in debate that he had little confidence in the practice of imposing a fundamental condition upon a state on its admission into the Union.[4]

On June 25, 1868, Congress passed the law which paved the way for the readmission of six states in a lump: North Carolina, South Carolina, Louisiana, Georgia, Alabama, and Florida.[5] The law recited that these states had fulfilled the provisions of the reconstruction acts, and declared "that each of the States . . . shall be entitled and admitted to representation in Congress as a State of the Union when the legislature . . . shall have . . . ratified the . . . [fourteenth] amendment," such readmission, however, to be subject to the "fundamental condition" already imposed upon Arkansas.[6]

With the exception of Georgia these six states promptly complied with the requirements, with the result that senators and representatives from Florida, Alabama, Louisiana, and the Carolinas had been seated by the latter part of July, 1868. New state officials being installed, the military commanders transferred the machinery of government to the state authorities.

2

Attention now turns to the four states in which reconstruction was retarded—Georgia, Mississippi, Virginia, and Texas. In general the reason for such retardation was the reluctance of the politically active elements in those states to fulfill the terms which Congress was imposing, a reluctance which taxed the ingenuity of the Radicals in inventing heroic devices to overcome the lack of harmony between actual conditions in the South and the measures which Congress had declared to be the law of the land.

In Mississippi a convention of Radical reconstructionists had framed in 1868 a constitution which aroused universal opposition among conservative whites. Its most hateful provision was the "franchise article" which required voters to take the test oath prescribed by the reconstruction acts and which denied office-holding to any who had promoted secession or supported the Confederacy. A conservative (Democratic) convention at Jackson in January, 1868, denounced the Radical constitution as the "nefarious design of the Republican party" and a "crime against the civilization of the age."[1] When put to the vote the constitution was rejected by a majority of over 7600; and at the same election the Democrats suc-

---

[4] *Ibid.*, 2859 (June 5, 1868).

[5] In passing this act over the President's veto the yeas in the House were 108, the nays 31, and the non-voters 55. *Ibid.*, 3484.

[6] *U. S. Stat. at Large*, XV, 73–74.

[1] J. W. Garner, *Reconstruction in Mississippi*, 202, 209.

ceeded in electing their governor, most of their congressmen, and about half the legislature. An investigating committee of the Radical convention, however, professed to find enough fraud in the Democratic votes to justify them in proclaiming the adoption of the constitution and the election of the Republican state ticket. The resulting confusion as to the status of reconstruction in Mississippi (a confusion typical of the period) caused the transference of the scene of controversy to Washington, where Radical Mississippi politicians congregated and where the subject was complicated by similar difficulties in Virginia and Texas. Congress now passed (April 10, 1869) an act which permitted the proscriptive clauses of the Mississippi constitution to be voted on separately from the main question of the adoption or rejection of the instrument. As a result the new constitution of Mississippi was adopted almost unanimously, but the sections proscribing ex-Confederates were overwhelmingly defeated. As a further condition of readmission the ratification of the fifteenth amendment, prohibiting the denial of suffrage on account of color, was required. When the new legislature had fulfilled the requirements, Mississippi was readmitted by act of February 23, 1870. Soon afterward, senators and representatives took their seats.

In Virginia the "restored government" under Pierpoint (the Unionist government which had moved its capital in 1863 from Wheeling to Alexandria) came into power at Richmond after the collapse of the Confederacy in 1865; but when the congressional program of reconstruction was applied in 1867 Pierpoint was discarded as not sufficiently "thorough" and the Radical H. H. Wells was made governor, while General Schofield was put in charge as military commander. This restored government had never been anything but Unionist, and had been deemed competent to act for the whole state in the creation of West Virginia. Yet its representatives had been excluded from Congress; and it was rejected as the agent of reconstruction. Under the régime of military rule a Radical convention under the presidency of John C. Underwood drafted in 1868 a constitution which conferred the privilege of voting and office-holding upon the colored race and disfranchised those whites who had supported the Confederacy.

At this point there occurred the intervention of conservative leaders, chief among whom was Alexander H. H. Stuart, who succeeded in gaining control of the reconstruction process.[2] The vote on the Underwood constitution was delayed while a double campaign was waged for the twofold purpose of educating the public mind in Virginia to the acceptance of Negro suffrage as inevitable, and of persuading Congress and President Grant, as a concession in return, to allow Virginia to come back to the fold without disfranchising ex-Confederates. A group of Virginians visited

_____

[2] But for the economic manipulations behind this political process, see below, pp. 630–631.

Washington to urge this adjustment. By act of Congress already mentioned (April 10, 1869) the people of Virginia were permitted to vote on the ratification or rejection of the state constitution and at the same time to vote separately on certain specific portions thereof, thus allowing a negative vote on the disqualifying clause and the test-oath article while the rest of the constitution was accepted. In the election of July, 1869, the constitution was adopted; but the test oath and disqualifying features were defeated. By act of January 26, 1870, Virginia was readmitted; shortly afterward her senators and representatives took their seats at Washington. State officers assumed their duties without taking the test oath; and Virginia, for practical purposes, escaped being reconstructed.

Opposition to the disqualification of Confederates beyond the provisions of the fourteenth amendment was one of the chief factors in delaying the reconstruction of Texas. Though hampered by Sheridan's watchful surveillance, the conservative whites in the state had perfected their organization and strengthened their power under the provisional government set up by President Johnson. By parliamentary skill and determined leadership they managed to defeat the drastic disfranchisement clause favored by the Radical majority in the 1868–1869 convention and carried a substitute proposal which merely provided that no one could vote or hold office who was disqualified by the Federal Constitution until such disqualification should be removed. With this moderate clause on the sensitive subject of disfranchisement the constitution was adopted in the election of November 30, 1869. In the first new state government organized under this constitution the Radicals had a majority; and they ratified the fourteenth and fifteenth amendments. Congress then admitted the state by act of March 30, 1870. There followed a period of Radical rule which ended in 1874, when Coke, newly elected Democratic governor, was inaugurated.

As to Georgia special action by Congress was found to be necessary. It will be recalled that it was one of the six states whose admission was provided for by act of June 25, 1868. The state government was formed, the governor inaugurated, the legislature organized, and members of both houses of the Federal Congress chosen. All these steps were deemed satisfactory by the distinguished military governor, George G. Meade, who withdrew the military forces which had been occupying the state. Subsequently, however, certain Negro members who had been elected to the legislature were denied seats, while ex-Confederates were granted seats in opposition to the reconstruction laws and the fourteenth amendment. Congress therefore passed a special act for Georgia, excluding from the legislature all who could not qualify under the amendment and prohibiting the exclusion of any member by reason of color. Severe penalties were imposed by this act upon anyone who should take oath falsely or hinder the taking of the oaths prescribed; and the President was authorized to use military force to execute its provisions. The reorganization of Georgia was effected under military direction, a board of officers being established to "inquire into" the eligibility of disputed members. By order of the commanding general those found ineligible by the military board were "prohibited" from taking part in the legislature, while as to those found eligible it was prescribed that no objections be made to their participation as members.[3] Proceedings in Congress concerning the enforcement of the fourteenth amendment in Georgia, the organization of a further military commission to inquire into the organization of the legislature, and like matters, are too complicated to be treated here. At length, after many parliamentary difficulties, a bill to admit the state was enacted into law (July 15, 1870).[4] Senators from Georgia took their seats on February 24, 1871, representatives having been previously admitted to the lower house.

3

Historians have generally called the ensuing period of Radical government in the South "Black Reconstruction" and have pictured it as an era in which illiterate Negroes, self-seeking Northern immigrants, called carpetbaggers, and a few vicious native whites, known as scalawags, ruled over and against the will of the large but disfranchised white majority in those states. "Saddled with an irresponsible officialdom," E. Merton Coulter writes, "the South was now plunged into debauchery, corruption, and private plundering unbelievable—suggesting that the government had been transformed into an engine of destruction. . . . The variety of means used to debauch government and plunder the public treasury bespeaks the vivid imagination and practical ability of the perpetrators." Witnessing the fearful exploitation of the South, Carl Schurz repented of his earlier Radicalism and termed the reconstruction governments "a usurpation such as this country has never seen, and probably no citizen of the United States ever dreamed of." [1]

Though it is extraordinarily difficult to generalize about an area where conditions differed so much from state to state and from year to year, it is clear that this conventional picture of "Black Reconstruction" needs major modifications. In the first place it must be stressed that these Radical governments in the South were never under Negro domination. Negroes never filled even the proportion of state offices to which their numbers entitled them. As Francis B. Simkins points out: "Only in South Carolina was the legislature dominated by blacks. Negroes became lieutenant governors in South Carolina, Mississippi, and Louisiana. . . . Only South Carolina had a justice of the supreme court who was a Negro. Not one was elected to a governorship. . . . Hiram R. Revels and Blanche K. Bruce, both of

[3] *Sen. Rep. No. 58,* 41 Cong., 2 sess., 6–8.
[4] *U. S. Stat. at Large,* XVI, 363.

[1] Coulter, *The South during Reconstruction,* 148, 161.

Mississippi, served in the United States Senate; only fifteen of their fellows were elected to the national House of Representatives during the Reconstruction period." [2]

It should be added that the few Negroes who served in high offices were mostly men of ability and integrity. The two Negro senators made very creditable records in Congress. Revels, the first Negro ever to sit in the Senate, was a Methodist minister, educated at Knox College, who later did important work in promoting the education of colored men in Mississippi. Pushed forward by the Radicals in the Senate, he made a generally favorable impression upon the country not merely by his modest behavior but by his advocacy of the repeal of the political disabilities which rested upon white Southerners. Bruce, the other Negro senator, was a man of greater force, who has been called "probably the most astute political leader the Negro ever had." After making his fortune as a planter in the Mississippi Delta, he entered politics, serving as election commissioner, county assessor, sheriff, tax collector, and superintendent of schools; in all these capacities his services were praised even by the white Democrats of his area. In the Senate he was very active, promoting "the improvement of the Mississippi River, the establishment of a more enlightened policy toward the Indians, the development of interracial harmony, and the clearing up of the affairs of the Freedmen's Bank." At the close of his senatorial term he was suggested for a place in President Garfield's cabinet, and some of the most prominent Mississippi Democrats, such as L. Q. C. Lamar, gave him their unqualified endorsement. Though he did not receive a cabinet post, he remained in the Federal civil service until his death in 1898.[3]

There are not sufficient available data to warrant sweeping generalizations about the Negroes who served in less conspicuous posts. It is, however, at least suggestive that the numerous colored men who served in the Mississippi legislature were of about average ability; as Vernon L. Wharton observes, they "sought no special advantages for their race, and in one of their very first acts they petitioned Congress to remove all political disabilities from the whites." The twelve Negro sheriffs in the same state have been called "moderately satisfactory; most of them were at least capable of exercising the functions of their office." Negro justices of the peace in Mississippi appear, on the whole, to have been "incompetent," and those who served on the county boards of supervisors "generally were dominated

---

[2] Simkins, *Hist. of the South*, 282–283. Simkins notes, however, that "the mulatto Pinckney Benton Stewart Pinchback served for a few weeks as acting governor of Louisiana and the Negro Alexander K. Davis frequently acted as governor of Mississippi during the absence of Governor Adelbert Ames."

[3] Samuel Denny Smith, "The Negro in the United States Senate," in Fletcher M. Green, ed., *Essays in Southern History*, 50–65; Vernon L. Wharton, *The Negro in Mississippi, 1865–1890*, 159–161.

by white Republicans, either natives or Northerners." "Although many of the Negro supervisors were ignorant and incompetent," Dr. Wharton adds, "little difference can be discovered in the administration of their counties and that of counties under Democratic control." [4]

There is a great deal of evidence to substantiate the familiar charge that these Radical governments in the South were corrupt. "Legislatures," as Professor Coulter points out, "piled up expenses against their impoverished states to fantastic heights. In Florida the cost of printing in 1869 was more than the entire cost of the state government in 1860; and the legislature sold for five cents an acre 1,100,000 acres of public land held in trust. The Georgia legislature bought from a favored agent in Atlanta an unfinished opera house for $250,000, previously sold for much less, to convert it into a capitol building. In Arkansas a Negro was given $9,000 for repairing a bridge which had originally cost $500. . . . In South Carolina the legislature bought for $700,000 land worth $100,000 for resale to Negroes; it issued $1,590,000 worth of bonds with which to redeem $500,000 worth of bank notes . . .; it voted extra compensation of $1,000 to the speaker for his efficient service when he lost $1,000 on a horse race; it paid for lunches, whiskies and wines, women's apparel, and coffins charged by the legislators to legislative expenses; and Governor Scott while drunk was induced by a fancy lady in a burlesque show to sign an issue of state bonds." [5] The list could be extended almost indefinitely.

With no attempt to minimize these frauds, the historian must attempt to put them in perspective. The entire postwar era, it must be remembered, was one of exploitation and graft; no political party and no section of the country escaped the malign influence. Corrupt officeholders in the South were deplorable, of course, yet when one compares their defalcations with those of the Whiskey Ring or the Tweed régime of New York their embezzlements seem relatively modest. Moreover, it is often forgotten that even in the South "no race, class, or party could lay a virtuous claim to clean hands." In exceedingly corrupt Louisiana all parties shared in the looting. "Why, damn it," exclaimed Henry Clay Warmoth, the carpetbag governor, "everybody is demoralizing down here. Corruption is the fashion." [6] In Mississippi fraud was rarer, but it also was nonpartisan. J. W. Garner was able to find only three cases of embezzlement during the five years of Radical rule. There was a Republican treasurer of a Natchez hospital who took $7,251; a colored librarian stole some books; and a native white Democratic state treasurer swindled the state more grandly to the sum of $61,952. [7] Nor was corruption a phenomenon that ended with the down-

[4] Wharton, 179, 172.
[5] Coulter, 148-149.
[6] Roger W. Shugg, *Origins of Class Struggle in Louisiana*, 226-227.
[7] Garner, *Reconstruction in Mississippi*, 322-323.

fall of the Radical régimes. In Mississippi shortly after the restoration of "home rule," the Democratic state treasurer stole $315,612.[8]

Opponents accused these Radical governments of being excessively expensive, and certainly they were so by comparison with the years before the Civil War. In Tennessee, for example, tax rates had to be quadrupled to meet the new expenditures.[9] Corruption accounted for some of this additional expense; sheer waste and inefficiency were responsible for much more of it. Most of the increase, however, was due to the imperative new demands made upon the state governments during the reconstruction period. The freeing of the slaves virtually doubled the civil population of many Southern states, for the Negroes were now entitled to receive schooling, to appear in courts, and to have eleemosynary care. In addition, extraordinary expenditures were required to rehabilitate the war-torn South. Public buildings had to be repaired; levees had to be rebuilt; schools, orphanages, and asylums had to be constructed. The heaviest drain upon the state finances was the assistance required to reconstruct and expand the transportation system, for, as Carter Goodrich points out, "not one of the eleven [Southern] states failed to use public money to promote the development of railroads." [10]

So pressing were these demands that any postwar government in the South had to meet them. Dr. Wharton notes that there was no significant variation between Democratic and Republican county administrations in Mississippi in respect to expenditures. In 1874 the average property tax rate in 39 counties under Democratic control was 12 7/13 mills, while that in 34 Republican counties was 13 7/17 mills. Postwar economic necessities recognized no party lines.[11]

The accusation is often made that these Radical régimes left the Southern states saddled with debts, but this is another stereotype which does not entirely hold upon closer study. Again and again, for example, critics have asserted that the Radicals piled up a $20,000,000 debt in Mississippi, even though, in fact, "Radicals contracted . . . only a nominal current sum of about $500,000, for the reason that the Radicals, over the protest of their Conservative opponents, put a clause into the Constitution of 1868 forbidding the pledging of state funds to aid corporations." [12]

Similarly, it is often said that Alabama Radicals left that state owing

[8] C. Vann Woodward, *Origins of the New South*, 70. For other cases of Democratic embezzlement in the post-reconstruction period, see *ibid.*, 68–73.
[9] Thomas B. Alexander, *Political Reconstruction in Tennessee*, 241.
[10] Goodrich, "Public Aid to Railroads in the Reconstruction South," *Political Science Quart.*, LXXI, 409.
[11] Wharton, 170.
[12] Howard K. Beale, "On Rewriting Reconstruction History," *Am. Hist. Rev.*, XLV, 816 (July, 1940).

$30,000,000 when their régime collapsed, and historians have sometimes become tearful over the economic consequences which this heavy burden had upon later generations. In fact, most of this "debt" consisted of bonds issued by the state government to support railroad construction and secured by a lien upon the property of the railroads. This, clearly, "would become a direct debt only in the event that the State foreclosed its mortgages upon the railroad property, leaving the State in debt, indeed, to bondholders, to the amount of the endorsements and loans, but at the same time possessed of the valuable railroad properties as compensation." After the Democrats regained power in 1874 they adjusted this "debt" upon terms highly favorable to the railroads, with which Democratic leaders had intimate financial connections. In his elaborate analysis of the evidence Horace Mann Bond concludes that the real debt of Alabama at the end of the Radical régime was about $12,000,000, of which $9,500,000 had been incurred before the Republicans gained office.[13]

While the defects of these Republican governments in the South are often pointed out, their achievements are seldom given full credit. On the positive side of the ledger one must note that these Radical régimes superintended the peaceful transformation of the Negro from a freedman to a first-class citizen; that they assisted in the physical reconstruction of the section; that they extended social services, such as general, compulsory education, in some states which had never before known them; and that their constitutions, usually drawn upon Northern models, were admirable documents, which many of the Southern states retained years after the white men had returned to exclusive political power.

4

The claim that these Radical governments were imposed upon the South against the will of the entire white population is demonstrably incorrect. According to the 1860 census figures, Negroes were in the majority only in South Carolina. Even if one accepts the guess that 150,000 whites were disfranchised by the fourteenth amendment, it is clear that such disqualification would produce Negro majorities only in South Carolina, Mississippi, and Louisiana. Fraudulent registration by Negroes and deliberate abstention from registering by whites may help explain the establishment of Radical régimes in the additional states of Alabama and Florida.[1] But in the rest of the South a majority of the voters were always white, and without considerable support from this group the Republican governments could never have been established.

It is difficult to generalize about these "scalawags" who cooperated with

[13] Bond, "Social and Economic Forces in Alabama Reconstruction," *Jour. of Negro Hist.*, XXIII, 336–343 (July, 1938).

[1] William A. Russ, Jr., "Registration and Disfranchisement under Radical Reconstruction," *M. V. H. R.*, XXI, 177–178 (Sept., 1934).

the carpetbaggers and the Negroes in the Republican program for the South. Some were unquestionably self-seeking adventurers, "renegades," "white men . . . [who] sold themselves for office." [2] In some cases, as W. E. B. DuBois suggests, they may have come from the "po' white trash" of the ante-bellum South, "ignorant, muddled and bewildered white men who had been disinherited of land and labor and fought a long battle with sheer subsistence, hanging on the edge of poverty, eating clay and chasing slaves," who now caught "a vision of democracy across racial lines." [3] In North Carolina and Alabama they appear to have been largely hill-country farmers, who had been opposed to the plantation-slavery system before the Civil War and had been disaffected toward the Confederacy during the war.

In most of the Southern states, however, these "scalawags" came from the planter, mercantile, and industrial classes. To understand their actions during reconstruction, one must go back to the pre-Civil War division of the South into Democrats and Whigs, the latter representing wealth and conservatism. During the 1850's many Southern Whigs had gradually been forced into the Democratic party, but the section still gave a large vote for John Bell in 1860. Reluctant to enter upon secession, most Southern Whigs had nevertheless "gone with their states" when the Confederacy was formed, and many had served with distinction in the Southern armies. These planters, bankers, merchants, and railroad men had never been happy about the disruption of the United States, and after Appomattox they began to reassert themselves as the natural, moderate leaders of their section on the road to reunion. They rallied loyally around the provisional governments set up by President Johnson. In the Tennessee constitutional convention of 1865, for example, of the 95 members whose antebellum political affiliations have been identified, 84 were Whigs. [4]

The overthrow of the Johnson régimes left these conservative leaders of the South in a quandary. Many continued to support the President in his contest with Congress, but others strongly objected to cooperating with their ancient enemies, the Democrats. In Tennessee, it was reported, Whigs "regard the Democratic party as the author of all their troubles, and . . . they hold the very name of Democracy as a synonym of disaster and defeat." [5] In Mississippi, Whigs protested that it would be absurd for them "to abandon their high conservative position, and aid in the reorganization of the Democratic party." [6] All over the South there was talk of reviving

[2] *Sen. Report No.* 527, 44 Cong., 1 sess., II, 1071.

[3] DuBois, *Black Reconstruction,* 347, 350.

[4] Thomas B. Alexander, "Whiggery and Reconstruction in Tennessee," *J.S.H.,* XVI, 293 (Aug., 1950).

[5] *Ibid.,* 301.

[6] David Donald, "The Scalawag in Mississippi Reconstruction," *ibid.,* X, 448–449 (Nov., 1944).

the old Whig party under some new name, such as "Conservative" or "Liberal."

When these third-party movements failed, many former Whigs joined the Republican party. Their motives are not too difficult to ascertain. They disliked the small farmers who made up the body of the Democratic party; because of their wealth they were not in direct social or economic competition with the freedmen; they believed that, as planters and former slave-masters, they could control the Negro vote; and they saw the Republican party, in the state as in the nation, as the best representative of the business community, of which they were part. From the state governments they desired financial assistance in the rebuilding of levees and railroads; they hoped for a reduction of land taxes; and they sought to work out arrangements for the leasing of convicts so as to have a steady labor supply. In consequence, during the early years of Radical reconstruction the Republican party in the South contained a high proportion of prominent white men who were old residents of their states. Representative of this class was James L. Alcorn, the first Republican governor of Mississippi, a rich delta planter and a former Whig. "His plan," as a close personal friend testified, was "to unite the old whigs . . . and through them control the negro." In order to attain his objectives, he was willing to guarantee to the Negro certain basic rights. "I propose," he announced, "to vote with [the Negro] . . .; to discuss political affairs with him; to sit, if necessary, in political counsel with him."

Unpalatable as these concessions were to many Southern whites, they were, nevertheless, accepted by a significant body of former Whigs. Although any figures for this difficult period must be regarded with skepticism, it has been estimated that from twenty-five to thirty per cent of the Mississippi white voters had by 1873 joined the Republican party.[7] In other states a similar pattern was evident.

As time went on, however, these old Whigs found it increasingly difficult to sustain their allegiance to the Republican party. They were constantly under attack by the Democrats, who argued that a horse thief was better than a scalawag and who said that the Southern man who cooperated with the Negro was "a beast in man's clothing" or "a traitor to his country."[8] What was more important, they found themselves unable to maintain their leadership in the Republican party. From the outset the carpetbaggers had suspected their aims. "Alcorn," exclaimed one irate Northern-born politician, "in some of his appointments . . . has put in his style of whig d—m rebels . . . and . . . he is fixing up a party of his own (whig) and using the negro for a blind."[9] Since the carpetbaggers had no property in the South, they could afford to make larger promises to

[7] *Ibid.,* 450.
[8] *Sen. Misc. Doc.,* No. 54, 44 Cong., 2 sess., 648.
[9] Donald, "The Scalawag in Mississippi Reconstruction," 451–452.

the Negroes than could these wealthy old Whigs; since these Northerners did not share the universal Southern aversion to social intercourse with the colored race, they were accepted by the Negroes as more truly their friends. It was symptomatic that when Alcorn, having resigned the Mississippi governorship to serve in the Senate, sought a new term in the governor's mansion in 1873, he was opposed by a carpetbagger, Adelbert Ames, and was soundly defeated.

Forced from the leadership of the Republican party, Southern merchants and planters made desperate efforts to establish a third party, which would avoid the excesses of both the Radicals and the Democrats. In Louisiana, for example, some of the principal businessmen of New Orleans, recognizing that racial strife was economically disastrous and hoping to end the extravagances of the Radical régime, tried to organize a "Unification Movement" which would attract both the Negroes and their former masters. To the old Whig element such a move offered a last opportunity to take control of the government and promote their own economic interests. To the Negroes the proposed organization pledged its guarantee of all their political rights and its opposition to discrimination in education, employment, and soil ownership. Such leaders of the white community as General P. G. T. Beauregard; James I. Day, president of the Sun Mutual Insurance Company; Isaac N. Marks, president of the Firemen's Charitable Association; and Auguste Bohn, president of the Mechanics' and Traders' Bank, pledged, in addition, "That we shall maintain and advocate the right of every citizen of Louisiana . . . to frequent at will all places of public resort, and to travel at will on all vehicles of public conveyance, upon terms of perfect equality. . . ." [10]

Such promising efforts toward interracial harmony proved abortive. The primary reason for the failure, as T. Harry Williams has shown, "was that its platform was not acceptable to the [majority of] the whites. They would not support the concessions made to the Negro because they were afraid that these concessions would lead to racial equality." [11] In addition, few colored men were attracted by the offer, partly because they distrusted their former masters, partly because the Radical carpetbaggers could offer them more. Increasingly as the Negroes gained political experience they became more self-assertive, and by the end of the reconstruction period they were demanding not merely a full share of the offices but, in many cases, social equality. Defeated in the Republican party, frustrated in their efforts to start up a third party, the white planters and businessmen were slowly and reluctantly forced to join the Democrats.

[10] T. Harry Williams, "The Louisiana Unification Movement of 1873," *J. S. H.*, XI, 356–361 (Aug., 1945).
[11] *Ibid.*, 367–368.

5

Behind these complex political developments of the reconstruction period in the South lay fierce economic rivalries. As necessity obliged the Southern state governments to assume increasing powers and to make additional expenditures, their economic favors became the objects of competing interest groups. In the ensuing struggles there was little to choose between parties or racial groups; all were out to make as much as they could from the state. Often these contests involved nothing more than a tug-of-war as to which newspaper was to receive the lucrative state printing contracts or which construction firm was to rebuild a bridge or a levee. Equally profitable were the state and county contracts for leasing criminals (mostly Negroes) to private employers. In Mississippi, for example, the military commander, General A. C. Gillem, "made a remarkable contract with Edmund Richardson, planter, capitalist, and speculator, under which Richardson received almost absolute control over the prisoners of the state until November, 1871. Richardson not only gained the labor of the convicts without cost, but also received from the state $18,000 yearly for their maintenance and almost $12,000 for their transportation." "There is little wonder," Vernon L. Wharton adds, "that he came to be known as the greatest cotton planter in the world, with a crop that in one year reached the amazing total of 11,500 bales." [1]

Around none of the favors given by the Southern state governments was there fiercer controversy than over the grants of land and money made to railroads. The necessity for state support in this area of activity was imperative, for the Southern rail system had been virtually destroyed during the war and the task of rebuilding could not be financed by private capital. It is important to note that, except in Mississippi, which had a constitutional restriction upon state assistance to corporations, every Southern government of the period, under both the Johnson and the Radical régimes, undertook to subsidize railroad building.[2] Naturally rival railroad interests fought bitterly over this state aid.

In Virginia, for example, where the reconstruction story is often told in terms of a struggle between conservatives and Radicals, it is probably more accurate to emphasize the fundamental conflict between the railroad aspirations of John W. Garrett, of the Baltimore & Ohio Railroad, and of William Mahone, of the Southside line. Garrett's idea was to funnel the trade of Virginia and the southwest through Baltimore; Mahone wanted to

[1] Wharton, *The Negro in Miss.*, 238.

[2] For an elaborate account of the varieties of state aid undertaken during this period see Carter Goodrich, "Public Aid to Railroads in the Reconstruction South," *Political Science Quart.*, LXXI, 407–442, esp. Table I, pp. 410–413. Even Mississippi, Dr. Goodrich notes, "found a variety of assets which could be transferred to the railroads without direct violation of the constitutional provision,"

build up rail connections which would make Norfolk a principal port for the European trade. Both men needed to gain control over the Virginia & Tennessee line, the one railroad running through the mountains to the southwest. State approval was required for the consolidation of this line into either Mahone's or Garrett's rival systems; for the legislature had to approve changes in the road's charter; moreover, the state still owned sizable blocks of its stock. Both Mahone and Garrett, therefore, set about winning over the government of Virginia.

Mahone was, in general, more successful. A native Virginian who was trying to build up one of the state's ports, he could also capitalize upon the fact that he had been a Confederate general, the "hero of the Crater." Tirelessly he worked behind the scenes in all parties to promote the interests of his project. In 1868, for example, seeing the nomination of the conservative Withers as part of "the design of the B. & O. road," he threw his support behind the Radical candidate for governor, H. H. Wells. When Wells, after his election, proved faithless to the Southside's interests, Mahone skillfully undermined his chances for re-election by pushing forward a Negro as his running mate in 1870, a move which he knew would alienate most white Republicans. Then he persuaded the Democrats to join these disaffected Republicans in backing a single candidate, Walker, to oppose Wells—a candidate who, incidentally, was a director of one of Mahone's railroads. In the ensuing contest Baltimore & Ohio money supported Wells; Southside funds backed Walker. Walker's victory has generally been spoken of as the restoration of "home rule" in Virginia; in fact, it would be more accurate to describe it as the triumph of the Southside Railroad, for on June 7, 1870, the Virginia legislature gave its approval to Mahone's scheme of consolidation.[3]

Similarly in Alabama, where the history of reconstruction is usually analyzed in terms of whites versus Negroes, the story of railroad rivalries is central. In this state the stake was rail access to the rich ore deposits of the Birmingham area, and the principal rivals for state favors were the North & South line, a subsidiary of the Louisville & Nashville Railroad, which was financed by August Belmont and Democratic capitalists of the North, and the Alabama & Chattanooga Railroad, which was backed by such Northern Republicans as Jay Cooke. There is not space here to trace the elaborately fraudulent operations of these competing interests as they wooed the state legislators. It is enough to say that officials of both rail lines operated with equal unscrupulousness, that both the Johnson provisional government and the subsequent Radical régime in Alabama showed themselves equally receptive to their blandishments, and that it would be impossible to distinguish between Democrats and Republicans in the legisla-

[3] Nelson M. Blake, *William Mahone of Virginia, Soldier and Political Insurgent*, 99–110. Cf. above, pp. 620–621.

ture as to willingness to accept their favors. Slightly to oversimplify a very complex story, one may say that when these two rail lines cooperated, reconstruction developments in Alabama were relatively tranquil, but that when they disagreed over the distribution of the loot, what has frequently been called "race war" broke out. It was no coincidence that 1873, which saw Jay Cooke go into bankruptcy during the panic, also witnessed the defeat of the Republican party in Alabama. The restoration of "home rule" meant the success of the North & South Railroad.[4]

[4] Horace Mann Bond, "Social and Economic Forces in Alabama Reconstruction," *Jour. of Negro Hist.*, XXIII, 290–348 (July, 1938).

CHAPTER 37

Postwar Politics
and Constitutional Change

I

WHILE THE SOUTH was thus being reconstructed, the Radicals were in power in Washington. Whatever these Republicans had earlier had in the way of idealism and a sense of mission had now largely vanished, and they were now concerned chiefly with the stakes of power. Many of the original Radicals had disappeared from the scene; the death of Thaddeus Stevens in 1868 cost the group its ablest leader. Power now fell into the hands of men like Oliver P. Morton of Indiana, John A. Logan of Illinois, and Benjamin F. Butler of Massachusetts, who used it with unscrupulous virtuosity to perpetuate themselves in office.

A notable characteristic of this period of Radical rule was its disregard for the Constitution. Nowhere was this attitude more clearly exhibited than in their disregard for form and procedure in the adoption of the fourteenth amendment. This amendment, it will be remembered, had been proposed in 1866 but had then failed of adoption.[1] In the reconstruction act of March 2, 1867, the Radicals resuscitated it, by providing that no state could be restored until its legislature under the new-formed Radical constitution should have ratified the amendment, and further that no state should be restored until the amendment had actually become a part of the Constitution. Taken in connection with other provisions in this law and its supplements, the congressional program required that a Southern state must declare its leaders disqualified from office-holding, establish Negro suffrage, create a constitution on a Radical pattern, elect a legislature on the basis of the new requirements, consent to a drastic modification of the existing scheme as to state and Federal powers, and, having taken these steps, must wait outside the Union until the hateful amendment, with its serious encroachment upon the principle of state sovereignty so dear to the

[1] See above, pp. 584–585.

South, should have been put into the Constitution by the carpetbaggers' reversal of the previous action of the Southern states, whose rejection of the amendment in 1866 was done with promptness and decision.

In reality Congress in 1867–1868 was not merely submitting an amendment to the states. It was creating fabricated governments in the South, to which there was given not an untrammeled opportunity of voting *Yes* or *No* on the proposed constitutional article, but only the alternative of voting *Yes* or being denied recognition as states in the Union. As a matter of constitutional law the method of amending the Constitution does not lie within the legislative power of Congress. It is prescribed in Article V of the Constitution; and the part which Congress has in the process is to frame the new article and adopt it, or call a convention of the states to perform this function, after which the amendment is submitted to the states, to be ratified either by conventions or by legislatures in three-fourths of them. It is for Congress to choose between the convention and legislative ratification, but not to create new factors or conditions as part of the amending process. In this case Congress submitted an amendment which was rejected by more than a fourth of the states; then in effect Congress changed the process, providing that ratification must be effected by a specified type of legislature, elected in a manner provided by Congress, a legislature chosen on the basis of Negro suffrage (though this was prior to the adoption of the fifteenth amendment, designed to force such suffrage), a legislature from which Confederates, regardless of their postwar attitude toward the Union, were to be excluded.

Maintaining that the Southern states were not in the Union until redeemed by Congress, the Radicals were driven to the absurd conclusion that the states could not qualify as members of the Union until after they had performed a function which only members can perform, i.e., ratify a Federal constitutional amendment. Another anomalous feature of the fourteenth amendment was that some of its provisions were anticipated before the amendment was adopted. The reconstruction act of March 2, 1867, provided that no person excluded from office-holding by the proposed amendment should be eligible to election as a member of the convention to frame a state constitution in the South, nor should any such person vote for members of the state constitutional convention. The Radicals were at the same time "proposing" an amendment to the Constitution and proceeding as if it were already adopted. In addition, by the civil rights act, Congress enacted into law some of the leading provisions of the amendment two years before the date accepted as the time of its adoption.

Carpetbag legislatures did ratify the amendment in the year 1868; and it became the duty of Secretary Seward, who doubted the validity of all these proceedings, to issue a proclamation declaring the amendment in force. His first proclamation on the subject (July 20, 1868) is something of a curiosity. Citing the law which requires the secretary of state to certify the adoption of a constitutional amendment,[2] Seward pointed out that the secretary is not authorized to decide doubtful questions as to the authenticity of state legislatures, or the right of a state to withdraw or rescind its act of ratification. He then announced that the amendment had been adopted by the legislatures of twenty-three states, and that it appeared to have been ratified by newly constituted bodies "avowing themselves to be and acting as" the legislatures of six Southern states, but that in two states (Ohio and New Jersey) the legislatures had passed resolutions withdrawing consent. Finally he declared: "Now, therefore, . . . I . . . certify that if the resolutions of the Legislatures of Ohio and New Jersey, ratifying the . . . amendment, are . . . of full force . . . notwithstanding the subsequent resolutions . . . [withdrawing ratification], then the . . . amendment has been ratified in the manner hereinbefore mentioned and so has become valid. . . ."[3]

This declaration that the amendment was valid "if [etc.]" did not satisfy Congress; and it would hardly have served as a basis for considering the amendment in force. Congress therefore passed a concurrent resolution which is also a curious constitutional document. It reads as follows: "Whereas the Legislatures of the States of Connecticut [etc.] . . ., being three fourths and more of the . . . States of the Union, have ratified the fourteenth article of amendment to the Constitution . . ., Therefore, Resolved, . . . That said fourteenth article is . . . declared to be a part of the Constitution . . . and it shall be duly promulgated as such by the Secretary of State."[4] This concurrent resolution was passed in haste. It was not referred to any committee, and discussion was cut off by use of the cloture. It was carried in the House by 127 out of 215 votes; but in the Senate the yeas and nays were not recorded, nor was the resolution even debated.[5]

In this resolution (one of the most important in American legal history, since it declared in force an amendment which has produced far-reaching constitutional and economic effects) twenty-seven states were named and were declared to be "three fourths and more of the several States of the Union." This was certainly incorrect if the Union, as conceived by Seward, included thirty-seven states in 1868. Nor could the Radicals consistently say that unless a state were officially "reconstructed" it could not be regarded as in the Union for the purpose of ratification; since in that case there would have been no need to go through the farce of having the amendment ratified in the states-to-be of the South.[6] Just what Congress

[2] Act of April 20, 1818, *U. S. Stat. at Large*, III, 439.
[3] *Ann. Cyc.*, 1868, 197–198.
[4] *Cong. Globe*, 40 Cong., 2 sess., 4295–4296 (July 21, 1868).
[5] *Ibid.*, 4266 (July 21, 1868).
[6] There was, of course, the further point, as noted above, that states of the former Confederacy, though unreconstructed, had been counted in the ratification

meant at this time by the phrase "States of the Union" is not clear, since the resolution was not subjected even to such deliberation as the Congress of 1868 could give it.

In addition to other questionable matters pertaining to the fourteenth amendment there was interjected a doubt as to whether Congress, by a concurrent resolution, has the power to put a constitutional amendment into effect against serious objections that the amendment has not been duly ratified. It was merely in obedience to congressional mandate that Seward issued (July 28, 1868) another proclamation listing the various ratifications and withdrawals of ratification (the list being different from that of the concurrent resolution) and certifying that the amendment had become valid.[7] Its validity has been usually dated from the time of Seward's second proclamation.

The present doctrine that an amendment automatically becomes a part of the Constitution by the ratification of three-fourths of the states [8] assumes that it is a simple matter, merely a ministerial function, to determine when such ratification has taken place. Ordinarily this is so; but in the reconstruction period it was far from simple. It involved the main issue of reconstruction, hinging as it did upon the question as to how many states were in the Union and as to the validity of organizations that purported to be state governments in the South. In these postwar years Congress did many unusual things; and the power of declaring an amendment valid as part of the Constitution has not been deemed a proper congressional function merely because it was exercised by the Congress of 1868. As to the fourteenth amendment, the abuses in connection with its adoption have long been tolerated; and its provisions, so vitally important in recent con-

---

of the thirteenth amendment and had been included in estimating the total number of states.

[7] *U. S. Stat. at Large*, XV, 708–711. The seceded states whose ratifications (by carpetbag governments) were counted in this proclamation of July 28 were Arkansas, Florida, North Carolina, Louisiana, South Carolina, Alabama, and Georgia.

[8] It is now recognized that the secretary of state has no option as to proclaiming an amendment in force, but is required to do so when official notice of ratifying action by three-fourths of the states has been received. (Fairchild *vs.* Hughes, 258 U. S. 126.) Notices of ratification are conclusive upon the secretary, and having been certified, are conclusive upon the courts. (Leser *vs.* Garnett, 258 U. S. 130.) It has been held that the eighteenth amendment became effective when ratification had been consummated, not when proclaimed by the secretary. (Dillon *vs.* Gloss, 256 U. S. 368.) It has also been held that no citizen has a right to enjoin the secretary from proclaiming an amendment in force, nor to use the Federal courts to obtain a determination whether a constitutional amendment, about to be adopted, will be valid. (Fairchild *vs.* Hughes, 258 U. S. 126.) These decisions would seem to leave unsettled the question as to how irregularities in the ratifying of amendments such as existed in the reconstruction period are to be legally avoided.

stitutional law, are as firmly placed in the Constitution as if those irregularities and abuses had not existed.

2

In the tense atmosphere of postwar controversy the presidential campaign of 1868 was waged. The Republicans had the advantage in the control of patronage, the power to admit or exclude the Southern states as their purposes might determine, the opportunity to shape legislation with an eye to votes, and the emotional appeal of a party that had conducted the administration during a tremendous war. The Democrats had many disadvantages: they had to live down as best they could the unfair accusation of alleged "disloyalty" during the war; their natural friendliness toward the South was misinterpreted; they suffered from the discrediting of Andrew Johnson, with whose policies they were associated; they were embarrassed by the Vallandigham element in their ranks; and they were handicapped by differences within their own household on financial matters, especially the questions of paper money and the payment of the huge government debt. The main issues before the country were the choice between Radical and moderate reconstruction and the problems of postwar finance.

The Republicans found it much easier to agree upon a candidate than the Democrats. Only three men seem to have been seriously considered—Chase, Colfax, and Grant—while a dozen or so candidates among the Democrats were prominently mentioned. For a time it appeared that both parties were minded to capture Grant. The Democrats had a reasonable claim to him by reason of previous political affiliations. Though not active in politics he and his father before him had been Democrats. In 1856 he had voted for Buchanan; in 1860, though casting no vote, he had favored and preferred Douglas. Months before the Republican convention of 1868, however, the impeachment row had started; Grant's break with the President had become definite; and in a rather passive manner, with little political thinking on his own part, he had "gone over" to the Radicals. At the Republican convention in Chicago (May 20–21) there was only one name presented for the presidency, and Grant was unanimously nominated on the first ballot. C. H. Coleman shows that the general showed no eagerness for the office. He told W. T. Sherman that he would avoid the nomination if he could.[1] According to the New York *World* he was "at first shy; he then wavered; then enveloped himself in . . . mystery; and at last, . . . changed his politics." [2] No such unanimity was manifest concerning the vice-presidential nomination; and it was not until the sixth ballot that the choice fell upon the Indiana Radical, Schuyler Colfax.

It would appear that until 1868 one of the chief contenders for the

[1] M. A. DeWolfe Howe, ed., *Home Letters of General Sherman*, 370.

[2] N. Y. *World*, Jan. 22, 1868, cited in C. H. Coleman, *The Election of 1868*, 87.

Republican nomination had been Chase. For some years the Ohio statesman had been a favorite of the Radicals, though he had not gone the full way with them in reconstruction politics, partly because he had in his character a saving quality of moderation, and partly because, since 1864, he had been Chief Justice of the United States. It is doubtful whether he could ever have satisfied the Radicals in any case; certainly from the time of the impeachment he was unmercifully denounced by them, and was, in fact, "virtually read out of the Republican party." [3]

Aside from nominations the matters most worthy of comment concerning the Republican convention were the presence of delegates from every state except Texas (illustrating thus early the activity of the Republicans in perfecting state organizations in the South), the savage attack upon the seven moderate Republican senators who had voted "Not Guilty" in the trial of Johnson, the declaration that Johnson was "properly pronounced guilty" (despite acquittal in the Senate), and the adoption of a resolution which "congratulate[d] the country" on the "success" of reconstruction. In "loyal States" suffrage was declared a state matter; in "the South" a matter of "guarantee by Congress." [4] The convention also paid tribute to Lincoln, inveighed against "corruption" under Johnson as sharply as if the outrageous accusations of Ashley had been proved, denounced financial repudiation, and caught the fancy of Irish-Americans by a "plank" denouncing England's efforts against naturalized American citizens. No mention was made of the tariff; nor did the convention extend the hand of friendship toward the South.

The Democratic delegates assembled in New York City in July. In their platform they declared that questions of slavery and secession had been settled for all time and that the return of peace demanded restoration of the states to their rights in the Union. In opposition to the Republican demand for penalties to be inflicted upon ex-Confederates, they advocated amnesty for past political offenses. Instead of Negro suffrage imposed by outside pressure they insisted that the regulation of the franchise belonged to the states. Adopting the "Ohio idea" associated with Pendleton, they urged that, where the law did not specify payment "in coin," the national debt be paid in "lawful money" (greenbacks); and they further urged government economy and prompt payment of the debt by taxation, including the taxation of government bonds. Abolition of the freedmen's bureau was urged; and the subordination of the military to the civil power was demanded "to the end that the usurpations of Congress and the despotism of the sword may cease." [5]

The difficulty of choosing a Democratic candidate was evident in the number of aspirants and the days of indeterminate balloting. Chase was a

[3] Coleman, 80.
[4] *Ibid.*, 91; *Ann. Cyc.*, 1868, 744–745.
[5] *Official Proceedings of the National Democratic Convention*, 1868, 59.

distinct possibility for the Democratic nomination; many of the delegates really favored him; and it appeared at various stages that the deadlocked convention might easily have turned to him with enthusiasm. His daughter Kate Chase Sprague, a lady famous for her beauty and social influence, was active at the convention, and it may be said that the month of July, 1868, marked the peak of Chase's chances for a presidential candidacy. On the other hand convention strategy worked against him, his own state did not support him, and his strength outside Ohio never had a chance to assert itself. Other leading Democratic contenders were President Johnson (whose name could hardly have been withheld from the convention in view of his reconstruction efforts and widespread popularity among Southern delegates), Pendleton, Hendricks, McClellan, Seymour, Frank Blair, and W. S. Hancock. Less likely possibilities included Charles Francis Adams (whose position was that of opposition to the Radicals rather than sympathy with the Democrats), W. T. Sherman (who, however, consistently avoided politics), D. G. Farragut, J. R. Doolittle, Sanford E. Church, Joel Parker, Thomas Ewing, and Reverdy Johnson.

On the first ballot Pendleton received 105 of the 317 votes, and Andrew Johnson 65, mostly from the South. Seymour was not even included in the balloting. Pendleton increased his lead as successive votes were cast, but without gaining a majority. Voting for Seymour of New York, president of the convention, began on the fourth ballot, after which his name was dropped on his own insistence that honor compelled him to withdraw, that he "must not be nominated," and that he could not accept the nomination if tendered.[6] The New Yorker's name reappeared, however, on the twenty-first ballot; and on the twenty-second McCook of Ohio urged that he be chosen on the ground that the convention should select the man "whom the presidency has sought and who has not sought the presidency." Meanwhile the vote for Hendricks had reached 132 on the twenty-first ballot and he seemed "within striking distance of victory."[7] The shift of Ohio to Seymour was a heavy factor. It effectually disposed of a possible stampede to Chase, and put Pendleton out of the running. Finally the protesting Seymour was hustled out of the convention hall by his friends, state after state shifted its vote to him, and, on the twenty-second ballot, he was nominated amid the wildest enthusiasm."[8] It was rumored that he had schemed to make himself the candidate; on the other hand it has been urged that his name had been dropped when vetoed by him, that it was revived against his genuine protest, and that he "was not a party to his nomination."[9] For vice-presidential candidate the choice fell upon Frank Blair.

[6] *Ann. Cyc.,* 1868, 748.
[7] Coleman, 239.
[8] *Ann. Cyc.,* 1868, 749.
[9] Coleman, 244.

The man whom the Democrats had selected had achieved prominence as wartime governor of New York and as an opponent of Lincoln, especially in the matter of conscription. Despite the fact that he "deplored" Lincoln's election, he made it clear in a speech at Utica in October, 1861, that he intended to give loyal and generous support to the President. In such a matter as the raising of volunteers, particularly at the time of Lee's invasion of the North in 1863, he acted energetically for the national cause; but he did not hesitate to assail the administration at Washington for what he termed its guilt in helping to bring on an avoidable war, its "unconstitutional" acts, and its tendency toward "military despotism." His conduct at the time of the draft riots in New York, when his attitude was definitely non-cooperative toward Lincoln, has already been noted.[10] In 1864 he supported McClellan, and after the war he became conspicuous as a caustic critic of the Republican scheme of reconstruction.

Though the military note was stressed by the Republicans, whose candidate was chosen for military distinction alone, it has been pointed out that "those soldiers with the highest war reputations took little active part in the campaign on either side." Sherman's indifference was a matter of concern to the Republican national committee. Thomas, Sheridan, and Meade were "inarticulate Republicans," while men such as Hancock, Franklin, McClellan, Buell, Slocum, McClernand, and Rosecrans, writes Coleman, were "Democrats in sympathy if not in campaign activity." [11]

In the final result the Democrats were unable to carry their candidate to victory. The popular vote was 2,703,000 for Seymour, 3,012,000 for Grant; the electoral vote 214 for Grant to 80 for Seymour. The Democrats carried New York, Delaware, Georgia, Kentucky, Louisiana, Maryland, New Jersey, and Oregon; the Republicans carried all the rest of the states except those in the South (Mississippi, Texas, and Virginia) in which no vote was recorded. Perhaps the most significant comment concerning the election is that "a majority of the white men of the country favored the Democratic party in 1868." [12] The number of Negro votes cast for Grant has been estimated at about 450,000 as compared to about 50,000 Negro votes estimated for Seymour, so that Grant's popular majority (less than 310,000) would have become a minority if all the Negro votes had been subtracted.[13] Coleman states that "the Republican popular majority in 1868

---

[10] See above, pp. 316–317.

[11] Coleman, 306–307.

[12] *Ibid.*, 369. (Large minorities for Seymour were recorded in the following states that were carried by Grant: Arkansas, California, Connecticut, Illinois, Indiana, Michigan, Missouri, Nevada, New Hampshire, North Carolina, Ohio, Pennsylvania, West Virginia, and Wisconsin.)

[13] Under the peculiar American system, however, the Republicans might conceivably have elected their candidate without a popular majority.

was dependent upon negro suffrage, and [that] this was probably true in most of the Presidential elections between the Civil and Spanish Wars." [14]

3

The matter of suffrage for the colored race underwent a process of evolution. At first it was feared that Northern sentiment would not support a program of nation-wide Negro suffrage; but the importance of the Negro vote to the Republican party North and South caused leading Radicals to keep their eye upon the issue. Thaddeus Stevens was quoted as saying that the Southern states ought never to be recognized until the Constitution was so amended as to "secure perpetual ascendancy to the party of the Union." Such a remark was typical of the general tendency of Republicans to perpetuate the fiction that the Democrats constituted the party of disunion. If the right of suffrage should be granted to persons of color, said Stevens, "there would always be Union [i.e., Republican] white men enough in the South, aided by the blacks, to . . . continue the Republican ascendancy." [1] According to Senator Howard, however, it was the opinion of the reconstruction committee in 1866 that three-fourths of the states could not be induced to grant the vote by constitutional amendment to the colored race. Gradually, however, as the Radicals felt their way, they found their power increasing. Step by step they were able to enact laws promoting Negro suffrage without an amendment, and finally to carry the suffrage amendment itself in the first year of Grant's administration.

An important step was taken in the establishment of Negro suffrage by national authority when the bill concerning the franchise in the District of Columbia was passed early in 1867. The supporters of Negro suffrage for the District, chiefly Radical Republicans, were embarrassed by the refusal of many Northern states to allow the Negroes to vote. In addition, the woman-suffrage question, which had hardly attained the dimensions of an "issue," was used by opponents of Negro suffrage, as when Reverdy Johnson of Maryland remarked that the women of America would reject the idea of having the suffrage conferred upon them, while Garrett Davis of Kentucky dwelt upon the inconsistency of "a frenzied party . . . clamoring to have suffrage given to the negro" while they "frown[ed] upon" female suffrage.[2] The chief objections to the proposal, however, were based upon the dense ignorance of the Negroes and the fact that the suffrage law was being forced upon the people without their consent. Among the leading advocates of the measure was Charles Sumner, who declared that the bill would complete emancipation by enfranchisement. "The courts [he said], and the rail-cars of the District, even the galleries of Congress, have been

[14] Coleman, 370.

[1] Hendricks, quoting Stevens, in U. S. Senate, *Cong. Globe*, 39 Cong., 1 sess., 878 (Feb. 16, 1866).

[2] *Ibid.*, 39 Cong., 2 sess., 79 (Dec. 12, 1866).

open to colored persons. It only remains that the ballot-box be opened to them." It must be remembered, however, that the people of the District, though governed by Congress, have no representation in that body, and no part in choosing a President. Their status is not comparable to that of a state, nor even of a territory.[3]

Having passed the two houses, the District suffrage bill was vetoed on January 7, 1867, by President Johnson. The President showed that the people of the District at a special election in 1865 had overwhelmingly voted against the proposal. He also showed that whereas the ratio of blacks to whites in Sumner's state was about 1 to 130, in the District the Negro race constituted about one-third of the population. The suffrage, he stated, was not necessary to the protection of Negro rights; and he feared that the imposition of suffrage qualifications from above, by weakening the minority party, might tend toward the concentration of all power in the Congress, with despotic results. Disregarding the President's objections, Congress passed the bill over the veto; and it became law January 8, 1867. A few days later (January 31) a measure was passed which imposed similar suffrage requirements upon the territories.

While these measures were being promoted the suffrage question had been considered also in connection with the bills to admit Colorado and Nebraska to the Union; for in both these states the constitutions confined the voting privilege to whites. Some Radicals, bent on increasing their power by adding new states, were willing to overlook this "defect"; others, especially Sumner, adhered to their philosophy of Negro equality and insisted upon Negro suffrage as a condition of admission. The Sumner principle prevailed and the suffrage condition was adopted by Congress for both states. As above noted, however, only Nebraska was admitted at this stage, while Johnson's veto was effective in the case of Colorado.[4]

These matters, and the suffrage provisions in the reconstruction acts, had revealed, even prior to Grant's election, a steady Radical movement toward giving the Negroes the vote; yet somehow for campaign purposes the issue was evaded, and the Republican platform of 1868 declared that suffrage remained with the states. Oberholtzer has pointed out that the Republicans avoided the Negro-suffrage question in the Grant-Seymour campaign, but that after Grant's election they "pretended to believe that they had received a mandate from the people in favor of the . . . enfranchisement of the African race."[5] Early in 1869 they launched a new constitutional amendment, worded as follows:

Section 1. The right of citizens of the United States to vote shall not be denied or abridged by the United States or by any State on account of race, color, or previous condition of servitude.

[3] Ibid., 107 (Dec. 13, 1866).
[4] See above, pp. 608–609.
[5] Oberholtzer, II, 204–205.

Section 2. The Congress shall have power to enforce this article by appropriate legislation.

As with the fourteenth amendment, ratification was enmeshed with congressional devices of reconstruction in the South. On March 30, 1870, the new article was proclaimed in force. It was not immediately effective in securing the vote to the Negro. Because the courts in early decisions interpreted the amendment as leaving suffrage to the states, which might prohibit the vote to Negroes on grounds other than race without a violation of its terms, Negro voting as practiced during the years of Radical rule was authorized by state and federal legislation, rather than by the amendment. Not until long afterward was the amendment invoked to strike down grandfather clauses, white primaries, and other discriminatory practices.[6]

4

In their effort to control all branches of government the Radicals showed a disposition to subject even the Supreme Court to their will, nor can it be said that the Court escaped the menace of congressional intimidation entirely without injury. It was in part shorn of jurisdiction, with a resulting loss of dignity. That it did not suffer more grievously was due chiefly to its acquiescence in the main body of reconstruction legislation. This was largely an acquiescence of silence, i.e., avoiding a review of the reconstruction acts on their merits.

The judicial decision which drew forth the most vociferous Radical curses was that of the Milligan case in 1866. As noted in a previous chapter,[1] the matter at issue involved the denial of ordinary processes of justice by the wartime use of a military commission for the trial of civilians in Indiana. When the Court, in a ringing opinion delivered by Justice David Davis, declared illegal the use of "martial law" in regions where courts were open and unobstructed, and denounced the application of military justice in 1864–1865 as "mere lawless violence," there followed a savage denunciation of the tribunal by Radical orators and editors. Such men as Wendell Phillips and John A. Bingham went so far as to threaten abolition of the Court itself.[2]

Those accused of conspiracy in the Lincoln assassination had been tried by military commission under methods which departed from traditional guarantees; and in the case of one of those executed, Mrs. Surratt, it has been the subsequent verdict of historians that a ghastly miscarriage of justice had taken place. In the trial and execution of Henry Wirz, the Swiss-American Confederate officer who commanded the infamous South-

[6] The leading cases are *Ex parte* Yarbrough, 110 U. S. 651 (1884); Quinn v. U. S., 238 U. S. 347 (1915); and Smith v. Allwright, 321 U. S. 649 (1944).

[1] See above, pp. 304–305.
[2] Oberholtzer, I, 465.

ern prison at Andersonville, the frustrations of justice were even more shocking. Wirz was tried by military commission, condemned, and executed on November 10, 1865. It was said in his defense that he was protected from arrest and prosecution under the terms of the surrender-on-parole of Johnston's army and that his prosecution was a violation of these terms.[3] Also it was urged that war conditions, not vindictive cruelty, were responsible for the frightful sufferings of the prisoners, that such sufferings arose from the failure of the Union and Confederate governments to agree upon a system of cartel, and that Northern prison pens were as deserving of condemnation as Southern. Postwar psychology, however, demanded the head of Wirz; and his destruction was promoted by Secretary of War Stanton, Judge Advocate General Holt, and even President Johnson, who approved the sentence of the military commission.

It was obvious that the doctrine of the Milligan decision would condemn as illegal the Wirz proceeding and the assassination trial;[4] and this will serve in part to explain the furious denunciation of the decision on the part of the Radicals. But this was not the whole point: even more important was the fact that under the reconstruction acts the South was subjected to a military régime in which the habeas corpus privilege and the safeguards of normal justice were swept aside.[5] Back in Lincoln's time the Chief Justice had declared the President guilty of executive usurpation in suppressing the processes of justice; and now it was strongly apprehended that, unless curbed in some manner, the Supreme Court might go to the extent of declaring the reconstruction acts unconstitutional and void. The Washington *Chronicle,* "semiofficial organ of the Republican Senate," was persistent in its denunciation of the Court in general and Davis in particular. It declared: "We have not met a Republican who does not speak with contempt of the language of Justice Davis." On the other hand, as Warren has pointed out, the Democratic papers generally applauded the decision.[6]

The annihilation of the Court itself was talked of by Republicans, while various other devices or expedients were also proposed, such as remodeling or "packing" the Court, reducing its membership to three, pro-

---

[3] Such violation was exceptional. As a rule Confederate officers and men included in the surrenders were unmolested as to criminal prosecutions after the war.

[4] It is difficult to see why the ordinary courts could not have been used for the trial of the assassins, as has been the regular American practice in similar cases. The danger that any guilty person could have escaped punishment if tried in the courts was negligible. If in the case of Wirz such a trial would have given a better chance of acquittal, that was all the more reason for giving him the normal protection of the law. The denial of this protection puts in clear focus the vindictive nature of the whole proceeding.

[5] Treating the Milligan decision as an endorsement of his policies, President Johnson promptly issued orders dismissing proceedings in military trials of civilians in the South. Charles Warren, *Sup. Court in U. S. History* (rev. ed.), II, 442.

[6] *Ibid.,* II, 433, 437.

hibiting it from taking jurisdiction in any case involving the reconstruction acts (Stevens's suggestion), placing various limitations upon its procedure as to quorum requirements, and the like. In order to take from President Johnson the power to make appointments on the Court a law was passed (July 23, 1866) which provided that vacancies among the associate justices should not be filled until the number of such justices should be reduced to six, making seven for the whole Court.[7]

A further attack upon the Court in 1868 reached the point where a bill requiring the agreement of two-thirds of the justices to effect a decision passed the House;[8] but the bill did not come to a vote in the Senate. One important measure, however, constituting a severe attack upon the judiciary, did become law when Congress on March 27, 1868, overriding the President's veto, took jurisdiction away from the Supreme Court in appeals from lower Federal courts where the habeas corpus right was involved.[9] The wording of the repeal clause was such as to obscure its real motive, which was, as Senator Hendricks said, to "reach the McCardle case."[10] A Mississippi editor, McCardle, had been placed under military arrest and put upon trial before a military commission for publishing criticisms of Radical reconstruction policy. When presented with a writ of habeas corpus intended to bring the question of the editor's detention before the Federal courts, the officer in charge declined to produce the prisoner, in which action he was sustained by a Federal circuit court in Mississippi. Appeal from the decision was pending in the Supreme Court of the United States when the legislation of March 27, 1868, deprived the Court of jurisdiction in this and similar suits. The case was being handled by able counsel and it was feared that the Court might declare the reconstruction acts unconstitutional, thus applying to the postwar South the same rule which it had already applied to the wartime North. The repeal turned the trick, and the Court bowed to the legislation, holding that while its appellate jurisdiction in general is derived from the Constitution, such jurisdiction is defined and limited by Congress.[11] Gideon Welles expressed disgust at the manner in which the justices had "caved in."[12] According to a statement attributed

[7] By act of March 3, 1863, the number had been raised to ten, the largest membership in the history of the Court. The act of July 23, 1866, fixed the number at nine, and prospectively (by the non-filling of vacancies) at seven. When Grant came in a law was promptly passed (April 10, 1869) raising the permanent membership to nine.

[8] *Cong. Globe,* 40 Cong., 2 sess., 489 (Jan. 13, 1868).

[9] This was done by the repeal of a former law which conferred jurisdiction in habeas corpus appeals. The trick was turned by an amendment which threw the opposition off their guard, and by the avoidance of free discussion. Robert C. Schenck, Republican congressman from Ohio, admitted that the purpose was to "clip the wings" of the Court. Warren, *Sup. Court,* II, 474–475.

[10] *Cong. Globe,* 40 Cong., 2 sess., 2116.

[11] *Ex parte* McCardle, 7 Wall. 506.

[12] Welles, *Diary,* III, 314, 320.

to Justice Field the acquiescence of the justices (with the exception of Grier and Field) in the congressional curtailment of their power was due to their disinclination to "run a race with Congress." To O. H. Browning it seemed that this "cowardice" and readiness to surrender to usurpation were "among the alarming symptoms of the times." [13]

In other cases the Supreme Court evaded fundamental decisions touching reconstruction. In *Mississippi* vs. *Johnson,* being asked in the name of Mississippi to enjoin President Johnson and the commanding general from executing the reconstruction acts, the Court held that such a judicial restraint upon the President was improper, and that it had "no jurisdiction . . . to enjoin the President in the performance of his official duties." [14] When another injunction was brought up with a similar object in *Georgia* vs. *Stanton* [15] the justices for similar reasons declined to assume jurisdiction. In *Cummings* vs. *Missouri* [16] the Court declared the unconstitutionality of a Missouri law which imposed upon officeholders, teachers, priests, etc., a test oath affirming that support had never been given by act or word to the enemies of the United States.[17] On the question of secession and the nature of the Union the Court took the orthodox view. In *Texas* vs. *White,*[18] in a matter concerning bonds issued by the state of Texas, it was held that the Union involved an indissoluble relation and that acts of secession were "absolutely null" and "utterly without operation in law." Though the history of reconstruction was reviewed in summarizing the facts of the case, the Court rather pointedly declined to pronounce judgment upon the reconstruction acts. The main point of the case was that Texas continued to remain a state in the Union despite the illegal transactions pertaining to secession.

5

Meanwhile the case against Jefferson Davis had dragged on year by year inconclusively until it was finally dropped. The rough treatment of the fallen Confederate leader involved a long military imprisonment followed by release to the Federal courts, where a fearsome indictment was brought; but there was never a trial on the indictment and the final dismissal of the proceedings early in 1869 was no more of a release to Davis himself, who insisted that the trial be pushed to a verdict, than to the government, to which the case had become a source of embarrassment.

[13] Browning, *Diary,* II, 191.
[14] 4 Wall. 475, especially 501.
[15] 6 Wall. 50.
[16] 71 U. S. 277 (1866).
[17] In *Ex parte* Garland (71 U. S. 333) a similar decision was reached in a case involving the right of an attorney to practice before the Supreme Court, whereas the Cummings case had reference to the imposition of the test oath upon priests in the Roman Catholic Church.
[18] 7 Wall. 700 (1868).

Davis's detention in military custody had begun in May, 1865, and continued for two years at Fort Monroe. It was only for a short period that he was kept in shackles. In the later stages of his imprisonment he was allowed considerable freedom within the fortress grounds and was given airy rooms in Carroll Hall, a building formerly used for officers' quarters. At the beginning visitors were denied him; but this rule was later relaxed. After earnest pleadings Mrs. Davis was allowed to visit her husband; and he was allowed to confer with counsel. His physician, John J. Craven, was given access to him, and in addition regular reports on his health were made by the military surgeon. Nevertheless, the two-year military imprisonment was a grievous hardship. Had he been under the civil courts he would have been released on bail while awaiting trial; and the government would have been under pressure to make out a case and proceed with the trial before a Virginia jury.

It is to be said to the credit of the Johnson administration that the proposal to subject Davis to a military trial was rejected, though in certain other respects it appears that the President and some of his advisers were minded to push forward the prosecution of the man who in popular imagination stood forth as the personification of the "rebellion." By writ of habeas corpus issued by the Federal circuit court at Richmond (May, 1867) Davis was released from military custody with the approval of the administration at Washington. He was then brought to the bar of the court, where an indictment for treason against the United States was pending against him. The prosecution not being ready for trial, Davis was admitted to bail, giving bond in the sum of $100,000. Gerrit Smith, Horace Greeley, and Cornelius Vanderbilt were among the sureties on the bail bond. Many delays ensued, with elaborate discussions among Radicals and loud denunciations of the Johnson administration for not proceeding more actively with the case. Meantime a new indictment, drawn by William M. Evarts and R. H. Dana, Jr., who had been assigned to the case by the President, had been voted by the grand jury in the Federal circuit court, in which Davis was elaborately and tautologically charged with treason against the United States under the statute of April 13, 1790, under which the penalty was death.

The complex issues involved in the case cannot be reviewed here; but it is to be noted that they involved the question whether Davis's "acts of war" could be deemed treason, and also whether the prosecution was not a violation of the fourteenth amendment. It was urged that, since the amendment imposed political disqualification upon ex-Confederates, any further pains and penalties were inadmissible.[1] Not death, nor even fine

[1] This argument concerning the fourteenth amendment in relation to the case was hit upon as the main point to be stressed by Davis's counsel; and the final proceedings had to do with the defense motion to quash the indictment on the ground of inconsistency with the amendment. On this point the Federal circuit court at

and imprisonment, was indicated as the constitutional penalty for Southern leaders, but only disqualification from holding office; and this disqualification was removable by Congress.[2]

If death for treason, said Davis's counsel, were to be imposed upon ex-Confederates, the disqualifications of the fourteenth amendment would become absurd. The government's own lawyers, especially Evarts and Dana, wavered in their determination to prosecute Davis; and time after time the government delayed proceedings, Chief Justice Chase meanwhile showing marked reluctance to be drawn into the case as presiding judge, as his circuit duties at Richmond required. Finally, after the circuit court at Richmond had disagreed, certifying their disagreement to the Supreme Court of the United States, the President's proclamation of unconditional amnesty (December 25, 1868) [3] was accepted as the basis for disposing finally of the case, which soon thereafter was dropped both at Richmond and at Washington.

Had the trial been pushed it seemed doubtful to competent observers that the Federal government could obtain a decision by the Supreme Court sustaining the indictment, and, following this, a verdict of conviction by a Virginia jury, even such a jury as was customary in reconstruction days. Had such conviction occurred, there still remained the probability of presidential pardon.[4] Release by dismissal of the indictment seemed the most reasonable way out, a release consonant not only with the common practice of amnesty for political offenses but also with the existing practice of the United States government concerning postwar accusations of treason and the like against those who had supported the Confederacy.[5]

Richmond disagreed. Chief Justice Chase favored quashing the indictment; while his colleague John C. Underwood (a Virginia Radical) decided that the indictment should stand. This was the question which was pending before the United States Supreme Court when the President's amnesty proclamation caused the final disposition of the case. Randall, *Constitutional Problems Under Lincoln,* chap. v.

[2] This constitutional disqualification persisted for decades after the war. In 1898 Congress removed the existing disability as to all who had supported the Confederacy, though the wording of the act seemed to recognize that similar disabilities would apply to a possible future insurrection or rebellion. *U. S. Stat. at Large,* XXX, 432.

[3] See above, p. 561.

[4] Evarts, who had become Johnson's attorney general, had advised in cabinet meeting against the prosecution of Davis and had said that if convicted he "would not be . . . and . . . ought not to be punished." Browning, *Diary,* II, 225.

[5] This account of Davis's case is based largely upon manuscript and archival sources, including Federal court records at Richmond, the attorney general's papers at Washington, the Stanton papers, and the Johnson manuscripts. See also Roy F. Nichols, "United States vs. Jefferson Davis, 1865–1869," *Am. Hist. Rev.,* XXXI, 266–284 (Jan., 1926); Samuel Shapiro, "Richard Henry Dana, Jr." (MS. doctoral dissertation, Columbia Univ., 1958), 233–238.

6

In its international dealings the Johnson administration presented a record of real achievement in such matters as the conclusion of the Mexican imbroglio, the suppression of Fenian disturbances, the "*Alabama* claims" with England,[1] the purchase of Alaska, and the notable Far Eastern diplomacy of Anson Burlingame. The end of the war found Sheridan in southwestern Texas with a force intended to put down the remaining opposition to the Union in that section. American disapproval of the French empire in Mexico had suffered no abatement; and border "incidents" were making it increasingly difficult to restrain the soldiers on the Rio Grande. Many persons in the United States favored open support for the Mexicans under Juarez; and it is at least interesting that Francis P. Blair, Sr., on a mission to Richmond (January, 1865) in which he conferred with Jefferson Davis, spoke of an armistice between North and South, with both sides joining to drive the French out of Mexico and establish the Juarez government in that country. Seward now pressed his inquiries as to French intentions; and in April, 1866, de Montholon, French minister at Washington, gave the pledge on the Emperor's authority that the French troops would be withdrawn in three detachments by November, 1867. When delays occurred in the fulfillment of this pledge, Seward sent vigorous notes.[2]

Napoleon meanwhile had lost interest in the Mexican venture, having failed to comply with certain promises to Maximilian; and in February, 1867, the last of the French troops left Mexico. Maximilian, who could have abdicated and escaped while French forces still guarded him, bravely decided to remain in the hope of obtaining better terms for the imperialists, who, however, were denied amnesty by the implacable Juarez, who could not forget that they had shed Mexican blood. Disappointed in his last heroic effort toward conciliation and captured by the republican forces, Maximilian was condemned to death and denied clemency despite earnest entreaties from outside nations. On June 19, 1867, the luckless but plucky monarch was executed at Querétaro. Nearly sixty years later (January, 1927) the long and tragic life of Empress Charlotte came to an end in a Belgian château.

Canadian border troubles had arisen from the use of American soil as a base for the activities of daring revolutionaries laboring for an Irish republic. An Irish-American organization known as the Fenian Brotherhood cooperated with the Phoenix Society in Ireland and did many provocative things inconsistent with American neutrality. Forces recruited on American soil actually invaded Canada on several occasions; and President Johnson

[1] Treated in the following chapter.
[2] See especially the dispatches of Seward to Bigelow under dates of Sept. 29, Oct. 8, and Nov. 23, 1866, *House Exec. Doc. No. 1*, 39 Cong., 2 sess., pt. 1, 358, 359, 366–367.

found it necessary to act vigorously in order to prevent the territory of the United States from becoming the base of hostile operations against a friendly nation. In performing this duty at a time when England was being criticized for unneutral acts during the late war, the President was considerably embarrassed by noisy American politicians who, in their angling for the anti-British vote, showed a feigned interest in the cause of Ireland and justified the troublemakers while assailing the administration. The President, however, succeeded in satisfactorily disposing of the matter. He issued a proclamation (June 6, 1866) warning all citizens to desist from taking part in or abetting these "unlawful proceedings," [3] caused offenders to be arrested, and sent General Meade with a military force to prevent further expeditions from setting out. The Fenian activities were thus effectively suppressed.

A treaty was negotiated under Seward for the annexation of the Danish islands of St. Thomas and St. John to the United States with the express consent of the people of the islands. In Denmark the treaty was ratified by the King and the Rigsdag; in the United States, however, it failed of ratification in the Senate, and annexation was deferred until the administration of Wilson. The Alaskan effort was more successful. Negotiations between Seward and Baron Stoeckl, Russian minister at Washington, were facilitated by Russian willingness, perhaps eagerness, to sell; and a treaty for the acquisition of this land in the far North had been completed and proclaimed by June, 1867. For the sum of $7,200,000 the United States obtained an immense area of more than half a million square miles, with rich undeveloped resources. At the time, however, the acquisition was treated as a joke and it was made to appear that Uncle Sam had been duped into paying money for valueless ice fields which the Czar would gladly have given away.

In oriental affairs Seward's diplomacy gave direction to both American and European policy for many decades to follow. Writing in 1922 Tyler Dennett stated that "no new principles . . . [had] been added to American Far Eastern policy since 1869." Reversing the traditional American policy as represented by Webster and other predecessors, Seward made a contribution to Asiatic diplomacy which exceeded that of Hay.[4] In general the essence of his policy was friendship toward China, cooperation with European powers combined with many an effort to restrain them in their oriental activities, promotion of the "open door" as to trade (though this idea antedated Seward), and the maintenance of Chinese integrity.

It is true that Seward allowed himself to be drawn into certain "un-American" attitudes. The joint show of force by various powers against Japan was participated in by the United States; the Convention of 1866

[3] Richardson, *Messages and Papers*, VI, 433.
[4] *Am. Hist. Rev.*, XXVIII, 45 (Oct., 1922).

with Japan was approved by Seward though "dictated from the gun-deck of a British flag-ship"; [5] and Korea was misjudged in an incident involving a stranded American ship.[6] It has been said, however, in Seward's defense that his "un-American actions . . . were the price he paid for co-operating with powers possessed of very different . . . purposes in the East." [7]

The best of Seward's Far Eastern transactions were associated with the diplomacy of Anson Burlingame, United States minister to China, whose policy was to induce the foreign powers to respect Chinese sovereignty, to win Chinese approval for measures deemed needful for the protection of foreigners and their property, and to avert European action looking toward the partition of Asia. Burlingame has been called "the most successful diplomat America has ever sent to Eastern lands." [8] Such was his influence in the East that he was actually made the Chinese envoy to foreign countries, and it was in this capacity, not as American representative, that he negotiated the famous Burlingame treaty of amity between the United States and China (1868). By this treaty Chinese integrity was recognized; the empire's acceptance of the principles of international law was proclaimed; interference in Chinese domestic matters was disclaimed by the United States; rights of travel, residence, and emigration were guaranteed; religious freedom was extended to Americans in China; and various privileges, including the appointment of consuls (but not including naturalization), were extended to the Chinese. The Chinese mission which Burlingame headed also endeavored to negotiate treaties of amity and commerce with European nations; it was while engaged in this duty that Burlingame died at St. Petersburg in 1870.

7

The Johnson administration drew to its close in an atmosphere of uncertainty, apprehension, and confusion, but not without a sense of pride and confidence that history would "set all right." Various projects, well advanced by the Johnson government, had to be referred to the succeeding administration. The thrill of the completion of the Union Pacific Railway was to redound to Grant's credit. In the closing weeks the Johnson cabinet was especially disturbed by reports from the South, which presented a condition of "anarchy . . . murders, assassinations, burnings, and general

[5] *Ibid.*, 49–50.

[6] Koreans sought to assist a stranded American ship, the *General Sherman*, in one of their rivers; but, being rudely handled owing to a misunderstanding of their intent, they attacked the vessel. Largely because of restraint at Paris a punitive expedition against Korea, in which Seward would have joined, was avoided. It should be added, however, that Seward was misinformed. L. M. Sears, *Hist. of Am. Foreign Relations*, 2nd ed., 336–337.

[7] Dennett, in *Am. Hist. Rev.*, XXVIII, 61.

[8] Sears, 337. See also Knight Biggerstaff, "The Official Chinese Attitude toward the Burlingame Mission," *Am. Hist. Rev.*, XLI, 682–702 (July, 1936).

insecurity. . . ." [1] In this situation there was presented one of the exquisite ironies of reconstruction, the spectacle of carpetbaggers appealing to President Johnson's administration for troops to protect them from the hostility of the Southern whites. In such matters the utmost caution was observed, with marked disinclination to use military force unless absolutely necessary to preserve order. Where possible, despite the reconstruction acts, the Johnson administration showed a conciliatory attitude toward the South. Heeding Evarts's advice that confiscations be no longer pursued, the "President and Cabinet gave . . . their unanimous consent" to the dismissal of such cases. When the wife of General Robert E. Lee requested that Arlington relics, handed down from Mount Vernon, be restored to her, the President and his advisers "unanimously determined" that this be done; [2] and one of the latest official acts of O. H. Browning, secretary of the interior, was to have the articles boxed for shipment to the Lees. On March 4, 1869, when the end of Johnson's term arrived, Browning confided to his diary his sense of pride in having struggled with the President "under great disadvantages . . . to restore peace . . . to a distracted . . . Country." "Had we had the . . . coöperation of Congress [he added] these desirable ends could have been attained." [3] The outgoing President and his cabinet were busy till after the hour of twelve examining bills requiring the President's approval. Without attending the ceremony of Grant's inauguration, they made their official adieus.

[1] Browning, *Diary,* II, 244, 222.
[2] *Ibid.,* II, 234–235, 241–242.
[3] *Ibid.,* II, 244.

CHAPTER 38

The Grant Era

I

THE GRANT ERA in American development was a period of conflicting tendencies. As energies were released to peacetime pursuits the nation showed marked exuberance and expanding power. The period was not lacking in enlightened striving; it produced notable humanitarian movements; it set the stage for material development hitherto unknown; it launched a fresh epoch of western expansion; it witnessed new triumphs of technology and business organization. Yet such was the coarseness of the era that its magnificence seemed cheap and tawdry. It has been branded as the "gilded age." In architecture it was the "parvenu period"; [1] but the extravagant dwellings were but a symptom. Tastes and standards were revealed not only in fancy *porte-cochères*, oriels, bay windows, and cast-iron dogs standing guard on formal lawns; they appeared also in a flaunting luxury among the new rich, a crassness of social attitudes, an unblushing partisanship among politicians, and an excessive flourish and patriotic unction among those who passed for statesmen. To use Harding's famous word, the period did not, in general, present a return to "normalcy." Postwar abnormality and excess were its most prominent characteristics.

Of Grant's conduct as President it may be said that, by consensus of opinion, he was unfitted for the duties of his lofty office and was so thoroughly involved in partisan politics that his administration became a national scandal. Professor Dunning refers to the era as the "nadir of national disgrace." [2] The spectacle of the inadequate President, betrayed by

[1] Thomas E. Tallmadge, *The Story of American Architecture*, chap. vi. Though the tastes of the time are usually related to American conditions, it is of interest to note that standards abroad were not dissimilar. In England "Tennyson and the Brownings . . . exchanged wax flowers . . . and antimacassars . . . ; . . . ladies laced and had the vapors; . . . young men wore Dundreary whiskers" (*ibid.*).

[2] W. A. Dunning, *Reconstruction, Political and Economic*, chap. xviii. Grant officially admitted his political incompetence and apologized for the "mistakes" of his administration. See Richardson, *Messages and Papers*, VII, 399–400.

men in whom he trusted, barely able to keep a cabinet together, and so bewildered by the complexities of his office that he hardly knew what it was all about, is in truth pathetic. Historians almost invariably express sympathy for the harassed Executive while presenting a condemnatory record of the trends that were manifest under his rule. The administration began with an undistinguished cabinet. Two of the appointees, Washburne for secretary of state and Rawlins for secretary of war, had been Grant's neighbors in Galena, Illinois. The millionaire merchant, A. T. Stewart, owner of a great department store in New York City, was nominated but found ineligible as head of the treasury department; A. E. Borie, Philadelphia merchant, a man almost unknown, was introduced to a puzzled nation as secretary of the navy. Other secretaries were Jacob D. Cox of Ohio, secretary of the interior; E. Rockwood Hoar of Massachusetts, attorney general; John A. J. Creswell of Maryland (follower of Henry Winter Davis), postmaster general. Most of these men did not remain at their posts; indeed the Grant administration became notable for its shifting cabinet personnel. It is not to our purpose even to mention all the cabinet appointments. G. S. Boutwell and W. A. Richardson of Massachusetts, B. H. Bristow of Kentucky, and Lot M. Morrill of Maine struggled at different times with the treasury portfolio. On the death of Rawlins in September, 1869, Grant appointed William T. Sherman secretary ad interim for a brief period; then he put in W. W. Belknap of Keokuk, Iowa. When Belknap resigned in 1876 under impeachment charges, he was succeeded by Alonzo Taft of Ohio, who in turn gave way to "Don" (James Donald) Cameron of Pennsylvania. Borie resigned during Grant's first year, and New Jersey's slightly known attorney general, George M. Robeson, was chosen for the naval secretaryship.

Of outstanding importance in the cabinet was Hamilton Fish of New York, who became secretary of state a week after the President's inauguration when Washburne resigned to become minister to France, and who remained in this important position to the end of Grant's second term. Amid cabinet squabbles, malignant attacks, knavery, and corruption Fish held steadfastly to his post, not only directing important international adjustments, but mediating in many an official or personal tangle, attending to confidential duties, and contributing the distinction of substantial statesmanship to an otherwise weak administration.

As Grant struggled with his official duties the Republican party swept with a rush into the public offices. In doing so they found their own tenure-of-office act, aimed at President Johnson, a considerable embarrassment. A bill repealing the act was passed by the House, whose members showed by this action that the original law was less a matter of constructive legislation than a partisan weapon. The Senate being unwilling to surrender its power, however, a troublesome legislative tangle followed. Repeal was thus defeated despite Grant's earnest desire for it, and a modified tenure act was preserved whose meaning was capable of "diametrically opposite" interpretations, but whose main effect was to have a law on the books which would not be heard of when Senate and President should be in party harmony,[3] but which might again be invoked if a future Senate should have a partisan motive to hinder presidential removals. It was not until March 5, 1887, under the administration of President Cleveland, that the tenure act was finally repealed.

In the related matter of civil service reform Grant's perfunctory recommendations brought no substantial result. He pointed out that the existing system of appointments did "not secure the best men, and often not even fit men, for public place," [4] and he appointed a commission of inquiry, headed by George William Curtis, which presented a striking exposé of degrading practices attending the spoils system; but men "laughed at such zeal," [5] and Curtis's reforms were defeated by congressional indifference and prevailing partisan philosophy.

2

The corruption of the Grant period was not of the President's making; it was not all centered at Washington; nor was it confined to one party. It seemed rather a characteristic of the times. In New York City Boss Tweed and his notorious Ring robbed and misgoverned with unblushing audacity. Seizing control of the city government with the assistance of a bribed legislature, and keeping themselves in power by the systematic herding of ignorant voters, the Ring made contracts in which the graft sometimes ran more than ninety per cent. Bills approved on one day by the gang's auditors exceeded $15,000,000 of which $14,000,000 was "sheer plunder." [1] By 1871 the outraged city, under the leadership of such men as Samuel J. Tilden the lawyer and Thomas Nast the cartoonist, was able to drive the Ring out of power and put Tweed himself in prison.

Another example of plunder on a colossal scale was the attempt of Jay Gould and James Fisk to corner the gold market, which resulted in the disastrous affair of "Black Friday." The scheme was to sweep the price of gold upward by an enormous bull movement (the connection of Gould and Fisk with purchasing contracts being carefully concealed) and to reap an unconscionable profit by compelling short sellers to buy from the conspirators. In less than three weeks the gold quotation was carried from 133 to 143; in one day it advanced from that figure to 163. Finally, the day of the crash (September 24, 1869) produced a panic in the Gold Room and on the Stock Exchange which resulted in the collapse of the syndicate and the ruin of many innocent dealers. By the simple process of repudiating

[3] Blaine, *Twenty Years*, II, 454–455.
[4] Richardson, *Messages and Papers*, VII, 109.
[5] Oberholtzer, II, 318.
[1] Nevins, *Emergence of Modern America*, 186.

their contracts Gould and Fisk escaped loss. Their avoidance of punishment was due to the use of thugs and bodyguards and to the failure of adequate legal prosecution. They moved in respectable circles, Fisk even having President Grant as a guest on one of his steamboats; and they lived to perpetrate another enormous swindle in their milking of the Erie Railroad. In this Erie affair their stock manipulation and their bribing of the legislature and judiciary, together with their huge profits, place them among the super-brigands of high finance.

In the national government one of the shocking scandals was that of the Crédit Mobilier. On the face of it the corporation which bore this fancy name was a joint stock company organized under the laws of Pennsylvania and ostensibly concerned with the construction of the Pacific railroad. The purpose of its promoters, however, was not to construct the road, but to get construction contracts from the Union Pacific and turn large portions of the money into the pockets of a few leading shareholders. By the "selling" of Crédit Mobilier shares to members of Congress far below their value legislative support was obtained which enabled the company to declare huge dividends. The fraudulent operations were exposed with permanent injury to the reputations of sundry congressmen, and for a time the chief concern of various public men seemed to be to explain away their connection with the affair. Aside from the exposure of many questionable dealings, the chief result was the passage in the House of Representatives of a resolution (February 27, 1873) [2] censuring Oakes Ames, who had formed the chief point of contact between Congress and the fraudulent company. It should, however, be remembered that the unsavory manipulations of the Crédit Mobilier belong to the year 1868, before the Grant administration began, and that the tendency to identify the scandal with the Grant régime arises from the fact that the investigation became public in 1872.

Other scandals followed with sickening effect. A bill was passed in Congress and signed by President Grant which was popularly known as the "salary grab." Existing congressional salaries (applying to both senators and representatives) amounted to $5000 a year; but by an act now passed (March 3, 1873) the compensation was raised to $7500 a year, with provision for two years' back pay, which would give each member a "bonus" of $5000 in addition to the regular increase. The salary of the President was at this time raised from $25,000 to $50,000. In 1874, after indignant protest over the country, the old congressional salary of $5000 was restored.

Both in petty transactions and in weightier things the low standards of official conduct were manifest. The very source of official authority was polluted in election frauds. Questionable favors were received by the secre-

[2] *Cong. Globe,* 42 Cong., 3 sess., 1833. In passing this resolution of censure there were 183 yeas, 36 nays, and 22 not voting.

AN 1872 CARTOON ATTACKING
THE LIBERAL REPUBLICANS
New York Public Library

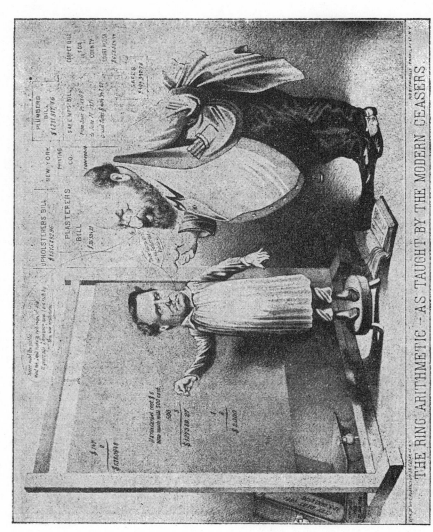

A CARTOON
AGAINST THE TWEED RING
New York Public Library

tary of the navy from men with profit-making axes to grind. The secretary of war, W. W. Belknap, "who had been receiving bribes from a trader at an Indian post," [3] resigned his office and was immediately thereafter impeached by the House of Representatives and tried by the Senate. A majority, but not the necessary two-thirds, voted for his conviction. The minority voted acquittal not on the ground of the secretary's innocence but because they considered that the Senate had no jurisdiction in the case of an officer who had resigned. One of the vilest scandals was the Whiskey Ring, a huge conspiracy by which hundreds of distillers, in collusion with treasury officials, evaded the internal revenue tax and defrauded the government. The suppression of the Ring with numerous convictions in the courts was largely the work of Grant's secretary of the treasury, Benjamin H. Bristow, who pushed the investigations with relentless vigor. In doing so, however, Bristow had scant sympathy from Grant, whose oft-quoted remark—"Let no guilty man escape"—was little more than a fine phrase.

In truth Grant had been duped by the corruptionists, and in particular he had both conferred and accepted social favors with marked publicity from the ring-leader, John McDonald. Furthermore, when it appeared that Grant's own private secretary, General Orville E. Babcock, was badly involved in the Ring, the President gave him aid and comfort and did much to save him from deserved punishment. That such a man could have been so intimate in the White House circle is a sufficient illustration of Grant's blindness to the qualities of his false friends. It has been said of Babcock that he "seems to have had intimate contacts with most of the corrupt men of a corrupt decade," and that he "fished for gold in every stinking cesspool." [4] His winnings from the Ring were estimated to include, besides other gifts, $25,000 in cash. Yet when his case came to the point of a civil trial, Grant obliged him with a deposition which aided materially in obtaining acquittal, though the serious charges had not been disproved. Though Grant himself was clear of any taint of venality, he had so obviously befriended the rascals who besmirched his administration, conferring upon them the gift of presidential approval, governmental office, and social prestige, that public confidence in the Chief Executive was seriously impaired. It was all too easy for corruptionists to win his sympathy with tears of outraged innocence and with the plea that insincere investigators were seeking to ruin the party and make political capital out of their "reforms."

3

The corruption and scandals that have been briefly sketched did not all occur during Grant's first term; but tendencies in this direction were

---

[3] Hesseltine, *Grant*, 395.
[4] *Ibid.*, 380–381.

sufficiently manifest to become an important factor in the presidential election of 1872. As the time for this election approached it became evident that, even within the Republican party, a strong anti-Grant movement would be developed. Already in 1870 the congressional election had registered a swing away from the President. Though falling short of Democratic supremacy, the ballots of that year showed a considerable Democratic increase and destroyed the two-thirds majority of the Republicans in the House.[1]

The state of Missouri now became the focal point for reorganization and change. Grant's manager in that state (Republican "boss" he might be called) was the notorious John McDonald who has been mentioned as the leader of the Whiskey Ring. Grant not only trusted him as to Missouri politics but honored him with an important Federal position as supervisor of internal revenue. Many Republicans, such as B. Gratz Brown and Carl Schurz, grew suspicious of McDonald, and at the same time the question of restoring citizenship rights to ex-Confederates became a burning issue and served further to divide the party in Missouri. The Brown and Schurz element, revolting from McDonald's domination, joined hands with the Democrats, and as a result the state Republican organization was split wide open, the Democrats gained the legislature in 1870, disqualifications were removed from ex-Confederates, and Gratz Brown became governor, Schurz having been sent to the United States Senate.

Soon the movement of Missouri liberals became associated with a larger crusade which was virtually nationwide, i.e., a movement to purge the Republican party of the spoils system, political corruption, and vindictiveness toward the South. Dissentients within the party came to be called Liberal Republicans, and they included, in addition to Brown and Schurz, such leaders as Horace Greeley, Theodore Tilton, David Dudley Field, A. K. McClure, John Wentworth, Leonard Swett, Gustave Koerner, Horace White, G. W. Julian, and Lyman Trumbull. Greeley, of course, brought to the movement the force of his powerful *Tribune,* and the *Times* now advertised itself as "the only Republican morning paper in New York." [2] As it became evident that Grant would be renominated by the regular Republicans, the signs indicated that enthusiasm for reform and opposition to Grantism would supply ammunition for a vigorous contest; but on the question of candidates there was great uncertainty. That there would be a

---

[1] In the Forty-First Congress elected in 1868 (taking the figures at the beginning of the first session and ignoring states not admitted to representation) the Senate had 55 Republicans and 10 Democrats, the House of Representatives 149 Republicans and 63 Democrats. In the Forty-Second Congress elected in 1870 there were in the Senate 57 Republicans and 17 Democrats; while the House had 138 Republicans and 103 Democrats. In the later career of this Congress the figures were somewhat different. *Tribune Almanac,* 1870, 44–45; *ibid.,* 1872, 51–52.

[2] Elmer Davis, *History of the New York Times, 1851–1921,* 117–118.

"Liberal Republican" ticket in the field, however, became evident as leaders in the various states responded to the call for a convention to be held at Cincinnati in May.

Naturally the liberals became associated with other discontented elements, and an alliance both with the Democrats and with a hopeful infant, the labor party, was sought. The National Labor Reform Convention at Columbus, Ohio, chose David Davis, Illinois millionaire and Supreme Court justice, as its candidate for the presidency; and Davis, eagerly accepting a nomination which seemed to many a joke,[3] laid his plans to capture the Cincinnati nomination. There was not much in Davis's reputation for liberal views beyond his opinion denouncing arbitrary military power in the Milligan case, but this in itself was a big factor. The decision had heartened liberals in proportion as it had angered vindictives. Davis's friends became overactive for him; his own purse supplied transportation for hundreds from central Illinois; and these noisy followers made themselves conspicuous at Cincinnati with their band playing, marching, and shouting.

Meanwhile the hopes of many earnest men centered in Charles Francis Adams. He was, however, connected with the Geneva arbitration which kept him out of the country most of the time in 1872; he was "an Adams"; he wrote a frigid letter which repelled support; and in the important state of Missouri, though favored by Schurz, he was hotly opposed by Gratz Brown and Blair. Even so Adams did receive a notable plurality on the first ballot; but his support failed to grow, and on the fourth ballot Horace Greeley was made the nominee. To numerous leaders of the movement (Carl Schurz and E. L. Godkin may be mentioned as examples) the painful anticlimax of Greeley's nomination was received with the deepest distress and chagrin. Efforts were made to persuade him to withdraw, but the editor took his candidacy most seriously; and soon the situation became the more remarkable when the Democratic convention at Baltimore also chose Greeley as their candidate. It was one of the strangest campaigns of history. Republicans excoriated a Republican President; Liberals labored without enthusiasm for a candidate whose choice was intolerable to them; Democrats supported a violent and abusive opponent; ex-Confederates in the South did battle for a foe who had denounced them as traitors and rebels.

With an "insignificant" platform [4] but a full campaign chest the Republicans swung into action for Grant; a "Southern Newspaper Union" supplied stereotypes to hundreds of papers; Ku Klux Klan prosecutions [5] were pushed in the South to discourage Democrats that might put too much

[3] H. E. Pratt, "David Davis, 1815–1886," *Transactions,* Ill. St. Hist. Soc., 1930, 175.

[4] Hesseltine, *Grant,* 277.

[5] See below, pp. 683–684.

pressure on Negroes; and the colored vote was rounded up by Union Leagues. As for Greeley one of the chief weapons against him in the North was ridicule. Yet, hopeless as was his case, there was something appealing in the spectacle of the veteran editor touring the country, denouncing corruption, pleading for the subordination of party motives, urging generosity toward the South, and declaring his own fitness for coming duties. Never a mere timeserver, he had labored for humanitarian causes and had been to millions an oracle and a prophet. To many among these very millions, however, party regularity was sacred; and election day gave Grant the victory by a majority larger than in 1868. The Republicans carried every Northern state and several in the South as well. The Greeley fusionists carried only Missouri, Tennessee, Texas, Georgia, Maryland, and Kentucky. Greeley had 2,834,000 of the popular ballots, Grant 3,597,000. In the congressional election the Republicans also made considerable gains.[6] The result gave an undue impression of Liberal and Democratic weakness; even supporters of the President thought that so overwhelming a victory was ominous of danger.[7] The defeated candidate bravely faced the future and tried to resume work on the *Tribune;* but he was exhausted by the strain of the canvass and crushed by the loss of his wife, whose death was nearly simultaneous with the election. Before the month of November, 1872, was out, Greeley lay dead.

4

American economic life at the time of Grant's second inauguration (1873) bore the superficial aspects of prosperous capitalism. Though obtaining their winnings largely with loaded dice, the magnates of big business were happy. In pyramiding their huge capitalistic structures with the connivance or encouragement of government, the wizards of industry displayed a bold resourcefulness which commands attention; but the unhealthiness of all this reckless advance of private greed was shown in exploitation of the country, riotous speculation, destruction of forests, waste of mineral wealth, private appropriation of essential products, and an unholy alliance of business and politics.

The haphazard nature of America's boom and the chaos inherent in the nation's uncoordinated business life were soon to bring their ugly con-

[6] The Forty-Third Congress, after the election of 1872, showed 49 Republican, 5 Liberal Republican, and 19 Democratic senators. This was a Republican loss; but in the House the figures showed 195 Republicans, 4 Liberal Republicans, and 88 Democrats. *Tribune Almanac*, 1874, 44–45. (For 1873 the *Tribune Almanac* [p. 41], counting Democrats as Liberals, gave the figures as follows: Senate, Administration 48, Liberals 24; House, Administration 193, Liberals 92.) For comparison with preceding Congresses, see above, p. 658, n. 1.

[7] Hesseltine, *Grant*, 289–290.

sequences. On September 18, 1873, following a series of previous failures, the New York office of Jay Cooke and Company, a highly respected firm of financiers whose mighty credits to railroad and industrial concerns had been so vital in the postwar boom, closed its doors. Immediately a startled country read that the Philadelphia and Washington offices had done likewise. Two days after the Cooke failure the New York Stock Exchange was closed. These events were merely symptoms of a general business collapse which extended through Grant's second term (1873–1877) and beyond.

The causes of the panic and the long resultant depression were varied, and the malady was almost worldwide. The aftermath of war, with its moral decline, its clamor for quick wealth, and its many economic dislocations, had much to do with the collapse in the United States; and it is also true that elsewhere in the world a "costly epidemic of wars" [1] (in an age of Bismarck, Lopez, and Napoleon III) created similar unsound conditions. Other causes were not far to seek. The strained and unnatural situation between the Federal government and the people of the South served as a discouragement to normal enterprise. The currency, whether badly "inflated" or not for expanding postwar needs, was unmistakably abnormal, while banking control had glaring defects. Critics of financial policy, especially in the West, considered the national banking system largely responsible for the panic, alleging that it "was created to give the capitalists and money kings . . . power to cause panics at will." [2] Industrial debts were enormous. Business loans had been expanded far beyond the credit facilities of the nation. The excessive railroad building which has just been noted was undoubtedly one of the major causes of the disturbance. With their bewildering mergers and plundering directors the railroads showed plainly that the opportunities of private gain in uncontrolled economy were not matched by a sense of business obligation.

The Fisks, Goulds, and Drews were too many, the Hewitts and Coopers too few; or, if not too few in number, they were insufficiently in command of the business structure. Confidence was woefully shaken. Investigations of government and private frauds and of shameful official extravagance had their unsettling effect. The public came to realize that it could no longer trust its servants. As for high-power businessmen, enough of them were brigands so that even the honest were likely to be unjustly suspected or innocently ruined. The easy economic optimism which assumed that abundance of free land in the West would absorb the unemployed of industry was shown to be without justification. Not until 1879, when "the return to the gold standard put a floor under prices and increased confidence; and poor crops abroad combined with bumper crops in the United

[1] Nevins, *Emergence of Modern America*, 291.
[2] George L. Anderson, "Western Attitudes toward National Banks, 1873–74," *M.V.H.R.*, XXIII, 209 (Sept., 1936).

States gave a powerful stimulus," did the nation get back on the road to prosperity.[3]

The depression, "the longest of which we have record," [4] had calamitous consequences for every segment of the American economy. Businessmen were badly hurt. Shaky banks collapsed; sound ones were wrecked by "runs"; currency payments were generally suspended; hundreds of factories closed; "indescribable" scenes were witnessed in financial marts; railroad building came to a halt; stock quotations fell; the "whole business of iron making" was deranged; [5] bankruptcies multiplied. Commercial failures for the year 1873 exceeded five thousand, with liabilities of $228,-000,000. These losses outnumbered those of 1872 by more than a hundred million; yet there was worse to follow. Failures in 1876 numbered nine thousand, those of 1877 about the same, those of 1878 over ten thousand.[6]

Labor also fared badly. Wages fell; hundreds of thousands were thrown out of work; bread lines were seen in the cities. "There was an alarming increase not merely in penury but in all that it entailed—illness, ignorance, discontent, crime." [7] The depression struck a body blow at labor organization. Hard times made it possible for employers to free themselves "from the restrictions that the trade unions had imposed upon them during the years preceding the crisis," and consequently they "added a systematic policy of lockouts, of blacklists, and of legal prosecution to the already crushing weight of hard times and unemployment." The total number of unionized workers dropped from 300,000 in 1870–1872 to perhaps 50,-000 in 1878. All over the country unions "either went to pieces, or retained a merely nominal existence." [8] The National Labor Union, which had held a commanding position under William Sylvis (1866–1869), had virtually disintegrated before the panic struck, and the Industrial Congress, formed in 1873, was a victim of the depression. Some workers sought to better their lot by supporting ineffectual third-party movements; others joined secret labor organizations, like the "Molly Maguires," who terrorized the mining communities, or the far more worthy Knights of Labor, who, however, did not attract many members until the return of prosperity. A series of fierce and bloody railroad strikes in 1877 showed the desperation to which the workers, unprotected by unions, were forced.

Similarly, farmers suffered greatly during the depression. A decline in agricultural prices had begun well before the panic of 1873, and they

[3] Rendigs Fels, "American Business Cycles, 1867–79," Am. Economic Rev., XLI, 349 (June, 1951).

[4] Ibid., 348.

[5] Oberholtzer, III, 93.

[6] Nevins, Emergence of Modern America, 298, 303–304.

[7] Ibid., 301.

[8] John R. Commons, ed., History of Labor in the United States, II, 195, 177.

continued to be low for most of the decade. Iowa corn, which had sold for 70 cents a bushel in 1864, brought only 24 cents in 1872; wheat dropped from $1.57 a bushel in 1867 to 77 cents in 1876.[9] Though the decline in farm income was not more drastic than that in other segments of the economy,[10] very many farmers, who had overextended their operations during the years of prosperity by borrowing money to buy land and machinery, were faced with fixed interest charges, which they could no longer meet. In addition, Westerners had a powerful grievance against the railroads, for they were plagued by "rate wars, long-and-short-haul discriminations, rebating, pooling arrangements, traffic associations, and the like." [11] The same depression which broke up labor unions caused farmers to organize. Looking for relief from their financial woes, thousands joined farmers' clubs and supported independent third parties. The chief of these farm organizations was the Patrons of Husbandry (the Grange),[12] which by 1874 had 268,000 members, chiefly in the North Central states and the South; by 1875 the number had reached 858,000. Though the Grange was prohibited by its constitution from taking a direct part in politics, its members often found it possible to adjourn their social and educational meetings in order to resume activities on the same spot as a farmers' political party. So effective were these organizations that the legislatures of Illinois, Wisconsin, Iowa, and Minnesota passed laws regulating railroad rates, measures which the Supreme Court upheld (Munn *vs.* Illinois) in 1877.

5

In addition to diverting attention from the South and its special problems, the economic difficulties of the 1870's served to bring new or neglected issues before the national government. After 1873 Congress spent less time talking of scalawags, carpetbaggers, Negroes, and rebels and more discussing tariffs, funding of the debt, and resumption of specie payments. These economic conflicts of the depression years have often been pictured as a struggle between Western agrarians and Eastern capitalists. There is, indeed, a good deal of merit in this view. The high protective tariffs adopted during the war received their principal backing in the East but were "decidedly unpopular in those parts of the West which were not distinctively wool growing regions." [1] Robert C. Schenck, of Ohio, spoke for the West in demanding "fair play" in this matter of protection. "I propose that we

[9] Mildred Throne, "The Grange in Iowa, 1868–1875," *Iowa Jour. of Hist.*, XLVII, 291 (Oct., 1949).

[10] "The estimated proportion of the national income going to agriculture . . . was 28 percent in both 1869 and 1879." O. V. Wells, "The Depression of 1873–79," *Agr. Hist.*, XI, 243 (July, 1937).

[11] Shannon, *Farmer's Last Frontier*, 300.

[12] See above, p. 542.

[1] Edward Stanwood, *American Tariff Controversies* . . . , II, 153.

wake up," he declared, addressing himself to his fellow congressmen from the Western states. "I propose that we try our hand at making tariffs, and see whether we cannot turn out possibly as good an article as these gentlemen who have manufactured it hitherto up in the manufacturing regions." [2]

Agitation over the national debt was also conducted largely upon sectional lines. In December, 1869, that debt stood at 2453 millions. In the long-term financing of this debt there arose a sharp difference of opinion between those who demanded payment in gold "dollar for dollar" (i.e., gold dollar for paper) and those who declared that this manner of payment would confer a special privilege upon the moneyed class and that the real obligation of the government consisted of "the value at the time in gold and silver . . . of the paper currency . . . paid to the Government on . . . [the] bonds." [3] Since most of the bonds were owned by Eastern financial interests, it is scarcely surprising that many Westerners argued against redemption of the bonds in gold at par; they said that the true policy would be to pay back gold only in proportion to the actual wartime value of the money which the treasury had received from the bondholders. The face-value-in-gold redemptionists won the battle; and their triumph was manifest in the passage at the outset of Grant's administration of an "Act to strengthen the public Credit" (March 18, 1869), which pledged the United States to the payment of its bonds "in coin or its equivalent" except where the law had expressly provided otherwise. [4] Though payment in gold was not specifically required, the law taken in connection with prevailing treasury policy produced this result.

The debt, however, required something beyond a pledge as to redemption. The war had left government obligations in an unsatisfactory state, and they needed refinancing on a long-term basis. For this purpose, by authority of the refunding act of July 14, 1870, payment was made for existing bonds at par and new bonds were issued at lower rates of interest. This measure, which an economist has called "the epitome of poor debt-management policy and short-sighted financial statesmanship," marked a clear-cut victory of East over West, for it guaranteed the capitalists' interest by placing a huge portion of the debt "out of reach so that for a generation it could not be called or redeemed, no matter how great the surplus of revenues or how firm the determination to reduce the debt." [5]

So keen was the antagonism between Eastern and Western interests over these economic issues that it reminded some observers of the sectional strife just before the Civil War. With something approaching satisfaction the Southern editor of the Petersburg (Va.) *Express* observed Easterners

[2] *Cong. Globe,* 39 Cong., 2 sess., 1606.
[3] *Ibid.,* 41 Cong., 1 sess., 67.
[4] *U. S. Stat. at Large,* XVI, 1.
[5] Robert T. Patterson, *Federal Debt-Management Policies, 1865–1879,* 88, 83.

and Westerners reviling each other. "Between these two great sections," he concluded, "there can be no congeniality. On the antagonism to slavery they were able to make a show of harmony. This link is now broken. New issues . . . begin to assert themselves. Finance, taxation, the tariff—all suggest issues to the Western States. . . . There is 'an irrepressible conflict' between the two sections—the bondholder in the East and the taxpayer in the West." [6]

6

It would, however, be a mistake to view the economic history of the reconstruction era as simply, or even primarily, a struggle between West and East. In actuality the story is far more confused and complex. Though anti-tariff and anti-monopoly sentiment was probably greatest in the West, one must remember that the headquarters of the American Free-Trade League and the National Anti-Monopoly Cheap Freight Railway League were in New York City. Even a phenomenon like the Grange, apparently so decidedly a Western manifestation, had Eastern antecedents.[1] Moreover, it must be noted that historians no longer regard the Grange as simply an expression of farmers' protests. The leaders of the Patrons of Husbandry were usually not working farmers but "large-scale landholders employing laborers or renting to tenants, or agricultural editors, produce merchants, real estate dealers, scale manufacturers, seedsmen, insurance agents, etc." Though farmers undoubtedly supplied the numerical strength of the Grange, the primary impetus for railroad regulation seems to have come from the merchants of the West, who had to pay the freight bills and were consequently "more directly affected by transportation charges and their fluctuations than agrarian interests." [2] In Iowa, for example, the leaders in securing the so-called Granger laws were "merchants and shippers . . . rebelling against the depressing effect which local rate discrimination had upon their trade at unfavored commercial centers." [3]

It is easy, too, to forget that the Eastern business community was anything but monolithic in its outlook upon economic issues. On the tariff question, for instance, Northeastern capitalists were badly split. As Stanley Coben points out, "The copper, iron, linseed, and woolen textile industries . . . were bitterly divided on crucial tariff schedules. The most significant split . . . was between certain high protectionist Pennsylvania interests on one side and influential low-tariff groups in New England and

[6] William A. Russ, Jr., "Was There Danger of a Second Civil War during Reconstruction?" *M. V. H. R.*, XXV, 57 (June, 1938).

[1] Frederick Merk, "Eastern Antecedents of the Grangers," *Agr. Hist.*, XXIII, 1–8 (Jan., 1949).

[2] Lee Benson, *Merchants, Farmers, and Railroads*, 257, 24.

[3] George H. Miller, "Origins of the Iowa Granger Law," *M.V.H.R.*, XL, 680 (Mar., 1954).

New York on the other." [4] The failure of Congress to enact significant tariff legislation during the entire Reconstruction period reflects the conflict between supporters and opponents of protection; since neither interest was able to triumph, tariff rates remained basically unchanged.[5]

Nowhere were the diversities within the Eastern business community more significantly revealed than in the disputes over the currency and finance which occupied so much of the time of Congress during the reconstruction years. Central to this issue was the problem of the greenback. The treasury's brief retirement program after the war reduced the amount to 356 millions, but in 1868 Congress took alarm at decreasing prices and suspended the process of further reduction. Still later, under Secretary Richardson, a policy of reissuing greenbacks was adopted which raised the amount to 382 millions. That depreciated paper, inconvertible into specie, should be the legal tender and should circulate in such large amounts as to constitute the money of the country was a matter of irritation to the sound-money men, who included most of the importers and exporters in the country, the Eastern bankers, and the manufacturing interests of New England. The fluctuating gold-paper ratio, they declared, made export trade "almost as uncertain as a ticket in a lottery," and the National Board of Trade protested that the greenback currency subjected businessmen to countless "inconveniences, losses, and evils." On the other hand, Western merchants, Eastern speculative investors, and the more dynamic segments of the manufacturing community were hostile to the contraction of the currency. The leaders of the iron and steel industries, finding that the gold premium served as a supplement to the protection afforded by the tariff, "through most of the greenback period . . . remained antagonistic to sound money." "Why," asked Jay Cooke, speaking for these soft-money interests, "should this Grand and Glorious Country be stunted and dwarfed—its activities chilled and its very life blood curdled by these miserable 'hard coin' theories—the musty theories of a by gone age." [6]

In the midst of all this controversy the greenback question had come up to the Supreme Court, and the economic importance of that high tri-

[4] Coben, "Northeastern Business and Radical Reconstruction: A Re-examination," *ibid.*, XLIV, 68 (June, 1959). And see above, p. 543.

[5] With minor modifications the high wartime protective rates were continued throughout the reconstruction era. In 1867 a moderate reform bill, drawn up by the economist David A. Wells, was defeated, and the only tariff legislation of the Johnson administration was a Wool and Woolens Act (1867), which gave increased protection to that industry. In 1870 Congress lowered duties on pig-iron, tea, coffee, and a few other commodities, and in 1872, as a pre-election gesture, made a general 10 per cent reduction of duties. But in 1875 Congress "repealed the ten per cent. reduction, and put duties back to where they had been before 1872." F. W. Taussig, *The Tariff History of the United States* (8th ed.), 174–190.

[6] Irwin Unger, "Business Men and Specie Resumption," *Political Science Quart.*, LXXIV, 47–48, 57, 61 (Mar., 1959).

bunal was impressively revealed. The case of *Hepburn* vs. *Griswold*, brought up from Kentucky, involved the question whether a debt contracted before 1862 could be legally discharged by the tendering of paper money notes. On February 7, 1870, Chief Justice Chase delivered the opinion that the legal tender law was unconstitutional.[7] He reasoned that making paper money legal tender was not within the express powers of Congress, that it was not "necessary" to carry into effect the war power, and that, being an impairment of contract, it was "inconsistent with the spirit of the Constitution." [8] When the country had time to reflect upon this four-to-three decision [9] it was realized that it went further than originally supposed because, though the facts of the case pertained only to contracts made before the passage of the act, the Court's reasoning was so broad as to apply the rule of unconstitutionality to contracts made after its passage. Plainly the whole question was in an unsatisfactory state and some further pronouncement was to be expected of the Court, if only to clarify the effect of the Hepburn decision.

Aside from this need of clarification there was also the naturally strong pressure in the country to have the Hepburn decision reversed so that the United States notes, which had been since 1862 the money of the country, should be upheld as valid for paying debts. Many thought that the road to sound money lay not in an invalidation of the notes as legal tender, but in the resumption policy which would make them equivalent to gold. On the day of the decision in the Hepburn case (February 7, 1870) Grant nominated two new members for the Court, William Strong of Pennsylvania and J. P. Bradley of New Jersey.[10] Next month they were confirmed, and in 1871 the Court reversed the Hepburn decision [11] and upheld the validity of the paper money act "in the broadest possible manner, . . . in respect to all contracts . . . made after or before the passage of the Acts." [12]

[7] 8 Wall. 603.

[8] He said "spirit" because the clause prohibiting the impairment of contracts is a limitation upon the states.

[9] The Court then had seven members. Chase, Nelson, Clifford, and Field held to the majority opinion; Miller, Swayne, and Davis dissented.

[10] There were two vacancies on the Court. Wayne had died in July, 1867, at a time when the law required the number of the Court to be decreased to seven; but (as stated in a previous chapter) the number was again raised to nine when Grant came in. Grier, in great feebleness, availed himself of a recent act permitting retirement on half pay. His resignation was effective February 1, 1870. Grant had appointed E. M. Stanton and E. Rockwood Hoar to the Court; but Stanton died soon after appointment and Hoar's nomination was not confirmed in the Senate.

[11] Legal Tender Cases, 11 Wall. 682; 12 Wall. 457. The decision was announced in May, 1871. The division was five to four: the affirmative justices were Strong and Bradley in addition to those who dissented in Hepburn *vs.* **Griswold;** the dissenters were the four who had concurred in the Hepburn decision.

[12] Warren, *Sup. Court in U. S. Hist.* (new and revised ed.), II, 525.

The reversal had been made possible by the appointment of the new members, and it was charged that the Court had been "packed," a thing genuinely shocking to the American judicial sense. After an exhaustive analysis of the evidence, Charles Fairman concludes that the charge is "supported by nothing more than the loose invective of political opponents and a semblance of plausibility arising from the unusual concatenation of events." [13] Grant did admit to Hamilton Fish his desire that the legal tender act should be sustained,[14] and it is also true that even prior to the Hepburn decision the attitude of possible Court appointees was studied in relation to the important paper money question; but, as to the constitutional position of Strong and Bradley, says Warren, it was that of "every prominent Republican lawyer" and of nearly all the state courts. Packing the Court to suit the Radicals would have been a thing very different from choosing Strong, who was a conservative; and the carpetbag senators were "ferocious" at the choice of Bradley. To "pack" the Court suggests increasing the statutory number of its membership, but this was not done in 1870. The President was, after all, filling two vacancies in a manner which bore no unworthy political taint, unless one should say that the selection of Republicans was unjustifiably partisan.

7

The raising of the paper dollar to parity with gold was now the motive of those in control; but it was realized that too great suddenness in accomplishing this object would be unfortunate. "Immediate resumption," said Grant in December, 1869, "if practicable, would not be desirable. It would compel the debtor class to pay, beyond their contracts, the premium on gold . . . and would bring . . . ruin to thousands." [1] If each paper dollar should become exchangeable for gold at par, those who owed debts would pay far more on settlement than the value which they had received. Prices would decline; each dollar would be worth more; buying would be slowed down; business would be depressed. As the minds of the country ranged themselves in opposite schools of thought, that school which favored the creditor and large bondholder came to be known as the school of "sound money," to which was attached all the prestige and dignity of social respect-

[13] Fairman, "Mr. Justice Bradley's Appointment to the Supreme Court and the Legal Tender Cases," *Harvard Law Rev.*, LIV, 1142 (May, 1941).

[14] Nevins, *Hamilton Fish*, 306–307. This evidence has caused Sidney Ratner to conclude that Grant chose Strong and Bradley "not only on account of their character, professional eminence, and fitness for office, but also because he believed they would sustain the constitutionality of the Legal Tender Acts." Ratner, "Was the Supreme Court Packed by President Grant?" *Political Science Quart.*, L, 351 (1935).

[1] Richardson, *Messages and Papers*, VII, 29.

ability; while the opposite school, which sought some concession to the obvious fact that depreciated greenbacks were the money of the people, were denounced as crack-brained and "unsound."

The general trend of currency policy was still unsettled when in the session of 1873–1874 the money question was canvassed most elaborately in a debate which, as Charles Francis Adams remarked, made Gibbon seem no longer voluminous.[2] The debate revealed the complex crosscurrents of economic forces at work in American politics. Firmly opposing any inflation of the currency were the New England businessmen, the academic economists, and the reformers of the E. L. Godkin variety. After a momentary wavering during the panic, both the Eastern banking interests and the mercantile community also strongly supported sound currency. On the other hand, the sections of the economy hardest hit by the depression clamorously demanded inflation. Western and Southern congressmen "spoke much of the plight of the agricultural debtor interests during a period of falling farm prices." Their voices were ably seconded by spokesmen for depressed business groups. The railroad interests, which had been the first victims of the panic, "were among the noisier disciples of currency relief." Ironmen were "convinced that only inflation could save them from ruin." Congressmen representing the coal and oil industries also favored an expansion of the currency.[3]

In the form which emerged from congressional wrangling the currency bill of 1874 fixed the greenback circulation at 400 millions and provided an increase of 46 millions in national banknote circulation. The limit for greenbacks was little more than the figure attained under Secretary Richardson (382 millions), while as to the banknotes it was urged that the small amount authorized would not necessarily be issued, and that if it were, it would not exceed the business needs of the country, which was then struggling in the morass of depression and could reasonably expect an upturn.[4]

After considerable delay, his attitude being meanwhile a matter of uncertainty, President Grant vetoed the "inflation bill." In conventional histories the veto has been hailed as a stalwart expression of "correct" monetary

[2] Adams pointed out that the currency speeches in this session covered 1700 columns of the *Congressional Record*. *No. Am. Rev.*, CXIX, 112, 120 (July, 1874).

[3] Irwin Unger, "Men, Money, and Politics: The Specie Resumption Issue, 1865–1879" (MS. doctoral dissertation, Columbia Univ., 1958), 144–160.

[4] "The ['inflation'] bill placed the maximum limit of both the greenbacks and the national banknotes at $400,000,000, . . . increasing the former by $18,000,000 and the latter by $46,000,000. Certain other provisions of the bill would have nullified a portion of this increase and it is extremely doubtful if it would have inflated the currency to any great extent." George LaVerne Anderson, "Western Attitude," *M.V.H.R.*, XXIII, 214–215 (Sept., 1936).

principles and an arresting of destructive and inflationary tendencies. This interpretation might be more convincing if it were not for a number of factors. For one thing, according to his own statement, Grant first prepared a message to justify approval of the bill. Furthermore, in his veto message he expressed doubt whether the bill "would give an additional dollar to the irredeemable paper currency of the country or not. . . ." [5] His objection was not so much to the actual inflation which the bill provided as to the probable clamor for more inflation which he said it would encourage. One need not conclude that Grant's veto was dictated by political motives, such as his desire for a third term or his wish to scotch the presidential ambitions of Morton or Logan by pleasing eastern bankers; but men of the time did not hesitate to raise such accusations. [6]

After the failure of the banknote circulation ("inflation") bill the main question of the resumption of specie payments was still pending and financial contests still raged. A bill fixing the greenback circulation at 382 millions was passed and became law by Grant's signature on June 20, 1874. In his annual message of December 7, 1874, Grant declared his belief that there could be no permanent revival of business without definite measures for a return to the specie basis. Though President and Congress had so recently differed in financial policy, and though the election of 1874 had resulted in a Democratic victory, the resumption movement succeeded, and Senator John Sherman's bill for this purpose became law on January 14, 1875. Among other things the law materially changed the number of national banks and the extent of banknote circulation. Abolishing existing limitations as to the total amount of national banknotes permitted for the whole country, it provided for the organization of new banking associations. Thus were met the objections of the South and West on the important matter of banknote currency.

As to resumption the act provided that on and after January 1, 1879, the treasury would redeem "in coin" all legal tender notes offered in amounts not less than $50. In preparation for such redemption the secretary of the treasury was authorized to issue United States bonds "to the extent necessary to carry . . . [the] act into full effect, ..." Though the law said "coin," the secretary favored redemption in gold. Thus by law, and by treasury policy supplemental to law, after seventeen years of irredeemable paper currency, greenbacks and gold were at a parity. Prior to the actual legal consummation of resumption the gold premium vanished and the Gold Exchange disappeared. The most abnormal features of wartime currency had been corrected.

[5] Richardson, *Messages and Papers*, VII, 269; Hesseltine, *Grant*, 335.

[6] *Ibid.*, 211; *Harper's Weekly*, July 4, 1874, p. 553; Kansas City (Mo.) *Times*, Apr. 24, 1874.

8

In foreign affairs the dealings of the Grant administration showed a mixture of expansionist intrigue, rash imperialism, and (where the hand of Fish was especially evident) real diplomacy. Along with other instances of questionable fishing in Caribbean waters the President made a persistent effort to annex Santo Domingo to the United States. Sympathetic attention was given to those speculative investments which were dignified by the term "American interests" in the region. The appropriate stage setting was supplied by warships dispatched to Dominican waters. The island leader Baez, who had not neglected his own private interests, was fêted and petted, while his doubtful position at home was strengthened by American naval force. Instead of intrusting the matter to his state department, Grant sent his notorious secretary, Orville E. Babcock, to investigate and report. In this irregular way and without prior cabinet approval, treaties were drawn up providing for the annexation of the republic to the United States and the leasing to the Federal government of the bay of Samaná.

When the matter was presented to the upper house, such leaders as Schurz and Sumner severely denounced Grant imperialism, while on the administration side the lack of popular enthusiasm was obvious. On June 30, 1870, ratification failed in the Senate. Grant persisted, however, and by strenuous efforts his legislative managers brought about the passage, against Sumner's fierce opposition, of a law creating a commission to investigate the question, albeit with an amendment declaring that Congress was not committed to the desirability of annexation. As was expected the commission advised annexation, and at this point the President was minded to push the scheme either by a treaty, which required a two-thirds vote of the Senate, or by a joint resolution of both houses, which required only a majority. Sumner again assailed the President's policy, however; the necessary legislative support could not be found; and, though the President continued to expound the magnificent benefits of annexation, the scheme was virtually a dead issue from and after the spring of 1871.

While the Dominican question occasioned fervid contests, the most important international problem under Grant was the liquidation of Civil War claims between the United States and England. Foremost in this category was the American demand for indemnity on account of the depredations of Confederate warships constructed, fitted out, and otherwise assisted by English interests. As the long dispute dragged on in the postwar years it became obvious that normal peaceful relations with England depended on the settlement of these "*Alabama* claims" as they were generally called. Yet a whole complex of factors threatened failure to the peacemakers. Excessive nationalism in the United States was met by Tory pride across the Atlantic. The rivalry of Tory and Liberal in England, Fenian troubles, American clamor for the annexation of Canada, the estrangement between Senator Sumner and the Grant administration (Sumner being chairman of the Senate committee on foreign relations), and the domestic need on each side for a face-saving "victory," were among the many vexatious elements in the controversy.

In its earlier phases the diplomatic negotiations were conducted by Secretary Seward. Ambitious to settle the dispute during the Johnson administration, Seward promoted negotiations which resulted at first in an abortive treaty signed by Lord Stanley, foreign secretary for England, and Reverdy Johnson, United States minister at London. By this treaty the disputes were to be referred to four commissioners, two each appointed by England and the United States, the four to choose an arbitrator whose decision would be final. The question of the *Alabama* was to be submitted merely on the basis of previous correspondence; no new evidence was to be presented; and no award was to be made unless by unanimous approval of the commissioners, or, failing this, by reference to some "sovereign head of a friendly state" as arbitrator. When this treaty was discussed in Johnson's cabinet Seward remarked that it "made him sick"; [1] but President Johnson saw a hopeful sign in Britain's willingness to arbitrate. Seward gave the instruction that the treaty be modified, whereupon the Johnson-Clarendon convention was concluded between Reverdy Johnson and Lord Clarendon, foreign secretary under Gladstone, who had just succeeded Disraeli as prime minister. In the revised treaty the introduction of new evidence concerning the *Alabama* question was not prohibited, and the appeal to a sovereign or head of state was to occur only on approval of the governments at London and Washington. Matters were at this stage, real progress having been made in the direction of peaceable adjustment, when Andrew Johnson gave way to Grant and Seward to Fish.

The Senate by a nearly unanimous vote (54 to 1), after listening to a bellicose speech by Sumner, rejected the Johnson-Clarendon convention; and Secretary Fish gave out the statement that he was in sympathy with Sumner's sentiments. Several changes in personnel now took place: Reverdy Johnson was followed by J. L. Motley, who soon became unacceptable to the Grant administration (chiefly because of his siding with Sumner) and was superseded by General Robert C. Schenck of Ohio. Fish's efforts to get along with Sumner failed; and at a time when matters were shaping toward a solution Sumner made a wild proposal which nearly wrecked the negotiation. In a memorandum to Fish (January 17, 1871) the Massachusetts senator argued that "all questions and sources of irritation between England and the United States should be removed absolutely and forever," and suggested "the withdrawal of the British flag . . . as a condition . . . of such a settlement. . . ." "To make the settlement complete [he added] the withdrawal should be from this hemisphere, including

[1] Browning, *Diary*, II, 228.

provinces and islands." [2] In making this demand, which he actually intended not "as a *conditio sine qua non*" but as "a desirable thing," [3] Sumner's motives were complex. In part he was merely following a goal which he had consistently cherished for nearly a quarter of a century.[4] In his own mind, moreover, he was attempting to preserve amicable Anglo-American relations; he recognized that large segments of the Northern population "thought that the United States should absorb all the area north of the Rio Grande and . . . dreaded the construction of a strong British nation in North America as a perpetual threat to their Republic," [5] and he thought that, by placing himself in the vanguard of annexationists, he could keep "the control of that question" rather than allowing demagogues to agitate the issue.[6] In some measure he was, no doubt unconsciously, motivated by a desire to embarrass Fish and Grant. Whatever Sumner's purposes, the Secretary of State found him impossible to work with. "I am convinced that he is crazy," Fish wrote; "vanity, conceit, ambition have disturbed the equilibrium of his mind . . . no wild bull ever dashed more violently at a red rag than he goes at any thing that he thinks the President is interested in." [7] So acute were the differences between the senator and Grant's government that progress toward a treaty with Great Britain became possible only when Sumner lost his place as chairman of the foreign relations committee of the Senate.

Under Fish's administration of international affairs the negotiation was transferred to Washington where specially appointed commissioners assembled. After six weeks of labor these men concluded the Treaty of Washington which provided the basis for successful arbitration. The main terms of the United States were embodied in the treaty: an expression of regret by England; a recognition of international duty in the matter of neutral obligations; and a promise of financial remuneration. The friendliness of Great Britain found expression in the preamble, which stated that Her Britannic Majesty was desirous of "an amicable settlement," and in the first article, which specifically mentioned the regret of Her Majesty's government for the escape of the *Alabama* and other vessels, and for their depredations.

Claims touching these vessels were referred by the terms of the treaty to a Tribunal of Arbitration consisting of five members, one each to be chosen by the President of the United States, Her Britannic Majesty, the King of Italy, the President of the Swiss Confederation, and the Emperor

[2] John Bassett Moore, *Hist. and Digest of . . . International Arbitrations . . .* , I, 525–526; Nevins, *Hamilton Fish*, 440–441.
[3] Carl Schurz, *Charles Sumner: An Essay*, 122.
[4] Donald, *Charles Sumner and the Coming of the Civil War*, 367.
[5] Donald F. Warner, *The Idea of Continental Union*, 98.
[6] John Rose to Lord Granville, Jan. 16, 1871, F. O. 5, Public Records Office.
[7] Fish to E. B. Washburne, Feb. 20, 1871, copy, Fish MSS., Lib. of Cong.

of Brazil. The Tribunal was to meet at Geneva, and its decisions were to be by a majority of the arbitrators. Of major importance was Article VI, which laid down three rules of neutral conduct which, in addition to the general principles of international law not inconsistent therewith, were to govern the decisions. The readiness of Great Britain to make a fair settlement was notably indicated in the wording of these rules, in which it was declared that a neutral government is bound "to prevent the fitting out, arming, or equipping, within its jurisdiction, of any vessel which it has reasonable ground to believe is intended to . . . carry on war against a Power with which it is at peace . . ."; to prevent the departure of such a vessel; and to refuse to permit a belligerent to use its ports or waters as naval bases or for the recruitment of men or the augmenting of military force.

These were distinctly put into the treaty as rules *ad hoc,* not as previously established principles. The parties agreed to consider the Tribunal's award as a "final settlement" of the controversy. In case a failure of neutral duty should be found, the award was to take the form of a sum in gross to be paid by Great Britain to the United States. In addition to the *Alabama* claims the Treaty of Washington also provided for the settlement of a series of other disputes, including the North Atlantic fisheries, the San Juan boundary, miscellaneous claims on both sides growing out of Civil War operations, and other matters. By the time the treaty reached the United States Senate Simon Cameron of Pennsylvania had succeeded Sumner as chairman of the committee on foreign relations. It was ratified on May 24, 1871.

The trial before the Geneva Tribunal began on December 15, 1871, and the case was not concluded until September 14, 1872.[8] The records, brief, arguments, and counterarguments were exceedingly voluminous. A perusal of the elaborate official volumes [9] which contain these records gives the impression, on the American side, of a truculent and tautological presentation which weakened the case with too much language, put undue emphasis on Great Britain's alleged unfriendliness,[10] and laid excessive

---

[8] The American member of the Tribunal was Charles Francis Adams, the British member Sir Alexander James Edmund Cockburn. The American "agent," appointed to represent the country "generally in all matters connected with the arbitration," was J. C. Bancroft Davis; counsel for the United States included William M. Evarts, Caleb Cushing, and Morrison R. Waite.

[9] *House Ex. Doc. No. 1,* part 1, 42 Cong., 3 sess. Under this document notation are found four volumes on the Geneva arbitration with the title "Papers relating to the Treaty of Washington." They are among the "Foreign Relations" documents for 1872.

[10] On this matter of Great Britain's unfriendliness during the war one should remember that regret was expressed in the Treaty of Washington in a manner intended to promote friendliness; that the very fact of arbitration, with a promise to pay damages, was sufficient to overcome any suspicion of continuing hostile

stress on legalistic abstractions concerning the nature of the Civil War. A prominent feature of the American case was a fantastic catalogue of "indirect" claims which pertained not to the depredations of the vessels in question before the Tribunal, but to general losses resulting from the "prolongation" of the war. The whole subject of secession was reviewed. The recognition of Confederate belligerency was bitterly attacked. The Queen's proclamation of May 13, 1861, was assailed, though the case before the Tribunal pertained to the correctness of Britain's "neutral" conduct, and this proclamation was, after all, but a declaration of neutrality. England's refusal to accept the American offer to adhere to the Declaration of Paris was denounced. The British government, it was said, erred in not treating the Southerners as insurgents and their ships as pirate craft.[11] The foreign enlistment (neutrality) act, it was argued, was either sufficient and should have been enforced, or insufficient and should have been amended.[12] British customs authorities, it was charged, winked at fraud and showed partiality to the Confederates.

In regard to a whole series of vessels it was urged that Great Britain had failed in its neutral obligations. Its government, said the American attorneys, did not use due diligence to prevent the construction of vessels for the Southern insurrectionists. It did not prevent the fitting out, arming, and equipping of warships within British jurisdiction. It did permit its ports and waters to be used as naval bases and as stations for the augmentation of supplies and the recruitment of men. It did not observe its own neutrality act. Its actions were deficient under international law; they did not conform to the rules of the Treaty of Washington. The government did not stop the construction or the departure of the *Alabama*. It did not arrest the Terceira expedition; it did not subsequently use "due diligence"

---

spirit; that the "rules" put into the treaty offered an adequate standard of neutral conduct without going into vague questions as to motives; and that in general it was the Confederacy, not the United States, which had cause to be deeply disappointed in the conduct of the British government. Furthermore, the whole purpose of the arbitration was to assess specific damages on the basis of concrete evidence, not to reopen wartime wrangles. At times the American arguments seemed to imply that the very existence of the war was due to the malignant influence of England.

[11] Britain was thus criticized for not adopting a procedure which the American government itself avoided in its own courts. See above, pp. 293–295, 448–449.

[12] On this point it may be noted that the "rules" given in the Treaty of Washington, whose formulation was a concession to the American point of view, specifically indicated the standard by which England's official conduct was to be judged by the Tribunal. In other words the arbitral court was definitely charged with applying specified rules; it was not sufficient for the judges to measure wartime conduct either by domestic neutrality laws or by the generally accepted principles of international law. In making these rules, England had herself conceded the main point as to this particular phase of the case. The function of the court was chiefly to make findings of fact as to the occurrences touching the warships and the extent of damage arising from these occurrences.

to prevent the departure of Semmes's warship from other British ports, such as Kingston, Cape Good Hope, and Singapore. In sum, its ministers, while demonstrating in the case of the Laird rams that the legal power existed, did not protect and enforce the government's neutrality.

Not only was it demanded that Britain pay damages owing directly to the depredations of the *Alabama* and other vessels; but to these were added the aforementioned "indirect" claims for reparations to cover expenses in pursuing the cruisers, losses in the transfer of ships to foreign registry, heavy insurance rates, and, most questionable of all, enormous expenditure and loss owing to the prolongation of the war. It was urged that the aggressive force of the Confederacy was crushed by July of 1863 and that the Southern cause was from that time sustained by a hope that the United States would become involved in a war with England. After Gettysburg and Vicksburg, it was argued, Confederate offensive operations were conducted only at sea; England was to blame for approximately the last half of the war.

Such was the indignation in England at these "preposterous" claims (which, though considered in the process of negotiation, had been purposely omitted from the Treaty of Washington) that the whole arbitration seemed on the point of breaking up. Here the diplomacy of Hamilton Fish and the common sense of Charles Francis Adams stood in good stead. Fish made it clear that indirect claims would not be insisted upon; Adams showed willingness to dismiss excessive American demands; and, after an ominous pause in the trial, the court agreed to rule out the indirect damages. The American agent, on behalf of the Grant administration, consented to this, and with "great relief" word came that the suspended arbitration was resumed.

The British case was presented with little rhetoric and with close attention to specific questions in dispute. The Tribunal, said Her Majesty's counsel, was simply to discover whether Great Britain had been guilty of a default of neutral duty, and if so to determine the extent of the loss and make an award. The Queen's proclamation was no grievance. It was simply a declaration of neutrality made necessary by Confederate privateering and Lincoln's proclamations of blockade, neither of which facts could be ignored by the British government. Britain's foreign enlistment act was modeled on the corresponding neutrality laws of the United States. The British government recognized Lincoln's blockade, and the Queen's subjects were warned that if they traded with the South, they did so at their own risk. Their government would not protect them against seizure and forfeiture. The good intentions of the government were shown in the detention of the *Alexandra* and the arrest of the Laird rams. As to the *Alabama*, it put to sea before it could be seized and received its armament on the high seas more than a thousand miles from England. If the ship committed depredations, that was due to the failure of the United States adequately to pursue the vessel. On the whole, it was urged, there was no fail-ure on Britain's part; while on the part of the United States there had been serious violations in filibustering attacks upon Cuba, in Fenian raids into Canada, and in the operations of Walker in Mexico and Central America.

In its decision and award the Tribunal determined that Great Britain had failed to use "due diligence" to enforce its neutrality in the cases of the *Alabama, Florida,* and *Shenandoah,* but had not so failed in regard to the *Georgia, Sumter, Nashville, Tallahassee,* and minor vessels. By a four-to-one vote (Cockburn dissenting) the Tribunal awarded the sum of $15,500,000 in gold as indemnity to be paid by Great Britain to the United States.[13] Numerous Civil War disputes separate from the *Alabama* claims (489 cases) were also adjudicated by the Geneva Tribunal, which gave this part of its decision in favor of Britain, decreeing that, for sundry damages to British subjects, the sum of $1,929,819 in gold was to be paid by the United States to Her Majesty's government.[14] Both these payments were promptly made; and at about the same time the San Juan boundary and the northeastern fisheries were satisfactorily arbitrated. With this liqui-dation of disputes remaining from the Civil War an impressive chapter in the judicial settlement of international controversies was concluded and a significant step taken in the maintenance of friendly relations between English-speaking peoples.

[13] Moore, *International Arbitrations,* I, 653–659.
[14] *Ibid.,* I, 698.

CHAPTER 39

The End of Reconstruction

I

LONG BEFORE the end of Grant's second term it was apparent that the program of Radical reconstruction was doomed. The majority of the Northern people turned against it. The Democrats, of course, had always opposed the Radicals, and, after the panic of 1873 renewed public interest in tariffs, currency reform, and antimonopoly legislation, their party made great gains in the North. In the 1874 elections the Democrats won a majority of seventy seats in the House of Representatives and nearly overturned Republican control of the Senate.

Equally significant was the fact that growing numbers of Northern Republicans began to oppose continuation of the Radical program. From the outset reformers interested in the civil service and better government had been dubious about the carpetbag régimes of the South. "The diminution of political corruption . . . is the great question of our time," announced E. L. Godkin's *Nation* as early as 1867. "It is greater than the suffrage, greater than reconstruction. . . ." [1] Most moderate Republicans, however, had gone along with the Radical program, partly fearing that lenient terms of reconstruction would imperil the rights of the freedmen, partly distrusting the machine-dominated Northern wing of the Democratic party. The scandals exposed during Grant's second administration, however, made it increasingly difficult for thinking men longer to maintain that the Democratic party should "be described as a common sewer and loathsome receptacle" and that the Republican party contained the "best elements in our national life." [2] By the 1870's the bogey that the Southern whites might attempt to re-enslave the Negroes was also viewed with skepticism. As Carl Schurz pointed out, ". . . there are vast numbers of Re-

[1] Ari A. Hoogenboom, "Outlawing the Spoils: A History of the Civil Service Reform Movement, 1865–1883" (MS. doctoral dissertation, Columbia Univ., 1957), 59.

[2] Buck, *Road to Reunion*, 88, 85.

publicans or men who used to vote the Republican ticket who have lost their fear of the return of the Rebellion to power." [3]

Powerful Northern economic interests also turned against the carpet-bag régimes. New York businessmen, never enthusiastic about the Radical program, came to view the continuation of the corrupt Republican administration, together with its Southern supporters, as more dangerous than a return of the Democrats to power. Despite a gesture toward civil service reform, the Grant régime carried the spoils system to a new extreme, and businessmen, especially those engaged in foreign commerce, suffered from its exactions and inefficiency. "With the aid of spies or inside informers," Matthew Josephson writes, "the experienced customhouse inspectors played for many years at a diverting game of trapping large mercantile houses with undervaluations or short weights, and by such measures wresting large fees from would-be defrauders of the Treasury. Under the terms of the law . . ., the entire value of an importation which had been falsely declared—not merely the amount of tax involved—was subject to forfeiture, the moiety, or half, going to the head of the New York Custom House as his fee and to cover legal expenses of collection." For example, agents of the New York collector, Chester A. Arthur, trapped the great metal importing firm of Phelps, Dodge & Co. in a small error involving several thousands of dollars, "whereupon the whole shipment of $1,750,000 of goods was declared subject to forfeiture." To escape costly litigation, William E. Dodge reluctantly settled the case out of court, paying some $271,017, the moiety of which was divided among the leading officers of the port. Of this sum $50,000 went to the "eminent legal counsel" employed by the collector, namely, to Radical senator Roscoe Conkling and to Radical congressman Benjamin F. Butler. [4]

Other Northern businessmen saw the uncertainties and disorder prevailing under Republican régimes in the South as the chief obstacles to the peaceful economic penetration of that section. "Had it not been for carpetbag mismanagement," declared the New York *Tribune* in 1872, "this country [i.e., the South] today would be filled with millions of Northern or foreign yeomanry carving out farms, or working in . . . iron, copper, coal, and marble." Increasingly, as William B. Hesseltine suggests, Northern "masters of capital were convinced that only the removal of this 'swarm of locusts' would make possible the economic exploitation of the section." [5]

All these pressures reflected the fact that the Civil War had now been over for nearly a decade and Northerners were coming to recover from their wartime hysteria. The worst sufferings of the conflict were growing

[3] Hoogenboom, 229–230.
[4] Josephson, *The Politicos, 1865–1896*, 96.
[5] Hesseltine, "Economic Factors in the Abandonment of Reconstruction," *M. V. H. R.*, XXII, 204 (Sept., 1935).

blurred in Northern memories. Wartime bitterness was vanishing. By 1874 even the *Atlantic Monthly,* in abolitionist Boston, could afford to publish writings of Southern apologists, such as George Cary Eggleston's charmingly sentimental *A Rebel's Recollections.* Some of the early and vehement Radicals came to lose much of their hatred for the South. Schurz became a reconciler; George W. Julian, who had once wanted to hang Jefferson Davis, now withdrew from the Republican party in disgust; Sumner, joining the Liberal Republicans, opposed all efforts "to aggravate the passions of a political conflict, and arrest the longing for concord." Though defeated in 1872, Greeley voiced the overwhelming desire of the Northern heart when he called for an end to "talk about rebels and traitors." "Fellow citizens," he asked, "are we never to be done with this? . . . You cannot afford to teach a part of your country to hate you, to feel that your success, your greatness is identical with their humiliation. . . . I ask you to take the hand held out to you by your [white] Southern brethren . . . and say . . . 'The war is ended, let us again be fellow countrymen, and forget that we have been enemies.' " [6]

Even the leaders of the Republican machine, who continued to support the carpetbag régimes because they had secured Grant's election in 1868 and would be necessary for a Republican victory in 1876, often did so with some aversion. Congressman Eugene Hale, a Republican from Maine, told his party's state convention in 1873 that he was "tired and sick of some of the carpet-bag governments." Postmaster General Marshall Jewell privately declared that the carpetbaggers did not have "among them one really first class man." [7] Grant himself, growing weary at the repeated demands these Southern régimes made for Federal protection, voiced a general sentiment in declaring that "the whole public are tired out with these . . . outbreaks in the South." [8]

2

At the same time that the Radical régimes were losing Northern support they were also being undermined in the South. At the outset the Republican governments in the ex-Confederate states had been characterized by some idealism, and they had during their first years in office brought about many needed social reforms. By Grant's second term, however, Radical rule, in the states which still remained under Republican control, had degenerated into a kind of racket. In part the change was due to the defection of the conservative native whites, who, as we have seen,[1] originally cooperated with these régimes but later left the Republican party. In part

[6] Buck, *Road to Reunion,* 95–97.
[7] Hesseltine, "Economic Factors," 207, 209.
[8] *Ann. Cyc.,* 1875, 516.

[1] See above, pp. 626–628.

it was attributable to the weariness and disillusionment of the more estimable of the carpetbaggers. Typical of this group was Adelbert Ames, the absolutely incorruptible Union general who served as senator from Mississippi and then was elected governor of the state. Sincerely believing that he had a mission to perform among the colored people, Ames was at first able to overcome his aversion to the South, with its "malarious atmosphere, with its baleful influence upon mind and body, the red clayey, turfless soil, filled with watercourses and gullies, the slothful indolence of all its people" and to conceal his irritation at the rudeness and hostility of the Southern whites, who made even the church "a place for annoyances and irritation" to Northerners. By 1874, however, he had come to give up his idea of remaking Mississippi upon a New England model. He painfully discovered that his Negro allies were both ignorant and corrupt; "the character of the material we have to work with," he wrote his wife with distaste, "gives me new cause to wish to be absolutely separated from it." His fellow carpetbaggers, he learned, were "an audacious, pushing crowd," out to loot the state. The native whites were hopeless. "Slavery blighted this people," he concluded, "then the war—then reconstruction—all piled upon such a basis destroyed the minds—at least impaired their judgment and consciousness to the extent that we cannot live among them." [2] Quietly but firmly he let it be known that he was unavailable for any further office after the expiration of his term as governor, and when the Democrats took over the state in 1876 and threatened to impeach him for imaginary crimes, he was, on the whole, glad to resign and leave the South entirely.

Behind the alienation of both the native whites and the better carpetbaggers was the fact that the Republican party in the South was increasingly dominated by unscrupulous manipulators who controlled the Negro vote. While one must not underestimate the significant progress made by the colored race during the postwar years, it must be admitted that they were largely ignorant and unprepared for their electoral responsibilities. Easily they fell under the sway of demagogues of both races. Elections in the South became a byword and a travesty. Thousands of illiterate Negroes cast their ballots without knowing even the names of the men for whom they were voting. Election laws were deliberately framed to open the way for fraud. Ballots were inspected before going into the box, and Negroes seeking to cast Democratic ballots were held up by objections and by an effort to change their votes. Registration lists showed Negroes in proportion to population at a much higher ratio than the actual fact. Vote-buying became so common that Negroes came to expect it; much of the bacon and ham mentioned as "relief" was distributed with an eye to election-day re-

[2] Blanche Butler Ames, ed., *Chronicles from the Nineteenth Century: Family Letters of Blanche Butler and Adelbert Ames,* I, 216, 397, 702; II, 14, 47.

sults. To colored voters in Florida, acting under instructions from Radical leaders, the motto seemed to be "Vote early and often." Starting in early morning they moved along in groups, voting "at every precinct" on a long "line of march," each time under assumed names.[3] In advance of the voting hour ballots would be fraudulently deposited in the box. Party conventions were manipulated by Radical leaders, and nominations were forced by the bosses (sometimes military officers) in control. Reporting on the election of 1872 in Louisiana a committee of Congress stated that in their determination to have a legislature of their own party, the Republican returning board juggled election returns, accepted false affidavits, and in some cases merely estimated "what the vote ought to have been." The whole proceeding was characterized as a "comedy of blunders and frauds."[4]

By 1867 the Union League had become strongly intrenched in the South; and it proved an effective instrument in the organization of the Radical Republican party among the Negroes. It was stated in October, 1867, that the League had eighty-eight chapters in South Carolina, and that almost every Negro in the state was enrolled in the order. According to a statement of a Leaguer, every member was oath-bound to vote for those nominated by the order. The League, he said, existed "for no other purpose than to carry the elections. . . ." The Leagues "voted the Negroes like 'herds of senseless cattle' " is the statement of competent observers, borne out by numerous instances similar to that of a South Carolina Negro who explained his vote by saying that the League was the "place where we learn the law." Another typical case was that of a Negro who was asked why he voted Republican and replied, "I can't read, and I can't write. . . . We go by instructions. We don't know nothing much."[5]

3

What the Republicans accomplished by fraud the Democrats did by intimidation. From the very beginning the majority of Southern whites, especially the small farmers of the hill country, had been unwilling to concede political rights to the Negroes. Regarding the Radical governments as an "unjust and tyrannical power" which "had filled their state with mourning, beggared them, freed their slaves and as a last insult and injury made the ex-slave a political equal," they "resisted by intimidation, violence and murder."[1] The most sensational, though not the most efficacious, aspect of this Southern white resistance to reconstruction was found in the fantastic and sinister operations of the Ku Klux Klan. From small beginnings as a frolicking secret lodge the institution spread rapidly, though in some-

[3] W. L. Fleming, ed., *Documentary History of Reconstruction*, II, 81–86.
[4] H. C. Warmoth, *War, Politics and Reconstruction: Stormy Days in Louisiana*, 225.
[5] Simkins and Woody, *South Carolina during Reconstruction*, 75 n., 79–80.
[1] Wharton, *Negro in Mississippi*, 197.

what haphazard fashion, throughout the South, attaining considerable dimensions within the years 1868 to 1871. Primarily the Klan was an answer to the Union League, a foil to the carpetbagger, and a means of suppressing Negro militia units. Its weird terminology included provinces, dominions, and realms, culminating in an empire. With a grand wizard and ten genii at the top, the order was governed by such officers as grand dragons and hydras, titans, furies, and night-hawks. In the local chapter (den) members were ghouls, the master a cyclops.

The activities of the order took less the form of a general conspiracy than of local efforts to destroy Radical political organizations by intimidation and terrorization. Night rides of white-robed and hooded men on sheeted and masked horses bore partly the aspect of frolicking pranks and partly that of ghostly intimidation of superstitious Negroes. Not infrequently, however, the victims, seeing through the disguise, were terrorized rather by real danger of violence than by the ghoulish affectation of supernatural power. Klansmen occupied themselves in destroying Union League councils, breaking up bands of roving Negroes, whipping Negro militiamen, forcing victims to pledge non-support of the Radical politicians, scaring black men away from the polls, and coercing individual carpetbaggers and scalawags.

The Klan was not successful in its attempt to overthrow Radical rule. In the first place, its efforts were too glaringly criminal, and they occurred at a time when Northern opinion still supported a thoroughgoing Radical policy toward the South. In a series of "enforcement acts" Congress moved to outlaw the Klan and other similar vigilante organizations. The first of these measures, commonly known as the "force bill," was that of May 31, 1870.[2] Designed to enforce the fifteenth amendment, it provided heavy penalties of fine and imprisonment where anyone by force, bribery, or intimidation should hinder or prevent citizens from voting. Cases of such hindrance were put under the jurisdiction of Federal courts, and for the better enforcement of court decisions the President was authorized to use the land or naval forces. By the same law congressional elections were taken under the wing of Federal regulation and abuses in connection therewith made punishable as crimes. These processes of Federal control were made more drastic by the second "force bill," passed on February 28, 1871.[3] This was similar to the act of the previous May; it merely went further in the same direction.

With the Klan particularly in mind, Congress passed the third "force bill" on April 20, 1871. In intolerably long sentences the statute listed activities such as those of the Klan (the forming of conspiracies, resisting officers, threatening or injuring witnesses, going abroad in disguise for

[2] *U. S. Stat. at Large*, XVI, 140–146.
[3] *Ibid.*, XVI, 433–440.

purposes of intimidation, et cetera), declared such acts to be high crimes, and fixed penalties. For the suppression of "armed combinations" the President was authorized to suspend the habeas corpus privilege, and the acts of the conspirators were declared tantamount to rebellion.[4] In putting the act into execution President Grant designated nine counties in South Carolina as regions in which lawlessness and terror prevailed, and suspended the habeas corpus process in those counties. This was followed by hundreds of arrests and court trials under charges of conspiracy to obstruct the exercise of rights under the fourteenth and fifteenth amendments. Meanwhile Federal troops were rushed to those areas where outlaw activity was most serious. In three sessions of the Federal circuit court in South Carolina (1871–1872) hundreds of indictments were registered and sentences of fine and imprisonment were imposed upon eighty-two persons, most of whom pleaded guilty. By such methods the Klan was effectively dispersed. Its existence virtually came to an end in 1871.[5]

A second reason for the failure of the Klan was the fact that its activities occurred at a period when, as we have seen, Southern planters and merchants were attempting to cooperate with the Radicals. The Klan flourished in the hill counties of the South, and in the eyes of the wealthy white Southerners it was composed of "low-type men," "a set of drunken and lawless vagabonds." To contemporary observers it seemed that its "primary motive . . . was the desire of the lower class whites to remove the Negro as a competitor in labor, and . . . in the renting of land." [6] Naturally Southern planters had no sympathy for such a program, and it is notable that in the exhaustive investigation which preceded the April, 1871, "force bill" many Southern conservatives strongly supported measures to suppress the menace and criminality of the Klan.

By 1873, however, most Southern whites had been obliged to give up any idea of working with the Republicans, and now planters and merchants joined the small farmers in devising new and more effective ways of subverting the Radical governments and terrorizing the Negroes. Typical of these developments was the "Mississippi Plan," devised in 1874 and put into practice in the elections of the following year. One part of the scheme had to do with arousing enthusiasm among the Democratic masses and with coercing the few remaining scalawags into leaving the Republican party. Its principal purpose, however, was to intimidate the Negroes.

Donning the red-shirt badge of Southern manhood, the whites formed rifle companies which drilled and marched in public. These were no secret

[4] *Ibid.*, XVII, 13–15.
[5] The later Klan of the Harding period was not so much a revival of the old order as a new organization in which the former terminology was borrowed and fine phrases concerning Americanism repeated, but in which the main motive seems to have been profit and political power for a few leaders.
[6] Simkins and Woody, 460, 462.

Ku Kluxers; they wanted the Negro and his friends to know that the entire white population of the state was against continuance of Republican rule. Republican meetings were disturbed by red-shirt horsemen who remarked loudly that "maybe they might kill a buck that day." Red-shirt companies fired cannon in the vicinity of Radical political rallies; some terrified Negroes were said to have believed that the war had begun again but most, no doubt, were simply aware of their own peril. The riflemen staged torchlight processions, made nocturnal raids against notorious carpetbaggers, and whipped Negroes who were politically conspicuous. They put the state under a kind of martial law. Even in the capital of Jackson, Governor Ames's wife reported, "the crack of the pistol or gun is as frequent as the barking of the dogs." The governor tried to organize his Negro supporters into militia companies, but he found that they had "not the courage or nerve—whatever it may be called—to act the part of soldiers." [7] In the dozen or so cases over the state when Negroes did resist, there occurred a race riot. In each instance the result was the same. Trained bands of white men were able to defeat the badly led Negroes; dozens of Negroes were killed, few if any whites were injured. So demoralized were Mississippi Republicans that the actual elections were unusually quiet. As one observer said, the Negroes were afraid to make any trouble and the whites did not need to. Virtually all the counties now passed under the control of native white administrations, and the Democrats gained heavy majorities in both houses of the legislature. Promptly they moved trumped-up impeachment charges against Governor Ames, only to be forestalled by his resignation.[8]

All over the South whites followed similar illegal or extralegal procedures. The result was the collapse of most of the remaining carpetbag régimes and the restoration of what is euphemistically called "home rule." Tennessee had passed under conservative control in 1869; Virginia and North Carolina followed in 1870; Democrats assumed power in Georgia in 1871; Arkansas, Alabama, and Texas were "redeemed" in 1874; Mississippi was "restored" in 1876. After that only Louisiana, South Carolina, and Florida had Radical governments, a situation fraught with significance, since their electoral votes might easily determine the outcome of the presidential election of 1876.[9]

4

The Republicans in 1876 held their national nominating convention in Cincinnati. Instead of choosing one of their strong regulars such as Ham-

---

[7] Ames, *Chronicles from the Nineteenth Century*, II, 259, 205–206.

[8] Donald, "Scalawag in Mississippi Reconstruction," 454–458.

[9] Various dates could be given for this "restoration of home rule" in each of the Southern states. For example, one might say that Mississippi was "redeemed" in 1874, when the "Mississippi Plan" was devised; in 1875, when the Democrats carried the election; or in 1876, when they actually took office and Ames resigned.

ilton Fish, or an independent of the reformer type such as Charles Francis Adams or B. H. Bristow, or a politician such as Blaine, Morton, or Conkling, the party delegates selected the less known Rutherford B. Hayes of Ohio, a Cincinnati lawyer who had risen in the Civil War to the brevet rank of major general and had served as congressman and later as governor of his state. He was a regular Republican with a difference. He had supported reconstruction measures and had been outspoken for hard money and the resumption of specie payments. That he was no spoilsman, however, was shown by his support of Bristow for the Republican nomination, while his unwillingness to take the vice-presidential candidacy on a ticket headed by Blaine was another sign of independence. It required seven ballots to get a majority for Hayes. Second place on the ticket was assigned to William A. Wheeler, a regular Republican from New York who had served in Congress.

As the opponent of Hayes the Democrats in convention at St. Louis chose Samuel J. Tilden of New York, a man of long experience whose chief fame had been won in the successful fight against the Tweed régime. Tilden's reputation as a reformer was not, in fact, entirely deserved, for he had for years been "friendly with Tweed and politically associated with him." "It was only after New York had turned on Tweed, and the 'Boss' began to totter," Mark D. Hirsh has shown, "that Tilden could be discerned in the fore" of the reformers.[1] Nevertheless, he had done excellent service in the final overthrow of the corrupt machine and, as a reward, had been elected governor of New York in 1874. While governor he had done much to suppress rascality, particularly in connection with an affair known as the "Canal Ring," whose promoters had shamefully turned government contracts to private gain. In their elaborate platform, which read like an indictment, the Democrats made their chief appeal on the issue of Republican abuse and the necessity of reform. For vice president the Democrats nominated T. A. Hendricks, of Indiana, whose soft-money policies might be expected to add to the party's strength in the West.

Even the Republicans sensed that Grantism was dying; and Governor Hayes took occasion in his letter of acceptance to advocate civil service reform and Southern autonomy in a manner that implied repudiation of Grant's policies. He also pledged that he would not be a candidate to succeed himself in 1880. The position of the Democrats, however, was much more clear-cut in demanding a house cleaning. With a reform candidate and an able national chairman (Abram S. Hewitt of New York) the supporters of Tilden faced the campaign of 1876 with high confidence. In an elaborate campaign textbook they popularized the conclusions touching government abuse which had been piled up in voluminous investigations. The Republicans, none too confident of success, countered by repeating

[1] Hirsch, "Samuel J. Tilden: The Story of a Lost Opportunity," *Am. Hist. Rev.*, LVI, 790 (July, 1951).

Civil War phrases, waving the bloody shirt, appealing to ex-soldiers, urging men to "vote as they shot," and declaring that if Tilden were chosen the South would return to power and the victory of the war would be lost. Meanwhile Grant, though at first cool toward Hayes, gave warm support to the campaign, dismissing Bristow men to the dismay of reformers, and "dispos[ing] of the offices at the requests of the party managers." [2]

5

Election day (November 7) came, and in reporting the result next morning the New York *Tribune* came out with the headline "Tilden Elected." The *Times,* however, then intensely Republican, suggested doubt in its first edition and gave a distinct note of Republican hope in the second.[1]

A remarkable situation now developed. As the returns came in it was obvious that Tilden was the choice of the voters who actually cast their ballots, having in the popular vote a majority over all of more than 150,000 with a margin over Hayes of about 250,000.[2] "In terms of the desires of the qualified voters in the election," Harry Barnard observes, "the truth never was and never will be told. . . . this count did not include, as it could not have included, votes *not* cast, because many qualified voters—

[2] Hesseltine, *Grant,* 409. The Republicans in 1876 sought, of course, to win over the reformers who had bolted four years before, and the candidacy of Hayes was an asset in this regard; but Grant's displeasure toward the liberals continued.

[1] The story is often told of a dramatic midnight conference (November 7–8) of *Times* editors, who deliberated as to "what should be said in the first edition" and framed a "deliberate plot to snatch the election from Tilden." Eckenrode, *Rutherford B. Hayes,* 178–179. One of the editors then got in touch with Zachariah Chandler, chairman of the Republican national committee, and persuaded him to issue his claim of victory; at the same time William E. Chandler was rushed off to the South in order to keep the returning boards in the disputed states firm. Though this story is essentially true, it would be naive to put too much emphasis upon this activity of the *Times* editorial council. "The claim of Democratic victory would have been challenged anyway," Harry Barnard points out, "if the results were at all close." Indeed, two days before the election Governor Kellogg of Louisiana had sent Zachariah Chandler a letter warning that Democrats were intimidating Negro voters. Thus "the Republicans had prepared a case for the charge of fraud even before Zach Chandler made his claim of victory." Barnard, *Rutherford B. Hayes and His America,* 321–322.

[2] The popular vote has been reported as follows: Tilden (Democrat), 4,284,-265; Hayes (Republican), 4,033,295; Peter Cooper (Greenback candidate), 81,-737; Green Clay Smith (Prohibition candidate), 9,522 (*Tribune Almanac,* 1877, 59). In addition, there were several thousand imperfect and scattering votes. For figures that vary only slightly from these totals, see Stanwood, *Hist. of the Presidency,* 383; *World Almanac,* 1914, 720; McKee, *National Conventions,* 179. All the figures show that, even if one concedes Republican claims as to disputed states, Tilden received a popular vote far in excess of that given to Hayes. A similar situation, of course, has happened in other presidential elections.

mainly Negroes—were scared off from attempting to vote." [3] But on the basis of this official count Tilden had 184 undisputed electoral votes; 185 were necessary to a choice. Hayes had 165 undisputed electors.[4] After the Republicans had developed their claims there was a serious dispute concerning nineteen electoral votes in the South. These included seven from South Carolina, four from Florida, and eight from Louisiana, both parties claiming to have "carried" those states. In addition, there was a minor dispute as to one Democratic electoral vote for Oregon (not included in the above-mentioned 184 for Tilden), where a Republican elector was chosen by the people, was constitutionally disqualified because of being a Federal officeholder (postmaster), and was superseded by a Democratic elector (the next highest in the popular voting) appointed by a Democratic governor.

The nub of the matter was the controversy as to the nineteen electors in the three disputed Southern states. If all nineteen should be assigned to Hayes, and the Oregon vote kept for him, he would have 185, a bare majority of one, and would thus be President. On the other hand, if only one of the votes in dispute were assigned to Tilden, he would have the needed majority. Confident of enough strength to obtain at least one of the controverted Southern states, the Democrats laid only minor stress on their questionable claim as to Oregon.[5]

As politicians proceeded with their calculations the Republicans began to see possibilities in the situation. Zachariah Chandler on November 8 issued his celebrated declaration: "Hayes has 185 electoral votes and is elected." He continued to "intone" this sentence till it became a kind of chant, "though there was no basis for such faith [writes Hayes's biographer] except Zach Chandler's boundless assurance." [6] Republican newspapers generally were soon claiming the election for Hayes; and their "visiting statesmen" appeared in the South, where they encouraged Republican man-

[3] Barnard, *Hayes*, 316–317.

[4] Counting the disputed Oregon elector for Hayes, he had, without Louisiana, Florida, and South Carolina, 166 electoral votes. It was conceded by the Republicans that Tilden had carried the states of the South except the three just mentioned. In addition he carried all the border states (including West Virginia) and, in the North, Connecticut, Indiana, New Jersey, and New York.

[5] It is sometimes pointed out that the Republicans were in a dilemma: if they were to make good their claim to the disputed electors in the South, they would be tempted to refuse to "go behind the returns"; but if this principle were applied to the case of Oregon, they would supposedly lose an elector in that state. A full discussion of all that is involved in this "dilemma" would be very involved and complicated; but there was enough Republican embarrassment in the situation to explain why the Democrats did not ignore their somewhat shaky Oregon elector. Having ample claims elsewhere, the friends of Tilden were willing, of course, to give up the Oregon elector if they could thus fix the principle that the validity of returns coming up from state officials could be made the subject of Federal inquiry.

[6] Eckenrode, *Hayes*, 184–185.

agers to "hold" their states, supervised the preparation of "returns," and saw to it that no oversight should occur by which a Hayes trick might be lost. Democratic politicians also made their way South, and their activities were as questionable as those of their opponents.

The three disputed Southern states now became the object of a tug of war, in which both contestants resorted to the most unscrupulous methods. "It is terrible to see the extent to which all classes go in their determination to win," wrote Republican Lew Wallace from Louisiana. "Conscience offers no restraint. Nothing is so common as the resort to perjury. . . . Money and intimidation can obtain the oath of white men as well as black to any required statement. A ton of affidavits could be carted into the state house tomorrow and not a word of truth in them. . . . Now what can come of such a state of things?" [7] The situation was made more complex because each of the disputed states had a curious legal device known as the "returning" (or "canvassing") board, which had been set up by the carpetbag governments to "review" the election returns and reject those polls in which unfair methods, in their judgment, had been used. Thoroughly partisan in motive and character, these returning boards were clothed with judicial power, and Radicals kept reiterating that their decision under state law was final in determining what the revised count should be.

6

A glance at the situation in each of the disputed Southern states is now necessary. It happened that political affairs in South Carolina gave unusual strength in 1876 to the Democratic party, which had been dormant since the establishment of carpetbag rule in 1868. From 1872 to 1874 the notorious and corrupt scalawag, Franklin J. Moses, Jr., had been governor. Up to the end of his rule the Democrats made no impression in political control of the state. Moses, however, was followed by a Radical of a different type, the reform governor D. H. Chamberlain (1874–1876); and the honest administration which he conducted, while incurring bitter opposition within his own Radical party, commanded respect among South Carolina whites. For a time the Democrats cooperated with the Chamberlain Radicals; but instead of doing so in 1876 they chose a "straightout" Democratic candidate for governor (Wade Hampton), and "the white population was for the first time in eight years united in a definite, fixed purpose." [1]

The ensuing campaign has been described as one of "force without violence." Democrats promised to protect the rights of the colored race, but in return they demanded that the Negroes abandon the Republican party. Hampton's rifle clubs openly displayed their might in order to intimidate

[7] Barnard, 327.
[1] Simkins and Woody, 495–496.

the Negroes. When President Grant ordered such extralegal military companies to disperse, one armed company in Columbia, which possessed field pieces and was trained to operate as a battery of horse artillery, "cheerfully announced that it was reorganized as 'the Hampton and Tilden Musical Club, with twelve four-pounder flutes.' Others renamed themselves 'Tilden's mounted baseball clubs.' Rifles and ammunition continued to arrive in shipments from outside, disguised in dry-goods boxes and provision barrels. . . . The Red Shirts . . . rode like the cavalry of Hampton's old brigades, paraded in towns, and attended meetings of both parties in impressive numbers. Radical speakers, Chamberlain included, found themselves repeatedly challenged before large audiences as 'liars, thieves and rascals.' " [2] In many communities whites "made a practice of giving certificates to qualified Negro Democrats. The idea was that Negroes holding such certificates would be given preference over Republicans in all employment and trade." In other areas the tactics were even more direct, for "each white voter was urged to pick one Negro and get him by bribery, threat, or persuasion either to vote for Hampton or not to vote at all." [3]

In these circumstances, with more ballots than voters, and with irregular practices in both parties, each side in South Carolina claimed victory in the 1876 election. The state board of canvassers showed no great concern to overthrow the majority for Hampton which was evident when returns from county canvassing boards came in, nor did they set aside the Democratic majority in the legislature; but in the presidential vote they reported in favor of the Hayes electors. The Democrats, refusing to admit defeat, sought unavailingly to overthrow the action of the board by court procedure and to establish the validity of the Tilden electors. Thus conflicting electoral reports came up from South Carolina, and meanwhile rivalry between Chamberlain and Hampton (both of whom were "inaugurated"),[4] together with the struggle of contesting legislatures, produced a condition of intolerable uncertainty and put Chamberlain in the light of a doubtful executive whose position depended upon Federal military support.

Conditions in Florida resembled those in South Carolina. There was intimidation via the "Mississippi plan," chiefly of a milder form. Though some of the "evidence" on the subject was "probably manufactured out of whole cloth," yet the fact of intimidation, writes P. L. Haworth, "rests upon an overwhelming mass of evidence." The board of state canvassers, according to Haworth, "did its work in an unpardonably partisan manner." With the encouragement of "visiting statesmen" its decision was announced in favor of the Hayes electors and also of a Republican state and congressional ticket. Haworth concludes that a "fair count" might have given the Florida

[2] Manly W. Wellman, *Giant in Gray: . . . Wade Hampton,* 265.
[3] Hampton M. Jarrell, *Wade Hampton and the Negro,* 70.
[4] The pretending Radical legislature declared Chamberlain elected despite the action of the board of canvassers which certified the election of Hampton.

electors to Tilden, but that a "free election" would have given them to Hayes and that "in equity" the vote belonged to the Republicans.[5] On the other hand Eckenrode states that "Tilden carried Florida" and that the canvassing board "falsified the returns." [6]

The most famous dispute, however, was in Louisiana. In that state the Warmoth (anti-Grant) faction of the Republicans, joining with the Democrats, had in 1872 supported John McEnery for governor; while the Radical Republicans, in league with the Grant administration, had supported a typical carpetbagger, William P. Kellogg. After an election which was reasonably peaceful both sides claimed victory; each side determined to grasp the government; and the row was on. The state returning board certified the election of the McEnery ticket in both the legislative and executive branches; but the Kellogg faction, having failed to "capture" the board, made up their own board which, "without having a single return from any poll in the State, proceeded to fabricate . . . what they claimed to be the result of the State election." [7] Using "pseudo-returns" [8] this board gave its declaration in favor of Kellogg and a majority of the Republican legislators. They also certified the choice of Grant and Wilson electors. The Kellogg organization, including its returning board, was denounced as a "bogus" [9] affair; but Congress did nothing to clear up the deadlock, and under these circumstances Grant chose the doubtful alternative of supporting the Kellogg faction, at the same time refusing a hearing to the McEnery element.

From that point the confused succession of events presented a sorry mixture of farce and tragedy. While the Democrats and liberal Republicans still claimed that McEnery and legislators of his party were the rightful and actual government of Louisiana, the Kellogg government was inaugurated and kept in power by the use of Federal troops. Defiance of the Kellogg government became so intense that actual civil war resulted in several localities. At Colfax in April, 1873, about fifty-nine Negroes and two whites were killed in a battle between a Kellogg sheriff and a band of pro-McEnery whites. At Coushatta in August, 1874, and at New Orleans in September of the same year similar outbreaks, with some loss of life, occurred. Each side, of course, put responsibility for the prevailing chaos upon the other.

[5] Haworth, *The Hayes-Tilden Disputed Presidential Election of 1876*, 57–58, 67, 76.

[6] Eckenrode, *Hayes*, 193. It is impossible to arrive at even a fairly satisfactory conclusion as to the votes of these states, the problem being how far Democratic intimidation offset Republican fraud. "The consensus of recent historical scholarship," C. Vann Woodward points out, "is that Hayes was probably entitled to the electoral votes of South Carolina and Louisiana, that Tilden was entitled to the four votes of Florida, and that Tilden was therefore elected by a vote of 188 to 181." Woodward, *Reunion and Reaction*, 19.

[7] Warmoth, 206.

[8] Rhodes, VII, 110.

[9] Warmoth, 212–213.

On the face of the returns in 1876, despite the efforts of the so-called "bogus" government, all the Democratic presidential electors in Louisiana had ample majorities, the lowest over 6000, the highest nearly 9000. Notwithstanding this the Republicans claimed the state and came forward with reams of arguments to support the claim. Emphasizing the activities of the White League, their investigators charged that criminal conspiracies, "by force . . . and intimidation, halting at no enormity of crime, . . . [had substituted] the rule of violence . . . [for] the will of . . . [the] majority." [10] Registration figures, so the argument ran, showed an excess of colored men; hence the Democrats could not rightly claim the state. As to the Kellogg government, Federal intervention was pictured by the Republicans as a virtue on the ground that "there had not been an hour since the inauguration of Governor Kellogg when the secret order of these men [elsewhere referred to as 'wolves . . . organized against the sheep'] would not have overthrown his authority . . . unless he were sustained by the power of the United States troops." [11] The whole authority for determining the vote in Louisiana, it was said, rested with the state returning board; that board "used their power in accordance with the . . . intent of the act that created them"; [12] thus the report of the election of November 7, 1876, in Louisiana was "promulgated by the proper authorities of . . . [the] State . . . and in conformity with the Constitution of the United States." [13]

Democratic congressional investigators emphatically refuted these Republican claims. On the matter of intimidation they showed that it was a prearranged plan in certain districts for Republicans to stay away from the polls and then, claiming intimidation, to urge the rejection of these districts in the final count.[14] Even with election machinery in Republican control, they stated, the actual returns gave a majority of several thousand to the Tilden electors. The Republican returning board then went to work. Calling in witnesses whose fees were paid by the United States government, using *ex parte* affidavits prepared (sometimes with fictitious names) by United States soldiers and government employees, rejecting evidence offered by Democrats and excluding their counsel, and conducting a purely arbitrary series of hearings, the board piled up a mass of so-called testimony and on this basis made out a Republican majority. As to Republican fraud in the election itself, it was pointed out that local registration officials were

[10] Report of the Republican minority of a select committee of the House of Representatives on the election in Louisiana, in *House Report No. 156*, 44 Cong., 2 sess., pt. 2, p. 1.

[11] *Ibid.*, 15.

[12] *Ibid.*, 20. The absolute truth of this statement presents a delicious example of unconscious humor.

[13] *Ibid.*, 26.

[14] J. F. Rhodes writes: "Undoubtedly the Republican frauds in registration offset Democratic intimidation." *Hist. of the U. S.*, VII, 235.

informed by Republican managers that the census showed a certain Republican (i.e., colored) vote, that they must get out the full vote and the required majority "without fail," and that if they did so their reward would be "ample and generous." [15]

There were four members of the important Louisiana returning board, and they were all Republicans. The law called for five members; but, though there was a vacancy, the board refused to fill it by the appointment of even one Democrat to their number. Not only the members, but all the clerks and employees of this allegedly "judicial" tribunal, were of one party. What is even more to the point is to note that the board's personnel comprised a "dishonest politician," a "corrupt local office-seeker," a man indicted for larceny, and a "colored ignoramus." [16] This was the group of men who, under orders to hold the state, and under terrific pressure, re-molded the election returns of Louisiana nearer to their hearts' desire. An example of their work may be seen in Ouachita parish, where, of the votes rejected by the board, less than 50 were Republican and over 1500 Democratic, or in East Baton Rouge parish, where they threw out 160 Republican and 1442 Democratic votes.

By the process of rejecting whole polls, sometimes whole parishes, the board reversed the result as reported by local election officials. P. L. Haworth, whose treatment is not unsympathetic to the Republican party, writes that the board did "some heroic work" to accomplish its purpose, took "an absurd view" to justify its party membership, and used "illegal" protests as a basis for its action. It "worked zealously," he said, "to evolve a Republican majority," and attained that result "by a series of grossly partisan and illegal acts." [17] This result in brief was the conversion of a Democratic majority of approximately 6000 to 9000 into a Republican majority of over 4000. In doing this the board got rid of over 13,000 Democratic votes.[18]

7

Though the legal process of choosing the President, as distinguished from party methods grafted on to the original system,[1] was prescribed in

[15] This paragraph summarizes the Democratic side of the congressional investigation. *House Report No. 156*, 44 Cong., 2 sess., pt. 1, pp. 5–6.

[16] Nevins, *Hewitt*, 327–328.

[17] Haworth, 101, 102, 112, 116. Haworth is clear and emphatic as to the partisan nature of the returning board's proceedings, but concludes that in a "free election" the state "would have" gone Republican by five to fifteen thousand (p. 121). He arrives at this conclusion by a statistical comparison of the election of 1874 with that of 1876.

[18] Rhodes, VII, 232.

[1] By provision of the Constitution (Article II, section 2) each state appoints as many "electors" as it has senators and representatives in the national Congress. These men vote for President and, on separate ballots, for Vice-President. Except

the Constitution, no part of that document offered a solution for the case of opposite returns of electoral votes being submitted from the same state. The Constitution provided that, in receiving electoral votes, the president of the Senate, in joint session of the two houses, should open the electors' certificates and that "the Votes . . . [should] then be counted." It was claimed in Republican circles that this gave the president of the Senate (T. W. Ferry, a Republican) the power of deciding disputes; and this was the "solution" which Republican leaders sought to apply for 1876. The Republicans themselves, however, had accepted no such solution in previous contests, but had set up the "twenty-second joint rule" of legislative procedure, by which, if either house objected to an electoral ballot, it should not be counted except by concurrent vote of the two houses. This was the rule used for the elections of 1864, 1868, and 1872. Now, however, the Republican Senate naturally refused to join with the Democratic House in re-enacting this joint resolution. Thus at a time of grave crisis the country lacked a method of determining the presidential count.

The constitutional provision that the House of Representatives shall choose the President if no majority is obtained for one man in the electoral college was applicable to a case where all the votes had been counted, but not to the existing predicament in which the very counting of the votes was the essence of the question. To appreciate the seriousness of the situation it must be remembered that weeks were passing while politicians maneuvered and clamored, and that there was real danger of March 4 arriving

---

in two elections (1800–1801 and 1824–1825) a clear majority of electoral votes has been given to one man, making him President; but where such a majority over all is not obtained the final choice from among the higher contestants is made by the House of Representatives, voting by states. Such in briefest outline is the constitutional road which every election must take. Two practices, however, have been grafted on to the original system which profoundly change the actual or effective method of choice: (1) the practice of party nominations, and (2) the "general ticket" method by which the people elect the electors. Each party nominates its candidates in national convention, and each elector is "bound" (in practice, not in law) to vote for the party nominee. Furthermore, by a movement that has extended over the country till it has become universal, each party puts before every voter in each state a full slate of the state's electors, these also being selected by party nomination; so that the party which "carries" the state, though it be by a small plurality, obtains all the electors (i.e. the full presidential vote) of that state, and the minority party obtains no vote that counts in the electoral college. Thus if a state has seven electors and if the popular ballots show 40,000 for the Republicans and 30,000 for the Democrats, the voting in the electoral college would not be four and three respectively, but seven for the Republicans and none for the Democrats. One party may have more of these wasted votes than the other, and thus it may lose the election though actually obtaining a majority in the popular ballots over the country. For a fuller view of the inequitable manner in which the clumsy system works, the reader should consult a treatise on the American government.

before a settlement could be reached. This might have resulted in two contending governments claiming to be the rightful authority at Washington — precisely the situation which Republican rule, matched by local resistance, had produced in more than one Southern state. On the Republican side there was talk of using the army; on the other side there were hotheads such as Henry Watterson, who threatened in a public speech that a hundred thousand Kentuckians would see justice done to Tilden. To some it looked like civil war; thoughtful men were deeply concerned at the possible "Mexicanization" of American elections.

Behind the scenes, however, there were powerful forces working for peaceful adjustment. Northern businessmen were emphatically opposed to any resort to violence. In New York, for example, there was held in December a conference "of a dozen or more of the wealthiest men in this city, equally divided as to politics, for the purpose of consulting as to what course ought to be or could be taken, to bring about . . . a settlement." [2] Equally important was the fact that the Southerners vetoed any talk of renewing civil war. As James A. Garfield reported to Hayes," . . . the leading southern Democrats in Congress . . . are saying that they have seen war enough, and don't care to follow the lead of their northern associates who . . . were 'invincible in peace and invisible in war.' " [3] Finally, one must stress the pacific tone adopted by Tilden himself. Imprudent action on his part might have set off another sectional conflict, but he declared cautiously: "It will not do to fight. We have just emerged from one civil war, and it will never do to engage in another civil war; it would end in the destruction of free government." [4]

With so many voices urging peaceful settlement, there was good reason to think that Hayes's supporters might be able to pick up enough strength among the Democrats to secure the election of their candidate. Three groups of Southerners proved particularly susceptible to Republican blandishments. The largest of these consisted of those congressmen who saw in the election controversy the opportunity of finally ending the carpetbag régimes in the South. They were aware that Hayes was already favorably disposed toward the claims of the Southern whites. They read eagerly an interview the Republican claimant had with a New Orleans editor, in which he was quoted as saying "that carpet bag government had not been successful; that the complaints of the southern people were just in this matter; that he would require absolute justice and fair play to the Negro, but that he was convinced this could be got best and most surely by trusting the honorable and influential southern whites." [5] They hoped, therefore, that Hayes, if elected through their support, would withdraw the few re-

[2] Barnard, 347.
[3] Woodward, *Reunion and Reaction*, 22.
[4] Barnard, 343.
[5] Woodward, 25.

maining Federal troops from the South and that, as a result, the Republican régimes of Florida, Louisiana, and South Carolina would collapse.[6]

A second group of Southerners, while sharing these desires, had also other objectives which they hoped to forward by supporting Hayes. These were the former Whigs, who, as we have seen, had been forced unwillingly into the Democratic party. They distrusted their new political associates, mostly small farmers with a tendency toward excessive democracy, and they hankered for a realignment of national parties which would permit them to join with the conservative business interests of the North. Remembering that the prewar Whig party had been just such a party and that most moderate Northern Republicans had been Whigs, they were prepared to do some shrewd horse trading. As negotiations took place it developed that in return for permitting Hayes to be counted in as President and for allowing the Republicans to organize the next House of Representatives, electing Garfield speaker, these Southern conservatives wanted promises that the incoming administration would abandon the carpetbag régimes, would appoint a former Southern Whig to the cabinet, and would assist in "laying the foundation for a revival of Republicanism in parts of the South under conservative native [i.e., white] leadership." [7]

Partly included in these two groups were other Southern congressmen who had economic rather than political objectives to promote. Throughout the South there was a general feeling that, in order to promote recovery from the war, the section needed Federal "appropriations, subsidies, grants, and bonds such as Congress had so lavishly showered upon capitalist enterprise in the North." [8] Some Southerners demanded subsidies to improve their harbors, levees, and canals, but the favorite Southern internal improvement project of the period was the grandiose plan of Thomas Scott, of the Pennsylvania Railroad, to connect the South by rail with California. His Texas & Pacific scheme, a revival of a decades-old Southern dream, enlisted the sympathies of Southerners of all classes. Legislatures in every Southern state except Louisiana and Virginia passed resolutions supporting the projected railroad. Even the National Grange, at a Southern domi-

---

[6] It has been argued that undue emphasis has been given to this Democratic objective, since the Democrats, already in control of the House of Representatives, were able to "write into the army appropriations bill, then still pending, a clause forbidding the use of troops to support the claims of any state government in the South until it should be recognized by Congress." When the Senate refused to accept this clause, the House Democrats held up all army appropriations and thus, it is said, made the withdrawal of troops inevitable even without a promise from Hayes. (Ibid., 8–9). This line of reasoning ignores the fact that failure to pay the troops did not mean the disbanding of the army; Hayes used unpaid troops to break strikes in the summer of 1877. In addition, Southerners wanted a Republican pledge against the future use of troops.

[7] Ibid., 174.

[8] Ibid., 55.

nated meeting held at Charleston, overcame its hostility to monopoly and endorsed the Texas & Pacific.

Hungry for Federal assistance in all these projects, Southerners, as C. Vann Woodward remarks, learned they had "arrived tardily at 'the Great Barbecue.'" After the exposure of the Crédit Mobilier and other scandals of the Grant administration, Congress was most reluctant to enter upon another orgy of public spending for private profit. Northern Democrats, especially those from the Granger states of the Middle West, took the lead in blocking congressional appropriations for railroads, canals, levees, and other internal improvements. To the marked irritation of their Southern brethren, Democrats like William S. Holman, of Indiana, made "Retrenchment and Reform" the party's watchword. It was no wonder, therefore, that Southerners began to say "that in the matter of internal improvements they had been much better treated by Republicans than they were likely to be by the Democrats" and to wonder whether Hayes, if elected, would promise to treat their projects "with kind consideration." [9]

Convinced that they could gain enough Southern votes from these three sources to secure the election of their candidate, Hayes's friends in Congress opposed any proposal to arbitrate the disputed election, but they were undercut by defections within their own party. Roscoe Conkling and other Stalwarts, partly representing the disturbed business community, partly reflecting their own distrust of Hayes's reform tendencies, joined Tilden's backers in creating, on January 29, 1877, an electoral commission to settle the dispute.[10] Composed of fifteen members (five from the House, five from the Senate, five from the Supreme Court), the commission was authorized to review conflicting returns submitted from any state and to decide "which is the true and lawful electoral vote of such State."

The establishment of this commission was generally regarded as a Democratic victory. The members were chosen according to their political affiliations. Three commissioners from the Senate were Republicans and two were Democrats; in the five from the House the proportion was reversed; and four of the justices were specified (by specifying their circuits) so that two were Republicans and two Democrats. It was expected that the fifteenth member would be David Davis of Illinois, a Liberal Republican of 1872, whom the Democrats believed to be favorable to Tilden or at least more open-minded than the other justices. At the last minute, however, Davis became unavailable on account of his election to the

---

[9] *Ibid.*, 60, 22.

[10] Taking congressmen and senators together, more Democrats than Republicans voted for the Electoral Commission bill. The measure could not have passed, however, without the support of both parties, for the House was Democratic and the Senate Republican. In the Senate 26 Democrats voted for the bill and 1 against it; 21 Republicans voted for and 16 against. In the House the yeas included 160 Democrats and 31 Republicans, the nays 17 Democrats and 69 Republicans.

United States Senate, and the role of fifteenth member fell to Justice Joseph P. Bradley of New Jersey.[11]

8

On February 1 the two houses of Congress met together to count the electoral votes, in accordance with the terms of the bill establishing the Electoral Commission. Ferry, the president of the Senate, proceeded to open the certificates from the states in alphabetical order. When he reached Florida, objection was made to the returns and immediately the subject was referred to the Commission, which then heard arguments from Democratic and Republican counsel. Democrats maintained that the Commission should arbitrate the points in controversy, that it had "full authority to investigate by all . . . legitimate means . . . the . . . fact . . ." as to disputed votes, and that, as between the two sets of electors, the Democrats had the "best legal title" and the "moral right." [1] On the Republican side the main argument was that of Evarts that the Commission could not "receive evidence in addition to the certificates . . .; that is, evidence that goes behind the State's record of its election, . . . certified by the governor. . . ." [2]

Eagerly the nation awaited the decision of the Commission. As to fourteen members it was generally understood that seven would vote Democratic and seven Republican: the one man about whom there was any doubt at the climax of this furious controversy was Justice Bradley. It is therefore of no little interest to read, in Abram Hewitt's "secret history" of the famous dispute, the dramatic account of how Bradley's decision was reached. In this narrative it is revealed that on the night preceding the Florida decision, an intimate friend visited the justice and reported to anxious Democratic leaders "that he had just left Judge Bradley after reading his [Bradley's] opinion in favor of counting the vote of the Democratic electors of the State of Florida," which of course would have insured the

[11] As finally constituted the Commission consisted of three Republican senators (G. F. Edmunds, O. P. Morton, and F. T. Frelinghuysen), two Democratic senators (T. F. Bayard and A. G. Thurman), three Democratic congressmen (H. B. Payne, E. Hunton, and J. G. Abbott), two Republican congressmen (J. A. Garfield and G. F. Hoar), and five justices (Nathan Clifford, S. F. Miller, S. J. Field, William Strong, and J. P. Bradley). The first four justices were designated as to circuit in the act, "which was to say that they should be Miller and Strong, Republicans, and Clifford and Field, Democrats" (Oberholtzer, III, 295). It may be said that the whole spirit of judicial arbitration and settlement was vitiated by this deliberate selection of the Court members as Democrats and Republicans. "It was pretended . . . , though none seems to have believed it, that the justices would rise above partisan feeling." (Ibid.)

[1] Electoral Count of 1877: Proceedings of the Electoral Commission . . . , 124 ff.

[2] Ibid., 118.

election of Tilden. Next day, however, Bradley voted Republican on the Florida question. "The change [writes Hewitt] was made between midnight and sunrise," and he charged that Bradley, having first been convinced of the validity of the Democratic electors in a case which involved the whole controversy and having gone so far as to write an opinion supporting this decision, yielded to political pressure, modified his position, and gave his decision in favor of the Hayes electors.[3] Other opponents of Bradley recalled that the justice had earlier given an extraordinary and favorable opinion in behalf of the Texas & Pacific Railroad and claimed that he was a creature of Thomas Scott. But, as Professor Woodward notes, "Bradley's accusers never brought forth proof of their charge that the justice yielded to improper pressure in changing his opinion. . . . The charge that the influence of Scott and his friends was decisive in determining Bradley's vote on the Electoral Commission was . . . the sort of charge that it is impossible to disprove and difficult to deny effectively." [4]

On February 9 it was announced that the Commission had refused to "go behind the returns" in the Florida case and had assigned the vote of that state to Hayes. The vote was eight to seven. Having thus taken a position which virtually avoided the controversy in the case of Florida, the Commission had a precedent for the same action in the cases of South Carolina and Louisiana. Its proceedings were concluded on February 23, by which time it had, in each instance by a vote of eight to seven, assigned every one of the disputed electors to Hayes.

Under the law the votes from all the states were opened in the presence of the two houses in joint session, and only those involving disputed returns were submitted to the Commission. Thus, even after the action of the Commission touching the disputed votes had signified the "defeat" of Tilden, the actual legal process of counting the votes in Congress was yet to be completed. In their indignation at the action of the Commission there were Democrats who talked of a filibuster which would obstruct the further proceedings of Congress, prevent the completion of the count, and leave Hayes without legal title. Some of those disposed to filibuster were cantankerous obstructionists; others, however, saw in the situation an opportunity to bargain with the incoming Hayes administration. Thus the whole range of bargaining opportunities, previously explored before the setting up of the Electoral Commission, was again opened up. At once railroad lobbyists for the Texas & Pacific became extraordinarily active; former Southern Whigs again put forth feelers; and Southern congressmen of all persuasions began to seek pledges concerning "home rule." Hayes's friends struck bargains with all three interests. It is impossible to say which of these three approaches was the most effective in winning Southern allies

[3] Nevins, *Hewitt*, 371–372.
[4] Woodward, 161–162.

for the Republicans; all three were both useful and necessary. It is clear, however, that historians have generally overrated the importance of a conference held at the Wormley Hotel in Washington on February 26, which has been credited with sealing a bargain between the Hayes Republicans and the Southern Democrats, by promising "home rule" to the latter in return for an end to the filibuster. The fundamental alignments had been made long before this conference and the basic decisions had already been taken. The Wormley conference, as Professor Woodward shows, "added nothing to the agreements . . ., but merely went over the same ground for the benefit of new participants." [5]

The terms of these several agreements can be briefly summarized, but it must be remembered that they were informal understandings, not written contracts. In return for calling off the filibuster and allowing Hayes to be counted in, the Democrats were promised that the new President would withdraw Federal troops from the South, that he would appoint a leading Southern ex-Whig to his cabinet, and that, without making a specific commitment as to the Texas & Pacific, he would be sympathetic to Southern demands for internal improvements. On these terms the heated dispute came to an end on March 2, and Senator Ferry announced that Hayes, with 185 votes, was duly elected President.

On March 5, 1877 (after a private swearing-in on the 4th, which fell on Sunday) Rutherford B. Hayes was peacefully inaugurated President. Recognizing that Radical reconstruction was a failure, the President proceeded to carry out his part in the agreements made by his friends during the recent contest. Even before he was inaugurated, the Republican régime in Florida had collapsed. On April 10 Federal troops in South Carolina were withdrawn from the state house at Columbia, and on the next day Governor Chamberlain, denouncing the action of the President, gave up his office and left Hampton undisputed governor. The same result was accomplished in Louisiana on April 24. The fact that Hayes's title to the presidency was bound up with these carpetbag governments in the disputed Southern states made it seem like giving away his whole case when these governments were abandoned and allowed to fall, but Hayes preferred conciliation to consistency.

The remaining parts of the bargain of 1877 were carried out with varying degrees of faithfulness. Hayes appointed David M. Key, a leading former Whig of Tennessee, as his postmaster general and tried to build up a native white Republican party in the South by giving appointments to "ex-Confederates and stanch Democrats, along with old-line Whigs and Douglas Democrats." [6] The Democrats failed to carry out their pledge (to which, however, only a small number of the Southerners had been privy)

[5] *Ibid.*, 196.
[6] *Ibid.*, 225.

to allow the Republicans to organize the House and name Garfield speaker; the Republicans failed to provide the internal improvement legislation the South demanded and killed Scott's railroad bill. The alliance was, consequently, weakened, but it was not ended. For many years thereafter the pattern of cooperation between conservative Southern Democrats and conservative Northern Republicans would continue.

The settlement of the disputed election of 1876–1877, therefore, is one of the great compromises of American history, deserving to rank along with the compromises of 1787, 1820, and 1850. It marked the end of force as an element in American political life and a return to the ways of conciliation. Never fully implemented, it failed to protect the rights of the Negro, and it did not produce a genuine native white Republican party in the South. It did, however, settle for many generations the pattern of race relations in the South, and it determined the political alignment of that section for generations. "The settlement," as Professor Woodward says, "was not ideal from any point of view, nor was it very logical either. But that is the way of compromises." [7]

[7] *Ibid.*, 4.

Bibliography

BIBLIOGRAPHICAL NOTE

The sources and literature of the Civil War and Reconstruction are of enormous proportions. The following list is therefore only a selection made with much sifting and with no claim to finality.[1] If the list appears long it must

[1] In the interest of compactness the following abbreviations for periodicals and serials have been employed: A.L.Q. (*Abraham Lincoln Quarterly*); Agr. H. (*Agricultural History*); Ala. H. Q. (*Alabama Historical Quarterly*); Ala. R. (*Alabama Review*); A.H.R. (*American Historical Review*); Ann. Rep. A.H.A. (*Annual Report of the American Historical Association*); Am. Q. (*American Quarterly*); Ark. H. Q. (*Arkansas Historical Quarterly*); Bus. Hist. Rev. (*Business History Review*); Cal. H. S. Q. (*California Historical Society Quarterly*); C.W.H. (*Civil War History*); Cincinnati Hist. Soc. Bull. (*Cincinnati Historical Society Bulletin*); Comp. Stud. in Soc. and Hist. (*Comparative Studies in Society and History*); Del. H. (*Delaware History*); Fla. H. Q. (*Florida Historical Quarterly*); Ga. H. Q. (*Georgia Historical Quarterly*); Ga. R. (*Georgia Review*); Ind. M. H. (*Indiana Magazine of History*); Iowa J. H. (*Iowa Journal of History*); Iowa J. H. & P. (*Iowa Journal of History and Politics*); J.A.H. (*Journal of American History*); J. Ec. H. (*Journal of Economic History*); J.I.S.H.S. (*Journal of the Illinois State Historical Society*); J. Miss. H. (*Journal of Mississippi History*); J.N.H. (*Journal of Negro History*); J. Pol. Econ. (*Journal of Political Economy*); J.S.H. (*Journal of Southern History*); Kans. H. Q. (*Kansas Historical Quarterly*); La. H. (*Louisiana History*); La. H. Q. (*Louisiana Historical Quarterly*); Mass. H. S. P. (*Massachusetts Historical Society Proceedings*); Md. H. M. (*Maryland Historical Magazine*); Mid-Am. (*Mid-America*); Mich. H. (*Michigan History*); Minn. H. (*Minnesota History*); M.V.H.R. (*Mississippi Valley Historical Review*); Mo. H. R. (*Missouri Historical Review*); N.C.H.R. (*North Carolina Historical Review*); N.E.Q. (*New England Quarterly*); N.J.H. (*New Jersey History*); N.Y.H. (*New York History*); N. Y. Hist. Soc. Q. (*New-York Historical Society Quarterly*); Ohio Arch. & H.Q. (*Ohio Archaeological and Historical Quarterly*); Ohio H. (*Ohio History*); Ohio H. Q. (*Ohio Historical Quarterly*); Ore. H. Q. (*Oregon Historical Quarterly*); Pac. H. R. (*Pacific Historical Review*); Pa. H. (*Pennsylvania History*); Penn. M. H. & B. (*Pennsylvania Magazine of History & Biography*); P.S.Q. (*Political Science Quarterly*); R.I.H. (*Rhode Island History*); S.A.Q. (*South Atlantic Quarterly*); S.C.M.H. (*South Carolina Magazine of History*); So. Econ. J. (*Southern Economic Journal*); So. Q. (*Southern Quarterly*); So. Speech Jour. (*Southern Speech Journal*); So. H. S. P. (*Southern Historical Society Papers*); Sw. H. Q. (*Southwestern Historical Quarterly*); Sw. Soc. Sci. Q. (*Southwestern Social Science Quarterly*); Tenn. H. Q. (*Tennessee Historical Quarterly*); Trans. Ill. S.H.S. (*Transactions of the Illinois State Historical Society*); Va. M. H. B. (*Virginia Magazine of History and Biography*); Wash. U. Stud. (*Washington University Studies*); W. Pa. H. M. (*Western Pennsylvania Historical Magazine*); W. Va. H. (*West Virginia History*); Wm. & M. Q. (*William and Mary Quarterly*); and Wisc. M. H. (*Wisconsin Magazine of History*).

be remembered that in its preparation thousands of items have been eliminated and that vast masses of material (archives, manuscripts, government publications, newspapers, et cetera) are omitted because it is impracticable to list them for so comprehensive a work as this. No attempt has been made to include here all the titles cited in the footnotes of the previous pages; readers are requested to use the index as a key to these citations. Nor has any effort been made to note all the editions through which a given work has passed; the publication dates throughout refer to the most convenient or the most useful edition of a book.

There is no one *vade mecum* for books and articles dealing with the Civil War era. Perhaps the nearest approach to a complete listing of books is the *Catalogue of Books Represented by Library of Congress Printed Cards* (167 v., 1942–46), its supplements, and its successor, *The National Union Catalog* (1961–date). The fullest listing of articles is in the series, *Writings on American History* (1904–date), which does not cover, however, the years 1941–47 and which as yet extends only through publications of 1958. Most students will prefer, at least at the beginning of their researches, a more compact bibliographical guide. Roy P. Basler and others have edited *A Guide to the Study of the United States of America* (1960), which is an annotated list of books dealing with all aspects of American thought and life. Because it is more comprehensive, the *Harvard Guide to American History,* edited by Oscar Handlin and others (1954), is more useful; though it now badly needs updating, every serious student of American history will make it his handbook. For students of the Civil War the new guide, *Civil War Books: A Critical Bibliography,* edited by Allan Nevins, James I. Robertson, Jr., and Bell I. Wiley (1967), promises to be invaluable; the first volume covers military aspects of the war, prisons, the Negro, naval operations, and diplomacy.

For unpublished doctoral dissertations on the Civil War-Reconstruction period see Warren F. Keuhl, *Dissertations in History* (1965), which lists such writings through 1960. For dissertations since that date see the periodical *Dissertation Abstracts*.

Manuscript collections for the period are voluminous. The best guides are Philip M. Hamer, ed., *A Guide to Archives and Manuscripts in the United States* (1961), and the *National Union Catalogue of Manuscript Collections* (5 v. to date, 1962–   ). Some large libraries—e.g., the Pennsylvania Historical Society and the Wisconsin State Historical Society—have published valuable annotated guides to their collections. Two comprehensive lists of manuscript collections, made by scholars who worked very widely in the field, can be found in Allan Nevins, *The Emergence of Lincoln,* II, 491–92, and in J. G. Randall, *Lincoln the President,* II, 349–53.

A superb guide to the bulky federal archives for the Civil War and Reconstruction years is Kenneth W. Munden and Henry P. Beers, *Guide to Federal Archives Relating to the Civil War* (1962).

Certain classes of published materials do not lend themselves readily to the enumeration of bibliographical titles. Such, for example, are the voluminous publications of the United States government, among which one should note the *Congressional Globe* (wherein the weighty speeches of solons appear with some self-editing), and the "Congressional Documents," which include the regular serial collections known as *House Miscellaneous Documents, House Executive Documents, House* [Committee] *Reports,* and corresponding issues for the Senate. The indispensable index to this enormous mass of material (an index for which the weary student often wishes a better editing) is Benjamin P. Poore's *Descriptive Catalogue of Government Publications, 1774–1881.* In addition to all this, however, there are many other classes of Federal government publications of high value—e.g., the journals of the House and Senate, hearings of committees, miscellaneous publications of the departments and bureaus, *United States Reports* (decisions of the Supreme Court of the United States), *Federal Cases* (decisions of the circuit and district courts), *United States Statutes at Large,* opinions of the attorneys general and the judge advocates general, et cetera. The serial issues for the years of war and Reconstruction are by no means sufficient; many publications pertaining to the period have appeared in recent years. The best guides to these voluminous sources are Annie M. Boyd, *United States Government Publications* (2nd ed., 1941), and Laurence F. Schmeckebier, *Government Publications and Their Use* (1936). But no list can give the full enumeration. A competent specialist on government documents is, in fact, necessary to advise as to available material.

State publications dealing with the subject matter of this book are of vast extent and great variety. They comprise codes or revised statutes, which commonly include state constitutions; session laws; legislative journals, including governors' messages; state "documents" (reports from executive officers and boards); reports of adjutants general (useful on conscription and military matters generally); handbooks or bluebooks; and court reports, e.g., *Illinois Reports* for the Illinois supreme court. A valuable guide and compilation is Herman V. Ames, *State Documents on Federal Relations, 1789–1861* (1907).

To begin an enumeration of newspapers would involve the embarrassing question of where to stop. Obviously this is an exceedingly important body of sources, albeit one to be used with caution and critical skepticism. J. G. Randall has treated newspapers during the Civil War in 33 *A.H.R.* 303–23. Newspaper opinion on the secession crisis has been conveniently presented in Dwight L. Dumond, ed., *Southern Editorials on Secession* (1931) and in Howard C. Perkins, ed., *Northern Editorials on Secession* (2 v., 1942). Besides reproducing a full and representative selection of editorials, these books offer a working guide to the journals of the period. There are, of course, histories of individual newspapers, the best being J. Cutler Andrews, *Pittsburgh's Post-Gazette* (1936), Harry W. Baehr, Jr., *The New York Tribune since the Civil War* (1936), Meyer Berger, *The Story of the New York Times* (1951), Philip Kinsley, *The Chicago Tribune: Its First Hundred Years* (3 v., 1943–46), and Allan Nevins, *The Evening Post* (1922). For a general account of newspapers during the period, see Frank L. Mott, *American Journalism* (rev. ed., 1950). To locate available files of newspapers, consult Winifred Gregory, ed., *American Newspapers, 1821–1936: A Union List . . .* (1937).

There is no adequate modern general treatment of the entire Civil War and Reconstruction era. James Schouler's *History of the United States of America under the Constitution* (7 v., 1894–1913) does cover the whole era (in vols. 5–7), but it is thinly researched, highly inaccurate, and narrowly political. Far more significant is James Ford Rhodes, *History of the United*

States from the Compromise of 1850 . . . [to 1877] (7 v., 1893–1900), a work of enormous scholarship and of real insight. But Rhodes's pro-Northern bias for the pre-Civil War era and his anti-Negro bias for the Reconstruction period have caused his work to become increasingly attacked and, in the light of recent monographic investigation, it has grown more and more inadequate as an authoritative treatment. For a critique of Rhodes's writings, see Raymond C. Miller, "James Ford Rhodes," in William T. Hutchinson, ed., *The Marcus W. Jernegan Essays in American Historiography* (1958), 171–90.

Fortunately Allan Nevins has underway a major history which will ultimately supersede Rhodes. The six volumes presently published—*Ordeal of the Union* (2 v., 1947); *The Emergence of Lincoln* (2 v., 1950); and *The War for the Union* (2 v., 1959–60)—cover the years 1850–1863. They are characterized by exhaustive research, great thoroughness, and literary excellence.

A number of general histories treat parts of the 1850–77 period. Those dealing solely with the war or with Reconstruction are discussed later. Herman E. Von Holst's *Constitutional and Political History of the United States* (8 v., 1889–92) treats the 1850's at great length, but it is marred by a violent antislavery bias and a profound ignorance of Southern conditions. Though scholarly and impartial on both prewar and Civil War years, Edward Channing's *History of the United States* (Vol. VI. *The War for Southern Independence*, 1925) is episodic, really a series of monographic investigations. Volumes 7 and 8 of John Bach McMaster's *History of the People of the United States* (1883–1913) contain vast amounts of undigested social history, as does his *History of the People of the United States during Lincoln's Administration* (1927), but all three are short on interpretation.

Of the shorter general works on the 1850's the most provocative is Avery Craven, *The Coming of the Civil War* (1942; rev. ed., 1957), a fresh and original work with decided pro-Southern sympathies. For other statements of Craven's interpretation, see his *The Repressible Conflict* (1939), his *Civil War in the Making* (1959), and his *An Historian and the Civil War* (1964). Narrower in scope, and even more pro-Southern, is Arthur Y. Lloyd, *The Slavery Controversy, 1831–1860* (1939). Henry H. Simms, *A Decade of Sectional Controversy, 1851–1861* (1942), is more temperate, but brief. U. B. Phillips, *The Course of the South to Secession*, ed. E. Merton Coulter (1939), a work of profound wisdom, was unfortunately left incomplete at its author's death. Arthur C. Cole, *The Irrepressible Conflict, 1850–1865* (1934), is particularly valuable on social and cultural changes. William Catton and Bruce Catton, *Two Roads to Sumter* (1963), is an attempt to polarize the era around the personalities of Lincoln and Jefferson Davis. Elbert B. Smith, *The Death of Slavery* (1967), is a very brief recent treatment. An excellent administrative history of the period is Leonard D. White's *The Jacksonians* (1954).

For the political history of the entire era two general works are invaluable: Eugene Roseboom, *History of Presidential Elections* (1957), and Edward Stanwood, *A History of the Presidency from 1788 to 1916* (2 v., 1916). Kirk H. Porter and Donald B. Johnson, eds., *National Party Platforms, 1840–1956* (1956), is an authoritative compilation. Richard C. Bain, *Convention Decisions and Voting Records* (1960), is a valuable guide to the nominating conventions. Most historians pay far too little attention to the actual election returns, which can be examined in *The Tribune Almanac for the Years 1838 to 1868, Inclusive* (2 v., 1868), and the supplements thereto, or, more conveniently, in W. Dean Burnham, *Presidential Ballots, 1836–1892* (1955). For excellent election maps, accompanied by informed commentary, see Charles O. Paullin, *Atlas of the Historical Geography of the United States,* ed. John K. Wright (1932).

BIOGRAPHIES AND AUTOBIOGRAPHIES: DIARIES, LETTERS, REMINISCENCES, AND COLLECTED WORKS

Some of the most important information about the Civil War-Reconstruction period is contained in biographies of its principal figures. The diaries and reminiscences of the leaders of the South and the North are equally important. Since in most cases these biographical writings relate to more than one of the subjects discussed in this book, it has seemed best to group them all together, listing them alphabetically by the name of the subject. Though long, this list is highly selective. Ephemera have been weeded out, along with many works that are now out of date. Articles which have been incorporated in later books by the same authors have been excluded.

For a fuller biographical bibliography, see Edward H. O'Neill, *Biography by Americans, 1658–1936* (1939). For an excellent bibliography of materials relating to the literary figures of the period (a category that includes Lincoln, Calhoun, and many other political leaders) see Robert E. Spiller, ed., *Literary History of the United States,* III (1948), and the *Supplement* edited by Richard M. Ludwig (1958). For a comprehensive, standard work of reference on the biographies of all prominent Americans, see *Dictionary of American Biography,* ed. by Allen Johnson and Dumas Malone (20 v. plus supplements, 1928–44).

ADAMS, CHARLES FRANCIS (1807–1886). Adams, Charles Francis, Jr., *Charles Francis Adams* (1909).
——. *Diary of Charles Francis Adams.* Vols. 1–2 ed. by Aïda DiPace Donald and David Donald; Vols. 3–4 ed. by Marc Friedlaender and L. H. Butterfield (1964–68).
——. Duberman, Martin B., *Charles Francis Adams, 1806–1886* (1961).
——. Ferris, Norman B., "An American Diplomatist . . . Confronts Victorian Society, 1861," 15 *History Today,* 550–58 (1965).
——. See also Henry Adams.
ADAMS, CHARLES FRANCIS (1835–1915), *Charles Francis Adams, 1835–1915: An Autobiography* . . . (1916).
——. Kirkland, Edward C., *Charles Francis Adams, Jr., 1835–1915: The Patrician at Bay* (1965).
ADAMS, HENRY, *The Education of Henry Adams: An Autobiography* (1918).
——. Ford, Worthington C., ed., *A Cycle of Adams Letters, 1861–1865* (2 v., 1920).
——. Samuels, Ernest, *Henry Adams: The Major Phase* (1964).
——. Samuels, Ernest, *Henry Adams: The Middle Years* (1958).
——. Samuels, Ernest, *The Young Henry Adams* (1948).

ADAMS, JOHN QUINCY, JR. Mirak, Robert, "John Quincy Adams, Jr., and the Reconstruction Crisis," 35 *N.E.Q.* 187–202 (1962).

AGASSIZ, LOUIS. Agassiz, Elizabeth Cary, *Louis Agassiz, His Life and Correspondence* (2 v., 1885).

——. Lurie, Edward, *Louis Agassiz* (1960).

——. Tharp, Louise H., *Adventurous Alliance: The Story of the Agassiz Family* (1959).

ALCORN, JAMES L. Pereyra, Lillian A., *James Lusk Alcorn: Persistent Whig* (1966).

——. Rainwater, P. L., ed., "Letters of James Lusk Alcorn," 3 *J.S.H.* 196–211 (1937).

——. Ringold, May S., "James Lusk Alcorn," 25 *J. Miss. H.* 1–14 (1963).

ALEXANDER, EDWARD P., *Military Memoirs of a Confederate: A Critical Narrative* (1907). New ed. with introduction by T. Harry Williams, 1962.

ALLEN, HENRY W. Cassidy, Vincent H., and Amos E. Simpson, *Henry Watkins Allen of Louisiana* (1964).

ALLISON, WILLIAM B. Sage, Leland L., *William Boyd Allison: A Study in Practical Politics* (1956).

AMES, ADELBERT. Ames, Blanche, *Adelbert Ames, 1835–1933: General, Senator, Governor* (1964).

——. Ames, Blanche B., ed., *Chronicles from the Nineteenth Century: Family Letters of Blanche Butler and Adelbert Ames* (2 v., 1957).

——. Buice, S. David, "The Military Career of Adelbert Ames," 2 *So. Q.* 236–46 (1964).

ANDERSON, JOSEPH R. Dew, Charles B., *Ironmaker to the Confederacy: Joseph R. Anderson and the Tredegar Iron Works* (1966).

ANDREW, JOHN A. Pearson, Henry G., *The Life of John A. Andrew, Governor of Massachusetts, 1861–1865* (2 v., 1904).

ANTHON·, SUSAN B. Harper, Ida H., *The Life and Work of Susan B. Anthony* (2 v., 1898–1908).

ASHBY, TURNER. Cunningham, Frank, *Knight of the Confederacy: Gen. Turner Ashby* (1960).

ASHLEY, JAMES M. Kahn, Maxine B., "Congressman Ashley in the Post-Civil War Years," 36 *Northwest Ohio Quarterly* 116–33, 194–210 (1964).

ATCHISON, DAVID R. Parrish, William E., *David Rice Atchison of Missouri, Border Politician* (1961).

AVARY, MYRTA L., ed., *A Virginia Girl in the Civil War* (1903).

BADGER, GEORGE E. London, Lawrence F., "George Edmund Badger, His Last Years in the United States Senate, 1851–1855," 15 *N.C.H.R.* 231–50 (1938).

BAKER, EDWARD D. Blair, Harry C., and Rebecca Tarshis, *Lincoln's Constant Ally: The Life of Colonel Edward D. Baker* (1960).

BANCROFT, GEORGE. Howe, M. A. De Wolfe, *The Life and Letters of George Bancroft* (2 v., 1908).

——. Nye, Russel B., *George Bancroft: Brahmin Rebel* (1945).

BANKS, NATHANIEL P. Harrington, Fred H., *Fighting Politician: Major General N. P. Banks* (1948).

——. Malin, James C., "Speaker Banks Courts the Free-Soilers," 12 *N.E.Q.* 103–12 (1939).

——. Williams, T. Harry, "General Banks and the Radical Republicans in the Civil War," 12 *N.E.Q.* 268–80 (1939).

BARKSDALE, ETHELBERT. Peterson, Owen M., "Ethelbert Barksdale in the Democratic National Convention of 1860," 14 *J. Miss. H.* 257–78 (1952).

BARNUM, PHINEAS T. Wallace, Irving, *The Fabulous Showman: the Life and Times of P. T. Barnum* (1959).

——. Werner, M. R., *Barnum* (1926).

BARTON, CLARA. Barton, W. E., *Life of Clara Barton* (2 v., 1922).

——. Ross, Ishbel, *Angel of the Battlefield: the Life of Clara Barton* (1956).

BATES, EDWARD. Beale, Howard K., ed., *The Diary of Edward Bates, 1859–1866* (1933).

——. Cain, Marvin R., *Lincoln's Attorney General: Edward Bates of Missouri* (1965).

——. Frank, John P., "Edward Bates, Lincoln's Attorney General," 10 *Am. J. of Legal Hist.* 34–50 (1966).

——. Klinkhamer, Marie C., "Lincoln's Attorney General," 41 *Univ. of Detroit Law J.* 507–24 (1964).

BAYARD, THOMAS F. Tansill, Charles C., *The Congressional Career of Thomas Francis Bayard, 1869–1885* (1946).

BEATTY, JOHN, *The Citizen-Soldier; Or, Memoirs of a Volunteer* (1879). New ed., 1946.

BEAUREGARD, P. G. T. Basso, Hamilton, *Beauregard: The Great Creole* (1933).

——. Williams, T. Harry, *P. G. T. Beauregard: Napoleon in Gray* (1955).

BEECHER, HENRY WARD. Abbott, Lyman, *Henry Ward Beecher* (1903).

——. Hibben, Paxton, *Henry Ward Beecher: An American Portrait* (1927).

BELKNAP, W. W. Jordan, Philip D., "The Domestic Finances of Secretary of War, W. W. Belknap," 52 *Ia. J. H.* 193–202 (1954).

BELL, JOHN. Caldwell, Joshua W., "John Bell of Tennessee: A Chapter of Political History," 4 *A.H.R.*, 652–64 (1899).

——. Parks, Joseph H., *John Bell of Tennessee* (1950).

BELLOWS, HENRY W. Chadwick, J. W., *Henry W. Bellows . . .* (1882).

BELMONT, AUGUST. Katz, Irving, *August Belmont: A Political Biography* (1968).

BENJAMIN, JUDAH P. Butler, Pierce, *Judah P. Benjamin* (1907).

——. Meade, Robert D., *Judah P. Benjamin: Confederate Statesman* (1943).

——. Osterweis, Rollin G., *Judah P. Benjamin: Statesman of the Lost Cause* (1933).

——. Padgett, James A., ed., "The Letters of Judah Philip Benjamin . . . ," 20 *La. H. Q.* 738–93 (1937).

——. Strode, Hudson, "Judah P. Benjamin's Loyalty to Jefferson Davis," 20 *Ga. R.* 251–60 (1966).

BENNETT, JAMES GORDON. Seitz, Don C., *The James Gordon Bennetts, Father and Son* (1928).

——. Starr, Louis M., "James Gordon Bennett—Beneficent Rascal," 6 *Am. Heritage* 32–37 (Feb., 1955).

BENNETT, JAMES GORDON. Voigt, David Q., " 'Too Pitchy To Touch'—President Lincoln and Editor Bennett," 6 *A.L.Q.* 139–61 (1950).

BENTON, THOMAS H. Chambers, William N., *Old Bullion Benton: Senator from the New West* (1956).

——. McCandless, Perry, "The Political Philosophy and Political Personality of Thomas Hart Benton," 50 *Mo. H. R.* 145–58 (1956).

——. McCandless, Perry, "The Rise of Thomas H. Benton in Missouri Politics," 50 *Mo. H. R.* 16–29 (1955).

——. Meigs, William M., *The Life of Thomas Hart Benton* (1904).

——. Merkel, Benjamin C., "The Slavery Issue and the Political Decline of Thomas Hart Benton, 1846–1856," 38 *Mo. H. R.* 388–407 (1944).

——. Smith, Elbert B., *Magnificent Missourian: The Life of Thomas Hart Benton* (1958).

——. Smith, Elbert B., "Thomas Hart Benton: Southern Realist," 58 *A.H.R.* 795–807 (1953).

BIGELOW, JOHN, *Retrospections of an Active Life* (5 v., 1909–13).

——. Clapp, Margaret, *Forgotten First Citizen: John Bigelow* (1947).

BIRNEY, JAMES G. Birney, William, *James G. Birney and His Times* (1890).

——. Dumond, Dwight L., ed., *Letters of James Gillespie Birney, 1831–1857* (2 v., 1938).

——. Fladelander, Betty, *James Gillespie Birney: Slaveholder to Abolitionist* (1955).

BLACK, JEREMIAH S. Auchampaugh, Philip G., ed., "Black, Thompson, and Stanton in 1864," 10 *Tyler's Quar. Hist. and Geneal. Mag.* 237–50 (1929).

——. Black, Chauncey F., ed., *Essays and Speeches of Jeremiah S. Black* (1885).

——. Brigance, William N., *Jeremiah Sullivan Black: A Defender of the Constitution and the Ten Commandments* (1934).

——. Brigance, William N., "Jeremiah Black and Andrew Johnson," 19 *M.V.H.R.* 205–18 (1932).

BLACKFORD, MARY B. M. Blackford, L. Minor, *Mine Eyes Have Seen the Glory: The Story of a Virginia Lady, Mary Berkeley Minor Blackford, 1802–1896 . . .* (1954).

BLACKFORD, WILLIAM W., *War Years with Jeb Stuart* (1945).

BLAINE, JAMES G., *Twenty Years of Congress: From Lincoln to Garfield* (2 v., 1884–86).

——. Muzzey, David S., *James G. Blaine, a Political Idol of Other Days* (1934).

——. Stanwood, Edward, *James Gillespie Blaine* (1905).

BLAIR, AUSTIN. Fennimore, Jean J. L., "Austin Blair," 48 *Mich. H.* 1–17, 130–66 (1964); 49 *ibid.* 193–227, 344–69 (1965).

BLAIR, FRANCIS P. Smith, William E., *The Francis Preston Blair Family in Politics* (2 v., 1933).

BOOTH, JOHN WILKES. Stern, Philip Van Doren, *The Man Who Killed Lincoln* (1939).

BORCKE, HEROS VON, *Memoirs of the Confederate War for Independence* (2 v., 1938).

BOUTWELL, GEORGE S., *Reminiscences of Sixty Years in Public Affairs* (2 v., 1902).

BOWLES, SAMUEL. Merriam, George S., *Life and Times of Samuel Bowles* (2 v., 1885).

BRADY, MATHEW B. Horan, James D., *Mathew Brady: Historian with a Camera* (1955).

——. Meredith, Roy, *Mr. Lincoln's Camera Man* (1946).

BRAGG, BRAXTON. Boom, Aaron M., ed., " 'We Sowed & We Have Reaped': A Postwar Letter from Braxton Bragg," 31 *J.S.H.* 75–79 (1965).

——. McWhiney, Grady, "Braxton Bragg at Shiloh," 21 *Tenn. H. Q.* 19–30 (1962).

——. Seitz, Don C., *Braxton Bragg, General of the Confederacy* (1924).

BRECKINRIDGE, JOHN C. Heck, Francis H., "John C. Breckinridge in the Crisis of 1860–61," 21 *J.S.H.* 316–46 (1955).

BRISTOW, BENJAMIN H. Webb, Ross A., "A Yankee from Dixie: Benjamin Helm Bristow," 10 *C.W.H.* 80–94 (1964).

——. Webb, Ross A., "Benjamin Helm Bristow (1832–1896): The Man Who Walked in Front of Destiny," 41 *Filson Club Hist. Q.* 105–26 (1967).

BROWN, ALBERT G. Ranck, James B., *Albert Gallatin Brown, Radical Southern Nationalist* (1937).

BROWN, B. GRATZ. Peterson, Norma L., *Freedom and Franchise: The Political Career of B. Gratz Brown* (1965).

BROWN, JOHN. Malin, James C., *John Brown and the Legend of Fifty-Six* (1942).

——. Ostrander, Gilman M., "Emerson, Thoreau, and John Brown," 39 *M.V.H.R.* 713–26 (1953).

——. Ruchames, Louis, ed., *A John Brown Reader* (1959).

——. Stutler, Boyd B., "The Hanging of John Brown," 6 *Am. Heritage* 4–9 (Feb., 1955).

——. Stutler, Boyd B., "John Brown and the Oberlin Lands," 12 *W. Va. H.* 183–99 (1951).

——. Villard, Oswald G., *John Brown, 1800–1859: A Biography Fifty Years After* (1910).

——. Whitridge, Arnold, "The John Brown Legend," 7 *Hist. Today* 211–20 (1957).

——. See also under Smith, Gerrit.

BROWN, JOSEPH E. Hill, Louise B., *Joseph E. Brown and the Confederacy* (1939).

BROWNING, ORVILLE H. Baxter, Maurice, *Orville H. Browning: Lincoln's Friend and Critic* (1957).

——. Pease, Theodore C., and J. G. Randall, eds., *The Diary of Orville Hickman Browning* (*Ill. Hist. Colls.,* XX, XXII, 1927–33).

BROWNLOW, WILLIAM G., *Sketches of the Rise, Progress, and Decline of Secession . . .* (1862). New ed. with introduction by Thomas B. Alexander, 1968.

——. Coulter, E. Merton, *William G. Brownlow: Fighting Parson of the Southern Highlands* (1937).

BRUCE, BLANCHE K. Urofsky, Melvin I., "Blanche K. Bruce, United States Senator, 1875–1881," 29 *J. Miss. H.* 118–41 (1967).

BUCHANAN, JAMES. Auchampaugh, Philip G., *James Buchanan and His Cabinet on the Eve of Secession* (1926).

——, *Mr. Buchanan's Administration on the Eve of the Rebellion* (1866).

——. Carlson, Robert E., "James Buchanan and Public Office," 81 *Penn. M. H. & B.* 255–79 (1957).

——. Curtis, George T., *Life of James Buchanan* (2 v., 1883).

——. Davis, Robert R., Jr., "James Buchanan and the Suppression of the Slave Trade, 1859–1861," 33 *Pa. H.* 446–60 (1966).

——. Klein, Philip S., *President James Buchanan* (1962).

——. Meerse, David E., "Buchanan, Corruption and the Election of 1860," 12 *C.W.H.* 116–31 (1966).

——. Moore, John B., ed., *The Works of James Buchanan* . . . (12 v., 1908–11).

BUCKNER, SIMON B., Stickles, Arndt M., *Simon Bolivar Buckner: Borderland Knight* (1940).

BULLOCH, JAMES D., *The Secret Service of the Confederate States in Europe* (2 v., 1884).

——. Roberts, William P., "James Dunwoody Bulloch and the Confederate Navy," 24 *N.C.H.R.* 315–66 (1947).

BURNSIDE, AMBROSE E. Poore, Ben: P., *The Life* . . . *of Ambrose E. Burnside* (1882).

BUTLER, BENJAMIN F., *Autobiography* . . . *of Benjamin F. Butler* . . . [*Butler's Book*] (1892).

——. Dabney, Thomas E., "The Butler Regime in Louisiana," 27 *La. H. Q.* 487–526 (1944).

——. Everett, Donald E., "Ben Butler and the Louisiana Native Guards, 1861–1862," 24 *J.S.H.* 202–17 (1958).

——. Holzman, Robert S., *Stormy Ben Butler* (1954).

——. Johnson, Howard P., "New Orleans under General Butler," 24 *La. H. Q.* 434–536 (1941).

——. Marshall, Jessie Ames, ed., *Private and Official Correspondence of General Benjamin F. Butler during the Period of the Civil War* (5 v., 1917).

——. Merrill, Louis T., "General Benjamin F. Butler in the Presidential Campaign of 1864," 33 *M.V.H.R.* 537–70 (1947).

——. Merrill, Louis T., "General Benjamin F. Butler in Washington," 39 *Columbia Hist. Soc. Rec.* 71–100 (1938).

——. Parton, James, *General Butler at New Orleans* (1892).

——. Trefousse, Hans L., *Ben Butler: The South Called Him Beast!* (1957).

——. Vernon, Manfred C., "General Benjamin Butler and the Dutch Consul," 5 *C.W.H.* 263–75 (1959).

——. West, Richard S., Jr., *Lincoln's Scapegoat General: A Life of Benjamin F. Butler, 1818–1893* (1965).

CALHOUN, JOHN C. Boucher, Chauncey S., and Robert P. Brooks, "Correspondence Addressed to John C. Calhoun, 1837–1847," *Ann. Rep. A.H.A.* 1929, 125–533, 551–70.

——. Capers, Gerald N., *John C. Calhoun—Opportunist: A Reappraisal* (1960).

——. Coit, Margaret L., *John C. Calhoun: American Portrait* (1950).

——. Crallé, R. K., ed., *Works of J. C. Calhoun* (6 v., 1851–55).

——. Current, Richard N., *John C. Calhoun* (1963).

——. Current, Richard N., "John C. Calhoun, Philosopher of Reaction," 3 *Antioch Rev.* 223–34 (1943).

——. Freehling, William W., "Spoilsmen and Interests in the Thought and Career of John C. Calhoun," 52 *J.A.H.* 25–42 (1965).

——. Hunt, Gaillard, *John C. Calhoun* (1908).

——. Jameson, James F., ed., "The Correspondence of John C. Calhoun," *Ann. Rep. A.H.A.* 1899, II.

——. Meigs, William M., *The Life of John Caldwell Calhoun* (2 v., 1917).

——. Meriwether, Robert L., and W. Edwin Hemphill, eds., *The Papers of John C. Calhoun* (3 v. to date, 1959–   ).

——. Silbey, Joel H., "John C. Calhoun and the Limits of Southern Congressional Unity, 1841–1850," 30 *Historian* 58–71 (1967).

——. Spain, August O., *The Political Theory of John C. Calhoun* (1951).

——. Thomas, John L., ed., *John C. Calhoun: A Profile* (1968).

——. Wiltse, Charles M., *John C. Calhoun* (3 v., 1944–51).

CALL, RICHARD K. Doherty, Herbert J., Jr., *Richard Keith Call: Southern Unionist* (1961).

CAMERON, SIMON. Bradley, Erwin S., *Simon Cameron, Lincoln's Secretary of War: A Political Biography* (1966).

——. Crippen, Lee F., *Simon Cameron: Ante-Bellum Years* (1942).

——. Kelley, Brooks M., "Simon Cameron and the Senatorial Nomination of 1867," 87 *Pa. M. H. & B.* 375–92 (1963).

CAMPBELL, JOHN A. Connor, Henry G., *John Archibald Campbell, Associate Justice of the United States Supreme Court, 1853–1861* (1920).

——. Holt, Thad, Jr., "The Resignation of Mr. Justice Campbell," 12 *Ala. R.* 105–18 (1959).

——. McPherson, James P., "The Career of John Archibald Campbell: A Study of Politics and the Law," 19 *Ala. R.* 53–63 (1966).

CARDOZO, FRANCIS L. Sweat, Edward F., "Francis L. Cardozo—Profile of Integrity in Reconstruction Politics," 46 *J.N.H.* 217–37 (1961).

CARDOZO, JACOB N. Leiman, Melvin M., *Jacob N. Cardozo: Economic Thought in the Antebellum South* (1966).

CAREY, HENRY C. Green, Arnold W., *Henry Charles Carey, Nineteenth-Century Sociologist* (1951).

——. Smith, George W., *Henry C. Carey and American Sectional Conflict* (1951).

CARNEGIE, ANDREW. Hendrick, Burton J., *The Life of Andrew Carnegie* (2 v., 1932).

CARPENTER, MATTHEW H. Thompson, E. Bruce, *Matthew Hale Carpenter, Webster of the West* (1954).

CARROLL, ANNA ELLA. Greenbie, Sydney, and Marjorie Barstow Greenbie, *Anna Ella Carroll and Abraham Lincoln* (1952). An account which exaggerates Miss Carroll's role and her influence. For criticisms, see F. Lauriston Bullard, "Anna Ella Carroll and Her 'Modest' Claim," 50 *Lincoln Herald* 2–10 (1948), and Kenneth P. Williams's review, 54 *Lincoln Herald* 54–56 (1952).

CARROLL, ANNA ELLA. Williams, Kenneth P., "The Tennessee River Campaign and Anna Ella Carroll," 46 *Ind. M. H.* 221–48 (1950).

CASS, LEWIS. McLaughlin, Andrew C., *Lewis Cass* (1899).

——. Stevens, Walter W., "Lewis Cass and the Presidency," 49 *Mich. H.* 123–34 (1965).

——. Woodford, Frank B., *Lewis Cass: The Last Jeffersonian* (1950).

CHAMBERLAIN, JOSHUA L., *The Passing of the Armies* (1915).

——. Wallace, Willard M., *Soul of the Lion: A Biography of General Joshua L. Chamberlain* (1960).

CHANDLER, WILLIAM E. Richardson, Leon B., *William E. Chandler, Republican* (1940).

CHANDLER, ZACHARIAH. Harbison, Winfred A., "Zachariah Chandler's Part in the Re-election of Abraham Lincoln," 22 *M.V.H.R.* 267–76 (1935). (Chandler's role as intermediary between Lincoln and Frémont.)

——. Harris, Wilmer C., *The Public Life of Zachariah Chandler, 1851–1875* (1917).

——. *Zachariah Chandler: An Outline Sketch of His Life and Public Services* (*Detroit Post and Tribune*, 1880).

CHASE, KATE (Mrs. William Sprague). See Sprague.

CHASE, SALMON P. Belden, Thomas Graham, and Marva Robins Belden, *So Fell the Angels* (1956).

——, *Diary and Correspondence of Salmon P. Chase* (1903). *Ann. Rep. A.H.A.*, 1902, II, 11–527.

——. Donald, David, ed., *Inside Lincoln's Cabinet: The Civil War Diaries of Salmon P. Chase* (1954).

——. Futch, Ovid L., "Salmon P. Chase and Civil War Politics in Florida," 32 *Fla. H. Q.* 163–88 (1954).

——. Hart, Albert B., ed., "Letters to Secretary Chase from the South, 1861," 4 *A.H.R.* 331–47 (1899).

——. Hart, Albert B., *Salmon Portland Chase* (1899).

——. Hughes, David F., "Salmon P. Chase, Chief Justice," 18 *Vanderbilt Law Rev.* 569–614 (1965).

——. Luthin, Reinhard H., "Salmon P. Chase's Political Career before the Civil War," 29 *M.V.H.R.* 517–40 (1943).

——. Nunns, Annie A., ed., "Some Letters of Salmon P. Chase, 1848–1865," 34 *A.H.R.* 536–55 (1929).

——. Perdue, M. Kathleen, "Salmon P. Chase and the Impeachment Trial of Andrew Johnson," 27 *Historian* 75–92 (1964).

——. Roseboom, Eugene H., "Salmon P. Chase and the Know Nothings," 25 *M.V.H.R.* 335–50 (1938).

——. Schuckers, J. W., *Life and Public Services of Salmon Portland Chase* (1874).

——. Sefton, James E., ed., "Chief Justice Chase as an Advisor on Presidential Reconstruction," 13 *C.W.H.* 242–64 (1967).

——. Smith, Donnal V., *Chase and Civil War Politics* (1931).

——. Smith, Donnal V., "Salmon P. Chase and the Election of 1860," 39 *Ohio Arch. and H. Q.* 514–607, 769–844 (1930).

——. Smith, Donnal V., "Salmon P. Chase and the Nomination of 1868," in

Avery O. Craven, ed., *Essays in Honor of William E. Dodd* (1935), 291–319.

——. Warden, Robert B., *Private Life and Public Services of Salmon P. Chase* (1874).

——. Wilson, Charles R., "The Original Chase Organization Meeting and *The Next Presidential Election*," 23 *M.V.H.R.* 61–79 (1936).

CHESNUT, MRS. MARY B. Martin, Isabella D., and Myrta L. Avary, *A Diary from Dixie, as Written by Mary Boykin Chesnut* . . . (1906). New ed., by Ben A. Williams, 1949.

CHILD, LYDIA MARIA. Baer, Helene G., *The Heart Is Like Heaven: The Life of Lydia Maria Child* (1964).

CHURCH, WILLIAM C. Bigelow, Donald N., *William Conant Church and the Army and Navy Journal* (1952).

CLAY, CASSIUS M., *Life, Memoirs, Writings, and Speeches* (1886). Title page indicates 2 v., but only one appeared.

——. Smiley, David L., *Lion of White Hall: The Life of Cassius M. Clay* (1962).

CLAY, HENRY. Colton, Calvin, ed., *The Private Correspondence of Henry Clay* (1855).

——. Colton, Calvin, ed., *The Works of Henry Clay* . . . (10 v., 1904).

——. Eaton, Clement, *Henry Clay and the Art of American Politics* (1957).

——. Hopkins, James F., and Mary W. M. Hargreaves, eds., *The Papers of Henry Clay* (3 v. to date, 1959–   ).

——. Poage, George R., *Henry Clay and the Whig Party* (1936).

——. Schurz, Carl, *Life of Henry Clay* (2 v., 1887).

——. Van Deusen, Glyndon G., *The Life of Henry Clay* (1937).

COBB, HOWELL. Brooks, Robert P., ed., "Howell Cobb Papers," *Ga. H. Q.*, V, VI (1921–22).

——. Davis, Ruby S., "Howell Cobb, President of the Provisional Congress of the Confederacy," 46 *Ga. H. Q.* 20–33 (1962).

——. Johnson, Zachary T., *Political Policies of Howell Cobb* (1929).

——. Montgomery, Horace, *Howell Cobb's Confederate Career* (1959).

——. See Toombs, Robert.

COBB, T. R. R., "The Correspondence of Thomas Reade Rootes Cobb, 1860–1862," *So. Hist. Assn. Pub.*, II, 147–328 *passim* (1907). Includes a sketch of Cobb by A. L. Hull (pp. 147–56).

——. Brown, Tom W., "The Military Career of Thomas R. R. Cobb," 45 *Ga. H. Q.* 345–62 (1961).

COLFAX, SCHUYLER. Hollister, O. J., *Life of Schuyler Colfax* (1886).

——. Smith, Willard H., *Schuyler Colfax: The Changing Fortunes of a Political Idol* (1952).

CONKLING, ROSCOE. Chidsey, Donald B., *The Gentleman from New York: A Life of Roscoe Conkling* (1935).

——. Conkling, Alfred R., *The Life and Letters of Roscoe Conkling, Orator, Statesman, Advocate* (1889).

CONNOLLY, JAMES A. Dunn, Frank K., ed., "Major James Austin Connolly," *Trans. Ill. S.H.S.*, 1928, 215–438. New ed., by Paul M. Angle, titled *Three Years in the Army of the Cumberland*, 1959.

CONWAY, MONCURE. Burtis, Mary E., *Moncure Conway, 1832–1907* (1952).
——, *Autobiography, Memories and Experiences of Moncure Daniel Conway* (2 v., 1904).
COOKE, JAY. Larson, Henrietta M., *Jay Cooke, Private Banker* (1936).
——. Oberholtzer, Ellis P., *Jay Cooke, Financier of the Civil War* (2 v., 1907).
COOKE, JOHN ESTEN. Beaty, John O., *John Esten Cooke, Virginian* (1922).
——, *Wearing of the Gray*, with introduction by Philip Van Doren Stern (1959).
——. Harwell, Richard B., "John Esten Cooke, Civil War Correspondent," 19 *J.S.H.* 501–16 (1953).
——. Hubbell, Jay B., ed., "The War Diary of John Esten Cooke," 7 *J.S.H.* 526–39 (1941).
COOPER, PETER. Lyon, Peter, "The Honest Man," 10 *Am. Heritage*, 4–11 ff. (Feb., 1959).
——. Mack, Edward C., *Peter Cooper, Citizen of New York* (1949).
——. See Hewitt, Abram S.
CORCORAN, WILLIAM W. Katz, Irving, "Confidant at the Capital: William W. Corcoran's Role in Nineteenth-Century American Politics," 29 *Historian* 546–64 (1967).
CORNING, ERASTUS. Neu, Irene D., *Erastus Corning: Merchant and Financier, 1794–1872* (1960).
CORWIN, THOMAS. Auer, J. Jeffrey, "Lincoln's Minister to Mexico," 59 *Ohio Arch. & H. Q.* 115–28 (1950).
——. Pendergraft, Daryl, "Thomas Corwin and the Conservative Republican Reaction, 1858–1861," 57 *Ohio Arch. & H. Q.* 1–23 (1948).
COX, JACOB D., *Military Reminiscences of the Civil War* (2 v., 1900).
COX, SAMUEL S., *Three Decades of Federal Legislation, 1855–1885: Personal and Historical Memories of Events . . .* (1885).
——. Lindsey, David, *"Sunset" Cox: Irrepressible Democrat* (1959).
CRITTENDEN, JOHN J. Coleman, Ann M. B., *The Life of John J. Crittenden* (2 v., 1871).
——. Kirwan, Albert D., *John J. Crittenden: The Struggle for the Union* (1962).
CULLOM, SHELBY M., *Fifty Years of Public Service: Personal Recollections* (1911).
——. Neilson, James W., *Shelby M. Cullom: Prairie State Republican* (1962).
CUMMING, KATE. Harwell, Richard B., ed., *Kate: The Journal of a Confederate Nurse* (1960).
CURRY, J. L. M. Alderman, Edwin A., and Armistead Gordon, *J. L. M. Curry: A Biography* (1911).
——. Rice, Jessie P., *J. L. M. Curry: Southerner, Statesman, and Educator* (1949).
CURTIN, ANDREW G. Albright, Rebecca G., "The Civil War Career of Andrew Gregg Curtin, Governor of Pennsylvania," 47 *Western Pa. Hist. Mag.* 323–41 (1964), 48 *ibid.* 19–42, 151–73 (1965).
CURTIS, BENJAMIN R. Benjamin R. Curtis, Jr., *A Memoir of Benjamin Robbins Curtis . . .* (2 v., 1879).
CURTIS, GEORGE W. Cary, Edward, *George William Curtis* (1894).

——. Milne, Gordon, *George William Curtis and the Genteel Tradition* (1956).
CUSHING, CALEB. Fuess, Claude M., *The Life of Caleb Cushing* (2 v., 1923).
——. Hodgson, Sister M. Michael Catherine, *Caleb Cushing: Attorney General of the United States, 1853–1857* (1955).
CUSTER, GEORGE A. Merington, Marguerite, ed., *The Custer Story: The Life and Intimate Letters of General George A. Custer and His Wife Elizabeth* (1950).
——. Monaghan, Jay, *Custer: The Life of General George Armstrong Custer* (1959).
DABNEY, THOMAS S. G. Smedes, Susan D., *Memorials of a Southern Planter* (1887). New ed. with introduction by Fletcher M. Green, 1965.
DAHLGREN, ULRIC. Stuart, Meriwether, "Colonel Ulric Dahlgren and Richmond's Union Underground, April 1864," 72 *Va. M. H. B.* 152–204 (1964).
DALY, MARIA L. Hammond, Harold E., ed., *Diary of a Union Lady, 1861–1865* (1962).
DANA, CHARLES A., *Recollections of the Civil War* . . . (1902).
——. Gertz, Elmer, "Charles A. Dana and *The Chicago Republican*," 45 *J.I.S.H.S.* 124–35 (1952).
DANA, RICHARD H. Adams, Charles F., *Richard Henry Dana: A Biography* (2 v., 1890).
——. Lucid, Robert F., *The Journal of Richard Henry Dana, Jr.* (3 v., 1968).
——. Shapiro, Samuel, *Richard Henry Dana, Jr., 1815–1882* (1961).
DANIEL, PETER V. Frank, John P., *Justice Daniel Dissenting: A Biography of Peter V. Daniel* (1964).
DAVIS, CHARLES H. Davis, Charles H., *Life of Charles Henry Davis, Rear-Admiral, 1807–1877* (1899).
DAVIS, DAVID. King, Willard L., *Lincoln's Manager, David Davis* (1960).
——. Pratt, Harry E., "David Davis, 1815–1886," *Trans. Ill. S.H.S.*, 1930, 157–83.
DAVIS, HENRY W. Steiner, Bernard C., *Life of Henry Winter Davis* (1916).
——. Tyson, Raymond W., "Henry Winter Davis, Orator for the Union," 58 *Md. H. M.* 1–19 (1963).
DAVIS, JEFFERSON. Alfriend, Frank H., *Life of Jefferson Davis* (1868).
——. Barbee, David R., "The Capture of Jefferson Davis," 29 *Tyler's Quar. Hist. and Geneal. Mag.* 6–42 (1947).
——. Craven, John J., *Prison Life of Jefferson Davis* (1905).
——. Cutting, Elisabeth, *Jefferson Davis, Political Soldier* (1930).
——. Davis, Varina Howell, *Jefferson Davis, Ex-President of the Confederate States of America: A Memoir by His Wife* (2 v., 1890).
——. Dimick, Howard T., "The Capture of Jefferson Davis," 9 *J. Miss. H.* 238–54 (1947).
——. Dodd, William E., *Jefferson Davis* (1907).
——. Eckenrode, Hamilton J., *Jefferson Davis, President of the South* (1923).
——. Ezell, John, "Jefferson Davis Seeks Political Vindication, 1851–1857," 26 *J. Miss. H.* 307–21 (1964).
——. McElroy, Robert, *Jefferson Davis: The Unreal and the Real* (2 v., 1937).

DAVIS, JEFFERSON. Pollard, Edward A., *Life of Jefferson Davis, with a Secret History of the Southern Confederacy* . . . (1869).

——. Rowland, Dunbar, ed., *Jefferson Davis, Constitutionalist: His Letters, Papers and Speeches* (10 v., 1923).

——. Shaw, Arthur M., ed., "Some Post-War Observations of Jefferson Davis Concerning Early Aspects of the Civil War," 10 *J.S.H.* 207–11 (1944).

——. Strode, Hudson, *Jefferson Davis* (3 v., 1955–64).

——. Strode, Hudson, ed., *Jefferson Davis: Private Letters, 1823–1889* (1966).

——. Tate, Allen, *Jefferson Davis, His Rise and Fall* (1929).

——. Vandiver, Frank E., "Jefferson Davis and Confederate Strategy," in *The American Tragedy: The Civil War in Retrospect* (1959), 19–32.

——. Walmsley, James E., ed., "Some Unpublished Letters of Burton N. Harrison," 8 *Pub. of Miss. H. S.* 81–85 (1904). These letters relate to the release of Davis from imprisonment.

——. Winston, Robert W., *High Stakes and Hair Trigger: The Life of Jefferson Davis* (1930).

DAVIS, VARINA H. (MRS. JEFFERSON DAVIS). Randall, Ruth P., *I Varina* (1962).

——. Ross, Ishbel, *First Lady of the South: The Life of Mrs. Jefferson Davis* (1958).

——. Rowland, Eron O., *Varina Howell, Wife of Jefferson Davis* (2 v., 1927–31).

DAWSON, SARAH M. Robertson, James I., Jr., ed., *A Confederate Girl's Diary* (1960).

DE BOW, J. D. B. Durden, Robert F., "J. D. B. De Bow: Convolutions of a Slavery Expansionist," 17 *J.S.H.* 441–61 (1951).

——. Skipper, Otis C., *J. D. B. De Bow: Magazinist of the Old South* (1958).

DE FOREST, JOHN W. Croushore, James H., and David M. Potter, eds., *A Union Officer in the Reconstruction* (1948).

——. Croushore, James H., ed., *A Volunteer's Adventures: A Union Captain's Record of the Civil War* (1946).

DE TROBRIAND, REGIS, *Four Years with the Army of the Potomac* (1889).

DEW, THOMAS R. Harrison, Lowell, "Thomas Roderick Dew: Philosopher of the Old South," 57 *Va. M. H. B.* 390–404 (1949).

——. Stampp, Kenneth M., "An Analysis of T. R. Dew's *Review of the Debates in the Virginia Legislature*," 27 *J.N.H.* 380–87 (1942).

DICKINSON, ANNA E. Chester, Giraud, *Embattled Maiden: The Life of Anna Dickinson* (1951).

——. Young, James Harvey, "Anna Elizabeth Dickinson and the Civil War: For and Against Lincoln," 31 *M.V.H.R.* 59–80 (1944).

DIX, DOROTHEA. Marshall, Helen E., *Dorothea Dix: Forgotten Samaritan* (1937).

——. Tiffany, Francis, *Life of Dorothea Lynde Dix* (1891).

DIX, JOHN A. Dix, Morgan, ed., *Memoirs of John Adams Dix* (2 v., 1883).

DODGE, GRENVILLE M. Farnham, Wallace D., "Grenville Dodge and the Union Pacific: A Study of Historical Legends," 51 *J.A.H.* 632–50 (1965).

——. Perkins, Jacob R., *Trails, Rails and War: The Life of General G. M. Dodge* (1929).

——. Hirshson, Stanley P., *Grenville M. Dodge: Soldier, Politician, Railroad Promoter* (1967).

DODGE, WILLIAM E. Lowitt, Richard, *A Merchant Prince of the Nineteenth Century: William E. Dodge* (1954).

DONNELLY, IGNATIUS. Ridge, Martin, *Ignatius Donnelly: The Portrait of a Politician* (1962).

DOOLEY, JOHN. Durkin, Joseph T., ed., *John Dooley, Confederate Soldier: His War Journal* (1945).

DOOLITTLE, JAMES R. Mowry, Duane, ed., "Post-bellum Days: Selections from the Correspondence of . . . James R. Doolittle [1865–1875]," 17 *Mag. of Hist.* 1–10 (1913).

——. Mowry, Duane, "Senator Doolittle and Reconstruction," 14 *Sewanee Rev.* 449–58 (1906).

DOUGLAS, HENRY KYD. Green, Fletcher M., ed., *I Rode with Stonewall: The War Experiences of the Youngest Member of Jackson's Staff* (1940).

DOUGLAS, STEPHEN A. Barbee, David R., and Milledge L. Bonham, Jr., eds., "The Montgomery Address [Nov. 2, 1860] of Stephen A. Douglas," 5 *J.S.H.* 527–52 (1939).

——. Capers, Gerald M., *Stephen A. Douglas: Defender of the Union* (1959).

——. Carpenter, John A., "Douglas and the Election of 1860," 2 *Topic* 5–15 (1961).

——. Hodder, Frank H., "Stephen A. Douglas," ed. James C. Malin, 8 *Kans. H. Q.* 227–37 (1939).

——. Johannsen, Robert W., ed., *The Letters of Stephen A. Douglas* (1961).

——. Johannsen, Robert W., "Stephen A. Douglas, Popular Sovereignty, and the Territories," 22 *Historian* 378–95 (1960).

——. Johnson, Allen, *Stephen A. Douglas: A Study in American Politics* (1908).

——. Milton, George F., *The Eve of Conflict: Stephen A. Douglas and the Needless War* (1934).

——. Nevins, Allan, "He Did Hold Lincoln's Hat," 10 *Am. Heritage,* 98–99 (Feb., 1959).

——. Nevins, Allan, "Stephen A. Douglas: His Weakness and His Greatness," 42 *J.I.S.H.S.* 385–410 (1949).

——. Sheahan, James W., *The Life of Stephen A. Douglas* (1860).

——. Stevens, Frank E., "Life of Stephen A. Douglas," 16 *J.I.S.H.S.* 243–673 (1924).

——. Taft, Robert, "The Appearance and Personality of Douglas," 21 *Kans. H. Q.* 8–33 (1954).

DOUGLASS, FREDERICK. Foner, Philip S., *The Life and Writings of Frederick Douglass* (4 v., 1950–55).

——. Quarles, Benjamin, *Frederick Douglass* (1948).

——. Quarles, Benjamin, ed., *Narrative of the Life of Frederick Douglass, an American Slave, Written by Himself* (1960).

——. Washington, Booker T., *Frederick Douglass* (1907).

DUDLEY, THOMAS H. Dyer, Brainerd, "Thomas H. Dudley," 1 *C.W.H.* 401–13 (1955).

EARLY, JUBAL A., *Autobiographical Sketch and Narrative of the War between the States* (1912). New ed., titled *War Memoirs* . . . , with introduction by Frank E. Vandiver, 1960.

——. Hoyt, William D., Jr., ed., "New Light on General Jubal A. Early after Appomattox," 9 *J.S.H.* 113–17 (1943).

——. Schmitt, Martin F., ed., "An Interview with General Jubal A. Early in 1889," 11 *J.S.H.* 547–63 (1945).

EGGLESTON, GEORGE C., *A Rebel's Recollections* (1874). New ed., with introduction by David Donald, 1959.

——, *Recollections of a Varied Life* (1910).

ELLIS, JOHN W. Tolbert, Noble J., ed., *The Papers of John Willis Ellis* (2 v., 1964).

ELLSWORTH, ELMER. Randall, Ruth Painter, *Colonel Elmer Ellsworth: A Biography of Lincoln's Friend and First Hero of the Civil War* (1960).

EMERSON, RALPH WALDO. Emerson, Edward W., and Waldo E. Forbes, eds., *Journals of Ralph Waldo Emerson* (10 v., 1909–14).

——, *Complete Works* (12 v., 1883–93).

——. Rusk, Ralph L., *The Life of Ralph Waldo Emerson* (1949).

ERICSSON, JOHN. Church, William C., *The Life of John Ericsson* (2 v., 1890).

——. White, Ruth, *Yankee from Sweden: The Dream and the Reality in the Days of John Ericsson* (1960).

EVARTS, WILLIAM M. Barrows, Chester L., *William M. Evarts: Lawyer, Diplomat, Statesman* (1941).

——. Dyer, Brainerd, *The Public Career of William M. Evarts* (1933).

——. Evarts, Sherman, ed., *Arguments and Speeches of William Maxwell Evarts* (3 v., 1919).

EVERETT, EDWARD. Frothingham, Paul R., *Edward Everett, Orator and Statesman* (1925).

EWELL, RICHARD S. Hamlin, Percy G., *"Old Bald Head"* (*General R. S. Ewell*): *The Portrait of a Soldier* (1940).

FAIRCHILD, LUCIUS. Ross, Sam, *The Empty Sleeve: A Biography of Lucius Fairchild* (1964).

FARRAGUT, DAVID. Farragut, Loyall, *The Life of David Glasgow Farragut* . . . (1882). First published, 1879.

——. Lewis, Charles L., *David Glasgow Farragut* (2 v., 1941–43).

——. Mahan, A. T., *Admiral Farragut* (1892).

FAY, EDWIN H. Wiley, Bell I., ed., *"This Infernal War": The Confederate Letters of Sgt. Edwin H. Fay* (1958).

FESSENDEN, WILLIAM P. Fessenden, Francis, *Life and Public Services of William Pitt Fessenden* . . . (2 v., 1907).

——. Jellison, Charles A., *Fessenden of Maine: Civil War Senator* (1962).

FIELD, CYRUS W. Carter, Samuel, *Cyrus Field: Man of Two Worlds* (1968).

——. Judson, Isabella F., *Cyrus W. Field: His Life and Work* (1896).

FIELD, STEPHEN J. Swisher, Carl B., *Stephen J. Field, Craftsman of the Law* (1930).

FILLMORE, MILLARD. Rayback, Robert J., *Millard Fillmore: Biography of a President* (1959).

——. Severance, Frank H., ed., *Millard Fillmore Papers* (Buffalo Hist. Soc. Pubs. X–XI, 1907).

FISH, HAMILTON. Nevins, Allan, *Hamilton Fish: The Inner History of the Grant Administration* (1936).

FISHER, SIDNEY G. Wainwright, Nicholas B., ed., *A Philadelphia Perspective: The Diary of Sidney George Fisher Covering the Years 1834–1871* (1967).

FISK, JIM. Swanberg, W. A., *Jim Fisk: the Career of an Improbable Rascal* (1959).

FITZHUGH, GEORGE. Leavelle, Arnaud B., and Thomas I. Cook, "George Fitzhugh and the Theory of American Conservatism," 7 *Jour. of Politics* 145–68 (1945).

——. Wish, Harvey, *George Fitzhugh: Propagandist of the Old South* (1943).

FLETCHER, WILLIAM A. Wiley, Bell I., ed., *Rebel Private Front and Rear* (1954).

FLOURNOY, JOHN J. Coulter, E. Merton, *John Jacobus Flournoy, Champion of the Common Man in the Ante-Bellum South* (1942).

FOOTE, HENRY S. Carter, John D., "Henry Stuart Foote in California Politics, 1854–1857," 9 *J.S.H.* 224–37 (1943).

——. Gonzales, John E., "Henry Stuart Foote: A Forgotten Unionist of the Fifties," 1 *So. Q.* 129–39 (1963).

——. Gonzales, John E., "Henry Stuart Foote: Confederate Congressman and Exile," 11 *C.W.H.* 384–95 (1965).

——. Gonzales, John E., "Henry Stuart Foote in Exile," 15 *J. Miss. H.* 90–98 (1953).

——. Gonzales, John E., "Reminiscences of a Mississippian," 22 *J. Miss. H.* 101–109 (1960).

FORBES, JOHN M. Hughes, Sarah F., ed., *Letters and Recollections of John Murray Forbes* (2 v., 1899).

——. Pearson, Henry G., *An American Railroad Builder: John Murray Forbes* (1911).

FORNEY, JOHN W., *Anecdotes of Public Men* (1877).

FORREST, NATHAN B. Henry, Robert S., ed., *As They Saw Forrest* (1956).

——. Henry, Robert S., *"First with the Most" Forrest* (1944).

——. Lytle, Andrew N., *Bedford Forrest and His Critter Company* (1931; new ed., 1960).

——. McCain, William D., "Nathan Bedford Forrest: An Evaluation," 24 *J. Miss. H.* 203–25 (1962).

——. Sheppard, Eric W., *Bedford Forrest, the Confederacy's Greatest Cavalryman* (1930).

——. Turner, Arlin, ed., "George W. Cable's Recollections of General Forrest," 21 *J.S.H.* 224–28 (1955).

——. Weller, Jac, "Nathan Bedford Forrest: An Analysis of Untutored Military Genius," 18 *Tenn. H. Q.* 213–51 (1959).

——. Wyeth, John A., *Life of General Nathan Bedford Forrest* (1899). New ed., titled *That Devil Forrest*, 1959.

FOX, GUSTAVUS V. Hoogenboom, Ari, "Gustavus Fox and the Relief of Fort Sumter," 9 *C.W.H.* 383–98 (1963).

——. Thompson, R. M., and R. Wainwright, eds., *Confidential Correspondence of Gustavus Vasa Fox, Assistant Secretary of the Navy, 1861–1865* (2 v., 1918–19).

FREMANTLE, ARTHUR J. L., *Three Months in the Southern States: April–June, 1863* (1864). New ed., by Walter Lord, titled *The Fremantle Diary . . .* , 1954.

FRÉMONT, JOHN C., *Memoirs of My Life* (1887). Title page indicates 2 v., but only one appeared.

——. Bartlett, Ruhl J., *John C. Frémont and the Republican Party* (1930).

——. Harrington, Fred H., "Frémont and the North Americans," 44 *A.H.R.* 842–48 (1939).

——. Nevins, Allan, *Frémont: Pathmaker of the West* (1955). A revision of *Frémont, the West's Greatest Adventurer . . .* (2 v., 1928).

GALES, JOSEPH. Eaton, Clement, "Winifred and Joseph Gales: Liberals in the Old South," 10 *J.S.H.* 461–74 (1944).

GAMBLE, HAMILTON R. Potter, Marguerite, "Hamilton R. Gamble, Missouri's War Governor," 35 *Mo. H. R.* 25–71 (1940).

GARFIELD, JAMES A. Brown, Harry J., and Frederick D. Williams, eds., *The Diary of James A. Garfield* (2 v., 1967).

——. Caldwell, Robert G., *James A. Garfield, Party Chieftain* (1931).

——. Smith, Theodore C., *The Life and Letters of James Abram Garfield* (2 v., 1925).

——. Williams, Frederick D., ed., *The Wild Life of the Army: Civil War Letters of James A. Garfield* (1964).

GARRISON, WILLIAM L. Garrison, F. J., and W. P. Garrison, *William Lloyd Garrison, 1805–1879: The Story of His Life* (4 v., 1885).

——. Korngold, Ralph, *Two Friends of Man: The Story of William Lloyd Garrison and Wendell Phillips* (1950).

——. Merrill, Walter M., *Against Wind and Tide: A Biography of William Lloyd Garrison* (1963).

——. Nelson, Truman, ed., *Documents of Upheaval: Selections from William Lloyd Garrison's The Liberator, 1831–1865* (1966).

——. Nye, Russel B., *William Lloyd Garrison and the Humanitarian Reformers* (1955).

——. Thomas, John L., *The Liberator: William Lloyd Garrison, a Biography* (1963).

——. Wentworth, Jean, " 'Not Without Honor'; William Lloyd Garrison," 62 *Md. H. M.* 318–36 (1967).

——. Williams, David A., "William Lloyd Garrison, the Historians, and the Abolitionist Movement," 98 *Essex Institute Historical Collections* 84–99 (1962).

——. Wyatt-Brown, Bertram, "William Lloyd Garrison and Antislavery Unity: A Reappraisal," 13 *C.W.H.* 5–24 (1967).

GEARY, JOHN W. Tinkcom, Harry M., *John White Geary, Soldier-Statesman, 1819–1873* (1940).

GIBBON, JOHN, *Personal Recollections of the Civil War* (1928).

GIDDINGS, JOSHUA R., *Speeches in Congress* (1853).

——. Julian, George W., *The Life of Joshua R. Giddings* (1892).

——. Long, Byron R., "Joshua Reed Giddings, a Champion of Political Freedom," 28 *Ohio Arch. & H. Q.* 1–47 (1919).

——. Ludlum, Robert P., "Joshua Giddings, Radical," 23 *M.V.H.R.* 49–60 (1936).

GILMORE, JAMES R., *Personal Recollections of Abraham Lincoln and the Civil War* (1898).

GODKIN, EDWIN L. Armstrong, William M., *E. L. Godkin and American Foreign Policy, 1865–1900* (1957).

——. Ogden, Rollo, *Life and Letters of Edwin Lawrence Godkin* (2 v., 1907).

GORDON, GEORGE H., *Brook Farm to Cedar Mountain in the War of the Great Rebellion, 1861–1862* (1883).

GORDON, JOHN B., *Reminiscences of the Civil War* (1903).

——. Tankersley, Allen P., *John B. Gordon: A Study in Gallantry* (1955).

GORDON, WILLIAM F. Gordon, Armistead C., *William Fitzhugh Gordon, a Virginian of the Old School . . .* (1909).

GORGAS, JOSIAH. Vandiver, Frank E., ed., *The Civil War Diary of General Josiah Gorgas* (1947).

——. Vandiver, Frank E., *Ploughshares into Swords: Josiah Gorgas and Confederate Ordnance* (1952).

GOULD, JAY. Grodinsky, Julius, *Jay Gould: His Business Career, 1867–1892* (1957).

GRAHAM, WILLIAM A. Hamilton, J. G. de R., ed., *The Papers of William Alexander Graham* (4 v., 1957–61).

GRANT, JULIA. Ross, Ishbel, *The General's Wife: The Life of Mrs. Ulysses S. Grant* (1959).

GRANT, ULYSSES S. Badeau, Adam, *Grant in Peace. From Appomattox to Mount McGregor . . .* (1887).

——. Badeau, Adam, *Military History of Ulysses S. Grant, from April, 1861, to April, 1865* (3 v., 1868–81).

——. Catton, Bruce, *Grant Moves South* (1960). A continuation of Lloyd Lewis's *Captain Sam Grant.*

——. Catton, Bruce, *U. S. Grant and the American Military Tradition* (1954).

——. Conger, A. L., *The Rise of U. S. Grant* (1931).

——. Coolidge, Louis A., *Ulysses S. Grant* (1917).

——. Cramer, Jesse G., ed., *Letters of U. S. Grant to His Father and His Youngest Sister, 1857–78* (1912).

——. Eaton, John, and Ethel O. Mason, *Grant, Lincoln and the Freedmen* (1907).

——. Fuller, John F. C., *The Generalship of Ulysses S. Grant* (1929). New ed., 1958.

——. *Personal Memoirs of U. S. Grant* (2 v., 1885–86). New ed., with introduction by E. B. Long, 1952.

——. Hesseltine, William B., *Ulysses S. Grant, Politician* (1935).

——. Lewis, Lloyd, *Captain Sam Grant* (1950).

——. Macartney, Clarence E., *Grant and His Generals* (1953).

GRANT, ULYSSES. Mallam, William D., "The Grant-Butler Relationship," 41 *M.V.H.R.* 259–76 (1954).

——. Meredith, Roy, ed., *Mr. Lincoln's General: U. S. Grant. An illustrated Autobiography* (1959).

——. Simon, John Y., ed., *The Papers of Ulysses S. Grant* (1 v. to date, 1967–   ).

——. Thomas, Benjamin P., ed., *Three Years with Grant, as Recalled by War Correspondent Sylvanus Cadwallader* (1955). For critical comment, see Ulysses S. Grant, III, "Civil War: Fact & Fiction," 2 *C.W.H.* 29–40 (1956).

——. Todd, Helen, *A Man Named Grant* (1940).

——. Wilson, James G., *General Grant* (1897).

——. Woodward, W. E., *Meet General Grant* (1928).

GRAY, JOHN CHIPMAN. Ford, Worthington C., ed., *War Letters, 1862–1865, of John Chipman Gray and John Codman Ropes* (1927).

GREELEY, HORACE. Bonner, Thomas N., "Horace Greeley and the Secession Movement," 38 *M.V.H.R.* 425–44 (1952).

——. Commons, John R., "Horace Greeley and the Working Class Origins of the Republican Party," 24 *P.S.Q.* 468–88 (1909).

——. Fahrney, Ralph R., *Horace Greeley and the Tribune in the Civil War* (1936).

——, *Recollections of a Busy Life* (1868).

——. Hale, William H., *Horace Greeley, Voice of the People* (1950).

——. Horner, Harlan H., *Lincoln and Greeley* (1953).

——. Isely, Jeter A., *Horace Greeley and the Republican Party* (1947).

——. Kirkwood, Robert, "Horace Greeley and Reconstruction, 1865," 40 *N.Y.H.* 270–80 (1959).

——. Ross, Earle D., "Horace Greeley and the South, 1865–1872," 16 *S.A.Q.* 324–38 (1917).

——. Seitz, Don C., *Horace Greeley, Founder of the New York Tribune* (1926).

——. Stoddard, Henry L., *Horace Greeley: Printer, Editor, Crusader* (1946).

——. Van Deusen, Glyndon G., *Horace Greeley: Nineteenth-Century Crusader* (1953).

GREEN, DUFF. Green, Fletcher M., "Duff Green, Militant Journalist of the Old School," 52 *A.H.R.* 247–64 (1947).

GREGG, WILLIAM. Mitchell, Broadus, *William Gregg, Factory Master of the Old South* (1928).

GRIMES, ABSALOM. Quaife, M. M., ed., *Absalom Grimes, Confederate Mail Runner* (1926).

GRIMES, JAMES W. Boeck, George A., "Senator Grimes and the Iowa Press, 1867–1868," 48 *Mid-Am.* 147–61 (1966).

——. Salter, William, *The Life of James W. Grimes* (1876).

GRIMKÉ, ANGELINA AND SARAH. Lerner, Gerda, *The Grimké Sisters from South Carolina: Rebels Against Slavery* (1967).

——. See T. D. Weld.

GROW, GALUSHA. DuBois, James T., and Gertrude S. Mathews, *Galusha A. Grow, Father of the Homestead Law* (1917).

GUROWSKI, ADAM. Fischer, LeRoy H., *Lincoln's Gadfly: Adam Gurowski* (1964).

——. *Diary* . . . (3 v., 1862–66).

HALE, JOHN P. Sewell, Richard H., *John P. Hale and the Politics of Abolition* (1965).

HALL, A. OAKEY. Bowen, Croswell, *The Elegant Oakey* (1956).

HALLECK, HENRY W. Ambrose, Stephen E., *Halleck: Lincoln's Chief of Staff* (1962).

——. Shutes, Milton H., "Henry Wager Halleck, Lincoln's Chief of Staff," 16 *Cal. H. S. Q.* 195–208 (1937).

HAMLIN, HANNIBAL. Hamlin, Charles E., *The Life and Times of Hannibal Hamlin* (1899).

HAMPTON, WADE. Jarrell, Hampton M., *Wade Hampton and the Negro: The Road Not Taken* (1949).

——. Wellman, Manly Wade, *Giant in Gray: A Biography of Wade Hampton of South Carolina* (1949).

HANCOCK, WINFIELD S. Tucker, Glenn, *Hancock the Superb* (1960).

HARDEE, WILLIAM J. Hughes, Nathaniel C., Jr., *General William J. Hardee: Old Reliable* (1965).

HARLAN, JAMES. Brigham, Johnson, *James Harlan* (1913).

HARRISON, BENJAMIN. Sievers, Harry J., *Benjamin Harrison* (3 v., 1966).

HASKELL, FRANK A., *The Battle of Gettysburg*, ed. by Bruce Catton (1958).

HAUPT, HERMAN, *Reminiscences* . . . (1901).

HAY, JOHN. Dennett, Tyler, *John Hay: From Poetry to Politics* (1933).

——. Dennett, Tyler, ed., *Lincoln and the Civil War in the Diaries and Letters of John Hay* (1939).

——, *Letters of John Hay and Extracts from Diary,* selected by Henry Adams and edited by Mrs. Hay (3 v., 1908).

——. Thayer, William R., *The Life and Letters of John Hay* (2 v., 1915).

HAYES, RUTHERFORD B. Barnard, Harry, *Rutherford B. Hayes and His America* (1954).

——. Eckenrode, H. J., *Rutherford B. Hayes, Statesman of Reunion* (1930).

——. Garrison, Curtis W., ed., "Conversations with Rutherford B. Hayes," 25 *M.V.H.R.* 369–80 (1938).

——. Williams, C. R., ed., *Diary and Letters of Rutherford Birchard Hayes* . . . (5 v., 1922–26).

——. Williams, C. R., *The Life of Rutherford Birchard Hayes* . . . (2 v., 1914).

——. Williams, T. Harry, *Hayes of the Twenty-Third: The Civil War Volunteer Officer* (1965).

——. Williams, T. Harry, ed., *Hayes: The Diary of a President, 1875–1881* (1964).

HEARTSILL, W. W. Wiley, Bell I., ed., *Fourteen Hundred and 91 Days in the Confederate Army: A Journal Kept by W. W. Heartsill* . . . (1954).

HELPER, HINTON R. Bailey, Hugh C., *Hinton Rowan Helper: Abolitionist-Racist* (1965).

——, *The Impending Crisis of the South: How to Meet It* (1857). New ed. by George Fredrickson, 1968.

HENRY, JOSEPH. Coulson, Thomas, *Joseph Henry: His Life and Work* (1950).

HERNDON, WILLIAM H. Donald, David, *Lincoln's Herndon* (1948).

HEWITT, ABRAM S. Nevins, Allan, *Abram S. Hewitt: With Some Account of Peter Cooper* (1935).

——. Nevins, Allan, ed., *Selected Writings of Abram S. Hewitt* (1937).

HICKS, THOMAS H. Radcliffe, George L. P., *Governor Thomas H. Hicks of Maryland and the Civil War* (1901).

HIGGINSON, THOMAS W. Higginson, Mary T., ed., *Letters and Journals of Thomas Wentworth Higginson, 1846–1906* (1921).

——, *Army Life in a Black Regiment* (1870).

——, *Cheerful Yesterdays* (1898).

——, *Part of a Man's Life* (1905).

——. Edelstein, Tilden G., *Strange Enthusiasm: A Life of Thomas Wentworth Higginson* (1968).

——. Wells, Anna M., *Dear Preceptor: The Life and Times of Thomas Wentworth Higginson* (1963).

HILL, A. P. Wheeler-Bennett, John, "A. P. Hill: A Study in Confederate Leadership," 37 *Va. Q. R.* 198–209 (1961).

HILL, BENJAMIN H. Pearce, Haywood J., Jr., *Benjamin H. Hill, Secession and Reconstruction* (1928).

HILL, DANIEL H. Bridges, Hal, *Lee's Maverick General: Daniel Harvey Hill* (1961).

HITCHCOCK, ETHAN A. Croffut, W. A., ed., *Fifty Years in Camp and Field: Diary of Major-General Ethan Allen Hitchcock, U.S.A.* (1909).

HITCHCOCK, HENRY. Howe, M. A. De Wolfe, ed., *Marching with Sherman: Passages from the Letters and Campaign Diaries of Henry Hitchcock . . .* (1927).

HOAR, EBENEZER R. Storey, Moorfield, and Edward W. Emerson, *Ebenezer Rockwood Hoar: A Memoir* (1911).

HOAR, GEORGE F. Gillett, Frederick H., *George Frisbie Hoar* (1934).

——, *Autobiography of Seventy Years* (2 v., 1903).

HOLDEN, W. W. Boyd, William K., ed., *Memoirs of W. W. Holden* (1911).

——. Folk, Edgar E., "W. W. Holden and the Election of 1858," 21 *N.C.H.R.* 294–318 (1944).

——. Raper, Horace W., "William W. Holden and the Peace Movement in North Carolina," 31 *N.C.H.R.* 493–516 (1954).

HOLMES, GEORGE F. Gillespie, Neal C., "The Spiritual Odyssey of George Frederick Holmes: A Study of Religious Conservatism in the Old South," 32 *J.S.H.* 291–307 (1966).

——. Wish, Harvey, "George Frederick Holmes and the Genesis of American Sociology," 46 *Am. Jour. of Sociology,* 698–707 (1941).

——. Wish, Harvey, "George Frederick Holmes and Southern Periodical Literature . . . ," 7 *J.S.H.* 343–56 (1941).

HOLMES, OLIVER W., JR., Howe, Mark De Wolfe, *Justice Oliver Wendell Holmes: The Shaping Years, 1841–1870* (1957).

——. Howe, Mark De Wolfe, ed., *Touched with Fire: Civil War Letters and Diary of Oliver Wendell Holmes, Jr., 1861–1864* (1946).

HOLT, JOSEPH. Bartman, Roger J., "Joseph Holt and Kentucky in the Civil War," 40 *Filson Club Hist. Q.* 105–22 (1966).

HONE, PHILIP. Nevins, Allan, ed., *The Diary of Philip Hone, 1828–1851* (2 v., 1927).

——. Tuckerman, Bayard, ed., *The Diary of Philip Hone, 1828–1851* (2 v., 1889).

HOOD, JOHN B. Dyer, John P., *The Gallant Hood* (1950).

——, *Advance and Retreat* (1880). New ed., with intro. by Richard N. Current, 1959.

——. O'Connor, Richard, *Hood: Cavalier General* (1949).

——. Vandiver, Frank E., "General Hood as Logistician," 16 *Military Affairs* 1–11 (1952).

HOOKER, JOSEPH. Hebert, Walter H., *Fighting Joe Hooker* (1944).

——. Shutes, Milton H., " 'Fighting Joe' Hooker," 16 *Cal. H. S. Q.* 304–20 (1937).

HOTZE, HENRY. Oates, Stephen B., "Henry Hotze: Confederate Agent Abroad," 27 *Historian* 131–54 (1965).

HOUSTON, SAMUEL. Day, Donald, and H. H. Ullom, eds., *The Autobiography of Sam Houston* (1954).

——. James, Marquis, *The Raven: A Biography of Sam Houston* (1929).

——. Maher, Edward R., Jr., "Sam Houston and Secession," 55 *Sw. H. Q.* 448–58 (1952).

——. Williams, Amelia W., and Eugene C. Barker, eds., *The Writings of Sam Houston* (8 v., 1938–43).

——. Wisehart, M. K., *Sam Houston, American Giant* (1962).

HOWARD, OLIVER O. Carpenter, John A., *Sword and Olive Branch: Oliver Otis Howard* (1964).

——, *Autobiography of Oliver Otis Howard* (2 v., 1903).

——. McFeely, William S., *Yankee Stepfather: General O. O. Howard and the Freedmen* (1968).

HOWE, JULIA W. Richards, Laura E., and Maud H. Elliott, *Julia Ward Howe* (2 v., 1916).

HOWE, SAMUEL G. Richards, Laura E., ed., *Letters and Journals of Samuel Gridley Howe* (2 v., 1906–09).

——. Schwartz, Harold, *Samuel Gridley Howe, Social Reformer, 1801–1876* (1956).

HOWE, TIMOTHY O. Russell, William H., "Timothy O. Howe, Stalwart Republican," 35 *Wisc. M. H.* 90–100 (1951).

HUNTER, R. M. T. Ambler, Charles H., ed., *Correspondence of Robert M. T. Hunter, 1826–1876* (1916).

——. Simms, Henry H., *Life of Robert M. T. Hunter: A Study in Sectionalism and Secession* (1935).

HYDE, THOMAS W., *Following the Greek Cross, or Memories of the Sixth Army Corps* (1894).

ISHERWOOD, BENJAMIN F. Sloan, Edward W., III, *Benjamin Franklin Isherwood, Naval Engineer: The Years as Engineer in Chief, 1861–1869* (1965).

JACKSON, THOMAS J. Chambers, Lenoir, *Stonewall Jackson* (2 v., 1959).

——. Davis, Burke, *They Called Him Stonewall* (1954).

——. Henderson, G. F. R., *Stonewall Jackson and the American Civil War* (2 v., 1919). New ed., 1936.

JACKSON, THOMAS J. Vandiver, Frank E., *Mighty Stonewall* (1957).

JENCKES, THOMAS A. Hoogenboom, Ari, "Thomas A. Jenckes and Civil Service Reform," 47 *M.V.H.R.* 636–58 (1961).

JOHNSON, ANDREW. Albjerg, Marguerite H., "The New York Press and Andrew Johnson," 26 *S.A.Q.* 404–16 (1927).

——. Barber, James D., "Adult Identity and Presidential Style: The Rhetorical Emphasis," 97 *Daedalus* 938–68 (1968).

——. Castel, Albert, "Andrew Johnson: His Historiographical Rise and Fall," 45 *Mid-Am.* 175–84 (1963).

——. Cox, John, and LaWanda Cox, "Andrew Johnson and His Ghost Writers," 48 *M.V.H.R.* 460–79 (1961).

——. DeWitt, David M., *Impeachment and Trial of Andrew Johnson* (1903). New ed. with introduction by Stanley I. Kutler, 1967.

——. Dunning, William A., "More Light on Andrew Johnson," 11 *A.H.R.* 574–94 (1906).

——. Graf, LeRoy P., "Andrew Johnson and the Coming of the War," 19 *Tenn. H. Q.* 208–21 (1960).

——. Graf, LeRoy P., and Ralph W. Haskins, eds., *The Papers of Andrew Johnson* (1 v. to date, 1967–   ).

——. Hall, Clifton R., *Andrew Johnson, Military Governor of Tennessee* (1916).

——. Haskins, Ralph W., "Andrew Johnson and the Preservation of the Union," *East Tenn. Hist. Soc. Pub.,* No. 33, 43–60 (1961).

——. Haskins, Ralph W., "Internecine Strife in Tennessee: Andrew Johnson versus Parson Brownlow," 24 *Tenn. H. Q.* 321–40 (1965).

——. Lomask, Milton, *Andrew Johnson: President on Trial* (1960).

——. McKitrick, Eric L., *Andrew Johnson and Reconstruction* (1960).

——. Milton, George F., *The Age of Hate: Andrew Johnson and the Radicals* (1930).

——. Moore, Frank, ed., *Speeches of Andrew Johnson . . .* (1865).

——. Nettels, Curtis, "Andrew Johnson and the South," 25 *S.A.Q.* 55–64 (1926).

——. Notaro, Carmen A., "History of the Biographic Treatment of Andrew Johnson in the Twentieth Century," 24 *Tenn. H. Q.* 143–55 (1965).

——. Robinson, Dan M., "Andrew Johnson on the Dignity of Labor," 23 *Tenn. H. Q.* 80–85 (1964).

——. Russell, Robert G., "Prelude to the Presidency: The Election of Andrew Johnson to the Senate," 26 *Tenn. H. Q.* 148–76 (1967).

——. Sioussat, St. George L., ed., "Notes of Colonel W. G. Moore, Private Secretary to President Johnson, 1866–1868," 19 *A.H.R.* 98–132 (1913).

——. Stampp, Kenneth M., *Andrew Johnson and the Failure of the Agrarian Dream* (1962).

——. Stryker, Lloyd P., *Andrew Johnson: A Study in Courage* (1929).

——. Thomas, Lately, *The First President Johnson* (1968).

——. Williams, Harry, "Andrew Johnson as a Member of the Committee on the Conduct of the War," *East Tenn. Hist. Soc. Pubs.* No. 12, 70–83 (1940).

——. Winston, Robert W., *Andrew Johnson, Plebeian and Patriot* (1928).

JOHNSON, HERSCHEL V. Flippin, Percy S., contributor, "From the Auto-biography of Herschel V. Johnson, 1856–1867," 30 *A.H.R.* 311–36 (1925).

——. Flippin, Percy S., *Herschel V. Johnson of Georgia, State Rights Unionist* (1931).

JOHNSON, REVERDY. Cook, Adrian, "Failure of a Mission: Reverdy Johnson in London, 1868–69," 61 *Md. H. M.* 120–45 (1966).

——. Steiner, Bernard C., *Life of Reverdy Johnson* (1914).

JOHNSTON, ALBERT S. Johnston, William P., *The Life of Gen. Albert Sidney Johnston* (1878).

——. Roland, Charles P., *Albert Sidney Johnston: Soldier of Three Republics* (1964).

JOHNSTON, JOSEPH E. Govan, Gilbert E., and James W. Livingood, *A Different Valor: The Story of General Joseph E. Johnston, C.S.A.* (1956).

——. James, Alfred P., "General Joseph Eggleston Johnston, Storm Center of the Confederate Army," 14 *M.V.H.R.* 342–59 (1927).

——, *Narrative of Military Operations . . . during the Late War between the States* (1874). New ed., with introduction by Frank E. Vandiver, 1959.

——. Sanger, Donald B., "Some Problems Facing Joseph E. Johnston in the Spring of 1863," in Avery O. Craven, ed., *Essays in Honor of William E. Dodd* (1935), 257–90.

JONES, JOHN BEAUCHAMP, *A Rebel War Clerk's Diary at the Confederate States Capital* (2 v., 1866). New ed., with introduction by Howard Swiggett, 1935.

JULIAN, GEORGE W. Clarke, Grace J., *George W. Julian* (1923).

——, *Political Recollections, 1840 to 1872* (1884).

——. Riddleberger, Patrick W., *George Washington Julian, Radical Republican: A Study in Nineteenth Century Politics and Reform* (1966).

KASSON, JOHN A. Younger, Edward, *John A. Kasson: Politics and Diplomacy from Lincoln to McKinley* (1955).

KEAN, ROBERT G. H. Younger, Edward, ed., *Inside the Confederate Government: The Diary of Robert Garlick Hill Kean* (1957).

KEARNY, PHILIP. Kearny, Thomas, *General Philip Kearny, Battle Soldier of Five Wars* (1937).

KELLEY, WILLIAM D. Brown, Ira V., "William D. Kelley and Radical Reconstruction," 85 *Pa. M. H. & B.* 316–29 (1961).

KELLOGG, WILLIAM P. Gonzales, John E., "William Pitt Kellogg, Reconstruction Governor of Louisiana, 1873–1877," 29 *La. H. Q.* 394–495 (1946).

KEMBLE, FRANCES A., *Journal of a Residence on a Georgia Plantation in 1838–39*, ed. John A. Scott (1961).

KENNEDY, JOHN P. Bohner, Charles H., *John Pendleton Kennedy: Gentleman from Baltimore* (1961).

——. Burton, Roland C., ed., "John Pendleton Kennedy and the Civil War: An Uncollected Letter," 29 *J.S.H.* 373–76 (1963).

——. Walhout, Clarence P., "John Pendleton Kennedy: Late Disciple of the Enlightenment," 32 *J.S.H.* 358–67 (1966).

KEY, DAVID M. Abshire, David M., *The South Rejects a Prophet: The Life of Senator D. M. Key, 1824–1900* (1967).

KING, WILLIAM R. Martin, John M., "William R. King and the Vice Presidency," 16 *Ala. R.* 35–54 (1963).

——. Martin, John M., "William R. King: Jacksonian Senator," 17 *Ala. R.* 243–68 (1965).

KIRBY SMITH, EDMUND. Parks, Joseph H., *General Edmund Kirby Smith* (1954).

KIRKWOOD, SAMUEL J. Clark, Dan E., *Samuel Jordan Kirkwood* (1917).

KOERNER, GUSTAVE. McCormack, Thomas J., ed., *Memoirs of Gustave Koerner, 1809–1896* . . . (2 v., 1909).

LAMAR, GAZAWAY B. Coddington, Edwin B., "The Activities and Interests of a Confederate Businessman: Gazaway B. Lamar," 9 *J.S.H.* 3–36 (1943).

——. Hay, Thomas R., "Gazaway Bugg Lamar, Confederate Banker and Business Man," 37 *Ga. H. Q.* 89–128 (1953).

LAMAR, L. Q. C. Cate, Wirt A., *Lucius Q. C. Lamar* (1935).

——. Dickey, Dallas C., "Lamar's Eulogy on Sumner: A Letter of Explanation," 20 *So. Speech Jour.* 316–22 (1955).

——. Mayes, Edward, *Lucius Q. C. Lamar: His Life, Times and Speeches, 1825–1893* (1896).

——. Mayne, John A., "L. Q. C. Lamar's 'Eulogy' of Charles Sumner: A Reinterpretation," 22 *Historian* 296–311 (1960).

——. Russell, Mattie, ed., "Why Lamar Eulogized Sumner," 21 *J.S.H.* 374–78 (1955).

——. Shanahan, Frank E., Jr., "L. Q. C. Lamar: An Evaluation," 26 *J. Miss. H.* 91–122 (1964).

LANE, JOSEPH. Hendrickson, James E., *Joe Lane of Oregon: Machine Politics and the Sectional Crisis, 1849–1861* (1967).

LEA, HENRY C. O'Brien, John M., "Henry Charles Lea: The Historian as Reformer," 19 *Am. Q.* 104–13 (1967).

LEAVITT, JOSHUA. McPherson, James M., "The Fight Against the Gag Rule: Joshua Leavitt and Antislavery Insurgency in the Whig Party, 1839–1842," 48 *J.N.H.* 177–95 (1963).

LE CONTE, EMMA. Miers, Earl S., ed., *When the World Ended: The Diary of Emma Le Conte* (1957).

LE CONTE, JOSEPH, *'Ware Sherman: A Journal of Three Months' Personal Experience in the Last Days of the Confederacy* (1937).

LEE, ROBERT E. Bradford, Gamaliel, *Lee the American* (1912).

——. Craven, Avery, ed., *To Markie: The Letters of Robert E. Lee to Martha Custis Williams* (1933).

——. Davis, Burke, *Gray Fox: Robert E. Lee and the Civil War* (1956).

——. Dowdey, Clifford, *Lee* (1965).

——. Dowdey, Clifford, and Louis H. Manarin, eds., *The Wartime Papers of R. E. Lee* (1961).

——. Fishwick, Marshall W., *Lee After the War* (1963).

——. Freeman, Douglas S., *R. E. Lee: A Biography* (4 v., 1934–35).

——. Freeman, Douglas S., ed., *Lee's Dispatches: Unpublished Letters of General Robert E. Lee* . . . *to Jefferson Davis* . . . (1915). New ed. with additional dispatches and foreword by Grady McWhiney, 1957.

——. Horn, Stanley F., ed., *The Robert E. Lee Reader* (1949).

——. Hoyt, William D., Jr., "Some Personal Letters of Robert E. Lee, 1850–1857," 12 *J.S.H.* 557–69 (1946).
——. Jones, J. William, *Life and Letters of Robert Edward Lee* (1906).
——. Lee, Robert E. [Jr.], *Recollections and Letters of General Robert E. Lee* (1924).
——. Maurice, Frederick, *Robert E. Lee, the Soldier* (1925).
——. Miers, Earl S., *Robert E. Lee: A Great Life in Brief* (1956).
——. Moger, Allen W., "General Lee's Unwritten 'History of the Army of Northern Virginia,'" 71 *Va. M. H. B.* 341–63 (1963).
——. Sanborn, Margaret, *Robert E. Lee* (2 v., 1966–67).
——. Stiles, Robert, *Four Years Under Marse Robert* (1903).
——. Taylor, Walter H., *General Lee: His Campaigns in Virginia, 1861–1865, with Personal Reminiscences* (1906).
LETCHER, JOHN. Boney, F. N., *John Letcher of Virginia: The Story of Virginia's Civil War Governor* (1966).
LIEBER, FRANCIS. Freidel, Frank, "Francis Lieber, Charles Sumner and Slavery," 9 *J.S.H.* 75–93 (1943).
——. Freidel, Frank, *Francis Lieber: Nineteenth Century Liberal* (1947).
LINCOLN, ABRAHAM. See separate listing, pp. 769–74.
LITTLEFIELD, MILTON S. Daniels, Jonathan, *Prince of Carpetbaggers* (1958).
LOGAN, JOHN A. Dawson, George F., *Life and Services of Gen. John A. Logan* . . . (1887).
——. Dickinson, John, "The Civil War Years of John Alexander Logan," 56 *J.I.S.H.S.* 212–32 (1963).
——. Jones, James P., *"Black Jack": John A. Logan and Southern Illinois in the Civil War Era* (1967).
——, *The Volunteer Soldier of America . . . with Memoir of the Author and Military Reminiscences from General Logan's Private Journal* (1877).
LOGAN, MRS. JOHN A., *Reminiscences of a Soldier's Wife: An Autobiography* (1913).
LONGSTREET, AUGUSTUS B. Wade, John D., *Augustus Baldwin Longstreet: A Study of the Development of Culture in the South* (1924).
LONGSTREET, JAMES. Eckenrode, H. J., and Bryan Conrad, *James Longstreet: Lee's War Horse* (1935).
——, *From Manassas to Appomattox: Memories of the Civil War in America* (1896). Rev. ed., 1903; new ed., with introduction by James I. Robertson, Jr., 1960.
——. Sanger, Donald B., and Thomas R. Hay, *James Longstreet* (1952).
LOVEJOY, OWEN. Haberkorn, Ruth E., "Owen Lovejoy in Princeton, Illinois," 36 *J.I.S.H.S.* 284–315 (1943).
——. Magdol, Edward, *Owen Lovejoy: Abolitionist in Congress* (1967).
LOWELL, JAMES R. Duberman, Martin, *James Russell Lowell* (1966).
——. Howard, Leon, *Victorian Knight-Errant: A Study of the Early Literary Career of James Russell Lowell* (1952).
——, *The Anti-slavery Papers of James Russell Lowell* (2 v., 1902).
——. Norton, Charles E., ed., *Letters of James Russell Lowell* (2 v., 1894).
——. Scudder, Horace E., *James Russell Lowell: A Biography* (2 v., 1901).

LUBBOCK, FRANCIS R. Raines, C. W., ed., *Six Decades in Texas, or Memoirs of Francis Richard Lubbock, Governor of Texas in War Time, 1861–1863* . . . (1900).

LYMAN, THEODORE. See George G. Meade.

LYON, NATHANIEL. Parrish, William E., "General Nathaniel Lyon, a Portrait," 49 *Mo. H. R.* 1–18 (1954).

MC CLELLAN, GEORGE B. Eckenrode, H. J., and Bryan Conrad, *George B. McClellan: The Man Who Saved the Union* (1951).

——. Hassler, Warren W., Jr., *General George B. McClellan: Shield of the Union* (1957).

——, *McClellan's Own Story* . . . (1887).

——. Michie, Peter S., *General McClellan* (1901).

——. Myers, William S., *A Study in Personality: General George Brinton McClellan* (1934).

MC CLELLAN, H. B., *I Rode with Jeb Stuart: The Life and Campaigns of Major General J. E. B. Stuart,* ed. by Burke Davis (1958).

MC CLERNAND, JOHN A. Hicken, Victor, "John A. McClernand and the House Speakership Struggle of 1859," 53 *J.I.S.H.S.* 163–78 (1960).

MC CLURE, ALEXANDER K., *Recollections of Half a Century* (1902).

——. Russell, William H., "A. K. McClure and the People's Party in the Campaign of 1860," 28 *Pa. H.* 335–45 (1961).

MC CORMICK, CYRUS H. Hutchinson, William T., *Cyrus Hall McCormick* (2 v., 1930–35).

MC CULLOCH, HUGH, *Men and Measures of Half a Century* . . . (1888).

——. Schell, Herbert S., "Hugh McCulloch and the Treasury Department, 1865–1869," 17 *M.V.H.R.* 404–21 (1930).

MC KIM, J. MILLER. Brown, Ira V., "Miller McKim and Pennsylvania Abolitionism," 30 *Pa.H.* 56–72 (1963).

MC KIM, RANDOLPH H., *A Soldier's Recollections: Leaves from the Diary of a Young Confederate* . . . (1910).

MC LEAN, JOHN. Weisenburger, Francis P., *The Life of John McLean, a Politician on the United States Supreme Court* (1937).

MC PHERSON, JAMES B. Whaley, Elizabeth J., *Forgotten Hero: General James B. McPherson* (1955).

MAHONE, WILLIAM. Blake, Nelson M., *William Mahone of Virginia, Soldier and Political Insurgent* (1935).

MALLORY, STEPHEN R. Clubbs, Occie, "Stephen Russell Mallory . . . ," 25 *Fla. H. Q.* 222–45, 295–318, and 26 *ibid.* 56–76 (1947).

——. Durkin, Joseph T., *Stephen R. Mallory: Confederate Navy Chief* (1954).

——. Jameson, J. Franklin, ed., "Letters of Stephen R. Mallory, 1861," 12 *A.H.R.* 103–108 (1906).

——. Melvin, Philip, "Stephen Russell Mallory, Southern Naval Statesman," 10 *J.S.H.* 137–60 (1944).

MARCY, WILLIAM L. Spencer, Ivor D., *The Victor and the Spoils: A Life of William L. Marcy* (1959).

MARSH, GEORGE P. Lowenthal, David, *George Perkins Marsh: Versatile Vermonter* (1958).

MARSHALL, CHARLES. Maurice, Frederick, ed., *An Aide-de-camp of Lee, Being the Papers of Col. Charles Marshall . . . 1862–1865* (1927).

MASON, JAMES M. Mason, Virginia, *The Public Life . . . of James M. Mason . . .* (1903).

MAURY, MATTHEW F. Lewis, Charles L., *Matthew Fontaine Maury, the Pathfinder of the Seas* (1927).

——. Williams, Frances L., *Matthew Fontaine Maury: Scientist of the Sea* (1963).

MEADE, GEORGE G. Agassiz, George R., ed., *Meade's Headquarters, 1863–1865: Letters of Colonel Theodore Lyman from the Wilderness to Appomattox* (1922).

——. Cleaves, Freeman, *Meade of Gettysburg* (1960).

——. Coddington, Edwin B., "The Strange Reputation of General Meade: A Lesson in Historiography," 23 *Historian* 145–66 (1961).

——. Hassler, Warren W., Jr., "George G. Meade and His Role in the Gettysburg Campaign," 32 *Pa. H.* 380–405 (1965).

——. Meade, George, *The Life and Letters of George Gordon Meade, Major-General United States Army* (2 v., 1913).

MEIGS, MONTGOMERY C. East, Sherrod D., "Montgomery C. Meigs and the Quartermaster Department," 25 *Military Affairs* 183–96 (1961–62).

——, "General M. C. Meigs on the Conduct of the Civil War," 26 *A.H.R.* 285–303 (1921).

——. Weigley, Russell F., *Quartermaster General of the Union Army: A Biography of M. C. Meigs* (1959).

MEMMINGER, C. G. Capers, H. D., *The Life and Times of C. G. Memminger* (1893).

MILLER, SAMUEL. Fairman, Charles, *Mr. Justice Miller and the Supreme Court, 1864–1890* (1939).

MOORE, ROBERT A. Silver, James W., ed., *A Life for the Confederacy: As Recorded in the Pocket Diaries of Pvt. Robert A. Moore, Co. G, 17th Mississippi Regiment, Confederate Guards, Holly Springs, Mississippi* (1959).

MORAN, BENJAMIN. Wallace, Sarah A., and Frances E. Gillespie, eds., *The Journal of Benjamin Moran, 1857–1865* (2 v., 1948–49).

MORGAN, EDWIN D. Rawley, James A., *Edwin D. Morgan, 1811–1883* (1955).

MORGAN, JOHN H. Holland, Cecil F., *Morgan and his Raiders: A Biography of the Confederate General* (1942).

——. Swiggett, Howard, *The Rebel Raider: A Life of John Hunt Morgan* (1937).

MORRILL, JUSTIN S. Parker, William B., *The Life and Public Services of Justin Smith Morrill* (1924).

MORTON, OLIVER P. Foulke, William D., *Life of Oliver P. Morton, Including His Important Speeches* (2 v., 1899).

MOSBY, JOHN S. Jones, Virgil C., *Ranger Mosby* (1944).

——, *Mosby's War Reminiscences and Stuart's Cavalry Campaigns* (1958).

——. Munson, John W., *Reminiscences of a Mosby Guerrilla* (1906).

——. Russell, Charles W., ed., *The Memoirs of Colonel John S. Mosby* (1917). New ed., with introduction by Virgil C. Jones, 1959.

MOTLEY, JOHN L. Curtis, George W., ed., *The Correspondence of John Lothrop Motley* (2 v., 1889).

——. Lynch, Sister Claire, *The Diplomatic Mission of John Lothrop Motley to Austria, 1861–1867* (1944).

MOTT, LUCRETIA. Cromwell, Otelia, *Lucretia Mott* (1958).

——. Hare, Lloyd C. M., *The Greatest American Woman: Lucretia Mott* (1937).

NAST, THOMAS. Keller, Morton, *The Art and Politics of Thomas Nast* (1968).

——. Paine, Albert B., *Thomas Nast: His Period and His Pictures* (1904).

NEESE, GEORGE M., *Three Years in the Confederate Horse Artillery* (1911).

NELSON, THOMAS A. R. Alexander, Thomas B., *Thomas A. R. Nelson of East Tennessee* (1956).

NORTHROP, LUCIUS. Felt, Jeremy P., "Lucius B. Northrop and the Confederacy's Subsistence Department," 69 *Va. M.H.B.* 181–93 (1961).

——. Hay, Thomas R., "Lucius B. Northrop: Commissary General of the Confederacy," 9 *C.W.H.* 5–23 (1963).

NORTON, CHARLES E. Norton, Sarah, and M. A. De Wolfe Howe, eds., *Letters of Charles Eliot Norton* (2 v., 1913).

OLMSTED, FREDERICK LAW. Mitchell, Broadus, *Frederick Law Olmsted, a Critic of the Old South* (1924).

——. Roper, Laura W., "Frederick Law Olmsted and the Port Royal Experiment," 31 *J.S.H.* 272–84 (1965).

——. Roper, Laura W., "Frederick Law Olmsted in the 'Literary Republic,' " 39 *M.V.H.R.* 459–82 (1952).

——. Schlesinger, Arthur M., "Was Olmsted an Unbiased Critic of the South?" 37 *J.N.H.* 173–87 (1952).

OPDYKE, GEORGE. Carson, Steven L., "Lincoln and the Mayor of New York," 67 *Lincoln Herald* 184–91 (1965).

OWEN, ROBERT D. Leopold, Richard W., *Robert Dale Owen: A Biography* (1940).

PALFREY, JOHN G. Gatell, Frank O., *John Gorham Palfrey and the New England Conscience* (1963).

PALMER, JOHN M. Palmer, George T., *A Conscientious Turncoat: The Story of John M. Palmer, 1817–1900* (1941).

PARKER, THEODORE. Commager, Henry S., *Theodore Parker* (1936).

——, *Works.* Centenary ed. (15 v., 1907–13).

——. Weiss, John, *Life and Correspondence of Theodore Parker* (2 v., 1864).

PATRICK, MARSENA R. Sparks, David S., ed., *Inside Lincoln's Army: The Diary of Marsena Rudolph Patrick, Provost Marshal General, Army of the Potomac* (1964).

PATRICK, ROBERT. Taylor, F. Jay, ed., *Reluctant Rebel: The Secret Diary of Robert Patrick, 1861–1865* (1959).

PATTERSON, ROBERT, *A Narrative of the Campaign in the Valley of the Shenandoah in 1861* (1865).

PEABODY, GEORGE F. Ware, Louise, *George Foster Peabody: Banker, Philanthropist, Publicist* (1951).

PEMBER, PHOEBE Y., *A Southern Woman's Story: Life in Confederate Richmond,* ed. by Bell I. Wiley (1959).

PEMBERTON, JOHN C. Pemberton, John C. [Jr.], *Pemberton: Defender of Vicksburg* (1942).

PENDLETON, ALEXANDER. Bean, W. G., *Stonewall's Man: Sandie Pendleton* (1959).

PEPPER, GEORGE W., *Personal Recollections of Sherman's Campaigns in Georgia and the Carolinas* (1866).

PERRY, BENJAMIN F. Kibler, Lillian A., *Benjamin F. Perry, South Carolina Unionist* (1946).

PETIGRU, JAMES L. Carson, James P., *Life, Letters and Speeches of James Louis Petigru, the Union Man of South Carolina* (1920).

PHILLIPS, WENDELL. Bartlett, Irving H., *Wendell Phillips, Brahmin Radical* (1961).

——, *Speeches, Lectures, and Letters* (2 v., 1863–91).

——. Sherwin, Oscar, *Prophet of Liberty: The Life and Times of Wendell Phillips* (1958).

——. See also William L. Garrison.

PICKETT, GEORGE E. Inman, Arthur C., ed., *Soldier of the South: General Pickett's War Letters to his Wife* (1928).

——. Pickett, La Salle C., *The Heart of a Soldier as Revealed in the Intimate Letters of Genl. George E. Pickett, C.S.A.* (1913).

PIERCE, FRANKLIN. Klement, Frank L., "Franklin Pierce and the Treason Charges of 1861–1862," 23 *Historian* 436–48 (1961).

——. Nichols, Roy F., *Franklin Pierce: Young Hickory of the Granite Hills* (1931). New ed., 1958.

——. Ray, P. Orman, ed., "Some Papers of Franklin Pierce, 1852–1862," 10 *A.H.R.* 110–27, 350–70 (1904).

PIERPONT, FRANCIS H. Ambler, Charles H., *Francis H. Pierpont: Union War Governor of Virginia and Father of West Virginia* (1937).

PIKE, ALBERT. Duncan, Robert L., *Reluctant General: The Life and Times of Albert Pike* (1961).

PIKE, JAMES, *The Scout and Ranger, Being the Personal Adventures of Corporal Pike* . . . (1865).

PIKE, JAMES S. Durden, Robert F., *James Shepherd Pike: Republicanism and the American Negro, 1850–1882* (1957).

PILLOW, GIDEON J. Stonesifer, Roy P., Jr., "Gideon J. Pillow (1806–78): A Study in Egotism," 25 *Tenn. H. Q.* 340–50 (1966).

PINCHBACK, P. B. S. Grosz, Agnes S., "The Political Career of Pickney Benton Stewart Pinchback," 27 *La. H. Q.* 527–612 (1944).

POLK, LEONIDAS. Parks, Joseph H., *General Leonidas Polk, C.S.A.: The Fighting Bishop* (1962).

——, Polk, William M., *Leonidas Polk, Bishop and General* (2 v., 1915).

PORTER, DAVID D., *Incidents and Anecdotes of the Civil War* (1886).

——. Soley, James R., *Admiral Porter* (1903).

——. West, Richard S., Jr., *The Second Admiral: A Life of David Dixon Porter* (1937).

PORTER, FITZ JOHN. Eisenschiml, Otto, *The Celebrated Case of Fitz John Porter: An American Dreyfus Affair* (1950).

PORTER, HORACE, *Campaigning with Grant* (1897).

PRICE, STERLING. Castel, Albert, *General Sterling Price and the Civil War in the West* (1968).

PRINGLE, CYRUS. Jones, Rufus M., ed., *The Record of a Quaker Conscience: Cyrus Pringle's Diary* (1918).

PRYOR, MRS. ROGER A., *Reminiscences of Peace and War* (1905).

PUBLIC MAN. "The Diary of a Public Man: Unpublished Passages of the Secret History of the American Civil War," 129 N. *Am. Rev.* 125–40, 259–73, 375–88, 484–96 (1879). New ed., with introduction by F. Lauriston Bullard, 1946. For the difficult question of the authorship and authenticity of this diary see 41 *A.H.R.* 277–79; Evelyn Page, "The Diary and the Public Man," 22 *N.E.Q.* 147–72 (1949); Benjamin M. Price, "That Baffling Diary," 54 *S.A.Q.* 56–64 (1955); Frank M. Anderson, *The Mystery of "A Public Man": A Historical Detective Story* (1948); Roy N. Lokken, "Has the Mystery of 'A Public Man' Been Solved?" 40 *M.V.H.R.* 419–40 (1953); Frank M. Anderson, "Has the Mystery of 'A Public Man' Been Solved?—A Rejoinder," 42 *M.V.H.R.* 101–107 (1955); Roy N. Lokken, "A Reply to 'A Rejoinder,'" 42 *M.V.H.R.* 107–109 (1955).

PUTNAM, GEORGE H., *Some Memories of the Civil War* (1924).

QUANTRILL, WILLIAM C. Castel, Albert, *William Clarke Quantrill: His Life and Times* (1962).

QUITMAN, JOHN A. Broussard, Ray, "Governor John A. Quitman and the Lopez Expeditions of 1851–1852," 28 *J. Miss. H.* 103–20 (1966).

——. Claiborne, J. F. H., *Life and Correspondence of John A. Quitman* (2 v., 1860).

——. Gonzales, John E., "John Anthony Quitman in the United States House of Representatives, 1855–1858," 4 *Southern Quarterly* 276–88 (1966).

——. McLendon, James H., "John A. Quitman, Fire-Eating Governor," 15 *J. Miss. H.* 73–89 (1953).

RANDOLPH, GEORGE W. Jones, Archer, "Some Aspects of George W. Randolph's Service as Confederate Secretary of War," 26 *J.S.H.* 299–314 (1960).

RAWLINS, JOHN A. Wilson, James H., *The Life of John A. Rawlins, Lawyer, Assistant Adjutant-General, Chief of Staff, Major General of Volunteers, and Secretary of War* (1916).

RAY, CHARLES H. Monaghan, Jay, *The Man Who Elected Lincoln* (1956).

RAYMOND, HENRY J. Brown, Francis, *Raymond of the Times* (1951).

——. Dodd, Dorothy, *Henry J. Raymond and the New York Times during Reconstruction* (1936).

REAGAN, JOHN H. McCaleb, Walter F., ed., *Memoirs, with Special Reference to Secession and the Civil War, by John H. Reagan* (1906).

——. Procter, Ben H., *Not Without Honor: The Life of John H. Reagan* (1962).

REID, WHITELAW. Cortissoz, Royal, *The Life of Whitelaw Reid* (2 v., 1921).

REYNOLDS, JOHN F. Keller, Oliver J., "Soldier General of the Army: John Fulton Reynolds," 4 *C.W.H.* 119–28 (1958).

——. Nichols, Edward J., *Toward Gettysburg: A Biography of General John F. Reynolds* (1958).

RHETT, ROBERT B. White, Laura A., *Robert Barnwell Rhett, Father of Secession* (1931).

RIDDLE, ALBERT G., *Recollections of War Times: Reminiscences of Men and Events in Washington, 1860–1865* (1895).

RIPLEY, EDWARD H. Eisenschiml, Otto, ed., *Vermont General: The Unusual War Experiences of Edward Hastings Ripley* (1862–1865) (1960).

ROCKEFELLER, JOHN D. Nevins, Allan, *Study in Power: John D. Rockefeller, Industrialist and Philanthropist* (2 v., 1953). This is a revised ed. of *John D. Rockefeller: The Heroic Age of American Enterprise* (1940).

ROSECRANS, WILLIAM S. Lamers, William M., *The Edge of Glory: A Biography of General William S. Rosecrans* (1961).

RUFFIN, EDMUND. Craven, Avery O., *Edmund Ruffin, Southerner: A Study in Secession* (1932).

——, "Extracts from the Diary of Edmund Ruffin," *Wm. & M. Q.* XIV, XX–XXIII (1905–1915).

——. Steinberg, Alfred, "Fire-eating Farmer of the Confederacy," 9 *Am. Heritage* 22–25 ff. (Dec., 1957).

RUFFIN, THOMAS. Hamilton, J. G. de Roulhac, ed., *The Papers of Thomas Ruffin* (4 v., 1918–20).

RUSSELL, WILLIAM HOWARD, *My Diary North and South* (1863).

SANFORD, HENRY S. Owsley, Harriet C., "Henry Shelton Sanford and Federal Surveillance Abroad, 1861–1865," 48 *M.V.H.R.* 211–28 (1961).

SAWYER, PHILETUS. Current, Richard N., *Pine Logs and Politics: A Life of Philetus Sawyer, 1816–1900* (1950).

SCHEIBERT, JUSTUS, *Seven Months in the Rebel States during the North American War, 1863.* Trans. by Joseph C. Haynes; ed. by Wm. S. Hoole (1958).

SCHOFIELD, JOHN M., *Forty-Six Years in the Army* (1897).

——. Weigley, Russell F., "The Military Thought of John M. Schofield," 23 *Military Affairs* 77–84 (1959).

SCHURZ, CARL. Bancroft, Frederic, ed., *Speeches, Correspondence and Political Papers of Carl Schurz* (6 v., 1913).

——. Easum, Chester V., *The Americanization of Carl Schurz* (1929).

——. Fuess, Claude M., *Carl Schurz, Reformer* (1829–1906) (1932).

——. Mahaffey, John H., ed., "Carl Schurz's Letters from the South," 35 *Ga. H. Q.* 222–56 (1951).

——. Schafer, Joseph, *Carl Schurz, Militant Liberal* (1930).

——. Schafer, Joseph, ed., *Intimate Letters of Carl Schurz, 1841–1869* (1928).

——, *The Reminiscences of Carl Schurz* (3 v., 1907–08).

SCOTT, THOMAS. Kamm, Samuel R., *The Civil War Career of Thomas A. Scott* (1940).

SCOTT, WINFIELD. Elliott, Charles W., *Winfield Scott: The Soldier and the Man* (1937).

——, *Memoirs of Lieut.-General Scott, LL.D., Written by Himself* (2 v., 1864).

SEDDON, JAMES A. Curry, Roy W., "James A. Seddon, a Southern Prototype," 63 *Va. M. H. B.* 123–50 (1955).

SEMMES, RAPHAEL. Bethel, Elizabeth, ed., "The Prison Diary of Raphael Semmes," 22 *J.S.H.* 498–511 (1956).

SEMMES, RAPHAEL. Gosnell, Harpur A., ed., *Rebel Raider: Being an Account of Raphael Semmes's Cruise in the C.S.S. Sumter* (1948).
——. Meriwether, Colyer, *Raphael Semmes* (1913).
——. Roberts, W. Adolphe, *Semmes of the Alabama* (1938).
——, *Service Afloat, or, The Remarkable Career of the Confederate Cruisers, Sumter and Alabama, during the War between the States* (1903).
SEWARD, FANNY. Johnson, Patricia C., ed., " 'I Have Supped Full on Horrors,' " 10 *Am. Heritage* 60–65 ff. (Oct., 1959).
SEWARD, FREDERICK W., *Reminiscences of a War-Time Statesman and Diplomat, 1830–1915* (1916).
SEWARD, WILLIAM H. Baker, George E., ed., *The Works of William H. Seward* (5 v., 1853–84).
——. Bancroft, Frederic, *The Life of William H. Seward* (2 v., 1900).
——. Conrad, Earl, *The Governor and His Lady: The Story of William Henry Seward and His Wife Frances* (1960).
——. Curran, Thomas J., "Seward and the Know-Nothings," 51 *N. Y. Hist. Soc. Q.* 141–59 (1967).
——. Hale, Edward E., Jr., *William H. Seward* (1910).
——. Seward, Frederick W., ed., *William H. Seward: An Autobiography from 1801 to 1834 with a Memoir of His Life, and Selections from His Letters* (3 v., 1891).
——. Sharrow, Walter G., "William Henry Seward and the Basis for American Empire, 1850–1860," 36 *Pac. H. R.* 325–42 (1967).
——. Van Deusen, Glyndon G., *William Henry Seward* (1967).
SEYMOUR, HORATIO. Murdock, Eugene C., "Horatio Seymour and the 1863 Draft," 11 *C.W.H.* 117–41 (1965).
——. Mitchell, Stewart, *Horatio Seymour of New York* (1938).
SHELBY, JOSEPH. O'Flaherty, Daniel, *General Jo Shelby, Undefeated Rebel* (1954).
SHERIDAN, PHILIP H. O'Connor, Richard, *Sheridan the Inevitable* (1953).
——, *Personal Memoirs* (2 v., 1888). New ed., 1904.
SHERMAN, JOHN. Burton, Theodore E., *John Sherman* (1906).
——. Randall, J. G., "John Sherman and Reconstruction," 19 *M.V.H.R.* 382–93 (1932).
——, *John Sherman's Recollections of Forty Years in the House, Senate and Cabinet: An Autobiography* (2 v., 1895).
——. See also W. T. Sherman.
SHERMAN, WILLIAM T. Burt, Jesse C., "Sherman, Railroad General," 2 *C.W.H.* 45–54 (1956).
——. Fleming, Walter L., *General W. T. Sherman as College President* (1912).
——. Howe, M. A. De Wolfe, ed., *Home Letters of General Sherman* (1909).
——. Lewis, Lloyd, *Sherman, Fighting Prophet* (1932).
——. Liddell Hart, Basil H., *Sherman: Soldier, Realist, American* (1929).
——. Miers, Earl S., *The General Who Marched to Hell: William Tecumseh Sherman and His March to Fame and Infamy* (1951).
——. Naroll, Raoul S., "Lincoln and the Sherman Peace Fiasco—Another Fable?" 20 *J.S.H.* 459–83 (1954).
——. Pfanz, Harry W., "The Surrender Negotiations between General John-

ston and General Sherman, April 1865," 16 *Military Affairs,* 61–70 (1952).

——, *Memoirs of General W. T. Sherman, Written by Himself* (2 v., 1875). Revised and corrected ed., 1887. New ed., with introduction by B. H. Liddell Hart, 1957. For a critique of the 1875 ed., see Henry Van Ness Boynton, *Sherman's Historical Raid* (1875).

——. Thorndike, Rachel S., ed., *The Sherman Letters: Correspondence between General and Senator Sherman from 1837 to 1891* (1894).

——. Walters, John B., "General William T. Sherman and Total War," 14 *J.S.H.* 447–80 (1948).

SICKLES, DANIEL. Swanberg, W. A., *Sickles the Incredible* (1956).

SIMMS, WILLIAM G. Higham, John W., "The Changing Loyalties of William Gilmore Simms," 9 *J.S.H.* 210–23 (1943).

——. Simms, Mary C., Alfred T. Odell and T. C. Duncan Eaves, eds., *The Letters of William Gilmore Simms* (5 v., 1952–56).

——. Trent, William P., *William Gilmore Simms* (1892).

——. Welsh, John R., "William Gilmore Simms, Critic of the South," 26 *J.S.H.* 201–14 (1960).

SIMPSON, MATTHEW. Clark, Robert D., *The Life of Matthew Simpson* (1956).

SLIDELL, JOHN. Sears, Louis M., *John Slidell* (1925).

——. Tregle, Joseph G., Jr., "The Political Apprenticeship of John Slidell," 26 *J.S.H.* 57–70 (1960).

——. Willson, Beckles, *John Slidell and the Confederates in Paris* (1862–65) (1932).

SMITH, GERRIT. Harlow, Ralph V., *Gerrit Smith: Philanthropist and Reformer* (1939).

——. Harlow, Ralph V., "Gerrit Smith and the John Brown Raid," 38 *A.H.R.* 32–60 (1932).

SMITH, GOLDWIN, "Letters of Goldwin Smith to Charles Eliot Norton [1863–1872]," 49 *Mass. H. S. P.* 106–60 (1915).

SMITH, MASON. Smith, Daniel E. H., and others, eds., *Mason Smith Family Letters, 1860–1868* (1950).

SMITH, WILLIAM. Fahrner, Alvin A., "William 'Extra Billy' Smith, Governor of Virginia, 1864–1865: A Pillar of the Confederacy," 74 *Va. M. H. B.* 68–87 (1966).

SMITH, WILLIAM F., *From Chattanooga to Petersburg under Generals Grant and Butler* (1893).

SORREL, G. MOXLEY, *Recollections of a Confederate Staff Officer* (1905). New ed., with introduction by Bell I. Wiley, 1958.

SOULÉ, PIERRE. Moore, J. Preston, "Pierre Soulé: Southern Expansionist and Promoter," 21 *J.S.H.* 203–23 (1955).

SPALDING, THOMAS. Coulter, E. Merton, *Thomas Spalding of Sapelo* (1940).

SPEED, JAMES. Speed, James [grandson], *James Speed: A Personality* (1914).

SPEED, JOSHUA F. Kinkaid, Robert L., "Joshua Fry Speed, Lincoln's Confidential Agent in Kentucky," 52 *Register Ky. Hist. Soc.* 99–110 (1954).

SPRAGUE, KATE CHASE. Belden, Thomas G., and Marva R. Belden, *So Fell the Angels* (1956).

SPRAGUE, KATE CHASE. Phelps, Mary M., *Kate Chase, Dominant Daughter: The Story of a Brilliant Woman and Her Famous Father* (1935).
——. Ross, Ishbel, *Proud Kate: Portrait of an Ambitious Woman* (1953).
STANTON, EDWIN M. Flower, Frank A., *Edwin McMasters Stanton, Lincoln's Great War Secretary* (1905).
——. Gorham, George C., *Life and Public Services of Edwin M. Stanton* (2 v., 1899).
——. Pratt, Fletcher, *Stanton: Lincoln's Secretary of War* (1953).
——. Schruben, Francis W., "Edwin M. Stanton and Reconstruction," 23 *Tenn. H. Q.* 145–68 (1964).
——. Thomas, Benjamin P., and Harold M. Hyman, *Stanton: The Life and Times of Lincoln's Secretary of War* (1962).
STANTON, ELIZABETH C. Stanton, Theodore, and Harriot S. Blatch, eds., *Elizabeth Cady Stanton* (2 v., 1922).
STEPHENS, ALEXANDER H. Cleveland, Henry, *Alexander H. Stephens, in Public and Private . . .* (1866).
——. Johnston, Richard M., and William H. Browne, *Life of Alexander H. Stephens* (1878).
——. Rabun, James Z., ed., *A Letter for Posterity: Alexander Stephens to His Brother Linton, June 3, 1864* (1954).
——. Rabun, James Z., "Alexander H. Stephens and Jefferson Davis," 58 *A.H.R.* 290–321 (1953).
——. Rabun, James Z., "Alexander H. Stephens and the Confederacy," 6 *Emory Univ. Q.* 129–46 (1950).
——. Richardson, E. Ramsay, *Little Aleck: A Life of Alexander H. Stephens, the Fighting Vice-President of the Confederacy* (1932).
——, *A Constitutional View of the Late War Between the States . . .* (2 v., 1868–70).
——, *Recollections of Alexander H. Stephens . . .* (1910).
——. Stephens, Robert G., Jr., "The Background and Boyhood of Alexander H. Stephens," 9 *Ga. R.* 386–97 (1955).
——. Von Abele, Rudolph, *Alexander H. Stephens: A Biography* (1946).
——. See Robert Toombs.
STEVENS, THADDEUS. Brodie, Fawn M., *Thaddeus Stevens: Scourge of the South* (1959).
——. Current, Richard N., *Old Thad Stevens: A Story of Ambition* (1942).
——. Korngold, Ralph, *Thaddeus Stevens: A Being Darkly Wise and Rudely Great* (1955).
STOCKWELL, ELISHA. Abernethy, Byron R., ed., *Private Elisha Stockwell, Jr., Sees the Civil War* (1958).
STONE, KATE. Anderson, John W., ed., *Brokenburn: The Journal of Kate Stone, 1861–1868* (1955).
STOWE, HARRIET B. Adams, John R., *Harriet Beecher Stowe* (1963).
——. Stowe, Charles E., and Lyman B. Stowe, *Harriet Beecher Stowe: The Story of Her Life* (1911).
——. Wagenknecht, Edward, *Harriet Beecher Stowe: The Known and the Unknown* (1965).

——. Wilson, Forrest, *Crusader in Crinoline: The Life of Harriet Beecher Stowe* (1941).

STRONG, GEORGE T. Nevins, Allan, and Milton H. Thomas, eds., *The Diary of George Templeton Strong, 1835–1875* (4 v., 1952).

STROTHER, DAVID H. Eby, Cecil D., Jr., *"Porte Crayon": The Life of David Hunter Strother* (1960).

——. Eby, Cecil D., Jr., ed., *A Virginia Yankee in the Civil War: The Diaries of David Hunter Strother* (1961).

STUART, A. H. H. Robertson, Alexander F., *Alexander Hugh Holmes Stuart, 1807–1891: A Biography* (1925).

STUART, JAMES E. B. Davis, Burke, *Jeb Stuart, the Last Cavalier* (1957).

——. Thomason, John W., Jr., *Jeb Stuart* (1930).

SUMNER, CHARLES. Donald, David, *Charles Sumner and the Coming of the Civil War* (1960). For hostile appraisals of this work, see Paul Goodman, "David Donald's *Charles Sumner* Reconsidered," 37 *N.E.Q.* 373–87 (1964), and Louis Ruchames, "The Pulitzer Prize Treatment of Charles Sumner," 2 *Massachusetts Review* 749–69 (1961).

——. Haynes, George H., *Charles Sumner* (1909).

——. Hogue, Arthur R., ed., *Charles Sumner: An Essay by Carl Schurz* (1951).

——. Pierce, Edward L., *Memoir and Letters of Charles Sumner* (4 v., 1877–93).

——. Ruchames, Louis, "Charles Sumner and American Historiography," 38 *J.N.H.* 139–60 (1953).

——, *Works* (15 v., 1870–83).

——. White, Laura A., "Charles Sumner and the Crisis of 1860–61," in Avery O. Craven, ed., *Essays in Honor of William E. Dodd* (1935), 131–93.

——. White, Laura A., "Was Charles Sumner Shamming, 1856–1859?" ed. Victor H. Cohen, 33 *N.E.Q.* 291–324 (1960).

SURRATT, MARY E. Moore, Guy W., *The Case of Mrs. Surratt* (1954).

SYLVIS, WILLIAM. Grossman, Jonathan, *William Sylvis, Pioneer of American Labor: A Study of the Labor Movement during the Era of the Civil War* (1945).

TANEY, ROGER B. Lewis, Walker, *Without Fear or Favor: A Biography of Chief Justice Roger Brooke Taney* (1965).

——. Smith, C. W., Jr., *Chief Justice Taney* (1935).

——. Steiner, Bernard C., *Life of Roger Brooke Taney* (1922).

——. Swisher, Carl B., *Roger B. Taney* (1935).

TAPPAN, ARTHUR. Southall, Eugene P., "Arthur Tappan and the Anti-Slavery Movement," 15 *J.N.H.* 162–97 (1930).

TAYLOR, RICHARD. Davis, Jackson B., "The Life of Richard Taylor," 24 *La. H. Q.* 49–126 (1941).

——, *Destruction and Reconstruction: Personal Experiences of the Late War* (1879). New ed., with introduction by Richard Harwell, 1955.

TAYLOR, ZACHARY. Dyer, Brainerd, *Zachary Taylor* (1946).

——. Hamilton, Holman, *Zachary Taylor* (2 v., 1941–51).

——. Lynch, William O., "Zachary Taylor as President," 4 *J.S.H.* 279–94 (1938).

TERRY, DAVID S. Buchanan, A. Russell, *David S. Terry of California: Duelling Judge* (1956).

THOMAS, GEORGE H. Cleaves, Freeman, *Rock of Chickamauga: The Life of General George H. Thomas* (1948).

——. Coppée, Henry, *General Thomas* (1893).

——. McKinney, Francis F., *Education in Violence: The Life of George H. Thomas and the History of the Army of the Cumberland* (1961).

——. O'Connor, Richard, *Thomas: Rock of Chickamauga* (1948).

——. Thomas, Wilbur, *General George H. Thomas: The Indomitable Warrior* (1964).

——. Van Horne, Thomas B., *The Life of Major-General George H. Thomas* (1882).

TILDEN, SAMUEL J. Bigelow, John, *The Life of Samuel J. Tilden* (2 v., 1895).

——. Flick, Alexander C., *Samuel Jones Tilden: A Study in Political Sagacity* (1939).

——. Hirsch, Mark D., "Samuel J. Tilden: The Story of a Lost Opportunity," 56 *A.H.R.* 788–802 (1951).

——. Kelley, Robert, "The Thought and Character of Samuel J. Tilden: The Democrat as Inheritor," 26 *Historian* 176–205 (1964).

TOOMBS, ROBERT. Phillips, Ulrich B., ed., "The Correspondence of Robert Toombs, Alexander H. Stephens, and Howell Cobb," *Ann. Rep. A.H.A.,* 1911, v. II.

——. Phillips, Ulrich B., *The Life of Robert Toombs* (1913).

——. Thompson, William Y., *Robert Toombs of Georgia* (1966).

TOURGÉE, ALBION W. Gross, Theodore L., *Albion W. Tourgée* (1963).

——. Keller, Dean H., ed., "A Civil War Diary of Albion W. Tourgée (May–Nov. 1863)" 74 *Ohio H.* 99–131 (1965).

——. Nye, Russel B., "Judge Tourgée and Reconstruction," 50 *Ohio Arch. & H. Q.* 101–114 (1941).

——. Olsen, Otto H., *Carpetbagger's Crusade: The Life of Albion Winegar Tourgée* (1965).

——. Weissbuch, Ted N., "Albion W. Tourgée, Propagandist and Critic of Reconstruction," 70 *Ohio H. Q.* 27–44 (1961).

TOWNSEND, GEORGE A., *Rustics in Rebellion: A Yankee Reporter on the Road to Richmond, 1861–65,* intro. by Lida Mayo (1950).

TRADER, JOHN W. Culmer, Frederic A., "Brigadier Surgeon John W. Trader's Recollections of the Civil War in Missouri," 46 *Mo. H. R.* 323–34 (1952).

TRUMBULL, LYMAN. Krug, Mark M., *Lyman Trumbull, Conservative Radical* (1965).

——. White, Horace, *The Life of Lyman Trumbull* (1913).

TWEED, WILLIAM M. Lynch, Denis T., *"Boss" Tweed* (1927).

——. Pratt, John W., "Boss Tweed's Public Welfare Program," 45 *N. Y. Hist. Soc. Q.* 396–411 (1961).

TYLER, JOHN. Chitwood, Oliver P., *John Tyler: Champion of the Old South* (1939).

——. Seager, Robert, II, *And Tyler Too: A Biography of John and Julia Gardiner Tyler* (1963).

——. Tyler, Lyon G., *The Letters and Times of the Tylers* (3 v., 1884–96).

TYLER, ROBERT. Auchampaugh, Philip G., *Robert Tyler, Southern Rights Champion, 1847–1866* . . . (1934).

TYLER, MASON W. Tyler, William S., ed., *Recollections of the Civil War . . . by* [Lt. Col.] *Mason Whiting Tyler* (1912).

UNDERWOOD, JOHN C. Hickin, Patricia, "John C. Underwood and the Anti-slavery Movement in Virginia, 1847–1860," 73 *Va. M. H. B.* 156–68 (1965).

UPSON, THEODORE F. Winther, Oscar O., ed., *With Sherman to the Sea: The Civil War Letters, Diaries & Reminiscences of Theodore F. Upson* (1943). New ed., 1958.

UPTON, EMORY. Ambrose, Stephen E., *Upton and the Army* (1964).

USHER, JOHN P. Richardson, Elmo R., and Alan W. Farley, *John Palmer Usher, Lincoln's Secretary of the Interior* (1960).

VALLANDIGHAM, CLEMENT L. Koenig, Louis W., " 'The Most Unpopular Man in the North,' " 15 *Am. Heritage* 12–15 ff. (Feb., 1964).

——. Klement, Frank L., "Clement L. Vallandigham's Exile in the Confederacy, May 25–June 17, 1863," 31 *J.S.H.* 149–63 (1965).

——. Klement, Frank L., "Vallandigham as an Exile in Canada, 1863–1864," 74 *Ohio H.* 151–68 (1965).

——, Vallandigham, James L., *A Life of Clement L. Vallandigham* (1872).

VANCE, ZEBULON B. Adler, Selig, "Zebulon B. Vance and the 'Scattered Nation,' " 7 *J.S.H.* 357–77 (1941).

——. Johnston, Frontis W., ed., *The Papers of Zebulon Baird Vance* (1 v. to date, 1963–   ).

——. Johnston, Frontis W., "Zebulon Baird Vance: A Personality Sketch," 30 *N.C.H.R.* 178–90 (1953).

——. Tucker, Glenn, *Zeb Vance: Champion of Personal Freedom* (1966).

——. Yates, Richard E., *The Confederacy and Zeb Vance* (1958).

——. Yates, Richard E., "Governor Vance and the Peace Movement," 17 *N.C.H.R.* 1–25, 89–113 (1940).

——. Yates, Richard E., "Zebulon B. Vance as War Governor of North Carolina, 1863–1865," 3 *J.S.H.* 43–75 (1937).

VANDERBILT, CORNELIUS. Croffut, W. A., *The Vanderbilts and the Story of Their Fortune* (1886).

——. Lane, Wheaton J., *Commodore Vanderbilt* (1942).

——. Smith, Arthur D. H., *Commodore Vanderbilt: An Epic of American Achievement* (1927).

VAN DORN, EARL. Hartje, Robert G., *Van Dorn: The Life and Times of a Confederate General* (1967).

VILLARD, HENRY, *Memoirs of Henry Villard, Journalist and Financier, 1835–1900* (2 v., 1904).

WADE, BENJAMIN F. Riddle, Albert G., *Life of Benjamin F. Wade* (1886).

——. Shover, Kenneth B., "Maverick at Bay: Ben Wade's Senate Re-election Campaign, 1862–1863," 12 *C.W.H.* 23–42 (1966).

——. Trefousse, Hans L., *Benjamin Franklin Wade: Radical Republican from Ohio* (1963).

WADE, BENJAMIN F. Williams, Harry, "Benjamin F. Wade and the Atrocity Propaganda of the Civil War," 48 *Ohio Arch. & H. Q.* 33–43 (1939).
——. Zornow, William F., " 'Bluff Ben' Wade in Lawrence, Kansas: The Issue of Class Conflict," 65 *Ohio H. Q.* 44–52 (1956).
WADSWORTH, JAMES S. Pearson, Henry G., *James S. Wadsworth of Geneseo, Brevet Major-General of United States Volunteers* (1913).
WAILES, BENJAMIN L. C. Sydnor, Charles S., *A Gentleman of the Old Natchez Region: Benjamin L. C. Wailes* (1938).
WAITE, MORRISON R. Magrath, C. Peter, *Morrison R. Waite: The Triumph of Character* (1963).
——. Trimble, Bruce R., *Chief Justice Waite, Defender of the Public Interest* (1938).
WALKER, LEROY P. Harris, William C., *Leroy Pope Walker, Confederate Secretary of War* (1962).
WALKER, ROBERT J. Dodd, William E., *Robert J. Walker, Imperialist* (1914).
——. Jordan, H. Donaldson, "A Politician of Expansion: Robert J. Walker," 19 *M.V.H.R.* 362–81 (1932).
——. Shenton, James P., *Robert John Walker: A Politician from Jackson to Lincoln* (1961).
WALKER, WILLIAM. Carr, Albert H., *The World and William Walker* (1963).
——. Greene, Laurence, *The Filibuster: The Career of William Walker* (1937).
WALLACE, LEW. McKee, Irving, *"Ben-Hur" Wallace: The Life of General Lew Wallace* (1947).
——, *Lew Wallace: An Autobiography* (2 v., 1906).
WARD, SAMUEL. Thomas, Lately, *Sam Ward: "King of the Lobby"* (1965).
WARMOTH, HENRY C., *War, Politics and Reconstruction: Stormy Days in Louisiana* (1930).
WARREN, GOUVERNEUR K. Taylor, Emerson G., *Gouverneur Kemble Warren: The Life and Letters of an American Soldier, 1830–1882* (1932).
WASHBURN, ISRAEL. Hunt, Gaillard, *Israel, Elihu, and Cadwallader Washburn* (1925).
WATKINS, SAM R., *Co. Aytch: A Side Show of the Big Show*, ed. by Bell I. Wiley (1954).
WATTERSON, HENRY. Wall, Joseph F., *Henry Watterson, Reconstructed Rebel* (1956).
——, *"Marse Henry": An Autobiography* (2 v., 1919).
WAYNE, JAMES M. Lawrence, Alexander A., *James Moore Wayne, Southern Unionist* (1943).
WEBSTER, DANIEL. Adams, Samuel H., *The Godlike Daniel* (1930).
——. Baxter, Maurice G., *Daniel Webster and the Supreme Court* (1966).
——. Brauer, Kinley J., "The Webster-Lawrence Feud: A Study in Politics and Ambitions," 29 *Historian* 34–59 (1966).
——. Current, Richard N., *Daniel Webster and the Rise of National Conservatism* (1955).
——. Curtis, George T., *The Life of Daniel Webster* (2 v., 1870).
——. Fisher, Sidney G., *The True Daniel Webster* (1911).

——. Fuess, Claude M., *Daniel Webster* (2 v., 1930).

——. Harvey, Peter, *Reminiscences and Anecdotes of Daniel Webster* (1877).

——. Johnson, Gerald W., "Great Man Eloquent," 9 *Am. Heritage* 74–79 ff. (Dec., 1957).

——. Lodge, Henry C., *Daniel Webster* (1883).

——. McIntyre, J. W., ed., *The Writings and Speeches of Daniel Webster* (18 v., 1903).

——. Nathans, Sydney, "Daniel Webster, Massachusetts Man," 39 *N.E.Q.* 161–81 (1966).

——. Parrish, Peter J., "Daniel Webster, New England, and the West," 54 *J.A.H.* 524–49 (1967).

——. Van Tyne, Claude H., ed., *The Letters of Daniel Webster . . .* (1902).

WEED, THURLOW. Van Deusen, Glyndon G., *Thurlow Weed: Wizard of the Lobby* (1947).

——, *Autobiography,* ed. by Harriet A. Weed. *Memoir of Thurlow Weed,* by Thurlow Weed Barnes. Though bearing separate titles, these books constitute vols. 1 and 2 of a set issued in 1883–84.

WELD, THEODORE D. Barnes, Gilbert H., and Dwight L. Dumond, eds., *Letters of Theodore Dwight Weld, Angelina Grimké Weld and Sarah Grimké, 1822–1844* (2 v., 1934).

——. Thomas, Benjamin P., *Theodore Weld: Crusader for Freedom* (1950).

WELLES, GIDEON. Beale, Howard K., "Is the Printed Diary of Gideon Welles Reliable?" 30 *A.H.R.* 547–52 (1925).

——. Muriel Bernitt, ed., "Two Manuscripts of Gideon Welles: President Lincoln Feels His Way and Welles *versus* Seward on Privateers," 11 *N.E.Q.* 576–605 (1938).

——. Meneely, A. Howard, ed., "Three Manuscripts of Gideon Welles," 31 *A.H.R.* 484–94 (1926).

——. Mordell, Albert, ed., *Selected Essays by Gideon Welles* (2 v., 1959–60).

——, *Diary of Gideon Welles, Secretary of the Navy under Lincoln and Johnson,* ed. by John T. Morse, Jr. (3 v., 1911). Morse's edition of the *Diary* included many later corrections and interpolations by Welles. Howard K. Beale, assisted by Alan W. Brownsword, issued a careful, scholarly edition of the *Diary* (3 v., 1960), showing both what Welles originally wrote and what he later wished he had written.

——. West, Richard S., Jr., *Gideon Welles: Lincoln's Navy Department* (1943).

WELLS, DAVID A. Ferleger, Herbert R., *David A. Wells and the American Revenue System, 1865–1870* (1942).

——. Joyner, Fred B., *David Ames Wells: Champion of Free Trade* (1939).

WELLS, JAMES M. Lowrey, Walter M., "The Political Career of James Madison Wells," 31 *La. H. Q.* 995–1123 (1948).

WENTWORTH, JOHN. Fehrenbacher, Don E., *Chicago Giant: A Biography of "Long John" Wentworth* (1957).

WHEAT, ROBERDEAU. Doufour, Charles L., *Gentle Tiger: The Gallant Life of Roberdeau Wheat* (1957).

WHEELER, JOSEPH. Dyer, John P., *"Fightin' Joe" Wheeler* (1941).

WHITE, ANDREW D., *Autobiography* (2 v., 1905).

WHITMAN, WALT. Allen, Gay W., *The Solitary Singer: A Critical Biography of Walt Whitman* (1955).

——. Lowenfels, Walter, ed., *Walt Whitman's Civil War* (1960).

WHITTIER, JOHN G. Albree, John, ed., *Whittier Correspondence . . . 1830–1892* (1911).

——. Pickard, Samuel T., *Life and Letters of John Greenleaf Whittier* (2 v., 1894).

——. Pollard, John A., *John Greenleaf Whittier, Friend of Man* (1949).

——. Scudder, Horace E., ed., *Writings of John Greenleaf Whittier* (7 v., 1894).

——. Wagenknecht, Edward, *John Greenleaf Whittier: A Portrait in Paradox* (1967).

WILKES, CHARLES. Henderson, Daniel, *The Hidden Coasts: A Biography of Admiral Charles Wilkes* (1953).

——. Jeffries, William W., "The Civil War Career of Charles Wilkes," 11 *J.S.H.* 324–48 (1945).

——. Long, John S., "Glory-Hunting off Havana: Wilkes and the *Trent* Affair," 9 *C.W.H.* 133–44 (1963).

WILLIAMS, ALPHEUS S. Quaife, Milo M., ed., *From the Cannon's Mouth: The Civil War Letters of General Alpheus S. Williams* (1959).

WILMOT, DAVID. Going, Charles B., *David Wilmot, Free-Soiler* (1924).

WILSON, HENRY. McKay, Ernest A., "Henry Wilson and the Coalition of 1851," 36 *N.E.Q.* 338–57 (1963).

——. McKay, Ernest A., "Henry Wilson: Unprincipled Know Nothing," 46 *Mid-America* 29–37 (1964).

——. Nason, Elias, and Thomas Russell, *The Life and Public Services of Henry Wilson, Late Vice-President of the United States* (1876).

WILSON, JAMES H., *Under the Old Flag: Recollections of Military Operations in the War for the Union, the Spanish War, the Boxer Rebellion . . .* (1912).

WINSLOW, JOHN A. Ellicott, John M., *The Life of John Ancrum Winslow, Rear Admiral United States Navy . . .* (1902).

WIRZ, HENRY. Rutman, Darrett B., "The War Crimes and Trial of Henry Wirz," 6 *C.W.H.* 117–33 (1960).

WISE, HENRY A. Eaton, Clement, "Henry A. Wise, a Liberal of the Old South," 7 *J.S.H.* 482–94 (1941).

——. Eaton, Clement, "Henry A. Wise and the Virginia Fire Eaters of 1856," 21 *M.V.H.R.* 495–512 (1935).

——. Wise, Barton H., *The Life of Henry A. Wise of Virginia, 1806–1876* (1899).

WISE, JOHN S., *The End of an Era* (1899).

WOOD, FERNANDO. Pleasants, Samuel A., *Fernando Wood of New York* (1948).

——. Richardson, James F., "Mayor Fernando Wood and the New York Police Force, 1855–187," 50 *N. Y. Hist. Soc. Q.* 5–40 (1966).

WOOD, WILLIAM N., *Reminiscences of Big I*, ed. by Bell I. Wiley (1956).

WOOL, JOHN E. Rezneck, Samuel, "The Civil War Role, 1861–1863, of a

Veteran New York Officer, Major General John E. Wool," 44 *N.Y.H.* 237–57 (1963).

WORTH, DANIEL. Tolbert, Noble J., "Daniel Worth: Tar Heel Abolitionist," 39 *N.C.H.R.* 284–304 (1962).

WORTH, JONATHAN. Hamilton, J. G. de R., ed., *The Correspondence of Jonathan Worth* (2 v., 1909).

——. Zuber, Richard L., *Jonathan Worth: A Biography of a Southern Unionist* (1965).

YANCEY, WILLIAM L. Draughon, Ralph B., Jr., "The Young Manhood of William L. Yancey," 19 *Ala. R.* 28–40 (1966).

——. DuBose, John W., *The Life and Times of William Lowndes Yancey* (1892).

——. Garner, Alto L., and Nathan Stott, "William Lowndes Yancey: Statesman of Secession," 15 *Ala. R.* 190–202 (1962).

——. McMillan, Malcolm C., "William L. Yancey and the Historians: One Hundred Years," 20 *Ala. R.* 163–86 (1967).

——. Venable, Austin L., "The Public Career of William Lowndes Yancey," 16 *Ala. R.* 200–12 (1963).

——. Venable, Austin L., "William L. Yancey's Transition from Unionism to State Rights," 10 *J.S.H.* 331–42 (1944).

YATES, RICHARD. Northrup, Jack, "Richard Yates: A Personal Glimpse of the Illinois Soldier's Friend," 56 *J.I.S.H.S.* 121–38 (1963).

——. Yates, Richard, and Catherine Y. Pickering, *Richard Yates: Civil War Governor*, ed. John H. Krenkel (1966).

A GROWING NATION

There is an enormous literature on the economic and social changes that affected the United States in the 1850's; only a small sampling can be attempted here. Works dealing with the ante-bellum South are reserved for later discussion. Note, too, that there is much information contained in the biographies of key industrialists and businessmen—e.g., Jay Cooke, Abram S. Hewitt, and Cornelius Vanderbilt.

The best general treatment of the social and cultural developments of the period remains Arthur C. Cole, *The Irrepressible Conflict.* A work of great insight is Thomas C. Cochran and William Miller, *The Age of Enterprise* (1940). George R. Taylor, *The Transportation Revolution, 1815–1860* (1951), is comprehensive and perceptive. Stuart Bruchey, *The Roots of American Economic Growth* (1965), is an admirable synthesis of recent scholarship. More technical, but provocative and useful, are two books by Douglass C. North: *The Economic Growth of the United States, 1790–1860* (1961), and *Growth and Welfare in the American Past* (1966). For economic theory during the ante-bellum period see Joseph Dorfman, *The Economic Mind in American Civilization, 1606–1918* (3 v., 1949). A vast body of source materials relating to almost every aspect of American economic life can be found in John R. Commons and others, eds., *A Documentary History of American Industrial Society* (10 v., 1910–11).

For any serious economic or demographic study the United States census reports are indispensable. See also the invaluable compilation, *Historical Statistics of the United States: Colonial Times to 1957* (1960). Charles O. Paullin's *Atlas of the Historical Geography of the United States,* previously cited, contains numerous useful maps on economic and social changes.

For business cycles that so profoundly affected the American economy see Walter B. Smith and Arthur H. Cole, *Fluctuations in American Business, 1790–1860* (1935). Also useful are Arthur H. Cole, *Wholesale Commodity Prices in the United States, 1700–1861* (1938), and Robert F. Martin, *National Income in the United States, 1799–1938* (1939). George W. Van Vleck, *The Panic of 1857* (1943), is inadequate. Edgar W. Martin, *The Standard of Living in 1860* (1942), is valuable.

Emory R. Johnson and others, *History of Domestic and Foreign Commerce of the United States* (2 v., 1915), is a standard work, as is Caroline E. MacGill and others, *History of Transportation in the United States before 1860* (1917). Seymour Dunbar, *A History of Travel in America* (4 v., 1915), is popular and readable. For conflicting views of the impact of the railroads on the American economy see Albert Fishlow, *American Railroads and the Transformation of the Ante-Bellum Economy* (1965), and Robert W. Fogel, *Railroads and American Economic Growth* (1964). Two local studies of special significance are Charles H. Ambler, *A History of Transportation in the Ohio Valley* (1932), and Louis C. Hunter, *Steamboats on the Western Rivers* (1949). Alfred D. Chandler, Jr., ed., *The Railroads: The Nation's First Big Business* (1965), is a thoughtfully edited collection of documents.

Victor S. Clark, *History of Manufactures in the United States* (3 v., 1929), is an invaluable compendium. Arthur H. Cole, *The American Wool Manufacture* (2 v., 1926), is a model history. On cotton manufacturing see Caroline F. Ware's thorough *The Early New England Cotton Manufacture* (1931) and Hannah Josephson's lively *The Golden Threads* (1949). Waldemar Kaempffert, ed., *A Popular History of American Invention* (2 v., 1924), is superficial; it should be supplemented by Dirk J. Struik, *Yankee Science in the Making* (1948).

Bray Hammond, *Banks and Politics in America* (1957), is a masterly study which replaces all previous works in its field. It can be supplemented at points, however, by Fritz Redlich, *The Molding of American Banking* (2 v., 1947–51).

The relation of the government to the American economy has been repeatedly analyzed. Still standard are Davis R. Dewey, *Financial History of the United States* (1903), and F. W. Taussig, *The Tariff History of the United States* (5th ed., 1910). Fuller on the Civil War era is Edward Stanwood, *American Tariff Controversies in the Nineteenth Century* (2 v., 1904). See also Richard Hofstadter, "The Tariff Issue on the Eve of the Civil War," 44 *A.H.R.* 50–55 (1938). Sidney Ratner, *Taxation and Democracy in America* (2nd ed., 1967), stands alone in its field. The myth of laissez-faire is effectively demolished in Carter Goodrich, *Government Promotion of American Canals and Railroads, 1800–1890* (1960), and in Goodrich's book of readings, *The Government and the Economy, 1783–1861* (1967). Four exemplary monographs deal with the relation between government and the economy in key states: Oscar and Mary F. Handlin, *Commonwealth* [Massachusetts]

BIBLIOGRAPHY 749

(1947); Louis Hartz, *Economic Policy and Democratic Thought* [Pennsylvania] (1948); Milton S. Heath, *Constructive Liberalism* [Georgia] (1954); and James N. Primm, *Economic Policy in the Development of a Western State* [Missouri] (1954). For other case studies see Harry H. Pierce, *Railroads of New York: A Study of Government Aid, 1826–1875* (1953); Merl E. Reed, "Government Investment and Economic Growth: Louisiana's Ante Bellum Railroads," 28 *J.S.H.* 183–201 (1962); Stephen Salsbury, *The State, the Investor, and the Railroad: The Boston and Albany, 1825–1867* (1967); and Harry N. Scheiber, *Ohio Canal Era: A Case Study of Government and Economy, 1820–1861* (1968). Daniel J. Elazar, *The American Partnership: Intergovernmental Co-operation in the Nineteenth-Century United States* (1962), deals with a neglected subject.

In the future analysis of all these economic developments will be easier because of the publication of *Trends in the American Economy in the Nineteenth Century* (1960), a massive and important work.

John R. Commons and others, *History of Labor in the United States* (4 v., 1918–35), is full and scholarly. Briefer treatments are Foster R. Dulles, *Labor in America* (1949), Joseph G. Rayback, *A History of American Labor* (1959), and Henry Pelling, *American Labor* (1960). Philip S. Foner, *History of the Labor Movement in the United States* (1947), has a left-wing bias. Norman Ware, *The Industrial Worker, 1840–1860* (1924), is an admirable monograph, by far the best treatment of this period of labor history. Also useful are William A. Sullivan, *The Industrial Worker in Pennsylvania* (1955), and Helene S. Zahler, *Eastern Workingmen and National Land Policy, 1829–1862* (1941).

The best general treatments of immigration are Oscar Handlin, *The Uprooted* (1951); Marcus L. Hansen, *The Atlantic Migration, 1607–1860* (1940); Maldwyn A. Jones, *American Immigration* (1960); and Carl Wittke, *We Who Built America* (1939). Three specialized studies are also of great importance: Rowland T. Berthoff, *British Immigrants in Industrial America, 1790–1950* (1953); Robert Ernst, *Immigrant Life in New York City, 1825–1863* (1949); and Oscar Handlin, *Boston's Immigrants, 1790–1880* (1959). See also Douglas T. Miller, "Immigration and Social Stratification in Pre-Civil War New York," 49 *N.Y.H.* 157–68 (1968).

Not enough attention has been given to the history of American cities. The best general treatments are Charles N. Glaab and A. Theodore Brown, *A History of Urban America* (1967); Constance M. Green, *American Cities in the Growth of the Nation* (1957); and Adna F. Weber, *The Growth of Cities in the Nineteenth Century* (1899), which is not confined to American history. Two valuable anthologies recapture the flavor of American urban life: Charles N. Glaab, ed., *The American City* (1963), and Wilson Smith, ed., *Cities of Our Past and Present* (1964). Among the outstanding histories of individual cities are Constance M. Green, *Holyoke, Massachusetts* (1939); Green, *Washington* (2 v., 1962–63); Blake McKelvey, *Rochester* (4 v., 1945–61); Bessie L. Pierce, *A History of Chicago* (3 v., 1937–57); and Bayrd Still, *Milwaukee* (1948). Stephan Thernstrom, *Poverty and Progress* (1964), is an enlightening study of social mobility in nineteenth-century Newburyport, Massachusetts.

Paul W. Gates, *The Farmer's Age* (1960), is an impressive, comprehensive work dealing with all aspects of agriculture in the period from 1815 to 1860. P. W. Bidwell and J. I. Falconer, *History of Agriculture in the Northern United States, 1620–1860* (1925), is authoritative. Reynold M. Wik, *Steam Power on the American Farm* (1953), is an illuminating monograph. Works on Southern agriculture are listed separately.

The literature on the West is extensive. The best general history, which contains an admirable bibliography, is Ray A. Billington, *Westward Expansion* (1949). Also useful are E. D. Branch's sprightly *Westward* (1930), Thomas D. Clark's accurate *Frontier America* (1959), and Robert E. Riegel's sober *America Moves West* (2nd ed., 1948). Ray A. Billington, *The Far Western Frontier, 1830–1860* (1956), is full and scholarly. The actual process of migration to the Northwest can be traced in Lois K. Matthews, *The Expansion of New England, 1620–1865* (1909), and in Stewart H. Holbrook, *Yankee Exodus* (1950). On the public lands the standard work is Roy M. Robbins, *Our Landed Heritage* (1942).

State and regional studies often offer valuable insights into the social and economic changes that were transforming the United States. For New England one must consult Samuel E. Morison, *The Maritime History of Massachusetts, 1783–1860* (1921); Edward C. Kirkland, *Men, Cities and Transportation* (2 v., 1948); and Harold F. Wilson, *The Hill Country of New England* (1936). On the Middle States Robert G. Albion, *The Rise of New York Port, 1815–1860* (1939), and Philip S. Foner, *Business and Slavery* (1941), are particularly useful. Of the many studies of the Old Northwest, the following are basic: John G. Clark, *The Grain Trade in the Old Northwest* (1966); A. L. Kohlmeier, *The Old Northwest as the Keystone of the Arch of American Federal Union* (1938); William A. Mabry, "Ante-Bellum Cincinnati and its Southern Trade," in David K. Jackson, ed., *American Studies in Honor of William Kenneth Boyd* (1940), 60–85; Wyatt W. Belcher, *The Economic Rivalry between St. Louis and Chicago, 1850–1880* (1947); and, especially, Homer C. Hubbart, *The Older Middle West, 1840–1880* (1936). See also Morton Rothstein, "Antebellum Wheat and Cotton Exports: Contrasts in Marketing Organization and Economic Development," 40 *Agr. H.* 91–100 (1965).

On American thought in the pre-Civil War decades there are four excellent general treatments: Irving H. Bartlett, *The American Mind in the Mid-Nineteenth Century* (1967); Merle E. Curti, *The Growth of American Thought* (1943); Ralph H. Gabriel, *The Course of American Democratic Thought* (1940); and Vernon L. Parrington, *Main Currents in American Thought* (3 v., 1927–30). Literary and cultural developments can be traced in Robert E. Spiller and others, *Literary History of the United States* (3 v., 1948), and in Van Wyck Brooks, *Makers and Finders* (5 v., 1936–52). Oliver W. Larkin, *Art and Life in America* (1949), is a richly rewarding study. W. W. Sweet, *The Story of Religion in America* (rev. ed., 1939), is a standard but not a very perceptive work. On popular culture see Carl Bode, *The American Lyceum* (1956), and Bode, *The Anatomy of American Popular Culture, 1840–1861* (1959). A satisfactory history of American education is badly needed. E. P. Cubberley, *Public Education in the United States* (rev. ed., 1934), contains many useful facts, but for its severe limitations see Lawrence A. Cremin, *The Wonderful World of Ellwood Patterson Cubberley*

(1965). Students are more likely to learn about what really went on in the schools from Ruth M. Elson's delightful *Guardians of Tradition: American Schoolbooks of the Nineteenth Century* (1964). Frederick Rudolph, *The American College and University* (1962), is an excellent general account, largely replacing Donald G. Tewksbury, *The Founding of American Colleges and Universities, before the Civil War* (1932). See also Richard Hofstadter and C. DeWitt Hardy, *The Development and Scope of Higher Education in the United States* (1952), and Hofstadter and Walter P. Metzger, *The Development of Academic Freedom in the United States* (1955).

Alice F. Tyler, *Freedom's Ferment* (1944), is the best introduction to the various reform movements which swept the country before 1860. There is not space to discuss most of them here, but Miss Tyler's excellent bibliography will serve as an introduction to the literature on woman's rights, temperance, etc. A briefer interpretation is C. S. Griffin, *The Ferment of Reform, 1830–1860* (1967). Griffin's thesis that "moral stewardship" was the concept underlying reform receives further elaboration in his *Their Brothers' Keepers* (1960). John L. Thomas, "Romantic Reform in America, 1815–1865," 17 *Am. Q.* 656–681 (1965), is an outstanding essay. See also two useful anthologies: David B. Davis, ed., *Ante-Bellum Reform* (1967), and Lorman Ratner, ed., *Pre-Civil War Reform* (1967).

The best general account of the antislavery movement is Louis Filler, *The Crusade against Slavery, 1830–1860* (1960). More ambitious but less successful is Dwight L. Dumond's *Antislavery: The Crusade for Freedom in America* (1961); for critical appraisals of this work see reviews by David Donald in 77 *P.S.Q.* 273–76 (1962), and C. Vann Woodward in 31 *American Scholar* 312–27 (1962). Dumond's *A Bibliography of Antislavery in America* (1961), is an unannotated listing of sources used in his book. Readers unable to complete Dumond's massive work will find his views more concisely presented in his *Antislavery Origins of the Civil War in the United States* (1939). Like Dumond, Gilbert H. Barnes in *The Antislavery Impulse, 1830–1844* (1933), plays down the activities of Garrison and his following and stresses the constructive work of Weld and the Tappan brothers. Henry H. Simms, *Emotion at High Tide* (1960), is an attack upon all abolitionists. The biographies listed above of Birney, Child, Garrison, the Grimké sisters, Phillips, and Weld are essential for an understanding of the antislavery crusade. See also two collections of their own writings: William H. and Jane H. Pease, eds., *The Antislavery Argument* (1965), and Louis Ruchames, ed., *The Abolitionists* (1964).

In recent years a principal interest of historians has been in the ideas advocated by abolitionists. For background on this topic David B. Davis, *The Problem of Slavery in Western Culture* (1966), is invaluable, though it does not carry the story far into the nineteenth century. Many of the essays in Martin Duberman, ed., *The Antislavery Vanguard* (1965), deal with this subject, though some are marred by a present-minded identification of abolitionism with the civil rights movement of the 1960's. Staughton Lynd, *Intellectual Origins of American Radicalism* (1968), connects abolitionism with a long tradition of radical dissent in England and America. Other significant studies which deal with antislavery ideology and rhetoric are: J. Jeffrey Auer, ed., *Antislavery and Disunion, 1858–1861* (1963); David B. Davis, "The Emergence of Immediatism in British and American Antislavery Thought," 49 *M.V.H.R.* 209–30 (1962); John Demos, "The Antislavery Movement and the Problem of Violent 'Means,' " 37 *N.E.Q.* 501–26 (1964); Leon F. Litwack, "The Abolitionist Dilemma: The Antislavery Movement and the Northern Negro," 34 *N.E.Q.* 50–73 (1961); Anne C. Loveland, "Evangelicalism and 'Immediate Emancipation' in American Antislavery Thought," 32 *J.S.H.* 172–88 (1966); and William H. and Jane H. Pease, "Antislavery Ambivalence: Immediatism, Expediency, Race," 17 *Am. Q.* 682–95 (1965).

Other historians have been more concerned with the social and institutional setting in which the abolitionists operated. Hazel C. Wolf, *On Freedom's Altar* (1952), conceived that antislavery leaders were motivated by a martyr complex. David Donald in *Lincoln Reconsidered,* 19–36, suggested that the abolitionists were a displaced elite. Robert A. Skotheim, in 25 *J.S.H.* 356–65 (1959), strongly criticized Donald's methods, and many of the contributors to Duberman, ed., *The Antislavery Vanguard,* deplored his conclusions. His interpretation was, however, upheld in Lawrence Lader, *The Bold Brahmins: New England's War against Slavery, 1831–1863* (1961). Meanwhile, Stanley M. Elkins, *Slavery,* 140–222, presented a view of abolitionists somewhat parallel to Donald's. It comes under vigorous attack in Aileen Kraditor, *Means and Ends in American Abolitionism* (1969). For other essays relating to these controversies see Robert W. Doherty, "Status Anxiety and American Reform: Some Alternatives," 19 *Am. Q.* 329–37 (1967); Martin B. Duberman, "The Abolitionists and Psychology," 47 *J.N.H.* 183–91 (1962); Betty Fladeland, "Who Were the Abolitionists?" 49 *J.N.H.* 99–115 (1964); and Staughton Lynd, "Rethinking Slavery and Reconstruction," 50 *J.N.H.* 198–209 (1965).

There are four full-length studies of the underground railroad: William Breyfogle, *Make Free* (1958); Henrietta Buckmaster, *Let My People Go* (1941); Wilbur H. Siebert, *Underground Railroad from Slavery to Freedom* (1899); and Horatio T. Strother, *The Underground Railroad in Connecticut* (1962). The findings of all four authors are strongly questioned in Larry Gara, *The Liberty Line: The Legend of the Underground Railroad* (1961).

Among much other valuable material on the antislavery movement there is here space to list only a few of the most important titles: Julian P. Bretz, "The Economic Background of the Liberty Party," 34 *A.H.R.* 250–64 (1929); Merton L. Dillon, "The Failure of the American Abolitionists," 25 *J.S.H.* 159–77 (1959); Benjamin Quarles, "Sources of Abolitionist Income," 32 *M.V.H.R.* 63–76 (1945); Russel B. Nye, *Fettered Freedom: Civil Liberties and the Slavery Controversy, 1830–1860* (2nd ed., 1964); Henry H. Simms, "A Critical Analysis of Abolition Literature, 1830–1840," 6 *J.S.H.* 368–82 (1940); and Lorenzo D. Turner, *Antislavery Sentiment in American Literature Prior to 1865* (1929).

The attitude of the clergy toward antislavery and other reform movements has been fully explored in John R. Bodo, *The Protestant Clergy and Public Issues, 1812–1848* (1954); Charles C. Cole, Jr., *The Social Ideas of the Northern Evangelists, 1826–1860* (1954); Donald G. Mathews, *Slavery and Methodism* (1965); and Timothy L. Smith, *Revivalism and Social Reform in*

Mid-Nineteenth Century America (1957). Whitney R. Cross, *The Burned-Over District* (1950), which integrates reform movements in upper New York state with concomitant social and economic changes, is a model study.

The best study of nativism, and particularly of the Know-Nothing movement, is Ray A. Billington, *The Protestant Crusade, 1800–1860* (1938). See also Billington, "The Know-Nothing Uproar," 10 *Am. Heritage,* 58–61 ff. (Feb., 1959). A popular, readable account is Carleton Beals, *Brass-Knuckle Crusade* (1960). Oscar Handlin's *Boston's Immigrants* is invaluable. W. Darrell Overdyke, *The Know-Nothing Party in the South* (1950), is a useful work. Other valuable studies include: Max Berger, "The Irish Emigrant and American Nativism," 70 *Pa. M. H. B.* 146–60 (1946); W. G. Bean, "Puritan Versus Celt, 1850–1860," 7 *N.E.Q.* 70–80 (1934); James H. Broussard, "Some Determinants of Know-Nothing Electoral Strength in the South, 1856," 7 *La. H.* 5–20 (1966); Harry J. Carman and Reinhard H. Luthin, "Some Aspects of the Know-Nothing Movement Reconsidered," 39 *S.A.Q.* 213–34 (1940); David B. Davis, "Some Ideological Functions of Prejudice in Ante-Bellum America," 15 *Am. Q.* 115–25 (1963); George H. Haynes, "A Chapter from the Local History of Knownothingism," 15 *New Eng. Mag.* 82–96 (1896–97); Haynes, "A Know Nothing Legislature," *Ann. Rep., A.H.A.,* 1896, I, 177–87; Ira M. Leonard, "The Rise and Fall of the American Republican Party in New York City, 1843–45," 50 *N.Y.H.* 151–92 (1966); Larry A. Rand, "The Know-Nothing Party in Rhode Island," 23 *R.I.H.* 102–16 (1964); Philip M. Rice, "The Know-Nothing Party in Virginia, 1854–1856," 55 *Va. M. H. B.* 61–75, 159–69 (1947); Louis D. Scisco, *Political Nativism in New York State* (1901); Leon C. Soule, *The Know Nothing Party in New Orleans* (1961); Arthur W. Thompson, "Political Nativism in Florida, 1848–1860: A Phase of Anti-Secessionism," 15 *J.S.H.* 39–65 (1949); and Ralph A. Wooster, "An Analysis of the Texas Know Nothings," 70 *Sw. H. Q.* 414–23 (1967).

THE OLD SOUTH

The literature on the ante-bellum South is extensive, and much of it is highly specialized. One way to approach it is through the historiography of the South. Wendell H. Stephenson's *The South Lives in History* (1955) and *Southern History in the Making* (1964) offer astute appraisals of some of the section's principal historians. For a superior guide to more recent scholarship see Arthur S. Link and Rembert W. Patrick, eds., *Writing Southern History* (1965); the essays on the historiography of the Old South by James C. Bonner, Herbert J. Doherty, Jr., and Charles E. Cauthen and Lewis P. Jones are highly recommended.

J. A. C. Chandler and others, *The South in the Building of the Nation* (12 v., 1909–10), is the fullest general history, but its scholarship is outdated. Of the shorter general histories Clement Eaton, *A History of the Old South* (2nd ed., 1966), William B. Hesseltine and David L. Smiley, *The South in American History* (2nd ed., 1960); and Francis B. Simkins, *A History of the South* (1953), can be enthusiastically recommended. R. S. Cotterill, *The Old South* (1936), is particularly useful on economic matters. A brief, brilliant interpretation is William E. Dodd, *The Cotton Kingdom* (1919). Clement Eaton, *The Growth of Southern Civilization* (1961), is a scholarly and balanced study, strongly emphasizing social and cultural developments. Charles S. Sydnor, *The Development of Southern Sectionalism, 1819–1848* (1948), is a profound, thoughtful book, by far the best account of the section in these crucial decades. Avery O. Craven, *The Growth of Southern Nationalism, 1848–1861* (1953), is less valuable on Southern internal developments but useful in appraising Southern reactions to national happenings. David M. Potter, *The South and the Sectional Conflict* (1968), is a collection of essays, united by the author's lively intelligence and his mastery of other social science disciplines. Six provocative interpretations of Southern history are: Thomas P. Govan, "Was the Old South Different?" 21 *J.S.H.* 447–55 (1955); U. B. Phillips, "The Central Theme of Southern History," 34 *A.H.R.* 30–43 (1928); Francis B. Simkins, *The Everlasting South* (1963); Earl E. Thorpe, *Eros and Freedom in Southern Life and Thought* (1967); T. Harry Williams, *Romance and Realism in Southern Politics* (1961); and C. Vann Woodward, "The Irony of Southern History," 19 *J.S.H.* 3–19 (1953). Also stimulating are the essays in Charles G. Sellers, Jr., ed., *The Southerner as American* (1960), and Frank E. Vandiver, ed., *The Idea of the South* (1964).

On the ante-bellum Southern economy the most accessible contemporary source is J. D. B. De Bow, *The Industrial Resources of the Southern and Western States* (3 v., 1852–53), composed of articles previously published in the influential *De Bow's Review*. The classic travel account is that by Frederick L. Olmsted, *The Cotton Kingdom;* the best edition is that with an introduction by Arthur M. Schlesinger (1953). For other travelers in the ante-bellum South see Thomas D. Clark, ed., *The Ante Bellum South, 1825–1860: Cotton, Slavery, and Conflict* (*Travels in the Old South: A Bibliography*, III, 1959). Laura A. White, "The South in the 1850's as Seen by British Consuls," 1 *J.S.H.* 29–48 (1935), is fresh and informative. Of the many contemporary accounts three merit special notice: Hinton R. Helper, *The Impending Crisis of the South* (1857; new ed. with introduction by George Fredrickson, 1968), a devastating critique by a Southern poor white; Daniel R. Hundley, *Social Relations in Our Southern States* (1860), one of the few books to achieve an understanding of the complex social structure of the region; and Thomas P. Kettell, *Southern Wealth and Northern Profits* (new ed. 1965, with introduction by Fletcher M. Green), which stresses the colonial economic status of the South. Two anthologies of contemporary materials deserve mention: Katharine M. Jones, ed., *The Plantation South* (1957), and Willard Thorp, ed., *A Southern Reader* (1955).

The classic account of the ante-bellum society and economy is Ulrich B. Phillips, *Life and Labor in the Old South* (1929), distinguished alike for its broad research and its felicitous style. In recent years Phillips's views have come under increasing attack. Richard Hofstadter, "U. B. Phillips and the Plantation Legend," 29 *J.N.H.* 109–24 (1944), R. F. Kugler, "U. B. Phillips' Use of Sources," 47 *J.N.H.* 153–68 (1962), and Sam E. Salem, "U. B. Phillips and the Scientific Tradition," 44 *Ga. H. Q.* 172–85 (1960), criticize his methodology, while Frank L. Owsley and a series of his students, using manuscript census returns, claim that Phillips ignored the prosperous agricultural middle class of the South. Owsley's views may be found in his *Plain Folk of the Old South* (1949) and in two articles written in collaboration with Harriet C. Owsley: "The Economic Basis of Society in the Late Ante-Bellum South," 6 *J.S.H.* 24–45 (1940); and "The Economic Structure of Rural Tennessee, 1850–1860," 8 *J.S.H.* 161–82 (1942). Studies by Owsley's students include Blanche H. Clark, *The Tennessee Yeoman, 1840–1860* (1942); Harry L. Coles, "Some Notes on Slaveownership and Landownership in Louisiana, 1850–1860," 9 *J.S.H.* 381–93 (1943); and Herbert Weaver, *Mississippi Farmers, 1850–1860* (1945). A powerful attack on Owsley's statistical competence is contained in Fabian Linden, "Economic Democracy in the Slave South," 31 *J.N.H.* 140–89 (1946). Robert R. Russel, "The Effects of Slavery upon Nonslaveholders in the Ante Bellum South," 15 *Agr. H.* 112–26 (1941), tends to agree with the Owsley view; James C. Bonner, "Profile of a Late Ante-Bellum Community," 49 *A.H.R.* 663–80 (1944), and Roger W. Shugg, *Origins of Class Struggle in Louisiana* (1939), tend to refute Owsley's findings.

The most recent major reinterpretation of the Southern social order is Eugene D. Genovese's thought-provoking *The Political Economy of Slavery* (1965), which shares the views, though not the values, presented in Phillips's work. Like Phillips, Genovese argues that the South had "a social system and a civilization with a distinct class structure, political community, economy, ideology, and set of psychological patterns" that made it different from the rest of the country.

On the Southern poor white (as distinguished from Owsley's "yeoman" farmer) see Paul H. Buck, "The Poor Whites of the Ante-Bellum South," 31 *A.H.R.* 41–54 (1925), and Shields McIlwaine, *The Southern Poor-White* (1939).

Lewis C. Gray, *History of Agriculture in the Southern United States to 1860* (2 v., 1933), is a magisterial study of great importance. For studies of individual crops see Stuart Bruchey, ed., *Cotton and the Growth of the American Economy, 1790–1860* (1967); David L. Cohn, *The Life and Times of King Cotton* (1956); Harold D. Woodman, *King Cotton and His Retainers* (1968); Donald L. Kemmerer, "The Pre-Civil War South's Leading Crop, Corn," 23 *Agr. H.* 236–39 (1949); James F. Hopkins, *A History of the Hemp Industry in Kentucky* (1951); J. Carlyle Sitterson, *Sugar Country* (1953); Joseph C. Robert, *The Tobacco Kingdom* (1938); and Robert, *The Story of Tobacco in America* (1949).

Agricultural methods are discussed by L. C. Gray and in William C. Bagley, Jr., *Soil Exhaustion and the Civil War* (1942), and in Avery O. Craven, *Soil Exhaustion as a Factor in the Agricultural History of Virginia and Maryland, 1606–1860* (1925). Efforts to reform Southern farming practices are presented in James C. Bonner, "Genesis of Agricultural Reform in the Cotton Belt," 9 *J.S.H.* 475–500 (1943), and in Craven's biography of Ruffin. For the view that these reforms were not, and could not be, successful, see Genovese, *The Political Economy of Slavery*, 124–53.

Several state studies round out the story of Southern agriculture: James C. Bonner, *A History of Georgia Agriculture, 1732–1860* (1964); Cornelius O. Cathey, *Agricultural Developments in North Carolina, 1783–1860* (1956);

Charles S. Davis, *The Cotton Kingdom in Alabama* (1939); John H. Moore, *Agriculture in Ante-Bellum Mississippi* (1958); and Alfred G. Smith, Jr., *Economic Readjustment of an Old Cotton State: South Carolina, 1820–1860* (1958).

Fully to understand Southern plantation life, one must at least sample the biographies and personal records of individual planters. The best collection is Ulrich B. Phillips, ed., *Plantation and Frontier,* being vols. I–II of John R. Commons and others, eds., *Documentary History of American Industrial Society.* For a charming memoir, see the biography of Thomas S. G. Dabney. Other valuable personal records include Edwin A. Davis, ed., *Plantation Life in the Florida Parishes of Louisiana, 1836–1846* . . . *the Diary of Bennett H. Barrow* (1943); J. H. Easterby, ed., *The South Carolina Rice Plantation as Revealed in the Papers of Robert F. W. Allston* (1945); Albert V. House, ed., *Planter Management and Capitalism in Ante-Bellum Georgia: The Journal of Hugh Fraser Grant, Ricegrower* (1954); Weymouth T. Jordan, *Hugh Davis and his Alabama Plantation* (1948); Ulrich B. Phillips and James D. Glunt, eds., *Florida Plantation Records from the Papers of George Noble Jones* (1927); J. Carlyle Sitterson, "Lewis Thompson, a Carolinian and his Louisiana Plantation, 1848–1888," in Fletcher M. Green, ed., *Essays in Southern History* (1949), 16–27; and Sitterson, "The William J. Minor Plantations," 9 *J.S.H.* 59–74 (1943).

William K. Scarborough, *The Overseer: Plantation Management in the Old South* (1966), attempts with considerable success to redeem the reputation of a much maligned element in Southern society.

On Southern transportation the standard work is Ulrich B. Phillips, *A History of Transportation in the Eastern Cotton Belt to 1860* (1908). See also James P. Baughman, "The Evolution of Rail-Water Transportation in the Gulf Southwest, 1836–1890," 34 *J.S.H.* 357–81 (1968); R. S. Cotterill, "The Beginnings of Railroads in the Southwest," 8 *M.V.H.R.* 318–26 (1922); Cotterill, "Southern Railroads, 1850–1860," 10 *M.V.H.R.* 396–405 (1924); and Merl E. Reed, *New Orleans and the Railroads* (1966).

The growth of Southern towns and cities deserves further attention from historians. See, however, the following very good studies: Gerald M. Capers, *Biography of a River Town: Memphis* (1939); Constance M. Green, *Washington: Village and Capital, 1800–1878* (1962); James D. Clayton, *Antebellum Natchez* (1968); and Robert C. Reinders, *End of an Era: New Orleans, 1850–1860* (1964). Richard C. Wade, *Slavery in the Cities: The South, 1820–1860* (1964), is also valuable. On the economic role played by the small town see Lewis E. Atherton, *The Southern Country Store, 1800–1860* (1949).

On Southern efforts to industrialize, see Lewis E. Atherton, "John McDonogh—New Orleans Mercantile Capitalist," 7 *J.S.H.* 451–81 (1941); Kathleen Bruce, *Virginia Iron Manufacture in the Slave Era* (1930); Philip G. Davidson, "Industrialism in the Ante-Bellum South," 27 *S.A.Q.* 405–25 (1928); Richard W. Griffin and Diffee W. Standard, "The Cotton Textile Industry in Ante-Bellum North Carolina . . . 1830–1860," 34 *N.C.H.R.* 131–64 (1957); Ernest M. Lander, Jr., "Charleston: Manufacturing Center of the Old South," 26 *J.S.H.* 330–51 (1960); Lander, "The Iron Industry in Ante-Bellum South Carolina," 20 *J.S.H.* 337–55 (1954); Fabian Linden, "Repercussions of Manufacturing in the Ante-Bellum South," 17 *N.C.H.R.* 313–31 (1940); Theodore R. Marmor, "Anti-Industrialism and the Old South: The Agrarian Perspective of John C. Calhoun," 9 *Comp. Stud. in Soc. and Hist.* 377–406 (1967); Thomas P. Martin, ed., "The Advent of William Gregg and the Graniteville Company," 11 *J.S.H.* 389–423 (1945); John H. Moore, "Mississippi's Ante-Bellum Textile Industry," 16 *J. Miss. H.* 81–98 (1954); Norris W. Preyer, "The Historian, the Slave, and the Ante-Bellum Textile Industry," 46 *J.N.H.* 67–82 (1961); Leonard P. Stavisky, "Industrialism in Ante Bellum Charleston," 36 *J.N.H.* 302–22 (1951). See also Dew's biography of Anderson and Mitchell's life of Gregg. Genovese, in *The Political Economy of Slavery,* 180–239, argues that these efforts to industrialize the Old South were doomed to failure.

For the westward movement of the Southern population before the war see Barnes F. Lathrop, "Migration into East Texas, 1835–1860," 52 *Sw. H. Q.* 1–31, 184–208, 325–48 (1948–49); William O. Lynch, "The Westward Flow of Southern Colonists before 1861," 9 *J.S.H.* 303–27 (1943); Tommy W. Rogers, "The Great Population Exodus from South Carolina, 1850–1860," 68 *S.C.M.H.* 14–21 (1967); Rogers, "Migration Patterns of Alabama's Population, 1850 and 1860," 28 *Ala. H. Q.* 45–50 (1966); and Frank L. Owsley, "The Pattern of Migration and Settlement on the Southern Frontier," 11 *J.S.H.* 147–76 (1945). Everett Dick, *The Dixie Frontier* (1948), is a vigorous account of life in the new, rough sections of the South.

A despised but vital function of the Southern economy is discussed in Frederic Bancroft, *Slave-Trading in the Old South* (1931). Wendell H. Stephenson, *Isaac Franklin, Slave Trader and Planter of the Old South* (1938), is a unique case study.

Five excellent studies of the way in which economic discontent shaped Southern sectional feeling are: Weymouth T. Jordan, *Rebels in the Making: Planters' Conventions and Southern Propaganda* (1958); Robert R. Russel, *Economic Aspects of Southern Sectionalism, 1840–1861* (1924); John G. Van Deusen, *The Ante-Bellum Southern Commercial Conventions* (1926); Van Deusen, *Economic Basis of Disunion in South Carolina* (1928); and Herbert Wender, *Southern Commercial Conventions, 1837–1859* (1930).

Both Eaton and Simkins offer good brief discussion of prewar Southern politics, and Sydnor and Craven give fuller accounts. See also biographies of major Southern statesmen, such as Albert G. Brown, John C. Calhoun, Henry Clay, Howell Cobb, Jefferson Davis, R. M. T. Hunter, Benjamin F. Perry, James M. Mason, Robert B. Rhett, Alexander H. Stephens, and Robert Toombs. William E. Dodd, *Statesmen of the Old South* (1911), uses three biographical sketches to trace the Southern road from "radicalism to conservative revolt." There is no book on the Democratic party in the South, but there are two excellent studies of the Whigs: Arthur C. Cole, *The Whig Party in the South* (1913), and Ulrich B. Phillips, "The Southern Whigs, 1834–1854," in *Essays . . . dedicated to Frederick Jackson Turner* (1910), 203–29. See also Charles G. Sellers, Jr., "Who Were the Southern Whigs?" 59 *A.H.R.* 335–46 (1954). In *Constitutional Development in the South Atlantic States, 1776–1860* (1930) and in "Democracy in the Old South," 12 *J.S.H.* 3–23 (1946),

Fletcher M. Green cogently argues that the South was becoming increasingly democratic.

Several state political studies are of great value. On Virginia one should consult Charles H. Ambler, *Sectionalism in Virginia from 1776 to 1861* (1910); Beverley B. Munford, *Virginia's Attitude Toward Slavery and Secession* (1910); Albert O. Porter, *County Government in Virginia* (1947); and Henry T. Shanks, *The Secession Movement in Virginia, 1847–1861* (1934). On North Carolina the best studies are: William K. Boyd, "North Carolina on the Eve of Secession," *Ann. Rep., A.H.A.,* 1910, 165–77; Clarence C. Norton, *The Democratic Party in Ante-Bellum North Carolina, 1835–1861* (1930); J. Carlyle Sitterson, "Economic Sectionalism in Ante-Bellum North Carolina," 16 *N.C.H.R.* 134–46 (1939); and Henry M. Wagstaff, *States Rights and Political Parties in North Carolina, 1776–1861* (1906). The special studies of South Carolina are particularly rewarding: Chauncey S. Boucher, "Sectionalism, Representation and the Electoral Question in Ante-Bellum South Carolina," *Wash. U. Stud.* IV, part 2, no. 1 (1916), and "The Secession and Coöperation Movements in South Carolina, 1848 to 1852," *Wash. U. Stud.* V, part 2, no. 2 (1918); Harold S. Schultz, *Nationalism and Sectionalism in South Carolina, 1852–1860* (1950); Nathaniel W. Stephenson, "Southern Nationalism in South Carolina in 1851," 36 *A.H.R.* 314–35 (1931); and Laura A. White, "The National Democrats in South Carolina, 1852 to 1860," 28 *S.A.Q.* 370–89 (1929). On Georgia politics one should read Horace Montgomery, *Cracker Parties* (1950); Paul Murray, *The Whig Party in Georgia, 1825–1853* (1948); and Ulrich B. Phillips, "Georgia and State Rights . . . ," *Ann. Rep. A.H.A.,* 1901, II, 3–224 (1902). The following studies deal with important Alabama political developments: Thomas B. Alexander *et al.,* "The Basis of Alabama's Ante-Bellum Two-Party System," 19 *Ala. R.* 243–76 (1966); Alexander *et al.,* "Who Were the Alabama Whigs?" 16 *Ala. R.* 5–19 (1963); Lewy Dorman, *Party Politics in Alabama from 1850 through 1860* (1935); Theodore H. Jack, *Sectionalism and Party Politics in Alabama, 1819–1842* (1919); Carlton Jackson, "The White Basis System and the Alabama Whiggery," 25 *Ala. H. Q.* 246–53 (1963); Allen W. Jones, "Party Nominating Machinery in Ante-Bellum Alabama," 20 *Ala. R.* 34–44 (1967); Malcolm C. McMillan, *Constitutional Development in Alabama, 1798–1901* (1955); and Grady McWhiney, "Were the Whigs a Class Party in Alabama?" 23 *J.S.H.* 510–22 (1957). On Mississippi see Percy L. Rainwater, *Mississippi: Storm Center of Secession, 1856–1861* (1938), and Donald M. Rawson, "Democratic Resurgence in Mississippi, 1852–1853," 26 *J. Miss. H.* 1–27 (1964). On Louisiana two useful works are Roger W. Shugg, *Origins of Class Struggle,* previously cited, and James K. Greer, "Louisiana Politics, 1845–1861," 12 *La. H. Q.* 381–425, 555–610 (1929), and 13 *ibid.* 67–116, 257–303, 444–83, 614–54 (1930). For Tennessee, see Thomas P. Abernethy, *From Frontier to Plantation in Tennessee* (1932); Mary E. R. Campbell, *The Attitude of Tennesseans toward the Union, 1847–1861* (1961); and Eric R. Lacy, *Vanquished Volunteers: East Tennessee Sectionalism from Statehood to Secession* (1965). On Missouri, consult John V. Mering, *The Whig Party in Missouri* (1967), and Jonas Viles, "Sections and Sectionalism in a Border State," 21 *M.V.H.R.* 3–22 (1934).

There is a rich literature about the cultural life of the Old South, which can only be suggested here. See the excellent bibliography in Curti, *Growth of American Thought,* 831–34. A brilliant interpretation is W. J. Cash, *The Mind of the South* (1941). More broad-ranging and more scholarly is Clement Eaton, *The Mind of the Old South* (rev. ed., 1967). See also Eaton's *The Civilization of the Old South* (1968), a collection of his most important essays, edited by Albert D. Kirwan. William R. Taylor, *Cavalier and Yankee* (1961), is a fascinating study of the South and the national character. Two important books emphasize the less happy aspects of Southern social and intellectual life: Clement Eaton, *The Freedom-of-Thought Struggle in the Old South* (rev. ed., 1964), and John H. Franklin, *The Militant South, 1800–1861* (1956). Rollin G. Osterweis, *Romanticism and Nationalism in the Old South* (1949), is useful but it rather overstates its principal thesis. Jesse T. Carpenter, *The South as a Conscious Minority, 1789–1861* (1930), is an acute study of Southern political theory.

For the various Southern defenses of slavery, see W. S. Jenkins, *Pro-Slavery Thought in the Old South* (1935). The serious student must also sample some of the contemporary polemical writings on this subject, e.g., J. D. B. De Bow, *The Interest in Slavery of the Southern Non-Slaveholder* (1860); E. N. Elliott, ed., *Cotton is King and Pro-Slavery Arguments* (1860); and George Fitzhugh, *Sociology for the South* (1854), and *Cannibals All!* (1857; new ed., with introduction by C. Vann Woodward, 1960). Eric L. McKitrick, ed., *Slavery Defended: The Views of the Old South* (1963), is a useful anthology. On the proslavery argument the following articles are important: Wilfred Carsel, "The Slaveholders' Indictment of Northern Wage Slavery," 6 *J.S.H.* 504–20 (1940); Alan Dowty, "Urban Slavery in Pro-Southern Fiction of the 1850's," 32 *J.S.H.* 25–41 (1966); Robert Gardner, "A Tenth-Hour Apology for Slavery," 26 *J.S.H.* 352–67 (1960); William B. Hesseltine, "Some New Aspects of the Pro-Slavery Argument," 21 *J.N.H.* 1–15 (1936); Ralph E. Morrow, "The Proslavery Argument Revisited," 48 *M.V.H.R.* 79–94 (1961); Lewis M. Purifoy, "The Southern Methodist Church and the Proslavery Argument," 32 *J.S.H.* 325–41 (1966); Kenneth M. Stampp, "An Analysis of T. R. Dew's *Review of the Debates in the Virginia Legislature,*" 27 *J.N.H.* 380–87 (1942); and Jeannette R. Tandy, "Pro-Slavery Propaganda in American Fiction of the Fifties," 21 *S.A.Q.* 41–50, 170–78 (1922). See also the biographical writings on Thomas R. Dew, George Fitzhugh, George F. Holmes, and Edmund Ruffin.

On Southern men of letters see the works by Van Wyck Brooks, Parrington, and Spiller, already cited, and also the biographies of J. P. Kennedy, A. B. Longstreet, and W. G. Simms. Jay B. Hubbell, *The South in American Literature, 1607–1900* (1954), is comprehensive. On Southern education, Edgar W. Knight, *Public Education in the South* (1922), is out of date, but his *A Documentary History of Education in the South before 1860* (5 v., 1949–53) is a mine of information. See also E. Merton Coulter's delightful *College Life in the Old South* (1928). Thomas C. Johnson, Jr., *Scientific Interests in the Old South* (1936), deals with a neglected aspect of the Southern mind. On Southern economic thought see Leiman's biography of J. N. Cardozo, already cited.

Seven articles, not easy to classify but all dealing with aspects of Southern culture, are especially provocative: James C. Bonner, "Plantation Architecture of the Lower South on the Eve of the Civil War," 11 *J.S.H.* 370–88 (1945); Guy A. Cardwell, "The Duel in the Old South: Crux of a Concept," 66 *S.A.Q.* 50–69 (1967); Herbert Collins, "The Southern Industrial Gospel before 1860," 12 *J.S.H.* 386–402 (1946); Clement Eaton, "Mob Violence in the Old South," 29 *M.V.H.R.* 351–70 (1942); Richard Shryock, "Cultural Factors in the History of the South," 5 *J.S.H.* 333–46 (1939); Charles S. Sydnor, "The Southerner and the Laws," 6 *J.S.H.* 3–23 (1940); and Paton Yoder, "Private Hospitality in the South, 1775–1850," 47 *M.V.H.R.* 419–33 (1960).

Several state and regional studies are very useful: Earl W. Fornell, *The Galveston Era: The Texas Crescent on the Eve of Secession* (1961); F. Garvin Davenport, *Ante-Bellum Kentucky* (1943) and *Cultural Life in Nashville on the Eve of the Civil War* (1941); Guion G. Johnson, *Ante-Bellum North Carolina* (1937) and *A Social History of the Sea Islands* (1930); Rosser H. Taylor, *Ante-Bellum South Carolina* (1942); and Jack K. Williams, *Vogues in Villainy: Crime and Retribution in Ante-Bellum South Carolina* (1959).

ANTE-BELLUM NEGROES IN SLAVERY AND IN FREEDOM

The best general history of the Negro in America is John H. Franklin's authoritative *From Slavery to Freedom* (3rd ed., 1967). An excellent shorter account is August Meier and Elliott Rudwick, *From Plantation to Ghetto* (1966). Saunders Redding, *The Lonesome Road* (1958), is episodic, and Benjamin Quarles, *The Negro in the Making of America* (1964), is brief. Richard Bardolph, *The Negro Vanguard* (1959), offers a perceptive study of Negro leadership. Oscar Handlin, *Race and Nationality in American Life* (1957), contains some provocative essays, and Thomas F. Gossett, *Race: The History of an Idea in America* (1963), William R. Stanton, *The Leopard's Spots* (1960), and J. C. Furnas, *Goodbye to Uncle Tom* (1956), are valuable on racial attitudes. Three useful documentary collections are: Herbert Aptheker, ed., *A Documentary History of the Negro People in the United States* (1951); Leslie H. Fishel, Jr., and Benjamin Quarles, eds., *The Negro American* (1967); and Gilbert Osofsky, ed., *The Burden of Race* (1967).

Four excellent and provocative introductions to the enormous literature on American Negro slavery are: Stanley M. Elkins, *Slavery* (1959), 1–26; Chase C. Mooney, "The Literature of Slavery," 47 *Ind. M. H.* 251–60 (1951); Kenneth M. Stampp, "The Historian and Southern Negro Slavery," 57 *A.H.R.* 613–24 (1952); and Bennett H. Wall, "African Slavery," in Arthur S. Link and Rembert W. Patrick, eds., *Writing Southern History* (1965), 175–97. See also David B. Davis's stimulating "Slavery," in C. Vann Woodward, ed., *The Comparative Approach to American History* (1968), 121–34. Allen Weinstein and Frank O. Gatell, eds., *American Negro Slavery* (1968), is a reader which includes many diverse interpretations.

Slaves tell their own story in B. A. Botkin, ed., *Lay My Burden Down* (1945), in Charles H. Nichols, *Many Thousand Gone: The Ex-Slaves' Account of Their Bondage and Freedom* (1963), and in Carter G. Woodson, ed.,

The Mind of the Negro as Reflected in Letters Written during the Crisis, 1800–1860 (1926). For a description of a little-used collection of such source materials see Norman R. Yetman, "The Background of the Slave Narrative Collection," 19 *Am. Q.* 534–53 (1967).

For many years the standard history of slavery was Ulrich B. Phillips, *American Negro Slavery* (1918), a work based upon vast research and characterized by sympathy toward the slaveholders. In recent years Phillips's views have come increasingly under attack, and Kenneth M. Stampp's authoritative *The Peculiar Institution* (1956) is a thorough-going refutation from a pronounced Northern point of view. Eugene D. Genovese has come strongly to Phillips's defense, writing a highly favorable introduction to a new edition of *American Negro Slavery* (1966), collecting and editing Phillips's scattered essays under the title, *The Slave Economy of the Old South* (1968), and publishing "Race and Class in Southern History: An Appraisal of the Work of Ulrich Bonnell Phillips," 41 *Agr. H.* 345–58 (1967). For evaluations of Genovese's attempts to rehabilitate Phillips, see the thoughtful comments by David M. Potter, Kenneth M. Stampp, and Stanley M. Elkins in 41 *Agr. H.* 359–72 (1967).

Meanwhile Stanley M. Elkins's *Slavery* has marked an attempt to change the ground of the argument by asking what effect slavery had upon the Negro's personality and by comparing American Negro slavery with servitude in other countries. It is clear that Elkins has overstrained his analogy between Southern slavery and life in the concentration camps of World War II; see George M. Fredrickson and Christopher Lasch, "Resistance to Slavery," 13 *C.W.H.* 315–29 (1967); Eugene D. Genovese, "Rebelliousness and Docility in the Negro Slave," 13 *C.W.H.* 293–314 (1967); and Mary A. Lewis, "Slavery and Personality," 19 *Am. Q.* 114–21 (1967). Elkins's call for comparative studies of slave systems has been met by Herbert S. Klein, *Slavery in the Americas: A Comparative Study of Virginia and Cuba* (1967), and Arnold A. Sio, "Interpretations of Slavery: The Slave Status in the Americas," 7 *Comp. Stud. in Soc. and Hist.* 289–308 (1965). In *The Problem of Slavery in Western Culture,* already cited, David B. Davis challenges Elkins's thesis that slavery in the United States was uniquely harsh.

The best local and state studies of slavery are: James C. Ballagh, *A History of Slavery in Virginia* (1902); John S. Bassett, *Slavery in the State of North Carolina* (1899); J. Winston Coleman, Jr., *Slavery Times in Kentucky* (1940); Lyle W. Dorsett, "Slaveholding in Jackson County, Missouri," 20 *Mo. Hist. Soc. Bull.* 25–37 (1963); Ralph B. Flanders, *Plantation Slavery in Georgia* (1933); Constance M. Green, *The Secret City: A History of Race Relations in the Nation's Capital* (1967); John S. Kendall, "New Orleans' 'Peculiar Institution,'" 23 *La. H. Q.* 864–86 (1940); Alton V. Moody, "Slavery on Louisiana Sugar Plantations," 7 *La. H. Q.* 191–301 (1924); Chase C. Mooney, *Slavery in Tennessee* (1957); Edward W. Phifer, "Slavery in Microcosm: Burke County, North Carolina," 28 *J.S.H.* 137–65 (1962); John Milton Price, "Slavery in Winn Parish," 8 *La. H.* 137–48 (1967); Walter Prichard, "Routine on a Louisiana Sugar Plantation under the Slavery Regime," 14 *M.V.H.R.* 168–78 (1927); Robert C. Reinders, "Slavery in New Orleans in the Decade before the Civil War," 44 *Mid-America* 211–20 (1962); James B.

Sellers, *Slavery in Alabama* (1950); Charles S. Sydnor, *Slavery in Mississippi* (1933); Joe G. Taylor, *Negro Slavery in Louisiana* (1963); Orville W. Taylor, *Negro Slavery in Arkansas* (1958); Rosser H. Taylor, *Slaveholding in North Carolina* (1926); Harrison A. Trexler, *Slavery in Missouri, 1804–1865* (1914); Edwin L. Williams, Jr., "Negro Slavery in Florida," 28 *Fla. H. Q.* 93–110 (1949). Of these, the works by Flanders, Mooney, Phifer, and Sydnor are outstanding. Richard C. Wade, *Slavery in the Cities: The South, 1820–1860* (1964), is an able and original study of the "peculiar institution" in Baltimore, Charleston, Louisville, Mobile, New Orleans, Norfolk, Richmond, St. Louis, Savannah, and Washington.

All these works contain information on the treatment of slaves. See also the excellent chapter in Nevins, *Ordeal of the Union,* I, 412–61. A special aspect of this subject is discussed in William D. Postell, *The Health of Slaves on Southern Plantations* (1951), and in Bennett H. Wall, "Medical Care of Ebenezer Pettigrew's Slaves," 37 *M.V.H.R.* 451–70 (1951). A vast amount of information on virtually every aspect of the slave system can be found in Helen T. Catterall, ed., *Judicial Cases Concerning American Slavery and the Negro* (5 v., 1926–37).

Too little attention has been given to nonagricultural employment of slaves. For exceptions, see S. Sydney Bradford, "The Negro Ironworker in Ante Bellum Virginia," 25 *J.S.H.* 194–206 (1959), and Kathleen Bruce, "Slave Labor in the Virginia Iron Industry," 7 *Wm. & M. Q.* 2 ser. 21–31 (1927). The works dealing with the industrialization of the South, listed above, also discuss the subject, at least in passing. The problem of the quasi-free slave, who was hired out, is treated in Clement Eaton, "Slave-Hiring in the Upper South," 46 *M.V.H.R.* 663–78 (1960), and in Richard B. Morris, "The Measure of Bondage in the Slave States," 41 *M.V.H.R.* 219–40 (1954). See also John H. Moore, "Simon Gray, Riverman: A Slave Who Was Almost Free," 49 *M.V.H.R.* 472–84 (1962).

Herbert Aptheker, *American Negro Slave Revolts* (1943), and Nicholas Halasz, *The Rattling Chains* (1966), are overstated accounts of discontent among slaves. That there was unrest, however, cannot be denied. Sometimes it took the form described in Raymond A. and Alice H. Bauer, "Day to Day Resistance to Slavery," 27 *J.N.H.* 388–419 (1942); sometimes it resulted in criminal action against the masters, as described in Marion J. Russell, "American Slave Discontent in Records of the High Courts," 31 *J.N.H.* 411–34 (1946). Rarely it erupted in the sort of conspiracies which are treated in Wendell G. Addington, "Slave Insurrections in Texas," 35 *J.N.H.* 408–34 (1950); Herbert Aptheker, *Nat Turner's Slave Rebellion, together with the Full Text of the So-called "Confessions" of Nat Turner* . . . (1966); William S. Drewry, *Slave Insurrections in Virginia* (1900); Drewry, *The Southampton Insurrection* (1900); Davidson B. McKibben, "Negro Slave Insurrections in Mississippi, 1800–1865," 34 *J.N.H.* 73–90 (1949); Charles S. Sydnor, "Slave Conspiracies in North Carolina," 5 *N.C.H.R.* 20–34 (1928); William W. White, "The Texas Slave Insurrection in 1860," 52 *Sw. H. Q.* 259–85 (1949); and Harvey Wish, "The Slave Insurrection Panic of 1856," 5 *J.S.H.* 206–22 (1939). Historians have difficulty in evaluating the factual basis for many of these alleged slave plots and conspiracies; for conflicting views on one of the most famous of these episodes see John Lofton, *Insurrection in South Carolina: The Turbulent World of Denmark Vesey* (1964), and Richard C. Wade, "The Vesey Plot: A Reconsideration," 30 *J.S.H.* 143–61 (1964).

Far too little has been written about the slave trade in the nineteenth century. See, however, W. E. B. DuBois, *The Suppression of the African Slave-Trade to the United States of America, 1638–1870* (1895); Peter Duignan and Clarence Clendenen, *The United States and the African Slave Trade, 1619–1862* (1963); Warren S. Howard, *American Slavers and the Federal Law, 1837–1862* (1963); and Daniel P. Mannix and Malcolm Cowley, *Black Cargoes: A History of the Atlantic Slave Trade, 1518–1865* (1962). Four essays dealing with the abortive attempt to reopen the slave trade are: Barton J. Bernstein, "Southern Politics and Attempts to Reopen the African Slave Trade," 51 *J.N.H.* 16–35 (1966); W. J. Carnathan, "The Proposal to Reopen the African Slave Trade in the South, 1854–1860," 25 *S.A.Q.* 410–29 (1926); Ronald Takaki, "The Movement to Reopen the African Slave Trade in South Carolina," 66 *S.C.H.M.* 38–54 (1965); and Harvey Wish, "The Revival of the African Slave Trade in the United States, 1856–1860," 27 *M.V.H.R.* 569–88 (1941). On the internal slave trade, see, in addition to Bancroft's *Slave-Trading* and Stephenson's *Isaac Franklin,* previously listed, Winfield H. Collins, *The Domestic Slave Trade of the Southern States* (1904), William T. Laprade, "The Domestic Slave Trade in the District of Columbia," 11 *J.N.H.* 17–34 (1926), and Charles H. Wesley, "Manifests of Slave Shipments along the Waterways, 1808–1864," 27 *J.N.H.* 155–74 (1942).

The profitability of slavery is a moot point among historians. U. B. Phillips gave a powerful argument against its profitability in *American Negro Slavery;* see also his "The Economic Cost of Slave Holding in the Cotton Belt," 20 *P.S.Q.* 257–75 (1905). Sydnor, in *Slavery in Mississippi,* also held that slavery brought in meager returns to the owners, as does Nevins in *Ordeal of the Union,* I, 462–97. Edward Saraydar, "A Note on the Profitability of Ante Bellum Slavery," 30 *So. Econ. J.* 325–32 (1964), reaches the same conclusion from an economist's point of view. Charles W. Ramsdell, "The Natural Limits of Slavery Expansion," 16 *M.V.H.R.* 151–71 (1929), argued that slavery was doomed because by the 1850's there was no territory into which it could profitably expand. Lewis C. Gray, *History of Agriculture in the Southern United States,* and Kenneth M. Stampp, *The Peculiar Institution,* oppose these conclusions. Further arguments that slavery was profitable can be found in Thomas P. Govan, "Was Plantation Slavery Profitable?" 8 *J.S.H.* 513–35 (1942); Alfred H. Conrad and John R. Meyer, "The Economics of Slavery in the Ante Bellum South," 66 *J. Pol. Econ.* 95–130 (1958); Robert W. Smith, "Was Slavery Unprofitable in the Ante-Bellum South?" 20 *Agr. H.* 62–64 (1946); and Richard Sutch, "The Profitability of Ante Bellum Slavery—Revisited," 31 *So. Econ. J.* 365–77 (1965). See also three articles by George R. Woolfolk: "Cotton Capitalism and Slave Labor in Texas," 37 *Sw. Soc. Sci. Q.* 43–52 (1956); "Planter Capitalism and Slavery," 41 *J.N.H.* 103–16 (1956); and "Taxes and Slavery in the Ante Bellum South," 26 *J.S.H.* 180–200 (1960).

The whole argument is carefully evaluated and the evidence reexamined in Harold D. Woodman, "The Profitability of Slavery: A Historical Perennial," 29 *J.S.H.* 303–25 (1963).

At the same time historians have disagreed as to the general effects of slavery upon Southern economic growth. For key statements on this issue see the symposium by Alfred H. Conrad, Douglas Dowd, Stanley Engerman, Eli Ginzberg, Charles Kelso, John R. Meyer, Harry N. Scheiber, and Richard Sutch on "Slavery as an Obstacle to Economic Growth in the United States," 27 *J. Ec. H.* 518–60 (1967); Stanley L. Engerman, "The Effects of Slavery upon the Southern Economy," 4 *Explorations in Entrepreneurial History* 2nd ser., 71–97 (1967); Robert Evans, Jr., "The Economics of American Negro Slavery," in *Aspects of Labor Economics* (1962), 183–256; John E. Moes, "Absorption of Capital in Slave Labor in the Ante-bellum South and Economic Growth," 20 *American Journal of Economics* 535–41 (1961); Robert R. Russel, "The General Effects of Slavery upon Southern Economic Progress," 4 *J.S.H.* 34–54 (1938); and Marvin Fischbaum and Julius Rubin, "Slavery and the Economic Development of the American South," 6 *Explorations in Entrepreneurial History,* 2nd ser., 116–27 (1968). For an intelligently edited collection of documents and readings on this topic see Harold D. Woodman, ed., *Slavery and the Southern Economy* (1966).

There are several rewarding studies of the free Negro in the South: J. Merton England, "The Free Negro in Ante-Bellum Tennessee," 9 *J.S.H.* 37–58 (1943); E. Horace Fitchett, "The Origin and Growth of the Free Negro Population of Charleston, South Carolina," 36 *J.N.H.* 421–37 (1941); John H. Franklin, *The Free Negro in North Carolina, 1790–1860* (1943); Luther P. Jackson, *Free Negro Labor and Property Holding in Virginia, 1830–1860* (1942); Leon Litwack, "The Federal Government and the Free Negro, 1790–1860," 43 *J.N.H.* 261–78 (1958); John H. Russell, *The Free Negro in Virginia, 1619–1865* (1913); Donald J. Senese, "The Free Negro and the South Carolina Courts, 1790–1860," 68 *S.C.H.M.* 140–53 (1967); Annie L. W. Stahl, "The Free Negro in Ante-Bellum Louisiana," 25 *La. H. Q.* 300–96 (1942); Charles S. Sydnor, "The Free Negro in Mississippi before the Civil War," 32 *A.H.R.* 769–88 (1927); James E. Winston, "The Free Negro in New Orleans, 1803–1860," 21 *La. H. Q.* 1075–85 (1938); and James M. Wright, *The Free Negro in Maryland, 1634–1860* (1921). A unique document is the diary of a Mississippi free Negro: William R. Hogan and Edwin A. Davis, eds., *William Johnson's Natchez* (1951). See also the biography of Johnson, *The Barber of Natchez,* by Edwin A. Davis and William R. Hogan (1954).

Because of prevailing racial prejudice, the lot of the free Negro was little better in the North than in the South. For white racist attitudes see the studies by Eric Foner and Eugene H. Berwanger, cited below in the section called "Wedges of Separation," and those by V. Jacque Voegeli and Forrest G. Wood, cited below in the section on "The Negro in the Civil War." Leon F. Litwack, *North of Slavery* (1961), is the authoritative study of the living and working conditions of Negroes in the free states before the Civil War. See also Lee Calligaro, "The Negro's Legal Status in Pre-Civil War New Jersey," 85 *N.J.H.* 167–80 (1967); Elmer Gertz, "The Black Laws of Illinois," 56 *J.I.S.H.S.*

454–73 (1963); Arvarh E. Strickland, "The Illinois Background of Lincoln's Attitude toward Slavery and the Negro," 56 *J.I.S.H.S.* 474–94 (1963); and Sylvestre C. Watkins, "Some of Early Illinois' Free Negroes," 56 *J.I.S.H.S.* 495–507 (1963). Efforts of Negroes to band together in separate colonies are discussed in William H. and Jane H. Pease, *Black Utopia: Negro Communal Experiments in America* (1963).

WEDGES OF SEPARATION

The essays in William N. Chambers and Walter D. Burnham, eds., *The American Party Systems* (1967), help put the political developments of the 1850's in a broader framework. Using computers to analyze congressional roll-calls, Thomas B. Alexander in *Sectional Stress and Party Strength* (1967) and Joel H. Silbey in *The Shrine of Party* (1967) have emphasized the continuing strength of party ties even in a time of sectional bitterness. See also Silbey's "The Civil War Synthesis in American Political History," 10 *C.W.H.* 130–40 (1964), and his *The Transformation of American Politics, 1840–1860* (1967).

On the Compromise of 1850 the standard monograph is Holman Hamilton's excellent *Prologue to Conflict* (1964). See also Hamilton's three significant articles: "Democratic Senate Leadership and the Compromise of 1850," 41 *M.V.H.R.* 403–18 (1954); "Texas Bonds and Northern Profits," 43 *M.V.H.R.* 579–94 (1957); and "The 'Cave of the Winds' and the Compromise of 1850," 23 *J.S.H.* 331–53 (1957). Other important articles are: Herman V. Ames, "John C. Calhoun and the Secession Movement of 1850," 28 *Am. Antiquarian Soc. Proc.* (new ser.) 19–50 (1918); Robert P. Brooks, "Howell Cobb and the Crisis of 1850," 4 *M.V.H.R.* 279–98 (1917); Herbert D. Foster, "Webster's Seventh of March Speech and the Secession Movement, 1850," 27 *A.H.R.* 245–70 (1922); George D. Harmon, "Douglas and the Compromise of 1850," 21 *J.I.S.H.S.* 453–99 (1929); Frank H. Hodder, "The Authorship of the Compromise of 1850," 22 *M.V.H.R.* 525–36 (1936); Joseph H. Parks, "John Bell and the Compromise of 1850," 9 *J.S.H.* 328–56 (1943); and Robert R. Russel, "What Was the Compromise of 1850?" 22 *J.S.H.* 292–309 (1956). Also valuable are the biographies of Bell, Blair, A. G. Brown, Calhoun, Cass, Chase, Clay, Douglas, H. V. Johnson, Seward, Stephens, Taylor, Toombs, Webster, and Wilmot, listed in an earlier section.

On Southern sentiment during and immediately after the crisis see the state studies listed above under "The Old South" and, especially, Cole, *The Whig Party in the South*, and Craven, *The Growth of Southern Nationalism*. Other useful studies are: Herbert J. Doherty, Jr., "Florida and the Crisis of 1850," 19 *J.S.H.* 32–47 (1953); John T. Hubbell, "Three Georgia Unionists [Howell Cobb, A. H. Stephens, and Toombs] and the Compromise of 1850," 51 *Ga. H. Q.* 307–23 (1967); Horace Montgomery, "The Crisis of 1850 and its Effect on Political Parties in Georgia," 24 *Ga. H. Q.* 293–322 (1940); Farrar Newberry, "The Nashville Convention and Southern Sentiment of 1850," 11 *S.A.Q.* 259–73 (1912); Richard Shryock, *Georgia and the Union in 1850* (1926); and St. George L. Sioussat, "Tennessee, the Compromise of 1850, and the Nashville Convention," 2 *M.V.H.R.* 313–47

(1915). For Northern reactions see Morton M. Rosenberg, "Iowa Politics and the Compromise of 1850," 56 *Iowa J. H.* 193–206 (1958), and David D. Van Tassel, "Gentlemen of Property and Standing: Compromise Sentiment in Boston in 1850," 23 *N.E.Q.* 307–19 (1950). Thomas O'Connor, *Lords of the Loom* (1968), describes the response of the conservative "Cotton Whigs."

On the Pierce administration as a whole see Nevins, *Ordeal of the Union,* Nichols, *Pierce,* and Spencer, *Marcy.* The problems of the Democratic party are well outlined in Roy F. Nichols, *The Democratic Machine, 1850–1854* (1923). On Southern political changes, see the works listed above under "The Old South." Party developments in key Northern states are traced in Donald, *Charles Sumner* (Massachusetts); Philip G. Auchampaugh, "Politics and Slavery, 1850–1860," 7 *Hist. of the State of N. Y.,* ed. by A. C. Flick, 63–97; Eugene H. Roseboom, *The Civil War Era, 1850–1873* [Ohio] (1944), 255–339; Roger H. Van Bolt, "Indiana in Political Transition, 1851–1853," 49 *Ind. M. H.* 131–60 (1953); Arthur C. Cole, *Era of the Civil War* [Illinois] (1919); and Erling Jorstad, "Personal Politics in the Origin of Minnesota's Democratic Party," 36 *Minn. H.* 259–71 (1959).

Nichols's *Pierce* is excellent on the foreign policy of the 1850's. See also A. A. Ettinger, *Mission to Spain of Pierre Soulé* (1932); Dexter Perkins, *Monroe Doctrine, 1826–1867* (1933); Basil Rauch, *American Interests in Cuba* (1948); L. B. Shippee, *Canadian-American Relations, 1849–1876* (1939); and Richard W. Van Alstyne, ed., "Anglo-American Relations, 1853–1857," 42 *A.H.R.* 491–500 (1937). Merle Curti, "Young America," 32 *A.H.R.* 34–55 (1926), William H. Goetzmann, *When the Eagle Screamed* (1966), Fred Somkin, *Unquiet Eagle* (1967), and A. K. Weinberg, *Manifest Destiny* (1935), treat the intellectual background to foreign policy.

The literature on the Kansas-Nebraska Act is large and controversial. The best guide to it, which also offers the most satisfactory explanation of the legislative history of the measure, is Roy F. Nichols, "The Kansas-Nebraska Act: A Century of Historiography," 43 *M.V.H.R.* 187–212 (1956). Nevins, *Ordeal of the Union,* gives a full analysis. Various views of Douglas's motives have been given in his biographies; see also Frank H. Hodder, "The Genesis of the Kansas-Nebraska Act," *Proc. St. Hist. Soc. of Wisc.,* 1912, 69–86 and "The Railroad Background of the Kansas-Nebraska Act," 12 *M.V.H.R.* 3–22 (1925); P. Orman Ray, *The Repeal of the Missouri Compromise* (1909); and Albert J. Beveridge, *Abraham Lincoln, 1809–1858* (1928). That issue now seems finally resolved with the publication of James C. Malin, "The Motives of Stephen A. Douglas in the Organization of Nebraska Territory: A Letter Dated December 17, 1853," 19 *Kans. H. Q.* 321–53 (1951). Malin's *The Nebraska Question, 1852–1854* (1953) is indispensable but difficult. For congressional debates on the Kansas-Nebraska bill, consult Robert R. Russel, "The Issues in the Congressional Struggle over the Kansas-Nebraska Bill, 1854," 29 *J.S.H.* 187–210 (1963). Also useful are the biographies of Bell, Benton, Cass, Chase, Douglas, Seward, and Sumner. Joseph H. Parks, "The Tennessee Whigs and the Kansas-Nebraska Bill," 10 *J.S.H.* 307–30 (1944), and Robert W. Johannsen, "The Kansas-Nebraska Act and the Pacific Northwest Frontier," 22 *Pac. H. R.* 129–42 (1953), are valuable. The fullest studies of transcontinental railroads as they affected politics are by Robert R. Russel: "The Pacific Railway

Issue in Politics Prior to the Civil War," 12 *M.V.H.R.* 187–201 (1925), and *Improvement of Communication with the Pacific Coast as an Issue in American Politics, 1783–1864* (1948).

Alice Nichols, *Bleeding Kansas* (1954), is a brief popular treatment of the incredibly complex history of Kansas during this period, but the serious student will learn more from Paul W. Gates, *Fifty Million Acres: Conflicts over Kansas Land Policy, 1854–1890* (1954), and from James C. Malin, *John Brown and the Legend of Fifty-Six* (1942). See also other biographies of Brown. An older general account is Leverett W. Spring, *Kansas: The Prelude to the War for the Union* (1885). On the New England Emigrant Aid Company see Horace Andrews, Jr., "Kansas Crusade: Eli Thayer and the New England Emigrant Aid Company," 35 *N.E.Q.* 497–514 (1962); W. H. Isely, "The Sharps Rifle Episode in Kansas History," 12 *A.H.R.* 546–66 (1907); Samuel A. Johnson, *The Battle Cry of Freedom* (1954); and Edgar Langsdorf, "S. C. Pomeroy and the New England Emigrant Aid Company, 1854–1858," 7 *Kans. H. Q.* 227–45 (1938). Other useful articles include Lester B. Baltimore, "Benjamin F. Stringfellow: The Fight for Slavery on the Missouri Border," 62 *Mo. H. R.* 14–29 (1967); Granville D. Davis, "Arkansas and the Blood of Kansas," 16 *J.S.H.* 431–56 (1950); Frank H. Hodder, "Some Aspects of the English Bill for the Admission of Kansas," *Ann. Rep. A.H.A.,* 1906, I, 201–10; Robert W. Johannsen, "The Lecompton Constitutional Convention: An Analysis of Its Membership," 23 *Kans. H. Q.* 225–43 (1957); Lloyd Lewis, "Propaganda and the Kansas-Missouri War," 34 *Mo. H. R.* 3–17 (1939); James C. Malin, "The Proslavery Background of the Kansas Struggle," 10 *M.V.H.R.* 285–305 (1923); Malin, "Judge Lecomte and the 'Sack of Lawrence,' May 21, 1856," 20 *Kans. H. Q.* 465–94, 553–97 (1953); Allan Nevins, "The Needless Conflict," 7 *Am. Heritage* 4–9 ff. (Aug., 1956); Floyd C. Shoemaker, "Missouri's Proslavery Fight for Kansas, 1854–1855," 48 *Mo. H. R.* 221–36, 325–40, and 49 *ibid.* 41–54 (1954); and Bernard A. Weisberger, "The Newspaper Reporter and the Kansas Embroglio," 36 *M.V.H.R.* 633–56 (1950).

It is impossible to understand the depth of emotion in the Northern outcry against Kansas-Nebraska without recognizing that it sprang not merely from a hostility toward slavery but in many cases from dislike and fear of the Negro. See Eric Foner, "Politics and Prejudices: The Free Soil Party and the Negro, 1849–1852," 50 *J.N.H.* 239–56 (1965); Foner, "Racial Attitudes of the New York Free Soilers," 46 *N.Y.H.* 311–29 (1965); Eugene H. Berwanger, *The Frontier Against Slavery: Western Anti-Negro Prejudice and the Slavery Extension Controversy* (1967); and Berwanger, "Western Prejudice and the Extension of Slavery," 12 *C.W.H.* 197–212 (1966).

The fullest account of the Sumner-Brooks affair is in Donald, *Charles Sumner and the Coming of the Civil War,* but see also the other biographies of Sumner.

Channing, Nevins, Rhodes, Schouler, and Von Holst all give accounts of the rise of the Republican party. The best general history is George H. Mayer, *The Republican Party, 1854–1964* (1964). Andrew W. Crandall, *The Early History of the Republican Party, 1854–1856* (1930) is now badly outdated. Consult the biographies of major Republican leaders, such as Banks, Blair,

Cameron, Chase, Frémont, Greeley, Grimes, Hale, McLean, Morgan, Stevens, Sumner, Trumbull, Wade, and Weed, and also the section titled "Lincolniana" below. For a lively, first-hand account of the 1856 nominations, see William B. Hesseltine and Rex G. Fisher, eds., *Trimmers, Trucklers & Temporizers: Notes of Murat Halstead from the Political Conventions of 1856* (1961). Among the special studies of significance on the 1856 campaign are: Fred H. Harrington, "Frémont and the North Americans," 44 *A.H.R.* 842–48 (1939); Jeter A. Isely, *Horace Greeley and the Republican Party* (1947); Clarence E. Macartney, "The First National Republican Convention," 20 *W. Pa. H. M.* 83–100 (1937); David S. Sparks, "The Birth of the Republican Party in Iowa, 1854–1856," 54 *Ia. J. H.* 1–34 (1956); Mildred C. Stoler, "The Democratic Element in the New Republican Party in Indiana," 36 *Ind. M. H.* 185–207 (1940); and Roger H. Van Bolt, "The Rise of the Republican Party in Indiana, 1855–1856," 51 *Ind. M. H.* 185–220 (1955).

For the political manifestations of nativism, so intimately related to the Republican party, see the bibliography for "A Growing Nation."

A HOUSE DIVIDING

The fullest and most vivid recreation of the 1857–1861 period is Allan Nevins, *The Emergence of Lincoln*. It should be supplemented by the excellent, more analytical account in Roy F. Nichols, *The Disruption of American Democracy* (1948).

On legal questions concerning slavery in the territories see Arthur Bestor, "State Sovereignty and Slavery: A Reinterpretation of Proslavery Constitutional Doctrine, 1846–1860," 54 *J.I.S.H.S.* 117–80 (1961); Mark DeWolfe Howe, "Federalism and Civil Rights," 77 *Mass. H. S. P.* 15–27 (1966); Allan Nevins, "The Constitution, Slavery and the Territories," in *The Caspar G. Bacon Lectures on the Constitution of the United States, 1940–1950* (1953), 95–141; and Robert R. Russel, "Constitutional Doctrines with Regard to Slavery in Territories," 32 *J.S.H.* 466–86 (1966). Further discussions may be found in Charles G. Haines and Foster H. Sherwood, *The Role of the Supreme Court in American Government and Politics, 1835–1864* (1957), and in Charles Warren, *The Supreme Court in United States History* (rev. ed., 2 v., 1947).

On the Dred Scott decision the standard monograph is Vincent C. Hopkins's admirable *Dred Scott's Case* (1951). Stanley I. Kutler, ed., *The Dred Scott Decision: Law or Politics?* (1967), is a useful collection of source materials. For an able review of the conflicting literature on this topic see Thomas B. Alexander, "Historical Treatments of the Dred Scott Case," *Proc. S. C. Hist. Assn.*, 1953, 37–60. Important articles include: Frederick S. Allis, Jr., "The Dred Scott Labyrinth," in *Teachers of History*, ed. H. Stuart Hughes (1954), 341–68; Philip G. Auchampaugh, "James Buchanan, the Court and the Dred Scott Case," 9 *Tenn. H. M.* 231–40 (1926); Helen T. Catterall, "Some Antecedents of the Dred Scott Case," 30 *A.H.R.* 56–71 (1924); Edward S. Corwin, "The Dred Scott Decision, in the Light of Contemporary Legal Doctrines," 17 *A.H.R.* 52–69 (1911); Walter Ehrlich, "Was the Dred Scott Case Valid?" 55 *J.A.H.* 256–65 (1968); Frank H. Hodder, "Some Phases of the Dred Scott Case," 16 *M.V.H.R.* 3–22 (1929); E. I. McCormac, "Justice

Campbell and the Dred Scott Decision," 19 *M.V.H.R.* 565–71 (1933); Richard R. Stenberg, "Some Political Aspects of the Dred Scott Case," 19 *M.V.H.R.* 571–77 (1933); Wallace Mendelson, "Dred Scott's Case—Reconsidered," 38 *Minn. Law Rev.* 16–28 (1953); and Carl B. Swisher, "Dred Scott One Hundred Years After," 19 *Jour. of Politics* 167–83 (1957). See also the biographies of Justices Campbell, Curtis, McLean, Taney, and Wayne. Appendix I of Nevins's *The Emergence of Lincoln,* II, 473–77, is particularly important.

On the Lincoln-Douglas debates see the subdivision "Lincolniana," which follows immediately. Also useful is Harry V. Jaffa, "Expediency and Morality in the Lincoln-Douglas Debates," *The Anchor Review,* No. 2 (1957), 179–204. Robert W. Johannsen, "Stephen A. Douglas, 'Harper's Magazine,' and Popular Sovereignty," 45 *M.V.H.R.* 606–31 (1959), deals with a sequel of the debates.

For John Brown's raid, consult the biographies of Brown and see Stephen B. Oates, "John Brown's Bloody Pilgrimage," 53 *Southwest Review* 1–22 (1968). Allan Keller, *Thunder at Harper's Ferry* (1958), is a vivid journalistic account. J. C. Furnas, *The Road to Harper's Ferry* (1959), is a more thorough-going exploration. For public reactions to the raid see C. Vann Woodward's perceptive essay in *The Burden of Southern History* (1960), 41–68, and John M. Ray, "Rhode Island Reactions to John Brown's Raid," 20 *R.I.H.* 97–108 (1961).

Other useful works on the late 1850's include W. G. Bean, "John Letcher and the Slavery Issue in Virginia's Gubernatorial Contest of 1858–1859," 20 *J.S.H.* 22–49 (1954); Ollinger Crenshaw, "The Speakership Contest of 1859–1860," 29 *M.V.H.R.* 323–38 (1942); Fred H. Harrington, "'The First Northern Victory' [Banks's election as speaker]," 5 *J.S.H.* 186–205 (1939); Robert W. Johannsen, *Frontier Politics and the Sectional Conflict: The Pacific Northwest on the Eve of the Civil War* (1955); Henry H. Simms, "The Controversy over the Admission of the State of Oregon," 32 *M.V.H.R.* 355–74 (1945); and Samuel Rezneck, "Depression and American Opinion, 1857–1859," 2 *J. Ec. H.* 1–23 (1942).

LINCOLNIANA

The literature about Abraham Lincoln is vast and of greatly varying quality; only a small selection of more significant works can be attempted here. The best bibliography is Jay Monaghan, ed., *Lincoln Bibliography, 1839–1939* (2 v., 1945), which is, however, all inclusive and therefore uncritical. For more selective lists see Paul M. Angle, *A Shelf of Lincoln Books* (1946), Ralph Newman, "Basic Lincolniana," 3 *C.W.H.* 199–208 (1957), and J. G. Randall, *Lincoln the President,* II, 343–400.

Any study of Lincoln must begin, and end, with his own writings. The definitive edition is that by Roy P. Basler and others, *The Collected Works of Abraham Lincoln* (9 v., 1953–55). For an appraisal of the technical merits of this edition, see the review by David Donald in 59 *A.H.R.* 142–49 (1953). Selections from Lincoln's writings are numerous; the best are Paul M. Angle and Earl S. Miers, eds., *The Living Lincoln* (1955), and Roy P. Basler, ed.,

Abraham Lincoln: His Speeches and Writings (1946). Though containing some spurious entries, Archer H. Shaw, ed., *The Lincoln Encyclopedia* (1950), is a convenient index to Lincoln's own words. For letters received by Lincoln, see David C. Mearns, ed., *The Lincoln Papers* (2 v., 1948).

Earl S. Miers, ed., *Lincoln Day by Day* (3 v., 1960), offers a full chronology of Lincoln's career; it is an invaluable tool.

Many important articles about Lincoln are contained in the Lincoln Centennial Association *Bulletins,* the Abraham Lincoln Association *Bulletins,* the *Papers* of the Abraham Lincoln Association, and, especially, the *Abraham Lincoln Quarterly.* Also highly valuable are the periodicals *Lincoln Lore, Lincoln Kinsman,* and the *Lincoln Herald.*

The best one-volume biography is Benjamin P. Thomas's *Abraham Lincoln* (1952), but Reinhard H. Luthin's *The Real Abraham Lincoln* (1960) is also excellent. John G. Nicolay and John Hay, *Abraham Lincoln: A History* (10 v., 1890), is the most complete multivolumed life. J. G. Randall, *Lincoln the President* (4 v., 1945–55; volume 4 completed by Richard N. Current), is both more selective and more critical. Carl Sandburg's *Abraham Lincoln: The Prairie Years* (2 v., 1926) and *Abraham Lincoln: The War Years* (4 v., 1939) together form the most flavorful and the most humanly interpretive of the Lincoln biographies. Albert J. Beveridge, *Abraham Lincoln, 1809–1858* (2 v., 1928), offers the fullest account of Lincoln's career in Illinois politics. Two useful anthologies are Paul M. Angle, ed., *The Lincoln Reader* (1947), and Courtland Canby, ed., *Lincoln and the Civil War* (1960).

Five books of essays deal with important and controversial aspects of Lincoln's career: O. Fritiof Ander, ed., *Lincoln Images* (1960); Richard N. Current, *The Lincoln Nobody Knows* (1958); David Donald, *Lincoln Reconsidered* (1956); Norman A. Graebner, ed., *The Enduring Lincoln* (1959); and J. G. Randall, *Lincoln the Liberal Statesman* (1947).

On Lincoln's ancestry, in addition to the biographies listed above, see W. E. Barton, *The Lineage of Lincoln* (1929) and *The Paternity of Abraham Lincoln* (1920); Marion D. Learned, *Abraham Lincoln: An American Migration* (1909); Waldo Lincoln, *History of the Lincoln Family* (1923); and Louis A. Warren, *Lincoln's Parentage and Childhood* (1926).

Material on Lincoln's childhood is sparse and generally unreliable. For a collection of reminiscences on this and other subjects, see Emanuel Hertz, ed., *The Hidden Lincoln* (1938). Louis A. Warren's *Lincoln's Youth . . . 1816–1830* (1960), is uncritical.

Lincoln's Illinois phase is much more elaborately documented. Benjamin P. Thomas, *Lincoln's New Salem* (rev. ed., 1954), is a charming book. Paul M. Angle's *"Here I Have Lived"* (1935) is a valuable history of Springfield in Lincoln's time. Lincoln's early career in the state legislature can be traced in William E. Baringer, *Lincoln's Vandalia* (1949), and in Paul Simon, *Lincoln's Preparation for Greatness* (1965). Harry E. Pratt, *The Personal Finances of Abraham Lincoln* (1943), is a mine of information. Lincoln's legal career is elaborately treated in John J. Duff, *A. Lincoln, Prairie Lawyer* (1960), John P. Frank, *Lincoln as a Lawyer* (1961), and Albert Woldman, *Lawyer Lincoln* (1936). See also Willard King, "Riding the Circuit with Lincoln," 6

Am. Heritage 48–49 ff. (Feb., 1955), and the biographies of David Davis and Herndon.

David Donald, *Lincoln's Herndon* (1948), is full on Lincoln's pre-presidential political activities. Donald W. Riddle's *Lincoln Runs for Congress* (1948) and *Congressman Abraham Lincoln* (1957) adequately cover their subject. Don E. Fehrenbacher, *Prelude to Greatness* (1962), is a major reinterpretation of Lincoln's re-emergence as a politician in the 1850's. See also William E. Baringer, *Lincoln's Rise to Power* (1937). On the Lincoln-Douglas debates one should read the full texts of the speeches in Edwin E. Sparks, ed., *The Lincoln-Douglas Debates of 1858* (1909), or in Paul M. Angle, ed., *Created Equal?* (1958). See also Arthur C. Cole, *Lincoln's "House Divided" Speech* (1923), Richard A. Heckman, *Lincoln vs Douglas: The Great Debates Campaign* (1967), and, especially, Fehrenbacher, *Prelude to Greatness* and Harry V. Jaffa, *Crisis of the House Divided* (1959).

For Lincoln's almost forgotten political activities in 1859, see Harry V. Jaffa and Robert W. Johannsen, eds., *In the Name of the People* (1959). The best monograph on Lincoln's role in the 1860 election is Reinhard H. Luthin's scholarly *The First Lincoln Campaign* (1944). William E. Baringer, *A House Dividing* (1945), is sprightly and informative on Lincoln as President-Elect. On Lincoln in the months after his election, see, in addition to the general works listed below, David M. Potter's authoritative *Lincoln and His Party in the Secession Crisis* (1942). The President's inaugural trip to Washington is chronicled in Victor Searcher, *Lincoln's Journey to Greatness* (1960). His rather ignominious entry into the capital can be followed in Norma B. Cuthbert, ed., *Lincoln and the Baltimore Plot* (1949), and Edward S. Lanis, "Allen Pinkerton and the Baltimore 'Assassination' Plot Against Lincoln," 45 *Md. H. M.* 1–13 (1950). John S. Tilley, *Lincoln Takes Command* (1941), is an unfriendly and unfair view of Lincoln's course in the Sumter crisis. Richard N. Current, *Lincoln and the First Shot* (1963), is balanced and scholarly.

After 1861 Lincoln's career tends to become identical with the history of the Union cause, and many of the works listed under special topics below are very useful. Note particularly the biographies of his leading contemporaries and of his cabinet members. Of course, the major Lincoln biographies by Luthin, Nicolay and Hay, Randall and Current, Sandburg, and Thomas continue to give full coverage to his war years.

On Lincoln's political role as President perhaps the best introduction is William B. Hesseltine, "Abraham Lincoln and the Politicians," 6 *C.W.H.* 43–55 (1960). Lincoln's relations with his cabinet are traced in Burton J. Hendrick, *Lincoln's War Cabinet* (1946), and in Clarence E. Macartney, *Lincoln and His Cabinet* (1931). Harry J. Carman and Reinhard H. Luthin, *Lincoln and the Patronage* (1943), shows the President as an adroit political manager. On Lincoln's struggle to achieve and maintain supremacy within his own party, three books are invaluable: William B. Hesseltine, *Lincoln and the War Governors* (1948); T. Harry Williams, *Lincoln and the Radicals* (1941); and William F. Zornow, *Lincoln and the Party Divided* (1954). Other significant works illustrating, in various ways, Lincoln's political astuteness are Arthur C. Cole, "Lincoln and the Presidential Election of 1864," *Trans. Ill. S.H.S.* 1917,

130–38, and "President Lincoln and the Illinois Radical Republicans," 4 *M.V.H.R.* 417–36 (1918); Winfred A. Harbison, "Lincoln and the Indiana Republicans, 1861–1864," 33 *Ind. M. H.* 277–303 (1937) and 34 *ibid.* 42–64 (1938); Earl S. Pomeroy, "Lincoln, the Thirteenth Amendment, and the Admission of Nevada," 12 *Pac. H. R.* 362–68 (1943); Milton H. Shutes, *Lincoln and California* (1943); and Vincent G. Tegeder, "Lincoln and the Territorial Patronage . . . ," 35 *M.V.H.R.* 77–90 (1948).

For Lincoln's efforts to shape military strategy Colin R. Ballard, *The Military Genius of Abraham Lincoln* (1926; rev. ed., 1952), and T. Harry Williams, *Lincoln and His Generals* (1952), are excellent. Clarence E. Macartney, *Lincoln and His Generals* (1925), is still useful. Robert V. Bruce, *Lincoln and the Tools of War* (1956), breaks new ground in showing Lincoln's minute attention to the details of Northern armament.

Jay Monaghan, *Diplomat in Carpet Slippers* (1945), is a vivid but somewhat overstated account of Lincoln's role in foreign policy. Albert A. Woldman, *Lincoln and the Russians* (1952), fully covers that topic. A. R. Tyrner-Tyrnauer, *Lincoln and the Emperors* (1962), deals principally with the President's relations with the Belgian and Austrian rulers.

On Lincoln's conception of his war powers and his relation to the Constitution the magisterial work is J. G. Randall, *Constitutional Problems under Lincoln* (rev. ed., 1951). It may be supplemented at points by David M. Silver, *Lincoln's Supreme Court* (1956).

Some idea of the abuse to which the President was subjected can be gained from Robert S. Harper, *Lincoln and the Press* (1951). George F. Milton, *Abraham Lincoln and the Fifth Column* (1942), shows how Lincoln dealt with subversives.

For Lincoln's personal life in the White House, in addition to John Hay's sprightly diary, one should read David H. Bates, *Lincoln in the Telegraph Office* (1907), Noah Brooks, *Washington in Lincoln's Time* (1895), Francis B. Carpenter, *Six Months at the White House* (1866), and Elizabeth Keckley, *Behind the Scenes* (1868). F. Lauriston Bullard, *Abraham Lincoln and the Widow Bixby* (1946), and John H. Cramer, *Lincoln under Enemy Fire* (1948), deal with two small but controversial subjects quite adequately. For Lincoln's Gettysburg address, see William E. Barton, *Lincoln at Gettysburg* (1930); J. W. Fesler, "Lincoln's Gettysburg Address," 40 *Ind. M. H.* 209–26 (1944); Robert Fortenbaugh, "Abraham Lincoln at Gettysburg . . . ," 5 *Pa. H.* 223–44 (1938); Allan Nevins, ed., *Lincoln and the Gettysburg Address* (1964); and Louis A. Warren, *Lincoln's Gettysburg Declaration* (1964).

Benjamin Quarles, *Lincoln and the Negro* (1962), is an excellent account of the President's changing views on race. William O. Douglas, *Mr. Lincoln and the Negroes* (1963), is superficial and inaccurate. In "Lincoln and Equal Rights," 32 *J.S.H.* 83–87 (1966), Ludwell H. Johnson challenges the authenticity of an alleged Lincoln letter pledging equal political and civil rights for the Negro. Harold M. Hyman, "Lincoln and Equal Rights for Negroes," 12 *C.W.H.* 258–66 (1966), attacks Johnson's conclusions but is effectively rebutted in Johnson's "Lincoln and Equal Rights: A Reply," 13 *C.W.H.* 66–73 (1967).

Lincoln's attitude toward his enemies is treated with sympathy and insight in J. G. Randall, *Lincoln and the South* (1946). W. M. Brewer, "Lincoln and the Border States," 34 *J.N.H.* 46–72 (1949), shows his tact in dealing with the Upper South. For two widely variant views of his plans for the postwar South, see Charles H. McCarthy, *Lincoln's Plan of Reconstruction* (1901), and William B. Hesseltine, *Lincoln's Plan of Reconstruction* (1960). Jonathan T. Dorris, *Pardon and Amnesty under Lincoln and Johnson* (1953), is an exhaustive treatment of a difficult subject.

For interpretations of Lincoln's political thought, see Gabor S. Borit, "Old Wine into New Bottles: Abraham Lincoln and the Tariff Reconsidered," 28 *Historian* 289–317 (1966); David Donald, *Lincoln Reconsidered*, 123–43; Richard Hofstadter, *The American Political Tradition and the Men Who Made It,* 92–134; Stanley Pargellis, "Lincoln's Political Philosophy," 3 *A.L.Q.* 275–90 (1945); Gerhard E. Mulder, "Abraham Lincoln and the Doctrine of Necessity," 66 *Lincoln Herald* 59–66 (1964); Vernon L. Parrington, *Main Currents in American Thought,* II, 152–60; Thomas J. Pressly, "Bullets and Ballots: Lincoln and the 'Right of Revolution,' " 67 *A.H.R.* 647–62 (1962); J. G. Randall, *Lincoln the Liberal Statesman,* 175–206; James A. Rawley, "The Nationalism of Abraham Lincoln," 9 *C.W.H.* 283–98 (1963); T. Harry Williams, "Abraham Lincoln: Principle and Pragmatism in Politics," 40 *M.V.H.R.* 89–106 (1953); and Edmund Wilson, "Abraham Lincoln: The Union as Religious Mysticism," in *Eight Essays* (1954). Richard N. Current, ed., *The Political Thought of Abraham Lincoln* (1967), is a useful anthology. Edward J. Kempf, *Abraham Lincoln's Philosophy of Common Sense* (3 v., 1965), is both ponderous and windy. For the development of Lincoln's literary style, see Herbert J. Edwards and John E. Hankins, *Lincoln the Writer* (1962).

On Lincoln's religion there are three excellent books: William E. Barton, *The Soul of Abraham Lincoln* (1920); Edgar D. Jones, *Lincoln and the Preachers* (1948); and William J. Wolf, *The Religion of Abraham Lincoln* (1963).

For contemporary letters and newspaper reports describing Lincoln, see Harry E. Pratt, ed., *Concerning Mr. Lincoln* (1944), and Herbert Mitgang, ed., *Lincoln as They Saw Him* (1956). Charles M. Segal, ed., *Conversations with Lincoln* (1961), is a collection of interviews with Lincoln.

On Lincoln's family the authoritative works are *Mary Lincoln: Biography of a Marriage* (1953) and *Lincoln's Sons* (1956), both by Ruth Painter Randall. William A. Evans, *Mrs. Abraham Lincoln* (1932), and Carl Sandburg and Paul M. Angle, *Mary Lincoln: Wife and Widow* (1949), are still useful.

Rather too much has been written about Lincoln's assassination. The best work is still David M. DeWitt, *The Assassination of Abraham Lincoln* (1909), but see also Jim Bishop, *The Day Lincoln Was Shot* (1955), George S. Bryan, *The Great American Myth* (1940), and the biographies of Booth and Fanny Seward. Otto Eisenschiml's *Why Was Lincoln Murdered?* (1937) and *In the Shadow of Lincoln's Death* (1940) contain much new data but are marred by an attempt to implicate Stanton in the assassination plot. The same can be said of Theodore Roscoe, *The Web of Conspiracy* (1960). Lloyd Lewis, *Myths after Lincoln* (1929), is a remarkable book.

The best guides to Lincoln historiography are Donald, *Lincoln's Herndon;*

D. E. Fehrenbacher, *The Changing Image of Lincoln in American Historiography* (1968); David M. Potter, *The Lincoln Theme and American National Historiography* (1948); J. G. Randall, "Has the Lincoln Theme Been Exhausted?" 41 *A.H.R.* 270–94 (1936); and, especially, Benjamin P. Thomas, *Portrait for Posterity* (1947). Roy P. Basler, *The Lincoln Legend* (1935), deals mostly with literary interpretations of Lincoln.

For pictures of Lincoln, see Charles Hamilton and Lloyd Ostendorf, *Lincoln in Photographs* (1963); Stephan Lorant, *Lincoln: A Picture Story of His Life* (1952); Frederick H. Meserve and Carl Sandburg, *The Photographs of Abraham Lincoln* (1944); and the biographies of Brady. Rufus R. Wilson, *Lincoln in Caricature* (1945), and F. Lauriston Bullard, *Lincoln in Marble and Bronze* (1952), also deserve mention.

THE ELECTION OF 1860

The election of 1860 is thoroughly treated in the general histories by Nevins and Channing and in Randall, *Lincoln the President*. Norman A. Graebner, ed., *Politics and the Crisis of 1860* (1961), is a collection of stimulating essays. See also the three following excellent monographs: Ollinger Crenshaw, *The Slave States in the Presidential Election of 1860* (1945); Emerson D. Fite, *The Presidential Campaign of 1860* (1911); and Luthin, *The First Lincoln Campaign*, cited above. There is much material also in the biographies of the several presidential hopefuls and candidates: Bates, Bell, Breckinridge, Cameron, Chase, Douglas, and Seward. For a vigorous firsthand account of the four nominating conventions read William B. Hesseltine, ed., *Three Against Lincoln: Murat Halstead Reports the Caucuses of 1860* (1960). On the Democratic conventions, see Owen M. Peterson, "The South in the Democratic National Convention of 1860," 20 *So. Speech Jour.* 212–23 (1955), and Austin L. Venable, "The Conflict between the Douglas and Yancey Forces in the Charleston Convention," 8 *J.S.H.* 226–41 (1942). On the Republican convention, consult P. Orman Ray, *The Convention That Nominated Lincoln . . .* (1916), and Glyndon G. Van Deusen, "Thurlow Weed's Analysis of William H. Seward's Defeat in the Republican Convention of 1860," 34 *M.V.H.R.* 101–104 (1947).

Economic issues in the campaign are discussed in Thomas D. Odle, "The Commercial Interests of the Great Lakes and the Campaign Issues of 1860," 40 *Mich. H.* 1–23 (1956), and in Thomas M. Pitkin, "Western Republicans and the Tariff in 1860," 27 *M.V.H.R.* 401–20 (1940). Something of the excitement of the campaign can be recaptured in William E. Baringer, "Campaign Technique in Illinois—1860," *Trans. Ill. S.H.S.*, 1932, 202–81, and in H. Preston James, "Political Pageantry in the Campaign of 1860 in Illinois," 4 *A.L.Q.* 313–47 (1947).

On the vexed question whether immigrants, and especially the Germans, supported the Republican ticket, see George H. Daniels, "Immigrant Vote in the 1860 Election: The Case of Iowa," 44 *Mid-America* 146–62 (1962); Andreas Dorpalen, "The German Element and the Issues of the Civil War," 29 *M.V.H.R.* 55–76 (1942); Paul J. Kleppner, "Lincoln and the Immigrant Vote," 48 *Mid-America* 176–95 (1966); Jay Monaghan, "Did Lincoln Receive the Illinois German Vote?" 35 *J.I.S.H.S.* 133–39 (1942); Joseph Schafer, "Who Elected Lincoln?" 47 *A.H.R.* 51–63 (1941); Donnal V. Smith, "The Influence of the Foreign-Born of the Northwest in the Election of 1860," 19 *M.V.H.R.* 192–204 (1932); and Robert P. Swierenga, "The Ethnic Voter and the First Lincoln Election," 11 *C.W.H.* 27–43 (1965).

For the Southern states in the 1860 election see, in addition to Crenshaw's monograph, Seymour M. Lipset, "The Emergence of the One-Party South— The Election of 1860," in his *Political Man* (1960), 344–54; Durward Long, "Economics and Politics in the 1860 Presidential Election in Alabama," 27 *Ala. H. Q.* 43–58 (1965); Long, "Political Parties and Propaganda in Alabama in the Presidential Election of 1860," 25 *Ala. H. Q.* 120–35 (1963); Jerry L. Tarver, "The Political Clubs of New Orleans in the Presidential Election of 1860," 4 *La. H.* 119–29 (1963); and David Y. Thomas, "Southern Non-Slaveholders in the Election of 1860," 26 *P.S.Q.* 222–37 (1911).

SECESSION AND THE SUMTER CRISIS

George H. Knoles, ed., *The Crisis of the Union, 1860–1861* (1965), consists of provocative essays on the secession crisis. The standard work on the secession of the Southern states is Dwight L. Dumond, *The Secession Movement, 1860–1861* (1931), which is ably supplemented by Dumond's *Southern Editorials on Secession*. Ralph A. Wooster, *The Secession Conventions of the South* (1962), is a careful statistical analysis of the membership in those bodies. The difficult question of popular support for secession is argued in William J. Donnelly, "Conspiracy or Popular Movement: The Historiography of Southern Support for Secession," 42 *N.C.H.R.* 70–84 (1965), and Ralph A. Wooster, "The Secession of the Lower South: An Examination of Changing Interpretations," 7 *C.W.H.* 117–27 (1961).

The biographies of Southern politicians help explain the actions taken by their states; see especially the lives of Bell, Breckinridge, A. G. Brown, J. E. Brown, Campbell, Howell Cobb, T. R. R. Cobb, Jefferson Davis, Houston, Memminger, Rhett, Ruffin, Stephens, Toombs, Robert Tyler, and Yancey. The various state studies, listed above under "The Old South," continue to be useful. In addition see: Thomas B. Alexander and Peggy J. Duckworth, "Alabama Black Belt Whigs during Secession," 17 *Ala. R.* 181–97 (1964); Dean A. Arnold, "The Ultimatum of Virginia Unionists: 'Security for Slavery or Disunion,' " 48 *J.N.H.* 115–29 (1963); William H. Brantley, Jr., "Alabama Secedes," 7 *Ala. R.* 165–85 (1954); T. Conn Bryan, "The Secession of Georgia," 31 *Ga. H. Q.* 89–111 (1947); Mary R. Campbell, "The Significance of the Unionist Victory in the Election of February 9, 1861, in Tennessee," *E. Tenn. Hist. Soc. Pubs.*, No. 14 (1942), 11–30; Willie M. Caskey, *Secession and Restoration of Louisiana* (1938); Charles E. Cauthen, "South Carolina's Decision to Lead the Secession Movement," 18 *N.C.H.R.* 360–72 (1941); Clarence P. Denman, *The Secession Movement in Alabama* (1933); J. Milton Henry, "The Revolution in Tennessee, February, 1861, to June, 1861," 18 *Tenn. H. Q.* 99–119 (1959); Milo B. Howard, Jr., ed., "A. B. Moore Correspondence Relating to Secession," 23 *Ala. H. Q.* 1–28 (1961); Lillian A. Kibler, "Unionist Sentiment in South Carolina in 1860," 4 *J.S.H.* 346–66

(1938); Durward Long, "Unanimity and Disloyalty in Secessionist Alabama," 11 *C.W.H.* 257–73 (1965); Robert J. Largent, "Virginia Takes the Road to Secession," 3 *W. Va. H.* 120–46 (1942); John A. May and Joan R. Faunt, *South Carolina Secedes* (1960); Van D. Odom, "The Political Career of Thomas Overton Moore, Secession Governor of Louisiana," 26 *La. H. Q.* 975–1054 (1943); Verton M. Queener, "East Tennessee Sentiment and the Secession Movement, November, 1860–June, 1861," *E. Tenn. Hist. Soc. Pubs.* No. 20 (1948), 59–83; Percy L. Rainwater, "An Analysis of the Secession Controversy in Mississippi, 1854–61," 24 *M.V.H.R.* 35–42 (1937); Henry T. Shanks, "Conservative Constitutional Tendencies in the Virginia Secession Convention," in Fletcher M. Green, ed., *Essays in Southern History,* 28–48; J. Carlyle Sitterson, *The Secession Movement in North Carolina* (1939); and James E. Walmsley, ed., "The Change of Secession Sentiment in Virginia in 1861," 31 *A.H.R.* 82–101 (1925).

Northern reactions to the Southern secession movement may be judged from Howard C. Perkins, ed., *Northern Editorials on Secession.* Kenneth M. Stampp, *And the War Came* (1950), is an acute analysis of Northern sentiment and its changing course during the crisis. See also the biographies of principal Northern political figures: C. F. Adams, Sr.; Bates; Black; Blair; Browning; Chandler; Chase; Dix; Douglas; Seward; Sumner; Wade; and Weed. Greeley's erratic course has evoked two articles, which reach opposing conclusions: Thomas N. Bonner, "Horace Greeley and the Secession Movement," 38 *M.V.H.R.* 425–44 (1951), and David M. Potter, "Horace Greeley and Peaceable Secession," 7 *J.S.H.* 145–59 (1941). For other Northern reactions see: Robert W. Johannsen, "The Douglas Democracy and the Crisis of Disunion," 9 *C.W.H.* 229–47 (1963); Johannsen, "The Sectional Crisis and the Frontier: Washington Territory, 1860–1861," 39 *M.V.H.R.* 415–40 (1952); Carl F. Krummel, "Henry J. Raymond and the New York Times in the Secession Crisis, 1860–61," 32 *N.Y.H.* 377–98 (1951); F. Paul Prucha, "Minnesota's Attitude toward the Southern Case for Secession," 24 *Minn. H.* 307–17 (1943); and Roman J. Zorn, "Minnesota Public Opinion and the Secession Controversy, December, 1860–April, 1861," 36 *M.V.H.R.* 435–56 (1949).

The difficulties of the Buchanan administration in the secession crisis are fully, if unsympathetically, treated in Nevins, *The Emergence of Lincoln,* and in Nichols, *The Disruption of American Democracy.* For defenses of Buchanan, see his biographies and Frank W. Klingberg, "James Buchanan and the Crisis of the Union," 9 *J.S.H.* 455–74 (1943).

No student should miss Henry Adams's memorable account of "The Great Secession Winter of 1860–61," 43 *Mass. H.S.P.* 660–87 (1910). Equally fascinating, but far less reliable, is the famous "Diary of a Public Man." For the literature on this "diary" consult the biographical section of this bibliography.

Efforts to avoid sectional hostilities are treated in Mary Scrugham, *The Peaceable Americans of 1860–1861 . . .* (1921). Lucius E. Chittenden gives a full *Report of the Debates and Proceedings . . . of the Conference Convention . . . held at Washington, D. C., in February, 1861* (1864). Three able monographs deal with this peace-keeping effort: Robert G. Gunderson, *Old Gentlemen's Convention* (1961); Jesse L. Keene, *The Peace Convention of 1861* (1961); and Samuel E. Morison, "The Peace Convention of February, 1861,"

73 *Mass. H.S.P.* 58–80 (1961). Also useful are Kenneth M. Stampp, ed., "Letters from the Washington Peace Conference of 1861," 9 *J.S.H.* 394–403 (1943), and Robert G. Gunderson, ed., "Letters from the Washington Peace Conference of 1861," 17 *J.S.H.* 382–92 (1951).

David M. Potter, *Lincoln and His Party in the Secession Crisis* (1942; new ed. with important introduction, 1962), is a perceptive study of the difficulties faced by the Republicans as they took power. Stampp's *And the War Came* continues to be valuable on this subject. See also the "Lincolniana" section listed above and the biography of Fox. An adverse view of Lincoln's Sumter policy is taken in Charles W. Ramsdell, "Lincoln and Fort Sumter," 3 *J.S.H.* 259–88 (1937); in Kenneth M. Stampp, "Lincoln and the Strategy of Defense in the Crisis of 1861," 11 *J.S.H.* 297–323 (1945); and in Tilley, *Lincoln Takes Command*. J. G. Randall offers a detailed defense of the new President in "When War Came in 1861," 1 *A.L.Q.* 3–42 (1940) and in *Lincoln the President*, I, 311–50. R. N. Current, in *The Lincoln Nobody Knows*, 104–30, and in *Lincoln and the First Shot*, previously cited, attempts a balanced appraisal of the evidence.

Less attention has been given to the forces which impelled the Confederates to fire on Sumter, but see Richard N. Current, "The Confederates and the First Shot," 7 *C.W.H.* 357–69 (1961); Grady McWhiney, "The Confederacy's First Shot," 14 *C.W.H.* 5–14 (1968); and Ludwell H. Johnson, "Fort Sumter and Confederate Diplomacy," 26 *J.S.H.* 441–77 (1960).

On the actual fighting at Fort Sumter see Samuel W. Crawford, *The History of the Fall of Fort Sumter* . . . (1898); Roy Meredith, *Storm Over Sumter* (1957); and W. A. Swanberg, *First Blood* (1958).

THE CAUSES OF THE CIVIL WAR

Virtually every writer listed in the pages of this bibliography has made at least an implicit judgment on the causes of the Civil War, and many have written at great length on this theme. It is obviously impracticable to enumerate all these books and articles here. Fortunately, however, there are two excellent guides to the enormous literature on this topics: Howard K. Beale, "What Historians Have Said About the Causes of the Civil War," in *Theory and Practice in Historical Study* (Social Science Research Council *Bulletin,* No. 54 [1946]), 55–102, which contains a full bibliography, and Thomas J. Pressly, *Americans Interpret Their Civil War* (1954). The following articles contain further bibliographical suggestions: Lee Benson and Cushing Strout, "Causation and the American Civil War: Two Appraisals," 1 *History and Theory* 163–85 (1961); Thomas N. Bonner, "Civil War Historians and the Needless War Doctrine," 17 *Jour. Hist. of Ideas* 193–216 (1956); A. E. Campbell, "An Excess of Isolation: Isolation and the American Civil War," 29 *J.S.H.* 161–74 (1963); Alan A. Conway, *The Causes of the American Civil War* (1961); David Donald, "American Historians and the Causes of the Civil War," 59 *S.A.Q.* 351–55 (1960); Donald, *An Excess of Democracy* (1960); William Dray, "Some Causal Accounts of the American Civil War," 91 *Daedalus* 578–98 (1962); Pieter Geyl, "The American Civil War and the Problem of Inevitability," 24 *N.E.Q.* 147–68 (1951); David M. Potter, "The Background of the Civil War," in *Interpreting and Teaching American History,* ed. W. H. Cartwright and Richard L. Watson, Jr. (1961), 87–119; Charles W. Ramsdell, "The Changing Interpretation of the Civil War," 3 *J.S.H.* 3–27 (1937); James G. Randall, "A Blundering Generation," 27 *M.V.H.R.* 3–28 (1940); Arthur M. Schlesinger, Jr., "The Causes of the Civil War: A Note on Historical Sentimentalism," 16 *Partisan Rev.* 969–81 (1949). Two useful anthologies, containing both primary and secondary writings on this theme, are Edwin C. Rozwenc, ed., *The Causes of the American Civil War* (1961), and Kenneth M. Stampp, ed., *The Causes of the Civil War* (1959).

THE CIVIL WAR: GENERAL WORKS

There is no entirely satisfactory general history of the Civil War. The multivolumed works of Channing, Rhodes, and Schouler are now badly out of date. So are John W. Burgess, *The Civil War and the Constitution, 1859–1865* (2 v., 1901), George C. Eggleston, *The History of the Confederate War* (2 v., 1910), and the two volumes by James K. Hosmer in the old American Nation series: *The Appeal to Arms, 1861–1863* (1907) and *Outcome of the Civil War, 1863–1865* (1907). Horace Greeley's compendious *The American Conflict* (2 v., 1964–66) remains surprisingly useful. Of the more recent works, Shelby Foote, *The Civil War* (2 v. to date, 1958–   ), is popular and readable but devoid of historical insight. Allan Nevins's massive, scholarly *The War for the Union* (2 v. to date, 1959–60), a continuation of his *Ordeal of the Union* series, as yet carries the story only through 1863 and concentrates almost exclusively upon the North. Perhaps the best large-scale work is Bruce Catton, *The Centennial History of the Civil War* (3 v., 1961–65), which is eloquent and imaginative but uneven in quality.

Among one-volume histories the best is Raimondo Luraghi, *Storia della Guerra Civile Americana* (1966), which overemphasizes military affairs. So, too, does Bruce Catton, *This Hallowed Ground* (1956). See also Catton's brief *America Goes to War* (1958), a series of lectures on the meaning of the Civil War experience. Roy F. Nichols, *The Stakes of Power* (1961), is a provocative interpretation by a leading scholar. James F. Rhodes condensed his massive researches in two briefer treatments, which have both the defects and the merits of the multivolumed work: *History of the Civil War, 1861–1865* (1917) and *Lectures on the American Civil War* (1913). Carl Sandburg's *Storm Over the Land* (1942) is an abridgment of *Abraham Lincoln: The War Years.* Carl R. Fish, *The American Conflict* (1937), is a thoughtful study, left incomplete at its author's death. Other short histories which deserve mention are: Alan Barker, *The Civil War in America* (1961); Roy P. Basler, *A Short History of the American Civil War* (1967); Harry Hansen, *The Civil War* (1961); George F. Milton, *Conflict* (1941); and Earl S. Miers, *The Great Rebellion* (1958). While not a general history, James A. Rawley, *Turning Points of the Civil War* (1966), deals intelligently with many aspects of the conflict.

Among the general interpretive essays dealing with the Civil War era, the best are Charles F. Adams, *Lee at Appomattox* (1902); Adams, *Studies, Military and Diplomatic, 1775–1865* (1911); Arthur Bestor, "The American Civil

War as a Constitutional Crisis," 69 *A.H.R.* 327–52 (1964); Avery O. Craven, "The Civil War and the Democratic Process," 4 *A.L.Q.* 269–92 (1947); Carl N. Degler, "One Among Many," 39 *Virginia Quarterly Review* 289–306 (1963); William A. Dunning, *Essays on the Civil War and Reconstruction* (1898; new ed. with introduction by David Donald, 1965); Allan Nevins, "A Major Result of the Civil War," 5 *C.W.H.* 237–50 (1959); Roy F. Nichols, "The Operation of American Democracy, 1861–1865: Some Questions," 25 *J.S.H.* 31–52 (1959); J. G. Randall, "The Civil War Re-studied," 6 *J.S.H.* 439–57 (1940); Denis W. Brogan, "A Fresh Appraisal of the Civil War," 220 *Harper's* 123–44 (1960); Frank E. Vandiver, "The Civil War as an Institutionalizing Force," in *Essays on the American Civil War,* ed. by Vandiver and others (1968), 73–87.

Special attention should be called to Karl Marx and Frederick Engels, *The Civil War in the United States* (1937), a provocative compilation of the wartime correspondence of the two communist leaders on the American problem. For a critical appraisal by an American Marxist, see Eugene D. Genovese, "Marxian Interpretations of the Slave South," in Barton J. Bernstein, ed., *Towards a New Past* (1968), 90–125. Views of Russian Marxists may be found in Ada M. Stoflet, translator, "The Civil War—Russian Version (I) from the Soviet Encyclopedia," 8 *C.W.H.* 357–64 (1962), and Joseph A. Lodgson, "The Civil War—Russian Version (II): The Soviet Historians," 8 *C.W.H.* 365–72 (1962).

There are several important reference works on the Civil War. The handiest is Mark M. Boatner, III, *The Civil War Dictionary* (1959), which contains brief, accurate articles on the major figures and engagements of the conflict. Edward McPherson, ed., *The Political History of the United States . . . during the Great Rebellion . . .* (1864), is a contemporary compilation of state papers, official reports, laws of Congress, etc. The volumes of Appleton's *American Annual Cyclopedia,* containing elaborate factual and statistical articles on a wide variety of topics, are very valuable for both the war and the Reconstruction years. Frank Moore, ed., *The Rebellion Record* (12 v., 1862–68), is a badly arranged but useful compilation of official papers, military accounts, newspaper reports, and even poetry.

The best of the Civil War anthologies are Paul M. Angle and Earl S. Miers, eds., *Tragic Years, 1860–1865* (2 v., 1960); Henry S. Commager, ed., *The Blue and the Gray* (2 v., 1950); Otto Eisenschiml and Ralph G. Newman, eds., *The American Iliad* (1947); and Richard B. Harwell, ed., *The Confederate Reader* (1957) and *The Union Reader* (1958); and William B. Hesseltine, ed., *The Tragic Conflict* (1962).

The most complete pictorial coverage of the conflict is Francis T. Miller, *The Photographic History of the Civil War* (10 v., 1911; new ed., with introduction by Henry S. Commager, 1957), but the photographs are badly reproduced. Better pictorial histories, using the best modern techniques of reproduction, are David Donald, ed., *Divided We Fought* (1952); Richard M. Ketchum, ed., *The American Heritage Picture History of the Civil War* (1960); Earl S. Miers, *The American Civil War* (1961); and Bell I. Wiley and Hirst D. Milhollen, *They Who Fought Here* (1959). See also the biographies of Mathew B. Brady.

Atlas to Accompany the Official Records of the Union and Confederate Armies (1891–95; new ed., with introduction by Henry S. Commager, 1958) is an invaluable tool. For modern battle maps, see Vincent J. Esposito, ed., *The West Point Atlas of American Wars* (2 v., 1959). The maps in Joseph B. Mitchell, *Decisive Battles of the Civil War* (1955), are especially designed to show present-day highway routes through the battlefields.

Edmund Wilson, *Patriotic Gore* (1962), is a profound analysis of the literature produced by the Civil War. In a lighter vein is Robert A. Lively, *Fiction Fights the Civil War* (1957). Brief but eloquent are Robert Penn Warren's reflections on the meaning of the conflict, *The Legacy of the Civil War* (1961).

THE CONFEDERACY AND ITS GOVERNMENT

On the historiography of the Confederacy see Douglas S. Freeman, *The South to Posterity* (1939), and Charles W. Ramsdell, "Some Problems Involved in Writing the History of the Confederacy," 2 *J.S.H.* 133–47 (1936). For a good guide to recent literature see Mary E. Massey, "The Confederate States of America: The Homefront," and John G. Barrett, "The Confederate States of America at War on Land and Sea," Chaps. 10 and 11 of *Writing Southern History,* ed. Arthur S. Link and Rembert W. Patrick (1965).

There are several distinguished general histories of the Confederacy. E. Merton Coulter, *The Confederate States of America, 1861–1865* (1950), is particularly good on social and economic developments. Clifford Dowdey, *The Land They Fought For* (1955), concentrates upon military events, with a decided anti-Davis interpretation. Clement Eaton, *A History of the Southern Confederacy* (1954), is the soundest and best balanced treatment of all phases of the subject. A straightforward narrative, emphasizing military campaigns, is Robert S. Henry, *The Story of the Confederacy* (1931). Nathaniel W. Stephenson, *The Day of the Confederacy* (1919), is an admirable brief interpretation. For a good, short synthesis of modern scholarship, see Charles P. Roland, *The Confederacy* (1960). Alfred H. Bill's *The Beleaguered City* (1946), a history of Richmond during the war, is also virtually a history of the Confederacy as seen from its capital. *The Confederacy* (1959), edited by Albert D. Kirwan, is an anthology of great value, especially on social and economic developments. Bell I. Wiley and Hirst D. Milhollen, *Embattled Confederates* (1964), is the best illustrated history.

Both the President and the Vice President of the Confederacy left memoirs: Jefferson Davis, *The Rise and Fall of the Confederate Government* (2 v., 1881; new ed., with introduction by Bell I. Wiley, 1958); and Alexander H. Stephens, *A Constitutional View of the Late War between the States* . . . (2 v., 1868–1870); both men concealed more than they revealed. J. L. M. Curry's *Civil History of the Government of the Confederate States* . . . (1900) is useful on internal affairs of the wartime South. Edward A. Pollard, *The Lost Cause* (1866), is a contemporary account marked by venomous anti-Davis sentiment. For the decision to move the capital of the Confederacy, see Jerrell Shofner and William W. Rogers, "Montgomery to Richmond," 10 *C.W.H.* 155–66 (1964).

The biographies of Davis and Stephens form important sources of information about the Confederate government. See also the biographies of Benjamin, Howell Cobb, T. R. R. Cobb, Foote, Hill, Hunter, Mallory, Memminger, Randolph, Reagan, Seddon, Toombs, L. P. Walker, and Yancey. Three Confederate diaries are of the greatest importance, those by Mrs. Chesnut, J. B. Jones, and R. G. H. Kean.

The rather spare official proceedings of the Confederate Congress may be found in the *Journal of the Congress of the Confederate States of America, 1861–1865* (7 v., 1904–1905, Sen. Doc. No. 234, 58 Cong., 2 sess.); fuller and livelier accounts of these debates are presented in the *Proceedings of the . . . Confederate Congress* (*So. Hist. Soc. Papers*, XLIV–LII, 1923–59; the last three volumes of these *Proceedings* are edited by Frank E. Vandiver). Other useful collections of documents are Douglas S. Freeman, ed., *A Calendar of Confederate Papers . . .* (1908); Rembert W. Patrick, ed., *The Opinions of the Confederate Attorneys General, 1861–1865* (1950); and James D. Richardson, ed., *A Compilation of the Messages and Papers of the Confederacy . . .* (2 v., 1905).

For full bibliographies of Confederate publications, see Marjorie L. Crandall, ed., *Confederate Imprints* (2 v., 1955), and Richard Harwell, ed., *More Confederate Imprints* (2 v., 1957).

Charles R. Lee, Jr., *The Confederate Constitutions* (1963), is authoritative. See also Albert N. Fitts, "The Confederate Convention," 2 *Ala. R.* 83–101, 189–210 (1949); Elmer D. Herd, Jr., "Laurence M. Keitt's Letters from the Provisional Congress of the Confederacy, 1861," 61 *S.C.H.M.* 19–25 (1960); William R. Leslie, "The Confederate Constitution," 2 *Michigan Quarterly Review* 153–65 (1963); H. C. Nixon and John C. Nixon, "The Confederate Constitution Today," 9 *Ga. R.* 369–97 (1955); and William M. Robinson, Jr., "A New Deal in Constitutions," 4 *J.S.H.* 449–61 (1938).

William M. Robinson, Jr., *Justice in Gray* (1941), is the definitive study of the judicial system of the Confederacy. It can be supplemented by two essays: S. D. Brummer, "The Judicial Interpretation of the Confederate Constitution," in *Studies in Southern History and Politics Inscribed to William Archibald Dunning* (1914), 105–33, and J. G. de R. Hamilton, "The State Courts and the Confederate Constitution," 4 *J.S.H.* 425–48 (1938).

Burton J. Hendrick, *Statesmen of the Lost Cause* (1939), and Rembert W. Patrick, *Jefferson Davis and His Cabinet* (1944), are two important studies of the Confederate executive departments. On Davis's role as President, see, in addition to his biographies, Robert D. Meade, "The Relations between Judah P. Benjamin and Jefferson Davis," 5 *J.S.H.* 468–78 (1939); Ralph Richardson, "The Choice of Jefferson Davis as Confederate President," 17 *J. Miss. H.* 161–76 (1955); Harrison A. Trexler, "Jefferson Davis and the Confederate Patronage," 28 *S.A.Q.* 45–58 (1929); and Trexler, "The Davis Administration and the Richmond Press, 1861–1865," 16 *J.S.H.* 177–95 (1950).

Studies of the workings of the Confederate war, navy, and state departments are cited below, under separate headings. On the Southern postal system there are three useful works: August Dietz, *The Postal Service of the Confederate States of America* (1929); Walter F. McCaleb, "The Organization of the Post-Office Department of the Confederacy," 12 *A.H.R.* 66–74 (1906);

and Cedric O. Reynolds, "The Postal System of the Southern Confederacy," 12 W. Va. H. 200–80 (1951). On Southern government employees in general, see Paul P. Van Riper and Harry N. Scheiber, "The Confederate Civil Service," 25 J.S.H. 448–70 (1959), and Monroe Haskell, "Early Confederate Political Patronage," 20 Ala. R. 45–61 (1967).

Wilfred B. Yearns, The Confederate Congress (1960), is a thorough study, but it can be supplemented by Richard E. Beringer, "A Profile of the Members of the Confederate Congress," 33 J.S.H. 518–41 (1967). See also the biographies of leading congressmen and Bell I. Wiley, ed., Letters of Warren Akin, Confederate Congressman (1960). Since there were no organized parties, politics in the Confederacy has been a neglected subject, but Thomas B. Alexander, "Persistent Whiggery in the Confederate South, 1860–1877," 27 J.S.H. 305–29 (1961), offers valuable insights.

For the relation between central and local governments May S. Ringold, The Role of the State Legislatures in the Confederacy (1966), is invaluable. Curtis A. Amlund, Federalism in the Southern Confederacy (1966), is also useful.

Virtually every historian of the Civil War has made at least an implicit judgment as to the reasons for the failure of the Confederacy. For the historiography of this subject see Robert D. Little, "Southern Historians and the Downfall of the Confederacy," 3 Ala. R. 243–62 (1950) and 4 ibid. 38–54 (1951). Other explicit discussions of the causes of the defeat of the South may be found in Henry S. Commager, ed., The Defeat of the Confederacy (1964); David Donald, ed., Why the North Won the Civil War (1960); Lawrence H. Gipson, "The Collapse of the Confederacy," 4 M.V.H.R. 437–58 (1918); Frank L. Owsley, "Local Defense and the Overthrow of the Confederacy," 11 M.V.H.R. 490–525 (1925); Charles H. Wesley, The Collapse of the Confederacy (1922); and Bell I. Wiley, The Road to Appomattox (1956).

THE CONFEDERACY: STATE STUDIES

There are a number of state and local studies which cast light on the problems of the Confederacy. There is no thorough study of Virginia; one must consult Hamilton J. Eckenrode, The Political History of Virginia during the Reconstruction (1904), Chaps. 1–2, and the biographies of Letcher and William Smith. Louis H. Manarin, ed., Richmond at War: The Minutes of the City Council, 1861–1865 (1966), is an important source.

On North Carolina the standard work is John G. Barrett, The Civil War in North Carolina (1963). See also J. G. de R. Hamilton, "The North Carolina Courts and the Confederacy," 4 N.C.H.R. 366–403 (1927), and the biographies of Ellis, Holden, and Vance.

Charles E. Cauthen, South Carolina Goes to War, 1861–1865 (1950), is an admirable monograph.

Georgia, too, has been thoroughly studied in T. Conn Bryan, Confederate Georgia (1953). Consult also J. Horace Bass, "Civil War Finance in Georgia," 26 Ga. H. Q. 213–24 (1942); Joseph H. Parks, "State Rights in a Crisis: Governor Joseph E. Brown versus President Jefferson Davis," 32 J.S.H. 3–24 (1966); John O. Sumner, contributor, "Georgia and the Confederacy, 1865,"

1 *A.H.R.* 97–102 (1895); and the biographies of Joseph E. Brown, Howell Cobb, Stephens, and Toombs. See also Alexander A. Lawrence, *A Present for Mr. Lincoln: The Story of Savannah from Secession to Sherman* (1961).

John E. Johns, *Florida during the Civil War* (1963), largely supersedes William W. Davis, *The Civil War and Reconstruction in Alabama* (1913), for the war years.

On Alabama the basic work is still Walter L. Fleming, *Civil War and Reconstruction in Alabama* (1905).

Mississippi is admirably treated in John K. Bettersworth, *Confederate Mississippi* (1943), John K. Bettersworth and James W. Silver, eds., *Mississippi in the Confederacy* (2 v., 1961), and Edwin C. Bearss, *Decision in Mississippi* (1962). See also James W. Silver, ed., "The Breakdown of Morale in Central Mississippi in 1864: Letters of Judge Robert S. Hudson," 16 *J. Miss. H.* 99–120 (1954).

On Tennessee, see Joseph H. Parks, "Memphis under Military Rule, 1862 to 1865," *E. Tenn. Hist. Soc. Pubs.*, No. 14 (1942), 31–58 (1942); Digby G. Seymour, *Divided Loyalties: Fort Sanders and the Civil War in East Tennessee* (1963); Oliver P. Temple, *East Tennessee and the Civil War* (1899); and the biographies of Brownlow and Andrew Johnson. Kentucky affairs are fully analyzed in E. Merton Coulter, *The Civil War and Readjustment in Kentucky* (1926). See also Wilson P. Shortridge, "Kentucky Neutrality in 1861," 9 *M.V.H.R.* 283–301 (1923) and Thomas Speed, *The Union Cause in Kentucky, 1860–1865* (1907).

Jefferson D. Bragg, *Louisiana in the Confederacy* (1941), is a work of admirable thoroughness, but John D. Winters, *The Civil War in Louisiana* (1963), is also valuable. See also Gerald M. Capers, *Occupied City: New Orleans under the Federals, 1862–1865* (1965); Jo Ann Carrigan, "Yankees versus Yellow Jack in New Orleans, 1862–1866," 9 *C.W.H.* 248–60 (1963); Elisabeth J. Doyle, "Greenbacks, Car Tickets, and the Pot of Gold," 5 *C.W.H.* 347–62 (1959); Doyle, "New Orleans Courts under Military Occupation, 1861–1865," 42 *Mid-Am.* 185–92 (1960); Doyle, "Nurseries of Treason: Schools in Occupied New Orleans," 26 *J.S.H.* 161–79 (1960); Roger W. Shugg, *Origins of Class Struggle;* and the biographies of Allen, Banks, and Butler.

The other trans-Mississippi states of the Confederacy have been less fully studied. Arthur R. Kirkpatrick, "Missouri's Secessionist Government, 1861–1865," 45 *Mo. H. R.* 124–37 (1951); Kirkpatrick, "The Admission of Missouri to the Confederacy," 55 *Mo. H. R.* 366–86 (1961); Kirkpatrick, "Missouri's Delegation in the Confederate Congress," 5 *C.W.H.* 188–98 (1959); and William H. Lyon, "Claiborne Fox Jackson and the Secession Crisis in Missouri," 58 *Mo. H. R.* 422–41 (1964), are good introductions to Confederate operations in that state. See also the discussion, below, of military operations in the trans-Mississippi West. On Arkansas one must use Allen W. Jones and Virginia A. Buttry, "Military Events in Arkansas during the Civil War, 1861–1865," 22 *Ark. H. Q.* 124–70 (1963), and Thomas S. Staples, *Reconstruction in Arkansas, 1862–1874* (1923), Chaps. 1–2. For Texas, see Stephen B. Oates, "Texas under the Secessionists," 67 *Sw. H. Q.* 167–212 (1963), and the biographies of Houston, Kirby Smith, and Lubbock.

A good deal has been written about the Confederacy and the Indian territory. The best general works are Annie H. Abel, *The American Indian as Slaveholder and Secessionist* (2 v., 1915–19), and Frank Cunningham, *General Stand Watie's Confederate Indians* (1959). Other useful accounts are Edward E. Dale, "The Cherokees in the Confederacy," 13 *J.S.H.* 159–85 (1947), and Dean Trickett, "The Civil War in the Indian Territory," 19 *Chronicles of Okla.* 55–69, 381–96 (1941).

THE CONFEDERACY: ECONOMIC AND SOCIAL STUDIES

The best treatment of financial and industrial developments in the wartime South is John C. Schwab's authoritative *The Confederate States of America, 1861–1865* (1901). Charles W. Ramsdell, *Behind the Lines in the Southern Confederacy* (1944), is a thoughtful treatment of developments on the homefront. The impact of the war on the ordinary citizens of the South is graphically described in Bell I. Wiley, *The Plain People of the Confederacy* (1943).

Richard C. Todd, *Confederate Finance* (1954), is a thorough, accurate treatment of a difficult subject. Three essays by Eugene M. Lerner are also of great importance in understanding Confederate economic difficulties: "Money, Prices, and Wages in the Confederacy," 63 *J. Pol. Econ.* 20–40 (1955); "Monetary and Fiscal Programs of the Confederate Government, 1861–65," 62 *J. Pol. Econ.* 506–22 (1954); and "Inflation in the Confederacy, 1861–1865," in Milton Friedman, ed., *Studies in the Quantity Theory of Money* (1956), 163–78. See also Ralph L. Andreano, "A Theory of Confederate Finance," 2 *C.W.H.* 21–28 (1956); James L. Nichols, "The Tax-in-Kind in the Department of the Trans-Mississippi," 5 *C.W.H.* 382–89 (1959); and John C. Schwab, "Prices in the Confederate States, 1861–65," 14 *P.S.Q.* 281–304 (1899).

On the relation of the Confederate government to industry see Lester J. Cappon, "Government and Private Industry in the Southern Confederacy," in *Humanistic Studies in Honor of John Calvin Metcalf* (1941), 151–89; Louise B. Hill, *State Socialism in the Confederate States of America* (1937); and Charles W. Ramsdell, "The Control of Manufacturing by the Confederate Government," 8 *M.V.H.R.* 231–49 (1921).

There is no general history of manufacturing in the Confederacy, but see Victor S. Clark, *History of Manufactures in the United States* (1929), II, 41–53. Charles B. Dew's admirable biography of Joseph R. Anderson is also a study of the South's most important iron works. See also Frank E. Vandiver, "The Shelby Iron Company in the Civil War," 1 *Ala. R.* 203–17 (1948).

Robert C. Black, III, *The Railroads of the Confederacy* (1952), is a richly rewarding study of one of the great failures of the Southern government. Angus J. Johnston, II, *Virginia Railroads in the Civil War* (1961), is able and intelligent. Other valuable studies of Southern railroads include Robert L. Clarke, "The Florida Railroad Company in the Civil War," 19 *J.S.H.* 180–92 (1953); Leo E. Huff, "The Memphis and Little Rock Railroad during the Civil War," 23 *Ark. H. Q.* 260–70 (1964); Charles L. Price, "North Carolina Railroads during the Civil War," 7 *C.W.H.* 298–309 (1961);

Charles W. Ramsdell, "The Confederate Government and the Railroads," 22 *A.H.R.* 794–810 (1917); Robert E. Riegel, "Federal Operation of Southern Railroads during the Civil War," 9 *M.V.H.R.* 126–38 (1922); Charles W. Turner, "The Virginia Central Railroad at War, 1861–1865," 12 *J.S.H.* 487–509 (1946); and Turner, "The Virginia Southwestern Railroad System at War, 1861–1865," 24 *N.C.H.R.* 467–84 (1947).

Southern trading activities are treated in E. Merton Coulter, "Commercial Intercourse with the Confederacy in the Mississippi Valley, 1861–1865," 5 *M.V.H.R.* 377–95 (1919); William Diamond, "Imports of the Confederate Government from Europe and Mexico," 6 *J.S.H.* 470–503 (1940); Joseph H. Parks, "A Confederate Trade Center under Federal Occupation: Memphis, 1862 to 1865," 7 *J.S.H.* 289–314 (1941); and Frank E. Vandiver, ed., *Confederate Blockade Running through Bermuda, 1861–1865* (1947).

Paul W. Gates, *Agriculture and the Civil War* (1965), gives extensive treatment to the South. See also D. Clayton James, "Mississippi Agriculture, 1861–1865," 24 *J. Miss. H.* 129–41 (1962), and Charles P. Roland, *Louisiana Sugar Plantations during the American Civil War* (1957).

Two books by Ella Lonn, *Foreigners in the Confederacy* (1940) and *Salt as a Factor in the Confederacy* (1933), are definitive treatments of their subjects, and both cast much light on the general economic and social problems of the South as well.

Other useful articles relating to economic conditions within the Confederacy are: Ralph W. Donnelly, "Confederate Copper," 1 *C.W.H.* 355–70 (1955); Edwin B. Coddington, "The Activities and Attitudes of a Confederate Businessman: Gazaway B. Lamar," 9 *J.S.H.* 3–36 (1943); William M. Robinson, Jr., "Prohibition in the Confederacy," 37 *A.H.R.* 50–58 (1931); James L. Sellers, "The Economic Incidence of the Civil War in the South," 14 *M.V.H.R.* 179–91 (1927); and Gordon Wright, "Economic Conditions in the Confederacy as Seen by the French Consuls," 7 *J.S.H.* 195–214 (1941).

Mary Elizabeth Massey's study of wartime shortages in the South, *Ersatz in the Confederacy* (1952), is both charmingly written and highly informative. Equally valuable is Miss Massey's *Refugee Life in the Confederacy* (1964).

Miss Massey's carefully researched *Bonnet Brigades: American Women and the Civil War* (1966), gives much attention to the women of the South. It largely replaces Francis B. Simkins and James W. Patton, *The Women of the Confederacy* (1936), and John L. Underwood, *The Women of the Confederacy* (1906). Still valuable are Katharine M. Jones, *Heroines of Dixie* (1955), and *Ladies of Richmond* (1962). See also the biographical entries under Myrta L. Avary, Mary B. Blackford, Mary B. Chesnut, Sarah M. Dawson, Emma LeConte, Phoebe Y. Pember, and Kate Stone.

Southern wartime medicine is elaborately treated in H. H. Cunningham, *Doctors in Gray* (1958), and more briefly in George W. Adams, "Confederate Medicine," 6 *J.S.H.* 151–66 (1940). These studies can be supplemented by two articles by Norman H. Franke: "Official and Industrial Aspects of Pharmacy in the Confederacy," 37 *Ga. H. Q.* 175–87 (1953), and "Pharmacy and Pharmacists in the Confederacy," 38 *Ga. H. Q.* 11–28 (1954).

Efforts of the Southern state governments to relieve destitution among the families of soldiers have been treated in Edwin B. Coddington, "Soldiers' Relief in the Seaboard States of the Confederacy," 37 *M.V.H.R.* 17–38 (1950); in Clyde O. Fisher, "The Relief of Soldiers' Families in North Carolina during the Civil War," 16 *S.A.Q.* 60–72 (1917); and in articles by William F. Zornow: "Aid for the Indigent Families of Soldiers in Virginia, 1861–1865," 66 *Va. M. H. B.* 454–58 (1958); "State Aid for Indigent Soldiers and Their Families in Florida, 1861–1865," 34 *Fla. H. Q.* 259–65 (1956); and "State Aid for Indigent Soldiers and Their Families in Louisiana, 1861–1865," 39 *La. H. Q.* 375–80 (1956).

For an excellent account of cultural life in the Confederacy, see Clement Eaton, *The Waning of the Old South Civilization* (1968).

The best book on religion in the Confederacy is James W. Silver, *Confederate Morale and Church Propaganda* (1957). Highly valuable are several articles by W. Harrison Daniel: "Bible Publication and Procurement in the Confederacy," 24 *J.S.H.* 191–201 (1958); "The Christian Association: A Religious Society in the Army of Northern Virginia," 69 *Va. M. H. B.* 93–100 (1961); "Protestant Clergy and Union Sentiment in the Confederacy," 23 *Tenn. H. Q.* 284–90 (1964); "Southern Protestantism—1861 and After," 5 *C.W.H.* 276–82 (1959); "Southern Protestantism and Army Missions in the Confederacy," 17 *Miss. Q.* 179–91 (1964); "Southern Protestantism and the Negro, 1860–1865," 41 *N.C.H.R.* 338–59 (1964); "Southern Presbyterians in the Confederacy," 44 *N.C.H.R.* 231–55 (1967); and "Virginia Baptists, 1861–1865," 72 *Va. M. H. B.* 94–114 (1964). Other useful studies are T. Conn Bryan, "The Churches in Georgia during the Civil War," 33 *Ga. H. Q.* 283–302 (1949); Joseph B. Cheshire, *The Church in the Confederate States: A History of the Protestant Episcopal Church* (1912); Walter L. Fleming, "The Churches of Alabama during the Civil War and Reconstruction," 7 *Gulf States Hist. Mag.* 105–27 (1902); Samuel Horst, *Mennonites in the Confederacy: A Study in Civil War Pacificism* (1967); Bertram W. Korn, "The Jews of the Confederacy," 13 *American Jewish Archives* 3–90 (1961); Oscar Lipscomb, "Catholics in Alabama, 1861–1865," 20 *Ala. R.* 278–88 (1967); Haskell Monroe, "South Carolinians and the Formation of the Presbyterian Church in the Confederate States of America," 42 *Journal of Presbyterian History* 219–43 (1964); Edgar L. Pennington, "The Confederate Episcopal Church in 1863," 52 *S. C. Hist. and Geneal. Mag.* 5–16 (1951); Sidney J. Romero, "The Confederate Chaplain," 1 *C.W.H.* 127–40 (1955); Romero, "Louisiana Clergy and the Confederate Army," 22 *La. H.* 277–300 (1961); and John Shepard, Jr., "Religion in the Army of Northern Virginia," 25 *N.C.H.R.* 341–76 (1948).

There is no full-scale study of Confederate journalism. Several articles, however, are suggestive: J. Cutler Andrews, "The Confederate Press and Public Morale," 32 *J.S.H.* 445–65 (1966); Andrews, "The Southern Telegraph Company, 1861–1865: A Chapter in the History of Wartime Communications," 30 *J.S.H.* 319–44 (1944); Thomas H. Baker, "Refugee Newspaper: The Memphis *Daily Appeal,* 1862–1865," 29 *J.S.H.* 326–44 (1963); Roy W. Curry, "The Newspaper Press and the Civil War in West Virginia," 6 *W. Va. H.* 225–64 (1945); Lawrence Huff, "Joseph Addison Turner: Southern Editor during the Civil War," 29 *J.S.H.* 469–85 (1963); John P. Jones, Jr., "The Confederate Press and the Government," 37 *Americana* 7–27 (1943);

Henry T. Malone, "Atlanta Journalism during the Confederacy," 37 *Ga. H. Q.*
210–19 (1953); William F. Swindler, "The Southern Press in Missouri,
1861–1864," 35 *Mo. H. R.* 394–400 (1941); and Bell I. Wiley, "Camp
Newspapers of the Confederacy," 20 *N.C.H.R.* 327–35 (1943). See also
Rabun L. Brantley, *Georgia Journalism of the Civil War Period* (1929).

THE CONFEDERACY: DISAFFECTION AND DISLOYALTY

Carleton Beals, *War Within a War: The Confederacy Against Itself*
(1965), is a popular treatment, of little scholarly merit.

One source of discontent with the Confederate government is admirably
and succinctly presented in Frank L. Owsley, *State Rights in the Confederacy*
(1925). The effect of conscription in lowering Confederate morale is analyzed
in Albert B. Moore, *Conscription and Conflict in the Confederacy* (1924).
The problem of desertions from the Southern armies is well handled in Ella
Lonn, *Desertion during the Civil War* (1928), and in Bessie Martin, *Desertion of Alabama Troops from the Confederate Army* (1932). See also Richard
Bardolph, "Inconstant Rebels: Desertion of North Carolina Troops in the Civil
War," 41 *N.C.H.R.* 163–89 (1964).

The best study of the peace movement in the South is Georgia L. Tatum,
Disloyalty in the Confederacy (1934). Frank W. Klingberg, *The Southern
Claims Commission* (1955), shows the extraordinary amount of Unionism
which persisted in the Confederacy.

A number of useful articles deal with aspects of Southern disaffection: Stephen E. Ambrose, "Yeoman Discontent in the Confederacy," 8 *C.W.H.* 259–
68 (1962); Hugh C. Bailey, "Disaffection in the Alabama Hill Country,
1861," 4 *C.W.H.* 183–94 (1958); Bailey, "Disloyalty in Early Confederate
Alabama," 23 *J.S.H.* 522–28 (1957); John K. Bettersworth, ed., "Mississippi
Unionism: The Case of the Reverend James A. Lyon," 1 *J. Miss. H.* 37–52
(1939); Norman D. Brown, "A Union Election in Civil War North Carolina,"
43 *N.C.H.R.* 381–400 (1966); Howard T. Dimick, "Peace Overtures of July,
1864," 29 *La. H. Q.* 1241–58 (1946); Claude Elliott, "Union Sentiment in
Texas, 1861–1865," 50 *Sw. H. Q.* 449–77 (1947); Walter L. Fleming, "The
Peace Movement in Alabama during the Civil War," 2 *S.A.Q.* 114–24, 246–
60 (1903); Harold M. Hyman, "Deceit in Dixie," 3 *C.W.H.* 65–82 (1957);
Angus J. Johnston, II, "Disloyalty on Confederate Railroads in Virginia," 63
Va. M. H. B. 410–26 (1955); Ludwell H. Johnson, "Contraband Trade during the Last Year of the Civil War," 49 *M.V.H.R.* 635–53 (1963); Frank W.
Klingberg, "The Case of the Minors: A Unionist Family within the Confederacy," 13 *J.S.H.* 27–45 (1947); Barnes F. Lathrop, "Disaffection in Confederate Louisiana: The Case of William Hyman," 24 *J.S.H.* 308–18 (1958); Durward Long, "Unanimity and Disloyalty in Secessionist Alabama," 11 *C.W.H.*
257–74 (1965); Eugene C. Murdock, "Was It a 'Poor Man's Fight'?" 10
C.W.H. 241–45 (1965); Horace W. Raper, "William W. Holden and the
Peace Movement in North Carolina," 31 *N.C.H.R.* 493–516 (1954); A. Sellew Roberts, "The Peace Movement in North Carolina," 11 *M.V.H.R.* 190–99
(1924); Henry T. Shanks, "Disloyalty to the Confederacy in Southwestern
Virginia, 1861–1865," 21 *N.C.H.R.* 118–35 (1944); J. Reuben Sheeler,

"The Development of Unionism in East Tennessee," 29 *J.N.H.* 166–203 (1944); Meriwether Stuart, "Samuel Ruth and General R. E. Lee: Disloyalty and the Line of Supply to Fredericksburg, 1862–1863," 71 *Va. M. H. B.* 35–109 (1963); Ethel Taylor, "Discontent in Confederate Louisiana," 2 *La. H.* 410–28 (1961); Rosser H. Taylor, ed., "Boyce-Hammond Correspondence," 3 *J.S.H.* 348–54 (1937); and Ted R. Worley, "The Arkansas Peace Society of 1861: A Study in Mountain Unionism," 24 *J.S.H.* 445–56 (1958). See also the biographies of Joseph E. Brown, Brownlow, Dahlgren, and Holden.

WARTIME GOVERNMENT IN THE NORTH

Most of the general histories of the Civil War give extended treatment to the Northern government and to Northern wartime politics. Nevins's *The War for the Union* and Rhodes's *History of the United States* are particularly full in this respect. The biographies and many of the special studies of Lincoln also deal with these matters. See the "Lincolniana" section above. Margaret Leech, *Reveille in Washington, 1860–1865* (1941), is an entertaining history of the Union war effort as seen from the national capital. See also P. J. Staudenraus, ed., *Mr. Lincoln's Washington* (1967), the dispatches of the Civil War correspondent Noah Brooks.

The diaries of Bates, Browning, Chase, Fisher, Gurowski, Hay, Strong, and Welles, listed in the biographical section of this bibliography, are of the greatest importance for an understanding of Northern wartime politics.

On Lincoln's cabinet, see, in addition to Hendrick, *Lincoln's War Cabinet,* and Macartney, *Lincoln and His Cabinet,* already cited, the biographies of Bates, Blair, Cameron, Chase, Fessenden, Harlan, Seward, James Speed, Stanton, Usher, and Welles.

There is no full study of the Northern Congress during the Civil War, but see Edward C. Boykin's disappointingly thin *Congress and the Civil War* (1955), and Maynard J. Brichford, "Congress at the Outbreak of the War," 3 *C.W.H.* 153–62 (1957). Leonard P. Curry, *Blueprint for Modern America: Nonmilitary Legislation of the First Civil War Congress* (1968), is an important pioneering study. See also the biographies of such leading Congressmen as Blaine, Browning, Zachariah Chandler, Conkling, S. S. Cox, H. W. Davis, Grimes, Hale, Reverdy Johnson, Julian, Lovejoy, E. D. Morgan, Morrill, Sprague, Stevens, Sumner, Trumbull, Wade, and Wood.

T. Harry Williams, *Lincoln and the Radicals,* previously cited, is the basic book on the wing of the Republican party often critical of Lincoln. In recent years the nature and definition of Republican "Radicalism" has been hotly debated by historians. See, for example, Allan G. Bogue, "Bloc and Party in the United States Senate, 1861–1863," 13 *C.W.H.* 221–41 (1967); David Donald, "Devils Facing Zionwards," in Grady McWhiney, ed., *Grant, Lee, Lincoln and the Radicals,* 72–91; Donald, *The Politics of Reconstruction, 1863–1867* (1965); Edward L. Gambill, "Who Were the Senate Radicals?" 11 *C.W.H.* 237–44 (1965); Glenn M. Linden, " 'Radicals' and Economic Policies: The House of Representatives, 1861–1873," 13 *C.W.H.* 51–65 (1967); Linden, " 'Radicals' and Economic Policies: The Senate, 1861–1873," 32 *J.S.H.* 189–99 (1966); and T. Harry Williams, "Lincoln and the Radicals: An Essay in

Civil War History and Historiography," in McWhiney, ed., *Grant, Lee, Lincoln and the Radicals,* 92–117. For conflicting appraisals of one of the principal Radical agencies, see William W. Pierson, Jr., "The Committee on the Conduct of the Civil War," 23 *A.H.R.* 550–76 (1918), and Hans L. Trefousse, "The Joint Committee on the Conduct of the War: A Reassessment," 10 *C.W.H.* 5–19 (1964).

So much attention has been given to the Radicals that the rest of the political spectrum has been largely neglected. See, however, William D. Mallam, "Lincoln and the Conservatives," 28 *J.S.H.* 31–45 (1962), and Leonard P. Curry, "Congressional Democrats, 1861–1863," 12 *C.W.H.* 213–29 (1966). The biographies of Crittenden continue to be useful on this topic, and Thomas B. Alexander, "Is Civil War History Polarized?" *East Tenn. Hist. Soc. Pubs.,* No. 29 (1957), 10–39, is thought-provoking.

Paul P. Van Riper and Keith A. Sutherland, "The Northern Civil Service, 1861–1865," 11 *C.W.H.* 351–69 (1965), is an important study in a neglected area.

On the judiciary under Lincoln, consult David M. Silver's excellent *Lincoln's Supreme Court* (1956), and the biographies of Justices Chase, Davis, Field, Miller, Taney, and Wayne. Samuel Klaus, ed., *The Milligan Case* (1929), is an extended treatment of one of the major cases which rose during the war, though the court's actual decision was not given until after hostilities had ceased. J. G. Randall's *Constitutional Problems under Lincoln* is indispensable to any understanding of the legal and judicial aspects of the war. See also Dean Sprague, *Freedom under Lincoln* (1965), and Harold M. Hyman, "Law and the Impact of the Civil War: A Review Essay," 14 *C.W.H.* 51–59 (1968).

The soldier vote during the Civil War has attracted a surprising amount of attention from historians. The fullest treatment is Josiah H. Benton, *Voting in the Field* (1915), but see also Lynwood G. Downs, "The Soldier Vote and Minnesota Politics, 1862–65," 26 *Minn. H.* 187–210 (1945); Walter N. Trenerry, "Votes for Minnesota's Civil War Soldiers," 36 *Minn. H.* 167–72 (1959); T. Harry Williams, "Voters in Blue," 31 *M.V.H.R.* 187–204 (1944); and Oscar O. Winther, "The Soldier Vote in the Election of 1864," 25 *N.Y.H.* 440–58 (1944).

Useful articles dealing with various aspects of Northern politics during the Civil War are: John D. Carter, "Abraham Lincoln and the California Patronage," 48 *A.H.R.* 495–506 (1943); Harold M. Dudley, "The Election of 1864," 18 *M.V.H.R.* 500–18 (1932); James F. Gloneck, "Lincoln, Johnson, and the Baltimore Ticket," 6 *A.L.Q.* 255–71 (1951); Winfred A. Harbison, "Indiana Republicans and the Re-election of President Lincoln," 34 *Ind. M. H.* 42–64 (1938); Harbison, "Lincoln and the Indiana Republicans, 1861–62," 33 *Ind. M. H.* 277–303 (1937); Reinhard H. Luthin, "A Discordant Chapter in Lincoln's Administration: The Davis-Blair Controversy," 39 *Md. H. M.* 25–48 (1944); Harry E. Pratt, "The Repudiation of Lincoln's War Policy in 1862—Stuart-Swett Congressional Campaign," 24 *J.I.S.H.S.* 129–40 (1931); Kenneth M. Stampp, "The Milligan Case and the Election of 1864 in Indiana," 31 *M.V.H.R.* 41–58 (1944).

THE WARTIME NORTH: STATE AND LOCAL STUDIES

William B. Weeden, *War Government, Federal and State, in Massachusetts, New York, Pennsylvania, and Indiana, 1861–1865* (1906), is a useful introduction to the important work done by the state governments of the North during the Civil War. William B. Hesseltine's *Lincoln and the War Governors,* previously cited, is also valuable. See, too, the biographies of such Northern war governors as Andrew, Austin Blair, Curtin, Gamble, Hicks, Kirkwood, E. D. Morgan, Morton, Pierpont, Seymour, and Yates.

Many of the Northeastern states during the Civil War era deserve further study. Edith E. Ware, *Political Opinion in Massachusetts during the Civil War and Reconstruction* (1916), though old, is still valuable. John Niven, *Connecticut for the Union* (1965), is an admirable treatment of that state's role in the war. Sidney D. Brummer, *Political History of New York State during the Period of the Civil War* (1911), is both thin and narrow. Some of its deficiencies are remedied in James A. Frost, "The Home Front in New York during the Civil War," 42 *N.Y.H.* 273–97 (1961), and Robert J. Rayback, "New York State in the Civil War," 42 *N.Y.H.* 56–70 (1961). For New Jersey, consult Charles M. Knapp, *New Jersey Politics during the Period of the Civil War and Reconstruction* (1924), and Earl S. Miers, ed., *New Jersey and the Civil War* (1964). The byzantine politics of Pennsylvania are analyzed in Stanton L. Davis, *Pennsylvania Politics, 1860–1863* (1935), and Erwin S. Bradley, *The Triumph of Militant Republicanism: A Study of Pennsylvania and Presidential Politics, 1860–1872* (1964). William Dusinberre, *Civil War Issues in Philadelphia, 1856–1865* (1965), is provocative and important. See also Winnifred Mackay, "Philadelphia during the Civil War, 1861–1865," 70 *Pa. M. H. & B.* 3–51 (1946); William L. Calderhead, "Philadelphia in Crisis, June–July, 1863," 28 *Pa. H.* 142–55 (1961); and the diary of Sidney G. Fisher.

The border states have been thoroughly studied. For a general treatment see Edward C. Smith, *The Borderland in the Civil War* (1927). Harold Hancock, *Delaware during the Civil War* (1961), is an objective and exhaustive political history. See also H. Clay Reed, "Lincoln's Compensated Emancipation Plan and Its Relation to Delaware," *Delaware Notes,* 7 ser. (Univ. of Del., 1931). On Maryland, see Charles B. Clark, "Politics in Maryland during the Civil War," 36 *Md. H. M.* 239–62, 381–93 (1941); 37 *ibid.* 171–92, 378–99 (1942); 38 *ibid.* 230–60 (1943); 39 *ibid.* 149–61, 315–31 (1944); 40 *ibid.* 233–41, 295–309 (1945); and 41 *ibid.* 132–58 (1946). Clark's "Suppression and Control of Maryland, 1861–1865 . . . ," 54 *Md. H. M.* 241–71 (1959), and Charles L. Wagandt, "Election by Sword and Ballot: The Emancipation Victory of 1863," 59 *Md. H. M.* 143–64 (1964), are also valuable. See, too, Wagandt's *The Mighty Revolution,* cited below in the section on "The Negro in the Civil War."

For West Virginia, Richard O. Curry, *A House Divided: A Study of Statehood Politics and the Copperhead Movement in West Virginia* (1964), replaces earlier studies, though Randall's *Constitutional Problems under Lincoln* continues to be valuable. See also George E. Moore, *A Banner in the Hills* (1963), and Boyd B. Stutler, *West Virginia in the Civil War* (1963). For Kentucky see, in addition to Coulter's admirable *The Civil War and Read-*

justment in Kentucky, William H. Townsend, *Lincoln and the Bluegrass* (1955).

William E. Parrish, *Turbulent Partnership: Missouri and the Union, 1861–1865* (1963), is a thorough study, largely superseding Sceva B. Laughlin, *Missouri Politics during the Civil War* (1930), and Walter W. Ryle, *Missouri: Union or Secession* (1931). Hans C. Adamson, *Rebellion in Missouri: 1861* (1961), is a high-spirited account of the opening of hostilities in that state. See also Marvin R. Cain, "Edward Bates and Hamilton R. Gamble: A Wartime Partnership," 56 *Mo. H. R.* 146–55 (1962); Arthur R. Kirkpatrick, "Missouri on the Eve of the Civil War," 55 *Mo. H. R.* 99–108 (1961); Bill R. Lee, "Missouri's Fight over Emancipation in 1863," 45 *Mo. H. R.* 256–74 (1951); and the works cited above in the section on "The Confederacy: State Studies." Albert Castel, *A Frontier State at War* (1958), is an admirable study of Kansas. See also Castel's "The Jayhawkers and Copperheads of Kansas," 5 *C.W.H.* 283–93 (1959), and Alan Conway, "The Sacking of Lawrence," 24 *Kans. H. Q.* 144–50 (1958). Military developments in both these states are discussed in a later section.

The states of the Old Northwest have been thoroughly and intelligently studied. H. C. Hubbart, *The Older Middle West, 1840–1880* (1936), is a book of great importance; it covers the social, economic, and political life of the whole region. Ohio has been carefully investigated in George H. Porter, *Ohio Politics during the Civil War Period* (1911), and in Eugene H. Roseboom, *The Civil War Era, 1850–1873* (1944). See also Roseboom's "Southern Ohio and the Union in 1863," 39 *M.V.H.R.* 29–44 (1952). Emma L. Thornbrough, *Indiana in the Civil War Era, 1850–1880* (1965), is thorough and able, while Kenneth M. Stampp's *Indiana Politics during the Civil War* (1949) is a model monograph, with an incisive interpretation. See also John D. Barnhart, "The Impact of the Civil War on Indiana," 57 *Ind. M. H.* 185–224 (1961).

For Illinois developments, see Arthur C. Cole's broad-ranging *The Era of the Civil War, 1848–1870* (1919) and Victor Hicken, *Illinois in the Civil War* (1966). Also useful is Jasper W. Cross, Jr., "The Civil War Comes to Egypt [Southern Illinois]," 44 *J.I.S.H.S.* 160–69 (1951). George S. May, ed., *Michigan Civil War History* (1961), is an annotated bibliography. Frank L. Klement, *Wisconsin and the Civil War* (1963), is brief but adequate. See also Walter S. Glazer, "Wisconsin Goes to War: April, 1861," 50 *Wisc. M. H.* 147–64 (1967), and James L. Sellers, "Republicanism and State Rights in Wisconsin," 17 *M.V.H.R.* 213–29 (1930).

O. B. Clark, *Politics of Iowa during the Civil War and Reconstruction* (1911), should be supplemented by the biographies of Dodge, Grimes, Kasson, and Kirkwood. Robert H. Jones, *The Civil War in the Northwest: Nebraska, Wisconsin, Iowa, Minnesota, and the Dakotas* (1960), covers territories often neglected by historians. For the states of the Far West, see Gilman M. Ostrander, *Nevada: The Great Rotten Borough* (1966); Royal A. Bennett, *All Quiet on the Yamhill: The Civil War in Oregon,* ed. by Gunter Barth (1959); John J. Earle, "The Sentiment of the People of California with Respect to the Civil War," *Ann. Rep. A.H.A.* 1907, I, 123–35; Benjamin F. Gilbert, "California and the Civil War: A Bibliographical Essay," 40 *Cal. H. S. Q.* 289–

307 (1961); Leo P. Kibby, "California, the Civil War, and the Indian Problem," 4 *Journal of the West* 183–209, 377–410 (1965); Kibby, "Some Aspects of California's Military Problems during the Civil War," 5 *C.W.H.* 251–62 (1959); and Kibby, "Union Loyalty of California's Civil War Governors," 44 *Cal. H. S. Q.* 311–21 (1965).

In a special category is Constance M. Green, *Washington: Village and Capital, 1800–1878* (1962), containing thoughtful and thoroughly researched chapters on the District of Columbia during wartime.

THE NORTH: ECONOMIC AND SOCIAL STUDIES

The best survey of economic and social developments in the wartime North is still Emerson D. Fite, *Social and Industrial Conditions in the North during the Civil War* (1910). A valuable anthology of firsthand accounts is George W. Smith and Charles Judah, eds., *Life in the North during the Civil War* (1966).

On the fiscal policies of the Federal government see, in addition to the biographies of Chase, the excellent discussion in Paul Studenski and Herman E. Krooss, *Financial History of the United States* (1952). Bray Hammond, "The North's Empty Purse," 67 *A.H.R.* 1–18 (1961), is a masterly analysis of the state of the treasury at the outbreak of hostilities. Bert W. Rein, *An Analysis and Critique of the Union Financing of the Civil War* (1962), is brief but useful. Paul B. Trescott, "Federal Government Receipts and Expenditures, 1861–1875," 26 *J. Ec. H.* 206–22 (1966), presents data not easily found elsewhere. Wesley C. Mitchell, *A History of the Greenbacks* . . . (1903), remains a classic in its field, but it can be supplemented at points by Don C. Barrett, *The Greenbacks and Resumption of Specie Payments* (1931), and Robert P. Sharkey, *Money, Class, and Party* (1959). The general tariff histories, cited above, continue to be useful; see also Reinhard H. Luthin, "Abraham Lincoln and the Tariff," 49 *A.H.R.* 609–29 (1944). Sidney Ratner, *Taxation and Democracy in America* (1967), is an excellent general presentation of Civil War imposts and their economic effects. Harry E. Smith, *The United States Federal Internal Tax History from 1861 to 1871* (1914), is for special students. Milton Friedman, "Price, Income and Monetary Changes in Three Wartime Periods," 42 *Am. Ec. Rev.* 612–25 (1952), and Marshall A. Robinson, "Federal Debt Management: Civil War, World War I, and World War II," 45 *Am. Ec. Rev.* 388–401 (1955), are stimulating reappraisals by two economists.

Recently historians have given much attention to the effect of the war upon Northern economic growth. Thomas C. Cochran, "Did the Civil War Retard Industrialization?" 48 *M.V.H.R.* 197–210 (1961), is a basic article which challenges the old stereotypes. It has provoked both controversy and further research: Carl M. Becker, "Entrepreneurial Invention and Innovation in the Miami Valley during the Civil War," 22 *Cincinnati Hist. Soc. Bull.* 5–28 (1964); Stanley L. Engerman, "The Economic Impact of the Civil War," 3 *Explorations in Entrepreneurial History*, 2nd series, 176–99 (1965); Harry N. Scheiber, "Economic Change in the Civil War Era: An Analysis of Recent Studies," 11 *C.W.H.* 396–411 (1965); Pershing Vartanian, "The Cochran Thesis: A Critique in Statistical Analysis," 51 *J.A.H.* 77–89 (1964); and

Richard F. Wacht, "A Note on the Cochran Thesis and the Small Arms Industry in the Civil War," 4 *Explorations in Entrepreneurial History*, 2nd series, 57–62 (1966). The topic is further pursued in two excellent collections: Ralph Andreano, ed., *The Economic Impact of the American Civil War* (1962), and David T. Gilchrist and W. David Lewis, eds., *Economic Change in the Civil War Era* (1965).

George E. Turner, *Victory Rode the Rails* (1953), treats both Northern and Southern railroads during the war. George B. Abdill, *Civil War Railroads* (1961), is a pictorial history. Thomas Weber, *The Northern Railroads in the Civil War, 1861–1865* (1952), is a careful work. On the Union Pacific Railroad see Wallace D. Farnham, "The Pacific Railroad Act of 1862," 43 *Nebraska History* 141–67 (1962); Farnham, " 'The Weakened Spring of Government,' " 68 *A.H.R.* 662–80 (1963); Robert W. Fogel, *The Union Pacific Railroad: A Case in Premature Enterprise* (1960); Wesley S. Griswold, *A Work of Giants* (1962); and James McCague, *Moguls and Iron Men* (1964). Other useful studies of Northern railroads include Carl R. Fish, "The Northern Railroads, April, 1861," 22 *A.H.R.* 778–93 (1917); Margaret L. Fitzsimmons, "Missouri Railroads during the Civil War and Reconstruction," 35 *Mo. H. R.* 188–206 (1941); Herman K. Murphey, "The Northern Railroads and the Civil War," 5 *M.V.H.R.* 324–38 (1918); Festus P. Summers, *The Baltimore and Ohio in the Civil War* (1939); Robert M. Sutton, "The Illinois Central: Thoroughfare for Freedom," 7 *C.W.H.* 273–87 (1961); and George R. Taylor and Irene D. Neu, *The American Railroad Network, 1861–1890* (1936).

On labor during the Civil War see, in addition to the general labor histories already cited, Norman J. Ware, *The Labor Movement in the United States, 1860–1895* (1929). Russell M. Nolen, "The Labor Movement in St. Louis from 1860 to 1890," 34 *Mo. H. R.* 157–81 (1940), and Albon P. Man, Jr., "Labor Competition and the New York Draft Riots of 1863," 36 *J.N.H.* 375–405 (1951), are helpful. See also Clarence D. Long, *Wages and Earnings in the United States, 1860–1890* (1960), and Reuben Kessel and Armen Alchian, "Real Wages in the North during the Civil War," 2 *J. of Law and Economics* (1959), 95–113.

On Northern agriculture, Paul W. Gates, *Agriculture and the Civil War* (1965), is basic. Frederick Merk, *Economic History of Wisconsin during the Civil War Decade* (1916), is invaluable for Middle Western farming. See also Wayne D. Rasmussen, "The Civil War: A Catalyst of Agricultural Revolution," 39 *Agr. H.* 187–95 (1965); Rasmussen, "The Impact of the Civil War on American Agriculture: A Review," 40 *Agr. H.* 319–21 (1966); Richard H. Sewell, "Michigan Farmers and the Civil War," 44 *Mich. H.* 353–74 (1960); David C. Smith, "Middle Range Farming in the Civil War Era," 48 *N.Y.H.* 352–69 (1967); and the biography of Cyrus H. McCormick.

There is a voluminous literature about the homestead act and its consequences which can only be suggested here. Some key articles are: Paul W. Gates, "The Homestead Law in an Incongruous Land System," 41 *A.H.R.* 652–81 (1936); Carter Goodrich and Sol Davidson, "The Wage-Earner in the Westward Movement," 50 *P.S.Q.* 161–85 (1935), and 51 *ibid.* 61–116 (1936); John B. Sanborn, "Some Political Aspects of Homestead Legislation,"

6 *A.H.R.* 19–37 (1900); and Fred A. Shannon, "The Homestead Act and the Labor Surplus," 41 *A.H.R.* 637–51 (1936).

On wartime immigration, see, in addition to the general histories of immigration listed above, Maurice G. Baxter, "Encouragement of Immigration to the Middle West during the Era of the Civil War," 46 *Ind. M. H.* 25–38 (1950), and Charlotte Erickson, *American Industry and the European Immigrant, 1860–1885* (1957).

The unsavory story of trading with the enemy during the Civil War is just beginning to be told. See four important articles by Ludwell H. Johnson: "The Butler Expedition of 1861–1862: The Profitable Side of War," 11 *C.W.H.* 229–36 (1965); "Commerce between Northeastern Ports and the Confederacy, 1861–1865," 54 *J.A.H.* 30–42 (1967); "Contraband Trade during the Last Year of the Civil War," 49 *M.V.H.R.* 635–53 (1963); and "Northern Profit and Profiteers: The Cotton Rings of 1864–1865," 12 *C.W.H.* 101–15 (1966).

The following articles deal with special aspects of Northern economic life during the Civil War: D. Balasubramanian, "Wisconsin's Foreign Trade in the Civil War Era," 46 *Wisc. M. H.* 257–62 (1963); Herbert Brinks, "The Effect of the Civil War in 1861 on Michigan Lumbering and Mining Industries," 44 *Mich. H.* 101–107 (1960); E. Merton Coulter, "Effects of Secession upon the Commerce of the Mississippi Valley," 3 *M.V.H.R.* 275–300 (1916); Dorothy J. Ernst, "Wheat Speculation in the Civil War Era," 47 *Wisc. M. H.* 125–35 (1963–64); Carl R. Fish, "Social Relief in the Northwest during the Civil War," 22 *A.H.R.* 309–24 (1917); Gerald Forbes, "The Civil War and the Beginning of the Oil Industry in West Virginia," 8 *W. Va. H.* 382–91 (1947); Katherine A. Harvey, "The Civil War and the Maryland Coal Trade," 62 *Md. H. M.* 361–80 (1967); Eugene M. Lerner, "Investment Uncertainty during the Civil War—A Note on the McCormick Brothers," 16 *J. Ec. H.* 34–40 (1956); A. Sellew Roberts, "The Federal Government and Confederate Cotton," 33 *A.H.R.* 262–75 (1927); Henry D. Shapiro, *Confiscation of Confederate Property in the North* (1962); and George W. Smith, "New England Business Interests in Missouri during the Civil War," 41 *Mo. H. R.* 1–18 (1946).

On religion in the wartime North see B. W. Korn, *American Jewry and the Civil War* (1951), W. W. Sweet, *The Methodist Episcopal Church and the Civil War* (1912), L. G. Vander Velde, *The Presbyterian Churches and the Federal Union, 1861–1869* (1932), and the December, 1960, issue of *Civil War History* (vol. VI). See also Rollin W. Quimby, "Congress and the Civil War Chaplaincy," 10 *C.W.H.* 246–59 (1964).

For a lavish and well-edited sampling of Northern propaganda efforts, see Frank Freidel, ed., *Union Pamphlets of the Civil War* (2 v., 1967). The following articles are also important: Frank Freidel, "The Loyal Publication Society: A Pro-Union Propaganda Agency," 26 *M.V.H.R.* 359–76 (1939); William B. Hesseltine, "The Propaganda Literature of Confederate Prisons," 1 *J.S.H.* 56–66 (1935); George W. Smith, "Broadsides for Freedom: Civil War Propaganda in New England," 21 *N.E.Q.* 291–312 (1948); and Smith, "The National War Committee of the Citizens of New York," 28 *N.Y.H.* 440–57 (1947).

The fullest account of Northern journalism during the war is J. Cutler Andrews, *The North Reports the Civil War* (1955). Three other spirited works deal with the same topic: Emmet Crozier, *Yankee Reporters, 1861–65* (1956); Louis M. Starr, *Bohemian Brigade* (1954); and Bernard A. Weisberger, *Reporters for the Union* (1953). See also Robert S. Harper, *Lincoln and the Press,* previously cited. The following articles are valuable: Robert S. Harper, "The Ohio Press in the Civil War," 3 *C.W.H.* 221–52 (1957); Sidney T. Matthews, "Control of the Baltimore Press during the Civil War," 36 *Md. H. M.* 150–70 (1941); J. G. Randall, "The Newspaper Problem . . . during the Civil War," 23 *A.H.R.* 303–23 (1918); Donald B. Sanger, "The Chicago Times and the Civil War," 17 *M.V.H.R.* 557–80 (1931). Consult also the biographies of such leading editors as Bennett, Bowles, Greeley, Pike, Ray, and Raymond.

On the role played by Northern women in the war, Mary Elizabeth Massey's *Bonnet Brigades,* previously cited, is invaluable.

For intellectual developments in the North two brilliant books are basic: Edmund Wilson, *Patriotic Gore,* already cited, and George M. Fredrickson, *The Inner Civil War: Northern Intellectuals and the Crisis of the Union* (1965). See also Lorraine A. Williams, "Northern Intellectual Attitudes towards Lincoln, 1860–1865," 67 *J.I.S.H.S.* 270–83 (1964), and Williams, "Northern Intellectual Reaction to Military Rule during the Civil War," 27 *Historian* 334–49 (1965).

THE NORTH: DISAFFECTION AND DISLOYALTY

The most comprehensive account of Northern disloyalty and subversion is Wood Gray, *The Hidden Civil War: The Story of the Copperheads* (1942). Like George F. Milton, whose *Abraham Lincoln and the Fifth Column* has been previously cited, Professor Gray thinks that the Copperheads posed a serious danger to the Northern war effort. On the other hand, Frank L. Klement, in *The Copperheads in the Middle West* (1960), argues that most Peace Democrats were opposed not so much to the war as to the advantages it gave to Eastern economic interests. See also Professor Klement's important essays: "Carrington and the Golden Circle Legend in Indiana during the Civil War," 61 *Ind. M. H.* 31–52 (1965); "Copperhead Secret Societies in Illinois during the Civil War," 48 *J.I.S.H.S.* 152–80 (1955); "Copperheads and Copperheadism in Wisconsin," 42 *Wis. M. H.* 182–92 (1959); "Economic Aspects of Middle Western Copperheadism," 14 *Historian* 27–44 (1951); "Middle Western Copperheadism and the Genesis of the Granger Movement," 38 *M.V.H.R.* 679–94 (1952); and "Middle Western Opposition to Lincoln's Emancipation Policy," 49 *J.N.H.* 169–83 (1964). See also the biographies of Vallandigham. For a review of the literature, consult Richard O. Curry, "The Union As It Was: A Critique of Recent Interpretations of the Copperheads," 13 *C.W.H.* 25–39 (1967).

Ollinger Crenshaw, "The Knights of the Golden Circle: The Career of George Bickley," 47 *A.H.R.* 23–50 (1941), is a good account of the founder of the principal antiwar society. Other general works on disloyalty include: William G. Carleton, "Civil War Dissidence in the North: The Perspective of a Century," 65 *S.A.Q.* 390–402 (1966); Charles H. Coleman, "The Use of the Term 'Copperhead' during the Civil War," 25 *M.V.H.R.* 263–64 (1938); William A. Dunning, "Disloyalty in Two Wars," 24 *A.H.R.* 625–30 (1919); Mayo Fesler, "Secret Political Societies in the North during the Civil War," 14 *Ind. M. H.* 183–286 (1918); and Bethania M. Smith, "Civil War Subversives," 45 *J.I.S.H.S.* 220–40 (1952).

The problem of disloyalty in the Northwestern states has been extensively explored. See, in addition to the works by Klement just cited, Curtis H. Morrow, *Politico-military Secret Societies of the Northwest, 1860–1865* (1929). The following state studies are important: Frank C. Arena, "Southern Sympathizers in Iowa during [the] Civil War Period," 30 *Annals of Iowa* (ser. 3) 486–538 (1951); A. B. Beitzinger, "The Father of Copperheadism in Wisconsin [Edward G. Ryan]," 39 *Wis. M. H.* 17–29 (1955); Florence L. Grayston, "Lambdin P. Milligan—a Knight of the Golden Circle," 43 *Ind. M. H.* 379–91 (1947); Stanley L. Jones, "Agrarian Radicalism in Illinois' Constitutional Convention of 1862," 48 *J.I.S.H.S.* 271–82 (1955); Ralph E. Morrow, "Methodists and 'Butternuts' in the Old Northwest," 49 *J.I.S.H.S.* 34–47 (1956); John W. Oliver, "Draft Riots in Wisconsin during the Civil War," 2 *Wis. M. H.* 334–36 (1919); Robert Rutland, "The Copperheads of Iowa: A Re-examination," 52 *Iowa J. H.* 1–30 (1954); and H. H. Wubben, "The Maintenance of Internal Security in Iowa, 1861–1865," 10 *C.W.H.* 401–15 (1964).

Disaffection and alleged disloyalty in the Eastern states have been far less extensively studied. See, however, John E. Talmadge, "A Peace Movement in Civil War Connecticut," 37 *N.E.Q.* 306–21 (1964); Nicholas B. Wainwright, "The Loyal Opposition in Civil War Philadelphia," 88 *Pa. M. H. & B.* 294–315 (1964); and the biographies of Pierce, Seymour, and Wood.

On the abortive movement to end the war by negotiation see Elbert J. Benton, "The Movement for Peace Without Victory during the Civil War," *Coll. West. Res. H. S.* no. 99, and Edward C. Kirkland, *The Peacemakers of 1864* (1927).

THE NEGRO IN THE CIVIL WAR

Benjamin Quarles, *The Negro in the Civil War* (1953), is the most comprehensive study. James M. McPherson, ed., *The Negro's Civil War* (1965), consists of documents skillfully woven into what amounts to a comprehensive history of how Negroes felt and acted during the war. See also Herbert Aptheker, *The Negro in the Civil War* (1938), and W. E. B. DuBois, "The Negro and the Civil War," 25 *Science and Society* 347–52 (1961).

Bell I. Wiley, *Southern Negroes, 1861–1865* (1938), is a scholarly and judicious treatment of all aspects of Negro life in the Confederacy. The following articles supplement Professor Wiley's work: Herbert Aptheker, "Notes on Slave Conspiracies in Confederate Mississippi," 29 *J.N.H.* 75–79 (1944); Mary F. Berry, "Negro Troops in Blue and Gray: The Louisiana Native Guards, 1861–1863," 8 *La. H.* 165–90 (1967); H. J. Eckenrode, "Negroes in Richmond in 1864," 46 *Va. M. H. B.* 193–200 (1938); Sing-Nan Fen, "Notes on the Education of Negroes at Norfolk and Portsmouth, Virginia, during the Civil War," 28 *Phylon* 197–207 (1967); Sing-Nan Fen, "Notes on the Education of Negroes in North Carolina during the Civil War," 36 *J. Negro Education* 24–31 (1967); Bernard H. Nelson, "Confederate Slave Impressment Legislation, 1861–1865," 31 *J.N.H.* 392–410 (1946); Nelson, "Legislative Control of the Southern Free Negro, 1861–1865," 32 *Catholic Hist. Rev.* 28–46 (1946); Nelson, "Some Aspects of Negro Life in North Carolina during the Civil War," 25 *N.C.H.R.* 143–66 (1948); Bill G. Reid, "Confederate Opponents of Arming the Slaves, 1861–1865," 22 *J. Miss. H.* 249–70 (1960); Robert D. Reid, "The Negro in Alabama during the Civil War," 35 *J.N.H.* 265–88 (1950); Nathaniel W. Stephenson, "The Question of Arming the Slaves," 18 *A.H.R.* 295–308 (1913); Joe G. Taylor, "Slavery in Louisiana during the Civil War," 8 *La. H.* 27–33 (1967); Harrison A. Trexler, "The Opposition of Planters to the Employment of Slaves as Laborers by the Confederacy," 27 *M.V.H.R.* 211–24 (1940); and Charles H. Wesley, "The Employment of Negroes as Soldiers in the Confederate Army," 4 *J.N.H.* 239–53 (1919).

Dudley T. Cornish, *The Sable Arm* (1956), is an excellent account of the use of Negroes in the Union army. George Washington Williams, *A History of the Negro Troops in the War of the Rebellion, 1861–65* (1888), though old, continues to be very valuable. See also Thomas W. Higginson, *Army Life in a Black Regiment* (1870), an account by a Massachusetts man who commanded Negro troops, and John H. Franklin, ed., *The Diary of James T. Ayers* (1947), the story of a man who recruited them. Henry Swint, ed., *Dear Ones at Home* (1966), is a collection of moving letters from contraband camps. Useful articles on this subject are Herbert Aptheker, "Negro Casualties in the Civil War," 32 *J.N.H.* 10–80 (1947); Aptheker, "The Negro in the Union Navy," 32 *J.N.H.* 169–200 (1947); Warren B. Armstrong, "Union Chaplains and the Education of the Freedmen," 52 *J.N.H.* 104–15 (1967); Martha M. Bigelow, "Freedmen of the Mississippi Valley, 1862–1865," 8 *C.W.H.* 38–47 (1962); Bigelow, "Vicksburg: Experiment in Freedom," 26 *J. Miss. H.* 28–44 (1964); Frederick M. Binder, "Pennsylvania Negro Regiments in the Civil War," 37 *J.N.H.* 383–417 (1952); John W. Blassingame, "The Recruitment of Colored Troops in Kentucky, Maryland and Missouri, 1863–1865," 29 *Historian* 533–45 (1967); Blassingame, "The Union Army as an Educational Institution for Negroes, 1862–1865," 34 *J. Negro Education* 152–59 (1965); Brainerd Dyer, "The Treatment of Colored Union Troops by the Confederates, 1861–1865," 20 *J.N.H.* 273–86 (1935); Victor Hicken, "The Record of Illinois' Negro Soldiers in the Civil War," 56 *J.I.S.H.S.* 529–51 (1963); Roland C. McConnell, ed., "Concerning the Procurement of Negro Troops in the South during the Civil War," 35 *J.N.H.* 320–35 (1950); L. D. Reddick, "The Negro Policy of the United States Army," 34 *J.N.H.* 9–29 (1949); Fred A. Shannon, "The Federal Government and the Negro Soldier, 1861–1865," 11 *J.N.H.* 563–83 (1926); Tinsley L. Spraggins, "Mobilization of Negro Labor for the Department of Virginia and North Carolina, 1861–1865," 24 *N.C.H.R.* 160–97 (1947); Charles L. Wagandt, "The Army Versus Maryland Slavery, 1862–1864," 10 *C.W.H.* 141–48 (1964); Bell I. Wiley, "Billy Yank and the Black Folk," 36 *J.N.H.* 35–52 (1951).

James M. McPherson, *The Struggle for Equality: Abolitionists and the Ne-*

gro in the Civil War and Reconstruction (1964), is an important work which stresses the idealistic motives of many antislavery groups in the North. The ugly racist ideas which were probably shared by more Northerners are presented in two excellent studies: V. Jacque Voegeli, *Free But Not Equal: The Midwest and the Negro during the Civil War* (1967), and Forrest G. Wood, *Black Scare: The Racist Response to Emancipation and Reconstruction* (1968). Charles L. Wagandt, *The Mighty Revolution: Negro Emancipation in Maryland, 1862–1864* (1964), is a close study of conflicting ideologies in a key state. Other useful articles on the Negro as a political issue in the wartime North are: Ray Abrams, "The Copperhead Newspapers and the Negro," 20 *J.N.H.* 131–52 (1935); William M. Armstrong, "The Freedmen's Movement and the Founding of the Nation," 53 *J.A.H.* 708–26 (1967); Albert Castel, "Civil War Kansas and the Negro," 51 *J.N.H.* 125–38 (1966); Leslie H. Fishel, Jr., "Wisconsin and Negro Suffrage," 46 *Wisc. M. H.* 180–96 (1963); Joseph E. Holliday, "Freemen's Aid Societies in Cincinnati, 1862–1870," 22 *Cincinnati Hist. Soc. Bull.* 169–85 (1964); Sidney Kaplan, "The Miscegenation Issue in the Election of 1864," 34 *J.N.H.* 274–343 (1949); Williston H. Lofton, "Northern Labor and the Negro during the Civil War," 34 *J.N.H.* 251–73 (1949); Emma L. Thornbrough, "The Race Issue in Indiana Politics during the Civil War," 47 *Ind. M. H.* 163–88 (1951); and Jacque Voegeli, "The Northwest and the Race Issue, 1861–1862," 50 *M.V.H.R.* 235–51 (1963).

Lincoln's attitude toward the Negro and emancipation has been elaborately treated in all the standard Lincoln biographies. Benjamin Quarles, *Lincoln and the Negro,* previously cited, is a balanced study. John H. Franklin, *The Emancipation Proclamation* (1963), is the standard monograph. For reactions to the proclamation see Mark M. Krug, "The Republican Party and the Emancipation Proclamation," 48 *J.N.H.* 98–114 (1963); Roland C. McConnell, "From the Preliminary to Final Emancipation: The First Hundred Days," 48 *J.N.H.* 260–76 (1963); Harold D. Moser, "Reaction in North Carolina to the Emancipation Proclamation," 44 *N.C.H.R.* 53–71 (1967); Lorraine A. Williams, "Northern Intellectual Reaction to the Policy of Emancipation," 46 *J.N.H.* 174–88 (1961).

P. J. Staudenraus, *The African Colonization Movement, 1816–1865* (1961), is the standard history of the efforts to colonize the free Negro outside of the United States. Other useful studies include: Frederic Bancroft, "The Colonization of American Negroes, 1801–1865," in Jacob E. Cooke, *Frederic Bancroft: Historian* (1957), 145–263; Warren A. Beck, "Lincoln and Negro Colonization in Central America," 6 *A.L.Q.* 162–83 (1950); Willis D. Boyd, "James Redpath and American Negro Colonization in Haiti, 1860–1862," 12 *The Americas* 169–82 (1955); N. A. N. Cleven, "Some Plans for Colonizing Liberated Negro Slaves in Hispanic America," 11 *J.N.H.* 35–49 (1926); Brainerd Dyer, "The Persistence of the Idea of Negro Colonization," 12 *Pac. H. R.* 53–67 (1943); Walter L. Fleming, "Deportation and Colonization: An Attempted Solution of the Race Problem," in *Studies in Southern History . . . Inscribed to William Archibald Dunning,* 3–30; Luveta W. Gresham, "Colonization Proposals for Free Negroes and Contrabands during the Civil War," 16 *Jour. Negro Education* 28–33 (1947); James M.

McPherson, "Abolitionist and Negro Opposition to Colonization during the Civil War," 26 *Phylon* 391–99 (1965); Walter A. Payne, "Lincoln's Caribbean Colonization Plan," 7 *Pacific Historian* 65–72 (1963); and Paul J. Scheips, "Lincoln and the Chiriqui Colonization Project," 37 *J.N.H.* 418–53 (1952).

WARTIME DIPLOMACY

Samuel Flagg Bemis and Grace G. Griffin, *Guide to the Diplomatic History of the United States, 1775–1921* (1935), is the best guide to the elaborate sources and voluminous secondary literature in this field; unfortunately, however, it is now much out of date. There is no satisfactory comprehensive account of Federal wartime diplomacy. See, however, the biographies of Seward and Samuel Flagg Bemis, ed., *The American Secretaries of State and Their Diplomacy* (10 v., 1927–29). The Confederacy has been more fortunate in this regard. James M. Callahan, *Diplomatic History of the Southern Confederacy* (1901), is still useful, and Frank L. Owsley, *King Cotton Diplomacy* (1931; rev. ed., 1959), is a thorough modern treatment. See also Henry Blumenthal, "Confederate Diplomacy: Popular Notions and International Realities," 32 *J.S.H.* 151–71 (1966).

Donaldson Jordan and Edwin J. Pratt, *Europe and the American Civil War* (1931), treats of the reactions of all the European states to the conflict. See also the interesting anthology of contemporary opinion, edited by Belle B. Sideman and Lillian Friedman, *Europe Looks at the Civil War* (1960), and Philip Van Doren Stern, *When the Guns Roared: World Aspects of the American Civil War* (1965).

Ephraim D. Adams, *Great Britain and the American Civil War* (2 v., 1925), though old, remains the authoritative work on Anglo-American relations during this crucial period. See also the briefer account of "Anglo-American Relations during the Civil War, 1860–1865," by A. P. Newton in A. W. Ward and G. P. Gooch, eds., *The Cambridge History of British Foreign Policy* (1923), 488–521. A recent comprehensive work is H. C. Allen, *Great Britain and the United States* (1955). Max Beloff, "Great Britain and the American Civil War," 37 *History* 40–48 (1952), is a thoughtful review of recent scholarship in this field. Robert H. Jones, "The American Civil War in the British Sessional Papers," 107 *Am. Philosophical Society Proc.* 415–26 (1963), is an invaluable guide to these official sources. See also Jones's "Anglo-American Relations, 1861–1865, Reconsidered," 45 *Mid-America* 36–49 (1963).

The best biographies of Lord Palmerston are those by Herbert C. F. Bell (2 v., 1936) and Donald Southgate (1966). For Earl Russell see the biography by Spenser Walpole (2 v., 1889), and G. P. Gooch, ed., *The Later Correspondence of Lord John Russell, 1840–1878* (2 v., 1925). Gladstone's position is analyzed in the biographies by Philip M. Magnus (1954) and John Morley (2 v., 1908) and in C. Collyer, "Gladstone and the American Civil War," 6 *Proc. Leeds Philosophical Soc.* (Pt. 8), 583–94. Cobden's friendship for the North is documented in John Morley, *The Life of Richard Cobden* (2 v., 1881), and in Edward L. Pierce, ed., "Letters of Richard Cobden to Charles Sumner, 1862–1865," 2 *A.H.R.* 306–19 (1897). For another powerful English friend of the Union cause see Herman Ausubel, *John Bright: Victorian Reformer* (1966), George M. Trevelyan, *The Life of John Bright* (1913), R. A. J. Walling, ed., *The Diaries of John Bright* (1931), and "Bright-Sumner Letters, 1861–1872," 46 *Mass. H. S. P.* 93–164 (1912). *The History of the [London] Times: The Tradition Established, 1841–1884* (1939) is a highly satisfactory account of the principal journalistic opponent of the Federals. Wilbur D. Jones, "The British Conservatives and the American Civil War," 58 *A.H.R.* 527–43 (1953), stresses that Palmerston's opponents did not make intervention a party issue. Robert Blake, *Disraeli* (1967), is a fascinating biography of one of the principal Conservatives. For the firsthand observations of another Tory, see Elisabeth J. Doyle, ed., "A Report on Civil War America: Sir James Fergusson's Five-Week Visit (Sept.–Oct. 1861)," 12 *C.W.H.* 357–62 (1966).

J. R. Pole, *Abraham Lincoln and the Working Classes of Britain* (1959), is a brief account of the group most hostile to the Confederacy. See also Royden Harrison, "British Labor and American Slavery," 25 *Science and Society* 291–319 (1961), and Gerald Runkle, "Karl Marx and the American Civil War," 6 *Comp. Stud. in Soc. and Hist.* 117–41 (1964).

The economic interpretation of English neutrality during the Civil War, as being based on the need for Northern wheat, was put forth by Louis B. Schmidt in "The Influence of Wheat and Cotton on Anglo-American Relations during the Civil War," 16 *Iowa J. H. & P.* 400–39 (1918). This theory has now been discredited by such scholars as Martin P. Claussen, "Peace Factors in Anglo-American Relations, 1861–1865," 26 *M.V.H.R.* 511–22 (1940), and Eli Ginzberg, "The Economics of British Neutrality during the American Civil War," 10 *Agr. H.* 147–56 (1936). For recent statements see Amos Khasigian, "Economic Factors and British Neutrality, 1861–1865," 25 *Historian* 241–65 (1963), and Robert H. Jones, "Long Live the King?" 37 *Agr. H.* 166–69 (1963).

Technical problems concerning neutrality, the right of search, and the efficacy of the blockade are presented in Charles F. Adams, *Seward and the Declaration of Paris* (1912); Alice M. McDiarmid, "American Civil War Precedents: The Nature, Application, and Extension," 34 *Am. Jour. Internat. Law* 220–37 (1940); Frank L. Owsley, "America and the Freedom of the Seas, 1861–1865," in Avery O. Craven, ed., *Essays in Honor of William E. Dodd* (1935), 194–256; and Edward A. Trescot, contributor, "The Confederacy and the Declaration of Paris," 23 *A.H.R.* 826–35 (1918). See also three important studies by James P. Baxter, 3rd: "The British Government and Neutral Rights, 1861–1865," 34 *A.H.R.* 9–29 (1928); "Papers Relating to Belligerent and Neutral Rights, 1861–1865," 34 *A.H.R.* 77–91 (1928); and "Some British Opinions as to Neutral Rights, 1861 to 1865," 23 *Am. Jour. Internat. Law,* 517–37 (1929).

A new scholarly study of the *Trent* affair is needed. Thomas L. Harris, *The Trent Affair* (1896), is old and partisan; Evan John, *Atlantic Impact, 1861* (1952), is superficial. See, however, the following useful articles: Charles F. Adams, "The Trent Affair," 17 *A.H.R.* 540–62 (1912); Victor H. Cohen, "Charles Sumner and the *Trent* Affair," 22 *J.S.H.* 205–19 (1956); Norman B. Ferris, "Abraham Lincoln and the *Trent* Affair," 49 *Lincoln Herald*

131–35 (1967); Ferris, "The Prince Consort, 'The Times,' and the Trent Affair," 6 *C.W.H.* 152–56 (1960); and Arnold Whitridge, "The Trent Affair, 1861," 4 *Hist. Today* 394–402 (1954). See also Harold E. Hancock and Norman B. Wilkinson, " 'The Devil to Pay!': Saltpeter and the Trent Affair," 10 *C.W.H.* 20–32 (1964).

Others aspects of Anglo-American relations are treated in Stuart L. Bernath, "Squall Across the Atlantic: The *Peterhoff* Episode," 34 *J.S.H.* 382–401 (1968); Milledge L. Bonham, *The British Consuls in the Confederacy* (1911); Edward W. Ellsworth, "Anglo-American Affairs in October of 1862," 66 *Lincoln Herald* 89–96 (1964); Ellsworth, "British Consuls in the Confederacy during 1862," 66 *Lincoln Herald,* 149–54 (1964); Ellsworth, "Lord John Russell and British Consuls in America in 1861," 66 *Lincoln Herald* 34–40 (1964); Don Higginbotham, "A Raider Refuels: Diplomatic Repercussions," 4 *C.W.H.* 129–42 (1958); J. Franklin Jameson, "The London Expenditures of the Confederate Secret Service," 35 *A.H.R.* 811–24 (1930); Wilbur D. Jones, *The Confederate Rams at Birkenhead* (1961); John H. Kiger, "Federal Government Propaganda in Great Britain during the American Civil War," 19 *Hist. Outlook* 204–209 (1929); Frank Merli, "Crown versus Cruiser: The Curious Case of the Alexandra," 9 *C.W.H.* 167–77 (1963); Frank J. Merli and Thomas W. Green, "Great Britain and the Confederate Navy, 1861–1865," 14 *Hist. Today* 687–95 (1964); Stephen B. Oates, "Henry Hotze: Confederate Agent Abroad," 27 *Historian* 131–54 (1965); and Arthur W. Silver, ed., "Henry Adams' 'Diary of a Visit to Manchester,' " 51 *A.H.R.* 74–89 (1945). Three scholarly essays by Douglas H. Maynard are of great interest: "The Forbes-Aspinwall Mission," 45 *M.V.H.R.* 67–89 (1958); "Plotting the Escape of the *Alabama,*" 20 *J.S.H.* 197–209 (1954); and "Union Efforts to Prevent the Escape of the 'Alabama,' " 41 *M.V.H.R.* 41–60 (1954). The following articles by Arnold Whitridge are popular but sound: "The Alabama, 1862–1864: A Crisis in Anglo-American Relations," 5 *Hist. Today* 174–85 (1955); "Anglo-American Trouble-Makers: J. G. Bennett and J. T. Delane," 6 *Hist. Today* 88–95 (1956); "The Peaceable Ambassadors," 8 *Am. Heritage* 40–43 ff. (Apr., 1957); and "British Liberals and the American Civil War," 12 *Hist. Today* 688–95 (1962).

On wartime relations with France the standard work is Henry Blumenthal, *A Reappraisal of Franco-American Relations, 1830–1871* (1959). See also Lynn M. Case, *French Opinion on the United States and Mexico, 1860–1867* (1936), and W. Reed West, *Contemporary French Opinion on the American Civil War* (1924). Hubert Galle, *La 'Famine du coton,' 1861–1865* (1967), suggests the economic pressures to which Napoleon was subjected. The best account of the French adventure in Mexico is Count Egon C. Corti, *Maximilian and Charlotte of Mexico* (2 v., 1928). Ralph Roeder, *Juarez and His Mexico* (2 v., 1947), is a standard work.

See also Paul P. du Bellet, *The Diplomacy of the Confederate Cabinet of Richmond and its Agents Abroad,* ed. William S. Hoole (1963); Serge Gavronsky, "American Slavery and the French Liberals," 51 *J.N.H.* 36–52 (1966); Kathryn A. Hanna, "The Roles of the South in the French Intervention in Mexico," 20 *J.S.H.* 3–21 (1954); Earl S. Pomeroy, "French Substitutes for American Cotton, 1861–1865," 9 *J.S.H.* 555–60 (1943); and

802 BIBLIOGRAPHY

Louis M. Sears, "A Confederate Diplomat at the Court of Napoleon III," 26 *A.H.R.* 255–81 (1921).

Benjamin P. Thomas, *Russo-American Relations, 1815–1867* (1930), and Albert A. Woldman, *Lincoln and the Russians* (1952), are both sound works. See also E. A. Adamov, ed., "Documents Relating to Russian Policy during the American Civil War," 2 *Jour. Mod. Hist.* 603–11 (1930); Adamov, "Russia and the United States at the Time of the Civil War," 2 *Jour. Mod. Hist.* 586–602 (1930); Harold E. Blinn, "Seward and the Polish Rebellion of 1863," 45 *A.H.R.* 828–33 (1940); and Frank A. Golder, "The American Civil War through the Eyes of a Russian Diplomat," 26 *A.H.R.* 454–63 (1921); and John Kutolowski, "The Effect of the Polish Insurrection of 1863 on the American Civil War Diplomacy," 27 *Historian* 560–77 (1965). The visit of the Russian fleet to America has been elaborately studied in Thomas A. Bailey, "The Russian Fleet Myth Re-Examined," 38 *M.V.H.R.* 81–90 (1951); Frank A. Golder, "The Russian Fleet and the Civil War," 20 *A.H.R.* 801–12 (1915); William E. Nagengast, "The Visit of the Russian Fleet to the United States: Were Americans Deceived?" 8 *Russian Rev.* 46–55 (1949); and Earl S. Pomeroy, "The Myth after the Russian Fleet, 1863," 31 *N.Y.H.* 169–76 (1950).

Robin Winks, *Canada and the United States: the Civil War Years* (1960), is scholarly and thorough. See also Arthur H. De Rosier, Jr., "The Confederates in Canada: A Survey," 3 *Southern Quarterly* 312–24 (1965); Ludwell H. Johnson, "Beverley Tucker's Canadian Mission, 1864–65," 29 *J.S.H.* 88–99 (1963); Fred Landon, "The American Civil War and Canadian Confederation," *Trans. of the Royal Society of Canada,* 3 ser., XXI, sec. II, 55–62 (1927), and Helen G. Macdonald, *Canadian Public Opinion on the American Civil War* (1926).

On Latin-American relations see Nathan L. Ferris, "The Relations of the United States with South America during the American Civil War," 21 *Hispanic Am. Hist. Rev.* 51–78 (1941), and Dexter Perkins's definitive *The Monroe Doctrine, 1826–1867* (1933).

Of course any study of foreign relations during the Civil War period must make heavy use of the biographies of American diplomats. See, in addition to the lives of Secretary Seward and Secretary Benjamin, the studies listed under Charles Francis Adams, Henry Adams, Bigelow, Bulloch, Cassius M. Clay, Corwin, Dudley, Evarts, Forbes, Lamar, Marsh, Mason, Moran, Motley, Sanford, Schurz, Slidell, Goldwin Smith, Sumner, and Robert J. Walker. For Lincoln's role in foreign affairs, consult Monaghan's *Diplomat in Carpet Slippers,* already cited.

MILITARY ACCOUNTS

Marcus Cunliffe, *Soldiers and Civilians: The Martial Spirit in America, 1775–1865* (1968), is a brilliant intellectual history, indispensable as background for a proper understanding of the military operations of the Civil War.

The basic source for the military history of the Civil War is the monumental *War of the Rebellion: . . . Official Records of the Union and Confederate Armies* (128 v., 1880–1901), an indispensable compendium of correspondence and battle reports from both armies. For the history of this important publication see Joseph L. Eisendrath, Jr., *"The Official Records*—Sixty-three Years in the Making," 1 *C.W.H.* 89–94 (1955), and Dallas D. Irvine, "The Genesis of the *Official Records*," 24 *M.V.H.R.* 221–29 (1937). Next to the *Official Records, Battles and Leaders of the Civil War,* ed. by Clarence C. Buel and Robert U. Johnson (4 v., 1887), is the most useful source, being a compilation of recollections by nearly all of the principal generals on both sides.

M. M. Boatner's *Civil War Dictionary,* previously cited, continues to be an invaluable reference tool. Ezra J. Warner, *Generals in Gray* (1959), and *Generals in Blue* (1964), contain good biographical sketches of all Confederate and Union commanders. See also William F. Amann, ed., *Personnel of the Civil War* (2 v., 1961). Frederick H. Dyer, *A Compendium of the War of the Rebellion* (1908), is an invaluable guide both to the engagements of the war and to the units which fought in them; there is a new edition in 3 vols., with introduction by Bell I. Wiley (1960). On Civil War casualties see William F. Fox, *Regimental Losses in the American Civil War, 1861–1865* (1889), and Thomas L. Livermore, *Numbers and Losses in the Civil War in America, 1861–1865* (1901; new ed., 1957).

Bibliography of State Participation in the Civil War, 1861–1866 (3rd ed., 1913), is an indispensable but incomplete and badly arranged guide. It is gradually being superseded by Charles E. Dornbusch, *Regimental Publications and Personal Narratives of the Civil War* (2 v. to date, 1961–   ).

Much of the best and most interesting writing on military aspects of the Civil War is contained in the biographies, autobiographies, and published letters of participants. For the principal Union commanders see the entries in the biographical section, listed above, under Ames, Banks, Burnside, Butler, Chamberlain, J. D. Cox, Custer, DeTrobriand, Ellsworth, Frémont, Garfield, Geary, Gibbon, Grant, Halleck, Hancock, Haupt, Hitchcock, Hooker, Howard, Kearny, Logan, Lyon, McClellan, McPherson, Meade, Meigs, Marsena Patrick, F. J. Porter, H. Porter, Rawlins, Reynolds, Rosecrans, Schofield, Schurz, Scott, Sheridan, W. T. Sherman, Sickles, W. F. Smith, Thomas, Upton, Wadsworth, Wallace, Warren, A. S. Williams, and J. H. Wilson. For Confederate biographies see the entries under Ashby, Beauregard, Bragg, Buckner, Early, Ewell, Forrest, J. B. Gordon, Gorgas, Hampton, Hardee, A. P. Hill, D. H. Hill, Hood, Jackson, A. S. Johnston, J. E. Johnston, Kirby Smith, Lee, Longstreet, Mahone, Mosby, Northrup, Pemberton, Pendleton, Pickett, Pike, Polk, Price, Shelby, Stuart, R. Taylor, Toombs, Van Dorn, Wheat, and Wheeler. Of these biographies Douglas S. Freeman's *R. E. Lee* is outstanding.

The lives of generals deal with weighty matters of strategy and tactics, but the autobiographies and letters of subordinate officers and privates give a better insight into the way the average Civil War soldier thought and felt. Among the best of these firsthand accounts are those (again listed in the biographical section above) of C. F. Adams, Beatty, Blackford, Connolly, Cooke, DeForest, Dooley, H. K. Douglas, Eggleston, Fay, Gray, Haskell, Heartsill, Higginson, H. Hitchcock, Holmes, Hyde, H. B. McClellan, McKim, Marshall, Moore, Neese, Patrick, Pepper, Pike, Sorrel, Stockwell, Trader, Upson, Watkins, and W. N. Wood.

Drawing upon such publications and upon large numbers of unpublished manuscript collections, Bell I. Wiley has written two fascinating studies of the common soldiers of the war: *The Life of Johnny Reb* (1943) and *The Life of Billy Yank* (1952). See also Fred A. Shannon, "The Life of the Common Soldier in the Union Army, 1861–1865," 13 *M.V.H.R.* 465–82 (1927). Three admirable modern unit histories are Alan T. Nolan, *The Iron Brigade* (1961); John J. Pullen, *The Twentieth Maine* (1957); and James I. Robertson, Jr., *The Stonewall Brigade* (1963).

Fred A. Shannon, *The Organization and Administration of the Union Army, 1861–1865* (2 v., 1928), is a standard work, stronger, however, on the demoralization of the early months of the war than on the relative efficiency of the later years. See the critique of this work in Kenneth P. Williams, *Lincoln Finds a General*, II, 796–803. A. H. Meneely, *The War Department, 1861* (1928), is an excellent account of the mismanagement of Cameron's regime. See also Brooks M. Kelley, "Fossildom, Old Fogeyism, and Red Tape," 40 *Pa. M. H. & B.* 93–114 (1966). Emory Upton's *The Military Policy of the United States* (1904), is both a general history and a biting criticism of American military practices. See Ambrose's biography of Upton, previously cited. Frank Freidel, "General Orders 100 and Military Government," 32 *M.V.H.R.* 541–56 (1946), describes the efforts of Francis Lieber and Henry W. Halleck to draw up a code of law regulating the practices of the Union armies. See also James G. Garner, "General Order 100 Revisited," 27 *Military Law R.* 1–48 (1965).

For Lincoln's relations with the Union generals and armies see the "Lincolniana" section, above, and especially T. Harry Williams, *Lincoln and His Generals*.

George W. Adams, *Doctors in Blue* (1952), George W. Smith, *Medicines for the Union Army* (1962), and Paul E. Steiner, *Physician-Generals in the Civil War* (1966), adequately cover medical aspects of the Union army. The invaluable work of the United States Sanitary Commission is well treated in William Q. Maxwell, *Lincoln's Fifth Wheel* (1956). See also the biographies of Clara Barton, Bellows, Dorothea Dix, and Walt Whitman.

For problems of intelligence and security see, in addition to Marsena R. Patrick's diary, previously cited, Edwin C. Fishel, "The Mythology of Civil War Intelligence," 10 *C.W.H.* 344–67 (1964); Wilton P. Moore, "The Provost Marshal Goes to War," 5 *C.W.H.* 62–71 (1959); and David S. Sparks, "General Patrick's Progress: Intelligence and Security in the Army of the Potomac," 10 *C.W.H.* 371–84 (1964).

The work of the quartermaster's department is admirably detailed in Weigley's biography of Meigs, previously cited. See also A. B. Warfield, "The Quartermaster's Department, 1861–1864," 8 *Quartermaster's Rev.* 43–46 (1928).

Robert V. Bruce, *Lincoln and the Tools of War* (1956), is a fine account of the President's efforts to prod the army ordnance department into action.

Other useful military studies include: Edward Hagerman: "From Jomini to Dennis Hart Mahan: The Evolution of Trench Warfare and the American Civil War," 13 *C.W.H.* 197–220 (1967); James A. Huston, "Logistical Support of Federal Armies in the Field," 7 *C.W.H.* 36–47 (1961); John K. Mahon, "Civil War Infantry Assault Tactics," 25 *Military Affairs*, 57–68

(1961); L. Van Loan Naisawald, *Grape and Canister: The Story of the Field Artillery of the Army of the Potomac, 1861–1865* (1960); Paul J. Scheips, "Union Signal· Communications: Innovation and Conflict," 9 *C.W.H.* 399– 421 (1963); Stephen Starr, "Cold Steel: The Saber and the Union Cavalry," 11 *C.W.H.* 142–59 (1963); and Roy P. Stonesifer, Jr., "The Union Cavalry Comes of Age," 11 *C.W.H.* 274–83 (1965).

The best account of the operations of the draft in the North is Jack F. Leach, *Conscription in the United States* (1952). Other important studies are Hugh G. Earnhart, "Commutation: Democratic or Undemocratic?" 12 *C.W.H.* 132–42 (1966); Carl R. Fish, "Conscription in the Civil War," 21 *A.H.R.* 100–103 (1915); Neil C. Kimmons, "Federal Draft Exemptions, 1863– 1865," 15 *Military Affairs* 25–33 (1951); Eugene C. Murdock, *Ohio's Bounty System in the Civil War* (1963); Murdock, *Patriotism Limited, 1862–1865: The Civil War Draft and the Bounty System* (1967); and Edward N. Wright, *Conscientious Objectors in the Civil War* (1931). James McCague, *The Second Rebellion* (1968), is a lively account of the riots provoked in New York City by the draft. See also A. Hunter Dupree and Leslie H. Fishel, Jr., eds., "An Eyewitness Account of the New York Draft Riots, July, 1863," 47 *M.V.H.R.* 472–79 (1960).

Ella Lonn, *Foreigners in the Union Army and Navy* (1951), is a massive and detailed work. It can be supplemented by Alan Conway, "Welshmen in the Union Armies," 4 *C.W.H.* 142–74 (1958); Robert L. Peterson and John A. Hudson, "Foreign Recruitment for Union Forces," 7 *C.W.H.* 176–89 (1961); William F. Raney, "Recruiting and Crimping in Canada for the Northern Forces, 1861–1865," 10 *M.V.H.R.* 21–33 (1923); and Robin W. Winks, "Creation of a Myth: Canadian Enlistments in the Northern Armies during the Civil War," 39 *Canadian Hist. Rev.* 24–40 (1958).

Frederick S. Haydon, *Aeronautics in the Union and Confederate Armies* . . . (1941), deals authoritatively with an almost forgotten aspect of the war. See also Eugene B. Block, *Above the Civil War: The Story of Thaddeus Lowe, Balloonist, Inventor, Railway Builder* (1966).

There is no magisterial study of the organization and administration of the Confederate army comparable to Shannon's treatment of the Northern forces. Frank E. Vandiver, *Rebel Brass* (1956), is a brief, brilliant critique of the Southern command system. Problems of Confederate supply are discussed in five important articles by Professor Vandiver: "Confederate Plans for Procuring Subsistence Stores," 27 *Tyler's Q. Hist. & Geneal. Mag.* 273–77 (1946); "The Food Supply of the Confederate Armies," 26 *Tyler's Q. Hist. & Geneal. Mag.* 77–89 (1944); "Makeshifts of Confederate Ordnance," 17 *J.S.H.* 180– 93 (1951); "A Sketch of Efforts . . . to Equip the Confederate Armory at Macon," 28 *Ga. H. Q.* 34–40 (1944); and "Texas and the Confederate Army's Meat Problem," 47 *Sw. H. Q.* 225–33 (1944). See also Charles W. Ramsdell, "General Robert E. Lee's Horse Supply, 1862–1865," 35 *A.H.R.* 758–77 (1930); Jac Weller, "The Confederate Use of British Cannon," 3 *C.W.H.* 135–52 (1957); and Weller, "Imported Confederate Shoulder Weapons," 5 *C.W.H.* 157–82 (1959).

The work ·of special branches of the Confederate armies is discussed in H. V. Canan, "Confederate Military Intelligence," 59 *Md. H. M.* 34–51

(1964); H. H. Cunningham, *Doctors in Gray,* previously cited; Ralph W. Donnelly, "Scientists of the Confederate Nitre and Mining Bureau," 2 *C.W.H.* 69–92 (1956); Bruce S. Eastwood, "Confederate Medical Problems in the Atlanta Campaign," 47 *Ga. H. Q.* 276–91 (1963); Robert P. Felgar, "The Ordnance Department of the Confederate States Army," 8 *Ala. H. Q.* 159–232 (1946); James L. Nichols, *Confederate Engineers* (1957); Nichols, *The Confederate Quartermaster in the Trans-Mississippi* (1964); Stephen B. Oates, "Recruiting Confederate Cavalry in Texas," 64 *Sw. H. Q.* 463–77 (1961); Richard P. Weinert, "The Confederate Regular Army," 26 *Military Affairs* 97–107 (1962); William T. Windham, "The Problem of Supply in the Trans-Mississippi Confederacy," 27 *J.S.H.* 149–68 (1961). See also the biographies of Gorgas and Northrup.

Conscription in the South is fully treated in A. B Moore's *Conscription and Conflict,* previously cited. See also Robert P. Brooks, "Conscription in the Confederate States of America, 1862–1865," 1 *Mil. Hist. and Econ.* 419–42 (1916); Memory F. Mitchell, *Legal Aspects of Conscription and Exemption in North Carolina, 1861–1865* (1965); and William L. Shaw, "The Confederate Conscription and Exemption Acts," 6 *Am. J. of Legal Hist.* 368–405 (1962).

To the actual military engagements of the war Richard E. Dupuy and Trevor N. Dupuy, *The Compact History of the Civil War* (1960), provides a good brief introduction. *Campaigns of the Civil War* (13 v., 1881–1883) is a cooperative work, whose volumes vary widely in quality. *History of the Civil War in America* by the Comte de Paris (Louis Phillippe Albert d'Orléans) (4 v., 1875–1888) is a work of remarkable ability, giving much stress to the organizational problems of the armies and their logistics. One of the best of the older histories is *The Story of the Civil War* (4 v., 1898–1913) by John C. Ropes and W. R. Livermore. Kenneth P. Williams, *Lincoln Finds a General* (5 v., 1949–1959), is a comprehensive and masterly study of the Northern armies and their commanders to 1864. Russell F. Weigley, *Towards an American Army: American Military Thought from Washington to Marshall* (1962), is a valuable analysis of the concepts of warfare held by Civil War generals. Warren W. Hassler, *Commanders of the Army of the Potomac* (1962), discusses those generals from a pro-McClellan point of view, while T. Harry Williams in "The Military Leadership of the North and South," in David Donald, ed., *Why the North Won the Civil War,* 33–54, and in *McClellan, Sherman and Grant* (1962), takes an opposite position. For a stimulating critique of strategy see Grady McWhiney, "Who Whipped Whom?" 11 *C.W.H.* 5–26 (1965).

The engagements of the American Civil War have had a considerable fascination for English historians and military men. For the best of these writings see Alfred H. Burne, *Lee, Grant and Sherman* (1938); Cyril Falls, *A Hundred Years of War* (1954); G. F. R. Henderson, *The Civil War, a Soldier's View* (1958); Frederick Maurice, *Statesmen and Soldiers of the Civil War* (1926); Garnet J. Wolseley, *The American Civil War: An English View,* ed. James A. Rawley (1964); and W. Birkbeck Wood and J. E. Edmonds, *A History of the Civil War in the United States, 1861–5* (1905). Henderson's *Jackson,* Liddell Hart's *Sherman,* and Ballard's *Military Genius of Abraham Lincoln,* all previously cited, also fall into this category. Jay Luvaas, *The Military Legacy of the*

Civil War (1959), is an acute study of the impact the American conflict had upon European military thought.

Virtually every major engagement of the Civil War has its own extensive and controversial literature, and only a few of the most important titles can be suggested here. The best introduction to Federal operations in the Eastern theater of the war is Bruce Catton's absorbing trilogy: *Mr. Lincoln's Army* (1951); *Glory Road* (1952); and *A Stillness at Appomattox* (1953). Douglas S. Freeman's *Lee's Lieutenants* (3 v., 1942–1944) is an equally fascinating account of Confederate operations in the same area.

Bull Run by Robert M. Johnston (1913) is still the best monograph on First Manassas. Clifford Dowdey, *The Seven Days: The Emergence of Lee* (1964), is superb military history. Edward J. Stackpole, *From Cedar Mountain to Antietam* (1959), is clear and accurate. Chancellorsville has been well studied by John Bigelow (1910) and by Edward J. Stackpole (1958). Fairfax Downey, *Clash of Cavalry* (1959), is a spirited narrative of the forgotten battle of Brandy Station.

Too much has been written about the battle of Gettysburg. The best modern accounts are Edwin B. Coddington, *The Gettysburg Campaign* (1968); Clifford Dowdey, *Death of a Nation* (1958); James S. Montgomery, *The Shaping of a Battle: Gettysburg* (1959); Wilbur S. Nye, *Here Come the Rebels!* (1965); Edward J. Stackpole, *They Met at Gettysburg* (1956); George R. Stewart, *Pickett's Charge* (1959); and Glenn Tucker, *High Tide at Gettysburg* (1958). See also extracts from ninety-two contemporary accounts in Earl S. Miers and Richard B. Brown, eds., *Gettysburg* (1948), and Haskell's memoir.

The 1864 encounters between Grant and Lee are admirably described in Clifford Dowdey's brilliant *Lee's Last Campaign* (1960) and in Edward Steere's thorough but technical *The Wilderness Campaign* (1960). Edward J. Stackpole, *Sheridan in the Shenandoah* (1961), is authoritative. Frank E. Vandiver, *Jubal's Raid* (1960), is a vigorous account of Early's attempt to seize the Federal capital. For the final days of the war in the East, see Philip Van Doren Stern, *An End to Valor* (1958), and Burke Davis, *To Appomattox* (1959). Rembert W. Patrick has briefly told of *The Fall of Richmond* (1960).

The literature about the war in the West is neither so extensive nor so distinguished. Archer Jones's provocative *Confederate Strategy from Shiloh to Vicksburg* (1961), defends both Secretary of War Randolph and General Joseph E. Johnston. Stanley F. Horn, *The Army of Tennessee* (1953), is pedestrian. Thomas L. Connelly, *Army of the Heartland: The Army of Tennessee, 1861–1862* (1967), makes a good beginning on a major subject. The best book on the Union armies at Vicksburg is Earl S. Miers, *Web of Victory* (1955); Peter F. Walker, *Vicksburg: A People at War, 1860–1865* (1960), tells the Confederate side of the same story. Edward C. Cunningham, *The Port Hudson Campaign, 1862–1863* (1963), is sound and readable. Fairfax Downey, *Storming the Gateway. Chattanooga, 1863* (1960), is meritorious. On Hood's final campaign see Stanley F. Horn, *The Decisive Battle of Nashville* (1956), and Thomas R. Hay, *Hood's Tennessee Campaign* (1929).

On the raids of John Hunt Morgan see, in addition to the biographies of Morgan, Dee A. Brown, *The Bold Cavaliers* (1959); Basil W. Duke, *A History of Morgan's Cavalry* (new ed., with introduction by Cecil F. Holland, 1960);

and John S. Still, "Blitzkrieg, 1863: Morgan's Raid and Rout," 3 *C.W.H.* 291–306 (1957). For the Federal counterpart of Morgan, read Dee A. Brown, *Grierson's Raid* (1954).

There are a number of important articles on Western military operations: Stephen E. Ambrose, "The Union Command System and the Donelson Campaign," 24 *Military Affairs,* 78–86 (1960); Edwin C. Bearss, "Unconditional Surrender: The Fall of Fort Donelson," 21 *Tenn. H. Q.* 47–65 (1962); Thomas R. Hay, "Confederate Leadership at Vicksburg," 11 *M.V.H.R.* 543–60 (1925); Hay, "The Davis-Hood-Johnston Controversy of 1864," 11 *M.V.H.R.* 54–84 (1924); Archer Jones, "Tennessee and Mississippi, Joe Johnston's Strategic Problem," 18 *Tenn. H. Q.* 134–47 (1959); Jones, "The Vicksburg Campaign," 29 *J. Miss. H.* 12–27 (1967); John L. Jordan, "Was There a Massacre at Fort Pillow?" 6 *Tenn. H. Q.* 99–133 (1947); Grady McWhiney, "Controversy in Kentucky: Braxton Bragg's Campaign of 1862," 6 *C.W.H.* 5–42 (1960); Ross H. Moore, "The Vicksburg Campaign of 1863," 1 *J. Miss. H.* 151–68 (1939); Charles P. Roland, "Albert Sidney Johnston and the Loss of Forts Henry and Donelson," 23 *J.S.H.* 45–69 (1957); Roland, "Albert Sidney Johnston and the Shiloh Campaign," 4 *C.W.H.* 355–82 (1958); and Jack B. Scroggs and Donald E. Reynolds, "Arkansas and the Vicksburg Campaign," 5 *C.W.H.* 390–401 (1959).

For Sherman's operations in Georgia see, in addition to the biographies of Sherman, J. E. Johnston, Hood, and their aides, the following essays: James C. Bonner, "Sherman at Milledgeville in 1864," 22 *J.S.H.* 273–91 (1956); Fred E. Brown, "The Battle of Allatoona," 6 *C.W.H.* 277–97 (1960); N. C. Hughes, Jr., "Hardee's Defense of Savannah," 47 *Ga. H. Q.* 43–67 (1963); Josef C. James, "Sherman at Savannah," 39 *J.N.H.* 127–36 (1954); James P. Jones, "The Battle of Atlanta and McPherson's Successor," 7 *C.W.H.* 393–405 (1961); Jones, "General Jeff C. Davis, U.S.A., and Sherman's Georgia Campaign," 47 *Ga. H. Q.* 231–48 (1963); Robert D. Little, "General Hardee and the Atlanta Campaign," 29 *Ga. H. Q.* 1–22 (1945); George C. Osborn, "The Atlanta Campaign, 1864," 34 *Ga. H. Q.* 271–87 (1950); and James F. Rhodes, "Sherman's March to the Sea," 6 *A.H.R.* 466–74 (1901). The last stages of Sherman's campaign are admirably treated in John C. Barrett, *Sherman's March through the Carolinas* (1956).

The best general account of operations in the trans-Mississippi area is Jay Monaghan, *Civil War on the Western Border, 1854–1865* (1955). The following books are also very useful: Wiley Britton, *The Civil War on the Border: A Narrative of Operations in Missouri, Kansas, Arkansas, and the Indian Territory during the Years 1861–65* (2 v., 1891–1899); Richard S. Brownlee, *Gray Ghosts of the Confederacy: Guerilla Warfare in the West, 1861–1865* (1958); Ray C. Colton, *The Civil War in the Western Territories: Arizona, Colorado, New Mexico and Utah* (1959); Martin H. Hall, *Sibley's New Mexico Campaign* (1960); Aurora Hunt, *The Army of the Pacific: Its Operations in California, Texas, Arizona, New Mexico, Utah, Nevada, Oregon, Washington, . . . etc., 1860–1866* (1951); Ludwell H. Johnson, *Red River Campaign* (1958); and Stephen B. Oates, *Confederate Cavalry West of the River* (1961).

Alwyn Barr has several significant essays on trans-Mississippi operations:

"Confederate Artillery in Arkansas," 22 *Ark. H. Q.* 238–72 (1963); "Confederate Artillery in the Trans-Mississippi," 27 *Military Affairs* 77–83 (1963); "Confederate Artillery in Western Louisiana, 1862–1863," 9 *C.W.H.* 74–85 (1963); and "Texas Coastal Defence, 1861–1865," 65 *Sw. H. Q.* 1–31 (1961). See also Edwin C. Bearss, "The Battle of Pea Ridge," 36 *Annals of Iowa,* 3rd ser., 569–89, 37 *ibid.,* 9–41, 121–55, 207–39, 304–17 (1963); Aurora Hunt, "The Civil War on the Western Seaboard," 9 *C.W.H.* 178–86 (1963); Albert Castel, "Order No. 11 and the Civil War on the Border," 57 *Mo. H. Q.* 357–68 (1963); Castel, "Quantrill's Bushwhackers: A Case Study in Partisan Warfare," 13 *C.W.H.* 40–50 (1967); Leo E. Huff, "The Union Expedition against Little Rock, August–September, 1863," 22 *Ark. H. Q.* 224–37 (1963); and Harold F. Smith, "The 1861 Struggle for Lexington, Missouri," 7 *C.W.H.* 155–66 (1961).

William B. Hesseltine, *Civil War Prisons: A Study in War Psychology* (1930), remains an outstanding study. See also Ovid L. Futch, *History of Andersonville Prison* (1968), and the entire June, 1962, issue of *Civil War History* (vol. VIII), which is devoted to war prisons, North and South.

THE NAVAL WAR

Official Records of the Union and Confederate Navies in the War of the Rebellion (30 v., 1894–1922) is the basic collection of printed sources for naval operations during the war.

The three volumes of *The Navy in the Civil War* (1883) provide the most comprehensive account of operations on the high seas and inland waters: Daniel Ammen, *The Atlantic Coast;* A. T. Mahan, *The Gulf and Inland Waters;* and James R. Soley, *The Blockade and the Cruisers.* Though old, Charles B. Boynton, *The History of the Navy during the Rebellion* (2 v., 1867–68), is still useful. Virgil C. Jones, *The Civil War at Sea* (3 v., 1960–62), is readable and comprehensive narrative. Bern Anderson, *By Sea and by River: The Naval History of the Civil War* (1962), is more analytical. For a recent French evaluation of the conflict see Adolphe A. M. Lepotier, *Mer contre terre: les leçons de l'histoire, 1861–1865* (1945).

The Naval History Division of the Navy Department has published a useful *Civil War Naval Chronology* (1963–66).

On the Southern navy the standard work is still J. T. Scharf, *History of the Confederate States Navy* (1887), a mine of information. See also the biographies of Bulloch, Mallory, Maury, and Semmes. William N. Still, Jr., has published four articles of great interest: "Confederate Naval Strategy: The Ironclad," 27 *J.S.H.* 330–43 (1961); "Confederate Navy Policy and the Ironclad," 9 *C.W.H.* 145–56 (1963); "Facilities for the Construction of War Vessels in the Confederacy," 31 *J.S.H.* 285–304 (1965); and "Selma and the Confederate States Navy," 15 *Ala. R.* 19–37 (1962). Also valuable are Joseph O. Baylen and William W. White, eds., "James M. Mason and the Failure of the Confederate Naval Effort in Europe, 1863–1864," 2 *La. Studies* 98–108 (1963); G. Melvin Herndon, "The Confederate States Naval Academy," 69 *Va. M. H. B.* 300–23 (1961); and James M. Merrill, "Confederate Shipbuilding at New Orleans," 28 *J.S.H.* 87–93 (1962).

For general accounts of the Union navy see Clarence E. Macartney, *Mr. Lincoln's Admirals* (1956); James M. Merrill, *The Rebel Shore: The Story of Union Sea Power in the Civil War* (1957); and Richard S. West, Jr., *Mr. Lincoln's Navy* (1957). Articles by Charles O. Paullin are very significant: "President Lincoln and the Navy," 14 *A.H.R.* 284–303 (1909), and "A Half Century of Naval Administration in America, 1861–1911," *U. S. Naval Inst. Proc.*, Dec., 1912; Mar., 1913. The biography and diaries of Gideon Welles are of great importance. See also the biographies of C. H. Davis, Ericsson, Farragut, Fox, Isherwood, Wilkes, and Winslow.

James P. Baxter, 3rd, *The Introduction of the Ironclad Warship* (1933), is a scholarly account of the revolution in naval architecture witnessed by the Civil War generation. For the first conspicuous clash of ironclads in the conflict see R. W. Daly, *How the "Merrimac" Won* (1957); T. Catesby Jones, "The Iron-Clad *Virginia*," 49 *Va. M. H. B.* 297–303 (1941); Robert S. McCordock, *The Yankee Cheese Box* (1938); Harrison A. Trexler, *The Confederate Ironclad "Virginia" ("Merrimac")* (1938); and William Chapman White and Ruth White, *Tin Can on a Shingle* (1957). For the story of another armored ship see Edwin C. Bearss, *Hardluck Ironclad: The Sinking and Salvage of the Cairo* (1966).

Milton F. Perry, *Infernal Machines: The Story of Confederate Submarine and Mine Warfare* (1965), is definitive.

For life aboard the Union navy blockading the South see Samuel P. Boyer, *Naval Surgeon: Blockading the South, 1862–1866*, ed. Elinor and James A. Barnes (1963). See also Rachel Minick, "New York Ferryboats in the Union Navy," 46 *N. Y. Hist. Soc. Q.* 422–36 (1962); 47 *ibid.* 173–219, 288–327, 437–62 (1963); and 48 *ibid.* 51–80 (1964).

On the career of the *Alabama* see, in addition to the biographies of Semmes, Edward Boykin, *Ghost Ship of the Confederacy* (1957); Edna and Frank Bradlow, *Here Comes the Alabama* (1958); Waldo G. Leland, contributor, *"Kearsarge* and *Alabama*: French Official Report, 1864," 23 *A.H.R.* 119–23 (1917); and William M. Robinson, Jr., "The Alabama-Kearsarge Battle: A Study in Original Sources," 40 *Essex Inst. Hist. Coll.* 97–120, 209–218 (1924). For other Confederate raiders see George W. Groh, "Last of the Rebel Raiders," 10 *Am. Heritage* 48–51 ff. (Dec. 1958); Benjamin F. Gilbert, "The Confederate Raider Shenandoah: The Elusive Destroyer in the Pacific and the Arctic," 14 *Journal of the West* 169–82 (1965); William S. Hoole, *Four Years in the Confederate Navy: The Career of Captain John Low . . .* (1964); James D. Horan, ed., *C.S.S. Shenandoah: The Memoirs of Lieutenant Commanding James I. Waddell* (1960); Stanley F. Horn, *Gallant Rebel: The Fabulous Cruise of the C.S.S. Shenandoah* (1947); Douglas H. Maynard, "The Confederacy's Super-'Alabama,'" 5 *C.W.H.* 80–95 (1959); Frank L. Owsley, Jr., *The C.S.S. Florida: Her Building and Operations* (1965); and Charles G. Sumersell, *The Cruise of C.S.S. Sumter* (1965). On the continuing effect of the damage wrought by these raiders upon the American carrying trade, consult George W. Dalzell, *The Flight from the Flag* (1940).

On privateering and prize cases see William M. Robinson, Jr., *The Con-*

federate Privateers (1928), and Madeline R. Robinton, *An Introduction to the Papers of the New York Prize Court, 1861–1865* (1945).

For blockade running see, in addition to the treatment in Owsley's *King Cotton Diplomacy*, previously cited, Francis B. Bradlee, *Blockade Running during the Civil War . . .* (1925); Hamilton Cochran, *Blockade Runners of the Confederacy* (1958); and Frank E. Vandiver, ed., *Confederate Blockade Running Through Bermuda, 1861–1865* (1947). Two useful articles on this topic are Kathryn A. Hanna, "Incidents of the Confederate Blockade," 11 *J.S.H.* 214–29 (1945), and Daniel O'Flaherty, "The Blockade That Failed," 6 *Am. Heritage,* 38–41 ff. (Aug., 1955).

The standard works on naval operations on the internal waters are H. Allen Gosnell, *Guns on the Western Waters* (1949), and John D. Milligan, *Gunboats down the Mississippi* (1965). See also Edwin C. Bearss, "A Federal Raid up the Tennessee River," 17 *Ala. R.* 261–70 (1964); John D. Milligan, "Charles Ellet and his Naval Steam Ram," 9 *C.W.H.* 121–32 (1963); and Richard S. West, Jr., "Gunboats in the Swamps: The Yazoo Pass Expedition," 9 *C.W.H.* 157–66 (1963).

RECONSTRUCTION: GENERAL WORKS

The best collection of printed sources on the postwar period is Walter L. Fleming, ed., *Documentary History of Reconstruction, Political, Social, Religious, Educational and Industrial, 1865 to the Present Time* (2 v., 1906; new ed. with introduction by David Donald, 1966); both because of Fleming's biases and the nature of the surviving sources the collection is pro-Bourbon and anti-Negro in emphasis, but it is also comprehensive, accurate, and invaluable. James P. Shenton, ed., *The Reconstruction* (1963), is a briefer documentary work. Edward McPherson, ed., *The Political History of the United States . . . during . . . Reconstruction* (1871), is a compilation of public documents.

The most comprehensive history of the Reconstruction period is Ellis P. Oberholtzer, *A History of the United States since the Civil War,* Vols. 1–3 (1926). Though containing much excellent general political history and some interesting material on social and economic conditions, Oberholtzer's work is badly prejudiced against both the Southern Negro and the Western farmer. The same can be said of Vols. 5–7 of James F. Rhodes's *History of the United States . . . ,* which cover the period.

Several one-volume histories of the Reconstruction era share essentially the same orientation; all stress Southern problems, minimize the achievements of the freedmen, and regard white supremacy as the normal political order in the South. The best of these works is William A. Dunning, *Reconstruction, Political and Economic, 1865–1877* (1907). For a hostile critique see Alan D. Harper, "William A. Dunning: The Historian as Nemesis," 10 *C.W.H.* 54–66 (1964). Walter L. Fleming, *The Sequel of Appomattox* (1919), is a brief, popular restatement of Dunning's views. Claude G. Bowers, *The Tragic Era* (1929), is a luridly colored anti-Republican tract. *The Story of Reconstruction,* by Robert S. Henry (1938), is a straightforward, essentially political narrative. In *The South during Reconstruction, 1865–1877* (1947) E. Merton

Coulter exhibits the biases of his predecessors but also adds much useful information on social and economic conditions in the ex-Confederate states. Hodding Carter, *The Angry Scar* (1959), makes an effort to be more fair to the Negro but does not alter the basic stereotypes of the period.

Equally prejudiced in the opposite direction are the Marxist historians. In *Black Reconstruction* (1935) W. E. Burghardt Du Bois stresses the accomplishments of the Negro and finds evidence of an abortive poor white-Negro proletarian alignment in the Southern states. See also Du Bois's "Reconstruction and Its Benefits," 15 *A.H.R.* 781–99 (1910). On the other hand, James S. Allen, in *Reconstruction: the Battle for Democracy, 1865–1876* (1937), while sharing Du Bois's enthusiasm for the Negro, believes that the Southern states were governed not by the proletariat but by "a bourgeois-democratic dictatorship."

Some of the books and articles which are outgrowths of the civil rights movement of the 1960's carry the rewriting of Reconstruction history even further, seeing the period as one of struggle between heroic Negroes and their idealistic white allies on the one hand and villainous white racists, North and South, on the other. Two examples of such present-minded distortion are Lerone Bennett, Jr., *Black Power, U.S.A.: The Human Side of Reconstruction, 1867–1877* (1967), and Henrietta Buckmaster, *Freedom Bound* (1965).

While drawing heavily upon the factual research of the Dunning-school writers and on the insights of the Marxists, a group of historians who can be called Revisionists have begun presenting a more balanced appraisal of the period. Rembert W. Patrick, *The Reconstruction of the Nation* (1967), is the most comprehensive of these studies, carefully balanced in judgment and rather like a textbook in tone. Kenneth M. Stampp, *The Era of Reconstruction, 1865–1877* (1965), is a far more satisfactory work, a broad interpretive synthesis of recent scholarship; brevity is its one defect. John H. Franklin, *Reconstruction: After the Civil War* (1961), is a Revisionist work which heavily stresses the role played by Negroes. The essays in Harold M. Hyman, ed., *New Frontiers of the American Reconstruction* (1966), also reflect Revisionist scholarship.

Much of the best Revisionist work is in the form of articles and monographs. For a useful selection from this literature see Kenneth M. Stampp and Leon Litwack, eds., *A Reconstruction Reader* (1969). Seven articles are invaluable guides to the newer writings on the period: Howard K. Beale, "On Rewriting Reconstruction History," 45 *A.H.R.* 807–27 (1940); John H. Franklin, "Whither Reconstruction Historiography?" 17 *Jour. Negro Education* 446–61 (1948); Francis B. Simkins, "New Viewpoints of Southern Reconstruction," 5 *J.S.H.* 49–61 (1939); A. A. Taylor, "Historians of Reconstruction," 23 *J.N.H.* 16–34 (1938); Bernard A. Weisberger, "The Dark and Bloody Ground of Reconstruction Historiography," 25 *J.S.H.* 427–47 (1959); Vernon L. Wharton, "Reconstruction," in Arthur S. Link and Rembert W. Patrick, eds., *Writing Southern History* (1965), 295–315; and T. Harry Williams, "An Analysis of Some Reconstruction Attitudes," 12 *J.S.H.* 469–86 (1946). Mark M. Krug, "On Rewriting of the Story of Reconstruction in the U.S. History Textbooks," 46 *J.N.H.* 133–53 (1961), is a distressing revelation of how small the impact of Revisionist scholarship has been upon the most widely read books about American history. For a pungent critique of Revisionism see Fletcher M. Green's "Introduction" to the 1964 edition of William W. Davis, *The Civil War and Reconstruction in Florida,* xiii–xliii.

Three important general works stand largely outside the historiographical controversies about the Reconstruction era. The first of these is Allan Nevins, *The Emergence of Modern America, 1865–1878* (1927), an excellent discussion of the social and economic changes experienced by the whole country. Leonard D. White, *The Republican Era, 1869–1901* (1958), is a thorough study of the administration of the federal government. In *The Road to Reunion, 1865–1900* (1937), Paul H. Buck, while not ignoring economic factors, stresses the cultural and social forces which reknit the bonds of national unity.

PRESIDENTIAL RECONSTRUCTION

All the Lincoln biographies discuss measures taken by the President during the war looking toward a restoration of the Southern states. See also Eben G. Scott, *Reconstruction during the Civil War* . . . (1895), and Herman Belz's important *Reconstructing the Union* (1969). The fullest treatment of this subject is Charles H. McCarthy, *Lincoln's Plan of Reconstruction* (1901). It has been challenged by William B. Hesseltine, in a book of the same title (1960), who argues that Lincoln had not one but many approaches to Reconstruction, all of them unsuccessful.

The biographies of Andrew Johnson deal extensively with the Reconstruction plans of Lincoln's successor. George Clemenceau, *American Reconstruction, 1865–1870* . . . (1928), is an important firsthand account. Charles E. Chadsey, *The Struggle between President Johnson and Congress over Reconstruction* (1897), is old and thin. The path-making monograph in this field has been Howard K. Beale, *The Critical Year: A Study of Andrew Johnson and Reconstruction* (1930; new ed., 1958), which stoutly defends the President and attributes economic motives to the Radicals. In recent years Beale's interpretation has come under severe attack. Eric L. McKitrick, *Andrew Johnson and Reconstruction,* already cited, blames Johnson's intransigency and political ineptitude for the breakup of the Republican party. LaWanda and John H. Cox, *Politics, Principle, and Prejudice, 1865–1866* (1963), stresses racism as the determinant of Johnson's unwise course. W. R. Brock, *An American Crisis: Congress and Reconstruction, 1865–1867* (1963), takes a friendly view of the Republican Radicals and stresses the rigidities of the American Constitution as leading to the deadlock between Johnson and the Congress. David Donald, *The Politics of Reconstruction, 1863–1867* (1965), attempts to explain the conduct of both Johnson and the Radical Republicans in terms of political expediency. Hans L. Trefousse, "Lincoln and Johnson," 5 *Topic* 63–75 (1965), contrasts the two Presidents, to the disadvantage of Johnson.

In a series of essays Gregg Phifer has made an elaborate study of Johnson's "Swing Around the Circle" in 1866: "Andrew Johnson Takes a Trip," 11 *Tenn. H. Q.* 3–22 (1952); "Andrew Johnson Argues a Case," 11 *ibid.* 148–70 (1952); "Andrew Johnson Delivers His Argument," 11 *ibid.* 212–34 (1952); and "Andrew Johnson Loses His Battle," 11 *ibid.* 291–328 (1952).

Other significant articles dealing with aspects of the Johnson period are William A. Dunning, "The Second Birth of the Republican Party," 16 *A.H.R.* 56–63 (1910); Lawrence H. Gipson, "The Statesmanship of President Johnson: A Study of the Presidential Reconstruction Policy," 2 *M.V.H.R.* 363–83 (1915); Jack D. L. Holmes, "The Underlying Causes of the Memphis Race Riot of 1866," 17 *Tenn. H. Q.* 195–221 (1958); John A. Krout, "Henry J. Raymond on the Republican Caucuses of July, 1866," 33 *A.H.R.* 835–42 (1928); Robert J. Moore, "Andrew Johnson: The Second Swing 'Round the Circle," *S. C. Hist. Assn. Proc.*, 1966, 40–48; Donald E. Reynolds, "The New Orleans Riot of 1866, Reconsidered," 5 *La. H.* 5–27 (1964); Joe M. Richardson, ed., "The Memphis Race Riot and its Aftermath: Report by a Northern Missionary," 24 *Tenn. H. Q.* 63–69 (1965); William A. Russ, Jr., "Was There Danger of a Second Civil War during Reconstruction?" 21 *M.V.H.R.* 163–80 (1934); and Thomas Wagstaff, "The Arm-in-Arm Convention," 14 *C.W.H.* 101–19 (1968).

Dunning's *Essays on the Civil War and Reconstruction,* previously cited, continues to be valuable for the constitutional issues of the Johnson period. Essential for understanding the background of the Reconstruction debates on constitutional issues is Herman Belz's excellent *Reconstructing the Union: Theory and Policy during the Civil War* (1969).

James E. Sefton, *The United States Army and Reconstruction, 1865–1877* (1967), is a scholarly treatment of the work performed by the troops occupying the South.

Jonathan T. Dorris, *Pardon and Amnesty under Lincoln and Johnson* (1953), is a monograph of great importance. See also Dorris, "Pardoning the Leaders of the Confederacy," 15 *M.V.H.R.* 3–21 (1928). William A. Russ's "The Struggle between President Lincoln and Congress over Disfranchisement of Rebels," 3 *Susquehanna Univ. Studies* 177–205 (1947) and 221–43 (1948), and "Registration and Disfranchisement under Radical Reconstruction," 21 *M.V.H.R.* 163–80 (1934), stress the fact that, contrary to a widespread misconception, relatively few ex-Confederates were denied the right to vote. See also James A. Rawley, "The General Amnesty Act of 1872," 47 *M.V.H.R.* 480–84 (1960).

It follows, therefore, that in most Southern states after the Civil War Negroes did not form a majority of the voters and could not have exercised political power without white cooperation. See Forrest G. Wood, "On Revising Reconstruction History: Negro Suffrage, White Disfranchisement, and Common Sense," 51 *J.N.H.* 98–113 (1966). For one significant group of white Republicans in the South see Allen W. Trelease, "Who Were the Scalawags?" 29 *J.S.H.* 445–68 (1963); David Donald's reply to Trelease, 30 *ibid.* 253–57 (1964); and Otto H. Olsen, "Reconsidering the Scalawags," 12 *C.W.H.* 304–20 (1966). Richard N. Current, *Three Carpetbag Governors* (1968), Current, "Carpetbaggers Reconsidered," in David H. Pinkney and Theodore Ropp, eds., *A Festschrift for Frederick B. Artz* (1964), 139–57, and David H. Overy, Jr., *Wisconsin Carpetbaggers in Dixie* (1961), discuss another group who worked with the Negroes in politics.

THE SOUTH AFTER THE WAR:
SOCIAL AND ECONOMIC CONDITIONS

Travel accounts are valuable in giving a general picture of the South after the war. Thomas D. Clark, ed., *Travels in the New South* (2 v., 1962), is an admirable bibliography and guide. The best-known travel accounts are Sidney Andrews, *The South since the War* (1866); John Dennett, *The South as It Is, 1865–1866,* ed. Henry M. Christman (1965); Edward King, *The Great South* (1875); Charles Nordhoff, *The Cotton States in the Spring and Summer of 1875* (1876); Whitelaw Reid, *After the War* (1866); Robert Somers, *The Southern States since the War* (1871); and John T. Trowbridge, *The Desolate South, 1865–1866* (1956). Wilbur D. Jones, ed., "A British Report on Postwar Virginia," 69 *Va. M. H. B.* 346–52 (1961), contains the informed opinions of Sir Frederick Bruce, the British minister to Washington, after an 1866 visit to the South. See also Myrta Lockett Avary, *Dixie after the War* (1906).

Fred A. Shannon, *The Farmer's Last Frontier* (1945), is an admirable presentation of the changes in Southern agriculture resulting from the war. See also "The Agrarian Revolution in Georgia, 1865–1912," in Gregor Sebba, ed., *Georgia Studies: Selected Writings of Robert Preston Brooks* (1952); Thomas D. Clark, "The Furnishing and Supply System in Southern Agriculture since 1865," 12 *J.S.H.* 24–44 (1946); Richard W. Griffin, "Problems of the Southern Cotton Planters after the Civil War," 39 *Ga. H. Q.* 103–17 (1955); Eugene M. Lerner, "Southern Output and Agricultural Income, 1860–1880," 33 *Agr. H.* 117–25 (1959); Theodore Saloutos, "Southern Agriculture and the Problems of Readjustment, 1865–1877," 30 *Agr. H.* 58–76 (1956); Bell I. Wiley, "Vicissitudes of Early Reconstruction Farming in the Lower Mississippi Valley," 3 *J.S.H.* 441–52 (1937); Harold D. Woodman, "The Decline of Cotton Factorage after the Civil War," 71 *A.H.R.* 1219–36 (1966); and Oscar Zeichner, "The Transition from Slave to Free Agricultural Labor in the Southern States," 13 *Agr. H.* 22–32 (1939).

For representative labor contracts consult Jesse M. Fraser, ed., "A Free Labor Contract, 1867," 6 *J.S.H.* 546–48 (1940); Albert V. House, Jr., "A Reconstruction Share-Cropper Contract on a Georgia Rice Plantation," 26 *Ga. H. Q.* 156–65 (1942); and Rosser H. Taylor, ed., "Post-Bellum Southern Rental Contracts," 17 *Agr. H.* 121–28 (1943).

Three firsthand accounts by Southern farmers are George C. Osborn, "The Life of a Southern Plantation Owner during Reconstruction as Revealed in the Clay Sharkey Papers," 6 *J. Miss. H.* 103–12 (1944); C. L. Marquette, ed., "Letters of a Yankee Sugar Planter," 6 *J.S.H.* 521–45 (1940); and Charles W. Turner, ed., "A Virginia Small Farmer's Life after the Civil War: The Journal of William J. Hart, 1871–1873," 63 *Va. M. H. B.* 286–305 (1955). For two informative case studies in postwar farming see Richard J. Amundson, "Oakley Plantation: A Post-Civil War Venture in Louisiana Sugar," 9 *La. H.* 21–42 (1968), and Thomas A. Belser, Jr., "Alabama Plantation to Georgia Farm: John Horry Dent and Reconstruction," 25 *Ala. H. Q.* 136–48 (1963).

On land tenure in the postwar South see Paul W. Gates, "Federal Land Policy in the South, 1866–1888," 6 *J.S.H.* 303–30 (1940); William E.

Highsmith, "Some Aspects of Reconstruction in the Heart of Louisiana," 13 *J.S.H.* 460–91 (1947); and Roger W. Shugg, "Survival of the Plantation System in Louisiana," 3 *J.S.H.* 311–25 (1937).

Further studies are needed of Southern industry during the Reconstruction period. See C. G. Belissary, "The Rise of Industry and the Industrial Spirit in Tennessee, 1865–1885," 19 *J.S.H.* 193–215 (1953); Justin Fuller, "Alabama Business Leaders, 1865–1900," 16 *Ala. R.* 279–86 (1963), and 17 *ibid.* 63–75 (1964); Richard W. Griffin, "Reconstruction of the North Carolina Textile Industry, 1865–1885," 41 *N.C.H.R.* 34–53 (1964); Broadus Mitchell, *The Rise of the Cotton Mills in the South* (1921); and J. Carlyle Sitterson, "Business Leaders in Post-Civil War North Carolina, 1865–1900," 39 *James Sprunt Studies in History and Political Science* 111–21 (1957).

John F. Stover, *The Railroads of the South, 1865–1900* (1955), is an excellent work. Also useful on this topic are E. G. Campbell, "Indebted Railroads — a Problem of Reconstruction," 6 *J.S.H.* 167–88 (1940); Leonard P. Curry, *Rail Routes South* (1968); James F. Doster, "The Georgia Railroad & Banking Company in the Reconstruction Era," 48 *Ga. H. Q.* 1–32 (1964); Doster, "Trade Centers and Railroad Rates in Alabama, 1873–1885," 18 *J.S.H.* 169–92 (1952); Doster, "Were the Southern Railroads Destroyed by War?" 7 *C.W.H.* 310–20 (1961); Carter Goodrich, "Public Aid to Railroads in the Reconstruction South," 71 *P.S.Q.* 407–42 (1956); Allan W. Moger, "Railroad Practices and Policies in Virginia after the Civil War," 59 *Va. M. H. B.* 423–57 (1951); A. B. Moore, "Railroad Building in Alabama during the Reconstruction Period," 1 *J.S.H.* 421–41 (1935); E. Dale Odom, "Vicksburg, Shreveport and Texas: The Fortunes of a Scalawag Railroad," 44 *Sw. Soc. Sc. Q.* 277–85 (1964); Maury Klein, "The Strategy of Southern Railroads," 73 *A.H.R.* 1052–68 (1968); Klein and Kozo Yamamura, "The Growth Strategies of Southern Railroads, 1865–1893," 41 *Bus. Hist. Rev.* 358–77 (1967); Charles W. Turner, "The Chesapeake and Ohio Railroad in Reconstruction, 1865–1873," 31 *N.C.H.R.* 150–72 (1954).

For Southern efforts to encourage immigration during the Reconstruction years see C. G. Belissary, "Tennessee and Immigration, 1865–1880," 7 *Tenn. H. Q.* 229–48 (1948); Rowland T. Berthoff, "Southern Attitudes Toward Immigration," 17 *J.S.H.* 328–60 (1951); Frank E. Dykema, ed., "An Effort to Attract Dutch Colonists to Alabama, 1869," 14 *J.S.H.* 247–61 (1948); Robert F. Futrell, "Efforts of Mississippians to Encourage Immigration, 1865–1880," 20 *J. Miss. H.* 59–76 (1958); and Robert H. Woody, "The Labor and Immigration Problem of South Carolina during Reconstruction," 18 *M.V.H.R.* 195–212 (1931).

A general study of the convict leasing system is needed. See Mark T. Carleton, "The Politics of the Convict Lease System in Louisiana, 1868–1901," 8 *La. H.* 5–25 (1967); Fletcher M. Green, "Some Aspects of the Convict Lease System in the Southern States," in Green, ed., *Essays in Southern History,* 112–23; Blake McKelvey, "Penal Slavery and Southern Reconstruction," 20 *J.N.H.* 153–79 (1935); and A. Elizabeth Taylor, "The Origin and Development of the Convict Lease System in Georgia," 26 *Ga. H. Q.* 113–28 (1942).

Fresh studies of education in the postwar South are also called for. Edgar W. Knight, *The Influence of Reconstruction on Education in the South*

(1913), is badly biased and out of date. Henry A. Bullock, *A History of Negro Education in the South from 1619 to the Present* (1967), is comprehensive and readable. Horace M. Bond, *Negro Education in Alabama* (1939), is fresh and provocative. Henry L. Swint, *The Northern Teacher in the South, 1862–1870* (1941), deals understandingly with the problems of these educational carpetbaggers. Also useful are Walter J. Frazer, Jr., "John Eaton, Jr., Radical Republican: Champion of the Negro and Federal Aid to Southern Education, 1869–1882," 25 *Tenn. H. Q.* 239–60 (1966); Louis R. Harlan, "Desegregation in New Orleans Public Schools during Reconstruction," 67 *A.H.R.* 663–75 (1962); Luther P. Jackson, "The Origin of Hampton Institute," 10 *J.N.H.* 131–49 (1925); William P. Vaughn, "Partners in Segregation: Barnas Sears and the Peabody Fund," 10 *C.W.H.* 260–74 (1964); Earl H. West, "The Peabody Educational Fund and Negro Education, 1867–1880," 6 *History of Education Quarterly* 3–21 (1966); Daniel J. Whitener, "Public Education in North Carolina during Reconstruction, 1865–1876," in Fletcher M. Green, ed., *Essays in Southern History*, 67–91; and Whitener, "The Republican Party and Public Education in North Carolina, 1867–1900," 37 *N.C.H.R.* 382–96 (1960). See also the biographies of Curry and the studies of the Freedmen's Bureau listed in the section of this bibliography on "The Negro during Reconstruction."

Three books trace the reactions of former Confederates to these changes: Nash K. Burger and John K. Bettersworth, *South of Appomattox* (1959); William B. Hesseltine, *Confederate Leaders in the New South* (1950); and William W. White, *The Confederate Veteran* (1962). See also Ray M. Atchison, *"The Land We Love:* A Southern Post-Bellum Magazine of Agriculture, Literature, and Military History," 37 *N.C.H.R.* 506–15 (1960). Many white Southerners found relief from harsh reality in humor; see Wade Hall, *The Smiling Phoenix: Southern Humor from 1865 to 1914* (1965).

STUDIES OF INDIVIDUAL SOUTHERN STATES
DURING RECONSTRUCTION

The basic state studies of Reconstruction belong to what is called the "Dunning School." Written by students of Professor William A. Dunning of Columbia University, or under similar inspiration at other universities, they are detailed, thorough, and generally accurate. Unfortunately they are also marked by hostility to the Negro, the carpetbagger, and the scalawag and by a tendency to equate the Democratic party and virtue. As a result these monographs need to be supplemented by the state Marxist and Revisionist accounts.

For Alabama the basic Dunning-school study is Walter L. Fleming, *Civil War and Reconstruction in Alabama* (1905). John W. DuBose, *Alabama's Tragic Decade,* ed. James K. Greer (1940), expresses much the same viewpoint. For Revisionist correctives see Thomas B. Alexander, "Persistent Whiggery in Alabama and the Lower South, 1860–1867," 12 *Ala. R.* 35–52 (1959); Horace M. Bond, "Social and Economic Forces in Alabama Reconstruction," 23 *J.N.H.* 290–348 (1928); Edward C. Williamson, "The Alabama Election of 1874," 17 *Ala. R.* 210–18 (1964); Robert S. Rhodes, "The Registration of Voters and the Election of Delegates to the Reconstruction Convention in Alabama," 8 *Ala. R.* 119–42 (1955); and four articles by Sarah Van V. Woolfolk: "Amnesty and Pardon and Republicanism in Alabama," 26 *Ala. H. Q.* 240–48 (1964); "Carpetbaggers in Alabama: Tradition versus Truth," 15 *Ala. R.* 133–44 (1962); "Five Men Called Scalawags," 17 *Ala. R.* 45–55 (1964); and "George E. Spencer: A Carpetbagger in Alabama," 19 *Ala. R.* 41–52 (1966).

On Arkansas the standard monographs are Thomas S. Staples, *Reconstruction in Arkansas, 1862–1874* (1923), and David Y. Thomas, *Arkansas in War and Reconstruction, 1861–1874* (1926). Consult also Powell Clayton, *The Aftermath of the Civil War in Arkansas* (1915), and J. M. Harrell, *The Brooks and Baxter War* (1893). Three recent articles are also valuable: John W. Graves, "Negro Disfranchisement in Arkansas," 26 *Ark. H. Q.* 199–225 (1967); Paul C. Palmer, "Miscegenation as an Issue in the Arkansas Constitutional Convention of 1868," 24 *Ark. H. Q.* 99–119 (1965); and Everette Swinney, "United States v. Powell Clayton: Use of the Federal Enforcement Acts in Arkansas," 26 *Ark. H. Q.* 143–54 (1967).

On the District of Columbia see James H. Whyte, *The Uncivil War: Washington during the Reconstruction, 1865–1878* (1958). See also Constance M. Green, *The Secret City,* and her *Washington: Village and Capital,* both previously cited.

The Dunning-type work on Florida is William W. Davis, *The Civil War and Reconstruction in Florida* (1913). John Wallace, *Carpet Bag Rule in Florida* (1888), is by a repentant Negro ex-Republican. Joe M. Richardson, *The Negro in the Reconstruction of Florida, 1865–1877* (1965), is an excellent Revisionist study. Important Revisionists essays include Marlin G. Cox, "Military Reconstruction in Florida," 46 *Fla. H. Q.* 219–33 (1968); Claude R. Flory, "Marcellus L. Stearns, Florida's Last Reconstruction Governor," 44 *Fla. H. Q.* 181–92 (1966); Ralph L. Peek, "Aftermath of Military Reconstruction, 1868–1869," 43 *Fla. H. Q.* 123–41 (1964); Peek, "Curbing of Voter Intimidation in Florida, 1871," 43 *Fla. H. Q.* 333–48 (1965); Peek, "Election of 1870 and the End of Reconstruction in Florida," 45 *Fla. H. Q.* 352–68 (1967); Derrell Roberts, "Social Legislation in Reconstruction Florida," 43 *Fla. H. Q.* 349–60 (1965); Jerrell H. Shofner, "The Constitution of 1868," 41 *Fla. H. Q.* 356–74 (1963); Shofner, "Political Reconstruction in Florida," 45 *Fla. H. Q.* 145–70 (1966); and George W. Smith, "Carpetbag Imperialism in Florida, 1862–1868," 27 *Fla. H. Q.* 99–130 (1948) and 260–99 (1949).

On Georgia, Edwin C. Woolley, *The Reconstruction of Georgia* (1901), is narrowly legalistic but surprisingly favorable to Radical Reconstruction. C. Mildred Thompson, *Reconstruction in Georgia* (1915), is one of the best of the Dunning studies, dealing with social and economic as well as with political issues. Manuel Gottlieb, "The Land Question in Georgia during Reconstruction," 3 *Science and Society* 356–88 (1939), is a Marxist view. Alan Conway, *The Reconstruction of Georgia* (1966), is a sweepingly Revisionist work. Elizabeth S. Nathans, *Losing the Peace: Georgia Republicans and Reconstruction, 1865–1871* (1968), and Olive H. Shadgett, *The Republican Party in Georgia: From Reconstruction through 1900* (1964), are valuable political studies. E. Merton Coulter has published careful, if basically hostile, biographical sketches of three principal Georgia Negro politicians: "Aaron Alpeoria

Bradley, Georgia Negro Politician during Reconstruction Times," 51 *Ga. H. Q.* 15–41, 154–74, 264–309 (1967); "Henry M. Turner: Georgia Negro Preacher-Politician during the Reconstruction Era," 48 *Ga. H. Q.* 371–410 (1964); and "Tunis G. Campbell, Negro Reconstructionist in Georgia," 51 *Ga. H. Q.* 401–24 (1967), and 52 *ibid.* 16–52 (1968). Also useful is William A. Russ, Jr., "Radical Disfranchisement in Georgia, 1867–1871," 19 *Ga. H. Q.* 175–209 (1935). See, in addition, the biographies of B. H. Hill, J. E. Brown, J. B. Gordon, Stephens, and Toombs. C. Vann Woodward, *Tom Watson, Agrarian Rebel* (1938), is a very important Revisionist work, but one which deals mostly with the post-Reconstruction period.

For Kentucky the standard work is E. Merton Coulter, *The Civil War and Readjustment in Kentucky* (1926). See also William A. Russ, Jr., "The Role of Kentucky in 1867," 1 *Susquehanna Univ. Studies* 106–14 (1933), and Thomas L. Connelly, "Neo-Confederatism or Power Vacuum: Post-War Kentucky Politics Reappraised," 64 *Register of the Kentucky Historical Society* 257–69 (1966).

John R. Ficklen, *History of Reconstruction in Louisiana (through 1868)* (1910), and Ella Lonn, *Reconstruction in Louisiana after 1868* (1918), are two standard Dunning-type monographs. They must be supplemented by Willie M. Caskey, *Secession and Restoration of Louisiana,* previously cited; Garnie W. McGinty, *Louisiana Redeemed: The Overthrow of the Carpet-bag Rule, 1876–1880* (1941); Stuart O. Landry, *The Battle of Liberty Place: The Overthrow of Carpetbag Rule in New Orleans* (1955); and Roger W. Shugg, *Origins of Class Struggle in Louisiana,* already cited. See also the biographies of Banks, Kellogg, Pinchback, Warmoth, and Wells, and the works on Louisiana cited above in the section on "The Confederacy: State Studies." There are many valuable articles on aspects of Louisiana Reconstruction: Fayette Copeland, "The New Orleans Press and the Reconstruction," 30 *La. H. Q.* 144–337 (1947); Donald W. Davis, "Ratification of the Constitution of 1868—Record of Votes," 6 *La. H.* 301–305 (1965); Charles L. Dufour, "The Age of Warmoth," 6 *La. H.* 335–64 (1965); Francis B. Harris, "Henry Clay Warmoth, Reconstruction Governor of Louisiana," 30 *La. H. Q.* 523–653 (1947); Joy Jackson, "Bosses and Businessmen in the Gilded Age of New Orleans Politics," 5 *La. H.* 387–400 (1964); Marguerite T. Leach, "The Aftermath of Reconstruction in Louisiana," 32 *La. H. Q.* 631–717 (1949); Hilda Mulvey McDaniel, "Francis Tillou Nicholls and the End of Reconstruction," 32 *La. H. Q.* 357–513 (1949); A. E. Perkins, "Some Negro Officers and Legislators in Louisiana," 14 *J.N.H.* 523–28 (1929); Althea D. Pitre, "The Collapse of the Warmoth Regime, 1870–72," 6 *La. H.* 161–87 (1965); Richard H. Wiggins, "Louisiana Press and the Lottery," 31 *La. H. Q.* 716–844 (1948); and T. Harry Williams, "The Louisiana Unification Movement of 1873," 11 *J.S.H.* 349–69 (1945).

The only study of Maryland is old and inadequate: W. S. Myers, *The Self-Reconstruction of Maryland, 1864–1867* (1909).

James W. Garner, *Reconstruction in Mississippi* (1901), is one of the best of the Dunning-school monographs, accurate, thorough, and generally impartial. See, however, *The Facts of Reconstruction* (1913), by John R. Lynch, the able Negro speaker of the Mississippi House of Representatives. The letters of

Adelbert and Blanche Ames, listed in the biographical section, are very valu-able. See also the biographies of Ames, Alcorn, Bruce, and L. Q. C. Lamar. Her-bert Aptheker, "Mississippi Reconstruction and the Negro Leader Charles Caldwell," 11 *Science and Society* 340–71 (1947), is a Marxist view. Two able Revisionist monographs are William C. Harris, *Presidential Reconstruc-tion in Mississippi* (1967), and Vernon L. Wharton, *The Negro in Missis-sippi, 1865–1890* (1947). Important Revisionist essays include Thomas B. Alexander, ed., "Persistent Whiggery in Mississippi: *The Hinds County Ga-zette,*" 23 *J. Miss. H.* 71–93 (1961); David Donald, "The Scalawag in Mis-sissippi Reconstruction," 10 *J.S.H.* 447–60 (1944); Winbourne M. Drake, "The Mississippi Reconstruction Convention of 1865," 21 *J. Miss. H.* 225–56 (1959); L. Marshall Hall, "William L. Sharkey and Reconstruction, 1866–1873," 27 *J. Miss. H.* 1–17 (1965); and William C. Harris, "Formulation of the First Mississippi Plan: The Black Code of 1865," 29 *J. Miss. H.* 181–201 (1967). Robert L. Brandfon, *Cotton Kingdom of the New South* (1967), contains revealing information about the connection between Mississippi poli-tics and land speculation in the rich Delta area.

The basic study of North Carolina is J. G. de Roulhac Hamilton, *Recon-struction in North Carolina* (1914). W. McKee Evans, *Ballots and Fence Rails: Reconstruction on the Lower Cape Fear* (1967), is a significant Revi-sionist study. Also valuable are the biographies of Holden, Littlefield, Tourgée, and Vance. Important articles include Leonard Bernstein, "The Participation of Negro Delegates in the Constitutional Convention of 1868 in North Caro-lina," 34 *J.N.H.* 391–409 (1949); James B. Browning, "The North Caro-lina Black Code," 15 *J.N.H.* 461–73 (1930); R. D. W. Connor, "The Reha-bilitation of a Rural Commonwealth," 36 *A.H.R.* 44–62 (1930); Douglass C. Dailey, "The Elections of 1872 in North Carolina," 40 *N.C.H.R.* 338–60 (1963); Cortez A. M. Ewing, "Two Reconstruction Impeachments," 15 *N.C.H.R.* 204–30 (1938); James R. Morrill, III, "North Carolina and the Administration of Brevet Major General Sickles," 42 *N.C.H.R.* 291–305 (1965); B. U. Ratchford, "The North Carolina Public Debt, 1870–1878," 10 *N.C.H.R.* 1–20 (1933); William A. Russ, Jr., "Radical Disfranchisement in North Carolina, 1867–1868," 11 *N.C.H.R.* 271–83 (1934); Kenneth E. St. Clair, "Debtor Relief in North Carolina during Reconstruction," 18 *N.C.H.R.* 215–35 (1941); and St. Clair, "Military Justice in North Carolina, 1865: A Microcosm of Reconstruction," 11 *C.W.H.* 341–50 (1965).

On Missouri there is an excellent monograph, William E. Parrish, *Mis-souri under Radical Rule* (1965). See also Fred DeArmond, "Reconstruction in Missouri," 61 *Mo. H. Q.* 364–77 (1967), and Norma Peterson's biography of B. Gratz Brown, already cited.

Conventional thinking about South Carolina during Reconstruction derives largely from *The Prostrate State* (1874), an anti-Negro account by the North-ern newspaperman, James S. Pike. For a critique of this work see Durden's ex-cellent biography of Pike and his long introduction to the 1968 edition of *The Prostrate State*. Neill W. Macaulay, Jr., "South Carolina Reconstruction His-toriography," 65 *S.C.H.M.* 20–32 (1964), offers a survey of the literature. John S. Reynolds, *Reconstruction in South Carolina, 1865–1877* (1905), is a strictly political narrative, written from the Bourbon point of view. Francis B.

Simkins and Robert H. Woody, *South Carolina during Reconstruction* (1932), is a massive Revisionist work, of the greatest importance. Willie Lee Rose, *Rehearsal for Reconstruction: The Port Royal Experiment* (1964), is a sensitively written study of Reconstruction on the Sea Islands. Joel Williamson, *After Slavery: The Negro in South Carolina during Reconstruction, 1861–1877* (1965), is a monograph which deals admirably with every aspect of its subject. Ernest M. Lander, *A History of South Carolina, 1865–1960* (1960), is a good general history. See also Gaillard Hunt, contributor, "Letter of William Henry Trescot on Reconstruction in South Carolina, 1867," 15 *A.H.R.* 574–82 (1910); John H. Wolfe, "The South Carolina Constitution of 1865 as a Democratic Document," *Proc. S. C. Hist. Assoc.*, 1942, 18–29; and R. H. Woody, ed., "Behind the Scenes in the Reconstruction Legislature of South Carolina: Diary of Joseph Woodruff," 2 *J.S.H.* 233–59 (1936). On the restoration of "home rule" in South Carolina see, in addition to the biographies of Wade Hampton, William A. Sheppard, *Red Shirts Remembered* (1940).

For Tennessee there are two Dunning-type monographs: James W. Fertig, *Secession and Reconstruction of Tennessee* (1898), and James W. Patton, *Unionism and Reconstruction in Tennessee, 1860–1869* (1934). These are supplemented and corrected by Thomas B. Alexander's significant Revisionist work, *Political Reconstruction in Tennessee* (1950). See also Alexander's "Neither Peace Nor War: Conditions in Tennessee in 1865," *East Tenn. Hist. Soc. Pubs.*, No. 21 (1949), 33–51 and "Whiggery and Reconstruction in Tennessee," 16 *J.S.H.* 291–305 (1950). James B. Campbell, "East Tennessee during the Radical Regime, 1865–1869," *East Tenn. Hist. Soc. Pubs.*, No. 20 (1948), 84–102, and E. G. Feistman, "Radical Disfranchisement and the Restoration of Tennessee, 1865–1866," 12 *Tenn. H. Q.* 135–51 (1953), are also useful. For the Republican party in Tennessee see three articles by Verton M. Queener: "A Decade of East Tennessee Republicanism, 1867–1876," *East Tenn. Hist. Soc. Pubs.*, No. 14 (1942), 59–85; "The East Tennessee Republicans as a Minority Party, 1870–1896," *East Tenn. Hist. Soc. Pubs.*, No. 15 (1943), 49–73; and "The Origin of the Republican Party in East Tennessee," *East Tenn. Hist. Soc. Pubs.*, No. 13 (1941), 66–90. See also Alexander's biography of T.A.R. Nelson and Coulter's life of Brownlow.

For Texas the Dunning-school monograph is Charles W. Ramsdell, *Reconstruction in Texas* (1910). Two important Revisionist studies are Paul C. Casdorph, *A History of the Republican Party in Texas, 1865–1965* (1965), and W. C. Nunn, *Texas under the Carpetbaggers* (1962). See also J. E. Ericson, "Delegates to the Texas Constitutional Convention of 1875: A Reappraisal," 67 *Sw. H. Q.* 22–27 (1963), and Robert W. Shook, "The Federal Military in Texas, 1865–1870," 6 *Texas Military History* 3–53 (1967). See also Procter's biography of Reagan.

H. J. Eckenrode, *The Political History of Virginia during Reconstruction* (1904), is the only comprehensive published work on its subject. See, however, Luther P. Jackson, *Negro Office-Holders in Virginia, 1865–1896* (1945); Richard Morton, *The Negro in Virginia Politics, 1865–1902* (1919); and A. A. Taylor's *The Negro in the Reconstruction of Virginia*, cited in the following section. Nelson M. Blake's biography of Mahone is important.

THE NEGRO DURING RECONSTRUCTION

Henderson H. Donald, *The Negro Freedman: . . . The American Negro in the Early Years after Emancipation* (1952), is the only comprehensive work on its subject, but it is marred by an uncritical willingness to accept any disreputable tale about the behavior of Negroes. We need more monographs like Willie Lee Rose's *Rehearsal for Reconstruction: The Port Royal Experiment,* and Joel Williamson's probing *After Slavery: The Negro in South Carolina during Reconstruction,* both previously cited. Other important state studies include Joe M. Richardson's *The Negro in the Reconstruction of Florida* and Vernon L. Wharton's *The Negro in Mississippi,* both of which have been previously mentioned, and three studies by Alrutheus A. Taylor: *The Negro in South Carolina during the Reconstruction* (1924); *The Negro in Tennessee, 1865–1880* (1941); and *The Negro in the Reconstruction of Virginia* (1926).

The continuing Northern idealistic and philanthropic interest in the Negro is the theme of James M. McPherson's *The Struggle for Equality: Abolitionists and the Negro in the Civil War and Reconstruction* (1964). See also Ira V. Brown, "Lyman Abbott and Freedmen's Aid, 1865–1869," 15 *J.S.H.* 22–38 (1949).

A major theme in the Reconstruction story is the continuing effort on the part of Southern whites to keep Negroes "in their place." At first they attempted this through restrictive legislation enacted by the Johnson provisional governments. Theodore B. Wilson, *The Black Codes of the South* (1965), is a general examination of these laws. See also the listings in the "Studies of Individual Southern States during Reconstruction," above. When these laws were struck down, terrorism followed. Stanley F. Horn, *Invisible Empire: The Story of the Ku Klux Klan, 1866–1871* (1939), which supersedes J. C. Lester and D. L. Wilson, *The Ku Klux Klan* (1905), is the best general study of this movement, but William P. Randel, *The Ku Klux Klan: A Century of Infamy* (1965), is also useful. Other valuable studies include Grady McWhiney and Francis B. Simkins, "The Ghostly Legend of the Ku-Klux Klan," 14 *Negro Hist. Bull.* 109–12 (1951); Otto H. Olsen, "The Ku Klux Klan: A Study in Reconstruction Politics and Propaganda," 39 *N.C.H.R.* 340–62 (1962); and Herbert Shapiro, "The Ku Klux Klan during Reconstruction: The South Carolina Episode," 49 *J.N.H.* 34–55 (1964). Claude H. Nolen, *The Negro's Image in the South: The Anatomy of White Supremacy* (1967), is a good summary of these developments.

George R. Bentley, *A History of the Freedmen's Bureau* (1955), is an authoritative work, which replaces Paul S. Peirce, *The Freedmen's Bureau* (1904). Martin Abbott, *The Freedmen's Bureau in South Carolina, 1865–1872* (1967), is an excellent state study. See also several revealing articles: Martin Abbott, "Free Land, Free Labor, and the Freedmen's Bureau," 30 *Agr. H.* 150–57 (1956); John and LaWanda Cox, "General O. O. Howard and the 'Misrepresented Bureau,' " 19 *J.S.H.* 427–56 (1953); and LaWanda Cox, "The Promise of Land for the Freedmen," 45 *M.V.H.R.* 413–40 (1958). Also useful are Walter Dyson, *Howard University* (1941), and Walter L. Fleming, *The Freedmen's Savings Bank* (1927). Several state studies give more details on the operations of the Bureau: Martin Abbott, "The Freedmen's Bureau and

Negro Schooling in South Carolina," 57 *S.C.H.M.* 65–81 (1956); William T. Alderson, Jr., "The Freedmen's Bureau and Negro Education in Virginia," 29 *N.C.H.R.* 64–90 (1952); Elizabeth Bethel, "The Freedmen's Bureau in Alabama," 14 *J.S.H.* 49–92 (1948); Claude Elliott, "The Freedmen's Bureau in Texas," 56 *Sw. H. Q.* 1–24 (1952); John C. Engelsman, "The Freedmen's Bureau in Louisiana," 32 *La. H. Q.* 145–224 (1949); J. G. de Roulhac Hamilton, "The Frenchmen's Bureau in North Carolina," 8 *S.A.Q.* 53–67, 154–63 (1909); Luther P. Jackson, "The Educational Efforts of the Freedmen's Bureau and Freedmen's Aid Societies in South Carolina, 1862–1872," 8 *J.N.H.* 1–40 (1923); Weymouth T. Jordan, "The Freedmen's Bureau in Tennessee," *East Tenn. Hist. Soc. Pubs.*, No. 11 (1939), 47–61; W. A. Lowe, "The Freedmen's Bureau and Civil Rights in Maryland," 37 *J.N.H.* 221–76 (1952); J. Thomas May, "The Freedmen's Bureau at the Local Level: A Study of a Louisiana Agent," 9 *La. H.* 5–19 (1968); Paul D. Phillips, "White Reaction to the Freedmen's Bureau in Tennessee," 25 *Tenn. H. Q.* 50–62 (1966); Joe M. Richardson, "The Freedmen's Bureau and Negro Education in Florida," 31 *J. of Negro Education* 460–67 (1962); Richardson, "An Evaluation of the Freedmen's Bureau in Florida," 46 *Fla. H. Q.* 223–38 (1963); and Henry L. Swint, ed., "Reports from Educational Agents of the Freedmen's Bureau in Tennessee, 1865–1870," 1 *Tenn. H. Q.* 51–80, 152–70 (1942).

Willis D. Boyd, "Negro Colonization in the Reconstruction Era, 1865–1870," 40 *Ga. H. Q.* 360–82 (1956), is a study of efforts to persuade the Negroes to emigrate from the South.

On the use of Negroes in the militia see Otis A. Singletary, *Negro Militia and Reconstruction* (1957), and J. G. Sproat, "Blueprint for Radical Reconstruction," 23 *J.S.H.* 25–44 (1957).

The political career of the Negro during Reconstruction is elaborately traced in the state studies listed above. See also Paul Lewinson, *Race, Class, and Party: A History of Negro Suffrage and White Politics in the South* (1932), and Samuel D. Smith, *The Negro in Congress, 1870–1901* (1940).

More work is needed on the Negro and the labor movement. Four suggestive studies are: Paul V. Black, "The Knights of Labor and the South, 1876–1893," 1 *So. Q.* 201–12 (1963); Herman D. Bloch, "Labor and the Negro, 1866–1910," 50 *J.N.H.* 163–84 (1965); Sidney H. Kessler, "The Organization of Negroes in the Knights of Labor," 37 *J.N.H.* 248–76 (1952); and Sumner E. Matison, "The Labor Movement and the Negro during Reconstruction," 33 *J.N.H.* 426–68 (1948).

The gradually hardening pattern of racial segregation in the South is brilliantly traced in C. Vann Woodward, *The Strange Career of Jim Crow.* A comparison of the first (1955) and second (1966) editions of this work will indicate the kinds of criticisms to which Woodward's work has been subjected. Charles E. Wynes, *Race Relations in Virginia, 1870–1902* (1961), largely supports Woodward's thesis, but see Williamson's *After Slavery* for a powerful dissent. Joel Williamson, ed., *The Origins of Segregation* (1968), is a fairminded presentation of arguments on both sides of the issue.

Leslie H. Fishel, Jr., "The Negro in Northern Politics, 1870–1900," 42 *M.V.H.R.* 466–89 (1955), opens up a neglected area of Negro history. See also Ira V. Brown, "Pennsylvania and the Rights of the Negro, 1865–1887,"

28 *Pa. H.* 45–57 (1961); Leslie H. Fishel, Jr., "Wisconsin and Negro Suffrage," 46 *Wisc. M. H.* 180–96 (1963); and Edgar A. Toppin, "Negro Emancipation in Historic Retrospect: Ohio. The Negro Suffrage Issue in Postbellum Ohio Politics," 11 *Journal of Human Relations* 232–46 (1963).

POST–CIVIL WAR POLITICS, 1867–1876:
REPUBLICAN RADICALISM AND THE GRANT ADMINISTRATION

Most of the recent work on National politics during the Reconstruction period has been concentrated upon the events of 1865–1867. See the listing of these important studies under "Presidential Reconstruction," above. Too little attention has been given to the years 1867–1876. For this reason the general histories of the period have special importance, as do the biographies of such men as Bayard, Blair, Blaine, Butler, W. E. Chandler, Zachariah Chandler, Chase, Colfax, Conkling, S. C. Cox, Doolittle, Fessenden, Grimes, T. O. Howe, Reverdy Johnson, Julian, Logan, Morton, Phillips, Seymour, Stanton, Stevens, Sumner, Tilden, Trumbull, Henry Wilson, and Welles.

One of the major problems in dealing with the political history of these years is the identification of a meaningful group that can be described as Radical Republicans. Conventional ideas about the Radicals are expressed in Margaret Shortreed, "The Anti-Slavery Radicals, 1840–1868," *Past and Present,* No. 16, 65–87 (Nov. 1959). For modern, more sophisticated attempts to delineate a Radical faction see the studies cited above under "Wartime Government in the North" and W. R. Brock's *An American Crisis* and David Donald's *The Politics of Reconstruction,* both previously cited. See also two useful essays by John G. Clark: "Historians and the Joint Committee on Reconstruction," 23 *Historian* 348–61 (1961), and "Radicals and Moderates on the Joint Committee on Reconstruction," 45 *Mid-Am.* 79–98 (1963). Hans L. Trefousse, *The Radical Republicans* (1969), is a scholarly group portrait which stresses the positive accomplishments of the Radicals.

Contrary to most previous interpretations, recent scholarship tends to question the degree of influence and power exerted by the Radicals over the course of Reconstruction legislation. Eric L. McKitrick, *Andrew Johnson and Reconstruction,* previously cited, shows that the Radicals were not in control immediately after the war and were not the principal shapers of the Fourteenth Amendment. Donald's *Politics of Reconstruction* demonstrates that the Military Reconstruction Act of 1867 was a compromise, not to the Radicals' liking. William Gillette, *The Right to Vote,* cited in full just below, points up Radical disappointment with the Fifteenth Amendment. Three articles show how Radicals had to compromise to get the Civil Rights Act of 1875: James M. McPherson, "Abolitionists and the Civil Rights Act of 1875," 52 *J.A.H.* 493–510 (1965); William P. Vaughn, "Separate but Unequal: The Civil Rights Act of 1875 and Defeat of the School Integration Clause," 48 *Sw. Soc. Sci. Q.* 146–54 (1967); and Bertram Wyatt-Brown, "The Civil Rights Act of 1875," 18 *Western Political Q.* 763–75 (1965).

At the same time historians have been analyzing the ideas of the Radicals. Harold M. Hyman, ed., *The Radical Republicans and Reconstruction, 1861–*

1870 (1967), presents an extensive sampling from their own writings. Lee A. Dew, "The Reluctant Radicals of 1866," 8 *Midwest Q.* 261–76 (1967), shows how very limited the objectives of most Radicals were at the end of the war. In the same vein is C. Vann Woodward, "Seeds of Failure in Radical Race Policy," 110 *Am. Phil. Soc. Proc.* 1–9 (1966). Patrick W. Riddleberger, "The Radicals' Abandonment of the Negro during Reconstruction," 45 *J.N.H.* 88–102 (1960), indicates how rapidly most Radicals dropped the civil rights issue. Eric McKitrick, "Reconstruction: Ultraconservative Revolution," in C. Vann Woodward, ed., *The Comparative Approach to American History* (1968), 146–59, suggests that there was very little interest anywhere in a general reorganization of American society. On the other hand, James McPherson, *The Struggle for Equality,* previously cited, proves the continuing interest that many former abolitionists maintained in the Negro during the postwar years. For other examinations of Radicals' ideas see Charles O. Lerche, Jr., "Congressional Interpretations of the Guarantee of a Republican Form of Government during Reconstruction," 15 *J.S.H.* 192–211 (1949), and Jack B. Scroggs, "Southern Reconstruction: A Radical View," 24 *J.S.H.* 407–39 (1958).

David Montgomery, *Beyond Equality: Labor and the Radical Republicans, 1862–1872* (1967), an important and provocative book, shows the role played by labor reformers in the postwar realignment of parties.

The powerful role played by the G.A.R. in backing the Radical program is revealed in Mary R. Dearing, *Veterans in Politics* (1952). See also Wallace E. Davies, *Patriotism on Parade* (1955); William H. Glasson, *Federal Military Pensions in the United States* (1918); Edward Noyes, "The Ohio G.A.R. and Politics from 1866 to 1900," 55 *Ohio Arch. & H. Q.* 79–105 (1946); and James N. Primm, "The G.A.R. in Missouri, 1866–1870," 20 *J.S.H.* 356–75 (1954).

Another powerful group supporting Radicalism is well portrayed in Ralph E. Morrow, *Northern Methodism and Reconstruction* (1956). See also William A. Russ, Jr., "The Influence of the Methodist Press upon Radical Reconstruction (1865–68)," 1 *Susquehanna Univ. Studies* 51–62 (1937).

The literature on the Democratic party during Reconstruction is less rewarding. See, however, two important essays by A. V. House: "Northern Congressional Democrats as Defenders of the South during Reconstruction," 6 *J.S.H.* 46–71 (1940), and "The Speakership Contest of 1875: Democratic Response to Power," 52 *J.A.H.* 252–74 (1965).

Surprisingly little has been written on Northern state politics during the postwar years. The best studies are Graham A. Cosmas, "The Democracy in Search of Issues: The Wisconsin Reform Party, 1873–1877," 46 *Wisc. M. H.* 93–108 (1962–63); Harris L. Dante, "Western Attitudes and Reconstruction Politics in Illinois, 1865–1872," 49 *J.I.S.H.S.* 149–62 (1956); Harriette M. Dilla, *The Politics of Michigan, 1865–1878* (1912); Frank B. Evans, *Pennsylvania Politics, 1872–1877: A Study in Political Leadership* (1966); Albert V. House, "Men, Morals, and Manipulation in the Pennsylvania Democracy of 1875," 23 *Pa. H.* 248–66 (1956); David Montgomery, "Radical Republicanism in Pennsylvania, 1866–1873," 85 *Pa. M. H. & B.* 439–57

(1961); Homer A. Stebbins, *A Political History of the State of New York, 1865–1869* (1913); and Helen J. and Harry Williams, "Wisconsin Republicans and Reconstruction, 1865–70," 23 *Wisc. M. H.* 17–39 (1939).

The literature on the Fourteenth Amendment is voluminous, specialized, and controversial. The best general treatment is Joseph B. James, *The Framing of the Fourteenth Amendment* (1959), which supersedes Horace E. Flack, *The Adoption of the Fourteenth Amendment* (1908). A basic source on this topic is Benjamin B. Kendrick, ed., *The Journal of the Joint Committee of Fifteen on Reconstruction* (1914). The "conspiracy theory" of the Fourteenth Amendment (the view that its framers designed to protect corporations from state regulation) is now discredited; see Louis B. Boudin, "Truth and Fiction about the Fourteenth Amendment," 16 *N. Y. Univ. Law Rev.* 19–82 (1938); Howard J. Graham, " 'Builded Better Than They Knew': The Framers, the Railroads, and the Fourteenth Amendment," 17 *Univ. of Pittsburgh Law Rev.* 537 ff. (1956); Graham, "The 'Conspiracy Theory' of the Fourteenth Amendment," 47 *Yale Law Rev.* 371–403 and 48 *ibid.* 171–94 (1938); Andrew C. McLaughlin, "The Court, the Corporation, and Conkling," 46 *A.H.R.* 45–63 (1940); and James F. S. Russell, "The Railroads in the 'Conspiracy Theory' of the Fourteenth Amendment," 41 *M.V.H.R.* 601–22 (1955). Charles Fairman, "Does the Fourteenth Amendment Incorporate the Bill of Rights?" 2 *Stanford Law Rev.* 5–139 (1949), deals with an important controversial topic. Recent scholarship stresses the antislavery background of the Fourteenth Amendment: John P. Frank and Robert Munro, "The Original Understanding of 'Equal Protection of the Laws,' " 50 *Columbia Law Rev.* 131–69 (1950); Howard J. Graham, "The Early Antislavery Backgrounds of the Fourteenth Amendment," *Wisc. Law Rev.* 479–507, 610–61 (1950); and Jacobus ten Broek, *The Antislavery Origins of the Fourteenth Amendment* (1951). On the intent of the framers of the Fourteenth Amendment with regard to segregation see Alexander M. Bickel, "The Original Understanding and the Segregation Decision," 69 *Harvard Law Rev.* 1–65 (1955); Howard J. Graham, "The Fourteenth Amendment and School Segregation," 3 *Buffalo Law Rev.* 1–24 (1953); and Alfred H. Kelly, "The Fourteenth Amendment Reconsidered: The Segregation Question," 54 *Mich. Law Rev.* 1049–86 (1956). For other aspects of the Fourteenth Amendment see Joseph L. Call, "The Fourteenth Amendment and its Skeptical Background," 24 *Alabama Lawyer* 82–98 (1963); R. Carter Pittman, "The Fourteenth Amendment: Its Intended Effect on Anti-Miscegenation Laws," 43 *N. C. Law Rev.* 92–109 (1964); and William W. Van Alstyne, "The Fourteenth Amendment, the 'Right' to Vote, and the Understanding of the Thirty-Ninth Congress," *Supreme Court Rev.* 33–86 (1965). For critiques of the process by which the amendment was ratified, see Ferdinand F. Fernandez, "Constitutionality of the Fourteenth Amendment," 39 *Southern Cal. Law Rev.* 378–407 (1966), and W. J. Suthron, Jr., "Dubious Origins of the Fourteenth Amendment," 28 *Tulane Law Rev.* 22–44 (1953).

In a series of articles Alfred Arvins has reexamined the legislative history of the Fourteenth Amendment with a view to questioning the constitutionality of recent civil rights legislation and to challenging recent Supreme Court rulings on civil rights: "Fourteenth Amendment Limitations on Banning Racial

Discrimination: The Original Understanding," 8 *Arizona Law Rev.* 236–59 (1967); "The Ku Klux Klan Act of 1871: Some Reflected Light on State Action and the Fourteenth Amendment," 11 *St. Louis Univ. Law J.* 331–81 (1967); "Racial Segregation in Public Accommodations: Some Reflected Light on the Fourteenth Amendment from the Civil Rights Act of 1875," 18 *Western Reserve Law Rev.* 1251–83 (1967); "Right to Bring Suit under the Fourteenth Amendment: The Original Understanding," 20 *Okla. Law Rev.* 284–300 (1967); "The Right to Hold Public Office and the Fourteenth and Fifteenth Amendments: The Original Understanding," 15 *Univ. of Kansas Law Rev.* 287–306 (1967); "The Right to Work and the Fourteenth Amendment: The Original Understanding," 18 *Labor Law J.* 15–28 (1967); and "Social Equality and the Fourteenth Amendment: The Original Understanding," 4 *Houston Law Rev.* 640–56 (1967).

William Gillette, *The Right to Vote: Politics and the Passage of the Fifteenth Amendment* (1965), is a first-rate study which combines constitutional and political history; it supersedes John M. Mathews, *Legislative and Judicial History of the Fifteenth Amendment* (1909). For a hostile evaluation of Gillette's study see LaWanda and John H. Cox, "Negro Suffrage and Republican Politics," 23 *J.S.H.* 303–30 (1967). Everette Swinney, "Enforcing the Fifteenth Amendment," 28 *J.S.H.* 202–18 (1962), is an excellent essay.

Harold M. Hyman, *Era of the Oath* (1954), is a careful scholarly study of the Radicals' attempt to regulate Southern loyalty through test oaths.

Stanley Kutler, *Judicial Power and Reconstruction Politics* (1968), is a thoughtful, comprehensive study which reverses the stereotype of judicial impotence during the postwar period. See also Kutler's "Ex Parte McCardle: Judicial Impotency? The Supreme Court and Reconstruction Reconsidered," 72 *A.H.R.* 835–51 (1967), and "Reconstruction and the Supreme Court: The Numbers Game Reconsidered," 32 *J.S.H.* 42–58 (1966). For other constitutional problems of the Reconstruction era see Sever L. Eubank, "The McCardle Case: A Challenge to Radical Reconstruction," 18 *J. Miss. H.* 111–27 (1956); Alfred K. Kelly, "The Congressional Controversy over School Segregation, 1867–1875," 64 *A.H.R.* 537–63 (1959); Samuel Klaus, ed., *The Milligan Case* (1929); R. Earl McClendon, "Status of the Ex-Confederate States as Seen in the Readmission of United States Senators," 41 *A.H.R.* 703–709 (1936); Lewis Mayers, "The Habeas Corpus Act of 1867: The Supreme Court as Legal Historian," 33 *Univ. of Chicago Law Rev.* 31–59 (1965); Roy F. Nichols, "United States vs. Jefferson Davis, 1865–1869," 31 *A.H.R.* 266–84 (1926); and Erwin C. Surrency, "The Legal Effects of the Civil War," 5 *Am. J. of Legal Hist.* 145–65 (1961).

On the impeachment and trial of President Johnson see the biographies of Johnson and the following articles: R. W. Bayless, "Peter G. Van Winkle and Waitman T. Willey in the Impeachment Trial of Andrew Johnson," 13 *W. Va. H.* 75–89 (1952); David Donald, "Why They Impeached Andrew Johnson," 8 *Am. Heritage* 20–25 ff. (Dec., 1956); Harold M. Hyman, "Johnson, Stanton, and Grant: A Reconstruction of the Army's Role in the Events Leading to Impeachment," 66 *A.H.R.* 85–100 (1960); Charles A. Jellison, "The Ross Impeachment Vote: A Need for Reappraisal," 41 *Sw. Soc. Sci. Q.* 150–55 (1960); Milton Lomask, "When Congress Tried to Rule," 11 *Am. Her-*

itage 60–61 ff. (Dec., 1959); James L. McDonough and William T. Alderson, eds., "Republican Politics and the Impeachment of President Johnson," 26 *Tenn. H. Q.* 177–83 (1967); Jerome Mushkat, ed., "The Impeachment of Andrew Johnson: A Contemporary View," 48 *N.Y.H.* 275–86 (1967); M. Kathleen Perdue, "Salmon P. Chase and the Impeachment Trial of Andrew Johnson," 27 *Historian* 75–92 (1964); Ralph J. Roske, "Republican Newspaper Support for the Acquittal of President Johnson," 11 *Tenn. H. Q.* 266–73 (1952); Roske, "The Seven Martyrs?" 64 *A.H.R.* 323–30 (1959); James E. Sefton, "The Impeachment of Andrew Johnson: A Century of Writing," 14 *C.W.H.* 120–47 (1968); and Hans L. Trefousse, "The Acquittal of Andrew Johnson and the Decline of the Radicals," 14 *C.W.H.* 148–61 (1968). See also the biographies of Black, B. R. Curtis, Evarts, and Nelson.

The standard work on the first election of Grant is Charles H. Coleman, *The Election of 1868* (1933). See also the biographies of Chase and Seymour and Edward S. Perzel, "Alexander Long, Salmon P. Chase and the Election of 1868," 23 *Cincinnati Hist. Soc. Bull.* 3–18 (1965).

Since little recent research has been done on the politics of the Grant administrations, the older accounts in Oberholtzer and Rhodes remain generally satisfactory. Of all the Grant biographies, only Hesseltine's concentrates on the presidential years. Allan Nevins's *Hamilton Fish* is an important source for the inner history of the Grant administrations. See also the biographies of Belknap, Boutwell, E. R. Hoar, and Rawlins. Matthew Josephson's *The Politicos, 1865–1896* (1938) is a spirited and cynical account of the whole era.

Grant's relation to the Supreme Court is debated in Charles Fairman, "Mr. Justice Bradley's Appointment to the Supreme Court and the Legal Tender Cases," 54 *Harvard Law Rev.* 977–1034 and 1128–55 (1941) and in Sidney Ratner, "Was the Supreme Court Packed by President Grant?" 50 *P.S.Q.* 343–58 (1935).

On the scandals of the Grant era see, in addition to the general works mentioned above, John A. Carpenter, "Washington, Pennsylvania and the Gold Conspiracy of 1869," 48 *W. Pa. H. M.* 345–53 (1965); Jay B. Crawford, *The Credit Mobilier of America* (1880); Fletcher M. Green, "Origins of the Credit Mobilier of America," 46 *M.V.H.R.* 238–51 (1959); Lucius E. Guese, "St. Louis and the Great Whiskey Ring," 36 *Mo. H. R.* 160–83 (1942); J. Martin Klotsche, "The Star Route Cases," 22 *M.V.H.R.* 406–18 (1935); David G. Loth, *Public Plunder: A History of Graft in America* (1938); Harry E. Resseguie, "Federal Conflict of Interest: The A. T. Stewart Case," 47 *N.Y.H.* 271–301 (1966); and Clark C. Spence, "Robert C. Schenck and the Emma Mine Affair," 68 *Ohio H. Q.* 141–60 (1959).

That such frauds and peculations were not confined to members of the Republican party is abundantly evidenced in Alexander B. Callow, Jr., *The Tweed Ring* (1966), and Seymour J. Mandelbaum, *Boss Tweed's New York* (1965). See also the biography of Tweed.

Carl R. Fish, *The Civil Service and the Patronage* (1904), gives an excellent survey of the abuses of the Grant period. Ari A. Hoogenboom, *Outlawing the Spoils: A History of the Civil Service Reform Movement, 1865–1883* (1961), a first-rate monograph, discusses the movement to eradicate those abuses. See also two significant essays by William Hartman: "The New York

Custom House: Seat of Spoils Politics," 34 *N.Y.H.* 149–63 (1953), and "Pioneer in Civil Service Reform: Silas W. Burt and the New York Custom House," 39 *N. Y. H. Soc. Q.* 369–79 (1955).

Earl D. Ross, *The Liberal Republican Movement* (1919), is an admirable account of the 1872 revolt against the Grant administration. See also Thomas S. Barclay, *The Liberal Republican Movement in Missouri* (1926), and Frederick E. Haynes, *Third Party Movements since the Civil War* (1916). John G. Sproat, *"The Best Men": Liberal Reformers in the Gilded Age* (1968), is a good study of men who led the drive against Grant. See also the following important articles: Donald W. Curl, "The Cincinnati Convention of the Liberal Republican Party," 24 *Cincinnati Hist. Soc. Bull.* 150–69 (1966); Matthew T. Downey, "Horace Greeley and the Politicians: The Liberal Republican Convention of 1872," 53 *J.A.H.* 727–50 (1967); Lena C. Logan, "Henry Watterson and the Liberal Convention of 1872," 40 *Ind. M. H.* 319–40 (1944); James M. McPherson, "Grant or Greeley: The Abolitionist Dilemma in the Election of 1872," 71 *A.H.R.* 43–61 (1965); Patrick W. Riddleberger, "The Break in the Radical Ranks: Liberals vs. Stalwarts in the Election of 1872," 44 *J.N.H.* 136–57 (1959); James G. Smart, "Whitelaw Reid and the Nomination of Horace Greeley," 49 *Mid-Am.* 227–43 (1967); and Mildred Throne, "The Liberal Republican Party in Iowa," 53 *Iowa J. H.* 121–52 (1955). Much valuable information can also be found in the biographies of such men as C. F. Adams, Henry Adams, B. Gratz Brown, G. W. Curtis, David Davis, Greeley, Julian, Reid, Schurz, Sumner, Trumbull, and Watterson.

POSTWAR DIPLOMACY

Many of the studies listed above under "Wartime Diplomacy" continue to be useful for the postwar period. The biographies of Seward, Fish, and Sumner are of great importance.

Dexter Perkins, *The Monroe Doctrine, 1867–1907* (1937), is the best general treatment of American relations with Latin America during this period. On the attitude of the United States toward the Maximilian regime see, in addition to the works previously cited, James M. Callahan, *American Foreign Policy in Mexican Relations* (1932); Percy F. Martin, *Maximilian in Mexico* (1914); and James F. Rippy, *The United States and Mexico* (1926).

The general expansionism of the postwar years is admirably treated in Joe P. Smith, *The Republican Expansionists of the Early Reconstruction Era* (1933), and in Donald F. Warner, *The Idea of Continental Union: Agitation for the Annexation of Canada to the United States, 1849–1893* (1960). Donald M. Dozer, "Anti-Expansionism during the Johnson Administration," 12 *Pac. H. R.* 253–76 (1943), deals with the opposition to this pervasive sentiment, and William M. Armstrong, *E. L. Godkin and American Foreign Policy, 1865–1900* (1957), discusses one of its principal critics.

The standard monograph on the purchase of Alaska is Victor Farrar, *The Annexation of Russian America to the United States* (1937), but it must be supplemented by several important articles: Thomas A. Bailey, "Why the United States Purchased Alaska," 3 *Pac. H. R.* 39–49 (1934); William A. Dunning, "Paying for Alaska: Some Unfamiliar Incidents in the Process," in his *Truth in History* (1937), 118–33; Frank A. Golder, "The Purchase of Alaska," 25 *A.H.R.* 411–25 (1920); Reinhard H. Luthin, "The Sale of Alaska," 16 *Slavic and East European Rev.* 168–82 (1937); Anatole G. Mazour, "The Prelude to Russia's Departure from America," 10 *Pac. H. R.* 311–19 (1941); Hunter Miller, "Russian Opinion on the Cession of Alaska," 48 *A.H.R.* 521–31 (1943); and Morgan B. Sherwood, "George Davidson and the Acquisition of Alaska," 28 *Pac. H. R.* 141–54 (1959). See also Morgan B. Sherwood, *Exploration of Alaska, 1865–1900* (1965). Archie W. Shiels, *The Purchase of Alaska* (1967), reprints most of the basic documents.

Other expansionist efforts of the Johnson period are discussed in Brainerd Dyer, "Robert J. Walker on Acquiring Greenland and Iceland," 27 *M.V.H.R.* 263–66 (1940); Halvdan Koht, "The Origins of Seward's Plan to Purchase the Danish West Indies," 50 *A.H.R.* 762–67 (1945); and Charles C. Tansill, *The Purchase of the Danish West Indies* (1932).

Nevins's *Fish* continues to be a basic source for the diplomatic history of the Grant era. On Grant's ill-advised attempt to annex Santo Domingo, see Charles C. Tansill, *The United States and Santo Domingo, 1798–1873* (1938), and Sumner Welles, *Naboth's Vineyard: The Dominican Republic* (2 v., 1928). Rayford W. Logan, *The Diplomatic Relations of the United States with Haiti, 1776–1891* (1941), deals with the adjacent nation.

John Bassett Moore, *History and Digest of the International Arbitrations to Which the United States Has Been a Party* (6 v., 1898), is a good introduction to the tangled problem of Anglo-American relations in the postwar years, involving the *Alabama* claims, the Fenian movement, and proposed annexation of Canada. The Canadian aspect of this story is well treated in Hugh L. Keenleyside and Gerald S. Brown, *Canada and the United States* (1952), and in Lester B. Shippee, *Canadian-American Relations, 1849–1874* (1939). The fullest account of the Fenian problem is Charles C. Tansill, *America and the Fight for Irish Freedom, 1866–1922* (1957), which is hostile to Great Britain. See also Thomas N. Brown, *Irish American Nationalism, 1870–1890* (1966); Homer Calkin, "St. Albans in Reverse: The Fenian Raid of 1866," 35 *Vermont History* 19–34 (1967); and Arthur H. DeRosier, Jr., "Importance in Failure: The Fenian Raids of 1866–1871," 3 *So. Q.* 181–97 (1965).

Adrian Cook, "A Lost Opportunity in Anglo-American Relations: The Alabama Claims, 1865–67," 12 *Australian Journal of Politics and History* 54–65 (1966), traces the failure of the Seward-Stanley negotiations. See also the biographies of Reverdy Johnson and Moran. R. C. Clark, "The Diplomatic Mission of Sir John Rose, 1871," 27 *Pacific Northwest Quart.* 227–42 (1936), deals with an important preliminary move which led to the ultimate settlement of Anglo-American disagreements. Andrew Lang's *Life, Letters, and Diaries of Sir Stafford Northcote* (2 v., 1890) treats of the work of one of the British joint high commissioners; see also James P. Baxter, 3rd, "The British High Commissioners at Washington in 1871," 65 *Mass. H. S. P.* 334–57 (1932–36). Donald G. Creighton, *John A. Macdonald* (2 v., 1953–56), discusses the role of the Canadian member of the commission. Goldwin Smith, *The Treaty of Washington, 1871* (1941), is an admirable study, which, however, concentrates upon consequences of the treaty for the reorganization of the

British empire. See also Maureen M. Robson, "The *Alabama* Claims and the Anglo-American Reconciliation, 1865–71," 42 *Canadian Historical Review* 1–22 (1961).

POSTWAR ECONOMIC PROBLEMS

The fluctuations of American business in the postwar era are admirably discussed in Rendigs Fels, *American Business Cycles, 1865–1897* (1959). See also Fels, "American Business Cycles, 1865–79," 41 *Am. Econ. Rev.* 325–49 (1951). On the great postwar depression see Ernest R. McCartney, *Crisis of 1873* (1935); Samuel Rezneck, "Distress, Relief and Discontent during the Depression of 1873–78," 58 *J. Pol. Econ.* 494–513 (1950); and O. V. Wells, "The Depression of 1873–79," 11 *Agr. H.* 237–49 (1937). For the explosive discontent of labor, see Robert V. Bruce, *1877: Year of Violence* (1959).

Edward C. Kirkland, *Industry Comes of Age: Business, Labor, and Public Policy, 1860–1897* (1961), is a comprehensive, well-informed history of all the nonagricultural sectors of the postwar economy. Thomas C. Cochran and William Miller, *The Age of Enterprise* (1942), demonstrates that good economic history is also good social history. Matthew Josephson, *The Robber Barons: The Great American Capitalists, 1861–1901* (1934), is a spirited, muckraking attack upon the captains of industry. For critiques of this view see Thomas C. Cochran, "The Legend of the Robber Barons," 74 *Pa. M. H. & B.* 307–21 (1950), and Edward C. Kirkland, "The Robber Barons Revisited," 66 *A.H.R.* 68–73 (1960). See also Allen Solganick, "The Robber Baron Concept and its Revisionists," 29 *Science and Society* 257–69 (1965), and Norman L. Hicks and Allen Solganick, "Robber Barons and Revisionism: A Discussion," 30 *Science and Society* 191–205 (1966).

There is not space here to list the literature on the growth of each individual American industry during the Reconstruction period, but a few representative titles may be suggested. George R. Woolfolk, *The Cotton Regency: the Northern Merchants and Reconstruction, 1865–1880* (1959), discusses the reknitting of economic ties between North and South. On Western railroads, which played such a large part in the economics and politics of the era, see Oscar Lewis, *The Big Four: The Story of Huntington, Stanford, Hopkins, and Crocker, and of the Building of the Central Pacific* (1945); Jacob R. Perkins, *Trails, Rails and War: The Life of General G. M. Dodge* (1929); and Robert E. Reigel, *The Story of the Western Railroads* (1926). Julius Grodinsky, *The Iowa Pool* (1950), discusses an early effort to stifle railroad competition. On the dynamic oil industry, see, in addition to Allan Nevins's biography of Rockefeller, Harold F. Williamson and Arnold R. Daum, *The American Petroleum Industry: The Age of Illumination, 1859–1899* (1959), and Paul H. Giddens, *The Birth of the Oil Industry* (1938).

For the rise of the city, most of the titles listed on this subject in the section of this bibliography called "A Growing Nation" continue to be valuable. See also Blake McKelvey, *The Urbanization of America, 1860–1915* (1963).

Many of the works on labor listed in that section also continue to be applicable. Norman J. Ware, *The Labor Movement in the United States, 1860–*

1890 (1929), is a classic in its field. Gerald N. Grob, *Workers and Utopia: A Study of Ideological Conflict in the American Labor Movement, 1865–1900* (1961), is a basic work. Wayne G. Broehl, *The Molly Maguires* (1965), deals with an explosive episode in labor history; for a critical judgment of this work see Ann J. Lane, "Recent Literature on the Molly Maguires," 30 *Science and Society* 309–19 (1966).

Sidney Fine, *Laissez Faire and the General Welfare State: A Study of Conflict in American Thought, 1865–1901* (1956), is an admirable study of economic ideas. See also Chester M. Destler, "The Opposition of American Businessmen to Social Control during the 'Gilded Age,' " 39 *M.V.H.R.* 641–72 (1953). Two books by Edward C. Kirkland cast much light upon the businessman's mind: *Business in the Gilded Age* (1952), and *Dream and Thought in the Business Community, 1860–1900* (1956).

Robert T. Patterson, *Federal Debt-Management Policies, 1867–1879* (1954), is an excellent, but technical, study.

For the view that Northeastern businessmen formed a monolithic bloc in support of the economic policies of the Republican party in the Reconstruction era, including the resumption of specie payments, the high tariff, and land grants to railroads, see Charles A. and Mary R. Beard, *The Rise of American Civilization*, Louis M. Hacker, *The Triumph of American Capitalism*, and Howard K. Beale, *The Critical Year*. Beale's "The Tariff and Reconstruction," 35 *A.H.R.* 276–94 (1930), is an explicit formulation of this interpretation. Recently this view has come under serious attack. For a general statement of newer views see Stanley Coben, "Northeastern Business and Radical Reconstruction: A Re-examination," 46 *M.V.H.R.* 67–90 (1959). Peter Kolchin, "The Business Press and Reconstruction, 1865–1868," 33 *J.S.H.* 183–96 (1967), shows how rarely organs of business endorsed Radical positions.

Some of the most searching criticisms of the Beard-Hacker-Beale view have been made in connection with studies of the resumption of specie payments, a highly technical question which has exercised an improbable fascination upon the minds of recent historians. For many years the standard works on this subject were those by Wesley C. Mitchell and Don C. Barrett, both previously cited, which assumed a strong anti-inflationist position. See also Wesley C. Mitchell, *Gold, Prices, and Wages under the Greenback Standard* (1908). For over a generation scholarship on this subject took the form of elaborating or slightly modifying the conclusions of Mitchell and Barrett. For examples of such useful studies see George L. Anderson, "The Proposed Resumption of Silver Payments in 1873," 8 *Pac. H. R.* 301–16 (1939); Anderson, "The South and Problems of Post-Civil War Finance," 9 *J.S.H.* 181–95 (1943); Anderson, "Western Attitudes toward National Banks, 1873–74," 23 *M.V.H.R.* 205–16 (1936); William G. Carleton, "The Money Question in Indiana Politics, 1865–1890," 42 *Ind. M. H.* 107–50 (1946); Frank D. Graham, "International Trade under Depreciated Paper. The United States, 1862–79," 36 *Quart. Jour. Econ.* 220–73 (1922); Reginald C. McGrane, "Ohio and the Greenback Movement," 11 *M.V.H.R.* 526–42 (1925); Roscoe C. Martin, "The Greenback Party in Texas," 30 *Sw. H. Q.* 161–77 (1927); and Max L. Shipley, "The Background and Legal Aspects of the Pendleton Plan," 24 *M.V.H.R.* 329–40 (1937).

Then historians began challenging the very foundations upon which this thesis rested. Chester M. Destler, *American Radicalism, 1865–1901* (1946), raised troublesome questions about the origins and significance of the Pendleton plan. Robert P. Sharkey, *Money, Class, and Party* (1959), demonstrated that businessmen held widely varying opinions upon the question of specie resumption, as did Radical Republicans, and that the views of both groups changed over time. Then Irwin Unger, in a brilliant exercise in both economic and intellectual history, showed in *The Greenback Era: A Social and Political History of American Finance, 1865–1879* (1964), how often ideological considerations rather than economic self-interest determined attitudes toward specie resumption. See also Unger's impressive articles: "Business and Currency in the Ohio Gubernatorial Campaign of 1875," 41 *Mid-Am.* 27–39 (1959); "The Business Community and the Origins of the 1875 Resumption Act," 35 *Bus. Hist. Rev.* 247–62 (1961); "Business Men and Specie Resumption," 74 *P.S.Q.* 46–70 (1959); and "Money and Morality: The Northern Calvinist Churches and the Reconstruction Finance Question," 10 *J. of Presbyterian Hist.* 38–55 (1962). For a concurring opinion see Richard H. Timberlake, Jr., "Ideological Factors in Specie Resumption, and Treasury Policy," 24 *J. Econ. H.* 29–52 (1964). On a related topic see Paul Barnett, "The Crime of 1873 Re-examined," 38 *Agr. H.* 178–81 (1964), and Allen Weinstein, "Was There a 'Crime of 1873'?" 54 *J.A.H.* 307–26 (1967). Walter T. K. Nugent, *The Money Question during Reconstruction* (1967), is a brief recent synthesis of all this scholarship.

Fred A. Shannon, *The Farmer's Last Frontier*, previously cited, is an admirable discussion of farm problems in the postwar years, giving sufficient attention to farm protest movement. These are discussed in more detail in two books by Solon J. Buck: *The Agrarian Crusade* (1920) and *The Granger Movement* (1913). Four recent articles supplement Buck's work: William D. Barns, "Oliver Hudson Kelley and the Genesis of the Grange: A Reappraisal," 41 *Agr. H.* 229–42 (1967); Roy V. Scott, "Grangerism in Champaign County, Illinois, 1873–1877," 43 *Mid-Am.* 139–63 (1961); Patricia Smith and Rhoda R. Gilman, "Oliver Hudson Kelley: Minnesota Pioneer, 1849–1868," 40 *Minn. H.* (1967); and Margaret L. Woodward, "The Northwestern Farmer, 1868–1876: A Tale of Paradox," 37 *Agr. H.* 134–42 (1963). Since Buck's work deals largely with Middle Western farm discontent, one must consult the articles on the Granger movement in the South: J. H. Easterby, "The Granger Movement in South Carolina," 1 *S. C. Hist. Assoc. Proc.* 21–32 (1931); James S. Ferguson, "Co-operative Activity of the Grange in Mississippi," 4 *J. Miss. H.* 3–19 (1942); Ferguson, "The Grange and Farmer Education in Mississippi," 8 *J.S.H.* 497–512 (1942); William W. Rogers, "The Alabama State Grange," 8 *Ala. R.* 104–18 (1955); Theodore Saloutos, "The Grange in the South, 1870–1877," 19 *J.S.H.* 473–87 (1953); and Ralph A. Smith, "The Granger Movement in Texas, 1873–1900," 42 *Sw. H. Q.* 297–315 (1939). Theodore Saloutos, *Farmer Movements in the South, 1865–1933* (1960), is a useful summary.

Very recently the basic assumptions behind the standard works on the Granger movement have been questioned: it has been suggested, for example, that the Grange had Eastern antecedents and that it was led not by farmers but by local businessmen. For the best of this revisionist work see Earl S. Beard, "The Background of State Railroad Regulation in Iowa," 51 *Iowa J. H.* 1–36 (1953); Lee Benson, *Merchants, Farmers, and Railroads: Railroad Regulation and New York Politics, 1850–1887* (1955); Frederick Merk, "Eastern Antecedents of the Grangers," 23 *Agr. H.* 1–8 (1949); George H. Miller, "Origins of the Iowa Granger Law," 40 *M.V.H.R.* 657–80 (1954); Mildred Throne, "The Grange in Iowa, 1868–1875," 47 *Iowa J. H.* 289–324 (1949); and Harold D. Woodman, "Chicago Businessmen and the 'Granger' Laws," 36 *Agr. H.* 16–24 (1962).

THE END OF RECONSTRUCTION

For many years Paul L. Haworth, *The Hayes-Tilden Disputed Presidential Election of 1876* (1906), has been a standard work, and as a study of the political aspects of the crisis it is not likely to be replaced. See, however, the biographies of Hewitt and the following essays: Harold Dippre, "Corruption and the Disputed Election Vote of Oregon in the 1876 Election," 67 *Ore. H. Q.* 257–72 (1966); Jerrell H. Shofner, "Fraud and Intimidation in the Florida Elections of 1876," 42 *Fla. H. Q.* 321–30 (1964); T. B. Tunnell, Jr., "The Negro, the Republican Party, and the Election of 1876 in Louisiana," 7 *La. H.* 101–16 (1966); and Jerome L. Sternstein, ed., "The Sickles Memorandum: Another Look at the Hayes-Tilden Election-Night Conspiracy," 32 *J.S.H.* 342–57 (1966).

Increasingly, however, historians have come to question the adequacy of Haworth's interpretation and to look behind the scenes for economic motives in the ending of Radical Reconstruction. William B. Hesseltine, "Economic Factors in the Abandonment of Reconstruction," 22 *M.V.H.R.* 191–210 (1935), was an important essay pointing in this direction. C. Vann Woodward's *Reunion and Reaction: The Compromise of 1877 and the End of Reconstruction* (1951) carried this revision much further, discrediting the Wormley conference as a factor in Hayes's selection and stressing the role of former Whigs and railroad magnates in the outcome. See also Woodward's *Origins of the New South, 1877–1913* (1951). Woodward's important new interpretation has received almost universal acceptance; see, for example, Harry Barnard's *Rutherford B. Hayes and His America* (1954).

Index

1 2 3 4 5 6 7 8 9 0

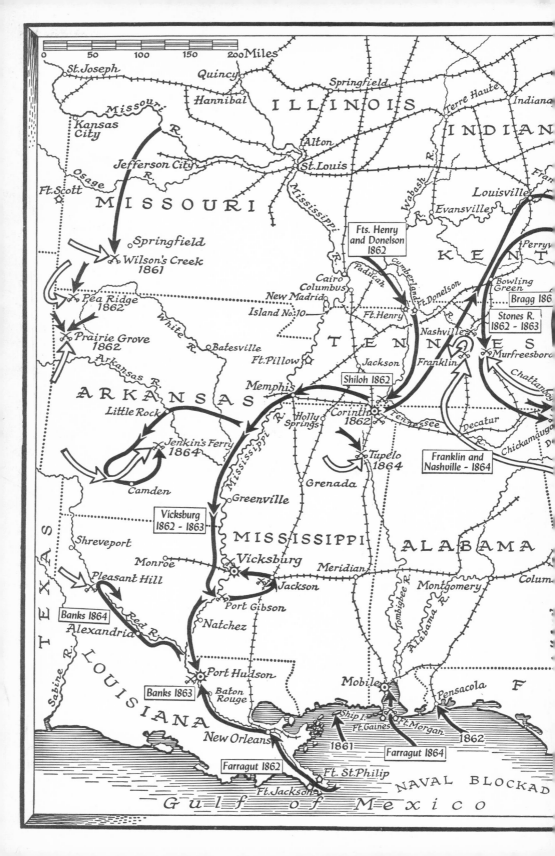